# CHAMBERS

# FACT FINDER

CHAMBERS

CHAMBERS
An imprint of Chambers Harrap Publishers Ltd
7 Hopetoun Crescent
Edinburgh, EH7 4AY

www.chambers.co.uk

First published by Chambers Harrap Publishers Ltd 2004



A CIP catalogue record for this book is available from the British Library.

ISBN 0550 10076 8

Image credits

Star images, p10
Copyright © 2002 by Houghton Mifflin Company. Adapted and reproduced by permission from *The American Heritage Student Science Dictionary*.

Cloud images, pp36–7
Copyright © 2002 by Houghton Mifflin Company. Reproduced by permission from *The American Heritage Student Science Dictionary*.

Electromagnetic spectrum image, p381
Copyright © 2002 by Houghton Mifflin Company. Reproduced by permission from *The American Heritage Student Science Dictionary*.

Muscles diagram, p390
Copyright © www.arttoday.com

Designed and typeset by Chambers Harrap Publishers Ltd, Edinburgh
Printed in Italy by Rotolito

# Contributors

**Editor**

Hazel Norris

**Managing Editor**

Una McGovern

**Publishing Manager**

Patrick White

**Contributors**

Gary Dexter
Camilla Rockwood

**Editorial Assistance**

Helen Bleck
Melanie Pepper

**Prepress**

Vienna Leigh
Claire Williamson

# Introduction

*Chambers Factfinder* is a brand-new addition to the Chambers family of reference books. It has been designed to be not only informative and reliable, but also easy to use and entertaining. The facts and figures have been specially chosen for their relevance, including some information often marginalized elsewhere, but which is nevertheless valuable for quizzes, crosswords, arguments and puzzles. Amusing 'fascinating fact' boxes pepper the text; from providing additional interesting material on a subject, to dropping in quirky, little-known or intriguing snippets of information, these fact boxes are a browser's delight and bring the subject areas to life.

A 'one-stop' approach has been taken, with careful and intuitive grouping of material so that all the data on a particular subject can be found in a single place. There are 28 major subject areas, within which are clearly-labelled individual subsections, arranged so as to take the user on a journey from the furthest realms of the universe to our own planet and the world around us, and then on to the world's people and the diverse fields of human culture and achievement.

Data is presented simply in tables and lists for clarity, aided by maps, diagrams, pie charts, pictures and boxes; introductory information is distinguished by background tints. Detailed contents pages at the front of the book and a handy index at the back guide the reader to the information sought.

*Chambers Factfinder* has been specially designed to be accessible, user-friendly and full of the information that really matters. Whether you are hoping to win a pub quiz, prove a point in an argument or just browsing inquisitively for fun, this book should satisfy your curiosity.

# ABBREVIATIONS

| | |
|---|---|
| a | acre(s) |
| abbrev. | abbreviation(s) |
| AD | Anno Domini |
| AU | astronomical unit(s) |
| BBC | British Broadcasting Corporation |
| BC | Before Christ |
| bu | bushel(s) |
| C | Celsius (Centigrade) |
| c | century |
| c. | circa |
| cc | cubic centimetre(s) |
| CIS | Commonwealth of Independent States |
| cl | centilitre(s) |
| cm | centimetre(s) |
| Co. | company |
| cu | cubic |
| cwt | hundredweight(s) |
| dB | decibel(s) |
| DC | District of Columbia |
| dm | decimetre(s) |
| E | east |
| e | estimate |
| eg | for example |
| etc | and so on (et cetera) |
| EU | European Union |
| F | Fahrenheit |
| fl. | floruit |
| fl oz | fluid ounce(s) |
| ft | foot (feet) |
| g | gram(s) |
| gal | gallon(s) |
| GB | gigabyte(s) |
| GMT | Greenwich Mean Time |
| ha | hectare(s) |
| hl | hectolitre(s) |
| HQ | headquarters |
| HRE | Holy Roman Empire |
| ie | that is (id est) |
| in | inch(es) |
| IVR | International Vehicle Registration |
| K | Kelvin |
| KB | kilobyte(s) |
| kg | kilogram(s) |
| km | kilometre(s) |
| kph | kilometre(s) per hour |
| kW | kilowatt(s) |
| l | litre(s) |
| lb | pound(s) |
| lbm | pound(s) mass |
| m | metre(s) |
| MB | megabyte(s) |
| mg | milligram(s) |
| mi | mile(s) |
| ml | millilitre(s) |
| mm | millimetre(s) |
| MP | Member of Parliament |
| mph | mile(s) per hour |
| Mt | Mount |
| N | north |
| n/a | not applicable |
| NASA | National Aeronautics and Space Administration |
| no. | number |
| oz | ounce(s) |
| pk | peck(s) |
| pop | population |
| p(p) | page(s) |
| Prot | Protestant |
| pt | pint(s) |
| qt | quart(s) |
| RC | Roman Catholic |
| S | south |
| sec | second(s) |
| SI | Système International (d'Unités) |
| sq | square |
| SS | Saints |
| St | Saint |
| st | stone(s) |
| TV | television |
| UK | United Kingdom |
| UN | United Nations |
| US | United States |
| USA | United States of America |
| USSR | Union of Soviet Socialist Republics |
| UT | Unified Team |
| v | versus |
| W | west |
| yd | yard(s) |
| ZIP | zone improvement plan |

Months are abbreviated to the first three letters (26 Nov 1976).

*Additional abbreviations can be found under individual sections in the text; for example, currency abbreviations are listed under* Economics.

# CONTENTS

# CONTENTS

**CONTENTS**



## POLITICS, LAW AND ORDER



## ANCIENT GREECE AND ROME

## RELIGIONS, BELIEFS AND FOLKLORE



## TIME



## SCIENCE

CONTENTS

## HUMAN BODY



## MATHEMATICS



## ECONOMICS



## MEASUREMENT, CONVERSION AND SIZE



## INVENTIONS, DISCOVERIES AND FIRSTS



## ARCHITECTURE AND ENGINEERING

## SOCIETY AND LEARNING



## LITERATURE



## ART



## FILM AND TELEVISION



## MUSIC



## FOOD AND DRINK

# CONTENTS

## LANGUAGE



## COMMUNICATION



## TRANSPORT



## SPORTS, COMPETITIONS AND GAMES

# THE SOLAR SYSTEM

## SUN

| | | | |
|---|---|---|---|
| **Age** | 4.5 billion–4.7 billion years | **Predicted total lifespan** | 10 billion years |
| **Distance from Earth (mean)** | 150 million km/93 million mi | **Surface area** | 6 087 billion sq km/ 2 350 billion sq mi |
| **Diameter** | 1 392 500km/864 950mi | **Volume** | $1.4122\times10^{18}$ cu km/ $3.388\times10^{17}$ cu mi |
| **Mass** | $1.989\times10^{30}$ kg/$4.385\times10^{30}$ lb | | |
| **Luminosity** | $3.83\times10^{27}$ kW | **Density (mean)** | 1.409g/cu cm/87.96 lbm/cu ft |
| **Temperature (core)** | 15 million K/15 million°C/ 27 million°F | **Surface gravity** | $2.740\times10^{4}$ cm/sq sec/1.787in/sq sec |
| **Rotation** | 26.8 days (of solar equator, as seen from Earth) | **Temperature (surface)** | 5 770 K/5 500°C/ 10 000°F |

### Composition of the Sun's photosphere

| Element | % weight |
|---|---|
| Hydrogen | 73.46 |
| Helium | 24.85 |
| Oxygen | 0.77 |
| Carbon | 0.29 |
| Iron | 0.16 |
| Neon | 0.12 |
| Nitrogen | 0.09 |
| Silicon | 0.07 |
| Magnesium | 0.05 |
| Sulphur | 0.04 |
| Others | 0.10 |

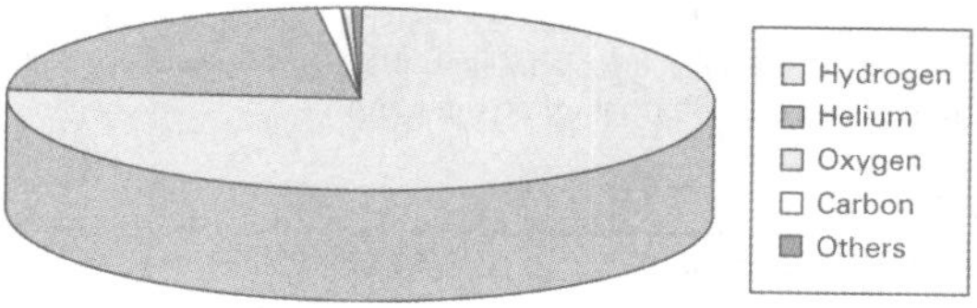


### *Exploding Energy*

The Sun's energy comes from nuclear fusion. It consumes hundreds of millions of tonnes of hydrogen every second, which reactions convert into helium. This generates as much energy every second as almost 91 billion tonnes, or 100 billion tons, of TNT exploding.

### Inside the Sun

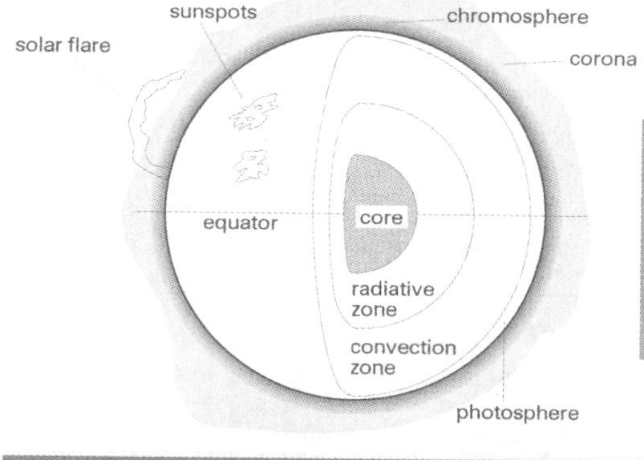


### *Sun Worship*

The Sun was worshipped by many early peoples. The sun god was called *Tezcatlipoca* by the Aztecs, *Helios* by the ancient Greeks, *Ra* or *Re* by the ancient Egyptians and *Sol* by the Romans.

# SOLAR SYSTEM

## SOLAR SYSTEM

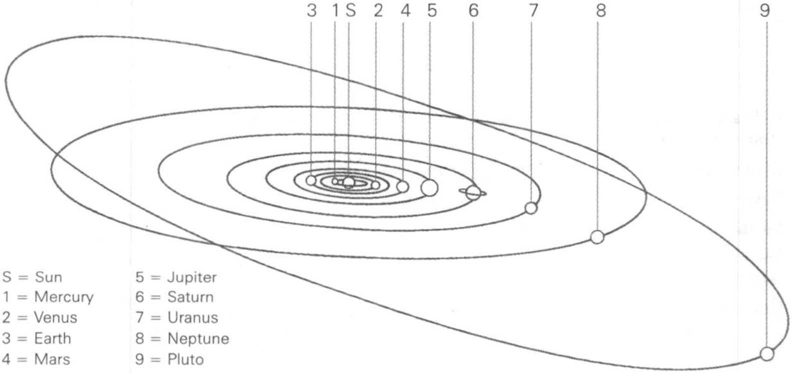


S = Sun
1 = Mercury
2 = Venus
3 = Earth
4 = Mars
5 = Jupiter
6 = Saturn
7 = Uranus
8 = Neptune
9 = Pluto

### Wandering Stars

*Planet* comes from the Greek word *planētēs*, meaning *wanderer*. Planets were known by the ancient Greeks as *astéres planêtai*, or *wandering stars*, because it was believed that they meandered about the skies.

## PLANETS

For satellites, the first figure gives the total number. The names of the major satellites are listed with the closest to the planet first; the year of discovery is given in parentheses. See separate section for information on the Earth.

### Mercury

| | |
|---|---|
| **Diameter at equator** | 4 878km/3 031mi |
| **Maximum distance from the Sun** | 69.4 million km/43 million mi |
| **Minimum distance from the Sun** | 46.8 million km/29 million mi |
| **Length of year** | 88 days |
| **Length of day** | 58 days 16 hours |
| **Atmosphere** | Almost none; traces of oxygen, sodium, and helium |
| **Surface gravity** | 370cm/sq sec/146in/sq sec |
| **Rings** | None |
| **Satellites** | None |

**Discovered**

Known in prehistory; named after the Roman god of merchants, the messenger of the gods, possibly because of its fast movement.

### Polar Planet

In 1991 radar observations indicated that Mercury may have water ice at its north and south poles.

## Venus

| | |
|---|---|
| **Diameter at equator** | 12 104km/7 521mi |
| **Maximum distance from the Sun** | 109 million km/67.6 million mi |
| **Minimum distance from the Sun** | 107.6 million km/66.7 million mi |
| **Length of year** | 224.7 days |
| **Length of day** | 243 days |
| **Atmosphere** | Mainly carbon dioxide and nitrogen; clouds of sulphuric acid |
| **Surface gravity** | 887cm/sq sec/349in/sq sec |
| **Rings** | None |
| **Satellites** | None |

**Discovered**

Known in prehistory; named after the Roman goddess of love, because of its brightness. Most of its surface features are named after female figures.

### *Sultry Venus*

Venus has an extreme greenhouse effect due to the high concentrations of carbon dioxide in its atmosphere. Temperatures on the surface are hot enough to melt lead.

**Earth** see separate section **THE EARTH**

## Mars

| | |
|---|---|
| **Diameter at equator** | 6 794km/4 222mi |
| **Maximum distance from the Sun** | 249.2 million km/154.5 million mi |
| **Minimum distance from the Sun** | 207.3 million km/128.5 million mi |
| **Length of year** | 687 days |
| **Length of day** | 24 hours 37 minutes 23 seconds |
| **Atmosphere** | Carbon dioxide, nitrogen, argon |
| **Surface gravity** | 371cm/sq sec/146in/sq sec |
| **Rings** | None |
| **Satellites** | 2: Phobos (1877), Deimos (1877) |

**Discovered**

Known in prehistory; named after the Roman god of war, because of its red colour.

### *Life on Mars*

Evidence of flooding on Mars billions of years ago suggests it once had rivers, lakes and seas. Life on Mars in the past is considered a distinct possibility, and some scientists think it may have 'seeded' Earth with life – meaning that we might all be Martians!

## Jupiter

| | |
|---|---|
| **Diameter at equator** | 142 800km/88 700mi |
| **Maximum distance from the Sun** | 817.4 million km/506.8 million mi |
| **Minimum distance from the Sun** | 741.6 million km/459.8 million mi |
| **Length of year** | 11.86 years |
| **Length of day** | 9 hours 50 minutes 30 seconds |
| **Atmosphere** | Mainly hydrogen and helium |
| **Surface gravity** | 2 312cm/sq sec/910in/sq sec |
| **Rings** | Yes |
| **Satellites** | Almost 60: Io (1610), Europa (1610), Ganymede (1610) and Callisto (1610) |

**Discovered**

Known in prehistory; named after the Roman god of the sky and its attributes (Sun, Moon, thunder, rain, etc).

### *Almost a Star*

Jupiter is a proto-star. If it had been 50–100 times more massive, hydrogen fusion in its interior would have caused it to shine like our Sun.

## Saturn

| | |
|---|---|
| **Diameter at equator** | 120 536km/74 900mi |
| **Maximum distance from the Sun** | 1.5 billion km/937.6 million mi |
| **Minimum distance from the Sun** | 1.3 billion km/834.6 million mi |
| **Length of year** | 29.46 years |
| **Length of day** | 10 hours 14 minutes |
| **Atmosphere** | Mainly hydrogen and helium |
| **Surface gravity** | 896cm/sq sec/353in/sq sec |
| **Rings** | Yes |
| **Satellites** | At least 30: Mimas (1789), Enceladus (1789), Tethys (1684), Dione (1684), Rhea (1672), Titan (1655), Hyperion (1848), Iapetus (1671) |

**Discovered**

Known in prehistory; named after the Roman god of fertility and agriculture.

### *Titanic Aliens*

Saturn's largest moon, Titan, is a little bigger than the planet Mercury. Scientists think there is a chance that the organic compounds in its atmosphere may indicate the presence of some form of life.

## Uranus

| | |
|---|---|
| **Diameter at equator** | 51 118km/31 765mi |
| **Maximum distance from the Sun** | 3 billion km/1.8 billion mi |
| **Minimum distance from the Sun** | 2.7 billion km/1.7 billion mi |
| **Length of year** | 84.01 years |
| **Length of day** | 16–28 hours[1] |
| **Atmosphere** | Hydrogen, helium, methane |
| **Surface gravity** | 869cm/sq sec/342in/sq sec |
| **Rings** | Yes |
| **Satellites** | At least 20: Ariel (1851), Umbriel (1851), Miranda (1948), Titania (1787), Oberon (1787) |

**Discovered**

1781; its discoverer, William Herschel, wanted to name it *Georgium Sidus* ('the Georgian planet') after the reigning British monarch, but the name Uranus came into more common use in around 1850. In Greek mythology Uranus was the god of the heavens.

[1] *Different latitudes rotate at different speeds.*

### Catastrophic Collision

Uranus orbits the Sun 'on its side' – that is, with its poles pointing toward the Sun. This may be the result of a catastrophic collision with a huge body such as a minor planet or asteroid.

## Neptune

| | |
|---|---|
| **Diameter at equator** | 49 492km/30 754mi |
| **Maximum distance from the Sun** | 4.5 million km/2.8 billion mi |
| **Minimum distance from the Sun** | 4.4 billion km/2.7 billion mi |
| **Length of year** | 164.79 years |
| **Length of day** | 18–20 hours[1] |
| **Atmosphere** | Methane, hydrogen, helium |
| **Surface gravity** | 1 100cm/sq sec/433in/sq sec |
| **Rings** | Yes |
| **Satellites** | 11: Proteus (1989), Triton (1846), Nereid (1949) |

**Discovered**

1846; the first planet to be discovered by mathematical calculations, rather than observation. Named after Neptune, the Roman god of the sea.

[1] *Different latitudes rotate at different speeds.*

### Far Out

Neptune is usually the eighth planet from the Sun, but for 20 of every 248 Earth years (most recently 1979–99) it becomes the ninth, the furthest planet, as Pluto's orbit takes it closer to the Sun.

## Pluto

| | |
|---|---|
| **Diameter at equator** | 2 300km/1 429mi |
| **Maximum distance from the Sun** | 7.3 billion km/4.5 billion mi |
| **Minimum distance from the Sun** | 4.4 billion km/2.7 billion mi |
| **Length of year** | 247.7 years |
| **Length of day** | 6 days 9 hours |
| **Atmosphere** | Almost none; probably seasonal traces of methane, nitrogen and carbon monoxide |
| **Surface gravity** | 60cm/sq sec/24in/sq sec |
| **Rings** | None |
| **Satellites** | 1: Charon (1978) |

**Discovered**

1930; named after the Roman god of the underworld.

### *Is it a Planet?*

Pluto may not actually be a planet at all. Some scientists believe instead that it is just the biggest of a large number of icy bodies known as the Kuiper belt. This orbiting belt is thought to be the origin of some of the solar system's comets.

## MOON

| | |
|---|---|
| **Diameter** | 3 476km/2 160mi |
| **Average distance from Earth** | 384 467km/238 908mi |
| **Orbital period** | 27.32 days |
| **Age** | c.4.6 billion years |
| **Atmosphere** | Trace elements only; water ice has however been detected at the poles |
| **Mean surface temperature** | 107°C (day), –153°C (night) |
| **Surface gravity** | 162cm/sq sec/64in/sq sec |
| **Mass** | $7.3483 \times 10^{22}$ kg/$16.2 \times 10^{22}$ lb |
| **Density** | 3.341g/cu cm/208.572 lbm/cu ft |

### *Moon Mystery*

No one knows for certain where the Moon comes from. The most probable theory suggests that a body approximately the size of Mars once hit the Earth, and the Moon is part of the debris from that collision. Others suggest that it may originally have been part of the Earth that broke away, or that it was separate and just happened to be caught by the Earth's gravity, or even that it formed gradually in orbit over time.

## Lunar seas

The Romans thought that the dark areas visible on the surface of the Moon were lunar 'maria', seas. Modern astronomy has shown instead that they are dry plains filled with volcanic rocks. However, how they formed is still problematic.

| Latin name | English name | Latin name | English name |
|---|---|---|---|
| Lacus Mortis | Lake of Death | Mare Serenitatis | Sea of Serenity |
| Lacus Somniorum | Lake of Dreams | Mare Smythii | Smyth's Sea |
| Mare Australe | Southern Sea | Mare Spumans | Foaming Sea |
| Mare Crisium | Sea of Crises | Mare Tranquillitatis | Sea of Tranquillity |
| Mare Fecunditatis | Sea of Fertility | Mare Undarum | Sea of Waves |
| Mare Frigoris | Sea of Cold | Mare Vaporum | Sea of Vapours |
| Mare Humboldtianum | Humboldt's Sea | Oceanus Procellarum | Ocean of Storms |
| Mare Humorum | Sea of Moisture | Palus Epidemiarum | Marsh of Epidemics |
| Mare Imbrium | Sea of Showers | Palus Nebularum | Marsh of Mists |
| Mare Ingenii[1] | Sea of Geniuses | Palus Putredinis | Marsh of Decay |
| Mare Marginis | Marginal Sea | Palus Somnii | Marsh of Sleep |
| Mare Moscoviense[1] | Moscow Sea | Sinus Aestuum | Bay of Heats |
| Mare Nectaris | Sea of Nectar | Sinus Iridum | Bay of Rainbows |
| Mare Nubium | Sea of Clouds | Sinus Medii | Central Bay |
| Mare Orientale[1] | Eastern Sea | Sinus Roris | Bay of Dew |

[1] *On the far side of the Moon.*

## Phases of the Moon

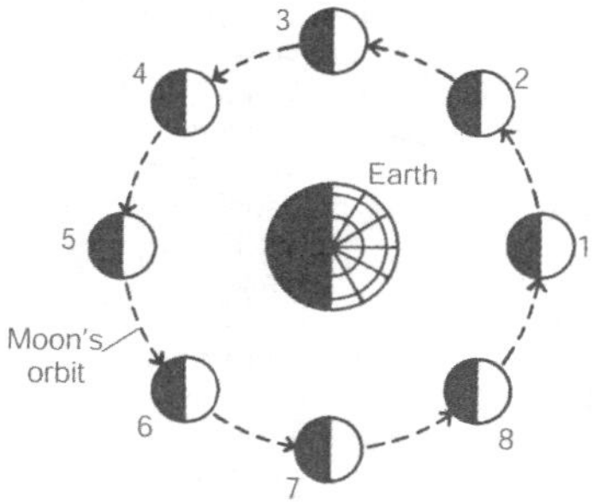


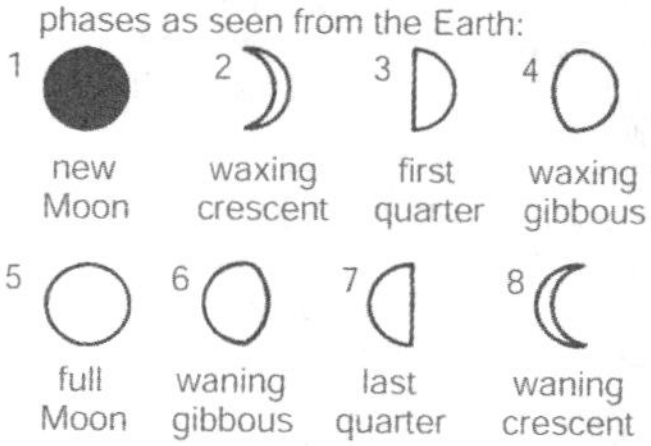


### *Lunar Diets*

Gravity on Earth is approximately six times greater than on the Moon. This means that someone standing on the surface of the Moon would weigh only one-sixth of his or her usual weight on Earth.

# The Universe

## STARS

### The constellations

A constellation is composed of stars which form a group as seen from the Earth. There are 88 constellations in total.

| Latin name | English name |
|---|---|
| Andromeda | Andromeda |
| Antlia | Air Pump |
| Apus | Bird of Paradise |
| Aquarius | Water Bearer |
| Aquila | Eagle |
| Ara | Altar |
| Aries | Ram |
| Auriga | Charioteer |
| Boötes | Herdsman |
| Caelum | Chisel |
| Camelopardalis | Giraffe |
| Cancer | Crab |
| Canes Venatici | Hunting Dogs |
| Canis Major | Great Dog |
| Canis Minor | Little Dog |
| Capricornus | Sea Goat |
| Carina | Keel |
| Cassiopeia | Cassiopeia |
| Centaurus | Centaur |
| Cepheus | Cepheus |
| Cetus | Whale |
| Chamaeleon | Chameleon |
| Circinus | Compasses |
| Columba | Dove |
| Coma Berenices | Berenice's Hair |
| Corona Australis | Southern Crown |
| Corona Borealis | Northern Crown |
| Corvus | Crow |
| Crater | Cup |
| Crux | Southern Cross |
| Cygnus | Swan |
| Delphinus | Dolphin |
| Dorado | Swordfish |
| Draco | Dragon |
| Equuleus | Little Horse |
| Eridanus | River Eridanus |
| Fornax | Furnace |
| Gemini | Twins |
| Grus | Crane |
| Hercules | Hercules |
| Horologium | Clock |
| Hydra | Sea Serpent |
| Hydrus | Water Snake |
| Indus | Indian |
| Lacerta | Lizard |
| Leo | Lion |
| Leo Minor | Little Lion |
| Lepus | Hare |
| Libra | Scales |
| Lupus | Wolf |
| Lynx | Lynx |
| Lyra | Harp |
| Mensa | Table |
| Microscopium | Microscope |
| Monoceros | Unicorn |
| Musca | Fly |
| Norma | Level |
| Octans | Octant |
| Ophiuchus | Serpent Bearer |
| Orion | Orion |
| Pavo | Peacock |
| Pegasus | Winged Horse |
| Perseus | Perseus |
| Phoenix | Phoenix |
| Pictor | Easel |
| Pisces | Fishes |
| Piscis Austrinus | Southern Fish |
| Puppis | Ship's Stern |
| Pyxis | Mariner's Compass |
| Reticulum | Net |
| Sagitta | Arrow |
| Sagittarius | Archer |
| Scorpius | Scorpion |
| Sculptor | Sculptor |
| Scutum | Shield |
| Serpens | Serpent |
| Sextans | Sextant |
| Taurus | Bull |
| Telescopium | Telescope |
| Triangulum | Triangle |
| Triangulum Australe | Southern Triangle |
| Tucana | Toucan |
| Ursa Major | Great Bear |
| Ursa Minor | Little Bear |
| Vela | Sails |
| Virgo | Virgin |
| Volans | Flying Fish |
| Vulpecula | Fox |

## Twinkle Twinkle Little Star

Because stars are so far away, starlight has to travel a great distance to reach Earth, and stars appear only as tiny points of light in the sky. They twinkle because of rapid changes in their brightness caused by moving air in the atmosphere which their light rays pass through. The scientific word for twinkling is *scintillation*. Planets are nearer to us, meaning that they appear larger in the sky, their light is stronger and less susceptible to atmospheric turbulence and so they don't twinkle.

### Brightest stars

The apparent brightness of a star is represented by a number called its magnitude. The larger the number, the fainter the star. The faintest stars visible to the naked eye are slightly fainter than magnitude six. Only approximately 6 000 of the billions of stars in the sky are visible to the naked eye. The table below gives the ten brightest stars visible from the Earth.

| Star name | Distance (light years) | Apparent magnitude | Absolute magnitude |
|---|---|---|---|
| Sirius A | 8.6 | –1.46 | +1.4 |
| Canopus | 98 | –0.72 | –8.5 |
| Arcturus | 36 | –0.06 | –0.3 |
| Alpha Centauri A | 4.3 | –0.01 | +4.4 |
| Vega | 26.5 | +0.04 | +0.5 |
| Capella | 45 | +0.05 | –0.7 |
| Rigel | 900 | +0.14 | –6.8 |
| Procyon A | 11.2 | +0.37 | +2.6 |
| Betelgeuse | 520 | +0.41 | –5.5 |
| Achernar | 118 | +0.51 | –1.0 |

### Nearest stars

| Star name | Distance (light years) | Apparent magnitude | Absolute magnitude |
|---|---|---|---|
| Proxima Centauri | 4.3 | +11.05 | +15.5 |
| Alpha Centauri A | 4.3 | –0.01 | +4.4 |
| Alpha Centauri B | 4.3 | +1.33 | +5.7 |
| Barnard's Star | 5.9 | +9.54 | +13.3 |
| Wolf | 3597.6 | +13.53 | +16.7 |
| Lalande 21185 | 8.1 | +7.50 | +10.5 |
| Sirius A | 8.6 | –1.46 | +1.4 |
| Sirius B | 8.6 | +8.68 | +11.6 |
| Luyten 726 | 8A8.9 | +12.45 | +15.3 |
| UV 726 8B | 8.9 | +12.95 | +15.3 |

## Biggest and Brightest Star

The *Pistol Star* is the largest and most powerful star known. Astronomers think it is approximately 100 times bigger than our Sun, and 10 million times brighter – it emits as much energy in just a few seconds as our Sun does in a whole year. The Pistol Star is only approximately 25 000 light years away from us, but it is hidden behind huge clouds of space dust, so despite its brightness isn't visible from the Earth.

## Star life cycle

A star is a sphere of matter held together entirely by its own gravitational field, generating energy by means of nuclear fusion reactions deep in its interior. Stars shine as a result of the heat and light energy generated by these reactions. A star will go through several different stages during its lifetime, which can be billions of years.

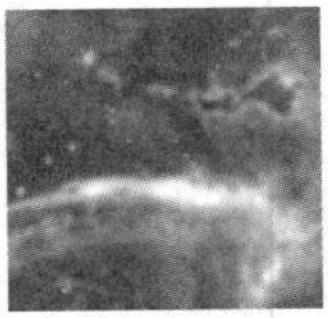

**nebula**

A cloud of gas and dust. As this matter contracts under gravity, the beginnings of the star are created.

### Dwarf Stars

As well as *white dwarf* and *black dwarf* stars, astronomers think that there may also be *brown dwarfs*, very large planets just below the critical mass needed to ignite a stellar nuclear reaction in their own interiors and turn them into stars.

**main-sequence star**

Eventually the star stops contracting and nuclear fusion reactions begin. The main reaction converts hydrogen into helium. The star begins to shine. Stars spend most of their life at this stage, during which their temperature and brightness will barely change. Our Sun is a main-sequence star.

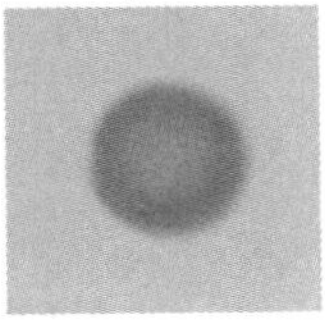

**red giant**

Eventually reactions in the star's core stop as all the hydrogen is exhausted. The star expands, and swells up greatly. It becomes cooler but brighter.

*smaller, less massive stars*

*larger stars*

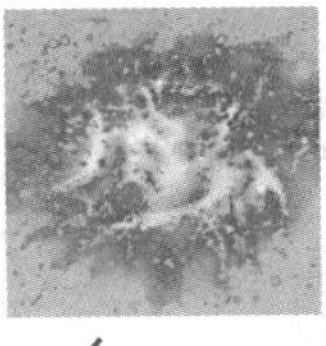

**supernova**

The star explodes, radiating enormous amounts of energy into space. But the core of the star can collapse under its own gravitational field.

**white dwarf**

The star implodes, collapsing into a small, very dense body. It is nearing the end of its life. The remains may eventually cool into a *black dwarf*, which no longer emits visible light.

**neutron star**

If a star has insufficient gravity to collapse entirely, it will become a tiny body, a mass of neutrons only a few miles across, but of very high density.

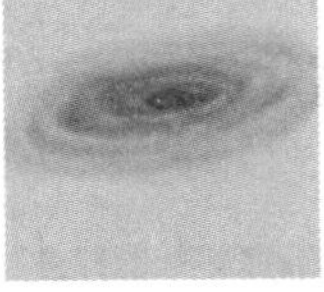

**black hole**

The core collapses in on itself to the point where its gravity is so strong that nothing, not even light, can escape.

## COMETS

**Origin**

*Short-period comets*, those which take less than 200 years to orbit the Sun, come from the Kuiper Belt, a large ring of icy bodies orbiting the Sun just beyond Neptune.

*Long-period comets* take much longer to orbit the Sun (up to 30 million years) and originate in the Oort cloud, a cloud of frozen comet nuclei approximately 100 000 astronomical units[1] away from the Sun. It is estimated that the Oort cloud contains approximately 10 trillion (10 000 000 000 000) comets.

**Number**

Over 850 recorded to date; approximately ten new comets are discovered each year.

**Size, structure and movement**

The solid nucleus of a comet is usually several kilometres in diameter, but may be several hundred kilometres; it consists of ice, dust and solid particles like a large, dirty snowball. When the comet passes close to the Sun, a cloud of gas and dust is ejected from the nucleus, forming a huge head or coma, many thousands of kilometres in diameter. The radiations from the Sun elongate the gas and dust to form one or more tails, often extending millions of kilometres in space. These tails point away from the Sun, but as the comet recedes, the tail will decrease in length until the comet returns to its latent dirty snowball state.

**Selected comets**

The date given is the year in which the comet was first seen.

Halley: 240BC, 76.1 year orbit
Tycho: 1577, orbit not known
Kirch[2]: 1680, 8 814 year orbit
De Chéseaux: 1744, orbit not known
Lexell: 1770, 5.6 year orbit
Encke: 1786, 3.3 year orbit
Flauergues: 1811, 3 094 year orbit
Pons-Winnecke: 1819, 6.34 year orbit
Great Comet: 1843, 512.6 year orbit
Donati: 1858, 1 950 year orbit
Tebbutt: 1861, 409.1 year orbit
Swift-Tuttle: 1862, 125 year orbit
Cruls: 1882, 758.4 year orbit
Wolf: 1884, 8.4 year orbit
Morehouse: 1908, orbit not known
Daylight Comet: 1910, orbit not known
Schwassmann-Wachmann 1: 1925, 15 year orbit
Arend-Roland: 1957, orbit not known
Mrkos: 1957, orbit not known
Humason: 1961, 3 000 year orbit
Seki-Lines: 1962, orbit not known
Ikeya-Seki: 1965, 880 year orbit
Tago-Sato-Kosaka: 1969, 420 000 year orbit
Bennett: 1970, 1 680 year orbit
Kohoutek: 1973, 75 000 year orbit
West: 1975, 500 000 year orbit
IRAS-Araki-Alcock: 1983, orbit not known
Hale-Bopp: 1995, 2 400 year orbit
Hyakutake: 1996, 18 000 year orbit

[1] *One astronomical unit is equal to the mean distance between the Earth and the Sun.*
[2] *Kirch is also known as Newton.*

### Halley's Comet

One of the best-known and brightest comets is Halley's comet. First recorded in 240BC, when it was seen over China, the comet is visible from Earth approximately every 76 years. Most famously it was visible during the Battle of Hastings in 1066, an event depicted in the Bayeux Tapestry. The comet was named after the English astronomer Edmond Halley (1656–1742), who successfully predicted the years in which it would return. Halley's comet was last seen in 1986, and will not be visible from Earth again until 2061.

# ASTEROIDS AND METEORS

## Annual meteor showers

Meteors appear to radiate from the named star region.

| Shower | Dates | Maximum activity |
|---|---|---|
| Quadrantids | 1–6 Jan | 3–4 Jan |
| Lyrids | 19–25 Apr | 22 Apr |
| Alpha-Scorpiids | 20 Apr–19 May | 28 Apr–10 May |
| Eta Aquariids | 1–8 May | 5 May |
| Delta Aquariids | 15 Jul–10 Aug | 28 Jul–5 Aug |
| Perseids | 27 Jul–17 Aug | 11–14 Aug |
| Orionids | 15–25 Oct | 21 Oct |
| Taurids | 25 Oct–25 Nov | 4–14 Nov |
| Leonids | 14–20 Nov | 17–18 Nov |
| Geminids | 8–14 Dec | 13–14 Dec |
| Ursids | 19–24 Dec | 22–23 Dec |

### *Falling Stars*

On the night of 16–17 Nov 1966, the Leonids put on a spectacular display between western North America and the eastern USSR. It is estimated that there were approximately 2 300 meteors every minute.

## Meteoroids and meteorites

**Origin**
Interplanetary; some may originate from the Asteroid Belt, others may have cometary origins.

**Average composition**
Rocky and/or metallic.

**Average size**
From a few micrometres to many metres or even kilometres; smaller meteoroids that burn up in the Earth's atmosphere are known popularly as 'shooting stars'; larger meteoroids that reach the Earth's surface are scientifically termed meteorites.

**Speed**
Meteorites can enter the Earth's atmosphere at speeds of up to 70km/sec, or 45mi/sec. They normally burn up at a height of approximately 100km/60mi.

**First recorded human injury from a meteorite**
Mrs Hewlett Hodges of Sylacauga, Alabama, USA, was badly bruised by a 3.5kg/8 lb meteorite which fell on her home on 30 Nov 1954.

**Heaviest known meteorite**
A meteorite found in Grootfontein, Namibia, in 1920 weighed 60 tonnes/59 tons. It was composed of nickel-rich iron and was almost 3m/9.8ft wide.

## Asteroids

**Origin**
The Asteroid Belt orbiting the Sun between Mars and Jupiter. This region may contain millions of asteroids.

**Number of catalogued asteroids**
Approximately 20 000.

**Largest asteroid**
Ceres (1801); 940km/584mi in diameter.

**Average composition**
Metallic rock with possible addition of water ice.

**First landing on an asteroid**
2001, on the asteroid Eros, by the unmanned NEAR Shoemaker spacecraft.

# ECLIPSES

## Solar eclipses

The eclipse begins in the first country named. In an annular eclipse, the apparent size of the Moon is too small for a total eclipse and a bright ring of Sun remains visible. Eclipse data is given for the years 2000–10.

| Date | Type of eclipse | Visibility path |
|---|---|---|
| 21 Jun 2001 | Total | southern Atlantic Ocean, southern Africa, Madagascar |
| 14 Dec 2001 | Annular | Pacific Ocean, Central America |
| 10 Jun 2002 | Annular | Indonesia, Pacific Ocean, Mexico |
| 4 Dec 2002 | Total | southern Africa, Indian Ocean, Australia |
| 31 May 2003 | Annular | Iceland, Greenland (Denmark), Scotland (UK) |
| 23 Nov 2003 | Total | Antarctica |
| 8 Apr 2005 | Annular/Total | Pacific Ocean, Panama, Venezuela |
| 3 Oct 2005 | Annular | Atlantic Ocean, Spain, Libya, Indian Ocean |
| 29 Mar 2006 | Total | Atlantic Ocean, Libya, Turkey, Russia |
| 22 Sep 2006 | Annular | Guyana, Atlantic Ocean, Indian Ocean |
| 7 Feb 2008 | Annular | Antarctica |
| 1 Aug 2008 | Total | Arctic, Siberia (Russia), China |
| 26 Jan 2009 | Annular | southern Atlantic Ocean, Indian Ocean, Borneo (Indonesia) |
| 22 Jul 2009 | Total | India, China, Pacific Ocean |
| 15 Jan 2010 | Annular | Africa, Indian Ocean, China |
| 11 Jul 2010 | Total | Pacific Ocean, southern Chile |

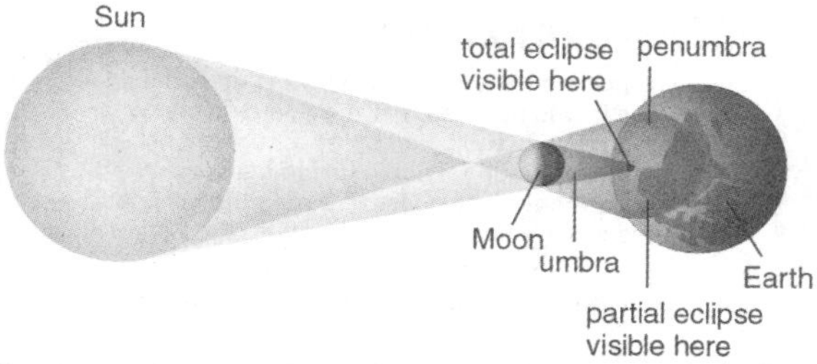

# ECLIPSES

## Lunar eclipses

Eclipse data is given for the years 2000–10.

| Date | Type of eclipse | Time of mid-eclipse (UT[1]) | Where visible |
|---|---|---|---|
| 21 Jan 2000 | Total | 04.45 | North America, part of South America, south-western Europe, western Africa |
| 16 Jul 2000 | Total | 13.57 | Pacific, Australia, south-eastern Asia |
| 9 Jan 2001 | Total | 20.22 | Europe, Asia, Africa |
| 5 Jul 2001 | Partial | 14.57 | Asia, Australia, Pacific |
| 16 May 2003 | Total | 03.41 | Americas, Europe, Africa |
| 9 Nov 2003 | Total | 01.20 | Americas, Europe, Africa, western Asia |
| 4 May 2004 | Total | 20.32 | Europe, Africa, Asia |
| 28 Oct 2004 | Total | 03.05 | Americas, Europe, Africa |
| 17 Oct 2005 | Partial | 12.05 | Eastern Asia, Pacific, North America |
| 7 Sep 2006 | Partial | 18.53 | Australia, Asia, eastern Africa |
| 3 Mar 2007 | Total | 23.22 | Europe, Asia, Africa |
| 28 Aug 2007 | Total | 10.39 | Australia, Pacific, part of North America |
| 21 Feb 2008 | Total | 03.27 | Americas, Europe, Africa |
| 16 Aug 2008 | Partial | 21.12 | Europe, Africa, western Asia |
| 31 Dec 2009 | Partial | 19.23 | Asia, Africa, Europe |
| 26 Jun 2010 | Partial | 11.39 | Pacific Rim |
| 21 Dec 2010 | Total | 08.17 | North and South America |

[1] *Universal Time, equivalent to Greenwich Mean Time (GMT).*

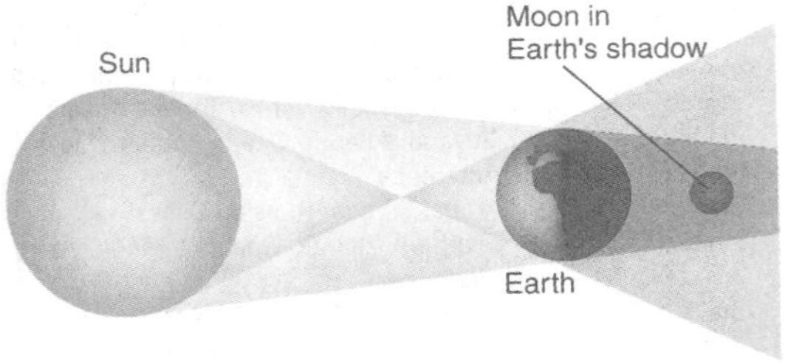


## *Moon-Eating Monsters*

In many ancient cultures eclipses were viewed with great fear. It was believed that the Sun or Moon was being attacked and swallowed up by a huge monster or demon, often a dragon. People would make as much noise and commotion as possible during the eclipse to scare the savage beast away and return the Sun or Moon to them safely.

# ASTRONOMY AND SPACE EXPLORATION

## ASTRONOMERS ROYAL

Astronomer Royal is an honorary title awarded to a distinguished British astronomer. Until 1972, the director of the Royal Observatory at Greenwich automatically became the Astronomer Royal, but the two posts have since been separate.

| Dates | Astronomer Royal |
|---|---|
| 1675–1719 | John Flamsteed |
| 1720–42 | Edmond Halley |
| 1742–62 | James Bradley |
| 1762–4 | Nathaniel Bliss |
| 1765–1811 | Nevil Maskelyne |
| 1811–35 | John Pond |
| 1835–81 | Sir George Airy |
| 1881–1910 | Sir William Christie |
| 1910–33 | Sir Frank Dyson |
| 1933–55 | Sir Harold Spencer Jones |
| 1956–71 | Sir Richard Woolley |
| 1972–82 | Sir Martin Ryle |
| 1982–90 | Sir Francis Graham Smith |
| 1991–5 | Sir Arnold Wolfendale |
| 1995– | Sir Martin Rees |

### Royal Raven Poo

The first Astronomer Royal, John Flamsteed, worked from the Tower of London until the building of the Royal Observatory at Greenwich was completed. Conditions at the Tower were not ideal for astronomy, however. The Tower's famous ravens found Flamsteed's telescopes to be excellent perches, and the unhappy astronomer had trouble gazing at the stars with his telescopes splattered with raven poo.

## SPACE FIRSTS

| Date | Event |
|---|---|
| 4 Oct 1957 | **First satellite** to orbit the Earth, Sputnik 1, is launched by the USSR. |
| 3 Nov 1957 | USSR's Sputnik 2 mission puts the **first living creature**, a dog called Laika, into space; Laika dies soon after launch from overheating and stress. |
| 2 Jan 1959 | USSR's Luna 1 mission **escapes Earth gravity**. |
| 14 Sep 1959 | USSR's Luna 2 mission makes a **lunar impact**. |
| 4 Oct 1959 | USSR's Luna 3 mission is launched and takes a **photo of the far side of the Moon**. |
| 12 Aug 1960 | **First communications satellite**, ECHO 1, is launched by the USA. |
| 31 Jan 1961 | **First 'chimponaut'**, a chimpanzee called Ham, enters space as part of the US Mercury programme. He survives. Previously monkeys, pigs, bears and mice had been used. |
| 12 Apr 1961 | Yuri Gagarin becomes the **first man in space**, making one orbit of the Earth aboard the USSR's Vostok 1 spacecraft. More than 400 people have since followed him. |
| 20 Feb 1962 | John Glenn becomes the **first American** to orbit the Earth. |

## SPACE FIRSTS

| **Date** | **Event** |
|---|---|
| 16 Jun 1963 | Valentina Tereshkova becomes the **first woman** in space aboard the USSR's Vostok 6 spacecraft. |
| 18 Mar 1965 | Alexei Leonov of the USSR's Voshkod 2 mission makes the **first spacewalk**. |
| 1 Mar 1966 | USSR robotic spacecraft Venera 3 lands on **Venus**. |
| 30 May 1966 | US spacecraft Surveyor 1 makes a soft landing on the **Moon**. |
| 21–27 Dec 1968 | Astronauts from the USA's Apollo 8 make the **first manned orbit** of the Moon (10 orbits). |
| 20 Jul 1969 | **First men set foot on the Moon**, landing at the Sea of Tranquillity; they are the USA's Apollo 11 crew members Neil Armstrong and Buzz Aldrin. Michael Collins remains on board the spacecraft. |
| 19 Apr 1971 | Salyut 1, the world's **first space station**, is launched by the USSR. |
| 27 Nov 1971 | Robotic probe from the USSR's Mars 2 mission makes the first crash landing on **Mars**. |
| 3 Mar 1972 | USA's Pioneer 10 spacecraft is launched; it later makes a Jupiter flyby, crosses Pluto's orbit and becomes the **first man-made object to escape the solar system**. |
| 17 Jul 1975 | Apollo (USA) and Soyuz (USSR) **spacecraft dock in space**. |
| 20 Jul 1976 | USA's Viking 1 spacecraft conducts operations on the surface of **Mars**. |
| 12 Apr 1981 | USA commences **space shuttle flights**. |
| 13 Mar 1986 | Robotic probe Giotto, launched by the European Space Agency, has a close-up rendezvous with **Halley's comet**. |
| 19 Feb 1986 | Main module of Mir, the **first space station designed for semi-permanent orbit**, is launched by the USSR. |
| 24 Apr 1990 | Hubble Space Telescope, the **first optical space-based telescope**, is launched. |
| 2 Dec 1990 | **First passenger pays to go into space** aboard a Russian Soyuz TM11 flight. |
| 18 May 1991 | Helen Sharman becomes the **first British person in space** with the Soyuz TM12 mission. |
| 31 Oct 2000 | **International Space Station** receives its first residents, from the USA, Russia, Europe, Canada and Japan. |
| 28 Apr 2001 | **First space tourist** visits the International Space Station. |
| 2 Jun 2003 | Beagle 2, **Britain's first Mars probe**, is launched as part of the European Space Agency's Mars Express programme. |

### *Astronomy Gastronomy*

During the eight days of the Apollo 11 mission in 1969, the astronauts had a choice of two meals. NASA says that 'Meal A was bacon squares, peaches, sugar cookie cubes, coffee and pineapple-grapefruit drink. Meal B included beef stew, cream of chicken soup, date fruitcake, grape punch and orange drink'.

## MOON LANDINGS

| Mission | Launch | Duration (hours: minutes) | Crew |
|---|---|---|---|
| Apollo 11 | 16–24 Jul 1969 | 195:18 | Neil A Armstrong, Michael Collins, Edwin E 'Buzz' Aldrin, Jr |
| On 20 Jul the first human beings land on the Moon, at the Sea of Tranquillity. Scientific instruments are deployed and 20kg/44lbs of moon rock brought back to Earth. | | | |
| Apollo 12 | 14–24 Nov 1969 | 244:36 | Charles 'Pete' Conrad, Jr, Richard F Gordon, Jr, Alan L Bean |
| The second landing is made on 19 Nov at the Ocean of Storms. Geological studies are undertaken and parts of the unmanned Surveyor 3 craft retrieved. | | | |
| Apollo 14 | 31 Jan–9 Feb 1971 | 216:02 | Alan B Shepard, Jr, Stuart A Roosa, Edgar D Mitchell |
| The third mission lands on 5 Feb in the Fra Mauro area, the area scheduled for the failed Apollo 13 mission (see below). The first golf shot on the Moon is played by Alan Shepard. | | | |
| Apollo 15 | 26 Jul–7 Aug 1971 | 295:12 | David R Scott, James B Irwin, Alfred M Worden |
| On 30 Jul the fourth landing takes place. The Lunar Roving Vehicle is used for the first time. Improved spacesuits give astronauts the longest stay so far, at almost 67 hours. | | | |
| Apollo 16 | 16–27 Apr 1972 | 265:51 | John W Young, Charles M Duke, Jr Thomas K Mattingly II |
| The fifth Moon landing is made on 20 Apr in the Descartes Highlands area. The first studies of lunar highland geology are undertaken. | | | |
| Apollo 17 | 7–19 Dec 1972 | 301:52 | Eugene A Cernan, Ronald E Evans, Harrison H 'Jack' Schmitt |
| The final and longest of the Apollo missions touches down successfully on 11 Dec in the Taurus–Littrow highlands and valley area. Harrison Schmitt is the first scientist–astronaut to walk on the Moon. | | | |

*Note: Apollo 13 (11–17 Apr 1970) was to have been the third Moon landing. Carrying James A Lovell, Jr, John L Swigert, Jr and Fred W Haise, Jr, the mission had to be aborted without landing on the Moon after an explosion in an oxygen tank. The mission lasted 142 hours and 54 minutes.*

### *Moon Landings Hoax?*

Conspiracy theorists suggest that perhaps human beings have never walked on the Moon, and that NASA faked the pictures from the lunar expeditions. Although these claims attracted a great deal of attention and made great headlines in the press, all the hoax theories have, in the past, been repudiated by scientists and experts.

## SPACE RECORDS

| | |
|---|---|
| Most time spent in space | Russian cosmonaut Sergei Avdeyev spent a total of 747 days 14 hours 22 minutes aboard the Mir space station, during three separate flights between Jul 1992 and Jul 1999. |
| Most space flights | US astronaut John W Young completed six space flights from Earth between 1962 and 1983, including acting as spacecraft commander for Apollo 16 (16–27 Apr 1972) and spacecraft commander of the first space shuttle flight (12–14 Apr 1981). |
| Longest space walk | US astronauts Susan Helms and Jim Voss both spent 8 hours 56 minutes in space outside the International Space Station on 11 Mar 2001. |
| Longest space shuttle flight | The space shuttle Columbia, with a crew of five, completed a mission of 17 days 15 hours 53 minutes between 19 Nov and 7 Dec 1996. |
| Shortest manned space flight | US astronaut Alan Shepard, aboard a Mercury–Redstone rocket, made a sub-orbital flight lasting 15 minutes 28 seconds on 5 May 1961. |
| Longest time spent on the surface of the Moon | During the Apollo 17 lunar mission (7–19 Dec 1972), the crew spent 74 hours 59 minutes on the Moon's surface. |
| Longest time spent in orbit around the Moon | During the Apollo 17 lunar mission (7–19 Dec 1972), Ronald E Evans spent 147 hours 41 minutes in orbit around the Moon. |
| Man-made object furthest from Earth | On 17 Feb 1998 Voyager 1, launched on 5 Sep 1977, became the most remote man-made object in the universe in its journey towards interstellar regions. |
| Oldest person in space | John Glenn, aged 77, went into space aboard the space shuttle Discovery on 15 Jan 1998. On 20 Feb 1962 he had become the first American to orbit the Earth. |
| Most isolated space traveller | During the USA's Apollo 15 lunar mission between 30 Jul and 1 Aug 1971, Alfred M Worden stayed in orbit around the Moon while his fellow crew members explored its surface, and travelled 3 596.4km/2 234.75mi from the nearest human being. |
| Most expensive individual space trip | Dennis Tito, a US businessman, reportedly paid the Russian space administration $20 million, the equivalent of £14 million, to go aboard the International Space Station from 28 Apr to 6 May 2001. |

### *One Small Step*

At 4:18pm (US Eastern Daylight Time) on 20 Jul 1969, the Apollo 11 lunar module touched down for the first time on the surface of the Moon and commander Neil Armstrong reported that 'the Eagle has landed'. At 10:56pm Armstrong stepped, left foot first, onto the Moon and declared 'That's one small step for a man, one giant leap for mankind'. He said the Moon has 'a stark beauty all its own'. The astronauts later spoke to the President in the White House, in what Nixon described as 'the most historic telephone call ever made', and left a plaque stating 'Here men from the planet Earth first set foot on the Moon. July 1969 AD. We came in peace for all mankind.'

# THE EARTH

There are no universally agreed estimates of many of the natural phenomena given in this section. Surveys make use of different criteria for identifying natural boundaries, and use different techniques of measurement. The sizes of continents, oceans, seas, deserts and rivers are particularly subject to variation.

## EARTH

| | |
|---|---|
| **Age** | 4.5 billion years (accurate to within a very small percentage of possible error) |
| **Distance from Sun (mean)** | 150 million km/93 million mi |
| **Surface area** | 510 069 120 sq km/196 938 800 sq mi |
| **Mass** | $5\,976 \times 10^{24}$ kg/$13\,175 \times 10^{24}$ lb |
| **Surface gravity** | 980cm/sq sec/386in/sq sec |
| **Land surface (approximate)** | 148 million sq km/57 million sq mi (c.29% of total area) |
| **Water surface (approximate)** | 361.6 million sq km/140 million sq mi (c.71% of total area) |
| **Circumference (equator)** | 40 076km/24 902mi |
| **Circumference (meridian)** | 40 000km/24 860mi |
| **Diameter (equator)** | 12 757km/7 927mi |
| **Diameter (meridian)** | 12 714km/7 900mi |
| **Period of axial rotation** | 23 hours 56 minutes 4.0966 seconds |
| **Temperature at core** | 4 500°C/8 100°F |

### *Ice Kingdom*

Ice permanently covers approximately 10% of the land surface of the Earth, with the majority of the ice cover at the South Pole. But there have been several great ice ages in the past, when a much larger part of the Earth's surface was covered with ice. The most famous, commonly known as 'the Ice Age', was during the Pleistocene period from approximately 2 million years ago to approximately 10 000 years ago.

## Composition of the Earth's crust

| Element | % weight |
|---|---|
| Oxygen | 46.60 |
| Silicon | 27.72 |
| Aluminium | 8.13 |
| Iron | 5.0 |
| Calcium | 3.63 |
| Sodium | 2.83 |
| Potassium | 2.59 |
| Magnesium | 2.09 |
| Others | 1.41 |

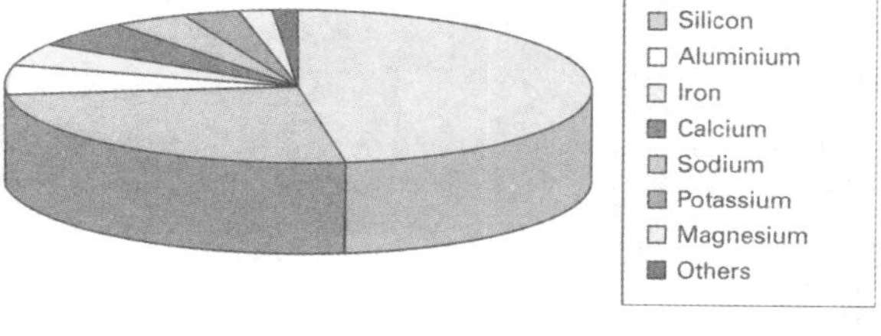

## Structure of the Earth

The outermost crust is approximately 10km/6mi thick under the oceans and 30km/19mi thick where there are continents.

A dozen or so crustal plates – the *lithosphere* – slide over the less rigid *asthenosphere*. Collisions between the plates produce folded mountains, and zones of seismic activity are concentrated along the plate boundaries.

Molten metallic core of iron and nickel, possibly with a solid core at the very centre at a temperature of around 4 000°C/7 200°F.

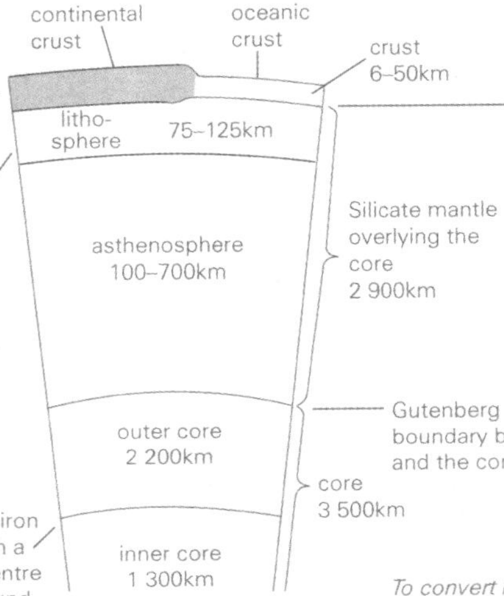


moho (Mohorovicic or Mohorovicician discontinuity, the boundary between the rocks of the Earth's crust and the different rock of the mantle)

Gutenberg discontinuity (the boundary between the mantle and the core)

*To convert kilometres to miles, multiply by 0.6214.*

## Atmosphere

**The Earth's atmosphere is composed of air, generally containing 78% nitrogen, 21% oxygen and 1% argon, together with carbon dioxide, hydrogen, ozone and methane, and traces of the other rare gases. The amount of water vapour present depends on the temperature and humidity. The temperature is the balance between convection and radiation. The amount of heat contained at any level depends on the pressure or density as well as the temperature. The temperature falls steadily as the influence of solar radiation lessens, reaching a minimum approximately 80km/50mi above the ground; then it increases again.**

| Gas | % volume |
|---|---|
| Nitrogen | 78.1 |
| Oxygen | 20.95 |
| Argon | 0.934 |
| Carbon dioxide | 0.031 |
| Neon | 0.00182 |
| Helium | 0.00052 |
| Methane | 0.0002 |
| Krypton | 0.00011 |
| Hydrogen | 0.00005 |
| Nitrous oxide | 0.00005 |
| Ozone | 0.00004 |
| Xenon | 0.000009 |

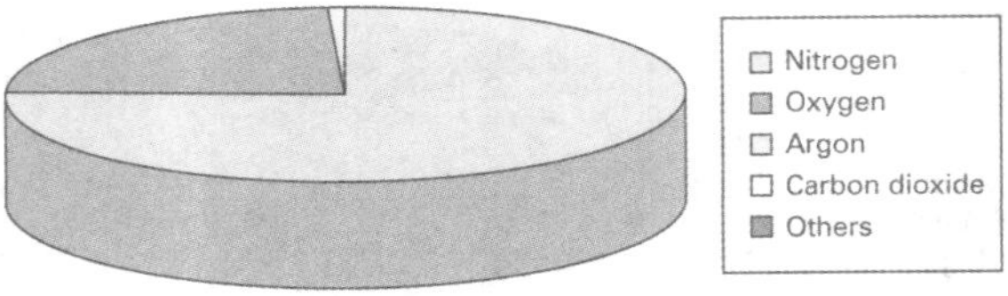

The atmosphere is divided into several layers:

**Thermosphere**
Air is very thin. Temperature increases with height. Composed of the *ionosphere*, which reflects radio waves back to Earth enabling signals to be transmitted around the curved surface of the Earth, the *ionopause* transitional layer, and the *exosphere*, the outermost layer of the Earth's atmosphere, approximately 500km above the surface, from which light gases can escape into space.

**Mesopause**
Transitional layer between the mesosphere and the thermosphere, approximately 80–85km above the surface.

**Mesosphere**
Middle atmosphere, up to approximately 85km above the surface. Temperature decreases with height.

**Stratopause**
Transitional layer, approximately 50–55km above the surface.

**Stratosphere**
Contains very few clouds. Aircraft usually fly in this layer above the weather disturbances in the troposphere. Temperatures increase with height, and typical pressure is only a hundredth of that on the surface. Also includes the *ozone layer*, approximately 20–40km above the surface.

**Tropopause**
Transitional layer.

**Troposphere**
Lower part of the atmosphere, from the surface up to a height varying from approximately 9km at the poles to 17km at the equator. Contains almost all of the clouds. Temperature decreases with height.

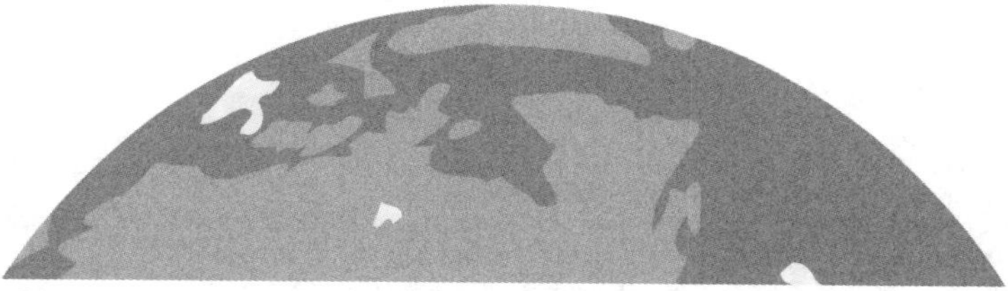

*Note: Diagram not to scale. To convert kilometres to miles, multiply by 0.6214.*

# EARTHQUAKE SEVERITY MEASUREMENT

## Modified Mercalli intensity scale (1956 revision)

The Mercalli scale measures the intensity of earthquake shocks in terms of the damage they cause. It was named after the Italian geologist Giuseppe Mercalli (1850–1914).

**Intensity value / description**

I Not felt; marginal and long-period effects of large earthquakes.

II Felt by persons at rest, on upper floors or favourably placed.

III Felt indoors; hanging objects swing; vibration like passing of light trucks; duration estimated; may not be recognized as an earthquake.

IV Hanging objects swing; vibration like passing of heavy trucks, or sensation of a jolt like a heavy ball striking the walls; standing cars rock; windows, dishes, doors rattle; glasses clink; crockery clashes; in the upper range of IV, wooden walls and frames creak.

V Felt outdoors; direction estimated; sleepers awoken; liquids disturbed, some spilled; small unstable objects displaced or upset; doors swing, close, open; shutters, pictures move; pendulum clocks stop, start, change rate.

VI Felt by all; many frightened and run outdoors; persons walk unsteadily; windows, dishes, glassware break; knick-knacks, books, etc, fall off shelves; pictures fall off walls; furniture moves or overturns; weak plaster and masonry D crack; small bells ring (church, school); trees, bushes shake visibly, or heard to rustle.

VII Difficult to stand; noticed by drivers; hanging objects quiver; furniture breaks; damage to masonry D, including cracks; weak chimneys broken at roof line; fall of plaster, loose bricks, stones, tiles, cornices, also unbraced parapets and architectural ornaments; some cracks in masonry C; waves on ponds, water turbid with mud; small slides and caving in along sand or gravel banks; large bells ring; concrete irrigation ditches damaged.

VIII Steering of cars affected; damage to masonry C and partial collapse; some damage to masonry B; none to masonry A; fall of stucco and some masonry walls; twisting, fall of chimneys, factory stacks, monuments, towers, elevated tanks; frame houses move on foundations if not bolted down; loose panel walls thrown out; decayed piling broken off; branches broken from trees; changes in flow or temperature of springs and wells; cracks in wet ground and on steep slopes.

IX General panic; masonry D destroyed; masonry C heavily damaged, sometimes with complete collapse; masonry B seriously damaged; general damage to foundations; frame structures, if not bolted, shift off foundations; frames racked; serious damage to reservoirs; underground pipes break; conspicuous cracks in ground; in alluviated areas sand and mud ejected, earthquake fountains, sand craters.

X Most masonry and frame structures destroyed with their foundations; some well-built wooden structures and bridges destroyed; serious damage to dams, dykes, embankments; large landslides; water thrown on banks of canals, rivers, lakes, etc; sand and mud shifted horizontally on beaches and flat land; rails bent slightly.

XI Rails bent greatly; underground pipelines completely out of service.

XII Damage nearly total; large rock masses displaced; lines of sight and level distorted; objects thrown into the air.

*Notes: Masonry type*

*A Good workmanship, mortar and design; reinforced, especially laterally, and bound together using steel, concrete, etc; designed to resist lateral forces.*

*B Good workmanship and mortar; reinforced, but not designed in detail to resist lateral forces.*

*C Ordinary workmanship and mortar; no extreme weakness like failing to tie in at corners, but neither reinforced nor designed against horizontal forces.*

*D Weak materials, such as adobe; poor mortar; low standards of workmanship; weak horizontally.*

## Richter scale

The Richter scale measures earthquake magnitude in terms of seismic energy released. It is logarithmic; a quake of magnitude 2 is barely perceptible, 5 is rather strong, and those over 7 are very strong. It was devised by US seismologist Dr Charles F Richter (1900–85).

| Magnitude | Relative amount of energy released | Magnitude | Relative amount of energy released |
|---|---|---|---|
| 1 | 1 | 6 | 29 million |
| 2 | 31 | 7 | 890 million |
| 3 | 960 | 8 | 28 billion |
| 4 | 30 000 | 9 | 850 billion |
| 5 | 920 000 | | |

### *Whole Lotta Shakin'*

The strongest earthquake ever recorded struck Chile on 22 May 1960, according to the US Geological Survey's Earthquake Hazards Program. The massive quake measured 9.5 on the Richter Scale.

## CONTINENTS

A continent is any of the seven main land masses of the world, namely Europe, Asia, North America, South America, Africa, Australia and Oceania and Antarctica. A continent's area also includes the submerged continental shelf around the edge of the exposed land mass.

| Continent | Area | Percentage of total land mass | Lowest point below sea level | Highest elevation |
|---|---|---|---|---|
| Africa | 30 293 000 sq km/ 11 696 000 sq mi | 20.2% | Lake Assal, Djibouti –156m/–512ft | Mt Kilimanjaro, Tanzania 5 895m/19 340ft |
| Antarctica | 13 975 000 sq km/ 5 396 000 sq mi | 9.3% | Bently sub-glacial trench –2 538m/–8 327ft | Vinson Massif 5 140m/16 864ft |
| Asia | 44 493 000 sq km/ 17 179 000 sq mi | 29.6% | Dead Sea, Israel/ Jordan/West Bank –400m/–1 312ft | Mt Everest, China/ Nepal 8 850m/29 035ft |
| Australia and Oceania[1] | 8 945 000 sq km/ 3 454 000 sq mi | 5.9% | Lake Eyre, Australia –15m/–49ft | Puncak Jaya, Indonesia 5 030m/16 503ft |
| Europe[2] | 10 245 000 sq km/ 3 956 000 sq mi | 6.8% | Caspian Sea, Iran/ Russia/Turkmenistan/ Kazakhstan/Azerbaijan –29m/–94ft | Mt Elbrus, Russia 5 642m/18 510ft |
| North America | 24 454 000 sq km/ 9 442 000 sq mi | 16.3% | Death Valley, California, USA –86m/–282ft | Mt McKinley, Alaska, USA 6 194m/20 322ft |
| South America | 17 838 000 sq km/ 6 887 000 sq mi | 11.9% | Península Valdés, Argentina –40m/–131ft | Aconcagua, Argentina 6 960m/22 835ft |

[1] *The land mass of Australia plus the wider continental area.*

[2] *Including the former western USSR.*

# OCEANS

## Continental drift

Continental drift is the theory that the continents were formed as a result of the breaking up of a single land mass into several smaller land masses, which slowly drifted apart across the Earth's surface. Arrows indicate the direction of drift.

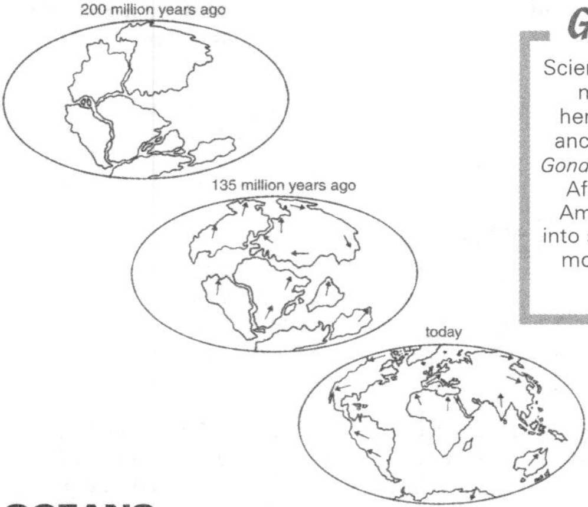


### Gondwana

Scientists believe that more than 200 million years ago the southern hemisphere was dominated by an ancient 'supercontinent', known as *Gondwana*, that connected Antarctica, Africa, Australia, India and South America. Gondwana disintegrated into smaller continents which are still moving – Australia heads north at about 5cm/2in each year.

## OCEANS

Water covers approximately 71% of the Earth's surface. Four oceans were traditionally recognized, with the International Hydrographic Organization (IHO) officially delimiting a fifth, the Southern Ocean, in 2000. However, the Atlantic Ocean and the Pacific Ocean are often divided (by the equator) into the North Atlantic and South Atlantic, and the North Pacific and South Pacific, leading to the recognition of seven oceans.

| Ocean | Area | Average depth | Greatest depth |
|---|---|---|---|
| Arctic | 14 056 000 sq km/ 5 427 021 sq mi | 1 330m/4 400ft | Molloy Deep 5 680m/18 400ft |
| Atlantic | 76 762 000 sq km/ 29 637 808 sq mi | 3 700m/12 100ft | Puerto Rico Trench 8 648m/28 372ft |
| Indian | 68 556 000 sq km/ 26 469 471 sq mi | 3 900m/12 800ft | Java Trench 7 725m/25 344ft |
| Pacific | 155 557 000 sq km/ 60 060 557 sq mi | 4 300m/14 100ft | Mariana Trench 11 040m/36 220ft |
| Southern | 20 327 000 sq km/ 7 848 254 sq mi | 4 500m/14 800ft | South Sandwich Trench 7 235m/32 737ft |

### Water Water Everywhere

The Pacific Ocean alone covers approximately 28% of the Earth's surface, making this single ocean bigger than all the land mass of the Earth.

## MAJOR OCEAN TRENCHES

Ocean trenches are long, narrow steep-sided depressions in an ocean floor. They are commonly found running parallel to a continent. There are more than 20 in total; the majority are found in the Pacific Ocean. Data for selected trenches is given.

| Trench | Ocean | Greatest depth |
|---|---|---|
| Cayman | Atlantic | 7 686m/25 216ft |
| Japan | Pacific | 8 513m/27 929ft |
| Java | Indian | 7 725m/25 344ft |
| Kermadec | Pacific | 10 047m/32 962ft |
| Kuril | Pacific | 10 542m/34 587ft |
| Mariana (Marianas) | Pacific | 11 040m/36 220ft |
| Middle America | Pacific | 6 669m/21 880ft |
| Nansei Shoto (Ryukyu) | Pacific | 7 507m/24 629ft |
| Palau | Pacific | 7 986m/26 200ft |
| Peru-Chile (Atacama) | Pacific | 8 065m/26 460ft |
| Philippine (Mindanao) | Pacific | 10 539m/34 578ft |
| Puerto Rico | Atlantic | 8 648m/28 372ft |
| Romanche | Atlantic | 7 758m/25 453ft |
| South Sandwich | Southern | 7 235m/32 737ft |
| Tonga | Pacific | 10 882m/35 702ft |
| Yap (West Caroline) | Pacific | 8 527m/27 976ft |

*Note: Other major trenches include the Aleutian, the Izu Bonin and the Bougainville, all in the Pacific Ocean.*

## LARGEST SEAS

Oceans are excluded.

| Sea | Area[1] |
|---|---|
| Coral Sea | 4 791 000 sq km/1 850 000 sq mi |
| Arabian Sea | 3 863 000 sq km/1 492 000 sq mi |
| South China (Nan) Sea | 3 685 000 sq km/1 423 000 sq mi |
| Mediterranean Sea | 2 516 000 sq km/971 000 sq mi |
| Bering Sea | 2 304 000 sq km/890 000 sq mi |
| Bay of Bengal | 2 172 000 sq km/839 000 sq mi |
| Sea of Okhotsk | 1 590 000 sq km/614 000 sq mi |
| Gulf of Mexico | 1 543 000 sq km/596 000 sq mi |
| Gulf of Guinea | 1 533 000 sq km/592 000 sq mi |
| Barents Sea | 1 405 000 sq km/542 000 sq mi |
| Norwegian Sea | 1 383 000 sq km/534 000 sq mi |
| Gulf of Alaska | 1 327 000 sq km/512 000 sq mi |
| Hudson Bay | 1 232 000 sq km/476 000 sq mi |
| Greenland Sea | 1 205 000 sq km/465 000 sq mi |
| Arafura Sea | 1 037 000 sq km/400 000 sq mi |
| Philippine Sea | 1 036 000 sq km/400 000 sq mi |
| Sea of Japan (East Sea) | 978 000 sq km/378 000 sq mi |
| East Siberian Sea | 901 000 sq km/348 000 sq mi |
| Kara Sea | 883 000 sq km/341 000 sq mi |
| East China Sea | 664 000 sq km/256 000 sq mi |

## LARGEST ISLANDS

| Sea | Area[1] |
|---|---|
| Andaman Sea | 565 000 sq km/218 000 sq mi |
| North Sea | 520 000 sq km/201 000 sq mi |
| Black Sea | 508 000 sq km/196 000 sq mi |
| Red Sea | 453 000 sq km/175 000 sq mi |
| Baltic Sea | 414 000 sq km/160 000 sq mi |
| Arabian Gulf | 239 000 sq km/92 000 sq mi |
| St Lawrence Gulf | 238 000 sq km/92 000 sq mi |

[1] *Areas are rounded to the nearest 1 000 sq km/sq mi.*

### *Seven Seas*

The term 'Seven Seas' is frequently used to refer to all the seas and oceans of the world. There are many suggestions as to the seas it specifically refers to, but it is commonly thought to refer to the oceans: Arctic, Antarctic, North Atlantic, South Atlantic, North Pacific, South Pacific and Indian Ocean.

## LARGEST ISLANDS

| Island | Area[1] |
|---|---|
| Australia[2] | 7 692 300 sq km/2 970 000 sq mi |
| Greenland | 2 175 600 sq km/840 000 sq mi |
| New Guinea | 790 000 sq km/305 000 sq mi |
| Borneo | 737 000 sq km/285 000 sq mi |
| Madagascar | 587 000 sq km/226 600 sq mi |
| Baffin | 507 000 sq km/195 800 sq mi |
| Sumatra | 425 000 sq km/164 100 sq mi |
| Honshu (Hondo) | 228 000 sq km/88 000 sq mi |
| Great Britain | 219 000 sq km/84 600 sq mi |
| Victoria, Canada | 217 300 sq km/83 900 sq mi |
| Ellesmere, Canada | 196 000 sq km/75 700 sq mi |
| Celebes | 174 000 sq km/67 200 sq mi |
| South Island, New Zealand | 151 000 sq km/58 300 sq mi |
| Java | 129 000 sq km/49 800 sq mi |
| North Island, New Zealand | 114 000 sq km/44 000 sq mi |
| Cuba | 110 900 sq km/42 800 sq mi |
| Newfoundland | 109 000 sq km/42 100 sq mi |
| Luzon | 105 000 sq km/40 500 sq mi |
| Iceland | 103 000 sq km/39 800 sq mi |
| Mindanao | 94 600 sq km/36 500 sq mi |
| Novaya Zemlya (two islands) | 90 600 sq km/35 000 sq mi |
| Ireland | 84 100 sq km/32 500 sq mi |
| Hokkaido | 78 500 sq km/30 300 sq mi |
| Hispaniola | 77 200 sq km/29 800 sq mi |
| Sakhalin | 75 100 sq km/29 000 sq mi |
| Tierra del Fuego | 71 200 sq km/27 500 sq mi |

[1] *Areas are rounded to the nearest 100 sq km/sq mi.*
[2] *Sometimes discounted, as a continent.*

## LARGEST LAKES

| Lake | Location | Area[1] |
|---|---|---|
| Caspian Sea | Iran/Russia/Turkmenistan/ Kazakhstan/Azerbaijan | 371 000 sq km/143 240 sq mi[2] |
| Superior | USA/Canada | 82 260 sq km/31 760 sq mi[3] |
| Aral Sea | Uzbekistan/Kazakhstan | 64 500 sq km/24 900 sq mi[2] |
| Victoria | east Africa | 62 940 sq km/24 300 sq mi |
| Huron | USA/Canada | 59 580 sq km/23 000 sq mi[3] |
| Michigan | USA | 58 020 sq km/22 400 sq mi |
| Tanganyika | east Africa | 32 000 sq km/12 360 sq mi |
| Baikal | Russia | 31 500 sq km/12 160 sq mi |
| Great Bear | Canada | 31 330 sq km/12 100 sq mi |
| Great Slave | Canada | 28 570 sq km/11 030 sq mi |
| Erie | USA/Canada | 25 710 sq km/9 930 sq mi[3] |
| Winnipeg | Canada | 24 390 sq km/9 420 sq mi |
| Malawi/Nyasa | east Africa | 22 490 sq km/8 680 sq mi |
| Balkhash | Kazakhstan | 17 000–22 000 sq km/6 560–8 490 sq mi[2] |
| Ontario | USA/Canada | 19 270 sq km/7 440 sq mi[3] |
| Ladoga | Russia | 18 130 sq km/7 000 sq mi |
| Maracaibo | Venezuela | 13 010 sq km/5 020 sq mi[4] |
| Patos | Brazil | 10 140 sq km/3 920 sq mi[4] |
| Chad | west Africa | 10 000–26 000 sq km/3 860–10 040 sq mi |
| Onega | Russia | 9 800 sq km/3 780 sq mi |
| Rudolf | east Africa | 9 100 sq km/3 510 sq mi |
| Eyre | Australia | 8 800 sq km/3 400 sq mi[4] |
| Titicaca | Peru/Bolivia | 8 300 sq km/3 200 sq mi |

*Note: The Caspian and Aral Seas, being entirely surrounded by land, are classified as lakes.*

[1] *Areas are rounded to the nearest 10 sq km/sq mi.*
[2] *Salt lakes.*
[3] *Average of areas given by Canada and USA.*
[4] *Salt lagoons.*

## GREAT LAKES

A group of five interconnected lakes, covering more than 244 000 sq km/94 000 sq mi, which separate eastern Canada from the USA. They contain approximately one-fifth of the Earth's fresh surface water.

| Great Lake | Location | Area | Volume |
|---|---|---|---|
| Superior | USA/Canada | 82 260 sq km/31 760 sq mi[1] | 12 100 cu km/2 900 cu mi |
| Huron | USA/Canada | 59 580 sq km/23 000 sq mi[1] | 3 540 cu km/850 cu mi |
| Michigan | USA | 58 020 sq km/22 400 sq mi | 4 920 cu km/1 180 cu mi |
| Erie | USA/Canada | 25 710 sq km/9 930 sq mi[1] | 484 cu km/116 cu mi |
| Ontario | USA/Canada | 19 270 sq km/7 440 sq mi[1] | 1 640 cu km/393 cu mi |

[1] *Average of areas given by Canada and USA.*

### Lovely Lake

Lake Ontario's name is said to come from an Iroquois word meaning 'beautiful lake'.

## LONGEST RIVERS

| River | Outflow | Length[1] |
|---|---|---|
| Nile–Kagera–Ruvuvu–Ruvusu–Luvironza | Mediterranean Sea (Egypt) | 6 690km/4 160mi |
| Amazon–Ucayali–Tambo–Ene–Apurimac | Atlantic Ocean (Brazil) | 6 570km/4 080mi |
| Mississippi–Missouri–Jefferson–Beaverhead–Red Rock | Gulf of Mexico (USA) | 6 020km/3 740mi |
| Chang Jiang (Yangtze) | East China Sea (China) | 5 980km/3 720mi |
| Yenisey–Angara–Selenga–Ider | Kara Sea (Russia) | 5 870km/3 650mi |
| Amur–Argun–Kerulen | Tartar Strait (Russia) | 5 780km/3 590mi |
| Ob–Irtysh | Gulf of Ob, Kara Sea (Russia) | 5 410km/3 360mi |
| Plata–Parana–Grande | Atlantic Ocean (Argentina/Uruguay) | 4 880km/3 030mi |
| Huang He (Yellow) | Yellow Sea (China) | 4 840km/3 010mi |
| Congo–Lualaba | South Atlantic Ocean (Angola/Democratic Republic of Congo) | 4 630km/2 880mi |
| Lena | Laptev Sea (Russia) | 4 400km/2 730mi |
| Mackenzie–Slave–Peace–Finlay | Beaufort Sea (Canada) | 4 240km/2 630mi |
| Mekong | South China Sea (Vietnam) | 4 180km/2 600mi |
| Niger | Gulf of Guinea (Nigeria) | 4 100km/2 550mi |

[1] *Lengths are given to the nearest 10km/mi, and include the river plus tributaries comprising the longest watercourse.*

## HIGHEST WATERFALLS

| Waterfall | Location | Height[1] |
|---|---|---|
| Angel (upper fall) | Venezuela | 807m/2 648ft |
| Itatinga | Brazil | 628m/2 060ft |
| Cuquenán | Guyana/Venezuela | 610m/2 001ft |
| Ormeli | Norway | 563m/1 847ft |
| Tysse | Norway | 533m/1 749ft |
| Pilao | Brazil | 524m/1 719ft |
| Ribbon | USA | 491m/1 611ft |
| Vestre Mardola | Norway | 468m/1 535ft |
| Kaieteur | Guyana | 457m/1 500ft |
| Cleve-Garth | New Zealand | 450m/1 476ft |

[1] *Height denotes individual leaps.*

### Niagara Falls

Almost 170 000 cu m/6 million cu ft of water per minute crashes over Niagara Falls, on the US–Canadian border. But it isn't just water that has gone over the Falls. The first person to make the 52m/170ft drop over the Horseshoe Falls in a barrel was 63-year old Annie Taylor, who pioneered the trip on 24 Oct 1901. She has since been followed by almost 20 others in various contraptions, some of whom have perished. The only man to survive without any protection is one Kirk Jones of Michigan, who took the plunge on 21 Oct 2003.

## DEEPEST CAVES

| Cave | Location | Depth |
|---|---|---|
| Jean Bernard | France | 1 494m/4 902ft |
| Snezhnaya | Georgia | 1 340m/4 396ft |
| Puertas de Illamina | Spain | 1 338m/4 390ft |
| Pierre-Saint-Martin | France | 1 321m/4 334ft |
| Sistema Huautla | Mexico | 1 240m/4 068ft |
| Berger | France | 1 198m/3 930ft |
| Vqerdi | Spain | 1 195m/3 921ft |
| Dachstein-Mammuthöhle | Austria | 1 174m/3 852ft |
| Zitu | Spain | 1 139m/3 737ft |
| Badalona | Spain | 1 130m/3 707ft |
| Batmanhöhle | Austria | 1 105m/3 625ft |
| Schneeloch | Austria | 1 101m/3 612ft |
| G E S Malaga | Spain | 1 070m/3 510ft |
| Lamprechstofen | Austria | 1 024m/3 360ft |

## LARGEST DESERTS

| Desert | Location | Area[1] |
|---|---|---|
| Sahara | north Africa | 8 600 000 sq km/3 320 000 sq mi |
| Arabian | south-west Asia | 2 330 000 sq km/900 000 sq mi |
| Gobi | Mongolia and north-east China | 1 166 000 sq km/450 000 sq mi |
| Patagonian | Argentina | 673 000 sq km/260 000 sq mi |
| Great Victoria | south-west Australia | 647 000 sq km/250 000 sq mi |
| Great Basin | south-west USA | 492 000 sq km/190 000 sq mi |
| Chihuahuan | Mexico | 450 000 sq km/174 000 sq mi |
| Great Sandy | north-west Australia | 400 000 sq km/154 000 sq mi |
| Sonoran | south-west USA | 310 000 sq km/120 000 sq mi |
| Kyzyl Kum | Kazakhstan | 300 000 sq km/116 000 sq mi |
| Takla Makan | northern China | 270 000 sq km/104 000 sq mi |
| Kalahari | south-west Africa | 260 000 sq km/100 000 sq mi |
| Kara Kum | Turkmenistan | 260 000 sq km/100 000 sq mi |
| Kavir | Iran | 260 000 sq km/100 000 sq mi |
| Syrian | Saudi Arabia/Jordan/Syria/Iraq | 260 000 sq km/100 000 sq mi |
| Nubian | The Sudan | 260 000 sq km/100 000 sq mi |
| Thar | India/Pakistan | 200 000 sq km/77 000 sq mi |
| Ust'-Urt | Kazakhstan | 160 000 sq km/62 000 sq mi |
| Bet-Pak-Dala | southern Kazakhstan | 155 000 sq km/60 000 sq mi |
| Simpson | central Australia | 145 000 sq km/56 000 sq mi |
| Dzungaria | China | 142 000 sq km/55 000 sq mi |
| Atacama | Chile | 140 000 sq km/54 000 sq mi |
| Namib | south-east Africa | 134 000 sq km/52 000 sq mi |
| Sturt | south-east Australia | 130 000 sq km/50 000 sq mi |
| Bolson de Mapimi | Mexico | 130 000 sq km/50 000 sq mi |
| Ordos | China | 130 000 sq km/50 000 sq mi |
| Alashan | China | 116 000 sq km/45 000 sq mi |

[1] *Desert areas are very approximate, because clear physical boundaries may not occur.*

## HIGHEST MOUNTAINS

| Mountain[1] | Location | Height[2] |
|---|---|---|
| Everest | China/Nepal | 8 850m/29 035ft |
| K2 (Qogir) | Jammu-Kashmir[3]/China | 8 610m/28 250ft |
| Kanchenjunga | India/Nepal | 8 590m/28 170ft |
| Lhotse | China/Nepal | 8 500m/27 890ft |
| Kangchenjunga South Peak | India/Nepal | 8 470m/27 800ft |
| Makalu I | China/Nepal | 8 470m/27 800ft |
| Kangchenjunga West Peak | India/Nepal | 8 420m/27 620ft |
| Lhotse East Peak | China/Nepal | 8 380m/27 500ft |
| Dhaulagiri | Nepal | 8 170m/26 810ft |
| Cho Oyu | China/Nepal | 8 150m/26 750ft |
| Manaslu | Nepal | 8 130m/26 660ft |
| Nanga Parbat | Kashmir-Jammu[3] | 8 130m/26 660ft |
| Annapurna I | Nepal | 8 080m/26 500ft |
| Gasherbrum I | Kashmir-Jammu[3] | 8 070m/26 470ft |
| Broad Peak I | Kashmir-Jammu[3] | 8 050m/26 400ft |
| Gasherbrum II | Kashmir-Jammu[3] | 8 030m/26 360ft |
| Gosainthan | China | 8 010m/26 290ft |
| Broad Peak Central | Kashmir-Jammu[3] | 8 000m/26 250ft |
| Gasherbrum III | Kashmir-Jammu[3] | 7 950m/26 090ft |
| Annapurna II | Nepal | 7 940m/26 040ft |
| Nanda Devi | India | 7 820m/25 660ft |
| Rakaposhi | Kashmir[3] | 7 790m/25 560ft |
| Kamet | India | 7 760m/25 450ft |
| Ulugh Muztagh | China (Tibet) | 7 720m/25 340ft |
| Tirichmir | Pakistan | 7 690m/25 230ft |
| Muz Tag Ata | China | 7 550m/24 760ft |
| Peak Ismoili Somoni | Tajikistan | 7 495m/24 590ft |
| Pobedy Peak | China/Kyrgyzstan | 7 439m/24 406ft |
| Aconcagua | Argentina | 6 960m/22 830ft |
| Ojos del Salado[4] | Argentina/Chile | 6 910m/22 660ft |

[1] *Mt, etc has not been included in the name.*
[2] *Heights are given to the nearest 10m/ft.*
[3] *Kashmir-Jammu is a disputed region on the border of India and Pakistan.*
[4] *Ojos del Salado is the world's highest volcano.*

## LONGEST MOUNTAIN RANGES

Mountain ranges over 3 000km/1 900mi are given.

| Mountains | Location | Length[1] |
|---|---|---|
| Andes | South America | 7 200km/4 500mi |
| Rocky Mountains | North America | 4 800km/3 000mi |
| Himalayas–Karakoram–Hindu Kush | Asia | 3 800km/2 400mi |
| Great Dividing Range | Australia | 3 600km/2 250mi |
| Trans-Antarctic Mountains | Antarctica | 3 500km/2 200mi |
| Atlantic Coast Range South | America | 3 000km/1 900mi |

[1] *Lengths are given to the nearest 100km/mi.*

## PHYSICAL EXTREMES

| | | |
|---|---|---|
| Highest mountain | Mt Everest, China/Nepal | 8 850m/29 035ft |
| Longest mountain range | Andes, South America | 7 200km/4 500mi |
| Highest cliffs | Near Molokai, Hawaii, USA | 1 010m/3 300ft |
| Lowest point on Earth | Dead Sea, Israel/Jordan/ West Bank (Palestine) | 400m/1 312ft below sea level |
| Deepest cave | Jean Bernard, France | 1 494m/4 902ft |
| Largest cave | Sarawak Chamber (Lubang Nasib Bagus), Malaysia | 700m/2 300ft long by 70m/230ft high by average 300m/985ft wide |
| Largest ocean | Pacific Ocean | 155 557 000 sq km/ 60 060 557 sq mi |
| Deepest point in the ocean | Challenger Deep, Mariana Trench, Pacific Ocean | 11 040m/36 220ft |
| Highest tides | Minas Basin, Bay of Fundy, Canada | 16m/53ft difference between high and low tide |
| Largest sea | Coral Sea | 4 791 000 sq km/ 1 850 000 sq mi |
| Largest lake | Caspian Sea, Iran/Russia/ Turkmenistan/Kazakhstan/ Azerbaijan | 371 000 sq km/143 240 sq mi |
| Deepest lake | Lake Baikal, Russia | 1 637m/5 371ft |
| Highest lake | In crater of Licancábur volcano, Chile/Bolivia | 5 930m/19 455ft |
| Highest navigable lake | Titicaca, Peru/Bolivia | 3 810m/12 500ft |
| Saltiest lake | Don Juan Pond, Antarctica | 40.2% salt by weight *(the Dead Sea has 23.1% and the ocean just 3.38%)* |
| Longest river | River Nile, Africa | 6 690km/4 160mi |
| Highest waterfall | Angel (upper fall), Venezuela | 807m/2 648ft |
| Largest island | Australia[1] | 7 692 300 sq km/2 970 000 sq mi |
| Largest desert | Sahara, north Africa | 8 600 000 sq km/3 320 000 sq mi |
| Largest glacier | Lambert Glacier, Antarctica | 1 000 000 sq km/386 102 sq mi |

[1] *Sometimes discounted, as a continent.*

### Mighty Mountain

The peak of Mauna Kea, Hawaii, USA reaches 4 205m/13 796ft above sea level. However, the base of the mountain is the seabed of the Pacific Ocean, and its full height from foot to summit is a mighty 10 205m/33 480ft – higher than Mt Everest.

### Mt Everest

Sir George Everest (1790–1866), was a Welsh military engineer. He became Surveyor-General of India in 1830 and completed a trigonometrical survey of the Indian subcontinent in 1841, being knighted in 1861. Mt Everest was named after him in 1865. Interestingly, Everest himself would not have recognised the modern pronunciation *ev-uh-rest*. He pronounced the name *eve-rest*.

# NATIONAL PARKS (UK)

## England and Wales

The National Parks and Access to the Countryside Act (1949) provided for the creation of National Parks in England and Wales. The Environment Act (1995) states their purpose as 'a) conserving and enhancing the natural beauty, wildlife and cultural heritage of the areas, and b) promoting opportunities for the understanding and enjoyment of the special qualities of those areas by the public'.

| National Park | Year designated (order) | Area | Terrain |
|---|---|---|---|
| Brecon Beacons | 1957 (10th) | 1 351 sq km/522 sq mi | Mountains/valleys |
| Dartmoor | 1951 (4th) | 954 sq km/368 sq mi | Moorland |
| Exmoor | 1954 (8th) | 693 sq km/268 sq mi | Moorland/coastline |
| Lake District | 1951 (2nd) | 2 292 sq km/885 sq mi | Mountains/valleys/ glaciated lakes |
| Northumberland | 1956 (9th) | 1 049 sq km/405 sq mi | Hills |
| North York Moors | 1952 (6th) | 1 432 sq km/554 sq mi | Woodland/moorland |
| Peak District | 1951 (1st) | 1 438 sq km/555 sq mi | Moorland/dales |
| Pembrokeshire Coast | 1952 (5th) | 620 sq km/239 sq mi | Cliffs/islands/ moorland |
| Snowdonia | 1951 (3rd) | 2 142 sq km/827 sq mi | Mountains/valleys |
| The Broads | 1989 (11th) | 303 sq km/117 sq mi | Waterways/fens |
| Yorkshire Dales | 1954 (7th) | 1 769 sq km/682 sq mi | Dales |

*Note: The South Downs and the New Forest are currently in the process of being designated as National Parks.*

## Scotland

The National Parks (Scotland) Act (2000) provided for the creation of National Parks in Scotland. The Act states their purpose as being 'a) to conserve and enhance the natural and cultural heritage of the area, b) to promote sustainable use of the natural resources of the area, c) to promote understanding and enjoyment (including enjoyment in the form of recreation) of the special qualities of the area by the public, and d) to promote sustainable economic and social development of the area's communities'.

| National Park | Year established (order) | Area | Terrain |
|---|---|---|---|
| Loch Lomond and The Trossachs | 2002 (1st) | 1 865 sq km/720 sq mi | Mountains/valleys/ lochs |
| Cairngorms | 2003 (2nd) | 3 800 sq km/1 467 sq mi | Mountains/moorland |

## *High Places*

England's highest mountain is Scafell Pike in the Lake District at 978m/3 209ft, the highest mountain in Wales is Snowdon at 1 085m/3 560ft, and Slieve Donard at 852m/2 795ft is Northern Ireland's highest point. All three are dwarfed by Scotland's highest mountain: Ben Nevis reaches a mighty 1 343m/4 406ft, but it is still a mere pimple compared to the world's highest peaks.

## BEAUFORT SCALE

| Beaufort number | Wind name | m/sec | Windspeed kph | Windspeed mph | Observable wind characteristics | Sea disturbance number | Average wave height m | Average wave height ft | Observable sea characteristics |
|---|---|---|---|---|---|---|---|---|---|
| 0 | Calm | 1 | <1 | <1 | Smoke rises vertically | 0 | 0 | 0 | Sea like a mirror |
| 1 | Light air | 1 | 1–5 | 1–3 | Wind direction shown by smoke drift, but not by wind vanes | 0 | 0 | 0 | Ripples like scales, without foam crests |
| 2 | Light breeze | 2 | 6–11 | 4–7 | Wind felt on face; leaves rustle; vanes moved by wind | 1 | 0.3 | 0–1 | More definite wavelets, but crests do not break |
| 3 | Gentle breeze | 4 | 12–19 | 8–12 | Leaves and small twigs in constant motion; wind extends light flag | 2 | 0.3–0.6 | 1–2 | Large wavelets; crests begin to break; scattered white horses |
| 4 | Moderate breeze | 7 | 20–28 | 13–18 | Raises dust, loose paper; | 3 | 0.6–1.2 | 2–4 | Small waves become longer; fairly frequent white horses |
| 5 | Fresh breeze | 10 | 29–38 | 19–24 | Small trees in leaf begin to sway; crested wavelets on inland waters | 4 | 1.2–2.4 | 4–8 | Moderate waves with a more definite long form; many white horses; some spray possible |
| 6 | Strong breeze | 12 | 39–49 | 25–31 | Large branches in motion; difficult to use umbrellas; whistling heard in telegraph wires | 5 | 2.4–4 | 8–13 | Large waves form; more extensive white foam crests; some spray probable |
| 7 | Near gale | 15 | 50–61 | 32–38 | Whole trees in motion; inconvenience walking against wind | 6 | 4–6 | 13–20 | Sea heaps up; streaks of white foam blown along |
| 8 | Gale | 18 | 62–74 | 39–46 | Breaks twigs off trees; impedes progress | 6 | 4–6 | 13–20 | Moderately high waves of greater length; well-marked streaks of foam |
| 9 | Strong gale | 20 | 75–8 | 47–54 | Slight structural damage occurs | 6 | 4–6 | 13–20 | High waves; dense streaks of foam; sea begins to roll; spray affects visibility |
| 10 | Storm | 26 | 89–102 | 55–63 | Trees uprooted; considerable damage occurs | 7 | 6–9 | 20–30 | Very high waves with long overhanging crests; dense streaks of foam blown along; generally white appearance of surface; heavy rolling |
| 11 | Violent storm | 30 | 103–117 | 64–72 | Widespread damage | 8 | 9–14 | 30–45 | Exceptionally high waves; long white patches of foam; poor visibility; ships lost to view behind waves |
| 12–17 | Hurricane | ≥30 | ≥118 | ≥73 | | 9 | 14 | >45 | Air filled with foam and spray; sea completely white; very poor visibility |

## WIND

A *cyclone* is a circulation of winds in the atmosphere which rotates anticlockwise round a depression in the northern hemisphere and clockwise in the southern hemisphere.

A *hurricane* is a rotating windstorm originating over tropical oceans, with winds in excess of 119kph/74mph. Hurricanes may be up to 645km/400mi wide, and can move forwards at up to 48kph/30mph, travelling up to 4 830km/3 000mi before becoming exhausted. Hurricanes occur between Jul and Oct in the northern hemisphere and between Nov and Mar in the southern hemisphere. They are named by the National Hurricane Center, USA, in alphabetical sequence as they occur each year. Since 1978 names given have been alternately male/female. In the Pacific they are known as *typhoons*, and in the Indian Ocean as *tropical cyclones*.

A *tornado* is a column of air rotating rapidly around a very low pressure centre.

### *Worst Windstorms*

Windstorms can cause terrible destruction. In the 20c over 20 windstorms caused damage totalling more than a billion dollars each, and it is estimated that Hurricane Andrew's 1992 visit to Florida, USA, left behind more than $20 billion, equivalent to £12.5 billion, worth of devastation.

## WIND CHILL TEMPERATURE INDEX

Exposed skin cools more rapidly when exposed to wind than at the same temperature in still conditions. This means that people feel colder on a windy day than they would on a still day at the same temperature. The wind chill temperature index takes account of the temperature and the wind speed to produce the equivalent temperature. The US National Weather Service defines wind chill temperature as 'a measure of the combined cooling effect of wind and temperature'.

*To convert Fahrenheit to Celsius, subtract 32, multiply by 5 and then divide the total by 9.*

**Outside temperature (°F)**

| Wind speed (mph) | Calm | 40 | 35 | 30 | 25 | 20 | 15 | 10 | 5 | 0 | –5 | –10 | –15 | –20 | –25 | –30 | –35 | –40 | –45 |
|---|---|---|---|---|---|---|---|---|---|---|---|---|---|---|---|---|---|---|---|
| | 5 | 36 | 31 | 25 | 19 | 13 | 7 | 1 | –5 | –11 | –16 | –22 | –28 | –34 | –40 | –46 | –52 | –57 | –63 |
| | 10 | 34 | 27 | 21 | 15 | 9 | 3 | –4 | –10 | –16 | –22 | –28 | –35 | –41 | –47 | –53 | –59 | –66 | –72 |
| | 15 | 32 | 25 | 19 | 13 | 6 | 0 | –7 | –13 | –19 | –26 | –32 | –39 | –45 | –51 | –58 | –64 | –71 | –77 |
| | 20 | 30 | 24 | 17 | 11 | 4 | –2 | –9 | –15 | –22 | –29 | –35 | –42 | –48 | –55 | –61 | –68 | –74 | –81 |
| | 25 | 29 | 23 | 16 | 9 | 3 | –4 | –11 | –17 | –24 | –31 | –37 | –44 | –51 | –58 | –64 | –71 | –78 | –84 |
| | 30 | 28 | 22 | 15 | 8 | 1 | –5 | –12 | –19 | –26 | –33 | –39 | –46 | –53 | –60 | –67 | –73 | –80 | –87 |
| | 35 | 28 | 21 | 14 | 7 | 0 | –7 | –14 | –21 | –27 | –34 | –41 | –48 | –55 | –62 | –69 | –76 | –82 | –89 |
| | 40 | 27 | 20 | 13 | 6 | –1 | –8 | –15 | –22 | –29 | –36 | –43 | –50 | –57 | –64 | –71 | –78 | –84 | –91 |
| | 45 | 26 | 19 | 12 | 5 | –2 | –9 | –16 | –23 | –30 | –37 | –44 | –51 | –58 | –65 | –72 | –79 | –86 | –93 |
| | 50 | 26 | 19 | 12 | 4 | –3 | –10 | –17 | –24 | –31 | –38 | –45 | –52 | –60 | –67 | –74 | –81 | –88 | –95 |
| | 55 | 25 | 18 | 11 | 4 | –3 | –11 | –18 | –25 | –32 | –39 | –46 | –54 | –61 | –68 | –75 | –82 | –89 | –97 |
| | 60 | 25 | 17 | 10 | 3 | –4 | –11 | –19 | –26 | –33 | –40 | –48 | –55 | –62 | –69 | –76 | –84 | –91 | –98 |

*Data source: US National Weather Service, Wind Chill Temperature Index (2001 revision).*

## WEATHER AND CLIMATE EXTREMES

| | |
|---|---|
| Hottest place | Dallol, Ethiopia, at 34.4°C/93.9°F (annual mean temperature). |
| Highest recorded temperature in the shade | 58°C/136.4°F at Al'Aziziyah, Libya, on 13 Sep 1922. |
| Coldest place | Plateau Station, Antarctica, at –56.6°C/–69.8°F (annual mean temperature). |
| Coldest recorded temperature | –89.2°C/–128.6°F at Vostok, Antarctica, on 21 Jul 1983. |
| Greatest temperature range | Verkhoyansk, Siberia, Russia, where temperatures can range from –68°C/–90.4°F to 37°C/98°F, a difference of 105°C/221°F. |
| Driest place | Atacama desert near Calama, Chile, where no rainfall was recorded in over 400 years to 1972. Today, the desert's average annual rainfall is just 0.1mm/0.0039in. |
| Most rain to fall in 24 hours | 1 870mm/74in which fell on Cilaos, Réunion, in the Indian Ocean, on 15–16 Mar 1952. |
| Most intense rainfall | 38.1mm/1.8in which fell in one minute at Basse Terre, Guadeloupe, Caribbean on 26 Nov 1970. |
| Most rainy days in a year | Mt Wai'ale'ale, Kauai, Hawaii, USA has an average of 350 days of rain each year. |
| Wettest place | Mawsynram, Meghalaya State, India, where the annual average rainfall is 11 870mm/467in; in Tutunendo, Colombia, the annual average rainfall is 11 770mm/464in. |
| Least amount of sunshine | North and South Poles, where the Sun does not rise for 182 days of winter. |
| Greatest amount of sunshine | Yuma, Arizona, USA, with a mean average of 4 055 hours of sun per year, or 91% of the possible hours of sunshine. |
| Greatest amount of snow to fall in twelve months | 31 102mm/1 225in, at Paradise, Mt Rainier, Washington, USA, in 1971–2. |
| Greatest amount of snow to fall in one day | 193cm/76in at Silver Lake, Colorado on 14 Apr 1921. |
| Highest recorded surface wind speed | 371.75kph/231mph, at Mt Washington, New Hampshire, USA, on 12 Apr 1934. |
| Most days of thunder in a year | Tororo, Uganda, had an average of 251 days of thunder per year between 1967 and 1976. |
| Most hail in a year | Keriche, Kenya has an average of 132 days of hail each year. |
| Heaviest hailstones | On 14 Apr 1986 hailstones weighing up to 1kg/2.2 lb fell in Gopalganj, Bangladesh, killing 92 people. On 5 Sep 1958 a hailstone weighing 142g/5oz fell at Horsham, West Sussex, the largest hailstone ever recorded in the UK. |

### *Stormy Weather*

Just one thunderstorm can produce 500 million litres, or 110 million gallons, of rain.

## CLOUDS

Clouds are formed by the condensation or freezing of water vapour on minute particles in the atmosphere when air masses move upward as a result of convection currents, unstable conditions, etc, and in so doing cool rapidly. Clouds are usually classified into ten main types according to their height and shape.

*Meteorologists use feet to measure cloud height; to convert to metres, multiply by 0.3048.*

### The Language of Clouds

The scientific study of clouds is called *nephology*, from the Greek word for cloud, *nephos*. The names of cloud types come from Latin: *cirrus* means a tuft or curl, *cumulus* means a heap, *stratus* means something spread out, *alto* means high and *nimbus* was the word for a rain-cloud.

### Low clouds

The base of low clouds is usually surface–7 000ft.

**Stratus (St)**

Cloud base: usually surface–1 500ft.
Colour: usually grey.

**Cumulonimbus (Cb)**

Cloud base: usually 1 000–5 000ft.
Colour: white above with dark underside.

**Cumulus (Cu)**

Cloud base: usually 1 200–6 000ft.
Colour: white in sunlight but dark underside.

**Stratocumulus (Sc)**

Cloud base: usually 1 200–7 000ft.
Colour: grey or white, with shading.

### Medium clouds

The base of medium clouds is usually 7 000–17 000ft, although Nimbostratus may be much lower.

**Nimbostratus (Ns)**

Cloud base: usually 1 500–10 000ft.
Colour: dark grey.

**Altocumulus (Ac)**

Cloud base: usually 7 000–17 000ft.
Colour: grey or white, with shading.

**Altostratus (As)**
Cloud base: usually 8 000–17 000ft.
Colour: greyish or bluish.

## High clouds

The base of high clouds is usually 17 000–35 000ft. High clouds are composed of ice crystals.

**Cirrus (Ci)**

Cloud base: usually 17 000–35 000ft.
Colour: white.

**Cirrocumulus (Cc)**

Cloud base: usually 17 000–35 000ft.
Colour: white.

**Cirrostratus (Cs)**

Cloud base: usually 17 000–35 000ft.
Colour: white.

### On Cloud Nine

Someone who is extremely pleased or happy has long been described as being 'on cloud nine'. The phrase is thought to come from the classification system used by the old US Weather Bureau, which divided clouds into nine types: 'cloud nine' was the dramatic cumulonimbus, towering many kilometres into the sky. Hence to be on cloud nine was to be magnificently high up. Unfortunately, however, cumulonimbus is a rain-cloud. So it might be a soggy, rather than a blissful, experience.

## ICEBERGS

Icebergs can pose a significant hazard to shipping and as a result are reported, tracked and monitored. They are divided into two shape categories: tabular, those with a flat top and steep vertical sides, and non-tabular, which is subdivided into groups including pinnacled, domed, drydocked and wedged.

| Iceberg | Height[1] (above water) | Length |
|---|---|---|
| growler | <1m | <5m |
| bergybit | 1–4m | 5–14m |
| small | 5–15m | 15–60m |
| medium | 16–45m | 61–120m |
| large | 46–75m | 121–200m |
| very large | >75m | >200m |

[1] *To convert metres to feet, multiply by 3.2808.*

## SHIPPING FORECAST AREAS

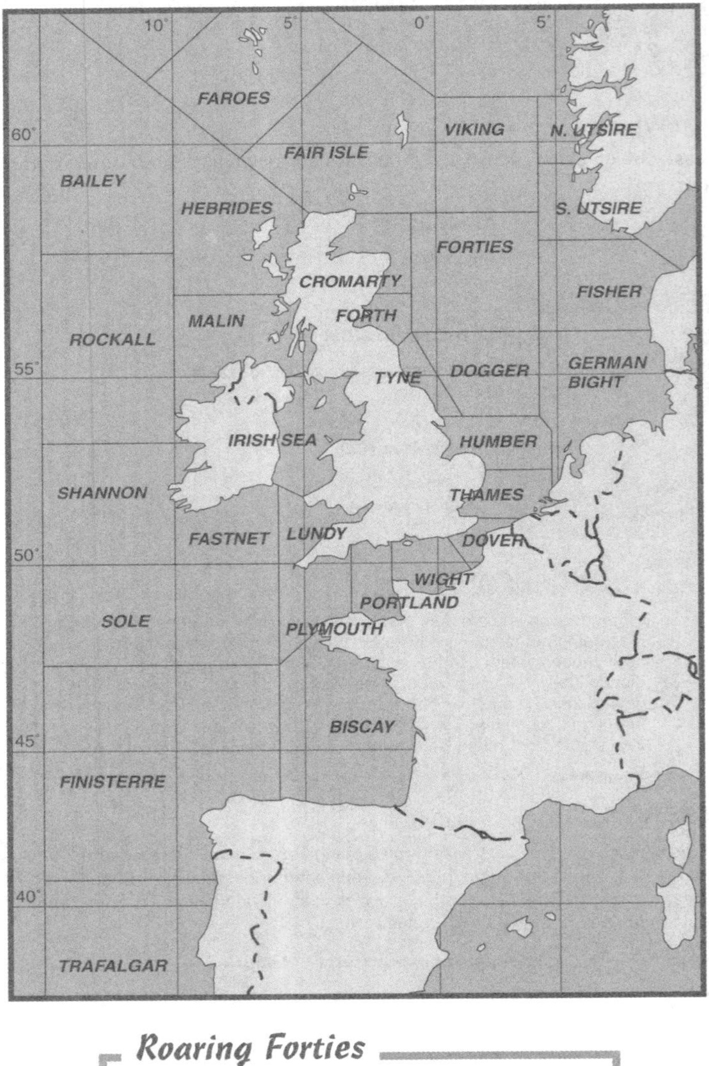


## *Roaring Forties*

This sailors' term refers to the tract of stormy west winds and high seas south of 40°S latitude. It is joined by the *Furious Fifties*, a similarly turbulent stretch of ocean.

## POINTS OF THE COMPASS

Naming the 32 compass points in order, in either or both directions, is called 'boxing the compass'.

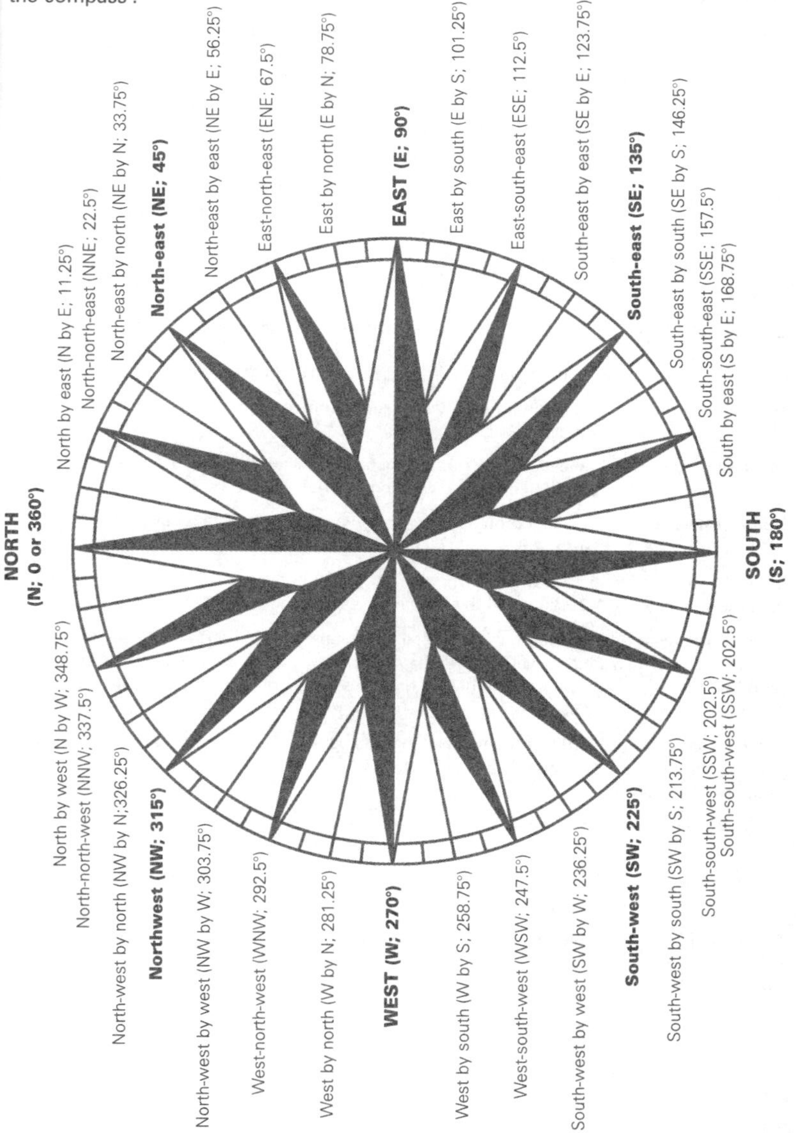

## FISH RECORDS

| | |
|---|---|
| Fastest | Over short distances, the sailfish can reach a speed of 110kph/68mph; however marlins are the fastest over longer distances, and can reach a burst speed of 68–80kph/40–50mph. |
| Largest | The whale shark is said to reach over 18m/59ft, with the largest on record being 12.65m/41ft 6in, weighing an estimated 21.5 tonnes/21.1 tons. |
| Smallest | The dwarf pygmy goby, found in the streams and rivers of Luzon in the Philippines, measures 7.5–9.9mm/0.3–0.4in and weighs 4–5mg/0.00014–0.00018oz. |
| Smallest in British waters | Guillet's goby reaches a maximum length of 24mm/0.95in. |
| Largest predatory | The great white shark reaches an average of 4.3–4.6m/14–15ft in length, and a weight of 520–770kg/1 150–1 700 lb. There are some reports of larger specimens up to 10m/33ft. |
| Most widespread | The distribution of the bristlemouths of genus *Cyclothone* is worldwide excluding the Arctic. |
| Most restricted | The devil's hole pupfish inhabits only a small area of water above a rock shelf in a spring-fed pool in Ash Meadows, Nevada, USA. |
| Deepest dweller | In 1970 a brotulid *Bassogigas profundissimus* was recovered from a depth of 8 299m/27 230ft, making it the deepest living vertebrate. |
| Largest fish ever caught on a rod | In 1959 a great white shark measuring 5.13m/16ft 10 in and weighing 1 208kg/2 664 lb was caught off southern Australia. |
| Largest freshwater fish found in Britain and Ireland | Reportedly, in 1815 a pike was taken from the River Shannon in Ireland weighing 41.7kg/92 lb; however there is evidence of a pike weighing 32.7kg/72 lb having been caught on Loch Ken, Scotland, in 1774. |
| Largest saltwater fish caught by anglers in the UK | In 1933 a tunny weighing 385.989kg/851 lb was caught near Whitby, Yorkshire. |
| Longest lived | Some specimens of the sturgeon are thought to be over 80 years old. |
| Shortest lived | Tooth carp of the suborder *Cyprinodontidae* live for only 8 months in the wild. |
| Greatest distance covered by a migrating fish | A bluefin tuna was tagged in 1958 off California, USA, and caught in 1963 in Japan; it had covered a distance of 9 335km/5 800mi. |
| Most eggs | The ocean sunfish can lay up to 30 million eggs at a time. Each egg measures approximately 1.3mm/0.05in in diameter. |

## BIRD RECORDS

| | |
|---|---|
| Largest | The ostrich can reach 2.75m/9ft in height and 156kg/345 lb in weight. |
| Smallest | The bee hummingbird of Cuba is under 6cm/2.4in long and weighs 3g/0.1oz. |
| Highest flier | Ruppell's griffon, a vulture, has been measured at 11 275m/36 991ft above sea level. |
| Fastest flier | The peregrine falcon can dive through the air at speeds up to 185kph/115mph. The fastest bird in level flight is the eider duck, which can reach 80kph/50mph. |
| Fastest animal on two legs | The ostrich can maintain a speed of 50kph/31mph for 15 minutes or more, and it may reach 65–70kph/40–43mph in short bursts, for example when escaping from predators. |
| Greatest wingspan | The wandering albatross can reach 3.65m/12ft. |
| Heaviest flying bird | The great bustard and the kori bustard both weigh up to 18kg/40 lb, with swans not far behind at approximately 16kg/35 lb. |
| Heaviest bird of prey | The Andean condor can reach 9–12kg/20–27 lb. |
| Deepest diver | The emperor penguin can reach a depth of 265m/870ft. The great northern diver or loon can dive to approximately 80m/262ft – deeper than any other flying bird. |
| Furthest migrator | The arctic tern travels up to 36 000km/22 400mi each year, flying from the Arctic to the Antarctic and back again. |
| Most abundant | Africa's red-billed quelea is the most numerous wild bird, with an estimated population of approximately 1.5 billion. The domestic chicken is the most abundant of all birds, numbering over 4 billion. |
| Largest egg | The ostrich lays the largest egg, with the heaviest specimen on record weighing 2.35kg/5 lb 2oz. |

### *Feathered Friends*

The greatest number of feathers counted on a bird was 25 216, on a swan.

## MAMMAL RECORDS

| | |
|---|---|
| Largest | The blue whale, up to 30m/98ft long and weighing up to 150 tonnes/148 tons, is the largest known mammal. The largest land mammal is the male African elephant, standing up to 3.3m/11ft at the shoulder and weighing up to 7 tonnes/6.89 tons. |
| Tallest | The giraffe stands up to 5.5m/18ft high. |
| Smallest | The pygmy white-toothed shrew, also called the Etruscan shrew, has a body approximately 5cm/2in long and weighs up to 2.5g/0.1oz. Some bats weigh even less. |
| Longest lived | Bowhead whales may be the oldest living mammals, with some specimens estimated at 177 to 245 years old at death. The next oldest are fin whales, at 114 years, and blue whales, at 110 years. |

## AMPHIBIAN RECORDS

| | |
|---|---|
| Loudest | Blue whales and fin whales can make calls that have been measured at 188 decibels and can travel for hundreds of kilometres through water. |
| Fastest on land | The cheetah can reach 100kph/62mph, but only in short bursts. The pronghorn can maintain speeds of 50kph/31mph for several kilometres. |
| Largest land carnivore | The Kodiak bear averages 2.4m/7.8ft in length and can weigh 680kg/1 500 lb. |
| Most prolific breeder | A North American meadow mouse can produce up to 17 litters in a single year (4–9 babies per litter). |
| Longest gestation period | The Asiatic elephant has the longest pregnancy, at 650–760 days. |
| Most widespread | Humans are the most widely distributed mammals, closely followed by the house mouse, which has accompanied humans to all parts of the world. |
| Most endangered | The Javan rhinoceros is now thought to number only around 60 specimens in the wild, with most in Indonesia and the remainder in Vietnam. |

### *Monkey Around*

The wonderful world of monkeys includes the sun-tailed monkey, purple-faced leaf monkey, greater white-nosed monkey, red-bellied monkey, yellow-tailed woolly monkey, moustached monkey, black-bearded saki, bald-faced saki, owl-faced monkey and red-handed howler.

## AMPHIBIAN RECORDS

| | |
|---|---|
| Largest | The Chinese giant salamander can grow up to 1.8m/5ft 11in long. |
| Smallest | The world's smallest amphibian is the frog *Eleutherodactylus limbatus* of Cuba, which is only 8.51mm/0.33–0.47in long when it reaches adulthood. |
| Largest frog | The Goliath frog can weigh up to 3.25kg/7.16 lb, and reach 32cm/12.6in in length. |
| Longest lived | The Japanese giant salamander, *Andrias japonicus*, has reached 55 years in captivity. |

## REPTILE RECORDS

| | |
|---|---|
| Largest | The estuarine or saltwater crocodile, which lives throughout tropical regions in Asia and the Pacific, can grow to over 7m/23ft long, although some eyewitness reports suggest crocodiles up to 10m/33ft in length. |
| Longest snake | The reticulated python of south-east Asia grows to an average of 6m/20ft, but the greatest length on record is 10m/32ft 9.5in. |
| Largest snake | The largest snake is probably the anaconda, which may not grow as long as the reticulated python but is thicker and heavier. Specimens have been known to reach 249kg/550 lb. |

| | |
|---|---|
| Smallest lizard | Two lizards are considered to be the smallest in the world: *Sphaerodactylus ariasiae* and the *Sphaerodactylus parthenopion*, which both measure an average of 16mm/0.6in. |
| Longest lived tortoise | Tortoises can reach ages of more than 100 years. The oldest specimen on record is a Madagascar giant tortoise that reputedly lived to 188 years, dying in 1965. |

## INSECT RECORDS

| | |
|---|---|
| Longest | The stick insect *Pharnacia serratipes*, living in Indonesia, can grow to 33cm/13in long. |
| Most massive | Females of the goliath beetle of the Congo in Africa can grow to 100g/0.25 lb and are around the same size as a clenched fist. |
| Greatest wingspan | The white witch moth, living in the rainforests of South and Central America, has a wingspan of up to 36cm/14in. |
| Fastest flying | Some dragonflies can fly at speeds of up to 75kmph/45mph. |
| Largest egg | The Malaysian stick insect lays eggs around 1.3cm/0.5in long, the size of a large jelly bean. Other insects lay even larger eggs, but these are cases containing a number of individual eggs. |
| Loudest | The African cicada produces a call that registers up to 106.7 decibels. |
| Shortest lived | Mayflies live for as little as an hour as adults with wings, although they may previously have lived for 2–3 years as nymphs in bodies of water. |

## SPIDER RECORDS

| | |
|---|---|
| Largest | Male Goliath bird-eating spiders, found in some rainforest regions of South America, can grow to have a leg span of 28cm/11in. |
| Smallest | Among the smallest spiders in the world are symphytognathid spiders from central Africa. Adult individuals reach an average of 0.5mm/0.02in across. |
| Largest web | The Golden Orb Web spider, living in tropical areas worldwide, makes webs which can extend to 6m/19ft 8in in height and 2m/6ft 7in in width. |

## WORM RECORDS

| | |
|---|---|
| Longest | The bootlace worm can reach 40m/131ft. |
| Longest tapeworm | The human tapeworm can grow as long as 15m/49ft 2in. |

## CRUSTACEAN RECORDS

| | |
|---|---|
| Largest | The Japanese spider crab can achieve a claw span of 3m/9ft 10in. |
| Heaviest | The American or North Atlantic lobster can weigh up to 20.14kg/44 lb 6oz. |
| Lightest | Water fleas are the smallest crustaceans, weighing as little as 0.00025g/0.0000088oz. |

## MOLLUSC RECORDS

| | |
|---|---|
| Largest cephalopod | The giant squid has been measured up to 18m/59ft in length and 900kg/1 980 lb in weight. It has never been observed in the wild and scientists have so far relied on measuring dead specimens. |
| Largest snail | The African giant snail is the largest land gastropod. The biggest specimen on record was 39.3cm/15.5in long and weighed 900g/2 lb. |
| Largest bivalve | The giant clam can measure more than 1.4–1.5m/4ft 7in–4ft 11in across and weigh up to 295kg/650 lb. |

## JELLYFISH RECORDS

| | |
|---|---|
| Largest | The Arctic giant jellyfish is reckoned to be the largest, with a body diameter of up to 2.2m/7ft 3in and a tentacle length of 35m/115ft. |
| Smallest | Polyp forms of various species of jellyfish may measure only around 1mm/0.039in across. |

### *Venomous Jelly*

The jellyfish with the deadliest venom is the box jellyfish, *Chironex fleckeri*. Also known as the sea wasp, it is found in the coastal waters of northern Australia from Nov to May. The 'bell' of the jellyfish can reach 30cm/12in across, while each of the sixty thick stinging tentacles trail up to 3m/10ft behind it; the translucent jellyfish is often almost impossible to spot in the water. Each one carries enough poison to kill 60 human adults; the venom not only attacks the nerves and heart but also destroys the skin, causing intense and excruciating pain before an agonizing death.

## PLANT RECORDS

| | |
|---|---|
| Largest living tree | The largest tree in terms of mass is the giant sequoia. The largest individual specimen is the 'General Sherman' in Sequoia National Park, California, USA, and is 83.82m/275ft tall. It is more than 10 times as massive as a blue whale. |
| Tallest living tree | The tallest tree is the coast redwood. The tallest individual specimen is the 'Stratosphere Giant' in the Humboldt Redwoods State Park, California, USA, and is 112.6m/369ft 4.8in tall. |
| Most massive plant | The largest individual plant in terms of mass so far discovered is a group of quaking aspen trees growing in the Wasatch Mountains, Utah, USA. Its roots extend over an area of 43ha/106 acres. |
| Largest fungi | A fungus known as the honey mushroom can extend over hundreds of hectares. The largest individual fungus of this type is thought to grow in the Malheur National Forest in the Blue Mountains of eastern Oregon, USA, and covers around 820ha/2 028 acres. |
| Oldest living tree | The tree that lives longest is estimated to be the bristlecone pine. The oldest individual yet found is named 'Methuselah' and grows in the White Mountains on the California-Nevada border in the USA. It is reckoned to be 4 767 years old. |
| Fastest growing plant | Bamboo can grow faster than any other plant, at up to 91cm/3ft per day. |

| | |
|---|---|
| Largest flower | The parasitic *Rafflesia arnoldi*, which grows on cissus vines in the south-east Asian rainforest, has the largest flowers. They can measure up to 91cm/3ft in width, with a weight of 11kg/24 lb. |
| Largest leaf | The largest leaves of any plant belong to the raffia palm of the Mascarene Islands, Indian Ocean, and the Amazonian bamboo palm of South America and Africa; both measure up to 20m/65ft 7in in length. |
| Largest seed | The giant fan palm, known as the double coconut or coco de mer, produces the largest seed, weighing up to 20kg/44 lb. |
| Longest root | Winter rye has been shown to have one of the most extensive yet tightly-packed root systems of any plant, with a single specimen producing 622.8km/387mi of roots in only 0.051cu m/1.8 cu ft of soil. |

## MOST POISONOUS ANIMALS

| | |
|---|---|
| Deadliest snake | The hook-nosed sea snake of seas and coastal waters in the Middle East, Asia and Australasia may be the world's deadliest snake. Its venom is 60 times more poisonous than a rattlesnake's. |
| Snake with most venom | The inland taipan, or fierce snake, of central Australia can deliver the greatest amount of venom per bite; 110mg/0.0038oz has been recorded, although 44mg/0.0015oz is more common. It is thought to be the most venomous land snake. |
| Snake responsible for most deaths | Russell's viper lives in habitats worldwide and is notably aggressive, with a deadly venom. It has probably killed more people than any other snake. |
| Most poisonous fish | The puffer fish of the Indian and Pacific oceans and Red Sea secretes a deadly poison that is present in its blood, organs and skin. A dose of less than 0.1g/0.004oz is sufficient to kill an adult human. |
| Most poisonous frog | The golden poison dart frog, living in western Colombia, secretes a poison which is the most toxic of any land animal known to science. Just 1g/0.035oz of it could kill 100 000 people. |

## MOST POISONOUS PLANTS

| | |
|---|---|
| Most poisonous in the world | The seeds of the castor bean plant, the source of castor oil, are highly toxic. Just 1mg/0.00004oz of their main toxin, ricin, can be enough to kill a human adult. Ricin is considered internationally to be a chemical and biological weapon. |
| Most poisonous in Europe | Monk's hood, also called wolfsbane, may be Europe's most poisonous plant. It was formerly used in traps to kill wolves. |
| Most poisonous in the USA | Western water hemlock is often cited as the most poisonous plant in the USA, and is a particular hazard to livestock. Small amounts of it are sufficient to kill a horse. |
| Most poisonous fungus | The death cap is the cause of most fatal poisonings from fungi. Whitish in colour, it is often mistaken for an edible mushroom. |
| Most poisonous edible fruit | The pith surrounding the ackee fruit is commonly cooked and eaten in Jamaica. The unripe pith, however, can be highly toxic, and may lead to serious illness, coma and death if ingested. |

## ANIMAL AGES

| Animal | Average age reached in captivity (years) | Animal | Average age reached in captivity (years) |
|---|---|---|---|
| bear | 15–30 | horse | 20–25 |
| camel | 12 | kangaroo | 4–7 |
| cat | 10–12 | lion | 10–15 |
| chimpanzee | 20 | monkey | 12–15 |
| cow | 9–15 | mouse | 3 |
| dog | 10–12 | pig | 10 |
| elephant | 30–40 | pigeon | 10–12 |
| fox | 7–10 | rabbit | 5–8 |
| giraffe | 10 | rhinoceros | 15–20 |
| goat | 8 | sheep | 12 |
| gorilla | 20 | squirrel | 8–10 |
| guinea pig | 4 | tiger | 16 |
| hippopotamus | 25–30 | zebra | 15 |

## CLOSE SEASONS (UK)

The close season is the time of the year when it is illegal to kill certain game or fish. Dates given are inclusive; for birds, the first dates refer to England, Scotland and Wales and the second to Northern Ireland, while for deer the first dates refer to England, Wales and Northern Ireland, the second to Scotland. Where only one set of dates is given the close season is the same across the UK.

**Fish**

Close season dates vary locally, according to byelaws, species of fish and type of water (lake, river, canal, etc).

**Birds**

| | | | |
|---|---|---|---|
| Capercaillie | 1 Feb–30 Sep | Woodcock | 1 Feb–30 Sep; 1 Feb–30 Sep |
| Partridge | 2 Feb–31 Aug; 1 Feb–31 Aug | Grouse[1] | 11 Dec–11 Aug; 1 Dec–11 Aug |
| Pheasant | 2 Feb–30 Sep; 1 Feb–30 Sep | Black game[2] | 11 Dec–19 Aug[3] |
| Common snipe | 1 Feb–11 Aug; 1 Feb–31 Aug | | |

[1] *Includes red grouse and ptarmigan.*
[2] *Black grouse.*
[3] *To 31 Aug in Somerset, Devon and the New Forest.*

**Deer**

| *Female* | | *Male* | |
|---|---|---|---|
| Red deer | 1 Mar–31 Oct; 16 Feb–20 Oct | Red deer | 1 May–31 Jul; 21 Oct–30 Jun |
| Fallow deer | 1 Mar–31 Oct; 16 Feb–20 Oct | Fallow deer | 1 May–31 Jul |
| Sika deer | 1 Mar–31 Oct; 16 Feb–20 Oct | Sika deer | 1 May–31 Jul; 21 Oct–30 Jun |
| Roe deer | 1 Mar–31 Oct; 1 Apr–20 Oct | Roe deer | 1 Nov–31 Mar; 21 Oct–31 Mar |

*Note: There is no statutory close season for muntjac or Chinese water deer.*

### MRS GREN

Scientists identify seven characteristics of living things, which can be remembered by the acronym MRS GREN: Movement, Respiration, Sensitivity, Growth, Reproduction, Excretion, Nutrition.

## COUNTRIES A–Z

### Introduction

**Names of countries and cities**
The official name of the country is given in English. Where appropriate the short form of the local name is given first, followed by the long form. English names of capital cities are given first, followed by the local name(s). Any notable names by which a country has been previously known in the 20c are listed with relevant dates.

**Area**
Area figures are for land mass only and do not include territorial waters (eg Kiribati covers c.3 million sq km/1.2 million sq mi but actual land area is only 717 sq km/277 sq mi).

**Chief towns**
If no chief towns are given the country is too small or sparsely populated to have major settlements.

**Population**
Population statistics are from the United Nations Population and Vital Statistics Report (Apr 2003 issue) or from government sources. Estimates are marked e; where a year alone is given the figure comes from the country's census of that year.

**Nationality**
Nationality gives the usual adjective form; exceptions are clearly marked.

**Time zone**
No allowance is made for daylight saving time.

**Country codes**
The country code shown is from the UN-recognized International Standards Organization (ISO) list.

**Climate**
Temperature figures are given in degrees Celsius. To convert to Fahrenheit multiply by 9, divide by 5 and add 32.

**National holidays**
The first part of each listing gives the holidays that occur on fixed dates (though it should be noted that holidays often vary according to local circumstances and the day of the week on which they fall). Most dates are accompanied by an indication of the purpose of the day, eg Independence = Independence Day; dates which have no gloss are either fixed dates within the Christian calendar (for which see below) or bank holidays. The second part of the listing gives holidays that vary, usually depending on religious factors. The most common of these are given in abbreviated form (see list below).

Where national holidays last for more than one day, the number of days devoted to the holiday is shown in parentheses. The listings do not include holidays that affect only certain parts of a country, half-day holidays, or Sundays. National holidays are subject to change.

The following fixed dates are shown without gloss:

| | |
|---|---|
| Jan 1 | New Year's Day |
| Jan 6 | Epiphany |
| Mar 21 | Novrus (Persian New Year; various spellings) |
| May 1 | Labour Day (often known by a different name, such as Workers' Day) |
| Aug 15 | Assumption of Our Lady |
| Nov 1 | All Saints' Day |
| Nov 2 | All Souls' Day |
| Dec 8 | Immaculate Conception |
| Dec 24 | Christmas Eve |
| Dec 25 | Christmas Day |
| Dec 26 | Boxing Day/St Stephen's Day |
| Dec 31 | New Year's Eve |

The following abbreviations are used for variable religious feast days:

| | |
|---|---|
| A | Ascension Thursday |
| Ad | Id-ul-Adha (also found with other spellings, especially Eid-ul-Adha; various names relating to this occasion are used in different countries, such as Tabaski, Id el-Kebir, Hari Raja Haji) |
| Ar | Arafa |
| As | Ashora (found with various spellings) |
| C | Carnival (immediately before Christian Lent, unless specified) |
| CC | Corpus Christi |
| D | Diwali/Deepavali |
| EM | Easter Monday |
| ER | End of Ramadan (known generally as Id/Eid-ul-Fitr, but various names relating to this occasion are used in different countries, such as Karite, Hari Raja Puasa) |
| ES | Easter Sunday |
| GF | Good Friday |
| HS | Holy Saturday |
| HT | Holy Thursday |
| NY | New Year |
| PB | Prophet's Birthday (known generally as Maul-id-al-Nabi in various forms and spellings) |
| R | First day of Ramadan |
| WM | Whit Monday |

**Dependencies**
Dependencies and other territories are listed by type then alphabetically.

**Political leaders**
Countries and organizations are listed alphabetically, with former or alternative names given in parentheses. Rulers are named chronologically since 1900 or (for new nations) since independence. For some major English-speaking nations, relevant details are also given of pre-20c rulers, along with a note of any political affiliation. Relevant details are also given of pre-20c rulers for some major monarchies, and other useful information, for example dynasties, is also included where appropriate. The list does not distinguish successive terms of office by a single ruler. Listings complete to Aug 2003.

There is no universally agreed way of transliterating proper names in non-Roman alphabets; variations from the spellings given are therefore to be expected, especially in the case of Arabic rulers. Minor variations in the titles adopted by Chiefs of State, or in the name of an administration, are not given; these occur most notably in countries under military rule.

**ABU DHABI** *see* **UNITED ARAB EMIRATES**

## AFGHANISTAN

| | | | |
|---|---|---|---|
| **Official name** | Islamic Transitional State of Afghanistan | **Nationality** | Afghan |
| **Local name** | Afqânestân (Dari), Afğānistān (Pashto) | **Languages** | Dari, Pashto |
| **Former name** | *as listed below under Political leaders* | **Ethnic groups** | Pashtun 38%, Tajik 25%, Hazara 19%, Uzbek 6%, others 12% |
| **Independence** | 1919 | **Religions** | Islam 99% (Sunni 74%, Shia 25%), others 1% |
| **Area** | 647 497 sq km/249 934 sq mi | **Time zone** | GMT +4.5 |
| **Capital** | Kabul; Kābul, Kâbol | **Currency** | 1 Afghani (Af) = 100 puls |
| **Chief towns** | Herat, Kandahar | **Telephone** | +93 |
| **Population** | 22 083 000 (2001e) | **Internet** | .af |
| | | **Country code** | AFG |

**Location**
A landlocked, mountainous republic in south-central Asia, bounded to the north by Turkmenistan, Uzbekistan and Tajikistan; to the east and south by Pakistan; to the west by Iran; and in the extreme north-east by China and India.

**Physical description**
Landlocked and mountainous, centred on the Hindu Kush system which reaches over 7 000m/23 000ft in centre and north-east; highest point is Nowshak (7 485m/24 557ft); north-west is the fertile valley of Herat; arid uplands in south; desert in south-west.

**Climate**
Continental climate with winter severity increased by altitude; summers are warm everywhere except on the highest peaks; protected from summer monsoons by the southern mountains; lower levels have a desert or semi-arid climate.

**National holidays**
Mar 21, Apr 28 (Victory of the Muslim Nation), May 1, 4 (Remembrance for Martyrs and Disabled), Aug 19 (Independence); Ad (3), Ar, As, ER (3), NY (Hindu), PB, R.

## Political leaders

### Afghan Empire

**Monarch**

| | |
|---|---|
| 1881–1901 | Abdur Rahman Khan |
| 1901–19 | Habibullah Khan |
| 1919–29 | Amanullah Khan |
| 1929 | Habibullah Ghazi |
| 1929–33 | Nadir Shah |
| 1933–73 | Zahir Shah |

### Republic of Afghanistan

**Prime Minister**

| | |
|---|---|
| 1973–8 | Mohammad Daoud Khan |

### Democratic Republic of Afghanistan

**President of Revolutionary Council**

| | |
|---|---|
| 1978–9 | Nour Mohammad Taraki |
| 1979 | Hafizullah Amin |

## Soviet invasion

| | |
|---|---|
| 1979–86 | Babrak Karmal |
| 1986–7 | Haji Mohammad Chamkani *Acting President* |
| 1987–92 | Mohammad Najibullah |
| 1992 | Sebghatullah Mojaddedi *Acting President* |

**General Secretary**

| | |
|---|---|
| 1978–86 | *As President* |
| 1986–92 | Mohammad Najibullah |

**Prime Minister**

| | |
|---|---|
| 1929–46 | Sardar Mohammad Hashim Khan |
| 1946–53 | Shah Mahmoud Khan Ghazi |
| 1953–63 | Mohammad Daoud |
| 1963–5 | Mohammad Yousef |
| 1965–7 | Mohammad Hashim Maiwandwal |
| 1967–71 | Nour Ahmad Etemadi |
| 1972–3 | Mohammad Mousa Shafiq |
| 1973–9 | *As President* |
| 1979–81 | Babrak Karmal |
| 1981–8 | Sultan Ali Keshtmand |

## Republic of Afghanistan (from 1987)

| | |
|---|---|
| 1988–9 | Mohammad Hasan Sharq |
| 1989–90 | Sultan Ali Keshtmand |
| 1990–2 | Fazal Haq Khaliqyar |
| 1992–3 | Abdul Sabour Fareed |
| 1993–6 | Gulbuddin Hekmatyar |

## Islamic State of Afghanistan

**President**

| | |
|---|---|
| 1992–2001 | Burhanuddin Rabbani[1] |

**Chairman of Interim Government**

| | |
|---|---|
| 2001–2 | Hamid Karzai |

## Islamic Transitional State of Afghanistan

**President**

| | |
|---|---|
| 2002– | Hamid Karzai |

[1] *Ousted by the Taliban in 1996, but remained titular head of state; Taliban de facto rulers 1996–2001.*

**AJMAN** *see* **UNITED ARAB EMIRATES**

# ALBANIA

| | |
|---|---|
| **Official name** | Republic of Albania |
| **Local name** | Shqipëria; Republika e Shqipërisë |
| **Former name** | Kingdom of Albania (1928–39), People's Republic of Albania (1946–76), People's Socialist Republic of Albania (until 1991) |
| **Independence** | 1912 |
| **Area** | 28 748 sq km/11 097 sq mi |
| **Capital** | Tirana; Tiranë |
| **Chief towns** | Shkodër, Durrës, Vlorë, Korçë, Elbasan |
| **Population** | 3 122 000 (2001e) |
| **Nationality** | Albanian |
| **Languages** | Albanian |
| **Ethnic groups** | Albanian 95%, Greek 3%, others 2% |
| **Religions** | Islam 60% (Sunni), none/unaffiliated 28%, Christianity 12% (Orthodox 8%, RC 4%) |
| **Time zone** | GMT +1 |
| **Currency** | 1 Lek (Lk) = 100 qindarka |
| **Telephone** | +355 |
| **Internet** | .al |
| **Country code** | ALB |

**Location**
A mountainous republic in the western part of the Balkan Peninsula, bounded to the west by the Adriatic Sea; to the north by Serbia and Montenegro; to the north-east by Macedonia; and to the south-east by Greece.

**Physical description**
Mountainous, relatively inaccessible and untravelled; highest point is Maja e Korabit (Golem Korab; 2 753m/9 032ft) on the Macedonian border; northern Albanian Alps rise to 2 692m/8 832ft; 50% of the population lives in 25% of the area (the low-lying west).

**Climate**
A Mediterranean-type climate: hot and dry on the plains in summer (average Jul temperature 24–25°C); winters are mild and damp (average Jan temperature 8–9°C), but often severe in the mountains.

**National holidays**
Jan 1, Mar 21, May 1, Nov 28 (Independence), 29 (Liberation), Dec 25; Ad, ER, ES, NY (Albanian), Orthodox Easter (Apr/May).

## Political leaders

### Monarch

| | |
|---|---|
| 1928–39 | Zog I (Ahmed Zogu) |
| 1939–44 | *Italian rule* |

### President

| | |
|---|---|
| 1944–85 | Enver Hoxha |
| 1985–92 | Ramiz Alia |
| 1992–7 | Sali Berisha |
| 1997–2002 | Rexhep Mejdani |
| 2002– | Alfred Moisiu |

### Prime Minister

| | |
|---|---|
| 1914 | Turhan Pashë Permëti |
| 1914 | Esad Toptani |
| 1914–18 | Abdullah Rushdi |
| 1918–20 | Turhan Pashë Permëti |
| 1920 | Sulejman Deluina |
| 1920–1 | Iljaz Bej Vrioni |
| 1921 | Pandeli Evangeli |
| 1921 | Xhafer Ypi |
| 1921–2 | Omer Vrioni |
| 1922–4 | Ahmed Zogu |
| 1924 | Iljaz Bej Vrioni |
| 1924–5 | Fan Noli |
| 1925–8 | Ahmed Zogu |
| 1928–30 | Koço Kota |
| 1930–5 | Pandeli Evangeli |
| 1935–6 | Mehdi Frashëri |
| 1936–9 | Koço Kota |
| 1939–41 | Shefqet Verlaci |
| 1941–3 | Mustafa Merlika-Kruja |
| 1943 | Eqrem Libohova |
| 1943 | Maliq Bushati |
| 1943 | Eqrem Libohova |
| 1943 | *Provisional Executive Committee* (Ibrahim Biçakçlu) |
| 1943 | *Council of Regents* (Mehdi Frashëri) |
| 1943–4 | Rexhep Mitrovica |
| 1944 | Fiori Dine |
| 1944–54 | Enver Hoxha |
| 1954–81 | Mehmed Shehu |
| 1981–91 | Adil Carcani |
| 1991 | Ylli Buffi |
| 1991 | Fatos Nano |
| 1991–2 | Vilson Ahmeti |
| 1992–7 | Aleksander Meksi |
| 1997 | Bashkim Fino |
| 1997–8 | Fatos Nano |
| 1998–9 | Pandeli Majko |
| 1999–2002 | Ilir Meta |
| 2002 | Pandeli Majko |
| 2002– | Fatos Nano |

## ALGERIA

| | | | |
|---|---|---|---|
| **Official name** | People's Democratic Republic of Algeria | **Population** | 29 100 867 (1998) |
| **Local name** | Al-Jazā'ir; Al-Jumhūriyya al-Jazā'iriyya ad-Dimuqratiyya ash-Sha'biyya (Arabic), Algérie; République Algérienne Démocratique et Populaire (French) | **Nationality** | Algerian |
| | | **Languages** | Arabic, Tamazight; French is also spoken |
| | | **Ethnic groups** | Arab 74%, Berber 25%, European 1% |
| | | **Religions** | Islam 99% (Sunni), others 1% |
| **Independence** | 1962 | **Time zone** | GMT +1 |
| **Area** | 2 460 500 sq km/949 753 sq mi | **Currency** | 1 Algerian Dinar (AD, DA) = 100 centimes |
| **Capital** | Algiers; Alger, El Djazâir, Al-Jazā'ir | **Telephone** | +213 |
| | | **Internet** | .dz |
| **Chief towns** | Constantine, Oran, Skikda, Annaba, Mostaganem, Blida, Tlemcen | **Country code** | DZA |

**Location**
A North African republic, bounded to the west by Morocco; to the south-west by Western Sahara, Mauritania and Mali; to the south-east by Niger; to the east by Libya; to the north-east by Tunisia; and to the north by the Mediterranean Sea.

**Physical description**
From the Mediterranean coast, where 91% of the population is located on the narrow coastal plain, the mountains rise to the Atlas Saharien; the Sahara Desert lies to the south; the Hoggar Mountains in the far south rise to 2 918m/9 573ft at Mt Tahat.

**Climate**
Typical Mediterranean climate on the north coast; snow on the higher ground; Algiers, representative of the coastal region, has average maximum daily temperatures of 15–29°C; elsewhere an essentially rainless Saharan climate.

**National holidays**
Jan 1, May 1, Jun 19 (Revolutionary Readjustment), Jul 5 (Independence), Nov 1 (Revolution); Ad (2), As, ER (2), NY (Muslim), PB.

## Political leaders

**President**

| | |
|---|---|
| 1962–5 | Ahmed Ben Bella |
| 1965–78 | Houari Boumédienne |
| 1979–92 | Chandli Benjedid |
| 1992 | *High Commission of State: Chair* Mohamed Boudiaf |
| 1992–4 | Ali Kafi |
| 1994–9 | Liamine Zeroual |
| 1999– | Abdelaziz Bouteflika |

**Prime Minister**

| | |
|---|---|
| 1962–3 | Ahmed Ben Bella |
| 1963–79 | *No Prime Minister* |
| 1979–84 | Mohamed Ben Ahmed Abdelghani |
| 1984–8 | Abdelhamid Brahimi |
| 1988–9 | Kasdi Merbah |
| 1989–91 | Mouloud Hamrouche |
| 1991–2 | Sid Ahmed Ghozali |
| 1992–3 | Belaid Abdessalam |
| 1993–4 | Redha Malek |
| 1994–5 | Mokdad Sifi |
| 1995–8 | Ahmed Ouyahia |
| 1998–9 | Ismail Hamdani |
| 1999–2000 | Ahmed Benbitour |
| 2000–3 | Ali Benflis |
| 2003– | Ahmed Ouyahia |

**AMERICAN SAMOA** *see* **UNITED STATES OF AMERICA**

## ANDORRA

| | | | |
|---|---|---|---|
| **Official name** | Principality of Andorra; also sometimes known as The Valleys of Andorra | **Languages** | Catalan; French and Spanish are also spoken |
| **Local name** | Andorra; Principat d'Andorra | **Ethnic groups** | Spanish 61%, Andorran 30%, French 6%, others 3% |
| **Area** | 468 sq km/181 sq mi | **Religions** | Christianity 95% (RC 94%, Prot 1%), none/ unaffiliated 5% |
| **Capital** | Andorra la Vella; Andorra la Vieja (Spanish), Andorre la Vielle (French), Andorra la Vella (Catalan) | **Time zone** | GMT +1 |
| **Population** | 66 000 (2001e) | **Currency** | 1 Euro (€) = 100 cents |
| **Nationality** | Andorran | **Telephone** | +376 |
| | | **Internet** | .ad |
| | | **Country code** | AND |

**Location**
A small, mountainous, semi-independent neutral state on the southern slopes of the central Pyrenees between France and Spain.

**Physical description**
A mountainous country, reaching 2 947m/9 669ft at Coma Pedrosa, occupying two valleys (del Norte and del Orient) of the River Valira.

**Climate**
Winters are cold but dry and sunny; the midsummer months are slightly drier than spring and autumn.

**National holidays**
Jan 1, 6, Mar 14 (Constitution), May 1, Jun 24 (People's Festival), Aug 15, Sep 8 (Our Lady of Meritxell), Nov 1, Dec 8, 21 (St Thomas), 25, 26; EM, GF, WM.

### Political leaders

There are two heads of state, called Co-Princes: the President of France (see entry for France) and the Bishop of Urgell, Spain (Joan Enric Vives Sicilia since 2003).

**President of the Executive Council**

| | | | |
|---|---|---|---|
| 1982–4 | Óscar Ribas Reig | 1990–4 | Óscar Ribas Reig |
| 1984–90 | Josep Pintat Solens | 1994– | Marc Forné Molné |

### *In the High Pyrenees*

Andorra, nestled among the mountains of the eastern Pyrenees, proudly claims to be Europe's highest inhabited country. The lowest point is a still-respectable 840m/2 756ft above sea level, while the highest mountain, Coma Pedrosa, reaches a sizeable 2 947m/9 669ft. Andorra manages to pack 65 peaks that reach higher than 2 500m/8 202ft into just 468 sq km/181 sq mi of land.

# ANGOLA

| | | | |
|---|---|---|---|
| **Official name** | Republic of Angola | **Languages** | Portuguese; many Bantu languages are also spoken |
| **Local name** | Angola; República de Angola | **Ethnic groups** | Ovimbundu 37%, Mbundu 25%, Bakongo 13%, others 25% |
| **Former name** | People's Republic of Angola (until 1992) | **Religions** | Christianity 81% (RC 69%, Prot 12%), traditional beliefs 19% |
| **Independence** | 1975 | **Time zone** | GMT +1 |
| **Area** | 1 245 790 sq km/480 875 sq mi | **Currency** | 1 Kwanza (Kz) = 100 lwei |
| **Capital** | Luanda | **Telephone** | +244 |
| **Chief towns** | Huambo, Benguela, Lobito, Namibe (Moçâmedes), Cabinda, Malanje, Lubango | **Internet** | .ao |
| **Population** | 12 768 000 (2001e) | **Country code** | AGO |
| **Nationality** | Angolan | | |

**Location**
A republic in south-west Africa, bounded to the south by Namibia; to the east by Zambia; and to the north by Democratic Republic of Congo; the separate province of Cabinda is enclosed by Congo and Democratic Republic of Congo.

**Physical description**
A narrow coastal plain, widening in the north towards the Congo Delta; high plateau inland with an average elevation of 1 200m/3 937ft; highest point is Serro Môco (2 619m/8 592ft); numerous rivers rise in the plateau but few are navigable for any length.

**Climate**
Mostly a tropical plateau climate; a single wet season Oct–Mar and a long dry season; average daily temperatures of 24–29°C in upland region; temperature and rainfall much reduced on the coast, which is semi-desert as far north as Luanda.

**National holidays**
Jan 1, 4 (Martyrs of the Colonial Repression), Feb 4 (Beginning of the Armed Struggle), Mar 8 (Women), May 1, Jun 1 (Children), Sep 17 (Nation's Founder/National Hero), Nov 2, 11 (Independence), Dec 25.

## Political leaders

**President**
1975–9 Antonio Agostinho Neto
1979– José Eduardo dos Santos

**Prime Minister**
1975–8 Lopo do Nasciemento
1978–91 *No Prime Minister*
1991–2 Fernando José de França van Dúnem
1992–6 Marcolino José Carlos Moco
1996–97 Fernando José de França van Dúnem
1999–2002 *No Prime Minister*
2002– Fernando da Piedade Dias dos Santos

**ANGUILLA** *see* **UNITED KINGDOM**

**ANTARCTIC TERRITORY, BRITISH** *see* **UNITED KINGDOM**

## ANTIGUA AND BARBUDA

| | | | |
|---|---|---|---|
| **Official name** | State of Antigua and Barbuda | **Religions** | Christianity 96% (Prot 87%, RC 9%), Rastafarianism 1%, none/unaffiliated 1%, others 2% |
| **Local name** | Antigua and Barbuda | **Time zone** | GMT –4 |
| **Independence** | 1981 | **Currency** | 1 East Caribbean Dollar (EC$) = 100 cents |
| **Area** | 442 sq km/171 sq mi | **Telephone** | +1 268 |
| **Capital** | St John's | **Internet** | .ag |
| **Chief towns** | Codrington (on Barbuda) | **Country code** | ATG |
| **Population** | 77 426 (2001) | | |
| **Nationality** | Antiguan, Barbudan | | |
| **Languages** | English | | |
| **Ethnic groups** | African descent 92%, British 4%, others 4% | | |

**Location**
An independent group of three tropical islands in the Leeward group of the Lesser Antilles in the eastern Caribbean Sea: Antigua, Barbuda and the uninhabited Redonda.

**Physical description**
The western part of Antigua rises to 402m/1 319ft at Boggy Peak; Barbuda is a flat, coral island reaching only 44m/144ft at its highest point, with a large lagoon on its western side.

**Climate**
Tropical, with temperatures ranging from 24°C in Jan to 27°C in Aug–Sep.

**National holidays**
Jan 1, Nov 1 (Independence), Dec 25, 26; EM, GF, WM, Labour (1st Mon in May), Emancipation (1st Mon and Tue in Aug).

### Political leaders

**Prime Minister**

1981–94 Vere Cornwall Bird
1994– Lester Bryant Bird

## ARGENTINA

| | | | |
|---|---|---|---|
| **Official name** | Argentine Republic | **Nationality** | Argentine, Argentinian |
| **Local name** | Argentina; República Argentina | **Languages** | Spanish |
| **Independence** | 1816 | **Ethnic groups** | European 85%, mestizo 14%, others 1% |
| **Area** | 3 761 274 sq km/ 1 451 852 sq mi | **Religions** | Christianity 92% (RC 90%, Prot 2%), Judaism 2%, others 6% |
| **Capital** | Buenos Aires | **Time zone** | GMT –3 |
| **Chief towns** | Córdoba, Rosario, Mendoza, La Plata, Mar del Plata, San Miguel de Tucumán | **Currency** | 1 Peso ($) = 100 centavos |
| **Population** | 36 223 947 (2001) | **Telephone** | +54 |
| | | **Internet** | .ar |
| | | **Country code** | ARG |

# ARGENTINA

**Location**
A republic in south-eastern South America, bounded to the east by the southern Atlantic Ocean; to the west by Chile; to the north by Bolivia and Paraguay; and to the north-east by Brazil and Uruguay.

**Physical description**
The Andes stretch the entire length, north to south, forming the boundary with Chile; the highest peak is Aconcagua (6 960m/22 835ft); the *pampa*, a grassy, treeless plain is to the east, with uneven, arid steppes to the south.

**Climate**
Most of Argentina lies in the rainshadow of the Andes; temperatures range from tropical to moderately cool (average annual temperature 16°C at Buenos Aires), with some desert; the south is directly influenced by strong prevailing westerlies.

**National holidays**
Jan 1, Apr 2 (Malvinas), May 1, 25 (National), Jun 20 (Flag), Jul 9 (Independence), Aug 17 (Death of General San Martín), Oct 12 (Americas Discovery), Dec 8, 25; GF, HT.

## Political leaders

**President**

| | |
|---|---|
| 1898–1904 | Julio Argentino Roca |
| 1904–6 | Manuel Quintana |
| 1906–10 | José Figueroa Alcorta |
| 1910–14 | Roque Sáenz Peña |
| 1914–16 | Victorino de la Plaza |
| 1916–22 | Hipólito Yrigoyen |
| 1922–8 | Marcelo T de Alvear |
| 1928–30 | Hipólito Yrigoyen |
| 1930–2 | José Félix Uriburu |
| 1932–8 | Augustin Pedro Justo |
| 1938–40 | Roberto M Ortiz |
| 1940–3 | Ramón S Castillo |
| 1943–4 | Pedro P Ramírez |
| 1944–6 | Edelmiro J Farrell |
| 1946–55 | Juan Perón |
| 1955–8 | Eduardo Lonardi |
| 1958–62 | Arturo Frondizi |
| 1962–3 | José María Guido |
| 1963–6 | Arturo Illia |
| 1966–70 | Juan Carlos Onganía |
| 1970–1 | Roberto Marcelo Levingston |
| 1971–3 | Alejandro Agustin Lanusse |
| 1973 | Héctor J Cámpora |
| 1973–4 | Juan Perón |
| 1974–6 | Martínez de Perón |
| 1976–81 | *Military Junta* (Jorge Rafaél Videla) |
| 1981 | *Military Junta* (Roberto Eduardo Viola) |
| 1981–2 | *Military Junta* (Leopoldo Galtieri) |
| 1982–3 | Reynaldo Bignone |
| 1983–8 | Raúl Alfonsín |
| 1988–99 | Carlos Saúl Menem |
| 1999–2001 | Fernando de la Rúa |
| 2001 | *Three Interim Presidents* |
| 2002–3 | Eduardo Duhalde |
| 2003– | Nestor Kirchner |

### Silver Country

The name *Argentina* comes from the Latin word *argentum*, meaning 'silver'. When Spanish explorers first reached the area in the early 16c the local people presented them with silver gifts, and the explorers returned home with tales of the *Sierra del Plata*, a mountain supposedly composed of silver. The main river estuary was christened *Río de la Plata*, or 'River of Silver'.

## ARMENIA

| | | | |
|---|---|---|---|
| **Official name** | Republic of Armenia | **Chief towns** | Vanadzor, Gyumri |
| **Local name** | Hayastan; Hayastany Hanrapetoutyun | **Population** | 3 458 303 (2001) |
| **Former name** | Transcaucasian Soviet Federated Socialist Republic (with Azerbaijan and Georgia, 1922–36), Armenian Soviet Socialist Republic (1920–2, 1936–90), within the Union of Soviet Socialist Republics (USSR; 1922–91) | **Nationality** | Armenian |
| | | **Languages** | Armenian; Russian is also widely spoken |
| | | **Ethnic group(s)** | Armenian 93%, Azeri 3%, Russian 2%, others 2% |
| | | **Religions** | Christianity 94% (Orthodox), others 6% |
| | | **Time zone** | GMT +4 |
| | | **Currency** | 1 Dram (Drm) = 100 lumas |
| **Independence** | 1991 | **Telephone** | +374 |
| **Area** | 29 800 sq km/11 500 sq mi | **Internet** | .am |
| | | **Country code** | ARM |
| **Capital** | Yerevan; Erevan | | |

**Location**
A republic in southern Transcaucasia, bounded to the north by Georgia; to the east and south-west by Azerbaijan; to the south-east by Iran; and to the north-west by Turkey.

**Physical description**
Mountainous, rising to 4 090m/13 418ft at Mt Aragats in the west; largest lake is Sevan.

**Climate**
Dry and cold in the summer, cold in the winter.

**National holidays**
Jan 1, 6 (Armenian Christmas), Apr 24 (Day of Remembrance of the Victims of the Genocide), May 28 (Declaration of the First Armenian Republic, 1918), Sep 21 (Independence), Dec 7 (Day of Remembrance of the Victims of the Earthquake); EM, ES, GF, HS.

## Political leaders

**President**

1991–8 Levon Ter-Petrossian
1998– Robert Kocharyan

**Prime Minister**

1991–2 Gagik Haroutunian
1992–3 Khosrov Haroutunian
1993–6 Hrand Bagratian
1996–7 Armen Sarkissian
1997–8 Robert Kocharyan
1998–9 Armen Darbinian
1999 Vazgen Sarkissian
1999–2000 Aram Sarkissian
2000– Andranik Markarian

### *Ancient Yerevan*

Yerevan was founded as a fortress settlement by King Argishti I in 782BC. The ruins of the first fortress are still visible, with an old inscription: ' ... I, Argishti, Son of Menua, erected this stronghold ... to the glory of the country of Biaina and to the fear of its enemies ...'

**ARUBA** *see* **NETHERLANDS, THE**

# AUSTRALIA

| | | | |
|---|---|---|---|
| **Official name** | Commonwealth of Australia | **Ethnic groups** | European 95%, Asian 4%, Aboriginal and others 1% |
| **Local name** | Australia | **Religions** | Christianity 73% (Prot 47%, RC 26%), none/ unaffiliated 17%, others 10% |
| **Independence** | 1901 | **Time zone** | GMT +8/10.5 |
| **Area** | 7 692 300 sq km/ 2 969 228 sq mi | **Currency** | 1 Australian Dollar ($A) = 100 cents |
| **Capital** | Canberra | **Telephone** | +61 |
| **Chief towns** | Melbourne, Brisbane, Perth, Adelaide, Sydney | **Internet** | .au |
| **Population** | 18 769 249 (2001) | **Country code** | AUS |
| **Nationality** | Australian | | |
| **Languages** | English; Aboriginal languages are also spoken | | |

**Location**
An independent country, the largest island and the smallest continent in the world, entirely in the southern hemisphere.

**Physical description**
Almost 40% of its land mass is north of the Tropic of Capricorn; Australian continent consists largely of plains and plateaux, most of which average 600m/1 968ft above sea level; the West Australian plateau occupies nearly half the whole area; most of the plateau is dry and barren desert; Great Dividing Range lies parallel to the eastern seaboard, rising to 2 228m/7 310ft at Mt Kosciusko (Australia's highest point); off the north-east coast, stretching for over 1 900km/1 200mi, is the Great Barrier Reef; the island of Tasmania rises to 1 617m/5 305ft at Mt Ossa; fertile land with a temperate climate and reliable rainfall is limited to the lowlands and valleys near the coast in the east and south-east, and to a small part of the south-west, and the population is concentrated in these two regions.

**Climate**
Half the country has a rainfall variability of more than 30%, with many areas experiencing prolonged drought; Darwin's average daily temperature is 26–34°C in Nov and 19–31°C in Jul; Melbourne's average daily temperature is 6–13°C in Jul and 14–26°C in Jan–Feb; in Tasmania, climatic conditions vary greatly between mountain and coast.

**National holidays**
Jan 1, 26 (Australia), Apr 25 (Anzac), Dec 25, 26; Queen's Birthday (Jun, *except Western Australia, Sept/Oct*), EM, GF, HS; *additional days vary between states*.

## Australian states and territories

| Name | Population (2001) | Area | Capital |
|---|---|---|---|
| Australian Capital Territory (ACT) | 309 184 | 2 432 sq km/939 sq mi | Canberra |
| New South Wales (NSW) | 6 311 168 | 801 427 sq km/309 431 sq mi | Sydney |
| Northern Territory (NT) | 202 729 | 1 346 200 sq km/519 768 sq mi | Darwin |
| Queensland (QLD) | 3 585 639 | 1 732 700 sq km/668 995 sq mi | Brisbane |
| South Australia (SA) | 1 458 912 | 984 376 sq km/380 070 sq mi | Adelaide |
| Tasmania (TAS) | 454 841 | 68 331 sq km/26 383 sq mi | Hobart |
| Victoria (VIC) | 4 612 097 | 227 600 sq km/87 876 sq mi | Melbourne |
| Western Australia (WA) | 1 832 008 | 2 525 500 sq km/975 096 sq mi | Perth |

## Overseas territories

### Norfolk Island

| | | | |
|---|---|---|---|
| **Location** | An island in the western Pacific Ocean, lying 1 488km/925mi north-east of Sydney. | | |
| **Area** | 35 sq km/14 sq mi | **Internet** | .nf |
| **Capital** | Kingston | **Country code** | NFK |
| **Population** | 2 000 (1986) | | |

### Heard and McDonald Islands

| | | | |
|---|---|---|---|
| **Location** | An island group comprising Heard Island, Shag Island and the McDonald Islands in the Southern Ocean, approximately 4 000km/2 500mi south-west of Fremantle. | | |
| **Area** | 412 sq km/159 sq mi | **Internet** | .hm |
| **Population** | uninhabited | **Country code** | HMD |

### Christmas Island

| | | | |
|---|---|---|---|
| **Location** | An island in the Indian Ocean, approximately 360km/224mi south of Java (Indonesia). | | |
| **Area** | 135 sq km/52 sq mi | **Internet** | .cx |
| **Capital** | The Settlement | **Country code** | CXR |
| **Population** | 430 (2003e) | | |

### Cocos (Keeling) Islands

| | | | |
|---|---|---|---|
| **Location** | Two separate groups of atolls in the Indian Ocean, 3 685km/2 290mi west of Darwin, comprising 27 islands; the main islands are West Island and Home Island. | | |
| **Area** | 14.2 sq km/5.5 sq mi | **Internet** | .cc |
| **Capital** | West Island | **Country code** | CCK |
| **Population** | 647 (1991) | | |

*Note: Australia also possesses the uninhabited Ashmore and Cartier Islands in the Indian Ocean and the Coral Sea Islands in the Coral Sea north-east of Australia.*

## Political leaders

Chief of State: British monarch, represented by Governor General.

**Prime Minister**

| | |
|---|---|
| 1901–3 | Edmund Barton *Prot* |
| 1903–4 | Alfred Deakin *Prot* |
| 1904 | John Christian Watson *Lab* |
| 1904–5 | George Houston Reid *Free* |
| 1905–8 | Alfred Deakin *Prot* |
| 1908–9 | Andrew Fisher *Lab* |
| 1909–10 | Alfred Deakin *Fus* |
| 1910–13 | Andrew Fisher *Lab* |
| 1913–14 | Joseph Cook *Lib* |
| 1914–15 | Andrew Fisher *Lab* |
| 1915–17 | William Morris Hughes *Nat Lab* |
| 1917–23 | William Morris Hughes *Nat* |
| 1923–9 | Stanley Melbourne Bruce *Nat* |
| 1929–32 | James Henry Scullin *Lab* |
| 1932–9 | Joseph Aloysius Lyons *Un* |

| | | | |
|---|---|---|---|
| 1939 | Earle Christmas Page *Co* | 1968–71 | John Grey Gorton *Lib* |
| 1939–41 | Robert Gordon Menzies *Un* | 1971–2 | William McMahon *Lib* |
| 1941 | Arthur William Fadden *Co* | 1972–5 | Edward Gough Whitlam *Lab* |
| 1941–5 | John Joseph Curtin *Lab* | 1975–83 | John Malcolm Fraser *Lib* |
| 1945 | Francis Michael Forde *Lab* | 1983–91 | Robert James Lee Hawke *Lab* |
| 1945–9 | Joseph Benedict Chifley *Lab* | 1991–6 | Paul Keating *Lab* |
| 1949–66 | Robert Gordon Menzies *Lib* | 1996– | John Howard *Lib* |
| 1966–7 | Harold Edward Holt *Lib* | | |
| 1967–8 | John McEwen *Co* | | |

*Co = Country*
*Con = Conservative*
*Free = Free Trade*
*Fus = Fusion*
*Lab = Labor*
*Lib = Liberal*
*Nat = Nationalist*
*Nat Lab = National Labor*
*Prot = Protectionist*
*Un = United*

## AUSTRIA

| | | | |
|---|---|---|---|
| **Official name** | Republic of Austria | **Nationality** | Austrian |
| **Local name** | Österreich; Republik Österreich | **Languages** | German |
| **Former name** | formerly part of Austria–Hungary (until 1918) | **Ethnic groups** | Austrian 98%, others 2% |
| **Independence** | 1955 | **Religions** | Christianity 84% (RC 77%, Prot 7%), none/unaffiliated 8%, Islam 2%, others 6% |
| **Area** | 83 854 sq km/32 368 sq mi | **Time zone** | GMT +1 |
| **Capital** | Vienna; Wien | **Currency** | 1 Euro (€) = 100 cents |
| **Chief town(s)** | Graz, Linz, Salzburg, Innsbruck, Klagenfurt | **Telephone** | +43 |
| **Population** | 8 065 465 (2001) | **Internet** | .at |
| | | **Country code** | AUT |

**Location**
A mountainous republic in central Europe, bounded to the north by Germany and the Czech Republic and Slovakia; to the south by Italy and Slovenia; to the west by Switzerland and Liechtenstein; and to the east by Hungary.

**Physical description**
Situated at the eastern end of the Alps, the country is almost entirely mountainous; highest point is Grossglockner, at 3 797m/12 457ft; most of the country is in the drainage basin of the River Danube.

**Climate**
Three climatic regions: the Alps (often sunny in winter but cloudy in summer); the Danube valley and the Vienna basin (the driest region); and the south-east, a region of heavy thunderstorms; most rain in summer; winters are cold.

**National holidays**
Jan 1, 6, May 1, Aug 15, Oct 26 (National), Nov 1, Dec 8, 25, 26; A, CC, EM, WM.

## Political leaders

### Monarch (Habsburg Dynasty)

| | | | |
|---|---|---|---|
| 1440–93 | Frederick III | 1519–58 | Karl V |
| 1493–1519 | Maximilian I | 1558–64 | Ferdinand I |

| | | | |
|---|---|---|---|
| 1564–76 | Maximilian II | 1742–5 | Karl VII |
| 1576–1612 | Rudolf II | 1745–65 | Franz I |
| 1612–19 | Matthias | 1765–90 | Josef II |
| 1619–37 | Ferdinand II | 1790–2 | Leopold II |
| 1637–57 | Ferdinand III | 1792–1835 | Franz II |
| 1658–1705 | Leopold I | 1835–48 | Ferdinand I |
| 1705–11 | Josef I | 1848–1916 | Franz Josef |
| 1711–40 | Karl VI | 1916–18 | Karl I |
| 1740–2 | *Interregnum* | | |

**President**

| | | | |
|---|---|---|---|
| 1918–20 | Karl Sätz | 1957–65 | Adolf Schärf |
| 1920–8 | Michael Hainisch | 1965–74 | Franz Jonas |
| 1928–38 | Wilhelm Miklas | 1974–86 | Rudolf Kirchsläger |
| 1938–45 | *German rule* | 1986–92 | Kurt Waldheim |
| 1945–50 | Karl Renner | 1992– | Thomas Klestil |
| 1950–7 | Theodor Körner | | |

**Chancellor**

| | | | |
|---|---|---|---|
| 1918–20 | Karl Renner | 1932–4 | Engelbert Dollfus |
| 1920–1 | Michael Mayr | 1934–8 | Kurt von Schuschnigg |
| 1921–2 | Johann Schober | 1938–45 | *German rule* |
| 1922 | Walter Breisky | 1945 | Karl Renner |
| 1922 | Johann Schober | 1945–53 | Leopold Figl |
| 1922–4 | Ignaz Seipel | 1953–61 | Julius Raab |
| 1924–6 | Rudolph Ramek | 1961–4 | Alfons Gorbach |
| 1926–9 | Ignaz Seipel | 1964–70 | Josef Klaus |
| 1929–30 | Ernst Streeruwitz | 1970–83 | Bruno Kreisky |
| 1930 | Johann Schober | 1983–6 | Fred Sinowatz |
| 1930 | Carl Vaugoin | 1986–97 | Franz Vranitzky |
| 1930–1 | Otto Ender | 1997–2000 | Viktor Klima |
| 1931–2 | Karl Buresch | 2000– | Wolfgang Schüssel |

## AZERBAIJAN

| | | | |
|---|---|---|---|
| **Official name** | Azerbaijani Republic | **Chief towns** | Gäncä, Sumqayit |
| **Local name** | Azərbaycan Respublikası | **Population** | 7 953 438 (1999) |
| **Former name** | Azerbaijan People's Republic (1918–20), Transcaucasian Soviet Federated Socialist Republic (with Armenia and Georgia, 1922–36), Azerbaijan Soviet Socialist Republic (1920–2, 1936–90), within the Union of Soviet Socialist Republics (USSR; 1922–91) | **Nationality** | Azerbaijani |
| | | **Languages** | Azeri |
| | | **Ethnic groups** | Azeri 83%, Russian 6%, Armenian 6%, Dagestani 3%, others 2% |
| | | **Religions** | Islam 93% (Shia), Christianity 5% (Orthodox), others 2% |
| | | **Time zone** | GMT +4 |
| | | **Currency** | 1 Manat = 100 gopik |
| **Independence** | 1991 | **Telephone** | +994 |
| **Area** | 86 600 sq km/33 428 sq mi | **Internet** | .az |
| **Capital** | Baku; Bakı | **Country code** | AZE |

**Location**
A republic in eastern Transcaucasia, bounded to the east by the Caspian Sea and to the south by Iran; Armenia splits the country in the south-west and forms the western boundary; Georgia and Russia lie to the north.

**Physical description**
Crossed by the Greater Caucasus in the north and the Lesser Caucasus in the south-west; they are separated by the plain of River Kura; the highest peak is Mt Bazar-Dyuzi (4 480m/14 698ft) in the north-east; 10.5% of total area is forested.

**Climate**
Continental; hot in summer, cold in winter.

**National holidays**
Jan 1, 20 (Martyrs), 8 Mar (Women), May 9 (Victory), 28 (Republic), Jun 15 (National Salvation), 26 (Army and Navy), Oct 18 (Independence), Nov 12 (Constitution), 17 (National Revival), Dec 31 (Azerbaijani Solidarity Worldwide); Ad, ER, NY (Muslim) (2).

## Political leaders

**President**

| | |
|---|---|
| 1991–2 | Ayaz Mutalibov |
| 1992 | Yakub Mamedov *Acting President* |
| 1992–3 | Abul Faz Elchibey |
| 1993– | Heydar Aliyev |

**Prime Minister**

| | |
|---|---|
| 1991–2 | Hassan Hasanov |
| 1992 | Feirus Mustafayev *Acting Prime Minister* |
| 1992–3 | Rakhim Guseinov |
| 1993 | Ali Masimov *Acting Prime Minister* |
| 1993 | Panakh Guseinov |
| 1993–4 | Surat Guseinov |
| 1994–6 | Fuad Kuliyev |
| 1996–2003 | Artur Rasizade |
| 2003– | Ilham Aliyev |

### *Azeri Proverbs*

Azerbaijan's many proverbs, known as 'father's words' include 'it's impossible to hold two watermelons in one hand', 'don't tie garlic on your head if you don't have a headache' and 'the dog is sleeping in the cart's shade but thinks it's his own'.

**AZORES** *see* **PORTUGAL**

## THE BAHAMAS

| | | | |
|---|---|---|---|
| **Official name** | Commonwealth of The Bahamas | **Ethnic groups** | black 85%, white 15% |
| **Local name** | Bahamas | **Religions** | Christianity 95% (Prot and others 74%, RC 21%), none/unaffiliated 3%, others 2% |
| **Independence** | 1973 | **Time zone** | GMT –5 |
| **Area** | 13 934 sq km/5 379 sq mi | **Currency** | 1 Bahamian Dollar (BA$, B$) = 100 cents |
| **Capital** | Nassau | **Telephone** | +1 242 |
| **Chief towns** | Freeport | **Internet** | .bs |
| **Population** | 303 611 (2000) | **Country code** | BHS |
| **Nationality** | Bahamian | | |
| **Languages** | English | | |

**Location**
An independent archipelago of c.700 low-lying islands and over 2 000 cays, forming a chain extending c.800km/500mi south-east from the coast of Florida.

**Physical description**
The coralline limestone islands of The Bahamas comprise the two oceanic banks of Little Bahama and Great Bahama; the highest point on the low-lying islands, Mt Alvernia on Cat Island, is only 63m/207ft above sea level.

**Climate**
Subtropical, with average temperatures of 21°C in winter and 27°C in summer; hurricanes are frequent in Jun–Nov.

**National holidays**
Jan 1, Jul 10 (Independence), Oct 12 (Discovery), Dec 25, 26; EM, GF, WM; Labour (1st Mon in Jun), Emancipation (1st Fri in Aug).

## Political leaders

Chief of State: British monarch, represented by Governor General.

**Prime Minister**

| | |
|---|---|
| 1973–92 | Lynden O Pindling |
| 1992–2002 | Hubert A Ingraham |
| 2002– | Perry Christie |

### *Islands of the Shallow Seas*

The Bahamas were first discovered by Europeans when Christopher Columbus arrived in 1492. The sailors were supposedly struck by the depth of the surrounding waters, and remarked '*baja mar*' – the Spanish for 'low water' or, loosely, 'shallow seas' – inadvertently christening the islands.

## BAHRAIN

| | |
|---|---|
| **Official name** | Kingdom of Bahrain |
| **Local name** | Al-Bahrayn; Mamlakat al-Bahrayn |
| **Former name** | State of Bahrain (until 2002) |
| **Independence** | 1971 |
| **Area** | 678 sq km/262 sq mi |
| **Capital** | Manama; Al Manāmah |
| **Chief towns** | Al Muharraq |
| **Population** | 650 604 (2001) |
| **Nationality** | Bahraini |
| **Languages** | Arabic |
| **Ethnic groups** | Bahraini 63%, Asian 13%, other Arab 10%, Iranian 8%, others 6% |
| **Religions** | Islam 95% (Shia 73%, Sunni 22%), others 5% |
| **Time zone** | GMT +3 |
| **Currency** | 1 Bahraini Dinar (BD) = 1 000 fils |
| **Telephone** | +973 |
| **Internet** | .bh |
| **Country code** | BHR |

**Location**
A group of 35 islands comprising a monarchy in the Arabian Gulf, midway between the Qatar Peninsula and mainland Saudi Arabia; a causeway (25km/16mi in length) connects Bahrain to Saudi Arabia.

**Physical description**
The island of Bahrain is c.48km/30mi long and 13–16km/8–10mi wide; highest point is Jabal Dukhan (135m/443ft); largely bare and infertile, though helped by many major drainage schemes since 1973.

**Climate**
Cool north/north-east winds, with a little rain in Dec–Mar; rest of the year dominated by either a moist north-east wind (the *Shamal*) or the hot, sand-bearing *Qaws* from the south; average temperature 36°C in summer, 19°C in Jan.

**National holidays**
Jan 1, Dec 16 (National); Ad (3), As, ER (3), NY (Muslim), PB.

## Political leaders

**Emir**

| | |
|---|---|
| 1971–99 | Isa Bin Salman Al-Khalifa |
| 1999–2002 | Hamad Bin Isa Al-Khalifa |

**Monarch**

| | |
|---|---|
| 2002– | Hamad Bin Isa Al-Khalifa |

**Prime Minister**

| | |
|---|---|
| 1971– | Khalifa Bin Salman Al-Khalifa |

### *Land of Immortality*

In the third millennium BC Bahrain was known as *Dilmun*, and was described in an ancient tale, the *Epic of Gilgamesh*, as the 'land of immortality' where the 'flower of eternal youth' might be found. The later name *Bahrain* comes from Arabic and means 'two seas'.

**BALEARIC ISLANDS** *see* **SPAIN**

## BANGLADESH

| | | | |
|---|---|---|---|
| **Official name** | People's Republic of Bangladesh | **Population** | 123 151 246 (2001) |
| **Local name** | Gana Prajatantri Bangladesh | **Nationality** | Bangladeshi |
| **Former name** | Part of the Indian states of Bengal (until 1905) and East Bengal (until 1947), then part of Pakistan as East Pakistan (until 1971) | **Languages** | Bangla (Bengali); English is the second language |
| **Independence** | 1971 | **Ethnic groups** | Bengali 98%, others 2% |
| **Area** | 143 998 sq km/55 583 sq mi | **Religions** | Islam 87% (mostly Sunni), Hinduism 12%, others 1% |
| **Capital** | Dhaka (formerly known as Dacca) | **Time zone** | GMT +6 |
| **Chief towns** | Chittagong, Khulna, Narayanganj | **Currency** | 1 Taka (TK) = 100 poisha |
| | | **Telephone** | +880 |
| | | **Internet** | .bd |
| | | **Country code** | BGD |

**Location**
An Asian republic lying between the foothills of the Himalayas and the Indian Ocean, bounded to the west, north-west and east by India; to the south-east by Myanmar; and to the south by the Bay of Bengal.

**Physical description**
Mainly a vast, low-lying alluvial plain, cut by a network of rivers and marshes; main rivers (including the Ganges and the Brahmaputra) join in the south to form the world's largest delta; frequent flooding; highest point is Keokradong (1 230m/4 035ft).

**Climate**
Tropical monsoon climate; hot season in Mar–Jun with heavy thunderstorms; very humid, with higher temperatures inland; main rainy season is Jun–Sep; cyclones in the Bay of Bengal cause widespread flooding of coastal areas.

**National holidays**
Feb 21 (Shaheed Dibash/International Mother Language), Mar 26 (Independence/National), May 1, Nov 7 (National Revolution and Solidarity), Dec 16 (Victory), 25; Ad (3), As, Buddha Purnima (Apr/May), Durgapuja (Jijaya Dashami), ER (3), Jamatul Wida, Janmashtami, NY (Bengali), PB, Shab-e-Barat, Shab-e-Qadr.

## Political leaders

**President**

| | |
|---|---|
| 1971–2 | Sayed Nazrul Islam *Acting President* |
| 1972 | Mujibur Rahman |
| 1972–3 | Abu Saeed Chowdhury |
| 1973–5 | Mohammad Mohammadullah |
| 1975 | Mujibur Rahman |
| 1975 | Khondaker Mushtaq Ahmad |
| 1975–7 | Abu Saadat Mohammad Sayem |
| 1977–81 | Zia Ur-Rahman |
| 1981–2 | Abdus Sattar |
| 1982–3 | Abdul Fazal Mohammad Ahsanuddin Chowdhury |
| 1983–90 | Hossain Mohammad Ershad |
| 1990–1 | Shehabuddin Ahmed *Acting President* |
| 1991–6 | Abdur Rahman Biswas |
| 1996–2001 | Shehabuddin Ahmed |
| 2001–2 | A Q M Badruddoza Chowdhury |
| 2002– | Iajuddin Ahmed |

**Prime Minister**

| | |
|---|---|
| 1971–2 | Tajuddin Ahmed |
| 1972–5 | Mujibur Rahman |
| 1975 | Mohammad Monsur Ali |
| 1975–9 | *Martial Law* |
| 1979–82 | Mohammad Azizur Rahman |
| 1982–4 | *Martial Law* |
| 1984–5 | Ataur Rahman Khan |
| 1986–8 | Mizanur Rahman Chowdhury |
| 1988–90 | Kazi Zafar Ahmed |
| 1991–6 | Khaleda Zia |
| 1996 | Mohammad Habibur Rahman |
| 1996–2001 | Sheikh Hasina Wajed |
| 2001– | Khaleda Zia |

### *Water Lilies and Jackfruit*

The national symbol of Bangladesh is the water lily, known in Bangla as the *shapla*, and the national fruit is the huge, distinctive jackfruit, called *kathal*. The little magpie robin, or *doel*, is the national bird. Bangladesh's national sport is *kabaddi*, a team sport that's popular across India and south-east Asia; it is a version of tag played barefoot by two teams of seven.

## BARBADOS

| | | | |
|---|---|---|---|
| **Official name** | Barbados | **Religions** | Christianity 71% (Prot and others 67%, RC 4%), none/unaffiliated 17%, others 12% |
| **Local name** | Barbados | **Time zone** | GMT –4 |
| **Independence** | 1966 | **Currency** | 1 Barbadian Dollar (BD$) = 100 cents |
| **Area** | 430 sq km/166 sq mi | **Telephone** | +1 246 |
| **Capital** | Bridgetown | **Internet** | .bb |
| **Chief towns** | Speightstown | **Country code** | BRB |
| **Population** | 268 000 (2001e) | | |
| **Nationality** | Barbadian or Bajan (*informal*) | | |
| **Languages** | English | | |
| **Ethnic groups** | black 80%, others 16%, white 4% | | |

**Location**
An independent state and the most easterly of the Caribbean Islands, situated in the Atlantic Ocean.

**Physical description**
A small, triangular island, 32km/20mi long (north-west to south-east); it rises to 340m/1 115ft at Mt Hillaby and is ringed by a coral reef.

**Climate**
Tropical, with an average annual temperature of 27°C.

**National holidays**
Jan 1, 21 (Errol Barrow), Apr 28 (National Heroes), May 1, Aug 1 (Emancipation), Dec 1 (Independence), Dec 25, 26; EM, GF, WM, Kadooment (Aug).

### Political leaders

**Prime Minister**

| | |
|---|---|
| 1966–76 | Errol Walton Barrow |
| 1976–85 | J M G (Tom) Adams |
| 1985–6 | H Bernard St John |
| 1986–7 | Errol Walton Barrow |
| 1987–94 | L Erskine Sandiford |
| 1994– | Owen Arthur |

### *Bearded Ones*

Bearded fig trees (*Ficus citrifolia*) used to be common in Barbados. When the Portuguese explorer Pedro a Campos visited in 1536, he named the island *Los Barbados*, meaning 'the bearded ones', in recognition of these trees. The tree is still featured on the national coat of arms, along with the national flower, the Pride of Barbados. The coat of arms also features a dolphin and a pelican, sugar cane and the motto 'Pride and Industry'. The national flag's ultramarine stripes represent the sea and sky and the golden centre represents the island's beautiful beaches. It also features the trident of Neptune, the ancient sea god.

**BARBUDA** *see* **ANTIGUA AND BARBUDA**

## BELARUS

| | | | |
|---|---|---|---|
| **Official name** | Republic of Belarus | | Bobruysk, Grodno, Brest |
| **Local name** | Belarus; Respublika Belarus | **Population** | 10 045 237 (1999) |
| **Former name** | Belorussian People's Republic (1918–19), Byelorussian or Belorussian Soviet Socialist Republic (until 1991), within the Union of Soviet Socialist Republics (USSR; 1922–91); sometimes also formerly known as Byelorussia, Belorussia, Byelarus or White Russia | **Nationality** | Belarusian |
| | | **Languages** | Belarusian, Russian |
| | | **Ethnic groups** | Belarusian 78%, Russian 13%, Polish 4%, Ukrainian 3%, others 2% |
| | | **Religions** | Christianity 72% (Orthodox 60%, RC 8%, Prot 4%), others 28% (including Islam and Judaism) |
| | | **Time zone** | GMT +2 |
| **Independence** | 1991 | **Currency** | 1 Belarusian Rouble (BR) = 100 kopeks |
| **Area** | 207 600 sq km/80 134 sq mi | **Telephone** | +375 |
| **Capital** | Minsk | **Internet** | .by |
| **Chief towns** | Gomel, Vitebsk, Mogilev, | **Country code** | BLR |

**Location**
A republic in eastern Europe, bounded to the west by Poland; to the north-west by Lithuania; to the north by Latvia; to the east by Russia; and to the south by the Ukraine.

**Physical description**
Largely flat, with low hills in the north-west rising to 345m/1 132ft at Dzyarzhynskaya Hara; c.11 000 lakes; one-third of the country is covered by forests.

**Climate**
Mild winters and cool summers.

**National holidays**
Jan 1, 7 (Orthodox Christmas), Mar 8 (Women), May 1, 6 (Memorial/Radounitsa), 9 (Victory), Jul 3 (Independence), Nov 7 (Oct Revolution), Dec 25; ES, Orthodox Easter Sunday.

## Political leaders

**Chair of Supreme Soviet**
1991–4 Stanislav Shushkevich
1994–6 Mecheslav Grib

**President**
1994– Alexander Lukashenko

**Prime Minister**
1990–4 Vyacheslav Kebich
1994–6 Mikhail Chigir
1996–2000 Sergei Ling
2000–1 Uladzimir Yarmoshyn
2001–3 Gennady Vasilyevich Novitsky
2003– Sergei Sidorsky *Acting Prime Minister*

**BELAU** *see* **PALAU**

## BELGIUM

| | | | |
|---|---|---|---|
| **Official name** | Kingdom of Belgium | **Languages** | Flemish (Dutch), French, German (mainly on the eastern border); Brussels is officially a bilingual city (French and Flemish) |
| **Local name** | Belgique; Royaume de Belgique (French), België; Koninkrijk België (Flemish), Belgien; Königreich Belgien (German) | **Ethnic groups** | Fleming 55%, Walloon 33%, Italian 2%, Moroccan 1%, others 9% |
| **Independence** | 1830 | **Religions** | Christianity 85% (RC 75%, Prot 10%), none/unaffiliated 10%, Islam 2%, others 3% |
| **Area** | 32 545 sq km/12 562 sq mi | **Time zone** | GMT +1 |
| **Capital** | Brussels; Bruxelles (French), Brussel (Flemish), Brüssel (German) | **Currency** | 1 Euro ( € ) = 100 cents |
| **Chief towns** | Antwerp, Ghent, Charleroi, Liège, Bruges, Namur, Mons | **Telephone** | +32 |
| **Population** | 10 273 000 (2001e) | **Internet** | .be |
| **Nationality** | Belgian | **Country code** | BEL |

**Location**
A kingdom in north-western Europe, bounded to the north by the Netherlands; to the south by France; to the east by Germany and Luxembourg; and to the west by the North Sea.

**Physical description**
Mostly low-lying fertile agricultural land, with some hills in the south-east (Ardennes); highest point is Signal de Botrange (694m/2 277ft); low-lying dune-fringed coastline; main rivers drain across the Dutch border and are linked by a network of canals.

**Climate**
Cool and temperate with strong maritime influences.

**National holidays**
Jan 1, May 1, Jul 21 (Independence), Aug 15, Nov 1, 11 (Armistice), Dec 25; A, EM, ES, WM; *also community holidays (Jul 11 Flemish, Sep 27 French, Nov 15 German).*

## Political leaders

Belgium became an independent kingdom in 1831. A national congress elected Prince Leopold of Saxe-Coburg as king.

**Monarch**

| | |
|---|---|
| 1831–65 | Léopold I |
| 1865–1909 | Léopold II |
| 1909–34 | Albert I |
| 1934–44 | Léopold III |
| 1944–50 | Prince Charles *Regent* |
| 1950–1 | Léopold III |
| 1951–93 | Baudouin |
| 1993– | Albert II |

**Prime Minister**

| | |
|---|---|
| 1899–1907 | Paul de Smet de Nayer |
| 1907–8 | Jules de Trooz |
| 1908–11 | Frans Schollaert |
| 1911–18 | Charles de Broqueville |
| 1918 | Gerhard Cooreman |
| 1918–20 | Léon Delacroix |
| 1920–1 | Henri Carton de Wiart |
| 1921–5 | Georges Theunis |

| | |
|---|---|
| 1925 | Alois van de Vyvere |
| 1925–6 | Prosper Poullet |
| 1926–31 | Henri Jaspar |
| 1931–2 | Jules Renkin |
| 1932–4 | Charles de Broqueville |
| 1934–5 | Georges Theunis |
| 1935–7 | Paul van Zeeland |
| 1937–8 | Paul Émile Janson |
| 1938–9 | Paul Spaak |
| 1939–45 | Hubert Pierlot |
| 1945–6 | Achille van Acker |
| 1946 | Paul Spaak |
| 1946 | Achille van Acker |
| 1946–7 | Camille Huysmans |
| 1947–9 | Paul Spaak |
| 1949–50 | Gaston Eyskens |
| 1950 | Jean Pierre Duvieusart |
| 1950–2 | Joseph Pholien |
| 1952–4 | Jean van Houtte |
| 1954–8 | Achille van Acker |
| 1958–61 | Gaston Eyskens |
| 1961–5 | Théodore Lefèvre |
| 1965–6 | Pierre Harmel |
| 1966–8 | Paul Vanden Boeynants |
| 1968–73 | Gaston Eyskens |
| 1973–4 | Edmond Leburton |
| 1974–8 | Léo Tindemans |
| 1978 | Paul Vanden Boeynants |
| 1979–81 | Wilfried Martens |
| 1981 | Marc Eyskens |
| 1981–91 | Wilfried Martens |
| 1992–9 | Jean-Luc Dehaene |
| 1999– | Guy Verhofstadt |

## BELIZE

| | |
|---|---|
| **Official name** | Belize |
| **Local name** | Belize |
| **Former name** | British Honduras (until 1973) |
| **Independence** | 1981 |
| **Area** | 22 963 sq km/8 864 sq mi |
| **Capital** | Belmopan |
| **Chief towns** | Belize City, Dangriga, Punta Gorda, San Ignacio |
| **Population** | 240 204 (2000) |
| **Nationality** | Belizean |
| **Languages** | English; Spanish and local Mayan, Carib and Creole languages are also spoken |
| **Ethnic groups** | mestizo 44%, Creole 30%, Maya 11%, Garifuna 7%, others 8% |
| **Religions** | Christianity 92% (RC 62%, Prot 30%), none/unaffiliated 2%, others 6% |
| **Time zone** | GMT –6 |
| **Currency** | 1 Belizean Dollar (BZ$) = 100 cents |
| **Telephone** | +501 |
| **Internet** | .bz |
| **Country code** | BLZ |

**Location**
An independent state in Central America, bounded to the north by Mexico; to the west and south by Guatemala; and to the east by the Caribbean Sea.

**Physical description**
An extensive coastal plain, swampy in the north, more fertile in the south; Maya Mountains extend almost to the east coast, rising to 1 120m/3 674ft at Victoria Peak; inner coastal waters are protected by the world's second longest barrier reef.

**Climate**
Generally subtropical but tempered by trade winds; coastal temperatures vary between 10°C and 36°C, with a greater range in the mountains; variable rainfall; dry season in Feb–May; hurricanes can cause severe damage.

**National holidays**
Jan 1, Mar 9 (Baron Bliss), May 1, 24 (Commonwealth), Sep 10 (St George's Caye), 21 (Independence), Oct 12 (Columbus), Nov 19 (Garifuna Settlement), Dec 25, 26; EM, GF, HS.

### Political leaders

Chief of State: British Monarch, represented by Governor General.

**Prime Minister**

| | |
|---|---|
| 1981–4 | George Cadle Price |
| 1985–9 | Manuel Esquivel |
| 1989–93 | George Cadle Price |
| 1993–8 | Manuel Esquivel |
| 1998– | Said Wilbert Musa |

### Flourishing in the Shade

The national motto of Belize is *Sub Umbra Florero*, which means 'Under the shade I flourish'. Belize's national tree is the mahogany and its national flower is the black orchid. The colourful keel-billed toucan is the national bird.

**BELORUSSIA** *see* **BELARUS**

## BENIN

| | | | |
|---|---|---|---|
| **Official name** | Republic of Benin | **Nationality** | Beninese |
| **Local name** | Bénin; République du Bénin | **Languages** | French; local languages are also spoken |
| **Former name** | Dahomey (until 1975); People's Republic of Benin (1975–90) | **Ethnic groups** | Fon 39%, Bariba 21%, Yoruba 10%, others 30% |
| **Independence** | 1960 | **Religions** | traditional beliefs 61%, Christianity 22% (RC 19%, Prot 3%), Islam 17% |
| **Area** | 112 622 sq km/43 472 sq mi | **Time zone** | GMT +1 |
| **Capital** | Porto Novo (administrative and constitutional) and Cotonou (economic and seat of government) | **Currency** | 1 CFA Franc (CFAFr) = 100 centimes |
| | | **Telephone** | +229 |
| | | **Internet** | .bj |
| **Chief towns** | Ouidah, Abomey, Kandi, Parakou, Natitingou | **Country code** | BEN |
| **Population** | 6 417 000 (2001e) | | |

**Location**
A republic in West Africa, bounded to the north by Niger; to the east by Nigeria; to the south by the Bight of Benin; to the west by Togo; and to the north-west by Burkina Faso.

**Physical description**
Rises from a 100km/62mi sandy coast with lagoons, to low-lying plains, then to a savannah plateau at c.400m/1 300ft; the Atakora Mountains rise to over 500m/1 640ft in the north-west; highest point is Mt Sokbaro (658m/2 159ft); several rivers.

**Climate**
Tropical climate, with three zones; south has rain throughout year, especially during the 'Guinea Monsoon' (May–Oct); centre has two rainy seasons (peaks in May–Jun and Oct); north has one (Jul–Sep).

**National holidays**
Jan 1, 10 (Traditional religions), May 1, Aug 1 (National), 15, Nov 1, Dec 25; A, Ad, EM, WM.

## Political leaders

### Dahomey

**President**

| | |
|---|---|
| 1960–3 | Hubert Coutoucou Maga |
| 1963–4 | Christophe Soglo |
| 1964–5 | Sourou Migan Apithy |
| 1965 | Justin Tométin Ahomadegbé |
| 1965 | Tairou Congacou |
| 1965–7 | Christophe Soglo |
| 1967–8 | Alphonse Amadou Alley |
| 1968–9 | Émile Derlin Zinsou |
| 1969–70 | *Presidential Committee* (Maurice Kouandété) |
| 1970–2 | *Presidential Committee* (Hubert Coutoucou Maga) |
| 1972–5 | Mathieu Kérékou |

**Prime Minister**

| | |
|---|---|
| 1958–9 | Sourou Migan Apithy |
| 1959–60 | Hubert Coutoucou Maga |
| 1960–4 | *As President* |
| 1964–5 | Justin Tométin Ahomadegbé |
| 1965–7 | *As President* |
| 1967–8 | Maurice Kouandété |
| 1968–75 | *As President* |

### People's Republic of Benin

**President and Prime Minister**

1975–90 Mathieu (*from 1980, sometimes called* Ahmed) Kérékou

### Republic of Benin

**President**

| | |
|---|---|
| 1990–1 | Mathieu Kérékou |
| 1991–6 | Nicéphore Soglo |
| 1996– | Mathieu Kérékou |

**Prime Minister**

| | |
|---|---|
| 1990–1 | Nicéphore Soglo |
| 1991–6 | *As President* |
| 1996–8 | Adrien Houngbedgi |
| 1998 | *Post abolished* |

**Cradle of Voodoo**

Benin has been described as 'the cradle of voodoo', the source of the beliefs which later flourished in the New World.

**BERMUDA** *see* **UNITED KINGDOM**

## BHUTAN

| | | | |
|---|---|---|---|
| **Official name** | Kingdom of Bhutan | **Ethnic groups** | Bhote 50%, Nepalese 35%, others 15% |
| **Local name** | Druk Yul | **Religions** | Buddhism 73%, Hinduism 22%, Islam 5% |
| **Area** | 46 600 sq km/18 000 sq mi | **Time zone** | GMT +6 |
| **Capital** | Thimphu | **Currency** | 1 Ngultrum (Nu) = 100 chetrum |
| **Chief towns** | Phuntsholing | **Telephone** | +975 |
| **Population** | 699 000 (2001e) | **Internet** | .bt |
| **Nationality** | Bhutanese | **Country code** | BTN |
| **Languages** | Dzongkha | | |

**Location**
A small state in the eastern Himalayas, bounded to the north by China and to the south by India.

**Physical description**
High peaks of the east Himalayas, reaching over 7 000m/22 966ft in the north; highest point is Kula Kangri (7 553m/24 780ft); forested mountain ridges with fertile valleys descend to low foothills in the south; many rivers flow to meet the River Brahmaputra.

**Climate**
Permanent snowfields and glaciers in the mountains; subtropical forest in the south; torrential rain is common.

**National holidays**
May 2 (Birthday of Jigme Dorji Wangchuk), Jun 2 (Coronation of Fourth Hereditary King), Jul 21 (First Sermon of Lord Buddha, Death of Jigme Dorji Wangchuk), Nov 11–13 (Birthday of HM Jigme Singye Wangchuk), Dec 17 (National).

## Political leaders

**Monarch (Druk Gyalpo)**

| | |
|---|---|
| 1907–26 | Uggyen Wangchuk |
| 1926–52 | Jigme Wangchuk |
| 1952–72 | Jigme Dorji Wangchuk |
| 1972– | Jigme Singye Wangchuk |

**Prime Minister**

| | |
|---|---|
| 1952–64 | Jigme Palden Dorji |
| 1964 | Lhendup Dorji *Acting Prime Minister* |
| 1964–98 | *No Prime Minister* |
| 1998–99 | Lyonpo Jigme Yozer Thinley |
| 1999–2000 | Lyonpo Sangye Ngedup |
| 2000–1 | Lyonpo Yeshey Zimba |
| 2001–2 | Lyonpo Khandu Wangchuk |

### *Land of the Thunder Dragon*

The name Bhutan is thought to come from the Sanskrit word *Bhu-uttan*, meaning 'high land'. However, the Bhutanese people call their country *Druk Yul*, meaning 'Land of the Thunder Dragon'.

## BOLIVIA

| | |
|---|---|
| **Official name** | Republic of Bolivia |
| **Local name** | Bolivia; República de Bolivia |
| **Independence** | 1825 |
| **Area** | 1 098 580 sq km/424 052 sq mi |
| **Capital** | La Paz (administrative) and Sucre (official and legislative) |
| **Chief towns** | Cochabamba, El Alto, Oruro, Potosí, Santa Cruz |
| **Population** | 8 274 325 (2001) |
| **Nationality** | Bolivian |
| **Languages** | Spanish, Quechua, Ayamará |
| **Ethnic groups** | mestizo 30%, Quechua 30%, Aymará 25%, European 10%, others 5% |
| **Religions** | Christianity 97% (RC 92%, Prot 5%), Baha'i 3% |
| **Time zone** | GMT –4 |
| **Currency** | 1 Boliviano ($b) = 100 centavos |
| **Telephone** | +591 |
| **Internet** | .bo |
| **Country code** | BOL |

**Location**
A landlocked republic in western central South America, bounded to the north and east by Brazil; to the west by Peru; to the south-west by Chile; to the south by Argentina; and to the south-east by Paraguay.

**Physical description**
Bounded to the west by the Andes, rising to 6 542m/21 463ft at Nevado Sajama; flat 400km/250mi Altiplano Plateau in the east which lies at 3 600m/11 811ft above sea level; major lakes are Titicaca on the Peruvian border and Poopó; several rivers.

**Climate**
Varies, according to altitude; humid and tropical in the lowlands, cold and semi-arid in the mountains.

**National holidays**
Jan 1, May 1, Aug 6 (Independence), Nov 2, Dec 25; C, CC, GF.

## Political leaders

**President**

| | |
|---|---|
| 1899–1904 | José Manuel Pando |
| 1904–9 | Ismael Montes |
| 1909–13 | Heliodoro Villazón |
| 1913–17 | Ismael Montes |
| 1917–20 | José N Gutiérrez Guerra |
| 1920–5 | Bautista Saavedra |
| 1925–6 | José Cabina Villanueva |
| 1926–30 | Hernando Siles |
| 1930 | Roberto Hinojusa *President of Revolutionaries* |
| 1930–1 | Carlos Blanco Galindo |
| 1931–4 | Daniel Salamanca |
| 1934–6 | José Luis Tejado Sorzano |
| 1936–7 | David Toro |
| 1937–9 | Germán Busch |
| 1939–40 | Carlos Quintanilla *(provisional)* |
| 1940–3 | Enrique Peñaranda y del Castillo |
| 1943–6 | Gualberto Villaroel |
| 1946 | Nestor Guillen |
| 1946–7 | Tomas Monje Gutiérrez |
| 1947–9 | Enrique Hertzog |
| 1949–51 | Mamerto Urriolagoitía |
| 1951–2 | Hugo Ballivián |
| 1952 | Hernán Siles Suazo |
| 1952–6 | Víctor Paz Estenssoro |
| 1956–60 | Hernán Siles Suazo |
| 1960–4 | Víctor Paz Estenssoro |
| 1964–5 | René Barrientos Ortuño |
| 1965–6 | René Barrientos Ortuño *and* Alfredo Ovando Candía |
| 1966 | Alfredo Ovando Candía |
| 1966–9 | René Barrientos Ortuño |
| 1969 | Luis Adolfo Siles Salinas |
| 1969–70 | Alfredo Ovando Candía |
| 1970 | Rogelio Mirando |
| 1970–1 | Juan José Torres Gonzales |
| 1971–8 | Hugo Banzer Suárez |
| 1978 | Juan Pereda Asbún |
| 1978–9 | *Military Junta* (David Padilla Arericiba) |
| 1979 | Walter Guevara Arze |
| 1979–80 | Lydia Gueiler Tejada |
| 1980–1 | *Military Junta* (Luis García Meza) |
| 1981–2 | *Military Junta* (Celso Torrelio Villa) |
| 1982 | Guido Vildoso Calderón |
| 1982–5 | Hernán Siles Suazo |
| 1985–9 | Víctor Paz Estenssoro |
| 1989–93 | Jaime Paz Zamora |
| 1993–97 | Gonzalo Sánchez de Lozada |
| 1997–2001 | Hugo Bánzer Suárez |
| 2001–2 | Jorge Quiroga Ramírez |
| 2002– | Gonzalo Sánchez de Lozada |

### Highest Capital

La Paz is the highest capital city in the world, with an altitude of 3 665 m/12 024ft. However it is dwarfed by Mt Illimani, which at 6 402m/21 004ft towers above the city to the south-east. La Paz was founded in 1548 by the Spanish.

## BOSNIA AND HERZEGOVINA

| | | | |
|---|---|---|---|
| **Official name** | Republic of Bosnia and Herzegovina; sometimes also known as Bosnia-Herzegovina | **Chief towns** | Banja Luka, Zenica, Tuzla, Mostar |
| **Local name** | Bosna i Hercegovina; Republika Bosna i Hercegovina | **Population** | 4 067 000 (2001e) |
| **Former name** | formerly part of the Kingdom of Serbs, Croats and Slovenes (until 1929), Kingdom of Yugoslavia (1929–41), Federal People's Republic of Yugoslavia (1945–63), Socialist Federal People's Republic of Yugoslavia (1963–92) | **Nationality** | Bosnian, Herzegovinian |
| **Independence** | 1992 | **Languages** | Bosnian, Serbian, Croatian |
| **Area** | 51 129 sq km/19 736 sq mi | **Ethnic groups** | Bosniak 40%, Serb 31%, Croat 19% |
| **Capital** | Sarajevo | **Religions** | Christianity 50% (Orthodox 31%, RC 15%, Prot 4%), Islam 40%, none/unaffiliated 1%, others 9% |
| | | **Time zone** | GMT +1 |
| | | **Currency** | 1 convertible Marka (KM) = 100 pfennige |
| | | **Telephone** | +387 |
| | | **Internet** | .ba |
| | | **Country code** | BIH |

**Location**
A republic in central Europe; bounded by the west and north by Croatia; and to the south and east by Serbia and Montenegro.

**Physical description**
Mountainous and includes part of the Dinaric Alps; highest point is Maglic (2 386m/7 828ft); it is noted for its limestone gorges.

**Climate**
Continental, with hot summers and cold winters.

**National holidays**
Jan 9 (Republic), Mar 1 (Independence), May 1, Nov 25 (Republic).

## Political leaders

See **Serbia and Montenegro** for political leaders of the former Yugoslavia.

### Republic

**Chairman of the Presidency**

| | |
|---|---|
| 1990–8 | Alija Izetbegović |
| 1998–9 | Živko Radišić |
| 1999–2000 | Ante Jelavić |
| 2000 | Alija Izetbegović |
| 2000–1 | Živko Radišić |
| 2001–2 | Jozo Križanović |
| 2002 | Beriz Belkić |
| 2002–3 | Mirko Šarović |
| 2003 | Borislav Paravac |
| 2003– | Dragan Čović |

*Note: Tripartite presidency rotates every eight months; at the time of going to press, Borislav Paravac (Serb), Sulejman Tihić (Muslim) and Dragan Čović (Croat).*

**Prime Minister**

| | |
|---|---|
| 1990–2 | Jure Pelivan |
| 1992–3 | Mile Akmadzic |
| 1993–6 | Haris Silajdžic |
| 1996–7 | Hasan Muratovic |
| 1997–9 | Boro Bosic *co-Prime Minister* |
| 1997–2000 | Haris Silajdžic *co-Prime Minister* |
| 1999–2000 | Svetozar Mihajlovic *co-Prime Minister* |
| 2000 | Spasoje Tusevljak |
| 2000–1 | Martin Raguz |
| 2001 | Bozidar Matic |
| 2001–2 | Zlatko Lagumdzija |
| 2002 | Dragan Mikerevic |
| 2002– | Adnan Terzic |

## Federation[1]

**President**

| | |
|---|---|
| 1994–7 | Krešimir Zubak |
| 1997 | Vladimir Šoljić |
| 1997–8 | Ejup Ganić |
| 1999–2000 | Ivo Andrić-Lužanski |
| 2000–1 | Ejup Ganić |
| 2001–2 | Karlo Filipović |
| 2002–3 | Safet Halilović |
| 2003– | Niko Lozančić |

**Prime Minister**

| | |
|---|---|
| 1994–6 | Haris Silajdžic |
| 1996 | Izudin Kapetanovic |
| 1996–2001 | Edhem Bicakcić |
| 2001 | Dragan Čović *Acting Prime Minister* |
| 2001–3 | Alija Behmen |
| 2003– | Ahmet Hadžipašić |

## Republika Srpska[2]

**President**

| | |
|---|---|
| 1992–6 | Radovan Karadzic |
| 1996–8 | Biljana Plavšic |
| 1998–9 | Nikola Poplašen |
| 2000–2 | Mirko Šarović |
| 2002– | Dragan Čavić |

**Prime Minister**

| | |
|---|---|
| 1992–3 | Branko Djeric |
| 1993–4 | Vladimir Lukic |
| 1994–5 | Dusan Kozic |
| 1995–6 | Rajko Kasagic |
| 1996–8 | Gojko Klickovic |
| 1998–2001 | Milorad Dodik |
| 2001–3 | Mladen Ivanic |
| 2003– | Dragan Mikerevic |

[1] *Bosnian Croat Federation.*
[2] *Bosnian Serb Republic.*

# BOTSWANA

| | |
|---|---|
| **Official name** | Republic of Botswana |
| **Local name** | Botswana |
| **Former name** | Bechuanaland (until 1966) |
| **Independence** | 1966 |
| **Area** | 582 096 sq km/224 689 sq mi |
| **Capital** | Gaborone |
| **Chief towns** | Francistown, Lobatse, Selebi-Phikwe, Orapa, Jwaneng |
| **Population** | 1 680 863 (2001) |
| **Nationality** | Motswana (singular noun), Batswana (plural noun), Tswana (adjective) |
| **Languages** | English, Setswana |
| **Ethnic groups** | Tswana 80%, Shona 12%, San 3%, others 5% |
| **Religions** | traditional beliefs 50%, Christianity 50% (predominantly Prot) |
| **Time zone** | GMT +2 |
| **Currency** | 1 Pula (P) = 100 thebe |
| **Telephone** | +267 |
| **Internet** | .bw |
| **Country code** | BWA |

**Location**
A landlocked republic in southern Africa, bounded to the south by South Africa; to the west and north by Namibia; and to the east by Zimbabwe.

**Physical description**
Kalahari Desert covers 84% of the land, at an average elevation of c.1 100m/3 609ft; most people live in the fertile east, bordered by the River Limpopo; highest point is Otse Mountain (1 491m/4 892ft); rich Okavango River delta in the north-west.

**Climate**
Largely subtropical, increasingly arid in the south and west; rainfall in the north and east falls almost totally in summer (Oct–Apr); average maximum daily temperatures 23–32°C; annual rainfall is erratic in the Kalahari Desert.

**National holidays**
Jan 1, 2, May 1, Jul 1 (Sir Seretse Khama), Sep 30 (Botswana), Dec 25, 26; A, EM, GF, HS, President's Day (Jul); Jul, Oct Public Holidays.

## Political leaders

**President**

| | |
|---|---|
| 1966–80 | Seretse Khama |
| 1980–98 | Ketumile Masire |
| 1998– | Festus Mogae |

### *Rain Shields*

The Botswanan unit of currency is the *pula*, which means *rain* in the Setswana language. In such a dry country, rain has a deep symbolic meaning. The smaller denomination is the *thebe*, which means *shield*.

**BOUVET ISLAND** *see* **NORWAY**

## BRAZIL

| | | | |
|---|---|---|---|
| **Official name** | Federative Republic of Brazil | **Languages** | Portuguese |
| **Local name** | Brasil; República Federativa do Brasil | **Ethnic groups** | white 55%, mixed 22%, black 12%, others 11% |
| **Independence** | 1822 | **Religions** | Christianity 94% (RC 87%, Prot 7%), none 3%, others 3% |
| **Area** | 8 511 965 sq km/ 3 285 618 sq mi | **Time zone** | GMT –2/5 |
| **Capital** | Brasília | **Currency** | 1 Real (R$) = 100 centavos |
| **Chief towns** | São Paulo, Rio de Janeiro, Belo Horizonte, Recife, Salvador | **Telephone** | +55 |
| **Population** | 169 799 170 (2000) | **Internet** | .br |
| **Nationality** | Brazilian | **Country code** | BRA |

**Location**
A republic in eastern and central South America, bounded to the north by French Guiana, Suriname, Guyana and Venezuela; to the north-west by Colombia; to the west by Peru, Bolivia and Paraguay; to the south-west by Argentina; to the south by Uruguay; and to the east by the Atlantic Ocean.

**Physical description**
The low-lying Amazon basin in the north is drained by rivers that carry one fifth of the earth's running water; the highest peak is Pico da Neblina (3 014m/9 888ft) in the south; 30% of the population live on a narrow coastal strip c.100km/62mi wide.

**Climate**
Almost entirely tropical; the Equator passes through the north, and the Tropic of Capricorn through the south-east; the Amazon basin has no dry season, with average midday temperatures of 27–32°C; long droughts in the north-east with daily temperatures 21–36°C; hot and tropical on the coast; seasonal, temperate climate in the far south.

**National holidays**
Jan 1, Apr 21 (Tiradentes), May 1, Sep 7 (Independence), Oct 12 (Our Lady of Aparecida), Nov 2, 15 (Proclamation of the Republic), Dec 25; C (5), CC, GF; *much local variation*.

## Political leaders

**President**

| | |
|---|---|
| 1898–1902 | Manuel Ferraz de Campos Sales |
| 1902–6 | Francisco de Paula Rodrigues Alves |
| 1906–9 | Alfonso Pena |
| 1909–10 | Nilo Peçanha |
| 1910–14 | Hermes Rodrigues da Fonseca |
| 1914–18 | Venceslau Brás Pereira Gomes |
| 1918–19 | Francisco de Paula Rodrigues Alves |
| 1919–22 | Epitácio Pessoa |
| 1922–6 | Artur da Silva Bernardes |
| 1926–30 | Washington Luís Pereira de Sousa |
| 1930–45 | Getúlio Dorneles Vargas |
| 1945–51 | Eurico Gaspar Dutra |
| 1951–54 | Getúlio Dorneles Vargas |
| 1954–5 | João Café Filho |
| 1955 | Carlos Coimbra da Luz |
| 1955–6 | Nereu de Oliveira Ramos |
| 1956–61 | Juscelino Kubitschek de Oliveira |
| 1961 | Jânio da Silva Quadros |
| 1961–3 | João Belchior Marques Goulart |
| 1963 | Pascoal Ranieri Mazilli |
| 1963–4 | João Belchior Marques Goulart |
| 1964 | Pascoal Ranieri Mazilli |
| 1964–7 | Humberto de Alencar Castelo Branco |
| 1967–9 | Artur da Costa e Silva |
| 1969–74 | Emílio Garrastazu Médici |
| 1974–9 | Ernesto Geisel |
| 1979–85 | João Baptista de Oliveira Figueiredo |
| 1985–90 | José Sarney |
| 1990–2 | Fernando Collor de Mello |
| 1992–4 | Itamar Franco |
| 1994–2002 | Fernando Henrique Cardoso |
| 2002– | Luiz Inacio Lula da Silva |

### *South American Giant*

Brazil is the largest country in South America, and covers almost half the total area of the continent. It is crossed by both the equator and the Tropic of Capricorn, has North Atlantic and South Atlantic coasts, and borders every other South American country except Ecuador and Chile.

**BRITISH ANTARCTIC TERRITORY** *see* **UNITED KINGDOM**

**BRITISH INDIAN OCEAN TERRITORY** *see* **UNITED KINGDOM**

**BRITISH VIRGIN ISLANDS** *see* **UNITED KINGDOM**

## BRUNEI DARUSSALAM

| | |
|---|---|
| **Official name** | State of Brunei, Abode of Peace |
| **Local name** | Brunei; Negara Brunei Darussalam |
| **Independence** | 1984 |
| **Area** | 5 765 sq km/2 225 sq mi |
| **Capital** | Bandar Seri Begawan |
| **Chief towns** | Kuala Belait, Seria, Muara, Bangar, Pekan Tutong |
| **Population** | 344 000 (2001e) |
| **Nationality** | Bruneian |
| **Language(s)** | Malay; English and Chinese are widely spoken |
| **Ethnic groups** | Malay 64%, Chinese 20%, others 16% |
| **Religion(s)** | Islam 65%, traditional beliefs and others 15%, Buddhism 12%, Christianity 8% |
| **Time zone** | GMT +8 |
| **Currency** | 1 Brunei Dollar (B$) = 100 cents |
| **Telephone** | +673 |
| **Internet** | .bn |
| **Country code** | BRN |

**Location**
A state on the north-west coast of Borneo, south-eastern Asia, bounded by the South China Sea in the north-west, and on all other sides by Malaysia's Sarawak and Sabah states.

**Physical description**
Swampy coastal plain rising through foothills to a mountainous region on the Malaysian border; highest point is Bukit Pagon (1 850m/6 098ft); 75% is equatorial rainforest; the Limbang River Valley in Sarawak divides the state into two.

**Climate**
Tropical climate, with high temperatures and humidity, and no marked seasons; average daily temperature 24–30°C; rainfall in the interior is twice as high as on the coast.

**National holidays**
Jan 1, Feb 23 (National), May 31 (Royal Brunei Armed Forces), Jul 15 (Sultan's Birthday), Dec 25; Ad, ER (2), Isra' Me'raj, NY (Chinese), NY (Muslim), PB, R, Revelation of the Koran.

## Political leaders

**Monarch (Sultan)**
1967– Muda Hassanal Bolkiah Mu'izzadin Waddaulah

### *The Royal Umbrella*

The red national crest of Brunei Darussalam is a striking feature in the centre of the state's yellow, white and black flag. The crest was developed from ancient royal symbols, and each element has a particular significance. At the top are the *bendera*, a small pennant, and the *payung ubor-ubor*, or royal umbrella, symbolizing the monarchy. Beneath is the *sayap*, two wings each with four feathers that represent the 'protection of justice, tranquillity, prosperity and peace', followed by the *bulan*, the crescent symbol of Islam, with the state's motto: 'always in service with God's guidance'. Finally, on each side of the crest is a *tangan* or *kimhap*, an outstretched hand, which the government explains as representing their 'pledge to promote welfare, peace and prosperity'. Beneath the crest is a scroll inscribed with the name Brunei Darussalam.

# BULGARIA

| | | | |
|---|---|---|---|
| **Official name** | Republic of Bulgaria | **Nationality** | Bulgarian |
| **Local name** | Bălgarija; Republika Bălgarija | **Languages** | Bulgarian |
| **Former name** | *as listed below under Political leaders* | **Ethnic groups** | Bulgarian 85%, Turk 9%, others 6% |
| **Independence** | 1908 | **Religions** | Christianity 80% (Orthodox), Islam 13%, none/unaffiliated 5%, Judaism 1%, others 1% |
| **Area** | 110 912 sq km/42 812 sq mi | **Time zone** | GMT +2 |
| **Capital** | Sofia; Sofija | **Currency** | 1 Lev (Lv) = 100 stotinki |
| **Chief towns** | Plovdiv, Varna, Ruse, Burgas, Stara Zagora, Pleven | **Telephone** | +359 |
| | | **Internet** | .bg |
| **Population** | 7 928 901 (2001) | **Country code** | BGR |

**Location**
A republic in the east of the Balkan Peninsula, south-eastern Europe, bounded to the north by Romania; to the west by Serbia and Montenegro and Macedonia; to the south-east by Turkey; to the south by Greece; and to the east by the Black Sea.

**Physical description**
Traversed west to east by the Balkan Mountains, rising to over 2 000m/6 562ft; Rhodope Mountains in the south-west rise to nearly 3 000m/9 842ft; highest point is Musala (2 925m/9 596ft); comparatively narrow lowlands stretch south from the River Danube.

**Climate**
Largely continental, with hot summers and cold winters, but to the south the climate is increasingly Mediterranean; winters are slightly warmer on the Black Sea coast.

**National holidays**
Jan 1, Mar 3 (National), May 1, 24 (Slavonic Script and Bulgarian Culture), Sep 6 (Unification), 22 (Independence), Dec 24, 25, 26; Orthodox Easter (Apr/May).

## Political leaders

### Tsardom of Bulgaria

**Monarch**

1887–1908 Ferdinand *Prince*
1908–18 Ferdinand I
1918–43 Boris III
1943–6 Simeon II

### People's Republic of Bulgaria

**President**

1946–7 Vasil Kolarov
1947–50 Mincho Naichev
1950–8 Georgi Damianov
1958–64 Dimitro Ganev
1964–71 Georgi Traikov
1971–89 Todor Zhivkov
1989–90 Petar Mladenov

**Premier**

1946–9 Georgi Dimitrov
1949–50 Vasil Kolarov
1950–6 Vulko Chervenkov
1956–62 Anton Yugov
1962–71 Todor Zhivkov
1971–81 Stanko Todorov

| | |
|---|---|
| 1981–6 | Grisha Filipov |
| 1986–90 | Georgy Atanasov |
| 1990 | Andrei Lukanov |
| 1990–1 | Dimitur Popov |

**First Secretary**

| | |
|---|---|
| 1946–53 | Vulko Chervenkov |
| 1953–89 | Todor Zhivkov |
| 1989–90 | Petar Mladenov |
| 1990 | Alexander Lilov |

## Republic of Bulgaria

**President**

| | |
|---|---|
| 1990–7 | Zhelyu Zhelev |
| 1997–2002 | Petar Stoyanov |
| 2002– | Georgi Parvanov |

**Prime Minister**

| | |
|---|---|
| 1991–2 | Filip Dimitrov |
| 1992–4 | Lyuben Berov |
| 1994–5 | Renate Indzhova *Acting Prime Minister* |
| 1995–7 | Zhan Videnov |
| 1997 | Stefan Sofiyanski *Acting Prime Minister* |
| 1997–2001 | Ivan Kostov |
| 2001– | Simeon Saxe-Coburg Gotha (Simeon II) |

### Return of the King

King Simeon II went into exile in 1946 when Bulgaria became a republic, and lived in Spain for more than 50 years. After the fall of communism he returned to Bulgaria in 2001 and was elected Prime Minister, becoming the first former eastern European monarch to regain his previous authority.

## BURKINA FASO

| | | | |
|---|---|---|---|
| **Official name** | Burkina Faso | **Ethnic groups** | Mossi 45%, Mande 10%, Fulani 9%, Bobo 7%, others 29% |
| **Local name** | Burkina Faso | **Religions** | traditional beliefs 45%, Islam 44%, Christianity 11% (RC 10%, others 1%) |
| **Former name** | Upper Volta (until 1984) | **Time zone** | GMT |
| **Independence** | 1960 | **Currency** | 1 CFA Franc (CFAFr) = 100 centimes |
| **Area** | 274 540 sq km/105 972 sq mi | **Telephone** | +226 |
| **Capital** | Ouagadougou | **Internet** | .bf |
| **Chief towns** | Bobo-Dioulasso, Koudougou, Ouahigouya, Tenkodogo | **Country code** | BFA |
| **Population** | 10 312 609 (1996) | | |
| **Nationality** | Burkinabé | | |
| **Languages** | French; many local languages are also spoken | | |

**Location**
A landlocked republic in West Africa, bounded to the north by Mali; to the east by Niger; to the south-east by Benin; to the south by Togo and Ghana; and to the south-west by Côte d'Ivoire.

**Physical description**
Low-lying plateau, falling away to the south; highest point is Tena Kourou (749m/2 457ft); many rivers (tributaries of the Volta or Niger) are unnavigable in the dry season; wooded savannahs in the south; semi-desert in the north.

**Climate**
Tropical climate; average temperature 27°C in the dry season (Dec–May); rainy season (Jun–Oct), with violent storms (Aug); the *harmattan* wind blows from the north-east (Dec–Mar); rainfall decreases from south to north.

**National holidays**
Jan 1, 3 (1966 Revolution), Mar 8 (Women), May 1, Aug 5 (Independence), 15, Nov 1, Dec 11 (National), 25; A, Ad, EM, ER, PB.

## Political leaders

### Upper Volta

**President**

| | |
|---|---|
| 1960–6 | Maurice Yaméogo |
| 1966–80 | Sangoulé Lamizana |
| 1980 | Saye Zerbo |
| 1982–3 | Jean-Baptiste Ouedraogo *Chairman of People's Salvation Council* |
| 1983–4 | Thomas Sankara *Chairman of National Revolutionary Council* |

### Burkina Faso

**President**

| | |
|---|---|
| 1984–7 | Thomas Sankara *Chairman* |
| 1987– | Blaise Compaoré |

**Prime Minister**

| | |
|---|---|
| 1992–4 | Youssouf Ouedraogo |
| 1994–6 | Roch Christian Kaboré |
| 1996–2000 | Kadré Désiré Ouedraogo |
| 2000– | Paramanga Ernest Yonli |

### *Land of Honest Men*

Previously known as Upper Volta, after the upper reaches of the River Volta, Burkina Faso was renamed in 1984 by the politician Thomas Sankara (1950–87). The new name came from the local languages and means 'Land of Honest Men' or 'Land of Upright Men'.

**BURMA** *see* **MYANMAR**

## BURUNDI

| | | | |
|---|---|---|---|
| **Official name** | Republic of Burundi | **Population** | 6 412 000 (2001e) |
| **Local name** | Burundi; République du Burundi (French), Republika y'UBurundi (Kirundi) | **Nationality** | Burundian |
| | | **Languages** | French, Kirundi; Swahili is also spoken |
| **Former name** | Urundi, as part of Ruanda-Urundi (with Rwanda, until 1962), Kingdom of Burundi (1962–6) | **Ethnic groups** | Hutu 85%, Tutsi 14%, others 1% |
| | | **Religions** | Christianity 70%, traditional beliefs 29%, Islam 1% |
| **Independence** | 1962 | **Time zone** | GMT +2 |
| **Area** | 27 834 sq km/10 744 sq mi | **Currency** | 1 Burundi Franc (BuFr, FBu) = 100 centimes |
| **Capital** | Bujumbura | **Telephone** | +257 |
| **Chief towns** | Bubanza, Ngozi, Muyinga, Muramvya, Gitega, Bururi, Rutana | **Internet** | .bi |
| | | **Country code** | BDI |

**Location**
A small landlocked republic in central Africa, bounded to the north by Rwanda; to the east and south by Tanzania; to the south-west by Lake Tanganyika; and to the west by Democratic Republic of Congo.

**Physical description**
Lies across the Nile–Congo watershed; bounded to the west by the narrow River Ruizi plain and Lake Tanganyika; River Akanyaru forms northern border; interior plateau at average height of c.1 500m/4 921ft; highest point is Mt Heha (2 670m/8 760ft).

**Climate**
Equatorial climate, varying with altitude and season; moderately wet, except during the dry season (Jun–Sep).

**National holidays**
Jan 1, May 1, Jul 1 (Independence), Aug 15, Sep 18 (Victory of Uprona), Nov 1, Dec 25; A.

## Political leaders

### Monarch

1962–6 Mwambutsa IV
1966 Ntare V

### President

1966–77 Michel Micombero
1977–87 Jean-Baptiste Bagaza
1987–93 *Military Junta* (Pierre Buyoya)
1993 Melchior Ndadaye
1994 Cyprien Ntaryamira
1994–6 Sylvestre Ntibantunganya
1996–2003 Pierre Buyoya
2003– Domitien Ndayizeye

### Prime Minister

1961 Joseph Cimpaye
1961 Louis Rwagasore
1962–3 André Muhirwa
1963–4 Pierre Ngendandumwe
1964–5 Albin Nyamoya
1965 Pierre Ngendandumwe
1965 Pie Masumbuko *Acting Prime Minister*
1965 Joseph Bamina
1965–6 Léopold Biha

| | |
|---|---|
| 1966–76 | Michel Micombero |
| 1976–8 | Edouard Nzambimana |
| 1978–87 | *No Prime Minister* |
| 1987–8 | Pierre Buyoya |
| 1988–93 | Adrien Sibomana |
| 1993–4 | Sylvie Kinigi |
| 1994–5 | Anatole Kanyenkiko |
| 1995–6 | Antoine Nduwayo |
| 1996–8 | Pascal-Firmin Ndimira |
| 1998– | *No Prime Minister* |

### *Swiss Africa*

Burundi's government suggests that Burundi is 'the heart of Africa', due to its central location in the continent. They also liken it to Switzerland, a 'Swiss Africa', and call it the 'country of the thousand and one hills' and the 'country of eternal spring'.

**BYELORUSSIA, BYELARUS** *see* **BELARUS**

**CAICOS ISLANDS** *see* **UNITED KINGDOM**

## CAMBODIA

| | |
|---|---|
| **Official name** | Kingdom of Cambodia |
| **Local name** | Kâmpuchéa; Preăh Réaché 'Anachâkr Kâmpuchéa |
| **Former name** | formerly part of Indochina (until 1953), Kingdom of Cambodia (1953–70), Khmer Republic (1970–6), Democratic Kampuchea (1976–79), People's Republic of Kampuchea (1979–89), State of Cambodia (1989–93) |
| **Independence** | 1953 |
| **Area** | 181 035 sq km/69 880 sq mi |
| **Capital** | Phnom Penh; Phnum Pénh |
| **Chief towns** | Battambang, Kâmpŏng Som, Kâmpŏng Chhnăng |
| **Population** | 11 437 656 (1998) |
| **Nationality** | Cambodian |
| **Languages** | Khmer; French is also widely spoken |
| **Ethnic groups** | Khmer 93%, Chinese 3%, Vietnamese 2%, others 2% |
| **Religions** | Buddhism 95%, Islam 2%, others 3% |
| **Time zone** | GMT +7 |
| **Currency** | 1 Riel (CRI) = 100 sen |
| **Telephone** | +855 |
| **Internet** | .kh |
| **Country code** | KHM |

**Location**
A republic in south-east Asia, bounded to the north-west by Thailand; to the north by Laos; to the east by Vietnam; and to the south and south-west by the Gulf of Thailand.

**Physical description**
Surrounds the Tonlé Sap (lake) on the Cambodian Plain, which is crossed by the floodplain of the Mekong River; Cardamom Mountains stretch 160km/100mi across the Thailand border, rising to 1 813m/5 948ft at Phnom Aural.

**Climate**
Tropical monsoon climate, with a wet season in May–Sep; heavy rainfall in the south-western mountains; high temperatures in the lowland region throughout the year.

**National holidays**
Jan 1, 7 (Victory over Genocide), Mar 8 (Women), Apr 3 (Culture), May 1, Jun 1 (Children), 18 (Queen's Birthday), Sep 24 (Constitution and Coronation), Oct 23 (Paris Peace Agreement), 30 (King's Birthday) (3), Nov 9 (Independence), Dec 10 (Human Rights); Cambodian New Year (Apr) (3), Pchum Ben (Sep) (3), Royal Ploughing Ceremony (May), Visakha Bochea (May), Water/Moon Festival (Nov) (3).

## Political leaders

**Monarch**

| | |
|---|---|
| 1941–55 | Norodom Sihanouk II |
| 1955–60 | Norodom Suramarit |

**Chief of State**

| | |
|---|---|
| 1960–70 | Prince Norodom Sihanouk |

**Khmer Republic Chief of State**

| | |
|---|---|
| 1970–2 | Cheng Heng *Acting Chief of State* |
| 1972–5 | Lon Nol |
| 1975–6 | Prince Norodom Sihanouk |
| 1976–81 | Khieu Samphan |
| 1981–91 | Heng Samrin |

**President of Government in exile (until 1991)**

| | |
|---|---|
| 1970–5 | Prince Norodom Sihanouk |
| 1982–93 | Prince Norodom Sihanouk |

**Monarch**

| | |
|---|---|
| 1993– | King Norodom Sihanouk |

**Prime Minister**

| | |
|---|---|
| 1945–6 | Son Ngoc Thanh |
| 1946–8 | Prince Monireth |
| 1948–9 | Son Ngoc Thanh |
| 1949–51 | Prince Monipong |
| 1951 | Son Ngoc Thanh |
| 1951–2 | Huy Kanthoul |
| 1952–3 | Norodom Sihanouk II |
| 1953 | Samdech Penn Nouth |
| 1953–4 | Chan Nak |
| 1954–5 | Leng Ngeth |
| 1955–6 | Prince Norodom Sihanouk |
| 1956 | Oum Chheang Sun |
| 1956 | Prince Norodom Sihanouk |
| 1956 | Khim Tit |
| 1956 | Prince Norodom Sihanouk |
| 1956 | Sam Yun |
| 1956–7 | Prince Norodom Sihanouk |
| 1957–8 | Sim Var |
| 1958 | Ek Yi Oun |
| 1958 | Samdech Penn Nouth *Acting Prime Minister* |
| 1958 | Sim Var |
| 1958–60 | Prince Norodom Sihanouk |
| 1960–1 | Pho Proung |
| 1961 | Samdech Penn Nouth |
| 1961–3 | Prince Norodom Sihanouk |
| 1963–6 | Prince Norodom Kantol |
| 1966–7 | Lon Nol |
| 1967–8 | Prince Norodom Sihanouk |
| 1968–9 | Samdech Penn Nouth |
| 1969–72 | Lon Nol |

**Khmer Republic Prime Minister**

| | |
|---|---|
| 1972 | Sisovath Sivik Matak |
| 1972 | Son Ngoc Thanh |
| 1972–3 | Hang Thun Hak |
| 1973 | In Tam |
| 1973–5 | Long Boret |
| 1975–6 | Samdech Penn Nouth |
| 1976–9 | Pol Pot |
| 1979–81 | Khieu Samphan |
| 1981–5 | Chan Si |
| 1985–93 | Hun Sen |

**Prime Minister (Government in exile until 1991)**

| | |
|---|---|
| 1970–3 | Samdech Penn Nouth |
| 1982–91 | Son Sann |
| 1993–7 | Norodom Ranariddh *First Prime Minister*<br>Hun Sen *Second Prime Minister* |
| 1997 | Ung Huot *First Prime Minister*<br>Hun Sen *Second Prime Minister* |
| 1998– | Hun Sen |

## CAMEROON

| | | | |
|---|---|---|---|
| **Official name** | Republic of Cameroon | **Population** | 15 429 000 (2001e) |
| **Local name** | Cameroun; République du Cameroun | **Nationality** | Cameroonian |
| **Former name** | Kamerun (until 1919), French Cameroon (until 1960) and British Cameroon (until 1961, when south part joined new Republic of Cameroon, north part joined Nigeria), Federal Republic of Cameroon (1961–72), United Republic of Cameroon (1972–84) | **Languages** | French, English; many local languages are also spoken |
| | | **Ethnic groups** | Fang 21%, Bamileke and Bamum 19%, Douala, Luanda and Bassa 15%, Fulani 10%, others 35% |
| | | **Religions** | Christianity 53% (RC 35%, Prot 18%), traditional beliefs 25%, Islam 22% |
| **Independence** | 1960 | **Time zone** | GMT +1 |
| **Area** | 475 439 sq km/183 519 sq mi | **Currency** | 1 CFA Franc (CFAFr) = 100 centimes |
| | | **Telephone** | +237 |
| **Capital** | Yaoundé | **Internet** | .cm |
| **Chief towns** | Douala | **Country code** | CMR |

**Location**
A republic in West Africa, bounded to the south-west by Equatorial Guinea; to the south by Gabon; to the south-east by Congo; to the east by the Central African Republic; to the north-east by Chad; and to the north-west by Nigeria.

**Physical description**
Equatorial forest on the coastal plain rising to a central plateau of over 1 300m/4 265ft; west is forested and mountainous; active volcano Mt Cameroon (4 070m/13 352ft) is the highest peak in West Africa; savannah and semi-desert towards Lake Chad.

**Climate**
North has a wet season in Apr–Sep, dry the rest of the year; northern plains are semi-arid; equatorial south has rain throughout the year, with two wet seasons and two dry seasons; maximum daily temperatures in the south average 27–30°C.

**National holidays**
Jan 1, Feb 11 (Youth), May 1, 20 (National), Aug 15, Dec 25; A, Ad, ER, GF.

## Political leaders

**President**

1960–82 Ahmadun Ahidjo
1982– Paul Biya

**Prime Minister**

1960 Ahmadou Ahidjo
1960–1 Charles Assalé
1961–75 *No Prime Minister*
1975–82 Paul Biya
1982–3 Bello Bouba Maigari
1983–4 Luc Ayang
1991–2 Sadou Hayatou
1992–6 Simon Achidi Achu
1996– Peter Mafany Musonge

### Prawn River

In 1472 the Portuguese sailor Fernando Po sailed up the River Wouri in Douala. He was amazed at the number of prawns in the river, and so named the place *Rio dos Camarões*, or 'River of Prawns'. From *camarões* the name Cameroon evolved.

## CANADA

| | |
|---|---|
| **Official name** | Canada |
| **Local name** | Canada |
| **Area** | 9 970 610 sq km/ 3 848 655 sq mi |
| **Capital** | Ottawa |
| **Chief towns** | Calgary, Edmonton, Montréal, Québec, Toronto, Vancouver, Victoria, Winnipeg |
| **Population** | 30 007 090 (2001) |
| **Nationality** | Canadian |
| **Languages** | English, French |
| **Ethnic groups** | British origin 39%, Canadian 31%, other European 25%, French origin 20%, Irish origin 13%, Amerindian 4%, others 7% *Percentages add to more than 100% as some people identify with more than one ethnicity.* |
| **Religions** | Christianity 77% (RC 43%, Prot 29%, Orthodox 2%, other 3%), none 16%, others 7% |
| **Time zone** | GMT –3.5/8 |
| **Currency** | 1 Canadian Dollar (C$, Can$) = 100 cents |
| **Telephone** | +1 |
| **Internet** | .ca |
| **Country code** | CAN |

**Location**
An independent country in North America, bounded to the south by the United States of America; to the west by the Pacific Ocean; to the north-west by Alaska; to the north by the Arctic Ocean and Baffin Bay; to the north-east by the Davis Strait; and to the east by the Labrador Sea and the Atlantic Ocean.

**Physical description**
North-east is dominated by the Canadian Shield; mountains of Nova Scotia and New Brunswick in the east; fertile lowlands in south Québec and Ontario; flat prairie country south and west of the Shield, stretching to the Western Cordillera, which includes the Rocky, Cassiar and Mackenzie mountains; Coast Mountains flank a rugged, heavily-indented coastline, rising to 5 950m/19 520ft at Mt Logan (highest peak); c.45% is forested; Great Lakes in south-east Ontario.

**Climate**
North coast is permanently ice-bound or obstructed by ice floes, except for Hudson Bay (frozen for c.9 months each year); cold air from the Arctic sweeps south and east in winter and spring; mild winters and warm summers on the west coast and some inland valleys of British Columbia; winter temperatures on the Atlantic shores are warmer than those of the interior, but summer temperatures are lower; much of the southern interior has warm summers and long, cold winters.

**National holidays**
Jan 1, Jul 1 (Canada), Nov 11 (Remembrance), Dec 25, 26; EM, GF, Labour (1st Mon in Sep), Thanksgiving (2nd Mon in Oct), Victoria (Mon preceding May 25).

### *Misdirected Names*

Canada gained its name when early 16c explorers were directed by local indigenous people to the nearest village: *kanata* was the Huron-Iroquois word for 'settlement'. The explorers later used *kanata* to refer to the whole of the local area, and then to the larger region, and finally to everywhere north of the St Lawrence River. By the 1700s the name referred to a vast swathe of the continent.

## Provinces of Canada

| Name | Population (2001) | Area | Capital |
|---|---|---|---|
| Alberta (AB) | 2 974 807 | 661 848 sq km/255 472 sq mi | Edmonton |
| British Columbia (BC) | 3 907 738 | 944 735 sq km/364 667 sq mi | Victoria |
| Manitoba (MB) | 1 119 583 | 647 797 sq km/250 050 sq mi | Winnipeg |
| New Brunswick (NB) | 729 498 | 72 908 sq km/28 142 sq mi | Fredericton |
| Newfoundland and Labrador (NL) | 512 930 | 405 212 sq km/156 412 sq mi | St John's |
| Northwest Territories (NT) | 37 360 | 1 346 106 sq km/519 597 sq mi | Yellowknife |
| Nova Scotia (NS) | 908 007 | 55 284 sq km/21 340 sq mi | Halifax |
| Nunavut (NU) | 26 745 | 2 093 190 sq km/807 971 sq mi | Iqaluit |
| Ontario (ON) | 11 410 046 | 1 076 395 sq km/415 488 sq mi | Toronto |
| Prince Edward Island (PE) | 135 294 | 5 660 sq km/2 185 sq mi | Charlottetown |
| Québec (QC) | 7 237 479 | 1 542 056 sq km/595 234 sq mi | Québec City |
| Saskatchewan (SK) | 978 933 | 651 036 sq km/251 300 sq mi | Regina |
| Yukon Territory (YT) | 28 674 | 482 443 sq km/186 223 sq mi | Whitehorse |

## Political leaders

Chief of State: British monarch, represented by Governor General.

**Prime Minister**

| | |
|---|---|
| 1867–73 | John A Macdonald *Con* |
| 1873–8 | Alexander Mackenzie *Lib* |
| 1878–91 | John A Macdonald *Con* |
| 1891–2 | John J C Abbot *Con* |
| 1892–4 | John S D Thompson *Con* |
| 1894–6 | Mackenzie Bowell *Con* |
| 1896 | Charles Tupper *Con* |
| 1896–1911 | Wilfrid Laurier *Lib* |
| 1911–20 | Robert Borden *Con/Un* |
| 1920–1 | Arthur Meighen *Un/Con* |
| 1921–6 | William Lyon Mackenzie King *Lib* |
| 1926 | Arthur Meighen *Con* |
| 1926–30 | William Lyon Mackenzie King *Lib* |
| 1930–5 | Richard Bedford Bennett *Con* |
| 1935–48 | William Lyon Mackenzie King *Lib* |
| 1948–57 | Louis St Laurent *Lib* |
| 1957–63 | John George Diefenbaker *Con* |
| 1963–8 | Lester Bowles Pearson *Lib* |
| 1968–79 | Pierre Elliott Trudeau *Lib* |
| 1979–80 | Joseph Clark *Con* |
| 1980–4 | Pierre Elliott Trudeau *Lib* |
| 1984 | John Turner *Lib* |
| 1984–93 | Brian Mulroney *Con* |
| 1993 | Kim Campbell *Con* |
| 1993– | Jean Chrétien *Lib* |

*Con = Conservative* *Un = Unionist* *Lib = Liberal*

### Long and Winding Road

The Trans-Canada Highway is the world's longest national highway. It runs 7 821km/ 4 860mi from St John's in Newfoundland and Labrador to Victoria in British Columbia.

### Beavers and Maple Leaves

The maple tree is the national tree of Canada, and the maple leaf its internationally recognized symbol. Ten species of maple tree grow in Canada: the *bigleaf*, *black*, *Douglas*, *Manitoba*, *mountain*, *red*, *silver*, *sugar*, *striped* and *vine maple*. The national animal is the beaver, upon which the prosperity of early trade settlements was based.

**CANARY ISLANDS** *see* **SPAIN**

## CAPE VERDE

| | | | |
|---|---|---|---|
| **Official name** | Republic of Cape Verde | **Ethnic groups** | mestizo 61%, African 29%, European 1%, others 9% |
| **Local name** | Cabo Verde; República de Cabo Verde | **Religions** | Christianity 98% (RC), none/unaffiliated 1%, others 1% |
| **Independence** | 1975 | **Time zone** | GMT –1 |
| **Area** | 4 033 sq km/1 557 sq mi | **Currency** | 1 Escudo Caboverdiano (CVEsc) = 100 centavos |
| **Capital** | Praia | **Telephone** | +238 |
| **Chief towns** | Mindelo | **Internet** | .cv |
| **Population** | 445 000 (2001e) | **Country code** | CPV |
| **Nationality** | Cape Verdean | | |
| **Languages** | Portuguese; Crioulo, a Creole language blending Portuguese and West African words, is spoken widely | | |

**Location**
An island group in the Atlantic Ocean which lies off the west coast of Africa.

**Physical description**
Islands are of volcanic origin, mostly mountainous; highest peak is Pico do Cano (2 829m/ 9 281ft), an active volcano on Fogo Island; coastal plains are semi-desert; savannah or thin forest lies on the mountains; fine, sandy beaches on most islands.

**Climate**
Located at the northern limit of the tropical rain belt; low and unreliable rainfall mainly in Aug and Sep; cooler and damper in the uplands; severe drought can occur; tropical heat; average temperatures at Praia range between 21°C (Jan) and 27°C (Oct).

**National holidays**
Jan 1, 13 (Democracy and Freedom), 20 (National Heroes), May 1, Jul 5 (Independence), Aug 15, Sep 12 (National), Nov 1, Dec 25; ES, GF, Ash Wednesday.

## Political leaders

**President**

| | |
|---|---|
| 1975–91 | Arístides Pereira |
| 1991–2001 | Antonio Mascarenhas Monteiro |
| 2001– | Pedro Pires |

**Prime Minister**

| | |
|---|---|
| 1975–91 | Pedro Pires |
| 1991–2000 | Carlos Wahnon Veiga |
| 2000–1 | António Gualberto do Rosário |
| 2001– | José Maria Neves |

### *Black Sands*

Volcanic Cape Verde is renowned for its beaches, such as that at Faja d'Agua on the small island of Brava, which have black sands. The black volcanic sand is rich in minerals, and is reputed to have beneficial medicinal qualities.

**CAYMAN ISLANDS** *see* **UNITED KINGDOM**

# CENTRAL AFRICAN REPUBLIC

| | | | |
|---|---|---|---|
| **Official name** | Central African Republic (CAR) | **Nationality** | Central African |
| **Local name** | République Centrafricaine (French), Ködörösêse tî Bêafrîka (Sango) | **Languages** | French, Sango |
| **Former name** | Ubangi Shari (until 1958), Central African Republic (1958–76), Central African Empire (1976-9) | **Ethnic groups** | Baya 34%, Banda 27%, Mandjia 21%, Sara 10%, others 8% |
| **Independence** | 1960 | **Religions** | Christianity 50% (Prot 25%, RC 25%), traditional beliefs 22%, Islam 14%, none/unaffiliated 13%, others 1% |
| **Area** | 626 780 sq km/241 937 sq mi | **Time zone** | GMT +1 |
| **Capital** | Bangui | **Currency** | 1 CFA Franc (CFAFr) = 100 centimes |
| **Chief towns** | Berbérati, Bouar, Bossangoa | **Telephone** | +236 |
| **Population** | 3 770 000 (2001e) | **Internet** | .cf |
| | | **Country code** | CAF |

**Location**
A republic in central Africa, bounded to the north by Chad; to the north-east by The Sudan; to the south by Democratic Republic of Congo and Congo; and to the west by Cameroon.

**Physical description**
On a plateau forming the watershed between the Chad and Congo river basins; highest ground is in the north-east (Massif des Bongos) and north-west; highest point is Mont Ngaoui (1 420m/4 659ft).

**Climate**
Single rainy season in the north between May and Sep; more equatorial climate in the south; average temperatures at Bangui are 24–27°C.

**National holidays**
Jan 1, Mar 29 (Death of President Boganda), May 1, Jun 1 (Mothers), Aug 13 (Independence), 15, Sep 1 (Arrival of the Military Committee for National Recovery), Nov 1, Dec 1 (Republic), 25; A, EM, WM.

## Political leaders

**President**

| | | | |
|---|---|---|---|
| 1960–6 | David Dacko | 1981–93 | André Kolingba |
| 1966–79 | Jean-Bédel Bokassa (*from 1977,* Emperor Bokassa I) | 1993–2003 | Ange-Félix Patasse |
| | | 2003– | François Bozizé |

**Prime Minister**

| | | | |
|---|---|---|---|
| 1991–2 | Edouard Frank | 1996–7 | Jean-Paul Ngoupandé |
| 1992–3 | Thimothée Malendoma | 1997–9 | Michel Gbezera-Bria |
| 1993 | Enoch Derant Lakoué | 1999–2001 | Anicet Georges Dologuélé |
| 1993–5 | Jean-Luc Mandaba | 2001–3 | Martin Ziguélé |
| 1995–6 | Gabriel Koyambounou | 2003– | Abel Goumba |

## CHAD

| | | | |
|---|---|---|---|
| **Official name** | Republic of Chad | **Ethnic groups** | Arab 26%, Sara 25%, Teda 18%, others 31% |
| **Local name** | Tchad; République du Tchad | **Religions** | Islam 50%, Christianity 25% (RC 20%, Prot 5%), traditional beliefs 25% |
| **Independence** | 1960 | **Time zone** | GMT +1 |
| **Area** | 1 284 640 sq km/495 871 sq mi | **Currency** | 1 CFA Franc (CFAFr) = 100 centimes |
| **Capital** | N'Djamena (also Ndjamena) | **Telephone** | +235 |
| **Chief towns** | Moundou, Sarh, Abéché | **Internet** | .td |
| **Population** | 8 322 000 (2001e) | **Country code** | TCD |
| **Nationality** | Chadian | | |
| **Languages** | French, Arabic; many local languages are also spoken | | |

**Location**
A landlocked republic in north central Africa, bounded to the north by Libya; to the east by The Sudan; to the south by Central African Republic; and to the west by Cameroon, Nigeria and Niger.

**Physical description**
A mostly arid, semi-desert plateau at the edge of the Sahara Desert; Lake Chad lies in the south-west; Tibesti Mountains rise to 3 415m/11 204ft at Emi Koussi; vegetation is generally desert scrub or steppe; most people live in the tropical south.

**Climate**
Moderately wet in the south between May and Oct, but dry for the rest of the year; hot and arid north is almost rainless; central plain is hot and dry, with a brief rainy season during Jun–Sep.

**National holidays**
Jan 1, May 1, 25 (OAU Foundation), Aug 11 (Independence), Nov 1, 28 (Republic), Dec 25; Ad, EM, ES, ER.

## Political leaders

**President**

| | |
|---|---|
| 1960–75 | François Tombalbaye |
| 1975–9 | *Supreme Military Council* (Félix Malloum) |
| 1979 | Goukouni Oueddi |
| 1979 | Mohammed Shawwa |
| 1979–82 | Goukouni Oueddi |
| 1982–90 | Hissène Habré |
| 1990– | Idriss Déby |

**Prime Minister**

| | |
|---|---|
| 1991–2 | Jean Alingue Bawoyeu |
| 1992–3 | Joseph Yodemane |
| 1993 | Fidèle Moungar |
| 1993–5 | Delwa Kassire Koumakoye |
| 1995–7 | Koibla Djimasta |
| 1997–9 | Nassour Ouaidou Guelendouksia |
| 1999–2002 | Negoum Yamassoum |
| 2002–3 | Haroun Kabadi |
| 2003– | Moussa Faki Mahamat |

**CHANNEL ISLANDS** *see* **UNITED KINGDOM**

# CHILE

| | | | |
|---|---|---|---|
| **Official name** | Republic of Chile | **Ethnic groups** | mestizo 94%, Amerindian 6% |
| **Local name** | Chile; República de Chile | **Religions** | Christianity 88% (RC 80%, Prot 8%), none/unaffiliated 11%, others 1% |
| **Independence** | 1818 | **Time zone** | GMT –4 |
| **Area** | 756 626 sq km/292 058 sq mi | **Currency** | 1 Chilean Peso (Ch$) = 100 centavos |
| **Capital** | Santiago | **Telephone** | +56 |
| **Chief towns** | Valparaíso, Concepción, Talcahuano, Antofagasta, Viña del Mar | **Internet** | .cl |
| **Population** | 15 402 000 (2001e) | **Country code** | CHL |
| **Nationality** | Chilean | | |
| **Languages** | Spanish | | |

**Location**
A republic in south-western South America, bounded to the west by the Pacific Ocean; to the east by Argentina; to the north-east by Bolivia; and to the north-west by Peru.

**Physical description**
Narrow coastal belt, backed by Andean mountains rising in the north to 6 723m/22 057ft at Llullaillaco; highest point is Ojos del Salado (6 910m/22 660ft); lower mountains in the centre and south; fertile central valley; Atacama Desert lies in the far north-west.

**Climate**
Highly varied (spans 37° of latitude; altitudes from the Andean peaks to the coastal plain); extreme aridity in the Atacama Desert; cold, wet and windy in the far south; Mediterranean climate in centre, with warm, wet winters and dry summers.

**National holidays**
Jan 1, May 1, 21 (Navy), Aug 15, Sep 18 (Independence), 19 (Armed Forces), Oct 12 (Americas), Dec 8, 25, 26; CC, GF, EM, Aug public holiday, May public holiday.

## Political leaders

**President**

1900–1 Federico Errázuriz Echaurren
1901 Aníbal Zañartu *Vice President*
1901–3 Germán Riesco
1903 Ramón Barros Luco *Vice President*
1903–6 Germán Riesco
1906–10 Pedro Montt
1910 Ismael Tocornal *Vice President*
1910 Elías Fernández Albano *Vice President*
1910 Emiliano Figueroa Larraín *Vice President*
1910–15 Ramón Barros Luco
1915–20 Juan Luis Sanfuentes
1920–4 Arturo Alessandri
1924–5 *Military Juntas*
1925 Arturo Alessandri
1925 Luis Barros Borgoño *Vice President*
1925–7 Emiliano Figueroa
1927–31 Carlos Ibáñez
1931 Pedro Opaso Letelier *Vice President*
1931 Juan Esteban Montero *Vice President*
1931 Manuel Trucco Franzani *Vice President*
1931–2 Juan Esteban Montero
1932 *Military Juntas*
1932 Carlos G Dávila *Provisional President*
1932 Bartolomé Blanche *Provisional President*
1932 Abraham Oyanedel *Vice President*
1932–8 Arturo Alessandri Palma
1938–41 Pedro Aguirre Cerda

| | | | |
|---|---|---|---|
| 1941–2 | Jerónimo Méndez Arancibia *Vice President* | 1964–70 | Eduardo Frei Montalva |
| 1942–6 | Juan Antonio Ríos Morales | 1970–3 | Salvador Allende Gossens |
| 1946–52 | Gabriel González Videla | 1973–90 | Augusto Pinochet Ugarte |
| 1952–8 | Carlos Ibáñez del Campo | 1990–3 | Patricio Aylwin Azócar |
| 1958–64 | Jorge Alessandri Rodríguez | 1993–9 | Eduardo Frei Ruíz-Tagle |
| | | 2000– | Ricardo Lagos Escobar |

## CHINA

| | |
|---|---|
| **Official name** | People's Republic of China (PRC) |
| **Local name** | Zhong Guo; Zhonghua Renmin Gongheguo |
| **Area** | 9 597 000 sq km/ 3 704 000 sq mi |
| **Capital** | Beijing (formerly known as Peking) |
| **Chief towns** | Shanghai, Tianjin, Shenyang, Wuhan, Guangzhou |
| **Population** | 1 295 330 000 (2000) |
| **Nationality** | Chinese |
| **Languages** | standard Chinese (Putonghua) or Mandarin, also Yue (Cantonese), Wu, Minbei, Minnan, Xiang, Gan, Hakka; minority languages |
| **Ethnic groups** | Han 92%, others 8% |
| **Religions** | none/unaffiliated 59%, Chinese folk religion 20%, Buddhism 6%, Islam 2%, others 13% |
| **Time zone** | GMT +8 |
| **Currency** | 1 Renminbi Yuan (RMBY, $, Y) = 10 jiao = 100 fen |
| **Telephone** | +86 |
| **Internet** | .cn |
| **Country code** | CHN |

**Location**
A socialist state in central and eastern Asia. Bounded to the north-west by Kyrgyzstan and Kazakhstan; to the north by Mongolia; to the north-east by Russia; to the east by North Korea, the Yellow Sea and the East China Sea; to the south by the South China Sea, Vietnam, Laos, Myanmar (Burma), India, Bhutan and Nepal; and to the west by India, Pakistan, Afghanistan and Tajikistan.

**Physical description**
Over two-thirds is upland, mountain and plateau; highest mountains are in the west, where the Tibetan Plateau rises to an average altitude of 4 000m/13 123ft; highest point is Mt Everest 8 850m/29 035ft; land descends to desert or semi-desert in Sinkiang and Inner Mongolia; broad fertile plains of Manchuria in the north-east and the densely forested Changpai Shan uplands; fertile southern plains and east coast are heavily populated.

**Climate**
Varied, with seven zones: (1) north-east has cold winters, with strong north winds and warm, humid summers; in Manchuria, the rivers are frozen for four to six months each year, and snow lies for 100–150 days; (2) centre has warm and humid summers, sometimes typhoons or tropical cyclones on the coast; (3) south, partly within the tropics, is the wettest area in summer; frequent typhoons (especially during Jul–Oct); (4) south-west has summer temperatures moderated by altitude, winters are mild with little rain; summers are wet on the mountains; (5) Tibet autonomous region, a high plateau surrounded by mountains, has severe winters with frequent light snow and hard frost, summers are warm, but nights are cold; (6) Xinjiang and the western interior has an arid desert climate with cold winters; (7) Inner Mongolia has an extreme continental-type climate, with cold winters and warm summers, and strong winds in winter and spring.

**National holidays**
Jan 1, May 1, Oct 1 (National) (2); Spring Festival (4) (Jan/Feb).

## Special Administrative Regions

### Hong Kong (HK)

| | | | |
|---|---|---|---|
| **Location** | Comprises the Kowloon/New Territories peninsula and more than 200 islands in the South China Sea. | | |
| **Local name** | Xianggang; Xianggang Tebie Xingzhengqu | **Population** | 6 708 389 (2001) |
| | | **Internet** | .hk |
| **Area** | 16 sq km/6 sq mi | **Country code** | HGK |

### Macao

| | | | |
|---|---|---|---|
| **Location** | Macao peninsula is linked by bridge and causeway to two islands in the South China Sea. | | |
| **Local name** | Aomen; Aomen Tebie Xingzhengqu; Macau (Portuguese) | **Population** | 435 200 (2001) |
| | | **Internet** | .mo |
| **Area** | 1 067 sq km/412 sq mi | **Country code** | MAC |

*Note: China also occupies the Paracel Islands in the South China Sea.*

## Political leaders

### Dynasties

| | |
|---|---|
| c.22–18cBC | Hsia |
| c.18–12cBC | Shang or Yin |
| c.1111–256BC | Chou |
| c.1111–770BC | Western Chou |
| 770–256BC | Eastern Chou |
| 770–476BC | Ch'un Ch'iu Period |
| 475–221BC | Warring States Period |
| 221–206BC | Ch'in |
| 206BC– AD220 | Han |
| 206BC– AD9 | Western Han |
| AD9–23 | Hsin Interregnum |
| AD25–220 | Eastern Han |
| AD220–265 | Three Kingdoms Period |
| AD265–420 | Chin |
| AD265–317 | Western Chin |
| AD317–420 | Eastern Chin |
| AD420–589 | Northern and Southern Dynasties |
| 581–618 | Sui |
| 618–907 | Tang |
| 907–960 | Five Dynasties and Ten Kingdoms Period |
| 960–1279 | Sung |
| 960–1127 | Northern Sung |
| 1127–1279 | Southern Sung |
| 1115–1234 | Chin (Jurchen Tartars) |
| 1279–1368 | Yuan (Mongol) |
| 1368–1644 | Ming |
| 1644–1912 | Ch'ing or Qing (Manchu) |

### Qing (Ch'ing) dynasty

**Emperor**

| | |
|---|---|
| 1875–1908 | Guangxu (Kuang-hsü) |
| 1908–12 | Xuantong (Hsüan-t'ung) |

**Prime Minister**

| | |
|---|---|
| 1901–3 | Ronglu (Jung-lu) |
| 1903–11 | Prince Qing (Ch'ing) |
| 1912 | Lu Zhengxiang (Lu Cheng-hsiang) |
| 1912 | Yuan Shikai (Yüan Shih-k'ai) |

## Republic of China

**President**

| | |
|---|---|
| 1912 | Sun Yat-sen (Sun Yixian) *Provisional* |
| 1912–16 | Yuan Shikai (Yüan Shih-k'ai) |
| 1916–17 | Li Yuanhong (Li Yüan-hung) |
| 1917–18 | Feng Guozhang (Feng Kuo-chang) |
| 1918–22 | Xu Shichang (Hsü Shih-ch'ang) |
| 1921–5 | Sun Yat-sen (Sun Yixian) *Canton Administration* |
| 1922–3 | Li Yuanhong (Li Yüan-hung) |
| 1923–4 | Cao Kun (Ts'ao K'un) |
| 1924–6 | Duan Qirui (Tuan Ch'i-jui) |
| 1926–7 | *Civil Disorder* |
| 1927–8 | Zhang Zuolin (Chang Tso-lin) |
| 1928–31 | Chiang K'ai-shek (Jiang Jieshi) |
| 1931–2 | Cheng Minxu (Ch'eng Ming-hsü) *Acting President* |
| 1932–43 | Lin Sen (Lin Sen) |
| 1940–4 | Wang Jingwei (Wang Ching-wei) *in Japanese-occupied territory* |
| 1943–9 | Chiang K'ai-shek (Jiang Jieshi) |
| 1945–9 | *Civil War* |
| 1949 | Li Zongren (Li Tsung-jen) |

**Premier**

| | |
|---|---|
| 1912 | Tang Shaoyi (T'ang Shao-i) |
| 1912–13 | Zhao Bingjun (Chao Ping-chün) |
| 1912–13 | Xiong Xiling (Hsiung Hsi-ling) |
| 1914 | Sun Baoyi (Sun Pao-chi) |
| 1915–16 | *no Premier* |
| 1916–17 | Duan Qirui (Tuan Ch'i-jui) |
| 1917–18 | Wang Shizhen (Wang Shih-chen) |
| 1918 | Duan Qirui (Tuan Ch'i-jui) |
| 1918–19 | Qian Nengxun (Ch'ien Neng-hsün) |
| 1919 | Gong Xinzhan (Kung Hsin-chan) |
| 1919–20 | Jin Yunpeng (Chin Yün-p'eng) |
| 1920 | Sa Zhenbing (Sa Chen-ping) |
| 1920–1 | Jin Yunpeng (Chin Yün-p'eng) |
| 1921–2 | Liang Shiyi (Liang Shih-i) |
| 1922 | Zhou Ziqi (Chow Tzu-ch'i) *Acting Premier* |
| 1922 | Yan Huiqing (Yen Hui-ch'ing) |
| 1922 | Wang Chonghui (Wang Ch'ung-hui) |
| 1922–3 | Wang Daxie (Wang Ta-hsieh) |
| 1923 | Zhang Shaozeng (Chang Shao-ts'eng) |
| 1923–4 | Gao Lingwei (Kao Ling-wei) |
| 1924 | Sun Baoyi (Sun Pao-ch'i) |
| 1924 | Gu Weijun (Ku Wei-chün) *Acting Premier* |
| 1924 | Yan Huiqing (Yen Hui-ch'ing) |
| 1924–5 | Huang Fu (Huang Fu) *Acting Premier* |
| 1925 | Duan Qirui (Tuan Ch'i-jui) |
| 1925–6 | Xu Shiying (Hsü Shih-ying) |
| 1926 | Jia Deyao (Chia Te-yao) |
| 1926 | Hu Weide (Hu Wei-te) |
| 1926 | Yan Huiqing (Yen Hui-ch'ing) |
| 1926 | Du Xigui (Tu Hsi-kuei) |
| 1926–7 | Gu Weijun (Ku Wei-chün) |
| 1927 | *Civil Disorder* |

**President of the Executive Council**

| | |
|---|---|
| 1928–30 | Tan Yankai (T'an Yen-k'ai) |
| 1930 | T V Soong (Sung Tzu-wen) *Acting President* |
| 1930 | Wang Jingwei (Wang Ching-wei) |
| 1930–1 | Chiang K'ai-shek (Jiang Jieshi) |
| 1931–2 | Sun Fo (Sun Fo) |
| 1932–5 | Wang Jingwei (Wang Ching-wei) |
| 1935–7 | Chiang K'ai-shek (Jiang Jieshi) |
| 1937–8 | Wang Chonghui (Wang Ch'ung-hui) *Acting President* |
| 1938–9 | Kong Xiangxi (K'ung Hsiang-hsi) |
| 1939–44 | Chiang K'ai-shek (Jiang Jieshi) |
| 1944–7 | T V Soong (Sung Tzu-wen) |
| 1945–9 | *Civil War* |
| 1948 | Wang Wenhao (Wong Wen-hao) |
| 1948–9 | Sun Fo (Sun Fo) |
| 1949 | He Yingqin (Ho Ying-ch'in) |
| 1949 | Yan Xishan (Yen Hsi-shan) |

## People's Republic of China

**President**

| | |
|---|---|
| 1949–59 | Mao Zedong (Mao Tse-tung) |
| 1959–68 | Liu Shaoqi |
| 1968–75 | Dong Biwu |
| 1975–6 | Zhu De |
| 1976–8 | Sung Qingling |
| 1978–83 | Ye Jianying |
| 1983–8 | Li Xiannian |
| 1988–93 | Yang Shangkun |
| 1993–2003 | Jiang Zemin |
| 2003– | Hu Jintao |

**Premier/Prime Minister**

| | |
|---|---|
| 1949–76 | Zhou Enlai (Chou En-lai) |
| 1976–80 | Hua Guofeng |
| 1980–7 | Zhao Ziyang |
| 1987–98 | Li Peng |
| 1998–2003 | Zhu Rongji |
| 2003– | Wen Jiabao |

**Chairman of the Communist Party**

| | |
|---|---|
| 1935–76 | Mao Zedong (Mao Tse-tung) |
| 1976–81 | Hua Guofeng |
| 1981–2 | Hu Yaobang |

**General Secretary of the Communist Party**

| | |
|---|---|
| 1982–7 | Hu Yaobang |
| 1987–9 | Zhao Ziyang |
| 1989–2002 | Jiang Zemin |
| 2002– | Hu Jintao |

*Note: Names are listed only in Pinyin transliterations for recent leaders.*

### Red for Go

The colour red is associated with the Communist party in China. During the Cultural Revolution (1966–76) it was reported that some over-zealous revolutionaries wanted the red light to mean 'go' at traffic lights, to symbolize the forward-thinking nature of the Communist regime.

**CHINA, REPUBLIC OF** *see* **TAIWAN**

**CHINESE TAIPEI** *see* **TAIWAN**

**CHRISTMAS ISLAND** *see* **AUSTRALIA**

**COCOS ISLANDS** *see* **AUSTRALIA**

**CIS** *see* **ARMENIA, AZERBAIJAN, BELARUS, GEORGIA, KAZAKHSTAN, KYRGYZSTAN, MOLDOVA, RUSSIA, TAJIKISTAN, TURKMENISTAN, UKRAINE, UZBEKISTAN** *and separate entry in* **POLITICS, LAW AND ORDER**

## COLOMBIA

| | |
|---|---|
| **Official name** | Republic of Colombia |
| **Local name** | Colombia; República de Colombia |
| **Independence** | 1810 (declared), 1819 (full) |
| **Area** | 1 140 105 sq km/440 080 sq mi |
| **Capital** | Bogotá, Santa Fé de Bogotá |
| **Chief towns** | Medellín, Cali, Barranquilla |
| **Population** | 43 071 000 (2001e) |
| **Nationality** | Colombian |
| **Languages** | Spanish |
| **Ethnic groups** | mestizo 58%, white 20%, mulatto 14%, black 4%, mixed black and Amerindian 3%, Amerindian 1% |
| **Religions** | Christianity 95% (RC), others 5% |
| **Time zone** | GMT –5 |
| **Currency** | 1 Colombian Peso (Col$) = 100 centavos |
| **Telephone** | +57 |
| **Internet** | .co |
| **Country code** | COL |

# COLOMBIA

**Location**
A republic in the north-west of South America. It is bounded to the north by Panama and the Caribbean Sea; to the west by the Pacific Ocean; to the east by Venezuela; to the south-east by Brazil; and to the south by Ecuador and Peru.

**Physical description**
Caribbean and Pacific coastlines, with several islands; Andes run north to south, branching into three dividing narrow coastal plains from forested Amazon basin lowlands; highest peaks are Pico Cristóbal Colón and Pico Simón Bolívar (both 5 775m/18 947ft) and Nevado del Huila (5 750m/18 864ft).

**Climate**
Hot and humid coastal plains in the north-west and west; drier period on the Caribbean coast (Dec–Apr); in the Andes rainfall is even throughout the year; hot and humid tropical lowlands in the east.

**National holidays**
Jan 1, 6, Mar 19 (St Joseph), May 1, Jun 29 (SS Peter and Paul), Jul 20 (Independence), Aug 7 (Battle of Boyacá), 15, Oct 12 (Columbus), Nov 1, 11 (Independence of Cartagena), Dec 8, 25; A, CC, GF, HT, Sacred Heart (Jun).

## Political leaders

**President**

| | |
|---|---|
| 1900–4 | José Manuel Marroquín *Vice President* |
| 1904–9 | Rafael Reyes |
| 1909–10 | Ramón González Valencia |
| 1910–14 | Carlos E Restrepo |
| 1914–18 | José Vicente Concha |
| 1918–21 | Marco Fidel Suárez |
| 1921–2 | Jorge Holguín *President Designate* |
| 1922–6 | Pedro Nel Ospina |
| 1926–30 | Miguel Abadía Méndez |
| 1930–4 | Enrique Olaya Herrera |
| 1934–8 | Alfonso López |
| 1938–42 | Eduardo Santos |
| 1942–5 | Alfonso López |
| 1945–6 | Alberto Lleras Camargo *President Designate* |
| 1946–50 | Mariano Ospina Pérez |
| 1950–3 | Laureano Gómez |
| 1953–7 | Gustavo Rojas Pinilla |
| 1957 | *Military Junta* |
| 1958–62 | Alberto Lleras Camargo |
| 1962–6 | Guillermo León Valencia |
| 1966–70 | Carlos Lleras Restrepo |
| 1970–4 | Misael Pastrana Borrero |
| 1974–8 | Alfonso López Michelsen |
| 1978–82 | Julio César Turbay Ayala |
| 1982–6 | Belisario Betancur |
| 1986–90 | Virgilio Barco Vargas |
| 1990–4 | César Gaviria Trujillo |
| 1994–8 | Ernesto Samper Pizano |
| 1998–2002 | Andrés Pastrana Arango |
| 2002– | Alvaro Uribe Velez |

### Orchids and Condors

The national flower of Colombia is the orchid, while the national tree is the wax palm, which only grows in the Colombian Andes and is the world's tallest palm tree, reaching up to 70m/230ft. The mighty condor is the national bird, a creature of great historical and cultural significance for the people. It lives high in the Andes and is known as the 'eternal bird' for its long lifespan.

# COMOROS

| | |
|---|---|
| **Official name** | Union of the Comoros |
| **Local name** | Comores; Union des Comores |
| **Former name** | Federal Islamic Republic of the Comoros (until 2001) |
| **Independence** | 1975 |
| **Area** | 1 862 sq km/719 sq mi |
| **Capital** | Moroni; Môrônî |
| **Population** | 726 000 (2001e) |
| **Nationality** | Comoran |
| **Languages** | French, Arabic; Shikomoro, or Comoran, a local Arabic-Swahili dialect, is also spoken |
| **Ethnic groups** | Comorian 97%, others 3% |
| **Religions** | Islam 86% (Sunni), Christianity 14% (RC) |
| **Time zone** | GMT +3 |
| **Currency** | 1 Comoran Franc (KMF) = 100 centimes |
| **Telephone** | +269 |
| **Internet** | .km |
| **Country code** | COM |

**Location**
A group of three volcanic islands, Grand Comore (Njazídja), Anjouan (Nzwani) and Mohéli (Mwali), at the northern end of the Mozambique Channel, between Mozambique and Madagascar.

**Physical description**
Interiors vary from steep mountains to low hills; highest point is the active volcano Le Karthala (2 360m/7 743ft) on Grand Comore.

**Climate**
Tropical; May–Oct is the dry season and Nov–Apr is the hot, humid season; average temperatures are 20°C in Jul and 28°C in Nov.

**National holidays**
May 9 (Islamic New Year), 18 (Ashoura), Jul 6 (Independence), 18 (Mouloud/Prophet's Birthday), Nov 17 (President Abdallah's Assassination), 28 (Leilat al-Meiraj/Ascension of the Prophet); Ad, ER, R.

## Political leaders

**President**

| | |
|---|---|
| 1976–78 | Ali Soilih |
| 1978–89 | Ahmed Abdallah Abderemane |
| 1989–96 | Said Mohammed Djohar |
| 1996–8 | Mohammed Taki Abdoulkarim |
| 1998–9 | Tadjiddine Ben Said Massounde *Interim President* |
| 1999–2002 | Azali Assoumani |
| 2002 | Hamada Madi Boléro *Interim President* |
| 2002– | Azali Assoumani |

**Prime Minister**

| | |
|---|---|
| 1976–8 | Abdallah Mohammed |
| 1978–82 | Salim Ben Ali |
| 1982–4 | Ali Mroudjae |
| 1984–92 | *No Prime Minister* |
| 1992 | Mohammed Taki Abdoulkarim |
| 1993 | Ibrahim Abdermane Halidi |
| 1993 | Said Ali Mohammed |
| 1993–4 | Ahmed Ben Cheikh Attoumane |
| 1994 | Mohammed Abdou Madi |
| 1994–5 | Halifa Houmadi |
| 1995–6 | Caambi el-Yachourtu |
| 1996 | Tadjiddine Ben Said Massounde |
| 1996–7 | Ahmed Abdou |
| 1997–8 | Nourdine Bourhane |
| 1998–9 | Abbas Djoussouf |
| 1999–2000 | Bianrifi Tarmidi |
| 2000–2 | Hamada Madi Boléro |
| 2002– | *No Prime Minister* |

# CONGO

| | | | |
|---|---|---|---|
| **Official name** | Republic of Congo; also sometimes known as Congo (Brazzaville) or Congo-Brazzaville | **Population** | 3 542 000 (2001e) |
| **Local name** | Congo; République du Congo | **Nationality** | Congolese, Congo |
| **Former name** | Middle Congo (until 1960), Republic of Congo (1960–70), People's Republic of Congo (1970–92) | **Languages** | French, Kikongo, Lingala |
| **Independence** | 1960 | **Ethnic groups** | Kongo 49%, Sangha 20%, Teke 17%, Mbosi 11%, others 3% |
| **Area** | 341 945 sq km/131 990 sq mi | **Religions** | Christianity 50% (RC), traditional beliefs 48%, Islam 2% |
| **Capital** | Brazzaville | **Time zone** | GMT +1 |
| **Chief towns** | Pointe-Noire, Loubomo, Nkayi | **Currency** | 1 CFA Franc (CFAFr) = 100 centimes |
| | | **Telephone** | +242 |
| | | **Internet** | .cg |
| | | **Country code** | COG |

**Location**
A west central African republic, bounded to the west by Gabon; to the north-west by Cameroon; to the north by the Central African Republic; to the east and south by Democratic Republic of the Congo; and to the south-west by the Atlantic Ocean.

**Physical description**
Short Atlantic coastline fringes a broad mangrove plain that rises inland to mountains reaching 900m/2 953ft; River Congo flows south-west to the coast; Monts de la Lékéti reach 1 040m/3 412ft; mainly covered by dense grassland, mangrove and forest.

**Climate**
Hot, humid, equatorial climate; rainfall decreases near the Atlantic coast and in the south; temperatures vary little, with average daily maximum temperatures at Brazzaville 28–33°C; dry season is Jun–Sep.

**National holidays**
Jan 1, Mar 18 (Day of the Supreme Sacrifice), May 1, Jul 31 (Revolution), Aug 13–15 (The Three Glorious Days), Nov 1 (Day of the Dead), Dec 25 (Children), 31 (Foundation of the Party and People's Republic).

## Political leaders

**President**

| | |
|---|---|
| 1960–3 | Abbé Fulbert Youlou |
| 1963–8 | Alphonse Massemba-Debat |
| 1968 | Marien Ngouabi |
| 1968 | Alphonse Massemba-Debat |
| 1968–9 | Alfred Raoul |
| 1969–77 | Marien Ngouabi |
| 1977–9 | Joachim Yhomby Opango |
| 1979–92 | Denis Sassou-Nguesso |
| 1992–7 | Pascal Lissouba |
| 1997– | Denis Sassou-Nguesso |

**Prime Minister**

| | |
|---|---|
| 1958 | Jacques Opangault |
| 1958–60 | Fulbert Youlou |
| 1960–3 | *No Prime Minister* |
| 1963–6 | Pascal Lissouba |
| 1966–8 | Ambroise Noumazalaye |
| 1968–9 | Alfred Raoul |
| 1969–73 | *No Prime Minister* |
| 1973–5 | Henri Lopès |
| 1975–84 | Louis Sylvain Goma |
| 1984–9 | Ange-Édouard Poungui |

| | |
|---|---|
| 1989–90 | Alphonse Poaty-Souchlaty |
| 1990–1 | Pierre Moussa *Acting Prime Minister* |
| 1991 | Louis Sylvain Goma |
| 1991–2 | André Milongo |
| 1992 | Stéphane Maurice Bongho-Nouarra |
| 1992–3 | Claude Antoine Dacosta |
| 1993–6 | Joachim Yhombi-Opango |
| 1996–7 | Charles David Ganao |
| 1997 | Bernard Kolelas |
| 1997– | *No Prime Minister* |

### Free French

During World War II Brazzaville served as the headquarters of the Free French forces led by General Charles de Gaulle. In the film *Casablanca* (1942), Rick and Captain Louis Renault head for the Free French garrison in Brazzaville at the end of the film and at the start of 'a beautiful friendship'.

## CONGO, DEMOCRATIC REPUBLIC OF

| | |
|---|---|
| **Official name** | Democratic Republic of Congo (DR Congo, DRC or DROC); also sometimes known as Congo (Kinshasa) or Congo-Kinshasa |
| **Local name** | Congo; République Démocratique du Congo |
| **Former name** | Congo Free State (until 1908), Belgian Congo (until 1960), Republic of the Congo (1960–4), Democratic Republic of Congo (1964–71), Zaïre (1971–97) |
| **Independence** | 1960 |
| **Area** | 2 343 950 sq km/904 765 sq mi |
| **Capital** | Kinshasa |
| **Chief towns** | Lubumbashi, Kisangani, Mbuji-Mayi, Kananga |
| **Population** | 49 785 000 (2001e) |
| **Nationality** | Congolese, Congo |
| **Languages** | French, Kikongo, Lingala |
| **Ethnic groups** | Bantu and Hamitic 44%, others 56% |
| **Religions** | Christianity 60% (RC 45%, Prot 15%), traditional beliefs 30%, Islam 10% |
| **Time zone** | GMT +1/2 |
| **Currency** | 1 Congolese Franc (CF) = 100 centimes |
| **Telephone** | +243 |
| **Internet** | .cd |
| **Country code** | COD |

**Location**
A central African republic, bounded to the west by Congo and the Atlantic Ocean; to the south-west by Angola; to the south-east by Zambia; to the east by Tanzania, Burundi, Rwanda and Uganda; to the north-east by The Sudan; and to the north and north-west by the Central African Republic.

**Physical description**
Rises in the east from a low-lying basin to a densely-forested plateau; Ruwenzori Mountains in the north-east rise to 5 110m/16 765ft at Pic Marguerite on Mt Ngaliema (Mt Stanley); chain of lakes in the Rift Valley; short 43km/27mi Atlantic coastline.

**Climate**
Crossed by the Equator and has a hot and humid climate; average maximum daily temperatures range between 28°C and 31°C.

**National holidays**
Jan 1, 4 (Martyrs of Independence), May 1, 20 (Mouvement Populaire de la Révolution), Jun 24 (Anniversary of Currency, Promulgation of the 1967 Constitution and Day of the Fishermen), 30 (Independence), Dec 25.

## Political leaders

**President**

| | |
|---|---|
| 1960–5 | Joseph Kasavubu |
| 1965–97 | Mobutu Sese Seko (*formerly* Joseph Mobutu) |
| 1997–2001 | Laurent Kabila |
| 2001– | Joseph Kabila |

**Prime Minister**

| | |
|---|---|
| 1960 | Patrice Lumumba |
| 1960 | Joseph Ileo |
| 1960–1 | *College of Commissioners* |
| 1961 | Joseph Ileo |
| 1961–4 | Cyrille Adoula |
| 1964–5 | Moïse Tshombe |
| 1965 | Evariste Kimba |
| 1965–6 | Mulamba Nyungu wa Kadima |
| 1966–77 | *As President* |
| 1977–80 | Mpinga Kasenga |
| 1980 | Bo-Boliko Lokonga Monse Mihambu |
| 1980–1 | Nguza Karl I Bond |
| 1981–3 | Nsinga Udjuu |
| 1983–6 | Léon Kengo Wa Dondo |
| 1986–8 | *No Prime Minister* |
| 1988 | Sambura Pida Nbagui |
| 1988–90 | Léon Kengo Wa Dondo |
| 1990–1 | Lunda Bululu |
| 1991 | Mulumba Lukeji |
| 1991 | Etienne Tshisekedi |
| 1991 | Bernardin Mungul Diaka |
| 1991–2 | Karl I Bond |
| 1992–3 | Etienne Tshisekedi |
| 1993–4 | Faustin Birindwa |
| 1994–7 | Léon Kengo Wa Dondo |
| 1997 | Etienne Tshisekedi |
| 1997 | Likulia Bolongo |
| 1997– | *No Prime Minister* |

### Mighty River

The River Congo is the second longest river in Africa, and the tenth longest in the world, at a massive 4 630km/2 880mi. It rises as the River Lualaba, crosses the Equator and becomes known as the River Congo, then flows in an arc across central Africa. The first European discovery of the river mouth was in 1482, but its extent was appreciated only in the 19c, with explorations by Stanley, Livingstone and others.

**COOK ISLANDS** *see* **NEW ZEALAND**

## COSTA RICA

| | |
|---|---|
| **Official name** | Republic of Costa Rica |
| **Local name** | Costa Rica; República de Costa Rica |
| **Independence** | 1821 |
| **Area** | 51 022 sq km/19 694 sq mi |
| **Capital** | San José |
| **Chief towns** | Cartago, Heredia, Liberia, Puntarenas, Limón |
| **Population** | 3 810 179 (2000) |
| **Nationality** | Costa Rican |
| **Languages** | Spanish |
| **Ethnic groups** | white and mestizo 95%, black and mulatto 3%, Amerindian 1%, Chinese 1% |
| **Religions** | Christianity 85% (RC), others 15% |
| **Time zone** | GMT –6 |
| **Currency** | 1 Costa Rican Colón (CR¢) = 100 céntimos |
| **Telephone** | +506 |
| **Internet** | .cr |
| **Country code** | CRI |

**Location**
The second smallest republic in Central America, bounded to the west by the Pacific Ocean; to the north by Nicaragua; to the east by the Caribbean; and to the south-east by Panama.

**Physical description**
A series of volcanic ridges form the backbone (some volcanoes active); highest peak is Chirripó Grande (3 819m/12 529ft); central plateau lies at an altitude of 800–1 400m/2 600–4 600ft; swampy near the coast, with tropical forest inland; some lowland savannah.

**Climate**
Tropical climate, with a small temperature range and abundant rainfall; more temperate in the central uplands; dry season is Dec–May; average annual temperature is 26–28°C.

**National holidays**
Jan 1, Mar 19 (St Joseph), Apr 11 (Battle of Rivas), May 1, Aug 15 (Mothers), 31 (International Black People), Sep 15 (Independence), Oct 12 (Culture), Nov 2, Dec 24, 25, 31; Holy Week.

## Political leaders

**President**

| | |
|---|---|
| 1894–1902 | Rafael Yglesias y Castro |
| 1902–6 | Ascención Esquivel Ibarra |
| 1906–10 | Cleto González Víquez |
| 1910–12 | Ricardo Jiménez Oreamuno |
| 1912–14 | Cleto González Víquez |
| 1914–17 | Alfredo González Flores |
| 1917–19 | Federico Tinoco Granados |
| 1919 | Julio Acosta García |
| 1919–20 | Juan Bautista Quiros |
| 1920–4 | Julio Acosta García |
| 1924–8 | Ricardo Jiménez Oreamuno |
| 1928–32 | Cleto González Víquez |
| 1932–6 | Ricardo Jiménez Oreamuno |
| 1936–40 | León Cortés Castro |
| 1940–4 | Rafael Ángel Calderón Guardia |
| 1944–8 | Teodoro Picado Michalski |
| 1948 | Santos Léon Herrera |
| 1948–9 | *Civil Junta* (José Figueres Ferrer) |
| 1949–52 | Otilio Ulate Blanco |
| 1952–3 | Alberto Oreamuno Flores |
| 1953–8 | José Figueres Ferrer |
| 1958–62 | Mario Echandi Jiménez |
| 1962–6 | Francisco José Orlich Bolmarcich |
| 1966–70 | José Joaquín Trejos Fernández |
| 1970–4 | José Figueres Ferrer |
| 1974–8 | Daniel Oduber Quirós |
| 1978–82 | Rodrigo Carazo Odio |
| 1982–6 | Luis Alberto Monge Álvarez |
| 1986–90 | Oscar Arias Sánchez |
| 1990–4 | Rafael Ángel Calderón Fournier |
| 1994–8 | José Maria Figueres Olsen |
| 1998–2002 | Miguel Angel Rodríguez Echevarría |
| 2002– | Abel Pacheco de la Espriella |

### *Pacifists on the Pacific*

Costa Rica is one of very few countries not to have an army. The military was abolished in 1948, and the government claims to have since invested the money saved into improving the quality of life and living standards of its people. But what Costa Rica lacks in military muscle, it makes up for in wildlife; the country estimates that it covers just 0.03% of the Earth's land surface, but contains approximately 6% of the world's biodiversity.

## CÔTE D'IVOIRE

| | | | |
|---|---|---|---|
| **Official name** | Republic of Côte d'Ivoire | **Languages** | French; many local languages are also spoken |
| **Local name** | Côte d'Ivoire; République de la Côte d'Ivoire | **Ethnic groups** | Akan 40%, Kru 17%, Voltaic 15%, Malinke 15%, Southern Mande 11%, others 2% |
| **Former name** | Ivory Coast (until 1986) | **Religions** | Islam 45%, traditional beliefs 30%, Christianity 25% |
| **Independence** | 1960 | **Time zone** | GMT |
| **Area** | 320 633 sq km/123 764 sq mi | **Currency** | 1 CFA Franc (CFAFr) = 100 centimes |
| **Capital** | Yamoussoukro (official) and Abidjan (administrative and economic) | **Telephone** | +225 |
| **Chief towns** | Bouaké, Daloa, Man, Korhogo, Gagnoa | **Internet** | .ci |
| **Population** | 16 939 000 (2001e) | **Country code** | CIV |
| **Nationality** | Ivorian | | |

**Location**
A republic in West Africa, bounded to the south-west by Liberia; to the north-west by Guinea; to the north by Mali and Burkina Faso; to the east by Ghana; and to the south by the Gulf of Guinea.

**Physical description**
Sandy beaches and lagoons, backed by a broad forest-covered coastal plain; land rises towards savannah at 300–350m/980–1 150ft; Mt Nimba massif in the north-west reaches 1 752m/5 748ft (highest point); rivers generally flow north to south.

**Climate**
Tropical, varying with distance from the coast; rainfall decreases towards the north; average temperatures are 25–27°C.

**National holidays**
Jan 1, May 1, Aug 15, Nov 1, Dec 7 (Independence), 24, 25, 31; A, Ad, EM, ER, GF, WM.

## Political leaders

**President**

| | |
|---|---|
| 1960–93 | Félix Houphouët-Boigny |
| 1993–9 | Henri Konan-Bédié |
| 1999–2000 | Robert Guëi |
| 2000– | Laurent Gbagbo |

**Prime Minister**

| | |
|---|---|
| 1958–9 | Auguste Denise |
| 1959–60 | Félix Houphouët-Boigny |
| 1960–90 | *No Prime Minister* |
| 1990–3 | Alassane Dramane Ouattara |
| 1993–9 | Daniel Kablan Duncan |
| 1999 | Robert Guëi |
| 2000 | Seydou Diarra |
| 2000–3 | Pascal Affi N'Guessan |
| 2003– | Seydou Diarra |

### *Cocoa Kings*

Côte d'Ivoire is the world's largest producer of cocoa. In 2002 it produced approximately 1 million tonnes/984 200 tons of cocoa beans, dwarfing its nearest competitor, Ghana, which produced only 380 000 tonnes/373 996 tons.

# CROATIA

| | | | |
|---|---|---|---|
| **Official name** | Republic of Croatia | **Chief towns** | Rijeka, Cakovec, Split, Zadar |
| **Local name** | Hrvatska; Republika Hrvatska | **Population** | 4 437 460 (2001) |
| **Former name** | formerly part of Kingdom of Serbs, Croats and Slovenes (until 1929), Kingdom of Yugoslavia (1929–41), Independent State of Croatia (1941–45), Federal People's Republic of Yugoslavia (1945–63), Socialist Federal People's Republic of Yugoslavia (1963–91) | **Nationality** | Croatian |
| | | **Languages** | Croatian |
| | | **Ethnic groups** | Croat 78%, Serb 12%, Bosniak 1%, others 9% |
| | | **Religions** | Christianity 88% (RC 77%, Orthodox 11%), Islam 1%, others 11% |
| | | **Time zone** | GMT +1 |
| | | **Currency** | 1 Kuna (Kn) = 100 lipa |
| **Independence** | 1991 | **Telephone** | +385 |
| **Area** | 56 538 sq km/21 824 sq mi | **Internet** | .hr |
| | | **Country code** | HRV |
| **Capital** | Zagreb | | |

**Location**
A republic in eastern Europe, bounded to the south-west and west by the Adriatic Sea; to the north by Slovenia; to the north-east by Hungary; to the east by Serbia and Montenegro; and to the south-east by Bosnia and Herzegovina.

**Physical description**
Mountainous, with islands on the Adriatic coast; highest point is Dinara (1 830m/6 004ft); inland terrain includes fertile plains.

**Climate**
Continental; hot summers and cold winters.

**National holidays**
Jan 1, May 1, 30 (National), Jun 22 (Antifascism), Aug 5 (National Thanksgiving), 15, Nov 1, Dec 25, 26; EM, GF.

## Political leaders

See **Serbia and Montenegro** for political leaders of the former Yugoslavia.

**President**

| | | | |
|---|---|---|---|
| 1992–9 | Franjo Tudjman | 2000 | Zlatko Tomčić *Acting President* |
| 1999–2000 | Vlatko Pavletić *Acting President* | 2000– | Stjepan Mesić |

**Prime Minister**

| | | | |
|---|---|---|---|
| 1990 | Stjepan Mesić | 1993–5 | Nikica Valentić |
| 1990–1 | Josip Manolić | 1995–2000 | Zlatko Mateša |
| 1991–2 | Franjo Gregurić | 2000– | Ivica Račan |
| 1992–3 | Hrvoje Šarinić | | |

## Martens and Lime Trees

*Kuna*, the name of the Croatian currency, means 'marten'. Historically, martens' pelts were used as payment in trading and bartering, and the *kuna* was first used on Croatian coins as far back as the 13c. *Lipa*, the name of the smaller currency unit, means 'lime tree'.

## CUBA

| | | | |
|---|---|---|---|
| **Official name** | Republic of Cuba | **Ethnic groups** | white 66%, mulatto 23%, black 11% |
| **Local name** | Cuba; República de Cuba | **Religions** | none/unaffiliated 55%, Christianity 43% (RC 40%, Prot 3%), traditional beliefs 2% |
| **Independence** | 1902 | **Time zone** | GMT –5 |
| **Area** | 110 860 sq km/42 792 sq mi | **Currency** | 1 Cuban Peso (Cub$) = 100 centavos |
| **Capital** | Havana; La Habana | **Telephone** | +53 |
| **Chief towns** | Santiago de Cuba, Camagüey, Holguín, Santa Clara, Guantánamo | **Internet** | .cu |
| **Population** | 11 230 000 (2001e) | **Country code** | CUB |
| **Nationality** | Cuban | | |
| **Languages** | Spanish | | |

**Location**
An island republic in the Caribbean Sea.

**Physical description**
An archipelago, comprising the island of Cuba, Isla de la Juventud and c.1 600 islets and cays; heavily indented coastline; highest peak is Pico Turquino (2 005m/6 578ft); mostly flat, with wide, fertile valleys and plains.

**Climate**
Subtropical, warm and humid; average annual temperature is 25°C; dry season is Nov–Apr; hurricanes usually occur between Jun and Nov.

**National holidays**
Jan 1 (Day of Liberation), May 1, Jul 25 (National Rebellion) (2), Oct 10 (Beginning of the Independence Wars).

## Political leaders

**President**

| | |
|---|---|
| 1902–6 | Tomas Estrada Palma |
| 1906–9 | *US rule* |
| 1909–13 | José Miguel Gómez |
| 1913–21 | Mario García Menocal |
| 1921–5 | Alfredo Zayas y Alfonso |
| 1925–33 | Gerardo Machado y Morales |
| 1933 | Carlos Manuel de Céspedes |
| 1933–4 | Ramón Grau San Martín |
| 1934–5 | Carlos Mendieta |
| 1935–6 | José A Barnet y Vinagres |
| 1936 | Miguel Mariano Gómez y Arias |
| 1936–40 | Federico Laredo Bru |
| 1940–4 | Fulgencio Batista |
| 1944–8 | Ramón Grau San Martín |
| 1948–52 | Carlos Prío Socarrás |
| 1952–9 | Fulgencio Batista |
| 1959 | Manuel Urrutia |
| 1959–76 | Osvaldo Dorticós Torrado |
| 1959–76 | Fidel Castro Ruz *Prime Minister and First Secretary* |
| 1976– | Fidel Castro Ruz *President* |

### Chatty Castro

Cuban President Fidel Castro holds the world record for the longest continuous speech at the United Nations. On 26 Sep 1960 Castro's speech denouncing imperialism and colonialism lasted an exhausting four and a half hours. He prefaced the speech by assuring those present that he would endeavour to be brief.

# CYPRUS

| | | | |
|---|---|---|---|
| **Official name** | Republic of Cyprus | **Languages** | Greek, Turkish, with English widely spoken |
| **Local name** | Kipros; Kypriaki Dimokratía (Greek), Kibris; Kibris Çumhuriyeti (Turkish) | **Ethnic groups** | Greek 78%, Turkish 18%, others 4% |
| **Independence** | 1960 | **Religions** | Christianity 78% (Orthodox), Islam 18%, others 4% |
| **Area** | 9 251 sq km/3 571 sq mi | **Time zone** | GMT +2 |
| **Capital** | Nicosia; Lefkosía (Greek), Lefkoşa (Turkish) | **Currency** | 1 Cyprus Pound (C£) = 100 cents; Turkish lira are used in the northern part under Turkish occupation |
| **Chief towns** | Larnaca, Limassol, Kyrenia; Famagusta (formerly the chief port) is under Turkish occupation and has been declared closed by the Cyprus government | **Telephone** | +357 |
| | | **Internet** | .cy |
| | | **Country code** | CYP |
| **Population** | 689 471 (2001) | | |
| **Nationality** | Cypriot | | |

**Location**
An island republic in the north-east Mediterranean Sea.

**Physical description**
Kyrenia Mountains extend along the north coast; forest-covered Troödos Mountains in the south-west rise to 1 951m/6 401ft at Mt Olympus; fertile plain across the island centre; indented coastline with several long, sandy beaches.

**Climate**
Typical Mediterranean climate with hot, dry summers and warm, wet winters; average daily temperatures (Jul–Aug) 22–29°C; winters are mild (average temperature 4°C in the mountains, 10°C on the plain); snow on higher land in winter.

**National holidays**
Jan 1, 6, Mar 25 (Greek National), Apr 1 (Greek Cypriot National), May 1, Aug 15, Oct 1 (Independence), 28 (Greek National Ochi), Dec 24, 25, 26; ES, Green Monday, Kataklysmos, Orthodox Easter (Apr/May) (3).

## Political leaders

**President**

| | |
|---|---|
| 1960–77 | Archbishop Makarios III |
| 1977–88 | Spyros Kyprianou |
| 1988–93 | Georgios Vassiliou |
| 1993–2003 | Glafcos Clerides |
| 2003– | Tassos Papadopoulos |

*Note: Turkey has occupied the northern third of Cyprus since 1974. It declared this area to be the Turkish Federated State of Cyprus in 1975 and the Turkish Republic of Northern Cyprus in 1983; the state is recognized only by Turkey. Since inception it has been led by Rauf Denktaş.*

# CZECH REPUBLIC

| | | | |
|---|---|---|---|
| **Official name** | Czech Republic | **Languages** | Czech |
| **Local name** | České Republiky, Česká Republika | **Ethnic groups** | Czech 82%, Moravian 13%, Slovak 3%, others 2% |
| **Former name** | formerly part of Czechoslovakia (until 1993) | **Religions** | Christianity 48% (RC 40%, Prot 5%, Orthodox 3%), none/unaffiliated 40%, others 12% |
| **Independence** | 1993 | **Time zone** | GMT +1 |
| **Area** | 78 864 sq km/30 441 sq mi | **Currency** | 1 Koruna (Kč) = 100 haléřů |
| **Capital** | Prague; Praha | **Telephone** | +420 |
| **Chief towns** | Brno, Plzen, Ostrava, Olomouc | **Internet** | .cz |
| **Population** | 10 292 933 (2001) | **Country code** | CZE |
| **Nationality** | Czech | | |

**Location**
A landlocked republic in eastern Europe, bounded to the west by Germany; to the north and east by Poland; to the south-east by Slovakia; and to the south by Austria.

**Physical description**
Bohemia and West Moravia are separated from East Moravia and Slovakia by the River Morava valley; western range of the Carpathians rise in the east; highest point is Sněžka (1 602m/5 256ft); many lakes and rivers; richly wooded.

**Climate**
Continental, with warm, humid summers and cold, dry winters.

**National holidays**
Jan 1, May 1, 8 (Liberation), Jul 5 (SS Cyril and Methodius), 6 (Martyrdom of Jan Hus), Sep 28 (Statehood), Oct 28 (Independence), Nov 17 (Fight for Freedom and Democracy), Dec 24, 25, 26; EM.

## Political leaders

### Czechoslovakia

**President**

| | |
|---|---|
| 1918–35 | Tomáš Garrigue Masaryk |
| 1935–8 | Edvard Beneš |
| 1938 | Emil Hácha |
| 1938–45 | Edvard Beneš *President in Exile (German Occupation)* |
| 1939–45 | Emil Hácha *State President (German Occupation)* |
| 1939–45 | Jozef Tiso *Slovak Republic President (German Occupation)* |
| 1945–8 | Edvard Beneš |
| 1948–53 | Klement Gottwald |
| 1953–7 | Antonín Zápotocký |
| 1957–68 | Antonín Novotný |
| 1968–75 | Ludvík Svoboda |
| 1975–89 | Gustáv Husák |
| 1989–93 | Václav Havel |

**Prime Minister**

| | |
|---|---|
| 1918–19 | Karel Kramář |
| 1919–20 | Vlastimil Tusar |
| 1920–1 | Jan Černý |
| 1921–2 | Edvard Beneš |
| 1922–6 | Antonín Švehla |
| 1926 | Jan Černý |
| 1926–9 | Antonín Švehla |
| 1929–32 | František Udržal |
| 1932–5 | Jan Malypetr |
| 1935–8 | Milan Hodža |

| | |
|---|---|
| 1938 | Jan Syrový |
| 1938–9 | Rudolf Beran |
| 1940–5 | Jan Šrámek *in exile* |
| 1945–6 | Zdeněk Fierlinger |
| 1946–8 | Klement Gottwald |
| 1948–53 | Antonín Zápotocký |
| 1953–63 | Viliám Široký |
| 1963–8 | Josef Lenárt |
| 1968–70 | Oldřich Černik |
| 1970–88 | Lubomír Štrougal |
| 1988–9 | Ladislav Adamec |
| 1989–92 | Marian Calfa |
| 1992 | Jan Strasky |

**First Secretary of the Communist Party**

| | |
|---|---|
| 1948–52 | Rudolf Slánsky |
| 1953–68 | Antonín Novotný |
| 1968–9 | Alexander Dubček |
| 1969–87 | Gustáv Husák |
| 1987–9 | Miloš Jakeš |
| 1989 | Karel Urbánek |
| 1989–93 | Ladislav Adamec |

In 1993 Czechoslovakia divided into two separate states, the Czech Republic and **Slovakia** (see separate entry).

## Czech Republic

**President**

| | |
|---|---|
| 1993–2003 | Václav Havel |
| 2003– | Václav Klaus |

**Prime Minister**

| | |
|---|---|
| 1993–7 | Václav Klaus |
| 1997–8 | Josef Tosovsky |
| 1998–2002 | Miloš Zeman |
| 2002– | Vladimír Špidla |

# DENMARK

| | |
|---|---|
| **Official name** | Kingdom of Denmark |
| **Local name** | Danmark; Kongeriget Danmark; also sometimes known as Rigsfællesskabet, the United Kingdom of Denmark, including the Faroe Islands and Greenland |
| **Area** | 43 076 sq km/16 627 sq mi |
| **Capital** | Copenhagen; København |
| **Chief towns** | Århus, Odense, Ålborg, Esbjerg, Randers, Kolding |
| **Population** | 5 294 860 (1998) |
| **Nationality** | Dane, Danish |
| **Languages** | Danish |
| **Ethnic groups** | Danish 96%, Faroese and Inuit 1%, others 3% |
| **Religions** | Christianity 93% (Prot 92%, RC 1%), none/unaffiliated 2%, others 5% |
| **Time zone** | GMT +1 |
| **Currency** | 1 Danish Krone (Dkr) = 100 øre |
| **Telephone** | +45 |
| **Internet** | .dk |
| **Country code** | DNK |

## DENMARK

**Location**
A kingdom in northern Europe, the smallest of the Scandinavian countries, comprising most of the Jutland Peninsula and 406 islands, including several in the Baltic Sea (the largest include Zealand, Fyn, Lolland, Falster and Bornholm), and some of the northern Frisian Islands in the North Sea.

**Physical description**
Uniformly low-lying; highest point (Ejer Bavnehøj) is only 173m/567ft; no large rivers and few lakes; shoreline is indented by many lagoons and fjords, the largest of which is Lim Fjord.

**Climate**
Much modified by the Gulf Stream, giving cold and cloudy winters, and warm, sunny summers.

**National holidays**
Jan 1, Jun 5 (Constitution), Dec 25, 26; A, EM, GF, HT, WM, General Prayer (Apr/May).

## Danish self-governing territories

### Faroe Islands

**Location**
The group of 18 islands and smaller islets lying between the Shetland Islands and Iceland, and subject to the Danish crown. Also spelt Faeroe Islands.

| | | | |
|---|---|---|---|
| **Local name** | Føroyar (Faeroese)/ Færøerne (Danish) | **Population** | 46 000 (2001e) |
| **Area** | 1 399 sq km/540 sq mi | **Internet** | .fo |
| **Capital** | Tórshavn (1999e) | **Country code** | FRO |

### Sheep Islands

The local name for the Faroes is *Føroyar*, which comes from an old Norse word meaning 'Sheep Islands'.

### Greenland

**Location**
The second-largest island in the world (after Australia), lying north-east of North America in the North Atlantic and Arctic oceans; autonomous with limited self-government but subject to the Danish crown.

| | | | |
|---|---|---|---|
| **Local name** | Kalaallit Nunaat (Inuit)/ Grønland (Danish) | **Population** | 56 000 (2001e) |
| **Area** | 2 175 600 sq km/ 839 780 sq mi | **Internet** | .gl |
| **Capital** | Nuuk (Inuit), Godthåb (Danish) | **Country code** | GRL |

## Political leaders

**Monarch**

| | |
|---|---|
| 1448–81 | Kristian I |
| 1481–1513 | Johan |
| 1513–23 | Kristian II |
| 1523–34 | Frederik I |
| 1534–59 | Kristian III |
| 1559–88 | Frederik II |
| 1588–1648 | Kristian IV |
| 1648–70 | Frederik III |
| 1670–99 | Kristian V |
| 1699–1730 | Frederik IV |
| 1730–46 | Kristian VI |
| 1746–66 | Frederik V |
| 1766–1808 | Kristian VII |
| 1808–39 | Frederik VI |
| 1839–48 | Kristian VIII |
| 1848–63 | Frederik VII |
| 1863–1906 | Kristian IX |
| 1906–12 | Frederik VIII |
| 1912–47 | Kristian X |
| 1947–72 | Frederik IX |
| 1972– | Margrethe II |

**Prime Minister**

| | |
|---|---|
| 1900–1 | Hannibal Sehested |
| 1901–5 | J H Deuntzer |
| 1905–8 | J C Christensen |
| 1908–9 | Niels Neergaard |
| 1909 | Ludvig Holstein-Ledreborg |
| 1909–10 | C Th Zahle |
| 1910–13 | Klaus Berntsen |
| 1913–20 | C Th Zahle |
| 1920 | Otto Liebe |
| 1920 | M P Friis |
| 1920–4 | Niels Neergaard |
| 1924–6 | Thorvald Stauning |
| 1926–9 | Thomas Madsen-Mygdal |
| 1929–42 | Thorvald Stauning |
| 1942 | Wilhelm Buhl |
| 1942–3 | Erik Scavenius |
| 1943–5 | *No government* |
| 1945 | Wilhelm Buhl |
| 1945–7 | Knud Kristensen |
| 1947–50 | Hans Hedtoft |
| 1950–3 | Erik Eriksen |
| 1953–5 | Hans Hedtoft |
| 1955–60 | H C Hansen |
| 1960–2 | Viggo Kampmann |
| 1962–8 | Jens Otto Krag |
| 1968–71 | Hilmar Baunsgaard |
| 1971–2 | Jens Otto Krag |
| 1972–3 | Anker Jørgensen |
| 1973–5 | Poul Hartling |
| 1975–82 | Anker Jørgensen |
| 1982–93 | Poul Schlüter |
| 1993–2001 | Poul Nyrup Rasmussen |
| 2001– | Anders Fogh Rasmussen |

# DJIBOUTI

| | |
|---|---|
| **Official name** | Republic of Djibouti |
| **Local name** | Djibouti; République de Djibouti (French), Jumhūriyya Jibūt (Arabic) |
| **Former name** | French Somaliland (until 1967), French Territory of the Afars and Issas (1966–77) |
| **Independence** | 1977 |
| **Area** | 23 310 sq km/8 998 sq mi |
| **Capital** | Djibouti; Djīboûtî |
| **Chief towns** | Tadjoura, Dikhil, Obock, Ali-Sabieh |
| **Population** | 681 000 (2001e) |
| **Nationality** | Djiboutian |
| **Languages** | Arabic, French |
| **Ethnic groups** | Issa 53%, Afar 36%, Arab 6%, others 5% |
| **Religions** | Islam 94% (Sunni), Christianity 6% (RC 4%, Prot 2%) |
| **Time zone** | GMT +3 |
| **Currency** | 1 Djibouti Franc (DF, DjFr) = 100 centimes |
| **Telephone** | +253 |
| **Internet** | .dj |
| **Country code** | DJI |

**Location**
A republic in north-east Africa, bounded to the north-west, west and south by Ethiopia; to the south-east by Somalia; and to the north by Eritrea and the Gulf of Aden.

**Physical description**
A series of plateaux dropping down from mountains to flat low-lying rocky desert; 350km/220mi of fertile coastal strip around the Gulf of Tadjoura, which juts deep into the country; highest point, Moussa Ali, rises to 2 020m/6 627ft in the north.

**Climate**
Semi-arid with a hot season (May–Sep); very hot on coastal plains, maximum average daily temperature dropping below 30°C for only three months (Dec–Feb); slightly lower temperatures in the interior highlands.

**National holidays**
Jan 1, May 1, Jun 27 (Independence) (2), Dec 25; Ad (2), ER (2), NY (Muslim), PB, Al-Isra Wal-Mira'age (Mar/Apr).

## Political leaders

**President**

| | |
|---|---|
| 1977–99 | Hassan Gouled Aptidon |
| 1999– | Ismaïl Omar Guelleh |

**Prime Minister**

| | |
|---|---|
| 1977–8 | Abdallah Mohammed Kamil |
| 1978–2001 | Barkat Gourad Hamadou |
| 2001– | Dileïta Mohamed Dileïta |

### Low-Lying Lake

Djibouti's Lake Assal is the lowest point in Africa, at –156m/–512ft. It lies in a rift valley, separated from the Gulf of Tadjourah that leads into the Gulf of Aden only by rocks made of ancient lava flows. These form a natural barrier and stop the lake being flooded by the salt waters of the Gulf.

## DOMINICA

| | |
|---|---|
| **Official name** | Commonwealth of Dominica |
| **Local name** | Dominica |
| **Independence** | 1978 |
| **Area** | 751 sq km/290 sq mi |
| **Capital** | Roseau |
| **Chief towns** | Portsmouth, Grand Bay |
| **Population** | 71 727 (2001) |
| **Nationality** | Dominican |
| **Languages** | English; French Creole is also spoken |
| **Ethnic groups** | African/mixed African-European 97%, Amerindian 2%, others 1% |
| **Religions** | Christianity 93% (RC 77%, Prot 16%), others 7% |
| **Time zone** | GMT –4 |
| **Currency** | 1 East Caribbean Dollar (EC$) = 100 cents |
| **Telephone** | +1 767 |
| **Internet** | .dm |
| **Country code** | DMA |

**Location**
An independent republic located in the Windward Islands, in the east Caribbean Sea.

**Physical description**
Roughly rectangular in shape, with a deeply-indented coastline; c.50km/30mi long and 26km/16mi wide, rising to 1 447m/4 747ft at Morne Diablotin; volcanic origin, with many fumaroles and sulphur springs; forestry covers 67% of its area.

**Climate**
Warm and humid; average monthly temperatures are 26–32°C; subject to hurricanes.

**National holidays**
Jan 1, May 1, Nov 3 (Independence), 4 (Community Service), Dec 25, 26; C (2), EM, GF, WM, August Monday (Aug).

## Political leaders

**President**

| | |
|---|---|
| 1978–9 | Louis Cools-Lartigue *Interim President* |
| 1979–80 | Frederick Degazon[1] |
| 1979–80 | Jenner Armour *Acting President* |
| 1980–3 | Aurelius Marie |
| 1983–93 | Clarence Augustus Seignoret |
| 1993–8 | Crispin Anselm Sorhaindo |
| 1998– | Vernon Shaw |

**Prime Minister**

| | |
|---|---|
| 1978–9 | Patrick Roland John |
| 1979–80 | Oliver Seraphine |
| 1980–95 | Mary Eugenia Charles |
| 1995–2000 | Edison James |
| 2000 | Rosie Douglas |
| 2000– | Pierre Charles |

[1] *Left Dominica Jun 1979 but did not officially resign until Feb 1980.*

## DOMINICAN REPUBLIC

| | |
|---|---|
| **Official name** | Dominican Republic (DR) |
| **Local name** | República Dominicana |
| **Independence** | 1844 |
| **Area** | 48 442 sq km/18 699 sq mi |
| **Capital** | Santo Domingo |
| **Chief towns** | Santiago, La Vega, San Juan, San Francisco de Macorís, La Romana |
| **Population** | 8 528 000 (2001e) |
| **Nationality** | Dominican |
| **Languages** | Spanish |
| **Ethnic groups** | mulatto 74%, white 16%, black 10% |
| **Religions** | Christianity 92% (RC), none/unaffiliated 7%, others 1% |
| **Time zone** | GMT –4 |
| **Currency** | 1 Dominican Republic Peso (RD$, DR$) = 100 centavos |
| **Telephone** | +1 809 |
| **Internet** | .do |
| **Country code** | DOM |

# DOMINICAN REPUBLIC

**Location**
A republic of the West Indies, comprising the eastern two-thirds of the island of Hispaniola, and bordering Haiti to the west.

**Physical description**
Crossed by the Cordillera Central, a heavily-wooded range with many peaks over 3 000m/9 840ft; Pico Duarte (3 175m/10 417ft) is the highest peak in the Caribbean; Lake Enriquillo lies in a broad valley in the south-west; wide coastal plain to the east.

**Climate**
Tropical maritime with a rainy season from May to Nov; average temperature at Santo Domingo ranges between 24°C (Jan) and 27°C (Jul); hurricanes may occur in Jun–Nov.

**National holidays**
Jan 1, 6, 21 (Our Lady of Altagracia), 26 (Duarte), Feb 27 (Independence), May 1, Aug 16 (Restoration of the Republic), Sep 24 (Our Lady of Mercy), Dec 25; CC, GF.

## Political leaders

**President**

| | |
|---|---|
| 1899–1902 | Juan Isidro Jiménez |
| 1902–3 | Horacio Vásquez |
| 1903 | Alejandro Wos y Gil |
| 1903–4 | Juan Isidro Jiménez |
| 1904–6 | Carlos Morales |
| 1906–11 | Ramon Cáceres |
| 1911–12 | Eladio Victoria |
| 1912–13 | Adolfo Nouel y Bobadilla |
| 1913–14 | José Bordas y Valdés |
| 1914 | Ramon Báez |
| 1914–16 | Juan Isidro Jiménez |
| 1916–22 | *US occupation* (Francisco Henríquez y Carrajal) |
| 1922–4 | *US occupation* (Juan Batista Vicini Burgos) |
| 1924–30 | Horacio Vásquez |
| 1930 | Rafael Estrella Urena |
| 1930–8 | Rafael Leónidas Trujillo y Molina |
| 1938–40 | Jacinto Bienvenudo Peynado |
| 1940–2 | Manuel de Jesus Troncoso de la Concha |
| 1942–52 | Rafael Leónidas Trujillo y Molina |
| 1952–60 | Hector Bienvenido Trujillo |
| 1960–2 | Joaquín Videla Balaguer |
| 1962 | Rafael Bonnelly |
| 1962 | *Military Junta* (Huberto Bogaert) |
| 1962–3 | Rafael Bonnelly |
| 1963 | Juan Bosch Gavino |
| 1963 | *Military Junta* (Emilio de los Santos) |
| 1963–5 | Donald Reid Cabral |
| 1965 | *Civil War* |
| 1965 | Elias Wessin y Wessin |
| 1965 | Antonio Imbert Barreras |
| 1965 | Francisco Caamaño Deñó |
| 1965–6 | Héctor Garcia Godoy Cáceres |
| 1966–78 | Joaquín Videla Balaguer |
| 1978–82 | Antonio Guzmán Fernández |
| 1982–6 | Salvador Jorge Blanco |
| 1986–96 | Joaquín Videla Balaguer |
| 1996–2000 | Leonel Fernández Reyna |
| 2000– | Hipólito Mejía |

### Hispaniola

The Dominican Republic comprises the east of the island of Hispaniola, an island first discovered by Europeans when Christopher Columbus visited it in 1492. It became the first Spanish colony in the Caribbean under the name Santo Domingo. The name Hispaniola is derived from *La Isla Española*, 'the Spanish island'.

**DUBAI** *see* **UNITED ARAB EMIRATES**

## EAST TIMOR

| | | | |
|---|---|---|---|
| **Official name** | Democratic Republic of East Timor | **Population** | 711 000 (2001e) |
| **Local name** | Timor-Leste; República Democrática de Timor-Leste (Portuguese), Timor Lorosa'e; Republika Demokratika Timor Lorosa'e (Tetum) | **Nationality** | Timorese |
| **Former names** | Portuguese Timor (until 1975), part of Indonesia (1976–2002) | **Languages** | Portuguese, Tetum; English and Indonesian are also spoken |
| **Independence** | 2002 | **Ethnic groups** | Malay, Papuan |
| **Area** | 14 874 sq km/5 743 sq mi | **Religions** | Christianity 93% (RC 90%, Prot 3%), Islam 4%, others 3% |
| **Capital** | Dili | **Time zone** | GMT +8 |
| **Chief towns** | Baucau, Pante Macassar | **Currency** | 1 US dollar ($) = 100 cents |
| | | **Telephone** | +670 |
| | | **Internet** | .tp |
| | | **Country code** | TLS |

**Location**
A republic in South-East Asia occupying the eastern half of the island of Timor and the enclave of Oecusse in the west of the island.

**Physical description**
Mountainous, with numerous rivers; highest peak is Tata Mailau (2 950m/9 678ft); also includes the smaller islands of Pulau Atauro and Jaco.

**Climate**
Hot and humid equatorial climate; dry season (Jun–Sep), rainy season (Dec–Mar); average temperature is 27°C on the coast, falling inland and with altitude.

**National holidays**
Jan 1, May 1, 20 (Independence), Aug 15, 30 (Constitution), Sep 20 (Liberation), Nov 1, 12 (Santa Cruz), Dec 8, 25; GF.

## Political leaders

**President**
2002– Xanana Gusmão

**Prime Minister**
2002– Mari Alkatiri

### *A New Country*

East Timor gained its independence on 20 May 2002, becoming the world's newest independent state and newest democracy. It became a member of the United Nations the same year.

## ECUADOR

| | | | |
|---|---|---|---|
| **Official name** | Republic of Ecuador | **Ethnic groups** | mestizo 50%, Amerindian 35%, white 10%, black 5% |
| **Local name** | Ecuador; República del Ecuador | **Religions** | Christianity 96% (RC 94%, Prot 2%), others 4% |
| **Independence** | 1822 | **Time zone** | GMT –5 |
| **Area** | 270 699 sq km/104 490 sq mi | **Currency** | 1 US dollar ($) = 100 cents |
| **Capital** | Quito | **Telephone** | +593 |
| **Chief towns** | Guayaquil, Cuenca, Riobamba, Esmeraldas | **Internet** | .ec |
| **Population** | 12 156 608 (2001) | **Country code** | ECU |
| **Nationality** | Ecuadorean or Ecuadorian | | |
| **Languages** | Spanish; Quechua is also spoken | | |

**Location**
A republic straddling the Equator in the north-west of South America. It is bounded to the north by Colombia; to the south and east by Peru; and to the west by the Pacific Ocean, and includes the Galápagos Islands (comprising six main volcanic islands).

**Physical description**
Coastal plain in west; Andean uplands in the centre, three main ranges which include Cotopaxi (5 896m/19 344ft), the world's highest active volcano; highest point is Mt Chimborazo (6 267m/20 560ft); forested alluvial plains in east; frequent earthquakes.

**Climate**
Hot and humid coast, rain throughout the year (especially Dec–Apr); temperatures are much reduced by altitude; Quito has warm days and chilly nights, with frequent heavy rain in the afternoon; hot and wet equatorial climate in the east.

**National holidays**
Jan 1, May 1, 24 (Battle of Pichincha), Aug 10 (Independence), Oct 9 (Independence of Guayaquil), Nov 2, 3 (Independence of Cuenca), Dec 25; GF.

## Political leaders

**President**

| | |
|---|---|
| 1895–1901 | Eloy Alfaro |
| 1901–5 | Leónides Plaza Gutiérrez |
| 1905–6 | Lizardo García |
| 1906–11 | Eloy Alfaro |
| 1911 | Emilio Estrada |
| 1911–12 | Carlos Freile Zaldumbide |
| 1912–16 | Leónides Plaza Gutiérrez |
| 1916–20 | Alfredo Baquerizo Moreno |
| 1920–4 | José Luis Tamayo |
| 1924–5 | Gonzálo S Córdova |
| 1925–6 | *Military Juntas* |
| 1926–31 | Isidro Ayora |
| 1931–2 | *Four Acting Presidents* |
| 1932–3 | Juan de Dios Martínez Mera |
| 1933–4 | Abelardo Montalvo |
| 1934–5 | José María Velasco Ibarra |
| 1935 | Antonio Pons |
| 1935–7 | Federico Páez |
| 1937–8 | Alberto Enríquez Gallo |
| 1938 | Manuel María Borrero |
| 1938–9 | Aurelio Mosquera Narváez |
| 1939–40 | Julio Enrique Moreno |
| 1940–4 | Carlos Alberto Arroya del Río |
| 1944–7 | José María Velasco Ibarra |
| 1947 | Carlos Mancheno |
| 1947–8 | Carlos Julio Arosemena Tola |
| 1948–52 | Galo Plaza Lasso |
| 1952–6 | José María Velasco Ibarra |
| 1956–60 | Camilo Ponce Enríquez |
| 1960–1 | José María Velasco Ibarra |

| | | | |
|---|---|---|---|
| 1961–3 | Carlos Julio Arosemena Monroy | 1984–8 | León Febres Cordero |
| 1963–6 | *Military Junta* | 1988–92 | Rodrigo Borja Cevallos |
| 1966 | Clemente Yerovi Indaburu | 1992–6 | Sixto Durán Ballén |
| 1966–8 | Otto Arosemena Gómez | 1996–7 | Abdalá Bucaram Ortiz |
| 1968–72 | José María Velasco Ibarra | 1997 | Rosalia Arteaga *Acting President* |
| 1972–6 | Guillermo Rodríguez Lara | 1997–8 | Fabián Alarcón Rivero |
| 1976–9 | *Military Junta* | 1998–2000 | Jamil Mahuad Witt |
| 1979–81 | Jaime Roldós Aguilera | 2000–3 | Gustavo Noboa Bejerano |
| 1981–4 | Oswaldo Hurtado Larrea | 2003– | Lucio Gutiérrez |

### *Incas and Volcanoes*

Quito sits at an altitude of 2 850m/9 350ft at the foot of Guagua Pichincha, an active volcano prone to showering the city with clouds of ash. Quito was an Inca capital, but was destroyed by followers of the Inca leader Atahualpa when it became clear that it would be captured by the Spanish in the early 1530s. It was refounded in 1534.

## EGYPT

| | | | |
|---|---|---|---|
| **Official name** | Arab Republic of Egypt | **Nationality** | Egyptian |
| **Local name** | Misr; Al-Jumhūriyya al-Miṣriyya al-'Arabiyya | **Languages** | Arabic |
| **Former name** | formerly part of the United Arab Republic, with Syria (1958–61; name retained until 1971) | **Ethnic groups** | Eastern Hamitic 91%, others 9% |
| **Independence** | 1922 | **Religions** | Islam 94% (mostly Sunni), Christianity 6% (mostly Coptic) |
| **Area** | 1 001 449 sq km/386 559 sq mi | **Time zone** | GMT +2 |
| **Capital** | Cairo; El Qāhirah | **Currency** | 1 Egyptian Pound (£E, LE) = 100 piastres |
| **Chief towns** | Alexandria, Port Said, Aswan, Suez, El Gîza | **Telephone** | +20 |
| **Population** | 59 312 914 (1996) | **Internet** | .eg |
| | | **Country code** | EGY |

**Location**
A republic in north-east Africa, bounded to the west by Libya; to the south by The Sudan; to the east by the Red Sea; to the north-east by Israel; and to the north by the Mediterranean Sea.

**Physical description**
River Nile flows north, dammed to create Lake Nasser; huge delta north of Cairo; Western Desert covers over two-thirds of the country; highest point is Gebel Katherîna (2 637m/8 651ft); 90% of the population lives on the Nile floodplain (c.3% of the country's area).

**Climate**
Mainly desert, except for an 80km/50mi wide Mediterranean coastal fringe; very hot on the coast when the dust-laden *khamsin* wind blows north from the Sahara (Mar–Jun).

**National holidays**
Apr 25 (Sinai Liberation), May 1, 23 (Revolution), Oct 6 (Armed Forces); Ad (2), Ar, ER (2), NY (Muslim), PB, Sham El Nessim (Apr/May).

## Political leaders

### Khedive

| | |
|---|---|
| 1895–1914 | Abbas Helmi II |

**Sultan**

| | |
|---|---|
| 1914–17 | Hussein Kamel |
| 1917–22 | Ahmed Fouad |

### Kingdom of Egypt

**Monarch**

| | |
|---|---|
| 1922–36 | Fouad I |
| 1936–7 | Farouk *Trusteeship* |
| 1937–52 | Farouk I |

### Republic of Egypt

**President**

| | |
|---|---|
| 1953–4 | Mohammed Najib |
| 1954–70 | Gamal Abdel Nasser |
| 1970–81 | Mohammed Anwar El-Sadat |
| 1981– | Mohammed Hosni Mubarak |

**Prime Minister**

| | |
|---|---|
| 1895–1908 | Mustafa Fahmy |
| 1908–10 | Butros Ghali |
| 1910–14 | Mohammed Said |
| 1914–19 | Hussein Rushdi |
| 1919 | Mohammed Said |
| 1919–20 | Yousuf Wahba |
| 1920–1 | Mohammed Tewfiq Nazim |
| 1921–2 | Adli Yegen |
| 1922 | Abdel Khaliq Tharwat |
| 1922–3 | Mohammed Tewfiq Nazim |
| 1923–4 | Yehia Ibrahim |
| 1924 | Saad Zaghloul |
| 1924–6 | Ahmed Zaywan |
| 1926–7 | Adli Yegen |
| 1927–8 | Abdel Khaliq Tharwat |
| 1928 | Mustafa An-Nahass |
| 1928–9 | Mohammed Mahmoud |
| 1929–30 | Adli Yegen |
| 1930 | Mustafa An-Nahass |
| 1930–3 | Ismail Sidqi |
| 1933–4 | Abdel Fattah Yahya |
| 1934–6 | Mohammed Tewfiq Nazim |
| 1936 | Ali Maher |
| 1936–7 | Mustafa An-Nahass |
| 1937–9 | Mohammed Mahmoud |
| 1939–40 | Ali Maher |
| 1940 | Hassan Sabri |
| 1940–2 | Hussein Sirry |
| 1942–4 | Mustafa An-Nahass |
| 1944–5 | Ahmed Maher |
| 1945–6 | Mahmoud Fahmy El-Nuqrashi |
| 1946 | Ismail Sidqi |
| 1946–8 | Mahmoud Fahmy El-Nuqrashi |
| 1948–9 | Ibrahim Abdel Hadi |
| 1949–50 | Hussein Sirry |
| 1950–2 | Mustafa An-Nahass |
| 1952 | Ali Maher |
| 1952 | Najib El-Hilali |
| 1952 | Hussein Sirry |
| 1952 | Najib El-Hilali |
| 1952 | Ali Maher |
| 1952–4 | Mohammed Najib |
| 1954 | Gamal Abdel Nasser |
| 1954 | Mohammed Najib |
| 1954–62 | Gamal Abdel Nasser |
| 1958–61 | *United Arab Republic* |
| 1962–5 | Ali Sabri |
| 1965–6 | Zakariya Mohyi Ed-Din |
| 1966–7 | Mohammed Sidqi Soliman |
| 1967–70 | Gamal Abdel Nasser |
| 1970–2 | Mahmoud Fawzi |
| 1972–3 | Aziz Sidki |
| 1973–4 | Mohammed Anwar El-Sadat |
| 1974–5 | Abdel Aziz Hijazy |
| 1975–8 | Mamdouh Salem |
| 1978–80 | Mustafa Khalil |
| 1980–1 | Mohammed Anwar El-Sadat |
| 1981–2 | Mohammed Hosni Mubarak |
| 1982–4 | Fouad Monyi Ed-Din |
| 1984 | Kamal Hassan Ali |
| 1985–6 | Ali Lotfi |
| 1986–96 | Atif Sidqi |
| 1996–1999 | Ahmed Kamal Al-Ganzouri |
| 1999– | Atef Muhammed Ebeid |

## Ancient Egyptian dynasties

All dates are BC.

| | | |
|---|---|---|
| c.3100–2890 | I | *Early Dynastic Period* |
| c.2890–2780 | II | (First use of stone in building; hieroglyphic script developed.) |
| c.2780–2613 | III | *Old Kingdom* |
| c.2613–2494 | IV | (The age of the great pyramid builders. Longest reign in history: Pepi II, 90 years.) |
| c.2494–2345 | V | |
| c.2345–2181 | VI | |
| c.2181–2173 | VII | *First Intermediate Period* |
| c.2173–2160 | VIII | (Social order upset; few monuments built.) |
| c.2160–2130 | IX | |
| c.2130–2040 | X | |
| c.2133–1991 | XI | |
| 1991–1786 | XII | *Middle Kingdom* |
| 1786–1633 | XIII | (Golden age of art and craftsmanship.) |
| 1786–c.1603 | XIV | *Second Intermediate Period* |
| 1674–1567 | XV | (Country divided into principalities.) |
| c.1684–1567 | XVI | |
| c.1660–1567 | XVII | |
| 1567–1320 | XVIII | *New Kingdom* |
| 1320–1200 | XIX | (Began with colonial expansion, ended in divided rule.) |
| 1200–1085 | XX | |
| 1085–945 | XXI | *Third Intermediate Period* |
| 945–745 | XXII | (Revival of prosperity and restoration of cults.) |
| 745–718 | XXIII | |
| 718–715 | XXIV | |
| 715–668 | XXV | |
| 664–525 | XXVI | *Late Period* |
| 525–404 | XXVII | (Completion of Nile Red Sea canal. Alexander the Great reached Alexandria in 332BC.) |
| 404–399 | XXVIII | |
| 399–380 | XXIX | |
| 380–343 | XXX | |
| 343–332 | XXXI | |

*See also* **EGYPTIAN GODS** *under* **RELIGIONS, BELIEFS AND FOLKLORE** *and* **SEVEN WONDERS OF THE WORLD** *under* **ANCIENT GREECE AND ROME**.

**ÉIRE** *see* **IRELAND, REPUBLIC OF**

## EL SALVADOR

| | |
|---|---|
| **Official name** | Republic of El Salvador |
| **Local name** | El Salvador; República de El Salvador |
| **Independence** | 1841 |
| **Area** | 21 476 sq km/8 290 sq mi |
| **Capital** | San Salvador |
| **Chief towns** | Santa Ana, San Miguel, Mejicanos |
| **Population** | 6 313 000 (2001e) |
| **Nationality** | Salvadoran |
| **Languages** | Spanish |
| **Ethnic groups** | mestizo 91%, Amerindian 8%, white 1% |
| **Religions** | Christianity 97% (RC 77%, Prot 20%), others 3% |
| **Time zone** | GMT –6 |
| **Currency** | 1 El Salvador Colón (¢) = 100 centavos/1 US Dollar ($, US$)=100 cents |
| **Telephone** | +503 |
| **Internet** | .sv |
| **Country code** | SLV |

**Location**
The smallest of the Central American republics, bounded to the north and east by Honduras; to the west by Guatemala; and to the south by the Pacific Ocean.

**Physical description**
Two volcanic ranges running east to west; highest volcano is Santa Ana (Ilamatepec) at 2 362m/7 749ft; terrain ranges from a narrow coastal belt in the south through upland valleys and plateaux to mountains in the north; highest point is Cerro El Pital (2 730m/8 957ft); many volcanic lakes; earthquakes are common.

**Climate**
Varies greatly with altitude; hot and tropical on the coastal lowlands; single rainy season (May–Oct); temperate uplands; average annual temperature at San Salvador is 23°C.

**National holidays**
Jan 1, May 1, 10 (Mothers), Aug 6 (El Salvador del Mundo) (2), Sep 15 (Independence), Nov 2, Dec 25, 31; GF, HT; *some local variation; public and private sector holidays may differ*.

## Political leaders

**President**

| | |
|---|---|
| 1899–1903 | Tomás Regalado |
| 1903–7 | Pedro José Escalon |
| 1907–11 | Fernando Figueroa |
| 1911–13 | Manuel Enrique Araujo |
| 1913–14 | Carlos Meléndez *President Designate* |
| 1914–15 | Alfonso Quiñónez Molina *President Designate* |
| 1915–18 | Carlos Meléndez |
| 1918–19 | Alfonso Quiñónez Molina *Vice President* |
| 1919–23 | Jorge Meléndez |
| 1923–7 | Alfonso Quiñónez Molina |
| 1927–31 | Pio Romero Bosque |
| 1931 | Arturo Araujo |
| 1931 | *Military Administration* |
| 1931–4 | Maximiliano H Martinez *Vice President* |
| 1934–5 | Andrés I Menéndez *Provisional President* |
| 1935–44 | Maximiliano H Martinez |
| 1944 | Andrés I Menéndez *Vice President* |
| 1944–5 | Osmin Aguirre y Salinas *Provisional President* |
| 1945–8 | Salvador Castaneda Castro |
| 1948–50 | *Revolutionary Council* |
| 1950–6 | Oscar Osorio |
| 1956–60 | José María Lemus |
| 1960–1 | *Military Junta* |

| | | | |
|---|---|---|---|
| 1961–2 | *Civil-Military Administration* | 1979–82 | *Military Juntas* |
| 1962 | Rodolfo Eusebio Cordón *Provisional President* | 1982–4 | *Government of National Unanimity* (Alvaro Magaña) |
| 1962–7 | Julio Adalberto Rivera | 1984–9 | José Napoleón Duarte |
| 1967–72 | Fidel Sánchez Hernández | 1989–94 | Alfredo Cristiani |
| 1972–7 | Arturo Armando Molina | 1994–9 | Armando Calderón Sol |
| 1977–9 | Carlos Humberto Romero | 1999– | Francisco Flores Perez |

**ENGLAND** *see* **UNITED KINGDOM**

## EQUATORIAL GUINEA

| | | | |
|---|---|---|---|
| **Official name** | Republic of Equatorial Guinea | **Languages** | Spanish, French; pidgin English and Fang are also spoken |
| **Local name** | Guinea Ecuatorial; República de Guinea Ecuatorial | **Ethnic groups** | Fang 82%, Bubi 11%, Ndowe 4%, others 3% |
| **Former name** | Spanish Guinea (until 1968) | **Religions** | Christianity 89% (RC), traditional beliefs 4%, none/unaffiliated 6%, Islam 1% |
| **Independence** | 1968 | **Time zone** | GMT +1 |
| **Area** | 26 016 sq km/10 042 sq mi | **Currency** | 1 CFA Franc (CFAFr) = 100 centimes |
| **Capital** | Malabo | **Telephone** | +240 |
| **Chief towns** | Bata and Evinayong on the mainland, Luba and Riaba on Bioko | **Internet** | .gq |
| **Population** | 468 000 (2001e) | **Country code** | GNQ |
| **Nationality** | Equatorial Guinean or Equatoguinean | | |

**Location**
A republic in western central Africa, comprising a mainland area (Río Muni) and several islands (notably Bioko and Annabón) in the Gulf of Guinea.

**Physical description**
Mainland rises sharply from a narrow coast of mangrove swamps towards the heavily-forested African plateau; Bioko Island, about 160km/100mi north-west of the mainland, is of volcanic origin, rising to 3 007m/9 865ft at Pico de Basilé.

**Climate**
Hot and humid equatorial; average maximum daily temperature is 29–32°C.

**National holidays**
Jan 1, May 1, Jun 5 (President's Birthday), Aug 3 (Armed Forces), Oct 12 (Independence), Dec 10 (Human Rights), 25; CC, GF, Constitution (Aug).

### Political leaders

**President**

1968–79 Francisco Macias Nguema
1979– Teodoro Obiang Nguema Mbasogo

**Prime Minister**

| | |
|---|---|
| 1963–8 | Bonifacio Ondó Edu |
| 1968–82 | *No Prime Minister* |
| 1982–92 | Cristino Seriche Bioko |
| 1992–6 | Silestre Siale Bileka |
| 1996–2001 | Ángel Serafín Seriche Dougan |
| 2001– | Candido Muatetema Rivas |

## ERITREA

| | | | |
|---|---|---|---|
| **Official name** | State of Eritrea | **Nationality** | Eritrean |
| **Local name** | Hagere Eretra, al-Dawla al-Iritra | **Languages** | Arabic, Tigrinya |
| **Former name** | formerly part of Ethiopia (until 1993) | **Ethnic groups** | Tigrinya 50%, Tigrean and Kunama 40%, Afar 4%, Saho 3%, others 3% |
| **Independence** | 1993 | **Religions** | Islam 50%, Christianity 50% (Coptic) |
| **Area** | 93 679 sq km/36 160 sq mi | **Time zone** | GMT +3 |
| **Capital** | Asmara; Asmera | **Currency** | 1 Nakfa (Nfa) = 100 cents |
| **Chief towns** | Assab, Massawa, Keren, Tessenai | **Telephone** | +291 |
| | | **Internet** | .er |
| **Population** | 3 847 000 (2001e) | **Country code** | ERI |

**Location**
A country in north-east Africa, bounded to the north and north-west by The Sudan; to the west and south-west by Ethiopia; to the south by Djibouti; and to the east by the Red Sea.

**Physical description**
Low-lying coastline stretching 1 000km/620mi along the Red Sea, rising to an inland plateau; highest point is Soira (3 018m/9 901ft).

**Climate**
Hot and dry along the Red Sea desert coast; cooler and wetter in the central highlands; semi-arid in the western hills and lowlands.

**National holidays**
Jan 1, 7 (Eritrean Christmas), 19 (Eritrean Epiphany), May 24 (Freedom), Jun 20 (Martyrs), Sep 1 (Start of the Armed Struggle), 11 (Eritrean Orthodox Church NY), 27 (Feast of the Cross); Eritrean Easter (Mar/Apr) (2), Eritrean Whit Sunday (Mar/Apr).

## Political leaders

**President**

1993– Isaias Afewerki

### Four Villages

It is believed that Asmara, the Eritrean capital, was originally four small villages. The original name was *Arbate Asmere*, meaning 'four united into one'.

# ESTONIA

| | | | |
|---|---|---|---|
| **Official name** | Republic of Estonia | **Languages** | Estonian |
| **Local name** | Eesti; Eesti Vabariik (Estonian), Estonskaya (Russia) | **Ethnic groups** | Estonian 68%, Russian 26%, Ukrainian 2%, Belarusian 1%, Finnish 1%, others 2% |
| **Former name** | Estonian Soviet Socialist Republic (1940–90), within the Union of Soviet Socialist Republics (USSR; 1940–91) | **Religions** | Christianity 100%, predominantly Lutheran protestant, also Orthodox, Baptist, Methodist and Pentecostal; Judaism |
| **Independence** | 1991 | **Time zone** | GMT +2 |
| **Area** | 45 100 sq km/17 409 sq mi | **Currency** | 1 Kroon (KR) = 100 sents |
| **Capital** | Tallinn | **Telephone** | +372 |
| **Chief towns** | Tartu, Narva, Kohtla-Järve, Pärnu | **Internet** | .ee |
| **Population** | 1 370 052 (2000) | **Country code** | EST |
| **Nationality** | Estonian | | |

**Location**
A republic in eastern Europe, bounded to the west by the Baltic Sea; to the north by the Gulf of Finland; to the east by Russia; and to the south by Latvia.

**Physical description**
Over 1 500 lakes in a fairly flat terrain; highest point is Suur Munamagi (318m/1 043ft); there are many islands on the coast, notably Saaremaa, Hiiumaa and Muhu; 36% of the area is forested.

**Climate**
Cool summers, wet winters.

**National holidays**
Jan 1, Feb 24 (Independence), May 1 (Spring), Jun 23 (Victory), 24 (St John/Midsummer), Aug 20 (Restoration of Independence), Dec 25, 26; GF, ES, Whit Sunday.

## Political leaders

**President**

| | |
|---|---|
| 1990–2 | Arnold Rüütel |
| 1992–2001 | Lennart Meri |
| 2001– | Arnold Rüütel |

**Prime Minister**

| | |
|---|---|
| 1990–2 | Edgar Savisaar |
| 1992 | Tiit Vähi |
| 1992–4 | Mart Laar |
| 1994–5 | Andres Tarand |
| 1995–7 | Tiit Vähi |
| 1997–9 | Mart Siimann |
| 1999–2002 | Mart Laar |
| 2002–3 | Siim Kallas |
| 2003– | Juhan Parts |

## ETHIOPIA

| | | | |
|---|---|---|---|
| **Official name** | Federal Democratic Republic of Ethiopia | **Languages** | Amharic; 70 local languages are also spoken |
| **Local name** | Ityopya; Ya'Ityopya Federalawi Dimokrasyawi Repeblik | **Ethnic groups** | Oromo 40%, Amhara and Tigrean 32%, Sidamo 9%, Shankella 6%, Somali 6%, others 7% |
| **Former name** | Abyssinia (until 1936), part of Italian East Africa (1936–41), People's Democratic Republic of Ethiopia (1987–91) | **Religions** | Christianity 42% (Coptic), Islam 40%, traditional beliefs 14%, others 4% |
| **Area** | 1 128 497 sq km/435 600 sq mi | **Time zone** | GMT +3 |
| **Capital** | Addis Ababa; Ādīs Ābeba, Addis Abeba | **Currency** | 1 Ethiopian Birr (EB) = 100 cents |
| **Chief towns** | Dire Dawa, Harer | **Telephone** | +251 |
| **Population** | 53 477 265 (1994) | **Internet** | .et |
| **Nationality** | Ethiopian | **Country code** | ETH |

**Location**
A republic in north-east Africa, bounded to the west and south-west by The Sudan; to the south by Kenya; to the east and north-east by Somalia; and to the north by Djibouti and Eritrea; the country is landlocked, having lost about 10% of its territory and all of its Red Sea coastline when the former province of Eritrea gained its independence in 1993.

**Physical description**
Dominated by a mountainous central plateau; split diagonally by the Great Rift Valley; highest point is Ras Dashen (4 620m/15 157ft); plateau is crossed east to west by the Blue Nile, which has its source in Lake Tana; north and east are relatively low-lying; in the north-east the Danakil Depression dips to 116m/381ft below sea level.

**Climate**
Tropical, moderated by higher altitudes; distinct wet season (Apr–Sep); temperatures warm, but rarely hot all year round; hot, semi-arid north-east and south-east lowlands; severe droughts in the 1980s caused widespread famine.

**National holidays**
Jan 7 (Ethiopian Christmas), 19 (Ethiopian Epiphany), Feb 18 (President), Mar 2 (Victory of Adwa), May 1, 28 (Downfall of the Dergue), Sep 27 (Finding of the True Cross); Ad, ER, NY (Ethiopian) (Sep), PB, Ethiopian Good Friday and Easter Sunday.

## Political leaders

**Monarch**

1889–1911 Menelik II
1911–16 Lij Iyasu (Joshua)
1916–28 Zawditu
1928–74 Haile Selassie *Emperor from 1930*

**Chairman of Provisional Military Administrative Council**

1974–7 Teferi Benti
1977–87 Mengistu Haile Mariam

**President**

| | |
|---|---|
| 1987–91 | Mengistu Haile Mariam |
| 1991 | Tesfaye Gebre Kidan *Acting President* |
| 1991–5 | Meles Zenawi |
| 1995–2001 | Negasso Gidada |
| 2001– | Girma Wolde-Giorgis |

**Prime Minister**

| | |
|---|---|
| 1987–9 | Fikre Selassie Wogderess |
| 1989–91 | Haile Yimenu *Acting Prime Minister* |
| 1991 | Tesfaye Dinka *Acting Prime Minister* |
| 1991–5 | Tamirat Layne *Acting Prime Minister* |
| 1995– | Meles Zenawi |

### Ancient Ethiopia

Ethiopia is the oldest independent country in sub-Saharan Africa and, except for a five-year occupation by Italy under Mussolini (1936–41), has never been colonized.

**FALKLAND ISLANDS** *see* **UNITED KINGDOM**

**FAROE ISLANDS** *see* **DENMARK**

## FIJI

| | |
|---|---|
| **Official name** | Republic of the Fiji Islands |
| **Local name** | Matanitu Ko Viti |
| **Former name** | Republic of Fiji (1987–98) |
| **Independence** | 1970 |
| **Area** | 18 333 sq km/7 076 sq mi |
| **Capital** | Suva |
| **Chief towns** | Lautoka, Ba, Labasa, Nadi, Nausori |
| **Population** | 775 077 (1996) |
| **Nationality** | Fijian |
| **Languages** | Fijian, Hindi |
| **Ethnic groups** | Fijian 51%, Indian 44%, others 5% |
| **Religions** | Christianity 46% (Prot 37%, mainly Methodist, RC 9%), Hinduism 38%, Islam 8%, Sikhism 1%, others 7% |
| **Time zone** | GMT +12 |
| **Currency** | 1 Fiji Dollar (F$) = 100 cents |
| **Telephone** | +679 |
| **Internet** | .fj |
| **Country code** | FJI |

**Location**
A Melanesian island group of 844 islands and islets in the south-west Pacific Ocean (c.100 permanently inhabited), forming an independent republic.

**Physical description**
Larger islands are generally mountainous; highest peak, Tomaniivi, is on Viti Levu (1 324m/4 348ft); smaller islands consist of limestone, with little vegetation; extensive coral reef (Great Sea Reef) stretches for 500km/300mi along western fringe.

**Climate**
Winds are variable in the wet season between Nov and Apr, with tropical cyclonic storms likely; temperatures average 23–27°C; humidity on the windward slopes averages 74%.

**National holidays**
Jan 1, Dec 25, 26; D, EM, GF, HS, PB, Queen's Birthday (Jun), National Youth (Apr/May), Ratu Sir Lala Sukuna (1st Mon in Jun), Fiji (Oct).

## Political leaders

Chief of State until 1987: British monarch, represented by Governor General.

**Governor General**

| | |
|---|---|
| 1970–3 | Robert Sidney Foster |
| 1973–83 | George Cakobau |
| 1983–7 | Penaia Ganilau |
| 1987 | *Military Administration* (Sitiveni Rabuka) |

**President**

| | |
|---|---|
| 1987–93 | Penaia Ganilau |
| 1993–2000 | Kamisese Mara |
| 2000 | *Interim Military Government* (Frank Bainimarama) |
| 2000– | Josefa Iloilovatu Uluivuda *Interim President until 2001* |

**Prime Minister**

| | |
|---|---|
| 1970–87 | Kamisese Mara |
| 1987 | Timoci Bavadra |
| 1987–92 | Kamisese Mara |
| 1992–9 | Sitiveni Rabuka |
| 1999–2000 | Mahendra Chaudhry |
| 2000 | Tevita Momoedonu *Acting Prime Minister* |
| 2000 | Epeli Nailatika *Interim Prime Minister* |
| 2000–1 | Laisenia Qarase |
| 2001 | Tevita Momoedonu |
| 2001– | Laisenia Qarase |

### Whales' Teeth

One of the national symbols of Fiji is the *tabua*, a whale's tooth. Historically very rare, the tabua is of supreme importance in Fijian traditions. Highly prized in ceremonies, it is regarded as a symbol of peace, understanding and love.

# FINLAND

| | | | |
|---|---|---|---|
| **Official name** | Republic of Finland | **Nationality** | Finnish |
| **Local name** | Suomi; Suomen Tasavalta (Finnish), Republiken Finland (Swedish) | **Languages** | Finnish, Swedish |
| **Independence** | 1917 | **Ethnic groups** | Finnish 93%, Swedish 6%, others 1% |
| **Area** | 338 145 sq km/130 524 sq mi | **Religions** | Christianity 91% (Prot 89%, Orthodox 1%, RC 1%), none/unaffiliated 9% |
| **Capital** | Helsinki (Finnish), Helsingfors (Swedish) | **Time zone** | GMT +2 |
| **Chief towns** | Tampere, Turku, Espoo, Vantaa | **Currency** | 1 Euro (€) = 100 cents |
| **Population** | 5 181 115 (2000) | **Telephone** | +358 |
| | | **Internet** | .fi |
| | | **Country code** | FIN |

**Location**
A republic in northern Europe, bounded to the east by Russia; to the south by the Gulf of Finland; to the west by the Gulf of Bothnia and Sweden; and to the north by Norway.

**Physical description**
A low-lying glaciated plateau; over one-third of the country is north of the Arctic Circle; highest peak is Halti (1 328m/4 356ft); over 60 000 shallow lakes in the south-east; Saaristomeri archipelago has over 17 000 islands; 65% is forest and 10% water.

**Climate**
Northern location is ameliorated by the Baltic Sea; western winds bring warm air currents in summer; Eurasian winds bring cold spells in winter and heatwaves in summer; during summer the sun stays above the horizon for over 70 days.

**National holidays**
Jan 1, 6, May 1, Nov 1, Dec 6 (Independence), 24, 25, 26; A, EM, ES, GF, Midsummer Day (Jun), Whitsun (May/Jun).

## Political leaders

### Monarch

Finland was under Swedish control from the 13c until it was ceded to Russia in 1809. Russian rulers then assumed the title of Grand Duke of Finland. In 1917 it became an independent monarchy. However in Nov 1918, after initially accepting the throne the previous month, Landgrave Frederick Charles of Hesse, the brother-in-law of the German Emperor William II, withdrew his acceptance because of the Armistice and the ensuing abdication of William II. The previous regent remained in power until a Republic was declared in Jul 1919.

| | |
|---|---|
| 1918 | Dr Pehr Evind Svinhufvud *Regent* |
| 1918 | Landgrave Frederick Charles of Hesse *(withdrew acceptance)* |
| 1918–19 | Dr Pehr Evind Svinhufvud *Regent* |

### President

| | |
|---|---|
| 1919–25 | Kaarlo Ståhlberg |
| 1925–31 | Lauri Relander |
| 1931–7 | Pehr Svinhufvud |
| 1937–40 | Kyösti Kallio |
| 1940–4 | Risto Ryti |
| 1944–6 | C G E Mannerheim |

| | |
|---|---|
| 1946–56 | Juho Paasikivi |
| 1956–82 | Urho Kekkonen |
| 1982–94 | Mauno Koivisto |
| 1994–2000 | Martti Ahtisaari |
| 2000– | Tarja Halonen |

**Prime Minister**

| | |
|---|---|
| 1917–18 | Pehr Svinhufvud |
| 1918 | Juho Paasikivi |
| 1918–19 | Lauri Ingman |
| 1919 | Kaarlo Castrén |
| 1919–20 | Juho Vennola |
| 1920–1 | Rafael Erich |
| 1921–2 | Juho Vennola |
| 1922 | Aino Cajander |
| 1922–4 | Kyösti Kallio |
| 1924 | Aino Cajander |
| 1924–5 | Lauri Ingman |
| 1925 | Antti Tulenheimo |
| 1925–6 | Kyösti Kallio |
| 1926–7 | Väinö Tanner |
| 1927–8 | Juho Sunila |
| 1928–9 | Oskari Mantere |
| 1929–30 | Kyösti Kallio |
| 1930–1 | Pehr Svinhufvud |
| 1931–2 | Juhu Sunila |
| 1932–6 | Toivo Kivimäki |
| 1936–7 | Kyösti Kallio |
| 1937–9 | Aino Cajander |
| 1939–41 | Risto Ryti |
| 1941–3 | Johann Rangell |
| 1943–4 | Edwin Linkomies |
| 1944 | Andreas Hackzell |
| 1944 | Urho Castrén |
| 1944–5 | Juho Paasikivi |
| 1946–8 | Mauno Pekkala |
| 1948–50 | Karl Fagerholm |
| 1950–3 | Urho Kekkonen |
| 1953–4 | Sakari Tuomioja |
| 1954 | Ralf Törngren |
| 1954–6 | Urho Kekkonen |
| 1956–7 | Karl Fagerholm |
| 1957 | Väinö Sukselainen |
| 1957–8 | Rainer von Fieandt |
| 1958 | Reino Kuuskoski |
| 1958–9 | Karl Fagerholm |
| 1959–61 | Väinö Sukselainen |
| 1961–2 | Martti Miettunen |
| 1962–3 | Ahti Karjalainen |
| 1963–4 | Reino Lehto |
| 1964–6 | Johannes Virolainen |
| 1966–8 | Rafael Paasio |
| 1968–70 | Mauno Koivisto |
| 1970 | Teuvo Aura |
| 1970–1 | Ahti Karjalainen |
| 1971–2 | Teuvo Aura |
| 1972 | Rafael Paasio |
| 1972–5 | Kalevi Sorsa |
| 1975 | Keijo Liinamaa |
| 1975–7 | Martti Miettunen |
| 1977–9 | Kalevi Sorsa |
| 1979–82 | Mauno Koivisto |
| 1982–7 | Kalevi Sorsa |
| 1987–91 | Harri Holkeri |
| 1991–5 | Esko Aho |
| 1995–2003 | Paavo Lipponen |
| 2003 | Anneli Jäätteenmäki |
| 2003– | Matti Vanhanen |

## FRANCE

| | |
|---|---|
| **Official name** | French Republic |
| **Local name** | France; République Française |
| **Area** | 551 000 sq km/213 000 sq mi |
| **Capital** | Paris |
| **Chief towns** | Marseilles, Lyons, Toulouse, Nice, Strasbourg |
| **Population** | 58 520 688 (1999) |
| **Nationality** | French |
| **Languages** | French |
| **Ethnic groups** | French 92%, North African 5%, Breton 1%, German 1%, others 1% |
| **Religions** | Christianity 84% (RC 80%, Prot 4%), none/unaffiliated 8%, Islam 6%, Judaism 1%, Buddhism 1% |
| **Time zone** | GMT +1 |
| **Currency** | 1 Euro (€) = 100 cents |
| **Telephone** | +33 |
| **Internet** | .fr |
| **Country code** | FRA |

**Location**
A republic in western Europe, bounded to the north and north-east by the English Channel, Belgium, Luxembourg and Germany; to the east by Switzerland, Italy and Monaco; to the south by the Mediterranean Sea, Spain and Andorra; and to the west by the Bay of Biscay; also includes the island of Corsica in the Mediterranean Sea.

**Physical description**
A country of low and medium-sized hills and plateaux deeply cut by rivers; bounded to the south and east by large mountain ranges; the Alps rise to 4 807m/15 771ft at Mont Blanc (the highest point) in the east, and the Pyrenees lie to the south; many major rivers.

**Climate**
South has a Mediterranean climate, with warm, moist winters and hot, dry summers; climate is maritime in the north-west; east has a continental climate.

**National holidays**
Jan 1, May 1, 8 (Victory), Jul 14 (Bastille), Aug 15, Nov 1, 11 (Armistice), Dec 25; A, EM, WM.

## Overseas departments

### French Guiana

| | | | |
|---|---|---|---|
| **Location** | Situated on the north-eastern coast of South America, it is bounded to the west by Suriname; to the east and south by Brazil; and to the north by the Atlantic Ocean. | | |
| **Local name** | Guyane | **Population** | 156 790 (1999) |
| **Area** | 90 909 sq km/35 091 sq mi | **Internet** | .gf |
| **Capital** | Cayenne | **Country code** | GUF |

### Guadeloupe

| | | | |
|---|---|---|---|
| **Location** | A group of seven islands in the central Lesser Antilles, in the east Caribbean Sea. | | |
| **Local name** | Guadeloupe | **Population** | 422 222 (1999) |
| **Area** | 1 779 sq km/687 sq mi | **Internet** | .gp |
| **Capital** | Basse-Terre | **Country code** | GLP |

### Martinique

| | | | |
|---|---|---|---|
| **Location** | An island in the Windward group of the Lesser Antilles, in the east Caribbean Sea, between Dominica and St Lucia. | | |
| **Local name** | Martinique | **Population** | 381 325 (1999) |
| **Area** | 1 079 sq km/416 sq mi | **Internet** | .mq |
| **Capital** | Fort-de-France | **Country code** | MTQ |

### Réunion

| | | | |
|---|---|---|---|
| **Location** | An island in the Indian Ocean, to the east of Madagascar. | | |
| **Local name** | Réunion | **Population** | 706 180 (1999) |
| **Area** | 2 510 sq km/969 sq mi | **Internet** | .re |
| **Capital** | St Denis | **Country code** | REU |

## Overseas territories

### French Polynesia

| | | | |
|---|---|---|---|
| **Location** | An island grouping of five scattered archipelagoes in the south-east Pacific Ocean, between the Cook Islands in the west and the Pitcairn Islands in the east. | | |
| **Local name** | Polynésie Française | **Population** | 219 521 (1996) |
| **Area** | 3 941 sq km/1 521 sq mi | **Internet** | .pf |
| **Capital** | Papeete | **Country code** | PYF |

### New Caledonia

| | | | |
|---|---|---|---|
| **Location** | A group of islands in the south-west Pacific Ocean, 1 100km/680mi east of Australia. | | |
| **Local name** | Nouvelle-Calédonie | **Population** | 196 836 (1996) |
| **Area** | 18 575 sq km/7 170 sq mi | **Internet** | .nc |
| **Capital** | Nouméa | **Country code** | NCL |

### French Southern and Antarctic Territories

| | | | |
|---|---|---|---|
| **Location** | A group of islands in the southern Indian Ocean and Adélie Land in Antarctica. | | |
| **Local name** | Terres australes et antarctiques françaises | **Population** | Scientific staff only |
| | | **Internet** | .tf |
| **Area** | 507 781 sq km/196 003 sq mi | **Country code** | ATF |

### Wallis and Futuna Islands

| | | | |
|---|---|---|---|
| **Location** | An island grouping (consisting principally of Wallis Island (Uvéa), Futuna and Alofi) in the south-central Pacific Ocean, lying north-east of Fiji. | | |
| **Local name** | Îles de Wallis et Futuna | **Population** | 14 166 (1996) |
| **Area** | 274 sq km/106 sq mi | **Internet** | .wf |
| **Capital** | Mata-Utui; Matâ'utu | **Country code** | WLF |

### DOM-TOM

French overseas departments and territories are collectively known as the *DOM-TOM*, *Départements d'outre-mer* and *Territoires d'outre-mer*. In contrast, the mainland of France is often known as *l'Hexagone*, a reference to its roughly hexagonal shape.

## Territorial collectivities

### Mayotte

| | | | |
|---|---|---|---|
| **Location** | A small island group of volcanic origin, east of Comoros, in the west Indian Ocean. | | |
| **Local name** | Mayotte | **Population** | 160 265 (2002) |
| **Area** | 374 sq km/144 sq mi | **Internet** | .yt |
| **Capital** | Mamoudzou | **Country code** | MYT |

### St Pierre and Miquelon

| | | | |
|---|---|---|---|
| **Location** | Two islands in the North Atlantic Ocean, south of Newfoundland (Canada). | | |
| **Local name** | St-Pierre-et-Miquelon | **Population** | 6 316 (1999) |
| **Area** | 240 sq km/93 sq mi | **Internet** | .pm |
| **Capital** | St Pierre | **Country code** | SPM |

*Note: France also possesses Bassas da India, Europa Island, the Glorioso Islands, Juan de Nova and Tromelin Island in the Indian Ocean and Clipperton Island in the Pacific Ocean, all largely uninhabited.*

## Political leaders

**Monarch**

| | |
|---|---|
| 987–996 | Hugh Capet |
| 996–1031 | Robert II |
| 1031–60 | Henry I |
| 1060–1108 | Philip I |
| 1108–37 | Louis VI |
| 1137–80 | Louis VII |
| 1180–1223 | Philip II Augustus |
| 1223–6 | Louis VIII |
| 1226–70 | Louis IX |
| 1270–85 | Philip III |
| 1285–1314 | Philip IV |
| 1314–16 | Louis X |
| 1316 | John I |
| 1316–22 | Philip V |
| 1322–8 | Charles IV |
| 1328–50 | Philip VI |
| 1350–64 | John II |
| 1364–80 | Charles V |
| 1380–1422 | Charles VI |
| 1422–61 | Charles VII |
| 1461–83 | Louis XI |
| 1483–98 | Charles VIII |
| 1498–1515 | Louis XII |
| 1515–47 | Francis I |
| 1547–59 | Henry II |
| 1559–60 | Francis II |
| 1560–74 | Charles IX |
| 1574–89 | Henry III |
| 1589–1610 | Henry IV (of Navarre) |
| 1610–43 | Louis XIII |
| 1643–1715 | Louis XIV |
| 1715–74 | Louis XV |
| 1774–92 | Louis XVI |
| 1793–1804 | *Republic* |
| 1804–14 | *Empire* (Napoleon Bonaparte) |
| 1814–24 | Louis XVIII |
| 1824–30 | Charles X |
| 1830–48 | Louis-Philippe |
| 1848 | *monarchy dissolved* |

### Royal Nicknames

Derogatory nicknames for early French kings include the Bald (Charles I, 823–77), the Fat (Charles II, 839–88) and the Simple (Charles III, 879–929). But they weren't all bad. There was also the Fair (Charles IV, 1294–1328), the Wise (Charles V, 1338–80), the Victorious (Charles VII, 1403–61), the Affable (Charles VIII, 1470–98), the Well-Beloved (Louis XV, 1710–74) and, of course, the Sun King himself, Louis XIV (1638–1715).

# FRANCE

## Third Republic

**President**

| | |
|---|---|
| 1899–1906 | Emile Loubet |
| 1906–13 | Armand Fallières |
| 1913–20 | Raymond Poincaré |
| 1920 | Paul Deschanel |
| 1920–4 | Alexandre Millerand |
| 1924–31 | Gaston Doumergue |
| 1931–2 | Paul Doumer |
| 1932–40 | Albert Lebrun |

**Prime Minister**

| | |
|---|---|
| 1899–1902 | Pierre Waldeck-Rousseau |
| 1902–5 | Emile Combes |
| 1905–6 | Maurice Rouvier |
| 1906 | Jean Sarrien |
| 1906–9 | Georges Clemenceau |
| 1909–11 | Aristide Briand |
| 1911 | Ernest Monis |
| 1911–12 | Joseph Caillaux |
| 1912–13 | Raymond Poincaré |
| 1913 | Aristide Briand |
| 1913 | Jean Louis Barthou |
| 1913–14 | Gaston Doumergue |
| 1914 | Alexandre Ribot |
| 1914–15 | René Viviani |
| 1915–17 | Aristide Briand |
| 1917 | Alexandre Ribot |
| 1917 | Paul Painlevé |
| 1917–20 | Georges Clemenceau |
| 1920 | Alexandre Millerand |
| 1920–1 | Georges Leygues |
| 1921–2 | Aristide Briand |
| 1922–4 | Raymond Poincaré |
| 1924 | Frédéric François-Marsal |
| 1924–5 | Édouard Herriot |
| 1925 | Paul Painlevé |
| 1925–6 | Aristide Briand |
| 1926 | Édouard Herriot |
| 1926–9 | Raymond Poincaré |
| 1929 | Aristide Briand |
| 1929–30 | André Tardieu |
| 1930 | Camille Chautemps |
| 1930 | André Tardieu |
| 1930–1 | Théodore Steeg |
| 1931–2 | Pierre Laval |
| 1932 | André Tardieu |
| 1932 | Édouard Herriot |
| 1932–3 | Joseph Paul-Boncour |
| 1933 | Édouard Daladier |
| 1933 | Albert Sarrault |
| 1933–4 | Camille Chautemps |
| 1934 | Édouard Daladier |
| 1934 | Gaston Doumergue |
| 1934–5 | Pierre-Étienne Flandin |
| 1935 | Fernand Bouisson |
| 1935–6 | Pierre Laval |
| 1936 | Albert Sarrault |
| 1936–7 | Léon Blum |
| 1937–8 | Camille Chautemps |
| 1938 | Léon Blum |
| 1938–40 | Édouard Daladier |
| 1940 | Paul Reynaud |
| 1940 | Philippe Pétain |

## Vichy Government

**President and Prime Minister**

| | |
|---|---|
| 1940–4 | Philippe Pétain |

## Provisional Government of the French Republic

**President and Prime Minister**

| | |
|---|---|
| 1944–6 | Charles de Gaulle |
| 1946 | Félix Gouin |
| 1946 | Georges Bidault |

## Fourth Republic

**President**

| | |
|---|---|
| 1947–54 | Vincent Auriol |
| 1954–8 | René Coty |

**Prime Minister**

| | |
|---|---|
| 1946–7 | Léon Blum |
| 1947 | Paul Ramadier |
| 1947–8 | Robert Schuman |
| 1948 | André Marie |

| | |
|---|---|
| 1948 | Robert Schuman |
| 1948–9 | Henri Queuille |
| 1949–50 | Georges Bidault |
| 1950 | Henri Queuille |
| 1950–1 | René Pleven |
| 1951 | Henri Queuille |
| 1951–2 | René Pleven |
| 1952 | Edgar Faure |
| 1952–3 | Antoine Pinay |
| 1953 | René Mayer |
| 1953–4 | Joseph Laniel |
| 1954–5 | Pierre Mendès-France |
| 1955–6 | Edgar Faure |
| 1956–7 | Guy Mollet |
| 1957 | Maurice Bourgès-Maunoury |
| 1957–8 | Félix Gaillard |
| 1958 | Pierre Pfimlin |
| 1958–9 | Charles de Gaulle |

## Fifth Republic

**President**

| | |
|---|---|
| 1958–69 | Charles de Gaulle |
| 1969–74 | Georges Pompidou |
| 1974–81 | Valéry Giscard d'Estaing |
| 1981–95 | François Mitterrand |
| 1995– | Jacques Chirac |

**Prime Minister**

| | |
|---|---|
| 1959–62 | Michel Debré |
| 1962–8 | Georges Pompidou |
| 1968–9 | Maurice Couve de Murville |
| 1969–72 | Jacques Chaban Delmas |
| 1972–4 | Pierre Mesmer |
| 1974–6 | Jacques Chirac |
| 1976–81 | Raymond Barre |
| 1981–4 | Pierre Mauroy |
| 1984–6 | Laurent Fabius |
| 1986–8 | Jacques Chirac |
| 1988–91 | Michel Rocard |
| 1991–2 | Édith Cresson |
| 1992–3 | Pierre Bérégovoy |
| 1993–5 | Édouard Balladur |
| 1995–7 | Alain Juppé |
| 1997–2002 | Lionel Jospin |
| 2002– | Jean-Pierre Raffarin |

**FRENCH GUIANA** *see* **FRANCE**

**FRENCH POLYNESIA** *see* **FRANCE**

**FRENCH SOUTHERN AND ANTARCTIC TERRITORIES** *see* **FRANCE**

**FUJAIRAH** *see* **UNITED ARAB EMIRATES**

# GABON

| | |
|---|---|
| **Official name** | Gabonese Republic |
| **Local name** | Gabon; République Gabonaise |
| **Former name** | French West Africa (1910–60) |
| **Independence** | 1960 |
| **Area** | 267 667 sq km/103 319 sq mi |
| **Capital** | Libreville |
| **Chief towns** | Lambaréné, Franceville, Port Gentil |
| **Population** | 1 237 000 (2001e) |
| **Nationality** | Gabonese |
| **Languages** | French; local languages are widely spoken |
| **Ethnic groups** | Fang 35%, Mpongwe 16%, Mbete 14%, Punu 11%, others 24% |
| **Religions** | Christianity 95% (RC 65%, Prot and others 30%), traditional beliefs 4%, Islam 1% |
| **Time zone** | GMT +1 |
| **Currency** | 1 CFA Franc (CFAFr) = 100 centimes |
| **Telephone** | +241 |
| **Internet** | .ga |
| **Country code** | GAB |

**Location**
A republic in west equatorial Africa, bounded to the south, east and north-east by Congo; to the north by Cameroon; to the north-west by Equatorial Guinea; and to the west by the Atlantic Ocean.

**Physical description**
On the Equator for 880km/550mi west to east; lagoons and estuaries on the coast; land rises towards the African central plateau, cut by several rivers, notably the Ogooué; highest point is Mont Iboundji (1 575m/5 167ft).

**Climate**
Typical equatorial climate, hot, wet and humid; Libreville has an average maximum daily temperature of 33–37°C.

**National holidays**
Jan 1, May 1, Aug 15, 16 (Independence) (2), Nov 1, Dec 25; Ad, EM, ER, WM.

## Political leaders

**President**

| | |
|---|---|
| 1960–7 | Léon M'ba |
| 1967– | Omar (*to 1973* Bernard-Albert) Bongo |

**Prime Minister**

| | |
|---|---|
| 1960–75 | *As President* |
| 1975–90 | Léon Mébiame (Mébiane) |
| 1991–3 | Casimir Oyé M'ba |
| 1993–8 | Paulin Obame-Nguema |
| 1999– | Jean-François Ntoutoume-Emane |

### *Hooded Cloak*

The name Gabon is thought to come from the Portuguese word *gabão*, meaning a hooded cloak with sleeves, coined in reference to the shape of the coast and river estuary by Portuguese explorers in the late 15c.

## THE GAMBIA

| | |
|---|---|
| **Official name** | Republic of The Gambia |
| **Local name** | Gambia |
| **Former name** | Senegambia (with Senegal, 1982–9) |
| **Independence** | 1965 |
| **Area** | 10 402 sq km/4 015 sq mi |
| **Capital** | Banjul |
| **Chief towns** | Serrekunda, Brikama, Bakau, Georgetown |
| **Population** | 1 420 000 (2001e) |
| **Nationality** | Gambian |
| **Languages** | English; Mandinka, Fula and Wolof are also spoken |
| **Ethnic groups** | Mandinka 40%, Fulani 18%, Wolof 16%, Dyola 10%, Soninke 8%, others 8% |
| **Religions** | Islam 95%, Christianity 4%, traditional beliefs 1% |
| **Time zone** | GMT |
| **Currency** | 1 Dalasi (D) = 100 butut |
| **Telephone** | +220 |
| **Internet** | .gm |
| **Country code** | GMB |

**Location**
A republic situated in west Africa, bounded on all sides by Senegal except for the Atlantic Ocean coastline in the west.

**Physical description**
A strip of land stretching 322km/200mi east to west along the River Gambia; flat country, not rising above 90m/295ft.

**Climate**
Tropical; rainy season Jun–Sep with rainfall decreasing inland; high humidity in the wet season with high night temperatures; average temperatures range from 23°C (Jan) to 27°C (Jul), rising inland to over 40°C.

**National holidays**
Jan 1, Feb 18 (Independence), May 1, Aug 15 (St Mary), Dec 25; Ad, As, ER (2), GF, PB.

## Political leaders

**President**

| | |
|---|---|
| 1965–94 | Dawda Kairaba Jawara |
| 1994– | Yahya Jammeh *Head of military junta 1994–6* |

**GAZA STRIP** *see* **PALESTINIAN AUTONOMOUS AREAS** *under* **ISRAEL**

## GEORGIA

| | | | |
|---|---|---|---|
| **Official name** | Georgia | **Population** | 5 224 000 (2001e) |
| **Local name** | Sak'art'velos Respublikis | **Nationality** | Georgian |
| **Former name** | Georgian Democratic Republic (1918–21), Transcaucasian Soviet Federated Socialist Republic (with Armenia and Azerbaijan, 1922–36), Georgian Soviet Socialist Republic (1936–90), within the Union of Soviet Socialist Republics (USSR; 1922–91) | **Languages** | Georgian, Russian |
| | | **Ethnic groups** | Georgian 70%, Armenian 8%, Russian 6%, Azeri 6%, Ossetian 3%, others 7% |
| | | **Religions** | Christianity 83% (Georgian Orthodox 65%, Russian Orthodox 10%, Armenian Orthodox 8%), Islam 11%, others 6% |
| **Independence** | 1991 | **Time zone** | GMT +3 |
| **Area** | 69 700 sq km/26 900 sq mi | **Currency** | 1 Lari (GEL) = 100 tetri |
| **Capital** | T'bilisi or Tbilisi; also sometimes called Tiflis | **Telephone** | +995 |
| | | **Internet** | .ge |
| **Chief towns** | Kutaisi, Rustavi, Batumi, Sukhumi, Poti | **Country code** | GEO |

**Location**
A republic in eastern Europe, occupying central and western Transcaucasia. It is bounded to the south-east by Azerbaijan; to the south by Armenia; to the south-west by Turkey; to the west by the Black Sea; and to the north by Russia.

**Physical description**
Contains the Greater Caucasus in the north and the Lesser Caucasus in the south; forest covers c.39% of the land; highest point is Mt Shkhara (5 608m/18 399ft).

**Climate**
Subtropical, warm and humid in the west; continental in the east with hot summers and cold winters.

**National holidays**
Jan 1, 7 (Orthodox Christmas), 19 (Orthodox Epiphany), Mar 3 (Mothers), Apr 9 (National), May 9 (National), 26 (Independence), Aug 28 (St Mary), Oct 14 (Mtskhetoba), Nov 23 (St Georgi); ES, EM.

## Political leaders

**President**

| | |
|---|---|
| 1991–2 | Zviad Gamsakhurdia |
| 1992 | *Military Council* |
| 1992– | Eduard Shevardnadze |

**Prime Minister**

| | |
|---|---|
| 1990–1 | Tengiz Sigua |
| 1991 | Murman Omanidze *Acting Prime Minister* |
| 1991–2 | Bessarion Gugushvili |
| 1992–3 | Tengiz Sigua |
| 1993 | Eduard Shevardnadze *Acting Prime Minister* |
| 1993–5 | Otar Patsatsia |

**State Minister**

| | |
|---|---|
| 1995–8 | Niko Lekishvili |
| 1998–2000 | Vazha Lordkipanidze |
| 2000–1 | Giorgi Arsenishvili |
| 2001– | Avtandil Jorbenadze |

**GEORGIA, SOUTH** *see* **UNITED KINGDOM**

## GERMANY

| | |
|---|---|
| **Official name** | Federal Republic of Germany |
| **Local name** | Deutschland; Bundesrepublik Deutschland |
| **Former name** | *as listed below under Political leaders* |
| **Area** | 357 868 sq km/138 137 sq mi |
| **Capital** | Berlin |
| **Chief towns** | Bonn, Hamburg, Munich, Cologne, Essen, Leipzig, Frankfurt (am Main) |
| **Population** | 82 357 000 (2001e) |
| **Nationality** | German |
| **Languages** | German; Sorbian (a Slavic language) is spoken by a few |
| **Ethnic groups** | German 92%, Turkish 2%, others 6% |
| **Religions** | Christianity 76% (Prot 39%, RC 37%), none/unaffiliated 15%, Islam 3%, others 6% |
| **Time zone** | GMT +1 |
| **Currency** | 1 Euro (€) = 100 cents |
| **Telephone** | +49 |
| **Internet** | .de |
| **Country code** | DEU |

**Location**
It is bounded to the east by Poland and the Czech Republic; to the south-east by Austria; to the south-west by Switzerland; to the west by France, Luxembourg, Belgium and the Netherlands; and to the north by the North Sea, Denmark and the Baltic Sea.

**Physical description**
Baltic coastline is backed by a fertile low-lying plain, low hills, and many glacial lakes; central uplands include the Black Forest; land rises in the south in several ranges, notably the Bavarian Alps; highest peak is the Zugspitze (2 962m/9 717ft); many major rivers.

**Climate**
Winters are mild but stormy in the north-west; elsewhere, the climate is continental (more temperate in the east); average winter temperatures 2°C (north) to –3°C (south); average summer temperature 16°C (north), slightly higher in the south.

**National holidays**
Jan 1, May 1, Oct 3 (Unity), Dec 25, 26; A, EM, GF, WM; *much regional variation*.

## Political leaders

### German Empire

**Emperor**

Modern Germany was united under Prussia in 1871.

| | |
|---|---|
| 1871–88 | Wilhelm I |
| 1888 | Friedrich |
| 1888–1918 | Wilhelm II *abdicated 1918* |

**Chancellor**

| | |
|---|---|
| 1909–17 | Theobald von Bethmann Hollweg |
| 1917 | Georg Michaelis |
| 1917–18 | Georg Graf von Hertling |
| 1918 | Prince Max von Baden |
| 1918 | Friedrich Ebert |

### German Republic

**President**

| | |
|---|---|
| 1919–25 | Friedrich Ebert |
| 1925–34 | Paul von Hindenburg |

**Reich Chancellor**

| | |
|---|---|
| 1919 | Philipp Scheidemann |
| 1919–20 | Gustav Bauer |
| 1920 | Hermann Müller |
| 1920–1 | Konstantin Fehrenbach |
| 1921–2 | Karl Joseph Wirth |
| 1922–3 | Wilhelm Cuno |
| 1923 | Gustav Stresemann |
| 1923–4 | Wilhelm Marx |
| 1925–6 | Hans Luther |
| 1926–8 | Wilhelm Marx |
| 1928–30 | Hermann Müller |
| 1930–2 | Heinrich Brüning |
| 1932 | Franz von Papen |
| 1932–3 | Kurt von Sleicher |
| 1933 | Adolf Hitler |

**Chancellor and Führer**

| | |
|---|---|
| 1933–45 | Adolf Hitler *Führer from 1934* |
| 1945 | Karl Dönitz |

### Allied Occupation

| | |
|---|---|
| 1945–9 | *Military Governors* |

## German Democratic Republic (East Germany)

**President**

| | |
|---|---|
| 1949–60 | Wilhelm Pieck |

**Chairman of the Council of State**

| | |
|---|---|
| 1960–73 | Walter Ernst Karl Ulbricht |
| 1973–6 | Willi Stoph |
| 1976–89 | Erich Honecker |
| 1989 | Egon Krenz |
| 1989–90 | Gregor Gysi *General Secretary as Chairman* |

**Premier**

| | |
|---|---|
| 1949–64 | Otto Grotewohl |
| 1964–73 | Willi Stoph |
| 1973–6 | Horst Sindermann |
| 1976–89 | Willi Stoph |
| 1989–90 | Hans Modrow |
| 1990 | Lothar de Maizière |

## German Federal Republic (West Germany)

**President**

| | |
|---|---|
| 1949–59 | Theodor Heuss |
| 1959–69 | Heinrich Lübke |
| 1969–74 | Gustav Heinemann |
| 1974–9 | Walter Scheel |
| 1979–84 | Karl Carstens |
| 1984–90 | Richard von Weizsäcker |

**Chancellor**

| | |
|---|---|
| 1949–63 | Konrad Adenauer |
| 1963–6 | Ludwig Erhard |
| 1966–9 | Kurt Georg Kiesinger |
| 1969–74 | Willy Brandt |
| 1974–82 | Helmut Schmidt |
| 1982–90 | Helmut Kohl |

## Germany

**President**

| | |
|---|---|
| 1990–4 | Richard von Weizsäcker |
| 1994–9 | Roman Herzog |
| 1999– | Johannes Rau |

**Chancellor**

| | |
|---|---|
| 1990–8 | Helmut Kohl |
| 1998– | Gerhard Schröder |

### German Feast

The German authorities estimate that there are over 550 sources of natural mineral water in Germany, and more than 1 200 breweries that produce over 5 000 different beers. German bakers have come up with more than 300 kinds of bread, and over 1 200 types of biscuit and cake. And, of course, Germany is the home of the sausage: regional specialities include the *Rotwurst* from Thüringia, the *Brawn* from Hesse, the *Bockwurst* from Berlin and the *Bauernseufzer* from Franconia. Not to mention the Westphalian soft smoked sausage, the Bavarian jellied white or black meat sausage, the liver sausage from Kassel or the speciality of Swabia, 'a black sausage spiced with thyme, cloves and nutmeg' as the German National Tourist Board describes it with barely-disguised culinary glee.

## GHANA

| | | | |
|---|---|---|---|
| **Official name** | Republic of Ghana | **Ethnic groups** | Akan 53%, Mossi 17%, Ewe 12%, Ga-Adangame 8%, Gurma 2%, others 8% |
| **Local name** | Ghana | **Religions** | Christianity 50% (Prot 32%, RC 18%), traditional beliefs 34%, Islam 10%, others 6% |
| **Former name** | British Gold Coast and British Togoland (until 1957) | **Time zone** | GMT |
| **Independence** | 1960 | **Currency** | 1 Cedi (¢) = 100 pesewas |
| **Area** | 238 686 sq km/92 133 sq mi | **Telephone** | +233 |
| **Capital** | Accra | **Internet** | .gh |
| **Chief towns** | Sekondi-Takoradi, Kumasi, Tamale | **Country code** | GHA |
| **Population** | 18 912 079 (2000) | | |
| **Nationality** | Ghanaian | | |
| **Languages** | English; several African languages are also spoken | | |

**Location**
A republic in West Africa, bounded to the west by Côte d'Ivoire; to the north by Burkina Faso; to the east by Togo; and to the south by the Gulf of Guinea.

**Physical description**
Coastline of sand bars and lagoons; low-lying plains inland, leading to the Ashanti plateau in the west and the River Volta basin in the east, dammed to form Lake Volta; mountains rise in the east to 885m/2 904ft at Afadjato.

**Climate**
Tropical climate, including a warm, dry coastal belt in the south-east, a hot, humid south-west corner, and hot, dry savannah in the north.

**National holidays**
Jan 1, Mar 6 (Independence), May 1, Jun 4 (Revolution), Jul 1 (Republic), Dec 1 (National Farmers), 25, 26; EM, GF.

## Political leaders

**President**
1960–6 Kwame Nkrumah

**Chairman of National Liberation Council**
1966–9 Joseph Arthur Ankrah
1969 Akwasi Amankwa Afrifa
1969–70 *Presidential Committee*

**President**
1970–2 Edward Akufo-Addo

**Chairman**
1972–8 *National Redemption Council* (Ignatius Kuti Acheampong)
1978–9 *Supreme Military Council* (Fred W Akuffo)
1979 *Armed Forces Revolutionary Council* (Jerry John Rawlings)

**President**
1979–81 Hilla Limann

**Chairman of Provisional National Defence Council**

1981–2001 Jerry John Rawlings *President from 1992*

**President**

2001– John Agyekum Kufuor

**Prime Minister**

| | | | |
|---|---|---|---|
| 1960–9 | *As President* | 1972–8 | *As President* |
| 1969–72 | Kufi Abrefa Busia | 1978– | *No Prime Minister* |

**GIBRALTAR** *see* **UNITED KINGDOM**

## GREECE

| | |
|---|---|
| **Official name** | Hellenic Republic |
| **Local name** | Ellas, Ellada; Elliniki Dimokratia |
| **Former name** | Kingdom of Greece (until 1924 and 1935–73), Republic of Greece (until 1935) |
| **Independence** | 1832 |
| **Area** | 131 957 sq km/50 935 sq mi |
| **Capital** | Athens; Athína |
| **Chief towns** | Thessaloniki, Patras, Heraklion, Volos, Larisa, Piraieus |
| **Population** | 10 020 000 (2001e) |
| **Nationality** | Greek |
| **Languages** | Greek |
| **Ethnic groups** | Greek 98%, others 2% |
| **Religions** | Christianity 98% (Orthodox), Islam 1%, others 1% |
| **Time zone** | GMT +2 |
| **Currency** | 1 Euro (€) = 100 cents |
| **Telephone** | +30 |
| **Internet** | .gr |
| **Country code** | GRC |

**Location**

A republic in south-eastern Europe, occupying the southern part of the Balkan Peninsula and numerous islands in the Aegean and Ionian seas.

**Physical description**

A large area of mainland, including the Peloponnese peninsula in the south, linked to the rest of the mainland by the narrow Isthmus of Corinth; over 1 400 islands, notably Crete, Euboea, Lesbos, Rhodes, Chios, Cephalonia, Lemnos, Samos, Naxos and Corfu; nearly 80% is mountainous or hilly; highest point is Mt Olympus (2 917m/9 570ft); several rivers and smaller lakes.

**Climate**

Mediterranean on the coast and islands, with mild, rainy winters and hot, dry summers; rainfall occurs almost entirely in the winter months.

**National holidays**

Jan 1, 6, Mar 25 (Independence), May 1, Aug 15, Oct 28 (Ochi), Dec 25, 26; GF, EM, ES, WM, Whit Sunday, Shrove Monday.

## Political leaders

**Monarch**

| | |
|---|---|
| 1832–62 | Otto of Bavaria |
| 1863–1913 | George I |
| 1913–17 | Constantine I |
| 1917–20 | Alexander |
| 1920–2 | Constantine I |
| 1922–3 | George II |
| 1923–4 | Paul Koundouriotis *Regent* |

**President**

| | |
|---|---|
| 1924–6 | Paul Koundouriotis |
| 1926 | Theodore Pangalos |
| 1926–9 | Paul Koundouriotis |
| 1929–35 | Alexander T Zaïmis |

**Monarch**

| | |
|---|---|
| 1935 | George Kondylis *Regent* |
| 1935–47 | George II |
| 1947–64 | Paul |
| 1964–7 | Constantine II |
| 1967–73 | *Military Junta* |
| 1973 | George Papadopoulos *Regent* |

**President**

| | |
|---|---|
| 1973 | George Papadopoulos |
| 1973–4 | Phaedon Gizikis |
| 1974–5 | Michael Stasinopoulos |
| 1975–80 | Constantine Tsatsos |
| 1980–5 | Constantine Karamanlis |
| 1985–90 | Christos Sartzetakis |
| 1990–5 | Constantine Karamanlis |
| 1995– | Constantine Stephanopoulos |

**Prime Minister**

| | |
|---|---|
| 1899–1901 | George Theotokis |
| 1901–2 | Alexander T Zaïmis |
| 1902–3 | Theodore Deligiannis |
| 1903 | George Theotokis |
| 1903 | Demetrius G Rallis |
| 1903–4 | George Theotokis |
| 1904–5 | Theodore Deligiannis |
| 1905 | Demetrius G Rallis |
| 1905–9 | George Theotokis |
| 1909 | Demetrius G Rallis |
| 1909–10 | Kyriakoulis P Mavromichalis |
| 1910 | Stephen N Dragoumis |
| 1910–15 | Eleftherios K Venizelos |
| 1915 | Demetrius P Gounaris |
| 1915 | Eleftherios K Venizelos |
| 1915 | Alexander T Zaïmis |
| 1915–16 | Stephen Skouloudis |
| 1916 | Alexander T Zaïmis |
| 1916 | Nicholas P Kalogeropoulos |
| 1916–17 | Spyridon Lambros |
| 1917 | Alexander T Zaïmis |
| 1917–20 | Eleftherios K Venizelos |
| 1920–1 | Demetrius G Rallis |
| 1921 | Nicholas P Kalogeropoulos |
| 1921–2 | Demetrius P Gounaris |
| 1922 | Nicholas Stratos |
| 1922 | Peter E Protopapadakis |
| 1922 | Nicholas Triandaphyllakos |
| 1922 | Sortirios Krokidas |
| 1922 | Alexander T Zaïmis |
| 1922–3 | Stylianos Gonatas |
| 1924 | Eleftherios K Venizelos |
| 1924 | George Kaphandaris |
| 1924 | Alexander Papanastasiou |
| 1924 | Themistocles Sophoulis |
| 1924–5 | Andreas Michalakopoulos |
| 1925–6 | Alexander N Chatzikyriakos |
| 1926 | Theodore Pangalos |
| 1926 | Athanasius Eftaxias |
| 1926 | George Kondylis |
| 1926–8 | Alexander T Zaïmis |
| 1928–32 | Eleftherios K Venizelos |
| 1932 | Alexander Papanastasiou |
| 1932 | Eleftherios K Venizelos |
| 1932–3 | Panagiotis Tsaldaris |
| 1933 | Eleftherios K Venizelos |
| 1933 | Nicholas Plastiras |
| 1933 | Alexander Othonaos |
| 1933–5 | Panagiotis Tsaldaris |
| 1935 | George Kondylis |
| 1935–6 | Constantine Demertzis |
| 1936–41 | John Metaxas |
| 1941 | Alexander Koryzis |
| 1941 | George II *Chairman of Ministers* |
| 1941 | *German Occupation* (Emmanuel Tsouderos) |
| 1941–2 | George Tsolakoglou |
| 1942–3 | Constantine Logothetopoulos |
| 1943–4 | John Rallis |
| 1941–4 | Emmanuel Tsouderos *Government in exile* |
| 1944 | Sophocles Venizelos *Government in exile* |
| 1944–5 | George Papandreou *Government in exile* |
| 1945 | Nicholas Plastiras |

| | |
|---|---|
| 1945 | Peter Voulgaris |
| 1945 | Damaskinos, Archbishop of Athens |
| 1945 | Panagiotis Kanellopoulos |
| 1945–6 | Themistocles Sophoulis |
| 1946 | Panagiotis Politzas |
| 1946–7 | Constantine Tsaldaris |
| 1947 | Demetrius Maximos |
| 1947 | Constantine Tsaldaris |
| 1947–9 | Themistocles Sophoulis |
| 1949–50 | Alexander Diomedes |
| 1950 | John Theotokis |
| 1950 | Sophocles Venizelos |
| 1950 | Nicholas Plastiras |
| 1950–1 | Sophocles Venizelos |
| 1951 | Nicholas Plastiras |
| 1952 | Demetrius Kiusopoulos |
| 1952–5 | Alexander Papagos |
| 1955 | Stephen C Stefanopoulos |
| 1955–8 | Constantine Karamanlis |
| 1958 | Constantine Georgakopoulos |
| 1958–61 | Constantine Karamanlis |
| 1961 | Constantine Dovas |
| 1961–3 | Constantine Karamanlis |
| 1963 | Panagiotis Pipinellis |
| 1963 | Stylianos Mavromichalis |
| 1963 | George Papandreou |
| 1963–4 | John Parskevopoulos |
| 1964–5 | George Papandreou |
| 1965 | George Athanasiadis-Novas |
| 1965 | Elias Tsirimokos |
| 1965–6 | Stephen C Stefanopoulos |
| 1966–7 | John Paraskevopoulos |
| 1967 | Panagiotis Kanellopoulos |
| 1967–74 | *Military Junta* |
| 1967 | Constantine Kollias |
| 1967–73 | George Papadopoulos |
| 1973 | Spyridon Markezinis |
| 1973–4 | Adamantios Androutsopoulos |
| 1974–80 | Constantine Karamanlis |
| 1980–1 | George Rallis |
| 1981–9 | Andreas Papandreou |
| 1989 | Tzannis Tzannetakis |
| 1989–90 | Xenofon Zolotas |
| 1990–3 | Constantine Mitsotakis |
| 1993–6 | Andreas Papandreou |
| 1996– | Kostas Simitis |

**GREENLAND** *see* **DENMARK**

## GRENADA

| | |
|---|---|
| **Official name** | State of Grenada |
| **Local name** | Grenada |
| **Independence** | 1974 |
| **Area** | 344 sq km/133 sq mi |
| **Capital** | St George's |
| **Chief towns** | Gouyave, Victoria, Grenville |
| **Population** | 101 000 (2001e) |
| **Nationality** | Grenadian or Grenadan |
| **Languages** | English |
| **Ethnic groups** | African descent 83%, mixed 13%, East Indian 3%, European 1% |
| **Religions** | Christianity 90% (RC 52%, Prot 38%), others 10% |
| **Time zone** | GMT –4 |
| **Currency** | 1 East Caribbean Dollar (EC$) = 100 cents |
| **Telephone** | +1 473 |
| **Internet** | .gd |
| **Country code** | GRD |

**Location**
An independent constitutional monarchy of the West Indies and the most southerly of the Windward Islands, in the eastern Caribbean Sea, comprising the main island of Grenada and the South Grenadines (including Carriacou), an arc of small islands extending from Grenada north to St Vincent.

**Physical description**
Main island of Grenada is 34km/21mi long and 19km/12mi wide, of volcanic origin, with a ridge of mountains along its entire length; highest point is Mt St Catherine, which rises to 843m/2 766ft.

**Climate**
Subtropical; the average annual temperature is 23°C.

**National holidays**
Jan 1, 2, Feb 7 (Independence), May 1, Aug 3 (Emancipation) (2), Oct 25 (Thanksgiving), Dec 25, 26; CC, EM, GF, WM.

## Political leaders

Chief of State: British monarch, represented by Governor General.

**Prime Minister**

| | |
|---|---|
| 1974–9 | Eric M Gairy |
| 1979–83 | Maurice Bishop |
| 1983–4 | Nicholas Brathwaite *Chairman of Interim Council* |
| 1984–9 | Herbert A Blaize |
| 1989–90 | Ben Jones |
| 1990–5 | Nicholas Brathwaite |
| 1995– | Keith Mitchell |

**GRENADINES** *see* **ST VINCENT AND THE GRENADINES**

**GUADELOUPE** *see* **FRANCE**

**GUAM** *see* **UNITED STATES OF AMERICA**

## GUATEMALA

| | |
|---|---|
| **Official name** | Republic of Guatemala |
| **Local name** | Guatemala; República de Guatemala |
| **Independence** | 1839 |
| **Area** | 108 889 sq km/42 031 sq mi |
| **Capital** | Guatemala City; La Ciudad de Guatemala |
| **Chief towns** | Quetzaltenango, Escuintla, Antigua, Mazatenango |
| **Population** | 11 237 196 (2002) |
| **Nationality** | Guatemalan |
| **Languages** | Spanish; many indigenous languages are also spoken |
| **Ethnic groups** | Amerindian 44%, mestizo (Ladino) 40%, white 5%, black 2%, others 9% |
| **Religions** | Christianity 95% (RC 73%, Prot 22%), traditional beliefs (Mayan) 5% |
| **Time zone** | GMT –6 |
| **Currency** | 1 Quetzal (Q) = 100 centavos |
| **Telephone** | +502 |
| **Internet** | .gt |
| **Country code** | GTM |

## GUATEMALA

**Location**
The northernmost of the central American republics, bounded to the north and west by Mexico; to the south-west by the Pacific Ocean; to the east by Belize and the Caribbean Sea; and to the south-east by Honduras and El Salvador.

**Physical description**
Over two-thirds mountainous with large forests; narrow Pacific coastal plain; highlands rise to 2 500–3 000m/8 200–9 840ft, with volcanoes on the southern edge; highest point is Tajumulco (4 220m/13 845ft); low undulating tableland in north.

**Climate**
Humid and tropical in the lowlands and on the Caribbean coast; rainy season from May to Oct; higher rainfall on exposed slopes; Guatemala City average temperatures are 17°C (Jan) and 21°C (Jul); subject to severe hurricanes and earthquakes.

**National holidays**
Jan 1, May 1, 10 (Mothers), Jun 30 (Army), Sep 15 (Independence), Oct 20 (Revolution), Nov 1, Dec 25, 31; GF, HT, Assumption (*date varies locally*).

## Political leaders

**President**

| | |
|---|---|
| 1898–1920 | Manuel Estrada Cabrera |
| 1920–2 | Carlos Herrera y Luna |
| 1922–6 | José María Orellana |
| 1926–30 | Lázaro Chacón |
| 1930 | Baudillo Palma |
| 1930–1 | Manuel María Orellana |
| 1931 | José María Reyna Andrade |
| 1931–44 | Jorge Ubico Castañeda |
| 1944 | Federico Ponce Vaidez |
| 1944–5 | Jacobo Arbenz Guzmán |
| 1945–51 | Juan José Arévalo |
| 1951–4 | Jacobo Arbenz Guzmán |
| 1954 | *Military Junta* (Carlos Díaz) |
| 1954 | Elfego J Monzón |
| 1954–7 | Carlos Castillo Armas |
| 1957 | *Military Junta* (Oscar Mendoza Azurdia) |
| 1957 | Luis Arturo González López |
| 1957–8 | *Military Junta* (Guillermo Flores Avendaño) |
| 1958–63 | Miguel Ydígoras Fuentes |
| 1963–6 | *Military Junta* (Enrique Peralta Azurdia) |
| 1966–70 | Julio César Méndez Montenegro |
| 1970–4 | Carlos Araña Osorio |
| 1974–8 | Kyell Eugenio Laugerua García |
| 1978–82 | Romeo Lucas García |
| 1982 | Angel Aníbal Guevara |
| 1982–3 | Efraín Rios Montt |
| 1983–6 | Oscar Humberto Mejía Victores |
| 1986–91 | Marco Vinicio Cerezo Arévalo |
| 1991–3 | Jorge Serrano Elias |
| 1993–6 | Ramiro de León Carpio |
| 1996–2000 | Álvaro Arzú Irigoyen |
| 2000– | Alfonso Portillo Cabrera |

### Resplendent Quetzal

The national bird of Guatemala is the quetzal, also known as the resplendent trogon. The quetzal has beautiful shimmering golden-green feathers, a crimson breast and brilliant iridescent tail feathers that may be up to 90cm/3ft long. It is steeped in myth and folklore, linked to the ancient Aztec god *Quetzalcoatl* and associated with freedom and liberty. The quetzal is immensely symbolic in Guatemala and has not only given its name to the national currency and to the major town of Quetzaltenango, but is depicted on the flag and the coat of arms and has appeared on postage stamps.

**GUIANA, FRENCH** *see* **FRANCE**

## GUINEA

| | | | |
|---|---|---|---|
| **Official name** | Republic of Guinea | **Languages** | French is the official language; eight local languages are also widely spoken |
| **Local name** | Guinée; République de Guinée | **Ethnic groups** | Fulani 40%, Malinke 30%, Soussou 12%, Kissi 9%, others 9% |
| **Former name** | French Guinea (until 1958), Republic of Guinea (1958–79), People's Revolutionary Republic of Guinea (1979–84) | **Religions** | Islam 85%, Christianity 8%, traditional beliefs 7% |
| **Independence** | 1958 | **Time zone** | GMT |
| **Area** | 246 048 sq km/94 974 sq mi | **Currency** | 1 Guinea Franc (GFr) = 100 centimes |
| **Capital** | Conakry | **Telephone** | +224 |
| **Chief towns** | Kankan, Kindia, Labé | **Internet** | .gn |
| **Population** | 8 242 000 (2001e) | **Country code** | GIN |
| **Nationality** | Guinean | | |

**Location**
A republic in West Africa, bounded to the north-west by Guinea-Bissau; to the north by Senegal and Mali; to the east by Côte d'Ivoire; to the south by Liberia and Sierra Leone; and to the south-west by the Atlantic Ocean.

**Physical description**
Coastal mangrove forests, rising to a forested and cultivated narrow coastal plain; massif beyond at c.900m/2 952ft; highest point is Mt Nimba (1 752m/5 748ft); savannah plains in the east; forested Guinea Highlands in the south rise above 1 000m/3 280ft.

**Climate**
Tropical climate (wet season May–Oct); average temperature in the dry season on the coast is 32°C, dropping to 23°C in the wet season; cooler inland.

**National holidays**
Jan 1, Apr 3 (Second Republic), May 1, Aug 15, Oct 2 (Independence), Dec 25; Ad, ER, PB.

## Political leaders

**President**

1961–84 Ahmed Sékou Touré
1984– Lansana Conté

**Prime Minister**

1958–72 Ahmed Sékou Touré
1972–84 Louis Lansana Beavogui
1984–5 Diarra Traore
1985–96 *No Prime Minister*
1996–9 Sidia Toure
1999– Lamine Sidime

### *Local Languages*

Although French is the official language of Guinea, the government estimates that only 15–20% of the country's people speak it. Instead, most people speak one of eight major national languages, of which the most important are Soussou, Malinke, Kissi, Peulh, Toma and Guerze.

## GUINEA-BISSAU

| | |
|---|---|
| **Official name** | Republic of Guinea-Bissau |
| **Local name** | Guiné-Bissau; República da Guiné-Bissau |
| **Former name** | Portuguese Guinea (1952–74) |
| **Independence** | 1973 (proclaimed), 1974 (recognized) |
| **Area** | 36 260 sq km/14 000 sq mi |
| **Capital** | Bissau |
| **Chief towns** | Bafatá, Bolama, Mansôa |
| **Population** | 1 407 000 (2001e) |
| **Nationality** | Guinea-Bissauan |
| **Languages** | Portuguese, Guinean Creole (Crioulo); many African languages are also spoken |
| **Ethnic groups** | Balante 26%, Fulani 24%, Malinke 13%, Mandyako 10%, Pepel 10%, others 17% |
| **Religions** | traditional beliefs 52%, Islam 42%, Christianity 6% |
| **Time zone** | GMT |
| **Currency** | 1 CFA Franc (CFAFr) = 100 centimes |
| **Telephone** | +245 |
| **Internet** | .gw |
| **Country code** | GNB |

**Location**
A republic in West Africa, bounded to the south-east by Guinea; to the north by Senegal; and to the south-west by the Atlantic Ocean.

**Physical description**
Indented coast with islands (including the heavily-forested Bijagós Archipelago) and mangrove-lined estuaries, backed by forested coastal plains; low-lying, with savannah-covered plateaux in the south and east, rising to 310m/1 017ft.

**Climate**
Tropical climate with a wet season (Jun–Oct); average annual temperature range at Bissau is 24–27°C.

**National holidays**
Jan 1, 20 (National Heroes), Feb 8 (BNG Anniversary and Monetary Reform), Mar 8 (Women), May 1, Aug 3 (Martyrs of Colonialism), Sep 12 (National), 24 (Establishment of the Republic), Nov 14 (Readjustment), Dec 25.

## Political leaders

**President**

| | |
|---|---|
| 1974–80 | Luis de Almeida Cabral |
| 1980–4 | *Revolutionary Council* (João Bernardo Vieira) |
| 1984–99 | João Bernardo Vieira |
| 1999–2000 | Malai Bacai Sanhá *Interim President* |
| 2000– | Kumba Yalla |

**Prime Minister**

| | |
|---|---|
| 1992–4 | Carlos Correia |
| 1994–7 | Manuel Saturnino da Costa |
| 1997–8 | Carlos Correia |
| 1998–2000 | Francisco Fadul |
| 2000–1 | Caetano N'Tchama |
| 2001 | Faustino Imbali |
| 2001–2 | Alamara Nhassé |
| 2002– | Mário Pires |

## GUYANA

| | | | |
|---|---|---|---|
| **Official name** | Co-operative Republic of Guyana | **Ethnic groups** | East Indian 49%, black 32%, mixed 12%, Amerindian 6%, Chinese 1% |
| **Local name** | Guyana | | |
| **Former name** | British Guiana (until 1966) | **Religions** | Christianity 55% (Prot 36%, RC 19%), Hinduism 35%, Islam 9%, others 1% |
| **Independence** | 1966 | | |
| **Area** | 214 969 sq km/82 978 sq mi | | |
| **Capital** | Georgetown | **Time zone** | GMT –4 |
| **Chief towns** | Linden, New Amsterdam | **Currency** | 1 Guyana Dollar (G$) = 100 cents |
| **Population** | 762 000 (2001e) | | |
| **Nationality** | Guyanese | **Telephone** | +592 |
| **Languages** | English; Hindi, Urdu and local dialects are also spoken | **Internet** | .gy |
| | | **Country code** | GUY |

**Location**
A republic on the northern coast of South America, bounded to the east by Suriname; to the west by Venezuela; to the south by Brazil; and to the north by the Atlantic Ocean.

**Physical description**
Inland forest covers c.85% of the land area; grass-covered savannah in the hinterland; coastal plain, below sea level at high tide, is protected by sea defences, canals and dams; highest peak is Mt Roraima (2 810m/9 219ft) in the Pakaraima Mountains.

**Climate**
Equatorial climate in the lowlands, hot, wet, with constant high humidity; temperatures of 23–34°C in coastal lowlands with two seasons of high rainfall (May–Jul, Nov–Jan); lower temperatures on the high plateau inland.

**National holidays**
Jan 1, Feb 23 (Republic), May 1, 26 (Independence), Aug 1 (Freedom), Dec 25, 26; Ad, D, EM, GF, PB, Phagwah (Mar), Caribbean (Jul).

## Political leaders

**President**

| | | | |
|---|---|---|---|
| 1970 | Edward A Luckhoo | 1992–7 | Cheddi Bharrat Jagan |
| 1970–80 | Arthur Chung | 1997 | Samuel Hinds |
| 1980–5 | Linden Forbes Sampson Burnham | 1997–9 | Janet Jagan |
| 1985–92 | Hugh Desmond Hoyte | 1999– | Bharrat Jagdeo |

**Prime Minister**

| | | | |
|---|---|---|---|
| 1966–85 | Linden Forbes Sampson Burnham | 1997 | Janet Jagan |
| 1985–92 | Hamilton Green | 1997– | Samuel Hinds |
| 1992–7 | Samuel Hinds | | |

### *Land of Many Waters*

The Atlantic Ocean pounds the coastline of northern Guyana and the country is criss-crossed by many rivers. Guyana also boasts the world's longest single-drop waterfall, Kaieteur Falls, where the Potaro River plunges 226m/741ft in one leap before continuing downward for another 231m/759ft. The name *Guyana* is believed to come from an Amerindian word meaning 'land of many waters'.

## HAITI

| | | | |
|---|---|---|---|
| **Official name** | Republic of Haiti | **Religions** | Christianity 95% (RC 80%, Prot 15%), none/ unaffiliated 1%, others 4% *Note: Around half the population practise voodoo* |
| **Local name** | Haïti; République d'Haïti | **Time zone** | GMT –5 |
| **Independence** | 1804 | **Currency** | 1 Gourde (G, Gde) = 100 centimes |
| **Area** | 27 750 sq km/10 712 sq mi | **Telephone** | +509 |
| **Capital** | Port-au-Prince | **Internet** | .ht |
| **Chief towns** | Port-de-Paix, Cap-Haïtien, Gonaïves, Les Cayes, Jacmel, Jérémie | **Country code** | HTI |
| **Population** | 8 132 000 (2001e) | | |
| **Nationality** | Haitian | | |
| **Languages** | French, Creole | | |
| **Ethnic groups** | black 95%, mulatto and white 5% | | |

**Location**
A republic in the West Indies. It occupies the western third of the island of Hispaniola in the Caribbean Sea, and also includes the islands of Gonâve off the west coast and Tortue off the north coast.

**Physical description**
Consists of two mountainous peninsulas separated by a deep structural depression; to the east is the Massif de la Selle, with Haiti's highest peak, La Selle (2 680m/8 792ft).

**Climate**
Tropical maritime; average monthly temperatures range from 24°C to 29°C; the wet season is May–Sep; hurricanes are common.

**National holidays**
Jan 1 (Independence), 2 (Ancestors), Apr 14 (Americas), May 1, 18 (Flag/University), Aug 15, Oct 17 (Death of Dessalines), 24 (United Nations), Nov 1, 2, 18 (Battle of Vertières), Dec 25; A, C, CC, GF.

## Political leaders

**President**

| | |
|---|---|
| 1896–1902 | P A Tirésias Simon Lam |
| 1902 | Boisrond Canal |
| 1902–8 | Alexis Nord |
| 1908–11 | Antoine Simon |
| 1911–12 | Michel Cincinnatus Leconte |
| 1912–13 | Tancrède Auge |
| 1913–14 | Michael Oreste |
| 1914 | Oreste Zamor |
| 1914–15 | Joseph Davilmare Théodore |
| 1915 | Jean Velbrun-Guillaume |
| 1915–22 | Philippe Sudre Dartiguenave |
| 1922–30 | Joseph Louis Bornó |
| 1930 | Étienne Roy |
| 1930–41 | Sténio Joseph Vincent |
| 1941–6 | Élie Lescot |
| 1946 | *Military Junta* (Frank Lavaud) |
| 1946–50 | Dumarsais Estimé |
| 1950 | *Military Junta* (Frank Lavaud) |
| 1950–6 | Paul E Magloire |
| 1956–7 | François Sylvain |
| 1957 | *Military Junta* |
| 1957 | Léon Cantave |
| 1957 | Daniel Fignolé |
| 1957 | Antoine Kebreau |
| 1957–71 | François Duvalier ('Papa Doc') |
| 1971–86 | Jean-Claude Duvalier ('Baby Doc') |
| 1986–8 | Henri Namphy |
| 1988 | Leslie Manigat |
| 1988 | Henri Namphy |
| 1988–90 | Prosper Avril |
| 1990–1 | Ertha Pascal-Trouillot |
| 1991 | Jean-Bertrand Aristide |

| | | | |
|---|---|---|---|
| 1991 | Raoul Cédras | 1994 | Émile Jonassaint |
| 1991–2 | Joseph Nérette | 1994–6 | Jean-Bertrand Aristide |
| 1992–3 | Marc-Louis Bazin | 1996–2000 | René Préval |
| 1993–4 | Jean-Bertrand Aristide | 2000– | Jean-Bertrand Aristide |

**Prime Minister**

| | | | |
|---|---|---|---|
| 1988 | Martial Célestin | 1994–5 | Smarck Michel |
| 1988–91 | *No Prime Minister* | 1995–6 | Claudette Werleigh |
| 1991 | René Préval | 1996–7 | Rosny Smarth |
| 1991–2 | Jean-Jacques Honorat *Interim Prime Minister* | 1998–2001 | Jacques-Édouard Alexis |
| 1992–3 | Marc Bazin | 2001–2 | Jean-Marie Cherestal |
| 1993–4 | Robert Malval | 2002– | Yvon Neptune |

### Slave Revolution

The Haitian Revolution of 1791–1804 was the only successful slave revolution in the New World. It created the world's first black-led republic, and meant that Haiti became the first Caribbean state to achieve independence. The revolution began in Aug 1791 with a slave revolt led by Toussaint L'Ouverture and culminated in the independence of Haiti in 1804 when a slave named Dessalines proclaimed himself Emperor of the independent country.

**HEARD AND MACDONALD ISLANDS** *see* **AUSTRALIA**

**HERZEGOVINA** *see* **BOSNIA AND HERZEGOVINA**

**HOLLAND** *see* **THE NETHERLANDS**

**HOLY SEE, THE** *see* **VATICAN**

## HONDURAS

| | | | |
|---|---|---|---|
| **Official name** | Republic of Honduras | **Languages** | Spanish; English is also spoken |
| **Local name** | Honduras; República de Honduras | **Ethnic groups** | mestizo 90%, Amerindian 7%, black 2%, white 1% |
| **Independence** | 1821 (from Spain), 1838 (as sovereign state) | **Religions** | Christianity 97% (RC 94%, Prot 3%), others 3% |
| **Area** | 112 088 sq km/43 266 sq mi | **Time zone** | GMT –6 |
| **Capital** | Tegucigalpa | **Currency** | 1 Lempira (L, La) = 100 centavos |
| **Chief towns** | San Pedro Sula, Choluteca, La Ceiba, El Progreso | **Telephone** | +504 |
| **Population** | 6 619 000 (2001e) | **Internet** | .hn |
| **Nationality** | Honduran | **Country code** | HND |

# HONDURAS

**Location**
A republic in Central America, bounded to the south-west by El Salvador; to the west by Guatemala; to the east and south-east by Nicaragua; to the north by the Caribbean Sea; and to the south by the Pacific Ocean; also comprises the Bay Islands in the Caribbean Sea and a group of nearly 300 islands in the Gulf of Fonseca.

**Physical description**
Southern coastal lands are separated from those of the Caribbean by mountains running north-west to south-east; southern plateau rises to 2 870m/9 416ft at Cerro Las Minas; Laguna Caratasca lies in the extreme north-east.

**Climate**
Tropical climate in coastal areas, temperate in the centre and west; two wet seasons in upland areas (May–Jul, Sep–Oct); variable temperatures in the interior, 15–24°C; on the coastal plains the average temperature is 30°C.

**National holidays**
Jan 1, May 1, Sep 15 (Independence), Oct 3 (Soldiers), 12 (Americas), 21 (Armed Forces), Dec 25; GF, HT.

## Political leaders

**President**

| | |
|---|---|
| 1900–3 | Terencio Sierra |
| 1903 | Juan Angel Arias |
| 1903–7 | Manuel Bonilla Chirinos |
| 1907–11 | Miguel R Dávila |
| 1912–15 | Manuel Bonilla Chirinos |
| 1915–20 | Francisco Bertrand |
| 1920–4 | Rafael López Gutiérrez |
| 1924–5 | Vicente Tosta Carrasco |
| 1925–8 | Miguel Paz Barahona |
| 1929–32 | Vicente Mejía Clindres |
| 1932–49 | Tiburcio Carías Andino |
| 1949–54 | Juan Manuel Gálvez |

**Head of State**

| | |
|---|---|
| 1954–6 | Julio Lozano Diaz |
| 1956–7 | *Military Junta* |

**President**

| | |
|---|---|
| 1958–63 | José Ramón Villeda Morales |

**Head of State**

| | |
|---|---|
| 1963–5 | Oswaldo López Arellano |

**President**

| | |
|---|---|
| 1965–71 | Oswaldo López Arellano |
| 1971–2 | Ramón Ernesto Cruz |

**Head of State**

| | |
|---|---|
| 1972–5 | Oswaldo López Arellano |
| 1975–8 | Juan Alberto Melgar Castro |
| 1978–82 | Policarpo Paz García |

**President**

| | |
|---|---|
| 1982–6 | Roberto Suazo Córdova |
| 1986–9 | José Azcona Hoyo |
| 1989–93 | Rafael Leonardo Callejas |
| 1993–7 | Carlos Roberto Reina |
| 1997–2002 | Carlos Roberto Flores Facussé |
| 2002– | Ricardo Maduro |

### Deep Blue Sea

Christopher Columbus arrived on the Caribbean coast of Honduras in 1502. He is reported to have exclaimed at how deep the coastal waters were, thus naming the country: *honduras* is the Spanish word for 'depths'. This was not the first time that Columbus's comments on the sea had resulted in a country name that would still be used 500 years later (see the fact box at The Bahamas).

**HONG KONG** *see* **CHINA**

## HUNGARY

| | | | |
|---|---|---|---|
| **Official name** | Republic of Hungary | **Chief towns** | Debrecen, Miskolc, Szeged, Pécs, Györ |
| **Local name** | Magyarorszag; Magyar Köztársaság | **Population** | 10 195 513 (2001) |
| **Former name** | formerly part of Austria-Hungary (until 1918), Hungarian People's Republic (1918, 1919, 1949–89), Hungarian Soviet Republic (1919), Hungarian State (1919–20, 1944–6), Hungarian Kingdom (1920–44), Hungarian Republic (1946–9) | **Nationality** | Hungarian |
| | | **Languages** | Magyar (Hungarian) |
| | | **Ethnic groups** | Magyar 90%, Romany 4%, German 3%, Serb 2%, others 1% |
| | | **Religions** | Christianity 79% (RC 58%, Prot 21%), none/unaffiliated 18%, Judaism 1%, others 2% |
| **Independence** | 1918 | **Time zone** | GMT +1 |
| **Area** | 93 030 sq km/35 910 sq mi | **Currency** | 1 Forint (Ft) = 100 fillér |
| | | **Telephone** | +36 |
| **Capital** | Budapest | **Internet** | .hu |
| | | **Country code** | HUN |

**Location**
A landlocked republic in the Danube basin, central Europe, bounded to the north by Slovakia; to the east by the Ukraine and Romania; to the south by Serbia and Montenegro; to the south-west by Croatia; and to the west by Slovenia and Austria.

**Physical description**
Drained by the River Danube and its tributaries (flowing north to south); frequent flooding; low spur of the Alps in the west, separating the Little Hungarian Plain from the Transdanubian downlands; highest peak is Kékes (1 014m/3 327ft).

**Climate**
Fairly extreme continental climate with a marked difference between summer and winter; wettest in spring and early summer; winters are cold and the Danube sometimes freezes over for long periods; frequent fog in settled winter weather.

**National holidays**
Jan 1, Mar 15 (Independence), May 1, Aug 20 (National/St Stephen), Oct 23 (Republic), Nov 1, Dec 25, 26; EM, WM.

## Political leaders

**Monarch**

1900–16 Franz Josef I
1916–18 Charles IV

**President**

1919 Mihály Károlyi
1919 *Revolutionary Governing Council* (Sándor Garbai)
1920–44 Miklós Horthy *Regent*
1944–5 *Provisional National Assembly*
1946–8 Zoltán Tildy
1948–50 Árpád Szakasits
1950–2 Sándor Rónai
1952–67 István Dobi
1967–87 Pál Losonczi
1987–8 Károly Németh
1988–9 Brunó Ferenc Straub
1989–90 Mátyás Szúrös
1990–2000 Árpád Göncz
2000– Ferenc Madl

**Premier**

| | | | |
|---|---|---|---|
| 1899–1903 | Kálmán Széll | 1944 | Döme Sztójay |
| 1903 | Károly Khuen-Héderváry | 1944 | Géza Lakatos |
| 1903–5 | István Tisza | 1944 | Ferenc Szálasi |
| 1905–6 | Géza Fejérváry | 1944–5 | *Provisional National Assembly* (Béla Dálnoki Miklós) |
| 1906–10 | Sándor Wekerle | 1945–6 | Zoltán Tildy |
| 1910–12 | Károly Khuen-Héderváry | 1946–7 | Ferenc Nagy |
| 1912–13 | Lázló Lukács | 1947–8 | Lajos Dinnyés |
| 1913–17 | István Tisza | 1948–52 | István Dobi |
| 1917 | Móric Esterházy | 1952–3 | Mátyás Rákosi |
| 1917–18 | Sándor Wekerle | 1953–5 | Imre Nagy |
| 1918–19 | Mihály Károlyi | 1955–6 | András Hegedüs |
| 1919 | Dénes Berinkey | 1956 | Imre Nagy |
| 1919 | *Revolutionary Governing Council* | 1956–8 | János Kádár |
| 1919 | Gyula Peidl | 1958–61 | Ferenc Münnich |
| 1919 | István Friedrich | 1961–5 | János Kádár |
| 1919–20 | Károly Huszár | 1965–7 | Gyula Kállai |
| 1920 | Sándor Simonyi-Semadam | 1967–75 | Jenö Fock |
| 1920–1 | Pál Teleki | 1975–87 | György Lázár |
| 1921–31 | István Bethlen | 1987–8 | Károly Grosz |
| 1931–2 | Gyula Károlyi | 1988–90 | Miklás Németh |
| 1932–6 | Gyula Gömbös | 1990–3 | József Antall |
| 1936–8 | Kálman Darányi | 1993–4 | Péter Boross |
| 1938–9 | Béla Imrédy | 1994–8 | Gyula Horn |
| 1939–41 | Pál Teleki | 1998–2002 | Viktor Orban |
| 1941–2 | Lázló Bárdossy | 2002– | Peter Medgyessy |
| 1942–4 | Miklós Kállay | | |

**First Secretary**

| | | | |
|---|---|---|---|
| 1949–56 | Mátyás Rákosi | 1956–88 | János Kádár |
| 1956 | Ernö Gerö | 1988–90 | Károly Grosz |

## ICELAND

| | | | |
|---|---|---|---|
| **Official name** | Republic of Iceland | **Nationality** | Icelandic |
| **Local name** | Ísland; Lyðveldið Ísland | **Languages** | Icelandic |
| **Former name** | formerly part of Denmark (to 1918), Kingdom of Iceland (1918–44) | **Ethnic groups** | Icelandic 94%, Danish 1%, others 5% |
| **Independence** | 1944 | **Religions** | Christianity 94% (Prot 93%, RC 1%), none/unaffiliated 6% |
| **Area** | 103 000 sq km/40 000 sq mi | **Time zone** | GMT |
| **Capital** | Reykjavík | **Currency** | 1 Króna (IKr, ISK) = 100 aurar |
| **Chief towns** | Akureyri, Húsavík, Akranes, Keflavík, Ísafjördur | **Telephone** | +354 |
| | | **Internet** | .is |
| **Population** | 285 000 (2001e) | **Country code** | ISL |

**Location**
An island state lying between the northern Atlantic Ocean and the Arctic Ocean, south-east of Greenland and 900km/550mi west of Norway.

**Physical description**
A volcanic island, with several active volcanoes; heavily indented coastline, with many long fjords; high ridges rise to 2 119m/6 952ft at Hvannadalshnúkur; large snowfields and glaciers cover much of the land area.

**Climate**
Changeable climate, with relatively mild winters; average daily temperatures are minimum −2°C (Jan), maximum 14°C (Jul–Aug); Reykjavík is generally ice-free throughout the year; summers are cool and cloudy.

**National holidays**
Jan 1, May 1, Jun 17 (National), Dec 25, 26; A, EM, ES, GF, HT, WM, Whit Sunday, First Day of Summer (Apr), Aug Holiday Monday.

## Political leaders

### President

| | |
|---|---|
| 1944–52 | Sveinn Björnsson |
| 1952–68 | Ásgeir Ásgeirsson |
| 1968–80 | Kristján Eldjárn |
| 1980–96 | Vigdís Finnbogadóttir |
| 1996– | Ólafur Ragnar Grimsson |

### Prime Minister

| | |
|---|---|
| 1900–1 | C Goos |
| 1901–4 | P A Alberti |
| 1904–9 | Hannes Hafstein |
| 1909–11 | Björn Jónsson |
| 1911–12 | Kristján Jónsson |
| 1912–14 | Hannes Hafstein |
| 1914–15 | Sigurđur Eggerz |
| 1915–17 | Einar Arnórsson |
| 1917–22 | Jón Magnússon |
| 1922–4 | Sigurđur Eggerz |
| 1924–6 | Jón Magnússon |
| 1926–7 | John þorláksson |
| 1927–32 | Tryggvi þórhallsson |
| 1932–4 | Ásgeir Ásgeirsson |
| 1934–42 | Hermann Jónasson |
| 1942 | Ólafur Thors |
| 1942–4 | Björn þórđarsson |
| 1944–7 | Ólafur Thors |
| 1947–9 | Stefán Jóhann Stefánsson |
| 1949–50 | Ólafur Thors |
| 1950–3 | Steingrímur Steinþórsson |
| 1953–6 | Ólafur Thors |
| 1956–8 | Hermann Jónasson |
| 1958–9 | Emil Jónsson |
| 1959–61 | Ólafur Thors |
| 1961 | Bjarni Benediktsson |
| 1961–3 | Ólafur Thors |
| 1963–70 | Bjarni Benediktsson |
| 1970–1 | Jóhann Hafstein |
| 1971–4 | Ólafur Jóhannesson |
| 1974–8 | Geir Hallgrímsson |
| 1978–9 | Ólafur Jóhannesson |
| 1979 | Benedikt Gröndal |
| 1980–3 | Gunnar Thoroddsen |
| 1983–7 | Steingrímur Hermannsson |
| 1987–8 | Thorsteinn Pálsson |
| 1988–91 | Steingrímur Hermannsson |
| 1991– | Davíd Oddsson |

## Geysers Galore

Iceland is famous for geysers – springs that periodically spout hot water and steam into the air. The most well-known is *Geysir*, meaning 'the gusher', which was first recorded in the year 1294 and from which the term *geyser* is derived. Others include *Strokkur* ('the churn'), *Smiđur* ('the carpenter'), *Fata* ('the bucket') and *Óþerrishola* ('the rainmaker').

## INDIA

| | | | |
|---|---|---|---|
| **Official name** | Republic of India | **Population** | 1 027 015 247 (2001) |
| **Local name** | Bhārat (Hindi) | **Nationality** | Indian |
| **Independence** | 1947 | **Languages** | Hindi, English and 17 others |
| **Area** | 3 166 829 sq km/ 1 222 396 sq mi | **Ethnic groups** | Indo-Aryan 72%, Dravidian 25%, others 3% |
| **Capital** | New Delhi; Nī Dillī | **Religions** | Hinduism 82%, Islam 12% (Sunni), Sikhism 2%, Christianity 2%, Jainism 1%, Buddhism 1% |
| **Chief towns** | Ahmadabad, Bangalore, Chennai, Hyderabad, Jaipur, Kanpur, Kolkata, Lucknow, Mumbai, Nagpur, Poona *India has renamed several of its cities and states in recent years, reverting to pre-colonial names. Thus, Bombay is now known as Mumbai, Calcutta as Kolkata and Madras as Chennai. Other such changes may follow.* | **Time zone** | GMT +5.5 |
| | | **Currency** | 1 Indian Rupee (Re, Rs) = 100 paise |
| | | **Telephone** | +91 |
| | | **Internet** | .in |
| | | **Country code** | IND |

**Location**
A federal republic in southern Asia, bounded to the north-west by Pakistan; to the north by China, Nepal and Bhutan; to the east by Myanmar and Bangladesh; to the south-east by the Bay of Bengal; and to the south-west by the Arabian Sea; the disputed area of Jammu and Kashmir lies to the north.

**Physical description**
The second largest state in Asia, bordered to the north by the Himalayas; highest peaks are over 7 000m/22 966ft; Kanchenjunga (8 598m/28 298ft) on the Nepalese border is the highest point; central river plains to the south (including the Ganges and Brahmaputra); best agricultural land is in the east; plateau in the southern peninsula; Thar Desert in the north-west is bordered by semi-desert; coastal plains are important areas of rice cultivation.

**Climate**
Dominated by the Asiatic monsoon; rains come from the south-west (Jun–Oct); rainfall decreases (Dec–Feb) with winds from the north, followed by drought until Mar or May; temperatures in the mountains vary greatly with altitude; desert conditions in the extreme west; south of the plateau is tropical, even in the cool season; west coast is subject to rain throughout the year, with high humidity in the south; cyclones and storms on the south-east coast (especially Oct–Dec), with high temperatures and humidity during the monsoon season.

**National holidays**
Jan 1 (*some states*), 26 (Republic), May 1 (*some states*), Jun 30, Aug 15 (Independence), Oct 2 (Mahatma Ghandi's Birthday), Dec 25, 31; NY (Parsi, Aug, *some states*).

## Political leaders

**President**

1950–62 Rajendra Prasad
1962–7 Sarvepalli Radhakrishnan
1967–9 Zakir Husain
1969 Varahagiri Venkatagiri *Acting President*

| | | | |
|---|---|---|---|
| 1969 | Mohammed Hidayatullah *Acting President* | 1982–7 | Giani Zail Singh |
| 1969–74 | Varahagiri Venkatagiri | 1987–92 | Ramaswami Venkataraman |
| 1974–7 | Fakhruddin Ali Ahmed | 1992–7 | Shankar Dayal Sharma |
| 1977 | B D Jatti *Acting President* | 1997–2002 | Kocheril Raman Narayanan |
| 1977–82 | Neelam Sanjiva Reddy | 2002– | A P J Abdul Kalam |

**Prime Minister**

| | | | |
|---|---|---|---|
| 1947–64 | Jawaharlal Nehru | 1980–4 | Indira Gandhi |
| 1964 | Gulzari Lal Nanda *Acting Prime Minister* | 1984–9 | Rajiv Gandhi |
| 1964–6 | Lal Bahadur Shastri | 1989–90 | Vishwanath Pratap Singh |
| 1966 | Gulzari Lal Nanda *Acting Prime Minister* | 1990–1 | Chandra Shekhar |
| 1966–77 | Indira Gandhi | 1991–6 | P V Narasimha Rao |
| 1977–9 | Morarji Desai | 1996 | Atal Behari Vajpayee |
| 1979–80 | Charan Singh | 1996–7 | H D Deve Gowda |
| | | 1997 | Inder Kumar Gujral |
| | | 1998– | Atal Behari Vajpayee |

**INDIAN OCEAN TERRITORY, BRITISH** *see* **UNITED KINGDOM**

## INDONESIA

| | | | |
|---|---|---|---|
| **Official name** | Republic of Indonesia | **Nationality** | Indonesian |
| **Local name** | Indonesia; Republik Indonesia | **Languages** | Bahasa Indonesia; English, Dutch and Javanese are also widely spoken, and 300 regional languages |
| **Former name** | Netherlands East Indies, Dutch East Indies (until 1949), Republic of the United States of Indonesia (1949–50) | **Ethnic groups** | Javanese 45%, others 25%, Sudanese 14%, Coastal Malays 8%, Madurese 8% |
| **Independence** | 1945 (declared), 1949 (legally) | **Religions** | Islam 87%, Christianity 9% (Prot 6%, RC 3%), Hinduism 2%, Buddhism 1%, others 1% |
| **Area** | 1 906 240 sq km/735 809 sq mi | | |
| **Capital** | Jakarta | **Time zone** | GMT +7/9 |
| **Chief towns** | Jayapura, Bandung, Semarang, Surabaya, Medan, Palembang | **Currency** | 1 Rupiah (Rp) = 100 sen |
| | | **Telephone** | +62 |
| | | **Internet** | .id |
| **Population** | 231 328 000 (2002e) | **Country code** | IDN |

**Location**
A republic in South-East Asia comprising the world's largest island group.

**Physical description**
Five main islands and 30 smaller archipelagos totalling 13 677 islands and islets, of which c.6 000 are inhabited; over 100 volcanic peaks on Java, of which 15 are active; highest point is Puncak Jaya (5 030m/16 503ft).

**Climate**
Hot and humid equatorial climate; dry season (Jun–Sep), rainy season (Dec–Mar), apart from the Moluccas (Jun–Sep); average temperature is 27°C on island coasts, falling inland and with altitude.

**National holidays**
Jan 1, Aug 17 (Independence), Dec 25; A, Ad, ER (2), GF, NY (Chinese), NY (Muslim), NY (Balinese Hindu), PB, Ascension of the Prophet, Waisak (May).

## Political leaders

**President**

| | | | |
|---|---|---|---|
| 1945–9 | Ahmed Sukarno | 1998–9 | B J Habibie |
| 1949–66 | Ahmed Sukarno | 1999–2001 | Abdurrahman Wahid |
| 1966–98 | T N J Suharto | 2001– | Megawati Sukarnoputri |

**Prime Minister**

| | | | |
|---|---|---|---|
| 1945 | R A A Wiranatakusumah | 1951–2 | Sukiman Wirjosandjojo |
| 1945–7 | Sutan Sjahrir | 1952–3 | Dr Wilopo |
| 1947–8 | Amir Sjarifuddin | 1953–5 | Ali Sastroamidjojo |
| 1948 | Mohammed Hatta | 1955–6 | Burhanuddin Harahap |
| 1948–9 | Sjarifuddin Prawiraranegara | 1956–7 | Ali Sastroamidjojo |
| 1949 | Susanto Tirtoprodjo | 1957–9 | Raden Haji Djuanda Kurtawidjaja |
| 1949 | Mohammed Hatta | 1959–63 | Ahmed Sukarno |
| 1950 | Dr Halim | 1963–6 | S E Subandrio |
| 1950–1 | Mohammed Natsir | 1966– | *No Prime Minister* |

### *Red and White Twins*

What do Indonesia and the tiny European principality of Monaco, thousands of miles away on the other side of the world, have in common? The answer is their flag. Both flags have a red upper half with white underneath. The only way of telling the two apart is by comparing the flags' proportions: the Indonesian flag is longer lengthways.

## IRAN

| | | | |
|---|---|---|---|
| **Official name** | Islamic Republic of Iran | | |
| **Local name** | Îrân; Jomhûri-ye-Eslâmi-ye-Îrân | | |
| **Former name** | Persia (until 1935) | | |
| **Independence** | 1925 | | |
| **Area** | 1 648 000 sq km/636 128 sq mi | | |
| **Capital** | Tehran; Tehrān | | |
| **Chief towns** | Mashhad, Isfahan, Tabriz, Shiraz, Abadan | | |
| **Population** | 60 055 488 (1996) | | |
| **Nationality** | Iranian | | |
| **Languages** | Farsi (Persian), with several minority languages spoken | | |
| **Ethnic groups** | Persian 51%, Azeri 24%, Gilaki and Mazandarani 8%, Kurdish 7%, others 10% | | |
| **Religions** | Islam 99% (Shia 91%, Sunni 8%), others 1% | | |
| **Time zone** | GMT +3.5 | | |
| **Currency** | Iranian Rial (Rls) | | |
| **Telephone** | +98 | | |
| **Internet** | .ir | | |
| **Country code** | IRN | | |

**Location**
A republic in south-west Asia, bounded to the north by Armenia, Azerbaijan, Turkmenistan and the Caspian Sea; to the east by Afghanistan and Pakistan; to the south by the Gulf of Oman and the Arabian Gulf; to the south-west by Iraq; and to the north-west by Turkey.

**Physical description**
A vast arid central plateau, average elevation 1 200 m/3 936ft, with many salt and sand basins; rimmed by mountain ranges that drop to narrow coastal lowlands; Elburz Mountains in the north rise to 5 670m/18 602ft at Mt Damavand.

**Climate**
Mainly a desert climate; average temperatures at Tehran are 2°C (Jan), 29°C (Jul); Caspian coastal strip is much wetter than the interior; hot and humid on the shores of the Arabian Gulf; frequent earthquakes.

**National holidays**
Feb 11 (Islamic Revolution), Mar 19 (Nationalization of Oil), 21, 31 (Islamic Republic), Apr 2 (13th Day of New Year), Jun 3 (Death of Imam Khomeini), 4 (Uprising); Ad, As, ER, PB, Eid Ghadir Khom, Tasooah, Arbaeen, Death of the Prophet, Martyrdom of Imam Reza, Birthday of Imam Ali, Ascension of the Prophet, Birthday of Imam Hussein, Birthday of the 12th living Imam, Martyrdom of Imam Ali, Death of Hadrath Zahra.

## Political leaders

**Shah**

1896–1907 Muzaffar Ad-Din
1907–9 Mohammed Ali
1909–25 Ahmad Mirza
1925–41 Mohammed Reza Khan
1941–79 Mohammed Reza Pahlavi

**Leader of the Islamic Revolution**

1979–89 Ruhollah Khomeini
1989– Sayed Ali Khamenei

**President**

1980–1 Abolhassan Bani-Sadr
1981 Mohammed Ali Rajai
1981–9 Sayed Ali Khamenei
1989–97 Ali Akbar Hashemi Rafsanjani
1997– Sayed Ayatollah Mohammad Khatami

**Prime Minister**

1979 Shahpur Bakhtiar
1979–80 Mehdi Bazargan
1980–1 Mohammed Ali Rajai
1981 Mohammed Javad Bahonar
1981 Mohammed Reza Mahdavi-Kani
1981–9 Mir Hossein Moussavi

## IRAQ

| | | | |
|---|---|---|---|
| **Official name** | Republic of Iraq | **Languages** | Arabic; Kurdish is also spoken |
| **Local name** | Al-Jumhūriyya al-'Iraqiyya | **Ethnic groups** | Arab 77%, Kurdish 18%, Turkmen, Assyrian and others 5% |
| **Former name** | part of the Ottoman Empire (until 1916), State of Iraq (1920–21), Iraqi Kingdom (1921–32), Kingdom of Iraq (1932–58) | **Religions** | Islam 96% (Shia 54%, Sunni 42%), Christianity 3%, others 1% |
| **Independence** | 1932 | **Time zone** | GMT +3 |
| **Area** | 434 925 sq km/167 881 sq mi | **Currency** | 1 Iraqi Dinar (ID) = 1 000 fils |
| **Capital** | Baghdad | **Telephone** | +964 |
| **Chief towns** | Basra, Kirkuk, Mosul | **Internet** | .iq |
| **Population** | 23 860 000 (2001e) | **Country code** | IRQ |
| **Nationality** | Iraqi | | |

**Location**
A republic in south-west Asia, bounded to the east by Iran; to the north by Turkey; to the north-west by Syria; to the west by Jordan; to the south-west and south by Saudi Arabia; and to the south-east by Kuwait and the Arabian Gulf.

**Physical description**
Largely comprises the vast alluvial tract of the Tigris–Euphrates lowland; the rivers join about 190km/118mi from the Arabian Gulf; lowland has swamp vegetation; mountains in the north-east rise to over 3 000m/9 840ft; highest point is Haji Ibrahim (3 600m/11 810ft); desert in other areas.

**Climate**
Mainly arid; summers are very hot and dry; winters are often cold; average temperatures at Baghdad are 10°C (Jan) and 35°C (Jul); rainfall is highest in the north-east.

**National holidays**
Jan 1, 6 (Army), Feb 8 (8 Feb Revolution), Mar 21, May 1, Jul 14 (14 Jul Revolution), 17 (17 Jul Revolution); Ad (4), As, ER (3), NY (Muslim), PB.

## Political leaders

**Monarch**

| | |
|---|---|
| 1921–33 | Faisal I |
| 1933–9 | Ghazi I |
| 1939–58 | Faisal II (*Regent* 1939–53, Abdul Illah) |

**Commander of the National Forces**

| | |
|---|---|
| 1958–63 | Abdul Karim Qassem |

**Head of Council of State**

| | |
|---|---|
| 1958–63 | Mohammed Najib Ar-Rubai |

**President**

| | |
|---|---|
| 1963–6 | Abd as-Salam Arif |
| 1966–8 | Abd ar-Rahman Arif |
| 1968–79 | Ahmad Hassan al-Bakr |
| 1979–2003 | Saddam Hussein[1] |
| 2003– | *Transitional administration* |

**Prime Minister**

| | |
|---|---|
| 1958–63 | Abdul Karim Qassem |
| 1963 | Ahmad Hassan al-Bakr |
| 1963–5 | Tahir Yahya |
| 1965 | Arif Abd ar-Razzaq |
| 1965–6 | Abd ar-Rahman al-Bazzaz |
| 1966–7 | Naji Talib |
| 1967 | Abd ar-Rahman Arif |
| 1967–8 | Tahir Yahya |
| 1968 | Abd ar-Razzaq an-Naif |
| 1968–79 | Ahmad Hassan al-Bakr |
| 1979–91 | Saddam Hussein |
| 1991 | Sadun Hammadi |
| 1991–3 | Mohammed Hamzah az-Zubaydi |
| 1993–4 | Ahmad Hussein Khudayir as-Samarrai |
| 1994–2003 | Saddam Hussein[1] |
| 2003– | *Transitional administration* |

[1] *Saddam Hussein's government was overthrown by a US-led military coalition in 2003; a US-controlled administration assumed power and subsequently appointed an Iraqi interim governing council; full Iraqi government is predicted but at the time of going to press no date had been agreed.*

# IRELAND

| | |
|---|---|
| **Official name** | Ireland |
| **Local name** | Éire |
| **Independence** | 1921 (treaty), 1922 (Irish Free State) |
| **Area** | 70 282 sq km/27 129 sq mi |
| **Capital** | Dublin; Baile Átha Cliath |
| **Chief towns** | Cork, Limerick, Waterford, Galway, Drogheda, Dundalk, Sligo |
| **Population** | 3 917 336 (2002) |
| **Nationality** | Irish |
| **Languages** | Irish, English; the Irish Gaelic-speaking areas, mostly in the west, are known as the *Gaeltacht* |
| **Ethnic groups** | Irish 95%, others 5% |
| **Religions** | Christianity 91% (RC 88%, Prot 3%), none/unaffiliated 5%, others 4% |
| **Time zone** | GMT |
| **Currency** | 1 Euro (€) = 100 cents |
| **Telephone** | +353 |
| **Internet** | .ie |
| **Country code** | IRL |

**Location**
A republic occupying southern, central and north-western Ireland, separated from Great Britain by the Irish Sea and St George's Channel, and bounded to the north-east by Northern Ireland, part of the UK.

**Physical description**
Mountainous landscapes in the west with quartzite peaks weathered into conical mountains; highest point is Carrantuohill (1 041m/3 415ft); mountains in the south create a landscape of ridges and valleys; eastern lowlands drained by slow-moving rivers.

**Climate**
Mild and equable, with few extremes of temperature; rainfall is heaviest in the west.

**National holidays**
Jan 1, Mar 17 (St Patrick), Dec 25, 26; EM, 1st Mon in May, 1st Mon in Jun, 1st Mon in Aug, last Mon in Oct public holidays.

## Political leaders

**Governor General**

| | |
|---|---|
| 1922–7 | Timothy Michael Healy |
| 1927–32 | James McNeill |
| 1932–6 | Donald Buckley |
| 1936–7 | Frank Fahy *and* Éamon de Valera *Acting heads of state* |

**President**

| | |
|---|---|
| 1937–8 | *Presidential Commission* |
| 1938–45 | Douglas Hyde |
| 1945–59 | Sean Thomas O'Kelly |
| 1959–73 | Éamon de Valera |
| 1973–4 | Erskine H Childers |
| 1974–6 | Carroll Daly |
| 1976–90 | Patrick J Hillery |
| 1990–7 | Mary Robinson |
| 1997– | Mary McAleese |

**Prime Minister**

| | |
|---|---|
| 1919–21 | Éamon de Valera |
| 1922 | Arthur Griffiths |
| 1922–32 | William Cosgrave |
| 1932–48 | Éamon de Valera |
| 1948–51 | John Aloysius Costello |
| 1951–4 | Éamon de Valera |
| 1954–7 | John Aloysius Costello |
| 1957–9 | Éamon de Valera |
| 1959–66 | Sean Lemass |
| 1966–73 | John Lynch |
| 1973–7 | Liam Cosgrave |
| 1977–9 | John Lynch |
| 1979–82 | Charles Haughey |
| 1982–7 | Garrett Fitzgerald |
| 1987–92 | Charles Haughey |
| 1992–4 | Albert Reynolds |
| 1994–7 | John Bruton |
| 1997– | Bertie Ahern |

**IRELAND, NORTHERN** *see* **UNITED KINGDOM**

**ISLE OF MAN** *see* **UNITED KINGDOM**

# ISRAEL

| | | | |
|---|---|---|---|
| **Official name** | State of Israel | **Nationality** | Israeli |
| **Local name** | Medinat Yisra'el, Dawlat Isrā'īl | **Languages** | Hebrew, Arabic |
| **Independence** | 1948 | **Ethnic groups** | Jewish 81%, Arab and others 19% |
| **Area** | 20 770 sq km/8 017 sq mi | **Religions** | Judaism 82%, Islam 14%, Druze 2%, Christianity 2% |
| **Capital** | Tel Aviv-Jaffa *Note: Israel claims Jerusalem as its capital, but this is not recognized internationally* | **Time zone** | GMT +2 |
| | | **Currency** | 1 Shekel (IS) = 100 agora |
| | | **Telephone** | +972 |
| **Chief towns** | Jerusalem, Haifa, Beersheba, Acre, Holon | **Internet** | .il |
| | | **Country code** | ISR |
| **Population** | 5 548 523 (1995) | | |

**Location**
A democratic republic in the Middle East, bounded to the north by Lebanon; to the north-east by Syria; to the east by Jordan (the River Jordan forms part of the border); to the south-west by Egypt; and to the west by the Mediterranean Sea.

**Physical description**
Extends 420km/260mi north to south; narrow coastal plain; mountainous interior, rising to 1 208m/3 963ft at Mt Meron; drops below sea level in the Jordan–Red Sea Rift Valley; Negev Desert in the south occupies c.60% of the country's area.

**Climate**
Typically Mediterranean in the north and centre, with hot, dry summers and warm, wet winters; average temperatures at Tel Aviv-Jaffa are 14°C (Jan) to 27°C (Jul); rainfall is heavier inland, with occasional snow; low rainfall in Negev Desert.

**National holidays**
Rosh Hashanah (Jewish NY; Sep/Oct), Yom Kippur (Sep/Oct), Sukkot (Sep/Oct), Hanukkah (Nov/Dec), Tu B'Shevat (Jan/Feb), Purim (Feb/Mar), Passover (Mar/Apr), Holocaust Martyrs and Heroes Remembrance (Apr/May), Remembrance for the Fallen of Israel's Wars (Apr/May), Independence (Apr/May), Lag B'omer (Apr/May), Jerusalem (May/Jun), Shavuot (May/Jun), Tisha B'Av (Jul/Aug) *Note: Israel's national holidays have fixed dates in the Jewish calendar; for example Hanukkah begins on 25 Kislev.*

## Political leaders

**President**

| | |
|---|---|
| 1948–52 | Chaim Weizmann |
| 1952–63 | Itzhak Ben-Zvi |
| 1963–73 | Zalman Shazar |
| 1973–8 | Ephraim Katzair |
| 1978–83 | Yitzhak Navon |
| 1983–93 | Chaim Herzog |
| 1993–2000 | Ezer Weizman |
| 2000– | Moshe Katsav |

**Prime Minister**

| | |
|---|---|
| 1948–53 | David Ben-Gurion |
| 1954–5 | Moshe Sharett |
| 1955–63 | David Ben-Gurion |
| 1963–9 | Levi Eshkol |
| 1969–74 | Golda Meir |
| 1974–7 | Yitzhak Rabin |
| 1977–83 | Menachem Begin |
| 1983–4 | Yitzhak Shamir |
| 1984–8 | Shimon Peres |
| 1988–92 | Yitzhak Shamir |
| 1992–5 | Yitzhak Rabin |
| 1995–6 | Shimon Peres *Acting Prime Minister* |
| 1996–9 | Binyamin Netanyahu |
| 1999–2001 | Ehud Barak |
| 2001– | Ariel Sharon |

## Palestinian autonomous areas

| | |
|---|---|
| **Local name** | Palestine; Qita Ghazzah (Gaza Strip), Daffah al-Gharbiyah (West Bank) |
| **Former name** | Palestine (under British mandate 1920–48) |
| **Area** | 6 231 sq km/2 406 sq mi (total) *Note: 412 sq km/159 sq mi is fully autonomous (352 sq km/136 sq mi Gaza Strip and 60 sq km/23 sq mi Jericho area of West Bank); 5 819 sq km/2 247sq mi is partially autonomous (West Bank)* |
| **Capital** | Gaza City *Note: Palestine claims East Jerusalem as its capital, but this is under Israeli occupation; Gaza City is the administrative capital* |
| **Chief towns** | Nablus, Hebron, Jericho, Ramallah, Bethlehem (West Bank); Khan Yunis, Rafah (Gaza Strip) |
| **Population** | 2 601 669 (1997) (excluding Jewish settlers) |
| **Nationality** | Palestinian |
| **Languages** | Arabic; Hebrew, English |
| **Ethnic groups** | Palestinian Arab and other 83%, Jewish 17% (West Bank); Palestinian Arab and other 99.4%, Jewish 0.6% (Gaza Strip) |
| **Religions** | Islam 75% (Sunni), Jewish 17%, Christian and other 8% (West Bank); Islam (Sunni) 98.7%, Christian 0.7%, Jewish 0.6% (Gaza Strip) |
| **Time zone** | GMT +2 |
| **Currency** | 1 Jordanian Dinar (JD) = 1 000 fils, 1 Israeli Shekel (IS) = 100 agora |
| **Telephone** | +970 |
| **Internet** | .ps |
| **Country code** | PSE |

**Location**
A disputed territory in the Middle East. It comprises the Gaza Strip, bordering the Mediterranean Sea to the west, Egypt to the south-west and otherwise surrounded by Israel; and the West Bank, a region separated from Jordan to the west by the River Jordan and the Dead Sea and otherwise surrounded by Israel.

**Physical description**
Gaza Strip is a low-lying, sandy coastal plain; highest point is Abu 'Awdah (105m/344ft); West Bank has a mountainous interior, dropping to below sea level (–400m/–1 312ft) at the Dead Sea; highest point is Tall Asur (1 022m/3 353ft).

**Climate**
Typically Mediterranean temperate climate, with hot, dry summers and warm, wet winters.

## Political leaders

The West Bank was previously administered by Jordan, but Israel took control of it after the Six Day War in 1967; Jordan's claims to the West Bank were ceded to the Palestine Liberation Organization (PLO) in 1974 and its legal and administrative links with the West Bank were cut in 1988. The Gaza Strip was administered by Egypt from 1949 until it was lost to the Israelis in the 1967 war. The Israeli military administered it until 1994. In 1993 negotiations between Israel and the PLO resulted in a 'Declaration of Principles on Interim Self Government Arrangements' concerning Palestinian self-rule in the occupied territories, and in May 1994 a transitional period of self-rule began in the Gaza Strip and the Jericho area of the West Bank under the Palestinian National Authority.

**Leader of the Palestinian National Authority**

1994– Yasser Arafat

**Prime Minister**

2003 Mahmoud Abbas (Abu Mazen)
2003– Ahmed Qurei (Abu Ala)

### *Ancient Jericho*

The West Bank city of Jericho is the site of the world's earliest known town, continuously occupied from c.9000–1850BC. Archaeological excavations of the mound of Tell es Sultan have revealed 20 successive settlement layers.

## ITALY

| | | | |
|---|---|---|---|
| **Official name** | Italian Republic | **Languages** | Italian; German, French and Slovene are also spoken in some parts |
| **Local name** | Italia; Repubblica Italiana | **Ethnic groups** | Italian 94%, others 6% |
| **Former name** | *as listed below under Political leaders* | **Religions** | Christianity 85% (RC), none/unaffiliated 14%, others 1% |
| **Area** | 301 225 sq km/116 273 sq mi | **Time zone** | GMT +1 |
| **Capital** | Rome; Roma | **Currency** | 1 Euro (€) = 100 cents |
| **Chief towns** | Milan, Turin, Genoa, Naples, Bologna, Palermo, Florence, Venice | **Telephone** | +39 |
| **Population** | 56 305 568 (2001) | **Internet** | .it |
| **Nationality** | Italian | **Country code** | ITA |

**Location**

A republic in southern Europe, comprising the boot-shaped peninsula extending south into the Mediterranean Sea, as well as Sicily, Sardinia and some smaller islands. It is bounded to the north-west by France; to the north by Switzerland and Austria; and to the north-east by Slovenia.

**Physical description**

Peninsula extends c.800km/500mi south-east; Alps in the north form an arc, with the highest peaks along the Swiss–French frontier at Mont Blanc (Monte Bianco; 4 807m/15 771ft) and the Matterhorn (4 477m/14 688ft); broad, fertile Lombardo–Venetian plain; several lakes at the foot of the Alps; three active volcanoes: Mt Etna (3 323m/10 902ft), Vesuvius (1 277m/4 190ft) and Stromboli (926m/3 038ft).

**Climate**
Great variation; north has hot, sunny summers and short, cold winters; higher areas are cold, wet, often snowy; coastal regions have a Mediterranean climate (warm, wet winters and hot, dry summers); long hours of summer sunshine in the extreme south.

**National holidays**
Jan 1, 6, Apr 25 (Liberation), May 1, Jun 2 (National), Aug 15, Nov 1, Dec 8, 25, 26; EM; *much local variation*.

## Political leaders

### Kingdom of Italy

**Monarch**

| | |
|---|---|
| 1861–78 | Victor-Emmanuel II |
| 1878–1900 | Humbert I |
| 1900–46 | Victor-Emmanuel III |
| 1946 | Humbert II |

**Prime Minister**

| | |
|---|---|
| 1900–1 | Giuseppe Saracco |
| 1901–3 | Giuseppe Zanardelli |
| 1903–5 | Giovanni Giolitti |
| 1905–6 | Alessandro Fortis |
| 1906 | Sydney Sonnino |
| 1906–9 | Giovanni Giolitti |
| 1909–10 | Sydney Sonnino |
| 1910–11 | Luigi Luzzatti |
| 1911–14 | Giovanni Giolitti |
| 1914–16 | Antonio Salandra |
| 1916–17 | Paolo Boselli |
| 1917–19 | Vittorio Emmanuele Orlando |
| 1919–20 | Francesco Saverio Nitti |
| 1920–1 | Giovanni Giolitti |
| 1921–2 | Ivanoe Bonomi |
| 1922 | Luigi Facta |
| 1922–43 | Benito Mussolini |
| 1943–4 | Pietro Badoglio |
| 1944–5 | Ivanoe Bonomi |
| 1945 | Ferrucio Parri |
| 1945 | Alcide de Gasperi |

### Italian Republic

**President**

| | |
|---|---|
| 1946–8 | Enrico de Nicola |
| 1948–55 | Luigi Einaudi |
| 1955–62 | Giovanni Gronchi |
| 1962–4 | Antonio Segni |
| 1964–71 | Giuseppe Saragat |
| 1971–8 | Giovanni Leone |
| 1978–85 | Alessandro Pertini |
| 1985–92 | Francesco Cossiga |
| 1992–9 | Oscar Luigi Scalfaro |
| 1999– | Carlo Azeglio Ciampi |

**Prime Minister**

| | |
|---|---|
| 1946–53 | Alcide de Gasperi |
| 1953–4 | Giuseppe Pella |
| 1954 | Amintore Fanfani |
| 1954–5 | Mario Scelba |
| 1955–7 | Antonio Segni |
| 1957–8 | Adone Zoli |
| 1958–9 | Amintore Fanfani |
| 1959–60 | Antonio Segni |
| 1960 | Fernando Tambroni |
| 1960–3 | Amintore Fanfani |
| 1963 | Giovanni Leone |
| 1963–8 | Aldo Moro |
| 1968 | Giovanni Leone |
| 1968–70 | Mariano Rumor |
| 1970–2 | Emilio Colombo |
| 1972–4 | Giulio Andreotti |
| 1974–6 | Aldo Moro |
| 1976–8 | Giulio Andreotti |
| 1979–80 | Francisco Cossiga |
| 1980–1 | Arnaldo Forlani |
| 1981–2 | Giovanni Spadolini |
| 1982–3 | Amintore Fanfani |
| 1983–7 | Bettino Craxi |
| 1987 | Amintore Fanfani |
| 1987–8 | Giovanni Goria |
| 1988–9 | Ciriaco de Mita |
| 1989–92 | Giulio Andreotti |
| 1992–3 | Giuliano Amato |

| | | | |
|---|---|---|---|
| 1993–4 | Carlo Azeglio Ciampi | 1998–2000 | Massimo D'Alema |
| 1994 | Silvio Berlusconi | 2000–1 | Giuliano Amato |
| 1995–6 | Lamberto Dini | 2001– | Silvio Berlusconi |
| 1996–8 | Romano Prodi | | |

**IVORY COAST** *see* **CÔTE D'IVOIRE**

## JAMAICA

| | | | |
|---|---|---|---|
| **Official name** | Jamaica | **Religions** | Christianity 61% (Prot 25%, Church of God 21%, RC 6%, others 9%), none/unaffiliated 18%, Rastafarianism 6%, others 15% |
| **Local name** | Jamaica | **Time zone** | GMT –5 |
| **Independence** | 1962 | **Currency** | 1 Jamaican Dollar (J$) = 100 cents |
| **Area** | 10 957 sq km/4 229 sq mi | **Telephone** | +1 876 |
| **Capital** | Kingston | **Internet** | .jm |
| **Chief towns** | Montego Bay, Spanish Town | **Country code** | JAM |
| **Population** | 2 621 000 (2001e) | | |
| **Nationality** | Jamaican | | |
| **Languages** | English; Jamaican Creole is also spoken | | |
| **Ethnic groups** | black 90%, mixed 7%, East Indian 2%, others 1% | | |

**Location**
An island nation of the West Indies in the Caribbean Sea.

**Physical description**
The third-largest island in the Caribbean Sea with a maximum length of 234km/145mi; mountainous and rugged particularly in the east, where the Blue Mountains rise to 2 256m/7 401ft at Blue Mountain Peak; more than 100 small rivers.

**Climate**
Humid and tropical climate at sea level, more temperate at higher altitudes; coastal temperatures range from 21°C to 34°C; virtually no rainfall on the south and south-west plains; lies within the hurricane belt.

**National holidays**
Jan 1, May 23 (Labour), Aug 1 (Emancipation), 6 (Independence), Oct 21 (National Heroes), Dec 25, 26; Ash Wednesday, EM, GF.

### *Land of Wood and Water*

Jamaica's name comes from *Xaymaca*, the name given to the island by its first inhabitants, the Taino people. In their language the name meant 'land of wood and water'.

## Political leaders

Chief of State: British monarch, represented by Governor General.

**Prime Minister**

| | |
|---|---|
| 1962–7 | William Alexander Bustamante |
| 1967 | Donald Burns Sangster |
| 1967–72 | Hugh Lawson Shearer |
| 1972–80 | Michael Norman Manley |
| 1980–9 | Edward Phillip George Seaga |
| 1989–92 | Michael Norman Manley |
| 1992– | Percival James Patterson |

**JAN MEYEN ISLAND** *see* **NORWAY**

# JAPAN

| | |
|---|---|
| **Official name** | Japan |
| **Local name** | Nihon |
| **Area** | 381 945 sq km/147 431 sq mi |
| **Capital** | Tokyo; Tōkyō, Tôkyô |
| **Chief towns** | Yokohama, Osaka, Nagoya, Sapporo, Kyoto, Kobe |
| **Population** | 126 925 843 (2000) |
| **Nationality** | Japanese |
| **Languages** | Japanese |
| **Ethnic groups** | Japanese 99%, others 1% |
| **Religions** | Shintoism and Buddhism 84%, others 15%, Christianity 1% |
| **Time zone** | GMT +9 |
| **Currency** | 1 Yen (Y, ¥) = 100 sen |
| **Telephone** | +81 |
| **Internet** | .jp |
| **Country code** | JPN |

**Location**
An island state off the east coast of Asia. It comprises the four large islands of Hokkaido (the northernmost island), Honshu (the largest island), Kyushu and Shikoku (in the south-west), and many small islands; the country tails off to the south into the Ryukyu chain of volcanic islands, of which Okinawa is the largest.

**Physical description**
Consists mainly of steep mountains with many volcanoes; Hokkaido has a central range rising to over 2 000m/6 562ft, falling to coastal uplands and plains; Honshu comprises parallel arcs of mountains bounded by narrow coastal plains and includes Mt Fuji (3 776m/12 388ft), Japan's highest point; heavily populated Kanto plain lies in the east; frequent earthquakes.

**Climate**
Oceanic climate, influenced by the Asian monsoon; short, warm summers, and severe winters with heavy snow in the north; average daily temperature at Akita (north Honshu) ranges from –5°C to 2°C (Jan), 19°C to 28°C (Aug); variable winter weather throughout; typhoons occur in summer and early autumn; mild, almost subtropical winters with light rainfall in south Honshu, Shikoku and Kyushu; summer heat is often oppressive.

**National holidays**
Jan 1, Feb 11 (National Foundation), Apr 29 (Greenery), May 3 (Constitution Memorial), 5 (Children), Sep 15 (Respect for the Aged), Nov 3 (Culture), 23 (Labour Thanksgiving), Dec 23 (Emperor's Birthday); Autumnal Equinox, Coming-of-Age (2nd Mon in Jan), Marine Day (Jul), Sports (2nd Mon in Oct), Vernal Equinox.

## Political leaders

**Chief of State (Emperor)**

| | |
|---|---|
| 660–585BC | Jimmu[1] |
| 581–549BC | Suizei[1] |
| 549–511BC | Annei[1] |
| 510–477BC | Itoku[1] |

| | |
|---|---|
| 475–393BC | Kosho[1] |
| 392–291BC | Koan[1] |
| 290–215BC | Korei[1] |
| 214–158BC | Kogen[1] |
| 158–98BC | Kaika[1] |
| 97–30BC | Sujin[1] |
| 29BC–70AD | Suinin[1] |
| AD71–130 | Keiko[1] |
| AD131–190 | Seimu[1] |
| AD192–200 | Chuai[1] |
| AD270–310 | Ojin[2] |
| AD313–399 | Nintoku[2] |
| AD400–405 | Richu[2] |
| AD406–410 | Hanzei[2] |
| AD412–453 | Ingyo[2] |
| AD453–456 | Anko[2] |
| AD456–479 | Yuryaku[2] |
| AD480–484 | Seinei[2] |
| AD485–487 | Kenzo[2] |
| AD488–498 | Ninken[2] |
| AD498–506 | Buretsu[2] |
| 507–531 | Keitai[2] |
| 531–535 | Ankan[2] |
| 535–539 | Senka[2] |
| 539–571 | Kimmei |
| 572–585 | Bidatsu |
| 585–587 | Yomei |
| 587–592 | Sushun |
| 592–628 | Suiko *(Empress)* |
| 629–641 | Jomei |
| 642–645 | Kogyoku *(Empress)* |
| 645–654 | Kotuko |
| 655–661 | Saimei *(Empress)* |
| 662–671 | Tenji |
| 671–672 | Kobun |
| 673–686 | Temmu |
| 686–697 | Jito *(Empress)* |
| 697–707 | Mommu |
| 707–715 | Gemmei *(Empress)* |
| 715–724 | Gensho *(Empress)* |
| 724–749 | Shomu |
| 749–758 | Koken *(Empress)* |
| 758–764 | Junnin |
| 764–770 | Shotoku *(Empress)* |
| 770–781 | Konin |
| 781–806 | Kammu |
| 806–809 | Heizei |
| 809–823 | Saga |
| 823–833 | Junna |
| 833–850 | Nimmyo |
| 850–858 | Montoku |
| 858–876 | Seiwa |
| 876–884 | Yozei |
| 884–887 | Koko |
| 887–897 | Uda |
| 897–930 | Daigo |
| 930–946 | Suzaku |
| 946–967 | Murakami |
| 967–969 | Reizei |
| 969–984 | En-yu |
| 984–986 | Kazan |
| 986–1011 | Ichijo |
| 1011–16 | Sanjo |
| 1016–36 | Go-Ichijo |
| 1036–45 | Go-Suzaku |
| 1045–68 | Go-Reizei |
| 1068–72 | Go-Sanyo |
| 1072–86 | Shirakawa |
| 1086–1107 | Horikawa |
| 1107–23 | Toba |
| 1123–41 | Sutoku |
| 1141–55 | Konoe |
| 1155–8 | Go-Shirakawa |
| 1158–65 | Nijo |
| 1165–8 | Rokujo |
| 1168–80 | Takakura |
| 1180–3 | Antoku |
| 1183–98 | Go-Toba |
| 1198–1210 | Tsuchimikado |
| 1210–21 | Juntoku |
| 1221 | Chukyo |
| 1221–32 | Go-Horikawa |
| 1232–42 | Shijo |
| 1242–6 | Go-Saga |
| 1246–59 | Go-Fukakusa |
| 1259–74 | Kameyama |
| 1274–87 | Go-Uda |
| 1287–98 | Fushimi |
| 1298–1301 | Go-Fushimi |
| 1301–8 | Go-Nijo |
| 1308–18 | Hanazono |
| 1318–39 | Go-Daigo |
| 1339–68 | Go-Murakami |
| 1368–83 | Chokei |
| 1383–92 | Go-Kameyama |

**Northern Court**

| | |
|---|---|
| 1331–3 | Kogon |
| 1336–48 | Komyo |
| 1348–51 | Suko |
| 1352–71 | Go-Kogon |
| 1371–82 | Go-Enyu |
| 1382–1412 | Go-Komatsu |
| 1412–28 | Shoko |
| 1428–64 | Go-Hanazono |
| 1464–1500 | Go-Suchimikado |
| 1500–26 | Go Kashiwabara |

| | |
|---|---|
| 1526–57 | Go-Nara |
| 1557–86 | Ogimachi |
| 1586–1611 | Go-Yozei |
| 1611–29 | Go-Mizuno-o |
| 1629–43 | Meisho *(Empress)* |
| 1643–54 | Go-Komyo |
| 1654–63 | Go-Sai |
| 1663–87 | Reigen |
| 1687–1709 | Higashiyama |
| 1709–35 | Nakamikado |
| 1735–47 | Sakuramachi |
| 1747–62 | Momozono |
| 1762–70 | Go-Sakuramachi |
| 1770–9 | Go-Momozono |
| 1779–1817 | Kokaku |
| 1817–46 | Ninko |
| 1846–66 | Komei |
| 1867–1912 | Mutsuhito (Meiji Era) |
| 1912–26 | Yoshihito (Taisho Era) |
| 1926–89 | Hirohito (Showa Era) |
| 1989– | Akihito (Heisei Era) |

[1] *The first 14 emperors (to Chuai) are regarded as legendary.*

[2] *The regnal dates for the 15th to the 28th emperor (Senka), taken from the early Japanese chronicle, 'Nihon shoki', are not considered to be authentic.*

**Prime Minister**

| | |
|---|---|
| 1900–1 | Hirobumi Ito |
| 1901–6 | Taro Katsura |
| 1906–8 | Kimmochi Saionji |
| 1908–11 | Taro Katsura |
| 1911–12 | Kimmochi Saionji |
| 1912–13 | Taro Katsura |
| 1913–14 | Gonnohyoe Yamamoto |
| 1914–16 | Shigenobu Okuma |
| 1916–18 | Masatake Terauchi |
| 1918–21 | Takashi Hara |
| 1921–2 | Korekiyo Takahashi |
| 1922–3 | Tomosaburo Kato |
| 1923–4 | Gonnohyoe Yamamoto |
| 1924 | Keigo Kiyoura |
| 1924–6 | Takaaki Kato |
| 1926–7 | Reijiro Wakatsuki |
| 1927–9 | Giichi Tanaka |
| 1929–31 | Osachi Hamaguchi |
| 1931 | Reijiro Wakatsuki |
| 1931–2 | Tsuyoshi Inukai |
| 1932–4 | Makoto Saito |
| 1934–6 | Keisuke Okada |
| 1936–7 | Koki Hirota |
| 1937 | Senjuro Hayashi |
| 1937–9 | Fumimaro Konoe |
| 1939 | Kiichiro Hiranuma |
| 1939–40 | Nobuyuki Abe |
| 1940 | Mitsumasa Yonai |
| 1940–1 | Fumimaro Konoe |
| 1941–4 | Hideki Tojo |
| 1944–5 | Kuniaki Koiso |
| 1945 | Kantaro Suzuki |
| 1945 | Naruhiko Higashikuni |
| 1945–6 | Kijuro Shidehara |
| 1946–7 | Shigeru Yoshida |
| 1947–8 | Tetsu Katayama |
| 1948 | Hitoshi Ashida |
| 1948–54 | Shigeru Yoshida |
| 1954–6 | Ichiro Hatoyama |
| 1956–7 | Tanzan Ishibashi |
| 1957–60 | Nobusuke Kishi |
| 1960–4 | Hayato Ikeda |
| 1964–72 | Eisaku Sato |
| 1972–4 | Kakuei Tanaka |
| 1974–6 | Takeo Miki |
| 1976–8 | Takeo Fukuda |
| 1978–80 | Masayoshi Ohira |
| 1980–2 | Zenko Suzuki |
| 1982–7 | Yasuhiro Nakasone |
| 1987–9 | Noburu Takeshita |
| 1989 | Sasuke Uno |
| 1989–91 | Toshiki Kaifu |
| 1991–93 | Kiichi Miyazawa |
| 1993 | Morihiro Hosokawa |
| 1994 | Tsutoma Hata |
| 1994–6 | Tomiichi Murayama |
| 1996–8 | Ryutaro Hashimoto |
| 1998–2000 | Keizo Obuchi |
| 2000 | Mikio Aoki *Acting Prime Minister* |
| 2000–1 | Yoshiro Mori |
| 2001– | Junichiro Koizumi |

## Growing Old Gracefully

Japan has the highest life expectancy in the world, at an average of 80.5 years, and in 2003 the Japanese government announced that Japan has more than 20 000 centenarians.

## JORDAN

| | | | |
|---|---|---|---|
| **Official name** | Hashemite Kingdom of Jordan | **Population** | 4 139 458 (1994) |
| **Local name** | Al'Urdunn; Al-Mamlaka al-Urdunniyya al-Hashimiyya | **Nationality** | Jordanian |
| **Former name** | Emirate of Transjordan (until 1946), Hashemite Kingdom of Transjordan (1946–9) | **Languages** | Arabic |
| **Independence** | 1946 | **Ethnic groups** | Arab 98%, others 2% |
| **Area** | 96 188 sq km/37 129 sq mi | **Religions** | Islam 94% (Sunni), Christianity 6% |
| **Capital** | Amman; 'Ammān | **Time zone** | GMT +2 |
| **Chief towns** | Irbid, Zarqa, Salt, Karak, Aqaba | **Currency** | 1 Jordanian Dinar (JD) = 1 000 fils |
| | | **Telephone** | +962 |
| | | **Internet** | .jo |
| | | **Country code** | JOR |

**Location**
A kingdom in the Middle East, bounded to the north by Syria; to the north-east by Iraq; to the east and south by Saudi Arabia; and to the west by Israel.

**Physical description**
Divided by the Red Sea–Jordan rift valley; lowest point is –400m/–1 312ft at the Dead Sea; sides of the rift rise through undulating hills; Syrian desert in the east, sandy in the south, hard and rocky further north; highest point is Jabal Rum (1 754m/5 755ft).

**Climate**
Desert covers c.90% of the country; summers are uniformly hot and sunny; typically Mediterranean climate elsewhere, with hot, dry summers and cool, wet winters; temperatures at Amman are 7°C (Jan), 25°C (Jul).

**National holidays**
Jan 1, May 1, 25 (Independence), Jun 9 (Accession of King Abdullah),10 (Great Arab Revolt), Nov 14 (late King Hussein's Birthday); Ad (4), R, ER (3), NY (Muslim), PB, Al-Isra' wal mi'raj.

## Political leaders

### Monarch

| | |
|---|---|
| 1921–51 | Abdullah ibn Hussein I |
| 1951–2 | Talal I |
| 1952–99 | Hussein ibn Talal |
| 1999– | Abdullah ibn Hussein II |

### Prime Minister

| | |
|---|---|
| 1921 | Rashid Tali |
| 1921 | Muzhir Ar-Raslan |
| 1921–3 | Rida Ar-Riqabi |
| 1923 | Muzhir Ar-Raslan |
| 1923–4 | Hassan Khalid |
| 1924–33 | Rida Ar-Riqabi |
| 1933–8 | Ibrahim Hashim |
| 1938–44 | Taufiq Abul-Huda |
| 1944–5 | Samir Ar-Rifai |
| 1945–7 | Ibrahim Hashim |
| 1947–50 | Taufiq Abul-Huda |
| 1950 | Said Al-Mufti |
| 1950–1 | Samir Ar-Rifai |
| 1951–3 | Taufiq Abul-Huda |
| 1953–4 | Fauzi Al-Mulqi |
| 1954–5 | Taufiq Abul-Huda |
| 1955 | Said Al-Mufti |
| 1955 | Hazza Al-Majali |
| 1955–6 | Ibrahim Hashim |
| 1956 | Samir Ar-Rifai |
| 1956 | Said Al-Mufti |
| 1956 | Ibrahim Hashim |
| 1956–7 | Suleiman Nabulsi |
| 1957 | Hussein Fakhri Al-Khalidi |
| 1957–8 | Ibrahim Hashim |
| 1958 | Nuri Pasha Al-Said |

| | |
|---|---|
| 1958–9 | Samir Ar-Rifai |
| 1959–60 | Hazza Al-Majali |
| 1960–2 | Bahjat Talhuni |
| 1962–3 | Wasfi At-Tall |
| 1963 | Samir Ar-Rifai |
| 1963–4 | Sharif Hussein Bin Nasir |
| 1964–5 | Bahjat Talhuni |
| 1965–7 | Wasfi At-Tall |
| 1967 | Sharif Hussein Bin Nasir |
| 1967 | Saad Jumaa |
| 1967–9 | Bahjat Talhuni |
| 1969 | Abdul Munem Rifai |
| 1969–70 | Bahjat Talhuni |
| 1970 | Abdul Munem Rifai |
| 1970 | *Military Junta* (Mohammed Daud) |
| 1970 | Mohamed Ahmed Tugan |
| 1970–1 | Wasfi At-Tall |
| 1971–3 | Ahmad Lozi |
| 1973–6 | Zeid Rifai |
| 1976–9 | Mudar Badran |
| 1979–80 | Sharif Abdul Hamid Sharaf |
| 1980 | Kassem Rimawi |
| 1980–4 | Mudar Badran |
| 1984–5 | Ahmad Ubayat |
| 1985–9 | Zeid Ar-Rifai |
| 1989 | Sharif Zaid ibn Shaker |
| 1989–91 | Mudar Badran |
| 1991 | Taher Al-Masri |
| 1991–3 | Sharif Zaid ibn Shaker |
| 1993–5 | Abdel Salam Al-Majali |
| 1995–7 | Abdul Karim Kabariti |
| 1997–8 | Abdel Salam Al-Majali |
| 1998–9 | Fayez Tarawneh |
| 1999–2000 | Abdul Raouf Rawabdeh |
| 2000– | Ali Abu al-Ragheb |

**KAMPUCHEA** *see* **CAMBODIA**

## KAZAKHSTAN

| | | | |
|---|---|---|---|
| **Official name** | Republic of Kazakhstan | **Nationality** | Kazakhstani |
| **Local name** | Qazaqstan Respūblīkasy | **Languages** | Kazakh; Russian is also widely spoken |
| **Former name** | Kazakh Soviet Socialist Republic (until 1991), within the Union of Soviet Socialist Republics (USSR; 1922–91) | **Ethnic groups** | Kazakh 46%, Russian 35%, Ukrainian 5%, German 4%, others 10% |
| **Independence** | 1991 | **Religions** | Islam 48%, Christianity 46% (Orthodox 44%, Prot 2%), others 6% |
| **Area** | 2 717 300 sq km/ 1 048 878 sq mi | **Time zone** | GMT +4/6 |
| **Capital** | Astana | **Currency** | 1 Tenge = 100 tiyn |
| **Chief towns** | Karaganda, Semipalatinsk, Chimkent, Petropavlovsk | **Telephone** | +7 |
| | | **Internet** | .kz |
| **Population** | 14 953 126 (1999) | **Country code** | KAZ |

**Location**
A republic in western Asia, bounded to the north by Russia; to the south by Turkmenistan, Uzbekistan and Kyrgyzstan; to the east by China; and to the west by the Caspian Sea.

**Physical description**
Steppeland in the north gives way to desert in the south; lowest point is near the eastern shore of the Caspian Sea (–132m/–433ft); mountain ranges in the east and south-east; highest point is Khan Tengri (6 995m/22 949ft) in the Tien Shan mountains; largest lake is Lake Balkhash; Aral Sea lies on the south border with Uzbekistan.

**Climate**
Continental; hot summers and cold winters.

**National holidays**
Jan 1, Mar 8 (Women), 21, May 1, 9 (Victory), Aug 30 (Constitution), Oct 25 (State Sovereignty), Dec 16 (Independence), 31.

## Political leaders

**President**

| | |
|---|---|
| 1991– | Nursultan Nazarbayev |

**Prime Minister**

| | |
|---|---|
| 1991–4 | Sergei Tereshchenko |
| 1994–7 | Akezhan Kazhageldin |
| 1997–9 | Nurlan Balgimbayev |
| 1999–2002 | Kasymzhomart Tokaev |
| 2002–3 | Imangali Tasmagambetov |
| 2003– | Daniyal Akhmetov |

**KEELING ISLANDS** *see* **AUSTRALIA**

# KENYA

| | |
|---|---|
| **Official name** | Republic of Kenya |
| **Local name** | Jamhuri ya Kenya |
| **Former name** | British East Africa Protectorate (until 1920) |
| **Independence** | 1963 |
| **Area** | 564 162 sq km/217 766 sq mi |
| **Capital** | Nairobi |
| **Chief towns** | Mombasa, Kisumu, Nakuru, Malindi |
| **Population** | 28 686 607 (1999) |
| **Nationality** | Kenyan |
| **Languages** | English and Swahili, with many tribal languages spoken |
| **Ethnic groups** | Kikuyu 22%, Luhya 14%, Luo 13%, Kalenjin 12%, Kamba 11%, others 28% |
| **Religions** | Christianity 66% (Prot 38%, RC 28%), traditional beliefs 26%, Islam 7%, others 1% |
| **Time zone** | GMT +3 |
| **Currency** | 1 Kenyan shilling (Ksh) = 100 cents |
| **Telephone** | +254 |
| **Internet** | .ke |
| **Country code** | KEN |

**Location**
A republic in East Africa, bounded to the south by Tanzania; to the west by Uganda; to the north-west by The Sudan; to the north by Ethiopia; to the north-east by Somalia; and to the east by the Indian Ocean.

**Physical description**
Crossed by the Equator; highest point is Mt Kenya (5 200m/17 060ft); Great Rift Valley in the west runs north to south; dry, arid semi-desert in the north; largest body of water is Lake Turkana in the north; Chalbi Desert lies south-east of the lake.

**Climate**
Tropical climate on the coast, with high temperatures and humidity; in Mombasa the average daily temperatures are 27–31°C; annual rainfall decreases from south to the far north; frost and snow lie in the high mountains.

**National holidays**
Jan 1, May 1, Jun 1 (Madaraka), Oct 10 (Moi), 20 (Kenyatta) (2), Dec 12 (Jamhuri), 25, 26; EM, ER, GF.

## Political leaders

**President**

| | |
|---|---|
| 1963–78 | Mzee Jomo Kenyatta |
| 1978–2002 | Daniel arap Moi |
| 2002– | Mwai Kibaki |

## KIRIBATI

| | | | |
|---|---|---|---|
| **Official name** | Republic of Kiribati | **Ethnic groups** | Micronesian 98%, others 2% |
| **Local name** | Kiribati; Ribaberikin Kiribati | **Religions** | Christianity 91% (RC 53%, Prot 38%), Baha'i 3%, others 6% |
| **Former name** | Gilbert Islands, as part of the Gilbert and Ellice Islands (until 1979) | **Time zone** | GMT +12/14 |
| **Independence** | 1979 | **Currency** | 1 Australian Dollar ($A) = 100 cents |
| **Area** | 717 sq km/277 sq mi | | |
| **Capital** | Tarawa | **Telephone** | +686 |
| **Population** | 77 658 (1995) | **Internet** | .ki |
| **Nationality** | I-Kiribati | **Country code** | KIR |
| **Languages** | English, I-Kiribati | | |

**Location**
A group of 33 low-lying coral islands scattered over c.3 million sq km/1.2 million sq mi of the central Pacific Ocean.

**Physical description**
Islands seldom rise to more than 4m/13ft and usually consist of a reef enclosing a lagoon; Banaba, a solid coral outcrop with a fringing reef, rises to 87m/285ft.

**Climate**
Maritime equatorial climate in the central islands; islands further north and south are tropical; average annual temperature is 27°C; rainy season from Nov to Apr; some islands suffer from periodic drought.

**National holidays**
Jan 1, Mar 8 (Women), Apr 17 (National Health), Jul 11 (Gospel), 12 (Independence) (3), Aug 6 (Youth), Dec 10 (Human Rights), 25, 26; GF, HS, EM, ES; *length of holidays varies locally*.

## Political leaders

**President**

| | |
|---|---|
| 1979–82 | Ieremia T Tabai |
| 1982–3 | *Council of State* (Rota Onorio) |
| 1983–91 | Ieremia T Tabai |
| 1991–4 | Teatao Teannaki |
| 1994 | *Council of State* (Tekire Tameura/Ata Teaotai) |
| 1994–2003 | Teburoro Tito |
| 2003 | *Council of State* (Tion Otang) |
| 2003– | Anote Tong |

### It's a Date

The International Date Line runs through the middle of Kiribati, meaning that the time difference between its easternmost and westernmost islands should be 24 hours. However, in 1995 the government 'bent' the Date Line to make the date the same everywhere, moving the line hundreds of kilometres east in a bulge big enough to include all the islands. An additional benefit of this was that Kiribati's Caroline Island, renamed Millennium Island, was the first place to see the sunrise on 1 Jan 2000, drawing attention and tourists from around the world.

## KOREA, NORTH

| | | | |
|---|---|---|---|
| **Official name** | Democratic People's Republic of Korea (DPRK) | **Languages** | Korean |
| **Local name** | Chosun; Chosun Minchu-chui In'min Kongwa-guk | **Ethnic groups** | Korean 100% |
| **Independence** | 1948 | **Religions** | none/unaffiliated 67%, traditional beliefs 16%, Chondogyo 14%, Buddhism 2%, Christianity 1% |
| **Area** | 122 098 sq km/47 130 sq mi | **Time zone** | GMT +9 |
| **Capital** | Pyongyang; P'yŏngyang | **Currency** | 1 Won (NKW) = 100 chon |
| **Chief towns** | Chongjin, Sinuiju, Wonsan, Kaesong | **Telephone** | +850 |
| **Population** | 22 409 000 (2001e) | **Internet** | .kp |
| **Nationality** | North Korean | **Country code** | PRK |

**Location**
A socialist state in eastern Asia, in the northern half of the Korean Peninsula, bounded to the north by China; to the north-east by Russia; to the west by Korea Bay and the Yellow Sea; to the east by the Sea of Japan (the East Sea); and to the south by South Korea, from which it is separated by a demilitarized zone.

**Physical description**
On a high plateau occupying the north of a mountainous peninsula which projects south-east from China; many areas rise to over 2 000m/6 562ft; highest point is Mt Paektu (2 744m/9 003ft); lower mountains in the south descend to coastal plains.

**Climate**
Temperate, with warm summers and severely cold winters; rivers freeze for 3–4 months, and ice blocks harbours; daily temperatures at Pyongyang in the west range from –3°C to –13°C (Jan), and from 20°C to 29°C (Jul–Aug).

**National holidays**
Jan 1, Feb 16 (Kim Jong Il's Birthday), Mar 8 (Women), Apr 15 (Kim Il Sung's Birthday), Apr 25 (Army Foundation), May 1, Jul 27 (Fatherland Liberation War Victory), Aug 15 (Liberation), Sep 9 (Foundation of the Republic), Oct 10 (Foundation of the Workers' Party), Dec 27 (Constitution).

## Political leaders

**President**

| | |
|---|---|
| 1948–57 | Kim Doo-bong |
| 1957–72 | Choi Yong-kun |
| 1972–94 | Kim Il Sung |
| 1994–7 | *Position vacant* |
| 1998– | Kim Il Sung (deceased) *Eternal President* |

**Chairman of National Defence Commission**

| | |
|---|---|
| 1993– | Kim Jong Il |

**Prime Minister**

| | |
|---|---|
| 1948–76 | Kim Il Sung |
| 1976–7 | Park Sung-chul |
| 1977–84 | Li Jong-ok |
| 1984–6 | Kang Song-san |
| 1986–8 | Yi Kun-mo |
| 1988–92 | Yon Hyong-muk |
| 1992–7 | Kang Song-san |
| 1997– | Hong Song-nam |

## KOREA, SOUTH

| | | | |
|---|---|---|---|
| **Official name** | Republic of Korea (ROK) | **Ethnic groups** | Korean 100% |
| **Local name** | Hanguk; Dae-han-min-guk | **Religions** | Christianity 51% (Prot 39%, RC 12%), Buddhism 47%, others 2% |
| **Independence** | 1948 | **Time zone** | GMT +9 |
| **Area** | 98 913 sq km/38 180 sq mi | **Currency** | 1 Won (W) = 100 jeon |
| **Capital** | Seoul; Sŏul | **Telephone** | +82 |
| **Chief towns** | Inchon, Pusan, Taegu | **Internet** | .kr |
| **Population** | 45 985 289 (2000) | **Country code** | KOR |
| **Nationality** | South Korean | | |
| **Languages** | Korean | | |

**Location**
A republic in eastern Asia occupying the southern half of the Korean Peninsula and about 3 000 islands off its west and south coasts; bounded to the west by the Yellow Sea; to the east by the Sea of Japan (the East Sea); to the south by the Korean Strait; and to the north by North Korea, from which it is separated by a demilitarized zone.

**Physical description**
Taebaek Sanmaek Range runs north to south along the east coast, reaching heights of over 900m/2 953ft; it descends through a series of ridges to broad, undulating coastal lowlands; highest peak is Halla-san (1 950m/6 398ft) on the island of Cheju do.

**Climate**
Extreme continental climate, with cold winters and hot summers; typhoons possible in the wettest months (Jun–Sep); average daily temperatures at Seoul range from –9°C to 0°C (Jan), 22°C to 31°C (Aug).

**National holidays**
Jan 1–3, Mar 1 (Independence Movement), 10 (Labour), Apr 5 (Arbor), May 5 (Children), Jun 6 (Memorial), Jul 17 (Constitution), Aug 15 (Liberation), Oct 1 (Armed Forces), 3 (National Foundation), 9 (Korean Alphabet), Dec 25; NY (Chinese) (Jan/Feb), Lord Buddha's Birthday (May), Moon Festival (Sep/Oct).

## Political leaders

**President**

| | |
|---|---|
| 1948–60 | Syngman Rhee |
| 1960 | Ho Chong *Acting President* |
| 1960 | Kwak Sang-hun *Acting President* |
| 1960 | Ho Chong *Acting President* |
| 1960–3 | Yun Po-sun |
| 1963–79 | Park Chung-hee |
| 1979–80 | Choi Kyu-hah |
| 1980 | Park Choong-hoon *Acting President* |
| 1980–8 | Chun Doo-hwan |
| 1988–93 | Roh Tae-woo |
| 1993–7 | Kim Young-sam |
| 1997–2003 | Kim Dae-jung |
| 2003– | Roh Moo-hyun |

**Prime Minister**

| | |
|---|---|
| 1948–50 | Lee Pom-sok |
| 1950 | Shin Song-mo *Acting Prime Minister* |
| 1950–1 | John M Chang |
| 1951–2 | Ho Chong *Acting Prime Minister* |
| 1952 | Lee Yun-yong *Acting Prime Minister* |
| 1952 | Chang Taek-sang |
| 1952–4 | Paik Too-chin |
| 1954–6 | Pyon Yong-tae |
| 1956–60 | Syngman Rhee |
| 1960 | Ho Chong |
| 1960–1 | John M Chang |
| 1961 | Chang To-yong |

| | |
|---|---|
| 1961–2 | Song Yo-chan |
| 1962–3 | Kim Hyun-chul |
| 1963–4 | Choe Tu-son |
| 1964–70 | Chung Il-kwon |
| 1970–1 | Paik Too-chin |
| 1971–5 | Kim Jong-pil |
| 1975–9 | Choi Kyu-hah |
| 1979–80 | Shin Hyun-hwak |
| 1980 | Park Choong-hoon *Acting Prime Minister* |
| 1980–2 | Nam Duck-woo |
| 1982 | Yoo Chang-soon |
| 1982–3 | Kim Sang-hyup |
| 1983–5 | Chin Lee-chong |
| 1985–8 | Lho Shin-yong |
| 1988 | Lee Hyun-jae |
| 1988–90 | Kang Young-hoon |
| 1990–1 | Ro Jai-bong |
| 1991–2 | Chung Won-shik |
| 1992–3 | Hyun Soong-jong |
| 1993 | Hwang In-sung |
| 1993–4 | Lee Hoi-chang |
| 1994 | Lee Yung-duck |
| 1994–5 | Yi Hong-ku |
| 1995–7 | Lee Soo-sung |
| 1997–8 | Koh Kun |
| 1998–2000 | Kim Jong-pil |
| 2000 | Park Tae-joon |
| 2000 | Lee Hun-jai *Acting Prime Minister* |
| 2000–2 | Lee Han-dong |
| 2002–3 | Kim Suk-soo |
| 2003– | Ko Kun |

## KUWAIT

| | | | |
|---|---|---|---|
| **Official name** | State of Kuwait | **Ethnic groups** | Kuwaiti 47%, other Arab 36%, South Asian 8%, Iranian 4%, others 5% |
| **Local name** | Dawlat al-Kuwayt | **Religions** | Islam 85% (Sunni 45%, Shia 40%), Hinduism 2%, others 13% |
| **Independence** | 1961 | **Time zone** | GMT +3 |
| **Area** | 17 818 sq km/6 878 sq mi | **Currency** | 1 Kuwaiti Dinar (KD) = 1 000 fils |
| **Capital** | Kuwait City; Al Kuwayt | **Telephone** | +965 |
| **Chief towns** | Shuwaikh, Mina al Ahmadi | **Internet** | .kw |
| **Population** | 1 575 570 (1995) | **Country code** | KWT |
| **Nationality** | Kuwaiti | | |
| **Languages** | Arabic; English is also widely spoken | | |

**Location**
An independent state at the head of the Arabian Gulf, bounded to the north and west by Iraq; to the south by Saudi Arabia; and to the east by the Arabian Gulf.

**Physical description**
Consists of the mainland and nine offshore islands; terrain is flat or gently undulating, rising in the south-west to 271m/889ft; Wadi al Batin runs along the western border with Iraq; terrain is generally stony with sparse vegetation.

**Climate**
Hot, dry climate; summer temperatures are very high, often above 45°C (Jul–Aug); winter daytime temperatures often exceed 20°C; humidity is generally high; sandstorms are common throughout the year.

**National holidays**
Jan 1, Feb 25 (National), 26 (Liberation); Mt Ararat and Ad (4), ER (3), NY (Muslim), PB, Ascension of the Prophet.

## Political leaders

**Emir**

*Family name: al-Sabah*

| | |
|---|---|
| 1896–1915 | Mubarak |
| 1915–17 | Jaber II |
| 1917–21 | Salem Al-Mubarak |
| 1921–50 | Ahmed Al-Jaber |
| 1950–65 | Abdallah Al-Salem |
| 1965–77 | Sabah Al-Salem |
| 1978– | Jaber Al-Ahmed Al-Jaber |

**Prime Minister**

| | |
|---|---|
| 1962–3 | Abdallah Al-Salem |
| 1963–5 | Sabah Al-Salem |
| 1965–78 | Jaber Al-Ahmed Al-Jaber |
| 1978–2003 | Saad Al-Abdallah Al-Salem |
| 2003– | Sabah Al-Ahmed Al-Jaber |

# KYRGYZSTAN[1]

| | |
|---|---|
| **Official name** | Kyrgyz Republic |
| **Local name** | Kyrgyz Respublikasy |
| **Former name** | Kyrgyz Soviet Socialist Republic (until 1990), within the Union of Soviet Socialist Republics (USSR; 1922–91) |
| **Independence** | 1991 |
| **Area** | 198 500 sq km/76 621 sq mi |
| **Capital** | Bishkek; Biškek |
| **Chief towns** | Osh, Przhevalsk, Kyzyl-Kiya |
| **Population** | 4 822 938 (1999) |
| **Nationality** | Kyrgyz |
| **Languages** | Kyrgyz, Russian |
| **Ethnic groups** | Kyrgyz 55%, Russian 21%, Uzbek 13%, Ukrainian 3%, German 2%, Tatar 2%, others 4% |
| **Religions** | Islam 75%, Christianity 20% (Orthodox), others 5% |
| **Time zone** | GMT +5 |
| **Currency** | 1 Som (Kgs) = 100 tyjyn[2] |
| **Telephone** | +996 |
| **Internet** | .kg |
| **Country code** | KGZ |

**Location**
A mountainous republic in north-east Middle Asia, bounded to the north by Kazakhstan; to the west by Uzbekistan; to the south and south-west by Tajikistan; and to the south-east and east by China.

**Physical description**
Largely occupied by the Tien Shan Mountains; highest point is Pobedy Peak (7 439m/24 406ft); Lake Issyk-Kul is the largest lake.

**Climate**
Varies according to location; sub-tropical in the south-west, dry in the north and west, continental to polar in the mountainous east.

**National holidays**
Jan 1, 7 (Russian Orthodox Christmas), Mar 8 (Women), 21, May 1, 5 (Constitution), 9 (Victory), Aug 31 (Independence); Ad, ER, Navroos.

[1] *Note: Kyrgyz sometimes also spelled Kirghiz; sometimes known as Kirghizia.*
[2] *Also sometimes transliterated as tyin or tyiyn.*

## Political leaders

**President**

1991– Askar Akayev

**Prime Minister**

| | |
|---|---|
| 1991 | Nasirdin Isanov |
| 1991–2 | Andrey Andreyevich Yordan *Acting Prime Minister* |
| 1992–3 | Tursunbek Chyngyshev |
| 1993–8 | Apas Jumagulov |
| 1998 | Kubanychbek Djumaliyev |
| 1998 | Boris Silayev *Acting Prime Minister* |
| 1998–9 | Jumabek Ibraimov |
| 1999 | Boris Silayev *Acting Prime Minister* |
| 1999–2000 | Amangeldy Muraliyev |
| 2000–2 | Kurmanbek Bakiyev |
| 2002– | Nikolai Tanayev |

### *Yurts in the Sun*

The national flag of Kyrgyzstan has a red background, symbolizing courage and audacity. In its centre is a golden sun, representing peace and wealth. Within the sun is a *tunduk*, the roof of a yurt, symbolizing home within the big wide world.

## LAOS

| | |
|---|---|
| **Official name** | Lao People's Democratic Republic |
| **Local name** | Lao; Sathalanalat Paxathipatai Paxaxôn Lao |
| **Former name** | Kingdom of Laos (1945–75) |
| **Independence** | 1949 |
| **Area** | 236 800 sq km/91 405 sq mi |
| **Capital** | Vientiane; Viangchan |
| **Chief towns** | Luang Prabang, Pakse, Savannakhét |
| **Population** | 5 403 000 (2001e) |
| **Nationality** | Lao or Laotian |
| **Languages** | Lao |
| **Ethnic groups** | Lao Loum 68%, Lao Theung 22%, Lao Soung 9%, others 1% |
| **Religions** | Buddhism 76%, traditional beliefs 20%, Christianity 2% (Prot 1%, RC 1%), Islam 1%, Chinese folk religion 1% |
| **Time zone** | GMT +7 |
| **Currency** | 1 Kip (Kp) = 100 at |
| **Telephone** | +856 |
| **Internet** | .la |
| **Country code** | LAO |

**Location**
A landlocked republic in south-east Asia, bounded to the east by Vietnam; to the south by Cambodia; to the west by Thailand and Myanmar; and to the north by China.

**Physical description**
On the Indochinese Peninsula; dense jungle and rugged mountains in the east; highest point is Phu Bia (2 820m/9 252ft); Mekong River flows north-west–south-east, following much of the west frontier with Thailand.

**Climate**
Monsoonal with heavy rain in May–Sep; hot and dry Feb–Apr; average annual temperatures in Vientiane are 14–34°C.

**National holidays**
Jan 1, 20 (Foundation of the Lao People's Revolutionary Army), Mar 8 (Women), 22 (Foundation of the Lao People's Revolutionary Party), May 1, Jun 1 (Children), Aug 23 (Declaration of Power), Oct 7 (Teachers), 12 (Independence), Dec 2 (National Foundation); New Year/Water Festival (Apr) (3), Boat Racing Festival (Oct), That Luang Festival (Nov), Makhabouxa (Feb), Visakhabouxa (May), Hokhaopadabdine (Aug), Hokhaosalak (Sep), Buddhist days (2).

## Political leaders

**Monarch**

| | |
|---|---|
| 1904–59 | Sisavang Vong |
| 1959–75 | Savang Vatthana |

**President**

| | |
|---|---|
| 1975–87 | Souphanouvong |
| 1987–91 | Phoumi Vongvichit |
| 1991–2 | Kaysone Phomvihane |
| 1992–8 | Nouhak Phoumsavan |
| 1998– | Khamtai Siphandon |

**Prime Minister**

| | |
|---|---|
| 1951–4 | Souvanna Phouma |
| 1954–6 | Katay Don Sasorith |
| 1956–8 | Souvanna Phouma |
| 1958–9 | Phoui Sahanikone |
| 1959–60 | Sunthone Patthamavong |
| 1960 | Kou Abhay |
| 1960 | Somsanith |
| 1960 | Souvana Phouma |
| 1960 | Sunthone Patthamavong |
| 1960 | Quinim Pholsena |
| 1960–2 | Boun Oum Na Champassac |
| 1962–75 | Souvanna Phouma |
| 1975–91 | Kaysone Phomvihane |
| 1991–8 | Khamtai Siphandon |
| 1998–2001 | Sisavath Keobounphan |
| 2001– | Boungnang Vorachit |

### Land of a Million Elephants

In 1353 King Fa Ngum unified various settlements along the Mekong River into a single state, which he named *Lane Xang*, the 'Land of A Million Elephants'. The nation's capital was at Luang Prabang, then called Xiengdong Xiengthong, but in 1560 the capital was moved to Vientiane where it was fortified. *Vientiane* means 'rampart of sandalwood'.

## LATVIA

| | |
|---|---|
| **Official name** | Republic of Latvia |
| **Local name** | Latvija; Latvijas Republika |
| **Former name** | Latvian Soviet Socialist Republic (1940–90), within the Union of Soviet Socialist Republics (USSR; 1940–91) |
| **Independence** | 1991 |
| **Area** | 63 700 sq km/24 600 sq mi |
| **Capital** | Riga; Rīga |
| **Chief towns** | Daugavpils, Liepaja |
| **Population** | 2 375 339 (2000) |
| **Nationality** | Latvian |
| **Languages** | Latvian |
| **Ethnic groups** | Latvian 57%, Russian 31%, Belarusian 5%, Ukrainian 4%, others 3% |
| **Religions** | Christianity, predominantly Lutheran Protestant, with Roman Catholic and Orthodox minorities |
| **Time zone** | GMT +2 |
| **Currency** | 1 Lat (Ls) = 100 santims |
| **Telephone** | +371 |
| **Internet** | .lv |
| **Country code** | LVA |

**Location**
A republic in north-eastern Europe, bounded to the west by the Baltic Sea; to the north-west by the Gulf of Riga; to the north by Estonia; to the east by Russia; and to the south-east by Belarus and Lithuania.

**Physical description**
A flat, glaciated area; north-west coast is indented by the Gulf of Riga; highest point is Gaizinkalns (312m/1 024ft); over 40% is forested.

**Climate**
Moderate winters; cool, rainy summers.

**National holidays**
Jan 1, May 1 (Convocation of the Constituent Assembly), Jun 23 (Ligo), 24 (Jani/Summer Solstice), Nov 18 (Proclamation of the Republic), Dec 25, 26, 31; EM, ES, GF, Mothers (2nd Sun in May).

## Political leaders

**President**

| | |
|---|---|
| 1990–3 | Anatolijs Gorbunovs |
| 1993–9 | Guntis Ulmanis |
| 1999– | Vaira Vike-Freiberga |

**Prime Minister**

| | |
|---|---|
| 1990–3 | Ivars Godmanis |
| 1993–4 | Valdis Birkavs |
| 1994–5 | Maris Gailis |
| 1995–7 | Andris Skele |
| 1997–8 | Guntars Krasts |
| 1998–9 | Vilis Kristopans |
| 1999–2000 | Andris Skele |
| 2000–2 | Andris Berzins |
| 2002– | Einars Repse |

### Crocodile Dundee?

A huge statue of an Australian saltwater crocodile is an unlikely find in the centre of a small Latvian village. But in the centre of Dundaga, north-east of Riga, is a crocodile statue that commemorates local man Arvids von Blumenfelds. Blumenfelds emigrated to Australia during World War II, where he lived in the outback and hunted crocodiles, and it is said that the film *Crocodile Dundee* (1986) was inspired by his exploits.

## LEBANON

| | |
|---|---|
| **Official name** | Republic of Lebanon |
| **Local name** | Al-Lubnān; Al-Jumhūriyya al-Lubnaniyya (Arabic), Liban; République Libanaise (French) |
| **Independence** | 1943 |
| **Area** | 10 452 sq km/4 034 sq mi |
| **Capital** | Beirut; Bayrūt |
| **Chief towns** | Tripoli, Saida, Zahle |
| **Population** | 3 537 000 (2001e) |
| **Nationality** | Lebanese |
| **Languages** | Arabic, French; English and Armenian are also spoken |
| **Ethnic groups** | Arab 95%, Armenian 4%, others 1% |
| **Religions** | Islam 69%, Christianity 30%, Druze 1% |
| **Time zone** | GMT +2 |
| **Currency** | 1 Lebanese Pound (LP, L£) = 100 piastres |
| **Telephone** | +961 |
| **Internet** | .lb |
| **Country code** | LBN |

**Location**
A republic on the eastern coast of the Mediterranean Sea, south-west Asia, bounded to the north and east by Syria, and to the south by Israel.

**Physical description**
Narrow Mediterranean coastal plain rises to the Lebanon Mountains, which extend along most of the country; peaks include the Qornet es-Sauda (3 090m/10 137ft); arid eastern slopes fall to the fertile El Beqaa plateau; Anti-Lebanon range lies in the east.

**Climate**
Mediterranean, varying with altitude, with hot, dry summers and warm, moist winters; average temperatures at Beirut are 13–27°C; much cooler and drier in the Beqaa valley and irrigation is essential.

**National holidays**
Jan 1, Feb 9 (St Maron), May 1, 6 (Martyrs), 25 (Resistance and Liberation), Aug 15, Nov 1, 22 (Independence), Dec 25; Ad (3), As, EM, GF, ER (3), NY (Muslim), PB.

## Political leaders

### President

| | |
|---|---|
| 1943–52 | Bishara Al-Khoury |
| 1952–8 | Camille Shamoun |
| 1958–64 | Fouad Shehab |
| 1964–70 | Charle Hilo |
| 1970–6 | Suleiman Frenjieh |
| 1976–82 | Elias Sarkis |
| 1982 | Bashir Gemayel |
| 1982–8 | Amin Gemayel |
| 1988–9 | *No President* |
| 1989 | Rene Muawad |
| 1989–98 | Elias Hrawi |
| 1998– | Emile Lahoud |

### Prime Minister

| | |
|---|---|
| 1943 | Riad Solh |
| 1943–4 | Henry Pharaon |
| 1944–5 | Riad Solh |
| 1945 | Abdul Hamid Karame |
| 1945–6 | Sami Solh |
| 1946 | Saadi Munla |
| 1946–51 | Riad Solh |
| 1951 | Hussein Oweini |
| 1951–2 | Abdullah Yafi |
| 1952 | Sami Solh |
| 1952 | Nazem Accari |
| 1952 | Saeb Salam |
| 1952 | Fouad Chehab |
| 1952–3 | Khaled Chehab |
| 1953 | Saeb Salam |
| 1953–5 | Abdullah Yafi |
| 1955 | Sami Solh |
| 1955–6 | Rashid Karami |
| 1956 | Abdullah Yafi |
| 1956–8 | Sami Solh |
| 1958–60 | Rashid Karami |
| 1960 | Ahmad Daouq |
| 1960–1 | Saeb Salam |
| 1961–4 | Rashid Karami |
| 1964–5 | Hussein Oweini |
| 1965–6 | Rashid Karami |
| 1966 | Abdullah Yafi |
| 1966–8 | Rashid Karami |
| 1968–9 | Abdullah Yafi |
| 1969–70 | Rashid Karami |
| 1970–3 | Saeb Salam |
| 1973 | Amin al-Hafez |
| 1973–4 | Takieddine Solh |
| 1974–5 | Rashid Solh |
| 1975 | Noureddin Rifai |
| 1975–6 | Rashid Karami |
| 1976–80 | Selim al-Hoss |
| 1980 | Takieddine Solh |
| 1980–4 | Chafiq al-Wazan |
| 1984–8 | Rashid Karami |
| 1988–90 | Michel Aoun/Selim al-Hoss |
| 1990–2 | Umar Karami |
| 1992–8 | Rafiq al-Hariri |
| 1998–2000 | Selim al-Hoss |
| 2000– | Rafiq al-Hariri |

## LESOTHO

| | | | |
|---|---|---|---|
| **Official name** | Kingdom of Lesotho | **Languages** | Sesotho, English; Zulu and Xhosa are also spoken |
| **Local name** | Lesotho; Mmuso wa Lesotho | **Ethnic groups** | Sotho 99%, others 1% |
| **Former name** | Basutoland (until 1966) | **Religions** | Christianity 94% (RC 45%, Prot 41%, others 8%), traditional beliefs 6% |
| **Independence** | 1966 | **Time zone** | GMT +2 |
| **Area** | 30 460 sq km/11 758 sq mi | **Currency** | 1 Loti (plural Maloti) (M, LSM) = 100 lisente |
| **Capital** | Maseru | **Telephone** | +266 |
| **Chief towns** | Mafeteng, Quthing | **Internet** | .ls |
| **Population** | 1 862 275 (1996) | **Country code** | LSO |
| **Nationality** | Mosotho (singular), Basotho (plural) | | |

**Location**
An African kingdom completely bounded by South Africa.

**Physical description**
Drakensberg Mountains in north-east and east include the highest peak, Thabana Ntlenyana (3 482m/11 424ft); Mulati Mountains running south to west form a steep escarpment; population mainly lives west of the highlands at altitude of 1 500–1 800m/ 4 920–5 900ft.

**Climate**
Mild, dry winters; warm summer season is Oct–Apr; lowland summer maximum temperature is 32°C, winter minimum is 7°C.

**National holidays**
Jan 1, Mar 11 (Moshoeshoe), Apr 4 (Heroes), May 1, Jul 17 (King's Birthday), Oct 4 (Independence), Dec 25, 26; A, EM, GF.

## Political leaders

**Monarch**
1966–70 Moshoeshoe II

**Head of State**
1970 Leabua Jonathan

**Monarch**
1970 'MaMohato Lerotholi *Queen Regent*
1970–90 Moshoeshoe II
1990 'MaMohato Lerotholi *Queen Regent*
1990–5 Letsie III
1996 'MaMohato Lerotholi *Queen Regent*
1995–6 Moshoeshoe II
1996– Letsie III

**Prime Minister**
1966–86 Leabua Jonathan

**Chairman of Military Council**
1986–91 Justin Metsing Lekhanya
1991–3 Elias Tutsoane Ramaema

**Prime Minister**
1993–4 Ntsu Mokhehle
1994 Hae Phoofolo (*interim*)
1994–8 Ntsu Mokhehle
1998– Pakalitha Mosisili

## LIBERIA

| | | | |
|---|---|---|---|
| **Official name** | Republic of Liberia | **Ethnic groups** | Kpelle 19%, Bassa 16%, Grebo 8%, Gio 8%, Kru 6%, Mano 6%, others 37% |
| **Local name** | Liberia | | |
| **Independence** | 1847 | | |
| **Area** | 113 370 sq km/43 760 sq mi | **Religions** | Christianity 68%, Islam 14%, traditional beliefs 10%, others 8% |
| **Capital** | Monrovia | | |
| **Chief towns** | Harper, Greenville, Buchanan, Robertsport | **Time zone** | GMT |
| **Population** | 3 099 000 (2001e) | **Currency** | 1 Liberian Dollar (L$) = 100 cents |
| **Nationality** | Liberian | **Telephone** | +231 |
| **Languages** | English; many local languages are also spoken | **Internet** | .lr |
| | | **Country code** | LBR |

**Location**
A tropical republic in West Africa, bounded to the north-west by Sierra Leone; to the north by Guinea; to the east by Côte d'Ivoire; and to the south by the Atlantic Ocean.

**Physical description**
Low coastal belt with lagoons, beaches, and mangrove marshes; rolling plateau (500–800m/1 640–2 624ft) with grasslands and forest; land rises inland to mountains; highest point is Mt Wuteve (1 380m/4 528ft); rivers cut south-west down through the plateau.

**Climate**
Equatorial climate, with high temperatures and abundant rainfall; rainfall declines from south to north; high humidity during the rainy season (Apr–Sep), especially on the coast.

**National holidays**
Jan 1, Feb 11 (Armed Forces), Mar 15 (J J Roberts), Apr 12 (Redemption), May 14 (National Unification), Jul 26 (Independence), Aug 24 (National Flag), Nov 29 (President Tubman's Birthday), Dec 25; Decoration (Mar), National Fast and Prayer (Apr), Thanksgiving (Nov).

## Political leaders

**President**

| | |
|---|---|
| 1900–4 | Garretson Wilmot Gibson |
| 1904–12 | Arthur Barclay |
| 1912–20 | Daniel Edward Howard |
| 1920–30 | Charles Dunbar Burgess King |
| 1930–43 | Edwin J Barclay |
| 1943–71 | William V S Tubman |
| 1971–80 | William Richard Tolbert |

**Chairman of People's Redemption Council**

1980–6 Samuel K Doe

**President**

1986–90 Samuel K Doe
1991–4 Amos Sawyer *Interim President*

**Chairman of Council of State**

1994–5 David Kpormakor
1996–7 Ruth Perry
1995–6 Wilton Sankawulo

**President**

| | |
|---|---|
| 1997–2003 | Charles Taylor |
| 2003 | Moses Blah *Interim President*[1] |

[1] *Charles Taylor went into exile in Aug 2003; Moses Blah handed power to a transitional government in Oct 2003.*

## *African Homeland*

Liberia is Africa's oldest republic. It was founded in 1822 by the American Colonization Society as a homeland for freed black American slaves. The capital was named Monrovia after US President James Monroe (1758–1831).

## LIBYA

| | |
|---|---|
| **Official name** | Great Socialist People's Libyan Arab Jamahiriya |
| **Local name** | Lībyā; Al-Jamāhīriyya Al-'Arabiyya Al-Lībiyya Ash-Sha'biyya Al-Ishtirākiyya |
| **Former name** | United Libyan Kingdom (1951–63), Libyan Kingdom (1963–9), Libyan Arab Republic (1969–77) |
| **Independence** | 1951 |
| **Area** | 1 758 610 sq km/678 823 sq mi |
| **Capital** | Tripoli; Tarābulus |
| **Chief towns** | Misratah, Benghazi, Tobruk |
| **Population** | 4 404 986 (1995) |
| **Nationality** | Libyan |
| **Languages** | Arabic |
| **Ethnic groups** | Arab and Berber 94%, others 6% |
| **Religions** | Islam 97% (Sunni), others 3% |
| **Time zone** | GMT +2 |
| **Currency** | 1 Libyan Dinar (LD) = 1 000 dirhams |
| **Telephone** | +218 |
| **Internet** | .ly |
| **Country code** | LBY |

**Location**
A north African state, bounded to the north-west by Tunisia; to the west by Algeria; to the south-west by Niger; to the south by Chad; to the south-east by The Sudan; to the east by Egypt; and to the north by the Mediterranean Sea.

**Physical description**
Mainly low-lying Saharan desert or semi-desert; land rises in the south to over 2 000m/6 561ft in the Tibesti Massif; highest point, Pic Bette (2 286m/7 500ft), lies on the Chad frontier; surface water is limited to infrequent oases.

**Climate**
Mediterranean climate on the coast; Tripoli, representative of the coastal region, has average maximum daily temperatures of 16–30°C; temperatures in the south are over 40°C for three months of the year.

**National holidays**
Mar 2 (Declaration of Establishment of Authority of People), 8 (National), 28 (Evacuation of British Troops), Jun 11 (Evacuation of US Troops), Jul 23 (National), Sep 1 (National), Oct 7 (Evacuation of Italian Fascists); Ad (4), ER (3), PB.

## Political leaders

**Monarch**

| | |
|---|---|
| 1951–69 | Mohammed Idris Al-Mahdi Al-Senussi |

**Chairman of Revolutionary Command Council**

| | |
|---|---|
| 1969–77 | Muammar Al-Gaddafi (Qaddafi) |

**Secretary General**

| | | | |
|---|---|---|---|
| 1977–9 | Muammar Al-Gaddafi | 1986–90 | Omar Al-Muntasir |
| 1979–84 | Abdul Ati Al-Ubaidi | 1990–4 | Abu Zayd 'Umar Durda |
| 1984–6 | Mohammed Az-Zaruq Rajab | 1994– | Zanati Mohammed Al-Zanati |

**Leader of the Revolution**

| | |
|---|---|
| 1969– | Muammar Al-Gaddafi |

# LIECHTENSTEIN

| | |
|---|---|
| **Official name** | Principality of Liechtenstein |
| **Local name** | Liechtenstein; Fürstentum Liechtenstein |
| **Independence** | 1719 (part of Holy Roman Empire to 1806) |
| **Area** | 160 sq km/62 sq mi |
| **Capital** | Vaduz |
| **Chief towns** | Schaan, Triesen, Balzers |
| **Population** | 33 000 (2001e) |
| **Nationality** | Liechtensteiner, Liechtenstein |
| **Languages** | German, spoken in the form of an Alemannic dialect |
| **Ethnic groups** | Liechtensteiner 62%, Swiss 17%, Austrian 8%, German 5%, others 8% |
| **Religions** | Christianity 88% (RC 80%, Prot 8%), others 12% |
| **Time zone** | GMT +1 |
| **Currency** | 1 Swiss Franc (SFr, SwF) = 100 centimes = 100 rappen |
| **Telephone** | +423 |
| **Internet** | .li |
| **Country code** | LIE |

**Location**

A small independent alpine principality in central Europe, lying between the Austrian state of Voralberg to the east and the Swiss cantons of St Gallen and Graubünden to the west.

**Physical description**

Bounded to the west by the River Rhine, its valley occupying c.40% of the country; much of the rest consists of forested mountains, rising to 2 599m/8 527ft in the Grauspitz.

**Climate**

Mild, influenced by a warm south wind (the *Föhn*); average maximum temperature of 20–28°C in summer.

**National holidays**

Jan 1, 2 (Berchtold), 6, Feb 2 (Candlemas), Mar 19 (St Joseph), May 1, Aug 15, Sep 8 (Nativity of Our Lady), Nov 1, Dec 8, 24, 25, 26, 31; A, C, CC, EM, ES, GF, WM, Whit Sunday.

### Commuter Heaven

Almost 13 000 of the 28 800 people employed in Liechtenstein are commuters from other countries who cross the border for work.

## Political leaders

**Prince**

| | |
|---|---|
| 1858–1929 | Johann II |
| 1929–38 | Franz von Paula |
| 1938–89 | Franz Josef II |
| 1989– | Hans Adam II |

**Prime Minister**

| | |
|---|---|
| 1928–45 | Franz Josef Hoop |
| 1945–62 | Alexander Friek |
| 1962–70 | Gérard Batliner |
| 1970–4 | Alfred J Hilbe |
| 1974–8 | Walter Kieber |
| 1978–93 | Hans Brunhart |
| 1993 | Markus Büchel |
| 1993–2001 | Mario Frick |
| 2001– | Otmar Hasler |

# LITHUANIA

| | |
|---|---|
| **Official name** | Republic of Lithuania |
| **Local name** | Lietuva; Lietuvos Respublika |
| **Former name** | Lithuanian Soviet Socialist Republic (1940–1990), within the Union of Soviet Socialist Republics (USSR; 1940–91) |
| **Independence** | 1990 (declared), 1991 (recognized) |
| **Area** | 65 200 sq km/25 167 sq mi |
| **Capital** | Vilnius |
| **Chief towns** | Kaunas, Klaipėda, Šiauliai |
| **Population** | 3 483 972 (2001) |
| **Nationality** | Lithuanian |
| **Languages** | Lithuanian |
| **Ethnic groups** | Lithuanian 81%, Russian 9%, Polish 7%, others 3% |
| **Religions** | Christianity (predominantly RC, with Lutheran Prot, Baptist and Orthodox minorities); also Judaism and Islam |
| **Time zone** | GMT +2 |
| **Currency** | 1 Litas (Lt) = 100 centas |
| **Telephone** | +370 |
| **Internet** | .lt |
| **Country code** | LTU |

**Location**
A republic in north-eastern Europe, bounded to the south-west by Poland and to the west by the Baltic Sea.

**Physical description**
Glaciated plains cover much of the area; highest point is Juozapine Hill (294m/965ft).

**Climate**
Varies between maritime and continental; wet, with moderate winters and summers.

**National holidays**
Jan 1, Feb 16 (Independence), Mar 11 (Restoration of Statehood), Jul 6 (Coronation of Mindaugas/Statehood), Aug 15, Nov 1, Dec 25, 26; ES; Mother's Day (1st Sun in May).

## Political leaders

**President**

| | |
|---|---|
| 1990–3 | Vytautas Landsbergis |
| 1993–8 | Algirdas Brazauskas |
| 1998–2003 | Valdas Adamkus |
| 2003– | Rolandas Paksas |

**Prime Minister**

| | |
|---|---|
| 1990–1 | Kazimiera Prunskienë |
| 1991 | Albertas Simenas |
| 1991–2 | Gediminas Vagnorius |
| 1992 | Aleksandras Abisala |
| 1992–3 | Bronislovas Lubys |
| 1993–6 | Adolfas Slezevicius |
| 1996 | Laurynas Stankevicius |
| 1996–9 | Gediminas Vagnorius |
| 1999 | Irena Degutienë *Acting Prime Minister* |
| 1999 | Rolandas Paksas |
| 1999 | Irena Degutienë *Acting Prime Minister* |
| 1999–2000 | Andrius Kubilius |
| 2000–1 | Rolandas Paksas |
| 2001– | Algirdas Brazauskas |

### *Amber Gold*

Amber, the yellowish fossil resin, was once known as 'Lithuania's gold' and was collected and traded for many centuries.

## LUXEMBOURG

| | |
|---|---|
| **Official name** | Grand Duchy of Luxembourg |
| **Local name** | Luxembourg; Grand-Duché de Luxembourg (French), Luxemburg; Grossherzogtum Luxemburg (German), Lëtzebuerg; Groussherzogtom Lëtzebuerg (Lëtzebuergesch) |
| **Independence** | 1867 |
| **Area** | 2 586 sq km/998 sq mi |
| **Capital** | Luxembourg; Luxembourg (French), Luxemburg (German), Lëtzebuerg (Lëtzebuergesch) |
| **Chief towns** | Esch-sur-Alzette, Dudelange, Differdange |
| **Population** | 439 539 (2001) |
| **Nationality** | Luxembourger, Luxembourg |
| **Languages** | French, German, Lëtzebuergesch |
| **Ethnic groups** | Luxembourger 72%, Portuguese 9%, Italian 5%, French 3%, Belgian 2%, German 2%, others 7% |
| **Religions** | Christianity 99% (RC 97%, Prot 2%), Judaism 1% |
| **Time zone** | GMT +1 |
| **Currency** | 1 Euro (€) = 100 cents |
| **Telephone** | +352 |
| **Internet** | .lu |
| **Country code** | LUX |

**Location**
An independent constitutional monarchy in north-western Europe, bounded to the east by Germany; to the west by Belgium; and to the south by France.

**Physical description**
Divided into two natural regions: Ösling in the north (wooded, hilly land) and flatter, more fertile Gutland; highest point is Buurgplaatz (559m/1 833ft); water resources developed by canalization of the River Mosel, hydroelectric dams on the River Our and reservoirs on the River Sûre.

**Climate**
Drier and sunnier in the south, but winters can be severe; summers and autumns are warm enough for cultivation of vines in the sheltered Mosel Valley.

**National holidays**
Jan 1, May 1, Jun 23 (National), Aug 15, Nov 1, 2, Dec 25, 26, 31; A, EM, WM, Shrove Monday.

## Political leaders

**Grand Dukes and Duchesses**

| | |
|---|---|
| 1890–1905 | Adolf of Nassau |
| 1905–12 | William IV |
| 1912–19 | Marie Adelaide |
| 1919–64 | Charlotte (*in exile* 1940–4) |
| 1964–2000 | Jean |
| 2000– | Henri |

**Prime Minister**

| | |
|---|---|
| 1889–1915 | Paul Eyschen |
| 1915 | Mathias Mongenast |
| 1915–16 | Hubert Loutsch |
| 1916–17 | Victor Thorn |
| 1917–18 | Léon Kaufmann |
| 1918–25 | Emil Reuter |
| 1925–6 | Pierre Prum |
| 1926–37 | Joseph Bech |
| 1937–53 | Pierre Dupong (*in exile* 1940–4) |
| 1953–8 | Joseph Bech |
| 1958–9 | Pierre Frieden |
| 1959–69 | Pierre Werner |
| 1969–79 | Gaston Thorn |
| 1979–84 | Pierre Werner |
| 1984–95 | Jacques Santer |
| 1995– | Jean-Claude Juncker |

### *On the Road*

Despite its relatively small size, Luxembourg has the highest number of passenger cars per person in the European Union, with 643 cars per 1 000 inhabitants. Greece has the fewest, at only 304 cars per 1 000 people, while the UK has 419 per 1 000.

**MACAO** *see* **CHINA**

## MACEDONIA

| | |
|---|---|
| **Official name** | Former Yugoslav Republic of Macedonia (FYRM or FYR Macedonia; *international name*); Republic of Macedonia (*local name*) |
| **Local name** | Makedonija; Republika Makedonija, Poranesna Jugoslovenska Republika Makedonija |
| **Former name** | formerly part of Kingdom of Serbs, Croats and Slovenes (until 1929), Kingdom of Yugoslavia (1929–41), Federal People's Republic of Yugoslavia (1945–63), Socialist Federal People's Republic of Yugoslavia (1963–91) |
| **Independence** | 1991 |
| **Area** | 25 713 sq km/9 925 sq mi |
| **Capital** | Skopje |
| **Chief towns** | Bitola, Gostivar, Tetovo, Kumanovo |
| **Population** | 1 949 644 (1994) |
| **Nationality** | Macedonian |
| **Languages** | Macedonian, Albanian |
| **Ethnic groups** | Macedonian 66%, Albanian 23%, Turkish 4%, others 7% |
| **Religions** | Christianity 67% (Orthodox), Islam 30%, others 3% |
| **Time zone** | GMT +1 |
| **Currency** | 1 Denar (D, den) = 100 deni |
| **Telephone** | +389 |
| **Internet** | .mk |
| **Country code** | MKD |

**Location**
A republic in southern Europe, bounded to the west by Albania; to the south by Greece; to the east by Bulgaria; and to the north by Serbia and Montenegro.

**Physical description**
Mountainous, covered with deep basins and valleys; bisected by the River Vardar; highest point is Golem Korab (Maja e Korabit; 2 753m/9 032ft) on the Albanian border.

**Climate**
Cold winters and warm, dry summers.

**National holidays**
Jan 1, 6 (Orthodox Christmas) (2), Mar 8 (Women), May 1, 24 (SS Cyril and Methodius), Aug 2 (St Elijah's Uprising), Sep 8 (Independence), Dec 25, 26; Ad, EM, ER, Old NY.

See **Serbia and Montenegro** for political leaders of the former Yugoslavia.

## Political leaders

**President**

| | |
|---|---|
| 1991–5 | Kiro Gligorov |
| 1995–8 | Stojan Andov *Acting President* |
| 1998–9 | Kiro Gligorov |
| 1999– | Boris Trajkovski |

**Prime Minister**

| | |
|---|---|
| 1991–2 | Branko Crvenkovski |
| 1992–6 | Petar Gosev |
| 1996–8 | Branko Crvenkovski |
| 1998–2002 | Ljubco Georgievski |
| 2002– | Branko Crvenkovski |

# MADAGASCAR

| | |
|---|---|
| **Official name** | Republic of Madagascar |
| **Local name** | Madagasikara; Repoblikan'i Madagasikara (Malagasy), Madagascar; République du Madagascar (French) |
| **Former name** | Malagasy Republic (1958–75), Democratic Republic of Madagascar (until 1992) |
| **Independence** | 1960 |
| **Area** | 592 800 sq km/228 821 sq mi |
| **Capital** | Antananarivo |
| **Chief towns** | Toamasina, Mahajanga, Fianarantsoa, Antsiranana, Toliara |
| **Population** | 16 439 000 (2001e) |
| **Nationality** | Malagasy |
| **Languages** | Malagasy, French |
| **Ethnic groups** | Merina 26%, Betsimisaraka 16%, Betsileo 12%, Tsimihety 7%, Sakalava 7%, others 32% |
| **Religions** | traditional beliefs 52%, Christianity 42% (RC 24%, Prot 18%), Islam 6% |
| **Time zone** | GMT +3 |
| **Currency** | 1 Ariary (A) = 5 Iraimbilanja *Note: The Ariary replaced the Malagasy Franc of 100 centimes in Jul 2003.* |
| **Telephone** | +261 |
| **Internet** | .mg |
| **Country code** | MDG |

**Location**
An island republic in the Indian Ocean, separated from East Africa by the Mozambique Channel.

**Physical description**
Ridge of mountains runs north to south, rising to 2 876m/9 436ft at Maromokotra; cliffs to the east drop down to a coastal plain through tropical forest; a terraced descent to the west through savannah to the coast, which is heavily indented in the north.

**Climate**
Temperate climate in the highlands; tropical coastal region.

**National holidays**
Jan 1, Mar 29 (Memorial), May 1, Jun 26 (Independence), Aug 15, Nov 1, Dec 25, 30 (National); A, EM, GF, WM.

## Political leaders

**President**

| | |
|---|---|
| 1960–72 | Philibert Tsiranana |
| 1972–5 | Gabriel Ramanantsoa |
| 1975 | Richard Ratsimandrava |
| 1975 | Gilles Andriamahazo |
| 1975–93 | Didier Ratsiraka |
| 1993–7 | Albert Zafy |
| 1997–2002 | Didier Ratsiraka |
| 2002– | Marc Ravalomanana |

**Prime Minister**

| | |
|---|---|
| 1960–75 | *As President* |
| 1975–6 | Joël Rakotomala |
| 1976–7 | Justin Rakotoriaina |
| 1977–88 | Désiré Rakotoarijaona |
| 1988–91 | Victor Ramahatra |
| 1991–3 | Guy Willy Razanamasy |
| 1993–5 | Francisque Ravony |
| 1995–6 | Emmanuel Rakotovahiny |
| 1996–7 | Norbert Ratsirahonana |
| 1997–8 | Paskal Rakotmavo |
| 1998–2002 | Tantely Andrianarivo |
| 2002– | Jacques Sylla |

**MADEIRA** *see* **PORTUGAL**

## MALAWI

| | | | |
|---|---|---|---|
| **Official name** | Republic of Malawi | **Languages** | English, Chichewa |
| **Local name** | Dziko la Malaŵi | **Ethnic groups** | Maravi 59%, Lomwe 20%, Yao 13%, Ngoni 6%, others 2% |
| **Former name** | Nyasaland (until 1964), part of the Federation of Rhodesia and Nyasaland (1953–63) | **Religions** | Christianity 70% (Prot 50%, RC 20%), Islam 21%, traditional beliefs 9% |
| **Independence** | 1964 | **Time zone** | GMT +2 |
| **Area** | 118 484 sq km/45 735 sq mi | **Currency** | 1 Kwacha (MK) = 100 tambala |
| **Capital** | Lilongwe | **Telephone** | +265 |
| **Chief towns** | Blantyre, Zomba, Limbe, Salima | **Internet** | .mw |
| **Population** | 9 933 868 (1998) | **Country code** | MWI |
| **Nationality** | Malawian | | |

**Location**
A republic in south-eastern Africa, bounded to the south-west and south-east by Mozambique; to the east by Lake Nyasa (Lake Malawi); to the north by Tanzania; and to the west by Zambia.

**Physical description**
Crossed north to south by the Great Rift Valley in which lies Africa's third-largest lake, Lake Nyasa (Lake Malawi); high plateaux on either side (900–1 200m/2 950–3 937ft); highlands in the south rise to 3 000m/9 840ft at Sapitwa Peak on Mt Mulanje.

**Climate**
Tropical climate in the south, with high year-round temperatures, 28–37°C; more moderate temperatures in centre; higher rainfall in the mountains overlooking Lake Nyasa.

**National holidays**
Jan 1, 15 (Chilembwe), Mar 3 (Martyrs), May 1, Jun 14 (Freedom), Jul 6 (Independence), Dec 25, 26; EM, ER, GF, Mothers (2nd Mon in Oct).

## Political leaders

**President**

| | |
|---|---|
| 1966–94 | Hastings Kamuzu Banda |
| 1994– | Bakili Muluzi |

### Get By in Chichewa

The Chichewa word for *hello* is *moni*, and *how are you?* is *muli bwanji?* Other useful words include *madzi* for *water*, *chakudya* for *food* and *chimbudzi* for *toilet*. If you hear a shout of *mkango*, it is either time to grab your camera or run for your life – it means *lion*.

## MALAYSIA

| | |
|---|---|
| **Official name** | Federation of Malaysia |
| **Local name** | Malaysia |
| **Independence** | 1957 |
| **Area** | 329 749 sq km/127 283 sq mi |
| **Capital** | Kuala Lumpur |
| **Chief towns** | George Town, Ipoh, Malacca, Johor Baharu, Kuching, Kota Kinabalu |
| **Population** | 23 274 690 (2000) |
| **Nationality** | Malaysian |
| **Languages** | Bahasa Malaysia (Malay); Chinese, English, Tamil and local languages are also spoken |
| **Ethnic groups** | Malay and indigenous 58%, Chinese 26%, Indian 7%, others 9% |
| **Religions** | Islam 53%, Buddhism 17%, Chinese folk religion 12%, Hinduism 7%, Christianity 6%, others 5% |
| **Time zone** | GMT +8 |
| **Currency** | 1 Malaysian Ringgit (dollar) (M$) = 100 cents |
| **Telephone** | +60 |
| **Internet** | .my |
| **Country code** | MYS |

# MALAYSIA

**Location**
An independent federation of states in south-east Asia. It includes mainland peninsular Malaysia, bounded to the north by Thailand and linked by a causeway to Singapore in the south, and also Sarawak and Sabah on the northern coast of the Indonesian island of Borneo, which completely enclose the state of Brunei Darussalam.

**Physical description**
Mainland peninsula (700km/435mi long) of mountains with narrow coastal plains; mostly tropical rainforest and mangrove swamp; Sarawak has a narrow, swampy coastal belt and mountainous interior; Sabah has a deeply indented coastline and narrow coastal plain, rising sharply into mountains reaching 4 094m/13 431ft at Mt Kinabalu, Malaysia's highest peak.

**Climate**
Tropical climate, with highest temperatures in coastal areas; strongly influenced by monsoon winds; high humidity.

**National holidays**
Jan 1 (*most states*), May 1, Jun 7 (Head of State's Birthday), Aug 31 (National), Dec 25; Ad (2), D (*most states*), ER (2), NY (Chinese) (Jan/Feb), NY (Muslim), PB, Wesak; *several local festivals*.

## Political leaders

### Chief of State (Yang di-Pertuan Agong)

| | |
|---|---|
| 1957–63 | Abdul Rahman |
| 1963–5 | Syed Putra Jamalullah |
| 1965–70 | Ismail Nasiruddin Shah |
| 1970–5 | Abdul Halim Muadzam Shah |
| 1975–9 | Yahya Petra Ibrahim |
| 1979–84 | Haji Ahmad Shah Al-Mustain Billah |
| 1984–9 | Mahmood Iskandar Shah |
| 1989–94 | Azlan Muhibuddin Shah |
| 1994–9 | Jaafar Ibni Abdul Rahman |
| 1999–2001 | Salehuddin Abdul Aziz Shah |
| 2001 | Mizal Zainal Abidin *Acting Chief of State* |
| 2001– | Syed Sirajuddin Syed Putra Jamalullail |

### Prime Minister

| | |
|---|---|
| 1957–70 | Abdul Rahman Putra Al-Haj |
| 1970–6 | Abdul Razak bin Hussein |
| 1976–9 | Haji Hussein bin Onn |
| 1979–97 | Mahathir bin Mohamad |
| 1997 | Anwar Ibrahim *Acting Prime Minister* |
| 1997– | Mahathir bin Mohamad |

### Malaysian Mud

The name of Malaysia's capital city, *Kuala Lumpur*, comes from Malay words meaning 'muddy estuary'.

## MALDIVES

| | | | |
|---|---|---|---|
| **Official name** | Republic of Maldives | **Ethnic groups** | Sinhalese majority; Arab and African minorities |
| **Local name** | Dhivehi Raajje; Dhivehi Rājjē Jumhūriyyā | **Religions** | Islam 100% (Sunni) |
| **Former name** | Maldive Islands | **Time zone** | GMT +5 |
| **Independence** | 1965 | **Currency** | 1 Rufiyaa (MRf, Rf) = 100 laarees |
| **Area** | 300 sq km/120 sq mi | **Telephone** | +960 |
| **Capital** | Malé; Daviyani | **Internet** | .mv |
| **Population** | 270 101 (2000) | **Country code** | MDV |
| **Nationality** | Maldivian | | |
| **Languages** | Dhivehi; English is spoken widely | | |

**Location**
A republic consisting of an island archipelago in the Indian Ocean. Fua Mulaku Island is the largest island, while Huvadhoo Atoll is the largest atoll.

**Physical description**
Small, low-lying islands, no more than 1.8m/6ft above sea level, with sandy beaches fringed with coconut palms. Of the 1 190 islands, spread over 26 coral atolls, fewer than 200 are inhabited.

**Climate**
Generally warm and humid; affected by south-west monsoons from Apr to Oct; average daily temperature is 22°C.

**National holidays**
Jan 1, May 3 (National), Jul 26 (Independence) (2), Nov 3 (Victory), 11 (Republic); Ad (4), Ar, ER (3), NY (Muslim), PB, R, Day the Maldives Embraced Islam.

### Political leaders

**Monarch (Sultan)**

1954–68 Mohammed Farid Didi

**President**

1968–78 Ibrahim Nasir
1978– Maumoon Abdul Gayoom

### *Maldives in the Dictionary*

The Maldives have contributed just one word to the English language: *atoll*, meaning a coral island with a circular belt of coral enclosing a central lagoon. The language of the Maldives, Dhivehi, is unusual in that it has no word for *hello* or *goodbye*. *Kihineh* is used instead of *hello*, meaning *how are you?*, while *dhanee!* or *I'm going!* is often used instead of *goodbye*.

## MALI

| | | | |
|---|---|---|---|
| **Official name** | Republic of Mali | **Languages** (cont.) | are spoken widely |
| **Local name** | Mali; République du Mali | **Ethnic groups** | Bambara 34%, Fulani 17%, Senufo 12%, Soninke 8%, Songhai 7%, Tuareg 7%, Malinke 6%, others 9% |
| **Former name** | French Sudan (until 1959), Mali Federation (until 1960) | **Religions** | Islam 85% (mostly Sunni), traditional beliefs 14%, Christianity 1% |
| **Independence** | 1960 | **Time zone** | GMT |
| **Area** | 1 240 192 sq km/478 714 sq mi | **Currency** | 1 CFA Franc (CFAFr) = 100 centimes |
| **Capital** | Bamako | **Telephone** | +223 |
| **Chief towns** | Ségou, Mopti, Sikasso, Kayes, Gao, Timbuktu | **Internet** | .ml |
| **Population** | 9 790 492 (1998) | **Country code** | MLI |
| **Nationality** | Malian | | |
| **Languages** | French; Bambara and other local languages are spoken widely | | |

**Location**
A landlocked republic in West Africa, bounded to the north-east by Algeria; to the north-west by Mauritania; to the west by Senegal; to the south-west by Guinea; to the south by Côte d'Ivoire; to the south-east by Burkina Faso; and to the east by Niger.

**Physical description**
On the fringe of the Sahara; lower part of the Hoggar massif is located in the north; arid plains between 300m/984ft and 500m/1 640ft; featureless desert land in the north with sand dunes; highest point is Hombori Tondo (1 155m/3 789ft); mainly savannah in the south.

**Climate**
Hot, dry climate with rainfall increasing from north to south; in the south the rainfall season lasts for five months (Jun–Oct); almost no annual average rainfall in the Saharan north.

**National holidays**
Jan 1, 20 (Memorial), Mar 26 (Martyrs), May 1, 25 (African Unity), Sep 22 (National), Dec 25; Ad, ER, PB, R.

## Political leaders

**President**

| | |
|---|---|
| 1960–8 | Modibo Keita |
| 1968–91 | Moussa Traoré[1] |
| 1991–2 | Amadou Toumani Touré[2] |
| 1992–2002 | Alpha Oumar Konaré |
| 2002– | Amadou Toumani Touré |

**Prime Minister**

| | |
|---|---|
| 1986–88 | Mamadou Dembelé |
| 1988–91 | *No Prime Minister* |
| 1991–2 | Soumana Sacko |
| 1992–3 | Younoussi Touré |
| 1993–4 | Abdoulaye Sekou Sow |
| 1994–2000 | Ibrahim Boubacar Keita |
| 2000–2 | Mande Sidibe |
| 2002– | Ahmed Mohamed ag Hamani |

**Far, Far Away ...**

Timbuktu is often used informally to mean any very distant place, but it is actually a real town in northern Mali, near the River Niger.

[1] *Chairman of Military Committee for the National Liberation until 1969; Head of State until 1979; President from 1979.*

[2] *Chairman of Military Committee for the Salvation of the People.*

# MALTA

| | | | |
|---|---|---|---|
| **Official name** | Republic of Malta | **Ethnic groups** | Maltese 98%, British 2% |
| **Local name** | Malta; Repubblika ta' Malta | **Religions** | Christianity 98% (RC 97%, Prot 1%), others 1%, none/unaffiliated 1% |
| **Independence** | 1964 | **Time zone** | GMT +1 |
| **Area** | 316 sq km/122 sq mi | **Currency** | 1 Maltese Lira (LM) = 100 cents = 1 000 mils |
| **Capital** | Valletta | **Telephone** | +356 |
| **Chief towns** | Sliema, Birkirkara, Qormi, Rabat, Victoria | **Internet** | .mt |
| **Population** | 395 000 (2001e) | **Country code** | MLT |
| **Nationality** | Maltese | | |
| **Languages** | English, Maltese; there are many Arabic words in the local vocabulary | | |

**Location**
An archipelago republic in the central Mediterranean Sea.

**Physical description**
Generally low-lying, rising to 253m/830ft; no rivers or mountains; well-indented coastline.

**Climate**
Dry summers and mild winters; average daily winter temperature is 13°C.

**National holidays**
Jan 1, Feb 10 (St Paul's Shipwreck), Mar 19 (St Joseph), 31 (Freedom), May 1, Jun 7 (Sette Giugno), 29 (SS Peter and Paul), Aug 15, Sep 8 (Our Lady of the Victories), 21 (Independence), Dec 8, 13 (Republic), 25; GF.

## Political leaders

**President**

| | |
|---|---|
| 1974–6 | Anthony Mamo |
| 1976–81 | Anton Buttigieg |
| 1981–2 | Albert Hyzler *Acting President* |
| 1982–7 | Agatha Barbara |
| 1987–9 | Paul Xuereb *Acting President* |
| 1989–94 | Vincent Tabone |
| 1994–9 | Ugo Mifsud Bonnici |
| 1999– | Guido de Marco |

**Prime Minister**

| | |
|---|---|
| 1962–71 | G Borg Olivier |
| 1971–84 | Dom Mintoff |
| 1984–7 | Carmelo Mifsud Bonnici |
| 1987–96 | Edward Fenech Adami |
| 1996–8 | Alfred Sant |
| 1998– | Edward Fenech Adami |

### *Maltese Medal*

In 1942 Malta was awarded the George Cross for its resistance to heavy air attacks in World War II.

**MALVINAS** *see* **FALKLAND ISLANDS** *under* **UNITED KINGDOM**

**MAN, ISLE OF** *see* **UNITED KINGDOM**

**MARIANA ISLANDS, NORTHERN** *see* **UNITED STATES OF AMERICA**

## MARSHALL ISLANDS

| | | | |
|---|---|---|---|
| **Official name** | Republic of the Marshall Islands (RMI) | **Languages** | Marshallese, English |
| **Local name** | Marshall Islands, Majol | **Ethnic groups** | Micronesian 97%, others 3% |
| **Former name** | formerly part of the Trust Territory of the Pacific Islands (1947–79) | **Religions** | Christianity 97% (Prot 90%, RC 7%), others 3% |
| **Independence** | 1986 | **Time zone** | GMT +12 |
| **Area** | c.180 sq km/70 sq mi | **Currency** | 1 US Dollar ($, US$) = 100 cents |
| **Capital** | Majuro | **Telephone** | +692 |
| **Population** | 50 848 (1999) | **Internet** | .mh |
| **Nationality** | Marshallese | **Country code** | MHL |

**Location**
An independent archipelago republic in the central Pacific Ocean.

**Physical description**
Coral limestone and sand islands, atolls and reefs, with few natural resources; low-lying, rising to no more than 10m/33ft.

**Climate**
Hot and humid; wet season is from May to Nov; occasional typhoons.

**National holidays**
Jan 1, Mar 1 (Nuclear Victims), May 1 (Constitution), Nov 17 (President), Dec 25; Fishermen (1st Fri in Jul), Workers (1st Fri in Sep), Customs (last Fri in Sep), Thanksgiving (3rd Thur in Nov), Gospel (1st Fri in Dec).

### Political leaders

**President**

| | |
|---|---|
| 1979–96 | Amata Kabua |
| 1996–7 | Kunio Lemari *Acting President* |
| 1997–2000 | Imata Kabua |
| 2000– | Kessai Note |

### The Real Bikini

The bikini swimsuit was named after Bikini Atoll in the Marshall Islands. The atoll was the scene of atom-bomb experiments in the late 1940s, and the bikini's effects on men were reputed to be similar. The real Bikini Atoll covers 6 sq km/2.3 sq mi of land and 594 sq km/229 sq mi of lagoon, and has 36 islets. The atoll's name is slightly different in Marshallese – had the word come into English in its original form, people might now be wearing a *pikinni* instead.

**MARTINIQUE** *see* **FRANCE**

## MAURITANIA

| | | | |
|---|---|---|---|
| **Official name** | Islamic Republic of Mauritania | **Languages** | Arabic; French is also widely spoken |
| **Local name** | Mauritanie; République Islamique de Mauritanie (French), Mūrītāniyā; Al-Jumhūriyya al-Islāmiyya al-Mawrītāniyya (Arabic) | **Ethnic groups** | Arab and Berber 72%, Wolof 6%, Tukulor 5%, Soninke 3%, Fulani 1%, others 13% |
| **Independence** | 1960 | **Religions** | Islam 99%, others 1% |
| **Area** | 1 029 920 sq km/397 549 sq mi | **Time zone** | GMT |
| **Capital** | Nouakchott | **Currency** | 1 Ouguiya (U, UM) = 5 khoums |
| **Chief towns** | Nouadhibou, Atar | **Telephone** | +222 |
| **Population** | 2 548 157 (2000) | **Internet** | .mr |
| **Nationality** | Mauritanian | **Country code** | MRT |

**Location**
A republic in north-west Africa, bounded to the south-west by Senegal; to the south and east by Mali; to the north-east by Algeria; to the north by Western Sahara; and to the west by the Atlantic Ocean.

**Physical description**
Saharan zone covers two thirds of the country with sand dunes, mountainous plateaux and occasional oases; coastal area has minimal rainfall and little vegetation; Senegal River is the chief agricultural region; highest point is Kediet Idjill (915m/3 002ft).

**Climate**
Dry and tropical with sparse rainfall; temperatures can rise to over 49°C in the Sahara.

**National holidays**
Jan 1, May 1, 25 (Celebration of the African Union), Nov 28 (National); Ad, ER, NY (Muslim), PB.

## Political leaders

**President**

1961–78 Mokhtar Ould Daddah
1978–9 Mustapha Ould Mohammed Salek
1979–80 Mohammed Mahmoud Ould Ahmed Louly
1980–4 Mohammed Khouna Ould Haydallah
1984– Maaouya Ould Sid'Ahmed Taya

**Prime Minister**

1992–6 Sidi Mohammed Ould Boubaker
1996–7 Cheikh el Avia Ould Mohammed Khouna
1997–8 Mohammed Lemine Ould Guig
1998–2003 Cheikh el Avia Ould Mohammed Khouna
2003– Sghaïr Ould M'Bareck

### *Place of Winds*

When Mauritania became independent in 1960 it lacked a capital, so a new city was built on the coast. It was named Nouakchott, supposedly meaning 'place of winds'.

## MAURITIUS

| | | | |
|---|---|---|---|
| **Official name** | Republic of Mauritius | | |
| **Local name** | Mauritius | **Religions** | Hinduism 52%, Christianity 28% (RC 26%, Prot 2%), Islam 17%, others 3% |
| **Independence** | 1968 | **Time zone** | GMT +4 |
| **Area** | 1 865 sq km/720 sq mi | **Currency** | 1 Mauritian Rupee (MR, MauRe) = 100 cents |
| **Capital** | Port Louis | **Telephone** | +230 |
| **Population** | 1 178 848 (2000) | **Internet** | .mu |
| **Nationality** | Mauritian | **Country code** | MUS |
| **Languages** | English; French is also spoken | | |
| **Ethnic groups** | Indo-Mauritian 68%, Creole 27%, others 5% | | |

**Location**
A small island nation in the Indian Ocean.

**Physical description**
Volcanic, with a central plateau; highest peak is Piton de la Petite Rivière Noire (828m/2 717ft); dry, lowland coast, with wooded savannah, mangrove swamp and bamboo; surrounded by coral reefs enclosing lagoons and sandy beaches.

**Climate**
Tropical-maritime, with temperatures averaging 22–26°C; wide variation in rainfall with most rain falling in the central plateau.

**National holidays**
Jan 1, 2, Feb 1 (Abolition of Slavery), Mar 12 (National), May 1, Nov 1, 2 (Arrival of Indentured Labourers), Dec 25; D, Chinese Spring Festival (Jan/Feb), ER, Ganesh Chathurti (Aug/Sep), Maha Shivaratree (Feb/Mar), Ougadi (Mar/Apr), Thaipoosam Cavadee (Jan/Feb).

## Political leaders

Chief of State until 1992: British monarch, represented by Governor General.

**Prime Minister**

1968–82 Seewoosagur Ramgoolam
1982–95 Anerood Jugnauth
1995–2000 Navin Ramgoolam
2000– Anerood Jugnauth

**President**

1992 Veerasamy Ringadoo
1992–2002 Cassam Uteem
2002 Angidi Chettiar
2002 Arianga Pillay *Interim President*
2002– Karl Offmann

### *Dead as a Dodo*

Perhaps the most famous native of Mauritius was the dodo, a clumsy flightless bird about the size of a turkey. The dodo was a source of amusement to explorers who first visited Mauritius in the early 16c, but when the Dutch set up permanent settlements on the island its demise was swift; hunting and newly-introduced animal predators meant it became extinct about the end of the 17c. *Dodo* comes from the Portuguese word *doudo*, meaning silly.

**MAYOTTE** *see* **FRANCE**

# MEXICO

| | | | |
|---|---|---|---|
| **Official name** | United Mexican States | **Languages** | Spanish; Native American languages are also spoken |
| **Local name** | México; Estados Unidos Méxicanos | **Ethnic groups** | mestizo 60%, Amerindian 25%, European 12%, others 3% |
| **Independence** | 1821 | **Religions** | Christianity 96% (RC 93%, Prot 3%), others 3%, none/unaffiliated 1% |
| **Area** | 1 978 800 sq km/763 817 sq mi | **Time zone** | GMT –6/8 |
| **Capital** | Mexico City; Ciudad de México | **Currency** | 1 Mexican Peso (Mex$) = 100 centavos |
| **Chief towns** | Guadalajara, Léon, Monterrey, Ciudad Juárez | **Telephone** | +52 |
| **Population** | 97 483 412 (2000) | **Internet** | .mx |
| **Nationality** | Mexican | **Country code** | MEX |

**Location**
A federal republic in the south of North America, bounded to the north by the United States of America; to the west by the Gulf of California; to the west and south-west by the Pacific Ocean; to the south by Guatemala and Belize; and to the east by the Gulf of Mexico.

**Physical description**
Bisected by the Tropic of Cancer; narrow coastal plains rise steeply to a central plateau, reaching a height of c.2 400m/7 874ft around Mexico City; volcanic peaks to the south, notably Citlaltépetl (also called Volcan Pico de Orizaba; 5 699m/18 697ft); Yucatán peninsula lowlands in south-east; subject to very severe earthquakes.

**Climate**
Great climatic variation between the coastlands and mountains; desert or semi-desert conditions in the north-west; typically tropical climate on the east coast; generally wetter on the south coast; extreme temperature variations in the north, very cold in winter, very warm in summer.

**National holidays**
Jan 1, Feb 5 (Constitution), Mar 21 (Birthday of Benito Juárez), May 1, 5 (Puebla Battle), Sep 1 (Presidential Report), 16 (Independence), Oct 12 (Columbus), Nov 2, 20 (Mexican Revolution), Dec 12 (Our Lady of Guadaloupe), 25, 31; HT, GF.

## Political leaders

**President**

| | |
|---|---|
| 1876–1911 | Porfirio Diaz |
| 1911 | Francisco León de la Barra |
| 1911–13 | Francisco I Madero |
| 1913–14 | Victoriano Huerta |
| 1914 | Francisco Carvajal |
| 1914 | Venustiano Carranza |
| 1914–15 | Eulalio Gutiérrez *Provisional President* |
| 1915 | Roque González Garza *Provisional President* |
| 1915 | Francisco Lagos Chazaro *Provisional President* |
| 1915–20 | Venustiano Carranza |
| 1920 | Adolfo de la Huerta |
| 1920–4 | Alvaro Obregón |
| 1924–8 | Plutarco Elías Calles |
| 1928–30 | Emilio Portes Gil |
| 1930–2 | Pascual Ortíz Rubio |
| 1932–4 | Abelardo L Rodríguez |
| 1934–40 | Lazaro Cardenas |

| | |
|---|---|
| 1940–6 | Manuel Avila Camacho |
| 1946–52 | Miguel Alemán |
| 1952–8 | Adolfo Ruiz Cortines |
| 1958–64 | Adolfo López Mateos |
| 1964–70 | Gustavo Díaz Ordaz |
| 1970–6 | Luis Echeverría |
| 1976–82 | José López Portillo |
| 1982–8 | Miguel de la Madrid Hurtado |
| 1988–94 | Carlos Salinas de Gortari |
| 1994–2000 | Ernesto Zedillo Ponce de León |
| 2000– | Vincente Fox Quesada |

### Aztec Capital

Mexico was at the centre of Mesoamerican civilizations for over 2 500 years. The Olmecs were based at La Venta; Zapotecs near Oaxaca; Mixtecs at Mitla; Toltecs at Tula; and Mayas in the Yucatán. Mexico City is the oldest capital in continental America and is built on the site of the Aztec capital, Tenochtitlán. In 1521 the Aztec city was captured and destroyed by the Spaniards under Hernán Cortés, and the new city built on the site.

## MICRONESIA, FEDERATED STATES OF

| | |
|---|---|
| **Official name** | Federated States of Micronesia (FSM) |
| **Local name** | Micronesia |
| **Former name** | formerly part of the Trust Territory of the Pacific Islands (1947–79) |
| **Independence** | 1991 |
| **Area** | 700 sq km/270 sq mi |
| **Capital** | Palikir (on Pohnpei) |
| **Chief towns** | Kolonia, Colonia, Weno, Lelu |
| **Population** | 105 506 (1994) |
| **Nationality** | Micronesian; also Chuukese, Kosraen, Pohnpeian, Yapese |
| **Languages** | English; eight major indigenous languages are also spoken |
| **Ethnic groups** | Chuukese 42%, Pohnpeian 27%, others 31% |
| **Religions** | Christianity 97% (RC 50%, Prot 47%), others 3% |
| **Time zone** | GMT +10/11 |
| **Currency** | 1 US Dollar (US$) = 100 cents |
| **Telephone** | +691 |
| **Internet** | .fm |
| **Country code** | FSM |

**Location**
A republic consisting of a group of 607 islands divided into four states – Yap, Chuuk (formerly Truk), Pohnpei (formerly Ponape) and Kosrae (formerly Kosaie) – in the western Pacific Ocean.

**Physical description**
Islands vary geologically, from low, coral atolls to high mountainous islands; Pohnpei, Kosrae and Chuuk have volcanic outcroppings; highest point is Totolom (791m/2 595ft).

**Climate**
Tropical; heavy rainfall all year round, especially in the eastern islands; subject to typhoons.

**National holidays**
Jan 1, May 10 (Proclamation of the Federated States of Micronesia), Oct 24 (United Nations Day), Nov 4 (National Day), Dec 25; *additional days vary between states*.

## Political leaders

**President**

| | | | |
|---|---|---|---|
| 1979–87 | Tosiwo Nakayama | 1997–9 | Jacob Nena |
| 1987–91 | John Haglelgam | 1999–2003 | Leo Falcam |
| 1991–7 | Bailey Olter | 2003– | Joseph Urusemal |

### *Stone Money*

The islanders of the Micronesian state of Yap still use traditional stone money as legal tender as well as the US dollar. The 'coins' are huge, doughnut-shaped stone discs, some taller than a person.

# MOLDOVA

| | | | |
|---|---|---|---|
| **Official name** | Republic of Moldova | **Population** | 4 276 000 (2001e) |
| **Local name** | Moldova; Republica Moldova | **Nationality** | Moldovan |
| | | **Languages** | Moldovan |
| **Former name** | formerly part of Romania (1918–40), Moldavia or Moldavian Soviet Socialist Republic (until 1991), within the Union of Soviet Socialist Republics (USSR; 1922–91) | **Ethnic groups** | Moldovan 65%, Ukrainian 14%, Russian 13%, Gagauzi 4%, Jewish 2%, others 2% |
| | | **Religions** | Christianity 98% (Orthodox), Judaism 2% |
| **Independence** | 1991 | **Time zone** | GMT +2 |
| **Area** | 33 700 sq km/13 000 sq mi | **Currency** | 1 Leu (Mld) = 100 bani |
| | | **Telephone** | +373 |
| **Capital** | Chisinau, Chişinău | **Internet** | .md |
| **Chief towns** | Tiraspol, Bendery, Beltsy | **Country code** | MDA |

**Location**
A republic in eastern Europe, bounded to the west by Romania, and to the north, east and south by the Ukraine.

**Physical description**
Terrain consists of a hilly plain, reaching a height of 429m/1 407ft at Mt Balanesti in the centre.

**Climate**
Moderate winters; warm summers.

**National holidays**
Jan 1, 7 (Orthodox Christmas) (2), Mar 8 (Women), May 1, 9 (Victory), Aug 27 (Independence), 31 (Limba Noastra/Our Language); EM, ES; 1st Mon after Easter.

## Political leaders

**President**

| | |
|---|---|
| 1991–6 | Mircea Snegur |
| 1996–2001 | Petru Lucinschi |
| 2001– | Vladimir Voronin |

**Prime Minister**

| | | | |
|---|---|---|---|
| 1991–2 | Valery Muravsky | 1999 | Ion Sturza |
| 1992–7 | Andrei Sangheli | 1999–2001 | Dumitru Barghis |
| 1997–9 | Ion Ciubuc | 2001– | Vasile Tarlev |

## MONACO

| | | | |
|---|---|---|---|
| **Official name** | Principality of Monaco | **Ethnic groups** | French 59%, Monégasque 17%, Italian 16%, others 8% |
| **Local name** | Monaco; Principauté de Monaco | **Religions** | Christianity 95% (RC 90%, Prot 5%), others 5% |
| **Area** | 1.9 sq km/0.75 sq mi | **Time zone** | GMT +1 |
| **Capital** | Monaco | **Currency** | 1 Euro (€) = 100 cents |
| **Chief towns** | Monte Carlo | **Telephone** | +377 |
| **Population** | 34 000 (2001e) | **Internet** | .mc |
| **Nationality** | Monégasque or Monacan | **Country code** | MCO |
| **Languages** | French | | |

**Location**
A small principality on the Mediterranean Riviera, close to the Italian frontier with France.

**Physical description**
Hilly, rugged and rocky, rising to 63m/206ft; almost entirely urban.

**Climate**
Warm, dry summers and mild winters.

**National holidays**
Jan 1, 27 (St Devote), May 1, Aug 15, Nov 1, 19 (National), Dec 8, 25; A, CC, EM, WM.

### Political leaders

**Head of State (Monarch)**

| | |
|---|---|
| 1889–1922 | Albert |
| 1922–49 | Louis II |
| 1949– | Rainier III |

## MONGOLIA

| | | | |
|---|---|---|---|
| **Official name** | State of Mongolia | **Nationality** | Mongolian |
| **Local name** | Mongol Uls | **Languages** | Khalkha Mongolian |
| **Former name** | Outer Mongolia (until 1924); People's Republic of Mongolia (1924–92) | **Ethnic groups** | Mongol 90%, Kazakh 4%, Chinese 2%, Russian 2%, others 2% |
| **Independence** | 1911 (declared), 1924 (republic) | **Religions** | Mainly Buddhism |
| **Area** | 1 564 619 sq km/604 099 sq mi | **Time zone** | GMT +8 |
| **Capital** | Ulan Bator; Ulaanbaatar | **Currency** | 1 Tugrug (T) = 100 möngö |
| **Chief towns** | Darhan, Erdenet | **Telephone** | +976 |
| **Population** | 2 373 943 (2000) | **Internet** | .mn |
| | | **Country code** | MNG |

**Location**
A landlocked republic in eastern central Asia, bounded to the north by Russia and on other sides by China.

**Physical description**
Mountainous, at an average height of 1 580m/5 184ft; highest point is Tavan Bogd (4 374m/14 350ft); high ground is mainly in the west, with mountains north-west to south-east, running into the Gobi Desert; lowland plains are mainly arid grasslands.

**Climate**
Continental, with hard and long-lasting frosts in winter; average temperature at Ulan Bator is 27°C in Jan and 9–24°C in Jul; rainfall is generally low; arid desert conditions prevail in the south.

**National holidays**
Jan 1, 2, Mar 8 (Women), May 1, Jul 10 (People's Revolution) (3), Nov 7 (Oct Revolution).

## Political leaders

**Prime Minister**

| | |
|---|---|
| 1924–8 | Tserendorji |
| 1928–32 | Amor |
| 1932–6 | Gendun |
| 1936–8 | Amor |
| 1939–52 | Korloghiin Choibalsan |
| 1952–74 | Yumsjhagiin Tsedenbal |

**Chairman of the Praesidium**

| | |
|---|---|
| 1948–53 | Gonchighlin Bumatsende |
| 1954–72 | Jamsarangiin Sambu |
| 1972–4 | Sonomyn Luvsan |
| 1974–84 | Yumsjhagiin Tsedenbal |
| 1984–90 | Jambyn Batmunkh |

**President**

| | |
|---|---|
| 1990–7 | Punsalmaagiyn Ochirbat |
| 1997– | Natsagiyn Bagabandi |

**Premier**

| | |
|---|---|
| 1974–84 | Jambyn Batmunkh |
| 1984–90 | Dumaagiyn Sodnom |
| 1990–2 | Dashiyn Byambasuren |
| 1992–6 | Puntsagiyn Jasray |
| 1996–8 | Mendsaihany Enkhsahan |
| 1998 | Tsahiagiyin Elbegdorj |
| 1998–9 | Janlaviyn Narantsatsralt |
| 1999–2000 | Rinchinnyamiyn Amarjagal |
| 2000– | Nambaryn Enkhbayar |

### Outer Mongolia

*Outer Mongolia* is sometimes used light-heartedly to describe anywhere very far away and isolated. But it is actually the official former name of Mongolia. Mongolia was originally the homeland of nomadic tribes, which united under Ghengis Khan in the 13c to become part of a great Mongol Empire. Mongolia was later assimilated into China, and divided into Inner and Outer Mongolia. Inner Mongolia remains an autonomous region of China, but Outer Mongolia declared itself independent in 1911.

**MONTENEGRO** *see* **SERBIA AND MONTENEGRO**

**MONTSERRAT** *see* **UNITED KINGDOM**

# MOROCCO

| | | | |
|---|---|---|---|
| **Official name** | Kingdom of Morocco | **Languages** | Arabic; Berber and French are also spoken |
| **Local name** | Al-Mamlaka Al-Maghribiyya | **Ethnic groups** | Arab and Berber 99%, European 1% |
| **Independence** | 1956 | **Religions** | Islam 99% (mostly Sunni), Christianity 1% |
| **Area** | 409 200 sq km/157 951 sq mi | **Time zone** | GMT |
| **Capital** | Rabat; Ar Ribāţ, Er Ribâţ | **Currency** | 1 Dirham (DH) = 100 centimes |
| **Chief towns** | Casablanca, Fez, Marrakesh, Tangier, Meknès, Kenitra, Tétouan, Oujda, Agadir | **Telephone** | +212 |
| **Population** | 26 019 280 (1994) | **Internet** | .ma |
| **Nationality** | Moroccan | **Country code** | MAR |

**Location**
A kingdom in North Africa, bounded to the south-west by Western Sahara, over which Morocco claims sovereignty; to the south-east and east by Algeria; to the north-east by the Mediterranean Sea; and to the west by the Atlantic Ocean.

**Physical description**
Dominated by a series of mountain ranges, rising in the High Atlas in the south to 4 165m/13 665ft at Mt Toubkal; Atlas Mountains descend south-east to the north-west edge of the Sahara Desert; has a broad coastal plain.

**Climate**
Mediterranean climate on the north coast; settled and hot in May–Sep; Sahara is virtually rainless, with extreme heat in summer but chilly winter nights; average maximum temperatures of 17–28°C on Atlantic coast; heavy winter snowfall in the High Atlas.

**National holidays**
Jan 1, 11 (Independence Manifest), May 1, Jul 30 (Feast of the Throne), Aug 14 (Qued-ed-Dahab Allegiance), Aug 21 (King and People), Nov 6 (Green Mar), 18 (Independence); Ad, ER, NY (Muslim), PB.

## Political leaders

**Monarch**

1927–61 Mohammed V
1961–99 Hassan II
1999– Mohammed VI

**Prime Minister**

1955–8 Si Mohammed Bekkai
1958 Ahmad Balfrej
1958–60 Abdullah Ibrahim
1960–3 *As Monarch*
1963–5 Ahmad Bahnini
1965–7 *As Monarch*
1967–9 Moulay Ahmed Laraki
1969–71 Mohammed Ben Hima
1971–2 Mohammed Karim Lamrani
1972–9 Ahmed Othman
1979–83 Maati Bouabid
1983–6 Mohammed Karim Lamrani
1986–92 Izz Id-Dien Laraki
1992–4 Mohammed Karim Lamrani
1994–8 Abdellatif Filali
1998–2002 Abderrahmane el-Yousifi
2002– Driss Jettou

## MOZAMBIQUE

| | |
|---|---|
| **Official name** | Republic of Mozambique |
| **Local name** | Moçambique; República de Moçambique |
| **Former name** | People's Republic of Mozambique (1975–90) |
| **Independence** | 1975 |
| **Area** | 789 800 sq km/304 863 sq mi |
| **Capital** | Maputo |
| **Chief towns** | Nampula, Beira, Pemba |
| **Population** | 15 521 090 (1997) |
| **Nationality** | Mozambican |
| **Languages** | Portuguese; Swahili and other African languages are widely spoken |
| **Ethnic groups** | Makua 47%, Tsonga 23%, Malawi 12%, Shona 11%, Yao 4%, others 3% |
| **Religions** | traditional beliefs 55%, Christianity 28% (RC 25%, others 3%), Islam 17% |
| **Time zone** | GMT +2 |
| **Currency** | 1 Metical (Mt, MZM) = 100 centavos |
| **Telephone** | +258 |
| **Internet** | .mz |
| **Country code** | MOZ |

**Location**
A republic in south-eastern Africa, bounded to the south by Swaziland; to the south and south-west by South Africa; to the west by Zimbabwe; to the north-west by Zambia and Malawi; to the north by Tanzania; and to the east by the Mozambique Channel and the Indian Ocean.

**Physical description**
South of the Zambezi River the low-lying coast has sandy beaches and mangroves; low hills of volcanic origin inland; coast north of the Zambezi is more rugged, with savannah plateau inland; highest peak is Mt Binga (2 436m/7 992ft).

**Climate**
Tropical, with relatively low rainfall in the coastal lowlands; maximum daily temperatures of 25–32°C in the central coast zone; rainfall decreases in the drier areas of the interior lowlands; one rainy season in Dec–Mar.

**National holidays**
Jan 1, Feb 3 (Heroes), Apr 7 (Mozambican Women), May 1, Jun 25 (Independence), Sep 7 (Victory), 25 (Armed Forces), Oct 4 (Peace and Reconciliation), Dec 25 (Christmas/Family).

## Political leaders

**President**

1975–86 Samora Moïses Machel
1986– Joaquim Alberto Chissano

**Prime Minister**

1986–94 Mario de Graça Machungo
1994– Pascoal Mocumbi

### *First Lady of Africa*

The first president of Mozambique, Samora Machel, was killed in an air crash in 1986. His widow, Graça Machel, is internationally respected for her work for women's and children's rights. She later married the former president of South Africa, Nelson Mandela.

## MYANMAR (BURMA)

| | |
|---|---|
| **Official name** | Union of Myanmar; still often referred to internationally as Burma |
| **Local name** | Myanmar; Pyidaungsu Myanmar Naingngandaw |
| **Former name** | Union of Burma (1948–74); Socialist Republic of the Union of Burma (1974–88), Union of Burma (1988–9) |
| **Independence** | 1948 |
| **Area** | 678 576 sq km/261 930 sq mi |
| **Capital** | Rangoon; Yangon |
| **Chief towns** | Mandalay, Henzada, Pegu, Myingyan |
| **Population** | 48 205 000 (2001e) |
| **Nationality** | Burmese or Myanmarese |
| **Languages** | Burmese; several minority languages are also spoken |
| **Ethnic groups** | Burman 68%, Shan 9%, Karen 7%, Rakhine 4%, Chinese 3%, Mon 2%, Kachin 1%, others 6% |
| **Religions** | Buddhism 89%, Christianity 6%, Islam 4%, Hindu 1% |
| **Time zone** | GMT +6.5 |
| **Currency** | 1 Kyat (K) = 100 pyas |
| **Telephone** | +95 |
| **Internet** | .mm |
| **Country code** | MMR |

**Location**
A republic in south-east Asia, bounded to the north and north-east by China; to the east by Laos and Thailand; to the north-west by India; to the west by Bangladesh; and to the south and west by the Bay of Bengal and the Andaman Sea.

**Physical description**
Rimmed in the north, east and west by mountains rising in the north to Hkakabo Razi (5 881m/19 294ft) and descending in a series of ridges and valleys; principal rivers run north to south; Irrawaddy River delta extends over 240km/150mi of tidal forest.

**Climate**
Tropical monsoon climate, with a marked change between the cooler, dry season of Nov–Apr and the hotter, wet season of May–Sep; lowlands are very hot all year round (especially Mar to May); high humidity on the coast.

**National holidays**
Jan 4 (Independence), Feb 12 (Union), Mar 2 (Peasants), 27 (Armed Forces), May 1, Jul 19 (Martyrs), Dec 25; Ad, D, 4 Full Moon days, National (Nov), NY (Burmese), NY (Kayin), Tazaungdaing Festival (Nov), Thingyan (Apr) (3–5).

## Political leaders

**President**

| | |
|---|---|
| 1948–52 | Sao Shwe Thaik |
| 1952–7 | Agga Maha Thiri Thudhamma Ba U |
| 1957–62 | U Wing Maung |
| 1962 | Sama Duwa Sinwa Nawng |

**Chairman of Revolutionary Council**

| | |
|---|---|
| 1962–74 | Ne Win |

**President**

| | |
|---|---|
| 1974–81 | Ne Win |
| 1981–8 | U San Yu |
| 1988 | U Sein Lwin |
| 1988 | Maung Maung |

**Chairman of State Law and Order Restoration Council**

| | |
|---|---|
| 1988–92 | Saw Maung |
| 1992–7 | Than Shwe |

**Chairman of State Peace and Development Council**

| | |
|---|---|
| 1997– | Than Shwe |

**Prime Minister**

| | |
|---|---|
| 1948–56 | U Nu |
| 1956–7 | U Ba Swe |
| 1957–8 | U Nu |
| 1958–60 | Ne Win |
| 1960–2 | U Nu |
| 1962–74 | Ne Win |
| 1974–7 | U Sein Win |
| 1977–8 | U Maung Maung Ka |
| 1988 | U Tun Tin |
| 1988–92 | Saw Maung |
| 1992– | Than Shwe |

## NAMIBIA

| | |
|---|---|
| **Official name** | Republic of Namibia |
| **Local name** | Namibia |
| **Former name** | South West Africa (until 1968) |
| **Independence** | 1990 |
| **Area** | 823 144 sq km/317 734 sq mi |
| **Capital** | Windhoek |
| **Chief towns** | Lüderitz, Keetmanshoop, Grootfontein |
| **Population** | 1 826 854 (2001) |
| **Nationality** | Namibian |
| **Languages** | English; Afrikaans, German and local languages are also widely spoken |
| **Ethnic groups** | Ovambo 50%, Kavango 9%, Damara 8%, Herero 8%, white 6%, Nama 5%, others 14% |
| **Religions** | Christianity 90%, traditional beliefs 10% |
| **Time zone** | GMT +1 |
| **Currency** | 1 Namibian Dollar (N$) = 100 cents |
| **Telephone** | +264 |
| **Internet** | .na |
| **Country code** | NAM |

**Location**
A republic in south-western Africa, bounded to the north by Angola; to the north-east by Zambia; to the east by Botswana; to the south by South Africa; and to the west by the Atlantic Ocean.

**Physical description**
Namib Desert runs along the Atlantic Ocean coast; inland plateau has a mean elevation of 1 500m/4 921ft; highest point is Konigstein peak on Brandberg (2 574m/8 445ft); Kalahari Desert lies to the east and south; Orange River forms the frontier with South Africa.

**Climate**
Low rainfall on the coast, higher in the interior; the average maximum daily temperature range at Windhoek, representative of the interior, is 20–30°C.

**National holidays**
Jan 1, Mar 21 (Independence), May 1, 4 (Cassinga), Aug 26 (Heroes), Dec 10 (Human Rights), Dec 25, 26 (Family); A, GF, EM.

### Political leaders

**President**

| | |
|---|---|
| 1990– | Sam Daniel Nujoma |

**Prime Minister**

| | |
|---|---|
| 1990–2002 | Hage Geingob |
| 2002– | Theo-Ben Gurirab |

## NAURU

| | | | |
|---|---|---|---|
| **Official name** | Republic of Nauru | **Ethnic groups** | Nauruan 58%, other Pacific Islanders 26%, Chinese and Vietnamese 8%, European 8% |
| **Local name** | Naoero (Nauruan), Nauru (English) | **Religions** | Christianity (predominantly Prot, with RC minority); also Buddhism |
| **Independence** | 1968 | **Time zone** | GMT +12 |
| **Area** | 21 sq km/8 sq mi | **Currency** | 1 Australian Dollar ($A) = 100 cents |
| **Capital** | There is no capital as such, but government offices are situated in Yaren District | **Telephone** | +674 |
| **Population** | 12 000 (2001e) | **Internet** | .nr |
| **Nationality** | Nauruan | **Country code** | NRU |
| **Languages** | Nauruan; English is also widely understood | | |

**Location**
An independent republic formed by a small, isolated island in the west-central Pacific Ocean, 42km/26mi to the south of the Equator and 4 000km/2 500mi north-east of Sydney, Australia.

**Physical description**
Ground rises from sandy beaches to form a fertile coastal belt, c.100–300m/330–980ft wide, the only cultivable soil; central plateau inland, which reaches 65m/213ft at its highest point, composed largely of phosphate-bearing rocks.

**Climate**
Tropical, with average daily temperatures of 24–34°C, and average humidity between 70% and 80%; rainfall mainly in the monsoon season from Nov to Feb, with marked yearly deviations.

**National holidays**
Jan 1, 31 (Independence), Feb 1, May 17 (Constitution), Oct 26 (Angam), Dec 25, 26; GF, EM (2).

## Political leaders

**President**

| | |
|---|---|
| 1968–76 | Hammer de Roburt |
| 1976–8 | Bernard Dowiyogo |
| 1978 | Lagumot Harris |
| 1978–86 | Hammer de Roburt |
| 1986 | Kennan Adeang |
| 1986–9 | Hammer de Roburt |
| 1989 | Kenas Aroi |
| 1989–95 | Bernard Dowiyogo |
| 1995–6 | Lagumot Harris |
| 1996 | Bernard Dowiyogo |
| 1996 | Kennan Adeang |
| 1996–7 | Rueben Kun |
| 1997–8 | Kinza Clodumar |
| 1998–9 | Bernard Dowiyogo |
| 1999–2000 | Rene Harris |
| 2000–1 | Bernard Dowiyogo |
| 2001–3 | Rene Harris |
| 2003 | Bernard Dowiyogo |
| 2003 | Derog Gioura *Acting President* |
| 2003 | Ludwig Scotty |
| 2003– | Rene Harris |

# NEPAL

| | | | |
|---|---|---|---|
| **Official name** | Kingdom of Nepal | **Ethnic groups** | Nepali 59%, Bihari 20%, Tamang 3%, Tharu 3%, Newar 3%, others 12% |
| **Local name** | Nepāl Adhirājya | **Religions** | Hinduism 90%, Buddhism 5%, Islam 3%, others 2% |
| **Area** | 145 391 sq km/56 121 sq mi | **Time zone** | GMT +5.75 |
| **Capital** | Kathmandu | **Currency** | 1 Nepalese Rupee (NRp, NRs) = 100 paise/pice |
| **Chief towns** | Patan, Bhadgaon | **Telephone** | +977 |
| **Population** | 23 151 423 (2001) | **Internet** | .np |
| **Nationality** | Nepalese | **Country code** | NPL |
| **Languages** | Nepali; around 70 local dialects and languages are also spoken | | |

**Location**
A landlocked independent kingdom lying along the southern slopes of the Himalayas in central Asia, bounded to the north by the Tibet region of China, and to the east, south and west by India.

**Physical description**
Rises steeply from the Ganges Basin; high fertile valleys in the hill country at 1 300m/4 265ft, such as the Vale of Kathmandu, are enclosed by mountains ranges; dominated by the glaciated peaks of the Himalayas; highest point is Mt Everest (8 850m/29 035ft).

**Climate**
Varies from subtropical lowland, with hot, humid summers and mild winters, to an alpine climate over 3 300m/10 827ft, with permanently snow-covered peaks; average temperatures at Kathmandu from 23°C (May–Aug) to 9°C (Jan); monsoon season during summer (Jun–Sep).

**National holidays**
Feb 19 (Democracy), Jul 8 (King's Birthday), Nov 8 (Constitution); NY (Nepalese) (Apr), Vijaya Dashami (Oct), Bhai Tika (Nov).

## Political leaders

**Monarch**

| | |
|---|---|
| 1881–1911 | Prithvi Bir Bikram Shah |
| 1911–50 | Tribhuvan Bir Bikram Shah |
| 1950–2 | Bir Bikram |
| 1952–5 | Tribhuvan Bir Bikram Shah |
| 1956–72 | Mahendra Bir Bikram Shah |
| 1972–2001 | Birendra Bir Bikram Shah Dev |
| 2001 | Dipendra Bir Bikram Shah Dev |
| 2001– | Gyanendra Bir Bikram Shah Dev |

**Prime Minister**

| | |
|---|---|
| 1901–29 | Chandra Sham Sher Jang Bahadur Rana |
| 1929–31 | Bhim Cham Sham Sher Jang Bahadur Rana |
| 1931–45 | Juddha Sham Sher Rana |
| 1945–8 | Padma Sham Sher Jang Bahadur Rana |
| 1948–51 | Mohan Sham Sher Jang Bahadur Rana |
| 1951–2 | Matrika Prasad Koirala |
| 1952–3 | *King also Prime Minister* |
| 1953–5 | Matrika Prasad Koirala |
| 1955–6 | Mahendra Bir Bikram Shah |
| 1956–7 | Tanka Prasad Acharya |
| 1957–9 | *King also Prime Minister* |
| 1959–60 | Sri Bishawa Prasad Koirala |
| 1960–3 | *No Prime Minister* |
| 1963–5 | Tulsi Giri |
| 1965–9 | Surya Bahadur Thapa |
| 1969–70 | Kirti Nidhi Bista |
| 1970–1 | *King also Prime Minister* |
| 1971–3 | Kirti Nidhi Bista |

| | | | |
|---|---|---|---|
| 1973–5 | Nagendra Prasad Rijal | 1997 | Lokendra Bahadur Chand |
| 1975–7 | Tulsi Giri | 1997 | Surya Bahadur Thapa |
| 1977–9 | Kirti Nidhi Bista | 1998–9 | Girija Prasad Koirala |
| 1979–83 | Surya Bahadur Thapa | 1999–2000 | Krishna Prasad Bhattari |
| 1983–6 | Lokendra Bahadur Chand | 2000–1 | Girija Prasad Koirala |
| 1986–91 | Marich Man Singh Shrestha | 2001–2 | Sher Bahadur Deuba |
| 1991–4 | Girija Prasad Koirala | 2002–3 | Lokendra Bahadur Chand |
| 1994–5 | Man Mohan Adhikari | 2003– | Surya Bahadur Thapa |
| 1995–7 | Sher Bahadur Deuba | | |

### *Nepalese Peoples*

Nepal is home to a diverse range of peoples, with more than 60 ethnic groups. These include the Sherpas, famous for their mountaineering skill, the Dolpa people, who live in probably the world's highest human settlements at around 4 000m/13 123ft, and the Gurungs, whose traditions include a colourful dancing season from Jan/Feb to Apr/May.

## THE NETHERLANDS

| | | | |
|---|---|---|---|
| **Official name** | Kingdom of the Netherlands; often known as Holland | **Languages** | Dutch; Frisian is spoken in Friesland, and English is widely spoken |
| **Local name** | Nederlanden; Koninkrijk der Nederlanden | **Ethnic groups** | Dutch 94%, others 6% |
| **Area** | 33 929 sq km/13 097 sq mi | **Religions** | Christianity 63% (RC 36%, Prot 27%), none/unaffiliated 32%, Islam 3%, others 2% |
| **Capital** | Amsterdam; The Hague (Den Haag) is the seat of government | **Time zone** | GMT +1 |
| | | **Currency** | 1 Euro (€) = 100 cents |
| **Chief towns** | Rotterdam, Utrecht, Haarlem, Eindhoven, Arnhem, Groningen | **Telephone** | +31 |
| | | **Internet** | .nl |
| **Population** | 16 044 000 (2001e) | **Country code** | NLD |
| **Nationality** | Dutch | | |

**Location**
A maritime kingdom in north-western Europe, bounded to the west and north by the North Sea; to the east by Germany; and to the south by Belgium.

**Physical description**
Generally low and flat, except in the south-east where hills rise to 321m/1 053ft; 24% of the land is below sea level, including much of the coast, which is protected by dunes and artificial dykes; many canals, totalling 6 340km/3 940mi in length.

**Climate**
Cool, temperate, maritime; average temperatures 1.7°C (Jan) and 17°C (Jul); rainfall is distributed fairly evenly throughout the year.

**National holidays**
Jan 1, Apr 30 (Queen), May 5 (Liberation), Dec 25, 26; A, EM, GF, WM.

## Netherlands overseas territories

### Netherlands Antilles (Dutch Antilles)

| | | | |
|---|---|---|---|
| **Location** | A group of islands in the Caribbean Sea, comprising the southern group of Curaçao and Bonaire north of the Venezuelan coast, and the northern group of St Maarten, St Eustatins and Saba, lying east of Puerto Rico (USA). | | |
| **Local name** | Nederlandse Antillen | **Population** | 175 653 (2001) |
| **Area** | 960 sq km/371 sq mi | **Internet** | .an |
| **Capital** | Willemstad | **Country code** | ANT |

### Aruba

| | | | |
|---|---|---|---|
| **Location** | An island in the Caribbean Sea, about 30km/19mi north of Venezuela, and 79km/44mi west of Curaçao (The Netherlands). | | |
| **Area** | 193 sq km/75 sq mi | **Internet** | .aw |
| **Capital** | Oranjestad | **Country code** | ABW |
| **Population** | 92 000 (2001e) | | |

## Political leaders

**Monarch (House of Orange-Nassau)**

| | |
|---|---|
| 1572–84 | William the Silent |
| 1584–1625 | Maurice |
| 1625–47 | Frederick Henry |
| 1647–50 | William II |
| 1672–1702 | William III |
| 1747–51 | William IV |
| 1751–95 | William V |
| 1806–10 | Louis Bonaparte |
| 1813–40 | William I |
| 1840–9 | William II |
| 1849–90 | William III |
| 1890–1948 | Wilhelmina |
| 1948–80 | Juliana |
| 1980– | Beatrix |

**Prime Minister**

| | |
|---|---|
| 1897–1901 | Nicholas G Pierson |
| 1901–5 | Abraham Kuyper |
| 1905–8 | Theodoor H de Meester |
| 1908–13 | Theodorus Heemskerk |
| 1913–18 | Pieter W A Cort van der Linden |
| 1918–25 | Charles J M Ruys de Beerenbrouck |
| 1925–6 | Hendrikus Colijn |
| 1926 | Dirk J de Geer |
| 1926–33 | Charles J M Ruys de Beerenbrouck |
| 1933–9 | Hendrikus Colijn |
| 1939–40 | Dirk J de Geer |
| 1940–5 | Pieter S Gerbrandy (*in exile*) |
| 1945–6 | Willem Schemerhorn/Willem Drees |
| 1946–8 | Louis J M Beel |
| 1948–51 | Willem Drees/Josephus R H van Schaik |
| 1951–8 | Willem Drees |
| 1958–9 | Louis J M Beel |
| 1959–63 | Jan E de Quay |
| 1963–5 | Victor G M Marijnen |
| 1965–6 | Joseph M L T Cals |
| 1966–7 | Jelle Zijlstra |
| 1967–71 | Petrus J S de Jong |
| 1971–3 | Barend W Biesheuvel |
| 1973–7 | Joop M Den Uyl |
| 1977–82 | Andreas A M van Agt |
| 1982–94 | Ruud F M Lubbers |
| 1994–2002 | Wim Kok |
| 2002– | Jan Peter Balkenende |

**NEVIS** *see* **ST KITTS AND NEVIS**

**NEW CALEDONIA** *see* **FRANCE**

## NEW ZEALAND

| | | | |
|---|---|---|---|
| **Official name** | New Zealand (NZ) | | |
| **Local name** | New Zealand (English), Aotearoa (Maori) | | |
| **Independence** | 1907 (from Britain), 1947 (full) | | |
| **Area** | 268 812 sq km/103 761 sq mi | **Religions** | Christianity 67% (Prot 52%, RC 15%), none/unaffiliated 16%, others 17% |
| **Capital** | Wellington; Te Whanganui-a-Tara | | |
| **Chief towns** | Auckland, Christchurch, Dunedin, Hamilton | **Time zone** | GMT +12 |
| **Population** | 3 618 303 (1996) | **Currency** | 1 New Zealand Dollar (NZ$) = 100 cents |
| **Nationality** | Kiwi (*informal*), New Zealand | **Telephone** | +64 |
| | | **Internet** | .nz |
| **Languages** | English, Maori | **Country code** | NZL |
| **Ethnic groups** | European 83%, Maori 15%, Pacific Islanders 6%, Asian 5% *Percentages add to more than 100% as some people identify with more than one ethnicity* | | |

**Location**
An independent state comprising a group of islands in the Pacific Ocean to the south-east of Australia; the two principal islands are North Island and South Island, separated by the Cook Strait; there is also Stewart Island, and several minor islands. The Cook Islands and Niue are New Zealand self-governing territories and Tokelau and the Ross Dependency are New Zealand non-self-governing territories.

**Physical description**
North Island is mountainous in the centre, with many hot springs; peaks rise to 2 797m/9 176ft at Mt Ruapehu; South Island is mountainous for its whole length, rising in the Southern Alps to 3 753m/12 312ft at Mt Cook, New Zealand's highest point; many glaciers and mountain lakes.

**Climate**
Highly changeable weather, with all months moderately wet; almost subtropical in the north and on the east coast, with mild winters and warm, humid summers; Auckland daily temperatures are 8–13°C (Jul), 16–23°C (Jan); generally cooler in South Island.

**National holidays**
Jan 1, 2, Feb 6 (Waitangi), Apr 25 (Anzac), Dec 25, 26; EM, GF, Queen's Birthday (Jun), Labour (Oct).

## Self-governing territories

### Cook Islands

| | | | |
|---|---|---|---|
| **Location** | A widely scattered group of 15 volcanic and coral islands in the South Pacific Ocean, c.3 200km/2 000mi north-east of New Zealand. | | |
| **Area** | 238 sq km/92 sq mi | **Internet** | .ck |
| **Chief town** | Avarua | **Country code** | COK |
| **Population** | 19 103 (1996) | | |

### Niue

| | | | |
|---|---|---|---|
| **Location** | A small island in the South Pacific Ocean, 2 140km/1 330mi north-east of New Zealand. | | |
| **Area** | 263 sq km/101 sq mi | **Internet** | .nu |
| **Chief town** | Alofi | **Country code** | NIU |
| **Population** | 2 088 (1997) | | |

## Non-self-governing territories

### Tokelau

| | | | |
|---|---|---|---|
| **Location** | Comprises three small atolls (Atafu, Nukunonu, Fakaofo) in the South Pacific Ocean, c.3 500km/2 200mi north-east of New Zealand. | | |
| **Area** | 10.1 sq km/3.9 sq mi | **Internet** | .tk |
| **Population** | 2 000 (2001e) | **Country code** | TKL |

### Ross Dependency

| | |
|---|---|
| **Location** | A territory in Antarctica. |
| **Area** | 413 540 sq km/159 626 sq mi (land); 336 770 sq km/129 993 sq mi (permanent shelf ice) |
| **Population** | Populated solely by scientists. |

## Political leaders

Chief of State: British monarch, represented by Governor General.

**Prime Minister**

| | |
|---|---|
| 1893–1906 | Richard John Seddon *Lib* |
| 1906 | William Hall-Jones *Lib* |
| 1906–12 | Joseph George Ward *Lib/Nat* |
| 1912 | Thomas Mackenzie *Nat* |
| 1912–25 | William Ferguson Massey *Ref* |
| 1925 | Francis Henry Dillon Bell *Ref* |
| 1925–8 | Joseph Gordon Coates *Ref* |
| 1928–30 | Joseph George Ward *Lib/Nat* |
| 1930–5 | George William Forbes *Un* |
| 1935–40 | Michael Joseph Savage *Lab* |
| 1940–9 | Peter Fraser *Lab* |
| 1949–57 | Sidney George Holland *Nat* |
| 1957 | Keith Jacka Holyoake *Nat* |
| 1957–60 | Walter Nash *Lab* |
| 1960–72 | Keith Jacka Holyoake *Nat* |
| 1972 | John Ross Marshall *Nat* |
| 1972–4 | Norman Eric Kirk *Lab* |
| 1974–5 | Wallace Edward Rowling *Lab* |
| 1975–84 | Robert David Muldoon *Nat* |
| 1984–89 | David Russell Lange *Lab* |
| 1989–90 | Geoffrey Palmer *Lab* |
| 1990 | Mike Moore *Lab* |
| 1990–7 | James Bolger *Nat* |
| 1997–9 | Jenny Shipley *Nat* |
| 1999– | Helen Clark *Lab* |

*Lab = Labor*
*Lib = Liberal*
*Nat = National*
*Ref = Reform*
*Un = United*

### Votes for Women

In 1893 New Zealand became the first country to give women the vote in national elections.

## NICARAGUA

| | |
|---|---|
| **Official name** | Republic of Nicaragua |
| **Local name** | Nicaragua; República de Nicaragua |
| **Independence** | 1821 |
| **Area** | 130 668 sq km/50 451 sq mi |
| **Capital** | Managua |
| **Chief towns** | León, Granada, Masaya, Chinandega, Matagalpa, Corinto |
| **Population** | 4 357 099 (1995) |
| **Nationality** | Nicaraguan |
| **Languages** | Spanish; English and local languages in Caribbean coastal areas |
| **Ethnic groups** | mestizo 69%, white 17%, black 9%, Amerindian 5% |
| **Religions** | Christianity 100% (RC 95%, Prot 5%) |
| **Time zone** | GMT –6 |
| **Currency** | 1 Córdoba (C$) = 100 centavos = 10 reales |
| **Telephone** | +505 |
| **Internet** | .ni |
| **Country code** | NIC |

**Location**
The largest of the Central American republics, bounded to the north by Honduras; to the east by the Caribbean Sea; to the south by Costa Rica; and to the west by the Pacific Ocean.

**Physical description**
Mountainous west with volcanic ranges rising to over 2 000m/6 562ft in the north-west; highest point is the Dipilto-Jalapa ridge (2 107m/6 913ft); two large lakes behind the coastal mountains; rolling uplands and forested plains to the east; many short rivers.

**Climate**
Tropical, with average annual temperatures ranging from 15–35°C according to altitude; there is a rainy season from May to Nov when humidity is high; subject to devastating hurricanes.

**National holidays**
Jan 1, May 1, Jul 19 (Sandinista Revolution), Sep 14 (Battle of San Jacinto), 15 (Independence), Dec 8, 25; GF, HT.

## Political leaders

**President**

| | |
|---|---|
| 1893–1909 | José Santos Zelaya |
| 1909–10 | José Madriz |
| 1910–11 | José Dolores Estrada |
| 1911 | Juan José Estrada |
| 1911–17 | Adolfo Díaz |
| 1912 | Luis Mena *rival President* |
| 1917–21 | Emiliano Chamorro Vargas |
| 1921–3 | Riego Manuel Chamorro |
| 1923–4 | Martínez Bartolo |
| 1925–6 | Carlos Solórzano |
| 1926 | Emiliano Chamorro Vargas |
| 1926–8 | Adolfo Díaz |
| 1926 | Juan Bautista Sacasa *rival President* |
| 1928–32 | José Marcia Moncada |
| 1933–6 | Juan Bautista Sacasa |
| 1936 | Carlos Brenes Jarquin |
| 1937–47 | Anastasio Somoza García |
| 1947 | Leonardo Argüello |
| 1947 | Benjamin Lascayo Sacasa |
| 1947–50 | Victor Manuel Román y Reyes |
| 1950–6 | Anastasio Somoza García |
| 1956–63 | Luis Somoza Debayle |
| 1963–6 | René Schick Gutiérrez |
| 1966–7 | Lorenzo Guerrero Gutiérrez |
| 1967–72 | Anastasio Somoza Debayle |
| 1972–4 | *Triumvirate* |
| 1974–9 | Anastasio Somoza Debayle |
| 1979–84 | *Government Junta of National Reconstruction* |

| | | | |
|---|---|---|---|
| 1984–90 | Daniel Ortega Saavedra | 1997–2001 | Arnoldo Alemán Lacayo |
| 1990–7 | Violeta Barrios de Chamorro | 2001– | Enrique Bolaños |

### Frangipani and Motmots

The national flower of Nicaragua is the red frangipani, known locally as *sacuanjoche*, while the national tree is the degame, known as *madroño*. The blue-crowned motmot is the national bird, called the *guardabarranco* in Spanish, a colourful creature with green body, scarlet and gold underparts, long dark bill and a striking blue head.

**NIUE** *see* **NEW ZEALAND**

## NIGER

| | | | |
|---|---|---|---|
| **Official name** | Republic of Niger | **Ethnic groups** | Hausa 56%, Djerma and Songhai 22%, Fulani 9%, Tuareg 8%, others 5% |
| **Local name** | Niger; République du Niger | **Religions** | Islam 80%, Christianity and traditional beliefs 20% |
| **Independence** | 1960 | **Time zone** | GMT +1 |
| **Area** | 1 186 408 sq km/ 457 953 sq mi | **Currency** | 1 CFA Franc (CFAFr) = 100 centimes |
| **Capital** | Niamey | **Telephone** | +227 |
| **Chief towns** | Agadès, Diffa, Dosso, Maradi, Tahoua, Zinder | **Internet** | .ne |
| **Population** | 11 134 000 (2001e) | **Country code** | NER |
| **Nationality** | Nigerien | | |
| **Languages** | French; Hausa and Djerma are spoken widely | | |

**Location**
A landlocked republic in West Africa, bounded to the north-east by Libya; to the north-west by Algeria; to the west by Mali; to the south-west by Burkina Faso; to the south by Benin and Nigeria; and to the east by Chad.

**Physical description**
Lies on the southern fringe of the Sahara Desert, on a high plateau; deserts in the east, centre and north; water in quantity is found only in the south-west around the River Niger and in the south-east around Lake Chad; highest point is Mt Greboun (2 310m/7 580ft).

**Climate**
One of the hottest countries in the world; marked rainy season in the south Jun–Oct; rainfall decreases in the north to almost negligible levels in desert areas; drought can occur.

**National holidays**
Jan 1, Apr 24 (Concord), May 1, Aug 3 (Independence), Dec 18 (Republic), 25; Ad, EM, ER, PB, Leilat-ul-kadr.

### Nomads of Niger

Northern Niger is home to several nomadic peoples, including the Bororo Fulani. In their traditional marriage rituals a young man must seduce his beloved, then 'kidnap' her, elope and travel widely. People gather at the annual Guérewol festival for – according to the Embassy of Niger – 'celebrations, engagements, kidnappings of wives and baptisms'.

## Political leaders

**President**

| | |
|---|---|
| 1960–74 | Hamani Diori |
| 1974–87 | Seyni Kountché |
| 1987–93 | Ali Saibou |
| 1993–6 | Mahamane Ousmane |
| 1996–9 | Ibrahim Baré Maïnassara |
| 1999 | Daouda Malam Wanke |
| 1999– | Tandja Mamadou |

**Prime Minister**

| | |
|---|---|
| 1957–8 | Djibo Bakary |
| 1958–60 | Hamani Diori |
| 1960–83 | *No Prime Minister* |
| 1983 | Mamane Oumarou |
| 1983–8 | Ahmid Algabid |
| 1988–9 | Mamane Oumarou |
| 1990–1 | Aliou Mahamidou |
| 1991–3 | Amadou Cheiffou |
| 1993–4 | Mahamadou Issoufou |
| 1994–5 | Abdoulaye Souley |
| 1995 | Amadou Boubacar Cissé |
| 1995–6 | Hama Amadou |
| 1996 | Boukary Adji |
| 1996–7 | Amadou Boubacar Cissé |
| 1997–2000 | Ibrahim Assane Mayaki |
| 2000– | Hama Amadou |

## NIGERIA

| | |
|---|---|
| **Official name** | Federal Republic of Nigeria |
| **Local name** | Nigeria |
| **Independence** | 1960 |
| **Area** | 923 768 sq km/356 574 sq mi |
| **Capital** | Abuja |
| **Chief towns** | Lagos, Ibadan, Ogbomosho, Kano, Oshogbo, Ilorin, Abeokuta, Port Harcourt |
| **Population** | 117 823 000 (2001e) |
| **Nationality** | Nigerian |
| **Languages** | English; Hausa, Yoruba, Edo and Igbo are also spoken |
| **Ethnic groups** | Yoruba 21%, Hausa 21%, Igbo 19%, Fulani 11%, Ibibio 6%, others 22% |
| **Religions** | Islam 50%, Christianity 40%, traditional beliefs 10% |
| **Time zone** | GMT +1 |
| **Currency** | 1 Naira (N,₦) = 100 kobo |
| **Telephone** | +234 |
| **Internet** | .ng |
| **Country code** | NGA |

**Location**
A republic in West Africa, bounded to the west by Benin; to the north by Niger; to the north-east by Chad; to the east by Cameroon; and to the south by the Gulf of Guinea and the Bight of Benin.

**Physical description**
Coastal strip dominated by the River Niger delta; tropical rainforest and oil palm bush lie north; dry central plateau of open woodland and savannah; edge of the Sahara Desert in the far north; numerous rivers; highest point is Mt Vogel (2 024m/6 640ft).

**Climate**
Two rainy seasons in the coastal areas; wettest part is the Niger delta and mountainous south-eastern frontier; Ibadan has an average daily maximum temperature of 31°C; only one rainy season in the north; dry season extends from Oct to Apr.

**National holidays**
Jan 1, May 1, 29 (Democracy), Oct 1 (National), Dec 25, 26; Ad, EM, ER, GF.

## Political leaders

**President**

| | |
|---|---|
| 1960–6 | Nnamdi Azikiwe |

**Prime Minister**

| | |
|---|---|
| 1960–6 | Abubakar Tafawa Balewa |

**Military Government**

| | |
|---|---|
| 1966 | J T U Aguiyi-Ironsi |
| 1966–75 | Yakubu Gowon |
| 1975–6 | Murtala R Mohamed |
| 1976–9 | Olusegun Obasanjo |

**President**

| | |
|---|---|
| 1979–83 | Alhaji Shehu Shagari |

**Military Government**

| | |
|---|---|
| 1983–5 | Mohammadu Buhari |
| 1985–93 | Ibrahim B Babangida |
| 1993 | Ernest Shonekan *Interim President* |
| 1993–8 | Sani Abacha |
| 1998–9 | Abdulsalami Abubakar |
| 1999– | Olusegun Obasanjo |

### *Agriculture, Peace and Unity*

The national flag of Nigeria has two stripes of emerald green, representing agriculture, and a white centre that symbolizes peace and unity. The flag is treated with the utmost dignity and respect, and its use is governed by laws; the government states that 'next to Mother Earth, it is the only national symbol worth dying for'. Strict rules govern the use of the flag – including when, where and by whom it may be flown – and infringement of these laws is an offence.

**NORFOLK ISLAND** *see* **AUSTRALIA**

**NORTHERN IRELAND** *see* **UNITED KINGDOM**

**NORTHERN MARIANA ISLANDS** *see* **UNITED STATES OF AMERICA**

**NORTH KOREA** *see* **KOREA, NORTH**

## NORWAY

| | |
|---|---|
| **Official name** | Kingdom of Norway |
| **Local name** | Norge; Kongeriket Norge |
| **Independence** | 1905 |
| **Area** | 323 895 sq km/125 023 sq mi |
| **Capital** | Oslo |
| **Chief towns** | Bergen, Trondheim, Stavanger, Kristiansand |
| **Population** | 4 513 000 (2001e) |
| **Nationality** | Norwegian |
| **Languages** | Norwegian, in the varieties of Bokmål and Nynorsk |
| **Ethnic groups** | Norwegian 96%, Lapp 1%, others 3% |
| **Religions** | Christianity 89% (Prot 88%, RC 1%), others and none/unaffiliated 11% |
| **Time zone** | GMT +1 |
| **Currency** | 1 Norwegian Krone (NKr) = 100 øre |
| **Telephone** | +47 |
| **Internet** | .no |
| **Country code** | NOR |

# NORWAY

**Location**
A kingdom in north-west Europe, bounded to the north by the Arctic Ocean; to the east by Sweden, Finland and Russia; to the west by the North Sea and Norwegian Sea; and to the south by the Skagerrak; includes the dependencies of Svalbard and Jan Mayen (Arctic) and Bouvet Island, Peter I Island and Queen Maud Land (Antarctica).

**Physical description**
Mountainous, with many ranges and extensive plateau regions, especially in the south-west and centre; much of the interior rises above 1 500m/4 921ft; highest point is Galdhøpiggen (2 469m/8 100ft); numerous lakes; irregular coastline with many small islands and long deep fjords.

**Climate**
Arctic winter climate in the interior highlands, with snow, strong winds and severe frosts; comparatively mild winter conditions on the coast; heavy rainfall on the west coast; colder winters and warmer, drier summers in southern lowlands.

**National holidays**
Jan 1, May 1, 17 (Constitution), Dec 25, 26; A, EM, GF, HT, WM.

## Bouvet Island

| | | | |
|---|---|---|---|
| **Location** | An inaccessible and uninhabited ice-covered island of volcanic origin in the South Atlantic ocean, lying approximately 1 370km/850mi to the south-west of the Cape of Good Hope, South Africa. | | |
| **Local name** | Bouvetøya | **Internet** | .bv |
| **Area** | 59 sq km/23 sq mi | **Country code** | BVT |

## Svalbard and Jan Meyen islands

| | | | |
|---|---|---|---|
| **Location** | Svalbard Islands lie to the north of Norway and to the east of Greenland (Denmark) at the eastern edges of the Barents Sea, south of the Arctic Ocean; Jan Meyen Island lies to the north-east of Iceland and east of Greenland between the Norwegian Sea and the Greenland Sea. | | |
| **Area** | 62 049 sq km/23 957 sq mi (Svalbard); 373 sq km/144 sq mi (Jan Meyen) | **Population** | 2 800 (Svalbard; 2003e); uninhabited (Jan Meyen) |
| | | **Internet** | .sj |
| **Capital** | Longyearbyen | **Country code** | SJM |

## Political leaders

**Monarch**

| | | | |
|---|---|---|---|
| 1872–1905 | Oscar II *union with Sweden* | 1957–91 | Olav V |
| 1905–57 | Haakon VII | 1991– | Harald V |

**Prime Minister**

| | | | |
|---|---|---|---|
| 1898–1902 | Johannes Steen | 1920–1 | Otto Bahr Halvorsen |
| 1902–3 | Otto Albert Blehr | 1921–3 | Otto Albert Blehr |
| 1903–5 | George Francis Hagerup | 1923 | Otto Bahr Halvorsen |
| 1905–7 | Christian Michelsen | 1923–4 | Abraham Berge |
| 1907–8 | Jørgen Løvland | 1924–6 | Johan Ludwig Mowinckel |
| 1908–10 | Gunnar Knudsen | 1926–8 | Ivar Lykke |
| 1910–12 | Wollert Konow | 1928 | Christopher Hornsrud |
| 1912–13 | Jens Bratlie | 1928–31 | Johan Ludwig Mowinckel |
| 1913–20 | Gunnar Knudsen | 1931–2 | Peder L Kolstad |

| | | | |
|---|---|---|---|
| 1932–3 | Jens Hundseid | 1973–6 | Trygve Bratteli |
| 1933–5 | Johan Ludwig Mowinckel | 1976–81 | Odvar Nordli |
| 1935–45 | Johan Nygaardsvold | 1981 | Gro Harlem Brundtland |
| 1945–51 | Einar Gerhardsen | 1981–6 | Kåre Willoch |
| 1951–5 | Oscar Torp | 1986–9 | Gro Harlem Brundtland |
| 1955–63 | Einar Gerhardsen | 1989–90 | Jan P Syse |
| 1963 | John Lyng | 1990–6 | Gro Harlem Brundtland |
| 1963–5 | Einar Gerhardsen | 1996–7 | Thorbjørn Jagland |
| 1965–71 | Per Borten | 1997–2000 | Kjell Magne Bondevik |
| 1971–2 | Trygve Bratteli | 2000–1 | Jens Stoltenberg |
| 1972–3 | Lars Korvald | 2001– | Kjell Magne Bondevik |

### *Midnight Sun and Northern Lights*

In the far north of Norway the sun never sets in summer, earning it the nickname 'the Land of the Midnight Sun', while in the winter the same area witnesses the Aurora Borealis or Northern Lights – luminous and shimmering colours and streamers of light in the dark night sky.

## OMAN

| | | | |
|---|---|---|---|
| **Official name** | Sultanate of Oman | **Ethnic groups** | Arab 74%, Pakistani 22%, others 4% |
| **Local name** | 'Umān; Saltanat 'Umān | **Religions** | Islam 86%, Hinduism 13%, others 1% |
| **Former name** | Sultanate of Muscat and Oman (until 1970) | **Time zone** | GMT +4 |
| **Area** | 300 000 sq km/115 800 sq mi | **Currency** | 1 Omani Rial (RO) = 1 000 baisas |
| **Capital** | Muscat; Masqaṭ | **Telephone** | +968 |
| **Chief towns** | Matrah, Nazwa, Salalah | **Internet** | .om |
| **Population** | 2 478 000 (2001e) | **Country code** | OMN |
| **Nationality** | Omani | | |
| **Languages** | Arabic | | |

**Location**

An independent state in the extreme south-eastern corner of the Arabian Peninsula. It is bounded to the north-west by the United Arab Emirates; to the north and west by Saudi Arabia; to the south-west by Yemen; to the north-east by the Gulf of Oman; and to the south-east and east by the Arabian Sea. The tip of the Musandam peninsula in the Strait of Hormuz is separated from the rest of the country by an 80km/50mi strip belonging to the United Arab Emirates.

**Physical description**

Hajar range runs north-west to south-east parallel to the coast; several peaks in the Jebal al Akhdar are over 3 000m/9 842ft; highest point is Jebel Shams (3 075m/10 088ft); alluvial plain of the Batinah lies east and north of the Hajar; a vast sand desert is to the north-east.

**Climate**

Desert climate with much regional variation; summer (Apr–Oct) is hot and humid on the coast (maximum temperature 47°C), hot and dry in the interior; relatively temperate in mountains; light monsoon rains in the south from Jun to Sep.

**National holidays**

Nov 18 (National) (2), Dec 31; Ad (5), ER (4), NY (Muslim), PB, Lailat al-Miraj (Mar/Apr).

## Political leaders

**Sultan**

| | |
|---|---|
| 1888–1913 | Faisal Bin Turki |
| 1913–32 | Taimur Bin Faisal |
| 1932–70 | Said Bin Taimur |
| 1970– | Qaboos Bin Said |

**Prime Minister**

| | |
|---|---|
| 1970–2 | Tariq Bin Taimur |
| 1972– | *As sultan* |

### Fragrant Oman

Incense-burning is an Omani tradition, and many villages will have a specialized craftsman who makes incense, known as *bokhur*, from local ingredients including ambergris, frankincense, myrrh, rosewater and sandalwood. Jasmine flowers are also used to perfume people's homes.

# PAKISTAN

| | |
|---|---|
| **Official name** | Islamic Republic of Pakistan |
| **Local name** | Pākistān; Islāmī Jamhūriya e Pākistān |
| **Former name** | formerly part of India (until 1947), Dominion of Pakistan (1947–56); known as West Pakistan (until 1971) |
| **Independence** | 1947 |
| **Area** | 803 943 sq km/310 322 sq mi |
| **Capital** | Islamabad; Islāmābād |
| **Chief towns** | Karachi, Lahore, Faisalabad, Rawalpindi |
| **Population** | 130 579 571 (1998) |
| **Nationality** | Pakistani |
| **Languages** | Urdu; English and several local languages are also spoken |
| **Ethnic groups** | Punjabi 55%, Sindhi 14%, Pashtun 14%, Mohajir 8%, Baluch 6%, others 3% |
| **Religions** | Islam 97% (Sunni 77%, Shia 20%), Hinduism 2%, Christianity 1% |
| **Time zone** | GMT +5 |
| **Currency** | 1 Pakistan Rupee (PRs, Rp) = 100 paisa |
| **Telephone** | +92 |
| **Internet** | .pk |
| **Country code** | PAK |

**Location**
An Asian state, bounded to the east by India; to the west by Afghanistan and Iran; and to the north by China; the disputed area of Jammu and Kashmir lies to the north.

**Physical description**
Largely centred on the alluvial floodplain of the River Indus; bounded to the north and west by mountains rising to 8 610m/28 251ft at K2 in the disputed Kashmir-Jammu region; mostly flat plateaux, low-lying plains, and arid desert to the south of the Karakoram range.

**Climate**
Dominated by the Asiatic monsoon; hottest season is Mar–Jun, with highest temperatures in south; rainy season is late Jun–early Oct; climate varies in the mountains and upland plateaux; Indus Valley is extremely hot in summer.

**National holidays**
Jan 1, Feb 5 (Kashmir), Mar 23 (Pakistan), May 1, Jul 1, Aug 14 (Independence), Nov 9 (Iqbal), Dec 25 (Christmas/Birthday of Quaid-e-Azam); Ad (2), As (2), ER (3), PB, R; *additional religious optional holidays*.

## Political leaders

**President**

| | |
|---|---|
| 1956–8 | Iskander Mirza |
| 1958–69 | Mohammad Ayoub Khan |
| 1969–71 | Agha Mohammad Yahya Khan |
| 1971–3 | Zulfikar Ali Bhutto |
| 1973–8 | Fazal Elahi Chawdry |
| 1978–88 | Mohammad Zia Ul-Haq |
| 1988–93 | Ghulam Ishaq Khan |
| 1993 | Wasim Sajjad *Acting President* |
| 1993–7 | Farooq Ahmad Khan Leghari |
| 1997–8 | Wasim Sajjad *Acting President* |
| 1998–2001 | Muhammed Rafiq Tarar |
| 2001– | Pervez Musharraf |

**Prime Minister**

| | |
|---|---|
| 1947–51 | Liaqat Ali Khan |
| 1951–3 | Khawaja Nazimuddin |
| 1953–5 | Mohammad Ali |
| 1955–6 | Chawdry Mohammad Ali |
| 1956–7 | Hussein Shahid Suhrawardi |
| 1957 | Ismail Chundrigar |
| 1957–8 | Malik Feroz Khan Noon |
| 1958 | Mohammad Ayoub Khan |
| 1958–73 | *No Prime Minister* |
| 1973–7 | Zulfikar Ali Bhutto |
| 1977–85 | *No Prime Minister* |
| 1985–8 | Mohammad Khan Junejo |
| 1988 | Mohammad Aslam Khan Khattak |
| 1988–90 | Benazir Bhutto |
| 1990 | Ghulam Mustafa Jatoi |
| 1990–3 | Mian Mohammad Nawaz Sharif |
| 1993–6 | Benazir Bhutto |
| 1996–7 | Meraj Khalid *Acting Prime Minister* |
| 1997–9 | Mian Mohammad Nawaz Sharif |
| 1999–2002 | *No Prime Minister* |
| 2002– | Mir Zafarullah Jamali |

# PALAU

| | |
|---|---|
| **Official name** | Republic of Palau |
| **Local name** | Belau; Belu'u era Belau |
| **Former name** | formerly part of the Trust Territory of the Pacific Islands (1917–79) |
| **Independence** | 1994 |
| **Area** | 494 sq km/191 sq mi |
| **Capital** | Koror |
| **Population** | 17 225 (1995) |
| **Nationality** | Palauan |
| **Languages** | Palauan, English |
| **Ethnic groups** | A composite of Polynesian, Malaysian and Melanesian peoples |
| **Religions** | Christianity 66% (mostly RC), traditional beliefs (Modekngei) 34% |
| **Time zone** | GMT +10 |
| **Currency** | 1 US Dollar ($, US$) = 100 cents |
| **Telephone** | +680 |
| **Internet** | .pw |
| **Country code** | PLW |

**Location**
A group of c.350 small islands and islets in the west Pacific Ocean, 960km/600mi east of the Philippines.

**Physical description**
Varies from the mountainous main island of Babelthuap to low-lying coral islands often surrounded by coral reefs; highest point is Mt Ngerchelchauus (242m/794ft).

**Climate**
Warm all year, with high humidity; average annual temperature is 27°C; typhoons are rare.

**National holidays**
Jan 1, Mar 15 (Youth), May 5 (Senior Citizens), Jun 1 (President), Jul 9 (Constitution), Oct 1 (Independence), 24 (United Nations), Dec 25; Labour Day (1st Mon in Sep), Thanksgiving (last Thurs in Nov).

## Political leaders

**President**

| | |
|---|---|
| 1981–5 | Haruo Remeliik |
| 1985 | Thomas Remengesau *Acting President* |
| 1985 | Alfonso Oiterong |
| 1985–8 | Lazarus Salii |
| 1988–9 | Thomas Remengesau |
| 1989–93 | Ngiratkel Etpison |
| 1993–2000 | Kuniwo Nakamura |
| 2001– | Tommy Remengesau |

### *Get By in Palauan*

The Palauan word for *hello* is *alii*, and *how are you?* is *ke ua ngerang? Goodbye* is *ak morolung*, while other useful phrases include *ngtecha ngklem?* for *what is your name?* and *bo momengur!* which means *have something to eat!*

**PALESTINE, PALESTINIAN AUTONOMOUS AREAS** *see* **ISRAEL**

## PANAMA

| | | | |
|---|---|---|---|
| **Official name** | Republic of Panama | **Ethnic groups** | mestizo 62%, black 13%, white 12%, mulatto 8%, Amerindian 5% |
| **Local name** | Panamá; República de Panamá | **Religions** | Christianity 89% (RC 84%, Prot 5%), Islam 5%, Baha'i 1%, others 5% |
| **Independence** | 1821 (from Spain), 1903 (from Gran Colombia union) | **Time zone** | GMT –5 |
| **Area** | 77 082 sq km/29 753 sq mi | **Currency** | 1 Balboa (B, Ba) = 100 centésimos; the US dollar is also in use |
| **Capital** | Panama City; La Ciudad de Panamá | **Telephone** | +507 |
| **Chief towns** | David, Colón, Santiago | **Internet** | .pa |
| **Population** | 2 839 177 (2000) | **Country code** | PAN |
| **Nationality** | Panamanian | | |
| **Languages** | Spanish | | |

**Location**
A republic occupying the south-eastern end of the isthmus of Central America, bounded to the north by the Caribbean Sea; to the south by the Pacific Ocean; to the west by Costa Rica; and to the east by Colombia.

**Physical description**
Mostly mountainous; Serranía de Tabasará in the west rises to over 2 000m/6 562ft; highest point is Barú volcano in Chiriqui (3 475m/11 400ft); Azuero peninsula lies to the south; lake-studded lowland cuts across the isthmus; dense tropical forests on the Caribbean coast; Panama Canal (c.80km/50mi long) links the Pacific and Caribbean coasts.

**Climate**
Tropical, with a mean annual temperature of 32°C.

**National holidays**
Jan 1, 9 (Martyrs), May 1, Nov 3 (Independence), 10 (First Call of Independence), 28 (Independence from Spain), Dec 8 (Mothers), 25; C, GF; *some local variation*.

## Political leaders

**President**

| | |
|---|---|
| 1904–8 | Manuel Amador Guerrero |
| 1908–10 | José Domingo de Obaldia |
| 1910 | Federico Boyd |
| 1910 | Carlos Antonio Mendoza |
| 1910–12 | Pablo Arosemena |
| 1912 | Rodolfo Chiari |
| 1912–16 | Belisario Porras |
| 1916–18 | Ramón Maximiliano Valdés |
| 1918 | Pedro Antonio Diaz |
| 1918 | Cirilo Luis Urriola |
| 1918–20 | Belisario Porras |
| 1920 | Ernesto T Lefevre |
| 1920–4 | Belisario Porras |
| 1924–8 | Rodolfo Chiari |
| 1928 | Tomás Gabriel Duque |
| 1928–31 | Florencio Harmodio Arosemena |
| 1931 | Harmodio Arias |
| 1931–2 | Ricardo Joaquín Alfaro |
| 1932–6 | Harmodio Arias |
| 1936–9 | Juan Demóstenes Arosemena |
| 1939 | Ezequiel Fernández Jaén |
| 1939–40 | Augusto Samuel Boyd |
| 1940–1 | Arnulfo Arias Madrid |
| 1941 | Ernesto Jaén Guardia |
| 1941 | José Pezet |
| 1941–5 | Ricardo Adolfo de la Guardia |
| 1945–8 | Enrique Adolfo Jiménez Brin |
| 1948–9 | Domingo Diaz Arosemena |
| 1949 | Daniel Chanis |
| 1949 | Roberto Francisco Chiari |
| 1949–51 | Arnulfo Arias Madrid |
| 1951–2 | Alcibiades Arosemena |
| 1952–5 | José Antonio Remón |
| 1955 | José Ramón Guizado |
| 1955–6 | Ricardo Manuel Arias Espinosa |
| 1956–60 | Ernesto de la Guardia |
| 1960–4 | Roberto Francisco Chiari |
| 1964–8 | Marco A Robles |
| 1968 | Arnulfo Arias Madrid |
| 1968 | *Military Junta* |
| 1968–9 | Omar Torrijos Herrera |
| 1969–78 | Demetrio Basilio Lakas |
| 1978–82 | Aristides Royo |
| 1982–4 | Ricardo de la Esoriella |
| 1984 | Jorge Enrique Illueca Sibauste |
| 1984–5 | Nicolás Ardito Barletta |
| 1985–8 | Eric Arturo Delvalle |
| 1988–9 | Manuel Solís Palma |
| 1989–94 | Guillermo Endara Galimany |
| 1994–9 | Ernesto Pérez Balladares |
| 1999– | Mireya Elisa Moscoso Rodriguez |

### *Fish and Butterflies*

The name *Panama* is widely believed to mean 'an abundance of fish' or 'an abundance of butterflies' in the local Amerindian language.

## PAPUA NEW GUINEA

| | |
|---|---|
| **Official name** | Independent State of Papua New Guinea (PNG) |
| **Local name** | Papua New Guinea; Gau Hedinarai ai Papua–Matamata Guinea |
| **Independence** | 1975 |
| **Area** | 462 840 sq km/178 656 sq mi |
| **Capital** | Port Moresby |
| **Chief towns** | Lae, Madang, Rabaul |
| **Population** | 5 190 786 (2000) |
| **Nationality** | Papua New Guinean |
| **Languages** | Pidgin English; approximately 800 other languages are spoken |
| **Ethnic groups** | Papuan 85%, Melanesian 1%, others 14% |
| **Religions** | Christianity 66% (Prot and others 44%, RC 22%), traditional beliefs 34% |
| **Time zone** | GMT +10 |
| **Currency** | 1 Kina (K) = 100 toea |
| **Telephone** | +675 |
| **Internet** | .pg |
| **Country code** | PNG |

**Location**
An independent island group in the south-west Pacific Ocean, comprising the eastern half of the island of New Guinea, bordering Indonesia to the west, and many smaller islands.

**Physical description**
Complex mountain system, with snow-covered peaks rising above 4 000m/13 123ft; highest point is Mt Wilhelm (4 509m/1 4793ft); mainly covered with tropical rainforest; coastal mangrove swamps; other islands are also mountainous and mostly volcanic.

**Climate**
Typically monsoonal, with temperatures and humidity constantly high; the average temperature range is 22–33°C; high rainfall.

**National holidays**
Jan 1, Jul 23 (Remembrance), Sep 16 (Independence), Dec 25, 26; EM, ES, GF, HS, Queen's Birthday (Jun).

## Political leaders

**Prime Minister**

| | |
|---|---|
| 1975–80 | Michael T Somare |
| 1980–2 | Julius Chan |
| 1982–5 | Michael T Somare |
| 1985–8 | Paias Wingti |
| 1988–92 | Rabbie Namaliu |
| 1992–4 | Paias Wingti |
| 1994–7 | Julius Chan |
| 1997 | John Giheno *Acting Prime Minister* |
| 1997 | Julius Chan |
| 1997–9 | Bill Skate |
| 1999–2002 | Mekere Morauta |
| 2002– | Michael T Somare |

### *Birds of Paradise*

The bird of paradise is important to many people in Papua New Guinea, and its beautiful feathers are used for decoration and in cultural and religious ceremonies. A yellow bird of paradise with trailing plumes is shown in flight on the national flag, while the national crest shows a striking crimson and gold bird with spread wings sitting on a ceremonial drum, with a traditional spear behind it.

## PARAGUAY

| | | | |
|---|---|---|---|
| **Official name** | Republic of Paraguay | **Ethnic groups** | mestizo 92%, white 2%, Amerindian 2%, others 4% |
| **Local name** | Paraguay; República del Paraguay | **Religions** | Christianity 99% (RC 90%, Prot 9%, mostly Mennonite), others 1% |
| **Independence** | 1811 | **Time zone** | GMT –4 |
| **Area** | 406 750 sq km/157 000 sq mi | **Currency** | 1 Guaraní (Gs) = 100 céntimos |
| **Capital** | Asunción | **Telephone** | +595 |
| **Chief towns** | Villarrica, Concepción | **Internet** | .py |
| **Population** | 5 604 000 (2001e) | **Country code** | PRY |
| **Nationality** | Paraguayan | | |
| **Languages** | Spanish, Guaraní | | |

**Location**
A landlocked country in central South America, bounded to the north-west by Bolivia; to the north and east by Brazil; to the south-west by Argentina; the River Paraná forms the Argentinian border in the south and east.

**Physical description**
Divided into two regions by the River Paraguay, lying mostly at altitudes below 450m/1476ft; west is mostly cattle country or scrub forest; more fertile in the east; higher Paraná Plateau is mainly wet, treeless savannah; highest point is Cerro Pero (842m/2 762ft).

**Climate**
Tropical in the north-west, with hot summers and warm winters; temperate in the south-east; temperature at Asunción ranges from 12°C in winter to 35°C in summer.

**National holidays**
Jan 1, Mar 1 (Battle of Cerro Corá), May 1, 15 (Independence), Jun 12 (Chaco Peace), Aug 15 (Foundation of Asunción), Dec 8, 25; GF, HT.

## Political leaders

**President**

| | |
|---|---|
| 1898–1902 | Emilio Aceval |
| 1902 | Héctor Carvallo |
| 1902–4 | Juan Antonio Escurra |
| 1904–5 | Juan Gaona |
| 1905–6 | Cecilio Baez |
| 1906–8 | Benigno Ferreira |
| 1908–10 | Emiliano González Navero |
| 1910–11 | Manuel Gondra |
| 1911 | Albino Jara |
| 1911 | Liberato Marcial Rojas |
| 1912 | Pedro Peña |
| 1912 | Emiliano González Navero |
| 1912–16 | Eduardo Schaerer |
| 1916–19 | Manuel Franco |
| 1919–20 | José P Montero |
| 1920–1 | Manuel Gondra |
| 1921 | Félix Paiva |
| 1921–3 | Eusebio Ayala |
| 1923–4 | Eligio Ayala |
| 1924 | Luis Alberto Riart |
| 1924–8 | Eligio Ayala |
| 1928–31 | José Particio Guggiari |
| 1931–2 | Emiliano González Navero |
| 1932 | José Particio Guggiari |
| 1932–6 | Eusebio Ayala |
| 1936–7 | Rafael Franco |
| 1937–9 | Félix Paiva |
| 1939–40 | José Félix Estigarribia |
| 1940–8 | Higino Moríñigo |
| 1948 | Juan Manuel Frutos |
| 1948–9 | Juan Natalicio González |
| 1949 | Raimundo Rolón |
| 1949 | Felipe Molas López |
| 1949–54 | Federico Chaves |
| 1954 | Tomás Romero Pareira |
| 1954–89 | Alfredo Stroessner |
| 1989–93 | Andrés Rodríguez |
| 1993–8 | Juan Carlos Wasmosy |
| 1998–9 | Raúl Cubas Grau |
| 1999–2003 | Luis González Mácchi |
| 2003– | Nicanor Duarte Frutos |

### Pleistocene Peccary

The Chacoan peccary is a hairy, pig-like creature that lives in the Gran Chaco, a vast area of arid scrublands, cacti and thorny vegetation in north-west Paraguay. The Chacoan peccary was thought to be extinct but had been described from fossil records of the Pleistocene period; the creature was discovered alive, to great scientific astonishment, in the 1970s.

# PERU

| | | | |
|---|---|---|---|
| **Official name** | Republic of Peru | **Ethnic groups** | Quechua 46%, mestizo 34%, white 12%, Aymara 5%, others 3% |
| **Local name** | Perú; República del Perú | **Religions** | Christianity 96% (RC 89%, Prot 7%), others 4% |
| **Independence** | 1821 | **Time zone** | GMT –5 |
| **Area** | 1 284 640 sq km/ 495 871 sq mi | **Currency** | 1 Nuevo Sol (Pes) = 100 cénts |
| **Capital** | Lima | **Telephone** | +51 |
| **Chief towns** | Arequipa, Chiclayo, Cuzco, Trujillo | **Internet** | .pe |
| **Population** | 26 347 000 (2001e) | **Country code** | PER |
| **Nationality** | Peruvian | | |
| **Languages** | Spanish, Quechua; Aymara is also widely spoken | | |

**Location**
A republic on the west coast of South America, bounded to the north by Ecuador; to the north-east by Colombia; to the east by Brazil and Bolivia; and to the south by Chile.

**Physical description**
Arid plains and foothills on the coast, with desert areas and fertile river valleys; 50% of the population lives on the central sierra, at an average altitude of 3 000m/9 842ft; highest point is Huascarán (6 768m/22 204ft); forested Amazon basin lies to the east; major rivers flow to the Amazon; Lake Titicaca lies on the Bolivian border.

**Climate**
Mild temperatures on the coast; dry, arid desert in the south; northern coastal region is affected by El Niño; Andean temperatures never rise above 23°C with a large daily range; the climate is typically wet and tropical in the Amazon basin.

**National holidays**
Jan 1, May 1, Jun 24 (Peasants), 29 (SS Peter and Paul), Jul 28 (Independence) (2), Aug 30 (St Rose of Lima), Oct 8 (Battle of Angamos), Nov 1, Dec 8, 25; GF, HT.

## Political leaders

**President**

| | |
|---|---|
| 1899–1903 | Eduardo López de Romaña |
| 1903–4 | Manuel Candamo |
| 1904 | Serapio Calderón |
| 1904–8 | José Pardo y Barreda |
| 1908–12 | Augusto B Leguía |
| 1912–14 | Guillermo Billinghurst |
| 1914–15 | Oscar R Benavides |
| 1915–19 | José Pardo y Barreda |
| 1919–30 | Augusto B Leguía |
| 1930 | Manuel Ponce |
| 1930–1 | Luis M Sánchez Cerro |
| 1931 | Leoncio Elías |
| 1931 | Gustavo A Jiménez |
| 1931 | David Samanez Ocampo |
| 1931–3 | Luis M Sánchez Cerro |
| 1933–9 | Oscar R Benavides |
| 1939–45 | Manuel Prado |
| 1945–8 | José Luis Bustamante y Rivero |
| 1948–56 | Manuel A Odría |
| 1956–62 | Manuel Prado |
| 1962–3 | *Military Junta* |
| 1963–8 | Fernando Belaúnde Terry |
| 1968–75 | *Military Junta* (Juan Velasco Alvarado) |
| 1975–80 | *Military Junta* (Francisco Morales Bermúdez) |

| | | | |
|---|---|---|---|
| 1980–5 | Fernando Belaúnde Terry | 2000–1 | Valentín Paniagua *Interim President* |
| 1985–90 | Alan García Pérez | 2001– | Alejandro Toledo Manrique |
| 1990–2000 | Alberto Keinya Fujimori | | |

**Prime Minister**

| | | | |
|---|---|---|---|
| 1900 | Enrique Coronel Zegarra y Cortés | 1935–6 | Manuel Esteban Rodríguez |
| 1900–1 | Domingo M Almenara Butler | 1936–9 | Ernesto Montagne Markholz |
| 1901–2 | Cesáreo Chacaltana Reyes | 1939 | Alberto Rey de Castro y Romaña |
| 1902 | Cesáreo Octavio Deustua Escarza | 1939–44 | Alfredo Solf y Muro |
| 1902–3 | Eugenio Larrabure y Unanue | 1944–5 | Manuel Cisneros Sánchez |
| 1903–4 | José Pardo y Barreda | 1945–6 | Rafael Belaúnde y Diez Canseco |
| 1904 | Alberto Elmore Fernández de Córdoba | 1946–7 | Julio Ernesto Portugal Escobedo |
| | | 1947 | José Alcamora |
| 1904–7 | Augusto B Leguía y Salcedo | 1948 | Roque Augusto Saldías Maninat |
| 1907 | Agustín Tovar | 1948 | Armando Revoredo Iglesias |
| 1907–8 | Carlos A Washburn Salas | 1948–54 | *No Prime Minister* |
| 1908–9 | Eulogio Romero Salcedo | 1954–6 | Roque Augusto Saldías Maninat |
| 1909–10 | Rafael Fernández de Villanueva Cortez | 1956–7 | Manuel Cisneros Sánchez |
| | | 1958–9 | Luis Gallo Porras |
| 1910 | Javier Prado y Ugarteche | 1959–61 | Pedro Gerardo Beltrán Espantos |
| 1910 | Germán Schreiber Waddington | 1961–2 | Carlos Moreyra y Paz Soldán |
| 1910 | José Salvador Cavero | 1962–3 | Nicolás Lindley López |
| 1910–11 | Enrique C Basadre Stevenson | 1963 | Julio Óscar Trelles Montes |
| 1911–12 | Agustín G Ganoza Cavero | 1963–5 | Fernando Schwalb López Aldana |
| 1912 | Elías Malpartida | 1965–7 | Daniel Becerra de la Flor |
| 1912–13 | Enrique Varela | 1967 | Edgardo Seoane Corrales |
| 1913 | Federico Luna y Peralta | 1967–8 | Raúl Ferrero Rebagliati |
| 1913 | Aurelio Sousa Matute | 1968 | Oswaldo Hercelles García |
| 1913–14 | Enrique Varela | 1968 | Miguel Mujica Gallo |
| 1914 | Pedro E Muñiz | 1968–73 | Ernesto Montagne Sánchez |
| 1914 | Manuel Melitón Carvajal | 1973–5 | Edgardo Mercado Jarrín |
| 1914 | Aurelio Sousa Matute | 1975 | Francisco Morales Bermúdez |
| 1914–15 | Germán Schreiber Waddington | 1975–6 | Óscar Vargas Prieto |
| 1915 | Carlos Isaac Abrill | 1976 | Jorge Fernández Maldonado Solari |
| 1915–17 | Enrique de la Riva-Agüero y Looz Corswaren | 1976–8 | Guillermo Arbulú Galliani |
| 1917–18 | Francisco Tudela y Varela | 1978–9 | Óscar Molina Pallochia |
| 1918–19 | Germán Arenas y Loayza | 1979–80 | Pedro Richter Prada |
| 1919 | Juan Manuel Zuloaga | 1980–3 | Manuel Ulloa Elías |
| 1919–22 | Germán Leguía y Martínez Jakeway | 1983–4 | Fernando Schwalb López Aldana |
| | | 1984 | Sandro Mariátegui Chiappe |
| 1922–4 | Julio Enrique Ego Aguirre | 1984–5 | Luis Pércovich Roca |
| 1924–6 | Alejandrino Maguiña | 1985–7 | Luis Alva Castro |
| 1926–9 | Pedro José Rada y Gamio | 1987–8 | Guillermo Larco Cox |
| 1929–30 | Benjamín Huamán de los Heros | 1988–9 | Armando Villanueva del Campo |
| 1930–1 | Fernando Sarmiento | 1989 | Luis Alberto Sánchez |
| 1931–2 | Germán Arenas y Loayza | 1989–90 | Guillermo Larco Cox |
| 1932 | Francisco R Lanatta | 1990–1 | Juan Carlos Hurtado Miller |
| 1932 | Luis A Flores | 1991 | Carlos Torres y Torres Lara |
| 1932 | Ricardo Rivadeneira | 1991–2 | Alfonso de los Heros |
| 1932–3 | José Matías Manzanilla Barrientos | 1992–3 | Óscar de la Puente Raygada |
| | | 1993–4 | Alfonso Bustamante y Bustamante |
| 1933 | Jorge Prado y Ugarteche | | |
| 1933–4 | José de la Riva-Agüero y Osma | 1994–5 | Efraín Goldenberg Schreiber |
| 1934–5 | Carlos Arenas y Loayza | 1995–6 | Dante Córdova Blanco |

| | | | |
|---|---|---|---|
| 1996–8 | Alberto Pandolfi | 2000 | Federico Salas Guevara |
| 1998 | Javier Valle Riestra | 2001 | Javier Perez de Cuellar |
| 1998–9 | Alberto Pandolfi | 2001–2 | Roberto Daniño Zapata |
| 1999 | Víctor Joy Way | 2002–3 | Luis Solari de la Fuente |
| 1999–2000 | Alberto Bustamante Belaúnde | 2003– | Beatriz Merino |

### *Peruvian Pisco*

Peru's national drink is *pisco*, an alcoholic grape liqueur made nowhere else in the world which is named after the Quechua word for 'bird'. Grape vines were introduced to Peru during Spanish colonization of South America in the 16c, but the Peruvians proved so adept at winemaking that worried Spanish vineyards banned the trade. The Peruvian producers therefore switched from wines to liqueurs, using ancient Inca earthenware, and created pisco.

## PHILIPPINES

| | |
|---|---|
| **Official name** | Republic of the Philippines |
| **Local name** | Pilipinas; Repúblika Ñg Pilipinas |
| **Independence** | 1946 |
| **Area** | 299 679 sq km/115 676 sq mi |
| **Capital** | Manila |
| **Chief towns** | Quezon City, Basilan, Cebu, Bacolod, Davao, Iloilo |
| **Population** | 76 498 735 (2000) |
| **Nationality** | Filipino (masculine), Filipina (feminine), Philippine |
| **Languages** | Pilipino; English and many local dialects are also spoken |
| **Ethnic groups** | Tagalog 30%, Cebuano 23%, Ilocano 9%, Ilongo 9%, Bicol 6%, Samar-Leyte 3%, others 20% |
| **Religions** | Christianity 92% (RC 83%, Prot 9%), Islam 5%, others 3% |
| **Time zone** | GMT +8 |
| **Currency** | 1 Philippine Peso (PHP) = 100 centavos |
| **Telephone** | +63 |
| **Internet** | .ph |
| **Country code** | PHL |

**Location**
A republic consisting of an archipelago of more than 7 100 islands and islets, situated to the north-east of Borneo (Indonesia) and to the south of Taiwan.

**Physical description**
Largely mountainous, with north to south ridges rising to over 2 500m/8 200ft; highest point is Mt Apo (2 954m/9 691ft); narrow coastal margins and broad interior plateaux; forests cover half the land area; some islands are ringed by coral reefs.

**Climate**
Lowlands have a warm and humid tropical climate throughout the year, with an average temperature of 27°C; lying astride the typhoon belt, the Philippines are affected by c.15 cyclonic storms annually.

**National holidays**
Jan 1, Apr 9 (Araw Ng Kagitingan), May 1, Jun 12 (Independence), Aug 30 (National Heroes), Nov 1, 2, 30 (Bonifacio), Dec 25, 30 (Rizal), 31; GF, HT.

## Political leaders

**President**

| | | | |
|---|---|---|---|
| 1935–44 | Manuel L Quezon (*in exile from 1942*) | 1957–61 | Carlos P Garcia |
| 1943–4 | José P Laurel (*Japanese occupation*) | 1961–5 | Diosdado Macapagal |
| 1944–6 | Sergio Osmeña | 1965–86 | Ferdinand E Marcos (*Martial law 1972–81*) |
| 1946–8 | Manuel A Roxas | 1986–92 | Corazon C Aquino |
| 1948–53 | Elpidio Quirino | 1992–8 | Fidel V Ramos |
| 1953–7 | Ramon Magsaysay | 1998–2001 | Joseph Estrada |
| | | 2001– | Gloria Macapagel-Arroyo |

### Seashells and Volcanoes

The Philippines Department of Tourism proudly reports that 488 of the world's 500 species of coral are found in its waters, along with seven of the eight known species of giant clam, five of the eight species of marine turtle and approximately 12 000 types of seashell. It adds that the province of Camiguin not only has more volcanoes per square kilometre than any other island in the world, but is 'the only place in the Philippines which has more volcanoes (seven) than towns (five)'.

**PITCAIRN ISLANDS** *see* **UNITED KINGDOM**

## POLAND

| | | | |
|---|---|---|---|
| **Official name** | Republic of Poland | **Nationality** | Pole, Polish |
| **Local name** | Polska; Rzeczpospolita Polska | **Languages** | Polish |
| **Former name** | People's Republic of Poland (1952–89) | **Ethnic groups** | Polish 98%, German 1%, others 1% |
| **Independence** | 1918 | **Religions** | Christianity 96% (RC 93%, Orthodox 2%, Prot 1%), none/unaffiliated 2%, others 2% |
| **Area** | 312 612 sq km/120 668 sq mi | | |
| **Capital** | Warsaw; Warszawa | **Time zone** | GMT +1 |
| **Chief towns** | Łódz, Kraków, Wrocław, Poznań, Gdańsk, Katowice, Lublin | **Currency** | 1 Złoty (Zl) = 100 groszy |
| | | **Telephone** | +48 |
| | | **Internet** | .pl |
| **Population** | 38 641 000 (2001e) | **Country code** | POL |

# POLAND

**Location**
A republic in central Europe, bounded to the north by Russia and the Baltic Sea; to the west by Germany; to the south-west by the Czech Republic; to the south by Slovakia; to the south-east by the Ukraine; and to the north-east by Belarus and Lithuania.

**Physical description**
Mostly part of the great European plain; mountains in the south rise in the High Tatra to 2 499m/8 199ft at Mt Rysy; Europe's richest coal basin lies in the west (Silesia); lowlands with many lakes in the north.

**Climate**
Continental climate, with severe winters and hot summers; rain falls chiefly in summer.

**National holidays**
Jan 1, May 1, 3 (National), Aug 15, Nov 1, 11 (Independence), Dec 25, 26; CC, EM.

## Political leaders

### Republic of Poland

**President**

| | |
|---|---|
| 1945–52 | Bolesław Bierut *Acting President until 1947* |
| 1952–64 | Aleksander Zawadzki |
| 1964–8 | Edward Ochab |
| 1968–70 | Marian Spychalski |
| 1970–2 | Józef Cyrankiewicz |
| 1972–85 | Henryk Jabłonski |
| 1985–90 | Wojciech Jaruzelski |
| 1990–5 | Lech Wałesa |
| 1995– | Aleksander Kwaśniewski |

**Prime Minister**

| | |
|---|---|
| 1947–52 | Józef Cyrankiewicz |
| 1952–4 | Bolesław Bierut |
| 1954–70 | Józef Cyrankiewicz |
| 1970–80 | Piotr Jecoszewicz |
| 1980 | Edward Babiuch |
| 1980–1 | Józef Pinkowski |
| 1981–5 | Wojciech Jaruzelski |
| 1985–8 | Zbigniew Messner |
| 1988–9 | Mieczyslaw Rakowski |
| 1989 | Czeslaw Kiszczak |
| 1989–90 | Tadeusz Mazowiecki |
| 1991 | Jan Krzysztof Bielecki |
| 1991–2 | Jan Olszewski |
| 1992 | Waldemar Pawlak |
| 1992–3 | Hanna Suchocka |
| 1993–5 | Waldemar Pawlak |
| 1995–6 | Józef Oleksy |
| 1996–7 | Wlodzimierz Cimoszewicz |
| 1997–2001 | Jerzy Buzek |
| 2001– | Leszek Miller |

**First Secretary**

| | |
|---|---|
| 1945–8 | Władysław Gomułka |
| 1948–56 | Bolesław Bierut |
| 1956 | Edward Ochab |
| 1956–70 | Władysław Gomułka |
| 1970–80 | Edward Gierek |
| 1980–1 | Stanisław Kania |
| 1981–9 | Wojciech Jaruzelski |
| 1989 | Mieczyslaw Rakowski |

**Polish Pines**

Forests cover about 27% of Poland, with pine trees the most abundant species.

**POLYNESIA, FRENCH** *see* **FRANCE**

# PORTUGAL

| | | | |
|---|---|---|---|
| **Official name** | Portuguese Republic | **Languages** | Portuguese |
| **Local name** | Portugal; República Portuguesa | **Ethnic groups** | Portuguese 99%, others 1% |
| **Former name** | Kingdom of Portugal (until 1910) | **Religions** | Christianity 96% (RC 94%, Prot 2%), none/unaffiliated 3%, others 1% |
| **Independence** | 1668 | | |
| **Area** | 88 500 sq km/34 200 sq mi | **Time zone** | GMT |
| **Capital** | Lisbon; Lisboa | **Currency** | 1 Euro (€) = 100 cents |
| **Chief towns** | Oporto, Setúbal, Coimbra | **Telephone** | +351 |
| **Population** | 10 355 824 (2001) | **Internet** | .pt |
| **Nationality** | Portuguese | **Country code** | PRT |

**Location**
A country in south-western Europe on the western side of the Iberian Peninsula, bounded to the north and east by Spain; and to the south and west by the Atlantic Ocean; also includes the islands of the Azores and Madeira.

**Physical description**
Several mountain ranges formed by the west spurs of the Spanish mountain system; chief range is the Serra da Estrêla in the north, rising to 1 991m/6 532ft; highest point is Mt Pico on Ilha do Pico (Pico Island) in the Azores (2 351m/7 713ft).

**Climate**
Basically a maritime climate, with increased variation between summer and winter temperatures inland; west coast is relatively cool in summer; most rainfall in winter.

**National holidays**
Jan 1, Apr 25 (Liberty), May 1, Jun 10 (Camões-Portugal), Aug 15, Oct 5 (Republic), Nov 1, Dec 1 (Independence), Dec 8, 24, 25; C, CC, GF.

## Azores

| | | | |
|---|---|---|---|
| **Location** | An island archipelago of volcanic origin in the North Atlantic ocean, lying 1 400–1 800km/870–1 100mi to the west of the Cabo da Roca on mainland Portugal. | | |
| **Area** | 2 300 sq km/900 sq mi | **Population** | 250 000 (1999e) |
| **Capital** | Ponta Delgada | | |

## Madeira

| | | | |
|---|---|---|---|
| **Location** | The main island in a Portuguese archipelago off the coast of North Africa, 990km/615mi south-west of Lisbon. | | |
| **Area** | 796 sq km/307 sq mi | **Population** | 275 000 (1999e) |
| **Capital** | Funchal | | |

## Political leaders

**Monarch**

1095–1112 Henry of Burgundy
1112–85 Alfonso I
1185–1211 Sancho I
1211–23 Alfonso II

| | |
|---|---|
| 1223–45 | Sancho II |
| 1245–79 | Alfonso III |
| 1279–1325 | Diniz |
| 1325–57 | Alfonso IV |
| 1357–67 | Peter I |
| 1367–83 | Ferdinand |
| 1383–5 | *disputed by John of Castile and John of Aviz* |
| 1385–1433 | John I of Aviz |
| 1433–8 | Edward |
| 1438–81 | Alfonso V |
| 1481–95 | John II |
| 1495–1521 | Manuel I |
| 1521–57 | John III |
| 1557–78 | Sebastian |
| 1578–80 | Henry |
| 1580–98 | Philip I (II of Spain) |
| 1598–1621 | Philip II (III of Spain) |
| 1621–40 | Philip III (IV of Spain) |
| 1640–56 | John IV of Braganza |
| 1656–83 | Alfonso VI |
| 1683–1706 | Peter II |
| 1706–50 | John V |
| 1750–77 | Joseph |
| 1777–1816 | Maria I |
| 1777–86 | Peter III (King Consort) |
| 1816–26 | John VI |
| 1826 | Peter IV (I of Brazil) |
| 1826–8 | Maria II |
| 1828–34 | Miguel |
| 1834–53 | Maria II |
| 1853–61 | Peter V |
| 1861–89 | Luis |
| 1889–1908 | Charles |
| 1908–10 | Manuel II |

## First Republic

**President**

| | |
|---|---|
| 1910–11 | Teófilo Braga |
| 1911–15 | Manuel José de Arriaga |
| 1915 | Teófilo Braga |
| 1915–17 | Bernardino Machado |
| 1917–18 | Sidónio Pais |
| 1918–19 | Joâo do Canto e Castro |
| 1919–23 | António José de Almeida |
| 1923–5 | Manuel Teixeira Gomes |
| 1925–6 | Bernardino Machado |

## New State

**President**

| | |
|---|---|
| 1926 | *Military Junta* (José Mendes Cabeçadas) |
| 1926 | *Military Junta* (Manuel de Oliveira Gomes da Costa) |
| 1926–51 | António Oscar Fragoso Carmona |
| 1951–8 | Francisco Craveiro Lopes |
| 1958–74 | Américo de Deus Tomás |

**Prime Minister**

| | |
|---|---|
| 1932–68 | António de Oliveira Salazar |
| 1968–74 | Marcelo Caetano |

## Second Republic

**President**

| | |
|---|---|
| 1974 | *Military Junta* (António Spínola) |
| 1974–6 | *Military Junta* (Francisco da Costa Gomes) |

**Prime Minister**

| | |
|---|---|
| 1974 | Adelino da Palma Carlos |
| 1974–5 | Vasco Gonçalves |
| 1975–6 | José Pinheiro de Azevedo |

## Third Republic

**President**

| | |
|---|---|
| 1976–86 | António dos Santos Ramalho Eanes |
| 1986–96 | Mário Soares |
| 1996– | Jorge Sampaio |

**Prime Minister**

| | |
|---|---|
| 1976–8 | Mário Soares |
| 1978 | Alfredo Nobre da Costa |
| 1978–9 | Carlos Alberto de Mota Pinto |
| 1979 | Maria de Lurdes Pintasilgo |
| 1980–1 | Francisco de Sá Carneiro |
| 1981–3 | Francisco Pinto Balsemão |
| 1983–5 | Mário Soares |
| 1985–95 | Aníbal Cavaço Silva |
| 1995–2001 | António Guterres |
| 2002– | José Manuel Durão Barroso |

**PRÍNCIPE** *see* **SÃO TOMÉ AND PRÍNCIPE**

**PUERTO RICO** *see* **UNITED STATES OF AMERICA**

## QATAR

| | |
|---|---|
| **Official name** | State of Qatar |
| **Local name** | Qatar; Dawlat Qatar |
| **Independence** | 1971 |
| **Area** | 11 437 sq km/4 415 sq mi |
| **Capital** | Doha; Ad Dawhah |
| **Chief towns** | Dukhan, Al Khawr, Umm Sai'd, Al Wakrah |
| **Population** | 522 023 (1997) |
| **Nationality** | Qatari |
| **Languages** | Arabic |
| **Ethnic groups** | Arab 40%, Pakistani 18%, Indian 18%, Iranian 10%, others 14% |
| **Religions** | Islam 95%, others 5% |
| **Time zone** | GMT +3 |
| **Currency** | 1 Qatari Riyal (QR) = 100 dirhams |
| **Telephone** | +974 |
| **Internet** | .qa |
| **Country code** | QAT |

**Location**
A low-lying state on the east coast of the Arabian Peninsula, comprising the Qatar Peninsula and numerous small offshore islands. It is bounded to the south by Saudi Arabia and the United Arab Emirates, and elsewhere by the Arabian Gulf.

**Physical description**
The peninsula, 160km/100mi long and 55–80km/34–50mi wide, slopes gently from the Dukhān Heights (98m/322ft) to the east shore; highest point is Qurayn Abu al Bawl (103m/338ft); barren terrain, mainly sand and gravel; coral reefs offshore.

**Climate**
Desert climate with average temperatures of 23°C in the winter and 35°C in the summer; high humidity; sparse annual rainfall.

**National holidays**
Sep 3 (Independence), Dec 31; Ad (4), ER (4).

### Political leaders

**Emir**

*Family name: al-Thani*

| | |
|---|---|
| 1971–2 | Ahmad Bin Ali |
| 1972–95 | Khalifa Bin Hamad |
| 1995– | Hamad Bin Khalifa |

**Prime Minister**

| | |
|---|---|
| 1971–95 | *As emir* |
| 1995–6 | *As emir* |
| 1996– | Abdullah Bin Khalifa |

**RAS AL-KHAIMAH** *see* **UNITED ARAB EMIRATES**

**REPUBLIC OF CHINA** *see* **TAIWAN**

**RÉUNION** *see* **FRANCE**

## ROMANIA

| | | | |
|---|---|---|---|
| **Official name** | Romania | **Nationality** | Romanian |
| **Local name** | România | **Languages** | Romanian |
| **Former name** | Kingdom of Romania (until 1947), People's Republic of Romania (1947–65), Socialist Republic of Romania (1965–89); known as Rumania in English until 1966 | **Ethnic groups** | Romanian 89%, Magyar 9%, Romany 1%, others 1% |
| | | **Religions** | Christianity 94% (Orthodox 82%, RC 6%, Prot 6%), none/unaffiliated 4%, Islam 1%, others 1% |
| **Independence** | 1878 | **Time zone** | GMT +2 |
| **Area** | 237 500 sq km/91 675 sq mi | **Currency** | 1 Leu (L) = 100 bani |
| **Capital** | Bucharest; București | **Telephone** | +40 |
| **Chief towns** | Brașov, Constanța, Iași, Timișoara, Cluj-Napoca | **Internet** | .ro |
| **Population** | 22 408 000 (2001e) | **Country code** | ROU |

**Location**
A republic in south-eastern Europe, bounded to the south by Bulgaria; to the west by Serbia and Montenegro and Hungary; to the east by Moldova and the Black Sea; and to the north and east by the Ukraine.

**Physical description**
Carpathian Mountains separate Old Romania from Transylvania, and form the heart of the country; highest peak is Mt Moldoveanu (2 544m/8 349ft); Romanian Plain in the south includes the richest arable area; over 25% of the land is forested.

**Climate**
Continental, with cold, snowy winters and warm summers; mildest area in winter is along the Black Sea coast; plains of the north and east can suffer from drought; average rainfall is higher in the mountains than in the Danube delta.

**National holidays**
Jan 1, 2, May 1, Dec 1 (National), 25, 26; Orthodox Easter (Apr/May) (2); *other major religions each have 2 days for festivals.*

## Political leaders

**Monarch**

| | |
|---|---|
| 1881–1914 | Carol I |
| 1914–27 | Ferdinand I |
| 1927–30 | Michael *Prince* |
| 1930–40 | Carol II |
| 1940–7 | Michael I |

**President**

| | |
|---|---|
| 1947–8 | Mihai Sadoveanu *Interim President* |
| 1948–52 | Constantin I Parhon |
| 1952–8 | Petru Groza |
| 1965–7 | Chivu Stoica |
| 1967–89 | Nicolae Ceaușescu |
| 1989–96 | Ion Iliescu |

| | |
|---|---|
| 1958–61 | Ion Georghe Maurer |
| 1961–5 | Georghe Gheorghiu-Dej |
| 1996–2000 | Emil Constantinescu |
| 2000– | Ion Iliescu |

**General Secretary**

| | |
|---|---|
| 1955–65 | Georghe Gheorghiu-Dej |
| 1965–89 | Nicolae Ceaușescu |

**Prime Minister**

| | |
|---|---|
| 1900–1 | Petre P Carp |
| 1901–6 | Dimitrie A Sturdza |
| 1906–7 | Gheorge Grigore Cantacuzino |
| 1907–9 | Dimitrie A Sturdza |
| 1909 | Ionel Brătianu |
| 1909–10 | Mihai Pherekyde |
| 1910–11 | Ionel Brătianu |
| 1911–12 | Petre P Carp |
| 1912–14 | Titu Maiorescu |
| 1914–18 | Ionel Brătianu |
| 1918 | Alexandru Averescu |
| 1918 | Alexandru Marghiloman |
| 1918 | Constantin Coandă |
| 1918 | Ionel Brătianu |
| 1919 | Artur Văitoianu |
| 1919–20 | Alexandru Vaida-Voevod |
| 1920–1 | Alexandru Averescu |
| 1921–2 | Take Ionescu |
| 1922–6 | Ionel Brătianu |
| 1926–7 | Alexandru Averescu |
| 1927 | Ionel Brătianu |
| 1927–8 | Vintila I C Brătianu |
| 1928–30 | Juliu Maniu |
| 1930 | Gheorghe C Mironescu |
| 1930 | Juliu Maniu |
| 1930–1 | Gheorghe C Mironescu |
| 1931–2 | Nicolae Iorga |
| 1932 | Alexandru Vaida-Voevod |
| 1932–3 | Juliu Maniu |
| 1933 | Alexandru Vaida-Voevod |
| 1933 | Ion G Duca |
| 1933–4 | Constantin Angelescu |
| 1934–7 | Gheorghe Tătărescu |
| 1937 | Octavian Goga |
| 1937–9 | Miron Cristea |
| 1939 | Armand Călinescu |
| 1939 | Gheorghe Argeșanu |
| 1939 | Constantine Argetoianu |
| 1939–40 | Gheorghe Tătărescu |
| 1940 | Ion Gigurtu |
| 1940–4 | Ion Antonescu |
| 1944 | Constantin Savbnătescu |
| 1944–5 | Nicolae Rădescu |
| 1945–52 | Petru Groza |
| 1952–5 | Gheorghe Gheorghiu-Dej |
| 1955–61 | Chivu Stoica |
| 1961–74 | Ion Gheorghe Maurer |
| 1974–80 | Manea Mănescu |
| 1980–3 | Ilie Verdet |
| 1983–9 | Constantin Dăscălescu |
| 1989–91 | Petre Roman |
| 1991–2 | Theodor Stolojan |
| 1992–6 | Nicolae Vacaroiu |
| 1996–8 | Victor Ciorbea |
| 1998 | Gavril Dejeu *Interim Prime Minister* |
| 1998–9 | Radu Vasile |
| 1999 | Alexandru Athanesiu *Interim Prime Minister* |
| 1999–2000 | Mugur Isarescu |
| 2000– | Adrian Nastase |

## Count Dracula's Castle

The classic vampire story *Dracula* (1897) by Bram Stoker is famed for its Transylvanian vampire. But while the mere mention of Transylvania conjures up images of tortuous mountain passes on dark, wild nights in the snow and sinister, cloaked aristocrats with sharp white teeth, it wasn't just a spectre of Stoker's twisted imagination: Transylvania is a real region of northern and central Romania, separated from the capital by the high Carpathian Mountains. The character of Dracula was inspired by one *Vlad Dracula*, a ruler of Romania in the mid-15c, whose nickname was Vlad the Impaler. Today the area thrives on the Dracula legend, with 'Dracula tours' taking in the real Dracula's birthplace in Sighisoara and his home at Castle Bran. Locals aren't averse to feeding off the fictional Count either, and the Borgo Pass now sports a 'Castle Dracula Hotel', which the tourist board coyly notes was 'built not so long ago, approximately where the fictional castle of the Count is supposed to be'.

**ROSS DEPENDENCY** *see* **NEW ZEALAND**

## RUSSIA

| | | | |
|---|---|---|---|
| **Official name** | Russian Federation | | Novosibirsk, Chelyabinsk, Kazan, Samara, Omsk |
| **Local name** | Rossiya; Rossiiskaya Federatsiya | **Population** | 144 400 000 (2001e) |
| **Former name** | Russian Empire (until 1917), Russian Republic (1917), Russian Socialist Federal Soviet Republic (until 1991), within the Union of Soviet Socialist Republics (USSR; 1922–91) | **Nationality** | Russian |
| | | **Languages** | Russian |
| | | **Ethnic groups** | Russian 82%, Tatar 4%, Ukrainian 3%, Chuvash 1%, others 10% |
| | | **Religions** | Christianity 75% (Orthodox), others including Islam 25% |
| **Independence** | 1991 | **Time zone** | GMT +2/12 |
| **Area** | 17 075 400 sq km/ 6 591 104 sq mi | **Currency** | 1 Rouble (R) = 100 kopeks |
| **Capital** | Moscow; Moskva | **Telephone** | +7 |
| **Chief towns** | St Petersburg, Nizhniy Novgorod, Rostov-on-Don, Volgograd, Yekaterinburg, | **Internet** | .ru |
| | | **Country code** | RUS |

**Location**
A republic occupying much of eastern Europe and northern Asia, bounded to the north by the Arctic Ocean; to the north-west by Norway, Finland, Estonia, Latvia, Belarus and the Ukraine; to the west by the Black Sea, Georgia and Azerbaijan; to the south-west by the Caspian Sea and Kazakhstan; to the south-east by China, Mongolia and North Korea; and to the east by the Sea of Okhotsk and the Bering Sea.

**Physical description**
Vast plains dominate the western half; Ural Mountains separate the East European Plain in the west from the West Siberian Lowlands in the east; Central Siberian Plateau lies east of the River Yenisei; further east lies the North Siberian Plain; over 20 000 lakes, the largest being the Caspian Sea, Lake Taymyr and Lake Baikal; highest point is Mt Elbrus (5 642m/18 510ft).

**Climate**
Several different climate regions; variable weather in the north and the centre; winter temperatures are increasingly severe in the east and north; Moscow average temperature is 9°C (Jan) and 18°C (Jul); Siberia has a continental climate, with very cold and prolonged winters and short, often warm summers.

**National holidays**
Jan 1, 2, 7 (Russian Orthodox Christmas), Feb 23 (Soldiers), Mar 8 (Women), May 1 (Spring and Labour) (2), 9 (Victory), Jun 12 (Independence), Aug 22 (Flag), Nov 7 (Accord and Conciliation), Dec 12 (Constitution); Russian Orthodox Easter (Apr/May).

## Political leaders

**Monarch (Tsar)**

| | |
|---|---|
| 1283–1303 | Daniel |
| 1303–25 | Yuri |
| 1325–41 | Ivan I |
| 1341–53 | Semeon |
| 1353–9 | Ivan II |
| 1359–89 | Dimitri Donskoy |
| 1389–1425 | Vasili I |
| 1425–62 | Vasili II |
| 1462–1505 | Ivan III (the Great) |
| 1505–33 | Vasili III |
| 1533–84 | Ivan IV (the Terrible) |
| 1584–98 | Feodor I |

| | |
|---|---|
| 1598–1605 | Boris Godunov |
| 1605 | Feodor II |
| 1605–6 | Dimitri II |
| 1606–10 | Vasili IV Shuisky |
| 1610–13 | *no Tsar* |
| 1613–45 | Michael Romanov |
| 1645–76 | Alexei |
| 1676–82 | Feodor III |
| 1682–96 | Ivan V *joint Tsar* |
| 1682–1725 | Peter I (the Great) *joint Tsar until 1696* |
| 1725–7 | Catherine I |
| 1727–30 | Peter II |
| 1730–40 | Anne |
| 1740–1 | Ivan VI |
| 1741–62 | Elizabeth |
| 1762 | Peter III |
| 1762–96 | Catherine II (the Great) |
| 1796–1801 | Paul |
| 1801–25 | Alexander I |
| 1825–55 | Nicholas I |
| 1855–81 | Alexander II |
| 1881–94 | Alexander III |
| 1894–1917 | Nicholas II |

See separate entry for the **USSR** for the period 1917–91.

**President**

| | |
|---|---|
| 1991–9 | Boris Yeltsin |
| 2000– | Vladimir Putin |

**Prime Minister**

| | |
|---|---|
| 1991–2 | Boris Yeltsin |
| 1992 | Yegor Gaidar *Acting Prime Minister* |
| 1992–8 | Viktor Chernomyrdin |
| 1998 | Sergei Kiriyenko |
| 1998 | Viktor Chernomyrdin *Acting Prime Minister* |
| 1998–9 | Yevgeny Primakov |
| 1999 | Sergei Stepashin |
| 1999–2000 | Vladimir Putin |
| 2000– | Mikhail Kasyanov |

### *White, Blue and Red*

Russia has had several flags – the Tsar's flag in the 19c, the Soviet flag and the current white, blue and red striped flag. The latter flag was first used in 1705 by Peter the Great, was used several times in the intervening centuries, and finally officially declared to be the modern Russian flag in 1993.

## RWANDA

| | |
|---|---|
| **Official name** | Republic of Rwanda |
| **Local name** | Rwanda; République Rwandaise, Republika y'u Rwanda |
| **Former name** | Ruanda, as part of Ruanda-Urundi (with Burundi, until 1962) |
| **Independence** | 1962 |
| **Area** | 26 338 sq km/10 166 sq mi |
| **Capital** | Kigali |
| **Chief towns** | Butare, Ruhengeri |
| **Population** | 8 066 000 (2001e) |
| **Nationality** | Rwandan |
| **Languages** | English, French, Kinyarwanda; Swahili is widely used in commerce |
| **Ethnic groups** | Hutu 90%, Tutsi 9%, others 1% |
| **Religions** | Christianity 74% (RC 65%, Prot 9%), Islam 1%, traditional beliefs and others 25% |
| **Time zone** | GMT +2 |
| **Currency** | 1 Rwanda Franc (RF, RWFr) = 100 centimes |
| **Telephone** | +250 |
| **Internet** | .rw |
| **Country code** | RWA |

**Location**
A landlocked republic in central Africa, bounded to the north by Uganda; to the east by Tanzania; to the south by Burundi; and to the west by Democratic Republic of Congo and Lake Kivu.

**Physical description**
Situated at a relatively high altitude; highest point is Karisimbi volcano (4 507m/14 787ft) in the Virunga range; western third of the country drains into Lake Kivu and then the River Congo, remainder drains towards the River Nile; many lakes.

**Climate**
A highland tropical climate; the two wet seasons run from Oct to Dec and Mar to May, with the highest rainfall in the west, decreasing in the central uplands and to the north and east.

**National holidays**
Jan 1, 28 (Democracy), May 1, Jul 1 (Independence), 5 (Peace), Aug 1 (Harvest), 15, Sep 25 (Referendum), Oct 26 (Armed Forces), Nov 1, Dec 25; A, EM, WM.

## Political leaders

**President**

| | |
|---|---|
| 1962–73 | Grégoire Kayibanda |
| 1973–94 | Juvénal Habyarimana |
| 1994 | Theodore Sindikubgabo *Interim President* |
| 1994–2000 | Pasteur Bizimungu |
| 2000– | Paul Kagame |

**Prime Minister**

| | |
|---|---|
| 1991–2 | Sylvestre Nsanzimana |
| 1992–4 | Dismas Nsengiyaremye |
| 1994 | Jean Kambanda *Acting Prime Minister* |
| 1994–5 | Faustin Twagiramungu |
| 1995–2000 | Pierre-Célestin Rwigyema |
| 2000– | Bernard Makuza |

**SAHARA, WESTERN** *see* **WESTERN SAHARA**

**ST HELENA** *see* **UNITED KINGDOM**

## ST KITTS AND NEVIS

| | |
|---|---|
| **Official name** | Federation of St Kitts and Nevis; also known as St Christopher and Nevis |
| **Local name** | St Kitts and Nevis |
| **Independence** | 1983 |
| **Area** | 269 sq km/104 sq mi |
| **Capital** | Basseterre |
| **Population** | 45 841 (2001) |
| **Nationality** | Kittitian, Nevisian |
| **Languages** | English |
| **Ethnic groups** | black 93%, mulatto 4%, white 1%, others 2% |
| **Religions** | Christianity 78% (Prot 71%, RC 7%), others 22% |
| **Time zone** | GMT –4 |
| **Currency** | 1 East Caribbean Dollar (EC$) = 100 cents |
| **Telephone** | +1 869 |
| **Internet** | .kn |
| **Country code** | KNA |

**Location**
An independent state in the North Leeward Islands in the eastern Caribbean Sea. It comprises the islands of St Kitts and Nevis.

**Physical description**
St Kitts is 37km/23mi long and has an area of 168 sq km/65 sq mi; a mountain range rises to 1 156m/3 793ft at Mt Liamuiga; Nevis, 3km/2mi south-east, has an area of 93 sq km/36 sq mi and is dominated by a central peak rising to 985m/3 232ft.

**Climate**
Warm, with an average annual temperature of 26°C; low humidity; subject to hurricanes.

**National holidays**
Jan 1, 2, Sep 19 (Independence), Dec 25, 26; EM, GF, WM, Labour (May), August Monday (Aug).

## Political leaders

Chief of State: British monarch, represented by Governor General.

**Prime Minister**

| | |
|---|---|
| 1983–95 | Kennedy A Simmonds |
| 1995– | Denzil Douglas |

### *Nelson on Nevis*

Lord Horatio Nelson (1758–1805), the British admiral, is popularly known for his exploits in naval battles in Europe. However, he spent much of his early career in the British navy in the Caribbean, and it was on Nevis that he met and married Frances Nisbet (1761–1831). Today there is a Nelson Museum on Nevis, which boasts 'the largest collection of Nelson memorabilia in the Americas'.

## ST LUCIA

| | | | |
|---|---|---|---|
| **Official name** | St Lucia | **Ethnic groups** | black 90%, mixed 6%, East Indian 3%, white 1% |
| **Local name** | St Lucia | **Religions** | Christianity 100% (RC 90%, Prot 10%) |
| **Area** | 616 sq km/238 sq mi | **Time zone** | GMT –4 |
| **Independence** | 1979 | **Currency** | 1 East Caribbean Dollar (EC$) = 100 cents |
| **Capital** | Castries | **Telephone** | +1 758 |
| **Chief towns** | Vieux Fort, Soufrière | **Internet** | .lc |
| **Population** | 158 147 (2001) | **Country code** | LCA |
| **Nationality** | St Lucian | | |
| **Languages** | English; French patois is also spoken | | |

**Location**
An independent constitutional monarchy and the second-largest of the Windward Islands, situated in the eastern Caribbean Sea.

**Physical description**
The island is 43km/27mi long and 23km/14mi wide; mountainous centre, rising to 950m/3 117ft at Mt Gimie; twin volcanic peaks of Gros and Petit Piton rise steeply from the sea on the south-west coast of the island.

**Climate**
Tropical; annual temperatures range from 18°C to 34°C; wet season is Jun–Dec.

**National holidays**
Jan 1, 2, Feb 22 (Independence), May 1, Dec 13 (National), Dec 25, 26; Emancipation (Aug).

## Political leaders

Chief of State: British monarch, represented by Governor General.

**Prime Minister**

| | |
|---|---|
| 1979 | John Compton |
| 1979–81 | Allan Louisy |
| 1981–3 | Winston Francis Cenac |
| 1983–96 | John Compton |
| 1996–7 | Vaughan Lewis |
| 1997– | Kenny Anthony |

### *Saints and Iguanas*

The Arawak Indians and Caribs were the first inhabitants of St Lucia, and knew the island as *Ioüanalao* and *Hewanorra*, meaning 'place where the iguana is found'. The island was renamed St Lucia by explorers in the late 16c, probably because it was first sighted on St Lucia's day (13 Dec).

**ST PIERRE AND MIQUELON** *see* **FRANCE**

## ST VINCENT AND THE GRENADINES

| | |
|---|---|
| **Official name** | St Vincent and the Grenadines |
| **Local name** | St Vincent and the Grenadines |
| **Independence** | 1979 |
| **Area** | 390 sq km/150 sq mi |
| **Capital** | Kingstown |
| **Population** | 109 202 (2001) |
| **Nationality** | St Vincentian or Vincentian |
| **Languages** | English; French patois is also spoken |
| **Ethnic groups** | black 81%, mixed 15%, others 4% |
| **Religions** | Christianity 81% (Prot 62%, RC 19%), others 19% |
| **Time zone** | GMT –4 |
| **Currency** | 1 East Caribbean Dollar (EC$) = 100 cents |
| **Telephone** | +1 784 |
| **Internet** | .vc |
| **Country code** | VCT |

**Location**
An island country in the Windward Islands, situated in the eastern Caribbean Sea.

**Physical description**
Comprises the island of St Vincent (length 29km/18mi; width 16km/10mi) and the northern Grenadine Islands; St Vincent is volcanic in origin; highest peak is Soufrière, an active volcano rising to a height of 1 234m/4 049ft.

**Climate**
Tropical, with an average annual temperature of 25°C.

**National holidays**
Jan 1, Mar 14 (National Heroes), May 1, Oct 27 (Independence), Dec 25, 26; C (Jul), EM, GF, WM, Caricom (Jul), Emancipation (Aug).

## Political leaders

Chief of State: British monarch, represented by Governor General.

**Prime Minister**

| | | | |
|---|---|---|---|
| 1979–84 | Milton Cato | 2000–1 | Arnhim Eustace |
| 1984–2000 | James Fitz-Allen Mitchell | 2001– | Ralph Gonsalves |

## SAMOA

| | | | |
|---|---|---|---|
| **Official name** | Independent State of Samoa | **Nationality** | Samoan |
| **Local name** | Samoa; 'O la Malo Tu To'atasi o Samoa | **Languages** | Samoan, English |
| **Former name** | Western Samoa (until 1997) | **Ethnic groups** | Samoan 92.6%, mixed 7%, European 0.4% |
| **Independence** | 1962 | **Religions** | Christianity 100% |
| **Area** | 2 842 sq km/1 097 sq mi | **Time zone** | GMT –11 |
| **Capital** | Apia | **Currency** | 1 Tala (ST$) = 100 sene |
| **Population** | 175 000 (2001e) | **Telephone** | +685 |
| | | **Internet** | .ws |
| | | **Country code** | WSM |

**Location**
An island nation in the south-west Pacific Ocean, 2 600km/1 600mi north-east of Auckland, New Zealand.

**Physical description**
Formed from ranges of mainly extinct volcanoes; many dormant volcanoes (last activity was between 1905 and 1911); highest point is Mt Silisili (1 857m/6 092ft); thick tropical vegetation; several coral reefs along the coast.

**Climate**
Tropical; rainy season is Dec–Apr; average annual temperatures are 22–30°C; hurricanes occur.

**National holidays**
Jan 1, May 12 (Anzac), Jun 1 (Mothers of Samoa), Aug 4 (Labour), Oct 12 (White Sunday) (2), Nov 7 (Arbor), Dec 25, 26; EM, GF.

## Political leaders

**President**

| | |
|---|---|
| 1962–3 | Tupua Tamesehe Mea'ole *and* Malietoa Tanumalfi II *Joint Presidents* |
| 1963– | Malietoa Tanumafili II |

**Prime Minister**

| | |
|---|---|
| 1962–1970 | Fiame Mata'afa Faumuina Mulinu'u II |
| 1970–6 | Tupua Tamasese Leolofi IV |
| 1976–82 | Tupuola Taisi Efi |
| 1982 | Va'ai Kolone |
| 1982 | Tupuola Taisi Efi |
| 1982–6 | Tofilau Eti Alesana |
| 1986–8 | Va'ai Kolone |
| 1988–98 | Tofilau Eti Alesana |
| 1998– | Tuilaepa Sailele Malielegaoi |

**SAMOA, AMERICAN** *see* **UNITED STATES OF AMERICA**

**SANDWICH ISLANDS, SOUTH** *see* **UNITED KINGDOM**

## SAN MARINO

| | |
|---|---|
| **Official name** | Republic of San Marino |
| **Local name** | San Marino; Repubblica di San Marino |
| **Area** | 61 sq km/24 sq mi |
| **Capital** | San Marino |
| **Chief towns** | Serravalle |
| **Population** | 27 000 (2001e) |
| **Nationality** | Sammarinese |
| **Languages** | Italian |
| **Ethnic groups** | Sammarinese 88%, Italian 11%, others 1% |
| **Religions** | Christianity 93% (RC), others and none/ unaffiliated 7% |
| **Time zone** | GMT +1 |
| **Currency** | 1 Euro (€) = 100 cents |
| **Telephone** | +378 |
| **Internet** | .sm |
| **Country code** | SMR |

**Location**
A very small landlocked republic completely surrounded by central Italy, lying 12mi/20km from the Adriatic Sea.

**Physical description**
Ruggedly mountainous, centred on the limestone ridges of Mt Titano (755m/2 477ft) and the valley of the River Ausa.

**Climate**
Temperate climate, with cool winters and warm summers (20–30°C); rainfall is moderate.

**National holidays**
Jan 1, 6, Feb 5 (Liberation and St Agatha), Mar 25 (Arengo), Apr 1 (Captain Regents' Ceremony), May 1, Jul 28 (Fall of Fascism), Aug 15, Sep 3 (San Marino and Republic), Oct 1 (Investiture of the New Captains Regent), Nov 1, 2 (Commemoration of the Dead), Dec 8, 25, 26.

## Political leaders

**Regent**

Heads of state are two *capitani reggenti* or 'Captain Regents' appointed every 6 months.

# SÃO TOMÉ AND PRÍNCIPE

| | | | |
|---|---|---|---|
| **Official name** | Democratic Republic of São Tomé and Príncipe | **Languages** | Portuguese |
| **Local name** | São Tomé e Príncipe; República Democrática de São Tomé e Príncipe | **Ethnic groups** | black 90%, Portuguese and Creole 10% |
| **Independence** | 1975 | **Religions** | Christianity 90% (RC 80%, Prot 5%, others 5%), others 10% |
| **Area** | 1 001 sq km/386 sq mi | **Time zone** | GMT |
| **Capital** | São Tomé | **Currency** | 1 Dobra (Db) = 100 céntimos |
| **Chief towns** | Santo António | **Telephone** | +239 |
| **Population** | 153 000 (2001e) | **Internet** | .st |
| **Nationality** | São Toméan, Santoméan | **Country code** | STP |

**Location**
An equatorial island republic in the Gulf of Guinea, off the coast of west Africa; São Tomé lies c.440km/275mi, and Príncipe c.200km/125mi, off the north coast of Gabon.

**Physical description**
Volcanic islands, heavily forested; São Tomé has an area of 860 sq km/332 sq mi and reaches a height of 2 024m/6 640ft at Pico de São Tomé; Príncipe, the smaller of the two islands, covers 140 sq km/54 sq mi and has similar terrain.

**Climate**
Tropical; average annual temperature is 27°C on the coast, 20°C in the mountains; rainy season from Oct to May.

**National holidays**
Jan 1, Feb 3 (Liberty Heroes), May 1, Jul 12 (National Independence), Sep 6 (Armed Forces), 30 (Agricultural Reform), Dec 21 (Power of the People), 25 (Family).

## Political leaders

**President**

| | |
|---|---|
| 1975–91 | Manuel Pinto da Costa |
| 1991–2001 | Miguel Trovoada |
| 2001– | Fradrique de Menezes |

**Prime Minister**

| | |
|---|---|
| 1974–5 | Leonel Maria d'Alva |
| 1975–8 | Miguel Trovoada |
| 1978–88 | *No Prime Minister* |
| 1988–91 | Celestino Rocha da Costa |
| 1991–2 | Daniel Lima dos Santos Daio |
| 1992–4 | Norberto José d'Alva Costa Alegre |
| 1994 | Evaristo Carvalho |
| 1994–5 | Carlos da Graça |
| 1995–6 | Armindo Vaz d'Almeida |
| 1996–9 | Raul Bragança |
| 1999–2002 | Guilherme Posser da Costa |
| 2002 | Gabriel Costa |
| 2002– | Maria das Neves |

### *Saints and Princes*

Portuguese explorers were the first Europeans to visit São Tomé, arriving on 21 Dec 1470, St Thomas's day – hence the name *São Tomé*, or St Thomas. By 17 Jan 1471 the explorers had reached a smaller island nearby, which they christened *Príncipe* – 'prince' – after a member of the Portuguese royal family.

## SAUDI ARABIA

| | | | |
|---|---|---|---|
| **Official name** | Kingdom of Saudi Arabia | **Ethnic groups** | Arab 90%, Afro-Asian 10% |
| **Local name** | Al-Mamlaka al-'Arabiyya as-Sa'ūdiyya | **Religions** | Islam 99% (mostly Sunni), Christianity and others 1% |
| **Area** | 2 331 000 sq km/ 899 766 sq mi | **Time zone** | GMT +3 |
| **Capital** | Riyadh; Ar Riyād | **Currency** | 1 Saudi Arabian Riyal (SR, SRls) = 20 qursh = 100 halala |
| **Chief towns** | Jeddah, Mecca, Medina, Ta'if, Ad Dammam, Abha | **Telephone** | +966 |
| **Population** | 22 829 000 (2001e) | **Internet** | .sa |
| **Nationality** | Saudi or Saudi Arabian | **Country code** | SAU |
| **Languages** | Arabic | | |

**Location**
An Arabic kingdom comprising about four-fifths of the Arabian Peninsula, bounded to the west by the Red Sea; to the north-west by Jordan; to the north by Iraq; to the north-east by Kuwait; to the east by the Arabian Gulf, Qatar and the United Arab Emirates; to the south-east and south by Oman; and to the south and south-west by Yemen.

**Physical description**
Red Sea coastal plain is bounded to the east by mountains; south-west highlands include Jabal Sawda', the highest peak (3 133m/10 278ft); Arabian Peninsula slopes north and east to the oil-rich Al Hasa plain on the Arabian Gulf; large areas of sand desert in the interior; numerous salt flats in the eastern lowlands.

**Climate**
Hot and dry, with average temperatures from 21°C (north) to 26°C (south); day temperatures may rise to 50°C in the interior deserts; night frosts are common in the north and highlands; Red Sea coast is hot and humid; average rainfall is low.

**National holidays**
Sep 23 (National); Ad (4), ER (3).

## Political leaders

### Monarch

*Family name: al-Saud*

| | |
|---|---|
| 1932–53 | Abdulaziz Bin Abdur-Rahman |
| 1953–64 | Saud Bin Abdulaziz |
| 1964–75 | Faisal Bin Abdulaziz |
| 1975–82 | Khalid Bin Abdulaziz |
| 1982–96 | Fahd Bin Abdulaziz |
| 1996 | Abdullah Bin Abdulaziz *Acting Monarch* |
| 1996– | Fahd Bin Abdulaziz |

### Heart of Islam

Saudi Arabia is famed as the birthplace of Islam. The holy cities of Mecca, the birthplace of Muhammad, and Medina, where his tomb lies, are both in Saudi Arabia, and Islam provides the foundation for the Saudi law and government. King Fahd holds the title 'Custodian of the Two Holy Mosques' in recognition of the country's role in protecting and supporting the holy shrines in Mecca and Medina.

**SCOTLAND** *see* **UNITED KINGDOM**

## SENEGAL

| | | | |
|---|---|---|---|
| **Official name** | Republic of Senegal | **Nationality** | Senegalese |
| **Local name** | Sénégal; République du Sénégal | **Languages** | French, Wolof |
| **Former name** | part of the Federation of Mali (1959–60); Senegambia (with The Gambia, 1982–9) | **Ethnic groups** | Wolof 43%, Fulani 24%, Serer 15%, Diola 4%, others 14% |
| **Independence** | 1960 | **Religions** | Islam 92% (Sunni), traditional beliefs 6%, Christianity 2% (RC) |
| **Area** | 196 840 sq km/75 980 sq mi | **Time zone** | GMT |
| **Capital** | Dakar | **Currency** | 1 CFA Franc (CFAFr) = 100 centimes |
| **Chief towns** | Thiès, Kaolack, St Louis, Ziguinchor | **Telephone** | +221 |
| | | **Internet** | .sn |
| **Population** | 9 803 000 (2001e) | **Country code** | SEN |

**Location**
A country in West Africa, bounded to the north by Mauritania; to the east by Mali; to the south by Guinea and Guinea-Bissau; and to the west by the Atlantic Ocean. It surrounds The Gambia on three sides.

**Physical description**
Most westerly country in mainland Africa; coast is characterized by dunes, mangrove forests and mudbanks; extensive low-lying basin of savannah and semi-desert vegetation lies to the north; south rises to c.500m/1 640ft.

**Climate**
Tropical with a rainy season Jun–Sep; high humidity levels and high night-time temperatures, especially on the coast; rainfall decreases from the south to the north; average temperature at Dakar ranges from 22°C to 28°C.

**National holidays**
Jan 1, Feb 1 (Senegambia), Apr 4 (National), May 1, Aug 15, Nov 1, Dec 25; Ad, EM, ER, NY (Muslim), PB, WM.

## Political leaders

**President**

| | |
|---|---|
| 1960–80 | Léopold Sédar Senghor |
| 1981–2000 | Abdou Diouf |
| 2000– | Abdoulaye Wade |

**Prime Minister**

| | |
|---|---|
| 1958–62 | Mamadou Dia |
| 1962–70 | *No Prime Minister* |
| 1970–80 | Abdou Diouf |
| 1981–3 | Habib Thiam |
| 1983 | Moustapha Niasse *Interim Prime Minister* |
| 1983–91 | *No Prime Minister* |
| 1991–8 | Habib Thiam |
| 1998–2000 | Mamadou Lamine Loum |
| 2000–1 | Moustapha Niasse |
| 2001–2 | Madior Boye |
| 2002– | Idrissa Seck |

## SERBIA AND MONTENEGRO

| | | | |
|---|---|---|---|
| **Official name** | Serbia and Montenegro | **Nationality** | Serbian, Montenegrin |
| **Local name** | Srbija i Crna Gora | **Languages** | Serbo-Croat |
| **Former name** | Kingdom of Serbs, Croats and Slovenes (until 1929), Kingdom of Yugoslavia (1929–41), Federal People's Republic of Yugoslavia (1945–63), Socialist Federal Republic of Yugoslavia (1963–92), Federal Republic of Yugoslavia (until 2003) | **Ethnic groups** | Serb 62%, Albanian 17%, Montenegrin 5%, Magyar 3%, others 13% |
| | | **Religions** | Christianity 70% (Orthodox 65%, RC 4%, Prot 1%), Islam 19%, others 11% |
| | | **Time zone** | GMT +1 |
| **Area** | 256 409 sq km/98 974 sq mi | **Currency** | 1 Dinar (D, Din) = 100 paras (Serbia); 1 Euro (€) = 100 cents (Montenegro) |
| **Capital** | Belgrade; Beograd | | |
| **Chief towns** | Priština, Subotica | **Telephone** | +381 |
| **Population** | 10 651 000 (2001e) | **Internet** | .yu |
| | | **Country code** | YUG |

**Location**
A federal union in the Balkan Peninsula of south-eastern Europe, consisting of the republics of Serbia and Montenegro. It is bounded to the west by Bosnia and Herzegovina and Croatia; to the north by Hungary; to the north-east by Romania; to the east by Bulgaria; and to the south by Macedonia and Albania.

**Physical description**
Dominated in the north by the Danube and other rivers; fertile plains in the north-east; drained in the centre by the River Morava; southern ranges cut by deep river valleys; several great lakes in the south; highest point is Daravica (2 656m/8 714ft).

**Climate**
Mediterranean climate on the Adriatic coast; continental climate in the north and north-east; rain falls throughout the year; colder upland climate, with winter snow.

**National holidays**
Jan 1, 2, 7 (Orthodox Christmas), Feb 15 (National) (Serbia), Apr 27 (Constitution), May 1 (2), 9 (Victory), Jul 13 (Uprising) (Montenegro); Orthodox Easter (Apr/May) (4).

## Political leaders

### Kingdom of Yugoslavia

**Monarch**
1921–34 Aleksandar II
1934–45 Petar II (*in exile from* 1941)

### Republic[1]

**Chairman**
1945–53 Ivan Ribar

**President**
1953–80 Josip Broz Tito

[1] *See* ***Former names*** *above for exact country names.*

**Collective Presidency**

| | |
|---|---|
| 1980 | Lazar Koliševski |
| 1980–1 | Cvijetin Mijatović |
| 1981–2 | Serghei Kraigher |
| 1982–3 | Petar Stambolić |
| 1983–4 | Mika Spiljak |
| 1984–5 | Veselin Đuranović |
| 1985–6 | Radovan Vlajković |
| 1986–7 | Sinan Hasani |
| 1987–8 | Lazar Mojsov |
| 1988–9 | Raif Dizdarević |
| 1989–90 | Janez Drnovsek |
| 1990–1 | Borisav Jovic |
| 1991 | *vacant* |
| 1991 | Stjepan Mesić |
| 1991–2 | Branko Kostic *Acting President* |

**Prime Minister**

| | |
|---|---|
| 1929–32 | Pear Živkovic |
| 1932 | Vojislav Marinković |
| 1932–4 | Milan Srškić |
| 1934 | Nikola Uzunović |
| 1934–5 | Bogoljub Jevtić |
| 1935–9 | Milan Stojadinović |
| 1939–41 | Dragiša Cvetković |
| 1941–2 | Dušan Simović |

**Prime Minister of government-in-exile**

| | |
|---|---|
| 1942–3 | Slobodan Jovanović |
| 1943 | Miloš Trifunović |
| 1943–4 | Božidar Purić |
| 1944–5 | Ivan Šubašić |
| 1945 | Drago Marušić |

**Prime Minister/Premier**

| | |
|---|---|
| 1941–4 | Milan Nedić |
| 1943–63 | Josip Broz Tito |
| 1963–7 | Petar Stambolić |
| 1967–9 | Mika Špiljak |
| 1969–71 | Mitja Ribičič |
| 1971–7 | Džemal Bijedić |
| 1977–82 | Veselin Đuranović |
| 1982–6 | Milka Planinc |
| 1986–9 | Branko Mikulić |
| 1989–91 | Ante Marković |
| 1992 | Aleksandar Mitrovic *Acting Prime Minister* |

## Communist Party

**Secretary-General**

| | |
|---|---|
| 1937–52 | Josip Broz Tito |

## League of Communists

**Secretary-General**

| | |
|---|---|
| 1952–63 | Josip Broz Tito |

**President of the Central Committee**

| | |
|---|---|
| 1963–80 | Josip Broz Tito |
| 1979–80 | Stevan Doronjski *Acting President* |
| 1980–1 | Lazar Mojsov |
| 1981–2 | Dušan Dragosavac |
| 1982–3 | Mitja Ribičič |
| 1983–4 | Dragoslav Marković |
| 1984–5 | Ali Sukrija |
| 1985–6 | Vidoje Žarkovic |
| 1986–7 | Milanko Renovica |
| 1987–8 | Boško Krunić |
| 1988–9 | Stipe Suvar |
| 1989–90 | Milan Pancevski |

## Federal Republic of Yugoslavia

**President**

| | |
|---|---|
| 1992–3 | Dobrica Cosic |
| 1993 | Milos Radulovic *Acting President* |
| 1993–7 | Zoran Lilic |
| 1997 | Srdja Bozovic *Acting President* |
| 1997–2000 | Slobodan Milosevic |
| 2000–3 | Vojislav Kostunica |

**Prime Minister**

| | |
|---|---|
| 1992–3 | Milan Panic |
| 1993–8 | Radoje Kontic |
| 1998–2000 | Momir Bulatovic |
| 2000–1 | Zoran Zizic |
| 2001–3 | Dragisa Pesic |

## Serbia and Montenegro

**President**

| | |
|---|---|
| 2003– | Svetozar Marović |

## Serbia

**President**

| | |
|---|---|
| 1992–7 | Slobodan Milosevic |
| 1997 | Dragan Tomic *Acting President* |
| 1997–2002 | Milan Milutinovic |
| 2002– | Nataša Mićić *Acting President* |

## Montenegro

**President**

| | |
|---|---|
| 1991–8 | Momir Bulatovic |
| 1998–2002 | Milo Djukanovic |
| 2002– | Filip Vujanović *Acting President until 2003* |

# SEYCHELLES

| | |
|---|---|
| **Official name** | Republic of Seychelles |
| **Local name** | Seychelles; République des Seychelles (French), Repiblik Sesel (Creole) |
| **Independence** | 1976 |
| **Area** | 453 sq km/175 sq mi |
| **Capital** | Victoria |
| **Population** | 75 876 (1997) |
| **Nationality** | Seychellois |
| **Languages** | Creole; French and English are spoken |
| **Ethnic groups** | mulatto 94%, Malagasy 3%, Chinese 2%, English 1% |
| **Religions** | Christianity 98% (RC 90%, Prot 8%), others (including Hinduism) 2% |
| **Time zone** | GMT +4 |
| **Currency** | 1 Seychelles Rupee (SR) = 100 cents |
| **Telephone** | +248 |
| **Internet** | .sc |
| **Country code** | SYC |

**Location**
An island group in the south-west Indian Ocean, north of Madagascar, comprising 115 islands.

**Physical description**
Two main groups; first, a compact group of 41 steep granitic islands, are mountainous, rising to 905m/2 969ft at Morne Seychellois on Mahé; steep forest-clad slopes; coastal lowlands of grass and dense scrub; second group are low-lying coralline islands and atolls situated to the south-west.

**Climate**
Tropical with a rainfall that varies with altitude and is higher on the southern sides of the islands; wettest months are Nov to Mar; rarely affected by tropical storms.

**National holidays**
Jan 1, 2, May 1, Jun 5 (Liberation), 18 (National), 29 (Independence), Aug 15, Nov 1, Dec 8, 25; CC, GF, HS.

## Political leaders

**President**

| | |
|---|---|
| 1976–7 | James R Mancham |
| 1977– | France-Albert René |

**SHARJAH** *see* **UNITED ARAB EMIRATES**

# SIERRA LEONE

| | | | |
|---|---|---|---|
| **Official name** | Republic of Sierra Leone | **Ethnic groups** | Mende 35%, Temne 32%, Limba 8%, Kuranko 4%, others 21% |
| **Local name** | Sierra Leone | **Religions** | traditional beliefs 52%, Islam 39% (Sunni), Christianity 9% |
| **Independence** | 1961 | **Time zone** | GMT |
| **Area** | 72 325 sq km/27 917 sq mi | **Currency** | 1 Leone (Le) = 100 cents |
| **Capital** | Freetown | **Telephone** | +232 |
| **Chief towns** | Bo, Sefadu, Makeni, Kenema, Lunsar | **Internet** | .sl |
| **Population** | 4 573 000 (2001e) | **Country code** | SLE |
| **Nationality** | Sierra Leonean | | |
| **Languages** | English, Mende, Temnel; Krio (a Creole language) is also widely spoken | | |

**Location**
A coastal republic in West Africa, bounded to the north by Guinea; to the south-east by Liberia; and to the south and south-west by the Atlantic Ocean.

**Physical description**
A low, narrow coastal plain; western half rises to an average height of 500m/1 640ft in the Loma Mountains; highest point is Loma Mansa (also called Bintimani; 1 948m/6 391ft); Tingi Mountains in the south-east rise to 1 853m/6 079ft.

**Climate**
Equatorial, with a rainy season from May to Oct; highest rainfall is on the coast; temperatures are uniformly high throughout the year, c.27°C.

**National holidays**
Jan 1, Apr 19 (Republic), Apr 27 (Independence), Dec 25, 26; Ad, EM, ER, GF, PB.

## Political leaders

**President**

| | |
|---|---|
| 1971 | Christopher Okero Cole |
| 1971–85 | Siaka Stevens |
| 1985–92 | Joseph Saidu Momoh |
| 1992–6 | Valentine Strasser |
| 1996–7 | Ahmad Tejan Kabbah |
| 1997 | *Military coup* |
| 1997 | Johnny Paul Koroma |
| 1998– | Ahmad Tejan Kabbah |

**Prime Minister**

| | |
|---|---|
| 1961–4 | Milton Margai |
| 1964–7 | Albert Michael Margai |
| 1967 | Siaka Stevens |
| 1967 | David Lansana |
| 1967 | Ambrose Genda |
| 1967–8 | *National Reformation Council* (Andrew Saxon-Smith) |
| 1968 | John Bangura |

| | | | |
|---|---|---|---|
| 1968–71 | Siaka Stevens | 1975–8 | Christian Alusine Kamara Taylor |
| 1971–5 | Sorie Ibrahim Koroma | 1978– | *No Prime Minister* |

## SINGAPORE

| | | | |
|---|---|---|---|
| **Official name** | Republic of Singapore | **Languages** | English, Chinese (Mandarin), Malay, Tamil; other Chinese dialects are also spoken |
| **Local name** | Singapore; Repablik Singapura (Malay), Singapur Kuṭiyara'su (Tamil), Xinjiapo Gongheguo (Chinese) | **Ethnic groups** | Chinese 76%, Malay 15%, Indian 7%, others 2% |
| **Former name** | part of Straits Settlement (until 1942), State of Singapore (1959–63), part of the Federation of Malaysia (1963–65) | **Religions** | Buddhism 28%, traditional beliefs 21%, none/unaffiliated 17%, Islam 16%, Taoism 13%, Hinduism 5% |
| **Independence** | 1965 | | |
| **Area** | 618 sq km/238 sq mi | **Time zone** | GMT +8 |
| **Capital** | Singapore; Singapura (Malay), Singapur (Tamil), Xinjiapo (Chinese) | **Currency** | 1 Singapore Dollar (S$) = 1 Ringgit = 100 cents |
| | | **Telephone** | +65 |
| **Population** | 4 017 700 (2000) | **Internet** | .sg |
| **Nationality** | Singaporean, Singapore | **Country code** | SGP |

**Location**
A republic at the southern tip of the Malay Peninsula, south-east Asia. It consists of the island of Singapore (linked to Malaysia by a causeway) and about 50 adjacent islets.

**Physical description**
Singapore Island measures c.42km/26mi by 22km/14mi at its widest; low-lying; highest point is Bukit Timah (177m/581ft); important deep-water harbour lies to the south-east.

**Climate**
Equatorial, with high humidity, and a daily temperature range from 21°C to 34°C.

**National holidays**
Jan 1, May 1, Aug 9 (National), Dec 25; Ad, D, ER, GF, NY (Chinese) (Jan/Feb) (2), Vesak.

## Political leaders

**President (Yang di-Pertuan Negara)**

| | | | |
|---|---|---|---|
| 1959–70 | Yusof bin Ishak | 1985–93 | Wee Kim Wee |
| 1970–81 | Benjamin Henry Sheares | 1993–9 | Ong Teng Cheong |
| 1981–5 | Chengara Veetil Devan Nair | 1999– | Sellapan Ramanathan Nathan |

**Prime Minister**

| | |
|---|---|
| 1959–90 | Lee Kuan Yew |
| 1990– | Goh Chok Tong |

# SLOVAKIA

| | | | |
|---|---|---|---|
| **Official name** | Republic of Slovakia or the Slovak Republic | **Languages** | Slovak |
| **Local name** | Slovensko; Slovenská Republika | **Ethnic groups** | Slovak 86%, Magyar 11%, Romany 2%, others 1% |
| **Former name** | formerly part of Czechoslovakia (until 1993) | **Religions** | Christianity 69% (RC 59%, Prot 6%, Orthodox 4%), none/unaffiliated 31% |
| **Independence** | 1993 | | |
| **Area** | 49 035 sq km/18 927 sq mi | **Time zone** | GMT +1 |
| **Capital** | Bratislava | **Currency** | 1 Koruna (Kčs) = 100 haléru |
| **Chief towns** | Košice, Banská Bystrica, Prešov | **Telephone** | +421 |
| | | **Internet** | .sk |
| **Population** | 5 379 455 (2001) | **Country code** | SVK |
| **Nationality** | Slovak | | |

**Location**
A landlocked republic in eastern Europe, bounded to the north by Poland; to the east by the Ukraine; to the south by Hungary; to the south-west by Austria; and to the west by the Czech Republic.

**Physical description**
Lowlands in the south; Tatra Mountains in the north rise to 2 655m/8 710ft at Gerlachovsky Stit, Slovakia's highest point.

**Climate**
Continental; hot in summer, cold in winter.

**National holidays**
Jan 1 (New Year/Establishment of Republic), 6, May 1, 8 (Triumph over Fascism), Jul 5 (SS Cyril and Methodius), Aug 29 (Slovak National Uprising), Sep 1 (Constitution), 15 (Our Lady of the Seven Sorrows), Nov 1, Dec 24, 25, 26; GF, EM.

## Political leaders

See entry for **Czech Republic** for political leaders prior to 1993.

**President**

1993–8 Michal Kovác
1998–9 *No President*
1999– Rudolf Schuster

**Prime Minister**

1993–4 Vladimír Mečiar
1994 Jozef Moravčik
1994–8 Vladimír Mečiar
1998– Mikuláš Dzurinda

### Thunder and Lightning

Slovakia's mighty Tatra mountains are commemorated in its national anthem, *Nad Tatrou sa blýska*, meaning 'Lightning over the Tatras'. It speaks of the lightning over the mountains and the roar of thunder reawakening the spirit of the Slovak people.

## SLOVENIA

| | | | |
|---|---|---|---|
| **Official name** | Republic of Slovenia | **Population** | 1 948 250 (2002) |
| **Local name** | Slovenija; Republika Slovenija | **Nationality** | Slovene, Slovenian |
| **Former name** | formerly part of Kingdom of Serbs, Croats and Slovenes (until 1929), Kingdom of Yugoslavia (1929–41), Federal People's Republic of Yugoslavia (1945–63), Socialist Federal People's Republic of Yugoslavia (1963–91) | **Languages** | Slovene |
| | | **Ethnic groups** | Slovene 91%, Croat 3%, Serb 2%, Bosniak 1%, others 3% |
| | | **Religions** | Christianity 72% (RC, including Uniate, 71%, Prot 1%), none/unaffiliated 5%, Islam 1%, others 21% |
| **Independence** | 1991 | **Time zone** | GMT +1 |
| **Area** | 20 251 sq km/7 817 sq mi | **Currency** | 1 Tolar (SIT) = 100 stotins |
| | | **Telephone** | +386 |
| **Capital** | Ljubljana | **Internet** | .si |
| **Chief towns** | Maribor, Kranj, Celje, Koper | **Country code** | SVN |

**Location**
A mountainous republic in central Europe, bounded to the north by Austria; to the west by Italy; to the south by Croatia; and to the east by Hungary.

**Physical description**
Forested and mountainous, linked to Austria by a number of pass roads; highest point is Mt Triglav (2 864m/9 396ft); drops down towards the Adriatic coast.

**Climate**
Hot summers and cold winters in the plateaux and valleys in the east; Mediterranean climate on the west coast.

**National holidays**
Jan 1, 2, Feb 8 (Culture), Apr 27 (National Resistance), May 1 (2), Jun 25 (National), Aug 15, Oct 31 (Reformation), Nov 1, Dec 25, 26 (Independence); EM.

## Political leaders

See **Serbia and Montenegro** for political leaders of the former Yugoslavia.

**President**
1991–2002 Milan Kučan
2002– Janez Drnovšek

**Prime Minister**
1990–2 Lojze Peterle
1992–2000 Janez Drnovšek
2000 Andrej Bajuk
2000–2 Janez Drnovšek
2002– Anton Rop

### *Slovenian Grammar*

The Slovene language is unusual in that it not only has singular and plural forms but also an additional *dual* form. While most languages distinguish whether one person is doing something or many people are doing it, Slovene also has different words and grammar for two people.

## SOLOMON ISLANDS

| | | | |
|---|---|---|---|
| **Official name** | Solomon Islands | **Languages** (cont.) | are also spoken |
| **Local name** | Solomon Islands | **Ethnic groups** | Melanesian 93%, Polynesian 4%, Micronesian 2%, others 1% |
| **Former name** | British Solomon Islands (until 1975) | **Religions** | Christianity 91% (Prot 62%, RC 19%, others 10%), others 9% |
| **Independence** | 1978 | **Time zone** | GMT +11 |
| **Area** | 27 556 sq km/10 637 sq mi | **Currency** | 1 Solomon Islands Dollar (SI$) = 100 cents |
| **Capital** | Honiara | **Telephone** | +677 |
| **Chief towns** | Gizo, Auki, Kirakira | **Internet** | .sb |
| **Population** | 450 000 (2001e) | **Country code** | SLB |
| **Nationality** | Solomon Islander (noun) | | |
| **Languages** | English; pidgin English and Melanesian dialects | | |

**Location**
An independent country consisting of an archipelago of several hundred islands in the south-west Pacific Ocean; the six main islands are Choiseul, Guadalcanal, Malaita, New Georgia, Makira and Santa Isabel.

**Physical description**
Larger islands have forested mountain ranges of mainly volcanic origin, deep, narrow valleys, and coastal belts lined with coconut palms; ringed by reefs; highest point is Mt Makarakomburu (2 477m/8 127ft) on Guadalcanal, the largest island.

**Climate**
Equatorial; average temperature is 27°C; high humidity.

**National holidays**
Jan 1, Jul 7 (Independence), Dec 25, 26; EM, GF, HS, WM, Queen's Birthday (Jun).

## Political leaders

Chief of State: British monarch, represented by Governor General.

**Prime Minister**

| | |
|---|---|
| 1978–82 | Peter Kenilorea |
| 1982–4 | Solomon Mamaloni |
| 1984–6 | Peter Kenilorea |
| 1986–9 | Ezekiel Alebua |
| 1989–93 | Solomon Mamaloni |
| 1993–4 | Francis Billy Hilly |
| 1994–7 | Solomon Mamaloni |
| 1997–2000 | Bartholomew Ulufa'alu |
| 2000–1 | Manasseh Sogavare |
| 2001– | Allan Kemakeza |

### *War in the Pacific*

The idyllic tropical islands, palm-fringed lagoons and sleepy islets of the Solomon Islands were the site of some of the fiercest fighting of World War II. Following the attacks on Pearl Harbor and Singapore (7–8 Dec 1941), Japan advanced into the South Pacific, reaching Guadalcanal in May 1942. US forces reinvaded and after six months of bitter fighting, in one of the crucial actions of the war, they halted the Japanese advance. Wreckage from the fighting can still be seen in the islands and surrounding waters.

## SOMALIA

| | | | |
|---|---|---|---|
| **Official name** | Somalia | **Chief towns** | Hargeysa, Berbera, Kismayu |
| **Local name** | Soomaaliya; Jamhuuriyadda Dimoqraadiya Soomaaliya | **Population** | 9 088 000 (2001e) |
| | | **Nationality** | Somali |
| **Former name** | British Somaliland (until 1960) and Italian Somalia (until 1936), Italian East Africa (1936–50), Somali Democratic Republic (1969–91) | **Languages** | Somali, Arabic; English and Italian are also spoken widely |
| | | **Ethnic groups** | Somalian 98%, Arab 2% |
| | | **Religions** | Islam 98% (Sunni), Christianity 2% |
| **Independence** | 1960 | **Time zone** | GMT +3 |
| **Area** | 686 803 sq km/265 106 sq mi | **Currency** | 1 Somali Shilling (SoSh) = 100 cents |
| **Capital** | Mogadishu; Muqdisho (Somali), Muqdishu (Arabic) | **Telephone** | +252 |
| | | **Internet** | .so |
| | | **Country code** | SOM |

**Location**
A north-east African republic, bounded to the north-west by Djibouti; to the west by Ethiopia; to the south-west by Kenya; to the east by the Indian Ocean; and to the north by the Gulf of Aden.

**Physical description**
Occupies the eastern Horn of Africa where a dry coastal plain broadens to the south and rises inland to a plateau at nearly 1 000m/3 280ft; forested mountains on the Gulf of Aden coast rise to 2 416m/7 926ft at Mt Shimbiris.

**Climate**
Considerable variation in climate; average maximum daily temperatures of 29–42°C (Berbera on the north coast) and 28–32°C (Mogadishu); higher rainfall on the east coast in Apr–Sep; serious and persistent threat of drought.

**National holidays**
Jan 1, May 1, Jun 26 (Independence), Jul 1 (Union), Oct 21 (Revolution) (2); Ad (2), ER (2), PB.

## Political leaders

**President**

| | |
|---|---|
| 1961–7 | Aden Abdallah Osman |
| 1967–9 | Abdirashid Ali Shermarke |
| 1969–80 | Mohammed Siad Barre *Supreme Revolutionary Council* |
| 1980–91 | Mohammed Siad Barre |
| 1991–2000 | *Civil War* |
| 2000 | Abdullahi Derow Isaq *Acting President* |
| 2000– | Abd-al-Qassim Salat Hasan |

**Prime Minister**

| | |
|---|---|
| 1960 | Mohammed Haji Ibrahim Egal |
| 1960–4 | Abdirashid Ali Shermarke |
| 1964–7 | Abdirizak Haji Hussein |
| 1967–9 | Mohammed Haji Ibrahim Egal |
| 1969–70 | Mohammed Siad Barre |
| 1970–87 | *No Prime Minister* |
| 1987–90 | Mohammed Ali Samater |
| 1990–1 | Mohammed Hawadie Madar |
| 1991 | Umar Arteh Ghalib |
| 1991–2000 | *Civil War* |
| 2000–1 | Ali Khalif Galaid |
| 2001– | Hassan Abshir Farah |

## SOUTH AFRICA

| | | | |
|---|---|---|---|
| **Official name** | Republic of South Africa (RSA) | **Languages** | Eleven official languages Afrikaans, English, IsiNdebele, IsiXosa, IsiZulu, Sepedi, Sosetho, SiSwati, Setswana, Tshivenda, Xitsonga |
| **Local name** | South Africa; Republiek van Suid-Afrika | | |
| **Independence** | 1931 (within Commonwealth), 1961 (republic) | **Ethnic groups** | black 75%, white 14%, mixed 9%, Asian 2% |
| **Area** | 1 233 404 sq km/ 476 094 sq mi | **Religions** | Christianity 62% (Prot and others 54%, RC 8%), traditional beliefs 35%, Hinduism 2%, Islam 1% |
| **Capital** | Pretoria (administrative), Bloemfontein (judicial) and Cape Town (Kaapstad) (legislative) | **Time zone** | GMT +2 |
| **Chief towns** | Durban, Johannesburg, Port Elizabeth | **Currency** | 1 Rand (R) = 100 cents |
| | | **Telephone** | +27 |
| **Population** | 40 583 573 (1996) | **Internet** | .za |
| **Nationality** | South African | **Country code** | ZAF |

**Location**
A republic in the south of the African continent. It is bounded to the north-west by Namibia; to the north by Botswana; to the north-east by Zimbabwe, Mozambique and Swaziland; to the east and south-east by the Indian Ocean; and to the south-west and west by the southern Atlantic Ocean; Lesotho is landlocked within its borders.

**Physical description**
Occupies the southern extremity of the African plateau, fringed by mountains and a lowland coastal margin; northern interior comprises the Kalahari Basin, scrub grassland and arid desert; highest point is Mafadi (3 451m/11 322ft).

**Climate**
Subtropical in the east, with lush vegetation; dry moistureless climate on the west coast; Cape Town has minimum daily temperatures of 7°C (Jul), to an average maximum of 26°C (Jan–Feb); desert region further north.

**National holidays**
Jan 1, Mar 21 (Human Rights), Apr 27 (Freedom Day), May 1, Jun 16 (Youth), Aug 9 (Women), Sep 24 (Heritage), Dec 16 (Reconciliation), 25, 26; GF, EM (Family).

### *Mineral Wealth*

South Africa enjoys great reserves of mineral wealth, and is famous for its diamonds. According to government figures, the country produces 20% of the world's gold, 62% of the world's vanadium, 48% of its chrome and is the leading producer of several other minerals. It is also the second biggest producer of platinum, titanium and zirconium.

## Political leaders

**Governor General**

| | |
|---|---|
| 1910–14 | Herbert, Viscount Gladstone |
| 1914–20 | Sydney, Earl Buxton |
| 1920–4 | Arthur, Duke of Connaught |
| 1924–31 | Alexander, Earl of Athlone |
| 1931–7 | George Herbert Hyde Villiers |
| 1937–43 | Patrick Duncan |
| 1943–5 | Nicolaas Jacobus de Wet |
| 1945–51 | Gideon Brand Van Zyl |
| 1951–9 | Ernest George Jansen |
| 1959 | Lucas Cornelius Steyn |
| 1959–61 | Charles Robberts Swart |

## Republic

**President**

| | |
|---|---|
| 1961–7 | Charles Robberts Swart |
| 1967 | Theophilus Ebenhaezer Dönges |
| 1967–8 | Jozua François Nandé |
| 1968–75 | Jacobus Johannes Fouché |
| 1975–8 | Nicolaas Diederichs |
| 1978–9 | Balthazar Johannes Vorster |
| 1979–84 | Marais Viljoen |
| 1984–89 | Pieter Willem Botha |
| 1989–94 | Frederick Willem de Klerk |
| 1994–9 | Nelson Rolihlahla Mandela |
| 1999– | Thabo Mbeki |

**Prime Minister**

| | |
|---|---|
| 1910–19 | Louis Botha *SAf* |
| 1919–24 | Jan Christiaan Smuts *SAf* |
| 1924–39 | James Barry Munnick Hertzog *Nat* |
| 1939–48 | Jan Christiaan Smuts *Un* |
| 1948–54 | Daniel François Malan *Nat* |
| 1954–8 | Johannes Gerardus Strijdom *Nat* |
| 1958–66 | Hendrik Frensch Verwoerd *Nat* |
| 1966–78 | Balthazar Johannes Vorster *Nat* |
| 1978–84 | Pieter Willem Botha *Nat* |
| 1984 | *post abolished* |

*Nat = National*
*SAf = South African Party*
*Un = United*

**SOUTHERN AND ANTARCTIC TERRITORIES, FRENCH** *see* **FRANCE**

**SOUTH GEORGIA** *see* **UNITED KINGDOM**

**SOUTH KOREA** *see* **KOREA, SOUTH**

**SOUTH SANDWICH ISLANDS** *see* **UNITED KINGDOM**

# SPAIN

| | |
|---|---|
| **Official name** | Kingdom of Spain |
| **Local name** | España; Reino de España |
| **Former name** | Spanish Republic (1931–9), Spanish State (1936–78) |
| **Area** | 492 431 sq km/190 078 sq mi |
| **Capital** | Madrid |
| **Chief towns** | Barcelona, Valencia, Seville, Zaragoza, Málaga |
| **Population** | 40 847 371 (2001) |
| **Nationality** | Spanish |
| **Languages** | Spanish (Castilian); Catalan, Galician (Gallego) and Basque (Euskera) are also spoken in certain regions |
| **Ethnic groups** | Castilian Spanish 72%, Catalan 17%, Galician 6%, others 3%, Basque 2% |
| **Religions** | Christianity 97% (RC), others 3% |
| **Time zone** | GMT +1 |
| **Currency** | 1 Euro (€) = 100 cents |
| **Telephone** | +34 |
| **Internet** | .es |
| **Country code** | ESP |

**Location**
A country in south-western Europe, bounded in the north by France across the Pyrenees, and in the west by Portugal. It also includes the Balearic Islands in the Mediterranean Sea and the Canary Islands in the Atlantic Ocean.

**Physical description**
Consists mainly of a furrowed central plateau (the Meseta, average height 700m/2 297ft) crossed by mountains; Andalusian or Baetic Mountains in the south-east rise to 3 478m/11 410ft at Mulhacén; Pyrenees in the north rise to 3 404m/11 168ft at Pico de Aneto; highest point is Pico de Teide (3 718m/12 198ft) on the island of Tenerife in the Canary Islands.

**Climate**
Meseta has a continental climate, with hot summers, cold winters and low rainfall; high rainfall in the mountains, with deep winter snow; south Mediterranean coast has the warmest winter temperatures on the European mainland.

**National holidays**
Jan 1, 6, May 1, Aug 15, Nov 1, Dec 6 (Constitution), 8, 25; GF, HT (*most areas*); *much regional variation*.

## Balearic Islands

| | | | |
|---|---|---|---|
| **Location** | An archipelago of five major islands (Majorca, Minorca, Ibiza, Formentera and Cabrera) and eleven islets in the west Mediterranean Sea, situated near the east coast of Spain. | | |
| **Area** | 5 014 sq km/1 935 sq mi | **Population** | 785 000 (1999e) |
| **Capital** | Palma de Mallorca | | |

## Canary Islands

| | | | |
|---|---|---|---|
| **Location** | An island archipelago of eight major islands (Tenerife, Gran Canaria, Fuerteventura, Lanzarote, La Palma, Hierro and Gomera) in the Atlantic Ocean, lying 100km/62mi off the north-west coast of Africa. | | |
| **Area** | 7 273 sq km/2 807 sq mi | **Population** | 1 605 000 (1999e) |
| **Capital** | Las Palmas | | |

# Political leaders

### Monarch

| | |
|---|---|
| 1516–56 | Charles I (Emperor Charles V) |
| 1556–98 | Philip II |
| 1598–1621 | Philip III |
| 1621–65 | Philip IV |
| 1665–1700 | Charles II |
| 1700–24 | Philip V |
| 1724 | Luis |
| 1724–46 | Philip V |
| 1746–59 | Ferdinand VI |
| 1759–88 | Charles III |
| 1788–1808 | Charles IV |
| 1808 | Ferdinand VII |
| 1808–14 | Joseph Bonaparte |
| 1814–33 | Ferdinand VII |
| 1833–68 | Isabella II |
| 1868–70 | *No monarchy* |
| 1870–3 | Amadeus of Savoy |
| 1873–4 | *Temporary republic* |
| 1874–85 | Alfonso XII |
| 1886–1931 | Alfonso XIII |

**President**

| | |
|---|---|
| 1931 | Niceto Alcalá Zamora y Torres |
| 1931 | Manuel Azaña y Díez |
| 1931–6 | Niceto Alcalá Zamora y Torres |
| 1936 | Diego Martínez Barrio *Acting President* |
| 1936–9 | Manuel Azaña y Díez *Civil War* |
| 1936–9 | Miguel Cabanellas Ferrer *Civil War* |

**Chief of State – Nationalist Government**

| | |
|---|---|
| 1936–75 | Francisco Franco Bahamonde |

**Monarch**

| | |
|---|---|
| 1975– | Juan Carlos I |

**Prime Minister**

| | |
|---|---|
| 1900–1 | Marcelo de Azcárraga y Palmero |
| 1901–2 | Práxedes Mateo Sagasta |
| 1902–3 | Francisco Silvela y Le-Vielleuze |
| 1903 | Raimundo Fernández Villaverde |
| 1903–4 | Antonio Maura y Montaner |
| 1904–5 | Marcelo de Azcárraga y Palmero |
| 1905 | Raimundo Fernández Villaverde |
| 1905 | Eugenio Montero Ríos |
| 1905–6 | Segismundo Moret y Prendergast |
| 1906 | José López Domínguez |
| 1906 | Segismundo Moret y Prendergast |
| 1906–7 | Antonio Aguilar y Correa |
| 1907–9 | Antonio Maura y Montaner |
| 1909–10 | Segismundo Moret y Prendergast |
| 1910–12 | José Canalejas y Méndez |
| 1912 | Álvaro Figueroa y Torres |
| 1912–13 | Manuel García Prieto |
| 1913–15 | Eduardo Dato y Iradier |
| 1915–17 | Álvaro Figueroa y Torres |
| 1917 | Manuel García Prieto |
| 1917 | Eduardo Dato y Iradier |
| 1917–18 | Manuel García Prieto |
| 1918 | Antonio Maura y Montaner |
| 1918 | Manuel García Prieto |
| 1918–19 | Álvaro Figueroa y Torres |
| 1919 | Antonio Maura y Montaner |
| 1919 | Joaquín Sánchez de Toca |
| 1919–20 | Manuel Allendesalazar |
| 1920–1 | Eduardo Dato y Iradier |
| 1921 | Gabino Bugallal Araujo *Acting Prime Minister* |
| 1921 | Manuel Allendesalazar |
| 1921–2 | Antonio Maura y Montaner |
| 1922 | José Sánchez Guerra y Martínez |
| 1922–3 | Manuel García Prieto |
| 1923–30 | Miguel Primo de Rivera y Oraneja |
| 1930–1 | Dámaso Berenguer y Fusté |
| 1931 | Juan Bautista Aznar-Cabañas |
| 1931 | Niceto Alcalá Zamora y Torres |
| 1931–3 | Manuel Azaña y Díez |
| 1933 | Alejandro Lerroux y García |
| 1933 | Diego Martínez Barrio |
| 1933–4 | Alejandro Lerroux y García |
| 1934 | Ricardo Samper Ibáñez |
| 1934–5 | Alejandro Lerroux y García |
| 1935 | Joaquín Chapaprieta y Terragosa |
| 1935–6 | Manuel Portela Valladares |
| 1936 | Manuel Azaña y Díez |
| 1936 | Santiago Casares Quiroga |
| 1936 | Diego Martínez Barrio |
| 1936 | José Giral y Pereyra |
| 1936–7 | Francisco Largo Caballero |
| 1937–9 | Juan Negrín |

**Chairman of the Council of Ministers**

| | |
|---|---|
| 1939–73 | Francisco Franco Bahamonde |

**Prime Minister**

| | |
|---|---|
| 1973 | Torcuato Fernández Miranda y Hevía *Acting Prime Minister* |
| 1973–6 | Carlos Arias Navarro |
| 1976–81 | Adolfo Suárez |
| 1981–2 | Calvo Sotelo |
| 1982–96 | Felipe González |
| 1996– | José María Aznar |

## SRI LANKA

| | | | |
|---|---|---|---|
| **Official name** | Democratic Socialist Republic of Sri Lanka | **Nationality** | Sri Lankan |
| **Local name** | Sri Lanka; Sri Lanka Prajatantrika Samajavadi Janarajaya | **Languages** | Sinhala, Tamil |
| **Former name** | Ceylon (until 1972) | **Ethnic groups** | Sinhalese 74%, Tamil 18%, Sri Lankan Moor 7%, others 1% |
| **Independence** | 1948 (from Britain), 1972 (republic) | **Religions** | Buddhism 69%, Hinduism 15%, Christianity 8%, Islam 8% |
| **Area** | 65 610 sq km/25 325 sq mi | **Time zone** | GMT +5.5 |
| **Capital** | Colombo (commercial capital) and Sri Jayawardenepura Kotte (administrative capital) | **Currency** | 1 Sri Lankan Rupee (SLR, SLRs) = 100 cents |
| **Chief towns** | Jaffna, Kandy, Galle, Trincomalee | **Telephone** | +94 |
| **Population** | 16 864 687 (2001) | **Internet** | .lk |
| | | **Country code** | LKA |

**Location**
An island state in the Indian Ocean situated off the south-east coast of India.

**Physical description**
Pear-shaped; low-lying areas in the north and south, surrounding the south-central uplands; highest peak is Pidurutalagala (2 524m/8 281ft); coastal plain is fringed by sandy beaches and lagoons; nearly half is tropical monsoon forest or open woodland.

**Climate**
High temperatures and humidity in the northern plains; average daily temperatures at Trincomalee are 24–33°C; temperatures in the interior are reduced by altitude; greatest rainfall on the south-west coast and in the mountains.

**National holidays**
Jan 15 (Tamil Thai Pongal), Feb 4 (National), May 1, Dec 25; Ad, D, ER, GF, NY (Sinhala/Tamil) (Apr) (2), PB, Mahasivarathri (Feb/Mar), Full Moon (*monthly*), day following Vesak Full Moon (May).

## Political leaders

### President

| | |
|---|---|
| 1972–8 | William Gopallawa |
| 1978–89 | Junius Richard Jayawardene |
| 1989–93 | Ranasinghe Premadasa |
| 1994– | Chandrika Bandaranaike Kumaratunga |

### Prime Minister

#### Ceylon

| | |
|---|---|
| 1947–52 | Don Stephen Senanayake |
| 1952–3 | Dudley Shelton Senanayake |
| 1953–6 | John Lionel Kotelawala |
| 1956–9 | Solomon West Ridgeway Dias Bandaranaike |
| 1959–60 | Vijayananda Dahanayake |
| 1960 | Dudley Shelton Senanayake |
| 1960–5 | Sirimavo Ratwatte Dias Bandaranaike |
| 1965–70 | Dudley Shelton Senanayake |

### Sri Lanka

| | |
|---|---|
| 1970–7 | Sirimavo Ratwatte Dias Bandaranaike |
| 1977–89 | Ranasinghe Premadasa |
| 1989–93 | Dingiri Banda Wijetunge |
| 1993–4 | Ranil Wickremasinghe |
| 1994 | Chandrika Bandaranaike Kumaratunga |
| 1994–2000 | Sirimavo Ratwatte Dias Bandaranaike |
| 2000–1 | Ratnasiri Wickremanayake |
| 2001– | Ranil Wickremasinghe |

#### Serendipity

*Serendipity* means the state of frequently making lucky or beneficial discoveries by accident. The word actually comes from an ancient name for Sri Lanka, *Serendip*. It made the jump from Sri Lanka to the English language through a Persian fairytale, 'The Three Princes of Serendip', whose heroes made many lucky discoveries by chance; the writer Horace Walpole then coined *serendipity* in reference to the tale.

## THE SUDAN

| | | | |
|---|---|---|---|
| **Official name** | Republic of The Sudan | **Nationality** | Sudanese |
| **Local name** | As-Sūdān; Al-Jumhūriyya as-Sūdān | **Languages** | Arabic |
| **Former name** | Anglo-Egyptian Sudan (until 1956), Democratic Republic of The Sudan (1969–85) | **Ethnic groups** | Arab 50%, Dinka 13%, Nuba 8%, Beja 6%, Nuer 5%, Azande 3%, others 15% |
| **Independence** | 1956 | **Religions** | Islam 70% (mostly Sunni), traditional beliefs 23%, Christianity 7% |
| **Area** | 2 504 530 sq km/ 966 749 sq mi | **Time zone** | GMT +2 |
| **Capital** | Khartoum; Al Khartūm, Al Khurtūm | **Currency** | 1 Sudanese Dinar (SD) = 10 pounds |
| **Chief towns** | Port Sudan, Wad Medani, Omdurman | **Telephone** | +249 |
| **Population** | 31 627 000 (2001e) | **Internet** | .sd |
| | | **Country code** | SDN |

**Location**
A north-east African republic, bounded to the north by Egypt; to the north-west by Libya; to the west by Chad; to the south-west by the Central African Republic; to the south by Democratic Republic of Congo; to the south-east by Uganda and Kenya; to the east by Ethiopia; and to the north by the Red Sea.

**Physical description**
Largest country on the African continent, astride the middle reaches of the River Nile; eastern edge formed by the Nubian Highlands and an escarpment rising to over 2 000m/ 6 562ft on the Red Sea; Imatong Mountains in the south rise to 3 187m/10 456ft at Kinyeti (the highest point); White Nile flows north to meet the Blue Nile at Khartoum.

**Climate**
Desert conditions in the north; in the hottest months (Jul–Aug), the temperature rarely falls below 24°C in the north.

**National holidays**
Jan 1 (Independence), Mar 3 (Unity), Apr 6 (Revolution), Dec 25; Ad (5), ER (5), NY (Muslim), PB, Sham al-Naseem (Apr/May).

## Political leaders

### Chief of State

| | |
|---|---|
| 1956–8 | *Council of State* |
| 1958–64 | Ibrahim Abboud |
| 1964–5 | *Council of Sovereignty* |
| 1965–9 | Ismail Al-Azhari |
| 1969–85 | Jaafar Mohammed Nimeiri *President from 1971* |
| 1993– | Omar Hassan Ahmed Al-Bashir *President* |

### Chairman of Transitional Military Council

| | |
|---|---|
| 1985–6 | Abd Al-Rahman Siwar Al-Dahab |

### Chairman of Supreme Council

| | |
|---|---|
| 1986–9 | Ahmad Al-Mirghani |

### Chairman of Revolutionary Command Council

| | |
|---|---|
| 1989–93 | Omar Hassan Ahmed Al-Bashir |

### Prime Minister

| | |
|---|---|
| 1955–6 | Ismail Al-Azhari |
| 1956–8 | Abdullah Khalil |
| 1958–64 | *As President* |
| 1964–5 | Serr Al-Khatim Al-Khalifa |
| 1965–6 | Mohammed Ahmed Mahjoub |
| 1966–7 | Sadiq Al-Mahdi |
| 1967–9 | Mohammed Ahmed Mahjoub |
| 1969 | Babiker Awadalla |
| 1969–76 | *As President* |
| 1976–7 | Rashid Al-Tahir Bakr |
| 1977–85 | *As Chief of State* |
| 1985–6 | *Transitional Military Council* (Al-Jazuli Dafallah) |
| 1986–9 | Sadiq Al-Mahdi *Military Council, Prime Minister* |
| 1989– | *No Prime Minister* |

### White and Blue Nile

Although Egypt is linked in the popular imagination to the River Nile, the mighty river actually crosses several countries, notably The Sudan. The principal tributaries of the River Nile itself are the White Nile, from Uganda, and the Blue Nile, from Ethiopia, which meet near Khartoum and flow north.

## SURINAME

| | | | |
|---|---|---|---|
| **Official name** | Republic of Suriname | **Ethnic groups** | Hindustani 37%, Creole 31%, Javanese 15%, black 9%, Amerindian 3%, Chinese 3%, others 2% |
| **Local name** | Suriname; Republiek Suriname | | |
| **Former name** | Netherlands Guiana, Dutch Guiana (until 1948) | **Religions** | Christianity 48% (Prot 25%, RC 23%), Hinduism 27%, Islam 21%, traditional beliefs 4% |
| **Independence** | 1975 | | |
| **Area** | 163 265 sq km/63 020 sq mi | | |
| **Capital** | Paramaribo | **Time zone** | GMT –3 |
| **Chief towns** | Brokopondo, Nieuw Amsterdam | **Currency** | 1 Surinamese Dollar (SRD, $) = 100 cents |
| **Population** | 429 000 (2001e) | **Telephone** | +597 |
| **Nationality** | Surinamese | **Internet** | .sr |
| **Languages** | Dutch; English, Hindi, Javanese and Sranang Tongo are also spoken | **Country code** | SUR |

**Location**
A republic in north-eastern South America, bounded to the west by Guyana; to the south by Brazil; to the east by French Guiana; and to the north by the Atlantic Ocean.

**Physical description**
Diverse natural regions, ranging from coastal lowland through savannah to mountainous upland; coastal strip is mostly covered by swamp; highland interior in the south is overgrown with dense tropical forest; highest point is Julianatop (1 230m/4 035ft).

**Climate**
Tropically hot and humid, with two rainy seasons in May–Jul and Nov–Jan; Paramaribo temperatures range from 22–33°C.

**National holidays**
Jan 1, May 1, Jul 1 (Freedom), Nov 25 (Independence), Dec 25, 26; EM, ER, GF, Holi Phagwa (Mar).

## Political leaders

**President**

1975–80 J H E Ferrier
1980–2 Henk Chin-a-Sen
1982–8 L F Ramdat-Musier *Acting President*
1988–90 Ramsewak Shankar
1990–1 Johan Kraag
1991–6 Ronald Venetiaan
1996–2000 Jules Wijdenbosch
2000– Ronald Venetiaan

**Chairman of National Military Council**

1980–7 Desi Bouterse
1987 Iwan Granoogst *Acting Prime Minister*

**Prime Minister**

1975–80 Henk Arron
1980 Henk Chin-a-Sen
1980–2 *No Prime Minister*
1982–3 Henry Weyhorst
1983–4 Errol Alibux
1984–6 Wim Udenhout

| | | | |
|---|---|---|---|
| 1986–7 | Pretaapnarain Radhakishun | 1990–1 | Jules Wijdenbosch |
| 1987–8 | Jules Wijdenbosch | 1991–6 | Jules Ajodhia |
| 1988–90 | Henk Arron | | |

**Vice President/Chairman of the Council of Ministers**

| | |
|---|---|
| 1996–2000 | Pretaapnarain Radhakishun |
| 2000– | Jules Ajodhia |

**SVALBARD ISLANDS** *see* **NORWAY**

# SWAZILAND

| | |
|---|---|
| **Official name** | Kingdom of Swaziland |
| **Local name** | Umbuso we Swatini |
| **Independence** | 1968 |
| **Area** | 17 363 sq km/6 702 sq mi |
| **Capital** | Mbabane (administrative) and Lobamba (legislative) |
| **Population** | 929 718 (1997) |
| **Nationality** | Swazi |
| **Languages** | English, Siswati |
| **Ethnic groups** | Swazi 84%, Zulu 10%, European 4%, Tsonga 2% |
| **Religions** | Christianity 60%, traditional beliefs 40% |
| **Time zone** | GMT +2 |
| **Currency** | 1 Lilangeni (plural Emalangeni) (Li, E) = 100 cents |
| **Telephone** | +268 |
| **Internet** | .sz |
| **Country code** | SWZ |

**Location**
A small monarchy in south-east Africa, bounded to the north, west, south and south-east by South Africa, and to the north-east by Mozambique.

**Physical description**
Mountainous Highveld in the west; highest point is Emblembe (1 862m/6 109ft); more populated Middleveld in the centre descends to 600–700m/1 970–2 300ft; rolling, bush-covered Lowveld in the east is irrigated by river systems.

**Climate**
Humid, near temperate climate in the west; subtropical and drier in the centre; tropical in the east, with relatively little rain (susceptible to drought); average annual temperature is 16°C in the west and 22°C in the east.

**National holidays**
Jan 1, Apr 19 (King's Birthday), 25 (National Flag), May 1, Sep 6 (Somhlolo), Dec 25, 26; A, EM, GF, Incwala (Dec/Jan), Umhlanga/Reed Dance (Aug/Sep), Jul public holiday.

## Political leaders

**Monarch**

| | | | |
|---|---|---|---|
| 1967–82 | Sobhuza II *Chief since 1921* | 1983–6 | Ntombi *Queen Regent* |
| 1982–3 | Dzeliwe *Queen Regent* | 1986– | Mswati III |
| 1983 | Sozisa Dlamini *Regent* | | |

**Prime Minister**

| | |
|---|---|
| 1967–78 | Prince Makhosini |
| 1978–9 | Prince Maphevu Dlamini |
| 1979–83 | Prince Mbandla Dlamini |
| 1983–6 | Prince Bhekimpi Dlamini |
| 1986–9 | Sotsha Dlamini |
| 1989–93 | Obed Dlamini *Acting Prime Minister* |
| 1993–6 | Jameson Mbilini Dlamini |
| 1996– | Sibusiso Barnabas Dlamini |

### Power Behind the Throne

Kings of Swaziland are permitted to have many wives, and King Sobhuza II, who ruled from 1921 to 1982, is thought to have had more than 60. Upon the death of a king, the Royal Council chooses one of his favourite senior wives to be the new Queen Mother, an important position that makes her the most influential woman in the country. One of her unmarried sons is then chosen to be the new king.

## SWEDEN

| | |
|---|---|
| **Official name** | Kingdom of Sweden |
| **Local name** | Sverige; Konungariket Sverige |
| **Area** | 411 479 sq km/158 830 sq mi |
| **Capital** | Stockholm |
| **Chief towns** | Gothenburg, Malmö, Uppsala, Norrköping, Västerås, Örebro, Linköping |
| **Population** | 8 860 000 (2001e) |
| **Nationality** | Swedish |
| **Languages** | Swedish |
| **Ethnic groups** | Swedish 91%, Finnish and Lapp 3%, others 6% |
| **Religions** | Christianity 93% (Prot 90%, RC 2%, others 1%), Islam 1%, others and none/unaffiliated 6% |
| **Time zone** | GMT +1 |
| **Currency** | 1 Swedish Krona (Skr) = 100 øre |
| **Telephone** | +46 |
| **Internet** | .se |
| **Country code** | SWE |

**Location**
A constitutional monarchy in northern Europe, occupying the eastern side of the Scandinavian Peninsula, bounded to the east by Finland, the Gulf of Bothnia and the Baltic Sea; to the south-west by the Skagerrak and Kattegat; and to the west and north-west by Norway.

**Physical description**
A large amount of inland water; many coastal islands; c.57% of the country is forested; Kjölen Mountains in the west form much of the boundary with Norway; highest peak is Kebnekaise (2 111m/6 926ft); many waterfalls.

**Climate**
Typically continental, with a considerable temperature range between summer and winter, except in the south-west where winters are warmer; average number of days with a mean temperature below freezing increases from 71 in Malmö to 184 near the Arctic Circle.

**National holidays**
Jan 1, 6, May 1, Nov 1, Dec 25, 26; A, EM, GF, WM, Midsummer (Jun).

## Political leaders

### Monarch

#### Vasa

| | |
|---|---|
| 1523–60 | Gustav I |
| 1560–8 | Erik XIV |
| 1568–92 | Johan III |
| 1592–9 | Sigismund |
| 1599–1611 | Karl IX |
| 1611–32 | Gustav II Adolf |
| 1632–54 | Kristina |

#### Zweibrucken

| | |
|---|---|
| 1654–60 | Karl X Gustav |
| 1660–97 | Karl XI |
| 1697–1718 | Karl XII |
| 1718–20 | Ulrika Eleonora |

#### Hesse

| | |
|---|---|
| 1720–51 | Fredrik |

#### Oldenburg-Holstein-Gottorp

| | |
|---|---|
| 1751–71 | Adolf Fredrik |
| 1771–92 | Gustav III |
| 1792–1809 | Gustav IV Adolf |
| 1809–18 | Karl XIII |

#### Bernadotte

| | |
|---|---|
| 1818–44 | Karl XIV Johan |
| 1844–59 | Oskar I |
| 1859–72 | Karl XV |
| 1872–1907 | Oskar II |
| 1907–50 | Gustav V |
| 1950–73 | Gustav VI Adolf |
| 1973– | Karl XVI Gustav |

### Prime Minister

| | |
|---|---|
| 1900–2 | Fredrik von Otter |
| 1902–5 | Erik Gustaf Boström |
| 1905 | Johan Ramstedt |
| 1905 | Christian Lundeberg |
| 1905–6 | Karl Staaf |
| 1906–11 | Arvid Lindman |
| 1911–14 | Karl Staaf |
| 1914–17 | Hjalmar Hammarskjöld |
| 1917 | Carl Swartz |
| 1917–20 | Nils Edén |
| 1920 | Hjalmar Branting |
| 1920–1 | Louis de Geer |
| 1921 | Oscar von Sydow |
| 1921–3 | Hjalmar Branting |
| 1923–4 | Ernst Trygger |
| 1924–5 | Hjalmar Branting |
| 1925–6 | Rickard Sandler |
| 1926–8 | Carl Gustaf Ekman |
| 1928–30 | Arvid Lindman |
| 1930–2 | Carl Gustaf Ekman |
| 1932 | Felix Hamrin |
| 1932–6 | Per Albin Hansson |
| 1936 | Axel Pehrsson-Branstorp |
| 1936–46 | Per Albin Hansson |
| 1946–69 | Tage Erlander |
| 1969–76 | Olof Palme |
| 1976–8 | Thorbjörn Fälldin |
| 1978–9 | Ola Ullsten |
| 1979–82 | Thorbjörn Fälldin |
| 1982–6 | Olof Palme |
| 1986–91 | Ingvar Carlsson |
| 1991–4 | Carl Bildt |
| 1994–6 | Ingvar Carlsson |
| 1996– | Göran Persson |

### *Crayfish Parties*

Every Aug, Swedes get together for big parties in celebration of crayfish. The crayfish party tradition began in the early 20c, when stocks of Swedish crayfish were threatened and fishing was restricted to Aug; the weeks when crayfish could be caught were celebrated with a big party at which crayfish were eaten. Today, silly hats, colourful decorations, songs in the honour of the crayfish and copious quantities of schnapps to wash the crustaceans down are all part of the raucous festivities.

## SWITZERLAND

| | |
|---|---|
| **Official name** | Swiss Confederation |
| **Local name** | Schweiz; Schweizerische Eidgenossenschaft (German), Suisse; Confédération Suisse (French), Svizzera; Confederazione Svizzera (Italian), Svizra; Confederaziun Svizra (Romansch) |
| **Area** | 41 228 sq km/15 914 sq mi |
| **Capital** | Berne; Bern, Berna |
| **Chief towns** | Zurich, Lucerne, St Gallen, Lausanne, Basle, Geneva |
| **Population** | 7 204 055 (2000) |
| **Nationality** | Swiss |
| **Languages** | German (65%), French (18%), Italian (12%) and Romansch (1%); many of the Swiss speak more than one of these |
| **Ethnic groups** | German 65%, French 18%, Italian 10%, Romansch 1%, others 6% |
| **Religions** | Christianity 86% (RC 46%, Prot 40%), none/unaffiliated 9%, Islam 2%, others 3% |
| **Time zone** | GMT +1 |
| **Currency** | 1 Swiss Franc (SFr, SwF) = 100 centimes = 100 rappen |
| **Telephone** | +41 |
| **Internet** | .ch |
| **Country code** | CHE |

**Location**
A landlocked European republic, bounded to the east by Liechtenstein and Austria; to the south by Italy; to the west by France; and to the north by Germany.

**Physical description**
Mountainous; the Alps run roughly east to west in the south; highest peak is Dufourspitze (4 634m/15 203ft); average height of the Pre-Alps in the north-west is 2 000m/6 562ft; central plateau, at an average altitude of 580m/1 903ft, is fringed by large lakes; c.3 000 sq km/1 160 sq mi of glaciers.

**Climate**
Temperate, varying greatly with relief and altitude; warm summers, with considerable rainfall; winter temperatures average 0°C; average annual temperature is 7–9°C; the *Föhn*, a warm wind, is noticeable in the Alps during late winter and spring.

**National holidays**
Jan 1, Aug 1 (National), Dec 25, 26; A, EM, GF, WM; *other canton and local holidays*.

## Political leaders

**President**

| | |
|---|---|
| 1900 | Walter Hauser |
| 1901 | Ernst Brenner |
| 1902 | Joseph Zemp |
| 1903 | Adolf Deucher |
| 1904 | Robert Comtesse |
| 1905 | Marc-Emile Ruchet |
| 1906 | Ludwig Forrer |
| 1907 | Eduard Müller |
| 1908 | Ernst Brenner |
| 1909 | Adolf Deucher |
| 1910 | Robert Comtesse |
| 1911 | Marc-Emile Ruchet |
| 1912 | Ludwig Forrer |
| 1913 | Eduard Müller |
| 1914 | Arthur Hoffmann |
| 1915 | Giuseppe Motta |
| 1916 | Camille Decoppet |
| 1917 | Edmund Schulthess |
| 1918 | Felix Calonder |
| 1919 | Gustave Ador |

| | | | |
|---|---|---|---|
| 1920 | Giuseppe Motta | 1962 | Paul Chaudet |
| 1921 | Edmund Schulthess | 1963 | Willy Spühler |
| 1922 | Robert Haab | 1964 | Ludwig von Moos |
| 1923 | Karl Scheurer | 1965 | Hans Peter Tschudi |
| 1924 | Ernest Chuard | 1966 | Hans Schaffner |
| 1925 | Jean-Marie Musy | 1967 | Roger Bonvin |
| 1926 | Heinrich Häberlin | 1968 | Willy Spühler |
| 1927 | Giuseppe Motta | 1969 | Ludwig von Moos |
| 1928 | Edmund Schulthess | 1970 | Hans Peter Tschudi |
| 1929 | Robert Haab | 1971 | Rudolf Gnägi |
| 1930 | Jean-Marie Musy | 1972 | Nello Celio |
| 1931 | Heinrich Häberlin | 1973 | Roger Bonvin |
| 1932 | Giuseppe Motta | 1974 | Ernst Brugger |
| 1933 | Edmund Schulthess | 1975 | Pierre Graber |
| 1934 | Marcel Pilet-Golaz | 1976 | Rudolf Gnägi |
| 1935 | Rudolf Minger | 1977 | Kurt Furgler |
| 1936 | Albert Meyer | 1978 | Willi Ritschard |
| 1937 | Giuseppe Motta | 1979 | Hans Hürlimann |
| 1938 | Johannes Baumann | 1980 | Georges-André Chevallaz |
| 1939 | Philipp Etter | 1981 | Kurt Furgler |
| 1940 | Marcel Pilet-Golaz | 1982 | Fritz Honegger |
| 1941 | Ernst Wetter | 1983 | Pierre Aubert |
| 1942 | Philipp Etter | 1984 | Leon Schlumpf |
| 1943 | Enrico Celio | 1985 | Kurt Furgler |
| 1944 | Walter Stampfli | 1986 | Alphons Egli |
| 1945 | Eduard von Steiger | 1987 | Pierre Aubert |
| 1946 | Karl Kobelt | 1988 | Otto Stich |
| 1947 | Philipp Etter | 1989 | Jean-Pascal Delamuraz |
| 1948 | Enrico Celio | 1990 | Arnold Koller |
| 1949 | Ernst Nobs | 1991 | Flavio Cotti |
| 1950 | Max Petitpierre | 1992 | René Felber |
| 1951 | Eduard von Steiger | 1993 | Adolf Ogi |
| 1952 | Karl Kobelt | 1994 | Otto Stich |
| 1953 | Philipp Etter | 1995 | Kaspar Villiger |
| 1954 | Rodolphe Rubattel | 1996 | Jean-Pascal Delamuraz |
| 1955 | Max Petitpierre | 1997 | Arnold Koller |
| 1956 | Markus Feldmann | 1998 | Flavio Cotti |
| 1957 | Hans Streuli | 1999 | Ruth Dreifuss |
| 1958 | Thomas Holenstein | 2000 | Adolf Ogi |
| 1959 | Paul Chaudet | 2001 | Moritz Leuenberger |
| 1960 | Max Petitpierre | 2002 | Kaspar Villinger |
| 1961 | Friedrich Wahlen | 2003 | Pascal Couchepin |

## Orson Welles on Switzerland

'In Italy for thirty years under the Borgias they had warfare, terror, murder, bloodshed – they produced Michelangelo, Leonardo da Vinci and the Renaissance. In Switzerland they had brotherly love, five hundred years of democracy and peace, and what did they produce? The cuckoo clock.'

**1949 Orson Welles (1915–85) US director and actor (from the film *The Third Man*).**

# SYRIA

| | | | |
|---|---|---|---|
| **Official name** | Syrian Arab Republic | **Nationality** | Syrian |
| **Local name** | As-Sūriyya; Al-Jumhūriyya Al-'Arabiyya as-Sūriyya | **Languages** | Arabic |
| **Former name** | formerly part of the United Arab Republic, with Egypt (1958–61) | **Ethnic groups** | Arab 90%, Kurdish 6%, Armenian and others 4% |
| **Independence** | 1946 | **Religions** | Islam 90% (Sunni 74%, others 16%), Christianity 10% |
| **Area** | 185 180 sq km/71 479 sq mi | **Time zone** | GMT +2 |
| **Capital** | Damascus; Dimashq | **Currency** | 1 Syrian Pound (LS, S$) = 100 piastres |
| **Chief towns** | Halab (Aleppo), Homs, Hama, Latakia | **Telephone** | +963 |
| **Population** | 13 782 315 (1994) | **Internet** | .sy |
| | | **Country code** | SYR |

**Location**
A republic in the Middle East, bounded to the west by the Mediterranean Sea and Lebanon; to the south-west by Israel and Jordan; to the east by Iraq; and to the north by Turkey.

**Physical description**
Behind a narrow coastal plain, the Jabal al Nusayriyah Mountains rise to c.1 500m/4 921ft; steep drop in the east to the Orontes River valley; Anti-Lebanon range in the south-west rises to 2 814m/9 232ft at Mt Hermon; open steppe and desert to the east.

**Climate**
Coastal Mediterranean climate, with hot, dry summers and mild, wet winters; 60% has a desert or semi-desert climate; the *khamsin* wind causes temperatures to rise to 43–49°C; in Damascus average temperatures from 7°C (Jan) to 27°C (Jul).

**National holidays**
Jan 1, Mar 8 (Revolution), Apr 17 (Evacuation), May 1, 6 (Martyrs), Jul 23 (Egyptian Revolution), Sep 1 (Libyan Unity), Oct 6 (Liberation), Dec 25; Ad (3), ER (4), ES, NY (Muslim), PB.

## Political leaders

### President

| | |
|---|---|
| 1943–9 | Shukri Al-Quwwatli |
| 1949 | Husni Az-Zaim |
| 1949–51 | Hashim Al-Atassi |
| 1951–4 | Adib Shishaqli |
| 1954–5 | Hashim Al-Atassi |
| 1955–8 | Shukri Al-Quwwatli |
| 1958–61 | *Part of United Arab Republic* |
| 1961–3 | Nazim Al-Qudsi |
| 1963 | Luai Al-Atassi |
| 1963–6 | Amin Al-Hafiz |
| 1966–70 | Nureddin Al-Atassi |
| 1970–1 | Ahmad Al-Khatib |
| 1971–2000 | Hafez Al-Assad |
| 2000– | Bashar Al-Assad |

### Prime Minister

| | |
|---|---|
| 1946–8 | Jamil Mardam Bey |
| 1948–9 | Khalid Al-Azm |
| 1949 | Husni Az-Zaim |
| 1949 | Muhsi Al-Barazi |
| 1949 | Hashim Al-Atassi |
| 1949 | Nazim Al-Qudsi |
| 1949–50 | Khalid Al-Azm |
| 1950–1 | Nazim Al-Qudsi |
| 1951 | Khalid Al-Azm |
| 1951 | Hassan Al-Hakim |
| 1951 | Maruf Ad-Dawalibi |
| 1951–3 | Fauzi As-Salu |

| | |
|---|---|
| 1953–4 | Adib Shishaqli |
| 1954 | Shewqet Shuqair |
| 1954 | Sabri Al-Asali |
| 1954 | Said Al-Ghazzi |
| 1954–5 | Faris Al-Khuri |
| 1955 | Sabri Al-Asali |
| 1955–6 | Said Al-Ghazzi |
| 1956–8 | Sabri Al-Asali |
| 1958–61 | *Part of United Arab Republic* |
| 1961 | Abd Al-Hamid As-Sarraj |
| 1961 | Mamun Kuzbari |
| 1961 | Izzat An-Nuss |
| 1961–2 | Maruf Ad-Dawalibi |
| 1962 | Bashir Azmah |
| 1962–3 | Khalid Al-Azm |
| 1963 | Salah Ad-Din Al-Bitaar |
| 1963 | Sami Al-Jundi |
| 1963 | Salah Ad-Din Al-Bitaar |
| 1963–4 | Amin Al-Hafez |
| 1964 | Salah Ad-Din Al-Bitaar |
| 1964–5 | Amin Al-Hafez |
| 1965 | Yousif Zeayen |
| 1966 | Salah Ad-Din Al-Bitaar |
| 1966–8 | Yousif Zeayen |
| 1968–70 | Nureddin Al-Atassi *Acting Prime Minister* |
| 1970–1 | Hafez Al-Assad |
| 1971–2 | Abdel Rahman Khleifawi |
| 1972–6 | Mahmoud Bin Saleh Al-Ayoubi |
| 1976–8 | Abdul Rahman Khleifawi |
| 1978–80 | Mohammed Ali Al-Halabi |
| 1980–7 | Abdel Rauof Al-Kasm |
| 1987–2000 | Mahmoud Al-Zubi |
| 2000– | Muhammad Mustafa Miro |

### Ancient City

Damascus claims to be the world's oldest continuously inhabited city. It dates back to at least the third millennium BC, or perhaps even to the seventh. Documented history shows that Damascus was an important regional centre by the second millennium BC. It has been suggested that the name Damascus may come from old Arabic *Dar Meshq*, meaning 'well-watered place'. In ancient times it was a great trade and commercial centre.

## TAIWAN

| | |
|---|---|
| **Official name** | Republic of China; also sometimes known as Chinese Taipei |
| **Local name** | T'ai-wan; Chung-hua Min-kuo |
| **Former name** | Formosa (until 1949) |
| **Independence** | 1949 (creation of republic) |
| **Area** | 36 000 sq km/13 896 sq mi |
| **Capital** | T'aipei |
| **Chief towns** | Chilung, Kaohsiung, Taichung |
| **Population** | 22 600 000 (2003e) |
| **Nationality** | Taiwanese, Chinese |
| **Languages** | Mandarin Chinese |
| **Ethnic groups** | Taiwanese Chinese (including Hakka) 84%, mainland Chinese 14%, Ainu 2% |
| **Religions** | Chinese folk religion 45%, Buddhism 42%, Christianity 5%, Islam 1%, others 7% |
| **Time zone** | GMT +8 |
| **Currency** | 1 New Taiwan Dollar (NT$) = 100 cents |
| **Telephone** | +886 |
| **Internet** | .tw |
| **Country code** | TWN |

# TAIWAN

**Location**
An island republic consisting of Taiwan Island and several smaller islands, lying c.80mi/130km off the south-east coast of China.

**Physical description**
Mountain range runs north to south, covering two thirds of Taiwan Island; highest peak is Yu Shan (3 997m/13 113ft); low-lying land is mainly on the west; crossed by the Tropic of Cancer.

**Climate**
Tropical monsoon-type climate; wettest period is May–Sep, when it is hot and humid; typhoons bring heavy rains in Jul–Sep; short mild winters; average daily temperature at T'aipei is 12–19°C (Jan), 24–33°C (Jul–Aug).

**National holidays**
Jan 1 (Foundation of the Republic of China), Feb 28 (Peace Memorial), Apr 5 (National Tomb Sweeping), May 1, Oct 10 (National); NY (Chinese) (Jan/Feb) (3), Dragon Boat Festival (Jun), Mid-Autumn Festival (Sep/Oct).

## Political leaders

**President**

| | |
|---|---|
| 1950–75 | Chiang Kai-shek |
| 1975–8 | Yen Chia-kan |
| 1978–87 | Chiang Ching-kuo |
| 1987–2000 | Lee Teng-hui |
| 2000– | Chen Shui-bian |

**President of Executive Council**

| | |
|---|---|
| 1950–4 | Ch'eng Ch'eng |
| 1954–8 | O K Yui |
| 1958–63 | Ch'eng Ch'eng |
| 1963–72 | Yen Chia-ken |
| 1972–8 | Chiang Ching-kuo |
| 1978–84 | Sun Yun-suan |
| 1984–9 | Yu Kuo-hwa |
| 1989–90 | Lee Huan |
| 1990–3 | Hau Pei-tsun |
| 1993–6 | Lien Chan |

**Prime Minister**

| | |
|---|---|
| 1996–7 | Lien Chan |
| 1997–2000 | Vincent Siew |
| 2000 | Tang Fei |
| 2000–2 | Chang Chun-hsiung |
| 2002– | Yu Shyi-kun |

### *What's in a Name?*

*Taiwan* is perhaps the most controversial country name in the world, for complex historical reasons. When the Communists took control of China in 1949, renaming it the People's Republic of China, the defeated Nationalist government fled to the island of Formosa and set up a 'Chinese government-in-exile'. They kept China's old name and so renamed the island Republic of China, which is still Taiwan's official name. Today there is a movement to rename the country simply as Taiwan and move on as an independent country. But China still claims that Taiwan is a Chinese province that should be under mainland Chinese control, and many people fear that renaming the country would be viewed by the Chinese authorities as an act of wilful independence that would provoke violent retaliation.

# TAJIKISTAN

| | | | |
|---|---|---|---|
| **Official name** | Republic of Tajikistan | **Nationality** | Tajik or Tadzhik, Tajikistani |
| **Local name** | Çumhurii Toçikiston | **Languages** | Tajik, Uzbek, Russian |
| **Former name** | Tajik Soviet Socialist Republic (until 1991), within the Union of Soviet Socialist Republics (USSR; 1929–91) | **Ethnic groups** | Tajik 66%, Uzbek 26%, Russian 3%, others 5% |
| **Independence** | 1991 | **Religions** | Islam 85% (Sunni 80%, Shia 5%), others 15% |
| **Area** | 143 100 sq km/55 200 sq mi | **Time zone** | GMT +5 |
| **Capital** | Dushanbe; Dušanbe | **Currency** | 1 Somoni (S) = 100 dirams |
| **Chief towns** | Khudzand, Kulyab, Kurgan-Tyube | **Telephone** | +992 |
| **Population** | 6 127 000 (2000) | **Internet** | .tj |
| | | **Country code** | TJK |

**Location**
A republic in south-eastern Middle Asia, bounded to the west and north by Uzbekistan; to the north by Kyrgyzstan; to the east by China; and to the south by Afghanistan.

**Physical description**
Tien Shan, Gissar-Alai and Pamir mountain ranges cover over 90% of the area; highest peak is Peak Ismoili Somoni (formerly Communism Peak; 7 495m/24 590ft); River Amudarya flows east to west along the southern border; largest lake is Lake Kara-Kul.

**Climate**
Predominantly continental; hot summers and mild winters.

**National holidays**
Jan 1, Mar 8 (Women), 21, May 9 (Victory), Sep 9 (Independence), Oct 14 (Formation of the Tajik Republic); ER.

## Political leaders

**President**

| | |
|---|---|
| 1991–2 | Rakhman Nabiev |
| 1992 | Akbarsho Iskandrov *Acting President* |
| 1992– | Imamoli Rakhmanov |

**Prime Minister**

| | |
|---|---|
| 1991–2 | Akbar Mirzoyev |
| 1992–3 | Abdumalik Abdullojanov |
| 1993–4 | Abduljalil Samadov *Acting Prime Minister* |
| 1994–6 | Jamshed Karimov |
| 1996–9 | Yahya Azimov |
| 1999– | Akil Akilov |

### Ice White

The flag of Tajikistan has three horizontal stripes of green, white and red, with a gold crown and seven stars above it. The green is said to represent the country's valleys and the white to symbolize not only the snow and ice of Tajikistan's many mountains but also cotton, a major export. The red stripe suggests the unified republic and sympathy with other countries.

# TANZANIA

| | | | |
|---|---|---|---|
| **Official name** | United Republic of Tanzania | **Languages** | Kiswahili, English |
| **Local name** | Tanzania | **Ethnic groups** | Nyamwezi and Sukuma 22%, Swahili 9%, Hehet and Bena 7%, Makonde 6%, Haya 6%, other tribes 50% |
| **Former name** | Republic of Tanganyika (1962–4), United Republic of Tanganyika and Zanzibar (1964) | **Religions** | Christianity 35%, Islam 33%, traditional beliefs 30%, others 2% |
| **Independence** | 1961 | **Time zone** | GMT +3 |
| **Area** | 939 652 sq km/362 706 sq mi | **Currency** | 1 Tanzanian Shilling (Tsh) = 100 cents |
| **Capital** | Dodoma | **Telephone** | +255 |
| **Chief towns** | Dar es Salaam, Zanzibar, Mwanza, Tanga, Arusha | **Internet** | .tz |
| **Population** | 34 569 232 (2002) | **Country code** | TZA |
| **Nationality** | Tanzanian | | |

**Location**
An East African republic, consisting of the mainland region of Tanganyika, and Zanzibar, just off the coast in the Indian Ocean, which includes Zanzibar Island, Pemba Island and some small islets.

**Physical description**
Largest East African country, just south of the Equator; central plateau at average elevation of 1 000m/3 281ft; high grasslands and mountain ranges to the centre and south; Rift Valley branches around Lake Victoria in the north; several high volcanic peaks, notably Mt Kilimanjaro, the highest point (5 895m/19 340ft); extensive Serengeti plain to the west.

**Climate**
Hot, humid and tropical on the coast and offshore islands; average temperature is c.23°C (Jun–Sept) and 27°C (Dec–Mar); hot and dry on the central plateau; semi-temperate at altitudes above 1 500m/4 921ft; permanent snow on high peaks.

**National holidays**
Jan 1, 12 (Zanzibar Revolution), Apr 26 (Union), May 1, Jul 7 (Industrial), Aug 8 (Farmers), Dec 9 (Independence/Republic), 25, 26; Ad, EM, ER (2), GF, PB.

## Political leaders

**President**

| | |
|---|---|
| 1964–85 | Julius Kambarage Nyerere |
| 1985–95 | Ali Hassan Mwinyi |
| 1995– | Benjamin William Mkapa |

**Prime Minister**

| | |
|---|---|
| 1964–72 | Rashid M Kawawa *Vice President* |
| 1972–7 | Rashid M Kawawa |
| 1977–80 | Edward M Sokoine |
| 1980–3 | Cleopa D Msuya |
| 1983–4 | Edward M Sokoine |
| 1984–5 | Salim A Salim |
| 1985–90 | Joseph S Warioba |
| 1990–4 | John Malecela |
| 1994–5 | Cleopa Msuya |
| 1995– | Frederick Tluway Sumaye |

# THAILAND

| | | | |
|---|---|---|---|
| **Official name** | Kingdom of Thailand | **Languages** | Thai |
| **Local name** | Prathet Thai | **Ethnic groups** | Thai 75%, Chinese 14%, others 11% |
| **Former name** | Siam (until 1939 and 1945–49) | **Religions** | Buddhism 95%, Islam 4%, others 1% |
| **Area** | 513 115 sq km/198 062 sq mi | **Time zone** | GMT +7 |
| **Capital** | Bangkok; Krung Thep | **Currency** | 1 Baht (B) = 100 satang |
| **Chief towns** | Chiang Mai, Nakhon Ratchasima | **Telephone** | +66 |
| **Population** | 60 617 200 (2000) | **Internet** | .th |
| **Nationality** | Thai | **Country code** | THA |

**Location**
A kingdom in south-east Asia, bounded to the west by the Andaman Sea; to the west and north-west by Myanmar (Burma); to the north-east and east by Laos; to the east by Cambodia; and to the south by Malaysia.

**Physical description**
Central agricultural region dominated by the Chao Phraya River floodplain; large north-eastern plateau; mountainous north rises to 2 595m/8 514ft at Doi Inthanon; low-lying south covered in tropical rainforest; mangrove-forested coastal islands.

**Climate**
Equatorial climate in the south; tropical monsoon climate in the north and centre.

**National holidays**
Jan 1, Apr 6 (Chakri), 13 (Songkran) (3), May 1, 5 (Coronation), Aug 12 (Queen's Birthday), Oct 23 (Chulalongkorn Memorial), Dec 5 (King's Birthday), 10 (Constitution), 31; Buddhist Lent (Jul), Makha Bucha (Feb), Visakha Bucha (May).

## Political leaders

### Monarch

| | |
|---|---|
| 1868–1910 | Chulalongkorn, Rama V |
| 1910–25 | Rama VI |
| 1925–35 | Rama VII |
| 1935–9 | Rama VIII (Ananda Mahidol) |
| 1939–46 | Nai Pridi Phanomyong *Regent* |
| 1946 | Rama IX |
| 1946–50 | Rangsit of Chainat *Regent* |
| 1950– | Bhumibol Adulyadej |

### Prime Minister

| | |
|---|---|
| 1932–3 | Phraya Manopakom |
| 1933–8 | Phraya Phahon Phonphahuyasena |
| 1938–44 | Luang Phibun Songgram |
| 1944–5 | Nai Khuang Aphaiwong |
| 1945 | Thawi Bunyaket |
| 1945–6 | Mom Rachawongse Seni Pramoj |
| 1946 | Nai Khuang Aphaiwong |
| 1946 | Nai Pridi Phanomyong |
| 1946–7 | Luang Thamrong Nawasawat |
| 1947–8 | Nai Khuang Aphaiwong |
| 1948–57 | Luang Phibun Songgram |
| 1957 | Sarit Thanarat |
| 1957 | Nai Pote Sarasin |
| 1957–8 | Thanom Kittikatchom |
| 1958–63 | Sarit Thanarat |
| 1963–73 | Thanom Kittikatchom |
| 1973–5 | Sanya Dharmasaki |
| 1975–6 | Mom Rachawongse Kukrit Pramoj |
| 1976 | Seni Pramoj |
| 1976–7 | Thanin Kraivichien |
| 1977–80 | Kriangsak Chammanard |
| 1980–7 | Prem Tinsulanonda |
| 1987–91 | Chatichai Choonhaven |
| 1991–2 | Anand Panyarachun |
| 1992 | Suchinda Kraprayoon |
| 1992 | Anand Panyarachun |

| | | | |
|---|---|---|---|
| 1992–5 | Chuan Leekpai | 1997–2001 | Chuan Leekpai |
| 1995–6 | Banharn Silpa-Archa | 2001– | Thaksin Shinawatra |
| 1996–7 | Chavalit Yongchaiyudh | | |

**TOBAGO** *see* **TRINIDAD AND TOBAGO**

## TOGO

| | | | |
|---|---|---|---|
| **Official name** | Republic of Togo (also Togolese Republic) | **Ethnic groups** | Ewe-Adja 41%, TemKabre 25%, Gurma 16%, others 18% |
| **Local name** | Togo; République Togolaise | **Religions** | traditional beliefs 55%, Christianity 30% (RC 23%, Prot 7%), Islam 15% |
| **Former name** | French Togoland (until 1956) | **Time zone** | GMT |
| **Independence** | 1960 | **Currency** | 1 CFA Franc (CFAFr) = 100 centimes |
| **Area** | 56 600 sq km/21 848 sq mi | **Telephone** | +228 |
| **Capital** | Lomé | **Internet** | .tg |
| **Chief towns** | Sokodé, Kpalimé, Atakpamé | **Country code** | TGO |
| **Population** | 4 686 000 (2001e) | | |
| **Nationality** | Togolese | | |
| **Languages** | French; many local languages are also spoken | | |

**Location**
A republic in West Africa, bounded to the west by Ghana; to the north by Burkina Faso; and to the east by Benin.

**Physical description**
Rises from the lagoon coast of the Gulf of Guinea, past low-lying plains to the Atakora Mountains, which run north-east to south-west across the north of the country; highest peak is Pic Baumann (Mt Agou; 986m/3 235ft); flat plains lie to the north-west.

**Climate**
Tropical; rain throughout the year in the south; one rainy season in the north Jul–Sep.

**National holidays**
Jan 1, 13 (National Liberation), 24 (Economic Liberation), Feb 2 (Triumphant Return), Apr 24 (Victory), 27 (Independence), May 1, Jun 1 (Trees), 21 (Pya Martyrs), Aug 15, 30 (Historical Address of Kpalimé), Sep 23 (Anniversary of Terrorist Aggression), Nov 1, 30 (Creation of the RPT), Dec 25; A, Ad, EM, WM.

## Political leaders

**President**

| | |
|---|---|
| 1960–3 | Sylvanus Olympio |
| 1963–7 | Nicolas Grunitzky |
| 1967– | Gnassingbé Eyadéma |

**Prime Minister**

| | | | |
|---|---|---|---|
| 1991–4 | Joseph Koukou Koffigoh | 1999–2000 | Eugene Koffi Adoboli |
| 1994–6 | Edem Kodjo | 2000–2 | Messan Agbeyome Kodjo |
| 1996–9 | Kwassi Klutse | 2002– | Koffi Sama |

**TOKELAU** *see* **NEW ZEALAND**

## TONGA

| | | | |
|---|---|---|---|
| **Official name** | Kingdom of Tonga; also sometimes known as the Friendly Islands | **Languages** | English, Tongan |
| **Local name** | Tonga; Pule'anga Fakatu'I 'O Tonga | **Ethnic groups** | Tongan 98%, others 2% |
| **Independence** | 1970 | **Religions** | Christianity 79% (Prot 63%, RC 16%), others 21% |
| **Area** | 646 sq km/249 sq mi | **Time zone** | GMT +13 |
| **Capital** | Nuku'alofa | **Currency** | 1 Pa'anga/Tongan Dollar (T$) = 100 seniti |
| **Population** | 97 784 (1996) | **Telephone** | +676 |
| **Nationality** | Tongan | **Internet** | .to |
| | | **Country code** | TON |

**Location**
An independent island group of 171 islands, 45 of which are inhabited, in the south-west Pacific Ocean.

**Physical description**
Divided into three main groups (coral formations of Ha'apai and Tongatapu-Eua, mountainous Vava'u); largest island is Tongatapu; western islands are mainly volcanic (some still active); highest point is the extinct volcano Kao (1 046m/3 432ft).

**Climate**
Semi-tropical; average annual temperature on Tongatapu is 23°C; occasional hurricanes in the summer months.

**National holidays**
Jan 1, Apr 25 (Anzac), May 4 (Birthday of Crown Prince Tupouto'a), Jun 4 (Emancipation), Jul 4 (King's Birthday), Nov 4 (Constitution), Dec 4 (King Tupou I), 25, 26; EM, GF.

## Political leaders

**Monarch**

| | |
|---|---|
| 1893–1918 | George Tupou II |
| 1918–65 | Salote Tupou III |
| 1965– | Taufa'ahau Tupou IV |

**Prime Minister**

| | |
|---|---|
| 1970–91 | Fatafehi Tu'ipelehake |
| 1991–2000 | Baron Vaea |
| 2000– | Prince 'Ulukalala Lavaka Ata |

### *Catching a Kingdom*

According to legend, Tonga was formed in ancient times by the Polynesian sun god Maui Fusi-Fonua, who was out fishing. The sun god's special tortoiseshell and whalebone fishhook became caught in the seabed, and as he pulled impatiently on the line to free it, he dragged a clump of land up from the ocean floor. Suddenly his hook snapped, and the land entangled on the hook broke up, scattering in pieces across the sea to create the islands of Tonga.

# TRINIDAD AND TOBAGO

| | | | |
|---|---|---|---|
| **Official name** | Republic of Trinidad and Tobago | **Ethnic groups** | black 40%, East Indian 40%, mixed 14%, others 6% |
| **Local name** | Trinidad and Tobago | **Religions** | Christianity 60% (RC 32%, Prot 28%), Hinduism 24%, Islam 6%, none/unaffiliated 5%, others 5% |
| **Independence** | 1962 | | |
| **Area** | 5 128 sq km/1 979 sq mi | | |
| **Capital** | Port of Spain | | |
| **Chief towns** | San Fernando, Arima, Scarborough | **Time zone** | GMT –4 |
| | | **Currency** | 1 Trinidad and Tobago Dollar (TT$) = 100 cents |
| **Population** | 1 294 000 (2001e) | | |
| **Nationality** | Trinidadian, Tobagonian | **Telephone** | +1 868 |
| **Languages** | English | **Internet** | .tt |
| | | **Country code** | TTO |

**Location**
A republic comprising the southernmost islands of the Lesser Antilles chain in the south-east Caribbean Sea, just off the South American mainland. Trinidad is separated from Venezuela in the south by the 11km/7mi wide Gulf of Paria, while Tobago lies 30km/19mi north-east of Trinidad.

**Physical description**
Trinidad is roughly rectangular; crossed by three mountain ranges; highest point is El Cerro del Aripo (940m/3 084ft); rest is low-lying, with large coastal mangrove swamps; Pitch Lake is the world's largest reservoir of natural asphalt; Tobago's Main Ridge extends along most of the island, rising to 576m/1 890ft.

**Climate**
Tropical, with an annual average temperature of 29°C.

**National holidays**
Jan 1, Mar 30 (Spiritual Baptist Liberation Shouter), May 30 (Indian Arrival), Jun 19 (Labour), Aug 1 (Emancipation), 31 (Independence), Dec 25, 26; CC, D, EM, ER, GF.

## Political leaders

**President**

| | |
|---|---|
| 1976–87 | Ellis Emmanuel Clarke |
| 1987–97 | Noor Mohammed Hassanali |
| 1997–2003 | Arthur Ray Robinson |
| 2003– | George Maxwell Richards |

**Premier**

| | |
|---|---|
| 1956–62 | Eric Williams |

**Prime Minister**

| | |
|---|---|
| 1962–81 | Eric Williams |
| 1981–6 | George Chambers |
| 1986–91 | Raymond Robinson |
| 1991–5 | Patrick Manning |
| 1995–2001 | Basdeo Panday |
| 2001– | Patrick Manning |

### *Steel Band Music*

The music of steel bands plays a central part in the culture of Trinidad and Tobago, and the government lists the steel pan as one of the national symbols alongside the national bird, the national flower, the state flag and the coat of arms.

# TUNISIA

| | | | |
|---|---|---|---|
| **Official name** | Republic of Tunisia | **Ethnic groups** | Arab and Berber 98%, European 1%, Jewish and others 1% |
| **Local name** | Tūnisiya; Al-Jumhūriyya at-Tūnisiyya | **Religions** | Islam 98%, Christianity 1%, others 1% |
| **Independence** | 1956 | **Time zone** | GMT +1 |
| **Area** | 164 150 sq km/63 362 sq mi | **Currency** | 1 Tunisian Dinar (TD, D) = 1 000 millimes |
| **Capital** | Tunis; Toûnis, Tunus | **Telephone** | +216 |
| **Chief towns** | Bizerta, Sousse, Sfax, Gabes | **Internet** | .tn |
| **Population** | 8 785 711 (1994) | **Country code** | TUN |
| **Nationality** | Tunisian | | |
| **Languages** | Arabic; French is also spoken | | |

**Location**
A north African republic, bounded to the west by Algeria; to the south-east by Libya; and to the north-east and north by the Mediterranean Sea.

**Physical description**
Atlas Mountains in the north-west rise to 1 544m/5 066ft at Djebel Chambi; central depression runs west to east, containing several salty lakes; dry, sandy upland lies to the south.

**Climate**
Mediterranean climate on the coast, with hot, dry summers and wet winters; daily maximum temperature is 14–33°C; higher rainfall in the Atlas Mountains; further south, rainfall decreases and temperatures can be extreme.

**National holidays**
Jan 1, 18 (Revolution), Mar 20 (Independence), Apr 9 (Martyrs), May 1, Jun 1 (Victory), 2 (Youth), Jul 25 (Republic), Aug 13 (Women), Sep 3 (3 Sep 1934), Oct 15 (Evacuation), Nov 7 (Election of President); Ad (2), ER (2), NY (Muslim), PB.

## Political leaders

**Bey**

1943–57 Muhammad VIII

**President**

1957–87 Habib Bourguiba
1987– Zine Al-Abidine Bin Ali

**Prime Minister**

1956–7 Habib Bourguiba
1957–69 *No Prime Minister*
1969–70 Bahi Ladgham
1970–80 Hadi Nouira
1980–6 Mohammed Mezali
1986–7 Rashid Sfar
1987 Zine Al-Abidine Bin Ali
1987–9 Hadi Baccouche
1989–99 Hamed Karoui
1999– Mohammed Ghannouchi

# TURKEY

| | | | |
|---|---|---|---|
| **Official name** | Republic of Turkey | **Ethnic groups** | Turkish 80%, Kurdish 16%, Arab 2%, others 2% |
| **Local name** | Türkiye; Türkiye Çumhuriyeti | **Religions** | Islam 99% (mostly Sunni), others 1% |
| **Area** | 779 452 sq km/300 868 sq mi | **Time zone** | GMT +2 |
| **Capital** | Ankara; Angora | **Currency** | 1 Turkish Lira (TL) = 100 kurus |
| **Chief towns** | Istanbul, Izmir, Adana, Bursa, Gaziantep | **Telephone** | +90 |
| **Population** | 68 610 000 (2001e) | **Internet** | .tr |
| **Nationality** | Turkish | **Country code** | TUR |
| **Languages** | Turkish | | |

**Location**
A republic lying partly in Europe and partly in Asia. The western area (Thrace) is bounded by the Aegean Sea and Greece, and to the north by Bulgaria and the Black Sea; the eastern area (Anatolia) is bounded by Georgia, Armenia, Azerbaijan and Iran, and to the south by Iraq, Syria and the Mediterranean Sea. The Turkish Straits (the Dardanelles, Sea of Marmara and Bosporus) connect the Black Sea in the north-east and the Mediterranean Sea in the south-west.

**Physical description**
Mountainous (average height 1 100m/3 609ft); average altitude of the central plateau is 1 000–2 000m/3 281–6 562ft; Taurus Mountains cover the entire southern part of Anatolia; highest peak is Mt Ararat (5 165m/16 945ft); alluvial coastal plains.

**Climate**
Typically Mediterranean climate on the Aegean and Mediterranean coasts, with hot, dry summers and warm, wet winters; further east along the Black Sea coast, rainfall becomes heavy in summer and autumn; low rainfall on the interior plateau, with cold winters and warm or hot summers.

**National holidays**
Jan 1, Apr 23 (National Sovereignty and Children), May 19 (Atatürk Commemoration/Youth and Sports), Aug 30 (Victory), Oct 29 (Republic); Ad (4), ER (3).

## Political leaders

### Sultan of the Ottoman Empire

1876–1909 Abdülhamit
1909–18 Mehmet Reşat
1918–22 Mehmet Vahideddin

### President

1923–38 Mustafa Kemal Atatürk
1938–50 İsmet İnönü
1950–60 Celal Bayar
1960–6 Cemal Gürsel
1966–73 Cevdet Sunay
1973–80 Fahri S Korutürk
1980 Ihsan Çaglayangil *Acting President*
1980–9 Kenan Evren *Chairman of National Security Council until 1982*
1989–93 Turgut Özal
1993–2000 Süleyman Demirel
2000– Ahmet Necdet Sezer

**Prime Minister**

| | |
|---|---|
| 1923–4 | İsmet İnönü |
| 1924–5 | Ali Fethi Okyar |
| 1925–37 | İsmet İnönü |
| 1937–9 | Celal Bayar |
| 1939–42 | Dr Refik Saydam |
| 1942–6 | Şükrü Saracoğlu |
| 1946–7 | Recep Peker |
| 1947–9 | Hasan Saka |
| 1949–50 | Şemşettin Günaltay |
| 1950–60 | Adnan Menderes |
| 1960–1 | Cemal Gürsel |
| 1961–5 | İsmet İnönü |
| 1965 | S Hayri Ürgüplü |
| 1965–71 | Süleyman Demirel |
| 1971–2 | Nihat Erim |
| 1972–3 | Ferit Melen |
| 1973–4 | Naim Talu |
| 1974 | Bülent Ecevit |
| 1974–5 | Sadi Irmak |
| 1975–7 | Süleyman Demirel |
| 1977 | Bülent Ecevit |
| 1977–8 | Süleyman Demirel |
| 1978–9 | Bülent Ecevit |
| 1979–80 | Süleyman Demirel |
| 1980–3 | Bülent Ülüsü |
| 1983–9 | Turgut Özal |
| 1989–91 | Yildrim Akbulut |
| 1991 | Mesut Yilmaz |
| 1991–3 | Süleyman Demirel |
| 1993–6 | Tansu Çiller |
| 1996 | Mesut Yilmaz |
| 1996–7 | Necmettin Erbakan |
| 1997–8 | Mesut Yilmaz |
| 1999–2002 | Bülent Ecevit |
| 2002–3 | Abdullah Gül |
| 2003– | Recep Tayyip Erdoğan |

## TURKMENISTAN

| | |
|---|---|
| **Official name** | Republic of Turkmenistan |
| **Local name** | Turkmenostan; Turkmenostan Respublikasy |
| **Former name** | Turkmen Soviet Socialist Republic (1924–91), within the Union of Soviet Socialist Republics (USSR; 1925–91) |
| **Independence** | 1991 |
| **Area** | 488 100 sq km/188 400 sq mi |
| **Capital** | Ashgabat; Ašgabat, Ašhabad |
| **Chief towns** | Chardzhou, Mary, Türkmenbashi, Nebit-Dag |
| **Population** | 4 483 251 (1995) |
| **Nationality** | Turkmen |
| **Languages** | Turkmen, Russian, Uzbek |
| **Ethnic groups** | Turkmen 77%, Uzbek 9%, Russian 7%, Kazakh 2%, others 5% |
| **Religions** | Islam 89% (mostly Sunni), Christianity 9% (Orthodox), others 2% |
| **Time zone** | GMT +5 |
| **Currency** | 1 Manat (TMM) = 100 tenesi |
| **Telephone** | +993 |
| **Internet** | .tm |
| **Country code** | TKM |

**Location**
A republic in south-west Middle Asia, bounded to the north by Kazakhstan and Uzbekistan; to the south by Iran and Afghanistan; and to the west by the Caspian Sea.

**Physical description**
Low-lying with hills in the south; mainly desert; highest point is Ayrybaba (3 139m/10 298ft).

**Climate**
Continental, hot and arid in the large desert areas.

**National holidays**
Jan 1, 12 (Remembrance/Anniversary of the Battle of Geok-Tepe), Feb 19 (President's Birthday), Mar 8 (Women), 21, May 9 (Victory); Ad, Day of Revival and Unity (May), Independence (Oct).

## Political leaders

**President**

| | |
|---|---|
| 1991– | Saparmurad Niyazov |

**Prime Minister**

| | |
|---|---|
| 1991–2 | Khan Akhmedov |
| 1992– | *As President* |

**TURKS AND CAICOS ISLANDS** *see* **UNITED KINGDOM**

# TUVALU

| | | | |
|---|---|---|---|
| **Official name** | Tuvalu | **Languages** | Tuvaluan, English |
| **Local name** | Tuvalu; Fakavae Aliki-Malo I Tuvalu | **Ethnic groups** | Polynesia 95%, others 5% |
| **Former name** | Ellice Islands, as part of the Gilbert and Ellice Islands (until 1975) | **Religions** | Christianity 98%, Baha'i 1%, others 1% |
| **Independence** | 1978 | **Time zone** | GMT +12 |
| **Area** | 26 sq km/10 sq mi | **Currency** | 1 Australian Dollar (A$) = 100 cents |
| **Capital** | Fongafale (on Funafuti) | **Telephone** | +688 |
| **Population** | 10 000 (2001e) | **Internet** | .tv |
| **Nationality** | Tuvaluan | **Country code** | TUV |

**Location**
An independent island group in the south-west Pacific, 1 050km/650mi north of Fiji.

**Physical description**
Comprises nine low-lying coral atolls, rising no higher than 5m/16ft, running north-west to south-east in a chain 580km/360mi long.

**Climate**
Hot and humid; average annual temperature is 30°C.

**National holidays**
Jan 1, May 13 (Gospel), Jun 14 (Queen's Birthday), Aug 5 (Children), Oct 1 (Independence), Dec 25, 26; EM, GF; Commonwealth Day (2nd Mon in Mar).

## Political leaders

Chief of State: British monarch, represented by Governor General.

**Prime Minister**

| | |
|---|---|
| 1978–81 | Toalipi Lauti |
| 1981–9 | Tomasi Puapua |
| 1989–93 | Bikenibeu Paeniu |
| 1993–6 | Kamuta Lataasi |
| 1996–9 | Bikenibeu Paeniu |
| 1999–2000 | Ionatana Ionatana |
| 2000–1 | Lagitupu Tuilimu *Acting Prime Minister* |
| 2001 | Faimalaga Luka |
| 2001–2 | Koloa Talake |
| 2002– | Saufatu Sopoanga |

### Rising Tide

Tuvalu is extremely low-lying – its highest point is barely 5m/16ft above sea level. Rising sea levels as a result of global warming are causing Tuvaluans a great deal of anxiety; some predictions suggest that the country could entirely disappear under the waves within the next 50 years.

# UGANDA

| | | | |
|---|---|---|---|
| **Official name** | Republic of Uganda | **Ethnic groups** | Ganda 19%, Banyoro 15%, Teso 9%, Banyan 8%, Basogo 8%, Bagisu 7%, Bachiga 7%, others 27% |
| **Local name** | Uganda | **Religions** | Christianity 66% (RC 33%, Prot 33%), traditional beliefs 18%, Islam 16% |
| **Independence** | 1962 | **Time zone** | GMT +3 |
| **Area** | 238 461 sq km/92 029 sq mi | **Currency** | 1 Uganda Shilling (USh) = 100 cents |
| **Capital** | Kampala | **Telephone** | +256 |
| **Chief towns** | Jinja, Mbale, Tororo, Soroti, Entebbe | **Internet** | .ug |
| **Population** | 22 788 000 (2001e) | **Country code** | UGA |
| **Nationality** | Ugandan | | |
| **Languages** | English; Swahili and other languages are also spoken | | |

**Location**
A landlocked East African republic, bounded to the south by Rwanda, Tanzania and Lake Victoria; to the east by Kenya; to the north by The Sudan; and to the west by Democratic Republic of Congo.

**Physical description**
Mainly on a plateau with an elevation of 900–1 000m/2 950ft–3 280ft; population is concentrated in the fertile Lake Victoria basin; highest point is Margherita Peak (5 110 m/16 765ft) in the Mt Stanley massif; main rivers are the upper reaches of the River Nile.

**Climate**
Highest rainfall is in the mountains to the west and south-west and along the shores of Lake Victoria; daily temperatures at Entebbe on the north shore of the lake are 24–28°C; central and north-eastern areas receive less rain.

**National holidays**
Jan 1, 26 (NRM Anniversary), Mar 8 (Women), May 1, Jun 3 (Martyrs), 9 (Heroes), Oct 9 (Independence), Dec 25, 26; Ad, EM, ER, GF.

## Antelope Hill

The name of Uganda's capital city, Kampala, comes from *Kasozi Kampala*, meaning 'the hill of antelopes'.

## Political leaders

**Governor-General**

1962–3 Walter Fleming Coutts

**President**

| | |
|---|---|
| 1963–6 | Edward Muteesa II |
| 1966–71 | Apollo Milton Obote |
| 1971–9 | Idi Amin |
| 1979 | Yusuf Kironde Lule |
| 1979–80 | Godfrey Lukongwa Binaisa |
| 1981–5 | Apollo Milton Obote |
| 1985–6 | *Military Council* (Tito Okello Lutwa) |
| 1986– | Yoweri Kaguta Museveni |

**Prime Minister**

| | |
|---|---|
| 1962–71 | Apollo Milton Obote |
| 1971–81 | *No Prime Minister* |
| 1981–5 | Eric Otema Alimadi |
| 1985 | Paulo Muwanga |
| 1985–6 | Abraham N Waliggo |
| 1986–91 | Samson B Kisekka |
| 1991–4 | George Cosmas Adyebo |
| 1994–9 | Kintu Musoke |
| 1999– | Apollo Nsibambi |

## UKRAINE

| | | | |
|---|---|---|---|
| **Official name** | Ukraine | **Nationality** | Ukrainian |
| **Local name** | Ukraïna | **Languages** | Ukrainian, Russian |
| **Former name** | Ukrainian Soviet Socialist Republic (1919–91), within the Union of Soviet Socialist Republics (USSR; 1922–91) | **Ethnic groups** | Ukrainian 73%, Russian 22%, Jewish 1%, others 4% |
| **Independence** | 1991 | **Religions** | Christianity 93% (Orthodox 76%, RC 14%, Prot 3%), Judaism 2%, others 5% |
| **Area** | 603 700 sq km/233 028 sq mi | **Time zone** | GMT +2 |
| **Capital** | Kiev; Kyïv | **Currency** | 1 Hryvnia = 100 kopiykas |
| **Chief towns** | Kharkov, Donetsk, Odessa, Dnepropetrovsk, Lvov, Zaporozhye, Krivoy Rog | **Telephone** | +380 |
| | | **Internet** | .ua |
| | | **Country code** | UKR |
| **Population** | 48 416 000 (2001) | | |

**Location**
A republic in eastern Europe, bounded to the south-west by Moldova and Romania; to the west by Hungary, Slovakia and Poland; to the north by Belarus; to the east by Russia; and to the south by the Black Sea.

**Physical description**
Generally a plain with high elevations in the west, south and south-east; Ukrainian Carpathian Mountains in the west rise to 2 061m/6 762ft at Hora Hoverla; Crimean Peninsula separates the Black Sea from the Sea of Azov; Crimean Mountains lie along the south coast of the peninsula; many reservoirs and lakes.

**Climate**
Temperate, continental; cold winters and warm summers.

**National holidays**
Jan 1, 7 (Eastern Orthodox Christmas), Mar 8 (Women), May 1 (2), 9 (Victory), Jun 28 (Constitution), Aug 24 (Independence); Orthodox Easter (Apr/May) (2).

## Political leaders

**President**

| | |
|---|---|
| 1991–4 | Leonid Kravchuk |
| 1994– | Leonid Kuchma |

**Prime Minister**

| | |
|---|---|
| 1990–2 | Vitold Fokin |
| 1992 | Valentin Symonenko |
| 1992–3 | Leonid Kuchma |
| 1993–4 | Yukhim Zvyahilski *Acting Prime Minister* |
| 1994–5 | Vitalii Masol |
| 1995–6 | Yevhenii Maruk |
| 1996–7 | Pavlo Lazarenko |
| 1997 | Vasyl Durdynets *Acting Prime Minister* |
| 1997–9 | Valery Pustovoytenko |
| 1999–2001 | Viktor Yushchenko |
| 2001–2 | Anatoli Kinakh |
| 2002– | Viktor Yanukovich |

**UMM AL-QAIWAIN** *see* **UNITED ARAB EMIRATES**

## UNITED ARAB EMIRATES

| | | | |
|---|---|---|---|
| **Official name** | United Arab Emirates (UAE) | **Nationality** | Emirati |
| **Local name** | Ittihād al-imārāt al-'Arabīyah | **Languages** | Arabic, English |
| **Former name** | Trucial States (until 1971) | **Ethnic groups** | Asian 52%, Emirian 18%, other Arab 24%, others 6% |
| **Independence** | 1971 | **Religions** | Islam 96%, others 4% |
| **Area** | 83 600 sq km/32 300 sq mi | **Time zone** | GMT +4 |
| **Capital** | Abu Dhabi; Abū Zhaby | **Currency** | 1 Dirham (DH) = 100 fils |
| **Chief towns** | Dubai, Sharjah, Ras al-Khaimah | **Telephone** | +971 |
| **Population** | 2 377 453 (1995) | **Internet** | .ae |
| | | **Country code** | ARE |

**Location**
A federation in the eastern central Arabian Peninsula comprising seven internally self-governing emirates: Abu Dhabi, Ajman, Dubai, Fujairah, Ras al-Khaimah, Sharjah and Umm al-Qaiwain. It is bounded to the north by the Arabian Gulf; to the east by Oman; and to the south and west by Saudi Arabia.

**Physical description**
Located along the southern shore of the Arabian Gulf; Fujairah has a coastline along the Gulf of Oman; salt marshes predominate on the coast; barren desert and gravel plain inland; Hajar Mountains in Fujairah rise to over 1 000m/3 280ft; highest point is Jabal Yibir (1 527m/5 010ft).

**Climate**
Hot with limited rainfall; winter temperatures average 21°C, with high humidity (in excess of 70%); less humid in summer, with maximum temperatures rising to 45°C; sandstorms are common.

**National holidays**
Jan 1, Aug 6 (Accession of Ruler), Dec 2 (National); Ad (4), Ascension of the Prophet, ER (3), NY (Muslim), PB, R.

## Political leaders

**President**
1971– Zayed Bin Sultan al-Nahayan

**Prime Minister**
1971–9 Maktoum Bin Rashid al-Maktoum
1979–91 Rashid Bin Said al-Maktoum
1991– Maktoum Bin Rashid al-Maktoum

### Abu Dhabi

*Tribe: al Bu Falah or al Nahyan (Bani Yas)*
*Family name: al-Nahyan*

**Sheikh**
1855–1909 Zayed
1909–12 Tahnoun
1912–22 Hamdan
1922–6 Sultan
1926–8 Saqr
1928–66 Shakhbout
1966– Zayed

## Ajman

*Tribe: al Bu Kharayban (Naim)*
*Family name: al-Nuaimi*

**Sheikh**

| | |
|---|---|
| 1900–10 | Abdel-Aziz |
| 1910–28 | Humaid |
| 1928–81 | Rashid |
| 1981– | Humaid |

## Dubai

*Tribe: al Bu Flasah (Bani Yas)*
*Family name: al-Maktoum*

**Sheikh**

| | |
|---|---|
| 1894–1906 | Maktoum |
| 1906–12 | Butti |
| 1912–58 | Said |
| 1958–90 | Rashid |
| 1990– | Maktoum |

## Fujairah

*Tribe: Sharqiyyin*
*Family name: al-Sharqi*

**Sheikh**

| | |
|---|---|
| 1952–75 | Mohammed |
| 1975– | Hamad |

## Ras al-Khaimah

*Tribe: Huwalah*
*Family name: al-Qasimi*

**Sheikh**

| | |
|---|---|
| 1921–48 | Sultan |
| 1948– | Saqr |

## Sharjah

*Tribe: Huwalah*
*Family name: al-Qasimi*

**Sheikh**

| | |
|---|---|
| 1883–1914 | Saqr |
| 1914–24 | Khaled |
| 1924–51 | Sultan |
| 1951–65 | Saqr |
| 1965–72 | Khaled |
| 1972–87 | Sultan |
| 1987 | Abdel-Aziz |
| 1987– | Sultan |

## Umm al-Qaiwain

*Tribe: al-Ali*
*Family name: al-Mualla*

**Sheikh**

| | |
|---|---|
| 1873–1904 | Ahmad |
| 1904–22 | Rashid |
| 1922–3 | Abdullah |
| 1923–9 | Hamad |
| 1929–81 | Ahmad |
| 1981– | Rashid |

# UNITED KINGDOM

| | | | |
|---|---|---|---|
| **Official name** | United Kingdom of Great Britain and Northern Ireland (UK) | **Ethnic groups** | white 94%, Asian 1%, West Indian 1%, Indian 1%, others 3% |
| **Local name** | United Kingdom | **Religions** | Christianity[1] 71.6%, none/unaffiliated 15.5%, unknown 7.3%, Islam 2.7%, Hinduism 1%, Sikhism 0.6%, Judaism 0.5%, Buddhism 0.3%, others 0.3% |
| **Area** | 244 755 sq km/94 475 sq mi | | |
| **Capital** | London | | |
| **Chief towns** | Birmingham, Leeds, Glasgow, Sheffield, Bradford, Edinburgh, Liverpool, Manchester, Cardiff, Belfast, Newcastle upon Tyne | **Time zone** | GMT |
| | | **Currency** | 1 Pound Sterling (£) = 100 pence |
| **Population** | 58 789 194 (2001) | **Telephone** | +44 |
| **Nationality** | British | **Internet** | .uk |
| **Languages** | English; Welsh and Gaelic are spoken by minorities | **Country code** | GBR |

**Location**
A kingdom in Western Europe, comprising England, Scotland, Wales and Northern Ireland.

**Climate**
Temperate maritime climate, moderated by prevailing south-west winds; generally wetter and warmer in the west.

[1] *2001 Census data; did not distinguish different Christian denominations.*

## Political leaders

### Monarch

### House of Stuart

1603–25 James I (VI of Scotland)
1625–49 Charles I

### Commonwealth and Protectorate

1649–53 *Council of State*
1653–8 Oliver Cromwell *Lord Protector*
1658–9 Richard Cromwell *Lord Protector*

### House of Stuart (restored)

1660–85 Charles II
1685–8 James II
1689–94 Mary II and William III (*jointly*)
1694–1702 William III (*alone*)
1702–14 Anne

### House of Hanover

1714–27 George I
1727–60 George II
1760–1820 George III
1820–30 George IV
1830–7 William IV
1837–1901 Victoria

## House of Saxe-Coburg

| | |
|---|---|
| 1901–10 | Edward VII |

## House of Windsor

| | |
|---|---|
| 1910–36 | George V |
| 1936 | Edward VIII |
| 1936–52 | George VI |
| 1952– | Elizabeth II |

**Prime Minister**

| | |
|---|---|
| 1721–42 | Robert Walpole *Whig* |
| 1742–3 | Earl of Wilmington (Spencer Compton) *Whig* |
| 1743–54 | Henry Pelham *Whig* |
| 1754–6 | Duke of Newcastle (Thomas Pelham-Holles) *Whig* |
| 1756–7 | Duke of Devonshire (William Cavendish) *Whig* |
| 1757–62 | Duke of Newcastle *Whig* |
| 1762–3 | Earl of Bute (John Stuart) *Tory* |
| 1763–5 | George Grenville *Whig* |
| 1765–6 | Marquess of Rockingham (Charles Watson Wentworth) *Whig* |
| 1766–70 | Duke of Grafton (Augustus Henry Fitzroy) *Whig* |
| 1770–82 | Lord North (Frederick North) *Tory* |
| 1782 | Marquess of Rockingham *Whig* |
| 1782–3 | Earl of Shelburne (William Petty-Fitzmaurice) *Whig* |
| 1783 | Duke of Portland (William Henry Cavendish Bentinck) *Coal* |
| 1783–1801 | William Pitt *Tory* |
| 1801–4 | Henry Addington *Tory* |
| 1804–6 | William Pitt *Tory* |
| 1806–7 | Lord Grenville (William Wyndham) *Whig* |
| 1807–9 | Duke of Portland (William Henry Cavendish Bentinck) *Tory* |
| 1809–12 | Spencer Perceval *Tory* |
| 1812–27 | Earl of Liverpool (Robert Banks Jenkinson) *Tory* |
| 1827 | George Canning *Tory* |
| 1827–8 | Viscount Goderich (Frederick John Robinson) *Tory* |
| 1828–30 | Duke of Wellington (Arthur Wellesley) *Tory* |
| 1830–4 | Earl Grey (Charles Grey) *Whig* |
| 1834 | Viscount Melbourne (William Lamb) *Whig* |
| 1834–5 | Robert Peel *Con* |
| 1835–41 | Viscount Melbourne *Whig* |
| 1841–6 | Robert Peel *Con* |
| 1846–52 | Lord John Russell *Lib* |
| 1852 | Earl of Derby (Edward George Smith Stanley) *Con* |
| 1852–5 | Lord Aberdeen (George Hamilton-Gordon) *Peelite* |
| 1855–8 | Viscount Palmerston (Henry John Temple) *Lib* |
| 1858–9 | Earl of Derby *Con* |
| 1859–65 | Viscount Palmerston *Lib* |
| 1865–6 | Lord John Russell *Lib* |
| 1866–8 | Earl of Derby *Con* |
| 1868 | Benjamin Disraeli *Con* |
| 1868–74 | William Ewart Gladstone *Lib* |
| 1874–80 | Benjamin Disraeli *Con* |
| 1880–5 | William Ewart Gladstone *Lib* |
| 1885–6 | Marquess of Salisbury (Robert Gascoyne-Cecil) *Con* |
| 1886 | William Ewart Gladstone *Lib* |
| 1886–92 | Marquess of Salisbury *Con* |
| 1892–4 | William Ewart Gladstone *Lib* |
| 1894–5 | Earl of Rosebery (Archibald Philip Primrose) *Lib* |
| 1895–1902 | Marquess of Salisbury *Con* |
| 1902–5 | Arthur James Balfour *Con* |
| 1905–8 | Henry Campbell-Bannerman *Lib* |
| 1908–15 | Herbert Henry Asquith *Lib* |
| 1915–16 | Herbert Henry Asquith *Coal* |
| 1916–22 | David Lloyd George *Coal* |
| 1922–3 | Andrew Bonar Law *Con* |
| 1923–4 | Stanley Baldwin *Con* |
| 1924 | James Ramsay MacDonald *Lab* |
| 1924–9 | Stanley Baldwin *Con* |
| 1929–31 | James Ramsay MacDonald *Lab* |
| 1931–5 | James Ramsay MacDonald *Nat* |
| 1935–7 | Stanley Baldwin *Nat* |
| 1937–40 | Arthur Neville Chamberlain *Nat* |
| 1940–5 | Winston Churchill *Coal* |
| 1945–51 | Clement Attlee *Lab* |
| 1951–5 | Winston Churchill *Con* |
| 1955–7 | Anthony Eden *Con* |
| 1957–63 | Harold Macmillan *Con* |
| 1963–4 | Alec Douglas-Home *Con* |
| 1964–70 | Harold Wilson *Lab* |
| 1970–4 | Edward Heath *Con* |
| 1974–6 | Harold Wilson *Lab* |
| 1976–9 | James Callaghan *Lab* |
| 1979–90 | Margaret Thatcher *Con* |
| 1990–7 | John Major *Con* |
| 1997– | Tony Blair *Lab* |

*Coal = Coalition* *Lib = Liberal* *Lab = Labour* *Con = Conservative* *Nat = Nationalist*

## England

| | | | |
|---|---|---|---|
| **Area** | 130 357 sq km/50 318 sq mi | **Population** | 49 138 831 (2001) |
| **Chief towns** | Birmingham, Bradford, Liverpool, Leeds, Manchester, Newcastle upon Tyne, Sheffield | **Capital** | London |
| | | **Nationality** | English |
| **Physical description** | Largely undulating lowland, rising in the south to the Mendips, Cotswolds, Chilterns and North Downs, in the north to the north–south ridge of the Pennines and in the north-west to the Cumbria Mountains; drained in the east by the Tyne, Tees, Humber, Ouse and Thames rivers, and in the west by the Eden, Ribble, Mersey and Severn rivers; Lake District in the north-west includes Derwent Water, Ullswater, Windermere and Bassenthwaite; highest point is Scafell Pike at 978m/3 209ft. | | |
| **National holidays** | Jan 1, Dec 25, 26; EM, GF, Early May, Spring (May) and Summer (Aug) Bank Holidays. | | |

**Monarch**

### West Saxon Kings

| | |
|---|---|
| 802–39 | Egbert |
| 839–58 | Æthelwulf |
| 858–60 | Æthelbald |
| 860–5 | Æthelbert |
| 866–71 | Æthelred |
| 871–99 | Alfred |
| 899–924 | Edward (the Elder) |
| 924–39 | Athelstan |
| 939–46 | Edmund |
| 946–55 | Edred |
| 955–9 | Edwy |
| 959–75 | Edgar |
| 975–8 | Edward (the Martyr) |
| 978–1016 | Æthelred (the Unready) |
| 1016 | Edmund (Ironside) |

### Danish Kings

| | |
|---|---|
| 1016–35 | Knut (Canute) |
| 1035–7 | Harold Regent |
| 1037–40 | Harold I (Harefoot) |
| 1040–2 | Hardaknut |
| 1042–66 | Edward (the Confessor) |
| 1066 | Harold II |

### House of Normandy

| | |
|---|---|
| 1066–87 | William I (the Conqueror) |
| 1087–1100 | William II (Rufus) |
| 1100–35 | Henry I |

### House of Blois

| | |
|---|---|
| 1135–54 | Stephen |

### House of Plantagenet

| | |
|---|---|
| 1154–89 | Henry II |
| 1189–99 | Richard I (the Lionheart) |
| 1199–1216 | John |
| 1216–72 | Henry III |
| 1272–1307 | Edward I |
| 1307–27 | Edward II |
| 1327–77 | Edward III |
| 1377–99 | Richard II |

### House of Lancaster

| | |
|---|---|
| 1399–1413 | Henry IV |
| 1413–22 | Henry V |
| 1422–61 | Henry VI |

### House of York

| | |
|---|---|
| 1461–70 | Edward IV |

### House of Lancaster

| | |
|---|---|
| 1470–1 | Henry VI |

### House of York

| | |
|---|---|
| 1471–83 | Edward IV |
| 1483 | Edward V |
| 1483–5 | Richard III |

### House of Tudor

| | |
|---|---|
| 1485–1509 | Henry VII |
| 1509–47 | Henry VIII |
| 1547–53 | Edward VI |
| 1553–8 | Mary I |
| 1558–1603 | Elizabeth I |

## Divorced, Beheaded, Died

King Henry VIII (1491–1547) is famous for his six wives who, as the school children's rhyme goes, were sequentially divorced, beheaded, died, divorced, beheaded and survived:

*Catherine of Aragon* (1485–1536) First married to Henry's brother Arthur, she was betrothed following his early death to her brother-in-law, Henry, who was then aged just 11. She married him in 1509. In 1527 Henry began a procedure for divorce, which he obtained in 1533. Catherine retired to lead an austere religious life until her death.

*Anne Boleyn* (c.1504–36) Secretly married to Henry in 1533, she was soon declared his legal wife but within months his passion for her had cooled. It was not revived by the birth of a daughter (later Elizabeth I), still less by that of a stillborn son. She was arrested and brought to the Tower, convicted of treason on fragile evidence and beheaded in 1536.

*Jane Seymour* (c.1509–37) A lady-in-waiting to Henry's first two wives, she married him 11 days after the execution of Anne Boleyn. She died soon after the birth of her son, the future Edward VI.

*Anne of Cleves* (1515–57) A Lutheran princess who became Henry's fourth queen in 1540, as part of a strategy to develop an alliance with German Protestant rulers. The marriage was declared null and void on grounds of non-consummation six months afterwards. On agreeing to the divorce, Anne was given a large income and she remained in England until her death.

*Catherine Howard* (c.1520–42) Became Queen in the same month as Anne of Cleves was divorced (Jul 1540). A year later she was charged with having had an affair before her marriage with a musician and a relation, and she was beheaded for treason.

*Catherine Parr* (1512–48) Married Henry in 1543. A learned, tolerant and tactful woman, she persuaded Henry to restore the succession to his daughters, and showed her stepchildren much kindness. Very soon after Henry's death in 1547 she married a former suitor and died in childbirth the following year.

## Northern Ireland

| | | | |
|---|---|---|---|
| **Area** | 14 120 sq km/5 450 sq mi | **Capital** | Belfast |
| **Chief towns** | Armagh, Londonderry | **Population** | 1 685 267 (2001) |
| **Nationality** | Northern Irish | | |
| **Physical description** | Northern Ireland occupies the north-eastern part of Ireland, and is centred on Lough Neagh; to the north and east are the Antrim Mountains; Mourne Mountains are in the south-east; highest point is Slieve Donard at 852m/2 795ft. | | |
| **National holidays** | Jan 1, Mar 17 (St Patrick), Dec 25, 26; GF, EM, Early May, Spring (May) Bank Holiday, Battle of the Boyne/Orangemen (Jul), Summer Bank Holiday (Aug). | | |

## Political leaders

**Devolved power was transferred to the Northern Ireland Assembly in Dec 1999. Devolution was suspended between Feb and May 2000, briefly in Aug 2001 and Sep 2001, and from Oct 2002.**

**First Minister**

| | |
|---|---|
| 1999–2001 | David Trimble *(First Minister designate from 1998)* |
| 2001 | Reg Empey *Acting First Minister* |
| 2001– | David Trimble |

## Scotland

| | | | |
|---|---|---|---|
| **Area** | 78 742 sq km/30 394 sq mi | **Capital** | Edinburgh |
| **Chief towns** | Aberdeen, Dundee, Glasgow, Inverness, Perth | **Population** | 5 062 011 (2001) |
| **Nationality** | Scottish | | |
| **Physical description** | Divided into the Southern Uplands (rising to 843m at Merrick), the Central Lowlands (the most densely populated area) and the Northern Highlands (divided by the fault line following the Great Glen); highest point is Ben Nevis (1 343m/4 406ft); 787 islands, most of which lie off the heavily-indented west coast and only c.60 exceed 8 sq km/3 sq mi; several wide estuaries on the east coast, primarily the Firths of Forth, Tay and Moray; interior has many freshwater lochs, the largest being Loch Lomond (70 sq km/27 sq mi) and the deepest Loch Morar (310m); longest river is the River Tay (192km/119mi). | | |
| **National holidays** | Jan 1, 2, Dec 25, 26; GF, Early May, Spring (May) and Summer (Aug) Bank Holidays; *local holidays may also be observed, in addition to or instead of the statutory days.* | | |

**Monarch**

| | |
|---|---|
| 1005–34 | Malcolm II |
| 1034–40 | Duncan I |
| 1040–57 | Macbeth |
| 1057–8 | Lulach |
| 1058–93 | Malcolm III |
| 1093–4 | Donald Bane |
| 1094 | Duncan II |
| 1094–7 | Donald Bane |
| 1097–1107 | Edgar |
| 1107–24 | Alexander I |
| 1124–53 | David I |
| 1153–65 | Malcolm IV |
| 1165–1214 | William I |
| 1214–49 | Alexander II |
| 1249–86 | Alexander III |
| 1286–90 | Margaret |
| 1290–2 | *Interregnum* |
| 1292–96 | John Balliol |
| 1296–1306 | *Interregnum* |
| 1306–29 | Robert I (the Bruce) |
| 1329–71 | David II |
| 1371–90 | Robert II |

| | | | |
|---|---|---|---|
| 1390–1406 | Robert III | 1488–1513 | James IV |
| 1406–37 | James I | 1513–42 | James V |
| 1437–60 | James II | 1542–67 | Mary Queen of Scots |
| 1460–88 | James III | 1567–1625 | James VI[1] |

[1] *In 1603, James VI succeeded Elizabeth I to the English throne and united the thrones of Scotland and England (Union of the Crowns).*

## Political leaders

The Scottish parliament was officially opened on 1 Jul 1999.

**First Minister**

| | | | |
|---|---|---|---|
| 1999–2000 | Donald Dewar | 2001 | Jim Wallace *Acting First Minister* |
| 2000 | Jim Wallace *Acting First Minister* | 2001– | Jack McConnell |
| 2000–1 | Henry McLeish | | |

## Wales

| | | | |
|---|---|---|---|
| **Area** | 20 761 sq km/8 014 sq mi | **Capital** | Cardiff |
| **Chief towns** | Swansea, Wrexham | **Population** | 2 903 085 (2001) |
| **Nationality** | Welsh | | |
| **Physical description** | Rises in the north-west to 1 085m/3 560ft at Snowdon in the Snowdonia range (the highest point); the Cambrian Mountains rise in the centre, and the Brecon Beacons in the south; drained by the Severn, Clwyd, Conwy, Dee, Dovey, Taff, Tawe, Teifi, Towy, Usk and Wye rivers. | | |
| **National holidays** | Jan 1, Dec 25, 26; EM, GF, Early May, Spring (May) and Summer (Aug) Bank Holidays. | | |

## Political leaders

The opening session of the Welsh Assembly was held in June 1999. The post of First Minister was called First Secretary until Oct 2000.

**First Minister**

| | |
|---|---|
| 1999–2000 | Alun Michael |
| 2000– | Rhodri Morgan |

## British islands[1]

### Channel Islands

| | | | |
|---|---|---|---|
| **Location** | An island group of the British Isles in the English Channel, west of the Cotentin Peninsula of Normandy. A dependent territory of the British Crown, it has individual legislative assemblies and legal system and is divided into the Bailiwicks of Jersey and of Guernsey. Main islands: Guernsey, Jersey, Alderney, Sark; other islands include Herm, Jethou, Brechou, the Caskets, the Minquiers and the Chauseys. | | |
| **Area** | 194 sq km/75 sq mi | **Language** | Both English and Norman-French are spoken |
| **Capital** | St Helier (Jersey); St Peter Port (Guernsey) | | |
| **Population** | 149 907 (2001e) | **Internet** | .gg (Guernsey), .je (Jersey) |

## Isle of Man

| | | | |
|---|---|---|---|
| **Location** | A British Crown Dependency in the Irish Sea, west of England and east of Northern Ireland. | | |
| **Area** | 572 sq km/221 sq mi | **Languages** | English; Manx is also spoken |
| **Capital** | Douglas | | |
| **Population** | 76 315 (2001) | **Internet** | .im |
| **Nationality** | Manx | **Country code** | XIM |

[1] *Part of the British Isles but not included in the United Kingdom.*

## UK dependent territories

### Anguilla

| | | | |
|---|---|---|---|
| **Location** | The most northerly of the Leeward Islands, in the east Caribbean Sea. | | |
| **Area** | 155 sq km/60 sq mi | **Nationality** | Anguillan |
| **Capital** | The Valley | **Internet** | .ai |
| **Population** | 11 430 (2001) | **Country code** | AIA |

### Bermuda

| | | | |
|---|---|---|---|
| **Location** | A group of c.150 low-lying, coral islands and islets situated in the west Atlantic Ocean c.900km/560mi east of Cape Hatteras, North Carolina (USA). | | |
| **Area** | 53 sq km/20 sq mi | **Nationality** | Bermudian |
| **Capital** | Hamilton | **Internet** | .bm |
| **Population** | 62 000 (2001e) | **Country code** | BMU |

### Bermuda Triangle

The *Bermuda Triangle* is an area in the Atlantic Ocean off the south-eastern USA where ships and aeroplanes have mysteriously disappeared. The points of the triangle are thought to be the city of Miami in Florida, the island of Bermuda and the city of San Juan, Puerto Rico. However the US Coast Guard reports rather sniffily that it 'is not impressed with supernatural explanations of disasters at sea'. It suggests that unpredictable weather, dangerous currents and seabed hazards are the more likely culprits. However, it does point out that the Bermuda Triangle area is one of only two places on Earth where a compass needle points to true north, rather than magnetic north. Inexperienced sailors who forget this may end up lost and miles off course.

### British Antarctic Territory

| | |
|---|---|
| **Location** | Includes the South Orkney Islands, the South Shetland Islands, the Antarctic Graham Land Peninsula, and the land mass extending to the South Pole. |
| **Area** | 6 sq km/2 sq mi |
| **Population** | Populated solely by scientists of the British Antarctic Survey. |

## British Indian Ocean Territory

| | | | |
|---|---|---|---|
| **Location** | Consists of 2 300 islands in the Chagos Archipelago in the Indian Ocean, 1 900km/1 180mi north-east of Mauritius; the largest island is Diego Garcia. | | |
| **Area** | 60 sq km/23 sq mi | **Internet** | .io |
| **Population** | Indigenous population relocated; military personnel and civilian support staff only. | **Country code** | IOT |

## British Virgin Islands

| | | | |
|---|---|---|---|
| **Location** | An island group at the north-western end of the Lesser Antilles chain in the east Caribbean Sea. | | |
| **Area** | 153 sq km/59 sq mi | **Nationality** | British Virgin Islander |
| **Capital** | Road Town | **Internet** | .vg |
| **Population** | 21 000 (2001e) | **Country code** | VGB |

## Cayman Islands

| | | | |
|---|---|---|---|
| **Location** | An island group in the west Caribbean Sea, comprising the islands of Grand Cayman, Cayman Brac and Little Cayman, c.240km/150mi south of Cuba. | | |
| **Area** | 260 sq km/100 sq mi | **Nationality** | Caymanian |
| **Capital** | George Town | **Internet** | .ky |
| **Population** | 41 000 (2001e) | **Country code** | CYM |

## Falkland Islands

| | | | |
|---|---|---|---|
| **Location** | Situated in the South Atlantic Ocean, c.650km/400mi north-east of the Magellan Strait. Also known as the Malvinas. | | |
| **Area** | 12 200 sq km/4 700 sq mi | **Nationality** | Falkland Islander |
| **Capital** | Stanley | **Internet** | .fk |
| **Population** | 2 913 (2001) | **Country code** | FLK |

## Gibraltar

| | | | |
|---|---|---|---|
| **Location** | The narrow peninsula rising steeply from the low-lying coast of south-west Spain at the eastern end of the Strait of Gibraltar, which is an important strategic point of control for the western Mediterranean. | | |
| **Area** | 5.9 sq km/2.3 sq mi | **Nationality** | Gibraltarian |
| **Capital** | Gibraltar | **Internet** | .gi |
| **Population** | 27 000 (2001e) | **Country code** | GIB |

## Montserrat

| | | | |
|---|---|---|---|
| **Location** | A volcanic island in the Leeward Islands, Lesser Antilles, in the east Caribbean Sea. | | |
| **Area** | 106 sq km/41 sq mi | **Population** | 3 000 (2001e) *Note: The population has dropped from 10 639 in 1991 as a result of an exodus after the 1997 eruption.* |
| **Capital** | Brades *Note: The original capital, Plymouth, lies within the Exclusion Zone – an area abandoned after a devastating volcanic eruption from the Soufriere Hills volcano in 1997 into which entry is prohibited.* | **Nationality** | Montserratian |
| | | **Internet** | .ms |
| | | **Country code** | MSR |

## Pitcairn Islands

| | | | |
|---|---|---|---|
| **Location** | An island group in the south-east Pacific Ocean, east of French Polynesia, comprising Pitcairn Island and the uninhabited islands of Ducie, Henderson and Oeno. | | |
| **Area** | 27 sq km/10 sq mi | **Nationality** | Pitcairn Islander |
| **Capital** | Adamstown | **Internet** | .pn |
| **Population** | 44 (2003e) | **Country code** | PCN |

## St Helena

| | | | |
|---|---|---|---|
| **Location** | A volcanic island in the South Atlantic Ocean, lying 1 920km/1 200mi from the south-west coast of Africa. | | |
| **Area** | 122 sq km/47 sq mi | **Nationality** | St Helenian |
| **Capital** | Jamestown | **Internet** | .sh |
| **Population** | 5 157 (1998) | **Country code** | SHN |

*Note: The islands of Ascension and Tristan da Cunha are dependencies of St Helena.*

## South Georgia

| | | | |
|---|---|---|---|
| **Location** | A barren, mountainous snow-covered island in the South Atlantic Ocean, about 500km/300mi east of the Falkland Islands. | | |
| **Area** | c.3 750 sq km/1 450 sq mi | **Internet** | .gs |

## South Sandwich Islands

| | | | |
|---|---|---|---|
| **Location** | A group of small, uninhabited islands in the South Atlantic Ocean, lying c.720km/450mi south-east of South Georgia. | | |
| **Area** | 1 152 sq km/445 sq mi | **Internet** | .gs |

## Turks and Caicos Islands

| | | | |
|---|---|---|---|
| **Location** | A pair of island groups which form the south-eastern archipelago of The Bahamas; they lie 920km/570mi south-east of Miami (USA). | | |
| **Area** | 500 sq km/200 sq mi | **Internet** | .tc |
| **Capital** | Cockburn Town | **Country code** | TCA |
| **Population** | 19 000 (2001e) | | |

# UNITED STATES OF AMERICA

| | | | |
|---|---|---|---|
| **Official name** | United States of America (USA) | **Languages** (cont.) | English; there is a sizeable Spanish-speaking minority |
| **Local name** | United States of America | **Ethnic groups** | white (including Hispanic) 84%, black 12%, Asian 3%, Amerindian 1% |
| **Independence** | 1776 | **Religions** | Christianity 84% (Prot 56%, RC 28%), none 10%, Judaism 2%, Islam 2%, others 2% |
| **Area** | 9 160 454 sq km/ 3 535 935 sq mi | **Time zone** | GMT –5/10 |
| **Capital** | Washington, DC (District of Columbia) | **Currency** | 1 US Dollar ($, US$) = 100 cents |
| **Chief towns** | New York City, Los Angeles, Chicago, Houston, Philadelphia, Phoenix, San Diego, Dallas, San Antonio, Detroit | **Telephone** | +1 |
| **Population** | 281 421 906 (2000) | **Internet** | .us |
| **Nationality** | American | **Country code** | USA |

**Location**
A federal republic in North America and the fourth-largest country in the world, divided into 50 states including the detached states of Alaska and Hawaii, plus the District of Columbia. The mainland is bounded to the north by Canada; to the east by the Atlantic Ocean; to the south by the Gulf of Mexico; and to the west by the Pacific Ocean.

**Physical description**
East Atlantic coastal plain is backed by the Appalachian Mountains from the Great Lakes in the north to Alabama in the south; this series of parallel ranges includes the Allegheny, Blue Ridge and Catskill mountains; to the south the plain broadens out towards the Gulf of Mexico and into the Florida Peninsula; to the west, the Gulf Plains stretch north to meet the higher Great Plains from which they are separated by the Ozark Mountains; further west, the Rocky Mountains rise to over 4 500m/14 760ft; highest point is Mt McKinley, Alaska, at 6 194m/20 322ft; lowest point is in Death Valley (–86m/–282ft); major rivers include the Hudson, Delaware, Potomac, Columbia, Colorado and the great Red River–Missouri–Mississippi River System.

**Climate**
Varies from conditions in hot tropical deserts (in the south-west) to those typical of Arctic continental regions; most regions are affected by westerly depressions that can bring changeable weather; rainfall is heaviest in the Pacific north-west, lightest in the south-west; in the Great Plains, wide temperature variation is the result of cold air from the Arctic as well as warm tropical air from the Gulf of Mexico; on the west coast the influence of the Pacific Ocean results in a smaller range of temperatures between summer and winter; on the east coast there is a gradual increase in winter temperatures southwards; the states bordering the Gulf of Mexico are subject to hurricanes and tornadoes moving north-east from the Caribbean Sea.

**National holidays**
Jan 1, Jul 4 (Independence), Nov 11 (Veterans), Dec 25; Martin Luther King's Birthday (3rd Mon in Jan), Washington's Birthday (3rd Mon in Feb), Memorial (last Mon in May), Labor (1st Mon in Sep), Columbus (2nd Mon in Oct), Thanksgiving (4th Thurs in Nov); *additional days vary between states.*

## States of the USA

| **State** (abbrev.; ZIP) | **Entry to Union** | **Population** (2000) | **Area** | **Capital** | **Inhabitant** | **Nickname** |
|---|---|---|---|---|---|---|
| **Alabama** (Ala; AL) | 1819 (22nd) | 4 447 100 | 131 443 sq km/50 750 sq mi | Montgomery | Alabamian | Camellia State, Heart of Dixie |
| **Alaska** (Alaska; AK) | 1959 (49th) | 626 932 | 1 477 268 sq km/570 373 sq mi | Juneau | Alaskan | Mainland State, The Last Frontier |
| **Arizona** (Ariz; AZ) | 1912 (48th) | 5 130 632 | 295 276 sq km/114 006 sq mi | Phoenix | Arizonan | Apache State, Grand Canyon State |
| **Arkansas** (Ark; AR) | 1836 (25th) | 2 673 400 | 137 754 sq km/53 187 sq mi | Little Rock | Arkansan | Bear State, Land of Opportunity |
| **California** (Calif; CA) | 1850 (31st) | 33 871 648 | 403 971 sq km/155 973 sq mi | Sacramento | Californian | Golden State |
| **Colorado** (Colo; CO) | 1876 (38th) | 4 301 261 | 268 658 sq km/103 729 sq mi | Denver | Coloradan | Centennial State |
| **Connecticut** (Conn; CT) | 1788 (5th) | 3 405 565 | 12 547 sq km/4 844 sq mi | Hartford | Nutmegger | Nutmeg State, Constitution State |
| **Delaware** (Del; DE) | 1787 (1st) | 783 600 | 5 133 sq km/1 985 sq mi | Dover | Delawarean | Diamond State, First State |
| **District of Columbia**[1] (DC; DC) | *Established* 1791 | 572 059 | 159 sq km/61 sq mi | Washington | Washingtonian | — |
| **Florida** (Fla; FL) | 1845 (27th) | 15 982 378 | 139 697 sq km/53 937 sq mi | Tallahassee | Floridian | Everglade State, Sunshine State |
| **Georgia** (Ga; GA) | 1788 (4th) | 8 186 453 | 152 571 sq km/58 908 sq mi | Atlanta | Georgian | Empire State of the South, Peach State |
| **Hawaii** (Hawaii; HI) | 1959 (50th) | 1 211 537 | 16 636 sq km/6 423 sq mi | Honolulu | Hawaiian | Aloha State |
| **Idaho** (Idaho; ID) | 1890 (43rd) | 1 293 953 | 214 325 sq km/82 751 sq mi | Boise | Idahoan | Gem State |
| **Illinois** (Ill; IL) | 1818 (21st) | 12 419 293 | 144 123 sq km/55 646 sq mi | Springfield | Illinoisan | Prairie State, Land of Lincoln |
| **Indiana** (Ind; IN) | 1816 (19th) | 6 080 485 | 92 903 sq km/35 870 sq mi | Indianapolis | Hoosier | Hoosier State |
| **Iowa** (Iowa; IA) | 1846 (29th) | 2 926 324 | 144 716 sq km/55 875 sq mi | Des Moines | Iowan | Hawkeye State, Corn State |

[1] *Not counted as one of the 50 states but included for reference.*

| State (abbrev.; ZIP) | Entry to Union | Population (2000) | Area | Capital | Inhabitant | Nickname |
|---|---|---|---|---|---|---|
| **Kansas** (Kans; KS) | 1861 (34th) | 2 688 418 | 211 922 sq km/81 823 sq mi | Topeka | Kansan | Sunflower State, Jayhawker State |
| **Kentucky** (Ky; KY) | 1792 (15th) | 4 041 769 | 102 907 sq km/39 732 sq mi | Frankfort | Kentuckian | Bluegrass State |
| **Louisiana** (La; LA) | 1812 (18th) | 4 468 976 | 112 836 sq km/43 566 sq mi | Baton Rouge | Louisianian | Pelican State, Sugar State, Creole State |
| **Maine** (Maine; ME) | 1820 (23rd) | 1 274 923 | 79 931 sq km/30 861 sq mi | Augusta | Downeaster | Pine Tree State |
| **Maryland** (Md; MD) | 1788 (7th) | 5 296 486 | 25 316 sq km/9 775 sq mi | Annapolis | Marylander | Old Line State, Free State |
| **Massachusetts** (Mass; MA) | 1788 (6th) | 6 349 097 | 20 300 sq km/7 838 sq mi | Boston | Bay Stater | Bay State, Old Colony |
| **Michigan** (Mich; MI) | 1837 (26th) | 9 938 444 | 150 544 sq km/58 125 sq mi | Lansing | Michigander | Wolverine State, Great Lake State |
| **Minnesota** (Minn; MN) | 1858 (32nd) | 4 919 479 | 206 207 sq km/79 617 sq mi | St Paul | Minnesotan | Gopher State, North Star State |
| **Mississippi** (Miss; MS) | 1817 (20th) | 2 844 658 | 123 510 sq km/47 687 sq mi | Jackson | Mississippian | Magnolia State |
| **Missouri** (Mo; MO) | 1821 (24th) | 5 595 211 | 178 446 sq km/68 898 sq mi | Jefferson City | Missourian | Bullion State, Show Me State |
| **Montana** (Mont; MT) | 1889 (41st) | 902 195 | 376 991 sq km/145 556 sq mi | Helena | Montanan | Treasure State, Big Sky Country |
| **Nebraska** (Nebr; NE) | 1867 (37th) | 1 711 263 | 199 113 sq km/76 878 sq mi | Lincoln | Nebraskan | Cornhusker State, Beef State |
| **Nevada** (Nev; NV) | 1864 (36th) | 1 998 257 | 273 349 sq km/105 540 sq mi | Carson City | Nevadan | Silver State, Sagebrush State |
| **New Hampshire** (NH; NH) | 1788 (9th) | 1 235 786 | 23 292 sq km/8 993 sq mi | Concord | New Hampshirite | Granite State |
| **New Jersey** (NJ; NJ) | 1787 (3rd) | 8 414 350 | 19 210 sq km/7 417 sq mi | Trenton | New Jerseyite | Garden State |
| **New Mexico** (N Mex; NM) | 1912 (47th) | 1 819 046 | 314 334 sq km/121 364 sq mi | Santa Fe | New Mexican | Sunshine State, Land of Enchantment |
| **New York** (NY; NY) | 1788 (11th) | 18 976 457 | 122 310 sq km/47 224 sq mi | Albany | New Yorker | Empire State |
| **North Carolina** (NC; NC) | 1789 (12th) | 8 049 313 | 126 180 sq km/48 718 sq mi | Raleigh | North Carolinian | Old North State, Tar Heel State |

| State (abbrev.; ZIP) | Entry to Union | Population (2000) | Area | Capital | Inhabitant | Nickname |
|---|---|---|---|---|---|---|
| **North Dakota** (N Dak; ND) | 1889 (39th) | 642 200 | 178 695 sq km/68 994 sq mi | Bismarck | North Dakotan | Flickertail State, Sioux State, Peace Garden State |
| **Ohio** (Ohio; OH) | 1803 (17th) | 11 353 140 | 106 067 sq km/40 952 sq mi | Columbus | Ohioan | Buckeye State |
| **Oklahoma** (Okla; OK) | 1907 (46th) | 3 450 654 | 177 877 sq km/68 678 sq mi | Oklahoma City | Oklahoman | Sooner State |
| **Oregon** (Oreg; OR) | 1859 (33rd) | 3 421 399 | 251 385 sq km/97 060 sq mi | Salem | Oregonian | Sunset State, Beaver State |
| **Pennsylvania** (Pa; PA) | 1787 (2nd) | 12 281 054 | 116 083 sq km/44 820 sq mi | Harrisburg | Pennsylvanian | Keystone State |
| **Rhode Island** (RI; RI) | 1790 (13th) | 1 048 319 | 2 707 sq km/1 045 sq mi | Providence | Rhode Islander | Little Rhody, Plantation State |
| **South Carolina** (SC; SC) | 1788 (8th) | 4 012 012 | 77 988 sq km/30 111 sq mi | Columbia | South Carolinian | Palmetto State |
| **South Dakota** (S Dak; SD) | 1889 (40th) | 754 844 | 196 576 sq km/75 898 sq mi | Pierre | South Dakotan | Sunshine State, Coyote State |
| **Tennessee** (Tenn; TN) | 1796 (16th) | 5 689 283 | 106 759 sq km/41 220 sq mi | Nashville | Tennessean | Volunteer State |
| **Texas** (Tex; TX) | 1845 (28th) | 20 851 820 | 678 358 sq km/261 914 sq mi | Austin | Texan | Lone Star State |
| **Utah** (Utah; UT) | 1896 (45th) | 2 233 169 | 212 816 sq km/82 168 sq mi | Salt Lake City | Utahn | Mormon State, Beehive State |
| **Vermont** (Vt; VT) | 1791 (14th) | 608 827 | 23 955 sq km/9 249 sq mi | Montpelier | Vermonter | Green Mountain State |
| **Virginia** (Va; VA) | 1788 (10th) | 7 078 515 | 102 558 sq km/39 598 sq mi | Richmond | Virginian | Old Dominion State, Mother of Presidents |
| **Washington** (Wash; WA) | 1889 (42nd) | 5 894 121 | 172 447 sq km/66 582 sq mi | Olympia | Washingtonian | Evergreen State, Chinook State |
| **West Virginia** (W Va; WV) | 1863 (35th) | 1 808 344 | 62 758 sq km/24 231 sq mi | Charleston | West Virginian | Panhandle State, Mountain State |
| **Wisconsin** (Wis; WI) | 1848 (30th) | 5 363 675 | 145 431 sq km/56 151 sq mi | Madison | Wisconsinite | Badger State, America's Dairyland |
| **Wyoming** (Wyo; WY) | 1890 (44th) | 493 782 | 251 501 sq km/97 105 sq mi | Cheyenne | Wyomingite | Equality State |

## US non-self-governing territories

### American Samoa (AS)

| | | | |
|---|---|---|---|
| **Location** | A group of islands in the South Pacific Ocean, some 3 500km/2 175mi north-east of New Zealand. | | |
| **Area** | 197 sq km/76 sq mi | **Nationality** | American Samoan |
| **Capital** | Pago Pago | **Internet** | .as |
| **Population** | 57 291 (2000) | **Country code** | ASM |

### Guam

| | | | |
|---|---|---|---|
| **Location** | The largest and southernmost island of the Mariana Islands, west Pacific Ocean. | | |
| **Area** | 541 sq km/209 sq mi | **Nationality** | Guamanian |
| **Capital** | Agaña | **Internet** | .gu |
| **Population** | 154 805 (2000) | **Country code** | GUM |

### Northern Mariana Islands

| | | | |
|---|---|---|---|
| **Location** | A group of 14 islands in the north-west Pacific Ocean, c.2 400km/1 500mi to the east of the Philippines. | | |
| **Area** | 471 sq km/182 sq mi | **Internet** | .mp |
| **Capital** | Saipan | **Country code** | MNP |
| **Population** | 69 221 (2000) | | |

### US Virgin Islands

| | | | |
|---|---|---|---|
| **Location** | A group of more than 50 islands in the south and west of the Virgin Islands group, Lesser Antilles, Caribbean Sea, 64km/40mi east of Puerto Rico (USA). There are three main islands: St Croix, St Thomas and St John. | | |
| **Area** | 342 sq km/132 sq mi | **Nationality** | Virgin Islander |
| **Capital** | Charlotte Amalie | **Internet** | .vi |
| **Population** | 108 612 (2000) | **Country code** | VIR |

## US associated commonwealths

### Puerto Rico

| | | | |
|---|---|---|---|
| **Location** | The easternmost island of the Greater Antilles, situated between the Dominican Republic in the west and the US Virgin Islands in the east, c.1 600km/1 000mi south-east of Miami (USA). | | |
| **Area** | 8 897 sq km/3 434 sq mi | **Nationality** | Puerto Rican, American |
| **Capital** | San Juan | **Internet** | .pr |
| **Population** | 3 808 610 (2000) | **Country code** | PRI |

*Note: The USA also possesses Baker Island, Howland Island, Johnston Atoll, Kingman Reef, Midway Island, Palmyra Atoll and Wake Island in the North Pacific Ocean, Jarvis Island in the South Pacific Ocean and Navassa Island in the Caribbean Sea, all largely uninhabited.*

## Political leaders

**President** *(Vice President in parentheses)*

1789–97 George Washington (1st) (John Adams)
1797–1801 John Adams (2nd) *Fed* (Thomas Jefferson)
1801–9 Thomas Jefferson (3rd) *Dem-Rep* (Aaron Burr, 1801–5) (George Clinton, 1805–9)
1809–17 James Madison (4th) *Dem-Rep* (George Clinton, 1809–12) *no Vice President* 1812–13 (Elbridge Gerry, 1813–14) *no Vice President* 1814–17
1817–25 James Monroe (5th) *Dem-Rep* (Daniel D Tompkins)
1825–9 John Quincy Adams (6th) *Dem-Rep* (John C Calhoun)
1829–37 Andrew Jackson (7th) *Dem* (John C Calhoun, 1829–32) *no Vice President* 1832–3 (Martin van Buren, 1833–7)
1837–41 Martin van Buren (5th) *Dem* (Richard M Johnson)
1841 William Henry Harrison (9th) *Whig* (John Tyler)
1841–5 John Tyler (10th) *Whig no Vice President*
1845–9 James Knox Polk (11th) *Dem* (George M Dallas)
1849–50 Zachary Taylor (12th) *Whig* (Millard Fillmore)
1850–3 Millard Fillmore (13th) *Whig no Vice President*
1853–7 Franklin Pierce (14th) *Dem* (William R King, 1853) *no Vice President* 1853–7
1857–61 James Buchanan (15th) *Dem* (John C Breckinridge)
1861–5 Abraham Lincoln (16th) *Rep* (Hannibal Hamlin, 1861–5) (Andrew Johnson, 1865)
1865–9 Andrew Johnson (17th) *Dem-Nat no Vice President*
1869–77 Ulysses Simpson Grant (18th) *Rep* (Schuyler Colfax, 1869–73) (Henry Wilson, 1873–5) *no Vice President* 1875–7
1877–81 Rutherford Birchard Hayes (19th) *Rep* (William A Wheeler)
1881 James Abram Garfield (20th) *Rep* (Chester A Arthur)
1881–5 Chester Alan Arthur (21st) *Rep no Vice President*
1885–9 Grover Cleveland (22nd) *Dem* (Thomas A Hendricks, 1885) *no Vice President* 1885–9
1889–93 Benjamin Harrison (23rd) *Rep* (Levi P Morton)
1893–7 Grover Cleveland (24th) *Dem* (Adlai E Stevenson)
1897–1901 William McKinley (25th) *Rep* (Garrat A Hobart, 1897–9) *no Vice President* 1899–1901 (Theodore Roosevelt, 1901)
1901–9 Theodore Roosevelt (26th) *Rep no Vice President* 1901–5 (Charles W Fairbanks, 1905–9)
1909–13 William Howard Taft (27th) *Rep* (James S Sherman, 1909–12) *no Vice President* 1912–13
1913–21 Woodrow Wilson (28th) *Dem* (Thomas R Marshall)
1921–3 Warren Gamaliel Harding (29th) *Rep* (Calvin Coolidge)

### Dead Presidents

John Adams, the 2nd President, and Thomas Jefferson, the 3rd President, both died on 4 Jul 1826 – the 50th anniversary of the Declaration of Independence.

1923–9 Calvin Coolidge (30th) *Rep no Vice President* 1923–5 (Charles G Dawes,1925–9)
1929–33 Herbert Clark Hoover (31st) *Rep* (Charles Curtis)
1933–45 Franklin Delano Roosevelt (32nd) *Dem* (John N Garner, 1933–41) (Henry A Wallace, 1941–5) (Harry S Truman, 1945)
1945–53 Harry S Truman (33rd) *Dem no Vice President* 1945-9 (Alben W Barkley, 1949–53)
1953–61 Dwight David Eisenhower (34th) *Rep* (Richard M Nixon)
1961–3 John Fitzgerald Kennedy (35th) *Dem* (Lyndon B Johnson)
1963–9 Lyndon Baines Johnson (36th) *Dem no Vice President* 1963–5 (Hubert H Humphrey, 1965–9)

| | |
|---|---|
| 1969–74 | Richard Milhous Nixon (37th) *Rep* (Spiro T Agnew, 1969–73) *no Vice President* 1973, Oct–Dec (Gerald R Ford, 1973–4) |
| 1974–7 | Gerald Rudolph Ford (38th) *Rep* *no Vice President* 1974, Aug–Dec (Nelson A Rockefeller, 1974–7) |
| 1977–81 | Jimmy Carter (39th) *Dem* (Walter F Mondale) |
| 1981–9 | Ronald Wilson Reagan (40th) *Rep* (George H W Bush) |
| 1989–93 | George Herbert Walker Bush (41st) *Rep* (J Danforth Quayle) |
| 1993–2001 | William Jefferson Blythe IV Clinton (42nd) *Dem* (Albert Gore) |
| 2001– | George Walker Bush (43rd) *Rep* (Richard B Cheney) |

*Dem = Democrat*
*Fed = Federalist*
*Nat = National Union*
*Rep = Republican*

### *Keeping It in the Family*

John Quincy Adams, the 6th President, was the son of John Adams, the 2nd President; Benjamin Harrison, the 23rd President, was the grandson of William Henry Harrison, the 9th President; Theodore Roosevelt, the 26th President, and Franklin D Roosevelt, the 32nd, were distant cousins; and George Bush, the 41st President, saw his son George W Bush become the 43rd President.

## URUGUAY

| | |
|---|---|
| **Official name** | Eastern Republic of Uruguay |
| **Local name** | Uruguay; República Oriental del Uruguay |
| **Independence** | 1828 |
| **Area** | 176 215 sq km/68 018 sq mi |
| **Capital** | Montevideo |
| **Chief towns** | Salto, Paysandú, Mercedes, Las Piedras |
| **Population** | 3 163 763 (1996) |
| **Nationality** | Uruguayan |
| **Languages** | Spanish; Portunol or Brazilero, a mix of Portuguese and Spanish, is also spoken on the Brazilian border |
| **Ethnic groups** | white 90%, mestizo 6%, black 4% |
| **Religions** | Christianity 63% (RC 60%, Prot 3%), Judaism 2%, others/unaffiliated 35% |
| **Time zone** | GMT –3 |
| **Currency** | 1 Uruguayan Peso (Ur$, Urug$) = 100 centésimos |
| **Telephone** | +598 |
| **Internet** | .uy |
| **Country code** | URY |

**Location**
A republic in eastern South America, bounded to the east by the Atlantic Ocean; to the north by Brazil; and to the west by the River Uruguay and Argentina.

**Physical description**
Grass-covered plains of the south rise north to a high sandy plateau; River Negro flows south to west to meet the River Uruguay on the Argentine frontier; highest point is Cerro Catedral (514m/1 686ft).

**Climate**
Temperate with warm summers and mild winters; the average temperature at Montevideo is 16°C.

**National holidays**
Jan 6 (Children), May 1, Jun 19 (Artigas's Birthday), Jul 18 (Constitution), Oct 12 (Americas), Dec 25; C (2), GF, HT.

## Political leaders

**President**

| | | | |
|---|---|---|---|
| 1899–1903 | Juan Lindolfo Cuestas | 1927–31 | Juan Capisteguy |
| 1903–7 | José Batlle y Ordóñez | 1931–8 | Gabriel Terra |
| 1907–11 | Claudio Williman | 1938–43 | Alfredo Baldomir |
| 1911–15 | José Batlle y Ordóñez | 1943–7 | Juan José de Amézaga |
| 1915–19 | Feliciano Viera | 1947 | Tomás Berreta |
| 1919–23 | Baltasar Brum | 1947–51 | Luis Batlle Berres |
| 1923–7 | José Serrato | 1951–5 | Andrés Martínez Trueba |

**President of the National Government Council**

| | | | |
|---|---|---|---|
| 1955–6 | Luis Batlle Berres | 1961–2 | Eduardo Victor Haedo |
| 1956–7 | Alberto F Zubiría | 1962–3 | Faustino Harrison |
| 1957–8 | Alberto Lezama | 1963–4 | Daniel Fernández Crespo |
| 1958–9 | Carlos L Fischer | 1964–5 | Luis Giannattasio |
| 1959–60 | Martín R Etchegoyen | 1965–6 | Washington Beltrán |
| 1960–1 | Benito Nardone | 1966–7 | Alberto Heber Usher |

**President**

| | | | |
|---|---|---|---|
| 1967 | Oscar Daniel Gestido | 1984–90 | Julio María Sanguinetti Cairolo |
| 1967–72 | Jorge Pacheco Areco | 1990–4 | Luis Alberto Lacalle Herrera |
| 1972–6 | Juan María Bordaberry Arocena | 1994–9 | Julio María Sanguinetti |
| 1976–81 | Aparicio Méndez | 1999– | Jorge Batlle Ibáñez |
| 1981–4 | Gregorio Conrado Álvarez Armelino | | |

# USSR (UNION OF SOVIET SOCIALIST REPUBLICS)

## Political leaders

No longer in existence, but included for reference. See separate entries for former constituent states of the USSR since 1990–91 (Armenia, Azerbaijan, Belarus, Estonia, Georgia, Kazakhstan, Kyrgyzstan, Latvia, Lithuania, Moldova, Russia, Tajikistan, Turkmenistan, Ukraine, Uzbekistan).

**President**

| | | | |
|---|---|---|---|
| 1917 | Leo Borisovich Kamenev | 1977–82 | Leonid Brezhnev |
| 1917–19 | Yakov Mikhailovich Sverlov | 1982–3 | Vasily Kuznetsov *Acting President* |
| 1919–46 | Mikhail Ivanovich Kalinin | 1983–4 | Yuri Andropov |
| 1946–53 | Nikolai Shvernik | 1984 | Vasily Kuznetsov *Acting President* |
| 1953–60 | Klimentiy Voroshilov | 1984–5 | Konstantin Chernenko |
| 1960–4 | Leonid Brezhnev | 1985 | Vasily Kuznetsov *Acting President* |
| 1964–5 | Anastas Mikoyan | 1985–8 | Andrei Gromyko |
| 1965–77 | Nikolai Podgorny | 1988–90 | Mikhail Gorbachev |

**Executive President**

| | |
|---|---|
| 1990–91 | Mikhail Gorbachev |
| 1991 | Gennady Yanayev *Acting President* |
| 1991 | Mikhail Gorbachev |

**Chairman of the Council of Ministers**

| | |
|---|---|
| 1917 | Georgy Evgenyevich Lvov |
| 1917 | Aleksandr Fyodorovich Kerensky |

**Chairman of the Council of People's Commissars**

| | | | |
|---|---|---|---|
| 1917–24 | Vladimir Ilyich Lenin | 1930–41 | Vyacheslav Mikhailovich Molotov |
| 1924–30 | Aleksei Ivanovich Rykov | 1941–53 | Josef Stalin |

**Chairman of the Council of Ministers**

| | | | |
|---|---|---|---|
| 1953–5 | Georgiy Malenkov | 1985–90 | Nikolai Ryzhkov |
| 1955–8 | Nikolai Bulganin | 1990–1 | Yuri Maslyukov *Acting Chairman* |
| 1958–64 | Nikita Khrushchev | 1991 | Valentin Pavlov |
| 1964–80 | Alexei Kosygin | 1991 | Ivan Silayev *Acting Chairman* |
| 1980–5 | Nikolai Tikhonov | | |

**General Secretary of the Communist Party**

| | | | |
|---|---|---|---|
| 1922–53 | Josef Stalin | 1982–4 | Yuri Andropov |
| 1953 | Georgiy Malenkov | 1984–5 | Konstantin Chernenko |
| 1953–64 | Nikita Khrushchev | 1985–91 | Mikhail Gorbachev |
| 1964–82 | Leonid Brezhnev | | |

**US VIRGIN ISLANDS** *see* **UNITED STATES OF AMERICA**

## UZBEKISTAN

| | | | |
|---|---|---|---|
| **Official name** | Republic of Uzbekistan | **Nationality** | Uzbek |
| **Local name** | Özbekiston; Özbekiston Respublikasia | **Languages** | Uzbek; Russian, Tajik and Kazakh are also spoken |
| **Former name** | Uzbek Soviet Socialist Republic (1924–91), within the Union of Soviet Socialist Republics (USSR; 1924–91) | **Ethnic groups** | Uzbek 71%, Russian 8%, Tajik 5%, Kazakh 4%, others 12% |
| **Independence** | 1991 | **Religions** | Islam 88% (Sunni), Christianity 9% (Orthodox), others/unaffiliated 3% |
| **Area** | 447 400 sq km/172 696 sq mi | **Time zone** | GMT +5 |
| **Capital** | Tashkent; Toškent, Taškent | **Currency** | 1 Sum = 100 tiyin |
| **Chief towns** | Samarkand, Andizhan, Namangan | **Telephone** | +998 |
| | | **Internet** | .uz |
| **Population** | 25 068 000 (2001e) | **Country code** | UZB |

**Location**
A republic in central and northern Middle Asia, bounded to the south by Afghanistan; to the south-west by Turkmenistan; to the west and north-east by Kazakhstan; to the north-west by the Aral Sea; and to the east by Kyrgyzstan and Tajikistan.

**Physical description**
Large area occupied by the Kyzyl-Kum desert; highest point is Beshtor Peak (4 299m/14 104ft).

**Climate**
Long, hot summers, mild winters.

**National holidays**
Jan 1, Mar 8 (Women), 21, May 9 (Memory and Respect), Sep 1 (Independence), Oct 1 (Teachers), Dec 8 (Constitution); Ad, ER.

### Political leaders

**President**

1991– Islam Karimov

**Prime Minister**

| | |
|---|---|
| 1991–5 | Abdulhashim Mutalov |
| 1995– | Otkir Sultonov |

## VANUATU

| | | | |
|---|---|---|---|
| **Official name** | Republic of Vanuatu | **Ethnic groups** | Melanesian 95%, others 5% |
| **Local name** | Vanuatu; Ripablik Blong Vanuatu, République de Vanuatu | **Religions** | Christianity 77% (Prot 52%, RC 15%, others 10%), traditional beliefs 8%, others 15% |
| **Former name** | New Hebrides (until 1980) | **Time zone** | GMT +11 |
| **Independence** | 1980 | **Currency** | 1 Vatu (V, VT) = 100 centimes |
| **Area** | 14 763 sq km/5 698 sq mi | **Telephone** | +678 |
| **Capital** | Port-Vila | **Internet** | .vu |
| **Population** | 202 000 (2001e) | **Country code** | VUT |
| **Nationality** | Ni-Vanuatu | | |
| **Languages** | Bislama, English, French | | |

**Location**
An independent republic comprising an irregular Y-shaped island chain in the south-west Pacific Ocean, 400km/250mi north-east of the French islands of New Caledonia.

**Physical description**
Mainly volcanic and rugged, with raised coral beaches fringed by reefs; highest peak (Tabwemasana on Espiritu Santo) rises to 1 888m/6 194ft; several active volcanoes; densely forested, with narrow strips of cultivated land on the coast.

**Climate**
Tropical, with a hot and rainy season in Nov–Apr when cyclones may occur; annual temperatures at Port-Vila are 16–33°C.

**National holidays**
Jan 1, Feb 21 (Memory of the Father of Independence), Mar 5 (Custom Chiefs), May 1, Jul 24 (Children), 30 (Independence), Aug 15, Oct 5 (Constitution), Nov 29 (Unity), Dec 25, 26; A, EM, ES, GF.

## Political leaders

**President**

| | |
|---|---|
| 1980–9 | George Sokomanu *(formerly* Kalkoa) |
| 1989–94 | Fred Timakata |
| 1994–9 | Jean-Marie Leye |
| 1999– | John Bani |

**Prime Minister**

| | |
|---|---|
| 1980–91 | Walter Lini |
| 1991 | Donald Kalpokas |
| 1991–5 | Maxime Carlot Korman |
| 1995–6 | Serge Vohor |
| 1996 | Maxime Carlot Korman |
| 1996–8 | Serge Vohor |
| 1998–9 | Donald Kalpokas |
| 1999–2001 | Barak Sopé |
| 2001– | Edward Natapei |

## VATICAN

| | | | |
|---|---|---|---|
| **Official name** | Vatican City State; the Holy See | **Languages** | Latin; Italian is widely spoken |
| **Local name** | Città del Vaticano; Stato della Citta del Vaticano; Santa Sede | **Ethnic groups** | predominantly European, especially Italian |
| **Independence** | 1929 (formally) | **Religions** | Christianity 100% (RC) |
| **Area** | 0.4 sq km/0.2 sq mi | **Time zone** | GMT +1 |
| **Capital** | Vatican City | **Currency** | 1 Euro (€) = 100 cents |
| **Population** | 1 000 (2001e) | **Telephone** | +39 |
| | | **Internet** | .va |
| | | **Country code** | VAT |

**Location**
A papal sovereign state, and the smallest independent state in the world. Surrounded on all sides by Rome, Italy, it is a World Heritage Site and includes St Peter's, the Vatican Palace and Museum, several buildings in Rome, and the Pope's summer villa at Castel Gandolfo.

**Physical description**
Landlocked, urban and entirely enclosed within the Italian city of Rome; reaches 75m/246ft at its highest point.

**Climate**
Mediterranean; hot summers and mild winters.

**National holidays**
Jan 1, 6, Feb 11 (Lateran Treaty), Mar 19 (St Joseph), May 1, Jun 29 (SS Peter and Paul), Aug 15, Oct 16 (Holy Father's Elevation), Oct 22 (Coronation of Pope John Paul II), Nov 1, 2, Dec 8, 25, 26; CC, EM, WM.

## Political leaders

The head of state is the Supreme Pontiff of the Roman Catholic Church, the pope, who is elected for life by the Sacred College of Cardinals and has full legislative, judicial and executive powers (see **Religions, Beliefs and Folklore** for lists of **popes**). The head of government is a Secretary of State appointed by the pope (since 1990, Cardinal Angelo Sodano).

### *Swiss Guards*

The Vatican and the pope himself are protected by the distinctive Swiss Guards, with their blue- and yellow-striped dress uniform and red-tufted helmets. The Swiss Guards were instituted as the papal police corps by Pope Julius II, pope from 1503 to 1513. Their distinctive uniform was designed by Michelangelo. To be admitted to the Swiss Guards, one must be Roman Catholic, of good moral and ethical background, have attended military school in Switzerland, be 19–30 years old, at least 1.74m/5.7ft tall, unmarried, hold a professional diploma or high school degree, and, of course, be Swiss.

# VENEZUELA

| | | | |
|---|---|---|---|
| **Official name** | Bolivarian Republic of Venezuela | | languages are also spoken |
| **Local name** | Venezuela; República Bolivariana de Venezuela | **Ethnic groups** | mestizo 69%, white 21%, black 9%, Amerindian 1% |
| **Independence** | 1830 | | |
| **Area** | 912 050 sq km/352 051 sq mi | **Religions** | Christianity 94% (RC 92%, Prot 2%), others/unaffiliated 6% |
| **Capital** | Caracas | | |
| **Chief towns** | Maracaibo, Ciudad Guayana, Valencia, Barquisimeto | **Time zone** | GMT –4 |
| | | **Currency** | 1 Bolívar (Bs) = 100 céntimos |
| **Population** | 24 632 000 (2001e) | **Telephone** | +58 |
| **Nationality** | Venezuelan | **Internet** | .ve |
| **Languages** | Spanish; indigenous | **Country code** | VEN |

**Location**
The most northerly country in South America, bounded to the north by the Caribbean Sea; to the east by Guyana; to the south by Brazil; and to the south-west and west by Colombia.

**Physical description**
Guiana Highlands in the south-east cover over half the country; Venezuelan Highlands in the west and along the coast reach heights of around 5 000m/16 400ft; highest point is Pico Bolívar (5 007m/16 427ft); lowlands around Lake Maracaibo and in the Orinoco River valley, which runs south to north-east.

**Climate**
Generally hot and humid; one rainy season from Apr to Oct; annual temperatures at Caracas are 13–27°C; very little rainfall on the coast around Lake Maracaibo, increasing in the east.

**National holidays**
Jan 1, Apr 19 (Independence), May 1, Jun 24 (Battle of Carabobo), Jul 5 (National), 24 (Bolívar's Birthday), Oct 12 (Discovery), Dec 17 (Liberator's Death), 25; C (2), GF, HT.

## Political leaders

**President**

| | |
|---|---|
| 1899–1908 | Cipriano Castro |
| 1908–36 | Juan Vicente Gomez |
| 1936–41 | Eleazar Lopez Contreras |
| 1941–5 | Isaias Medina Angarita |
| 1945–7 | *Military Junta* (Rómulo Betancourt) |
| 1947–8 | Romulo Gallegos |
| 1948–50 | *Military Junta* (Carlos Delgado Chalbaud) |
| 1950–9 | *Military Junta* (Marcos Pérez Jiménez) |
| 1959–64 | Rómulo Betancourt |
| 1964–9 | Raul Leoni |
| 1969–74 | Rafael Caldera Rodriguez |
| 1974–9 | Carlos Andres Pérez |
| 1979–84 | Luis Herrera Campins |
| 1984–9 | Jaime Lusinchi |
| 1989–93 | Carlos Andres Pérez |
| 1994–8 | Rafael Caldera Rodríguez |
| 1998–2002 | Hugo Chávez Frías |
| 2002 | Pedro Carmona *Head of Transitional Government* |
| 2002– | Hugo Chávez Frías |

# VIETNAM

| | | | |
|---|---|---|---|
| **Official name** | Socialist Republic of Vietnam (SRV) | **Population** | 76 324 753 (1999) |
| **Local name** | Viêt Nam; Công-Hòa Xã-Hôi Chu-Nghĩ Viêt Nam | **Nationality** | Vietnamese |
| **Former name** | formerly part of Indochina (until 1945), *post-1945 as listed below under Political leaders* | **Languages** | Vietnamese |
| **Independence** | 1945 (declared), 1976 (republic) | **Ethnic groups** | Vietnamese 86%, Chinese 3%, Thai 2%, others 9% |
| **Area** | 329 566 sq km/127 213 sq mi | **Religions** | Buddhism 55%, none/ unaffiliated 15%, Christianity 7%, others 23% |
| **Capital** | Hanoi; Hà Nội | **Time zone** | GMT +7 |
| **Chief towns** | Ho Chi Minh City (formerly Saigon), Haiphong, Da Nang, Nha Trang | **Currency** | 1 Dông (D) = 10 hào = 100 xu |
| | | **Telephone** | +84 |
| | | **Internet** | .vn |
| | | **Country code** | VNM |

**Location**
An independent socialist state in south-east Asia, bounded to the east by the South China Sea (including the Gulf of Tongking in the north); to the west by Laos and Cambodia; and to the north by China.

**Physical description**
Occupies a narrow strip along the coast of the Gulf of Tongking and the South China Sea; broader at the Mekong River Delta, in the south, and along the Red River Valley to the north; highest peak is Fan si Pan (3 143m/10 312ft).

**Climate**
Tropical monsoon-type, dominated by south to south-east winds during May–Sep and north to north-east winds during Oct–Apr; high humidity in the rainy season; temperatures are high in the south during Oct–Apr.

**National holidays**
Jan 1, Apr 30 (Saigon Liberation), May 1, Sep 2 (National); NY (Vietnamese) (4).

## Political leaders

### Democratic Republic of Vietnam (North Vietnam)

**President**

1945–69 Ho Chi Minh
1969–76 Ton Duc Thang

**Prime Minister**

1945–55 *As President*
1955–76 Pham Van Dong

### State of Vietnam (South Vietnam)

**Chief of State**

1949–55 Bao Dai

**Prime Minister**

| | |
|---|---|
| 1949–50 | Nguyen Van Xuan |
| 1950 | Nguyen Phan Long |
| 1950–2 | Tran Van Huu |
| 1952 | Tran Van Huong |
| 1952–3 | Nguyen Van Tam |
| 1953–4 | Buu Loc |
| 1954–5 | Ngo Dinh Diem |

## Republic of Vietnam (South Vietnam)

**President**

| | |
|---|---|
| 1955–63 | Ngo Dinh Diem |
| 1963–4 | Duong Van Minh |
| 1964 | Nguyen Khanh |
| 1965–75 | Nguyen Van Thieu |
| 1975 | Tran Van Huong |
| 1975 | Duong Van Minh |
| 1975–6 | *Provisional Revolutionary Government* (Huynh Tan Phat) |

**Prime Minister**

| | |
|---|---|
| 1955–63 | Ngo Dinh Diem |
| 1963–4 | Nguyen Ngoc Tho |
| 1964 | Nguyen Khan |
| 1964–5 | Tran Van Huong |
| 1965 | Phan Huy Quat |
| 1965–7 | Nguyen Cao Ky |
| 1967–8 | Nguyen Van Loc |
| 1968–9 | Tran Van Huong |
| 1969–75 | Tran Thien Khiem |
| 1975 | Nguyen Ba Can |
| 1975–6 | Vu Van Mau |

## Socialist Republic of Vietnam

**President**

| | |
|---|---|
| 1976–80 | Ton Duc Thang |
| 1980–1 | Nguyen Hun Tho *Acting President* |
| 1981–7 | Truongh Chinh |
| 1987–92 | Vo Chi Cong |
| 1992–7 | Le Duc Anh |
| 1997– | Tran Duc Luong |

**Premier**

| | |
|---|---|
| 1976–87 | Pham Van Dong |
| 1987–8 | Pham Hung |
| 1988 | Vo Van Kiet *Acting Premier* |
| 1988–91 | Do Muoi |
| 1991–7 | Vo Van Kiet |
| 1997– | Phan Van Khai |

**General Secretary**

| | |
|---|---|
| 1976–86 | Le Duan |
| 1986 | Truong Chinh |
| 1986–91 | Nguyen Van Linh |
| 1991–7 | Do Muoi |
| 1997–2001 | Le Kha Phieu |
| 2001– | Nong Duc Manh |

### *Vietnamese Customs*

Chewing betel and areca is an old Vietnamese custom. Betel and areca nuts are shared for enjoyment at weddings, are a source of comfort at funerals, are used during ancestor worship, and as a symbol of friendship during festivals. Betel is a relaxant and intoxicant; the chewed quid often comprises a mixture of betel bark, areca leaf, chay root and hydrated lime, giving a mixture of hot, sweet, bitter and pungent tastes.

**VIRGIN ISLANDS, BRITISH** *see* **UNITED KINGDOM**

**VIRGIN ISLANDS, US** *see* **UNITED STATES OF AMERICA**

**WALES** *see* **UNITED KINGDOM**

**WALLIS AND FUTUNA ISLANDS** *see* **FRANCE**

**WEST BANK** *see* **PALESTINIAN AUTONOMOUS AREAS** *under* **ISRAEL**

## WESTERN SAHARA

| | | | |
|---|---|---|---|
| **Official name** | Saharawi Arab Democratic Republic; Saharan Arab Democratic Republic; claimed by Morocco | **Population** | 293 000 (2001e) |
| | | **Nationality** | Sahrawi, Sahraoui; Sahrawian, Sahraouian |
| | | **Languages** | Arabic; French, Berber and Spanish are also spoken |
| **Local name** | Sahara Occidental; République Arabe Saharouie Démocratique | **Ethnic groups** | Arab, Berber |
| **Former name** | Spanish Sahara (until 1976) | **Religions** | Islam (Sunni) 100% |
| | | **Time zone** | GMT |
| **Area** | 252 126 sq km/97 321 sq mi | **Currency** | 1 Moroccan Dirham (DH) = 100 centimes |
| **Capital** | El Aaiún; Laâyoune, La 'Youn | **Telephone** | +212 |
| | | **Internet** | .eh |
| **Chief towns** | Smara, Bu Craa, Dakhla | **Country code** | ESH |

**Location**
A disputed non-self-governing territory in north-west Africa, administered by Morocco. It is bounded by Morocco in the north, Algeria in the north-east, to the east and south by Mauritania, and to the west by the Atlantic Ocean. It is crossed by the Tropic of Cancer.

**Physical description**
Low, flat desert terrain, composed principally of plains and low plateaux; rises in the south to hills; rocky desert in the northeast, rising to steep hills; highest point reaches 463m/1 519ft; ergs and sand dunes inland, with sparse desert vegetation.

**Climate**
Hot, dry climate, with little rainfall; coastal fog, mists and dew; subject to the hot, dry *sirocco* wind in winter and spring.

## Political leaders

Disputed; Morocco claims sovereignty and views Western Sahara as Moroccan provinces administered by the Moroccan government (see Morocco). The Western Saharan independence movement, the Polisario Front, proclaimed a government-in-exile in 1976 (see below).

## Saharawi Arab Democratic Republic

**Chairman of Revolutionary Council**

| | |
|---|---|
| 1976 | El Wali Mustafa Sayed |
| 1976 | Mahfoud Ali Beiba *Acting Chairman* |

**Chairman of Revolutionary Command Council**

| | |
|---|---|
| 1976–82 | Mohamed Abdelaziz |

**President**

| | |
|---|---|
| 1982– | Mohamed Abdelaziz |

**Prime Minister**

| | |
|---|---|
| 1976–82 | Mohamed Lamine Ould Ahmed |
| 1982–5 | Mahfoud Ali Beiba |
| 1985–8 | Mohamed Lamine Ould Ahmed |
| 1988–93 | Mahfoud Ali Beiba |
| 1993–5 | Bouchraya Hammoudi Bayoune |
| 1995–9 | Mahfoud Ali Beiba |
| 1999– | Bouchraya Hamoudi Bayoune |

### *Coming of the Camel*

It is thought that the camel first arrived in Western Sahara in the 1c AD.

**WESTERN SAMOA** *see* **SAMOA**

# YEMEN

| | | | |
|---|---|---|---|
| **Official name** | Republic of Yemen | **Nationality** | Yemeni |
| **Local name** | Al-Yamaniyya; Al-Jumhūriyya Al-Yamaniyya | **Languages** | Arabic |
| **Former name** | *as listed below under Political leaders* | **Ethnic groups** | Arab 96%, others 4% |
| **Independence** | 1990 (united republic) | **Religions** | Islam 97% (Shia 56%, Sunni 41%), others 3% |
| **Area** | 531 570 sq km/205 186 sq mi | **Time zone** | GMT +3 |
| **Capital** | Sana'a; Şan'ā', Sanaa | **Currency** | 1 Yemeni Riyal (YR, YRI) = 100 fils |
| **Chief towns** | Ta'iz | **Telephone** | +967 |
| **Population** | 14 587 807 (1994) | **Internet** | .ye |
| | | **Country code** | YEM |

**Location**
A republic in the south of the Arabian Peninsula, bounded to the north by Saudi Arabia; to the west by the Red Sea; to the south by the Gulf of Aden; and to the east by Oman.

**Physical description**
Narrow desert plain bordering the Red Sea rises abruptly to mountains at 3 000–3 700m/9 840–12 140ft; highest point is Jabal an Nabi Shu'ayb (3 760m/12 336ft); to the north, a plateau merges with the gravel plains and sand of the Rub al Khali Basin.

**Climate**
Hot and humid on the western coastal strip, with an annual temperature of 29°C; milder in the highlands; rainfall is highest in the north and west; hot all year round in the south, with maximum temperatures over 40°C (Jul–Aug) and very high humidity.

**National holidays**
May 1, 22 (National), Sep 26 (Revolution), Oct 14 (Revolution), Nov 30 (Independence); Ad (5), ER (5), NY (Muslim).

## Political leaders

### Yemen Arab Republic (North Yemen)

**Monarch (Imam)**

| | |
|---|---|
| 1918–48 | Yahya Mohammed Bin Mohammed |
| 1948–62 | Ahmed Bin Yahya |
| 1962–70 | Mohammed Bin Ahmed |
| 1962 | *Civil War* |

**President**

| | |
|---|---|
| 1962–7 | Abdullah Al-Sallal |
| 1967–74 | Abdur Rahman Al-Iriani |
| 1974–7 | *Military Command Council* (Ibrahim Al- Hamadi) |
| 1977–8 | Ahmed Bin Hussein Al-Ghashmi |
| 1978–90 | Ali Abdullah Saleh |

**Prime Minister**

| | |
|---|---|
| 1964 | Hamud Al-Jaifi |
| 1965 | Hassan Al-Amri |
| 1965 | Ahmed Mohammed Numan |
| 1965 | *As President* |
| 1965–6 | Hassan Al-Amri |
| 1966–7 | *As President* |
| 1967 | Muhsin Al-Aini |
| 1967–9 | Hassan Al-Amri |
| 1969–70 | Abd Allah Kurshumi |
| 1970–1 | Muhsin Al-Aini |
| 1971 | Abdel Salam Sabra *Acting Prime Minister* |
| 1971 | Ahmed Mohammed Numan |
| 1971 | Hassan Al-Amri |
| 1971–2 | Muhsin Al-Aini |
| 1972–4 | Qadi Abdullah Al-Hijri |
| 1974 | Hassan Makki |
| 1974–5 | Muhsin Al-Aini |
| 1975 | Abdel Latif Deifallah *Acting Prime Minister* |
| 1975–90 | Abdel-Aziz Abdel-Ghani |

### People's Democratic Republic of Yemen (South Yemen)

**President**

| | |
|---|---|
| 1967–9 | Qahtan Mohammed Al-Shaabi |
| 1969–78 | Salim Ali Rubai |
| 1978 | Ali Nasir Mohammed Husani |
| 1978–80 | Abdel Fattah Ismail |
| 1980–6 | Ali Nasir Mohammed Husani |
| 1986–90 | Haidar Abu Bakr Al-Attas |

**Prime Minister**

| | |
|---|---|
| 1969 | Faisal Abd Al-Latif Al-Shaabi |
| 1969–71 | Mohammed Ali Haithem |
| 1971–85 | Ali Nasir Mohammed Husani |
| 1985–6 | Haidar Abu Bakr Al-Attas |
| 1986–90 | Yasin Said Numan |

### Republic of Yemen

**President**

| | |
|---|---|
| 1990– | Ali Abdullah Saleh |

**Prime Minister**

| | |
|---|---|
| 1990–3 | Haidar Abu Bakr Al-Attas |
| 1993–7 | Abdel-Aziz Abdel-Ghani |
| 1997 | Farag Said Ben Ghanem |
| 1998–2001 | Abdul Ali Al-Karim Al-Iryani |
| 2001– | Abd al-Qadir Abd al-Rahman Bajammal |

**YUGOSLAVIA** *see* **SERBIA AND MONTENEGRO**

**ZAÏRE** *see* **CONGO, DEMOCRATIC REPUBLIC OF**

# ZAMBIA

| | | | |
|---|---|---|---|
| **Official name** | Republic of Zambia | **Languages** | English; local languages are also spoken |
| **Local name** | Zambia | **Ethnic groups** | Bemba 35%, Maravi 19%, Tonga 14%, others 32% |
| **Former name** | Northern Rhodesia (until 1964), part of the Federation of Rhodesia and Nyasaland (1953–63) | **Religions** | Christianity 68% (Prot 35%, RC 27%, African Christian 6%), traditional beliefs 31%, Islam and Hinduism 1% |
| **Independence** | 1964 | **Time zone** | GMT +2 |
| **Area** | 752 613 sq km/290 509 sq mi | **Currency** | 1 Kwacha (K) = 100 ngwee |
| **Capital** | Lusaka | **Telephone** | +260 |
| **Chief towns** | Ndola, Kitwe, Kabwe, Livingstone | **Internet** | .zm |
| **Population** | 10 285 631 (2000) | **Country code** | ZMB |
| **Nationality** | Zambian | | |

**Location**
A landlocked republic in southern Africa, bounded to the west by Angola; to the south by Namibia; to the south-east by Zimbabwe and Mozambique; to the east by Malawi; to the north-east by Tanzania; and to the north-west by Democratic Republic of Congo.

**Physical description**
Occupies a high plateau at an altitude of 1 000–1 400m/3 280–4 590ft; highest point is 2 067m/6 781ft south-east of Mbala; Zambezi River rises in the north extremity of North-West Province.

**Climate**
Temperate climate on upland plateau; rainy season is Oct–Mar; at Lusaka the maximum average daily temperatures range between 23°C and 35°C; tropical climate in the lower river valleys.

**National holidays**
Jan 1, May 1, 25 (Africa Freedom), Oct 24 (Independence), Dec 25; EM, GF, HS, Youth (2nd Mon in Mar), Heroes (1st Mon in Jul), Unity (1st Tues in Jul), Farmers (1st Mon in Aug).

## Political leaders

**President**

1964–91 Kenneth Kaunda
1991–2002 Frederick Chiluba
2002– Levy Mwanawasa

**Prime Minister**

1964–73 Kenneth Kaunda
1973–5 Mainza Chona
1975–7 Elijah Mudenda
1977–8 Mainza Chona
1978–81 Daniel Lisulu
1981–5 Nalumino Mundia
1985–9 Kebby Musokotwane
1989–91 Malimba Masheke
1991– *No Prime Minister*

### Smoke that Thunders

Zambia is renowned for the Victoria Falls, the waterfalls on the Zambezi River which lie on the border with Zimbabwe. The falls are 61–108m/200–350ft high and 1 688m/5 538ft wide. In 1855 the explorer David Livingstone became the first European to see the falls, which he named after Queen Victoria. However, the indigenous Kololo people knew the falls as *Mosi oa Tunya*, 'the smoke that thunders', while the Leya people called the falls *Shongwe*, meaning 'rainbow'.

## ZIMBABWE

| | | | |
|---|---|---|---|
| **Official name** | Republic of Zimbabwe | | |
| **Local name** | Zimbabwe | | |
| **Former name** | Southern Rhodesia (until 1965), part of the Federation of Rhodesia and Nyasaland (1953–63), Rhodesia (1965–80) | | |
| **Independence** | 1980 | | |
| **Area** | 391 090 sq km/150 961 sq mi | | |
| **Capital** | Harare | | |
| **Chief towns** | Bulawayo, Gweru, Mutare | | |
| **Population** | 12 960 000 (2001e) | | |
| **Nationality** | Zimbabwean | | |
| **Languages** | English; Shona, Sindebele and other local languages are also spoken | | |
| **Ethnic groups** | Shona 71%, Ndebele 16%, other Bantu-speaking peoples 11%, white 1%, mixed and Asian 1% | | |
| **Religions** | Christianity 45% (Prot 33%, RC 12%), traditional beliefs 40%, Islam 1%, others 14% | | |
| **Time zone** | GMT +2 | | |
| **Currency** | 1 Zimbabwe Dollar (Z$) = 100 cents | | |
| **Telephone** | +263 | | |
| **Internet** | .zw | | |
| **Country code** | ZWE | | |

**Location**
A landlocked republic in southern Africa, bounded to the south by South Africa; to the south-west by Botswana; to the north-west by Zambia; and to the north-east, east and south-east by Mozambique.

**Physical description**
High plateau country, with the Middleveld at 900–1 200m/2 950–3 940ft and the Highveld at 1 200–1 500m/3 940–4 920ft; lower towards the Zambezi River in the north and the Limpopo River in the south; mountains in the east rise to 2 592m/8 504ft at Mt Inyangani.

**Climate**
Generally subtropical, strongly influenced by altitude; warm and dry in the lowlands; average maximum daily temperatures at Harare, in the Highveld, range between 21°C and 29°C.

**National holidays**
Jan 1, Apr 18 (Independence), May 1, 25 (Africa), Aug 11 (Heroes), 12 (Defence Forces), Dec 22 (Unity), 25, 26; EM, ES, GF, HS.

## Political leaders

**President**

1980–7 Canaan Sodindo Banana
1987– Robert Gabriel Mugabe

**Prime Minister**

1980–7 Robert Gabriel Mugabe

### *Politicians and Chiefs*

Zimbabwe's capital was founded in 1890 and was named Salisbury after the British Prime Minister of the time, Lord Salisbury. After Zimbabwe gained its independence the capital was renamed Harare in 1982, this time after Chief Neharawa, a former indigenous ruler of the area.

# HISTORICAL EMPIRES

For the Roman Empire see **Ancient Greece and Rome**, for ancient Chinese dynasties see **China** in **Countries A–Z**, for ancient Egyptian dynasties see **Egypt** in **Countries A–Z** and for ancient Japanese emperors see **Japan** in **Countries A–Z**.

## Holy Roman Empire

The establishment of the Holy Roman Empire (HRE) is usually dated to the coronation of Charlemagne in 800 as emperor over most of Christian Western Europe. It was known as the Roman Empire and the Holy Empire before its full title was adopted in 1254. It was always based principally in the territory of modern-day Germany, though its full extent fluctuated considerably. It was at its zenith in the early Middle Ages, but remained officially in existence until 1806, when it was abolished by Francis II.

| | |
|---|---|
| 800–814 | Charlemagne (Charles I) |
| 814–840 | Louis I (the Pious) |
| 840–843 | *Civil War* |
| 843–855 | Lothair I |
| 855–875 | Louis II |
| 875–877 | Charles II (the Bald) |
| 877–881 | *Interregnum* |
| 881–887 | Charles III (the Fat) |
| 887–891 | *Interregnum* |
| 891–894 | Guido of Spoleto |
| 892–898 | Lambert of Spoleto[1] |
| 896–899 | Arnulf[2] |
| 901–905 | Louis III |
| 905–924 | Berengar |
| 911–918 | Conrad I[2, 4] |
| 919–936 | Henry I, the Fowler[4] |
| 936–973 | Otto I (the Great) |
| 973–983 | Otto II |
| 983–1002 | Otto III |
| 1002–24 | Henry II (the Saint) |
| 1024–39 | Conrad II |
| 1039–56 | Henry III (the Black) |
| 1056–1106 | Henry IV |
| 1077–80 | Rudolf of Rheinfelden[2, 4] |
| 1081–93 | Hermann[2, 4] |
| 1093–1101 | Conrad[2, 4] |
| 1106–25 | Henry V |
| 1125–37 | Lothair II |
| 1138–52 | Conrad III[4] |
| 1152–90 | Frederick I (Barbarossa) |
| 1190–7 | Henry VI |
| 1198–1214 | Otto IV |
| 1198–1208 | Philip[2, 4] |
| 1215–50 | Frederick II |
| 1246–7 | Henry Raspe[2, 4] |
| 1247–56 | William of Holland[2, 4] |
| 1250–4 | Conrad IV[4] |
| 1254–73 | *Great Interregnum* |
| 1257–72 | Richard[2, 4] |
| 1257–75 | Alfonso (Alfonso X of Castile)[2, 4] |
| 1273–91 | Rudolf I[4] |
| 1292–8 | Adolf[4] |
| 1298–1308 | Albert[4] |
| 1308–13 | Henry VII |
| 1314–26 | Frederick (III)[3, 4] |
| 1314–46 | Louis IV |
| 1346–78 | Charles IV |
| 1378–1400 | Wenceslas[4] |
| 1400–10 | Rupert[4] |
| 1410–37 | Sigismund |
| 1438–9 | Albert II[4] |
| 1440–93 | Frederick III |
| 1493–1519 | Maximilian I[4] |
| 1519–56 | Charles V[4] |
| 1556–64 | Ferdinand I[4] |
| 1564–76 | Maximilian II[4] |
| 1576–1612 | Rudolf II[4] |
| 1612–19 | Matthias[4] |
| 1619–37 | Ferdinand II[4] |
| 1637–57 | Ferdinand III[4] |
| 1658–1705 | Leopold I[4] |
| 1705–11 | Joseph I[4] |
| 1711–40 | Charles VI[4] |
| 1740–42 | *Interregnum* |
| 1742–5 | Charles VII[4] |
| 1745–65 | Francis I[4] |
| 1765–90 | Joseph II[4] |
| 1790–2 | Leopold II[4] |
| 1792–1806 | Francis II[4, 5] |

[1] *Co-emperor.*
[2] *Rival.*
[3] *Co-regent.*
[4] *Ruler not crowned at Rome; therefore, strictly speaking, only King of Germany.*
[5] *The threat that Napoleon I might endeavour to appropriate the Holy Roman title in an attempt to establish a European hegemony led Francis II to abolish the HRE and restyle himself Emperor of Austria.*

# HISTORICAL EMPIRES

## Inca Empire

The Incas were originally a small group of Quechua-speaking Indians living in the Cuzco Basin of the central Andean highlands. In the 11c the Inca established their capital at Cuzco, the Sacred City of the Sun, where they built huge stone temples and fortresses, and occasionally covered important buildings in sheets of gold. During the 15c they brought together much of the Andean area, stretching along the entire western length of South America, from near the present Ecuador–Columbia border to south central Chile, and occupied much of the Andean region of Bolivia as well. They ruled more than 12 million people. The Inca emperor was a despotic ruler of a highly stratified society, and a quasi-religious figure thought to be a direct descendant of the sun god, Inti. In 1532 Spanish invaders under Pizarro encountered the Incas. They captured the emperor, Atahualpa, whom they later murdered, and seized control of the empire. By the 1570s Inca power was totally destroyed.

*Note: The earliest Inca emperors are considered to be mythical, rather than historical figures. Dates are not known for the early emperors. The Spanish names, rather than the Inca names, of the emperors are given.*

| | |
|---|---|
| dates unknown | Manco Capac |
| dates unknown | Sinchi Roca |
| dates unknown | Lloque Yupanqui |
| dates unknown | Mayta Capac |
| dates unknown | Capac Yupanqui |
| dates unknown | Inca Roca |
| dates unknown | Yahuar Huacac |
| dates unknown | Viracocha Inca |
| dates unknown | Inca Urcon |
| 1438–71 | Pachacuti Inca Yupanqui |
| 1471–93 | Topa Inca Yupanqui |
| 1493–1525 | Huayna Capac |
| 1525–32 | Huascar |
| 1532–3 | Atahualpa |
| 1533 | Topa Huallpa |
| 1533–45 | Manco Inca Yupanqui |
| 1545–60 | Sayri Tupac |
| 1560–71 | Titu Cusi Yupanqui |
| 1571–2 | Tupac Amaru |

## Mughal Empire

The Mughal Empire was an important Indian Muslim state, founded in 1526 by Babur. The empire was extended during the 16c and 17c, but its last great emperor was Aurangzeb and by the mid-18c it ruled only a small area around Delhi, although its administrative forms and culture continued to have great influence.

| | |
|---|---|
| 1526–30 | Babur |
| 1530–56 | Humayun[1] |
| 1556–1605 | Akbar |
| 1605–27 | Jahangir |
| 1627–58 | Shah Jahan |
| 1658–1707 | Aurangzeb (Alamgir) |
| 1707–12 | Bahadur Shah I (or Shah Alam I) |
| 1712–13 | Jahandar Shah |
| 1713–19 | Farruksiyar |
| 1719 | Rafid-ud-Darajat |
| 1719 | Rafi-ud-Daulat |
| 1719 | Nekusiyar |
| 1719 | Ibrahim |
| 1719–48 | Muhammad Shah |
| 1748–54 | Ahmad Shah |
| 1754–9 | Alamgir II |
| 1759–1806 | Shah Alam II |
| 1806–37 | Akbar II |
| 1837–57 | Bahadur Shah II[2] |

[1] *Humayun lost his throne to the Afghan chieftain Sher Shah in 1540, became a fugitive, and did not regain his title until 1555.*

[2] *Bahadur Shah II was exiled by the British to Rangoon after the Indian Uprising of 1857–8.*

## WORLD POLITICAL MAPS

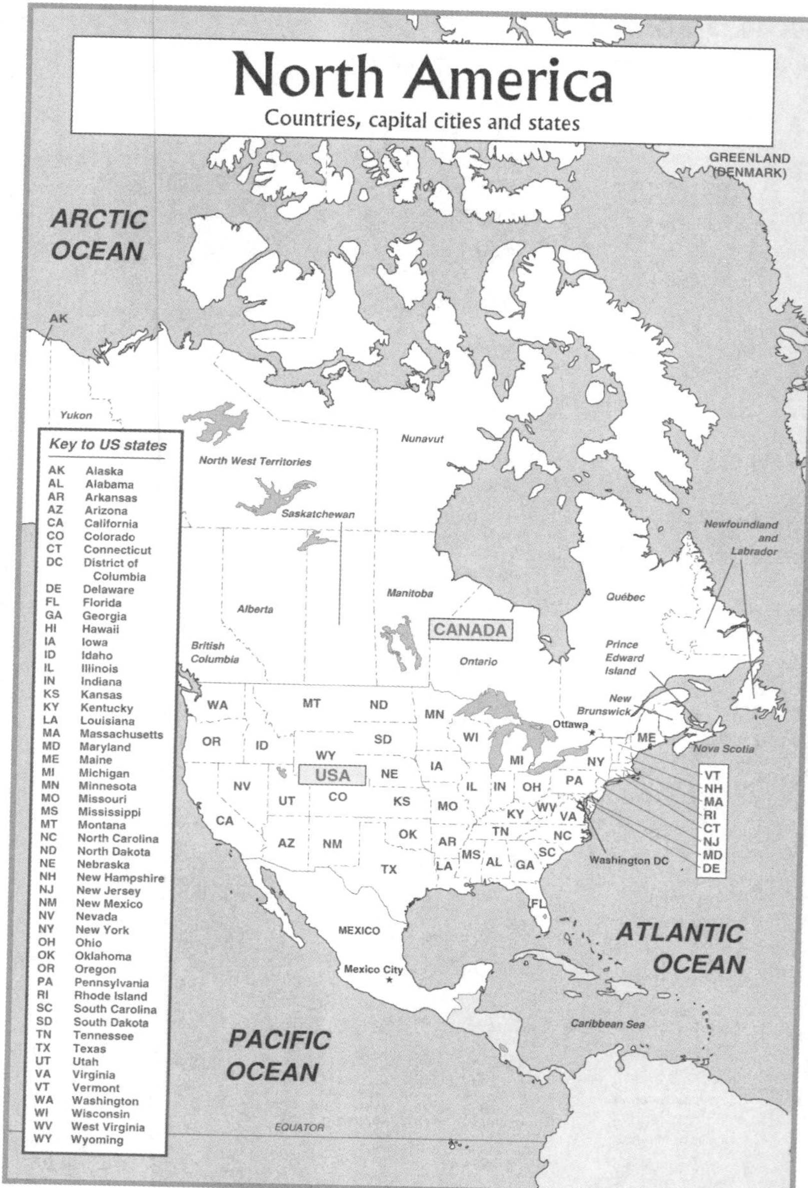
North America
Countries, capital cities and states
ARCTIC OCEAN
GREENLAND (DENMARK)
AK
Yukon
Nunavut
North West Territories
Saskatchewan
Newfoundland and Labrador
Manitoba
Québec
Alberta
CANADA
British Columbia
Ontario
Prince Edward Island
New Brunswick
Ottawa
Nova Scotia
Key to US states
AK Alaska
AL Alabama
AR Arkansas
AZ Arizona
CA California
CO Colorado
CT Connecticut
DC District of Columbia
DE Delaware
FL Florida
GA Georgia
HI Hawaii
IA Iowa
ID Idaho
IL Illinois
IN Indiana
KS Kansas
KY Kentucky
LA Louisiana
MA Massachusetts
MD Maryland
ME Maine
MI Michigan
MN Minnesota
MO Missouri
MS Mississippi
MT Montana
NC North Carolina
ND North Dakota
NE Nebraska
NH New Hampshire
NJ New Jersey
NM New Mexico
NV Nevada
NY New York
OH Ohio
OK Oklahoma
OR Oregon
PA Pennsylvania
RI Rhode Island
SC South Carolina
SD South Dakota
TN Tennessee
TX Texas
UT Utah
VA Virginia
VT Vermont
WA Washington
WI Wisconsin
WV West Virginia
WY Wyoming
WA
MT
ND
MN
OR
ID
SD
WI
ME
WY
MI
NY
USA
NE
IA
VT
NH
MA
RI
CT
NJ
MD
DE
NV
IL
IN
OH
PA
UT
CO
KS
MO
KY
WV
VA
CA
TN
NC
OK
AR
AZ
NM
MS
AL
GA
SC
TX
LA
Washington DC
FL
MEXICO
ATLANTIC OCEAN
Mexico City
Caribbean Sea
PACIFIC OCEAN
EQUATOR

# Central & South America

Countries and capital cities

# Asia and the Middle East

Countries and capital cities

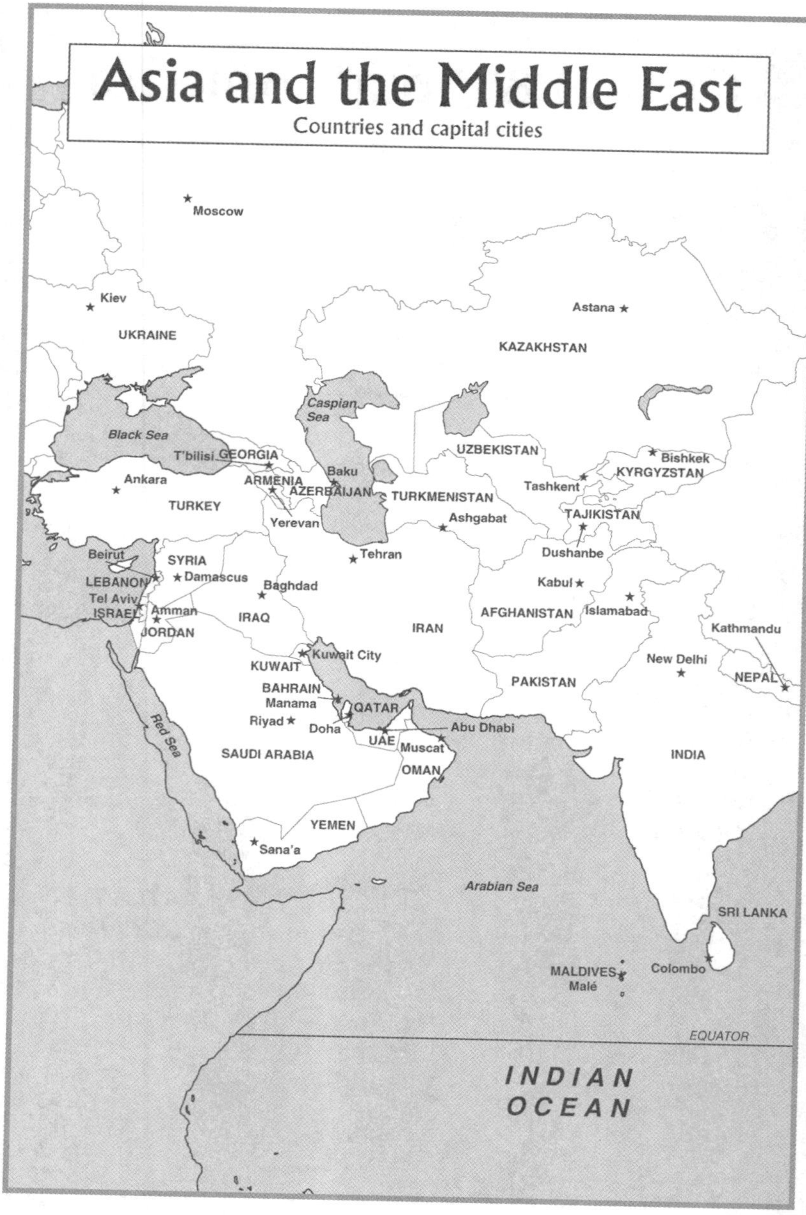

# Far East

Countries and capital cities

# Australasia and Indonesia

Countries, states and territories and capital cities

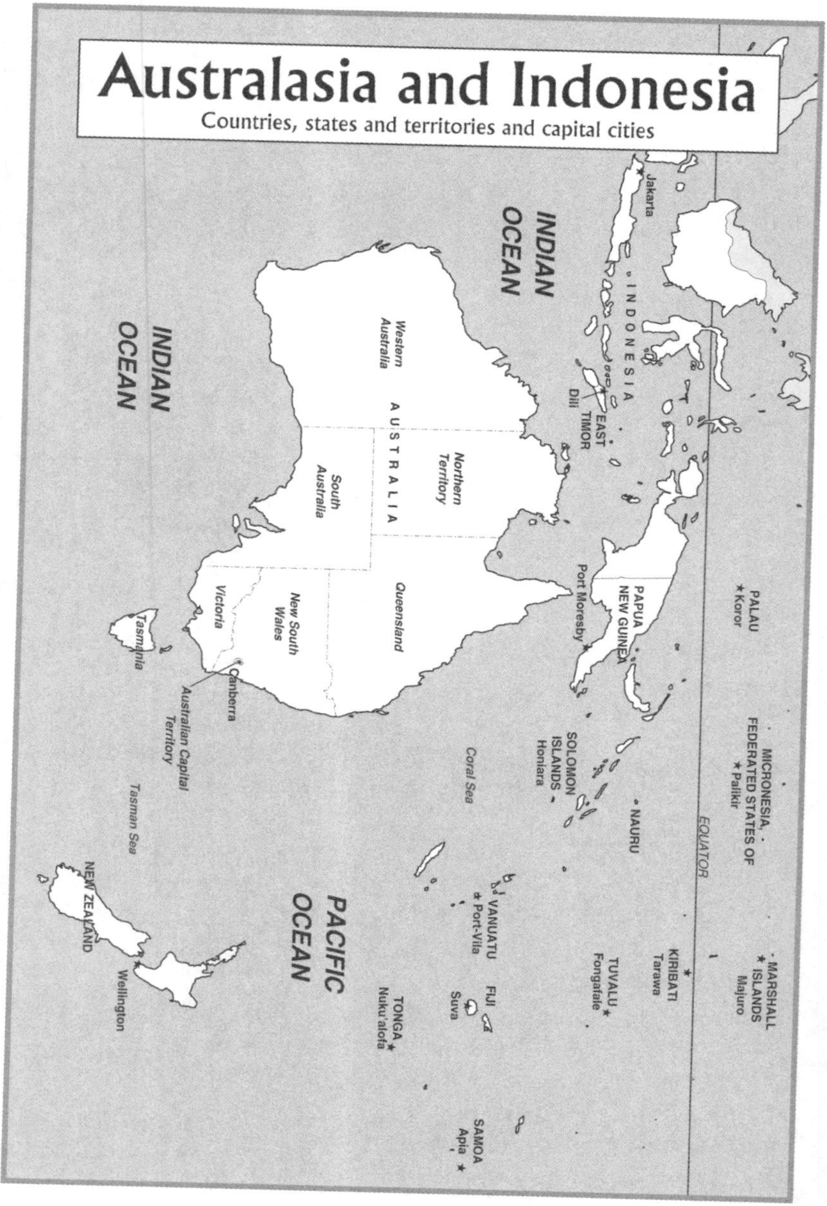

# Africa

Countries and capital cities

## LARGEST COUNTRIES

The ten largest countries in the world by area:

| Country | Area |
|---|---|
| Russia | 17 075 400 sq km/6 591 104 sq mi |
| Canada | 9 970 610 sq km/3 848 655 sq mi |
| China | 9 597 000 sq km/3 704 000 sq mi |
| United States of America | 9 160 454 sq km/3 535 935 sq mi |
| Brazil | 8 511 965 sq km/3 285 618 sq mi |
| Australia | 7 692 300 sq km/2 969 228 sq mi |
| Argentina | 3 761 274 sq km/1 451 852 sq mi |
| India | 3 166 829 sq km/1 222 396 sq mi |
| Kazakhstan | 2 717 300 sq km/1 048 878 sq mi |
| The Sudan | 2 504 530 sq km/966 749 sq mi |

## SMALLEST COUNTRIES

The ten smallest countries in the world by area:

| Country | Area |
|---|---|
| Vatican | 0.4 sq km/0.2 sq mi |
| Monaco | 1.9 sq km/0.75 sq mi |
| Nauru | 21 sq km/8 sq mi |
| Tuvalu | 26 sq km/10 sq mi |
| San Marino | 61 sq km/24 sq mi |
| Liechtenstein | 160 sq km/62 sq mi |
| Marshall Islands | 180 sq km/70 sq mi |
| St Kitts and Nevis | 269 sq km/104 sq mi |
| Maldives | 300 sq km/120 sq mi |
| Malta | 316 sq km/122 sq mi |

## MOST POPULOUS COUNTRIES

The ten most populous countries in the world:

| Country | Population |
|---|---|
| China | 1 295 330 000 (2000) |
| India | 1 027 015 247 (2001) |
| United States of America | 281 421 906 (2000) |
| Indonesia | 231 328 000 (2002e) |
| Brazil | 169 799 170 (2000) |
| Russia | 144 400 000 (2001e) |
| Pakistan | 130 579 571 (1998) |
| Japan | 126 925 843 (2000) |
| Bangladesh | 123 151 246 (2001) |
| Nigeria | 117 823 000 (2001e) |

## LEAST POPULOUS COUNTRIES

The ten least populous countries in the world:

| Country | Population |
|---|---|
| Vatican | 1 000 (2001e) |
| Tuvalu | 10 000 (2001e) |
| Nauru | 12 000 (2001e) |
| Palau | 17 225 (1995) |
| San Marino | 27 000 (2001e) |
| Monaco | 32 017 (2000) |
| Liechtenstein | 33 000 (2001e) |
| St Kitts and Nevis | 45 841 (2001) |
| Dominica | 71 727 (2001) |
| Antigua and Barbuda | 77 426 (2001) |

### *Oldest and Youngest*

Monaco has the oldest overall population in the world, with 10.8% of its people aged 75 years or older in 1995. The youngest population is that of the United Arab Emirates, where just 0.2% of the population in 1995 were 75 or older.

## COUNTRY POPULATION ESTIMATES

The world's six most populous countries compared for 2050 against 1950 in medium-variant predictions.

| | *1950* | | *2000* | | *2050* | |
|---|---|---|---|---|---|---|
| | **Country** | **Population estimate[1]** | **Country** | **Population estimate[1]** | **Country** | **Population estimate[1]** |
| 1 | China | 554 760 000 | China | 1 275 133 000 | India | 1 572 055 000 |
| 2 | India | 357 561 000 | India | 1 008 937 000 | China | 1 462 058 000 |
| 3 | USA | 157 813 000 | USA | 283 230 000 | USA | 397 063 000 |
| 4 | Russia | 102 702 000 | Indonesia | 212 092 000 | Pakistan | 344 170 000 |
| 5 | Japan | 83 625 000 | Brazil | 170 406 000 | Indonesia | 311 335 000 |
| 6 | Indonesia | 79 538 000 | Russia | 145 491 000 | Nigeria | 278 788 000 |

[1] *Population figures are rounded to the nearest 1 000. Data source: United Nations Population Division.*

## WORLD POPULATION

World population estimates (medium variant predictions).

| Date (AD) | Millions[1] | Date (AD) | Millions[1] |
|---|---|---|---|
| 1 | 300 | 1960 | 3 021 |
| 1000 | 310 | 1970 | 3 692 |
| 1250 | 400 | 1980 | 4 435 |
| 1500 | 500 | 1990 | 5 264 |
| 1750 | 790 | 2000 | 6 071 |
| 1800 | 980 | 2010 | 6 830 |
| 1850 | 1 260 | 2020 | 7 540 |
| 1900 | 1 650 | 2030 | 8 130 |
| 1950 | 2 519 | 2040 | 8 594 |
| | | 2050 | 8 919 |

[1] *Population figures are rounded to the nearest 1 000 000. Data source: United Nations Population Division.*

### People Galore

The world's population is growing by 1.2 per cent annually – equivalent to an increase of 77 million people per year. In 2000 there were approximately 6.1 billion of us on Earth.

## CAPITAL CITIES

The principal English names of capital cities are listed. For local names, names in other languages and alternative spellings, see the entry for the country in **Countries A–Z**. Capitals of states, provinces, dependencies, overseas possessions and other territories are not listed.

| Capital city | Country |
|---|---|
| Abidjan | Côte d'Ivoire *(administrative and economic capital)* |
| Abu Dhabi | United Arab Emirates |
| Abuja | Nigeria |
| Accra | Ghana |
| Addis Ababa | Ethiopia |
| Algiers | Algeria |
| Amman | Jordan |
| Amsterdam | The Netherlands |
| Andorra la Vella | Andorra |
| Ankara | Turkey |
| Antananarivo | Madagascar |
| Apia | Samoa |
| Ashgabat | Turkmenistan |
| Asmara | Eritrea |
| Astana | Kazakhstan |
| Asunción | Paraguay |
| Athens | Greece |
| Baghdad | Iraq |
| Baku | Azerbaijan |
| Bamako | Mali |
| Bandar Seri Begawan | Brunei Darussalam |
| Bangkok | Thailand |
| Bangui | Central African Republic |
| Banjul | The Gambia |
| Basseterre | St Kitts and Nevis |
| Beijing | China |
| Beirut | Lebanon |
| Belgrade | Serbia and Montenegro |
| Belmopan | Belize |
| Berlin | Germany |
| Berne | Switzerland |
| Bishkek | Kyrgyzstan |
| Bissau | Guinea-Bissau |
| Bloemfontein | South Africa *(judicial capital)* |
| Bogotá | Colombia |
| Brasília | Brazil |

| Capital city | Country |
|---|---|
| Bratislava | Slovakia |
| Brazzaville | Congo |
| Bridgetown | Barbados |
| Brussels | Belgium |
| Bucharest | Romania |
| Budapest | Hungary |
| Buenos Aires | Argentina |
| Bujumbura | Burundi |
| Cairo | Egypt |
| Canberra | Australia |
| Cape Town | South Africa *(legislative capital)* |
| Caracas | Venezuela |
| Castries | St Lucia |
| Chisinau | Moldova |
| Colombo | Sri Lanka *(commercial capital)* |
| Conakry | Guinea |
| Copenhagen | Denmark |
| Cotonou | Benin *(seat of government and economic capital)* |
| Dakar | Senegal |
| Damascus | Syria |
| Dhaka | Bangladesh |
| Dili | East Timor |
| Djibouti | Djibouti |
| Dodoma | Tanzania |
| Doha | Qatar |
| Dublin | Ireland |
| Dushanbe | Tajikistan |
| El Aaiún | Western Sahara |
| Fongafale | Tuvalu |
| Freetown | Sierra Leone |
| Gaborone | Botswana |
| Georgetown | Guyana |
| Guatemala City | Guatemala |
| Hanoi | Vietnam |
| Harare | Zimbabwe |
| Havana | Cuba |
| Helsinki | Finland |
| Honiara | Solomon Islands |
| Islamabad | Pakistan |
| Jakarta | Indonesia |
| Kabul | Afghanistan |
| Kampala | Uganda |
| Kathmandu | Nepal |
| Khartoum | The Sudan |
| Kiev | Ukraine |
| Kigali | Rwanda |
| Kingston | Jamaica |
| Kingstown | St Vincent and the Grenadines |
| Kinshasa | Democratic Republic of Congo |
| Koror | Palau |
| Kuala Lumpur | Malaysia |
| Kuwait City | Kuwait |
| La Paz | Bolivia *(administrative capital)* |

| Capital city | Country |
|---|---|
| Libreville | Gabon |
| Lilongwe | Malawi |
| Lima | Peru |
| Lisbon | Portugal |
| Ljubljana | Slovenia |
| Lobamba | Swaziland *(legislative capital)* |
| Lomé | Togo |
| London | United Kingdom |
| Luanda | Angola |
| Lusaka | Zambia |
| Luxembourg | Luxembourg |
| Madrid | Spain |
| Majuro | Marshall Islands |
| Malabo | Equatorial Guinea |
| Malé | Maldives |
| Managua | Nicaragua |
| Manama | Bahrain |
| Manila | Philippines |
| Maputo | Mozambique |
| Maseru | Lesotho |
| Mbabane | Swaziland *(administrative capital)* |
| Mexico City | Mexico |
| Minsk | Belarus |
| Mogadishu | Somalia |
| Monaco | Monaco |
| Monrovia | Liberia |
| Montevideo | Uruguay |
| Moroni | Comoros |
| Moscow | Russia |
| Muscat | Oman |
| Nairobi | Kenya |
| Nassau | The Bahamas |
| N'Djamena | Chad |
| New Delhi | India |
| Niamey | Niger |
| Nicosia | Cyprus |
| Nouakchott | Mauritania |
| Nuku'alofa | Tonga |
| Oslo | Norway |
| Ottawa | Canada |
| Ouagadougou | Burkina Faso |
| Palikir | Micronesia, Federated States of |
| Panama City | Panama |
| Paramaribo | Suriname |
| Paris | France |
| Phnom Penh | Cambodia |
| Port Louis | Mauritius |
| Port Moresby | Papua New Guinea |
| Port of Spain | Trinidad and Tobago |
| Port-au-Prince | Haiti |
| Porto Novo | Benin *(administrative and constitutional capital)* |
| Port-Vila | Vanuatu |

## CAPITAL CITIES

| Capital city | Country |
|---|---|
| Prague | Czech Republic |
| Praia | Cape Verde |
| Pretoria | South Africa *(administrative capital)* |
| Pyongyang | Korea, North |
| Quito | Ecuador |
| Rabat | Morocco |
| Rangoon | Myanmar (Burma) |
| Reykjavík | Iceland |
| Riga | Latvia |
| Riyadh | Saudi Arabia |
| Rome | Italy |
| Roseau | Dominica |
| St George's | Grenada |
| St John's | Antigua and Barbuda |
| San José | Costa Rica |
| San Marino | San Marino |
| San Salvador | El Salvador |
| Sana'a | Yemen |
| Santiago | Chile |
| Santo Domingo | Dominican Republic |
| São Tomé | São Tomé and Príncipe |
| Sarajevo | Bosnia and Herzegovina |
| Seoul | Korea, South |
| Singapore | Singapore |
| Skopje | Macedonia |
| Sofia | Bulgaria |
| Sri Jayaward-enepura Kotte | Sri Lanka *(administrative capital)* |
| Stockholm | Sweden |
| Sucre | Bolivia *(official capital)* |

| Capital city | Country |
|---|---|
| Suva | Fiji |
| T'aipei | Taiwan |
| Tallinn | Estonia |
| Tarawa | Kiribati |
| Tashkent | Uzbekistan |
| T'bilisi | Georgia |
| Tegucigalpa | Honduras |
| Tehran | Iran |
| Tel Aviv-Jaffa[1] | Israel |
| Thimphu | Bhutan |
| Tirana | Albania |
| Tokyo | Japan |
| Tripoli | Libya |
| Tunis | Tunisia |
| Ulan Bator | Mongolia |
| Vaduz | Liechtenstein |
| Valletta | Malta |
| Vatican City | Vatican |
| Victoria | Seychelles |
| Vienna | Austria |
| Vientiane | Laos |
| Vilnius | Lithuania |
| Warsaw | Poland |
| Washington, DC | United States of America |
| Wellington | New Zealand |
| Windhoek | Namibia |
| Yamoussoukro | Côte d'Ivoire *(official capital)* |
| Yaoundé | Cameroon |
| Yaren District[2] | Nauru |
| Yerevan | Armenia |
| Zagreb | Croatia |

[1] *Israel claims Jerusalem as its capital, but this is not recognized internationally.*

[2] *There is no capital as such, but government offices are situated in this area.*

### City of the North

Reykjavík, founded in 874, is the most northerly capital city in the world.

## CAPITAL CITIES ON RIVERS

Information for selected major capital cities is given. Capital cities that are sea ports or that lie on bays, estuaries, lakes or other water expanses are not included.

| Capital city | Country | River |
|---|---|---|
| Amman | Jordan | Zarqa |
| Amsterdam | The Netherlands | Amstel (and the Ijsselmeer) |
| Ankara | Turkey | a tributary of the Ova |
| Baghdad | Iraq | Tigris |
| Bangkok | Thailand | Chao Phraya |
| Belgrade | Serbia and Montenegro | Danube, Sava |
| Berlin | Germany | Spree, Havel (and others) |

| Capital city | Country | River |
|---|---|---|
| Bratislava | Slovakia | Danube |
| Brussels | Belgium | Senne |
| Bucharest | Romania | Dambovit |
| Budapest | Hungary | Danube |
| Buenos Aires | Argentina | Plate |
| Cairo | Egypt | Nile |
| Canberra | Australia | Molonglo |
| Damascus | Syria | Barada |
| Dhaka | Bangladesh | Meghna |
| Dublin | Ireland | Liffey |
| Hanoi | Vietnam | Red |
| Islamabad | Pakistan | Jhelum |
| Jakarta | Indonesia | Liwung |
| Kiev | Ukraine | Dnieper |
| Lima | Peru | Rímac |
| Lisbon | Portugal | Tagus |
| Ljubljana | Slovenia | Sava, Ljubljanica |
| London | United Kingdom | Thames |
| Luxembourg | Luxembourg | Alzette and Petrusse |
| Madrid | Spain | Manzanares |
| Manila | Philippines | Pasig |
| Minsk | Belarus | Svisloch |
| Moscow | Russia | Moskva |
| New Delhi | India | Yamuna (Old Delhi) |
| Ottawa | Canada | Ottawa, Rideau |
| Paris | France | Seine |
| Phnom Penh | Cambodia | Mekong (at confluence with the Tonlé Sap lake) |
| Prague | Czech Republic | Vltava |
| Pyongyang | Korea, North | Taedong |
| Rabat | Morocco | Bou Regreg |
| Riga | Latvia | Daugava |
| Rome | Italy | Tiber |
| Santiago | Chile | Mapocho |
| Sarajevo | Bosnia and Herzegovina | Miljacka |
| Seoul | Korea, South | Han |
| Skopje | Macedonia | Vardar |
| Tokyo | Japan | Sumida |
| Vienna | Austria | Danube |
| Vilnius | Lithuania | Vilnya |
| Warsaw | Poland | Vistula |
| Washington, DC | United States of America | Potomac, Anacostia |
| Zagreb | Croatia | Sava |

## Skinny-Dipping Presidents

Rivers in capital cities are liable to receive unexpected visitors. John Quincy Adams (1767–1848), the sixth president of the United States of America, reportedly swam naked in the Potomac every day.

## CAPITAL CITY POPULATION

| Capital city | Population[1] |
|---|---|
| Abidjan | 3 956 000 |
| Abu Dhabi | 471 000 |
| Abuja | 420 000 |
| Accra | 1 925 000 |
| Addis Ababa | 2 753 000 |
| Algiers | 2 861 000 |
| Amman | 1 181 000 |
| Amsterdam | 1 105 000 |
| Andorra la Vella | 21 000 |
| Ankara | 3 208 000 |
| Antananarivo | 1 689 000 |
| Apia | 35 000 |
| Ashgabat | 558 000 |
| Asmara | 503 000 |
| Astana | 328 000 |
| Asunción | 1 302 000 |
| Athens | 3 120 000 |
| Baghdad | 4 958 000 |
| Baku | 1 964 000 |
| Bamako | 1 161 000 |
| Bandar Seri Begawan | 46 000 |
| Bangkok | 7 527 000 |
| Bangui | 666 000 |
| Banjul | 418 000 |
| Basseterre | 12 000 |
| Beijing | 10 836 000 |
| Beirut | 2 115 000 |
| Belgrade | 1 687 000 |
| Belmopan | 9 000 |
| Berlin | 3 319 000 |
| Berne | 316 000 |
| Bishkek | 736 000 |
| Bissau | 292 000 |
| Bloemfontein | 364 000 |
| Bogotá | 6 957 000 |
| Brasília | 2 073 000 |
| Bratislava | 464 000 |
| Brazzaville | 1 360 000 |
| Bridgetown | 136 000 |
| Brussels | 1 134 000 |
| Bucharest | 1 998 000 |
| Budapest | 1 812 000 |
| Buenos Aires | 12 106 000 |
| Bujumbura | 346 000 |
| Cairo | 9 586 000 |
| Canberra | 387 000 |
| Cape Town | 2 993 000 |
| Caracas | 3 177 000 |
| Castries | 57 000 |
| Chisinau | 662 000 |
| Colombo[2] | 681 000 |
| Conakry | 1 272 000 |
| Copenhagen | 1 332 000 |
| Cotonou | 650 660 (2000) |
| Dakar | 2 160 000 |
| Damascus | 2 195 000 |
| Dhaka | 13 181 000 |
| Dili | 56 000 |
| Djibouti | 542 000 |
| Dodoma | 180 000 |
| Doha | 285 000 |
| Dublin | 993 000 |
| Dushanbe | 522 000 |
| El Aaiún | 207 000 |
| Fongafale | 5 000 |
| Freetown | 837 000 |
| Gaborone | 225 000 |
| Georgetown | 280 000 |
| Guatemala City | 3 366 000 |
| Hanoi | 3 822 000 |
| Harare | 1 868 000 |
| Havana | 2 268 000 |
| Helsinki | 936 000 |
| Honiara | 78 000 |
| Islamabad | 636 000 |
| Jakarta | 11 429 000 |
| Kabul | 2 734 000 |
| Kampala | 1 274 000 |
| Kathmandu | 755 000 |
| Khartoum | 2 853 000 |
| Kiev | 2 488 000 |
| Kigali | 412 000 |
| Kingston | 672 000 |
| Kingstown | 28 000 |
| Kinshasa | 5 253 000 |
| Koror | 14 000 |
| Kuala Lumpur | 1 410 000 |
| Kuwait City | 888 000 |
| La Paz | 1 499 000 |
| Libreville | 573 000 |
| Lilongwe | 523 000 |
| Lima | 7 594 000 |
| Lisbon | 3 942 000 |
| Ljubljana | 250 000 |
| Lomé | 732 000 |
| London | 7 640 000 |
| Luanda | 2 819 000 |
| Lusaka | 1 718 000 |
| Luxembourg | 82 000 |
| Madrid | 3 969 000 |
| Majuro | 25 000 |
| Malabo | 33 000 |
| Malé | 84 000 |
| Managua | 1 039 000 |
| Manama | 150 000 |
| Manila (Metro) | 10 069 000 |
| Maputo | 1 134 000 |
| Maseru | 271 000 |

| Capital city | Population[1] | Capital city | Population[1] |
|---|---|---|---|
| Mbabane[3] | 80 000 | St John's | 24 000 |
| Mexico City | 18 268 000 | San José | 983 000 |
| Minsk | 1 664 000 | San Marino | 5 000 |
| Mogadishu | 1 212 000 | San Salvador | 1 381 000 |
| Monaco | 34 000 | Sana'a | 1 410 000 |
| Monrovia | 491 000 | Santiago | 5 551 000 |
| Montevideo | 1 329 000 | Santo Domingo | 2 629 000 |
| Moroni | 49 000 | São Tomé | 67 000 |
| Moscow | 8 316 000 | Sarajevo | 552 000 |
| Muscat | 540 000 | Seoul | 9 862 000 |
| Nairobi | 2 343 000 | Singapore | 4 108 000 |
| Nassau | 220 000 | Skopje | 437 000 |
| Nauru[4] | 13 000 | Sofia | 1 187 000 |
| N'Djamena | 735 000 | Stockholm | 1 626 000 |
| New Delhi | 301 297 (1991) | Sucre | 183 000 |
| Niamey | 821 000 | Suva (Greater) | 203 000 |
| Nicosia | 199 000 | T'aipei[6] | 2 640 322 (1999) |
| Nouakchott | 626 000 | Tallinn | 401 000 |
| Nuku'alofa | 33 000 | Tarawa | 32 000 |
| Oslo | 787 000 | Tashkent | 2 157 000 |
| Ottawa | 1 094 000 | T'bilisi | 1 406 000 |
| Ouagadougou | 862 000 | Tegucigalpa | 980 000 |
| Palikir | <1 000[5] | Tehran | 7 038 000 |
| Panama City | 1 20 0002 | Tel Aviv-Jaffa[7] | 348 300 (1998) |
| Paramaribo | 240 000 | Thimphu | 32 000 |
| Paris | 9 658 000 | Tirana | 299 000 |
| Phnom Penh | 1 109 000 | Tokyo | 26 546 000 |
| Port-au-Prince | 1 838 000 | Tripoli | 1 776 000 |
| Port Louis | 176 000 | Tunis | 1 927 000 |
| Port Moresby | 259 000 | Ulan Bator | 781 000 |
| Port of Spain | 54 000 | Vaduz | 5 000 |
| Porto Novo | 225 000 | Valletta | 82 000 |
| Port-Vila | 31 000 | Vatican City | 1 000 |
| Prague | 1 202 000 | Victoria | 30 000 |
| Praia | 82 000 | Vienna | 2 066 000 |
| Pretoria | 1 651 000 | Vientiane | 663 000 |
| Pyongyang | 3 164 000 | Vilnius | 579 000 |
| Quito | 1 660 000 | Warsaw | 2 282 000 |
| Rabat | 1 668 000 | Washington, DC | 3 997 000 |
| Rangoon | 4 504 000 | Wellington | 345 000 |
| Reykjavík | 175 000 | Windhoek | 216 000 |
| Riga | 756 000 | Yamoussoukro | 106 786 (1988) |
| Riyadh | 4 761 000 | Yaoundé | 1 481 000 |
| Rome | 2 651 000 | Yerevan | 1 420 000 |
| Roseau | 26 000 | Zagreb | 1 081 000 |
| St George's | 36 000 | | |

[1] *Population figures are rounded to the nearest 1 000; 2001e except where otherwise marked.*
[2] *No accurate figure available for Sri Jayawardenepura Kotte, Sri Lanka's administrative capital.*
[3] *No accurate figure available for Lobamba, Swaziland's royal and legislative capital.*
[4] *There is no capital of Nauru as such, although the government offices are located in Yaren District. Figure given is for the entire island.*
[5] *Estimated population under 1 000.*
[6] *Figure for T'aipei may contain rural areas, as well as the urban centre.*
[7] *Israel claims Jerusalem as its capital, but this is not recognized internationally.*
*Data source: United Nations Population Division.*

# LARGEST CITIES

## World

UN population estimates for the world's ten largest urban agglomerations ranked by population size. The agglomeration includes not only the city itself but also its urban hinterland – the greater metropolitan area. This means that the figures given will vary from the population estimates for the city alone. Population estimates also vary substantially according to the criteria used in their calculation.

| City | Country | Population (2000e)[1] |
|---|---|---|
| Tokyo | Japan | 26 444 000 |
| Mexico City | Mexico | 18 066 000 |
| São Paulo | Brazil | 17 962 000 |
| New York City | United States of America | 16 732 000 |
| Mumbai (Bombay) | India | 16 086 000 |
| Los Angeles | United States of America | 13 213 000 |
| Kolkata (Calcutta) | India | 13 058 000 |
| Shanghai | China | 12 887 000 |
| Dhaka | Bangladesh | 12 519 000 |
| Delhi | India | 12 441 000 |

[1] *Population figures are rounded to the nearest 1 000. Data source: United Nations Population Division.*

## UK

The ten largest cities in the United Kingdom ranked by population size.

| City | Population (2001) |
|---|---|
| London | 7 172 036 |
| Birmingham | 977 091 |
| Leeds | 715 404 |
| Glasgow | 577 869 |
| Sheffield | 513 234 |
| Bradford | 467 668 |
| Edinburgh | 448 624 |
| Liverpool | 439 476 |
| Manchester | 392 819 |
| Kirklees | 388 576 |

*Data source: ONS, © Crown copyright, 2001.*

## Cities of the Future

People are increasingly living in cities in the modern world. The United Nations predicts that more than half of the world's population will live in urban areas by 2008 – compared to just 2% of people in 1800, 30% in 1950 and 47% in 2000.

## USA

The ten largest cities in the United States of America ranked by population size.

| City | State | Population (2002e) |
|---|---|---|
| New York City | New York | 8 084 316 |
| Los Angeles | California | 3 798 981 |
| Chicago | Illinois | 2 886 251 |
| Houston | Texas | 2 009 834 |
| Philadelphia | Pennsylvania | 1 492 231 |
| Phoenix | Arizona | 1 371 960 |
| San Diego | California | 1 259 532 |
| Dallas | Texas | 1 211 467 |
| San Antonio | Texas | 1 194 222 |
| Detroit | Michigan | 925 051 |

*Data source: Population Division, US Census Bureau.*

## City Life

New York City was the first city in the world to have more than ten million citizens (including its urban agglomeration). But others caught up fast. By 1975 there were five cities boasting more than ten million inhabitants, by 2000 that figure had risen to 19 and by 2015 the United Nations estimates that 23 cities will have reached the ten million mark.

## UNITED NATIONS (UN)

An organization formed to maintain world peace and foster international co-operation, formally established on 24 Oct 1945 with 51 founder countries. It has six 'principal organs': the General Assembly, the Security Council, the Secretariat, the International Court of Justice, the Economic and Social Council and the Trusteeship Council.

### United Nations membership

The United Nations has 191 member states. Countries are grouped according to year of entry; only the country's current name is given, although its name may have changed during its membership (for example Belarus joined the UN in 1945 as Byelorussia). For information on former names see each country's entry in **Countries A–Z** under **Human Geography**.

| | |
|---|---|
| 1945 | Argentina, Australia, Belarus, Belgium, Bolivia, Brazil, Canada, Chile, China[1], Colombia, Costa Rica, Cuba, Czechoslovakia (until 1992), Denmark, Dominican Republic, Ecuador, Egypt, El Salvador, Ethiopia, France, Greece, Guatemala, Haiti, Honduras, India, Iran, Iraq, Lebanon, Liberia, Luxembourg, Mexico, The Netherlands, New Zealand, Nicaragua, Norway, Panama, Paraguay, Peru, Philippines, Poland, Russia, Saudi Arabia, South Africa, Syria, Turkey, Ukraine, United Kingdom, United States of America, Uruguay, Venezuela, Yugoslavia (until 1992) |
| 1946 | Afghanistan, Iceland, Sweden, Thailand |
| 1947 | Pakistan, Yemen[2] |
| 1948 | Myanmar (Burma) |
| 1949 | Israel |
| 1950 | Indonesia |
| 1955 | Albania, Austria, Bulgaria, Cambodia, Finland, Hungary, Ireland, Italy, Jordan, Laos, Libya, Nepal, Portugal, Romania, Spain, Sri Lanka |
| 1956 | Japan, Morocco, The Sudan, Tunisia |
| 1957 | Ghana, Malaysia |
| 1958 | Guinea |
| 1960 | Benin, Burkina Faso, Cameroon, Central African Republic, Chad, Congo, Congo (Democratic Republic of), Côte d'Ivoire, Cyprus, Gabon, Madagascar, Mali, Niger, Nigeria, Senegal, Somalia, Togo |
| 1961 | Mauritania, Mongolia, Sierra Leone, Tanzania[3] |
| 1962 | Algeria, Burundi, Jamaica, Rwanda, Trinidad and Tobago, Uganda |
| 1963 | Kenya, Kuwait |
| 1964 | Malawi, Malta, Zambia |
| 1965 | The Gambia, Maldives, Singapore |
| 1966 | Barbados, Botswana, Guyana, Lesotho |
| 1968 | Equatorial Guinea, Mauritius, Swaziland |
| 1970 | Fiji |
| 1971 | Bahrain, Bhutan, Oman, Qatar, United Arab Emirates |

| | |
|---|---|
| 1973 | The Bahamas, East Germany (until 1990), Germany |
| 1974 | Bangladesh, Grenada, Guinea-Bissau |
| 1975 | Cape Verde, Comoros, Mozambique, Papua New Guinea, São Tomé and Príncipe, Suriname |
| 1976 | Angola, Samoa, Seychelles |
| 1977 | Djibouti, Vietnam |
| 1978 | Dominica, Solomon Islands |
| 1979 | St Lucia |
| 1980 | St Vincent and the Grenadines, Zimbabwe |
| 1981 | Antigua and Barbuda, Belize, Vanuatu |
| 1983 | St Kitts and Nevis |
| 1984 | Brunei Darussalam |
| 1990 | Liechtenstein, Namibia |
| 1991 | Estonia, Korea (North), Korea (South), Latvia, Lithuania, Marshall Islands, Micronesia (Federated States of) |
| 1992 | Armenia, Azerbaijan, Bosnia and Herzegovina, Croatia, Georgia, Kazakhstan, Kyrgyzstan, Moldova, San Marino, Slovenia, Tajikistan, Turkmenistan, Uzbekistan |
| 1993 | Andorra, Czech Republic, Eritrea, Macedonia, Monaco, Slovakia |
| 1994 | Palau |
| 1999 | Kiribati, Nauru, Tonga |
| 2000 | Tuvalu, Serbia and Montenegro |
| 2002 | East Timor, Switzerland |

[1] *Taiwan, as the Republic of China, represented China at the UN until 25 Oct 1971, when the People's Republic of China was recognized instead; Taiwan has not since been a member of the UN.*
[2] *North Yemen joined the UN in 1947 and South Yemen joined in 1967; since unification in 1990 as Yemen the UN has considered 1947 to be the state's date of joining.*
[3] *Tanganyika joined the UN in 1961 and Zanzibar joined in 1963; since unification in 1964 as Tanzania the UN has considered 1961 to be the state's date of joining.*

### Blue Berets for Peace

Between Oct 1945, when the United Nations was founded, and Oct 2003, UN peacekeepers took part in 56 operations, and are currently deployed in 14 ongoing missions. The UN calculates that peacekeeping for the year Jun 2002–Jun 2003 cost a whopping $2.63 billion. However, that's small change in comparison with the big money that governments worldwide spend on weapons of war – the UN estimates that $839 billion was spent on arms in 2001 alone.

## United Nations Secretaries-General

**The United Nations Secretariat, under the Secretary-General, employs some 4 700 full-time members of staff at the UN's headquarters and around 8 700 worldwide. The Secretary-General is often a significant figure in international diplomacy.**

**Secretary-General**

| | |
|---|---|
| 1946–53 | Trygve Lie *Norway* |
| 1953–61 | Dag Hammarskjöld *Sweden* |
| 1962–71 | U Thant *Burma* |
| 1972–81 | Kurt Waldheim *Austria* |
| 1982–91 | Javier Pérez de Cuéllar *Peru* |
| 1992–6 | Boutros Boutros-Ghali *Egypt* |
| 1997– | Kofi Annan *Ghana* |

## United Nations Security Council

The 15-member United Nations Security Council is dominated by the five permanent members who each have the power of veto over any resolutions; the remaining ten are elected for two-year periods. The primary role of the Council is to maintain international peace and security; its decisions are binding on all other members. It is empowered to order mandatory sanctions, call for ceasefires, and establish peacekeeping forces. The use of the veto has prevented it from intervening in a number of disputes, such as the Vietnam War. The permanent members are:

China
France
Russia
United Kingdom
United States of America

## United Nations organizations

In addition to the bodies established under the UN Charter there is a range of subsidiary agencies, many with their own constitutions and membership. There are also a number of functional and regional commissions and research and training institutes.

### UN specialized agencies

Food and Agriculture Organization of the United Nations (FAO)
International Civil Aviation Organization (ICAO)
International Fund for Agricultural Development (IFAD)
International Labour Organization (ILO)
International Maritime Organization (IMO)
International Monetary Fund (IMF)
International Telecommunication Union (ITU)
United Nations Economic, Scientific and Cultural Organization (UNESCO)
United Nations Industrial Development Organization (UNIDO)
Universal Postal Union (UPU)
World Bank Group[1]
World Health Organization (WHO)
World Intellectual Property Organization (WIPO)
World Meteorological Organization (WMO)

[1] *Includes the International Bank for Reconstruction and Development (IBRD), the International Development Association (IDA), the International Finance Corporation (IFC), the Multilateral Investment Guarantee Agency (MIGA) and the International Centre for Settlement of Investment Disputes (ICSID).*

### UN programmes and funds

International Trade Centre (ITC)
Office of the United Nations High Commissioner for Refugees (UNHCR)
United Nations Children's Fund (UNICEF)
United Nations Conference on Trade and Development (UNCTAD)
United Nations Development Fund for Women (UNIFEM)
United Nations Development Programme (UNDP)
United Nations Drug Control Programme (UNDCP)
United Nations Environment Programme (UNEP)
United Nations Human Settlements Programme (UNHSP/UN-Habitat)
United Nations Population Fund (UNFPA)
United Nations Relief and Works Agency for Palestine Refugees in the Near East (UNRWA)
United Nations Volunteers (UNV)
World Food Programme (WFP)

### Other UN entities

Joint United Nations Programme on HIV/AIDS (UNAIDS)
Office of the United Nations High Commissioner for Human Rights (OHCHR)
United Nations Office for Project Services (UNOPS)
United Nations System Staff College (UNSSC)
United Nations University (UNU)

### UN related organizations

International Atomic Energy Agency (IAEA)
Organization for the Prohibition of Chemical Weapons (OPCW)
World Tourism Organization (WTO tourism)
World Trade Organization (WTO trade)

### *International HQ*

Deep in the heart of New York City in the United States of America lie 7.3 hectares/18 acres of foreign land. The United Nations headquarters on Manhattan Island is an 'international territory', owned by the UN and beyond US jurisdiction.

## THE COMMONWEALTH

The Commonwealth is a voluntary organization of autonomous states which have in the past been imperial possessions of Britain. Its head is the reigning British monarch. It was formally established by the Statute of Westminster (1931) and meets frequently to discuss matters of mutual interest and concern. There are 54 members.

### Commonwealth membership

| Member countries are grouped by year of entry. | |
|---|---|
| 1931 | Australia, Canada, New Zealand, United Kingdom, South Africa (left 1961, rejoined 1994) |
| 1947 | India, Pakistan (left 1972, rejoined 1989; suspended 1999) |
| 1948 | Sri Lanka |
| 1957 | Ghana, Malaysia |
| 1960 | Nigeria (suspended 1995, readmitted 1999) |
| 1961 | Cyprus, Sierra Leone, Tanzania |
| 1962 | Jamaica, Trinidad and Tobago, Uganda |
| 1963 | Kenya |
| 1964 | Malawi, Malta, Zambia |
| 1965 | The Gambia, Singapore |
| 1966 | Barbados, Botswana, Guyana, Lesotho |
| 1968 | Mauritius, Nauru, Swaziland |
| 1970 | Tonga, Samoa, Fiji (left 1987, rejoined 1997; suspended 2000, readmitted 2001) |
| 1972 | Bangladesh |
| 1973 | The Bahamas |
| 1974 | Grenada |
| 1975 | Papua New Guinea |
| 1976 | Seychelles |
| 1978 | Dominica, Solomon Islands, Tuvalu |
| 1979 | Kiribati, St Lucia, St Vincent and the Grenadines |
| 1980 | Vanuatu, Zimbabwe (suspended 2002) |

| | |
|---|---|
| 1981 | Antigua and Barbuda, Belize |
| 1982 | Maldives |
| 1983 | St Kitts and Nevis |
| 1984 | Brunei Darussalam |
| 1990 | Namibia |
| 1995 | Cameroon, Mozambique[1] |

*The Republic of Ireland resigned from the Commonwealth in 1949.*

[1] *Although Mozambique is a former Portuguese colony it was allowed to join the Commonwealth because of its close relationship with the Commonwealth since its independence.*

### Commonwealth Secretaries-General

**Secretary-General**

| | |
|---|---|
| 1965–75 | Arnold Smith *Canada* |
| 1975–90 | Shridath Ramphal *Guyana* |
| 1990–2000 | Emeka Anyaoku *Nigeria* |
| 2000– | Donald C McKinnon *New Zealand* |

## THE EUROPEAN UNION (EU)

### European Union membership

Member countries are listed by year of entry.

| | |
|---|---|
| 1958 | Belgium, France, Germany, Italy, Luxembourg, The Netherlands |
| 1973 | Denmark, Republic of Ireland, United Kingdom |
| 1981 | Greece |
| 1986 | Portugal, Spain |
| 1995 | Austria, Finland, Sweden |

*Cyprus, Czech Republic, Estonia, Hungary, Latvia, Lithuania, Malta, Poland, Slovakia and Slovenia intend to join the EU in 2004. Bulgaria, Romania and Turkey are candidates for subsequent entry.*

### European Union Commission presidents

The European Commission is an executive body composed of 20 Commissioners from EU member countries led by a president.

**President**

| | |
|---|---|
| 1958–67 | Walter Hallstein *West Germany* |
| 1967–70 | Jean Rey *Belgium* |
| 1970–2 | Franco Maria Malfatti *Italy* |
| 1972–3 | Sicco L Mansholt *The Netherlands* |
| 1973–7 | François-Xavier Ortoli *France* |
| 1977–81 | Roy Jenkins *United Kingdom* |
| 1981–5 | Gaston Thorn *Luxembourg* |
| 1985–95 | Jacques Delors *France* |
| 1995–9 | Jacques Santer *Luxembourg* |
| 1999– | Romano Prodi *Italy* |

*Note: The current Commission's term of office will end on 31 Oct 2004.*

### Bendy Bananas and Cucumber Confusion

The British press loves a good yarn about Brussels bureaucrats apparently destroying the very fabric of British life by regulating, relabelling and prohibiting. And nothing annoys EU officials more than the misrepresentation of their attempts to standardize and simplify across the continent. The bendiness of bananas, the curvature of cucumbers, a proposal to rename chocolate as *vegelate* and plans to refer to fish by their Latin names are all stories that have hit the UK headlines in recent years, only to be vehemently denied by the exasperated Europeans.

## AFRICAN UNION (AU)

The Organization of African Unity (OAU) was established in 1963 and changed its name to the African Union (AU) in 2002. Its stated aim is to promote accelerated socio-economic integration of the continent, leading to greater unity and solidarity between African countries and peoples. It has 52 member states.

Algeria
Angola
Benin
Botswana
Burkina Faso
Burundi
Cameroon
Cape Verde
Central African Republic
Chad
Comoros
Congo
Congo, Democratic Republic of
Côte d'Ivoire
Djibouti
Egypt
Equatorial Guinea
Eritrea
Ethiopia
Gabon
The Gambia
Ghana
Guinea
Kenya
Lesotho
Liberia
Libya
Madagascar
Malawi
Mali
Mauritania
Mauritius
Mozambique
Namibia
Niger
Nigeria
Rwanda
São Tomé and Príncipe
Senegal
Seychelles
Sierra Leone
Somalia
South Africa
The Sudan
Swaziland
Tanzania
Togo
Tunisia
Uganda
Western Sahara
Zambia
Zimbabwe

## ARAB LEAGUE

The League of Arab States, known as the Arab League, was established in 1945 and has 22 members from the Middle East and Africa. It exists primarily to promote political and economic co-operation, and its charter forbids its members from resorting to force against each other. Seven countries originally signed the treaty. Member countries are listed by year of entry.

| | |
|---|---|
| 1945 | Egypt, Iraq, Jordan, Lebanon, Saudi Arabia, Syria, Yemen |
| 1953 | Libya |
| 1956 | The Sudan |
| 1958 | Morocco, Tunisia |
| 1961 | Kuwait |
| 1962 | Algeria |
| 1971 | Bahrain, Oman, Qatar, United Arab Emirates |
| 1973 | Mauritania |
| 1974 | Somalia |
| 1976 | Palestine |
| 1977 | Djibouti |
| 1993 | Comoros |

### *Atlantic Ocean, Arabian Sea*

The Arab League estimates that the Arabic world covers approximately 14.2 million sq km/ 5.5 million sq mi, stretching across two continents from northern Africa's Atlantic coast to the Middle East and Asia, and encompassing a population of approximately 273 million people.

## ASSOCIATION OF SOUTH EAST ASIAN NATIONS (ASEAN)

The Association of South East Asian Nations (ASEAN) comprises ten member nations and was established in 1967. Its stated aims are 'to accelerate economic growth, social progress and cultural development in the region' and 'to promote regional peace and stability'. Five countries originally signed the treaty. Member countries are listed by year of entry.

| | |
|---|---|
| 1967 | Indonesia, Malaysia, Philippines, Singapore, Thailand |
| 1984 | Brunei Darussalam |
| 1995 | Vietnam |
| 1997 | Laos, Myanmar (Burma) |
| 1999 | Cambodia |

## CENTRAL AMERICAN INTEGRATION SYSTEM (SICA)

SICA (the *Sistema de la Integración Centroamericana*, or Central American Integration System) is a trade and customs union among the nations of Central America. It emerged in 1991 from a previous union, the Organization of Central American States (ODECA). SICA is designed to facilitate the eventual economic and political integration of Central America. There are seven current members:

Belize
Costa Rica
El Salvador
Guatemala
Honduras
Nicaragua
Panama

## COMMONWEALTH OF INDEPENDENT STATES (CIS)

The Commonwealth of Independent States (CIS) is a grouping of twelve independent states formed in 1991 from the 15 republics which previously made up the USSR. Each member state has sovereign equality, and in 1993 all states signed an agreement to co-ordinate policies on taxation, customs, labour movement and other aspects of economic activity. Eleven countries originally joined the CIS in 1991; Georgia joined in 1993.

Armenia
Azerbaijan
Belarus
Georgia
Kazakhstan
Kyrgyzstan
Moldova
Russia
Tajikistan
Turkmenistan
Ukraine
Uzbekistan

## GROUP OF EIGHT (G8)

The present Group of Eight (G8) leading industrialized democracies has its origins in an economic summit called in 1975 by President Valéry Giscard d'Estaing of France. The annual meetings of the G8 have a wide remit, dealing with economic, political and social issues on a global level. At other times these and other economically powerful countries have met to discuss matters of mutual interest as the Group of Five (G5), Seven (G7), Ten (G10), etc, always including France, the United Kingdom, Germany, the United States of America and Japan. Six countries attended the original summit. Current member countries are listed by year of entry.

| | |
|---|---|
| 1975 | France, Germany, Italy, Japan, United Kingdom, United States of America |
| 1976 | Canada |
| 1998 | Russia |

## NORTH ATLANTIC TREATY ORGANIZATION (NATO)

The North Atlantic Treaty Organization (NATO) comprises 19 countries from Europe and North America. It was created from the signatories to the North Atlantic Treaty in 1949. Its stated aim is to 'safeguard the freedom and security of its member countries by political and military means'. Twelve countries originally signed the treaty. Member countries are listed by year of entry.

| | |
|---|---|
| 1949 | Belgium, Canada, Denmark, France, Iceland, Italy, Luxembourg, The Netherlands, Norway, Portugal, United Kingdom, United States of America |
| 1952 | Greece, Turkey |
| 1955 | Germany |
| 1982 | Spain |
| 1999 | Czech Republic, Hungary, Poland |

*Bulgaria, Estonia, Latvia, Lithuania, Romania, Slovakia and Slovenia were invited to join NATO in 2002; the process is expected to be completed in 2004.*

## ORGANIZATION OF AMERICAN STATES (OAS)

The Organization of American States (OAS), created in 1948, comprises 35 countries of North and South America and the Caribbean. Its aims are wide-ranging, seeking to promote unity and co-operation on economic, social and political issues. Twenty-one countries originally joined the organization. Member countries are listed by year of entry.

| | |
|---|---|
| 1948 | Argentina, Bolivia, Brazil, Chile, Colombia, Costa Rica, Cuba[1], Dominican Republic, Ecuador, El Salvador, Guatemala, Haiti, Honduras, Mexico, Nicaragua, Panama, Paraguay, Peru, United States of America, Uruguay, Venezuela |
| 1967 | Barbados, Trinidad and Tobago |
| 1969 | Jamaica |
| 1975 | Grenada |
| 1977 | Suriname |
| 1979 | Dominica, St Lucia |
| 1981 | Antigua and Barbuda, St Vincent and the Grenadines |
| 1982 | The Bahamas |
| 1984 | St Kitts and Nevis |
| 1990 | Canada |
| 1991 | Belize, Guyana |

[1] *Since 1962 the current government of Cuba, while remaining a member, has been excluded from participation in the OAS.*

### *Panama and Pan American*

The Organization of American States traces its history back to the Congress of Panama in 1826, which first considered creating an association of states in the Americas. But it wasn't until 1890 that the International Union of American Republics was established, led by a secretariat known as the Commercial Bureau of the American Republics; this became the Pan American Union in 1910 and finally the OAS was created in 1948.

## ORGANIZATION OF PETROLEUM EXPORTING COUNTRIES (OPEC)

The Organization of Petroleum Exporting Countries (OPEC) comprises eleven countries from Africa, Asia, the Middle East and Latin America which are reliant on oil exports as their main source of income. It was formed in 1960 with five founder members. Member countries are listed by year of entry.

| | |
|---|---|
| 1960 | Iran, Iraq, Kuwait, Saudi Arabia, Venezuela |
| 1961 | Qatar |
| 1962 | Indonesia, Libya |
| 1967 | United Arab Emirates |
| 1969 | Algeria |
| 1971 | Nigeria |

### *Black Gold*

The world's thirst for oil shows no signs of abating. OPEC calculates that the total world demand in 2000 was 76 million barrels per day, approximately 40% of which was from OPEC countries. Saudi Arabia is the world's biggest crude oil producer, pumping out almost 7.9 million barrels every day.

## WARSAW PACT

The Warsaw Pact was a military alliance, formed in 1955, comprising the USSR and the Communist states of Eastern Europe (excluding Yugoslavia). It was intended as a counterbalance to the NATO alliance of Western Europe and the United States of America. The Warsaw Pact was dissolved in 1991 after the break-up of the USSR. Its members were:

Albania (seceded 1968)
Bulgaria
Czechoslovakia
East Germany (from 1990 part of united Germany)
Hungary
Poland
Romania
USSR

## GENEVA CONVENTIONS

The four Geneva Conventions and two additional Protocols are a series of international agreements regulating the treatment of victims of war. They deal with such matters as torture, deportation, treatment of women and children, hostage-taking and the use of chemical and biological weapons, and are signed by most states and some non-governmental bodies.

| Convention/ Protocol | Date | Application |
|---|---|---|
| Convention I | 12 Aug 1949 | For the amelioration of the condition of the wounded and sick in armed forces in the field. |
| Convention II | 12 Aug 1949 | For the amelioration of the condition of wounded, sick and shipwrecked members of armed forces at sea. |

| Convention/ Protocol | Date | Application |
|---|---|---|
| Convention III | 12 Aug 1949 | Relative to the treatment of prisoners of war. |
| Convention IV | 12 Aug 1949 | Relative to the protection of civilian persons in time of war. |
| Protocol I | 8 Jun 1977 | Additional to the Geneva Conventions of 12 Aug 1949, and relating to the protection of victims of international armed conflicts. |
| Protocol II | 8 Jun 1977 | Additional to the Geneva Conventions of 12 Aug 1949, and relating to the protection of victims of non-international armed conflicts. |

## NOBEL PEACE PRIZE

**Nobel prizes were established by a bequest in the will of Alfred Nobel (1833–96) to honour 'those who, during the preceding year, shall have conferred the greatest benefit on mankind'. The Nobel peace prize is awarded annually to a person or organization who has 'done the most or the best work for fraternity between nations, for the abolition or reduction of standing armies and for the holding and promotion of peace congresses'; first awarded in 1901.**

| | |
|---|---|
| 1901 | Henri Dunant, Frédéric Passy |
| 1902 | Élie Ducommun, Albert Gobat |
| 1903 | Randal Cremer |
| 1904 | Institute of International Law |
| 1905 | Bertha von Suttner |
| 1906 | Theodore Roosevelt |
| 1907 | Ernesto Teodoro Moneta, Louis Renault |
| 1908 | Klas Pontus Arnoldson, Fredrik Bajer |
| 1909 | Auguste Beernaert, Paul Henri d'Estournelles de Constant |
| 1910 | Permanent International Peace Bureau |
| 1911 | Tobias Asser, Alfred Fried |
| 1912 | Elihu Root |
| 1913 | Henri La Fontaine |
| 1914 | *no award* |
| 1915 | *no award* |
| 1916 | *no award* |
| 1917 | International Committee of the Red Cross |
| 1918 | *no award* |
| 1919 | Woodrow Wilson |
| 1920 | Léon Bourgeois |
| 1921 | Hjalmar Branting, Christian Lange |
| 1922 | Fridtjof Nansen |
| 1923 | *no award* |
| 1924 | *no award* |
| 1925 | Sir Austen Chamberlain, Charles G Dawes |
| 1926 | Aristide Briand, Gustav Stresemann |
| 1927 | Ferdinand Buisson, Ludwig Quidde |
| 1928 | *no award* |
| 1929 | Frank B Kellogg |
| 1930 | Nathan Söderblom |
| 1931 | Jane Addams, Nicholas Murray Butler |
| 1932 | *no award* |
| 1933 | Sir Norman Angell |
| 1934 | Arthur Henderson |
| 1935 | Carl von Ossietzky |
| 1936 | Carlos Saavedra Lamas |
| 1937 | Robert Cecil |
| 1938 | Nansen International Office for Refugees |
| 1939 | *no award* |
| 1940 | *no award* |
| 1941 | *no award* |
| 1942 | *no award* |
| 1943 | *no award* |
| 1944 | International Committee of the Red Cross |
| 1945 | Cordell Hull |
| 1946 | Emily Greene Balch, John R Mott |
| 1947 | Friends Service Council, American Friends Service Committee |
| 1948 | *no award* |
| 1949 | Lord Boyd Orr |
| 1950 | Ralph Bunche |
| 1951 | Léon Jouhaux |
| 1952 | Albert Schweitzer |
| 1953 | George C Marshall |

| | |
|---|---|
| 1954 | Office of the United Nations High Commissioner for Refugees |
| 1955 | *no award* |
| 1956 | *no award* |
| 1957 | Lester Bowles Pearson |
| 1958 | Georges Pire |
| 1959 | Philip Noel-Baker |
| 1960 | Albert Lutuli |
| 1961 | Dag Hammarskjöld |
| 1962 | Linus Pauling |
| 1963 | International Committee of the Red Cross, League of Red Cross Societies |
| 1964 | Martin Luther King |
| 1965 | United Nations Children's Fund |
| 1966 | *no award* |
| 1967 | *no award* |
| 1968 | René Cassin |
| 1969 | International Labour Organization |
| 1970 | Norman Borlaug |
| 1971 | Willy Brandt |
| 1972 | *no award* |
| 1973 | Henry Kissinger, Le Duc Tho |
| 1974 | Seán MacBride, Eisaku Sato |
| 1975 | Andrei Sakharov |
| 1976 | Betty Williams, Mairead Corrigan |
| 1977 | Amnesty International |
| 1978 | Anwar al-Sadat, Menachem Begin |
| 1979 | Mother Teresa |
| 1980 | Adolfo Pérez Esquivel |
| 1981 | Office of the United Nations High Commissioner for Refugees |
| 1982 | Alva Myrdal, Alfonso García Robles |
| 1983 | Lech Walesa |
| 1984 | Desmond Tutu |
| 1985 | International Physicians for the Prevention of Nuclear War |
| 1986 | Elie Wiesel |
| 1987 | Oscar Arias Sánchez |
| 1988 | United Nations Peacekeeping Forces |
| 1989 | The 14th Dalai Lama |
| 1990 | Mikhail Gorbachev |
| 1991 | Aung San Suu Kyi |
| 1992 | Rigoberta Menchú Tum |
| 1993 | Nelson Mandela, F W de Klerk |
| 1994 | Yasser Arafat, Shimon Peres, Yitzhak Rabin |
| 1995 | Joseph Rotblat, Pugwash Conferences on Science and World Affairs |
| 1996 | Carlos Filipe Ximenes Belo, José Ramos-Horta |
| 1997 | International Campaign to Ban Landmines, Jody Williams |
| 1998 | John Hume, David Trimble |
| 1999 | Médecins Sans Frontières |
| 2000 | Kim Dae-jung |
| 2001 | United Nations, Kofi Annan |
| 2002 | Jimmy Carter |
| 2003 | Shirin Ebadi |

### *Winning Ways*

The Office of the United Nations High Commissioner for Refugees has won the Nobel peace prize twice, in 1954 and 1981. But the organization with the most Nobel peace prizes gathering dust on the mantelpiece is the International Committee of the Red Cross, which was first honoured in 1917 and subsequently picked up the award in 1944 and 1963.

## RANKS OF THE POLICE

**UK-wide police service**

Chief Constable
Deputy Chief Constable
Assistant Chief Constable
Chief Superintendent
Superintendent
Chief Inspector
Inspector
Sergeant
Constable

**Metropolitan Police**

Commissioner
Deputy Commissioner
Assistant Commissioner
Deputy Assistant Commissioner
Commander
Chief Superintendent
Superintendent
Chief Inspector
Inspector
Sergeant
Constable

## PRECEDENCE OF LAW COURTS

Courts are listed from highest to lowest. The European Court of Justice is the recourse for cases concerning European Community law in the UK.

### Criminal law

**England and Wales**
House of Lords
Court of Appeal
Crown Court
Magistrates' Court

**Scotland**
High Court of Justiciary
Sheriff's Court
District Court

**Northern Ireland**
House of Lords
Northern Ireland Court of Appeal
Crown Court
Magistrates' Court

### Civil law

**England and Wales**
House of Lords
Court of Appeal
High Court of Justice
County Court
Magistrates' Court

**Scotland**
House of Lords
Court of Session
Sheriff's Principal Court
Sheriff's Court

**Northern Ireland**
House of Lords
Northern Ireland Court of Appeal
High Court Of Justice
County Court
Magistrates' Court

## MILITARY RANKS

### UK officer ranks

| Army | Air Force | Navy |
|---|---|---|
| Field Marshal | Marshal of the Royal Air Force | Admiral of the Fleet |
| General | Air Chief Marshal | Admiral |
| Lieutenant-General | Air Marshal | Vice-Admiral |
| Major-General | Air Vice-Marshal | Rear-Admiral |
| Brigadier | Air Commodore | Commodore Admiral |
| Colonel | Group Captain | Captain RN |
| Lieutenant-Colonel | Wing Commander | Commander |
| Major | Squadron Leader | Lieutenant Commander |
| Captain | Flight Lieutenant | Lieutenant |
| Lieutenant | Flying Officer | Sub-Lieutenant |
| Second-Lieutenant | Pilot Officer | Midshipman |

### USA officer ranks

| Army | Air Force | Navy |
|---|---|---|
| General of the Army | General of the Air Force | Fleet Admiral |
| General | General | Admiral |
| Lieutenant General | Lieutenant General | Vice Admiral |
| Major General | Major General | Rear Admiral (Upper Half) |
| Brigadier General | Brigadier General | Rear Admiral (Lower Half) |
| Colonel | Colonel | Captain |
| Lieutenant Colonel | Lieutenant Colonel | Commander |
| Major | Major | Lieutenant Commander |
| Captain | Captain | Lieutenant |
| First Lieutenant | First Lieutenant | Lieutenant Junior Grade |
| Second Lieutenant | Second Lieutenant | Ensign |

## PARLIAMENT (UK)

All information is for the year 2003–4 unless otherwise stated. For British prime ministers, monarchs and first ministers of devolved regional governments see **United Kingdom** in **Countries A–Z** under **Human Geography**.

| | |
|---|---|
| Number of MPs (House of Commons) | 659 |
| Number of peers (House of Lords) | 689 (May 2003) |
| MP's annual parliamentary salary | £56 358 |
| Prime minister's annual salary | £175 414 (inclusive of MP's salary) |
| Days that the House of Commons sits | 155 (annual average) |
| Days that the House of Lords sits | 148 (annual average) |
| Father of the House | A traditional title given to the MP who has the 'longest unbroken service in the Commons'. Tam Dalyell MP became the Father of the House in Jun 2001; he entered Parliament in 1962. |
| Speaker | The person who presides over the debates in the House of Commons. The Rt Hon Michael Martin MP became the 156th Speaker in Oct 2000. |
| Women MPs | 119 (2003) |
| Maximum length of a Parliament | 5 years, as decreed by the Parliament Act (1911); this term has only been extended twice, during World War I and World War II. |
| Palace of Westminster | The current Palace of Westminster dates to the mid-19c; it was built 1840–70 after the previous Palace was destroyed by a fire in 1834. |
| Big Ben | Big Ben weighs 13.8 tonnes/13.6 tons. It is believed that the bell was named after one Sir Benjamin Hall, the Commissioner of Works at the Houses of Parliament (1855–8), whose name is engraved on the bell. The famous clock tower that houses Big Ben is 96.3m/316ft tall. |
| Voting | Women aged 30 years and over were given the vote in 1918. In 1928 women aged 21 and over were allowed to vote, giving them equality with men. The voting age was reduced to 18 in 1969. |

### *Boozy Budgets*

According to an old House of Commons tradition, the Chancellor of the Exchequer is 'permitted to fortify himself with the liquid refreshment of his choice' (in the words of the House of Commons Information Office) while delivering the budget speech, although alcohol is not usually drunk in the House. Tipples of choice are reputed to have included brandy and water (Disraeli), sherry mixed with beaten egg (Gladstone), gin and tonic (Geoffrey Howe), neat whisky (Kenneth Clarke) and, simply, mineral water (Gordon Brown). Although the latter's speeches have hovered around the one hour mark, some of his predecessors must surely have required fortification: Gladstone holds the record for the longest continuous budget speech, having orated for 4 hours 45 minutes in Apr 1853.

## US CONSTITUTIONAL AMENDMENTS

The US Constitution was framed in 1787 and came into effect in 1789. Amendments to the Constitution were later proposed, and the following is a list of those that have been ratified. The first ten Amendments collectively are known as the Bill of Rights.

| Amendment | Date | Main areas of application |
|---|---|---|
| I | 1791 | Freedom of religion, speech, the press, assembly and petition |
| II | 1791 | Right to bear arms |
| III | 1791 | Restrictions on the quartering of troops |
| IV | 1791 | Restrictions on search and seizure |
| V | 1791 | Grand jury trial, double jeopardy, self-incrimination, due process |
| VI | 1791 | Criminal prosecutions, jury trial, right to confront and to counsel |
| VII | 1791 | Common law suits, jury trial |
| VIII | 1791 | Excess bail or fines, cruel and unusual punishment |
| IX | 1791 | Non-enumerated rights |
| X | 1791 | Rights reserved to states |
| XI | 1795 | Suits against a state |
| XII | 1804 | Election of the president and vice-president |
| XIII | 1865 | Abolition of slavery |
| XIV | 1868 | Privileges and immunities, due process, equal protection, apportionment of representatives, Civil War disqualification and debt |
| XV | 1870 | Rights not to be denied on account of race |
| XVI | 1913 | Income tax |
| XVII | 1913 | Election of senators |
| XVIII | 1919 | Prohibition |
| XIX | 1920 | Women's right to vote |
| XX | 1933 | Presidential term and succession |
| XXI | 1933 | Repeal of prohibition |
| XXII | 1951 | Two term limit on president |
| XXIII | 1961 | Presidential voting powers |
| XXIV | 1964 | Poll tax |
| XXV | 1967 | Presidential succession |
| XXVI | 1971 | Right to vote at age 18 |
| XXVII | 1992 | Compensation of members of Congress |

### *Constitutional Prohibition*

The only constitutional amendment ever to have been repealed is the 18th, relating to Prohibition, which was ratified in Jan 1919. It stated that 'after one year ... the manufacture, sale, or transportation of intoxicating liquors within, the importation thereof into, or the exportation thereof from the United States ... for beverage purposes is hereby prohibited'. It was repealed by the 21st amendment, ratified in Dec 1933, but both remain in the Constitution.

# ANCIENT GREECE AND ROME

## GREEK GODS

| | |
|---|---|
| **Adonis** | God of vegetation and rebirth |
| **Aeolus** | God of the winds |
| **Alphito** | Barley goddess of Argos |
| **Aphrodite** | Goddess of love and beauty |
| **Apollo** | God of prophecy, music, youth, archery and healing |
| **Ares** | God of war |
| **Arethusa** | Goddess of springs and fountains |
| **Artemis** | Goddess of fertility, chastity and hunting |
| **Asclepius** | God of healing |
| **Athene** | Goddess of prudence and wise council; protectress of Athens |
| **Atlas** | A Titan who bears up the Earth |
| **Attis** | God of vegetation |
| **Boreas** | God of the north wind |
| **Cronus** | Father of Zeus |
| **Cybele** | Goddess of the earth |
| **Demeter** | Goddess of the harvest |
| **Dionysus** | God of wine, vegetation and ecstasy |
| **Eos** | Goddess of the dawn |
| **Eros** | God of love |
| **Gaia** | Goddess of the earth |
| **Ganymede** | God of rain |
| **Hades** | God of the underworld |
| **Hebe** | Goddess of youth |
| **Hecate** | Goddess of the moon |
| **Helios** | God of the sun |
| **Hephaestus** | God of fire |
| **Hera** | Goddess of marriage and childbirth; queen of heaven |
| **Hermes** | Messenger of the gods |
| **Hestia** | Goddess of the hearth |
| **Hypnos** | God of sleep |
| **Iris** | Goddess of the rainbow |
| **Morpheus** | God of dreams |
| **Nemesis** | God of destiny |
| **Nereus** | A sea god |
| **Nike** | Goddess of victory |
| **Oceanus** | God of the river Oceanus |
| **Pan** | God of male sexuality and of herds |
| **Persephone** | Goddess of the underworld and of corn |
| **Poseidon** | God of the sea |
| **Rhea** | The original mother goddess; wife of Cronus |
| **Selene** | Goddess of the moon |
| **Thanatos** | God of death |
| **Zeus** | Overlord of the Olympian gods and goddesses; god of the sky and all its properties |

**Principal Greek gods**

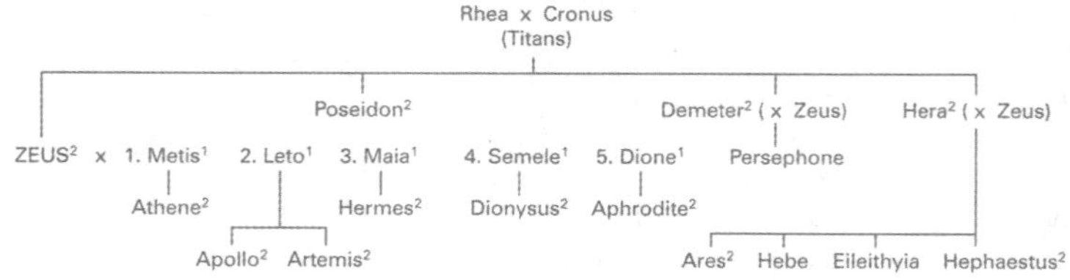


[1] A consort of Zeus.
[2] One of the twelve Olympians in the 'central group' of gods on the Parthenon frieze.

## *Cruel Immortality*

Eos, the Greek goddess of the dawn, abducted several mortal men to be her lovers. One of these handsome young men was Tithonus, who was granted immortality by Zeus at Eos's request. However, she forgot to ask for perpetual youth, so Tithonus became immensely old and decrepit, and finally Eos shut him away. Eventually the gods took pity on his plight and changed him into a cicada, a grasshopper-like insect. The myth inspired the poem *Tithonus* by Tennyson.

## ROMAN GODS

| | |
|---|---|
| **Apollo** | God of the sun |
| **Bacchus** | God of wine and ecstasy |
| **Bellona** | Goddess of war |
| **Ceres** | Goddess of corn |
| **Consus** | God of seed sowing |
| **Cupid** | God of love |
| **Diana** | Goddess of fertility and hunting |
| **Egreria** | Goddess of fountains and childbirth |
| **Epona** | Goddess of horses |
| **Fauna** | Goddess of fertility |
| **Faunus** | God of crops and herbs |
| **Feronia** | Goddess of spring flowers |
| **Fides** | God of honesty |
| **Flora** | Goddess of fruitfulness and flowers |
| **Fortuna** | Goddess of chance and fate |
| **Genius** | Protective god of individuals, groups and the state |
| **Janus** | God of entrances, travel and the dawn |
| **Juno** | Goddess of marriage, childbirth and light |
| **Jupiter** | God of the sky and its attributes (Sun, Moon, thunder, rain, etc) |
| **Lares** | Gods of the house |
| **Liber Pater** | God of agricultural and human fertility |
| **Libitina** | Goddess of funeral rites |
| **Luna** | Goddess of the moon |
| **Maia** | Goddess of fertility |
| **Mars** | God of war |
| **Mercury** | Messenger of the gods; also god of merchants |
| **Minerva** | Goddess of war, craftsmen, education and the arts |
| **Mithras** | Sun god; also god of regeneration |
| **Neptune** | God of the sea |
| **Ops** | Goddess of the harvest |
| **Orcus** | God of death |
| **Pales** | Goddess of flocks |
| **Penates** | Gods of food and drink |
| **Picus** | God of woods |
| **Pluto** | God of the underworld |
| **Pomona** | Goddess of fruit trees |
| **Portunus** | God of husbands |
| **Proserpina** | Goddess of the underworld |
| **Rumina** | Goddess of nursing mothers |
| **Saturn** | God of fertility and agriculture |
| **Silvanus** | God of trees and forests |
| **Venus** | Goddess of spring, gardens and love |
| **Vertumnus** | God of fertility |
| **Vesta** | Goddess of the hearth |
| **Victoria** | Goddess of victory |
| **Vulcan** | God of fire |

**Principal Roman gods**

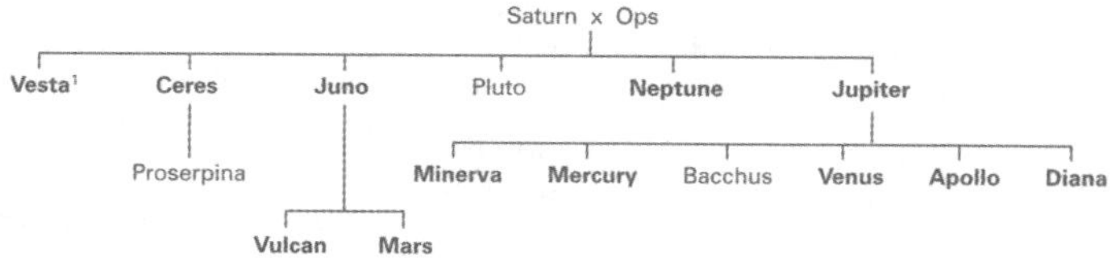


The twelve major gods of Olympus are shown in **bold** type.
[1] In some accounts, Vesta is supplanted by Bacchus.

## ROMAN EMPERORS

Dates overlap where there are periods of joint rule (eg Marcus Aurelius and Lucius Verus) and where the government of the empire divides between east and west. All dates are AD unless otherwise indicated.

| Regnal dates | Name |
|---|---|
| 27BC–AD14 | Augustus (Caesar Augustus) |
| 14–37 | Tiberius |
| 37–41 | Caligula (Gaius Caesar) |
| 41–54 | Claudius |
| 54–68 | Nero |
| 68–69 | Galba |

## ROMAN EMPERORS

| Regnal dates | Name | Regnal dates | Name |
|---|---|---|---|
| 69 | Otho | 282–283 | Carus |
| 69 | Vitellius | 283–285 | Carinus |
| 69–79 | Vespasian | 283–284 | Numerian |
| 79–81 | Titus | 284–305 | Diocletian (East) |
| 81–96 | Domitian | 286–305 | Maximian (West) |
| 96–98 | Nerva | 305–311 | Galerius (East) |
| 98–117 | Trajan | 305–306 | Constantius I |
| 117–138 | Hadrian | 306–307 | Severus (West) |
| 138–161 | Antoninus Pius | 306–312 | Maxentius (West) |
| 161–180 | Marcus Aurelius | 306–337 | Constantine I |
| 161–169 | Lucius Verus | 308–324 | Licinius (East) |
| 176–192 | Commodus | 337–340 | Constantine II |
| 193 | Pertinax | 337–350 | Constans I |
| 193 | Didius Julianus | 337–361 | Constantius II |
| 193–211 | Septemius Severus | 350–351 | Magnentius |
| 198–217 | Caracalla | 360–363 | Julian |
| 209–212 | Geta | 364–375 | Valentinian I (West) |
| 217–218 | Macrinus | 364–378 | Valens (East) |
| 218–222 | Elagabalus | 365–366 | Procopius (East) |
| 222–235 | Alexander Severus | 375–383 | Gratian (West) |
| 235–238 | Maximin | 375–392 | Valentinian II (West) |
| 238 | Gordian I | 379–395 | Theodosius I |
| 238 | Gordian II | 395–408 | Arcadius (East) |
| 238 | Maximus | 395–423 | Honorius (West) |
| 238 | Balbinus | 408–450 | Theodosius II (East) |
| 238–244 | Gordian III | 421–423 | Constantius III (West) |
| 244–249 | Philip | 423–455 | Valentinian III (West) |
| 249–251 | Decius | 450–457 | Marcian (East) |
| 251 | Hostilian | 455 | Petronius Maximus (West) |
| 251–253 | Gallus | 455–456 | Avitus (West) |
| 253 | Aemilian | 457–474 | Leo I (East) |
| 253–260 | Valerian | 457–461 | Majorian (West) |
| 253–268 | Gallienus | 461–467 | Libius Severus (West) |
| 268–269 | Claudius II (the Goth) | 467–472 | Anthemius (West) |
| 269–270 | Quintillus | 472–473 | Olybrius (West) |
| 270–275 | Aurelian | 474–480 | Julius Nepos (West) |
| 275–276 | Tacitus | 474 | Leo II (East) |
| 276 | Florian | 474–491 | Zeno (East) |
| 276–282 | Probus | 475–476 | Romulus Augustus (West) |

### *Fiddling While Rome Burned*

Nero, the Roman emperor from AD54–68, lived a wild and violent life. His reign was infamous for its debauchery, extravagance and tyranny. He caused his stepbrother to be poisoned, murdered his mother and his first wife and subsequently murdered his second wife in a fit of passion. He then proposed marriage to his murdered stepbrother's daughter, had her executed when she refused, and finally married a third wife after murdering her husband. Nero was also said to have been responsible for the fire which destroyed two-thirds of Rome in Jul AD64, but this is doubtful, as is the story that he admired the spectacle from a distance while reciting his poetry and playing his lyre. He finally met his end in AD68, when the army and guards rose against him; he fled Rome and committed suicide.

## ROMAN KINGS

According to Roman literary tradition, Rome was founded by Romulus.

| | | | |
|---|---|---|---|
| 753–715BC | Romulus | 616–578BC | Tarquinius Priscus |
| 715–673BC | Numa Pompilius | 578–534BC | Servius Tullius |
| 673–642BC | Tullus Hostilius | 534–509BC | Tarquinius Superbus |
| 642–616BC | Ancus Marcius | | |

## SEVEN WONDERS OF THE WORLD

Originally compiled by Antipater of Sidon, a Greek poet, c.100BC. Modern locations are shown in italics.

| | |
|---|---|
| **Pyramids of Egypt** *Egypt* | Oldest and only surviving 'wonder'. Built c.2000BC as royal tombs, about 80 are still standing. The largest, the Great Pyramid of Cheops, at el-Gizeh, is approximately 146m/482ft high, covering 5.3 hectares/13 acres at the base. |
| **Hanging Gardens of Babylon** *Iraq* | Terraced gardens adjoining Nebuchadnezzar's palace, said to rise 23–91m/75–300ft. Supposedly built by the king c.600BC to please his wife, a princess from the mountains, they are also associated with the Assyrian Queen Semiramis. |
| **Statue of Zeus at Olympia** *Greece* | Carved by Phidias, the 12m/40ft statue marked the site of the original Olympic Games c.400BC. It was constructed of ivory and gold, and showed Zeus (Jupiter) on his throne. |
| **Temple of Artemis (Diana) at Ephesus** *Turkey* | Constructed of Parian marble and more than 122m/400ft long with over 100 columns 18m/60ft high, it was begun c.350BC and took some 120 years to build. Destroyed by the Goths in AD262. |
| **Mausoleum at Halicarnassus** *Turkey* | Erected by Queen Artemisia in memory of her husband King Mausolus of Caria (in Asia Minor), who died 353BC. It stood 43m/140ft high. All that remains are a few pieces in the British Museum. |
| **Colossus of Rhodes** *Greece* | Gigantic bronze statue of sun god Helios (or Apollo); stood about 36m/117ft high, dominating the harbour entrance at Rhodes. The sculptor Chares supposedly laboured for twelve years before he completed it in 280BC. It was destroyed by an earthquake in 224BC. |
| **Pharos of Alexandria** *Egypt* | Marble lighthouse and watchtower built c.270BC on the island of Pharos in Alexandria's harbour. Possibly standing 122m/400ft high, it was destroyed by an earthquake in 1375. |

## SEVEN HILLS OF ROME

The ancient city of Rome was built around seven hills.

| | | |
|---|---|---|
| **Aventine** | **Cælian** | **Capitoline** |
| **Esquiline** | **Quirinal** *or* **Colline** | |
| **Palatine** | **Viminal** | |

### *Language Legacy*

The monument to King Mausolus at Halicarnassus was destroyed centuries ago, but his name still lives on in the English word *mausoleum*, a magnificent tomb or monument.

## FURIES

Three Greek goddesses, inhabitants of hell who were responsible for punishing bloody crimes; represented as winged spirits with long hair entwined with snakes, carrying whips and torches; they tortured their victims and made them mad. Also known as *Erinyes*.

**Alecto** **Megara** **Tisiphone**

## FATES

Three Greek goddesses, daughters of Zeus; the first spun a thread which signified birth, the second unravelled the thread, symbolizing the unravelling of life, and the third cut the thread, signifying death. Also known as *Moerae*.

**Atropos** **Clotho** **Lachesis**

## THREE GRACES

In Greek mythology, three daughters of Zeus and Hera; embodied beauty and social accomplishments.

**Aglaia** **Euphrosyne** **Thalia**

## TWELVE LABOURS OF HERCULES

Hercules, also known as Heracles, was a Greek hero famous for his great strength. The son of Zeus and Alcmene, he demonstrated his strength from birth, choking the serpents sent by the jealous Hera, Zeus's wife. He undertook the twelve famous labours for Eurystheus of Tiryns.

**To kill and flay the Nemean lion**

**To kill the monster Hydra**

**To capture the Arcadian stag**

**To destroy the Erymanthian boar**

**To clean the stables of Augeas, King of Elis, in a day**

**To destroy the man-eating birds of the Stymphalian marshes**

**To capture the Cretan bull**

**To catch the savage horses of the Thracian king Diomedes**

**To obtain the golden girdle of the Amazonian queen Hippolyta**

**To steal the oxen of the giant Geryon**

**To fetch the golden apples of the Hesperides**

**To capture Cerberus, the three-headed dog of Hades, the underworld**

## MUSES

Nine Greek goddesses, daughters of Zeus, each with the vocation to promote an area of the arts; they favoured communication, delighted the gods and inspired poets.

**Calliope**
*epic poetry*

**Erato**
*lyric poetry and hymns*

**Melpomene**
*tragedy*

**Terpsichore**
*dance and lyric poetry*

**Clio**
*history and lyre-playing*

**Euterpe**
*flute-playing*

**Polyhymnia**
*dance, mime and acting*

**Thalia**
*comedy and idyllic poetry*

**Urania**
*astronomy*

## SEVEN AGAINST THEBES

Seven Greek champions who attacked Thebes to deprive Eteocles of his kingship; defeated by another seven champions at the seven gates of Thebes; all were killed in battle, except for Amphiarus, whom the earth swallowed alive, and Adrastus, who escaped.

**Adrastus** *or* **Eteoklos** **Amphiarus** **Capaneus**

**Hippomedon** **Parthenopaeus**

**Polynices** **Tydeus**

# RELIGIONS, BELIEFS AND FOLKLORE

For Greek and Roman gods see **Ancient Greece and Rome**.

## NORSE GODS

| | |
|---|---|
| **Aegir** | God of the sea |
| **Aesir** | Race of warlike gods |
| **Alcis** | Twin gods of the sky |
| **Balder** | Odin's son; favourite of the gods |
| **Bor** | Father of Odin |
| **Bragi** | God of poetry |
| **Fafnir** | Dragon god |
| **Fjorgynn** | Mother of Thor |
| **Frey** | God of fertility |
| **Freyja** | Goddess of libido |
| **Frigg** | Goddess of fertility; wife of Odin |
| **Gefion** | Goddess who received virgins after death |
| **Heimdall** | Guardian of the bridge Bifrost |
| **Hel** | Goddess of death; Queen of Niflheim, the land of mists |
| **Hermod** | Son of Odin |
| **Hoder** | Blind god who killed Balder |
| **Hoenir** | Companion to Odin and Loki |
| **Idunn** | Guardian goddess of the golden apples of youth |
| **Kvasir** | God of wise utterances |
| **Logi** | Fire god |
| **Loki** | God of mischief |
| **Mimir** | God of wisdom |
| **Nanna** | Goddess wife of Balder |
| **Nehallenia** | Goddess of plenty |
| **Nerthus** | Goddess of earth |
| **Njord** | God of ships and the sea |
| **Norns** | Goddesses of destiny |
| **Odin, Woden, Wotan** | Chief of the Aesir family of gods, the 'father' god; the god of battle, death, inspiration |
| **Otr** | Otter god |
| **Ran** | Goddess of the sea |
| **Sif** | Goddess wife of Thor |
| **Sigyn** | Goddess wife of Loki |
| **Thor, Donar** | God of thunder and sky; good crops |
| **Tyr** | God of battle |
| **Ull** | Stepson of Thor, an enchanter |
| **Valkyries** | Female helpers of the gods of war |
| **Vanir** | Race of benevolent gods |
| **Vidar** | Slayer of the wolf, Fenrir |
| **Weland, Volundr** | Craftsman god |

### World Tree

In Norse mythology the World Tree, a giant ash known as *Yggdrasil*, supported the sky, held the different realms of gods and men in its branches and had its roots in the Underworld. Odin created *Asgard*, the home of the gods, in the upper branches of the World Tree. Asgard was reached from earth by the rainbow bridge *Bifrost*, guarded by Heimdall, the watchman of the gods.

## EGYPTIAN GODS

| | |
|---|---|
| **Amun-Re** | Universal god |
| **Anubis** | God of funerals |
| **Apis** | God of fertility |
| **Aten** | Unique god |
| **Geb** | God of the earth |
| **Hathor** | Goddess of love |
| **Horus** | God of light |
| **Isis** | Goddess of magic |
| **Khnum** | Goddess of creation |
| **Khonsou** | Son of Amun-Re |
| **Maat** | Goddess of order |
| **Nephthys** | Goddess of funerals |
| **Nut** | God of the sky |
| **Osiris** | God of vegetation |
| **Ptah** | God of creation |
| **Re, Ra** | Sun god (later Amun-Re) |
| **Sekhmet** | Goddess of might |
| **Seth** | God of evil |
| **Thoth** | Supreme scribe |

### Gods and Beasts

The gods of Ancient Egypt were often portrayed with human bodies but the heads of animals, for example Anubis (the head of a jackal), Hathor (cow), Horus (falcon), Sekhmet (lioness), and Thoth (ibis or baboon). Re was depicted as a falcon with the Sun's disc on his head during the day, while at night he appeared as a ram-headed god who sailed through the Underworld.

## CELTIC GODS

Selected Celtic gods are listed below. Many were known by different names by different Celtic peoples; where names differ, the British spelling is given.

| | |
|---|---|
| **Anna** | Mother goddess of fecundity and plenty |
| **Arianrhod** | Earth goddess |
| **Badhbh** | Goddess of war |
| **Boann** | River goddess |
| **Bel, Beli, Belinus** | God of the sun, light and fire |
| **Blodeuwedd** | Goddess of love and generosity |
| **Brigantia, Brighid** | Goddess of livestock, agriculture, midwifery, poetry and crafts |
| **Cernunnos** | Ruler of all the animals and lord of the Underworld |
| **Cerridwen** | Goddess of the Underworld |
| **Cliodna** | Goddess of peace and beauty |
| **Dea Arduinna** | Goddess of wild animals |
| **Don** | The chief of the Irish gods; the lord of the Otherworld |
| **Dylan** | God of the sea |
| **Édain, Étain** | Goddess of the Otherworld |
| **Epona** | Goddess of horses |
| **Flidhais** | Goddess of wild animals |
| **Gofannon** | God of smiths and of strength |
| **Grannos** | God of healing |
| **Llyr, Lir** | God of the sea |
| **Lleu** | Hero god, deity of crafts, commerce and (in some traditions) youth and games |
| **Macha** | Goddess of horses |
| **Mabon** | God of youth, healing, music and hunting |
| **Manawydan, Manawyddan** | God of wisdom and patience |
| **Matres, Matronae** | Trio of goddesses associated with Earth, fecundity and motherhood |
| **Medhbh** | Warrior-goddess representing sexuality |
| **Merlin** | Guardian god of the land |
| **Modron** | Mother goddess |
| **Morríghan** | Goddess of war |
| **Nemhain** | Goddess of war |
| **Ogmia** | God of strength and eloquence |
| **Rhiannon** | Goddess of horses, birds and the moon, known as the Great Queen |
| **Silvanus, Sucellus** | God of the Underworld |
| **Taran** | God of thunder and war |

### *Talking Heads*

In Celtic mythology Bran was a gigantic god who featured in the Welsh tales *The Mabinogion* (14c) as King of Britain. He died in Ireland, and his severed head provided his followers with advice and entertainment for 80 years. It was finally buried at the site of the Tower of London, from where it protected Britain from invaders until it was eventually dug up.

## BAHA'I

| | |
|---|---|
| **Founded** | 1863 |
| **Founder** | Mirza Husayn Ali (1817–92) |
| **Sacred texts** | Most Holy Book, The Seven Valleys, The Hidden Words, The Bayan. |
| **Place of worship** | Shrine, temple |
| **Beliefs** | The oneness of God, the unity of all faiths, the inevitable unification of humankind, universal education and obedience to government. |
| **Organization** | There is a network of elected local and national level bodies, and an elected international governing body. There is little formal ritual. |
| **Divisions** | No major divisions. |

## BUDDHISM

| | |
|---|---|
| **Founded** | c.500BC |
| **Founder** | Prince Siddhartha Gautama (c.563–c.483BC) |
| **Sacred texts** | The Pali Canon or Tripitaka. Other texts include the Mahayana Sutras, the Milindapanha (Questions of Milinda) and the Bardo Thodol (Tibetan Book of the Dead). |
| **Place of worship** | Temple |
| **Beliefs** | The Four Noble Truths concerning suffering and freedom from it; the Eightfold Path leading to Nirvana; the law of Karma. |
| **Organization** | Monastic system; numerous festivals and ceremonies for the laity. |
| **Divisions** | Two main historical divisions: Theravada and Mahayana. Other schools include Zen, Lamaism, Tendai, Nichiren and Soka Gakkai. |

### The Enlightened One

Buddha was born in c.563BC as Prince Siddhartha Gautama, the son of the rajah in a ruling tribe in Nepal. When he was about 30 he left the luxuries of the court, his beautiful wife and all earthly ambitions in exchange for the life of an ascetic; after six years of extreme self-mortification he saw in the contemplative life the perfect way to self-enlightenment. According to tradition, he achieved enlightenment when sitting beneath a banyan tree near Buddh Gaya in Bihar. For the next 40 years he taught, gaining many disciples and followers. He died aged about 80 in c.483BC.

## DALAI LAMAS

**Dalai Lama is the title given to the spiritual and political leader of Tibetan Buddhists. Each successive Dalai Lama is held to be a reincarnation of the previous one, and is also regarded as a manifestation of the Bodhisattva Avalokiteshavara, the Buddha of Compassion.**

| | |
|---|---|
| 1391–1475 | Gedun Truppa |
| 1475–1542 | Gedun Gyatso |
| 1543–88 | Sonam Gyatso |
| 1589–17 | Yonten Gyatso |
| 1617–82 | Ngawang Lobzang Gyatso |
| 1683–1706 | Tsang-yang Gyatso |
| 1708–57 | Kezang Gyatso |
| 1758–1804 | Jampel Gyatso |
| 1806–15 | Luntok Gyatso |
| 1816–37 | Tshultrim Gyatso |
| 1838–56 | Khedrup Gyatso |
| 1856–75 | Trinle Gyatso |
| 1876–1933 | Thupten Gyatso |
| 1935– | Tenzin Gyatso |

### Ocean-like Guru

The name *Dalai Lama* comes from the Mongolian word *dalai*, meaning ocean, and the Tibetan word *lama*, high priest, and is sometimes translated as 'ocean-like guru' or 'ocean of wisdom'. The Panchen Lama, the Tibetan religious leader second in importance to the Dalai Lama, is named from the Tibetan *pandita chen-po*, meaning 'great scholar'.

## FOUR NOBLE TRUTHS

The Four Noble Truths are a summary of the central teachings of Buddha.

Suffering is always present in life.
The origin of suffering is desire.
By ceasing to desire one ceases to suffer.
The Eightfold Path is the way of achieving release from desire and suffering.

## EIGHTFOLD PATH

The fourth of Buddha's Four Noble Truths, prescribing the way to enlightenment.

| | |
|---|---|
| Right views | Right livelihood |
| Right thoughts | Right effort |
| Right speech | Right mindfulness |
| Right action | Right concentration |

## CHRISTIANITY

| | | | |
|---|---|---|---|
| **Founded** | 1c AD | **Founder** | Jesus Christ, 'the Son of God' (c.4BC–c.30AD) |

**Sacred texts** The Bible consisting of the Old and New Testaments.

*Old Testament:* Genesis, Exodus, Leviticus, Numbers, Deuteronomy, Joshua, Judges, Ruth, 1 Samuel, 2 Samuel, 1 Kings, 2 Kings, 1 Chronicles, 2 Chronicles, Ezra, Nehemiah, Esther, Job, Psalms, Proverbs, Ecclesiastes, Song of Solomon, Isaiah, Jeremiah, Lamentations, Ezekiel, Daniel, Hosea, Joel, Amos, Obadiah, Jonah, Micah, Nahum, Habakkuk, Zephaniah, Haggai, Zechariah, Malachi.

*New Testament:* Matthew, Mark, Luke, John, Acts of the Apostles, Romans, 1 Corinthians, 2 Corinthians, Galatians, Ephesians, Philippians, Colossians, 1 Thessalonians, 2 Thessalonians, 1 Timothy, 2 Timothy, Titus, Philemon, Hebrews, James, 1 Peter, 2 Peter, 1 John, 2 John, 3 John, Jude, Revelation. Apocrypha (Revised standard version 1957): 1 Esdras, 2 Esdras, Tobit, Judith, Additions to Esther, Wisdom of Solomon, Ecclesiasticus, Epistle of Jeremiah, Baruch, Prayer of Azariah and the Song of the Three Young Men, (History of) Susanna, Bel and the Dragon, Prayer of Manasseh, 1 Maccabees, 2 Maccabees. (The Authorized version incorporates Jeremiah into Baruch; The prayer of Azariah is simply called the Song of the Three Holy Children. The Roman Catholic Church includes Tobit, Judith, all of Esther, Maccabees 1 and 2, Wisdom of Solomon, Ecclesiasticus and Baruch in its canon.)

**Place of worship** Cathedral, chapel, church

**Beliefs** Monotheistic: centred on the life and works of Jesus of Nazareth. Christians believe that Jesus was crucified and resurrected from the dead.

**Organization** Various priestly hierarchies, often involving bishops and lesser clergy, ultimately deriving from the traditions of the Apostles and their successors.

**Divisions** Major divisions are the Orthodox or Eastern Church, the Roman Catholic Church, acknowledging the Bishop of Rome as head, and the Protestant Churches stemming from the split with the Roman Church in the 16c.

# POPES

Antipopes (who claimed to be pope in opposition to those canonically chosen) are given in square brackets. All dates listed are AD.

| | |
|---|---|
| until c.64 | Peter |
| c.64–c.76 | Linus |
| c.76–c.90 | Anacletus |
| c.90–c.99 | Clement I |
| c.99–c.105 | Evaristus |
| c.105–c.117 | Alexander I |
| c.117–c.127 | Sixtus I |
| c.127–c.137 | Telesphorus |
| c.137–c.140 | Hyginus |
| c.140–c.154 | Pius I |
| c.154–c.166 | Anicetus |
| c.166–c.175 | Soter |
| 175–89 | Eleutherius |
| 189–98 | Victor I |
| 198–217 | Zephyrinus |
| 217–22 | Callistus I |
| [217–c.235 | Hippolytus] |
| 222–30 | Urban I |
| 230–5 | Pontian |
| 235–6 | Anterus |
| 236–50 | Fabian |
| 251–3 | Cornelius |
| [251–c.258 | Novatian] |
| 253–4 | Lucius I |
| 254–7 | Stephen I |
| 257–8 | Sixtus II |
| 259–68 | Dionysius |
| 269–74 | Felix I |
| 275–83 | Eutychianus |
| 283–96 | Caius |
| 296–304 | Marcellinus |
| 304–8 | *interregnum* |
| 308–9 | Marcellus I |
| 310 | Eusebius |
| 311–14 | Miltiades |
| 314–35 | Sylvester I |
| 336 | Mark |
| 337–52 | Julius I |
| 352–66 | Liberius |
| [355–65 | Felix II] |
| 366–84 | Damasus I |
| [366–7 | Ursinus] |
| 384–99 | Siricius |
| 399–401 | Anastasius I |
| 402–17 | Innocent I |
| 417–18 | Zosimus |
| 418–22 | Boniface I |
| [418–19 | Eulalius] |
| 422–32 | Celestine I |
| 432–40 | Sixtus III |
| 440–61 | Leo I |
| 461–8 | Hilarus |
| 468–83 | Simplicius |
| 483–92 | Felix III (II) |
| 492–6 | Gelasius I |
| 496–8 | Anastasius II |
| 498–514 | Symmachus |
| [498, 501–5 | Laurentius] |
| 514–23 | Hormisdas |
| 523–6 | John I |
| 526–30 | Felix IV (III) |
| 530–2 | Boniface II |
| [530 | Dioscorus] |
| 533–5 | John II |
| 535–6 | Agapetus I |
| 536–7 | Silverius |
| 537–55 | Vigilius |
| 556–61 | Pelagius I |
| 561–74 | John III |
| 575–9 | Benedict I |
| 579–90 | Pelagius II |
| 590–604 | Gregory I |
| 604–6 | Sabinianus |
| 607 | Boniface III |
| 608–15 | Boniface IV |
| 615–18 | Deusdedit *or* Adeodatus I |
| 619–25 | Boniface V |
| 625–38 | Honorius I |
| 640 | Severinus |
| 640–2 | John IV |
| 642–9 | Theodore I |
| 649–55 | Martin I |
| 654–7 | Eugenius I[1] |
| 657–72 | Vitalian |
| 672–6 | Adeodatus II |
| 676–8 | Donus |
| 678–81 | Agatho |
| 682–3 | Leo II |
| 684–5 | Benedict II |
| 685–6 | John V |
| 686–7 | Cono |
| [687 | Theodore] |
| [687–92 | Paschal] |
| 687–701 | Sergius I |
| 701–5 | John VI |
| 705–7 | John VII |
| 708 | Sisinnius |
| 708–15 | Constantine |
| 715–31 | Gregory II |
| 731–41 | Gregory III |

## POPES

| | | | |
|---|---|---|---|
| 741–52 | Zacharias | 936–9 | Leo VII |
| 752 | Stephen II (*not consecrated*) | 939–42 | Stephen IX |
| 752–7 | Stephen II (III) | 942–6 | Marinus II |
| 757–67 | Paul I | 946–55 | Agapetus II |
| [767–9 | Constantine II] | 955–64 | John XII |
| [768 | Philip] | [963–5 | Leo VIII] |
| 768–72 | Stephen III (IV) | 964 | Benedict V |
| 772–95 | Hadrian I | 965–72 | John XIII |
| 795–816 | Leo III | 973–4 | Benedict VI |
| 816–17 | Stephen IV (V) | [974, 984–5 | Boniface VII] |
| 817–24 | Paschal I | 974–83 | Benedict VII |
| 824–7 | Eugenius II | 983–4 | John XIV |
| 827 | Valentine | 985–96 | John XV |
| 827–44 | Gregory IV | 996–9 | Gregory V |
| [844 | John] | [997–8 | John XVI] |
| 844–7 | Sergius II | 999–1003 | Sylvester II |
| 847–55 | Leo IV | 1003 | John XVII |
| 855–8 | Benedict III | 1004–9 | John XVIII |
| [855 | Anastasius Bibliothecarius] | 1009–12 | Sergius IV |
| 858–67 | Nicholas I | 1012–24 | Benedict VIII |
| 867–72 | Hadrian II | [1012 | Gregory] |
| 872–82 | John VIII | 1024–32 | John XIX |
| 882–4 | Marinus I | 1032–44 | Benedict IX |
| 884–5 | Hadrian III | 1045 | Sylvester III |
| 885–91 | Stephen V (VI) | 1045 | Benedict IX (*second reign*) |
| 891–6 | Formosus | 1045–6 | Gregory VI |
| 896 | Boniface VI | 1046–7 | Clement II |
| 896–7 | Stephen VI (VII) | 1047–8 | Benedict IX (*third reign*) |
| 897 | Romanus | 1048 | Damasus II |
| 897 | Theodore II | 1048–54 | Leo IX |
| 898–900 | John IX | 1055–7 | Victor II |
| 900–3 | Benedict IV | 1057–8 | Stephen IX (X) |
| 903 | Leo V | [1058–9 | Benedict X] |
| [903–4 | Christopher] | 1059–61 | Nicholas II |
| 904–11 | Sergius III | 1061–73 | Alexander II |
| 911–13 | Anastasius III | [1061–72 | Honorius II] |
| 913–14 | Lando | 1073–85 | Gregory VII |
| 914–28 | John X | [1080, 1084–1100 | Clement VII] |
| 928 | Leo VI | 1086–7 | Victor III |
| 928–31 | Stephen VII (VIII) | 1088–99 | Urban II |
| 931–5 | John XI | 1099–1118 | Paschal II |

### Choosing the Pope

Upon the death of the pope a set of ancient ceremonies are held to choose a successor. Firstly, the *camerlengo* (papal treasurer) strikes the dead pope's forehead three times with a silver hammer and calls him by his real name to ensure he is truly dead. All the cardinals of the Roman Catholic church who are younger than 80 years then assemble in a *conclave*. The cardinals are locked into a specially prepared area of the Vatican palace, guarded and unable to leave or communicate with the outside world; the door will not be reopened until a successor has been elected, which may take days. The election itself is by secret ballot in the Sistine Chapel; the ballot papers are burned with chemicals after each inconclusive round of voting, sending black smoke into the air above the Vatican, while burning of the ballots alone after a successful vote sends up white smoke and signals to the waiting crowds outside that a new pope has been chosen.

| | |
|---|---|
| [1100–2 | Theodoric] |
| [1102 | Albert] |
| [1105–11 | Sylvester IV] |
| 1118–19 | Gelasius II |
| [1118–21 | Gregory VIII] |
| 1119–24 | Callistus II |
| 1124–30 | Honorius II |
| [1124 | Celestine II] |
| 1130–43 | Innocent II |
| [1130–8 | Anacletus II] |
| [1138 | Victor IV][2] |
| 1143–4 | Celestine II |
| 1144–5 | Lucius II |
| 1145–53 | Eugenius III |
| 1153–4 | Anastasius IV |
| 1154–9 | Hadrian IV |
| 1159–81 | Alexander III |
| [1159–64 | Victor IV][2] |
| [1164–8 | Paschal III] |
| [1168–78 | Callistus III] |
| [1179–80 | Innocent III] |
| 1181–5 | Lucius III |
| 1185–7 | Urban III |
| 1187 | Gregory VIII |
| 1187–91 | Clement III |
| 1191–8 | Celestine III |
| 1198–1216 | Innocent III |
| 1216–27 | Honorius III |
| 1227–41 | Gregory IX |
| 1241 | Celestine IV |
| 1241–3 | *interregnum* |
| 1243–54 | Innocent IV |
| 1254–61 | Alexander IV |
| 1261–4 | Urban IV |
| 1265–8 | Clement IV |
| 1268–71 | *interregnum* |
| 1271–6 | Gregory X |
| 1276 | Innocent V |
| 1276 | Hadrian V |
| 1276–7 | John XXI[3] |
| 1277–80 | Nicholas III |
| 1281–5 | Martin IV |
| 1285–7 | Honorius IV |
| 1288–92 | Nicholas IV |
| 1292–4 | *interregnum* |
| 1294 | Celestine V |
| 1294–1303 | Boniface VIII |
| 1303–4 | Benedict XI |
| 1304–5 | *interregnum* |
| 1305–14 | Clement V |
| 1314–16 | *interregnum* |
| 1316–34 | John XXII |
| [1328–30 | Nicholas V] |
| 1334–42 | Benedict XII |
| 1342–52 | Clement VI |
| 1352–62 | Innocent VI |
| 1362–70 | Urban V |
| 1370–8 | Gregory XI |
| 1378–89 | Urban VI |
| [1378–94 | Clement VII] |
| 1389–1404 | Boniface IX |
| [1394–1423 | Benedict XIII] |
| 1404–6 | Innocent VII |
| 1406–15 | Gregory XII |
| [1409–10 | Alexander V] |
| [1410–15 | John XXIII] |
| 1416 | *interregnum* |
| 1417–31 | Martin V |
| [1423–9 | Clement VIII] |
| [1425–30 | Benedict XIV] |
| 1431–47 | Eugenius IV |
| [1439–49 | Felix V] |
| 1447–55 | Nicholas V |
| 1455–8 | Callistus III |
| 1458–64 | Pius II |
| 1464–71 | Paul II |
| 1471–84 | Sixtus IV |
| 1484–92 | Innocent VIII |
| 1492–1503 | Alexander VI |
| 1503 | Pius III |
| 1503–13 | Julius II |
| 1513–21 | Leo X |
| 1522–3 | Hadrian VI |
| 1523–34 | Clement VII |
| 1534–49 | Paul III |
| 1550–5 | Julius III |
| 1555 | Marcellus II |
| 1555–9 | Paul IV |
| 1559–65 | Pius IV |
| 1566–72 | Pius V |
| 1572–85 | Gregory XIII |
| 1585–90 | Sixtus V |
| 1590 | Urban VII |
| 1590–1 | Gregory XIV |
| 1591 | Innocent IX |
| 1592–1605 | Clement VIII |
| 1605 | Leo XI |
| 1605–21 | Paul V |
| 1621–3 | Gregory XV |
| 1623–44 | Urban VIII |
| 1644–55 | Innocent X |
| 1655–67 | Alexander VII |
| 1667–9 | Clement IX |
| 1670–6 | Clement X |
| 1676–89 | Innocent XI |
| 1689–91 | Alexander VIII |
| 1691–1700 | Innocent XII |
| 1700–21 | Clement XI |
| 1721–4 | Innocent XIII |
| 1724–30 | Benedict XIII |

| | | | |
|---|---|---|---|
| 1730–40 | Clement XII | 1878–1903 | Leo XIII |
| 1740–58 | Benedict XIV | 1903–14 | Pius X |
| 1758–69 | Clement XIII | 1914–22 | Benedict XV |
| 1769–74 | Clement XIV | 1922–39 | Pius XI |
| 1775–99 | Pius VI | 1939–58 | Pius XII |
| 1800–23 | Pius VII | 1958–63 | John XXIII |
| 1823–9 | Leo XII | 1963–78 | Paul VI |
| 1829–30 | Pius VIII | 1978 | John Paul I |
| 1831–46 | Gregory XVI | 1978– | John Paul II |
| 1846–78 | Pius IX | | |

[1] *Elected during the banishment of Martin I.*

[2] *Different individuals.*

[3] *There was no John XX.*

## ARCHBISHOPS OF YORK

| | | | |
|---|---|---|---|
| 627–33 | Paulinus[1] | 1286–96 | John le Romeyn (Romanus) |
| 644–69 | Chad (Ceadda)[1] | 1298–9 | Henry of Newark |
| 669–77 | Wilfrid I (St Wilfrid)[1] | 1300–4 | Thomas of Corbridge |
| 678–705 | Bosa[1] | 1306–16 | William Greenfield |
| 705–14 | John (St John of Beverley)[1] | 1317–40 | William of Melton |
| 718–32 | Wilfrid II[1] | 1342–52 | William le Zouche |
| 735–66 | Egbert | 1352–73 | John of Thoresby |
| 767–80 | Ethelbert | 1374–88 | Alexander Neville |
| 780–96 | Eanbald I | 1388–96 | Thomas Arundel |
| 796–808 | Eanbald II | 1396–8 | Robert Waldby |
| 808–37 | Wulfsige | 1398–1407 | Richard le Scrope |
| 837–54 | Wigmund | 1407–23 | Henry Bowet |
| 854–900 | Wulfhere | 1425–52 | John Kempe |
| 900–4 | Ethelbald | 1452–64 | William Booth |
| 904–31 | Hrotheweard (or Lodeward) | 1465–76 | George Neville |
| 931–56 | Wulfstan I | 1476–80 | Lawrence Booth |
| 958–71 | Oskytel | 1480–1500 | Thomas Rotheram (or Scott) |
| 971 | Edwald (or Ethelwold) | 1501–7 | Thomas Savage |
| 972–92 | Oswald | 1508–14 | Christopher Bainbridge |
| 992–1002 | Ealdulf (Abbot of Peterborough) | 1514–30 | Thomas Wolsey |
| 1003–23 | Wulfstan II | 1531–44 | Edward Lee |
| 1023–51 | Aelfric Puttoc | 1545–54 | Robert Holgate |
| 1051–60 | Cynesige | 1555–60 | Nicholas Heath |
| 1061–9 | Ealdred | 1561–8 | Thomas Young |
| 1070–1100 | Thomas I | 1570–6 | Edmund Grindal |
| 1101–8 | Gerard | 1577–88 | Edwin Sandys |
| 1109–14 | Thomas II | 1589–94 | John Piers |
| 1119–40 | Thurstan | 1595–1606 | Matthew Hutton |
| 1143–7 | William Fitzherbert | 1606–28 | Tobias Matthew |
| 1147–53 | Henry Fitzherbert/William Fitzherbert | 1628 | George Monteigne |
| | | 1628–31 | Samuel Harsnett |
| 1154 | William Fitzherbert | 1632–40 | Richard Neile |
| 1154–81 | Roger of Pont-L'Eveque | 1641–50 | John Williams |
| 1181–91 | Geoffrey Plantagenet | 1660–4 | Accepted Frewen |
| 1215–55 | Walter de Grey | 1664–83 | Richard Sterne |
| 1256–8 | Sewal de Bovill | 1683–6 | John Dolben |
| 1258–65 | Godfrey of Ludham (or Kineton) | 1688–91 | Thomas Lamplugh |
| 1265–79 | Walter Giffard | 1691–1714 | John Sharp |
| 1279–85 | William Wickwane | 1714–24 | Sir William Dawes |

| | |
|---|---|
| 1724–43 | Lancelot Blackburne |
| 1743–7 | Thomas Herring |
| 1747–57 | Matthew Hutton |
| 1757–61 | John Gilbert |
| 1761–76 | Robert Hay Drummond |
| 1777–1807 | William Markham |
| 1807–47 | Edward Venables Vernon (afterwards Harcourt) |
| 1847–60 | Thomas Musgrave |
| 1860–2 | Charles Thomas Longley |
| 1862–90 | William Thomson |
| 1890–1 | William Connor Magee |
| 1891–1908 | William Dalrymple |
| 1908–28 | Cosmo Gordon Lang |
| 1929–42 | William Temple |
| 1942–55 | Cyril Forster Garbett |
| 1956–61 | Arthur Michael Ramsey |
| 1961–74 | Frederic Donald Coggan |
| 1975–83 | Stuart Yarworth Blanch |
| 1983–95 | John Stapylton Habgood |
| 1995– | David Hope |

[1] *Bishop of York; the first Archbishop was Egbert in 735.*

*Note: Gaps in the chronology indicate that the see was vacant or subject to conflict.*

## ARCHBISHOPS OF CANTERBURY

The date given is the date of succession.

| | |
|---|---|
| 597 | Augustine |
| 604 | Laurentius |
| 619 | Mellitus |
| 624 | Justus |
| 627 | Honorius |
| 655 | Deusdedit |
| 668 | Theodore |
| 693 | Berhtwald |
| 731 | Tatwine |
| 735 | Nothelm |
| 740 | Cuthbert |
| 761 | Bregowine |
| 765 | Jaenbert |
| 793 | Ethelhard |
| 805 | Wulfred |
| 832 | Feologeld |
| 833 | Ceolnoth |
| 870 | Ethelred |
| 890 | Plegmund |
| 914 | Athelm |
| 923 | Wulfhelm |
| 942 | Oda |
| 959 | Aelfsige |
| 959 | Brithelm |
| 960 | Dunstan |
| 990 | Sigeric |
| 995 | Aelfric |
| c.988 | Ethelgar |
| 1005 | Alphege |
| 1013 | Lyfing |
| 1020 | Ethelnoth |
| 1038 | Eadsige |
| 1051 | Robert of Jumieges |
| 1052 | Stigand |
| 1070 | Lanfranc |
| 1093 | Anselm |
| 1114 | Ralph d'Escures |
| 1123 | William de Corbeil |
| 1139 | Theobald |
| 1162 | Thomas à Becket |
| 1174 | Richard (of Dover) |
| 1184 | Baldwin |
| 1193 | Hubert Walter |
| 1207 | Stephen Langton |
| 1229 | Richard le Grant |
| 1234 | Edmund of Abingdon |
| 1245 | Boniface of Savoy |
| 1273 | Robert Kilwardby |
| 1279 | John Peckham |
| 1294 | Robert Winchelsey |
| 1313 | Walter Reynolds |
| 1328 | Simon Meopham |
| 1333 | John de Stratford |
| 1349 | Simon Islip |
| 1349 | Thomas Bradwardine |
| 1366 | Simon Langham |
| 1368 | William Whittlesey |
| 1375 | Simon Sudbury |
| 1381 | William Courtenay |
| 1396 | Thomas Arundel |
| 1398 | Roger Walden |
| 1399 | Thomas Arundel (*restored*) |
| 1414 | Henry Chichele |
| 1443 | John Stafford |
| 1452 | John Kempe |
| 1454 | Thomas Bourchier |
| 1486 | John Morton |
| 1501 | Henry Deane |
| 1503 | William Warham |
| 1533 | Thomas Cranmer |
| 1556 | Reginald Pole |
| 1559 | Matthew Parker |
| 1576 | Edmund Grindal |
| 1583 | John Whitgift |

## APOSTLES

| | |
|---|---|
| 1604 | Richard Bancroft |
| 1611 | George Abbot |
| 1633 | William Laud |
| 1660 | William Juxon |
| 1663 | Gilbert Sheldon |
| 1678 | William Sancroft |
| 1691 | John Tillotson |
| 1695 | Thomas Tenison |
| 1716 | William Wake |
| 1737 | John Potter |
| 1747 | Thomas Herring |
| 1757 | Matthew Hutton |
| 1758 | Thomas Secker |
| 1768 | Frederick Cornwallis |
| 1783 | John Moore |
| 1805 | Charles Manners-Sutton |
| 1828 | William Howley |
| 1848 | John Sumner |
| 1862 | Charles Longley |
| 1868 | Archibald Tait |
| 1883 | Edward Benson |
| 1896 | Frederick Temple |
| 1903 | Randall Davidson |
| 1928 | William Lang |
| 1942 | William Temple |
| 1945 | Geoffrey Fisher |
| 1961 | Arthur Ramsey |
| 1974 | Frederick Coggan |
| 1980 | Robert Runcie |
| 1991 | George Carey |
| 2002 | Rowan Williams |

### *Chair of St Augustine*

The post of Archbishop of Canterbury is known as the 'Chair of St Augustine', after the first Archbishop. St Augustine was probably born in Rome, where he became the prior of a Benedictine monastery. In 596 he was sent by Pope Gregory I to convert the Anglo-Saxons to Christianity, and it is recorded that he baptized 1 000 people in the River Swale in a single day. Augustine became Bishop of the English in 597 and established his church at Canterbury, where he died in 604.

## APOSTLES

In Christianity, the Apostles were Christ's twelve chosen followers. The apostles are generally taken to include the twelve original followers of Christ (excluding Judas Iscariot in some versions), who witnessed the resurrected Jesus and were charged with proclaiming his gospel.

**Peter** (brother of Andrew)

**Andrew** (brother of Peter)

**James, son of Zebedee** (brother of John)

**John** (brother of James)

**Philip**

**Bartholomew**

**Thomas**

**Matthew**

**James of Alphaeus**

**Simon the Canaanite** (*in Matthew and Mark*) or **Simon the Zealot** (*in Luke and Acts*)

**Judas Iscariot**

*The twelfth apostle is Thaddeus in the biblical gospels of Matthew and Mark; in Luke and Acts it is Judas or James. Matthias succeeded to Judas's place.*

## FATHERS OF THE CHURCH

'Father of the Church' is a title usually applied to the leaders of the early Christian Church. Recognized as eminent teachers of the faith, they were characterized by orthodoxy of doctrine and personal holiness, and were usually beatified.

*Note: The title has also been subsequently awarded by the Roman Catholic church to later Christian writers.*

## Apostolic Fathers

The Apostolic Fathers were the immediate disciples and fellow labourers of the Apostles, more especially those who have left writings. The three major Fathers are:

**St Clement of Rome**

**St Ignatius of Antioch**

**St Polycarp of Smyrna**

## Doctors of the Church

A small number of especially revered early ecclesiastical writers are known as Doctors of the Church. There were eight from medieval times, originally four from the Greek Church and four from the Latin Church.

| | |
|---|---|
| **St Basil the Great** | **St Ambrose** |
| **St Gregory Nazianzen** | **St Jerome** |
| **St John Chrysostom** | **St Augustine** |
| **St Gregory the Great** | **St Athanasius** |

## TEN COMMANDMENTS

In the Bible, the ten commandments given by God to Moses on Mount Sinai, as described in the Old Testament Book of Exodus.

| | |
|---|---|
| I | I am the Lord your God, who brought you out of the land of Egypt, out of the house of bondage. You shall have no other gods before me. |
| II | You shall not make for yourself a graven image. You shall not bow down to them or serve them. |
| III | You shall not take the name of the Lord your God in vain. |
| IV | Remember the sabbath day, to keep it holy. |
| V | Honour your father and your mother. |
| VI | You shall not kill. |
| VII | You shall not commit adultery. |
| VIII | You shall not steal. |
| IX | You shall not bear false witness against your neighbour. |
| X | You shall not covet. |

*The Ten Commandments appear in two different places in the Bible – Exodus 20.17 and Deuteronomy 5.6–21. Most Protestant, Anglican and Orthodox Christians enumerate the Commandments differently from Roman Catholics and Lutherans.*

## CHAMPIONS OF CHRISTENDOM

In medieval times the patron saints of seven nations were known as the Champions of Christendom. Their supposed exploits were celebrated in *The Famous History of the Seven Champions of Christendom*, published c.1597 by Richard Johnson (1573–c.1659).

| | |
|---|---|
| **St George of England** | **St Denys of France** |
| **St Andrew of Scotland** | **St James of Spain** |
| **St Patrick of Ireland** | **St Anthony of Italy** |
| **St David of Wales** | |

## PATRON SAINTS

A patron saint is a saint regarded as the protector of a particular group.

| | |
|---|---|
| Accountants | Matthew |
| Actors | Genesius, Vitus |
| Advertisers | Bernardino of Siena |
| Architects | Thomas (Apostle) |
| Artists | Luke, Angelico |
| Astronauts | Joseph (Cupertino) |
| Astronomers | Dominic |
| Athletes | Sebastian |
| Authors | Francis de Sales |
| Aviators | Our Lady of Loreto |
| Bakers | Honoratus |
| Bankers | Bernardino (Feltre) |
| Barbers | Cosmas and Damian |
| Blacksmiths | Eligius |
| Bookkeepers | Matthew |
| Book trade | John of God |
| Brewers | Amand, Wenceslaus |
| Builders | Barbara, Thomas (Apostle) |
| Butchers | Luke |
| Carpenters | Joseph |
| Chemists | Cosmas and Damian |
| Comedians | Vitus |
| Çooks | Lawrence, Martha |
| Dancers | Vitus |
| Dentists | Apollonia |
| Doctors | Cosmas and Damian, Luke |
| Editors | Francis de Sales |
| Farmers | Isidore |
| Firemen | Florian |
| Fishermen | Andrew, Peter |
| Florists | Dorothy, Thérèse of Lisieux |
| Gardeners | Adam, Fiacre |
| Glassworkers | Luke, Lucy |
| Gravediggers | Joseph of Arimathea |
| Grocers | Michael |
| Hotelkeepers | Amand, Julian the Hospitaler |
| Housewives | Martha |
| Jewellers | Eligius |
| Journalists | Francis de Sales |
| Labourers | James, John Bosco |
| Lawyers | Ivo, Thomas More |
| Librarians | Jerome, Catherine of Alexandria |
| Merchants | Francis of Assisi |
| Messengers | Gabriel |
| Metalworkers | Eligius |
| Midwives | Raymond Nonnatus |
| Miners | Anne, Barbara |
| Motorists | Christopher |
| Musicians | Cecilia, Gregory the Great |
| Nurses | Camillus de Lellis, John of God |
| Philosophers | Thomas Aquinas, Catherine of Alexandria |
| Poets | Cecilia, David |
| Police | Michael |
| Politicians | Thomas More |
| Postal Workers | Gabriel |
| Priests | Jean-Baptiste Vianney |
| Printers | John of God |
| Prisoners | Leonard |
| Radio Workers | Gabriel |
| Sailors | Christopher, Erasmus, Francis of Paola |
| Scholars | Thomas Aquinas |
| Scientists | Albert the Great |
| Sculptors | Luke, Louis |
| Secretaries | Genesius |
| Servants | Martha, Zita |
| Shoemakers | Crispin, Crispinian |
| Singers | Cecilia, Gregory |
| Soldiers | George, Joan of Arc, Martin of Tours, Sebastian |
| Students | Thomas Aquinas |
| Surgeons | Luke, Cosmas and Damian |
| Tailors | Homobonus |
| Tax Collectors | Matthew |
| Taxi Drivers | Fiacre |
| Teachers | Gregory the Great, John Baptiste de la Salle |
| Theologians | Augustine, Alphonsus Liguori, Thomas Aquinas |
| Television Workers | Gabriel |
| Undertakers | Dismas, Joseph of Arimathea |
| Waiters | Martha |
| Writers | Lucy |

### *Politicians' Patron*

In 2000 Pope John Paul II declared the martyr Sir Thomas More (1478–1535) to be the patron saint of politicians and statesmen. More was Speaker of the House of Commons and Lord Chancellor under King Henry VIII; he was beheaded in 1535.

## SAINTS

Information on selected well-known saints is given below. The official recognition of saints, and the choice of a saint's day, varies greatly between different branches of Christianity, calendars and localities. Where there are major variations, the dates given below refer to the dates in the Western church calendar.

| **Saint** | **Lived** | **Saint's Day** |
|---|---|---|
| **Alban** | 3c AD | 22 Jun |

The first Christian martyr in Britain, he was a pagan living in the town of Verulamium who was scourged and beheaded around AD300 for helping a fugitive Christian priest who had converted him. A monastery was founded on the site in 793, and the place was renamed St Albans.

| | | |
|---|---|---|
| **Andrew** | 1c AD | 30 Nov |

One of the twelve Apostles of Jesus Christ, he was a fisherman who preached the Gospel in Asia Minor, and was crucified in Greece. The belief that his cross was X-shaped dates only from the 14c. He is a patron saint not only of Scotland but of Greece and Russia.

| | | |
|---|---|---|
| **Bernard** | 923–1008 | 28 May or 15 Jun |

Also known as the Apostle of the Alps, he founded hospices in Alpine passes which were named after him, as were St Bernard dogs, trained by the monks to go to the aid of travellers.

| | | |
|---|---|---|
| **Catherine** | died AD307 | 25 Nov |

Born in Alexandria, she is said to have publicly confessed the Gospel at a sacrificial feast appointed by Emperor Maximinus, and was consequently beheaded, after being tortured on a spiked wheel (later known as a 'catherine wheel').

| | | |
|---|---|---|
| **Christopher** | 3c AD | 25 Jul |

He was, according to tradition, a man some 3.5m/11.5ft tall. His name in Greek (*Christophoros*) means 'Christ-bearing', which gave rise to the legend that he had carried the Christ-child (and all the weight of the world's sin) across a river. He is the patron saint of travellers.

| | | |
|---|---|---|
| **David** | c.520–601 | 1 Mar |

He presided over two Welsh synods and is believed to have died in 601 as Bishop of Moni Judeorum, or Menevia, afterwards St David's. He is the patron saint of Wales.

| | | |
|---|---|---|
| **George** | early 4c AD | 23 Apr |

Little is known about him, the date of his death is uncertain, and he has been confused with others; his name was soon obscured by fables and myth. The famous story of his fight with the dragon cannot be traced much earlier than the 13c. He is the patron saint of England and Portugal.

| | | |
|---|---|---|
| **Nicholas** | 4c AD | 6 Dec |

In legend he gave gifts of gold to three poor girls for their dowries, which gave rise to the custom of giving gifts on his feast day. His identification with Father Christmas began in Europe and spread to the USA. He is a patron saint of Greece and Russia, and also of children, scholars, merchants, sailors, travellers and thieves.

**Pancras** died AD304 12 May

He was killed in persecutions while still a child, and is one of the patron saints of children.

**Patrick** 5c 17 Mar

In AD432 it is thought he was sent by the Pope as a missionary to Ireland. He converted his old master Milchu and other chiefs, and after 20 years spent in missionary work fixed his see at Armagh (AD454). He is the patron saint of Ireland.

**Stephen** 1c AD 26 Dec

All we know is from the Bible, Acts 6–7. He was appointed by the Apostles to manage the finances and alms of the early Church, was tried for blasphemy and stoned to death.

**Swithin** died 862 15 Jul

An English ecclesiastic, he was made Bishop of Winchester in 852. When the monks exhumed his body in 971 to bury it in the rebuilt cathedral, the removal, which was to have taken place on 15 Jul, is said to have been delayed by violent rain. This led to the belief that if it rains on his feast day it will rain for a further 40 days.

**Valentine** died AD269 14 Feb

He is said to have been executed during Roman persecutions, but claims have been made for another St Valentine who was martyred in Rome. Neither is associated with romance, hardly surprisingly; the custom of sending love letters on his feast day originated in the Middle Ages, when it was thought the birds' mating season started then.

### *Death of Saints*

Many early saints met a premature end through martyrdom. Their gruesome fates include being rolled over burning coals (St Agatha, died AD251), tortured on a spiked wheel and beheaded (St Catherine, died AD307), pressed to death (St Margaret Clitherow, c.1556–86), tied to a tree and shot to death with arrows by the Danes (St Edmund, c.841–70), murdered by a heathen daughter-in-law (St Ludmilla, died 921), impaled or crucified head downward (St Peter, 1c AD), beaten to death with rods (St Sebastian, died AD288) and being killed, along with 11 000 virgin companions, by a horde of Huns (St Ursula, 4c AD).

## DAYS OF CHRISTMAS

According to the old song, 'my true love' gave a present on each of the twelve days of Christmas:

| Day | Gift | Day | Gift |
|---|---|---|---|
| 1st | Partridge in a pear tree | 7th | Swans a-swimming |
| 2nd | Turtle doves | 8th | Maids a-milking |
| 3rd | French hens | 9th | Ladies dancing |
| 4th | Calling birds | 10th | Lords a-leaping |
| 5th | Gold rings | 11th | Pipers piping |
| 6th | Geese a-laying | 12th | Drummers drumming |

### *Christmas Birds*

It is thought that 'calling birds' is a corruption of the older 'colly birds' – a dialect word for blackbirds. 'Gold rings' may also be ring-necked birds, rather than jewellery, meaning that the first seven gifts are all birds.

## TRIBES OF ISRAEL

In the Bible (Genesis 49), a confederacy of twelve tribes generally traced to Jacob's twelve sons – six by Leah (Reuben, Simeon, Levi, Judah, Issachar, Zebulun), two by Rachel (Joseph, Benjamin), two by Rachel's maid Bilhah (Dan, Naphtali), and two by Leah's maid Zilpah (Gad, Asher). Joseph's sons Ephraim and Manasseh gave rise to two tribes; the Tribe of Levi is not conventionally listed as they served in the Holy Temple rather than owning land. Jacob had received the name Israel (Genesis 32.28) when he wrestled with a divine being.

| | | |
|---|---|---|
| **Reuben** | **Simeon** | **Gad** |
| **Judah** | **Issachar** | **Zebulun** |
| **Ephraim** | **Manasseh** | **Benjamin** |
| **Dan** | **Asher** | **Naphtali** |

## PLAGUES OF EGYPT

Ten Biblical plagues, described in the book of Exodus, that afflicted the Egyptians as a result of the Pharaoh's refusal to release the Israelites from captivity.

| | |
|---|---|
| **Water turns to blood** | **Boils** |
| **Frogs** | **Hail** |
| **Lice** | **Locusts** |
| **Flies** | **Darkness** |
| **Cattle disease** | **Death of first-born** |

## SEVEN DEADLY SINS

| | | |
|---|---|---|
| **Pride** *or* **vanity** | **Envy** | **Gluttony** |
| **Lust** | **Anger** *or* **wrath** | **Sloth** |
| **Avarice, greed** *or* **covetousness** | | |

## VIRTUES

### Cardinal virtues

Also known as the natural virtues.

| | | |
|---|---|---|
| **Justice** | **Prudence** | **Temperance** |
| **Fortitude** | | |

### Theological virtues

Also known as the supernatural or Christian virtues.

| | | |
|---|---|---|
| **Faith** | **Hope** | **Charity** |

## SEVEN SLEEPERS

The Seven Sleepers of Ephesus in medieval legend were seven persecuted Christians who fled into a cave at the time of the emperor Decius (AD250). They slept for 200 years, emerging in AD447 at the time of Theodosius II. The story was thought to confirm the resurrection of Christ.

| | | |
|---|---|---|
| **Achillides** | **Diomedes** | **Diogenus** |
| **Probatus** | **Stephanus** | **Sambatus** |
| **Quiriacus** | | |

## HORSEMEN OF THE APOCALYPSE

The symbolic biblical characters described in Revelation 6 and Zechariah 6.1–7, who signal the beginning of the messianic age. Each comes on a steed of different colour, symbolizing devastations associated with the end of the world, except for the white horse's rider, who is given a crown and sent to conquer (Revelation 6.2).

| | |
|---|---|
| **Black horse** | **Famine** |
| **Red** | **Bloodshed and War** |
| **Pale** | **Pestilence and Death** |
| **White** | **various interpretations** |

## WISE MEN

In the Bible, a group who came from 'the East' guided by a star (Matthew 2.1–12) to visit the infant Jesus in Bethlehem. They brought three gifts:

| | | |
|---|---|---|
| **gold** | **frankincense** | **myrrh** |

### We Three Kings

The three wise men are a Christian tradition. But the Bible doesn't specify how many wise men there were: the belief that there were three developed in later centuries. Tradition also suggests the three were called Balthasar, Gaspar and Melchior. The wise men are sometimes known as the 'three kings', after the Christmas carol. They are also known as the *Magi*. The word is the plural of *magus*, which comes from the Old Persian word for magician.

## CONFUCIANISM

| | | | |
|---|---|---|---|
| **Founded** | 6c BC | **Organization** | Confucianism is not an institution and has no church or clergy. Weddings and funerals follow a tradition handed down by Confucian scholars. |
| **Founder** | K'ung-fu-tzu (Confucius) (c.551–479BC), a Chinese philosopher | **Divisions** | Two major divisions: the first is associated with Confucius and Hsun Tzu (c.298–238BC), and the second with Mencius (c.371–289BC) and medieval neo-Confucians. |
| **Sacred texts** | Shih Ching, Li Ching, Shu Ching, Chu'un Ch'iu, I Ching. | | |
| **Place of worship** | Temple | | |
| **Beliefs** | Confucius was concerned with the best way to live and behave in this world and was not concerned with the afterlife. He laid particular emphasis on the family. | | |

### *Act Wisely*

'Man has three ways of acting wisely. First, on meditation; that is the noblest. Secondly, on imitation; that is the easiest. Thirdly, on experience; that is the bitterest.'

**From *The Analects* (c.479BC), a collection of the sayings and doings of Confucius.**

## HINDUISM

| | | | |
|---|---|---|---|
| **Founded** | c.1500BC | **Organization** | A Brahmanic priesthood officiates at prayer and festivals. |
| **Founder** | No single founder | **Divisions** | The three major living traditions are those devoted to Vishnu, Shiva and the goddess Shakti. Many folk traditions exist. |
| **Sacred texts** | The Vedas ('knowledge') including the Upanishads, the Ramayana and the Mahabharata, the Bhagavad Gita, the Agamas. | | |
| **Place of worship** | Temple | | |
| **Beliefs** | Many diverse religious beliefs and practices, including dharma (right living), the law of karma and reincarnation; numerous gods. | | |

## HINDU GODS

| | |
|---|---|
| **Agni** | God of fire |
| **Brahma** | God of creation |
| **Durga** | Shiva's wife |
| **Ganesh** | Elephant-headed son of Shiva |
| **Garuda** | Bird that carries Shiva |
| **Hanuman** | Monkey god |
| **Indra** | God of storms and war |
| **Iswara** | God of nature and the soul |
| **Kali** | Goddess of destruction and wife of Shiva |
| **Kama** | God of lust and desire |
| **Kartikeya** | Six-headed war god mounted on a peacock |
| **Krishna** | Incarnation of Vishnu |

| | |
|---|---|
| **Kurma** | Incarnation of Vishnu in the form of a tortoise |
| **Lakshmana** | Half-brother of Rama |
| **Lakshmi** | Goddess of wealth and good luck |
| **Narada** | Incarnation of Vishnu |
| **Narasimha** | Incarnation of Vishnu as a lion-man |
| **Nataraja** | Aspect of Shiva as the Lord of Dance |
| **Parvati** | Shiva's wife |
| **Pushan** | God of enlightenment |
| **Radha** | Goddess of love and consort of Krishna |
| **Rama** | Incarnation of Vishnu |
| **Rudra** | Destructive aspect of Shiva |
| **Sarasvati** | Mother goddess representing art, learning and music |
| **Shakti** | Female principle of power and energy |
| **Shani** | Bringer of bad luck |
| **Shiva** | God of creation and destruction |
| **Sita** | Rama's wife |
| **Soma** | God of speech and deity of the soma creeper |
| **Surya** | God of the sun |
| **Varuna** | God of the sea |
| **Vishnu** | God of creation |
| **Yama** | God of death |

## HINDU CALENDAR

The Indian classical calendar was based on the sun for purposes of astrology, but the lunar one was necessary for the sacred calendar. In the 6c AD the practice of dating years relative to the revolutions of the orbit of Jupiter was introduced, creating a 60-year cycle. In recent times the National Calendar of India was introduced in 1957, using Gregorian dates alongside the Saka era calendar (calculated from AD78, each year beginning on 22 Mar, or 21 Mar in a leap year). Other calendars in use include the Vikrama era calendar (calculated from 58BC) and the Kalacuri era calendar (calculated from AD248). Other important Hindu eras include the Gupta era (AD320) and Harsa era (AD606).

**Months (solar days)**

*Basis: Moon*

Chaitra (29 or 30)
Vaisakha (29 or 30)
Jyaistha (29 or 30)
Asadha (29 or 30)
Dvitiya Asadha (*certain leap years*)
Sravana (29 or 30)
Dvitiya Sravana (*certain leap years*)
Bhadrapada (29 or 30)
Asvina (29 or 30)
Karttika (29 or 30)
Margasirsa (29 or 30)
Pausa (29 or 30)
Magha (29 or 30)
Phalguna (29 or 30)

**Saka era**

| Year | Gregorian equivalents (AD) |
|---|---|
| 1917 | (22 Mar 1995–20 Mar 1996) |
| 1918 | (21 Mar 1996–21 Mar 1997) |
| 1919 | (22 Mar 1997–21 Mar 1998) |
| 1920 | (22 Mar 1998–21 Mar 1999) |
| 1921 | (22 Mar 1999–20 Mar 2000) |
| 1922 | (21 Mar 2000–21 Mar 2001) |
| 1923 | (22 Mar 2001–21 Mar 2002) |
| 1924 | (22 Mar 2002–21 Mar 2003) |
| 1925 | (22 Mar 2003–20 Mar 2004) |
| 1926 | (21 Mar 2004–21 Mar 2005) |
| 1927 | (22 Mar 2005–21 Mar 2006) |
| 1928 | (22 Mar 2006–21 Mar 2007) |
| 1929 | (22 Mar 2007–20 Mar 2008) |
| 1930 | (21 Mar 2008–21 Mar 2009) |
| 1931 | (22 Mar 2009–21 Mar 2010) |
| 1932 | (22 Mar 2010–21 Mar 2011) |
| 1933 | (22 Mar 2011–20 Mar 2012) |
| 1934 | (21 Mar 2012–21 Mar 2013) |
| 1935 | (22 Mar 2013–21 Mar 2014) |
| 1936 | (22 Mar 2014–21 Mar 2015) |
| 1937 | (22 Mar 2015–20 Mar 2016) |
| 1938 | (21 Mar 2016–21 Mar 2017) |
| 1939 | (22 Mar 2017–21 Mar 2018) |
| 1940 | (22 Mar 2018–21 Mar 2019) |
| 1941 | (22 Mar 2019–20 Mar 2020) |

**Vikrama era**

| Year | Gregorian equivalents (AD) | Year | Gregorian equivalents (AD) |
|---|---|---|---|
| 2052 | (14 Mar 1995–13 Mar 1996) | 2065 | (14 Mar 2008–13 Mar 2009) |
| 2053 | (14 Mar 1996–13 Mar 1997) | 2066 | (14 Mar 2009–13 Mar 2010) |
| 2054 | (14 Mar 1997–13 Mar 1998) | 2067 | (14 Mar 2010–13 Mar 2011) |
| 2055 | (14 Mar 1998–13 Mar 1999) | 2068 | (14 Mar 2011–13 Mar 2012) |
| 2056 | (14 Mar 1999–13 Mar 2000) | 2069 | (14 Mar 2012–13 Mar 2013) |
| 2057 | (14 Mar 2000–13 Mar 2001) | 2070 | (14 Mar 2013–13 Mar 2014) |
| 2058 | (14 Mar 2001–13 Mar 2002) | 2071 | (14 Mar 2014–13 Mar 2015) |
| 2059 | (14 Mar 2002–13 Mar 2003) | 2072 | (14 Mar 2015–13 Mar 2016) |
| 2060 | (14 Mar 2003–13 Mar 2004) | 2073 | (14 Mar 2016–13 Mar 2017) |
| 2061 | (14 Mar 2004–13 Mar 2005) | 2074 | (14 Mar 2017–13 Mar 2018) |
| 2062 | (14 Mar 2005–13 Mar 2006) | 2075 | (14 Mar 2018–13 Mar 2019) |
| 2063 | (14 Mar 2006–13 Mar 2007) | 2076 | (14 Mar 2019–13 Mar 2020) |
| 2064 | (14 Mar 2007–13 Mar 2008) | | |

## ISLAM

| | |
|---|---|
| **Founded** | 7c AD |
| **Founder** | Muhammad (c.570–c.632) |
| **Sacred texts** | The Koran (the word of God as revealed to Muhammad) and the Hadith (a collection of the prophet's sayings). |
| **Place of worship** | Mosque |
| **Beliefs** | Monotheistic: God is the creator of all things and holds absolute power over man; the perfect word of God was revealed to the prophet Muhammad. |
| **Organization** | No organized priesthood, but great respect is accorded to descendants of Muhammad and holy men, scholars and teachers such as mullahs and ayatollahs. |
| **Divisions** | Two main groups: the Sunni (the majority and the more orthodox) and the Shiites. Other sub-sects include the Sufis, the Ismailis and the Wahhabis. |

## PILLARS OF ISLAM

Islam has five essential religious duties:

| | |
|---|---|
| **Shahada** | Profession of faith, the sincere recitation of the two-fold creed, 'There is no god but God' and 'Muhammad is the Messenger of God'. |
| **Salat** | Formal prayer, to be performed at fixed hours five times a day while facing towards the holy city of Mecca. |
| **Zakat** | Almsgiving, through the payment of zakat, is the duty of sharing one's wealth out of gratitude for God's favour, according to the uses laid down in the Koran. |
| **Saum** | Fasting, during the hours of daylight of the month of Ramadan. |
| **Hajj** | Pilgrimage to Mecca, to be performed if at all possible at least once during one's lifetime. |

## ISLAMIC CALENDAR

The Islamic calendar is calculated from the Hegira (the year Muhammad migrated from Mecca to Medina, and the beginning of the Muslim era) in AD622. Still used by Muslims for religious purposes, it has twelve lunar months, with no intercalations.

**Months (solar days)**

*Basis: Moon*

Muharram (30)
Safar (29)
Rabi I (30)
Rabi II (29)
Jumada I (30)
Jumada II (29)
Rajab (30)
Shaban (29)
Ramadan (30)
Shawwal (29)
Dhu al-Qadah (30)
Dhu al-Hijjah (29 or 30)

| Year | Gregorian equivalents (AD) |
|---|---|
| 1416 | (31 May 1995–18 May 1996) |
| 1417 | (19 May 1996–8 May 1997) |
| 1418 | (9 May 1997–27 Apr 1998) |
| 1419 | (28 Apr 1998–16 Apr 1999) |
| 1420 | (17 Apr 1999–5 Apr 2000) |
| 1421 | (6 Apr 2000–25 Mar 2001) |
| 1422 | (26 Mar 2001–14 Mar 2002) |
| 1423 | (15 Mar 2002–3 Mar 2003) |
| 1424 | (4 Mar 2003–21 Feb 2004) |
| 1425 | (22 Feb 2004–9 Feb 2005) |
| 1426 | (10 Feb 2005–30 Jan 2006) |
| 1427 | (31 Jan 2006–20 Jan 2007) |
| 1428 | (21 Jan 2007–9 Jan 2008) |
| 1429 | (10 Jan 2008–28 Dec 2008) |
| 1430 | (29 Dec 2008–17 Dec 2009) |
| 1431 | (18 Dec 2009–6 Dec 2010) |
| 1432 | (7 Dec 2010–26 Nov 2011) |
| 1433 | (27 Nov 2011–14 Nov 2012) |
| 1434 | (15 Nov 2012–4 Nov 2013) |
| 1435 | (5 Nov 2013–24 Oct 2014) |
| 1436 | (25 Oct 2014–13 Oct 2015) |
| 1437 | (14 Oct 2015–1 Oct 2016) |
| 1438 | (2 Oct 2016–21 Sep 2017) |
| 1439 | (22 Sep 2017–10 Sep 2018) |
| 1440 | (11 Sep 2018–31 Aug 2019) |
| 1441 | (1 Sep 2019–19 Aug 2020) |

### One God

Allah is simply the Arabic name for 'God'. Muslims, Christians and Jews all worship this same God.

## JAINISM

| | |
|---|---|
| **Founded** | 6C BC |
| **Founder** | Vardhamana Mahavira (c.540–468BC) |
| **Sacred texts** | The Svetambara canon of scripture and Digambara texts. |
| **Place of worship** | Temple |
| **Beliefs** | Salvation and freedom from the working of karma can be acquired by ascetic practices. All living things are sacred and must not be harmed. |
| **Organization** | Jain monks and nuns have a strong relationship with lay people and officiate at temple rituals. |
| **Divisions** | Svetambara and Digambara. |

## JUDAISM

| | |
|---|---|
| **Founded** | c.2000BC |
| **Founder** | Abraham (c.2000–1650BC) and Moses (c.1500–1300BC) |
| **Sacred texts** | The Hebrew Bible: Torah (Pentateuch): Genesis, Exodus, Leviticus, Numbers, Deuteronomy. Also the books of the Prophets, Psalms, Chronicles and Proverbs, as well as the Talmud (made up of the Mishna, the oral law, and the Gemara, an extensive commentary). The Zohar (Book of Splendour) is a famous Cabalistic book. |
| **Place of worship** | Synagogue |
| **Beliefs** | Monotheistic: God created the world, delivered the Israelites out of bondage in Egypt, and chose them to be a light to all humankind. |
| **Organization** | Hierarchy of chief rabbis, rabbis and congregations. |
| **Divisions** | Today most Jews are descendants of either the Ashkenazim or the Sephardim. |

## CHIEF RABBIS

Chief Rabbi of the United Hebrew Congregations of the Commonwealth is the title given to the spiritual leader of the Jewish community in the UK. The Chief Rabbinate consists of the Chief Rabbi and his Cabinet.

| | |
|---|---|
| 1704–56 | Aaron Hart |
| 1756–8 | *post vacant* |
| 1758–64 | Hart Lyon |
| 1765–91 | David Tevele Schiff |
| 1791–1802 | *post vacant* |
| 1802–42 | Solomon Hirschell |
| 1842–5 | *post vacant* |
| 1845–91 | Nathan Marcus Adler |
| 1891–1911 | Hermann Marcus Adler |
| 1911–13 | *post vacant* |
| 1913–46 | Joseph Herman Hertz |
| 1946–8 | *post vacant* |
| 1948–65 | Israel Brodie |
| 1966–91 | Immanuel Jakobovits |
| 1991– | Jonathan Sacks |

## JEWISH CALENDAR

The Jewish religious calendar dates in its modern form from the Babylonian Exile in the 6c BC, when the Jews adopted the Babylonian calendar. This was lunar-solar, with a lunar year of 354 days and a solar year (important to agriculture) of 365 days. By the 4c BC an accurate system of intercalation had been devised. Each month starts with the new moon, but each day begins at sunset. These features were retained in the Jewish calendar. The year count of the Jewish era is calculated from 3761BC, said to be the year of the creation of the world.

**Months (solar days)**

*Basis: Moon*

Tishri (30)
Heshvan (29 or 30)
Kislev (29 or 30)
Tevet (29)
Shevat (30)
Adar (29 or 30)
Adar Sheni (*leap years only*)
Nisan (30)
Iyar (29)
Sivan (30)
Tammuz (29)
Av (30)
Elul (29)

| Year | Gregorian equivalents (AD) | Year | Gregorian equivalents (AD) |
|---|---|---|---|
| 5756 | (25 Sep 1995–13 Sep 1996) | 5769 | (30 Sep 2008–18 Sep 2009) |
| 5757 | (14 Sep 1996–1 Oct 1997) | 5770 | (19 Sep 2009–8 Sep 2010) |
| 5758 | (2 Oct 1997–20 Sep 1998) | 5771 | (9 Sep 2010–28 Sep 2011) |
| 5759 | (21 Sep 1998–10 Sep 1999) | 5772 | (29 Sep 2011–16 Sep 2012) |
| 5760 | (11 Sep 1999–29 Sep 2000) | 5773 | (17 Sep 2012–4 Sep 2013) |
| 5761 | (30 Sep 2000–17 Sep 2001) | 5774 | (5 Sep 2013–24 Sep 2014) |
| 5762 | (18 Sep 2001–6 Sep 2002) | 5775 | (25 Sep 2014–13 Sep 2015) |
| 5763 | (7 Sep 2002–26 Sep 2003) | 5776 | (14 Sep 2015–2 Oct 2016) |
| 5764 | (27 Sep 2003–15 Sep 2004) | 5777 | (3 Oct 2016–20 Sep 2017) |
| 5765 | (16 Sep 2004–3 Oct 2005) | 5778 | (21 Sep 2017–9 Sep 2018) |
| 5766 | (4 Oct 2005–22 Sep 2006) | 5779 | (10 Sep 2018–29 Sep 2019) |
| 5767 | (23 Sep 2006–12 Sep 2007) | 5780 | (30 Sep 2019–18 Sep 2020) |
| 5768 | (13 Sep 2007–29 Sep 2008) | | |

## SHINTOISM

| | |
|---|---|
| **Founded** | 8c AD |
| **Founder** | No single founder |
| **Sacred texts** | Kojiki and Nihon Shoki |
| **Place of worship** | Shrine |
| **Beliefs** | Founded on Japanese folk religions, Shinto is made up of many elements, including animism, veneration of nature and ancestor worship. |
| **Organization** | Shamans originally performed the ceremonies; in the 8c the imperial family were ascribed divine origins and state Shintoism was established. |
| **Divisions** | In the 19c Shinto was divided into Shrine (jinga) Shinto and Sectarian (kyoko) Shinto. Jinga was a state cult until 1945. |

## SIKHISM

| | |
|---|---|
| **Founded** | 15c |
| **Founder** | Guru Nanak (1469–1539) |
| **Sacred texts** | Adi Granth |
| **Place of worship** | Temple |
| **Beliefs** | Monotheistic; a fusion of Brahmanism and Islam, preaching tolerance and equality in the sight of God; initiates wear the Five Ks. |
| **Organization** | No priestly caste. All Sikhs are empowered to perform rituals connected with births, marriages and deaths. |
| **Divisions** | There are several religious orders of Sikhs based either on disputes over the succession of gurus or points of ritual and tradition. |

## FIVE KS OF SIKHISM

The Five Ks are the symbols of a Sikh's spiritual and cultural allegiance to Sikhism, worn by baptized Sikhs.

**Kesh** (uncut hair)

**Kanga** (comb)

**Kara** (steel bangle symbolizing the one God)

**Kirpan** (ceremonial dagger to fight injustice)

**Kaccha** (short trousers signifying willingness to ride into battle)

## TAOISM

| | |
|---|---|
| **Founded** | c.600BC |
| **Founder** | Lao-tzu (6c BC) |
| **Sacred texts** | Chuang-tzu, Lao-tzu (Tao-te-ching) |
| **Place of worship** | Temple |
| **Beliefs** | Tao ('the way') stresses harmony with nature, meditation, worship of a pantheon of gods and spirits and the theory of Yin-Yang. |
| **Organization** | Monastic orders and priests practise temple worship and divination, including the I ching. |
| **Divisions** | Taoism emerged from many sects, each emphasizing different aspects such as worship of the Immortals, exorcism, faith healing, alchemy or meditative practice. |

## TEMPLETON PRIZE

Awarded for progress towards research or discoveries about spiritual realities.

| | |
|---|---|
| 1973 | Mother Teresa |
| 1974 | Brother Roger |
| 1975 | Sarvepalli Radhakrishnan |
| 1976 | Leon Joseph Suenens |
| 1977 | Chiara Lubich |
| 1978 | Thomas F Torrance |
| 1979 | Nikkyo Niwano |
| 1980 | Ralph Wendell Burhoe |
| 1981 | Dame Cecily Saunders |
| 1982 | Billy Graham |
| 1983 | Aleksandr Solzhenitsyn |
| 1984 | Michael Bourdeaux |
| 1985 | Alister Hardy |
| 1986 | James I McCord |
| 1987 | Stanley L Jaki |
| 1988 | Inamullah Khan |
| 1989 | Lord MacLeod of Fiunary; Carl Friedrich von Weizsäcker |
| 1990 | Baba Amte; L Charles Birch |
| 1991 | Lord Jakobovits |
| 1992 | Kyung-Chik Han |
| 1993 | Charles W Colson |
| 1994 | Michael Novak |
| 1995 | Paul Charles William Davies |
| 1996 | William Rohl Bright |
| 1997 | Pandurang Shastri Athavale |
| 1998 | Sigmund Sternberg |
| 1999 | Ian Graeme Barbour |
| 2000 | Freeman J Dyson |
| 2001 | Arthur Peacocke |
| 2002 | John C Polkinghorne |
| 2003 | Holmes Rolston III |

## SIGNS OF THE ZODIAC

The zodiac is the band of sky, about 18° wide, through the centre of which the Sun appears to move. It forms the background for the motions of the Sun, Moon and major planets, and is divided into twelve equal parts of 30°, each of which once contained one of the zodiacal constellations. The passing of time means that the Sun no longer passes through each constellation on the accepted dates.

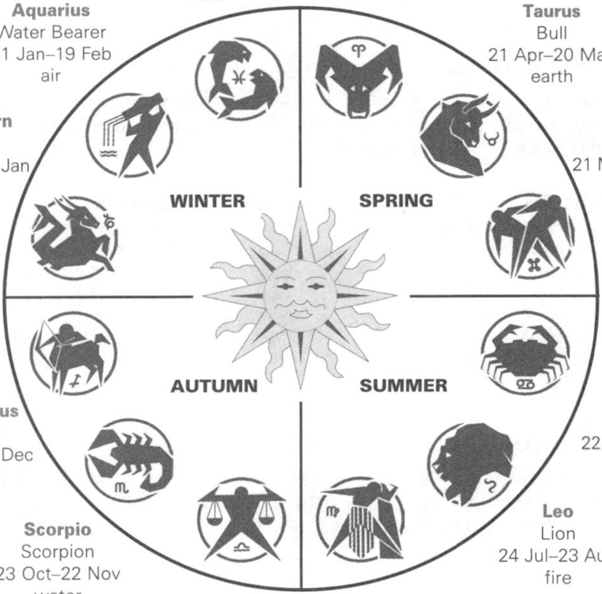


### *Sky Figures*

The word *zodiac* comes from the French word *zodiaque* but is originally from the Greek word *zōidion*, a small carved or painted figure, which itself comes from the word *zōion*, an animal.

## BIRTH STONES

In many Western countries, the months are traditionally associated with gemstones. There is considerable variation between countries; the following combinations are widely recognized in North America and the UK.

| **Month** | **Gemstone** | **Month** | **Gemstone** |
|---|---|---|---|
| Jan | Garnet | Jul | Ruby |
| Feb | Amethyst | Aug | Peridot, Sardonyx |
| Mar | Aquamarine, Bloodstone | Sep | Sapphire |
| Apr | Diamond | Oct | Opal, Tourmaline |
| May | Emerald | Nov | Topaz |
| Jun | Alexandrite, Moonstone, Pearl | Dec | Turquoise, Zircon |

## BIRTH FLOWERS

In many Western countries, the months are traditionally associated with flowers. There is considerable variation between countries; the following combinations are widely recognized in North America and the UK.

| **Month** | **Flower** | **Month** | **Flower** |
|---|---|---|---|
| Jan | Carnation, Snowdrop | Jul | Larkspur, Water Lily |
| Feb | Primrose, Violet | Aug | Gladiolus, Poppy |
| Mar | Jonquil, Violet | Sep | Aster, Morning Glory |
| Apr | Daisy, Sweet Pea | Oct | Calendula, Cosmos |
| May | Hawthorn, Lily of the Valley | Nov | Chrysanthemum |
| Jun | Honeysuckle, Rose | Dec | Holly, Narcissus, Poinsettia |

## KNIGHTS OF THE ROUND TABLE

Tradition has it that King Arthur and his knights sat at the Round Table, a table shaped so that no individual knight should have precedence. Lists of the knights vary considerably; below are those recorded on the Winchester Round Table:

Sir Alymere
King Arthur
Sir Bedivere
Sir Bleoberis
Sir Bors de Ganis
Sir Brunor le Noir
La Cote Male Taile
Sir Dagonet
Sir Degore
Sir Ector de Maris
Sir Galahad
Sir Gareth
Sir Gawaine
Sir Kay
Sir Lamorak
Sir Lancelot (Launcelot) Du Lac
Sir Le Bel Desconneu
Sir Lionell
Sir Lucan
Sir Mordred
Sir Palomedes
Sir Pelleas
Sir Percivale
Sir Safer
Sir Tristan (Tristram)

## SANTA'S REINDEER

Clement Clarke Moore (1779–1863) christened Santa's reindeer in his poem 'A Visit from St Nicholas' (1823), popularly known as ''Twas the Night Before Christmas'. They are:

Blitzen
Comet
Cupid
Dasher
Dancer
Donder[1]
Prancer
Vixen

[1] *Donder is also known as Donner.*

### *Rudolph the Red-Nosed Reindeer*

Shopping chains and promotional gimmicks might not seem to have anything to do with the spirit of Christmas. However, Rudolph, the famous reindeer with the 'very shiny nose', was originally devised as a character in a storybook to be given away as a Christmas freebie in 1939 to customers of Montgomery Ward department stores in Chicago, USA. His creator, Robert L May, supposedly went through a number of names before settling on Rudolph: Santa's red-nosed pal was nearly called Rollo, or even Reginald.

## SEASONS

### Northern hemisphere

| Season | Duration |
|---|---|
| Spring | From vernal equinox (c.21 Mar) to summer solstice (c.21 Jun) |
| Summer | From summer solstice (c.21 Jun) to autumnal equinox (c.23 Sep) |
| Autumn | From autumnal equinox (c.23 Sep) to winter solstice (c.21 Dec) |
| Winter | From winter solstice (c.21 Dec) to vernal equinox (c.21 Mar) |

### Southern hemisphere

| Season | Duration |
|---|---|
| Spring | From vernal equinox (c.23 Sep) to summer solstice (c.21 Dec) |
| Summer | From summer solstice (c.21 Dec) to autumnal equinox (c.21 Mar) |
| Autumn | From autumnal equinox (c.21 Mar) to winter solstice (c.21 Jun) |
| Winter | From winter solstice (c.21 Jun) to vernal equinox (c.23 Sep) |

## MONTHS

| Month | Days | Name origin |
|---|---|---|
| January | 31 | From the Latin *Jānuārius* (*mēnsis*), the month dedicated to Janus, the god of gates, doorways, and beginnings, usually depicted with a two-faced head. |
| February | 28 or 29 | From the Latin *Februārius* (*mēnsis*) the month of expiation, and *februa* the feast of expiation. |
| March | 31 | From the Latin *Martius* (*mēnsis*) the month dedicated to Mars, the Roman god of war. |
| April | 30 | From the Latin *Aprīlis*, probably from Latin *aperire*, to open. |
| May | 31 | From the Old French *Mai*, from Latin *Māius* (*mēnsis*), probably meaning the month sacred to Māia, the Roman goddess of fertility. |
| June | 30 | From the Latin *Jūnius* (*mēnsis*) the month of Juno, the Roman goddess of marriage, childbirth and light. |
| July | 31 | From the Latin *Jūlius*, from the Roman emperor Julius Caesar, who was born in it. |
| August | 31 | From the first Roman emperor, Augustus, who amended the Roman calendar in 8BC. |
| September | 30 | From the Latin *September*, from *septem* seven; in the original Roman calendar, September was the seventh month of a ten-month year. |
| October | 31 | From the Latin *Octōber*, from *octō* eight; in the original Roman calendar, October was the eighth month of a ten-month year. |
| November | 30 | From the Latin *November*, from *novem* nine; in the original Roman calendar, November was the ninth month of a ten-month year. |
| December | 31 | From the Latin *December*, from *decem* ten; in the original Roman calendar, December was the tenth month of a ten-month year. |

For the Hindu, Islamic and Jewish calendars and months see **Religions, Beliefs and Folklore**.

## Gregorian Calendar

The calendar in general use throughout the world is the Gregorian New Style calendar. The calendar was reformed by Pope Gregory XIII in 1582.

The Julian calendar that was previously in use had a shortcoming in that the value of 365¼ days placed on the solar year was too long by 11 minutes and 14 seconds. By 1545 the vernal equinox, used by the Church to determine the date of Easter, had moved ten days. It took time for astronomers to work out a satisfactory method of correction, but finally the Pope instructed that ten days should be omitted from Oct 1582.

Britain didn't adopt the new calendar until 1752. At that time the difference between the two calendars was eleven days. The changeover meant that 2 Sep was immediately followed by 14 Sep, leading to popular protests, as people felt swindled out of the missing days, shouting 'Give us back our eleven days!'

## DAYS

| **Day** | **Name origin** |
|---|---|
| Sunday | From the Old English *sunnan dæg*, a translation of the Latin *dīēs sōlis*, meaning day of the Sun. |
| Monday | From the Old English *mōnandæg*, from *mōnan*, *mōna* meaning Moon, and *dæg* meaning day, a translation of the Latin *dīēs lūnae*, Moon's day. |
| Tuesday | From the Old English *Tīwes dæg*, the day of Tīw, the god of war, corresponding to the Latin *dīēs Martis*, the day of Mars. |
| Wednesday | From the Old English *Wōdnes dæg*, the day of Woden, or Odin, the chief god. |
| Thursday | From the Old English *Thunres dæg*, the day of Thunor, the thunder god, and the Old Norse *Thōrsdagr*, Thor's day. |
| Friday | From the Old English *Frīgedæg*, the day of *Frīg*, the goddess of married love, corresponding to the Latin *dīēs Veneris*, the day of Venus. |
| Saturday | From the Old English *Sæterdæg* or *Sætern(es)dæg*, a translation of the Latin *dīēs Saturni*, the day of Saturn. |

## Hot Dogs

The hottest days of the year are known as the *dog days*, and are associated with the rising of the Dog Star (Sirius). The definition of this period varies, but it is generally reckoned to last from 3 Jul to 11 Aug. According to ancient superstition, disease and disaster were rife at this time and dogs were at their most susceptible to rabies: in some towns and cities all dogs had to wear muzzles in public places for the duration.

## QUARTER DAYS

**Traditionally, the quarter days were those days in each of the year's quarters on which rent or interest was due to be paid.**

| **England, Wales and Ireland** | | **Scotland**[1] | |
|---|---|---|---|
| Lady Day | 25 Mar | Candlemas | 28 Feb |
| Midsummer Day | 24 Jun | Whitsunday | 28 May |
| Michaelmas Day | 29 Sep | Lammas | 28 Aug |
| Christmas Day | 25 Dec | Martinmas | 28 Nov |

[1] *As defined in the Term and Quarter Days (Scotland) Act 1990.*

## FRENCH REVOLUTIONARY CALENDAR

The French Revolutionary Calendar, also known as the French Republican Calendar, was introduced in 1793 to herald the beginning of a new age for France. It attempted to move the organization of the calendar away from all religious connections. Instead, Year 1 dated from the declaration of the First Republic on 22 Sep 1792 (the autumnal equinox of that year). Twelve 30-day months were introduced, named to be appropriate to the season, and were divided into three ten-day weeks called *decadi*. Five supplementary days (or six in leap years) were known as *sans-culottides*. The calendar worked well enough in France but caused problems for international communications, and Napoleon I replaced it with the Gregorian calendar in 1805.

| Month | Derivation of name |
|---|---|
| Vendémiaire | vintage |
| Brumaire | mist |
| Frimaire | frost |
| Nivôse | snow |
| Pluviôse | rain |
| Ventôse | wind |
| Germinal | seed |
| Floréal | blossom |
| Prairial | meadow |
| Messidor | harvest |
| Thermidor | heat |
| Fructidor | fruits |

## CHINESE ANIMAL YEARS AND TIMES

Data is given for the years 1960–2019.

| Chinese | English | Years | | | | | Time of day (hours) |
|---|---|---|---|---|---|---|---|
| Shu | Rat | 1960 | 1972 | 1984 | 1996 | 2008 | 2300–0100 |
| Niu | Ox | 1961 | 1973 | 1985 | 1997 | 2009 | 0100–0300 |
| Hu | Tiger | 1962 | 1974 | 1986 | 1998 | 2010 | 0300–0500 |
| Tu | Hare | 1963 | 1975 | 1987 | 1999 | 2011 | 0500–0700 |
| Long | Dragon | 1964 | 1976 | 1988 | 2000 | 2012 | 0700–0900 |
| She | Serpent | 1965 | 1977 | 1989 | 2001 | 2013 | 0900–1100 |
| Ma | Horse | 1966 | 1978 | 1990 | 2002 | 2014 | 1100–1300 |
| Yang | Sheep | 1967 | 1979 | 1991 | 2003 | 2015 | 1300–1500 |
| Hou | Monkey | 1968 | 1980 | 1992 | 2004 | 2016 | 1500–1700 |
| Ji | Cock | 1969 | 1981 | 1993 | 2005 | 2017 | 1700–1900 |
| Gou | Dog | 1970 | 1982 | 1994 | 2006 | 2018 | 1900–2100 |
| Zhu | Boar | 1971 | 1983 | 1995 | 2007 | 2019 | 2100–2300 |

## WEDDING ANNIVERSARIES

In many Western countries, wedding anniversaries have become associated with gifts of different materials. There is some variation between countries.

| Anniversary | Traditional gift | Modern gift |
|---|---|---|
| 1st | paper | clocks |
| 2nd | cotton | china |
| 3rd | leather | crystal, glass |
| 4th | fruit, flowers | appliances |
| 5th | wood | silverware |
| 6th | sugar, iron | wood |
| 7th | copper, wool | desk sets |
| 8th | bronze, pottery | linen, lace |
| 9th | pottery, willow | leather |
| 10th | tin, aluminium | diamond jewellery |
| 11th | steel | fashion jewellery |
| 12th | silk, linen | pearl |
| 13th | lace | textiles, fur |
| 14th | ivory | gold jewellery |
| 15th | crystal | watches |
| 20th | china | platinum |
| 25th | silver | silver |
| 30th | pearl | diamond |
| 35th | coral | jade |
| 40th | ruby | ruby |
| 45th | sapphire | sapphire |
| 50th | gold | gold |
| 55th | emerald | emerald |
| 60th | diamond | diamond |
| 70th | platinum | platinum |

### *A Call from the Queen*

It is well known that the monarch will send congratulations to centenarians upon their 100th birthday, a tradition that dates back to 1917. But the sovereign will also send royal best wishes to couples reaching their diamond wedding anniversary, and also to husbands and wives celebrating 65 years of marriage, 70 years, and every subsequent anniversary.

# SCIENCE

## CHEMICAL ELEMENTS

Chemical elements with atomic numbers between 1 and 109 are given below.

| Symbol | Element | Derived from | Atomic no |
|---|---|---|---|
| Ac | actinium | Greek *aktis* = ray | 89 |
| Ag | silver | Old English *silfer* | 47 |
| Al | aluminium | Latin *alumen* = alum | 13 |
| Am | americium | America | 95 |
| Ar | argon | Greek *argon* = inactive | 18 |
| As | arsenic | Greek *arsenikon* = yellow orpiment | 33 |
| At | astatine | Greek *astatos* = unstable | 85 |
| Au | gold | Old English *gold* | 79 |
| B | boron | Arabic *buraq* = borax | 5 |
| Ba | barium | Greek *barys* = heavy | 56 |
| Be | beryllium | Greek *beryllos* = beryl | 4 |
| Bh | bohrium | Bohr, Danish physicist | 107 |
| Bi | bismuth | German (origin unknown) | 83 |
| Bk | berkelium | Berkeley, California | 97 |
| Br | bromine | Greek *bromos* = stink | 35 |
| C | carbon | Latin *carbo* = coal | 6 |
| Ca | calcium | Latin *calx* = lime | 20 |
| Cd | cadmium | Greek *kadmeia* = calamine | 48 |
| Ce | cerium | asteroid Ceres | 58 |
| Cf | californium | California | 98 |
| Cl | chlorine | Greek *chloros* = pale green | 17 |
| Cm | curium | Curie, French physicists | 96 |
| Co | cobalt | German *Kobold* = demon | 27 |
| Cr | chromium | Greek *chroma* = colour | 24 |
| Cs | caesium | Latin *caesius* = bluish-grey | 55 |
| Cu | copper | Cyprus | 29 |
| Db | dubnium | Dubna, Russia | 105 |
| Dy | dysprosium | Greek *dysprositos* = difficult to reach | 66 |
| Er | erbium | Ytterby, Sweden | 68 |
| Es | einsteinium | Einstein, US physicist | 99 |
| Eu | europium | Europe | 63 |
| F | fluorine | Latin *fluor* = flow | 9 |
| Fe | iron | Old English *iren* | 26 |
| Fm | fermium | Fermi, Italian physicist | 100 |
| Fr | francium | France | 87 |
| Ga | gallium | Latin *Gallia* = France, or *gallus* = cock | 31 |
| Gd | gadolinium | Gadolin, Finnish chemist | 64 |

| Symbol | Element | Derived from | Atomic no |
|---|---|---|---|
| Ge | germanium | Germany | 32 |
| H | hydrogen | Greek *hydor* = water + *gennaein* = to produce | 1 |
| He | helium | Greek *helios* = sun | 2 |
| Hf | hafnium | Latin *Hafnia* = Copenhagen | 72 |
| Hg | mercury | Latin *Mercurius* | 80 |
| Ho | holmium | N Latin *Holmia* = Stockholm | 67 |
| Hs | hassium | Latin *Hassias* = Hesse | 108 |
| I | iodine | Greek *ioeides* = violet-coloured | 53 |
| In | indium | indigo lines in the spectrum | 49 |
| Ir | iridium | Latin *iris* = rainbow goddess | 77 |
| K | potassium | potash | 19 |
| Kr | krypton | Greek *kryptein* = to hide | 36 |
| La | lanthanum | Greek *lanthanein* = to escape notice | 57 |
| Li | lithium | Greek *lithos* = stone | 3 |
| Lr | lawrencium | Lawrence, US physicist | 103 |
| Lu | lutetium | Latin *Lutetia* = Paris | 71 |
| Md | mendelevium | Mendeleev, Russian scientist | 101 |
| Mg | magnesium | Magnesia, Thessaly, Greece | 12 |
| Mn | manganese | Latin *magnesia* | 25 |
| Mo | molybdenum | Greek *molybdos* = lead | 42 |
| Mt | meitnerium | Meitner, Austrian physicist | 109 |
| N | nitrogen | Greek *nitron* = sodium carbonate + *gennaein* = to produce | 7 |
| Na | sodium | soda | 11 |
| Nb | niobium | Niobe (Greek myth) | 41 |
| Nd | neodymium | Greek *neos* = new + *didymos* = twin | 60 |
| Ne | neon | Greek *neos* = new | 10 |
| Ni | nickel | German *Kupfernickel* = niccolite | 28 |
| No | nobelium | Nobel Institute | 102 |
| Np | neptunium | planet Neptune | 93 |
| O | oxygen | Greek *oxys* = acid + *gennaein* = to produce | 8 |
| Os | osmium | Greek *osme* = smell | 76 |
| P | phosphorus | Greek *phosphoros* = light-bearer | 15 |
| Pa | protactinium | Greek *protos* = first + *actinium* (see above) | 91 |
| Pb | lead | Old English *lead* | 82 |
| Pd | palladium | minor planet Pallas | 46 |
| Pm | promethium | Prometheus (Greek myth) | 61 |
| Po | polonium | Poland | 84 |
| Pr | praseodymium | Greek *prasios* = leek green + *didymos* = twin | 59 |

# CHEMICAL ELEMENTS

| Symbol | Element | Derived from | Atomic no |
|---|---|---|---|
| Pt | platinum | Spanish *plata* = silver | 78 |
| Pu | plutonium | planet Pluto | 94 |
| Ra | radium | Latin *radius* = ray | 88 |
| Rb | rubidium | Latin *rubidus* = red | 37 |
| Re | rhenium | Latin *Rhenus* = the Rhine | 75 |
| Rf | rutherfordium | Rutherford, British physicist | 104 |
| Rh | rhodium | Greek *rhodon* = rose | 45 |
| Rn | radon | radium | 86 |
| Ru | ruthenium | Latin *Ruthenia* = Russia | 44 |
| S | sulphur | Latin *sulphur* | 16 |
| Sb | antimony | Latin *antimonium* | 51 |
| Sc | scandium | Scandinavian | 21 |
| Se | selenium | Greek *selene* = moon | 34 |
| Sg | seaborgium | Seaborg, US physicist | 106 |
| Si | silicon | Latin *silex* = flint | 14 |
| Sm | samarium | Samarski, Russian engineer | 62 |
| Sn | tin | Old English *tin* | 50 |
| Sr | strontium | Strontian, Scotland | 38 |
| Ta | tantalum | Tantalus (Greek myth) | 73 |
| Tb | terbium | Ytterby, Sweden | 65 |
| Tc | technetium | Greek *technetos* = artificial | 43 |
| Te | tellurium | Latin *tellus* = earth | 52 |
| Th | thorium | Scandinavian god Thor | 90 |
| Ti | titanium | Greek *Titan* = Titan | 22 |
| Tl | thallium | Greek *thallos* = a young shoot | 81 |
| Tm | thulium | Latin *Thule* = an island in the extreme north | 69 |
| U | uranium | planet Uranus | 92 |
| V | vanadium | Old Norse *Vanadis* = goddess Freya | 23 |
| W | tungsten | Swedish *tungsten* = heavy stone | 74 |
| Xe | xenon | Greek *xenos* = stranger | 54 |
| Y | yttrium | Ytterby, Sweden | 39 |
| Yb | ytterbium | Ytterby, Sweden | 70 |
| Zn | zinc | German *zink* | 30 |
| Zr | zirconium | Persian *zargun* = gold-coloured | 40 |

## Radioactive Family

Element number 96, curium, is named after the French physicists Pierre (1859–1906) and Marie Curie (1867–1934). Marie coined the word 'radioactivity' in 1898, and together they isolated radium and polonium. They were jointly awarded the Nobel prize for physics in 1903; Marie later received the Nobel prize for chemistry (1911). Their daughter, Irène Joliot-Curie (1897–1956), and her husband, Frédéric (1900–58), also won the Nobel prize for chemistry in 1935.

# PERIODIC TABLE

element symbol — atomic number
element name

| | | | | | | | | | | | | | | | | | |
|---|---|---|---|---|---|---|---|---|---|---|---|---|---|---|---|---|---|
| H 1 hydrogen | | | | | | | | | | | | | | | | | He 2 helium |
| Li 3 lithium | Be 4 beryllium | | | | | | | | | | | B 5 boron | C 6 carbon | N 7 nitrogen | O 8 oxygen | F 9 fluorine | Ne 10 neon |
| Na 11 sodium | Mg 12 magnesium | | | | | | | | | | | Al 13 aluminium | Si 14 silicon | P 15 phos-phorus | S 16 sulphur | Cl 17 chlorine | Ar 18 argon |
| K 19 potassium | Ca 20 calcium | Sc 21 scandium | Ti 22 titanium | V 23 vanadium | Cr 24 chromium | Mn 25 manganese | Fe 26 iron | Co 27 cobalt | Ni 28 nickel | Cu 29 copper | Zn 30 zinc | Ga 31 gallium | Ge 32 germanium | As 33 arsenic | Se 34 selenium | Br 35 bromine | Kr 36 krypton |
| Rb 37 rubidium | Sr 38 strontium | Y 39 yttrium | Zr 40 zirconium | Nb 41 niobium | Mo 42 moly-bdenum | Tc 43 technetium | Ru 44 ruthenium | Rh 45 rhodium | Pd 46 palladium | Ag 47 silver | Cd 48 cadmium | In 49 indium | Sn 50 tin | Sb 51 antimony | Te 52 tellurium | I 53 iodine | Xe 54 xenon |
| Cs 55 caesium | Ba 56 barium | 57–71 * | Hf 72 hafnium | Ta 73 tantalum | W 74 tungsten | Re 75 rhenium | Os 76 osmium | Ir 77 iridium | Pt 78 platinum | Au 79 gold | Hg 80 mercury | Tl 81 thallium | Pb 82 lead | Bi 83 bismuth | Po 84 polonium | At 85 astatine | Rn 86 radon |
| Fr 87 francium | Ra 88 radium | 89–103 ** | Rf 104 ruther-fordium | Db 105 dubnium | Sg 106 sea-borgium | Bh 107 bohrium | Hs 108 hassium | Mt 109 meitnerium | Uun 110 ununnilium | Uuu 111 unununium | Uub 112 ununbium | | | | | | |

| | | | | | | | | | | | | | | | |
|---|---|---|---|---|---|---|---|---|---|---|---|---|---|---|---|
| *Lanthanide series | La 57 lanthanum | Ce 58 cerium | Pr 59 praseo-dymium | Nd 60 neo-dymium | Pm 61 pro-methium | Sm 62 samarium | Eu 63 europium | Gd 64 gadolinium | Tb 65 terbium | Dy 66 dysprosium | Ho 67 holmium | Er 68 erbium | Tm 69 thulium | Yb 70 ytterbium | Lu 71 lutetium |
| **Actinide series | Ac 89 actinium | Th 90 thorium | Pa 91 pro-tactinium | U 92 uranium | Np 93 neptunium | Pu 94 plutonium | Am 95 americium | Cm 96 curium | Bk 97 berkelium | Cf 98 californium | Es 99 einsteinium | Fm 100 fermium | Md 101 men-delevium | No 102 nobelium | Lr 103 law-rencium |

## SUBATOMIC PARTICLES

Subatomic particles are those that constitute the atom.

**hadrons**

**baryons**
proton
neutron

**mesons**
pion
kaon
J/psi
upsilon

**quarks**
up quark
down quark
charmed quark
strange quark
bottom quark
top quark

**leptons**
electron
positron
muon
tau lepton
neutrino (electron)
neutrino (muon)
neutrino (tau)

**gauge bosons**
photon
W
Z
gluon
gravitron

### *Flavours of Quark*

The language of *quarks* is one of the quirkier areas of particle physics. It is thought that there are six types of quark, known as *flavours* – *up*, *down*, *top*, *bottom*, *strange* and *charmed*. *Bottom* is sometimes also known as *beauty*, and *top* as *truth*. Each flavour of quark is also believed to have an antiparticle known as an *antiquark*. Flavours of quark come in three *colours*: red, blue and green; and for antiquarks, three *anticolours*. The term *quark* was coined by the writer James Joyce (1882–1941) in *Finnegans Wake* (1939), and adopted for scientific use by the American physicist Murray Gell-Mann (born 1929).

## DECIBEL SCALE

A decibel is a term used to express a level of sound. It is the tenth part of a bel, a measure for comparing the intensity of noises, named after Alexander Graham Bell (1847–1922), the inventor of the telephone.

| Source | Decibel level (dB) |
|---|---|
| Breathing | 10 |
| Whisper | 20 |
| Conversation | 50–60 |
| Vacuum cleaner | 80 |
| Traffic | 60–90 |
| Pneumatic drill | 110 |
| Jet aircraft | 120 |
| Space vehicle launch | 140–170 |

## WENTWORTH SCALE

The Wentworth scale is one of the main scales used in geology to describe the general dimensions of grains in a rock, especially sediment. It was devised by Chester K Wentworth (1891–1969), a US geologist.

| Name | Dimension[1] |
|---|---|
| boulder | greater than 256mm |
| cobble | 64–256mm |
| pebble | 4–64mm |
| gravel | 2–4mm |
| sand | $^1/_{16}$–2mm |
| silt | $^1/_{256}$–$^1/_{16}$mm |
| clay | less than $^1/_{256}$mm |

[1] *To convert millimetres to inches, multiply by 0.0394.*

## MOHS' HARDNESS SCALE

The relative hardness of solids can be expressed using a scale of numbers from 1 to 10, each relating to a mineral (1 representing talc, 10 representing diamond). The method was devised by Friedrich Mohs (1773–1839), a German mineralogist. Sets of hardness pencils are used to test specimens to see what will scratch them; other useful instruments for testing include: fingernail (2.5), copper coin (3.5), steel knife (5.5), glass (6.0).

| | | | | | | | |
|---|---|---|---|---|---|---|---|
| Talc | 1 | Fluorite | 4 | Quartz | 7 | Diamond | 10 |
| Gypsum | 2 | Apatite | 5 | Topaz | 8 | | |
| Calcite | 3 | Orthoclase | 6 | Corundum | 9 | | |

## pH SCALE

pH or pH value is a number used to express degrees of acidity or alkalinity in solutions. The title comes from the German word *potenz* meaning power, and *H* the symbol for hydrogen.

*The scale ranges from 0 to 14; a pH below 7 indicates acidity, and one above 7 alkalinity. A solution with a pH of 7 is neutral.*

## ELECTROMAGNETIC SPECTRUM

The electromagnetic spectrum ranges from short to long wavelengths, ie including gamma rays, X-rays, ultraviolet radiation, visible light, infrared radiation, microwaves and radio waves. *To convert metres to feet multiply by 3.2808.*

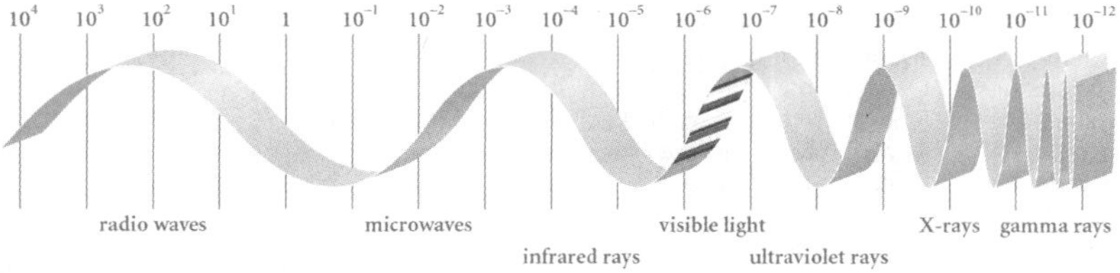


### Light Speed

The speed of light is $2.99792458 \times 10^8$m/sec, equivalent to 300 000km, or 186 000mi, per second. The speed of sound is a tardy 331.4m/sec, or 1 193kph/741mph.

## SI PREFIXES

| Factor | Prefix | Symbol | Factor | Prefix | Symbol |
|---|---|---|---|---|---|
| $10^{24}$ | yotta | Y | $10^{-1}$ | deci | d |
| $10^{21}$ | zetta | Z | $10^{-2}$ | centi | c |
| $10^{18}$ | exa | E | $10^{-3}$ | milli | m |
| $10^{15}$ | peta | P | $10^{-6}$ | micro | µ |
| $10^{12}$ | tera | T | $10^{-9}$ | nano | n |
| $10^9$ | giga | G | $10^{-12}$ | pico | p |
| $10^6$ | mega | M | $10^{-15}$ | femto | f |
| $10^3$ | kilo | k | $10^{-18}$ | atto | a |
| $10^2$ | hecto | h | $10^{-21}$ | zepto | z |
| $10^1$ | deca | da | $10^{-24}$ | yocto | y |

## GEMSTONES

Nearly all gemstones are minerals, as are those in this table. The four non-mineral gems are amber, coral, jet and pearl. The hardness of solid substances is expressed on the Mohs' scale.

| Mineral | Colour | Mohs of hardness |
|---|---|---|
| agate | brown, red, blue, green, yellow | 7.0 |
| alexandrite | green, red | 8.5 |
| amethyst | violet | 7.0 |
| aquamarine | sky blue, greenish blue | 7.5 |
| beryl | green, blue, pink | 7.5 |
| bloodstone | green with red spots | 7.0 |
| chalcedony | all colours | 7.0 |
| chrysoprase | apple green | 7.0 |
| citrine | yellow | 7.0 |
| diamond | colourless, tints of various colours | 10.0 |
| emerald | green | 7.5 |
| garnet | red and other colours | 6.5–7.25 |
| jade | green, whitish, mauve, brown | 7.0 |
| jasper | dark red, multi-coloured | 7.0 |
| lapis lazuli | deep blue | 5.5 |
| malachite | dark green banded | 3.5 |
| moonstone | whitish with blue shimmer | 6.0 |
| onyx | various colours with straight coloured bands | 7.0 |
| opal | black, white, orange-red, rainbow coloured | 6.0 |
| peridot | green | 6.5 |
| ruby | red | 9.0 |
| sapphire | blue and other colours | 9.0 |
| serpentine | red and green | 3.0 |
| soapstone | white, may be stained with impurities | 2.0 |
| sunstone | whitish red-brown flecked with golden particles | 6.0 |
| topaz | blue, green, pink, yellow, colourless | 8.0 |
| tourmaline | brown-black, blue, pink, red, violet-red, yellow, green | 7.5 |
| turquoise | greenish grey, sky blue | 6.0 |
| zircon | all colours | 7.5 |

## DRUGS DERIVED FROM PLANTS

A selection of commonly prescribed drugs of plant origin are given below.

| Drug | Plant | Effect |
|---|---|---|
| aspirin | white willow | pain relief |
| atropine | deadly nightshade (Belladonna) | anticholinergic (blocks nerve impulses, as in antidepressants and antispasmodics) |
| cocaine | coca | local anaesthetic/central nervous system stimulant |
| codeine | opium poppy | pain relief |
| curare | various tropical American plants | muscle relaxant |
| digitalis | foxglove | heart stimulant |
| L-dopa | velvet bean | mitigation of Parkinson's disease |
| morphine | opium poppy | pain relief/narcotic |
| penicillin | *Penicillium notatum* fungus | antibiotic |
| quinine | yellow cinchona | antimalarial |
| strychnine | Nux vomica (*Strychnos nux-vomica*) | central nervous system stimulant |

## MEASURING DEVICES

| Device | Measures |
|---|---|
| accelerometer | acceleration |
| altimeter | height |
| ammeter | electric current |
| anemometer | wind |
| barometer | atmospheric pressure |
| calorimeter | heat capacities, etc |
| chronometer | time |
| cryometer | low temperatures |
| decelerometer | deceleration |
| dosimeter | radiation |
| dynamometer | force |
| evaporimeter, evaporometer | rate of evaporation |
| flowmeter | rate of flow of a fluid in a pipe |
| focimeter | focal length of a lens |
| galvanometer | electric currents |
| Geiger counter | radioactivity |
| geothermometer | subterranean temperatures |
| gravimeter | variations in the Earth's surface gravity |
| hyetometer, ombrometer, pluviometer | rain |
| hygrometer | humidity of the air or of other gases |
| inclinometer | slopes |
| interferometer | wavelengths, wave speeds, angles, etc |
| luxmeter | illumination |
| magnetometer | strength/direction of a magnetic field |
| mileometer, milometer | miles that a vehicle, etc has travelled |
| odometer, hodometer | distance travelled by a wheeled vehicle |
| ohmmeter | electrical resistance |
| optometer | vision |
| pedometer | paces (approximate distance walked) |
| photometer | luminous intensity |
| pulsimeter | strength or quickness of the pulse |
| pyrometer | high temperatures |
| respirometer | breathing |
| seismometer | intensity and duration of earthquakes |
| spectrometer | refractive indices |
| speedometer | speed at which a vehicle is travelling |
| sphygmomanometer, sphygmometer | arterial blood pressure |
| tachometer | velocity |
| theodolite | horizontal and vertical angles |
| thermometer | temperature |
| vaporimeter | vapour pressure or vapour |
| velocimeter | velocity |
| vibrograph, vibrometer | vibrations |
| viscometer, viscosimeter | viscosity |
| voltmeter | electromotive force |
| volumeter | volumes of gases and liquids |
| wattmeter | circuit power |
| wavemeter | wavelengths |

### *Unusual Measuring Devices*

In the realm of science there are instruments to measure almost everything. Some of the less common are the *cyanometer* (measures the blueness of the sky or ocean), *diaphanometer* (the transparency of the air), *drosometer* (dew), *konimeter* (dust in the air), *oenometer* (the alcoholic strength of wines), *Nilometer* (the height of the River Nile), *weatherometer* (the weather-resisting properties of paints or other surfaces) and *xylometer* (the specific gravity of wood). The specific gravity, relative density and purity or richness of milk are measured by the *galactometer*, *lactometer* and *lactoscope* respectively, while the *plethysmograph* measures variations in the size of body parts, for example when varying amounts of blood flow through them.

## NOBEL PRIZE FOR PHYSICS

Nobel prizes were established by a bequest in the will of Alfred Nobel (1833–96) to honour 'those who, during the preceding year, shall have conferred the greatest benefit on mankind'. The Nobel prize for physics is awarded annually to a person who has 'made the most important discovery or invention within the field of physics'; first awarded in 1901.

| | |
|---|---|
| 1901 | Wilhelm Conrad Röntgen |
| 1902 | Hendrik A Lorentz, Pieter Zeeman |
| 1903 | Henri Becquerel, Pierre Curie, Marie Curie |
| 1904 | Lord Rayleigh |
| 1905 | Philipp Lenard |
| 1906 | J J Thomson |
| 1907 | Albert A Michelson |
| 1908 | Gabriel Lippmann |
| 1909 | Guglielmo Marconi, Ferdinand Braun |
| 1910 | Johannes Diderik van der Waals |
| 1911 | Wilhelm Wien |
| 1912 | Gustaf Dalén |
| 1913 | Heike Kamerlingh Onnes |
| 1914 | Max von Laue |
| 1915 | William Bragg, Lawrence Bragg |
| 1916 | *no award* |
| 1917 | Charles Glover Barkla |
| 1918 | Max Planck |
| 1919 | Johannes Stark |
| 1920 | Charles Edouard Guillaume |
| 1921 | Albert Einstein |
| 1922 | Niels Bohr |
| 1923 | Robert A Millikan |
| 1924 | Manne Siegbahn |
| 1925 | James Franck, Gustav Hertz |
| 1926 | Jean Baptiste Perrin |
| 1927 | Arthur H Compton, C T R Wilson |
| 1928 | Owen Willans Richardson |
| 1929 | Louis de Broglie |
| 1930 | Venkata Raman |
| 1931 | *no award* |
| 1932 | Werner Heisenberg |
| 1933 | Erwin Schrödinger, Paul A M Dirac |
| 1934 | *no award* |
| 1935 | James Chadwick |
| 1936 | Victor F Hess, Carl D Anderson |
| 1937 | Clinton Davisson, George Paget Thomson |
| 1938 | Enrico Fermi |
| 1939 | Ernest Lawrence |
| 1940 | *no award* |
| 1941 | *no award* |
| 1942 | *no award* |
| 1943 | Otto Stern |
| 1944 | Isidor Isaac Rabi |
| 1945 | Wolfgang Pauli |
| 1946 | Percy W Bridgman |
| 1947 | Edward V Appleton |
| 1948 | Patrick M S Blackett |
| 1949 | Hideki Yukawa |
| 1950 | Cecil Powell |
| 1951 | John Cockcroft, Ernest T S Walton |
| 1952 | Felix Bloch, E M Purcell |
| 1953 | Frits Zernike |
| 1954 | Max Born, Walther Bothe |
| 1955 | Willis E Lamb, Polykarp Kusch |
| 1956 | William B Shockley, John Bardeen, Walter H Brattain |
| 1957 | Chen Ning Yang, Tsung-Dao Lee |
| 1958 | Pavel A Cherenkov, Il´ja M Frank, Igor Y Tamm |
| 1959 | Emilio Segrè, Owen Chamberlain |
| 1960 | Donald A Glaser |
| 1961 | Robert Hofstadter, Rudolf Mössbauer |
| 1962 | Lev Landau |
| 1963 | Eugene Wigner, Maria Goeppert-Mayer, J Hans D Jensen |
| 1964 | Charles H Townes, Nicolay G Basov, Aleksandr M Prokhorov |
| 1965 | Sin-Itiro Tomonaga, Julian Schwinger, Richard P Feynman |
| 1966 | Alfred Kastler |
| 1967 | Hans Bethe |
| 1968 | Luis Alvarez |
| 1969 | Murray Gell-Mann |
| 1970 | Hannes Alfvén, Louis Néel |
| 1971 | Dennis Gabor |
| 1972 | John Bardeen, Leon N Cooper, Robert Schrieffer |
| 1973 | Leo Esaki, Ivar Giaever, Brian D Josephson |
| 1974 | Martin Ryle, Antony Hewish |
| 1975 | Aage N Bohr, Ben R Mottelson, James Rainwater |
| 1976 | Burton Richter, Samuel C C Ting |
| 1977 | Philip W Anderson, Sir Nevill F Mott, John H van Vleck |
| 1978 | Pyotr Kapitsa, Arno Penzias, Robert Woodrow Wilson |
| 1979 | Sheldon Glashow, Abdus Salam, Steven Weinberg |

| | |
|---|---|
| 1980 | James Cronin, Val Fitch |
| 1981 | Nicolaas Bloembergen, Arthur L Schawlow, Kai M Siegbahn |
| 1982 | Kenneth G Wilson |
| 1983 | Subramanyan Chandrasekhar, William A Fowler |
| 1984 | Carlo Rubbia, Simon van der Meer |
| 1985 | Klaus von Klitzing |
| 1986 | Ernst Ruska, Gerd Binnig, Heinrich Rohrer |
| 1987 | J Georg Bednorz, K Alex Müller |
| 1988 | Leon M Lederman, Melvin Schwartz, Jack Steinberger |
| 1989 | Norman F Ramsey, Hans G Dehmelt, Wolfgang Paul |
| 1990 | Jerome I Friedman, Henry W Kendall, Richard E Taylor |
| 1991 | Pierre-Gilles de Gennes |
| 1992 | Georges Charpak |
| 1993 | Russell A Hulse, Joseph H Taylor Jr |
| 1994 | Bertram N Brockhouse, Clifford G Shull |
| 1995 | Martin L Perl, Frederick Reines |
| 1996 | David M Lee, Douglas D Osheroff, Robert C Richardson |
| 1997 | Steven Chu, Claude Cohen-Tannoudji, William D Phillips |
| 1998 | Robert B Laughlin, Horst L Störmer, Daniel C Tsui |
| 1999 | Gerardus 't Hooft, Martinus JG Veltman |
| 2000 | Zhores I Alferov, Herbert Kroemer, Jack S Kilby |
| 2001 | Eric A Cornell, Wolfgang Ketterle, Carl E Wieman |
| 2002 | Raymond Davis Jr, Masatoshi Koshiba, Riccardo Giacconi |
| 2003 | Alexei A Abrikosov, Vitaly L Ginzburg, Anthony J Leggett |

### Bragging About Physics

Lawrence Bragg (1890–1971) was just 25 years old when he won the Nobel prize for physics, making him the youngest ever winner of a Nobel award. Bragg's long and illustrious career went on to include a professorship at Cambridge University, directorship of the Royal Institution and involvement in the discovery of DNA and the creation of the new field of molecular biology. He was knighted in 1941.

## NOBEL PRIZE FOR CHEMISTRY

**Nobel prizes were established by a bequest in the will of Alfred Nobel (1833–96) to honour 'those who, during the preceding year, shall have conferred the greatest benefit on mankind'. The Nobel prize for chemistry is awarded annually to a person who has 'made the most important chemical discovery or improvement'; first awarded in 1901.**

| | |
|---|---|
| 1901 | Jacobus H van't Hoff |
| 1902 | Emil Fischer |
| 1903 | Svante Arrhenius |
| 1904 | Sir William Ramsay |
| 1905 | Adolf von Baeyer |
| 1906 | Henri Moissan |
| 1907 | Eduard Buchner |
| 1908 | Ernest Rutherford |
| 1909 | Wilhelm Ostwald |
| 1910 | Otto Wallach |
| 1911 | Marie Curie |
| 1912 | Victor Grignard, Paul Sabatier |
| 1913 | Alfred Werner |
| 1914 | Theodore W Richards |
| 1915 | Richard Willstätter |
| 1916 | *no award* |
| 1917 | *no award* |
| 1918 | Fritz Haber |
| 1919 | *no award* |
| 1920 | Walther Nernst |
| 1921 | Frederick Soddy |
| 1922 | Francis W Aston |
| 1923 | Fritz Pregl |
| 1924 | *no award* |

# NOBEL PRIZE FOR CHEMISTRY

| | |
|---|---|
| 1925 | Richard Zsigmondy |
| 1926 | The Svedberg |
| 1927 | Heinrich Wieland |
| 1928 | Adolf Windaus |
| 1929 | Arthur Harden, Hans von Euler-Chelpin |
| 1930 | Hans Fischer |
| 1931 | Carl Bosch, Friedrich Bergius |
| 1932 | Irving Langmuir |
| 1933 | *no award* |
| 1934 | Harold C Urey |
| 1935 | Frédéric Joliot, Irène Joliot-Curie |
| 1936 | Peter Debye |
| 1937 | Norman Haworth, Paul Karrer |
| 1938 | Richard Kuhn |
| 1939 | Adolf Butenandt, Leopold Ruzicka |
| 1940 | *no award* |
| 1941 | *no award* |
| 1942 | *no award* |
| 1943 | George de Hevesy |
| 1944 | Otto Hahn |
| 1945 | Artturi Virtanen |
| 1946 | James B Sumner, John H Northrop, Wendell M Stanley |
| 1947 | Sir Robert Robinson |
| 1948 | Arne Tiselius |
| 1949 | William F Giauque |
| 1950 | Otto Diels, Kurt Alder |
| 1951 | Edwin M McMillan, Glenn T Seaborg |
| 1952 | Archer J P Martin, Richard L M Synge |
| 1953 | Hermann Staudinger |
| 1954 | Linus Pauling |
| 1955 | Vincent du Vigneaud |
| 1956 | Sir Cyril Hinshelwood, Nikolay Semenov |
| 1957 | Lord Todd |
| 1958 | Frederick Sanger |
| 1959 | Jaroslav Heyrovsky |
| 1960 | Willard F Libby |
| 1961 | Melvin Calvin |
| 1962 | Max F Perutz, John C Kendrew |
| 1963 | Karl Ziegler, Giulio Natta |
| 1964 | Dorothy Crowfoot Hodgkin |
| 1965 | Robert B Woodward |
| 1966 | Robert S Mulliken |
| 1967 | Manfred Eigen, Ronald G W Norrish, George Porter |
| 1968 | Lars Onsager |
| 1969 | Derek Barton, Odd Hassel |
| 1970 | Luis Leloir |
| 1971 | Gerhard Herzberg |
| 1972 | Christian Anfinsen, Stanford Moore, William H Stein |
| 1973 | Ernst Otto Fischer, Geoffrey Wilkinson |
| 1974 | Paul J Flory |
| 1975 | John Cornforth, Vladimir Prelog |
| 1976 | William Lipscomb |
| 1977 | Ilya Prigogine |
| 1978 | Peter Mitchell |
| 1979 | Herbert C Brown, Georg Wittig |
| 1980 | Paul Berg, Walter Gilbert, Frederick Sanger |
| 1981 | Kenichi Fukui, Roald Hoffmann |
| 1982 | Aaron Klug |
| 1983 | Henry Taube |
| 1984 | Bruce Merrifield |
| 1985 | Herbert A Hauptman, Jerome Karle |
| 1986 | Dudley R Herschbach, Yuan T Lee, John C Polanyi |
| 1987 | Donald J Cram, Jean-Marie Lehn, Charles J Pedersen |
| 1988 | Johann Deisenhofer, Robert Huber, Hartmut Michel |
| 1989 | Sidney Altman, Thomas R Cech |
| 1990 | Elias James Corey |
| 1991 | Richard R Ernst |
| 1992 | Rudolph A Marcus |
| 1993 | Kary B Mullis, Michael Smith |
| 1994 | George A Olah |
| 1995 | Paul J Crutzen, Mario J Molina, F Sherwood Rowland |
| 1996 | Robert F Curl Jr, Sir Harold Kroto, Richard E Smalley |
| 1997 | Paul D Boyer, John E Walker, Jens C Skou |
| 1998 | Walter Kohn, John Pople |
| 1999 | Ahmed Zewail |
| 2000 | Alan Heeger, Alan G MacDiarmid, Hideki Shirakawa |
| 2001 | William S Knowles, Ryoji Noyori, K Barry Sharpless |
| 2002 | John B Fenn, Koichi Tanaka, Kurt Wüthrich |
| 2003 | Peter Agre, Roderick MacKinnon |

## NOBEL PRIZE FOR PHYSIOLOGY OR MEDICINE

Nobel prizes were established by a bequest in the will of Alfred Nobel (1833–96) to honour 'those who, during the preceding year, shall have conferred the greatest benefit on mankind'. The Nobel prize for physiology or medicine is awarded annually to a person who has 'made the most important discovery within the domain of physiology or medicine'; first awarded in 1901.

| | |
|---|---|
| 1901 | Emil von Behring |
| 1902 | Ronald Ross |
| 1903 | Niels Ryberg Finsen |
| 1904 | Ivan Pavlov |
| 1905 | Robert Koch |
| 1906 | Camillo Golgi, Santiago Ramón y Cajal |
| 1907 | Alphonse Laveran |
| 1908 | Ilya Mechnikov, Paul Ehrlich |
| 1909 | Theodor Kocher |
| 1910 | Albrecht Kossel |
| 1911 | Allvar Gullstrand |
| 1912 | Alexis Carrel |
| 1913 | Charles Richet |
| 1914 | Robert Bárány |
| 1915 | *no award* |
| 1916 | *no award* |
| 1917 | *no award* |
| 1918 | *no award* |
| 1919 | Jules Bordet |
| 1920 | August Krogh |
| 1921 | *no award* |
| 1922 | Archibald V Hill, Otto Meyerhof |
| 1923 | Frederick G Banting, John Macleod |
| 1924 | Willem Einthoven |
| 1925 | *no award* |
| 1926 | Johannes Fibiger |
| 1927 | Julius Wagner-Jauregg |
| 1928 | Charles Nicolle |
| 1929 | Christiaan Eijkman, Sir Frederick Hopkins |
| 1930 | Karl Landsteiner |
| 1931 | Otto Warburg |
| 1932 | Sir Charles Sherrington, Edgar Adrian |
| 1933 | Thomas H Morgan |
| 1934 | George H Whipple, George R Minot, William P Murphy |
| 1935 | Hans Spemann |
| 1936 | Sir Henry Dale, Otto Loewi |
| 1937 | Albert Szent-Györgyi |
| 1938 | Corneille Heymans |
| 1939 | Gerhard Domagk |
| 1940 | *no award* |
| 1941 | *no award* |
| 1942 | *no award* |
| 1943 | Henrik Dam, Edward A Doisy |
| 1944 | Joseph Erlanger, Herbert S Gasser |
| 1945 | Sir Alexander Fleming, Ernst B Chain, Sir Howard Florey |
| 1946 | Hermann J Muller |
| 1947 | Carl Cori, Gerty Cori, Bernardo Houssay |
| 1948 | Paul Müller |
| 1949 | Walter Hess, Egas Moniz |
| 1950 | Edward C Kendall, Tadeus Reichstein, Philip S Hench |
| 1951 | Max Theiler |
| 1952 | Selman A Waksman |
| 1953 | Hans Krebs, Fritz Lipmann |
| 1954 | John F Enders, Thomas H Weller, Frederick C Robbins |
| 1955 | Hugo Theorell |
| 1956 | André F Cournand, Werner Forssmann, Dickinson W Richards |
| 1957 | Daniel Bovet |
| 1958 | George Beadle, Edward Tatum, Joshua Lederberg |
| 1959 | Severo Ochoa, Arthur Kornberg |
| 1960 | Sir Frank Macfarlane Burnet, Peter Medawar |
| 1961 | Georg von Békésy |
| 1962 | Francis Crick, James Watson, Maurice Wilkins |
| 1963 | Sir John Eccles, Alan L Hodgkin, Andrew F Huxley |
| 1964 | Konrad Bloch, Feodor Lynen |
| 1965 | François Jacob, André Lwoff, Jacques Monod |
| 1966 | Peyton Rous, Charles B Huggins |
| 1967 | Ragnar Granit, Haldan K Hartline, George Wald |
| 1968 | Robert W Holley, H Gobind Khorana, Marshall W Nirenberg |
| 1969 | Max Delbrück, Alfred D Hershey, Salvador E Luria |
| 1970 | Sir Bernard Katz, Ulf von Euler, Julius Axelrod |
| 1971 | Earl W Sutherland, Jr |
| 1972 | Gerald M Edelman, Rodney R Porter |
| 1973 | Karl von Frisch, Konrad Lorenz, Nikolaas Tinbergen |

# NOBEL PRIZE FOR PHYSIOLOGY OR MEDICINE

1974 Albert Claude, Christian de Duve, George E Palade
1975 David Baltimore, Renato Dulbecco, Howard M Temin
1976 Baruch S Blumberg, D Carleton Gajdusek
1977 Roger Guillemin, Andrew V Schally, Rosalyn Yalow
1978 Werner Arber, Daniel Nathans, Hamilton O Smith
1979 Allan M Cormack, Godfrey N Hounsfield
1980 Baruj Benacerraf, Jean Dausset, George D Snell
1981 Roger W Sperry, David H Hubel, Torsten N Wiesel
1982 Sune K Bergström, Bengt I Samuelsson, John R Vane
1983 Barbara McClintock
1984 Niels K Jerne, Georges JF Köhler, César Milstein
1985 Michael S Brown, Joseph L Goldstein
1986 Stanley Cohen, Rita Levi-Montalcini
1987 Susumu Tonegawa
1988 Sir James W Black, Gertrude B Elion, George H Hitchings
1989 J Michael Bishop, Harold E Varmus
1990 Joseph E Murray, E Donnall Thomas
1991 Erwin Neher, Bert Sakmann
1992 Edmond H Fischer, Edwin G Krebs
1993 Richard J Roberts, Phillip A Sharp
1994 Alfred G Gilman, Martin Rodbell
1995 Edward B Lewis, Christiane Nüsslein-Volhard, Eric F Wieschaus
1996 Peter C Doherty, Rolf M Zinkernagel
1997 Stanley B Prusiner
1998 Robert F Furchgott, Louis J Ignarro, Ferid Murad
1999 Günter Blobel
2000 Arvid Carlsson, Paul Greengard, Eric R Kandel
2001 Leland H Hartwell, Tim Hunt, Sir Paul Nurse
2002 Sydney Brenner, H Robert Horvitz, John E Sulston
2003 Paul C Lauterbur, Sir Peter Mansfield

# HUMAN BODY

## SKELETON

Human beings have an internal skeleton or endoskeleton made of bone or cartilage. It supports the tissues and organs of the body, and protects soft internal organs such as the lungs. The muscles are attached to the bones of the skeleton by means of tendons, and when they contract they pull against the bones, causing them to move. The point of articulation or contact between two or more bones of the skeleton is known as a joint, different types of joint allowing varying degrees of movement. In total, the adult human skeleton has 206 bones; some are illustrated below.

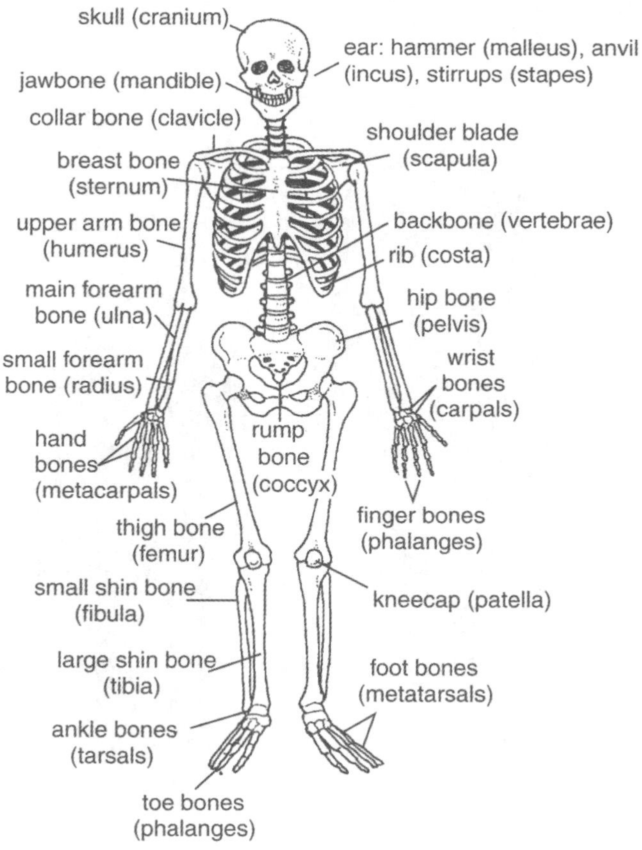

## MUSCLES

Muscles consist of bundles of small fibres, each of which is in turn composed of many protein myofibrils, which lengthen or shorten as their filaments slide past each other. This movement, which occurs in response to a stimulus from the nervous system, or a hormonal signal, causes contraction of the whole muscle. *Voluntary muscle*, which is under conscious control, produces voluntary movements by pulling against the bones of the skeleton, to which it is attached by means of tendons, so that contractions of such muscles cause the bones to move. *Involuntary muscle* (also called *smooth muscle*) maintains the movements of the internal body systems, and forms part of many internal organs, such as the intestines and uterus. *Cardiac muscle*, found only in the heart, does not become fatigued, and continues to contract rhythmically even when it is disconnected from the nervous system. Some of the body's major superficial muscles are illustrated below.

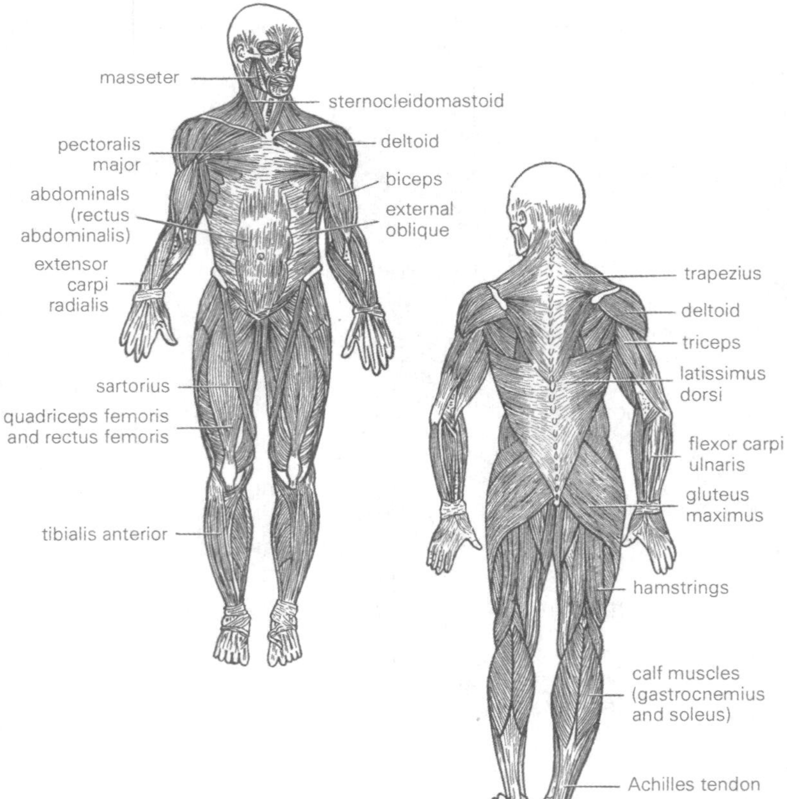

# TEETH

In humans, the first set of teeth, consisting of 20 deciduous or milk teeth, is gradually replaced from about six years of age by 32 permanent teeth. These consist of chisel-shaped incisors for cutting, situated at the front of each jaw, and behind them the pointed canine teeth, for tearing food. Behind the canines are the molars and premolars, which have uneven surfaces for grinding and chewing food.

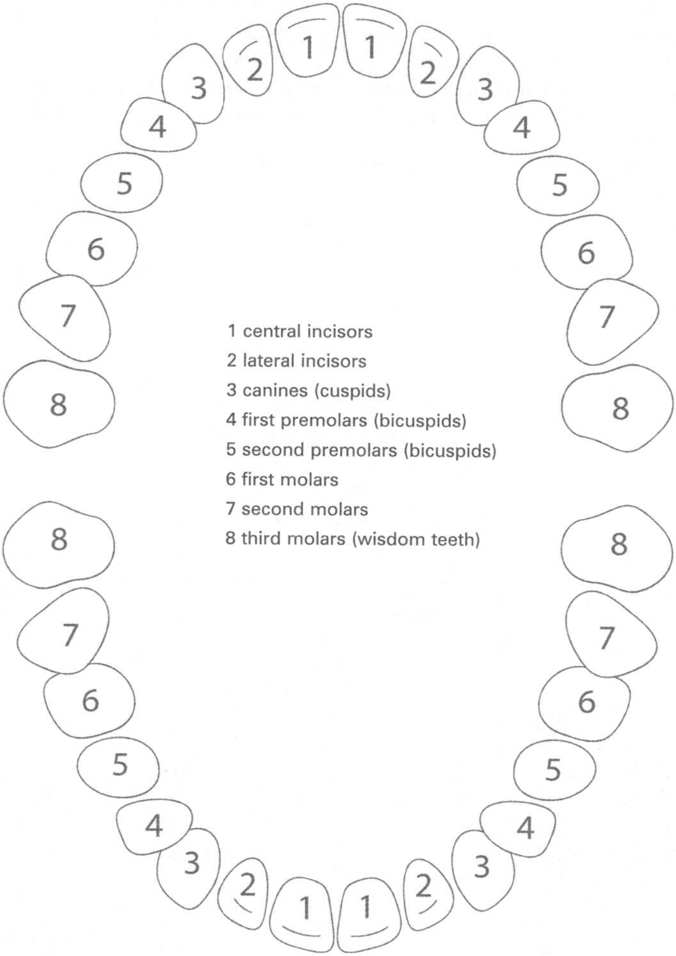

## HUMAN BODY DATA

| | |
|---|---|
| Number of bones | 206 |
| Number of muscles | approximately 650 |
| Number of chromosomes | 22 pairs and two sex chromosomes |
| Average body temperature | 37°C/98.6°F |
| Average pulse rate | 72 beats per minute (men), 80 beats per minute (women) |
| Average weight of brain | 1 400g/49.42oz |
| Number of nerve cells in the brain | more than 10 billion |
| Total surface area of the skin of an adult | approximately 1.86 sq m/20 sq ft |
| Total dead skin cells shed per person per lifetime | approximately 18kg/40lb |
| Total surface area of the alveoli in the lungs | 70 sq m/753 sq ft |

# MATHEMATICS

## FIELDS MEDAL

The Fields Medal is the world's highest award for achievement in mathematics. Named after a Canadian mathematician, Professor J C Fields (1863–1932), the medals are awarded at the International Congress of Mathematicians (ICM) to 'recognize outstanding mathematical achievement' in a mathematician of no older than 40 years. Up to four medals may be awarded on each occasion.

| | |
|---|---|
| 1936 | Lars Valerian Ahlfors, Jesse Douglas |
| 1950 | Laurent Schwartz, Atle Selberg |
| 1954 | Kunihiko Kodaira, Jean-Pierre Serre |
| 1958 | Klaus Friedrich Roth, René Thom |
| 1962 | Lars Hörmander, John Willard Milnor |
| 1966 | Michael Francis Atiyah, Paul Joseph Cohen, Alexander Grothendieck, Stephen Smale |
| 1970 | Alan Baker, Heisuke Hironaka, Serge Novikov, John Griggs Thompson |
| 1974 | Enrico Bombieri, David Bryant Mumford |
| 1978 | Pierre René Deligne, Charles Louis Fefferman, Gregori Alexandrovitch Margulis, Daniel G Quillen |
| 1982 | Alain Connes, William P Thurston, Shing-Tung Yau |
| 1986 | Simon K Donaldson, Gerd Faltings, Michael H Freedman |
| 1990 | Vladimir Drinfeld, Vaughan F R Jones, Shigefumi Mori, Edward Witten |
| 1994 | Jean Bourgain, Pierre-Louis Lions, Jean-Christophe Yoccoz, Efim Zelmanov |
| 1998 | Richard E Borcherds, W Timothy Gowers, Maxim Kontsevich, Curtis T McMullen |
| 2002 | Laurent Lafforgue, Vladimir Voevodsky |

### *Fermat's Last Theorem*

The most famous problem in mathematics was scrawled by the French mathematician Pierre de Fermat (1601–65) in the margin of a page of a book.

Fermat had studied law at Toulouse University, where he became a councillor of parliament, but his passion was mathematics. Most of his work was communicated in letters to friends, containing results without proof.

In what became known as his 'Last Theorem', Fermat stated that it is impossible to find a solution to the equation

$$x^n + y^n = z^n$$

if $n$ is greater than 2. He added tantalizingly that 'I have a truly marvellous demonstration of this proposition which this margin is too narrow to contain'.

The puzzle to find Fermat's proof went on to baffle and outwit mathematicians for almost 350 years. The proof was finally announced in 1993 by the US mathematician Andrew Wiles, and revised by him in 1994. Wiles was just too old to qualify for the Fields Medal, so the International Mathematical Union instead honoured him with a silver plaque as a special tribute.

## NUMERALS

| Arabic | Roman | Greek | Binary numbers |
|---|---|---|---|
| 1 | I | α′ | 1 |
| 2 | II | β′ | 10 |
| 3 | III | γ′ | 11 |
| 4 | IV | δ′ | 100 |
| 5 | V | ε′ | 101 |
| 6 | VI | ς′ | 110 |
| 7 | VII | ζ′ | 111 |
| 8 | VIII | η′ | 1000 |
| 9 | IX | θ′ | 1001 |
| 10 | X | ι′ | 1010 |
| 11 | XI | ια′ | 1011 |
| 12 | XII | ιβ′ | 1100 |
| 13 | XIII | ιγ′ | 1101 |
| 14 | XIV | ιδ′ | 1110 |
| 15 | XV | ιε′ | 1111 |
| 16 | XVI | ις′ | 10000 |
| 17 | XVII | ιζ′ | 10001 |
| 18 | XVIII | ιη′ | 10010 |
| 19 | XIX | ιθ′ | 10011 |
| 20 | XX | κ′ | 10100 |
| 30 | XXX | λ′ | 11110 |
| 40 | XL | μ′ | 101000 |
| 50 | L | ν′ | 110010 |
| 60 | LX | ξ′ | 111100 |
| 70 | LXX | ο′ | 1000110 |
| 80 | LXXX | π′ | 1010000 |
| 90 | XC | ,ο′ | 1011010 |
| 100 | C | ρ′ | 1100100 |
| 200 | CC | σ′ | 11001000 |
| 300 | CCC | τ′ | 100101100 |
| 400 | CD | ν′ | 110010000 |
| 500 | D | φ′ | 111110100 |
| 1 000 | M | ,α | 1111101000 |
| 5 000 | $\bar{V}$ | ,ε | 1001110001000 |
| 10 000 | $\bar{X}$ | ,ι | 10011100010000 |
| 100 000 | $\bar{C}$ | ,ρ | 11000011010100000 |

## FRACTIONS AND DECIMALS

| % | Decimal | Fraction | % | Decimal | Fraction |
|---|---|---|---|---|---|
| 1 | 0.01 | $^{1}/_{100}$ | 11 | 0.11 | $^{11}/_{100}$ |
| 2 | 0.02 | $^{1}/_{50}$ | 12 | 0.12 | $^{3}/_{25}$ |
| 3 | 0.03 | $^{3}/_{100}$ | $12^{1}/_{2}$ | 0.125 | $^{1}/_{8}$ |
| 4 | 0.04 | $^{1}/_{25}$ | 13 | 0.13 | $^{13}/_{100}$ |
| 5 | 0.05 | $^{1}/_{20}$ | 14 | 0.14 | $^{7}/_{50}$ |
| 6 | 0.06 | $^{3}/_{50}$ | 15 | 0.15 | $^{3}/_{20}$ |
| 7 | 0.07 | $^{7}/_{100}$ | 16 | 0.16 | $^{4}/_{25}$ |
| 8 | 0.08 | $^{2}/_{25}$ | $16^{1}/_{3}$ | 0.167 | $^{1}/_{6}$ |
| $8^{1}/_{3}$ | 0.083 | $^{1}/_{12}$ | 17 | 0.17 | $^{17}/_{100}$ |
| 9 | 0.09 | $^{9}/_{100}$ | 18 | 0.18 | $^{9}/_{50}$ |
| 10 | 0.10 | $^{1}/_{10}$ | 19 | 0.19 | $^{19}/_{100}$ |

| % | Decimal | Fraction | % | Decimal | Fraction |
|---|---|---|---|---|---|
| 20 | 0.20 | 1/5 | 40 | 0.40 | 2/5 |
| 21 | 0.21 | 21/100 | 41 | 0.41 | 41/100 |
| 22 | 0.22 | 11/50 | 42 | 0.42 | 21/50 |
| 23 | 0.23 | 23/100 | 43 | 0.43 | 43/100 |
| 24 | 0.24 | 6/25 | 44 | 0.44 | 11/25 |
| 25 | 0.25 | 1/4 | 45 | 0.45 | 9/20 |
| 26 | 0.26 | 13/50 | 46 | 0.46 | 23/50 |
| 27 | 0.27 | 27/100 | 47 | 0.47 | 47/100 |
| 28 | 0.28 | 7/25 | 48 | 0.48 | 12/25 |
| 29 | 0.29 | 29/100 | 49 | 0.49 | 49/100 |
| 30 | 0.30 | 3/10 | 50 | 0.50 | 1/2 |
| 31 | 0.31 | 31/100 | 55 | 0.55 | 11/20 |
| 32 | 0.32 | 8/25 | 60 | 0.60 | 3/5 |
| 33 | 0.33 | 33/100 | 65 | 0.65 | 13/20 |
| 33 1/3 | 0.333 | 1/3 | 70 | 0.70 | 7/10 |
| 34 | 0.34 | 17/50 | 75 | 0.75 | 3/4 |
| 35 | 0.35 | 7/20 | 80 | 0.80 | 4/5 |
| 36 | 0.36 | 9/25 | 85 | 0.85 | 17/20 |
| 37 | 0.37 | 37/100 | 90 | 0.90 | 9/10 |
| 38 | 0.38 | 19/50 | 95 | 0.95 | 19/20 |
| 39 | 0.39 | 39/100 | 100 | 1.00 | 1 |

| Fraction | Decimal | Fraction | Decimal | Fraction | Decimal |
|---|---|---|---|---|---|
| 1/2 | 0.5000 | 8/9 | 0.8889 | 15/16 | 0.9375 |
| 1/3 | 0.3333 | 1/10 | 0.1000 | 1/20 | 0.0500 |
| 2/3 | 0.6667 | 3/10 | 0.3000 | 3/20 | 0.1500 |
| 1/4 | 0.2500 | 7/10 | 0.7000 | 7/20 | 0.3500 |
| 3/4 | 0.7500 | 9/10 | 0.9000 | 9/20 | 0.4500 |
| 1/5 | 0.2000 | 1/11 | 0.0909 | 11/20 | 0.5500 |
| 2/5 | 0.4000 | 2/11 | 0.1818 | 13/20 | 0.6500 |
| 3/5 | 0.6000 | 3/11 | 0.2727 | 17/20 | 0.8500 |
| 4/5 | 0.8000 | 4/11 | 0.3636 | 19/20 | 0.9500 |
| 1/6 | 0.1667 | 5/11 | 0.4545 | 1/32 | 0.0312 |
| 5/6 | 0.8333 | 6/11 | 0.5454 | 3/32 | 0.0937 |
| 1/7 | 0.1429 | 7/11 | 0.6363 | 5/32 | 0.1562 |
| 2/7 | 0.2857 | 8/11 | 0.7272 | 7/32 | 0.2187 |
| 3/7 | 0.4286 | 9/11 | 0.8181 | 9/32 | 0.2812 |
| 4/7 | 0.5714 | 10/11 | 0.9090 | 11/32 | 0.3437 |
| 5/7 | 0.7143 | 1/12 | 0.0833 | 13/32 | 0.4062 |
| 6/7 | 0.8571 | 5/12 | 0.4167 | 15/32 | 0.4687 |
| 1/8 | 0.1250 | 7/12 | 0.5833 | 17/32 | 0.5312 |
| 3/8 | 0.3750 | 11/12 | 0.9167 | 19/32 | 0.5937 |
| 5/8 | 0.6250 | 1/16 | 0.0625 | 21/32 | 0.6562 |
| 7/8 | 0.8750 | 3/16 | 0.1875 | 23/32 | 0.7187 |
| 1/9 | 0.1111 | 5/16 | 0.3125 | 25/32 | 0.7812 |
| 2/9 | 0.2222 | 7/16 | 0.4375 | 27/32 | 0.8437 |
| 4/9 | 0.4444 | 9/16 | 0.5625 | 29/32 | 0.9062 |
| 5/9 | 0.5556 | 11/16 | 0.6875 | 31/32 | 0.9687 |
| 7/9 | 0.7778 | 13/16 | 0.8125 | | |

## MULTIPLICATION TABLE

| | 2 | 3 | 4 | 5 | 6 | 7 | 8 | 9 | 10 | 11 | 12 | 13 | 14 | 15 | 16 | 17 | 18 | 19 | 20 | 21 | 22 | 23 | 24 | 25 |
|---|---|---|---|---|---|---|---|---|---|---|---|---|---|---|---|---|---|---|---|---|---|---|---|---|
| **2** | 4 | 6 | 8 | 10 | 12 | 14 | 16 | 18 | 20 | 22 | 24 | 26 | 28 | 30 | 32 | 34 | 36 | 38 | 40 | 42 | 44 | 46 | 48 | 50 |
| **3** | 6 | 9 | 12 | 15 | 18 | 21 | 24 | 27 | 30 | 33 | 36 | 39 | 42 | 45 | 48 | 51 | 54 | 57 | 60 | 63 | 66 | 69 | 72 | 75 |
| **4** | 8 | 12 | 16 | 20 | 24 | 28 | 32 | 36 | 40 | 44 | 48 | 52 | 56 | 60 | 64 | 68 | 72 | 76 | 80 | 84 | 88 | 92 | 96 | 100 |
| **5** | 10 | 15 | 20 | 25 | 30 | 35 | 40 | 45 | 50 | 55 | 60 | 65 | 70 | 75 | 80 | 85 | 90 | 95 | 100 | 105 | 110 | 115 | 120 | 125 |
| **6** | 12 | 18 | 24 | 30 | 36 | 42 | 48 | 54 | 60 | 66 | 72 | 78 | 84 | 90 | 96 | 102 | 108 | 114 | 120 | 126 | 132 | 138 | 144 | 150 |
| **7** | 14 | 21 | 28 | 35 | 42 | 49 | 56 | 63 | 70 | 77 | 84 | 91 | 98 | 105 | 112 | 119 | 126 | 133 | 140 | 147 | 154 | 161 | 168 | 175 |
| **8** | 16 | 24 | 32 | 40 | 48 | 56 | 64 | 72 | 80 | 88 | 96 | 104 | 112 | 120 | 128 | 136 | 144 | 152 | 160 | 168 | 176 | 184 | 192 | 200 |
| **9** | 18 | 27 | 36 | 45 | 54 | 63 | 72 | 81 | 90 | 99 | 108 | 117 | 126 | 135 | 144 | 153 | 162 | 171 | 180 | 189 | 198 | 207 | 216 | 225 |
| **10** | 20 | 30 | 40 | 50 | 60 | 70 | 80 | 90 | 100 | 110 | 120 | 130 | 140 | 150 | 160 | 170 | 180 | 190 | 200 | 210 | 220 | 230 | 240 | 250 |
| **11** | 22 | 33 | 44 | 55 | 66 | 77 | 88 | 99 | 110 | 121 | 132 | 143 | 154 | 165 | 176 | 187 | 198 | 209 | 220 | 231 | 242 | 253 | 264 | 275 |
| **12** | 24 | 36 | 48 | 60 | 72 | 84 | 96 | 108 | 120 | 132 | 144 | 156 | 168 | 180 | 192 | 204 | 216 | 228 | 240 | 252 | 264 | 276 | 288 | 300 |
| **13** | 26 | 39 | 52 | 65 | 78 | 91 | 104 | 117 | 130 | 143 | 156 | 169 | 182 | 195 | 208 | 221 | 234 | 247 | 260 | 273 | 286 | 299 | 312 | 325 |
| **14** | 28 | 42 | 56 | 70 | 84 | 98 | 112 | 126 | 140 | 154 | 168 | 182 | 196 | 210 | 224 | 238 | 252 | 266 | 280 | 294 | 308 | 322 | 336 | 350 |
| **15** | 30 | 45 | 60 | 75 | 90 | 105 | 120 | 135 | 150 | 165 | 180 | 195 | 210 | 225 | 240 | 255 | 270 | 285 | 300 | 315 | 330 | 345 | 360 | 375 |
| **16** | 32 | 48 | 64 | 80 | 96 | 112 | 128 | 144 | 160 | 176 | 192 | 208 | 224 | 240 | 256 | 272 | 288 | 304 | 320 | 336 | 352 | 368 | 384 | 400 |
| **17** | 34 | 51 | 68 | 85 | 102 | 119 | 136 | 153 | 170 | 187 | 204 | 221 | 238 | 255 | 272 | 289 | 306 | 323 | 340 | 357 | 374 | 391 | 408 | 425 |
| **18** | 36 | 54 | 72 | 90 | 108 | 126 | 144 | 162 | 180 | 198 | 216 | 234 | 252 | 270 | 288 | 306 | 324 | 342 | 360 | 378 | 396 | 414 | 432 | 450 |
| **19** | 38 | 57 | 76 | 95 | 114 | 133 | 152 | 171 | 190 | 209 | 228 | 247 | 266 | 285 | 304 | 323 | 342 | 361 | 380 | 399 | 418 | 437 | 456 | 475 |
| **20** | 40 | 60 | 80 | 100 | 120 | 140 | 160 | 180 | 200 | 220 | 240 | 260 | 280 | 300 | 320 | 340 | 360 | 380 | 400 | 420 | 440 | 460 | 480 | 500 |
| **21** | 42 | 63 | 84 | 105 | 126 | 147 | 168 | 189 | 210 | 231 | 252 | 273 | 294 | 315 | 336 | 357 | 378 | 399 | 420 | 441 | 462 | 483 | 504 | 525 |
| **22** | 44 | 66 | 88 | 110 | 132 | 154 | 176 | 198 | 220 | 242 | 264 | 286 | 308 | 330 | 352 | 374 | 396 | 418 | 440 | 462 | 484 | 506 | 528 | 550 |
| **23** | 46 | 69 | 92 | 115 | 138 | 161 | 184 | 207 | 230 | 253 | 276 | 299 | 322 | 345 | 368 | 391 | 414 | 437 | 460 | 483 | 506 | 529 | 552 | 575 |
| **24** | 48 | 72 | 96 | 120 | 144 | 168 | 192 | 216 | 240 | 264 | 288 | 312 | 336 | 360 | 384 | 408 | 432 | 456 | 480 | 501 | 528 | 552 | 576 | 600 |
| **25** | 50 | 75 | 100 | 125 | 150 | 175 | 200 | 225 | 250 | 275 | 300 | 325 | 350 | 375 | 400 | 425 | 450 | 475 | 500 | 525 | 550 | 575 | 600 | 625 |

## SQUARES AND ROOTS

| Number | Square | Cube | Square root | Cube root |
|---|---|---|---|---|
| 1 | 1 | 1 | 1.000 | 1.000 |
| 2 | 4 | 8 | 1.414 | 1.260 |
| 3 | 9 | 27 | 1.732 | 1.442 |
| 4 | 16 | 64 | 2.000 | 1.587 |
| 5 | 25 | 125 | 2.236 | 1.710 |
| 6 | 36 | 216 | 2.449 | 1.817 |
| 7 | 49 | 343 | 2.646 | 1.913 |
| 8 | 64 | 512 | 2.828 | 2.000 |
| 9 | 81 | 729 | 3.000 | 2.080 |
| 10 | 100 | 1 000 | 3.162 | 2.154 |
| 11 | 121 | 1 331 | 3.317 | 2.224 |
| 12 | 144 | 1 728 | 3.464 | 2.289 |
| 13 | 169 | 2 197 | 3.606 | 2.351 |
| 14 | 196 | 2 744 | 3.742 | 2.410 |
| 15 | 225 | 3 375 | 3.873 | 2.466 |
| 16 | 256 | 4 096 | 4.000 | 2.520 |
| 17 | 289 | 4 913 | 4.123 | 2.571 |
| 18 | 324 | 5 832 | 4.243 | 2.621 |
| 19 | 361 | 6 859 | 4.359 | 2.668 |
| 20 | 400 | 8 000 | 4.472 | 2.714 |
| 25 | 625 | 15 625 | 5.000 | 2.924 |
| 30 | 900 | 27 000 | 5.477 | 3.107 |
| 40 | 1 600 | 64 000 | 6.325 | 3.420 |
| 50 | 2 500 | 125 000 | 7.071 | 3.684 |

## POLYGONS

A polygon is a many-sided plane figure.

| Sides | Polygon | Sides | Polygon |
|---|---|---|---|
| n | n-gon | 12 | dodecagon |
| 3 | trigon, triangle | 13 | tridecagon, triskaidecagon |
| 4 | tetragon, quadrilateral | 14 | tetradecagon, tetrakaidecagon |
| 5 | pentagon | 15 | pentadecagon, pentakaidecagon |
| 6 | hexagon | 16 | hexadecagon, hexakaidecagon |
| 7 | heptagon | 17 | heptadecagon, heptakaidecagon |
| 8 | octagon | 18 | octadecagon, octakaidecagon |
| 9 | enneagon, nonagon | 19 | enneadecagon, enneakaidecagon |
| 10 | decagon | | |
| 11 | hendecagon, undecagon | 1 000 | chiliagon |

*Other names have been proposed for larger polygons using a system of prefixes but the form n-gon, eg 76-gon for a figure with 76 sides, is more common. The name* myriagon *has been proposed for a polygon with 10 000 sides.*

## LARGE NUMBERS

The names of large numbers formerly differed between the UK and the USA. In the UK, a billion was one million millions, rather than one thousand millions, as below. International economics has led to the US system becoming increasingly used worldwide. The US system is given below; to find the former British equivalents, increase the power by 6 each time (hence one billion becomes $10^{12}$, one trillion becomes $10^{18}$ and one centillion $10^{600}$).

| | | |
|---|---|---|
| thousand | $10^3$ | 1 000 |
| million | $10^6$ | 1 000 000 |
| billion | $10^9$ | 1 000 000 000 |
| trillion | $10^{12}$ | 1 000 000 000 000 |
| quadrillion | $10^{15}$ | 1 000 000 000 000 000 |
| quintillion | $10^{18}$ | 1 000 000 000 000 000 000 |
| sextillion | $10^{21}$ | 1 000 000 000 000 000 000 000 |
| septillion | $10^{24}$ | 1 000 000 000 000 000 000 000 000 |
| octillion | $10^{27}$ | 1 000 000 000 000 000 000 000 000 000 |
| nonillion | $10^{30}$ | 1 000 000 000 000 000 000 000 000 000 000 |
| decillion | $10^{33}$ | 1 000 000 000 000 000 000 000 000 000 000 000 |
| googol | $10^{100}$ | 1 followed by 100 zeros |
| centillion | $10^{303}$ | 1 followed by 303 zeros |
| googolplex | 10 to the power of a googol | 1 followed by a googol of zeros |

### Googol, Google®

The popular internet search engine Google® is named after the *googol*, one followed by 100 zeros. The company's world headquarters in Mountain View, California, USA, is affectionately known as 'the Googleplex'.

# ECONOMICS

## NOBEL PRIZE FOR ECONOMICS

Nobel prizes were established by a bequest in the will of Alfred Nobel (1833–96) to honour 'those who, during the preceding year, shall have conferred the greatest benefit on mankind'. However, the prize for economics was not such a bequest. Instead, it was instituted by the Bank of Sweden and is officially called the 'Bank of Sweden Prize in Economic Sciences in Memory of Alfred Nobel'; first awarded 1969.

| | |
|---|---|
| 1969 | Ragnar Frisch, Jan Tinbergen |
| 1970 | Paul A Samuelson |
| 1971 | Simon Kuznets |
| 1972 | John R Hicks, Kenneth J Arrow |
| 1973 | Wassily Leontief |
| 1974 | Gunnar Myrdal, Friedrich August von Hayek |
| 1975 | Leonid Vitaliyevich Kantorovich, Tjalling C Koopmans |
| 1976 | Milton Friedman |
| 1977 | Bertil Ohlin, James E Meade |
| 1978 | Herbert A Simon |
| 1979 | Theodore W Schultz, Sir Arthur Lewis |
| 1980 | Lawrence R Klein |
| 1981 | James Tobin |
| 1982 | George J Stigler |
| 1983 | Gerard Debreu |
| 1984 | Richard Stone |
| 1985 | Franco Modigliani |
| 1986 | James M Buchanan Jr |
| 1987 | Robert M Solow |
| 1988 | Maurice Allais |
| 1989 | Trygve Haavelmo |
| 1990 | Harry M Markowitz, Merton H Miller, William F Sharpe |
| 1991 | Ronald H Coase |
| 1992 | Gary S Becker |
| 1993 | Robert W Fogel, Douglass C North |
| 1994 | John C Harsanyi, John F Nash Jr, Reinhard Selten |
| 1995 | Robert E Lucas Jr |
| 1996 | James A Mirrlees, William Vickrey |
| 1997 | Robert C Merton, Myron S Scholes |
| 1998 | Amartya Sen |
| 1999 | Robert A Mundell |
| 2000 | James J Heckman, Daniel L McFadden |
| 2001 | George A Akerlof, A Michael Spence, Joseph E Stiglitz |
| 2002 | Daniel Kahneman, Vernon L Smith |
| 2003 | Robert F Engle, Clive W J Granger |

## STOCK EXCHANGE INDICES

The world's major indices include:

| **Index** | **Country** |
|---|---|
| FTSE 100 | United Kingdom |
| Dow Jones Industrial Average | United States of America |
| Nasdaq | United States of America |
| Nikkei 225 | Japan |
| Hang Seng | Hong Kong |
| Dax | Germany |
| CAC 40 | France |

# BANKNOTE DESIGNS

## Bank of England

Banknotes featuring people were first issued by the Bank in 1970. The notable figures are:

| | |
|---|---|
| £50 | Sir John Houblon (1632–1711, first Governor of the Bank of England) |
| £20 | Sir Edward Elgar (1857–1934) |
| £10 | Charles Darwin (1809–82) |
| £5 | Elizabeth Fry (1780–1845) |

*Previous figures have included Sir Christopher Wren (£50), William Shakespeare (£20), Michael Faraday (£20), Charles Dickens (£10), Florence Nightingale (£10), George Stephenson (£5), the Duke of Wellington (£5) and Sir Isaac Newton (£1).*

## Bank of Scotland

All banknotes feature Sir Walter Scott (1771–1832) on the front. On the back are illustrations of various aspects of Scottish industry, commerce and culture.

| | |
|---|---|
| £100 | Leisure and tourism |
| £50 | Arts and culture |
| £20 | Education and research |
| £10 | Distilling and brewing |
| £5 | Oil and energy |

## Royal Bank of Scotland

All banknotes feature Lord Ilay (1682–1761), first Governor of the Bank. On the back are illustrations of some of Scotland's famous castles.

| | |
|---|---|
| £100 | Balmoral Castle |
| £20 | Brodick Castle |
| £10 | Glamis Castle |
| £5 | Culzean Castle |
| £1 | Edinburgh Castle |

## Clydesdale Bank

Banknotes feature a notable figure on the front. On the back are relevant scenes from the person's life.

| | |
|---|---|
| £100 | Lord Kelvin (1824–1907) |
| £50 | Adam Smith (1723–90) |
| £20 | King Robert the Bruce (1274–1329) |
| £10 | Mary Slessor (1848–1915) |
| £5 | Robert Burns (1759–96) |

## POUND COIN INSCRIPTIONS

### First Trust Bank

All banknotes feature generic people of Northern Ireland on the front. On the back are coastal scenes or designs featuring the Spanish Armada.

| | |
|---|---|
| £100 | The Armada |
| £50 | A commemorative medal |
| £20 | The chimney at Lagada Point |
| £10 | The ship *Girona* |
| £5 | Dunluce Castle |

### Northern Bank

All banknotes except the £5 feature a notable figure on the front and a representation of Belfast City Hall on the back.

| | |
|---|---|
| £100 | Sir James Martin (1893–1981) |
| £50 | Sir Samuel Davidson (1846–1921) |
| £20 | Harry Ferguson (1884–1960) |
| £10 | John Boyd Dunlop (1840–1921) |
| £5 | US space shuttle |

### Ulster Bank

Banknotes are in £50, £20, £10 and £5 denominations. All notes feature a view of Belfast City Harbour, flanked by landscape views. On the back of each is the Bank's coat of arms.

### Bank of Ireland

Banknotes are in £100, £50, £20, £10 and £5 denominations. All notes feature a seated woman representing Hibernia on the front. On the back of each is a view of Queens University Belfast.

### Million Pound Notes

The Bank of England is obliged to back notes issued by the Scottish and Northern Irish banks on a 'pound for pound' basis. The Bank calculates that over a billion pounds is needed to do so – far too much money to be stored in normal Bank of England notes. To get round the problem, they issue special £1 000 000 notes for the purpose. But it is unlikely that most people will ever see one: the Bank sternly declares that the notes 'are for internal use only and are never seen outside the Bank'.

## POUND COIN INSCRIPTIONS

**Scotland**

*nemo me impune lacessit*
no one provokes me with impunity
(from the Motto of the Order of the Thistle)

**Wales**

*pleidiol wyf i'm gwlad*
true am I to my Country
(from the Welsh National Anthem)

**England, Northern Ireland, United Kingdom**
*decus et tutamen*
an ornament and a safeguard
(from Virgil's *Aeneid*)

## BRITISH PRE-DECIMAL CURRENCY

| Coins | Nickname | Value |
|---|---|---|
| Farthing | Jenny | 1/4 penny |
| Half penny | Ha'penny | 1/2 penny |
| Penny | Copper | 1/240 pound, 1/12 shilling |
| Three pence | Thruppence, throppence, threppence, thruppenny bit, joey | 3 pence, 1/4 shilling, 1/80 pound |
| Six pence | Tanner | 6 pence, 1/2 shilling, 1/40 pound |
| Shilling | Bob | 12 pence, 1/20 pound |
| Florin | Two bob | 24 pence, 2 shillings, 1/10 pound |
| Half crown | Half a crown, two and six | 30 pence, 2 shillings and 6 pence, 1/2 pound |
| Crown | Five bob | 60 pence, 5 shillings, 1/4 pound |
| **Notes** | **Nickname** | **Value** |
| Ten shilling note | Half a quid | 120 pence, 10 shillings, ½ pound |
| Pound note | Quid | 240 pence, 20 shillings |

## CURRENCY ABBREVIATIONS

For currency by country see **Human Geography**.

| Abbrev. | Country | Currency |
|---|---|---|
| AED | United Arab Emirates | Dirham |
| AFA | Afghanistan | Afghani |
| ALL | Albania | Lek |
| AMD | Armenia | Dram |
| AON | Angola | Kwanza |
| ARS | Argentina | Peso |
| AUD | Australia | Dollar |
| AZM | Azerbaijan | Manat |
| BAM | Bosnia and Herzegovina | Convertible Marka |
| BBD | Barbados | Dollar |
| BDT | Bangladesh | Taka |
| BGL | Bulgaria | Lev |
| BHD | Bahrain | Dinar |
| BIF | Burundi | Franc |
| BND | Brunei Darussalam | Dollar |
| BOB | Bolivia | Boliviano |
| BRL | Brazil | Real |
| BSD | The Bahamas | Dollar |
| BTN | Bhutan | Ngultrum |
| BWP | Botswana | Pula |
| BYR | Belarus | Rouble |
| BZD | Belize | Dollar |
| CAD | Canada | Dollar |
| CDF | Congo, Democratic Republic of | Franc |

# CURRENCY ABBREVIATIONS

| Abbrev. | Country | Currency |
|---|---|---|
| CHF | Switzerland | Franc |
| CLP | Chile | Peso |
| CNY | China | Renminbi Yuan |
| COP | Colombia | Peso |
| CRC | Costa Rica | Colón |
| CUP | Cuba | Peso |
| CVE | Cape Verde | Escudo Caboverdiano |
| CYP | Cyprus | Pound |
| CZK | Czech Republic | Koruna |
| DJF | Djibouti | Franc |
| DKK | Denmark | Krone |
| DOP | Dominican Republic | Peso |
| DZD | Algeria | Dinar |
| EEK | Estonia | Kroon |
| EGP | Egypt | Pound |
| ERN | Eritrea | Nakfa |
| ETB | Ethiopia | Birr |
| EUR | Euro member countries | Euro |
| FJD | Fiji | Dollar |
| GBP | United Kingdom | Pound |
| GEL | Georgia | Lari |
| GHC | Ghana | Cedi |
| GMD | The Gambia | Dalasi |
| GNF | Guinea | Franc |
| GTQ | Guatemala | Quetzal |
| GYD | Guyana | Dollar |
| HNL | Honduras | Lempira |
| HRK | Croatia | Kuna |
| HTG | Haiti | Gourde |
| HUF | Hungary | Forint |
| IDR | Indonesia | Rupiah |
| ILS | Israel | Shekel |
| INR | India | Rupee |
| IQD | Iraq | Dinar |
| IRR | Iran | Rial |
| ISK | Iceland | Króna |
| JMD | Jamaica | Dollar |
| JOD | Jordan | Dinar |
| JPY | Japan | Yen |
| KES | Kenya | Shilling |
| KGS | Kyrgyzstan | Som |
| KHR | Cambodia | Riel |
| KMF | Comoros | Franc |
| KPW | Korea (North) | Won |
| KRW | Korea (South) | Won |
| KWD | Kuwait | Dinar |
| KZT | Kazakhstan | Tenge |
| LAK | Laos | Kip |
| LBP | Lebanon | Pound |
| LKR | Sri Lanka | Rupee |
| LRD | Liberia | Dollar |
| LSL | Lesotho | Loti |
| LTL | Lithuania | Litas |
| LVL | Latvia | Lat |

| Abbrev. | Country | Currency |
|---|---|---|
| LYD | Libya | Dinar |
| MAD | Morocco | Dirham |
| MDL | Moldova | Leu |
| MGA | Madagascar | Ariary |
| MKD | Macedonia | Denar |
| MMK | Myanmar (Burma) | Kyat |
| MNT | Mongolia | Tugrik |
| MRO | Mauritania | Ouguiya |
| MTL | Malta | Lira |
| MUR | Mauritius | Rupee |
| MVR | Maldives | Rufiyaa |
| MWK | Malawi | Kwacha |
| MXN | Mexico | Peso |
| MYR | Malaysia | Ringgit |
| MZM | Mozambique | Metical |
| NAD | Namibia | Dollar |
| NGN | Nigeria | Naira |
| NIO | Nicaragua | Córdoba |
| NOK | Norway | Krone |
| NPR | Nepal | Rupee |
| NZD | New Zealand | Dollar |
| OMR | Oman | Rial |
| PAB | Panama | Balboa |
| PEN | Peru | Nuevo Sol |
| PGK | Papua New Guinea | Kina |
| PHP | Philippines | Peso |
| PKR | Pakistan | Rupee |
| PLN | Poland | Złoty |
| PYG | Paraguay | Guaraní |
| QAR | Qatar | Rial |
| ROL | Romania | Leu |
| RUR | Russia | Roubles |
| RWF | Rwanda | Franc |
| SAR | Saudi Arabia | Riyal |
| SBD | Solomon Islands | Dollar |
| SCR | Seychelles | Rupee |
| SDD | The Sudan | Dinar |
| SEK | Sweden | Krona |
| SGD | Singapore | Dollar |
| SIT | Slovenia | Tolar |
| SKK | Slovakia | Koruna |
| SLL | Sierra Leone | Leone |
| SOS | Somalia | Shilling |
| SRD | Suriname | Dollar |
| STD | São Tomé and Príncipe | Dobra |
| SVC | El Salvador | Colón |
| SYP | Syria | Pound |
| SZL | Swaziland | Lilangeni |
| THB | Thailand | Baht |
| TJS | Tajikistan | Somoni |
| TMM | Turkmenistan | Manat |
| TND | Tunisia | Dinar |
| TOP | Tonga | Pa'anga |
| TRL | Turkey | Lira |

## CURRENCY ABBREVIATIONS

| Abbrev. | Country | Currency |
|---|---|---|
| TTD | Trinidad and Tobago | Dollar |
| TWD | Taiwan | New Dollar |
| TZS | Tanzania | Shilling |
| UAH | Ukraine | Hryvnia |
| UGS | Uganda | Shilling |
| USD | United States of America | Dollar |
| UYU | Uruguay | New Peso |
| UZS | Uzbekistan | Sum |
| VEB | Venezuela | Bolívar |
| VND | Vietnam | Dông |
| VUV | Vanuatu | Vatu |
| WST | Samoa | Tala |
| XAF | African Financial Community, *Communauté Financière Africaine* (CFA); Bank of Central African States (BEAC) | Franc |
| XCD | East Caribbean states | Dollars |
| XOF | African Financial Community *Communauté Financière Africaine* (CFA); Central Bank of West African States (BCEAO) | Franc |
| XPF | Pacific Financial Community, *Comptoirs Français du Pacifique* (CFP) | Franc |
| YER | Yemen | Riyal |
| YUM | Serbia | New Dinar |
| ZAR | South Africa | Rand |
| ZMK | Zambia | Kwacha |
| ZWD | Zimbabwe | Dollar |

*Note: Countries which use the currency of another (for example Liechtenstein uses the Swiss Franc) do not have a separate currency code.*

### *Money Madness*

The Association for Payment Clearing Services estimates that in 2002 each adult in the UK owned an average of at least three credit and debit cards – a total of 146 million plastic cards! They calculate that the amount spent on plastic cards was £211 billion, a figure that is rising all the time; spending on plastic is likely to leap to a massive £415 billion by 2012.

# MEASUREMENT, CONVERSION AND SIZE

Figures in tables are rounded to two decimal places.

## LENGTH

All miles are statute miles. See **Nautical Measurements** below for nautical miles.

### Metric units

1 millimetre (mm)
10 millimetres (mm) = 1 centimetre (cm)
10 centimetres (cm) = 1 decimetre (dm)
100 centimetres (cm) = 1 metre (m)
1 000 metres (m) = 1 kilometre (km)

### Imperial units

1 inch (in)
12 inches (in) = 1 foot (ft)
3 feet (ft) = 1 yard (yd)
1 760 yards (yd) = 1 mile (mi)

### Exact conversions

1 mm = 0.03937in
1 cm = 0.3937in
1 cm = 0.0328ft
1 cm = 0.0109yd
1 dm = 3.937in
1 m = 39.37in
1 m = 3.2808ft
1 m = 1.0936yd
1 m = 0.00062mi
1 km = 3 280.8ft
1 km = 1 093.6yd
1 km = 0.6214mi

1 in = 25.4mm
1 in = 2.54cm
1 in = 0.254dm
1 in = 0.0254m
1 ft = 30.48cm
1 ft = 0.3048m
1 ft = 0.0003km
1 yd = 91.44cm
1 yd = 0.9144m
1 yd = 0.0009km
1 mi = 1 609.3m
1 mi = 1.6093km

**Inches to centimetres**

| *in* | *cm* |
|---|---|
| 1/8 | 0.31 |
| 1/4 | 0.64 |
| 3/8 | 0.95 |
| 1/2 | 1.27 |
| 5/8 | 1.59 |
| 3/4 | 1.91 |
| 7/8 | 2.22 |
| 1 | 2.54 |
| 2 | 5.08 |
| 3 | 7.62 |
| 4 | 10.16 |
| 5 | 12.70 |
| 6 | 15.24 |
| 7 | 17.78 |
| 8 | 20.32 |
| 9 | 22.86 |
| 10 | 25.40 |
| 11 | 27.94 |
| 12 | 30.48 |

**Centimetres to inches**

| *cm* | *in* |
|---|---|
| 1 | 0.39 |
| 2 | 0.79 |
| 3 | 1.18 |
| 4 | 1.57 |
| 5 | 1.97 |
| 6 | 2.36 |
| 7 | 2.76 |
| 8 | 3.15 |
| 9 | 3.54 |
| 10 | 3.94 |
| 20 | 7.87 |
| 30 | 11.81 |
| 40 | 15.75 |
| 50 | 19.69 |
| 60 | 23.62 |
| 70 | 27.56 |
| 80 | 31.50 |
| 90 | 35.43 |
| 100 | 39.37 |

**Inches to millimetres**

| *in* | *mm* |
|---|---|
| 1/8 | 3.18 |
| 1/4 | 6.35 |
| 3/8 | 9.53 |
| 1/2 | 12.70 |
| 5/8 | 15.88 |
| 3/4 | 19.05 |
| 7/8 | 22.23 |
| 1 | 25.40 |
| 2 | 50.80 |
| 3 | 76.20 |
| 4 | 101.60 |
| 5 | 127.00 |
| 6 | 152.40 |
| 7 | 177.80 |
| 8 | 203.20 |
| 9 | 228.60 |
| 10 | 254.00 |
| 11 | 279.40 |
| 12 | 304.80 |

**Millimetres to inches**

| *mm* | *in* |
|---|---|
| 1 | 0.04 |
| 2 | 0.08 |
| 3 | 0.12 |
| 4 | 0.16 |
| 5 | 0.20 |
| 6 | 0.24 |
| 7 | 0.28 |
| 8 | 0.31 |
| 9 | 0.35 |
| 10 | 0.39 |
| 20 | 0.79 |
| 30 | 1.18 |
| 40 | 1.58 |
| 50 | 1.97 |
| 60 | 2.36 |
| 70 | 2.76 |
| 80 | 3.15 |
| 90 | 3.55 |
| 100 | 3.94 |

**Feet to metres**

| ft | m |
|---|---|
| 1 | 0.30 |
| 2 | 0.61 |
| 3 | 0.91 |
| 4 | 1.22 |
| 5 | 1.52 |
| 6 | 1.83 |
| 7 | 2.13 |
| 8 | 2.44 |
| 9 | 2.74 |
| 10 | 3.05 |
| 20 | 6.10 |
| 30 | 9.14 |
| 40 | 12.19 |
| 50 | 15.24 |
| 75 | 22.86 |
| 100 | 30.48 |
| 200 | 60.96 |
| 300 | 91.44 |
| 400 | 121.92 |
| 500 | 152.40 |
| 1 000 | 304.80 |
| 2 000 | 609.60 |
| 3 000 | 914.40 |
| 4 000 | 1 219.20 |
| 5 000 | 1 524.00 |

**Metres to feet**

| m | ft |
|---|---|
| 1 | 3.28 |
| 2 | 6.56 |
| 3 | 9.84 |
| 4 | 13.12 |
| 5 | 16.40 |
| 6 | 19.68 |
| 7 | 22.97 |
| 8 | 26.25 |
| 9 | 29.53 |
| 10 | 32.81 |
| 20 | 65.62 |
| 30 | 98.42 |
| 40 | 131.23 |
| 50 | 164.04 |
| 75 | 246.06 |
| 100 | 328.08 |
| 200 | 656.16 |
| 300 | 984.24 |
| 400 | 1 312.32 |
| 500 | 1 640.40 |
| 1 000 | 3 280.80 |
| 2 000 | 6 561.60 |
| 3 000 | 9 842.40 |
| 4 000 | 13 123.20 |
| 5 000 | 16 404.00 |

**Yards to metres**

| yd | m |
|---|---|
| 1 | 0.91 |
| 2 | 1.83 |
| 3 | 2.74 |
| 4 | 3.66 |
| 5 | 4.57 |
| 6 | 5.49 |
| 7 | 6.40 |
| 8 | 7.32 |
| 9 | 8.23 |
| 10 | 9.14 |
| 20 | 18.29 |
| 30 | 27.43 |
| 40 | 36.58 |
| 50 | 45.72 |
| 75 | 68.58 |
| 100 | 91.44 |
| 200 | 182.88 |
| 300 | 274.32 |
| 400 | 365.76 |
| 500 | 457.20 |
| 1 000 | 914.40 |
| 2 000 | 1 828.80 |
| 3 000 | 2 743.20 |
| 4 000 | 3 657.60 |
| 5 000 | 4 572.00 |

**Metres to yards**

| m | yd |
|---|---|
| 1 | 1.09 |
| 2 | 2.19 |
| 3 | 3.28 |
| 4 | 4.37 |
| 5 | 5.47 |
| 6 | 6.56 |
| 7 | 7.66 |
| 8 | 8.75 |
| 9 | 9.84 |
| 10 | 10.94 |
| 20 | 21.87 |
| 30 | 32.81 |
| 40 | 43.74 |
| 50 | 54.68 |
| 75 | 82.02 |
| 100 | 109.36 |
| 200 | 218.72 |
| 300 | 328.08 |
| 400 | 437.44 |
| 500 | 546.80 |
| 1 000 | 1 093.60 |
| 2 000 | 2 187.20 |
| 3 000 | 3 280.80 |
| 4 000 | 4 374.40 |
| 5 000 | 5 468.00 |

**Miles to kilometres**

| mi | km | mi | km |
|---|---|---|---|
| 1 | 1.61 | 50 | 80.47 |
| 2 | 3.22 | 75 | 120.70 |
| 3 | 4.83 | 100 | 160.93 |
| 4 | 6.44 | 200 | 321.86 |
| 5 | 8.05 | 300 | 482.79 |
| 6 | 9.66 | 400 | 643.72 |
| 7 | 11.27 | 500 | 804.65 |
| 8 | 12.87 | 1 000 | 1 609.30 |
| 9 | 14.48 | 2 000 | 3 218.60 |
| 10 | 16.09 | 3 000 | 4 827.90 |
| 20 | 32.19 | 4 000 | 6 437.20 |
| 30 | 48.28 | 5 000 | 8 046.50 |
| 40 | 64.37 | | |

**Kilometres to miles**

| km | mi | km | mi |
|---|---|---|---|
| 1 | 0.62 | 50 | 31.07 |
| 2 | 1.24 | 75 | 46.61 |
| 3 | 1.86 | 100 | 62.14 |
| 4 | 2.49 | 200 | 124.28 |
| 5 | 3.11 | 300 | 186.42 |
| 6 | 3.73 | 400 | 248.56 |
| 7 | 4.35 | 500 | 310.70 |
| 8 | 4.97 | 1 000 | 621.40 |
| 9 | 5.59 | 2 000 | 1 242.80 |
| 10 | 6.21 | 3 000 | 1 864.20 |
| 20 | 12.43 | 4 000 | 2 485.60 |
| 30 | 18.64 | 5 000 | 3 107.00 |
| 40 | 24.86 | | |

# AREA

## Metric units

1 square millimetre (sq mm)
100 square millimetres (sq mm) = 1 square centimetre (sq cm)
100 square centimetres (sq cm) = 1 square decimetre (sq dm)
100 square decimetres (sq dm) = 1 square metre (sq m)
10 000 square centimetres (sq cm) = 1 square metre (sq m)
10 000 square metres (sq m) = 1 hectare (ha)
100 hectares (ha) = 1 square kilometre (sq km)
1 000 000 square metres (sq m) = 1 square kilometre (sq km)

## Imperial units

1 square inch (sq in)
144 square inches (sq in) = 1 square foot (sq ft)
9 square feet (sq ft) = 1 square yard (sq yd)
4 840 square yards (sq yd) = 1 acre (a)
640 acres (a) = 1 square mile (sq mi)

## Exact conversions

1 sq mm = 0.0016 sq in
1 sq cm = 0.155 sq in
1 sq cm = 0.0011 sq ft
1 sq dm = 15.5 sq in
1 sq m = 1 550 sq in
1 sq m = 10.7639 sq ft
1 sq m = 1.196 sq yd
1 sq m = 0.0002 a
1 ha = 2.471 a
1 ha = 11 959.9 sq yd
1 ha = 0.0039 sq mi
1 sq km = 0.3861 sq mi
1 sq km = 247.1 a

1 sq in = 645.16 sq mm
1 sq in = 6.4516 sq cm
1 sq in = 0.0645 sq dm
1 sq in = 0.0006 sq m
1 sq ft = 929.03 sq cm
1 sq ft = 0.0929 sq m
1 sq yd = 0.8361 sq m
1 sq yd = 0.00008 ha
1 a = 4 046.85 sq m
1 a = 0.4047 ha
1 a = 0.0016 sq km
1 sq mi = 258.9988 ha
1 sq mi = 2.5899 sq km

| Square inches to square centimetres | | Square centimetres to square inches | | Square feet to square metres | | Square metres to square feet | |
|---|---|---|---|---|---|---|---|
| *sq in* | *sq cm* | *sq cm* | *sq in* | *sq ft* | *sq m* | *sq m* | *sq ft* |
| 1 | 6.45 | 1 | 0.16 | 1 | 0.09 | 1 | 10.76 |
| 2 | 12.90 | 2 | 0.31 | 2 | 0.19 | 2 | 21.53 |
| 3 | 19.35 | 3 | 0.47 | 3 | 0.28 | 3 | 32.29 |
| 4 | 25.81 | 4 | 0.62 | 4 | 0.37 | 4 | 43.06 |
| 5 | 32.26 | 5 | 0.78 | 5 | 0.46 | 5 | 53.82 |
| 6 | 38.71 | 6 | 0.93 | 6 | 0.56 | 6 | 64.58 |
| 7 | 45.16 | 7 | 1.09 | 7 | 0.65 | 7 | 75.35 |
| 8 | 51.61 | 8 | 1.24 | 8 | 0.74 | 8 | 86.11 |
| 9 | 58.06 | 9 | 1.40 | 9 | 0.84 | 9 | 96.88 |
| 10 | 64.52 | 10 | 1.55 | 10 | 0.93 | 10 | 107.64 |
| 11 | 70.97 | 11 | 1.71 | 11 | 1.02 | 11 | 118.40 |
| 12 | 77.42 | 12 | 1.86 | 12 | 1.11 | 12 | 129.17 |
| 13 | 83.87 | 13 | 2.02 | 13 | 1.21 | 13 | 139.93 |
| 14 | 90.32 | 14 | 2.17 | 14 | 1.30 | 14 | 150.69 |
| 15 | 96.77 | 15 | 2.33 | 15 | 1.39 | 15 | 161.46 |
| 16 | 103.23 | 16 | 2.48 | 16 | 1.49 | 16 | 172.22 |
| 17 | 109.68 | 17 | 2.64 | 17 | 1.58 | 17 | 182.99 |
| 18 | 116.13 | 18 | 2.79 | 18 | 1.67 | 18 | 193.75 |
| 19 | 122.58 | 19 | 2.95 | 19 | 1.77 | 19 | 204.51 |
| 20 | 129.03 | 20 | 3.10 | 20 | 1.86 | 20 | 215.28 |
| 25 | 161.29 | 25 | 3.88 | 25 | 2.32 | 25 | 269.10 |
| 50 | 322.58 | 50 | 7.75 | 50 | 4.65 | 50 | 538.20 |
| 75 | 483.87 | 75 | 11.63 | 75 | 6.97 | 75 | 807.29 |
| 100 | 645.16 | 100 | 15.50 | 100 | 9.29 | 100 | 1 076.39 |
| | | | | 250 | 23.23 | 250 | 2 690.98 |
| | | | | 500 | 46.45 | 500 | 5 381.95 |
| | | | | 750 | 69.68 | 750 | 8 072.93 |
| | | | | 1 000 | 92.90 | 1 000 | 10 763.90 |

**Acres to hectares**

| *a* | *ha* |
|---|---|
| 1 | 0.40 |
| 2 | 0.81 |
| 3 | 1.21 |
| 4 | 1.62 |
| 5 | 2.02 |
| 6 | 2.43 |
| 7 | 2.83 |
| 8 | 3.24 |
| 9 | 3.64 |
| 10 | 4.05 |
| 11 | 4.45 |
| 12 | 4.86 |
| 13 | 5.26 |
| 14 | 5.67 |
| 15 | 6.07 |
| 16 | 6.47 |
| 17 | 6.88 |
| 18 | 7.28 |
| 19 | 7.69 |
| 20 | 8.09 |
| 25 | 10.12 |
| 50 | 20.23 |
| 75 | 30.35 |
| 100 | 40.47 |
| 250 | 101.17 |
| 500 | 202.34 |
| 750 | 303.51 |
| 1 000 | 404.69 |

**Hectares to acres**

| *ha* | *a* |
|---|---|
| 1 | 2.47 |
| 2 | 4.94 |
| 3 | 7.41 |
| 4 | 9.88 |
| 5 | 12.36 |
| 6 | 14.83 |
| 7 | 17.30 |
| 8 | 19.77 |
| 9 | 22.24 |
| 10 | 24.71 |
| 11 | 27.18 |
| 12 | 29.65 |
| 13 | 32.12 |
| 14 | 34.59 |
| 15 | 37.07 |
| 16 | 39.54 |
| 17 | 42.01 |
| 18 | 44.48 |
| 19 | 46.95 |
| 20 | 49.42 |
| 25 | 61.78 |
| 50 | 123.55 |
| 75 | 185.33 |
| 100 | 247.10 |
| 250 | 617.75 |
| 500 | 1 235.50 |
| 750 | 1 853.25 |
| 1 000 | 2 471.00 |

**Square miles to square kilometres**

| *sq mi* | *sq km* |
|---|---|
| 1 | 2.59 |
| 2 | 5.18 |
| 3 | 7.77 |
| 4 | 10.36 |
| 5 | 12.95 |
| 6 | 15.54 |
| 7 | 18.13 |
| 8 | 20.72 |
| 9 | 23.31 |
| 10 | 25.90 |
| 20 | 51.80 |
| 30 | 77.70 |
| 40 | 103.60 |
| 50 | 129.50 |
| 100 | 258.99 |
| 200 | 517.98 |
| 300 | 776.97 |
| 400 | 1 035.96 |
| 500 | 1 294.95 |
| 1 000 | 2 589.90 |
| 1 500 | 3 884.85 |
| 2 000 | 5 179.80 |

**Square kilometres to square miles**

| *sq km* | *sq mi* |
|---|---|
| 1 | 0.39 |
| 2 | 0.77 |
| 3 | 1.16 |
| 4 | 1.54 |
| 5 | 1.93 |
| 6 | 2.32 |
| 7 | 2.70 |
| 8 | 3.09 |
| 9 | 3.47 |
| 10 | 3.86 |
| 20 | 7.72 |
| 30 | 11.58 |
| 40 | 15.44 |
| 50 | 19.31 |
| 100 | 38.61 |
| 200 | 77.22 |
| 300 | 115.83 |
| 400 | 154.44 |
| 500 | 193.05 |
| 1 000 | 386.10 |
| 1 500 | 579.15 |
| 2 000 | 772.20 |

## VOLUME

### Metric units

1 cubic centimetre (cu cm[1])
1 000 cubic centimetres (cu cm) = 1 cubic decimetre (cu dm)
1 000 cubic decimetres (cu dm) = 1 cubic metre (cu m)

[1] *Cubic centimetres sometimes abbreviated as cc.*

### Imperial units

1 cubic inch (cu in)
1 728 cubic inches (cu in) = 1 cubic foot (cu ft)
27 cubic feet (cu ft) = 1 cubic yard (cu yd)

### Exact conversions

1 cu cm = 0.0610 cu in
1 cu dm = 61.024 cu in
1 cu m = 61 023.74 cu in
1 cu m = 35.3147 cu ft
1 cu m = 1.308 cu yd

1 cu in = 16.3871 cu cm
1 cu in = 0.0164 cu dm
1 cu in = 0.000016 cu m
1 cu ft = 0.0283 cu m
1 cu yd = 0.7646 cu m

**Cubic inches to cubic centimetres**

| cu in | cu cm |
|---|---|
| 1 | 16.39 |
| 2 | 32.77 |
| 3 | 49.16 |
| 4 | 65.55 |
| 5 | 81.93 |
| 6 | 93.32 |
| 7 | 114.71 |
| 8 | 131.10 |
| 9 | 147.48 |
| 10 | 163.87 |
| 15 | 245.81 |
| 20 | 327.74 |
| 50 | 819.35 |
| 100 | 1 638.71 |

**Cubic centimetres to cubic inches**

| cu cm | cu in |
|---|---|
| 1 | 0.06 |
| 2 | 0.12 |
| 3 | 0.18 |
| 4 | 0.24 |
| 5 | 0.30 |
| 6 | 0.37 |
| 7 | 0.43 |
| 8 | 0.49 |
| 9 | 0.55 |
| 10 | 0.61 |
| 15 | 0.92 |
| 20 | 1.22 |
| 50 | 3.05 |
| 100 | 6.10 |

**Cubic feet to cubic metres**

| cu ft | cu m |
|---|---|
| 1 | 0.03 |
| 2 | 0.06 |
| 3 | 0.08 |
| 4 | 0.11 |
| 5 | 0.14 |
| 6 | 0.17 |
| 7 | 0.20 |
| 8 | 0.23 |
| 9 | 0.25 |
| 10 | 0.28 |
| 15 | 0.42 |
| 20 | 0.57 |
| 50 | 1.41 |
| 100 | 2.83 |

**Cubic metres to cubic feet**

| cu m | cu ft |
|---|---|
| 1 | 35.31 |
| 2 | 70.63 |
| 3 | 105.94 |
| 4 | 141.26 |
| 5 | 176.57 |
| 6 | 211.89 |
| 7 | 247.20 |
| 8 | 282.52 |
| 9 | 317.83 |
| 10 | 353.15 |
| 15 | 529.72 |
| 20 | 706.29 |
| 50 | 1 765.74 |
| 100 | 3 531.47 |

**Cubic yards to cubic metres**

| cu yd | cu m | cu yd | cu m |
|---|---|---|---|
| 1 | 0.76 | 8 | 6.12 |
| 2 | 1.53 | 9 | 6.88 |
| 3 | 2.29 | 10 | 7.65 |
| 4 | 3.06 | 15 | 11.47 |
| 5 | 3.82 | 20 | 15.29 |
| 6 | 4.59 | 50 | 38.23 |
| 7 | 5.35 | 100 | 76.46 |

**Cubic metres to cubic yards**

| cu m | cu yd | cu m | cu yd |
|---|---|---|---|
| 1 | 1.31 | 8 | 10.46 |
| 2 | 2.62 | 9 | 11.77 |
| 3 | 3.92 | 10 | 13.08 |
| 4 | 5.23 | 15 | 19.62 |
| 5 | 6.54 | 20 | 26.16 |
| 6 | 7.85 | 50 | 65.40 |
| 7 | 9.16 | 100 | 130.80 |

# CAPACITY

## Liquid capacity measures

### Metric units

1 millilitre (ml)
10 millilitres (ml) = 1 centilitre (cl)
100 centilitres (cl) = 1 litre (l)
100 litres (l) = 1 hectolitre (hl)

### Imperial units

1 fluid ounce (fl oz)
20 fluid ounces (fl oz) = 1 pint (pt)
2 pints (pt) = 1 quart (qt)
8 pints (pt) = 1 gallon (gal)
4 quarts (qt) = 1 gallon (gal)

### Exact conversions

1 ml = 0.035 fl oz
1 cl = 0.352 fl oz
1 l = 35.196 fl oz
1 l = 1.7598pt
1 l = 0.220gal
1 hl = 22gal

1 fl oz = 28.41ml
1 fl oz = 2.84cl
1 fl oz = 0.0284 l
1 pt = 0.5682 l
1 qt = 1.14 l
1 gal = 4.546 l

# CAPACITY

## US measures

8 fl oz = 1 cup

1 fl oz = 0.0296 l
1 pt = 0.4732 l
1 gal = 3.7854 l

1 l = 33.8140 fl oz
1 l = 2.1134pt
1 l = 0.2642gal

1 pt (UK) = 1.20pt (US)
1 pt (US) = 0.83pt (UK)

1 gal (UK) = 1.200929gal (US)
1 gal (US) = 0.832688gal (UK)

### UK fluid ounces to litres

| *UK fl oz* | *l* |
|---|---|
| 1 | 0.03 |
| 2 | 0.06 |
| 3 | 0.09 |
| 4 | 0.11 |
| 5 | 0.14 |
| 6 | 0.17 |
| 7 | 0.20 |
| 8 | 0.23 |
| 9 | 0.26 |
| 10 | 0.28 |
| 11 | 0.31 |
| 12 | 0.34 |
| 13 | 0.37 |
| 14 | 0.40 |
| 15 | 0.43 |
| 20 | 0.57 |
| 50 | 1.42 |
| 100 | 2.84 |

### US fluid ounces to litres

| *US fl oz* | *l* |
|---|---|
| 1 | 0.03 |
| 2 | 0.06 |
| 3 | 0.09 |
| 4 | 0.12 |
| 5 | 0.15 |
| 6 | 0.18 |
| 7 | 0.21 |
| 8 | 0.24 |
| 9 | 0.27 |
| 10 | 0.30 |
| 11 | 0.33 |
| 12 | 0.36 |
| 13 | 0.39 |
| 14 | 0.41 |
| 15 | 0.44 |
| 20 | 0.59 |
| 50 | 1.48 |
| 100 | 2.96 |

### Litres to fluid ounces

| *l* | *UK fl oz* | *US fl oz* |
|---|---|---|
| 1 | 35.20 | 33.81 |
| 2 | 70.39 | 67.63 |
| 3 | 105.59 | 101.44 |
| 4 | 140.78 | 135.26 |
| 5 | 175.98 | 169.07 |
| 6 | 211.18 | 202.88 |
| 7 | 246.37 | 236.70 |
| 8 | 281.57 | 270.51 |
| 9 | 316.76 | 304.33 |
| 10 | 351.96 | 338.14 |
| 11 | 387.16 | 371.95 |
| 12 | 422.35 | 405.77 |
| 13 | 457.55 | 439.58 |
| 14 | 492.75 | 473.40 |
| 15 | 527.94 | 507.21 |
| 20 | 703.92 | 676.28 |
| 50 | 1 759.81 | 1 690.70 |
| 100 | 3 519.61 | 3 381.40 |

### UK pints to litres

| *UK pt* | *l* |
|---|---|
| 1 | 0.57 |
| 2 | 1.14 |
| 3 | 1.70 |
| 4 | 2.27 |
| 5 | 2.84 |
| 6 | 3.41 |
| 7 | 3.98 |
| 8 | 4.55 |
| 9 | 5.11 |
| 10 | 5.68 |
| 11 | 6.25 |
| 12 | 6.82 |
| 13 | 7.38 |
| 14 | 7.95 |
| 15 | 8.52 |
| 20 | 11.36 |
| 50 | 28.41 |
| 100 | 56.82 |

### US pints to litres

| *US pt* | *l* |
|---|---|
| 1 | 0.47 |
| 2 | 0.95 |
| 3 | 1.42 |
| 4 | 1.89 |
| 5 | 2.37 |
| 6 | 2.84 |
| 7 | 3.31 |
| 8 | 3.78 |
| 9 | 4.26 |
| 10 | 4.73 |
| 11 | 5.20 |
| 12 | 5.68 |
| 13 | 6.15 |
| 14 | 6.62 |
| 15 | 7.10 |
| 20 | 9.46 |
| 50 | 23.66 |
| 100 | 47.32 |

### Litres to pints

| *l* | *UK pt* | *US pt* |
|---|---|---|
| 1 | 1.76 | 2.11 |
| 2 | 3.52 | 4.23 |
| 3 | 5.28 | 6.34 |
| 4 | 7.04 | 8.45 |
| 5 | 8.80 | 10.57 |
| 6 | 10.56 | 12.68 |
| 7 | 12.32 | 14.79 |
| 8 | 14.08 | 16.91 |
| 9 | 15.84 | 19.02 |
| 10 | 17.60 | 21.13 |
| 11 | 19.36 | 23.25 |
| 12 | 21.12 | 25.36 |
| 13 | 22.88 | 27.47 |
| 14 | 24.64 | 29.59 |
| 15 | 26.40 | 31.70 |
| 20 | 35.20 | 105.67 |
| 50 | 87.99 | 211.34 |
| 100 | 175.98 | 422.68 |

**UK gallons to litres**

| *UK gal* | *l* |
|---|---|
| 1 | 4.55 |
| 2 | 9.09 |
| 3 | 13.64 |
| 4 | 18.18 |
| 5 | 22.73 |
| 6 | 27.28 |
| 7 | 31.82 |
| 8 | 36.37 |
| 9 | 40.91 |
| 10 | 45.46 |
| 11 | 50.01 |
| 12 | 54.55 |
| 13 | 59.10 |
| 14 | 63.64 |
| 15 | 68.19 |
| 16 | 72.74 |
| 17 | 77.28 |
| 18 | 81.83 |
| 19 | 86.37 |
| 20 | 90.92 |
| 25 | 113.65 |
| 50 | 227.30 |
| 75 | 340.96 |
| 100 | 454.61 |

**US gallons to litres**

| *US gal* | *l* |
|---|---|
| 1 | 3.78 |
| 2 | 7.57 |
| 3 | 11.36 |
| 4 | 15.14 |
| 5 | 18.93 |
| 6 | 22.71 |
| 7 | 26.50 |
| 8 | 30.28 |
| 9 | 34.07 |
| 10 | 37.85 |
| 11 | 41.64 |
| 12 | 45.42 |
| 13 | 49.21 |
| 14 | 52.99 |
| 15 | 56.78 |
| 16 | 60.57 |
| 17 | 64.35 |
| 18 | 68.14 |
| 19 | 71.92 |
| 20 | 75.71 |
| 25 | 94.63 |
| 50 | 189.27 |
| 75 | 283.90 |
| 100 | 378.54 |

**Litres to gallons**

| *l* | *UK gal* | *US gal* |
|---|---|---|
| 1 | 0.22 | 0.26 |
| 2 | 0.44 | 0.53 |
| 3 | 0.66 | 0.79 |
| 4 | 0.88 | 1.06 |
| 5 | 1.10 | 1.32 |
| 6 | 1.32 | 1.58 |
| 7 | 1.54 | 1.85 |
| 8 | 1.76 | 2.11 |
| 9 | 1.98 | 2.38 |
| 10 | 2.20 | 2.64 |
| 11 | 2.42 | 2.91 |
| 12 | 2.64 | 3.17 |
| 13 | 2.86 | 3.43 |
| 14 | 3.08 | 3.70 |
| 15 | 3.30 | 3.96 |
| 16 | 3.52 | 4.23 |
| 17 | 3.74 | 4.49 |
| 18 | 3.96 | 4.76 |
| 19 | 4.18 | 5.02 |
| 20 | 4.40 | 5.28 |
| 25 | 5.50 | 6.60 |
| 50 | 11.00 | 13.20 |
| 75 | 16.50 | 19.81 |
| 100 | 22.00 | 26.42 |

**UK gallons to US gallons**

| *UK gal* | *US gal* |
|---|---|
| 1 | 1.20 |
| 2 | 2.40 |
| 3 | 3.60 |
| 4 | 4.80 |
| 5 | 6 |
| 6 | 7.21 |
| 7 | 8.41 |
| 8 | 9.61 |
| 9 | 10.81 |
| 10 | 12.01 |
| 11 | 13.21 |
| 12 | 14.41 |
| 13 | 15.61 |
| 14 | 16.81 |
| 15 | 18.01 |
| 20 | 24.02 |
| 25 | 30.02 |
| 50 | 60.05 |

**US gallons to UK gallons**

| *US gal* | *UK gal* |
|---|---|
| 1 | 0.83 |
| 2 | 1.67 |
| 3 | 2.50 |
| 4 | 3.33 |
| 5 | 4.16 |
| 6 | 5.00 |
| 7 | 5.83 |
| 8 | 6.66 |
| 9 | 7.49 |
| 10 | 8.33 |
| 11 | 9.16 |
| 12 | 9.99 |
| 13 | 10.82 |
| 14 | 11.66 |
| 15 | 12.49 |
| 20 | 16.65 |
| 25 | 20.82 |
| 50 | 41.63 |

## CAPACITY

# Dry capacity measures

## Metric units

Cubic metres (cu m) see **Volume** above.
Litres (l) see **Liquid capacity measures** above.

## Imperial units

1 gallon (gal)
2 gallons (gal) = 1 peck (pk)
4 pecks (pk) = 1 bushel (bu)
8 gallons (gal) = 1 bushel (bu)

## Exact conversions

1 cu m = 219.97gal
1 cu m = 109.98pk
1 cu m = 27.4962bu
1 l = 0.2200gal
1 l = 0.1100pk
1 l = 0.0275bu
1 gal = 0.0045 cu m
1 gal = 4.546 l
1 pk = 0.0091 cu m
1 pk = 9.0919 l
1 bu = 0.0369 cu m
1 bu = 36.3677 l

## US measures

1 cu m = 227.02gal
1 cu m = 113.51pk
1 cu m = 28.3776bu
1 l = 0.227gal
1 l = 0.1135pk
1 l = 0.0284bu
1 gal = 0.0044 cu m
1 gal = 4.4049 l
1 pk = 0.0088 cu m
1 pk = 8.8095 l
1 bu = 0.9353 cu m
1 bu = 35.2381 l
1 qt = 1 101.22 cu cm
1 qt = 0.0011012 cu m
1 qt = 1.1012 l
1 pt = 550.61 cu cm
1 pt = 0.0006 cu m
1 pt = 0.5506 l
1 cu cm = 0.0009qt
1 cu m = 908.08qt
1 l = 0.908qt
1 cu cm = 0.0018pt
1 cu m = 1 816.17pt
1 l = 1.816pt

**UK bushels to cubic metres and litres**

| *UK bu* | *cu m* | *l* |
|---|---|---|
| 1 | 0.04 | 36.37 |
| 2 | 0.07 | 72.74 |
| 3 | 0.11 | 109.10 |
| 4 | 0.15 | 145.47 |
| 5 | 0.18 | 181.84 |
| 10 | 0.37 | 363.68 |

**US bushels to cubic metres and litres**

| *US bu* | *cu m* | *l* |
|---|---|---|
| 1 | 0.04 | 35.24 |
| 2 | 0.07 | 70.48 |
| 3 | 0.11 | 105.71 |
| 4 | 0.14 | 140.95 |
| 5 | 0.18 | 176.19 |
| 10 | 0.35 | 352.38 |

**Cubic metres to bushels**

| *cu m* | *UK bu* | *US bu* |
|---|---|---|
| 1 | 27.50 | 28.38 |
| 2 | 54.99 | 56.76 |
| 3 | 82.49 | 85.13 |
| 4 | 109.98 | 113.51 |
| 5 | 137.48 | 141.89 |
| 10 | 274.96 | 283.78 |

**Litres to bushels**

| *l* | *UK bu* | *US bu* |
|---|---|---|
| 1 | 0.03 | 0.03 |
| 2 | 0.06 | 0.06 |
| 3 | 0.08 | 0.09 |
| 4 | 0.11 | 0.11 |
| 5 | 0.14 | 0.14 |
| 10 | 0.28 | 0.28 |

**UK pecks to litres**

| *UK pk* | *l* |
|---|---|
| 1 | 9.09 |
| 2 | 18.18 |
| 3 | 27.28 |
| 4 | 36.37 |
| 5 | 45.46 |
| 10 | 90.92 |

**US pecks to litres**

| *US pk* | *l* |
|---|---|
| 1 | 8.81 |
| 2 | 17.62 |
| 3 | 26.43 |
| 4 | 35.24 |
| 5 | 44.05 |
| 10 | 88.10 |

**Litres to pecks**

| *l* | *UK pk* | *US pk* |
|---|---|---|
| 1 | 0.11 | 0.11 |
| 2 | 0.22 | 0.23 |
| 3 | 0.33 | 0.34 |
| 4 | 0.44 | 0.45 |
| 5 | 0.55 | 0.57 |
| 10 | 1.10 | 1.14 |

**US dry quarts to cubic centimetres and litres**

| *US qt* | *cu cm* | *l* |
|---|---|---|
| 1 | 1 101 | 1.1 |
| 2 | 2 202 | 2.2 |
| 3 | 3 304 | 3.3 |
| 4 | 4 405 | 4.4 |
| 5 | 5 506 | 5.5 |
| 10 | 11 012 | 11.0 |

**US dry pints to cubic centimetres and litres**

| *US pt* | *cu cm* | *l* |
|---|---|---|
| 1 | 551 | 0.55 |
| 2 | 1 101 | 1.10 |
| 3 | 1 652 | 1.65 |
| 4 | 2 202 | 2.20 |
| 5 | 2 753 | 2.75 |
| 10 | 5 506 | 5.51 |

## WEIGHT

All ounces are avoirdupois.

### Metric units

1 gram (g)
1 000 grams (g) = 1 kilogram (kg)
1 000 kilograms (kg) = 1 tonne[1]

[1] *The tonne is sometimes known as the metric ton.*

### Imperial units

1 ounce (oz)
16 ounces (oz) = 1 pound (lb)
14 pounds (lb) = 1 stone (st)
8 stones (st) = 1 hundredweight[1] (cwt)
20 hundredweights (cwt) = 1 ton[2]

1 pound (lb) = 0.0714 stones (st)
1 hundredweight (cwt) = 112 pounds (lb)
1 ton = 2 240 pounds (lb)
1 ton = 160 stone (st)

[1] *The UK hundredweight of 112 lb is sometimes known as the long hundredweight.*
[2] *The UK ton of 2 240 lb is sometimes known as the long ton.*

### Exact conversions

1 g = 0.0353oz
1 kg = 35.274oz
1 kg = 2.2046 lb
1 kg = 0.1575st
1 kg = 0.0197cwt
1 tonne = 157.5st
1 tonne = 19.684cwt
1 tonne = 0.9842 tons

1 oz = 28.3495g
1 lb = 0.4536kg
1 st = 6.350kg
1 cwt = 50.8023kg
1 cwt = 0.0508 tonnes
1 ton = 1 016.06kg
1 ton = 1.0160 tonnes

### US measures

100 pounds (lb) = 1 hundredweight[1] (cwt)
2 000 pounds (lb) = 1 ton[2]
20 hundredweights (cwt) = 1 ton

1 kg = 0.0220 cwt
1 tonne = 1.1023 tons

1 cwt = 45.3592 kg
1 ton = 0.9072 tonnes

1 cwt (UK) = 1.1199 cwt (US)
1 cwt (US) = 0.8929 cwt (UK)
1 ton (UK) = 1.1199 tons (US)
1 ton (US) = 0.8929 ton (UK)

[1] *The US hundredweight of 100 lb is sometimes known as the short hundredweight.*
[2] *The US ton of 2 000 lb is sometimes known as the short ton.*

## WEIGHT

**Ounces to grams**

| *oz* | *g* |
|---|---|
| 1 | 28.35 |
| 2 | 56.70 |
| 3 | 85.05 |
| 4 | 113.40 |
| 5 | 141.75 |
| 6 | 170.10 |
| 7 | 198.45 |
| 8 | 226.80 |
| 9 | 255.15 |
| 10 | 283.50 |
| 11 | 311.84 |
| 12 | 340.19 |
| 13 | 368.54 |
| 14 | 396.89 |
| 15 | 425.24 |
| 16 | 453.59 |

**Grams to ounces**

| *g* | *oz* |
|---|---|
| 1 | 0.04 |
| 2 | 0.07 |
| 3 | 0.11 |
| 4 | 0.14 |
| 5 | 0.18 |
| 6 | 0.21 |
| 7 | 0.25 |
| 8 | 0.28 |
| 9 | 0.32 |
| 10 | 0.35 |
| 20 | 0.71 |
| 30 | 1.06 |
| 40 | 1.41 |
| 50 | 1.76 |
| 60 | 2.12 |
| 70 | 2.47 |
| 80 | 2.82 |
| 90 | 3.18 |
| 100 | 3.53 |

**Pounds to kilograms**

| *lb* | *kg* |
|---|---|
| 1 | 0.45 |
| 2 | 0.91 |
| 3 | 1.36 |
| 4 | 1.81 |
| 5 | 2.27 |
| 6 | 2.72 |
| 7 | 3.18 |
| 8 | 3.63 |
| 9 | 4.08 |
| 10 | 4.54 |
| 11 | 4.99 |
| 12 | 5.44 |
| 13 | 5.90 |
| 14 | 6.35 |
| 15 | 6.80 |
| 16 | 7.26 |
| 17 | 7.71 |
| 18 | 8.16 |
| 19 | 8.62 |
| 20 | 9.07 |
| 30 | 13.61 |
| 40 | 18.14 |
| 50 | 22.68 |
| 100 | 45.36 |
| 200 | 90.72 |
| 250 | 113.40 |
| 500 | 226.80 |
| 750 | 340.19 |
| 1 000 | 453.59 |

**Kilograms to pounds**

| *kg* | *lb* |
|---|---|
| 1 | 2.21 |
| 2 | 4.41 |
| 3 | 6.62 |
| 4 | 8.82 |
| 5 | 11.03 |
| 6 | 13.23 |
| 7 | 15.44 |
| 8 | 17.64 |
| 9 | 19.85 |
| 10 | 22.05 |
| 11 | 24.26 |
| 12 | 26.46 |
| 13 | 28.67 |
| 14 | 30.87 |
| 15 | 33.08 |
| 16 | 35.28 |
| 17 | 37.49 |
| 18 | 39.69 |
| 19 | 41.90 |
| 20 | 44.10 |
| 30 | 66.15 |
| 40 | 88.20 |
| 50 | 110.25 |
| 100 | 220.50 |
| 200 | 441.00 |
| 250 | 551.25 |
| 500 | 1 102.50 |
| 750 | 1 653.75 |
| 1 000 | 2 205.00 |

**Stones to kilograms**

| *st* | *kg* |
|---|---|
| 1 | 6.35 |
| 2 | 12.70 |
| 3 | 19.05 |
| 4 | 25.40 |
| 5 | 31.75 |
| 6 | 38.10 |
| 7 | 44.45 |
| 8 | 50.80 |
| 9 | 57.15 |
| 10 | 63.50 |

**Kilograms to stones**

| *kg* | *st* |
|---|---|
| 1 | 0.16 |
| 2 | 0.32 |
| 3 | 0.47 |
| 4 | 0.63 |
| 5 | 0.79 |
| 6 | 0.95 |
| 7 | 1.10 |
| 8 | 1.26 |
| 9 | 1.42 |
| 10 | 1.58 |

**Stones to pounds**

| *st* | *lb* |
|---|---|
| 1 | 14 |
| 2 | 28 |
| 3 | 42 |
| 4 | 56 |
| 5 | 70 |
| 6 | 84 |
| 7 | 98 |
| 8 | 112 |
| 9 | 126 |
| 10 | 140 |
| 11 | 154 |
| 12 | 168 |
| 13 | 182 |
| 14 | 196 |
| 15 | 210 |
| 16 | 224 |
| 17 | 238 |
| 18 | 252 |
| 19 | 266 |
| 20 | 280 |

**Pounds to stones**

| *lb* | *st* |
|---|---|
| 1 | 0.07 |
| 2 | 0.14 |
| 3 | 0.21 |
| 4 | 0.29 |
| 5 | 0.36 |
| 6 | 0.43 |
| 7 | 0.50 |
| 8 | 0.57 |
| 9 | 0.64 |
| 10 | 0.71 |
| 11 | 0.79 |
| 12 | 0.86 |
| 13 | 0.93 |
| 14 | 1.00 |

**UK hundredweights to kilograms**

| *UK cwt* | *kg* |
|---|---|
| 1 | 50.80 |
| 2 | 101.60 |
| 3 | 152.41 |
| 4 | 203.21 |
| 5 | 254.01 |
| 10 | 508.02 |
| 20 | 1 016.05 |
| 50 | 2 540.12 |
| 75 | 3 810.17 |
| 100 | 5 080.23 |

**US hundredweights to kilograms**

| *US cwt* | *kg* |
|---|---|
| 1 | 45.36 |
| 2 | 90.72 |
| 3 | 136.08 |
| 4 | 181.44 |
| 5 | 226.80 |
| 10 | 453.59 |
| 20 | 907.18 |
| 50 | 2 267.96 |
| 75 | 3 401.94 |
| 100 | 4 535.92 |

**Kilograms to hundredweights**

| *kg* | *UK cwt* | *US cwt* |
|---|---|---|
| 1 | 0.02 | 0.02 |
| 2 | 0.04 | 0.04 |
| 3 | 0.06 | 0.07 |
| 4 | 0.08 | 0.09 |
| 5 | 0.10 | 0.11 |
| 10 | 0.20 | 0.22 |
| 20 | 0.40 | 0.44 |
| 50 | 0.99 | 1.10 |
| 75 | 1.48 | 1.65 |
| 100 | 1.97 | 2.20 |

**UK hundredweights to US hundredweights**

| *UK cwt* | *US cwt* |
|---|---|
| 1 | 1.12 |
| 2 | 2.24 |
| 3 | 3.36 |
| 4 | 4.48 |
| 5 | 5.60 |
| 10 | 11.20 |
| 20 | 22.40 |
| 50 | 56.00 |
| 75 | 83.99 |
| 100 | 111.99 |

**US hundredweights to UK hundredweights**

| *US cwt* | *UK cwt* |
|---|---|
| 1 | 0.89 |
| 2 | 1.79 |
| 3 | 2.68 |
| 4 | 3.57 |
| 5 | 4.46 |
| 10 | 8.93 |
| 20 | 17.86 |
| 50 | 44.64 |
| 75 | 66.96 |
| 100 | 89.29 |

**UK tons to tonnes**

| *UK tons* | *tonnes* |
|---|---|
| 1 | 1.02 |
| 2 | 2.03 |
| 3 | 3.05 |
| 4 | 4.06 |
| 5 | 5.08 |
| 10 | 10.16 |
| 20 | 20.32 |
| 50 | 50.80 |
| 75 | 76.20 |
| 100 | 101.60 |

**US tons to tonnes**

| *US tons* | *tonnes* |
|---|---|
| 1 | 0.91 |
| 2 | 1.81 |
| 3 | 2.72 |
| 4 | 3.63 |
| 5 | 4.54 |
| 10 | 9.07 |
| 20 | 18.14 |
| 50 | 45.36 |
| 75 | 68.04 |
| 100 | 90.72 |

**Tonnes to tons**

| *tonnes* | *UK tons* | *US tons* |
|---|---|---|
| 1 | 0.98 | 1.10 |
| 2 | 1.97 | 2.20 |
| 3 | 2.95 | 3.30 |
| 4 | 3.94 | 4.40 |
| 5 | 4.92 | 5.50 |
| 10 | 9.84 | 11.02 |
| 20 | 19.68 | 22.05 |
| 50 | 49.21 | 55.11 |
| 75 | 73.82 | 82.67 |
| 100 | 98.42 | 110.23 |

**UK tons to US tons**

| *UK tons* | *US tons* |
|---|---|
| 1 | 1.12 |
| 2 | 2.24 |
| 3 | 3.36 |
| 4 | 4.48 |
| 5 | 5.60 |
| 10 | 11.20 |
| 20 | 22.40 |
| 50 | 56.00 |
| 75 | 83.99 |
| 100 | 111.99 |

**US tons to UK tons**

| *US tons* | *UK tons* |
|---|---|
| 1 | 0.89 |
| 2 | 1.79 |
| 3 | 2.68 |
| 4 | 3.57 |
| 5 | 4.46 |
| 10 | 8.93 |
| 20 | 17.86 |
| 50 | 44.64 |
| 75 | 66.96 |
| 100 | 89.29 |

## TYRE PRESSURES

1 pound per square inch = 0.070307 kilogram per square centimetre.

| *lb per sq in* | *kg per sq cm* | *lb per sq in* | *kg per sq cm* |
|---|---|---|---|
| 10 | 0.70 | 26 | 1.83 |
| 15 | 1.05 | 28 | 1.97 |
| 20 | 1.41 | 30 | 2.11 |
| 24 | 1.69 | 40 | 2.81 |

# TEMPERATURE

## Temperature conversion

Carry out operations in sequence.

| To convert | To | Equation |
|---|---|---|
| °Fahrenheit | °Celsius[1] | –32, ×5, ÷9 |
| °Fahrenheit | °Rankine | +459.67 |
| °Fahrenheit | °Réaumur | –32, ×4, ÷9 |
| °Celsius[1] | °Fahrenheit | ×9, ÷5, +32 |
| °Celsius[1] | Kelvin | +273.15 |
| °Celsius[1] | °Réaumur | ×4, ÷5 |
| Kelvin | °Celsius[1] | –273.15 |
| °Rankine | °Fahrenheit | –459.67 |
| °Réaumur | °Fahrenheit | ×9, ÷ 4, +32 |
| °Réaumur | °Celsius[1] | ×5, ÷4 |

[1] *Celsius also known as Centigrade.*

## Fahrenheit to Celsius (Centigrade)

| °F | °C | °F | °C | °F | °C | °F | °C |
|---|---|---|---|---|---|---|---|
| 1 | –17.2 | 31 | –0.5 | 61 | 16.1 | 91 | 32.8 |
| 2 | –16.7 | 32 | 0.0 | 62 | 16.7 | 92 | 33.3 |
| 3 | –16.1 | 33 | 0.5 | 63 | 17.2 | 93 | 33.9 |
| 4 | –15.5 | 34 | 1.1 | 64 | 17.8 | 94 | 34.4 |
| 5 | –15.0 | 35 | 1.7 | 65 | 18.3 | 95 | 35.0 |
| 6 | –14.4 | 36 | 2.2 | 66 | 18.9 | 96 | 35.5 |
| 7 | –13.9 | 37 | 2.8 | 67 | 19.4 | 97 | 36.1 |
| 8 | –13.3 | 38 | 3.3 | 68 | 20.0 | 98 | 36.7 |
| 9 | –12.8 | 39 | 3.9 | 69 | 20.5 | 99 | 37.2 |
| 10 | –12.2 | 40 | 4.4 | 70 | 21.1 | 100 | 37.8 |
| 11 | –11.6 | 41 | 5.0 | 71 | 21.7 | 101 | 38.3 |
| 12 | –11.1 | 42 | 5.5 | 72 | 22.2 | 102 | 38.9 |
| 13 | –10.5 | 43 | 6.1 | 73 | 22.8 | 103 | 39.4 |
| 14 | –10.0 | 44 | 6.7 | 74 | 23.3 | 104 | 40.0 |
| 15 | –9.4 | 45 | 7.2 | 75 | 23.9 | 105 | 40.5 |
| 16 | –8.9 | 46 | 7.8 | 76 | 24.4 | 106 | 41.1 |
| 17 | –8.3 | 47 | 8.3 | 77 | 25.0 | 107 | 41.7 |
| 18 | –7.8 | 48 | 8.9 | 78 | 25.5 | 108 | 42.2 |
| 19 | –7.2 | 49 | 9.4 | 79 | 26.1 | 109 | 42.8 |
| 20 | –6.7 | 50 | 10.0 | 80 | 26.7 | 110 | 43.3 |
| 21 | –6.1 | 51 | 10.5 | 81 | 27.2 | 111 | 43.9 |
| 22 | –5.5 | 52 | 11.1 | 82 | 27.8 | 112 | 44.4 |
| 23 | –5.0 | 53 | 11.7 | 83 | 28.3 | 113 | 45.0 |
| 24 | –4.4 | 54 | 12.2 | 84 | 28.9 | 114 | 45.5 |
| 25 | –3.9 | 55 | 12.8 | 85 | 29.4 | 115 | 46.1 |
| 26 | –3.3 | 56 | 13.3 | 86 | 30.0 | 116 | 46.7 |
| 27 | –2.8 | 57 | 13.9 | 87 | 30.5 | 117 | 47.2 |
| 28 | –2.2 | 58 | 14.4 | 88 | 31.1 | 118 | 47.8 |
| 29 | –1.7 | 59 | 15.0 | 89 | 31.7 | 119 | 48.3 |
| 30 | –1.1 | 60 | 15.5 | 90 | 32.2 | 120 | 48.9 |

| °F | °C | °F | °C | °F | °C | °F | °C |
|---|---|---|---|---|---|---|---|
| 121 | 49.4 | 144 | 62.2 | 167 | 75.0 | 190 | 87.8 |
| 122 | 50.0 | 145 | 62.8 | 168 | 75.5 | 191 | 88.3 |
| 123 | 50.5 | 146 | 63.3 | 169 | 76.1 | 192 | 88.8 |
| 124 | 51.1 | 147 | 63.9 | 170 | 76.7 | 193 | 89.4 |
| 125 | 51.7 | 148 | 64.4 | 171 | 77.2 | 194 | 90.0 |
| 126 | 52.2 | 149 | 65.0 | 172 | 77.8 | 195 | 90.5 |
| 127 | 52.8 | 150 | 65.5 | 173 | 78.3 | 196 | 91.1 |
| 128 | 53.3 | 151 | 66.1 | 174 | 78.9 | 197 | 91.7 |
| 129 | 53.9 | 152 | 66.7 | 175 | 79.4 | 198 | 92.2 |
| 130 | 54.4 | 153 | 67.2 | 176 | 80.0 | 199 | 92.8 |
| 131 | 55.0 | 154 | 67.8 | 177 | 80.5 | 200 | 93.3 |
| 132 | 55.5 | 155 | 68.3 | 178 | 81.1 | 201 | 93.9 |
| 133 | 56.1 | 156 | 68.9 | 179 | 81.7 | 202 | 94.4 |
| 134 | 56.7 | 157 | 69.4 | 180 | 82.2 | 203 | 95.0 |
| 135 | 57.2 | 158 | 70.0 | 181 | 82.8 | 204 | 95.6 |
| 136 | 57.8 | 159 | 70.5 | 182 | 83.3 | 205 | 96.1 |
| 137 | 58.3 | 160 | 71.1 | 183 | 83.9 | 206 | 96.7 |
| 138 | 58.9 | 161 | 71.7 | 184 | 84.4 | 207 | 97.2 |
| 139 | 59.4 | 162 | 72.2 | 185 | 85.0 | 208 | 97.8 |
| 140 | 60.0 | 163 | 72.8 | 186 | 85.5 | 209 | 98.3 |
| 141 | 60.5 | 164 | 73.3 | 187 | 86.1 | 210 | 98.9 |
| 142 | 61.1 | 165 | 73.9 | 188 | 86.7 | 211 | 99.4 |
| 143 | 61.7 | 166 | 74.4 | 189 | 87.2 | 212 | 100.0 |

## Celsius (Centigrade) to Fahrenheit

| °C | °F | °C | °F | °C | °F | °C | °F |
|---|---|---|---|---|---|---|---|
| 1 | 33.8 | 26 | 78.8 | 51 | 123.8 | 76 | 168.8 |
| 2 | 35.6 | 27 | 80.6 | 52 | 125.6 | 77 | 170.6 |
| 3 | 37.4 | 28 | 82.4 | 53 | 127.4 | 78 | 172.4 |
| 4 | 39.2 | 29 | 84.2 | 54 | 129.2 | 79 | 174.2 |
| 5 | 41.0 | 30 | 86.0 | 55 | 131.0 | 80 | 176.0 |
| 6 | 42.8 | 31 | 87.8 | 56 | 132.8 | 81 | 177.8 |
| 7 | 44.6 | 32 | 89.6 | 57 | 134.6 | 82 | 179.6 |
| 8 | 46.4 | 33 | 91.4 | 58 | 136.4 | 83 | 181.4 |
| 9 | 48.2 | 34 | 93.2 | 59 | 138.2 | 84 | 183.2 |
| 10 | 50.0 | 35 | 95.0 | 60 | 140.0 | 85 | 185.0 |
| 11 | 51.8 | 36 | 96.8 | 61 | 141.8 | 86 | 186.8 |
| 12 | 53.6 | 37 | 98.6 | 62 | 143.6 | 87 | 188.6 |
| 13 | 55.4 | 38 | 100.4 | 63 | 145.4 | 88 | 190.4 |
| 14 | 57.2 | 39 | 102.2 | 64 | 147.2 | 89 | 192.2 |
| 15 | 59.0 | 40 | 104.0 | 65 | 149.0 | 90 | 194.0 |
| 16 | 60.8 | 41 | 105.8 | 66 | 150.8 | 91 | 195.8 |
| 17 | 62.6 | 42 | 107.6 | 67 | 152.6 | 92 | 197.6 |
| 18 | 64.4 | 43 | 109.4 | 68 | 154.4 | 93 | 199.4 |
| 19 | 66.2 | 44 | 111.2 | 69 | 156.2 | 94 | 201.2 |
| 20 | 68.0 | 45 | 113.0 | 70 | 158.0 | 95 | 203.0 |
| 21 | 69.8 | 46 | 114.8 | 71 | 159.8 | 96 | 204.8 |
| 22 | 71.6 | 47 | 116.6 | 72 | 161.6 | 97 | 206.6 |
| 23 | 73.4 | 48 | 118.4 | 73 | 163.4 | 98 | 208.4 |
| 24 | 75.2 | 49 | 120.2 | 74 | 165.2 | 99 | 210.2 |
| 25 | 77.0 | 50 | 122.0 | 75 | 167.0 | 100 | 212.0 |

## ASTRONOMICAL MEASUREMENTS

1 astronomical unit (AU) = 149 598 073 kilometres = 92 955 933 miles[1]
1 light year = 9 460 753 090 819 kilometres = 5 878 639 427 505 miles
1 parsec = 30 856 780 000 000 kilometres = 19 173 514 177 205 miles

[1] *The astronomical unit is equivalent to the mean distance between the Sun and the Earth.*

## BREWING MEASUREMENTS

4.5 gallons = 1 pin
2 pins = 9 gallons = 1 firkin
4 firkins = 1 barrel = 36 gallons
6 firkins = 1 hogshead = 54 gallons
4 hogsheads = 1 tun

## CLOTH MEASUREMENTS

1 ell = 45 inches
1 bolt = 120 feet = 32 ells

## CRUDE OIL MEASUREMENTS (PETROLEUM)

1 barrel = 35 UK gallons = 42 US gallons

## HORSES MEASUREMENTS

The height of horses is measured in hands.

1 hand = 4 inches = 10 centimetres

## NAUTICAL MEASUREMENTS

1 span = 9 inches = 23 centimetres
8 spans = 1 fathom = 6 feet
1 cable's length = $^1/_{10}$ nautical mile
1 nautical mile (old) = 6 080 feet
1 nautical mile (international) = 6 076.1 feet = 1.151 statute mile = 1 852 metres[1]
60 nautical mile = 1 degree
3 nautical mile = 1 league (nautical)
1 knot = 1 nautical mile per hour
1 ton (shipping) = 42 cubic feet
1 ton (displacement) = 35 cubic feet
1 ton (register) = 100 cubic feet

[1] *1 kilometre = 0.54 nautical miles.*

## PRINTING MEASUREMENTS

1 point = 0.3515 millimetres
1 pica = 4.2175 millimetres
1 pica = 12 points

## TIMBER MEASUREMENTS

1 000 millisteres = 1 stere = 1 cubic metre
1 board foot = 144 cubic inches (12 × 12 × 1 inches)
1 cord foot = 16 cubic feet
1 cord = 8 cord feet
1 hoppus foot = 4/π cubic feet (round timber)
1 Petrograd standard = 165 cubic feet

## COMPUTER MEMORY SIZES

1 byte = 8 bits
1 kilobyte (KB) = 1 024 bytes
1 megabyte (MB) = 1 024 kilobytes = 1 048 576 bytes
1 gigabyte (GB) = 1 024 megabytes = 1 048 576 kilobytes = 1 073 741 824 bytes

## CLOTHING SIZES

Size equivalents are approximate, and may display some variation between manufacturers.

### Women's suits/dresses

| UK | USA | UK/continent |
|---|---|---|
| 8 | 6 | 36 |
| 10 | 8 | 38 |
| 12 | 10 | 40 |
| 14 | 12 | 42 |
| 16 | 14 | 44 |
| 18 | 16 | 46 |
| 20 | 18 | 48 |
| 22 | 20 | 50 |
| 24 | 22 | 52 |

### Adults' shoes – women

| UK | USA | UK/continent |
|---|---|---|
| 3 | 4½ | 36 |
| 3½ | 5 | 37 |
| 4 | 5½ | 37 |
| 4½ | 6 | 38 |
| 5 | 6½ | 38 |
| 5½ | 7 | 39 |
| 6 | 7½ | 39 |
| 6½ | 8 | 40 |
| 7 | 8½ | 41 |
| 7½ | 9 | 42 |

### Adults' shoes – men

| UK | USA | UK/continent |
|---|---|---|
| 6½ | 7 | 40 |
| 7 | 7½ | 41 |
| 7½ | 8 | 41 |
| 8 | 8½ | 42 |
| 8½ | 9 | 43 |
| 9 | 9½ | 43 |
| 9½ | 10 | 44 |
| 10 | 10½ | 44 |
| 10½ | 11 | 45 |
| 11 | 11½ | 45 |

### Children's shoes

| UK/USA | UK/continent |
|---|---|
| 0 | 15 |
| ½ | 16 |
| 1 | 17 |
| 2 | 18 |
| 3 | 19 |
| 4 | 20 |
| 4½ | 21 |
| 5 | 22 |
| 6 | 23 |
| 7 | 24 |
| 8 | 25 |
| 8½ | 26 |
| 9 | 27 |
| 10 | 28 |
| 11 | 29 |
| 12 | 30 |
| 12½ | 31 |
| 13 | 32 |

### Women's hosiery

| UK/USA | continent | UK/USA | continent |
|---|---|---|---|
| 8 | 0 | 9½ | 3 |
| 8½ | 1 | 10 | 4 |
| 9 | 2 | 10½ | 5 |

### Men's suits and overcoats

| UK/USA | continent | UK/USA | continent |
|---|---|---|---|
| 36 | 46 | 42 | 52 |
| 38 | 48 | 44 | 54 |
| 40 | 50 | 46 | 56 |

### Men's socks

| UK/USA | continent | UK/USA | continent |
|---|---|---|---|
| 9½ | 38–39 | 11 | 41–42 |
| 10 | 39–40 | 11½ | 42–43 |
| 10½ | 40–41 | | |

### Men's shirts

| UK/USA | UK/continent | UK/USA | UK/continent |
|---|---|---|---|
| 12 | 30–31 | 15 | 38 |
| 12½ | 32 | 15½ | 39–40 |
| 13 | 33 | 16 | 41 |
| 13½ | 34–35 | 16½ | 42 |
| 14 | 36 | 17 | 43 |
| 14½ | 37 | 17½ | 44–45 |

## EGG SIZES

There are four weight grades for Class A eggs ('fresh eggs') as follows:

| | | | |
|---|---|---|---|
| XL | Very large (73g and above) | M | Medium (53g–63g) |
| L | Large (63g–73g) | S | Small (under 53g) |

## *Egg Science*

Dr Charles Williams of the School of Physics at the University of Exeter has worked out a scientific formula to calculate the exact cooking time needed to produce a perfect soft-boiled egg. His investigation concluded that the equation is:

$$t = aM^{2/3}\log_e\left[2\times\frac{(T_{egg}-T_{water})}{(T_{yolk}-T_{water})}\right]$$

where: $t$ is the total cooking time in minutes;
$a$ is a constant which depends on the egg's specific heat capacity and thermal conductivity (use a = 16 s $g^{-2/3}$ for eggs that are a week or two old – very fresh eggs will need a higher value, old eggs may need a lower value);
$M$ is the mass of the egg in grams;
$T_{egg}$ is the temperature in °C of the egg at the beginning;
$T_{yolk}$ is the temperature in °C at which the egg is ready to be eaten (for soft-boiled eggs use 45°C);
$T_{water}$ is the temperature in °C of the boiling water.

## PAPER SIZES

All sizes in these series have sides in the proportion of $1:\sqrt{2}$.

**A series** Used for writing paper, books and magazines.

| | *mm* | *in* | | *mm* | *in* |
|---|---|---|---|---|---|
| A0 | 841×1 189 | 33.11×46.81 | A6 | 105×148 | 4.13×5.83 |
| A1 | 594×841 | 23.39×33.11 | A7 | 74×105 | 2.91×4.13 |
| A2 | 420×594 | 16.54×23.39 | A8 | 52×74 | 2.05×2.91 |
| A3 | 297×420 | 11.69×16.54 | A9 | 37×52 | 1.46×2.05 |
| A4 | 210×297 | 8.27×11.69 | A10 | 26×37 | 1.02×1.46 |
| A5 | 148×210 | 5.83×8.27 | | | |

**B series** Used for posters.

| | *mm* | *in* | | *mm* | *in* |
|---|---|---|---|---|---|
| B0 | 1 000×1 414 | 39.37×55.67 | B6 | 125×176 | 4.92×6.93 |
| B1 | 707×1 000 | 27.83×39.37 | B7 | 88×125 | 3.46×4.92 |
| B2 | 500×707 | 19.68×27.83 | B8 | 62×88 | 2.44×3.46 |
| B3 | 353×500 | 13.90×19.68 | B9 | 44×62 | 1.73×2.44 |
| B4 | 250×353 | 9.84×13.90 | B10 | 31×44 | 1.22×1.73 |
| B5 | 176×250 | 6.93×9.84 | | | |

**C series** Used for envelopes.

| | *mm* | *in* | | *mm* | *in* |
|---|---|---|---|---|---|
| C0 | 917×1 297 | 36.00×51.20 | C6 | 114×162 | 4.50×6.40 |
| C1 | 648×917 | 25.60×36.00 | C7 | 81×114 | 3.19×4.50 |
| C2 | 458×648 | 18.00×25.60 | DL | 110×220 | 4.33×8.66 |
| C3 | 324×458 | 12.80×18.00 | C7/6 | 81×162 | 3.19×6.38 |
| C4 | 229×324 | 9.00×12.80 | | | |
| C5 | 162×229 | 6.40×9.00 | | | |

### Writing paper sizes

25 sheets = 1 quire
20 quires = 1 ream
500 sheets = 1 ream

## PENCIL HARDNESS

Pencil lead classification uses *black*, abbreviated to B, to indicate softness in quality and darkness in use, and *hard*, abbreviated to H, to indicate durability in quality and faintness in use.

**9H** extremely hard and faint

**HH** *or* **2H** very hard

**H** hard

**HB** hard black

**B** black

**BB** *or* **2B** very black

**9B** extremely soft and dark

## INVENTIONS, DISCOVERIES AND FIRSTS

| Date | Invention, discovery or first |
|---|---|
| c.4000BC | **Lock** is invented in Mesopotamia. |
| c.3500BC | **Wheel** is invented in Mesopotamia. |
| c.3000BC | **Writing** (pictography) is invented in Egypt. |
| c.2500BC | **Soap** is invented in Sumer, Babylonia. |
| c.2250BC | **Maps** are invented in Mesopotamia. |
| 245BC | **Gun** is invented by Ctesibius (fl.2c BC). |
| 2c BC | **Cannon** is invented by Archimedes (c.287–212BC). |
| c.2c BC | **Parachute** is invented in China. |
| 59BC | **Newspaper** is invented by Julius Caesar (100 or 102–44BC). |
| 25BC | **Suspension bridge** is invented in China. |
| 1c | **Discovery of magnetite** leads to the invention of the **compass** in China. |
| 1c | **Concrete** is invented in Rome. |
| AD105 | **Paper** is invented in China. **Parchment** had been invented by Eumenes II of Pergamon (died 159BC) in the 2c BC. |
| c.600 | **Windmill** is invented in Syria. |
| 725 | **Mechanical clock** is invented in China. |
| c.10c | **Vaccination** is invented in Turkey and China. |
| c.980–1020 | Coast of **America** is explored by first European, Leif Erikson (fl.1000). |
| 1232 | **Rocket** is invented by the Mongols in China. |
| c.1450 | **Wooden printing press** is invented by Johannes Gutenberg (1400–68). |
| 1513 | **Pacific Ocean** is sighted by Vasco Nuñez de Balboa (1475–1519). |
| 1519–22 | First **circumnavigation of the world** by crew members of Ferdinand Magellan's (c.1480–1521) expedition. |
| 1590 | **Microscope** is invented by Zacharias Janssen (1580–1638). |
| 1608 | **Refractor telescope** is invented by Hans Lippershey (c.1570–c.1619). |
| 1620 | **Submarine** is invented by Cornelis Drebbel (c.1572–1633). |
| 1628 | **Blood circulation** is discovered by William Harvey (1578–1677). |
| 1643 | **Barometer** is invented by Evangelista Torricelli (1608–47). |
| 1657 | **Pendulum clock** is invented by Christiaan Huygens (1629–93). |
| 1675 | **Protozoa** are observed by Anton van Leeuwenhoek (1632–1723). |
| 1675 or 1684 | **Red corpuscles** are observed by Anton van Leeuwenhoek (1632–1723). |
| 1677 | **Spermatozoa** are observed by Anton van Leeuwenhoek (1632–1723). |
| 1680 | **Match** is invented by Robert Boyle (1627–91). |
| 1698 | **Steam engine** is invented by Thomas Savery (c.1650–1715); it is later refined by Thomas Newcomen (1663–1729) and James Watt (1736–1819). |
| 1714 | **Mercury thermometer** is invented by Daniel Fahrenheit (1686–1736). The **thermometer** itself had been invented by Ctesibius (fl.2c BC) in the 2c BC. |
| 1718 | **Machine gun** is invented by James Puckle (dates unknown). |
| 1720 | **Pianoforte** is invented by Bartolomeo Cristofori (1655–1731). |
| 1735 | **Chronometer** is invented by John Harrison (1693–1776). |
| c.1740 | **Lemon juice treatment** for scurvy is developed by James Lind (1716–94). |
| 1751 | **Nickel** is discovered by Baron Axel Fredrik Cronstedt (1722–65). |
| 1766 | **Existence of carbon dioxide** and **hydrogen** in atmospheric air is demonstrated by Henry Cavendish (1731–1810). |
| 1770–80 | **Use of oxygen in respiration** is discovered by Antoine Lavoisier (1743–94). |
| 1771 | **Fluorine** is discovered by Carl Wilhelm Scheele (1742–86). |
| 1772 | **Nitrogen** is discovered by Daniel Rutherford (1749–1819). |
| 1774 | **Oxygen** is discovered by Joseph Priestley (1733–1804). |
| 1774 | **Chlorine** is discovered by Carl Wilhelm Scheele (1742–86). |

INVENTIONS, DISCOVERIES AND FIRSTS

| Date | Invention, discovery or first |
|---|---|
| 1776 | **Nitrous oxide** (laughing gas) is discovered by Joseph Priestley (1733–1804). Its analgesic and laughter-provoking effects are later discovered by Humphry Davy (1778–1829). |
| 1783 | **Balloon** able to carry human passengers is invented by Jacques (1745–99) and Joseph (1740–1810) Montgolfier. |
| 1789 | **Uranium** is discovered by Martin Heinrich Klaproth (1743–1817). |
| 1789 | **Titanium** is discovered by William Gregor (1761–1817). |
| 1795 | **Pencil** is invented by Nicholas Jacques Conté (1755–1805). |
| 1796 | **Smallpox vaccination** is discovered by Edward Jenner (1749–1823). |
| 1800 | **Electric battery** is invented by Alessandro Volta (1745–1827). |
| 1804 | **Railed locomotive** is invented by Richard Trevithick (1771–1833). |
| 1807 | **Potassium** and **sodium** are discovered by Humphry Davy (1778–1829). |
| 1808 | **Barium** and **calcium** are discovered by Humphry Davy (1778–1829). |
| 1811 | **Iodine** is discovered by Bernard Courtois (1777–1838). |
| 1816 | **Photography** (on metal) is invented by Nicéphore Niepce (1765–1833). In 1838 William Henry Fox Talbot (1800–77) invents photography on paper. Colour photography is invented by James Clerk Maxwell (1831–79) in 1861. |
| 1817 | **Lithium** is discovered by Johan August Arfvedson (1792–1841). |
| 1823 | **Silicon** is discovered by Jöns Jacob Berzelius (1779–1848). |
| 1828 | **Aluminium** is discovered by Friedrich Wöhler (1800–82). |
| 1829 | **Magnesium** is discovered by Antoine Alexandre Brutus Bussy (1794–1882). |
| 1829 | A basic **typewriter**, called a typographer, is invented by William Burt (1792–1858). The first practical working typewriter was patented in 1868 by Christopher Sholes (1819–90). The electric typewriter was invented by Thomas Alva Edison (1847–1931) in 1872. |
| 1835 | '**Difference engine**', considered to be the first computer, is invented by Charles Babbage (1791–1871). |
| 1835 | **Revolver** is invented by Samuel Colt (1814–62). |
| 1837 | **Telegraph code** is invented by Samuel Morse (1791–1872). |
| 1839–40 | **Bicycle** is invented by Kirkpatrick Macmillan (1813–78). |
| c.1840 | **General anaesthetic** is invented; priority is claimed by Crawford Long (1815–78), Gardner Cotton (1814–98), Horace Wells (1815–48) and Charles Jackson (1805–80). **Local anaesthetic** had been described centuries before in *Natural History* by Pliny the Elder (23–79AD). |
| 1844 | **Ship with a metal hull and propeller** is built by Isambard Kingdom Brunel (1806–59). |
| 1846 | **Ether** is discovered by William Thomas Morton (1819–68). |
| 1847 | **Anaesthetic properties of chloroform** are discovered by James Young Simpson (1811–70). |
| 1851 | **Mechanical lift** is invented by Elisha G Otis (1811–61). |
| 1855 | **Cellular division** is discovered by Rudolph Virchow (1821–1902). |
| 1858 | **Theory of evolution** is presented by Charles Darwin (1809–82). |
| 1859 | Synthesization of **aspirin** by Hermann Kolbe (1818–84). Aspirin is introduced into medicine by Felix Hoffmann (1868–1946) in 1899. |
| 1863 | **Pasteurization** is invented by Louis Pasteur (1822–95). |
| 1865 | **Heredity** is discovered by Gregor Johann Mendel (1822–84). |
| 1865 | **Antisepsis** is developed by Joseph Lister (1827–1912). |
| 1866 | **Dynamite** is invented by Alfred Nobel (1833–96). |
| 1868 | **Plastics** are invented by John Wesley Hyatt (1837–1920). |
| 1870 | **DC electric motor** is invented by Zenobe Gramme (1826–1901). |
| 1875 | **Fertilization** is discovered by Oskar Hertwig (1849–1922). |
| 1876 | **Telephone** is invented by Alexander Graham Bell (1847–1922). |
| 1877 | **Phonograph** and the **gramophone** are invented by Thomas Alva Edison (1847–1931). |

| Date | Invention, discovery or first |
|---|---|
| 1879 | **Electric light bulb** is invented by Thomas Alva Edison (1847–1931). |
| 1880 | **Staphylococcus** and **Streptococcus** are observed by Louis Pasteur (1822–95). |
| 1881 | **Transmission of yellow fever by mosquito** is described by Ronald Ross (1857–1932) and Carlos Juan Finlay (1833–1915). |
| 1884 | First practical working **fountain pen** is patented by Lewis Waterman (1837–1901). It is not until 1938 that Laszlo Biró (1899–1985) invents the **ballpoint pen**. |
| 1885 | **Car** is built using a high-speed internal combustion engine by Gottlieb Daimler (1834–1900). |
| 1885 | **Rabies vaccination** is pioneered by Louis Pasteur (1822–95). |
| 1885 | **Motorcycle** is invented by Gottlieb Daimler (1834–1900). |
| 1886 | **Petrol engine** is pioneered by Karl Benz (1844–1929). |
| 1887 | **Contact lenses** are invented by Adolph E Fick (1829–1901). |
| 1888 | **Chromosomes** are discovered by Thomas Hunt Morgan (1866–1945). |
| 1888 | **Radio telegraphy** is invented by Heinrich Hertz (1857–94). |
| 1888 | **AC electric motor** is invented by Nikola Tesla (1856–1943). |
| 1889 | **Photographic film** is invented by George Eastman (1854–1932). |
| 1892 | **Diesel engine** is invented by Rudolf Diesel (1858–1913). |
| 1892 | **Serum against diphtheria** is developed by Emil Adolf von Behring (1854–1917), Shibasaburo Kitasato (1852–1931) and Pierre Émile Roux (1853–1933). |
| 1892 | **X-rays** are discovered by Heinrich Hertz (1857–94). Their properties are discovered by Wilhelm Konrad von Röntgen (1845–1923) in 1895. |
| 1895 | **Helium** is discovered by William Ramsay (1852–1916). |
| 1895 | **Cinema** is pioneered by Auguste (1862–1954) and Louis (1865–1948) Lumière. |
| 1895 | **Safety razor** is invented by King Camp Gillette (1855–1932). The **electric razor** was invented by Jacob Schick (1878–1937) in 1928. |
| 1898 | **Radium** is discovered by Marie (1867–1934) and Pierre (1859–1906) Curie. |
| 1898 | **Neon** is discovered by William Ramsay (1852–1916) and Morris William Travers (1872–1961). |
| 1900 | **Rigid airship** is invented by Graf Ferdinand von Zeppelin (1838–1917). |
| 1901 | **Adrenaline** is discovered by Jokichi Takamine (1854–1922) based on work by Edward Sharpey-Schafer (1850–1935) and George Oliver (1841–1915). |
| 1901 | **Blood groups** A, O, B and AB are discovered by Karl Landsteiner (1868–1943). |
| 1901 | **Radio** (transatlantic) is invented by Guglielmo Marconi (1874–1937). |
| 1903 | **Aeroplane** is invented by Orville (1897–1948) and Wilbur (1867–1912) Wright. |
| 1906 | **Necessity of vitamins** in diet is demonstrated by Sir Frederick Gowland Hopkins (1861–1947). |
| 1907 | Electric **washing machine** is invented by Hurley Machine Co. |
| 1909 | **North Pole** is reached by Robert Edwin Peary (1856–1920). |
| 1909 | First **cross-Channel flight** is made by Louis Blériot (1872–1936). |
| 1911 | **South Pole** is reached by Roald Amundsen (1872–1928). |
| 1919 | First **nonstop transatlantic flight** is made by John Alcock (1892–1919) and Arthur Whitten Brown (1886–1948). |
| 1921 | **Insulin** is isolated by Frederick Grant Banting (1891–1941), Charles Herbert Best (1899–1978) and John James McLeod (1876–1935). |
| 1926 | **Television** is invented by John Logie Baird (1888–1946). Peter Goldmark (1906–77) went on to invent **colour television** in 1940. |
| 1927 | First **solo transatlantic flight** is made by Charles Lindbergh (1902–74). The first solo transatlantic flight by a woman was made by Amelia Earhart (1897–1937) in 1932. |
| 1928 | **Turbojet** is invented by Frank Whittle (1907–96). |
| 1928 | **Penicillin** is discovered by Alexander Fleming (1881–1955). |
| 1933 | First **solo round-the-world flight** is made by Wiley Post (1900–35). |
| 1935 | **Sulphonamides** (the first **antibiotics**) are discovered by Gerhard (Johannes Paul) Domagk (1895–1964). |
| 1937 | **Nylon** is invented by Wallace H Carothers (1896–1937). |

# INVENTIONS, DISCOVERIES AND FIRSTS

| Date | Invention, discovery or first |
|---|---|
| 1938 | **Xerography** is invented by Chester Carlson (1906–68). |
| 1939–45 | **Atomic bomb** is invented by Otto Frisch (1904–79). |
| 1940 | **Plutonium** is discovered by Glenn Theodore Seaborg (1912–99), Edwin Mattison McMillan (1907–91) and others. |
| 1943 | **Streptomycin** (an antibiotic against tuberculosis) is discovered by Selman Abraham Waksman (1888–1973). |
| 1945 | **Microwave oven** is invented by Percy L Spencer (1894–1970). |
| 1947 | **Polaroid camera** is invented by Edwin Land (1909–91). |
| 1947 | First **piloted supersonic flight** is made by Charles E Yeager (born 1923). |
| 1948 | **Transistor** is invented by John Bardeen (1908–91). |
| 1950 | **Californium** is discovered by Glenn Theodore Seaborg (1912–99) and others. |
| 1950 | **Contraceptive pill** is invented by Gregor Pincus (1903–67) and others. |
| 1952 | **Chemical regulation by genes** is discovered by Jacques Monod (1910–76) and Edwin Joseph Cohn (1892–1953). |
| 1953 | **Structure of DNA** is unravelled by Francis Crick (born 1916) and James D Watson (born 1928). |
| 1953 | First people to reach the **summit of Mt Everest** are Edmund Hillary (born 1919) and Tenzing Norgay (1914–86). |
| 1955 | **Hovercraft** is invented by Christopher Cockerell (1910–99). |
| 1956 | **Video recorder** is invented by Ampex Co. |
| 1957 | First **satellite** to orbit the Earth, Sputnik 1, is launched by the USSR. |
| 1958 | **Microchip** is invented by Jack Kilby (born 1923). |
| 1960 | The first working **laser** is invented by Theodore Maiman (born 1927); the laser was patented by Arthur L Schawlow (1921–99) and Charles H Townes (born 1915). |
| 1961 | First **human being in space** as Yuri Gagarin (1934–68) makes one orbit of the Earth. |
| 1961 | **Silicon chip** is invented by Texas Instruments. |
| 1969 | First **human beings to walk on the moon** are Neil Armstrong (born 1930) and Buzz Aldrin (born 1930) of the Apollo 11 mission. |
| 1971 | **Microprocessor** is invented by Marcian E Hoff (born 1937). |
| 1979 | **Compact disc** is invented by the Philips and Sony companies. |
| 1981 | **AIDS** (Acquired Immune Deficiency Syndrome) is identified by scientists in Los Angeles. |
| 1981 | **Space shuttle flights** are commenced by the USA. |
| 1983 | **HIV** (the Human Immuno-Deficiency Virus) is isolated by Luc Montagnier (born 1932) and others. |
| 1989 | **World Wide Web** is invented by Tim Berners-Lee (born 1955). |
| 1990 | **Hubble Space Telescope** (the first optical space-based telescope) is launched by NASA. |
| 1999 | First **nonstop round-the-world balloon flight** is completed by Bertrand Piccard (born 1958) and Brian Jones (born 1947). |
| 2001 | First **space tourist** visits the International Space Station. |
| 2003 | First **solo crossing of the Atlantic in an open basket balloon** is made by David Hempleman-Adams (born 1956). |

## Interesting Inventions

Other inventions that we now take for granted include the *aerosol* (Erik Rotheim, 1926), the *burglar alarm* (Edwin T Holmes, 1858), *chocolate* (François-Louis Cailler, 1819), the *credit card* (Ralph Scheider, 1950), the *crossword* (Arthur Wynne, 1913), the *automatic dishwasher* (Mrs W A Cockran, 1889), the *escalator* (Jesse W Reno, 1892), *instant coffee* (Nestlé, 1937), *jeans* (Levi-Strauss, 1872), the *lawnmower* (Edwin Beard Budding, 1830), the *paperclip* (Johann Vaaler, 1900), the *safety pin* (Walter Hunt, 1849), the *toaster* (Charles Strite, 1927), *automatic traffic lights* (Alfred Benesch, 1914), the *travel agency* (Thomas Cook, 1841) and the *zip* (Whitcomb L Judson, 1893).

# ARCHITECTURE AND ENGINEERING

## TALLEST BUILDINGS

### Tallest structures

| Name | Location | Height | Date completed |
|---|---|---|---|
| KVLY-TV Mast | Blanchard, North Dakota, USA | 629m/2 063ft | 1963 |
| CN Tower | Toronto, Canada | 553m/1 815ft | 1975 |

### Tallest inhabited buildings

| Name | Location | Height | Date completed |
|---|---|---|---|
| Taipei 101 | Taipei, Taiwan | 508m/1 667ft | 2003 |
| Petronas I | Kuala Lumpur, Malaysia | 452m/1 483ft | 1998 |
| Petronas II | Kuala Lumpur, Malaysia | 452m/1 483ft | 1998 |
| Sears Tower | Chicago, USA | 442m/1 450ft | 1974 |
| Jin Mao Building | Shanghai, China | 421m/1 381ft | 1998 |
| Two International Finance Centre | Hong Kong, China | 415m/1 361ft | 2003 |
| CITIC Plaza | Guangzhou, China | 391m/1 282ft | 1997 |
| Shun Hing Square | Shenzhen, China | 384m/1 260ft | 1996 |
| Empire State Building | New York City, USA | 381m/1 250ft | 1931 |
| Central Plaza | Hong Kong, China | 374m/1 227ft | 1992 |
| Bank of China | Hong Kong, China | 367m/1 204ft | 1990 |
| Emirates Office Tower | Dubai, United Arab Emirates | 355m/1 164ft | 2000 |
| Tuntex Sky Tower | Kaohsiung, China | 348m/1 141ft | 1997 |
| Aon Center | Chicago, USA | 346m/1 135ft | 1973 |

### *Towering Craziness*

The CN Tower has had its fair share of wild and wacky climbers. Records have been set for carrying a piano, lugging a 91kg/200lb pumpkin, driving a motorbike and bouncing on a pogo stick up the Tower's many stairs. World records have also been set for the descent, notably in 1984 when a stuntman tumbled his way to the bottom, falling down the 1 760-odd steps in just under two hours.

## LONGEST BRIDGES

Figures refer to main unsupported spans. All bridges are of the suspension type.

| Name | Location | Length | Date completed |
|---|---|---|---|
| Akashi-Kaikyo | Honshu–Shikoku, Japan | 1 990m/6 527ft | 1998 |
| Great Belt East (Storebaelt) | Halsskov–Kudshoved, Denmark | 1 624m/5 327ft | 1998 |
| Humber Estuary | Hull–Grimsby, UK | 1 410m/4 625ft | 1981 |
| Jiangyin | Jiangsu Province, China | 1 385m/4 543ft | 1999 |
| Tsing Ma | Hong Kong, China | 1 377m/4 516ft | 1997 |
| Verrazano Narrows | Brooklyn–Staten Island, New York Harbour, USA | 1 298m/4 257ft | 1964 |
| Golden Gate | San Francisco, California, USA | 1 280m/4 198ft | 1937 |

| Name | Location | Length | Date completed |
|---|---|---|---|
| Höga Kusten | Kramfors, Sweden | 1 210m/3 969ft | 1997 |
| Mackinac | Mackinaw City–St Ignace, Michigan, USA | 1 158m/3 799ft | 1957 |
| Minami Bisan-Seto | Honshu–Shikoku, Japan | 1 100m/3 608ft | 1988 |
| Bosporus II | Istanbul, Turkey | 1 090m/3 575ft | 1988 |
| Bosporus | Istanbul, Turkey | 1 074m/3 523ft | 1973 |
| George Washington | Hudson River, New York City, USA | 1 067m/3 500ft | 1931 |
| Kurushima-3 | Onomichi–Imabari, Japan | 1 030m/3 378ft | 1999 |
| Kurushima-2 | Onomichi–Imabari, Japan | 1 020m/3 346ft | 1999 |
| Ponte 25 de Abril | Lisbon, Portugal | 1 013m/3 323ft | 1966 |
| Forth Road | Edinburgh, UK | 1 006m/3 300ft | 1964 |
| Kita Bisan-seto | Kojima–Sakaide, Japan | 990m/3 247ft | 1988 |
| Severn | Bristol, UK | 988m/3 240ft | 1966 |
| Yichang | Hubei Province, China | 960m/3 149ft | 2001 |

## LONGEST TUNNELS

| Name | Location | Length | Type | Date completed |
|---|---|---|---|---|
| Seikan | Honshu–Hokkaido, Japan | 53.9km/33.4mi | rail | 1985 |
| Channel | Cheriton, England–Coquelles, France | 49.9km/30.9mi | rail | 1994 |
| Moscow subway | Moscow, Russia | 37.9km/23.5mi | rail | 1990 |
| Northern tube line | London, UK | 27.8km/17.2mi | rail | 1926 |
| Iwate Ichinohe | Tanigawa Mountains, Japan | 25.8km/16.0mi | rail | 2002 |
| Laerdal | Laerdal–Aurland, Norway | 24.5km/15.2mi | road | 2000 |
| Dai-shimizu | Honshu, Japan | 22.2km/13.8mi | rail | 1979 |
| Simplon I & II | Brigue, Switzerland–Iselle, Italy | 19.8km/12.3mi | rail | 1906, 1922 |
| Kanmon | Kanmon Strait, Japan | 19.3km/12.0mi | rail | 1975 |
| Vereina | Klosters–Sagliains, Switzerland | 19.1km/11.8mi | rail | 1999 |
| Qinling I-II | Qinling Mountains, China | 18.5km/11.5mi | rail | 2002 |
| Apennine | Vernio, Italy | 18.5km/11.5mi | rail | 1934 |
| St Gotthard (road) | Göschenen, Switzerland–Airolo, Italy | 16.3km/10.1mi | road | 1980 |
| Rokko | Osaka–Köbe, Japan | 16.1km/10.0mi | rail | 1972 |
| Furka Base | Andermatt–Brig, Switzerland | 15.4km/9.5mi | rail | 1982 |
| Haruna | Gunma Prefecture, Japan | 15.4km/9.5mi | rail | 1982 |
| Severomuyskiy | Baikal–Amur, Russia | 15.3km/9.4mi | rail | 2001 |
| Gorigamine | Takasaki–Nagano, Japan | 15.2km/9.4mi | rail | 1997 |
| Monte Santomarco | Paola–Cosenza, Italy | 15.0km/9.3mi | rail | 1987 |
| St Gotthard (rail) | Göschenen, Switzerland–Airolo, Italy | 14.9km/9.2mi | rail | 1882 |
| Nakayama | Nakayama Pass, Hokkaido, Japan | 14.9km/9.2mi | rail | 1982 |
| Romeriksporten | Oslo–Gardermoen airport, Norway | 14.6km/9.1mi | rail | 1999 |
| Mount MacDonald | British Columbia, Canada | 14.6km/9.1mi | rail | 1989 |
| Lotschberg | Thun–Brig, Switzerland | 14.5km/9.0mi | rail | 1913 |
| Hokuriku | Sea of Japan coast, Japan | 14.5km/9.0mi | rail | 1962 |
| Dayaoshan | Nanling Mountains, China | 14.3km/8.9mi | rail | 1987 |
| Arlberg | Austrian Alps | 14.0km/8.7mi | rail | 1979 |
| Frejus (Mont Cenis) | Modane, France–Bardonecchia, Italy | 13.5km/8.4mi | rail | 1871 |
| Shin shimizu | Mikuni Mountains, Japan | 13.5km/8.4mi | rail | 1961 |

## HIGHEST DAMS

This table gives those dams completed at the time of going to press. Several dams currently under construction are planned to be among the world's highest: they include the Three Gorges dam on the Yangtze River in China, due for completion in 2009, which is expected to be the world's largest and highest dam.

| Name | River, country | Structural height | Date completed |
|---|---|---|---|
| Nurek | Vakhsh, Tajikistan | 300m/984ft | 1980 |
| Grande Dixence | Dixence, Switzerland | 285m/935ft | 1962 |
| Inguri | Inguri, Georgia | 272m/892ft | 1984 |
| Vaiont | Vaiont, Italy | 262m/859ft | 1961 |
| Manuel M Torres | Grijalva, Mexico | 261m/856ft | 1981 |
| Alvaro Obregon | Tenasco, Mexico | 260m/853ft | 1946 |
| Mauvoisin | Drance de Bagnes, Switzerland | 250m/820ft | 1957 |
| Alberto Lleras | Guavio, Colombia | 243m/797ft | 1989 |
| Mica | Columbia, Canada | 243m/797ft | 1972 |
| Sayano-Shushensk | Yenisei, Russia | 242m/794ft | 1980 |
| Ertan | Yangtze/Yalong, China | 240m/787ft | 1999 |
| La Esmeralda | Batá, Colombia | 237m/777ft | 1975 |

## STIRLING PRIZE

The Stirling Prize of the Royal Institute of British Architects (RIBA) is awarded annually to the architects of the building which is judged to have made the greatest contribution to British architecture in the foregoing year. The building must be sited within the European Union and the architects must be RIBA members. The prize is named after the architect Sir James Stirling (1926–92). The first prize is £20 000.

| Date | Building | Architects |
|---|---|---|
| 1996 | University of Salford Centenary Building, Salford, UK | Hodder Associates |
| 1997 | Staatliche Hochschule für Musik und Darstellende Kunst, Stuttgart, Germany | Michael Wilford and Partners |
| 1998 | American Air Museum, Duxford, UK | Foster and Partners |
| 1999 | Natwest Media Centre, Lord's Cricket Ground, London, UK | Future Systems |
| 2000 | Peckham Library and Media Centre, London, UK | Alsop and Stormer |
| 2001 | Magna Centre, Rotherham, UK | Wilkinson Eyre |
| 2002 | Millennium Bridge, Gateshead, UK | Wilkinson Eyre |
| 2003 | Laban dance centre, London, UK | Herzog and de Meuron |

## LIBERAL ARTS

In the Middle Ages, the *trivium* and *quadrivium* were studied:

| Trivium | Quadrivium |
|---|---|
| grammar | arithmetic |
| rhetoric | geometry |
| logic | astronomy |
| | music |

## OXFORD UNIVERSITY COLLEGES

Oxford University has 39 official colleges and seven permanent private halls.

| College | Date founded |
|---|---|
| All Souls College | 1438 |
| Balliol College | 1263 |
| Blackfriars Hall[3] | 1994 |
| Brasenose College | 1509 |
| Campion Hall | 1896 |
| Christ Church | 1546 |
| Corpus Christi College | 1517 |
| Exeter College | 1314 |
| Green College[1] | 1979 |
| Greyfriars Hall[3] | 1957 |
| Harris Manchester College[3] | 1889 |
| Hertford College | 1282 |
| Jesus College | 1571 |
| Keble College | 1870 |
| Kellogg College[3] | 1994 |
| Lady Margaret Hall | 1878 |
| Linacre College[1] | 1962 |
| Lincoln College | 1427 |
| Magdalen College | 1448 |
| Mansfield College | 1886 |
| Merton College | 1264 |
| New College | 1379 |
| Nuffield College[1] | 1937 |
| Oriel College | 1326 |
| Pembroke College | 1624 |
| Queen's College, The | 1341 |
| Regent's Park College | 1810 |
| St Anne's College | 1952 |
| St Antony's College[1] | 1950 |
| St Benet's Hall | 1897 |
| St Catherine's College | 1962 |
| St Cross College[1] | 1965 |
| St Edmund Hall | c.1278 |
| St Hilda's College[2] | 1893 |
| St Hugh's College | 1886 |
| St John's College | 1555 |
| St Peter's College | 1929 |
| St Stephen's House | 1876 |
| Somerville College | 1879 |
| Templeton College[1] | 1965 |
| Trinity College | 1555 |
| University College | 1249 |
| Wadham College | 1609 |
| Wolfson College[1] | 1965 |
| Worcester College | 1714 |
| Wycliffe Hall | 1877 |

[1] *Graduates only.*

[2] *Women only.*

[3] *Date that Private Hall status was granted, or that the College or Hall joined the University; may been established previously.*

### Old Oxford

Oxford University is the oldest university in Britain, having its origins in informal groups of masters and students that gathered in Oxford in the 12c. The closure of the University of Paris to the English in 1167 accelerated Oxford's development. Cambridge is the second oldest university; its first college, Peterhouse, was founded in 1284.

## CAMBRIDGE UNIVERSITY COLLEGES

Cambridge University has 31 official colleges and halls.

| College | Date founded |
|---|---|
| Christ's College | 1505 |
| Churchill College | 1960 |
| Clare College | 1326 |
| Clare Hall[1] | 1965 |
| Corpus Christi College | 1352 |
| Darwin College[1] | 1964 |
| Downing College | 1800 |
| Emmanuel College | 1584 |
| Fitzwilliam College | 1966 |
| Girton College | 1869 |
| Gonville & Caius College | 1348 |
| Homerton College | 1976 |
| Hughes Hall | 1885 |
| Jesus College | 1497 |
| King's College | 1441 |
| Lucy Cavendish College[2] | 1965 |
| Magdalene College | 1428 |
| New Hall[2] | 1954 |
| Newnham College[2] | 1871 |
| Pembroke College | 1347 |
| Peterhouse | 1284 |
| Queens' College | 1448 |
| Robinson College | 1979 |
| St Catharine's College | 1473 |
| St Edmund's College | 1896 |
| St John's College | 1511 |
| Selwyn College | 1882 |
| Sidney Sussex College | 1596 |
| Trinity College | 1546 |
| Trinity Hall | 1350 |
| Wolfson College | 1965 |

[1] *Graduates only.*
[2] *Women only.*

## IVY LEAGUE

The Ivy League is a group of eight long-established universities, of particular academic and social prestige, in the north-eastern USA . The league was formally established in 1956 to oversee inter-collegiate sports.

**Brown University**

**Columbia University**

**Cornell University**

**Dartmouth College**

**Harvard University**

**Princeton University**

**University of Pennsylvania**

**Yale University**

## PRESIDENTS OF THE ROYAL SOCIETY

The Royal Society was founded in 1660 and is the UK's foremost body for the encouragement of research and development in science, engineering and technology. Since the late 19c the president has been appointed for a five-year term.

| Dates | Names |
|---|---|
| 1662–77 | William, Viscount Brouncker |
| 1677–80 | Sir Joseph Williamson |
| 1680–2 | Sir Christopher Wren |
| 1682–3 | Sir John Hoskins |
| 1683–4 | Sir Cyril Wyche |
| 1684–6 | Samuel Pepys |
| 1686–9 | John Vaughan, Earl of Carbery |
| 1689–90 | Thomas Herbert, Earl of Pembroke |
| 1690–5 | Sir Robert Southwell |
| 1695–8 | Charles Montagu (afterwards Earl of Halifax) |
| 1698–1703 | John, Lord Somers |
| 1703–27 | Sir Isaac Newton |

| Dates | Names |
|---|---|
| 1727–41 | Sir Hans Sloane |
| 1741–52 | Martin Folkes |
| 1752–64 | George Parker, Earl of Macclesfield |
| 1764–8 | James Douglas, Earl of Morton |
| 1768 | James (afterwards Sir James) Burrow |
| 1768–72 | James West |
| 1772–8 | Sir John Pringle |
| 1778–1820 | Sir Joseph Banks |
| 1820 | William Hyde Wollaston |
| 1820–7 | Sir Humphry Davy |
| 1827–30 | Davies Gilbert (formerly Giddy) |
| 1830–8 | Augustus Frederick, Duke of Sussex |
| 1838–48 | Joshua Alwyne Compton, Marquess of Northampton |
| 1848–54 | William Parsons, Earl of Rosse |
| 1854–8 | John, Lord Wrottesley |
| 1858–61 | Sir Benjamin Collins Brodie |
| 1861–71 | Sir Edward Sabine |
| 1871–3 | Sir George Biddell Airy |
| 1873–8 | Sir Joseph Dalton Hooker |
| 1878–83 | William Spottiswoode |
| 1883–5 | Thomas Henry Huxley |
| 1885–90 | Sir George Gabriel Stokes |
| 1890–5 | Sir William Thomson, Lord Kelvin |
| 1895–1900 | Joseph, Lord Lister |
| 1900–5 | Sir William Huggins |
| 1905–8 | John William Strutt, Lord Rayleigh |

| Dates | Names |
|---|---|
| 1908–13 | Sir Archibald Geikie |
| 1913–15 | Sir William Crookes |
| 1915–20 | Sir Joseph John Thomson |
| 1920–5 | Sir Charles Scott Sherrington |
| 1925–30 | Ernest Rutherford, Lord Rutherford of Nelson |
| 1930–5 | Sir Frederick Gowland Hopkins |
| 1935–40 | Sir William Henry Bragg |
| 1940–5 | Sir Henry Dale |
| 1945–50 | Sir Robert Robinson |
| 1950–5 | Edgar Douglas Adrian (afterwards Lord Adrian of Cambridge) |
| 1955–60 | Sir Cyril Hinshelwood |
| 1960–5 | Sir Howard Florey (afterwards Lord Florey of Adelaide and Marston) |
| 1965–70 | Patrick Maynard Stuart Blackett (afterwards Lord Blackett of Chelsea) |
| 1970–5 | Sir Alan Hodgkin |
| 1975–80 | Alexander Robertus Todd, Lord Todd of Trumpington |
| 1980–5 | Sir Andrew Huxley |
| 1985–90 | George Porter, Lord Porter of Luddenham |
| 1990–5 | Sir Michael Atiyah |
| 1995–2000 | Sir Aaron Klug |
| 2000– | Sir Robert May |

## RANKS OF THE ARISTOCRACY (UK)

**king**

**prince**

**duke**

**marquess**

**earl**

**viscount**

**baron**

## ROYAL SUCCESSION (UK)

**The Prince of Wales**

**Prince William of Wales**

**Prince Henry of Wales**

**The Duke of York**

**Princess Beatrice of York**

**Princess Eugenie of York**

**The Earl of Wessex**

**The Lady Louise Windsor**

**The Princess Royal**

**Peter Phillips**

## POETS LAUREATE

The Poet Laureate is a poet appointed to a lifetime post in the royal household. He or she is required to compose poems for state occasions, etc. The date given is the date of appointment.

| | |
|---|---|
| 1617 | Ben Jonson |
| 1638 | Sir William Davenant |
| 1668 | John Dryden |
| 1689 | Thomas Shadwell |
| 1692 | Nahum Tate |
| 1715 | Nicholas Rowe |
| 1718 | Laurence Eusden |
| 1730 | Colley Cibber |
| 1757 | William Whitehead |
| 1785 | Thomas Warton |
| 1790 | Henry Pye |
| 1813 | Robert Southey |
| 1843 | William Wordsworth |
| 1850 | Alfred, Lord Tennyson |
| 1896 | Alfred Austin |
| 1913 | Robert Bridges |
| 1930 | John Masefield |
| 1968 | Cecil Day-Lewis |
| 1972 | Sir John Betjeman |
| 1984 | Ted Hughes |
| 1999 | Andrew Motion |

## CHILDREN'S LAUREATE

The title of Children's Laureate is awarded once every two years to an eminent writer or illustrator of children's books.

| | |
|---|---|
| 1999 | Quentin Blake |
| 2001 | Anne Fine |
| 2003 | Michael Morpurgo |

## PLAYS OF SHAKESPEARE

William Shakespeare (1564–1616) was an English playwright and poet, born in Stratford-upon-Avon. He is considered to be the greatest English dramatist.

| Title | Date | Category |
|---|---|---|
| The Two Gentlemen of Verona | 1590–1 | comedy |
| Henry VI Part One | 1592 | history |
| Henry VI Part Two | 1592 | history |
| Henry VI Part Three | 1592 | history |
| Titus Andronicus | 1592 | tragedy |
| Richard III | 1592–3 | history |
| The Taming of the Shrew | 1593 | comedy |
| The Comedy of Errors | 1594 | comedy |
| Love's Labour's Lost | 1594–5 | comedy |
| Richard II | 1595 | history |
| Romeo and Juliet | 1595 | tragedy |
| A Midsummer Night's Dream | 1595 | comedy |
| King John | 1596 | history |
| The Merchant of Venice | 1596–7 | comedy |
| Henry IV Part One | 1596–7 | history |
| The Merry Wives of Windsor | 1597–8 | comedy |
| Henry IV Part Two | 1597–8 | history |

| Title | Date | Category |
|---|---|---|
| Much Ado About Nothing | 1598 | dark comedy |
| Henry V | 1598–9 | history |
| Julius Caesar | 1599 | tragedy |
| As You Like It | 1599–1600 | comedy |
| Hamlet, Prince of Denmark | 1600–1 | tragedy |
| Twelfth Night | 1601 | comedy |
| Troilus and Cressida | 1602 | tragedy |
| Measure for Measure | 1603 | dark comedy |
| Othello | 1603–4 | tragedy |
| All's Well That Ends Well | 1604–5 | dark comedy |
| Timon of Athens | 1605 | romantic drama |
| The Tragedy of King Lear | 1605–6 | tragedy |
| Macbeth | 1606 | tragedy |
| Antony and Cleopatra | 1606 | tragedy |
| Pericles | 1607 | romance |
| Coriolanus | 1608 | tragedy |
| The Winter's Tale | 1609 | romance |
| Cymbeline | 1610 | comedy |
| The Tempest | 1611 | comedy |
| Henry VIII | 1613 | history |

## *Writers on Shakespeare*

The remarkable thing about Shakespeare is that he is really very good – in spite of all the people who say he is very good.
**Robert Graves, 1964 Attributed.**

I have tried lately to read Shakespeare, and found it so intolerably dull that it nauseated me.
**Charles Darwin, 1860 Autobiography.**

Shakespeare one gets acquainted with without knowing how. It is part of an Englishman's constitution. His thoughts and beauties are so spread abroad that one touches them everywhere, one is intimate with him by instinct.
**Jane Austen, 1814 *Mansfield Park*, chapter 34.**

## NOBEL PRIZE FOR LITERATURE

Nobel prizes were established by a bequest in the will of Alfred Nobel (1833–96) to honour 'those who, during the preceding year, shall have conferred the greatest benefit on mankind'. The Nobel prize for literature is awarded annually to a person who has 'produced in the field of literature the most outstanding work in an ideal direction'; first awarded in 1901.

| | |
|---|---|
| 1901 | Sully Prudhomme |
| 1902 | Theodor Mommsen |
| 1903 | Bjørnstjerne Bjørnson |
| 1904 | Frédéric Mistral, José Echegaray |
| 1905 | Henryk Sienkiewicz |
| 1906 | Giosuè Carducci |
| 1907 | Rudyard Kipling |
| 1908 | Rudolf Eucken |
| 1909 | Selma Lagerlöf |
| 1910 | Paul Heyse |
| 1911 | Maurice Maeterlinck |
| 1912 | Gerhart Hauptmann |
| 1913 | Rabindranath Tagore |
| 1914 | *no award* |
| 1915 | Romain Rolland |
| 1916 | Verner von Heidenstam |

# NOBEL PRIZE FOR LITERATURE

| | |
|---|---|
| 1917 | Karl Gjellerup, Henrik Pontoppidan |
| 1918 | *no award* |
| 1919 | Carl Spitteler |
| 1920 | Knut Hamsun |
| 1921 | Anatole France |
| 1922 | Jacinto Benavente |
| 1923 | William Butler Yeats |
| 1924 | Wladyslaw Reymont |
| 1925 | George Bernard Shaw |
| 1926 | Grazia Deledda |
| 1927 | Henri Bergson |
| 1928 | Sigrid Undset |
| 1929 | Thomas Mann |
| 1930 | Sinclair Lewis |
| 1931 | Erik Axel Karlfeldt |
| 1932 | John Galsworthy |
| 1933 | Ivan Bunin |
| 1934 | Luigi Pirandello |
| 1935 | *no award* |
| 1936 | Eugene O'Neill |
| 1937 | Roger Martin du Gard |
| 1938 | Pearl S Buck |
| 1939 | Frans Eemil Sillanpää |
| 1940 | *no award* |
| 1941 | *no award* |
| 1942 | *no award* |
| 1943 | *no award* |
| 1944 | Johannes V Jensen |
| 1945 | Gabriela Mistral |
| 1946 | Hermann Hesse |
| 1947 | André Gide |
| 1948 | Thomas Stearns Eliot |
| 1949 | William Faulkner |
| 1950 | Bertrand Russell |
| 1951 | Pär Lagerkvist |
| 1952 | François Mauriac |
| 1953 | Winston Churchill |
| 1954 | Ernest Hemingway |
| 1955 | Halldór Kiljan Laxness |
| 1956 | Juan Ramón Jiménez |
| 1957 | Albert Camus |
| 1958 | Boris Pasternak |
| 1959 | Salvatore Quasimodo |
| 1960 | Saint-John Perse |
| 1961 | Ivo Andric |
| 1962 | John Steinbeck |
| 1963 | Giorgos Seferis |
| 1964 | Jean-Paul Sartre |
| 1965 | Michail Sholokhov |
| 1966 | Samuel Agnon, Nelly Sachs |
| 1967 | Miguel Angel Asturias |
| 1968 | Yasunari Kawabata |
| 1969 | Samuel Beckett |
| 1970 | Alexander Solzhenitsyn |
| 1971 | Pablo Neruda |
| 1972 | Heinrich Böll |
| 1973 | Patrick White |
| 1974 | Eyvind Johnson, Harry Martinson |
| 1975 | Eugenio Montale |
| 1976 | Saul Bellow |
| 1977 | Vicente Aleixandre |
| 1978 | Isaac Bashevis Singer |
| 1979 | Odysseus Elytis |
| 1980 | Czeslaw Milosz |
| 1981 | Elias Canetti |
| 1982 | Gabriel García Márquez |
| 1983 | William Golding |
| 1984 | Jaroslav Seifert |
| 1985 | Claude Simon |
| 1986 | Wole Soyinka |
| 1987 | Joseph Brodsky |
| 1988 | Naguib Mahfouz |
| 1989 | Camilo José Cela |
| 1990 | Octavio Paz |
| 1991 | Nadine Gordimer |
| 1992 | Derek Walcott |
| 1993 | Toni Morrison |
| 1994 | Kenzaburo Oe |
| 1995 | Seamus Heaney |
| 1996 | Wislawa Szymborska |
| 1997 | Dario Fo |
| 1998 | José Saramago |
| 1999 | Günter Grass |
| 2000 | Gao Xingjian |
| 2001 | V S Naipaul |
| 2002 | Imre Kertész |
| 2003 | J M Coetzee |

## *Sinclair's Speech*

'Our American professors like their literature clear and cold and pure and very dead.'

**Sinclair Lewis (1885–1951), Nobel prize address, 12 Dec 1930.**

## BOOKER PRIZE

The prize is awarded for the year's best novel, and is open to all citizens of Commonwealth countries or the Republic of Ireland. It was established in 1968 in the UK; known as the Man Booker Prize from 2002.

| | |
|---|---|
| 1969 | P H Newby *Something To Answer for* |
| 1970 | Bernice Rubens *The Elected Member* |
| 1971 | V S Naipaul *In a Free State* |
| 1972 | John Berger *G* |
| 1973 | J G Farrell *The Siege of Krishnapur* |
| 1974 | Nadine Gordimer *The Conservationist* |
| 1975 | Ruth Prawer Jhabvala *Heat and Dust* |
| 1976 | David Storey *Saville* |
| 1977 | Paul Scott *Staying on* |
| 1978 | Iris Murdoch *The Sea, The Sea* |
| 1979 | Penelope Fitzgerald *Offshore* |
| 1980 | William Golding *Rites of Passage* |
| 1981 | Salman Rushdie *Midnight's Children* |
| 1982 | Thomas Keneally *Schindler's Ark* |
| 1983 | J M Coetzee *Life and Times of Michael K* |
| 1984 | Anita Brookner *Hotel du Lac* |
| 1985 | Keri Hulme *The Bone People* |
| 1986 | Kingsley Amis *The Old Devils* |
| 1987 | Penelope Lively *Moon Tiger* |
| 1988 | Peter Carey *Oscar and Lucinda* |
| 1989 | Kazuo Ishiguro *The Remains of the Day* |
| 1990 | A S Byatt *Possession* |
| 1991 | Ben Okri *The Famished Road* |
| 1992 | Michael Ondaatje *The English Patient* and Barry Unsworth *Sacred Hunger* |
| 1993 | Roddy Doyle *Paddy Clarke, Ha Ha Ha* |
| 1994 | James Kelman *How Late It Was, How Late* |
| 1995 | Pat Barker *The Ghost Road* |
| 1996 | Graham Swift *Last Orders* |
| 1997 | Arundhati Roy *The God of Small Things* |
| 1998 | Ian McEwan *Amsterdam* |
| 1999 | J M Coetzee *Disgrace* |
| 2000 | Margaret Atwood *The Blind Assassin* |
| 2001 | Peter Carey *True History of the Kelly Gang* |
| 2002 | Yann Martel *Life of Pi* |
| 2003 | D B C Pierre *Vernon God Little* |

### Booze and Curtains

After his win in 1986 Kingsley Amis (1922–95) declared 'I used to say that the Booker Prize was a bit artificial, but I have changed my mind in the last 15 minutes. Now I feel it is a wonderful indication of literary merit'. When asked what he intended to spend the prize money on, his answer was 'Booze, of course, and then curtains'.

## ORANGE PRIZE FOR FICTION

Awarded for the year's best English-language novel by a female author. It was established in 1996 in reaction to the perceived male domination of other literary awards.

| | |
|---|---|
| 1996 | Helen Dunmore *A Spell of Winter* |
| 1997 | Anne Michaels *Fugitive Pieces* |
| 1998 | Carol Shields *Larry's Party* |
| 1999 | Suzanne Berne *A Crime in the Neighborhood* |
| 2000 | Linda Grant *When I Lived in Modern Times* |
| 2001 | Kate Grenville *The Idea of Perfection* |
| 2002 | Ann Patchett *Bel Canto* |
| 2003 | Valerie Martin *Property* |

## WHITBREAD BOOK AWARDS

Since its establishment in 1971 in the UK, prizes have been awarded in several varying categories. Today there are five: Novel, First Novel, Biography, Poetry and Children's Book. Since 1985, one book has been chosen from these winners to be Whitbread Book of the Year.

| | |
|---|---|
| 1985 | Douglas Dunn *Elegies* (Poetry) |
| 1986 | Kazuo Ishiguro *An Artist of the Floating World* (Novel) |
| 1987 | Christopher Nolan *Under the Eye of the Clock* (Biography) |
| 1988 | Paul Sayer *The Comforts of Madness* (First Novel) |
| 1989 | Richard Holmes *Coleridge: Early Visions* (Biography) |
| 1990 | Nicholas Mosley *Hopeful Monsters* (Novel) |
| 1991 | John Richardson *A Life of Picasso* (Biography) |
| 1992 | Jeff Torrington *Swing Hammer Swing!* (First Novel) |
| 1993 | Joan Brady *Theory of War* (Novel) |
| 1994 | William Trevor *Felicia's Journey* (Novel) |
| 1995 | Kate Atkinson *Behind the Scenes at the Museum* (First Novel) |
| 1996 | Seamus Heaney *The Spirit Level* (Poetry) |
| 1997 | Ted Hughes *Tales from Ovid* (Poetry) |
| 1998 | Ted Hughes *Birthday Letters* (Poetry) |
| 1999 | Seamus Heaney *Beowulf* (Poetry) |
| 2000 | Matthew Kneale *English Passengers* (Novel) |
| 2001 | Philip Pullman *The Amber Spyglass* (Children's Book) |
| 2002 | Claire Tomalin *Samuel Pepys: The Unequalled Self* (Biography) |
| 2003 | Mark Haddon *The Curious Incident of the Dog in the Night-time* (Novel) |

### Lengthy Literature

The French novelist Marcel Proust (1871–1922) wrote what is widely considered to be the world's longest novel, *À la recherche du temps perdu* ('Remembrance of Times Past'; published between 1913 and 1927). Guinness World Records® estimate that the novel, originally published in 13 volumes, contains a whopping 9 609 000 letters. Proust was a semi-invalid all his life, pampered by his mother; her death in 1905, when he was 34 years old, caused him to withdraw from society and hide himself away in a soundproof apartment, where he abandoned himself entirely to introspection.

## PRIX GONCOURT

The Académie Goncourt was founded in the will of Edmond de Goncourt (1822–96), to further the aims of the 'Brothers Goncourt' – Goncourt and his brother Jules (1830–70). Its purpose is to foster fiction with the annual Prix Goncourt for 'the best imaginary prose work of the year'; first awarded in France in 1903.

| | |
|---|---|
| 1903 | John-Antoine Nau *Force ennemie* |
| 1904 | Léon Frapié *La maternelle* |
| 1905 | Claude Farrère *Les civilisés* |
| 1906 | Jérôme et Jean Tharaud *Dingley, l'illustre écrivain* |
| 1907 | Émile Moselly *Terres lorraines* |
| 1908 | Francis de Miomandre *Écrit sur de l'eau* |
| 1909 | Marius et Ary Leblond *En France* |
| 1910 | Louis Pergaud *De Goupil à Margot* |
| 1911 | Alphonse de Châteaubriant *Monsieur des Lourdines* |
| 1912 | André Savignon *Filles de la pluie* |
| 1913 | Marc Elder *Le peuple de la mer* |
| 1914 | Adrien Bertrand *L'appel du sol*[1] |
| 1915 | René Benjamin *Gaspard* |
| 1916 | Henri Barbusse *Le feu* |
| 1917 | Henri Malherbe *La flamme au poing* |
| 1918 | Georges Duhamel *Civilisation* |
| 1919 | Marcel Proust *A l'ombre des jeunes filles en fleurs* |
| 1920 | Ernest Pérochon *Nêne* |
| 1921 | René Maran *Batouala* |
| 1922 | Henri Béraud *Le vitriol de lune* |

1923 Lucien Fabre *Rabevel ou le mal des ardents*
1924 Thierry Sandre *Le chèvrefeuille*
1925 Maurice Genevoix *Raboliot*
1926 Henry Deberly *Le supplice de Phèdre*
1927 Maurice Bedel *Jérôme, 60° latitude Nord*
1928 Maurice Constantin-Weyer *Un homme se penche sur son passé*
1929 Marcel Arland *L'ordre*
1930 Henri Fauconnier *Malaisie*
1931 Jean Fayard *Mal d'amour*
1932 Guy Mazeline *Les loups*
1933 André Malraux *La condition humaine*
1934 Roger Vercel *Capitaine Conan*
1935 Joseph Peyré *Sang et lumières*
1936 Maxence Van der Meersch *L'empreinte du Dieu*
1937 Charles Plisnier *Faux passeports*
1938 Henri Troyat *L'araigne*
1939 Philippe Hériat *Les enfants gâtés*
1940 Francis Ambrière *Les grandes vacances*
1941 Henri Pourrat *Vent de mars*
1942 Marc Bernard *Pareils à des enfants*
1943 Marius Grout *Passage de l'homme*
1944 Elsa Triolet *Le premier accroc coûte deux cents francs*
1945 Jean-Louis Bory *Mon village à l'heure allemande*
1946 Jean-Jacques Gautier *Histoire d'un fait divers*
1947 Jean-Louis Curtis *Les forêts de la nuit*
1948 Maurice Druon *Les grandes familles*
1949 Robert Merle *Week-end à Zuydcoote*
1950 Paul Colin *Les jeux sauvages*
1951 Julien Gracq *Le rivage des Syrtes*
1952 Béatrice Beck *Léon Morin, prêtre*
1953 Pierre Gascar *Les bêtes, Le temps des morts*
1954 Simone de Beauvoir *Les Mandarins*
1955 Roger Ikor *Les eaux mêlées* (volume two of *Les fils d'Avrom*)
1956 Romain Gary *Les racines du ciel*
1957 Roger Vailland *La loi*
1958 Francis Walder *Saint-Germain ou la négociation*
1959 André Schwartz-Bart *Le dernier des justes*
1960 Vintila Horia *Dieu est né en exil*[2]
1961 Jean Cau *La pitié de Dieu*
1962 André Langfus *Les bagages de sable*
1963 Armand Lanoux *Quand la mer se retire*
1964 Georges Conchon *L'état sauvage*
1965 Jacques Borel *L'adoration*
1966 Edmonde Charles-Roux *Oublier Palerme*
1967 André Pieyre de Mandiargues *La marge*
1968 Bernard Clavel *Les fruits de l'hiver*
1969 Félicien Marceau *Creezy*
1970 Michel Tournier *Le roi des aulnes*
1971 Jacques Laurent *Les bétises*
1972 Jean Carrière *L'épervier de Maheux*
1973 Jacques Chessex *L'ogre*
1974 Pascal Laîné *La dentellière*
1975 Émile Ajar *La vie devant soi*
1976 Patrick Grainville *Les flamboyants*
1977 Didier Decoin *John l'Enfer*
1978 Patrick Modiano *Rue des boutiques obscures*
1979 Antonine Maillet *Pélagie-la-Charrette*
1980 Yves Navarre *Le jardin d'acclimatation*
1981 Lucien Bodard *Anne-Marie*
1982 Dominique Fernandez *Dans la main de l'ange*
1983 Frédérick Tristan *Les égarés*
1984 Marguerite Duras *L'amant*
1985 Yann Queffélec *Les noces barbares*
1986 Michel Host *Valet de nuit*
1987 Tahar Ben Jelloun *La nuit sacrée*
1988 Erik Orsenna *L'exposition coloniale*
1989 Jean Vautrin *Un grand pas vers le Bon Dieu*
1990 Jean Rouaud *Les champs d'honneur*
1991 Pierre Combescot *Les filles du calvaire*
1992 Patrick Chamoiseau *Texaco*
1993 Amin Maalouf *Le rocher de Tanios*
1994 Didier Van Cauwelaert *Un aller simple*
1995 Andreï Makine *Le testament français*
1996 Pascale Roze *Le chasseur Zéro*
1997 Patrick Rambaud *La bataille*
1998 Paule Constant *Confidence pour confidence*
1999 Jean Echenoz *Je m'en vais*
2000 Jean-Jacques Schuhl *Ingrid Caven*
2001 Jean-Christophe Rufin *Rouge Brésil*
2002 Pascal Quignard *Les ombres errantes*
2003 Jacques-Pierre Amette *La maîtresse de Brecht*

[1] *Prize awarded retrospectively in 1916 as a result of disruption caused by World War I.*
[2] *Horia refused the prize as a result of political pressure.*

## PULITZER PRIZE IN LETTERS: FICTION

Pulitzer Prizes, first awarded in the United States of America in 1917, are given annually for literature, drama, music and journalism. Established in the will of Joseph Pulitzer (1847–1911); first prize for fiction was awarded in 1918; prize was known as the prize for a novel, rather than fiction, until 1948.

| | |
|---|---|
| 1917 | *no award* |
| 1918 | Ernest Poole *His Family* |
| 1919 | Booth Tarkington *The Magnificent Ambersons* |
| 1920 | *no award* |
| 1921 | Edith Wharton *The Age of Innocence* |
| 1922 | Booth Tarkington *Alice Adams* |
| 1923 | Willa Cather *One of Ours* |
| 1924 | Margaret Wilson *The Able McLaughlins* |
| 1925 | Edna Ferber *So Big* |
| 1926 | Sinclair Lewis *Arrowsmith* |
| 1927 | Louis Bromfield *Early Autumn* |
| 1928 | Thornton Wilder *The Bridge of San Luis Rey* |
| 1929 | Julia Peterkin *Scarlet Sister Mary* |
| 1930 | Oliver Lafarge *Laughing Boy* |
| 1931 | Margaret Ayer Barnes *Years of Grace* |
| 1932 | Pearl S Buck *The Good Earth* |
| 1933 | T S Stribling *The Store* |
| 1934 | Caroline Miller *Lamb in His Bosom* |
| 1935 | Josephine Winslow Johnson *Now in November* |
| 1936 | Harold L Davis *Honey in the Horn* |
| 1937 | Margaret Mitchell *Gone With the Wind* |
| 1938 | John Phillips Marquand *The Late George Apley* |
| 1939 | Marjorie Kinnan Rawlings *The Yearling* |
| 1940 | John Steinbeck *The Grapes of Wrath* |
| 1941 | *no award* |
| 1942 | Ellen Glasgow *In This Our Life* |
| 1943 | Upton Sinclair *Dragon's Teeth* |
| 1944 | Martin Flavin *Journey in the Dark* |
| 1945 | John Hersey *A Bell for Adano* |
| 1946 | *no award* |
| 1947 | Robert Penn Warren *All the King's Men* |
| 1948 | James A Michener *Tales of the South Pacific* |
| 1949 | James Gould Cozzens *Guard of Honor* |
| 1950 | A B Guthrie, Jr *The Way West* |
| 1951 | Conrad Richter *The Town* |
| 1952 | Herman Wouk *The Caine Mutiny* |
| 1953 | Ernest Hemingway *The Old Man and the Sea* |
| 1954 | *no award* |
| 1955 | William Faulkner *A Fable* |
| 1956 | MacKinlay Kantor *Andersonville* |
| 1957 | *no award* |
| 1958 | James Agee *A Death In The Family* |
| 1959 | Robert Lewis Taylor *The Travels of Jaimie McPheeters* |
| 1960 | Allen Drury *Advise and Consent* |
| 1961 | Harper Lee *To Kill A Mockingbird* |
| 1962 | Edwin O'Connor *The Edge of Sadness* |
| 1963 | William Faulkner *The Reivers* |
| 1964 | *no award* |
| 1965 | Shirley Ann Grau *The Keepers Of The House* |
| 1966 | Katherine Anne Porter *Collected Stories* |
| 1967 | Bernard Malamud *The Fixer* |
| 1968 | William Styron *The Confessions of Nat Turner* |
| 1969 | N Scott Momaday *House Made of Dawn* |
| 1970 | Jean Stafford *Collected Stories* |
| 1971 | *no award* |
| 1972 | Wallace Stegner *Angle of Repose* |
| 1973 | Eudora Welty *The Optimist's Daughter* |
| 1974 | *no award* |
| 1975 | Michael Shaara *The Killer Angels* |
| 1976 | Saul Bellow *Humboldt's Gift* |
| 1977 | *no award* |
| 1978 | James Alan McPherson *Elbow Room* |
| 1979 | John Cheever *The Stories of John Cheever* |
| 1980 | Norman Mailer *The Executioner's Song* |
| 1981 | John Kennedy *A Confederacy of Dunces* |
| 1982 | John Updike *Rabbit is Rich* |
| 1983 | Alice Walker *The Color Purple* |
| 1984 | William Kennedy *Ironweed* |
| 1985 | Alison Lurie *Foreign Affairs* |
| 1986 | Larry McMurtry *Lonesome Dove* |
| 1987 | Peter Taylor *A Summons to Memphis* |
| 1988 | Toni Morrison *Beloved* |
| 1989 | Anne Tyler *Breathing Lessons* |
| 1990 | Oscar Hijuelos *The Mambo Kings Play Songs of Love* |

1991 John Updike *Rabbit at Rest*
1992 Jane Smiley *A Thousand Acres*
1993 Robert Olen Butler *A Good Scent From A Strange Mountain*
1994 E Annie Proulx *The Shipping News*
1995 Carol Shields *The Stone Diaries*
1996 Richard Ford *Independence Day*
1997 Martin Dressler *The Tale of an American Dreamer*
1998 Philip Roth *American Pastoral*
1999 Michael Cunningham *The Hours*
2000 Jhumpa Lahiri *Interpreter of Maladies*
2001 Michael Chabon *The Amazing Adventures of Kavalier & Clay*
2002 Richard Russo *Empire Falls*
2003 Jeffrey Eugenides *Middlesex*

### You Only Live Twice

Ernest Hemingway (1899–1961), the Pulitzer prize winner in 1953, cheated death more than once and had the strange pleasure of reading his own obituary twice.

## LIBRARY BOOKS

### Most borrowed authors in the UK

Most Borrowed Adult Fiction Author: Catherine Cookson
Most Borrowed Children's Author: Jacqueline Wilson
Most Borrowed Classic Author: J R R Tolkien

### Library Queen

Catherine Cookson has spent 17 consecutive years at the top of the UK Most Borrowed Author charts.

### Top ten borrowed authors in the UK

Catherine Cookson
Danielle Steel
Josephine Cox
Jacqueline Wilson[1]
R L Stine[1]
Dick Francis
Mick Inkpen[1]
Agatha Christie
Jack Higgins
Janet and Allan Ahlberg[1]

[1] *Children's author.*

### Most borrowed books in the UK

Most Borrowed Fiction Title: Josephine Cox *Looking Back*
Most Borrowed Children's Fiction Title: J K Rowling *Harry Potter and the Chamber of Secrets*
Most Borrowed Non-Fiction Title: Bill Bryson *Down Under*

### Top ten borrowed books in the UK

*Harry Potter and the Chamber of Secrets* J K Rowling
*Looking Back* Josephine Cox
*Scarlet Feather* Maeve Binchy
*Harry Potter and the Prisoner of Azkaban* J K Rowling
*The Silent Lady* Catherine Cookson
*Rosie of the River* Catherine Cookson
*The Blind Years: a novel* Catherine Cookson
*Harry Potter and the Goblet of Fire* J K Rowling
*Second Wind* Dick Francis
*Let it Shine* Josephine Cox

### Riveting Reads

Thirteen authors had over 1 million loans in the UK in 2001–2: Janet and Allan Ahlberg, Agatha Christie, Catherine Cookson, Patricia Cornwell, Josephine Cox, Lucy Daniels, Dick Francis, Jack Higgins, Audrey Howard, Mick Inkpen, Danielle Steel, R L Stine and Jacqueline Wilson.

*Data compiled and supplied by Public Lending Right, Stockton-on-Tees. Information given is for Jul 2001–Jun 2002.*

## FICTIONAL LITERARY PLACES

Some fictional places from literature are given below.

| Place | Author | Book |
|---|---|---|
| Airstrip One | George Orwell (1903–50) | *Nineteen Eighty-Four* (1949) |
| Ankh-Morpork | Terry Pratchett (1948– ) | Discworld® books (since 1983) |
| Barchester | Anthony Trollope (1815–82) | Barsetshire Novels (1855–67) |
| Barset | Anthony Trollope (1815–82) | Barsetshire Novels (1855–67) |
| Barsetshire | Anthony Trollope (1815–82) | Barsetshire Novels (1855–67) |
| Brobdingnag | Jonathan Swift (1667–1745) | *Gulliver's Travels* (1726) |
| Celestial City | John Bunyan (1628–88) | *The Pilgrim's Progress* (1678–84) |
| Christminster | Thomas Hardy (1840–1928) | various novels (1871–95[1]), especially *Jude the Obscure* (1895) |
| Discworld® | Terry Pratchett (1948– ) | Discworld® books (since 1983) |
| Earthsea | Ursula Le Guin (1929– ) | Earthsea Tetralogy (1968–91) |
| Emerald City | L Frank Baum (1856–1919) | *The Wonderful Wizard of Oz* (1900) |
| Erehwon | Samuel Butler (1612–80) | *Erehwon* (1872) |
| Eurasia | George Orwell (1903–50) | *Nineteen Eighty-Four* (1949) |
| Gormenghast | Mervyn Peake (1911–68) | Gormenghast Trilogy (1946–59) |
| Lake Wobegon | Garrison Keillor (1942– ) | various (since 1985) |
| Laputa | Jonathan Swift (1667–1745) | *Gulliver's Travels* (1726) |
| Lilliput | Jonathan Swift (1667–1745) | *Gulliver's Travels* (1726) |
| Llaregyb | Dylan Thomas (1914–53) | *Under Milk Wood* (1954) |
| Looking-Glass Land | Lewis Carroll (1832–98) | *Through the Looking-Glass* (1872) |
| Maple White Land | Arthur Conan Doyle (1859–1930) | *The Lost World* (1912) |
| Maycomb | Harper Lee (1926– ) | *To Kill a Mockingbird* (1960) |
| Middle-Earth | J R R Tolkien (1892–1973) | *The Hobbit, The Lord of the Rings* (1937, 1954–5) |
| Narnia | C S Lewis (1898–1963) | *Chronicles of Narnia* (1950–6) |
| Never-Never Land | J M Barrie (1860–1937) | *Peter Pan* (1904 play; 1911 book) |
| Oceania | George Orwell (1903–50) | *Nineteen Eighty-Four* (1949) |
| Oz | L Frank Baum (1856–1919) | *The Wonderful Wizard of Oz* (1900) |
| Rivendell | J R R Tolkien (1892–1973) | *The Hobbit, The Lord of the Rings* (1937, 1954–5) |
| Shangri-la | James Hilton (1900–54) | *Lost Horizon* (1933) |
| The Shire | J R R Tolkien (1892–1973) | *The Hobbit, The Lord of the Rings* (1937, 1954–5) |
| Toyland | Enid Blyton (1897–1968) | *Noddy Goes to Toyland* (1949) |
| Treasure Island | Robert Louis Stevenson (1850–94) | *Treasure Island* (1883) |
| Utopia | Thomas More (1478–1535) | *Utopia* (1516) |
| Vanity Fair | John Bunyan (1628–88) | *The Pilgrim's Progress* (1678–84) |
| Wessex | Thomas Hardy (1840–1928) | various (1871–95[1]) |
| Wonderland | Lewis Carroll (1832–98) | *Alice's Adventures in Wonderland* (1865) |
| Xanadu | Samuel Taylor Coleridge (1772–1834) | 'Kubla Khan: A Vision in a Dream' (1816) |
| Yoknapatawpha County | William Faulkner (1897–1962) | various (1929–62[2]) |
| Zenda | Anthony Hope (1863–1933) | *The Prisoner of Zenda* (1894) |

[1] *Years between which he published novels, not those specifically set in Christminster or Wessex.*

[2] *Specifically covers period of works set in Yoknapatawpha County.*

## AUTHORS' REAL NAMES

Selected authors' real names are given below.

| Pseudonym | Real name |
|---|---|
| Bachman, Richard | Stephen King |
| Bell, Acton | Anne Brontë |
| Bell, Currer | Charlotte Brontë |
| Bell, Ellis | Emily Brontë |
| Burgess, Anthony | John Anthony Burgess Wilson |
| Carroll, Lewis | Charles Lutwidge Dodgson |
| Charteris, Leslie | Leslie Charles Bowyer Yin |
| Conrad, Joseph | Józef Teodor Konrad Nalecz Korzeniowski |
| Coolidge, Susan | Sarah Chauncy Woolsey |
| Dinesen, Isak | Karen Blixen |
| Eliot, George | Mary Ann *or* Marian Evans |
| Farrell, M J | Molly Keane, *originally* Mary Nesta Skrine |
| Ford, Ford Madox | Ford Hermann Hueffer |
| France, Anatole | Anatole François Thibault |
| Gibbon, Lewis Grassic | James Leslie Mitchell |
| Gorky, Maxim | Aleksei Maksimovich Peshkov |
| Henry, O | William Sydney Porter |
| Higgins, Jack | Harry Patterson |
| Hite, Shere | Shirley Diana Gregory |
| Kincaid, Jamaica | Elaine Potter Richardson |
| Le Carré, John | David John Moore Cornwell |
| London, Jack | John Griffith Chaney |
| McBain, Ed | Salvatore A Lambino |
| Molière | Jean Baptiste Poquelin |
| Morrison, Toni | Chloe Anthony Morrison, *née* Wofford |
| Orwell, George | Eric Arthur Blair |
| Peters, Ellis | Edith Mary Pargeter |
| Queen, Ellery | Frederick Dannay *and* Manfred B Lee |
| Rhys, Jean | Gwen Williams |
| Robbins, Harold | Francis Kane |
| Saki | Hector Hugh Munro |
| Salten, Felix | Siegmund Salzmann |
| Sand, George | Amandine Aurore Lucie Dupin, Baronne Dudevant |
| Sapper | Herman Cyril McNeile |
| Seuss, Dr | Theodor Seuss Geisel |
| Shute, Nevil | Nevil Shute Norway |
| Smith, Stevie | Florence Margaret Smith |
| Stern, Daniel | Marie de Flavigny, Comtesse d'Agoult |
| Stoppard, Tom | Thomas Straussler |
| Tey, Josephine | Elizabeth Mackintosh |
| Twain, Mark | Samuel Langhorne Clemens |
| Voltaire | François Marie Arouet |
| Weldon, Fay | Franklin Birkinshaw |
| Wesley, Mary | Mary Aline Siepmann, *née* Farmar |
| West, Dame Rebecca | Cecily Isabel Andrews, *née* Fairfield |
| West, Nathanael | Nathan Wallenstein Weinstein |
| Westmacott, Mary | Dame Agatha Christie, *née* Miller |
| Williams, Tennessee | Thomas Lanier |
| Wyndham, John | John Wyndham Parkes Lucas Beynon Harris |

## THREE MUSKETEERS

The three musketeers appear in the novel *The Three Musketeers* (1844) by Alexandre Dumas (1802–70). As the novel progresses, the three are joined by d'Artagnan.

**Aramis**

**Athos**

**Porthos**

## SNOW WHITE'S DWARFS

In the fairy tale by the Brothers Grimm the seven dwarfs are not mentioned by name, but the following names were used in the Walt Disney animated film of 1937.

**Bashful**

**Doc**

**Dopey**

**Grumpy**

**Happy**

**Sleepy**

**Sneezy**

## SUPERHEROES' REAL NAMES

| Superhero | Real name |
|---|---|
| Batman | Bruce Wayne |
| Captain America | Steve Rogers |
| Captain Marvel | Billy Batson |
| Daredevil | Matt Murdock |
| The Incredible Hulk | Dr Robert Bruce Banner |
| Spiderman | Peter Parker |
| Superman | Kel-El (on Krypton); Clark Kent (on Earth) |
| Wonder Woman | Diana Prince |

### *Speeding Bullets*

'Faster than a speeding bullet! More powerful than a locomotive! Able to leap tall buildings in a single bound!'
**Jerome Siegel, Introduction for the Superman radio serial. Quoted in *Time*, 14 Mar 1988.**

# ART

## TURNER PRIZE

**The Turner prize was founded in 1984 by the Patrons of New Art. It is an award of £20 000 given to a contemporary British artist under the age of 50 for an 'outstanding exhibition of work in the past 12 months'.**

| | |
|---|---|
| 1984 | Malcolm Morley, painter |
| 1985 | Sir Howard Hodgkin, painter |
| 1986 | Gilbert and George (Gilbert Proesch and George Passmore), performance and photopiece artists |
| 1987 | Richard Deacon, sculptor |
| 1988 | Tony Cragg, sculptor |
| 1989 | Richard Long, land artist |
| 1990 | *no award* |
| 1991 | Anish Kapoor, sculptor |
| 1992 | Grenville Davey, sculptor |
| 1993 | Rachel Whiteread, sculptor |
| 1994 | Antony Gormley, sculptor |
| 1995 | Damien Hirst, painter and conceptual and installation artist |
| 1996 | Douglas Gordon, video artist |
| 1997 | Gillian Wearing, photographer and video artist |
| 1998 | Chris Ofili, painter |
| 1999 | Steve McQueen, video artist |
| 2000 | Wolfgang Tillmans, photographer |
| 2001 | Martin Creed, conceptual and installation artist |
| 2002 | Keith Tyson, conceptual and installation artist |
| 2003 | Grayson Perry, potter |

### *Angel of the North*

Antony Gormley, the Turner prize winner in 1994, went on to create the largest sculpture in the UK with his *Angel of the North* (1998) in Gateshead. Weighing 200 tonnes/197 tons, the *Angel* stands 20m/65ft high and has a wingspan of 54m/175ft. Gateshead council reckons that it must be one of the world's most viewed works of art, as a result of its prominent location by the A1 road and the east coast railway line. It is estimated that the *Angel* is seen by 33 million people each year, which works out at at least one person every second.

## FAMOUS WORKS OF ART

A selection of some famous works of art are listed.

| Art work | Artist or sculptor | Location | Date |
|---|---|---|---|
| *The Age of Bronze* | Auguste Rodin | Leeds City Art Gallery, Leeds, UK | 1877 |
| *The Ambassadors* (properly *Jean de Dinteville and Georges de Selve*) | Hans Holbein the Younger | National Gallery, London, UK | 1533 |
| *Angel of the North* | Antony Gormley | Gateshead, UK | 1998 |
| *The Artist's Mother* (also known as *Arrangement in Grey and Black: the Artist's Mother*) | James Abbott McNeill Whistler | Musée d'Orsay, Paris, France | 1871–2 |

# FAMOUS WORKS OF ART

| Art work | Artist or sculptor | Location | Date |
|---|---|---|---|
| *At the Moulin Rouge* | Henri de Toulouse-Lautrec | Art Institute of Chicago, USA | 1895 |
| *The Birth of Venus* | Sandro Botticelli | Uffizi Gallery, Florence, Italy | c.1485 |
| *Campbell's Soup Cans* | Andy Warhol | Museum of Modern Art, New York City, USA | 1962 |
| *Christ of St John of the Cross* | Salvador Dalí | St Mungo Museum of Religious Life And Art, Glasgow, UK | 1951 |
| *David* | Michelangelo | Accademia Gallery, Florence, Italy | 1504 |
| *Le Déjeuner sur l'herbe* | Edouard Manet | Musée d'Orsay, Paris, France | 1863 |
| *Les Demoiselles d'Avignon* | Pablo Picasso | Museum of Modern Art, New York City, USA | 1907 |
| *The Fighting Téméraire* (properly *The Fighting Temeraire tugged to her Last Berth to be broken up, 1838*) | J M W Turner | National Gallery, London, UK | 1839 |
| *Girl with a Pearl Earring* | Jan Vermeer | Mauritshuis, The Hague, The Netherlands | c.1665 |
| *Guernica* | Pablo Picasso | Reina Sofia, Madrid, Spain | 1937 |
| *Haystacks* | Claude Monet | various collections worldwide | 1890–1 |
| *The Hay Wain* | John Constable | National Gallery, London, UK | 1821 |
| *Impression: Rising Sun* | Claude Monet | Marmottan Monet Museum, Paris, France | 1872 |
| *The Kiss* | Auguste Rodin | Rodin Museum, Paris, France | 1888–9 |
| *The Kiss* | Gustav Klimt | Österreichische Galerie Belvedere, Vienna, Austria | 1907–08 |
| *The Last Supper* | Leonardo da Vinci | Santa Maria delle Grazie, Milan, Italy | completed c.1498 |
| *Mona Lisa* | Leonardo da Vinci | Louvre, Paris, France | 1503–6 |
| *Night Café* | Vincent van Gogh | Yale University Art Gallery, New Haven, USA | 1888 |
| *The Night Watch* (properly *The Company of of Frans Banning Cocq and Willem van Ruytenburch*) | Rembrandt | Rijksmuseum, Amsterdam, The Netherlands | 1642 |
| *The Persistence of Memory* (also known as *Limp Watches*) | Salvador Dalí | Museum of Modern Art, New York City, USA | 1931 |
| *The Potato Eaters* | Vincent van Gogh | Van Gogh Museum, Amsterdam, The Netherlands | 1885 |
| *Rain, Steam and Speed* (properly *Rain, Steam, and Speed – The Great Western Railway*) | J M W Turner | National Gallery, London, UK | before 1844 |
| *Reverend Robert Walker Skating on Duddingston Loch* | Henry Raeburn | National Gallery of Scotland, Edinburgh, UK | 1784 |
| *Rouen Cathedral* | Claude Monet | various collections worldwide | 1892–4 |
| *St George and the Dragon* | Paolo Uccello | National Gallery, London, UK | c.1470 |
| *The Scream* | Edvard Munch | National Gallery, Oslo, Norway | 1893 |
| *The Starry Night* | Vincent van Gogh | Museum of Modern Art, New York City, USA | 1889 |

| Art work | Artist or sculptor | Location | Date |
|---|---|---|---|
| *Sunflowers* | Vincent van Gogh | Van Gogh Museum, Amsterdam, The Netherlands (and other versions elsewhere) | 1889 |
| *The Thinker* | Auguste Rodin | Rodin Museum, Paris, France (and other versions elsewhere) | 1881 |
| *36 Views of Mount Fuji* | Hokusai | various collections worldwide | c.1826–33 |
| *The Three Graces* | Antonio Canova | shared between the Victoria & Albert Museum, London, UK and the National Gallery of Scotland, Edinburgh, UK | 1814 |
| *The Toilet of Venus* (also known as '*The Rokeby Venus*') | Diego Velázquez | National Gallery, London, UK | 1647-51 |
| *Venus de Milo* (also known as *Aphrodite of Melos*) | unknown | Louvre, Paris, France | c.100BC |
| *Water Lilies* | Claude Monet | various collections worldwide | 1899–1906 |

## MUSEUMS AND ART GALLERIES

| Museum/Gallery | City | Country |
|---|---|---|
| Acropolis Museum | Athens | Greece |
| Ashmolean Museum of Art and Archaeology | Oxford | United Kingdom |
| Guggenheim Museum | New York | United States of America |
| Louvre | Paris | France |
| Metropolitan Museum of Art | New York | United States of America |
| Musée d'Orsay | Paris | France |
| Museum of Modern Art (MoMa) | New York | United States of America |
| Museum of Modern Art at the Pompidou Centre | Paris | France |
| National Gallery | London | United Kingdom |
| Prado Museum | Madrid | Spain |
| Reina Sofia | Madrid | Spain |
| Rijksmuseum | Amsterdam | The Netherlands |
| Stedelijk Museum of Modern Art | Amsterdam | The Netherlands |
| Tate Gallery | London | United Kingdom |
| Tate Modern | London | United Kingdom |
| Uffizi Gallery | Florence | Italy |
| Van Gogh Museum | Amsterdam | The Netherlands |
| Victoria and Albert Museum | London | United Kingdom |

### Just Another Paint Job

Michelangelo's famous paintings that decorate the ceiling of the Sistine Chapel (1508–12) are widely viewed today as a masterpiece. Michelangelo himself was rather more down to earth about the work. He commented in a letter written to his father after 18 months of painting the ceiling: 'I've finished that chapel I was painting. The Pope is quite satisfied.'

## ACADEMY AWARDS®

Awarded annually by the Academy of Motion Picture Arts and Sciences. Popularly known as Oscars®. Best Actor and Best Actress awards are for performance in a leading role.

| Year | Best Film (director) | Best Actor | Best Actress | Best Director |
|---|---|---|---|---|
| 1927/8 | *Wings* (William A Wellman) | Emil Jannings *The Last Command*, *The Way of All Flesh* | Janet Gaynor *7th Heaven*, *Street Angel*, *Sunrise* | Lewis Milestone *Two Arabian Knights*; Frank Borzage *7th Heaven* |
| 1928/9 | *The Broadway Melody* (Harry Beaumont) | Warner Baxter *In Old Arizona* | Mary Pickford *Coquette* | Frank Lloyd *The Divine Lady* |
| 1929/30 | *All Quiet on the Western Front* (Lewis Milestone) | George Arliss *Disraeli* | Norma Shearer *The Divorcee* | Lewis Milestone *All Quiet on the Western Front* |
| 1930/1 | *Cimarron* (Wesley Ruggles) | Lionel Barrymore *A Free Soul* | Marie Dressler *Min and Bill* | Norman Taurog *Skippy* |
| 1931/2 | *Grand Hotel* (Edmund Goulding) | Wallace Beery *The Champ*; Fredric March *Dr Jeckyll and Mr Hyde* | Helen Hayes *The Sin of Madame Claudet* | Frank Borzage *Bad Girl* |
| 1932/3 | *Cavalcade* (Frank Lloyd) | Charles Laughton *The Private Life of Henry VIII* | Katharine Hepburn *Morning Glory* | Frank Lloyd *Cavalcade* |
| 1934 | *It Happened One Night* (Frank Capra) | Clark Gable *It Happened One Night* | Claudette Colbert *It Happened One Night* | Frank Capra *It Happened One Night* |
| 1935 | *Mutiny on the Bounty* (Frank Lloyd) | Victor Laglen *The Informer* | Bette Davis *Dangerous* | John Ford *The Informer* |
| 1936 | *The Great Ziegfeld* (Robert Z Leonard) | Paul Muni *The Story of Louis Pasteur* | Luise Rainer *The Great Ziegfeld* | Frank Capra *Mr Deeds Goes to Town* |
| 1937 | *The Life of Emile Zola* (William Dieterle) | Spencer Tracy *Captains Courageous* | Luise Rainer *The Good Earth* | Leo McCarey *The Awful Truth* |
| 1938 | *You Can't Take It with You* (Frank Capra) | Spencer Tracy *Boys Town* | Bette Davis *Jezebel* | Frank Capra *You Can't Take It with You* |
| 1939 | *Gone With the Wind* (Victor Fleming) | Robert Donat *Goodbye, Mr Chips* | Vivien Leigh *Gone with the Wind* | Victor Fleming *Gone with the Wind* |
| 1940 | *Rebecca* (Alfred Hitchcock) | James Stewart *The Philadelphia Story* | Ginger Rogers *Kitty Foyle* | John Ford *The Grapes of Wrath* |

| Year | Best Film (director) | Best Actor | Best Actress | Best Director |
|---|---|---|---|---|
| 1941 | *How Green Was My Valley* (John Ford) | Gary Cooper *Sergeant York* | Joan Fontaine *Suspicion* | John Ford *How Green Was My Valley* |
| 1942 | *Mrs Miniver* (William Wyler) | James Cagney *Yankee Doodle Dandy* | Greer Garson *Mrs Miniver* | William Wyler *Mrs Miniver* |
| 1943 | *Casablanca* (Michael Curtiz) | Paul Lukas *Watch on the Rhine* | Jennifer Jones *The Song of Bernadette* | Michael Curtiz *Casablanca* |
| 1944 | *Going My Way* (Leo McCarey) | Bing Crosby *Going My Way* | Ingrid Bergman *Gaslight* | Leo McCarey *Going My Way* |
| 1945 | *The Lost Weekend* (Billy Wilder) | Ray Milland *The Lost Weekend* | Joan Crawford *Mildred Pierce* | Billy Wilder *The Lost Weekend* |
| 1946 | *The Best Years of Our Lives* (William Wyler) | Fredric March *The Best Years of Our Lives* | Olivia de Havilland *To Each His Own* | William Wyler *The Best Years of Our Lives* |
| 1947 | *Gentleman's Agreement* (Elia Kazan) | Ronald Colman *A Double Life* | Loretta Young *The Farmer's Daughter* | Elia Kazan *Gentleman's Agreement* |
| 1948 | *Hamlet* (Laurence Olivier) | Laurence Olivier *Hamlet* | Jane Wyman *Johnny Belinda* | John Huston *The Treasure of the Sierra Madre* |
| 1949 | *All the King's Men* (Robert Rossen) | Broderick Crawford *All the King's Men* | Olivia de Havilland *The Heiress* | Joseph L Mankiewicz *A Letter to Three Wives* |
| 1950 | *All About Eve* (Joseph L Mankiewicz) | José Ferrer *Cyrano de Bergerac* | Judy Holliday *Born Yesterday* | Joseph L Mankiewicz *All About Eve* |
| 1951 | *An American in Paris* (Vincente Minnelli) | Humphrey Bogart *The African Queen* | Vivien Leigh *A Streetcar Named Desire* | George Stevens *A Place in the Sun* |
| 1952 | *The Greatest Show on Earth* (Cecil B DeMille) | Gary Cooper *High Noon* | Shirley Booth *Come Back, Little Sheba* | John Ford *The Quiet Man* |
| 1953 | *From Here to Eternity* (Fred Zinnemann) | William Holden *Stalag 17* | Audrey Hepburn *Roman Holiday* | Fred Zinnemann *From Here to Eternity* |
| 1954 | *On the Waterfront* (Elia Kazan) | Marlon Brando *On the Waterfront* | Grace Kelly *The Country Girl* | Elia Kazan *On the Waterfront* |
| 1955 | *Marty* (Delbert Mann) | Ernest Borgnine *Marty* | Anna Magnani *The Rose Tattoo* | Delbert Mann *Marty* |
| 1956 | *Around the World in 80 Days* (Michael Anderson) | Yul Brynner *The King and I* | Ingrid Bergman *Anastasia* | George Stevens *Giant* |

## ACADEMY AWARDS®

| Year | Best Film (director) | Best Actor | Best Actress | Best Director |
|---|---|---|---|---|
| 1957 | *The Bridge on the River Kwai* (David Lean) | Alec Guinness *The Bridge on the River Kwai* | Joanne Woodward *The Three Faces of Eve* | David Lean *The Bridge on the River Kwai* |
| 1958 | *Gigi* (Vincente Minnelli) | David Niven *Separate Tables* | Susan Hayward *I Want To Live!* | Vincente Minnelli *Gigi* |
| 1959 | *Ben-Hur* (William Wyler) | Charlton Heston *Ben-Hur* | Simone Signoret *Room at the Top* | William Wyler *Ben-Hur* |
| 1960 | *The Apartment* (Billy Wilder) | Burt Lancaster *Elmer Gantry* | Elizabeth Taylor *Butterfield 8* | Billy Wilder *The Apartment* |
| 1961 | *West Side Story* (Robert Wise, Jerome Robbins) | Maximilian Schell *Judgment at Nuremberg* | Sophia Loren *Two Women* | Robert Wise, Jerome Robbins *West Side Story* |
| 1962 | *Lawrence of Arabia* (David Lean) | Gregory Peck *To Kill a Mockingbird* | Anne Bancroft *The Miracle Worker* | David Lean *Lawrence of Arabia* |
| 1963 | *Tom Jones* (Tony Richardson) | Sidney Poitier *Lilies of the Field* | Patricia Neal *Hud* | Tony Richardson *Tom Jones* |
| 1964 | *My Fair Lady* (George Cukor) | Rex Harrison *My Fair Lady* | Julie Andrews *Mary Poppins* | George Cukor *My Fair Lady* |
| 1965 | *The Sound of Music* (Robert Wise) | Lee Marvin *Cat Ballou* | Julie Christie *Darling* | Robert Wise *The Sound of Music* |
| 1966 | *A Man for All Seasons* (Fred Zinnemann) | Paul Scofield *A Man for All Seasons* | Elizabeth Taylor *Who's Afraid of Virginia Woolf?* | Fred Zinnemann *A Man for All Seasons* |
| 1967 | *In the Heat of the Night* (Norman Jewison) | Rod Steiger *In the Heat of the Night* | Katharine Hepburn *Guess Who's Coming to Dinner* | Mike Nichols *The Graduate* |
| 1968 | *Oliver!* (Carol Reed) | Cliff Robertson *Charly* | Katharine Hepburn *The Lion in Winter;* Barbra Streisand *Funny Girl* | Carol Reed *Oliver!* |
| 1969 | *Midnight Cowboy* (John Schlesinger) | John Wayne *True Grit* | Maggie Smith *The Prime of Miss Jean Brodie* | John Schlesinger *Midnight Cowboy* |
| 1970 | *Patton* (Franklin J Schaffner) | George C Scott *Patton* | Glenda Jackson *Women in Love* | Franklin J Schaffner *Patton* |
| 1971 | *The French Connection* (William Friedkin) | Gene Hackman *The French Connection* | Jane Fonda *Klute* | William Friedkin *The French Connection* |
| 1972 | *The Godfather* (Francis Ford Coppola) | Marlon Brando *The Godfather* | Liza Minnelli *Cabaret* | Bob Fosse *Cabaret* |

| Year | Best Film (director) | Best Actor | Best Actress | Best Director |
|---|---|---|---|---|
| 1973 | *The Sting* (George Roy Hill) | Jack Lemmon *Save the Tiger* | Glenda Jackson *A Touch of Class* | George Roy Hill *The Sting* |
| 1974 | *The Godfather Part II* (Francis Ford Coppola) | Art Carney *Harry and Tonto* | Ellen Burstyn *Alice Doesn't Live Here Anymore* | Francis Ford Coppola *The Godfather Part II* |
| 1975 | *One Flew Over the Cuckoo's Nest* (Milos Forman) | Jack Nicholson *One Flew Over the Cuckoo's Nest* | Louise Fletcher *One Flew Over the Cuckoo's Nest* | Milos Forman *One Flew Over the Cuckoo's Nest* |
| 1976 | *Rocky* (John G Avildsen) | Peter Finch *Network* | Faye Dunaway *Network* | John G Avildsen *Rocky* |
| 1977 | *Annie Hall* (Woody Allen) | Richard Dreyfuss *The Goodbye Girl* | Diane Keaton *Annie Hall* | Woody Allen *Annie Hall* |
| 1978 | *The Deer Hunter* (Michael Cimino) | Jon Voight *Coming Home* | Jane Fonda *Coming Home* | Michael Cimino *The Deer Hunter* |
| 1979 | *Kramer vs. Kramer* (Robert Benton) | Dustin Hoffman *Kramer vs Kramer* | Sally Field *Norma Rae* | Robert Benton *Kramer vs Kramer* |
| 1980 | *Ordinary People* (Robert Redford) | Robert De Niro *Raging Bull* | Sissy Spacek *Coal Miner's Daughter* | Robert Redford *Ordinary People* |
| 1981 | *Chariots of Fire* (Hugh Hudson) | Henry Fonda *On Golden Pond* | Katharine Hepburn *On Golden Pond* | Warren Beatty *Reds* |
| 1982 | *Gandhi* (Richard Attenborough) | Ben Kingsley *Gandhi* | Meryl Streep *Sophie's Choice* | Richard Attenborough *Gandhi* |
| 1983 | *Terms of Endearment* (James L Brooks) | Robert Duvall *Tender Mercies* | Shirley MacLaine *Terms of Endearment* | James L Brooks *Terms of Endearment* |
| 1984 | *Amadeus* (Milos Forman) | F Murray Abraham *Amadeus* | Sally Field *Places in the Heart* | Milos Forman *Amadeus* |
| 1985 | *Out of Africa* (Sydney Pollack) | William Hurt *Kiss of the Spider Woman* | Geraldine Page *The Trip to Bountiful* | Sydney Pollack *Out of Africa* |
| 1986 | *Platoon* (Oliver Stone) | Paul Newman *The Color of Money* | Marlee Matlin *Children of a Lesser God* | Oliver Stone *Platoon* |
| 1987 | *The Last Emperor* (Bernardo Bertolucci) | Michael Douglas *Wall Street* | Cher *Moonstruck* | Bernardo Bertolucci *The Last Emperor* |
| 1988 | *Rain Man* (Barry Levinson) | Dustin Hoffman *Rain Man* | Jodie Foster *The Accused* | Barry Levinson *Rain Man* |
| 1989 | *Driving Miss Daisy* (Bruce Beresford) | Daniel Day-Lewis *My Left Foot* | Jessica Tandy *Driving Miss Daisy* | Oliver Stone *Born on the Fourth of July* |

# ACADEMY AWARDS®

| Year | Best Film (director) | Best Actor | Best Actress | Best Director |
|---|---|---|---|---|
| 1990 | *Dances With Wolves* (Kevin Costner) | Jeremy Irons *Reversal of Fortune* | Kathy Bates *Misery* | Kevin Costner *Dances With Wolves* |
| 1991 | *The Silence of the Lambs* (Jonathan Demme) | Anthony Hopkins *The Silence of the Lambs* | Jodie Foster *The Silence of the Lambs* | Jonathan Demme *The Silence of the Lambs* |
| 1992 | *Unforgiven* (Clint Eastwood) | Al Pacino *Scent of a Woman* | Emma Thompson *Howards End* | Clint Eastwood *Unforgiven* |
| 1993 | *Schindler's List* (Steven Spielberg) | Tom Hanks *Philadelphia* | Holly Hunter *The Piano* | Steven Spielberg *Schindler's List* |
| 1994 | *Forrest Gump* (Robert Zemeckis) | Tom Hanks *Forrest Gump* | Jessica Lange *Blue Sky* | Robert Zemeckis *Forrest Gump* |
| 1995 | *Braveheart* (Mel Gibson) | Nicolas Cage *Leaving Las Vegas* | Susan Sarandon *Dead Man Walking* | Mel Gibson *Braveheart* |
| 1996 | *The English Patient* (Anthony Minghella) | Geoffrey Rush *Shine* | Frances McDormand *Fargo* | Anthony Minghella *The English Patient* |
| 1997 | *Titanic* (James Cameron) | Jack Nicholson *As Good As It Gets* | Helen Hunt *As Good As It Gets* | James Cameron *Titanic* |
| 1998 | *Shakespeare in Love* (Guy Madden) | Roberto Benigni *Life Is Beautiful* | Gwyneth Paltrow *Shakespeare in Love* | Steven Spielberg *Saving Private Ryan* |
| 1999 | *American Beauty* (Sam Mendes) | Kevin Spacey *American Beauty* | Hilary Swank *Boys Don't Cry* | Sam Mendes *American Beauty* |
| 2000 | *Gladiator* (Ridley Scott) | Russell Crowe *Gladiator* | Julia Roberts *Erin Brockovich* | Steven Soderbergh *Traffic* |
| 2001 | *A Beautiful Mind* (Ron Howard) | Denzel Washington *Training Day* | Halle Berry *Monster's Ball* | Ron Howard *A Beautiful Mind* |
| 2002 | *Chicago* (Rob Marshall) | Adrien Brody *The Pianist* | Nicole Kidman *The Hours* | Roman Polanski *The Pianist* |

## Most Successful

*It Happened One Night* (1934), *One Flew Over the Cuckoo's Nest* (1975) and *The Silence of the Lambs* (1991) are members of a very exclusive club: the only three films to have won all of the five most prestigious Oscars® (for Best Film, Actor, Actress, Director and Writing).

## Hi Ho, Hi Ho

When *Snow White and the Seven Dwarfs* (1937) won an honorary Oscar® at the 11th Academy Awards®, the award comprised one normal-sized statuette – and seven miniature Oscars, one for each of the dwarfs.

## BRITISH ACADEMY FILM AWARDS

The British Film Academy was founded in 1947, and in 1975 changed its name to the British Academy of Film and Television Arts (BAFTA). Best Actor and Best Actress awards are for performance in a leading role.

| Year | **Best Film** (director) | **Best Actor** | **Best Actress** | **Best Direction** |
|---|---|---|---|---|
| 1947 | *The Best Years of our Lives* (William Wyler) | | | |
| 1948 | Hamlet (Laurence Olivier) | | | |
| 1949 | *The Bicycle Thief* (Vittorio De Sica) | | | |
| 1950 | *All About Eve* (Joseph L Mankiewicz) | | | |
| 1951 | *La Ronde* (Max Ophuls) | | | |
| 1952 | *The Sound Barrier* (David Lean) | Ralph Richardson *The Sound Barrier* | Vivien Leigh *A Streetcar Named Desire* | |
| 1953 | *Forbidden Games* (René Clément) | John Gielgud *Julius Caesar* | Audrey Hepburn *Roman Holiday* | |
| 1954 | *The Wages of Fear* (Henri-Georges Clouzot) | Kenneth More *Doctor in the House* | Yvonne Mitchell *The Divided Heart* | |
| 1955 | *Richard III* (Laurence Olivier) | Laurence Olivier *Richard III* | Katie Johnson *The Ladykillers* | |
| 1956 | *Gervaise* (René Clément) | Peter Finch *A Town Like Alice* | Virginia McKenna *A Town Like Alice* | |
| 1957 | *The Bridge on the River Kwai* (David Lean) | Alec Guinness *The Bridge on the River Kwai* | Heather Sears *The Story of Esther Costello* | |
| 1958 | *Room at the Top* (Jack Clayton) | Trevor Howard *The Key* | Irene Worth *Orders to Kill* | |
| 1959 | *Ben-Hur* (William Wyler) | Peter Sellers *I'm All Right Jack* | Audrey Hepburn *The Nun's Story* | |
| 1960 | *The Apartment* (Billy Wilder) | Peter Finch *The Trials of Oscar Wilde* | Rachel Roberts *Saturday Night and Sunday Morning* | |
| 1961 | *Ballad of a Soldier* (Grigori Chukhraj); *The Hustler* (Robert Rossen) | Peter Finch *No Love for Johnnie* | Dora Bryan *A Taste of Honey* | |
| 1962 | *Lawrence of Arabia* (David Lean) | Peter O'Toole *Lawrence of Arabia* | Leslie Caron *The L-shaped Room* | |

## BRITISH ACADEMY FILM AWARDS

| Year | **Best Film** (director) | **Best Actor** | **Best Actress** | **Best Direction** |
|---|---|---|---|---|
| 1963 | *Tom Jones* (Tony Richardson) | Dirk Bogarde *The Servant* | Rachel Roberts *This Sporting Life* | |
| 1964 | *Dr Strangelove* (Stanley Kubrick) | Richard Attenborough *Séance on a Wet Afternoon, Guns at Batasi* | Audrey Hepburn *Charade* | |
| 1965 | *My Fair Lady* (George Cukor) | Dirk Bogarde *Darling* | Julie Christie *Darling* | |
| 1966 | *Who's Afraid of Virginia Woolf?* (Mike Nichols) | Richard Burton *The Spy Who Came in from the Cold* | Elizabeth Taylor *Who's Afraid of Virginia Woolf?* | |
| 1967 | *A Man for All Seasons* (Fred Zinnemann) | Paul Scofield *A Man for All Seasons* | Edith Evans *The Whisperers* | |
| 1968 | *The Graduate* (Mike Nichols) | Spencer Tracy *Guess Who's Coming to Dinner?* | Katharine Hepburn *Guess Who's Coming to Dinner?, The Lion in Winter* | Mike Nichols *The Graduate* |
| 1969 | *Midnight Cowboy* (John Schlesinger) | Dustin Hoffman *Midnight Cowboy, John and Mary* | Maggie Smith *The Prime of Miss Jean Brodie* | John Schlesinger *Midnight Cowboy* |
| 1970 | *Butch Cassidy and the Sundance Kid* (George Roy Hill) | Robert Redford *Butch Cassidy and the Sundance Kid, Tell Them Willie Boy is Here, Downhill Racer* | Katharine Ross *Butch Cassidy and the Sundance Kid, Tell Them Willie Boy is Here* | George Roy Hill *Butch Cassidy and the Sundance Kid* |
| 1971 | *Sunday, Bloody Sunday* (John Schlesinger) | Peter Finch *Sunday, Bloody Sunday* | Glenda Jackson *Sunday, Bloody Sunday* | John Schlesinger *Sunday, Bloody Sunday* |
| 1972 | *Cabaret* (Bob Fosse) | Gene Hackman *The French Connection, The Poseidon Adventure* | Liza Minnelli *Cabaret* | Bob Fosse *Cabaret* |
| 1973 | *Day for Night* (François Truffaut) | Walter Matthau *Pete 'n' Tillie, Charley Varrick* | Stéphane Audran *The Discreet Charm of the Bourgeoisie, Just Before Nightfall* | François Truffaut *Day for Night* |
| 1974 | *Lacombe Lucien* (Louis Malle) | Jack Nicholson *Chinatown, The Last Detail* | Joanne Woodward *Summer Wishes, Winter Dreams* | Roman Polanski *Chinatown* |
| 1975 | *Alice Doesn't Live Here Anymore* (Martin Scorsese) | Al Pacino *Dog Day Afternoon, The Godfather II* | Ellen Burstyn *Alice Doesn't Live Here Anymore* | Stanley Kubrick *Barry Lyndon* |
| 1976 | *One Flew Over the Cuckoo's Nest* (Milos Forman) | Jack Nicholson *One Flew Over the Cuckoo's Nest* | Louise Fletcher *One Flew Over the Cuckoo's Nest* | Milos Forman *One Flew Over the Cuckoo's Nest* |
| 1977 | *Annie Hall* (Woody Allen) | Peter Finch *Network* | Diane Keaton *Annie Hall* | Woody Allen *Annie Hall* |

## BRITISH ACADEMY FILM AWARDS

| Year | **Best Film** (director) | **Best Actor** | **Best Actress** | **Best Direction** |
|---|---|---|---|---|
| 1978 | *Julia* (Fred Zinnemann) | Richard Dreyfuss *The Goodbye Girl* | Jane Fonda *Julia* | Alan Parker *Midnight Express* |
| 1979 | *Manhattan* (Woody Allen) | Jack Lemmon *The China Syndrome* | Jane Fonda *The China Syndrome* | Francis Ford Coppola *Apocalypse Now* |
| 1980 | *The Elephant Man* (Jonathan Sanger) | John Hurt *The Elephant Man* | Judy Davis *My Brilliant Career* | Akira Kurosawa *Kagemusha* |
| 1981 | *Chariots of Fire* (Hugh Hudson) | Burt Lancaster *Atlantic City* | Meryl Streep *The French Lieutenant's Woman* | Louis Malle *Atlantic City* |
| 1982 | *Gandhi* (Richard Attenborough) | Ben Kingsley *Gandhi* | Katharine Hepburn *On Golden Pond* | Richard Attenborough *Gandhi* |
| 1983 | *Educating Rita* (Lewis Gilbert) | Michael Caine *Educating Rita* | Julie Walters *Educating Rita* | Bill Forsyth *Local Hero* |
| 1984 | *The Killing Fields* (Roland Joffe) | Haing S Ngor *The Killing Fields* | Maggie Smith *A Private Function* | Wim Wenders *Paris, Texas* |
| 1985 | *The Purple Rose of Cairo* (Woody Allen) | William Hurt *Kiss of the Spider Woman* | Peggy Ashcroft *A Passage to India* | *no award* |
| 1986 | *A Room With a View* (James Ivory) | Bob Hoskins *Mona Lisa* | Maggie Smith *A Room With a View* | Woody Allen *Hannah and Her Sisters* |
| 1987 | *Jean de Florette* (Claude Berri) | Sean Connery *The Name of the Rose* | Anne Bancroft *84 Charing Cross Road* | Oliver Stone *Platoon* |
| 1988 | *The Last Emperor* (Bernardo Bertolucci) | John Cleese *A Fish Called Wanda* | Maggie Smith *The Lonely Passion of Judith Hearne* | Louis Malle *Au Revoir Les Enfants* |
| 1989 | *Dead Poets Society* (Peter Weir) | Daniel Day-Lewis *My Left Foot* | Pauline Collins *Shirley Valentine* | Kenneth Branagh *Henry V* |
| 1990 | *Goodfellas* (Martin Scorsese) | Philippe Noiret *Cinema Paradiso* | Jessica Tandy *Driving Miss Daisy* | Martin Scorsese *Goodfellas* |
| 1991 | *The Commitments* (Alan Parker) | Anthony Hopkins *The Silence of the Lambs* | Jodie Foster *The Silence of the Lambs* | Alan Parker *The Commitments* |
| 1992 | *Howards End* (James Ivory) | Robert Downey Jnr *Chaplin* | Emma Thompson *Howards End* | Robert Altman *The Player* |
| 1993 | *Schindler's List* (Steven Spielberg) | Anthony Hopkins *The Remains of the Day* | Holly Hunter *The Piano* | Steven Spielberg *Schindler's List* |
| 1994 | *Four Weddings and a Funeral* (Mike Newell) | Hugh Grant *Four Weddings and a Funeral* | Susan Sarandon *The Client* | Mike Newell *Four Weddings and a Funeral* |
| 1995 | *Sense and Sensibility* (Ang Lee) | Nigel Hawthorne *The Madness of King George* | Emma Thompson *Sense and Sensibility* | Michael Radford *Il Postino* |

## BRITISH ACADEMY FILM AWARDS

| Year | **Best Film** (director) | Best Actor | Best Actress | Best Direction |
|---|---|---|---|---|
| 1996 | *The English Patient* (Anthony Minghella) | Geoffrey Rush *Shine* | Brenda Blethyn *Secrets and Lies* | Joel Coen *Fargo* |
| 1997 | *The Full Monty* (Peter Cattaneo) | Tom Wilkinson *The Full Monty* | Judi Dench *Mrs Brown* | Baz Luhrmann *Romeo and Juliet* |
| 1998 | *Shakespeare in Love* (John Madden) | Roberto Benigni *Life is Beautiful* | Cate Blanchett *Elizabeth* | Peter Weir *The Truman Show* |
| 1999 | *American Beauty* (Sam Mendes) | Kevin Spacey *American Beauty* | Annette Bening *American Beauty* | Pedro Almodovar *All About My Mother* |
| 2000 | *Gladiator* (Ridley Scott) | Jamie Bell *Billy Elliot* | Julia Roberts *Erin Brockovich* | Ang Lee *Crouching Tiger Hidden Dragon* |
| 2001 | *Lord of the Rings* (Peter Jackson) | Russell Crowe *A Beautiful Mind* | Judi Dench *Iris* | Peter Jackson *Lord of the Rings* |
| 2002 | *The Pianist* (Roman Polanski) | Daniel Day-Lewis *Gangs of New York* | Nicole Kidman *The Hours* | Roman Polanski *The Pianist* |

### Continuity Chaos

Sharp-eyed movie buffs are constantly on the lookout for continuity errors, anachronisms and other mistakes in films. From camera crews reflected in plate-glass windows to Roman centurions wearing watches, some of the worst howlers have passed into film legend. These include the Von Trapp family fleeing over the mountains straight into enemy Germany at the end of *The Sound of Music* (1965), Dorothy's hair varying in length in *The Wizard of Oz* (1939), and a passenger in a lifeboat wearing a digital watch in *Titanic* (1997). Other classic gaffes include a distant aeroplane flying past in one scene in *Ben-Hur* (1959), a storm trooper banging his head in *Star Wars* (1977) and a building marked 'Est. 1953' in World War II film *Pearl Harbor* (2001). Scenes involving food, drink and cigars or cigarettes are also a continuity nightmare for filmmakers: watch the fluctuating levels of alcohol in the wine glasses in *The Godfather* (1972) and the half-eaten hamburgers in *Pulp Fiction* (1994), not to mention the lit, unlit and relit cigarettes and cigars in almost every film featuring a smoker. Fans can also spot an anachronism a mile off. One of the best known is in *The Rocky Horror Picture Show*, in which US President Richard Nixon's resignation speech can be heard on a car radio. Nixon resigned in August – but the narrator solemnly intones that the events of the film take place 'on a late November evening'.

## PALME D'OR

The Cannes Film Festival began in 1946 and is the world's leading festival of its kind. The *Palme d'Or* (Golden Palm) for best film has been awarded every year since 1955. The director is given in brackets.

1955 *Marty* (Delbert Mann)
1956 *The Silent World* (*Le Monde du Silence*) (Jacques-Yves Cousteau)
1957 *Friendly Persuasion* (William Wyler)
1958 *The Cranes are Flying* (*Letiat Zhuravli*) (Mikhail Kalatozov)
1959 *Black Orpheus* (*Orfeu Negro*) (Marcel Camus)
1960 *La Dolce Vita* (Federico Fellini)
1961 *Viridiana* (Luis Buñuel); *Une Aussi Longue Absence* (Henri Colpi)
1962 *The Given Word* (*O Pagador de Promessas*) (Anselmo Duarte)
1963 *The Leopard* (*Il Gattopardi*) (Luchino Visconti)
1964 *The Umbrellas of Cherbourg* (*Les Parapluies de Cherbourg*) (Jacques Demy)
1965 *The Knack...And How to Get It* (Richard Lester)
1966 *A Man and a Woman* (*Un Homme et Une Femme*) (Claude Lelouch)
1967 *Blow-Up* (Michelangelo Antonioni)
1968 *festival cancelled*
1969 *If...* (Lindsay Anderson)
1970 *M*A*S*H* (Robert Altman)
1971 *The Go-Between* (Joseph Losey)
1972 *The Mattei Affair* (*Il Caso Mattei*) (Francesco Rossi); *The Working Class Go to Heaven* (*La Classe Operaia Va in Paradiso*) (Elio Petri)
1973 *Scarecrow* (Jerry Schatzberg); *The Hireling* (Alan Bridges)
1974 *The Conversation* (Francis Ford Coppola)
1975 *Chronicle of the Years of Embers* (*Ahdat Sanawouach Eldjamr*) (Mohammed Lakhdar Hamina)
1976 *Taxi Driver* (Martin Scorsese)
1977 *Padro Padrone* (Paolo and Vittorio Taviani)
1978 *The Tree of Wooden Clogs* (*L'Albero degli Zoccoli*) (Ermanno Olmi)
1979 *Apocalypse Now* (Francis Ford Coppola); *The Tin Drum* (*Die Blechtrommel*) (Volker Schlöndorff)
1980 *Kagemusha* (Akira Kurosawa); *All That Jazz* (Bob Fosse)
1981 *Man of Iron* (*Czolowieck z Zelaza*) (Andrzej Wajda)
1982 *Missing* (Costa-Gavras); *Yol* (Yilmaz Güney)
1983 *The Ballad of Narayama* (*Narayama Bushi Ko*) (Shohei Imamura)
1984 *Paris, Texas* (Wim Wenders)
1985 *When Father was Away on Business* (*Otak Na Sluzbenom Putu*) (Emir Kusturica)
1986 *The Mission* (Roland Joffe)
1987 *Under Satan's Sun* (*Sous le Soleil de Satan*) (Maurice Pialat)
1988 *Pelle the Conquerer* (*Pell Erobreren*) (Bille August)
1989 *Sex, lies and videotape* (Steven Soderbergh)
1990 *Wild at Heart* (David Lynch)
1991 *Barton Fink* (Joel and Ethan Coen)
1992 *The Best Intentions* (*Den Goda Vilijan*) (Bille August)
1993 *The Piano* (Jane Campion); *Farewell my Concubine* (Chen Kaige)
1994 *Pulp Fiction* (Quentin Tarantino)
1995 *Underground* (Emir Kusturica)
1996 *Secrets and Lies* (Mike Leigh)
1997 *The Eel* (*Unagi*) (Shohei Imamura); *A Taste of Cherry* (*Ta'me Guilass*) (Abbas Kiarostami)
1998 *Eternity and a Day* (*Mia Eoniotita Ke Mia Mera*) (Theo Angelopoulos)
1999 *Rosetta* (Luc and Jean-Pierre Dardenne)

| | |
|---|---|
| 2000 | *Dancer in the Dark* (Lars von Trier) |
| 2001 | *The Son's Room* (*La Stanza del Figlio*) (Nanni Moretti) |
| 2002 | *The Pianist* (Roman Polanski) |
| 2003 | *Elephant* (Gus Van Sant) |

## MAJOR FILM FESTIVALS

| Festival | Location | Prize |
|---|---|---|
| Bangkok | Bangkok, Thailand | Golden Kinnaree |
| Berlin | Berlin, Germany | Golden Bear |
| Cairo | Cairo, Egypt | Golden Pyramid |
| Cannes | Cannes, France | Palme d'Or |
| Cartagena | Cartagena, Colombia | Golden India Catalina |
| Chicago | Chicago, Illinois, USA | Gold Hugo |
| Cleveland | Cleveland, Ohio, USA | Best Film |
| Copenhagen | Copenhagen, Denmark | Golden Swan |
| Edinburgh | Edinburgh, Scotland, UK | Audience Award |
| Havana | Havana, Cuba | Grand Coral |
| Istanbul | Istanbul, Turkey | Golden Tulip |
| Locarno | Locarno, Switzerland | Golden Leopard |
| London | London, England, UK | Sutherland Trophy |
| Melbourne | Melbourne, Australia | Best Film |
| Montreal | Montreal, Canada | Grand Prix des Amériques |
| Moscow | Moscow, Russia | Golden St George |
| Paris | Paris, France | Grand Prix |
| Rotterdam | Rotterdam, The Netherlands | Tiger Award |
| San Francisco | San Francisco, California, USA | Golden Gate |
| San Sebastian | San Sebastian, Spain | Golden Seashell |
| Seattle | Seattle, Washington, USA | Golden Space Needle |
| Stockholm | Stockholm, Sweden | Bronze Horse |
| Sundance | Park City, Utah, USA | Grand Jury Prize |
| Tokyo | Tokyo, Japan | Grand Prix |
| Toronto | Toronto, Canada | People's Choice Award |
| Venice | Venice, Italy | Golden Lion |
| Vevey | Vevey, Switzerland | Golden Cane |

## ACTORS' REAL NAMES

Real names of selected actors are given below.

| Pseudonym | Real name |
|---|---|
| Alda, Alan | Alphonso Joseph d'Abruzzo |
| Allen, Woody | Allen Stewart Konigsberg |
| Andrews, Dame Julie | Julia Elizabeth Wells |
| Astaire, Fred | Frederick Austerlitz |
| Bacall, Lauren | Betty Perske |
| Bancroft, Anne | Anna Maria Louisa Italiano |
| Bardot, Brigitte | Camille Javal |
| Bernhardt, Sarah | Sarah-Marie-Henriette Rosine Bernard |
| Bogarde, Sir Dirk | Derek Jules Ulric Niven van den Bogaerde |
| Bronson, Charles | Charles Buchinsky |
| Brooks, Mel | Melvin Kaminsky |
| Burton, Richard | Richard Walter Jenkins |
| Cage, Nicolas | Nicholas Coppola |
| Caine, Sir Michael | Maurice Micklewhite |
| Cher | Cheryl Sarkisian La Pier |
| Coltrane, Robbie | Robin McMillan |
| Crawford, Joan | Lucille Le Sueur |
| Crosby, Bing | Harry Lillis Crosby |
| Cruise, Tom | Tom Cruise Mapother IV |
| Curtis, Tony | Bernard Schwartz |
| Day, Doris | Doris Kappelhoff |
| Deneuve, Catherine | Catherine Dorléac |
| Dietrich, Marlene | Maria Magdalena Von Losch |

| Pseudonym | Real name |
|---|---|
| Dors, Diana | Diana Fluck |
| Douglas, Kirk | Issur Danielovich |
| Fairbanks, Douglas | Douglas Elton Ullman |
| Fields, W C | William Claude Dukenfield |
| Flynn, Errol | Leslie Thomson Flynn |
| Foster, Jodie | Alicia Christian Foster |
| Garbo, Greta | Greta Lovisa Gustafsson |
| Gardner, Ava | Lucy Johnson |
| Garland, Judy | Frances Ethel Gumm |
| Gish, Lillian Diana | Lillian de Guiche |
| Goldberg, Whoopi | Caryn Johnson |
| Grant, Cary | Archibald Leach |
| Grant, Richard E | Richard Grant Esterhuysen |
| Hardy, Oliver | Norvell Hardy Junior |
| Harlow, Jean | Harlean Carpentier |
| Hayworth, Rita | Margarita Carmen Cansino |
| Hepburn, Audrey | Edda Van Heemstra Hepburn-Ruston |
| Heston, Charlton | Charles Carter |
| Hill, Benny | Alfred Hawthorne Hill |
| Holm, Sir Ian | Ian Holm Cuthbert |
| Irving, Sir Henry | John Henry Brodribb |
| Jacques, Hattie | Josephine Edwina Jacques |
| Jason, David | David John White |
| Jolson, Al | Asa Yoelson |
| Karloff, Boris | William Henry Pratt |
| Keaton, Diane | Diane Hall |
| Keith, Penelope | Penelope Hatfield |
| Kingsley, Ben | Krishna Bhanji |
| Lancaster, Burt | Stephen Burton Lancaster |
| Laurel, Stan | Arthur Stanley Jefferson |
| Leigh, Vivien | Vivian Mary Hartley |
| Lindsay, Robert | Robert Lindsay Stevenson |
| Lombard, Carole | Jane Alice Peters |
| Loren, Sophia | Sofia Scicolone |
| Lugosi, Bela | Bela Ferenc Denzso Blasko |
| MacLaine, Shirley | Shirley MacLean Beaty |
| Matthau, Walter | Walter Matuschanskavasky |
| Mirren, Helen | Helen Lydia Mironoff |
| Monroe, Marilyn | Norma Jean Mortenson |
| Montand, Yves | Ivo Livi |
| Moore, Demi | Demi Guynes |
| Moore, Julianne | Julie Anne Smith |
| Neeson, Liam | William John Neeson |
| Niven, David | James David Graham Nevins |
| Pickford, Mary | Gladys Mary Smith |
| Robinson, Edward G | Emanuel Goldenberg |
| Rogers, Ginger | Virginia Katherine McMath |
| Russell, Lillian | Helen Louise Leonard |
| Ryder, Winona | Winona Horowitz |
| Scales, Prunella | Prunella Margaret Rumney Illingworth |
| Shepard, Sam | Samuel Shepard Rogers |
| Spacey, Kevin | Kevin Fowler |
| Stanwyck, Barbara | Ruby Stevens |
| Streisand, Barbra | Barbara Joan Rosen |
| Swanson, Gloria | Gloria May Josephine Svensson |
| Turner, Lana | Julia Jean Mildred Frances Turner |
| Valentino, Rudolph | Rodolpho Alphonso Guglielmi di Valentina d'Antonguolla |
| Wayne, John | Marion Michael Morrison |
| Welch, Raquel | Raquel Tejada |
| Wood, Natalie | Natasha Gurdin |
| York, Susannah | Susannah Yolande-Fletcher |

### Cameo Leach

Cary Grant used to enjoy sneaking his real name into his films. In *His Girl Friday* (1940) Grant refers in conversation to a man named Archie Leach, while the same name appears on a tombstone behind Grant in a graveyard scene in *Arsenic and Old Lace* (1944).

## FILM RECORDS

| | |
|---|---|
| First film | Thomas Edison and William Dickson pioneered the Kinetoscope in the early 1890s, showing short films such as 'The Sneeze' (1894); in 1895 Auguste and Louis Lumière patented the Cinematograph which they demonstrated in public with such short films as 'Arrival of Train at Station'. |
| First feature film with sound | *The Jazz Singer* (1927) featured short spoken clips and music, though other experiments with sound had been made with shorter films. |

| | |
|---|---|
| Oldest star | Jeanne Louise Calment appeared as herself in the film *Vincent And Me* (1990) at the age of 114. She lived to the age of 122. |
| Youngest star | Leroy Overacker appeared in the film *A Bedtime Story* (1933) at the age of 6 months, and received star billing. |
| Most leading roles in Hollywood films | John Wayne played leading roles in 142 Hollywood films, and appeared in 153. Adoor Bhasi appeared in 549 Bollywood films. |
| Longest shot in a feature film | *Russian Ark* (2001) consists entirely of one long shot lasting 96 minutes. |
| Highest box office gross | *Titanic* (1997) is the most successful film of all time, and was the first to gross more than $1 billion internationally. |
| Film with most Academy Awards® | *Ben-Hur* (1959) and *Titanic* (1997) have both won 11 Academy Awards. |
| Most Academy Awards® for Best Actress | Katharine Hepburn won four Academy Awards for Best Actress, in 1932, 1967, 1968 and 1981. |
| Most Academy Awards® for Best Actor | Seven actors have won two Academy Awards for Best Actor: Spencer Tracy, Gary Cooper, Marlon Brando, Jack Nicholson, Fredric March, Dustin Hoffman and Tom Hanks. |
| Most Academy Awards® in total | Walt Disney won 26 Academy Awards. |
| Most Academy Award® nominations | Walt Disney had 64 nominations, while John Williams is the most nominated person today with 41. |

### *Play It Again, Sam*

Perhaps the most famous line associated with *Casablanca* (1942), 'Play it again, Sam', was never actually spoken by either star. Rick, played by Humphrey Bogart, declares 'Play it!' while Ingrid Bergman's character Ilsa requests 'Play it, Sam. Play *As Time Goes By*' – but neither ever utters the famous line.

## BRITISH ACADEMY TELEVISION AWARDS

**The British Academy of Film and Television Arts (BAFTA) has awarded prizes for outstanding work in television entertainment since 1954. Programmes associated with the awards are given from 1968.**

| Year | Best Actress | Best Actor |
|---|---|---|
| 1954 | Googie Withers | Paul Rogers |
| 1955 | Virginia McKenna | Peter Cushing |
| 1956 | Rosalie Crutchley | Michael Gough |
| 1957 | *no award* | Michael Hordern |
| 1958 | Gwen Watford | Donald Pleasance |
| 1959 | Catherine Lacey | Patrick McGoohan |
| 1960 | Billie Whitelaw | Lee Montague |
| 1961 | Ruth Dunning | Rupert Davies |
| 1962 | Brenda Bruce | Harry H Corbett |
| 1963 | Vivien Merchant | Alan Badel |
| 1964 | Katherine Blake | Patrick Wymark |
| 1965 | Gwen Watford | Alan Badel |
| 1966 | Vanessa Redgrave | Warren Mitchell |

## BRITISH ACADEMY TELEVISION AWARDS

| Year | Best Actress | Best Actor |
|---|---|---|
| 1967 | Judi Dench | Eric Porter |
| 1968 | Wendy Craig *Not in Front of the Children* | Roy Dotrice *Brief Lives* |
| 1969 | Margaret Tyzack *The First Churchills* | Edward Woodward *Callan, A Dream Divided* (Omnibus), *A Bit of a Holiday* |
| 1970 | Annette Crosbie *The Six Wives of Henry VIII* | Keith Michell *The Six Wives of Henry VIII, An Ideal Husband* |
| 1971 | Patricia Hayes *Edna, the Inebriate Woman* | John Le Mesurier *Traitor* |
| 1972 | Billie Whitelaw *The Sextet* (eight plays) | Anthony Hopkins *War and Peace* |
| 1973 | Celia Johnson *Mrs Palfrey at the Claremont* | Frank Finlay *The Adventures of Don Quixote, Candide, The Death of Adolf Hitler* |
| 1974 | Lee Remick *Jennie* | Peter Barkworth *Crown Matrimonial* |
| 1975 | Annette Crosbie *Edward the Seventh* | John Hurt *The Naked Civil Servant, Nijinsky, God of the Dance* |
| 1976 | Sian Phillips *I Claudius* | Derek Jacobi *I Claudius* |
| 1977 | Penelope Keith *The Norman Conquests, Saving It for Albie* | Peter Barkworth *Professional Foul, The Country Party* |
| 1978 | Francesca Annis *Lillie, The Comedy of Errors* | Edward Fox *Edward and Mrs Simpson* |
| 1979 | Cheryl Campbell *Testament of Youth, The Duke of Wellington, Malice Aforethought* | Alec Guinness *Tinker Tailor Soldier Spy* |
| 1980 | Peggy Ashcroft *Caught on a Train, Cream in My Coffee* | Denholm Elliott *Gentle Folk/In Hiding/Blade on the Feather/The Stinker* |
| 1981 | Judi Dench *Going Gently, A Fine Romance, The Cherry Orchard* | Anthony Andrews *Brideshead Revisited* |
| 1982 | Beryl Reid *Smiley's People* | Alec Guinness *Smiley's People* |
| 1983 | Coral Browne *An Englishman Abroad* | Alan Bates *An Englishman Abroad* |
| 1984 | Peggy Ashcroft *The Jewel in the Crown* | Tim Pigott-Smith *The Jewel in the Crown* |
| 1985 | Claire Bloom *Shadowlands* | Bob Peck *Edge of Darkness* |
| 1986 | Anna Massey *Hotel Du Lac* | Michael Gambon *The Singing Detective* |
| 1987 | Emma Thompson *Fortunes of War, Tutti Frutti* | David Jason *Porterhouse Blue* |
| 1988 | Thora Hird *A Cream Cracker under the Settee* | Ray McAnally *A Very British Coup* |
| 1989 | Diana Rigg *Mother Love* | John Thaw *Inspector Morse* |
| 1990 | Geraldine McEwan *Oranges are not the Only Fruit* | Ian Richardson *House of Cards* |
| 1991 | Helen Mirren *Prime Suspect* | Robert Lindsay *G.B.H.* |
| 1992 | Helen Mirren *Prime Suspect 2* | John Thaw *Inspector Morse* |
| 1993 | Helen Mirren *Prime Suspect 3* | Robbie Coltrane *Cracker* |
| 1994 | Juliet Aubrey *Middlemarch* | Robbie Coltrane *Cracker* |
| 1995 | Jennifer Ehle *Pride and Prejudice* | Robbie Coltrane *Cracker* |
| 1996 | Gina McKee *Our Friends in the North* | Nigel Hawthorne *The Fragile Heart* |
| 1997 | Daniela Nardini *This Life* | Simon Russell Beale *A Dance to the Music of Time* |
| 1998 | Thora Hird *Waiting for the Telegram* | Tom Courtenay *A Rather English Marriage* |
| 1999 | Thora Hird *Lost for Words* | Michael Gambon *Wives and Daughters* |
| 2000 | Judi Dench *Last of the Blonde Bombshells* | Michael Gambon *Longitude* |
| 2001 | Julie Walters *My Beautiful Son* | Michael Gambon *Perfect Strangers* |
| 2002 | Julie Walters *Murder* | Albert Finney *The Gathering Storm* |

## SOAP OPERA PLACES

| Soap opera | Setting |
|---|---|
| The Archers | Ambridge, South Borsetshire, UK |
| The Bill | Sun Hill, Canley, London, UK |
| Brookside | Brookside Close, Liverpool, UK |
| Casualty | Holby City Hospital, Holby, UK |
| Coronation Street | Weatherfield, Manchester, UK |
| EastEnders | Albert Square, Walford, London, UK |
| Emmerdale | Emmerdale, Yorkshire, UK |
| Holby City | Holby City Hospital, Holby, UK |
| Hollyoaks | Hollyoaks, Chester, UK |
| Home and Away | Summer Bay, Australia |
| Neighbours | Ramsay Street, Erinsborough, Australia |
| River City | Montego Street, Shieldinch, Glasgow, UK |

### Soap and Beer

The pubs in television soaps are some of the best known in the country. From The Bull (*The Archers*) to The Rover's Return (*Coronation Street*) and The Woolpack (*Emmerdale*), the characters in soap operas are often found having a pint and mulling over their problems at their local. Perhaps the most famous imaginary pub is *EastEnders*' Queen Vic. The BBC says that the booze served in the Vic is real, albeit low-alcohol, beer.

## ORCHESTRAS

### Orchestra layout

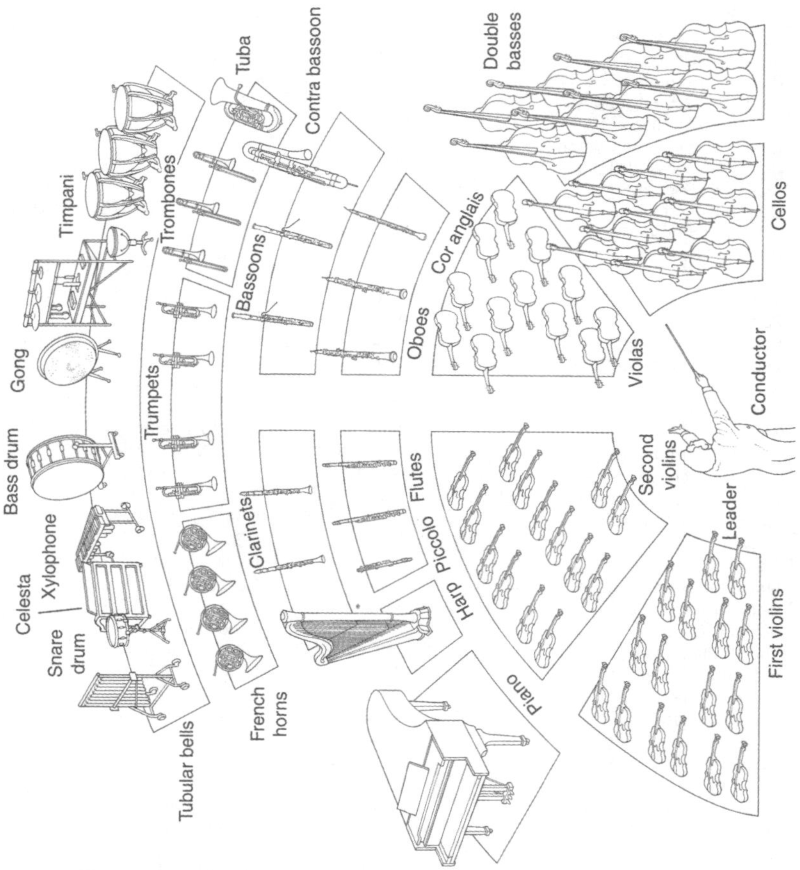


## *Empty Orchestra*

Karaoke and classical orchestras might not seem to have much in common. However, the Japanese word *karaoke* literally means 'empty orchestra'.

## Major orchestras

| Name | Date founded | Location |
|---|---|---|
| Academy of Ancient Music | 1973 | UK (London) |
| Academy of St Martin-in-the-Fields | 1959 | UK (London) |
| Australian Chamber | 1975 | Sydney |
| BBC Philharmonic | 1934 | UK (Manchester) |
| BBC Scottish Symphony | 1935 | UK (Glasgow) |
| BBC Symphony | 1930 | UK (London) |
| BBC Welsh Symphony | 1935 | UK (Cardiff) |
| Berliner Philharmonic | 1882 | Germany |
| Boston Symphony | 1881 | USA |
| Bournemouth Symphony | 1893 | UK |
| Chicago Symphony | 1891 | USA |
| City of Birmingham Symphony | 1920 | UK |
| City of Glasgow Philharmonic | 1990 | UK |
| Cleveland Symphony | 1918 | USA |
| Concertgebouw | 1888 | The Netherlands (Amsterdam) |
| Detroit Symphony | 1914 | USA |
| English Chamber | 1948 | UK (London) |
| Hallé | 1858 | UK (Manchester) |
| Israel Philharmonic | 1936 | Israel (Tel Aviv) |
| London Philharmonic | 1904 | UK |
| London Symphony | 1904 | UK |
| Los Angeles Philharmonic | 1904 | USA |
| Melbourne Symphony | 1906 | Australia |
| Milan La Scala | 1778 | Italy |
| Minnesota | 1903 | USA (Minneapolis) |
| National Symphony | 1931 | USA (Washington DC) |
| NBC Symphony | 1937–54 | USA (New York) |
| New Orleans Philharmonic Symphony | 1936 | USA |
| New York Philharmonic | 1842 | USA |
| New York Symphony | 1878 | USA |
| Northern Sinfonia | 1958 | UK (Newcastle upon Tyne) |
| Orchestre Symphonique de Montréal | 1842 | Canada |
| Oslo Philharmonic | 1919 | Norway |
| Philadelphia | | 1900 USA |
| The Philharmonia | 1945 | UK (London) |
| Pittsburgh Symphony | 1926 | USA |
| Royal Liverpool Philharmonic | 1840 | UK |
| Royal Philharmonic | 1946 | UK (London) |
| Royal Scottish National | 1891 | UK (Glasgow) |
| St Petersburg Philharmonic | 1921 | Russia |
| San Francisco | 1911 | USA |
| Santa Cecelia Academy | 1895 | Italy (Rome) |
| Scottish Chamber | 1974 | UK (Edinburgh) |
| Seattle Symphony | 1903 | USA |
| Staatskapelle | 1923 | Germany (Dresden) |
| Sydney Symphony | 1934 | Australia |
| Toronto Symphony | 1922 | Canada |
| Ulster | 1966 | UK (Belfast) |
| Vienna Philharmonic | 1842 | Austria |
| Vienna Symphony | 1900 | Austria |

## OPERAS AND OPERETTAS

| Name | Composer | Date | Name | Composer | Date |
|---|---|---|---|---|---|
| Aïda | Verdi | 1871 | Manon | Massenet | 1884 |
| Andrea Chénier | Umberto Giordano | 1896 | Manon Lescaut | Puccini | 1893 |
| Ariadne auf Naxos | Richard Strauss | 1916 | The Marriage of Figaro | Mozart | 1786 |
| Un Ballo in Maschera | Verdi | 1859 | The Merry Wives of Windsor | Otto Nicolai | 1849 |
| The Barber of Seville | Rossini | 1816 | The Midsummer Marriage | Tippett | 1955 |
| The Bartered Bride | Smetana | 1866 | The Mikado | Gilbert and Sullivan | 1885 |
| La Bohème | Puccini | 1896 | Moses und Aron | Schönberg | 1954 |
| Boris Godunov | Mussorgsky | 1874 | Nabucco | Verdi | 1842 |
| Carmen | Bizet | 1875 | Nixon in China | Peter Adams | 1990 |
| Cavalleria Rusticana | Mascagni | 1890 | Norma | Bellini | 1831 |
| Così Fan Tutte | Mozart | 1790 | Orfeo ed Euridice | Gluck | 1762 |
| The Cunning Little Vixen | Janácek | 1924 | Orpheus in the Underworld | Offenbach | 1858 |
| Dido and Aeneas | Purcell | 1689 | Otello | Verdi | 1887 |
| Don Carlos | Verdi | 1867 | Pagliacci | Leoncavallo | 1892 |
| Don Giovanni | Mozart | 1787 | Parsifal | Wagner | 1882 |
| Don Pasquale | Donizetti | 1843 | Pelléas et Mélisande | Debussy | 1902 |
| Duke Bluebeard's Castle | Bartók | 1918 | Peter Grimes | Britten | 1945 |
| Einstein on the Beach | Philip Glass | 1976 | Porgy and Bess | Gershwin | 1935 |
| Elektra | Richard Strauss | 1909 | The Rake's Progress | Stravinsky | 1951 |
| Eugene Onegin | Tchaikovsky | 1879 | Rigoletto | Verdi | 1851 |
| Falstaff | Verdi | 1893 | The Ring | Wagner | 1876 |
| Faust | Gounod | 1859 | Salome | Richard Strauss | 1911 |
| Fidelio | Beethoven | 1814 | Samson et Dalila | Saint-Saëns | 1877 |
| La Fille du Régiment | Donizetti | 1840 | Simon Boccanegra | Verdi | 1857 |
| Die Fledermaus | Johann Strauss | 1874 | La Sonnambula | Bellini | 1831 |
| The Flying Dutchman | Wagner | 1843 | The Tales of Hoffman | Offenbach | 1881 |
| Hansel and Gretel | Humperdinck | 1893 | Tannhäuser | Wagner | 1845 |
| HMS Pinafore | Gilbert and Sullivan | 1878 | The Threepenny Opera | Weill | 1928 |
| Jenufa | Janácek | 1904 | Tosca | Puccini | 1900 |
| King Priam | Tippett | 1962 | La Traviata | Verdi | 1853 |
| Lady Macbeth of Mtsensk | Shostakovich | 1934 | Tristan und Isolde | Wagner | 1865 |
| Lohengrin | Wagner | 1850 | Il Trovatore | Verdi | 1853 |
| The Love for Three Oranges | Prokofiev | 1920 | Turandot | Puccini | 1926 |
| Lucia di Lammermoor | Donizetti | 1835 | The Turn of the Screw | Britten | 1954 |
| Lulu | Berg | 1937 | Werther | Massenet | 1892 |
| Macbeth | Verdi | 1847 | William Tell | Rossini | 1829 |
| Madame Butterfly | Puccini | 1904 | Wozzeck | Berg | 1925 |
| The Magic Flute | Mozart | 1791 | | | |

### Coward on Opera

'People are wrong when they say the opera isn't what it used to be. It is what it used to be. That's what's wrong with it.'

**Sir Noël Coward (1899–1973), *Design for Living*, 1933.**

## BALLETS

| Ballet | Composer | Choreographer | First performance |
|---|---|---|---|
| Bolero | Ravel | Bejart | 1961 |
| Cinderella | Prokofiev | Ashton | 1948 |
| Coppélia | Delibes | St Léon | 1870 |
| La Fille mal gardée | Various (French popular songs and airs) | Dauberval | 1789 |
| The Firebird | Stravinsky | Fokine | 1910 |
| Giselle | Adam | Coralli and Perro (later revised by Petipa) | 1841 |
| Manon | Massenet | MacMillan | 1974 |
| The Nutcracker | Tchaikovsky | Ivanov | 1892 |
| Romeo and Juliet | Prokofiev | Lavrovsky | 1940 |
| Le Sacré du printemps (The Rite of Spring) | Stravinsky, Roerich | Nijinsky | 1913 |
| Schéhérazade | Rimsky-Korsakov | Fokine | 1910 |
| The Sleeping Beauty | Tchaikovsky | Petipa | 1890 |
| 'Still Life' at the Penguin Café | Bintley | Jeffes | 1988 |
| Swan Lake | Tchaikovsky | Petipa and Ivanov | 1895 |
| La Sylphide | Løvenskjold | Bournonville | 1836 |

### Manuscript Millions

Original manuscripts of works by renowned composers are highly sought after by collectors and can fetch millions at auction. In May 2003 the working manuscript of Beethoven's 'Ninth Symphony' was sold for £2 133 600, setting a new record price both for a work by Beethoven and for a single musical manuscript. Described by Sotheby's as 'perhaps the single most important musical work ever to appear at auction', the pages, dating from 1826, have Beethoven's handwritten revisions scrawled throughout, including frustrated comments to his copyist such as *du verfluchter Kerl!* – 'you damned fool!' The record for the highest price ever paid for a manuscript was set in May 1987, when nine complete Mozart symphonies reached almost £2.6 million.

## GRAMMY® AWARDS

**Grammy® awards are awarded annually, in a number of categories, by the US National Academy of Recording Arts and Sciences to 'to honor excellence in the recording arts and sciences'. They were first awarded in 1958.**

| Year | Best record | Best album |
|---|---|---|
| 1958 | Domenico Modugno 'Nel Blu Dipinto Di Blu (Volare)' | Henry Mancini *Peter Gunn* |
| 1959 | Bobby Darin 'Mack the Knife' | Frank Sinatra *Come Dance with Me* |
| 1960 | Percy Faith 'Theme from *A Summer Place*' | Bob Newhart *Button Down Mind* |
| 1961 | Henry Mancini 'Moon River' | Judy Garland *Judy at Carnegie Hall* |
| 1962 | Tony Bennett 'I Left My Heart in San Francisco' | Vaughn Meader *The First Family* |
| 1963 | Henry Mancini 'The Days of Wine and Roses' | Barbra Streisand *The Barbra Streisand Album* |

| Year | Best record | Best album |
|---|---|---|
| 1964 | Stan Getz, Astrud Gilberto 'The Girl from Ipanema' | Stan Getz, João Gilberto *Getz/Gilberto* |
| 1965 | Herb Alpert 'A Taste of Honey' | Frank Sinatra *September of My Years* |
| 1966 | Frank Sinatra 'Strangers in the Night' | Frank Sinatra *A Man and His Music* |
| 1967 | 5th Dimension 'Up, Up and Away' | The Beatles *Sgt Pepper's Lonely Hearts Club Band* |
| 1968 | Simon and Garfunkel 'Mrs Robinson' | Glen Campbell *By the Time I Get to Phoenix* |
| 1969 | 5th Dimension 'Aquarius/Let the Sunshine In' | Blood, Sweat and Tears *Blood, Sweat and Tears* |
| 1970 | Simon and Garfunkel 'Bridge Over Troubled Water' | Simon and Garfunkel *Bridge Over Troubled Water* |
| 1971 | Carole King 'It's Too Late' | Carole King *Tapestry* |
| 1972 | Roberta Flack 'The First Time Ever I Saw Your Face' | Various *The Concert for Bangladesh* |
| 1973 | Roberta Flack 'Killing Me Sofly with His Song' | Stevie Wonder *Innervisions* |
| 1974 | Olivia Newton-John 'I Honestly Love You' | Stevie Wonder *Fulfillingness' First Finale* |
| 1975 | Captain and Tennille 'Love Will Keep Us Together' | Paul Simon *Still Crazy After All These Years* |
| 1976 | George Benson 'This Masquerade' | Stevie Wonder *Songs in the Key of Life* |
| 1977 | Eagles 'Hotel California' | Fleetwood Mac *Rumours* |
| 1978 | Billy Joel 'Just the Way You Are' | Bee Gees *Saturday Night Fever* |
| 1979 | The Doobie Brothers 'What a Fool Believes' | Billy Joel *52nd Street* |
| 1980 | Christopher Cross 'Sailing' | Christopher Cross *Christopher Cross* |
| 1981 | Kim Carnes 'Bette Davis Eyes' | John Lennon, Yoko Ono *Double Fantasy* |
| 1982 | Toto 'Rosanna' | Toto *Toto IV* |
| 1983 | Michael Jackson 'Beat It' | Michael Jackson *Thriller* |
| 1984 | Tina Turner 'What's Love Got to Do with It' | Lionel Richie *Can't Slow Down* |
| 1985 | USA for Africa 'We Are the World' | Phil Collins *No Jacket Required* |
| 1986 | Steve Winwood 'Higher Love' | Paul Simon *Graceland* |
| 1987 | Paul Simon 'Graceland' | U2 *The Joshua Tree* |
| 1988 | Bobby McFerrin 'Don't Worry, Be Happy' | George Michael *Faith* |
| 1989 | Bette Midler 'Wind Beneath My Wings' | Bonnie Raitt *Nick of Time* |
| 1990 | Phil Collins 'Another Day in Paradise' | Quincy Jones *Back on the Block* |
| 1991 | Natalie Cole with Nat 'King' Cole 'Unforgettable' | Natalie Cole with Nat 'King' Cole *Unforgettable* |
| 1992 | Eric Clapton 'Tears in Heaven' | Eric Clapton *Unplugged* |
| 1993 | Whitney Houston 'I Will Always Love You' | Whitney Houston *The Bodyguard* |
| 1994 | Sheryl Crow 'All I Wanna Do' | Tony Bennett *MTV Unplugged* |
| 1995 | Seal 'Kiss From a Rose' | Alanis Morissette *Jagged Little Pill* |
| 1996 | Eric Clapton 'Change the World' | Celine Dion *Falling into You* |
| 1997 | Shawn Colvin 'Sunny Came Home' | Bob Dylan *Time Out of Mind* |
| 1998 | Celine Dion 'My Heart Will Go On' | Lauryn Hill *The Miseducation of Lauryn Hill* |
| 1999 | Santana, featuring Rob Thomas 'Smooth' | Santana *Supernatural* |
| 2000 | U2 'Beautiful Day' | Steely Dan *Two Against Nature* |
| 2001 | U2 'Walk On' | Various *O Brother, Where Art Thou?* |
| 2002 | Norah Jones 'Don't Know Why' | Norah Jones *Come Away With Me* |
| 2003 | Coldplay 'Clocks' | Outkast *Speakerboxxx/The Love Below* |

## EUROVISION SONG CONTEST

The Eurovision Song Contest is held annually to choose a winning pop song from among those entered by the participating countries. Open to member countries of the European Broadcasting Union; first held in 1956.

| | |
|---|---|
| 1956 | Switzerland |
| 1957 | The Netherlands |
| 1958 | France |
| 1959 | The Netherlands |
| 1960 | France |
| 1961 | Luxembourg |
| 1962 | France |
| 1963 | Denmark |
| 1964 | Italy |
| 1965 | Luxembourg |
| 1966 | Austria |
| 1967 | UK |
| 1968 | Spain |
| 1969 | France, The Netherlands, Spain and UK[1] |
| 1970 | Ireland |
| 1971 | Monaco |
| 1972 | Luxembourg |
| 1973 | Luxembourg |
| 1974 | Sweden |
| 1975 | The Netherlands |
| 1976 | UK |
| 1977 | France |
| 1978 | Israel |
| 1979 | Israel |
| 1980 | Ireland |
| 1981 | UK |
| 1982 | Germany |
| 1983 | Luxembourg |
| 1984 | Sweden |
| 1985 | Norway |
| 1986 | Belgium |
| 1987 | Ireland |
| 1988 | Switzerland |
| 1989 | Yugoslavia |
| 1990 | Italy |
| 1991 | Sweden |
| 1992 | Ireland |
| 1993 | Ireland |
| 1994 | Ireland |
| 1995 | Norway |
| 1996 | Ireland |
| 1997 | UK |
| 1998 | Israel |
| 1999 | Sweden |
| 2000 | Denmark |
| 2001 | Estonia |
| 2002 | Latvia |
| 2003 | Turkey |

[1] *Four-way tie.*

### *La La Land*

Eurovision entries are not usually noted for their lyrical brilliance. Silly Eurovision song titles have included 'Bana Bana' (Turkey, 1989), 'Boom Bang-a-Bang' (UK, 1969), 'Diggi-Loo-Diggi-Ley' (Sweden, 1984), 'A-Ba-Ni-Bi' (Israel, 1978), and 'Ding Dinge Dong' (The Netherlands, 1975), while Spain's 1968 entry 'La La La ...' contained almost 140 instances of the word 'la'.

## JAMES BOND FILM THEME SONGS

| Year | Film | Song | Artist |
|---|---|---|---|
| 1962 | Dr No | 'The James Bond Theme' | John Barry and orchestra |
| 1963 | From Russia with Love | 'From Russia With Love' | Matt Munro |
| 1964 | Goldfinger | 'Goldfinger' | Shirley Bassey |
| 1965 | Thunderball | 'Thunderball' | Tom Jones |
| 1967 | You Only Live Twice | 'You Only Live Twice' | Nancy Sinatra |
| 1969 | On Her Majesty's Secret Service | 'We Have All the Time in the World' | Louis Armstrong |

| Year | Film | Song | Artist |
|---|---|---|---|
| 1971 | Diamonds Are Forever | 'Diamonds Are Forever' | Shirley Bassey |
| 1973 | Live and Let Die | 'Live and Let Die' | Paul McCartney and Wings |
| 1974 | The Man With the Golden Gun | 'The Man with the Golden Gun' | Lulu |
| 1977 | The Spy Who Loved Me | 'Nobody Does It Better' | Carly Simon |
| 1979 | Moonraker | 'Moonraker' | Shirley Bassey |
| 1981 | For Your Eyes Only | 'For Your Eyes Only' | Sheena Easton |
| 1983 | Octopussy | 'All Time High' | Rita Coolidge |
| 1985 | A View to a Kill | 'A View to a Kill' | Duran Duran |
| 1987 | The Living Daylights | 'The Living Daylights' | A-Ha |
| 1989 | Licence to Kill | 'Licence to Kill' | Gladys Knight |
| 1995 | GoldenEye | 'GoldenEye' | Tina Turner |
| 1997 | Tomorrow Never Dies | 'Tomorrow Never Dies' | Sheryl Crow |
| 1999 | The World Is Not Enough | 'The World Is Not Enough' | Garbage |
| 2002 | Die Another Day | 'Die Another Day' | Madonna |

### *The Name's Norman*

The famous signature tune of the James Bond movies, 'The James Bond Theme', was composed by Londoner Monty Norman (born 1928). Norman, who insists that it was only the all-expenses paid trip to the *Dr No* set in Jamaica that convinced him to take on the project, based the theme on a song that he had written for a long-since abandoned musical. He reworked the song's simple melody into the now instantly recognizable riff that he describes as 'Dum de-de-dum-dum, dum dum dum, dum de-de dum dum, dum dum dum ...'. The theme was then orchestrated by John Barry, who went on to have a lasting involvement in later Bond film scores. More than 25 million copies of the theme tune have since been sold worldwide.

## MUSICAL REAL NAMES

| Pseudonym | Real name |
|---|---|
| Bennett, Tony | Anthony Dominick Benedetto |
| Berlin, Irving | Israel Baline |
| Bizet, Georges | Alexandre Césare Léopold |
| Black, Cilla | Priscilla Maria Veronica White |
| Bo Diddley | Elias Bates, later McDaniel |
| Bon Jovi, Jon | John Francis Bongiovi, Jnr |
| Bono | Paul Hewson |
| Bowie, David | David Robert Jones |
| Boy George | George O'Dowd |
| Bygraves, Max | Walter William Bygraves |
| Charles, Ray | Ray Charles Robinson |
| Cher | Cheryl Sarkisian La Pier |
| Clark, Petula | Sally Owen |
| Cline, Patsy | Virginia Petterson Hensley |
| Cole, Nat 'King' | Nathaniel Adams Coles |
| Cooper, Alice | Vincent Damon Furnier |
| Costello, Elvis | Declan Patrick McManus |
| Crosby, Bing | Harry Lillis Crosby |
| Dylan, Bob | Robert Allen Zimmerman |
| The Edge | David Evans |
| Eminem | Marshall Mathers III |
| Fields, Dame Gracie | Grace Stansfield |
| Gershwin, George | Jacob Gershvin |
| Gershwin, Ira | Israel Gershvin |
| Holiday, Billie | Eleanora Fagan |
| Holly, Buddy | Charles Hardin |
| Howlin' Wolf | Chester Arthur Burnett |
| John, Sir Elton Hercules | Reginald Kenneth Dwight |
| Jones, Tom | Thomas Jones Woodward |

# MUSICAL REAL NAMES

| Pseudonym | Real name |
|---|---|
| King, B B | Riley B King |
| Laine, Dame Cleo | Clementina Dinah Campbell |
| Lanza, Mario | Alfredo Arnold Coccozza |
| Leadbelly | Huddie William Ledbetter |
| Little Richard | Richard Wayne Penniman |
| Lulu | Marie McDonald McLaughlin Lawrie |
| Lynn, Dame Vera | Vera Margaret Welch |
| Madonna | Madonna Louise Veronica Ciccone |
| Manilow, Barry | Barry Allen Pincus |
| Manson, Marilyn | Brian Warner |
| Meat Loaf | Marvin Lee Aday |
| Mercury, Freddie | Frederick Bulsara |
| Michael, George | Georgios Kyriacos Panayiotou |
| Miranda, Carmen | Maria do Carmo Miranda Da Cunha |
| Morton, Jelly Roll | Ferdinand Joseph La Menthe or Lamothe |
| Novello, Ivor | David Ivor Davies |
| Offenbach, Jacques | Jakob Eberst |
| Osbourne, Ozzy | John Osbourne |
| Piaf, Edith | Edith Giovanna Gassion |
| Pop, Iggy | James Newell Osterberg |
| Prince | Prince Rogers Nelson |
| Rainey, Ma | Gertrude Pridgett Rainey *née* Pridgett |
| Reed, Lou | Louis Firbank |
| Richard, Sir Cliff | Harry Rodger Webb |
| Ross, Diana | Diane Earle |
| Rotten, Johnny | John Lydon |
| Scott, Ronnie | Ronald Schatt |
| Simone, Nina | Eunice Kathleen Waymon |
| Sly Stone | Sylvester Stewart |
| Solti, Sir Georg | György Stern |
| Springfield, Dusty | Mary O'Brien |
| Starr, Ringo | Richard Starkey |
| Steele, Tommy | Thomas Hicks |
| Stevens, Cat | Stephen Demetre Georgiou |
| Sting | Gordon Matthew Sumner |
| Streisand, Barbra | Barbara Joan Rosen |
| Turner, Tina | Annie Mae Bullock |
| Vicious, Sid | John Simon Ritchie |
| Washington, Dinah | Ruth Jones |
| Waters, Muddy | McKinley Morganfield |
| Wonder, Stevie | Steveland Judkins |
| Wyman, Bill | William Perks |
| Wynette, Tammy | Virginia Wynette Pugh |

## Musical Monikers

Musicians, not content with renaming themselves, are also renowned for the intriguing and often unusual names with which they christen their offspring. In the 1960s, Keith Richards of the Rolling Stones named his daughter *Dandelion*, Sonny Bono and Cher christened their daughter *Chastity* and Frank Zappa famously called his daughter *Moon Unit*. From the 1970s came the euphonious *Zowie Bowie* (son of David) and *Rolan Bolan* (son of Marc). More recent additions to the pop world's second generation include children named after places (Victoria Beckham's son *Brooklyn*, Madonna's daughter *Lourdes* and Michael Jackson's daughter *Paris*), musical heroes (Liam Gallagher's son *Lennon*), and wonderful names such as *Blue Angel* (U2's The Edge), *Fifi Trixibelle*, *Peaches Honeyblossom* and *Pixie* (Bob Geldof), *Heavenly Hiraani Tiger Lily* (Michael Hutchence) and *Phoenix Chi* (the Spice Girls' Mel B).

# FOOD AND DRINK

## VITAMINS

Vitamins are any of numerous organic substances present in minute quantities in nutritive foods, and are essential for the health of animals. The main types of vitamin are:

### Fat soluble vitamins

| Vitamin | Chemical name | Source |
|---|---|---|
| A | retinol (carotene) | milk, butter, cheese, egg yolk, liver, fatty fish, dark green vegetables, yellow/red fruits and vegetables, especially carrots |
| D | cholecalciferol | egg yolk, liver, fatty fish; made on skin in sunlight |
| E | tocopherols | vegetable oils |
| K | phytomenadione | green leafy vegetables, beef, liver |

### Water soluble vitamins

| Vitamin | Chemical name | Source |
|---|---|---|
| $B_1$ | thiamin | germ and bran of seeds, grains, yeast |
| $B_2$ | riboflavin | liver, milk, cheese, eggs, green leafy vegetables, pulses, yeast |
| $B_6$ | pyridoxine | liver, meats, fruits, cereals, leafy vegetables |
| | pantothenic acid | widespread in plants and animals; destroyed in heavily-processed food |
| | biotin | liver, kidney, yeast extract; made by micro-organisms in large intestine |
| $B_{12}$ | cyanocobalamin | liver, kidney, milk; none found in plants |
| | folic acid | liver, green leafy vegetables, peanuts; cooking and processing can cause serious losses in food |
| C | ascorbic acid | blackcurrants, citrus fruits, other fruits, green leafy vegetables, potatoes; losses occur during storage and cooking |

## MINERALS

The main trace minerals are:

| Mineral | Source |
|---|---|
| calcium | milk, butter, cheese, sardines, green leafy vegetables, citrus fruits |
| chromium | brewer's yeast, black pepper, liver, wholemeal bread, beer |
| copper | green vegetables, fish, oysters, liver |
| fluorine | fluoridated drinking water, seafood, tea |
| iodine | seafood, saltwater fish, seaweed, iodized salt, table salt |
| iron | liver, kidney, green leafy vegetables, egg yolk, dried fruit, potatoes, molasses |
| magnesium | green leafy vegetables (eaten raw), nuts, whole grains |
| manganese | legumes, cereal grains, green leafy vegetables, tea |
| molybdenum | legumes, cereal grains, liver, kidney, some dark green vegetables |
| phosphorus | meat, poultry, fish, eggs, dried beans and peas, milk products |
| potassium | fresh vegetables, meat, orange juice, bananas, bran |
| selenium | seafood, cereals, meat, egg yolk, garlic |
| sodium | table salt, other naturally occurring salts (very rare) |
| zinc | meat, whole grains, legumes, oysters, milk |

## WINE BOTTLE SIZES

| Name | Capacity[1] | Equivalent (standard bottles) |
|---|---|---|
| wine bottle | 75cl | 1 |
| magnum | 1.5 l | 2 |
| jeroboam | 3 l | 4 |
| rehoboam | 4.5 l | 6 |
| methuselah | 6 l | 8 |
| salmanazar | 9 l | 12 |
| balthazar | 12 l | 16 |
| nebuchadnezzar | 15 l | 20 |

[1] *To convert litres to pints, multiply by 0.56821.*

*Note: A flagon of wine contains 1.13 l/2pt.*

### Biblical Bottles

Many of the larger bottle sizes are named after well-known Old Testament figures. The *balthazar* and the *nebuchadnezzar* were both so-called after kings of Babylon, the *methuselah* was named after a patriarch said to have lived 969 years, the *salmanazar* received its name by allusion to Shalmaneser, king of Assyria, and the *jeroboam* and *rehoboam* are both named after figures in the Book of Kings. In contrast, the *magnum* simply comes from the Latin word for 'big'.

## EUROPEAN CHEESES

**Belgium**

Limburger

**Cyprus**

halloumi

**England**

Cheddar
Cheshire
Derby
double Gloucester
Ilchester
Lancashire
Red Leicester
Stilton®
Wensleydale

**Denmark**

Danish blue

**France**

Brie
Camembert
Cantal
Coulommiers
Munster
Pont l'Évêque
Port Salut
reblochon
Roquefort
St Paulin
vacherin

**Germany**

Cambozola®
Münster
Tilsit

**Greece**

feta

**Italy**

bel paese
dolcelatte
Fontina
Gorgonzola
mascarpone
mozzarella
Parmesan
pecorino
provolone
ricotta
Romano
stracchino
Taleggio

**The Netherlands**

Edam
Gouda

**Norway**

Jarlsberg®

**Scotland**

crowdie
Dunlop

**Spain**

Manchego

**Switzerland**

Emmenthal
Gruyère
sapsago

**Wales**

Caerphilly

### Red Hot Chilli Peppers

The heat of chilli peppers is measured by the Scoville scale, which was developed by pharmacologist Wilbur Scoville in 1912. Although originally a taste test, today the test scientifically measures the amount of capsaicin – the substance that makes chillis taste hot – in each pepper. The higher the number of Scoville units, the hotter the pepper; pure capsaicin measures a sizzling 16 million Scoville units. A bell pepper measures 0 Scoville units, a jalapeño pepper measures between 2 500 and 5 000 units, and cayenne pepper measures between 30 000 and 50 000 units. Guinness World Records® states that the world's hottest chilli pepper is the Red Savina habañero, which can contain up to an eye-watering 570 000 Scoville units; most habañero peppers peak at around 325 000 to 350 000.

## COCKTAILS

A selection of the best-known cocktails is given. There are many variations; only the most common ingredients are listed.

| Cocktail | Alcohol | Other common ingredients |
|---|---|---|
| Bellini | chilled champagne | peach nectar or peach schnapps |
| Between the Sheets | rum, brandy, Cointreau® | lemon juice |
| Black Russian | vodka, Kahlúa® | none |
| Bloody Mary | vodka | tomato juice and seasoning |
| Brandy Alexander | brandy, crème de cacao | cream |
| Bullshot | vodka | beef consommé |
| Caipirinha | cachaça | crushed lime and sugar |
| Champagne Cocktail | champagne, brandy | sugar and Angostura bitters |
| Collins | a spirit, for example vodka or whisky | lemon or lime juice, sugar and soda water |
| Cosmopolitan | vodka, orange liqueur | lime juice and cranberry juice |
| Daiquiri | rum | lime juice |
| Gimlet | gin or vodka | lime juice |
| Harvey Wallbanger | Galliano, vodka | orange juice |
| Horse's Neck | brandy | ginger ale and a twist of lemon |
| Mai tai | rum, triple sec, grenadine | lime juice |
| Manhattan | vermouth, whisky and sometimes curaçao or maraschino | Angostura bitters |
| Margarita | tequila, orange liqueur | lime or lemon juice |
| Martini | vermouth, gin, sometimes vodka | bitters, etc and a twist of lemon |
| Moscow Mule | vodka | ginger ale and lemon juice |
| Old Fashioned | whisky | bitters, water and sugar |
| Pink Lady | gin, grenadine | cream, egg white and lemon juice |
| Planter's Punch | rum | lime or lemon juice and sugar |
| Rickey | gin or vodka | lime juice and soda water with ice |
| Rusty Nail | whisky and Drambuie® | |
| Sazerac® | Pernod and whisky | |
| Screwdriver | vodka | orange juice |
| Sea Breeze | vodka | cranberry juice and grapefruit juice |
| Sidecar | brandy, orange liqueur | lemon juice |
| Singapore Sling | brandy, gin, Cointreau®, Benedictine and grenadine | orange juice, lime juice |
| Slammer | tequila | |
| Sour | gin or whisky | lemon or lime juice |
| Stinger | brandy and white crème de menthe | |
| Tequila Sunrise | tequila, grenadine | orange juice |
| Tom Collins | gin | lime juice, soda and sugar or syrup |
| White Lady | gin, orange liqueur | lemon juice |
| White Russian | vodka, Kahlúa® | milk |

### *Cocktail Salvation*

'The greatest of all the contributions of the American way of life to the salvation of humanity.'

**H L Mencken on the cocktail. Quoted by William Grimes in 'The American Cocktail', *Americana*, Dec 1992.**

## LIQUEURS

A liqueur is a potent alcoholic preparation that is flavoured or perfumed and sweetened.

| Liqueur | Description |
|---|---|
| absinthe | a bitter, green, aniseed-flavoured liqueur containing (originally) extract of wormwood |
| advocaat | a liqueur containing raw eggs and flavourings |
| amaretto | an Italian liqueur flavoured with almonds |
| anisette | a liqueur prepared from anise seed (aromatic seeds, of a flavour similar to liquorice) |
| Benedictine | a liqueur resembling Chartreuse, distilled at Fécamp in Normandy, formerly by Benedictine monks |
| Chartreuse | a green or yellow liqueur, manufactured at La Grande Chartreuse monastery near Grenoble, France, by the monks which is made from aromatic herbs, flowers and brandy |
| cherry brandy | a liqueur made by steeping Morello cherries in brandy |
| Cointreau® | an orange-flavoured liqueur |
| crème de cacao | a chocolate-flavoured liqueur |
| crème de menthe | a green peppermint-flavoured liqueur |
| curaçao | a liqueur flavoured with bitter orange peel |
| Drambuie® | Scotch whisky liqueur |
| eau des creoles | a fine Martinique liqueur, made by distilling the flowers of the mammee-apple with alcohol |
| Frangelico | an Italian liqueur flavoured with hazelnuts |
| Galliano | an Italian liqueur flavoured with anise |
| Grand Marnier® | an orange-flavoured liqueur with a cognac base |
| Kahlúa® | a Mexican liqueur made from coffee beans, cocoa beans and vanilla |
| kirsch | a liqueur made from the wild cherry |
| kümmel | a liqueur flavoured with cumin and caraway seeds |
| maraschino | a liqueur distilled from a cherry grown in the Croatian region of Dalmatia |
| mirabelle | a colourless liqueur distilled from mirabelle plums |
| noyau | a liqueur made from brandy flavoured with bitter almonds or peach kernels |
| ouzo | an aniseed liqueur |
| ratafia | a cordial or liqueur flavoured with fruit kernels |
| rum shrub | a liqueur of rum, sugar, lime or lemon juice, etc |
| sambuca | an Italian liquorice-flavoured liqueur made from aniseed |
| Southern Comfort® | a whisky liqueur originally produced in the southern US |
| Strega® | a sweet, orange-flavoured Italian liqueur |
| Tia Maria® | a coffee-flavoured liqueur |
| Triple sec | a clear orange-flavoured liqueur |
| Van der Hum | a South African liqueur flavoured with tangerines |

### *What's in a Name?*

Liqueur names come from a variety of sources. Some reflect the liqueur's origin, for example *curaçao*, named after the island in the Caribbean where it was first made, or *Benedictine* after the Benedictine monks who first created it. Other names are derived from the taste of the liqueur, for example *amaretto*, which comes from the Italian word *amaro* meaning 'bitter'. And some are named after their ingredients, such as *maraschino* from the Italian *marasca*, 'sour cherry', and *absinthe*, from the Greek word *apsinthion* meaning 'wormwood'. *Advocaat*, however, comes from Dutch *advokaatenborrel* which means 'advocate's dram', as a clearer of the throat.

## PROVERBS

The proverbs below are arranged alphabetically by key words (which are shown in *italic*). In each case the proverb is followed by the century in which it first occurred in print in English in a recognizable form. In many cases related sentiments are attested earlier, often in Greek and Latin, and a number of other proverbs are derived from medieval French sources. Some of the uses are not in the precise form given here, as proverbs often appear in many forms.

**Proverb / Date / Notable uses**

*absence* makes the heart grow fonder 19c
*actions* speak louder than words 17c
*all's* well that ends well 14c
an *apple* a day keeps the doctor away 19c
don't throw the *baby* out with the bathwater 19c *Thomas Carlyle*
*beauty* is in the eye of the beholder 18c *David Hume*
*beauty* is only skin deep 17c
*beggars* can't be choosers 16c
the early *bird* catches the worm 17c
a *bird* in the hand is worth two in the bush 15c
*birds* of a feather flock together 16c *Bible, Ecclesiasticus 27*
once *bitten*, twice shy 19c
when the *blind* lead the blind, both shall fall into the ditch 9c *Bible, Matthew 15*
you can't get *blood* from a stone 17c
*blood* is thicker than water 19c
*brevity* is the soul of wit 17c *Shakespeare, Hamlet*
you can't make *bricks* without straw 17c *Bible, Exodus 5*
don't cross your *bridges* until you come to them 19c
a new *broom* sweeps clean 16c
you can't have your *cake* and eat it 16c
if the *cap* fits, wear it 18c
when the *cat's* away, the mice will play 17c
a *change* is as good as a rest 19c *Arthur Conan Doyle*
*charity* begins at home 14c *John Wycliffe*
don't count your *chickens* before they are hatched 16c
*clothes* make the man 15c
every *cloud* has a silver lining 19c
cut your *coat* according to your cloth 16c
too many *cooks* spoil the broth 16c
*curiosity* killed the cat 20c
there's none so *deaf* as those that will not hear 16c
needs must when the *devil* drives 15c *Shakespeare, All's Well that Ends Well*
the *devil* finds work for idle hands to do 14c *Geoffrey Chaucer*
the *devil* looks after his own 17c
better the *devil* you know than the devil you don't 16c
*discretion* is the better part of valour 16c *Shakespeare, Henry IV Part One*
give a *dog* a bad name and hang him 18c

**Proverb / Date / Notable uses**

you can't teach an old *dog* new tricks 16c
let sleeping *dogs* lie 14c *Geoffrey Chaucer*
barking *dogs* seldom bite 16c
to *err* is human, to forgive divine 16c
the *exception* proves the rule 17c
*familiarity* breeds contempt 14c
there are as good *fish* in the sea as ever came out of it 16c
a *fool* and his money are soon parted 16c
there's no *fool* like an old fool 16c
*fools* rush in where angels fear to tread 18c *Alexander Pope*
*forewarned* is forearmed 15c
a *friend* in need is a friend indeed 11c
those who live in *glass* houses shouldn't throw stones 14c *Geoffrey Chaucer*
all that *glitters* is not gold 13c *Shakespeare, Merchant of Venice, as 'all that glisters ...'*
don't teach your *grandmother* to suck eggs 18c
the *grass* is always greener on the other side of the fence 20c
old *habits* die hard 18c *Benjamin Franklin*
many *hands* make light work 14c
first you catch your *hare* 19c *William Makepeace Thackeray*
more *haste* less speed 14c
he who *hesitates* is lost 18c
there is *honour* among thieves 17c
never look a gift *horse* in the mouth 16c
you may take a *horse* to water but you can't make him drink 12c
*hunger* is the best sauce 16c
where *ignorance* is bliss, 'tis folly to be wise 18c *Thomas Gray*
strike while the *iron* is hot 14c *Geoffrey Chaucer*
a little *knowledge* is a dangerous thing 18c *Alexander Pope*
better *late* than never 14c
he who *laughs* last, laughs longest 20c
*least* said, soonest mended 15c
a *leopard* doesn't change its spots 16c *Bible, Jeremiah 13.23*
many a *little* makes a mickle 13c
half a *loaf* is better than no bread 16c
*look* before you leap 14c
one man's *meat* is another man's poison 16c
it's no use crying over spilt *milk* 17c
a *miss* is as good as a mile 17c
if the *mountain* won't come to Mahomet, Mahomet must go to the mountain 17c *Francis Bacon*
*necessity* is the mother of invention 16c
no *news* is good news 17c *James I*
don't cut off your *nose* to spite your face 16c
*nothing* ventured, nothing gained 17c
great *oaks* from little acorns grow 14c *Geoffrey Chaucer*
you can't make an *omelette* without breaking eggs 19c
*out* of sight, out of mind 13c

**Proverb / Date / Notable uses**

the *pen* is mightier than the sword 16c
take care of the *pence* and the pounds will take care of themselves 18c
in for a *penny*, in for a pound 17c
he that pays the *piper* calls the tune 19c
little *pitchers* have large ears 16c
there's no *place* like home 16c
a watched *pot* never boils 19c *Mrs Gaskell*
*practice* makes perfect 16c
*prevention* is better than cure 17c
*pride* goes before a fall 14c
*procrastination* is the thief of time 18c *Bible, Proverbs 16*
the *proof* of the pudding is in the eating 14c
you can't make a silk *purse* out of a sow's ear 16c
it never *rains* but it pours 18c
the *road* to hell is paved with good intentions 16c
spare the *rod* and spoil the child 11c *Bible, Proverbs 13*
*Rome* was not built in a day 16c
when in *Rome*, do as the Romans do 15c
better *safe* than sorry 19c
there is *safety* in numbers 17c *Bible, Proverbs 11*, and *John Bunyan*
what's *sauce* for the goose is sauce for the gander 17c
as well to be hanged for a *sheep* as a lamb 17c
there's no *smoke* without fire 14c
*speech* is silver, but silence is golden 19c *Thomas Carlyle*
it's no use shutting the *stable* door after the horse has bolted 14c
a *stitch* in time saves nine 18c
a rolling *stone* gathers no moss 14c
it's the last *straw* that breaks the camel's back 17c
little *strokes* fell great oaks 15c
one *swallow* doesn't make a summer 16c
what you lose on the *swings* you gain on the roundabouts 20c
you can have too much of a good *thing* 15c
little *things* please little minds 16c
*time* and tide wait for no man 14c *Geoffrey Chaucer, in Latin*
don't put off till *tomorrow* what you can do today 14c *Geoffrey Chaucer*
it's better to *travel* hopefully than to arrive 19c *Robert Louis Stevenson*
the *tree* is known by its fruit 16c *Bible, Matthew 12*
*trouble* shared is trouble halved 20c *Dorothy L Sayers*
there's many a good *tune* played on an old fiddle 20c *Samuel Butler*
one good *turn* deserves another 15c
*variety* is the spice of life 18c
all things come to those who *wait* 16c
*waste* not, want not 8c

## Fat Ladies Singing

While some proverbs are thousands of years old, others are more recent arrivals in the language. One modern proverb, 'It ain't over 'til the fat lady sings', is thought to have been coined as recently as 1978 by Dan Cook, a Texan journalist, in the form 'the opera ain't over 'til the fat lady sings'. Although it has been suggested that the phrase was older and was simply popularized by Cook, it has certainly caught on in the public imagination and in collections it is found alongside proverbs coined many centuries before.

## SIMILES

**A simile is a figure of speech in which a person or thing is described by being explicitly likened to another.**

as bald as a coot
as black as ink *or* pitch
as blind as a bat
as blue as the sky
as bold as brass
as bright as a button
as brown as a berry
as calm as a millpond
as clean as a whistle
as clear as a bell *or* as crystal *or* *(ironically)* as mud
as cold as charity *or* ice
as cool as a cucumber
as cross as two sticks
as daft as a brush
as dead as a dodo *or* a doornail *or* as mutton
as deaf as a post
as different as chalk and cheese
as drunk as a lord *or* a piper
as dry as a bone
as dull as ditchwater
as easy as falling off a log *or* as winking
as fair as a rose
as fit as a fiddle
as flat as a pancake
as free as a bird
as fresh as a daisy *or* as paint
as good as gold
as green as grass
as happy as a lark *or* as a sandboy *or* as Larry *or* as the day is long
as hard as nails
as high as a kite
as innocent as a lamb
as keen as mustard
as large as life
as light as a feather *or* as down
as like as two peas in a pod *or (ironically)* chalk and cheese
as lively as a cricket
as mad as a hatter *or* a March hare
as merry as a grig
as near as a touch
as neat as ninepence
as often as not
as old as Adam *or* Methuselah *or* the hills
as plain as a pikestaff
as pleased as Punch
as poor as a church mouse
as proud as a peacock
as pure as the driven snow
as quick as lightning
as quiet as a mouse
as red as a beetroot
as regular as clockwork
as rich as Croesus
as right as a trivet *or* as rain
as ripe as a cherry
as safe as houses
as sharp as a razor
as sick as a dog *or* a parrot
as silent as the grave
as slippery as an eel
as sober as a judge
as soft as a baby's bottom
as sound as a bell *or* a roach
as steady as a rock
as stiff as a poker
as straight as a die
as strong as a horse
as stubborn as a mule
as sure as a gun *or* as eggs is eggs
as thick *(= conspiratorial)* as thieves
as thick *(= stupid)* as a plank *or* as two short planks
as thin as a rake
as tough as leather *or* old boots
as ugly as sin
as warm as toast
as weak as a kitten
as white as a sheet *or* as snow
as wise as an owl

### *Common as a Simile*

'One thing that literature would be greatly the better for
Would be a more restricted employment by authors of simile and metaphor.'
**Ogden Nash, *Many Long Years Ago*, 'Very Like A Whale', 1945.**

## INTERESTING OLOGIES

An 'ology' is a science whose name ends in *-logy* or *-ology*. This ending comes from the Greek word *logos*, meaning 'word' or 'reason'.

| Ology | Study of ... |
|---|---|
| acarology | mites |
| agrostology | grasses |
| aristology | dining |
| astacology | crayfish |
| autology | oneself |
| balneology | bathing and mineral springs |
| batology | brambles |
| bryology | mosses |
| caliology | birds' nests |
| campanology | bells and bellringing |
| carcinology | crustaceans |
| chaology | chaos or chaos theory |
| chirology | the language of gesture, and the hand |
| codicology | manuscript volumes |
| conchology | molluscs and their shells |
| coprology | the use of obscenity in speech, literature and art |
| cryptology | codes |
| cryptozoology | creatures, such as the Loch Ness monster, that are generally regarded as mythical |
| dactyliology | rings or engraved gems |
| deltiology | picture postcards |
| demonology | demons and their ways |
| garbology | a society's waste materials |
| graphology | handwriting |
| hagiology | saints' legends |
| helminthology | worms, especially parasitic ones |
| heortology | religious feasts |
| hepaticology | liverworts |
| heresiology | heresies |
| hierology | sacred matters |
| hippology | horses |
| hoplology | weapons |
| hymnology | hymns |
| hypnology | sleep |
| irenology | peace |
| koniology | dust in the air |
| limacology | slugs |
| malacology | molluscs |
| missiology | religious missions |
| myrmecology | ants |
| odonatology | dragonflies |
| oenology | wines |
| oneirology | dreams |
| oology | birds' eggs |
| ophiology | snakes |
| orchidology | orchids |
| orology or oreology | mountains |
| paroemiology | proverbs |
| phycology | algae |
| podology | feet |
| pomology | fruit-growing |
| pseudology | lying |
| pteridology | ferns |
| scatology | excrement |
| sindonology | the Turin shroud |
| spectrology | ghosts |
| speleology | caves |
| sphygmology | the pulse |
| storiology | folk tales |
| thaumatology | miracles |
| timbrology | stamp collecting |
| ufology | UFOs |
| vexillology | flags |
| xylology | the structure of wood |
| zymology | the science of fermentation |

### *Mysterious Creatures*

One of the more exciting 'ologies' is *cryptozoology*, the study and attempted discovery of creatures that are generally regarded as mythical. The Loch Ness monster, the Bigfoot or sasquatch, the Yeti and numerous other big cats, sea monsters and unexplained beasts – such as the unlikely-sounding Mongolian Death Worm – are all the somewhat elusive targets of cryptozoologists.

## ISMS

Most of the words included here denote beliefs and practices. Some, however, denote aspects of discrimination; these include **ageism** and **sexism**. Etymological information is given in parentheses.

| | |
|---|---|
| **ageism** | discrimination on the grounds of age |
| **agnosticism** | belief in the impossibility of knowing God (Greek *agnostos* unknown, unknowable) |
| **alcoholism** | addiction to alcohol |
| **altruism** | unselfish concern for the welfare of others (Latin *alteri huic* to this other) |
| **atavism** | reversion to an earlier type (Latin *atavus* ancestor) |
| **atheism** | belief that God does not exist (Greek *atheos* without god) |
| **barbarism** | state of being coarse or uncivilized (Greek *barbaros* foreign, stammering) |
| **behaviourism** | basis of psychology in behaviour of people and animals |
| **cannibalism** | practice of eating human flesh (Spanish *Canibal* Carib) |
| **capitalism** | economic system based on the private ownership of wealth and resources |
| **communism** | political and economic system based on collective ownership of wealth and resources |
| **conservatism** | inclination to preserve the status quo |
| **consumerism** | economic policy of encouraging spending and consuming |
| **cubism** | artistic movement using geometrical shapes to represent objects |
| **cynicism** | belief in the worst in others (Greek *kynikos* dog-like) |
| **defeatism** | belief in the inevitability of defeat |
| **dogmatism** | tendency to present statements of opinion as if unquestionable (Greek *dogma* opinion) |
| **dynamism** | state of having limitless energy and enthusiasm |
| **egoism** | principle that self-interest is the basis of morality (Latin *ego* I) |
| **elitism** | belief in the natural superiority of some people (Latin *eligere* to elect) |
| **empiricism** | theory that knowledge can only be gained through experiment and observation (Greek *empeiria* experience) |
| **environmentalism** | concern to protect the natural environment |
| **escapism** | tendency to escape from unpleasant reality into fantasy |
| **evangelism** | practice of trying to persuade someone to adopt a particular belief or cause (Greek *evangelion* good news) |
| **exhibitionism** | tendency to behave so as to attract attention to oneself |
| **existentialism** | philosophy emphasizing freedom of choice and personal responsibility for one's actions |
| **expressionism** | artistic movement emphasizing expression of emotions over representation of external reality |
| **extremism** | adherence to fanatical or extreme opinions |
| **fanaticism** | excessive enthusiasm for something (Latin *fanaticus* filled with a god, frenzied) |
| **favouritism** | practice of giving unfair preference to a person or group |
| **feminism** | advocacy of equal rights and opportunities for women |
| **feudalism** | social system based on tenants' allegiance to a lord |
| **functionalism** | theory that the intended use of something should determine its design |
| **hedonism** | belief in the importance of pleasure above all else (Greek *hedone* pleasure) |
| **heroism** | quality of showing great courage in one's actions |
| **holism** | theory that any complex being or system is more than the sum of its parts (Greek *holos* whole) |
| **humanism** | philosophy emphasizing human responsibility for moral behaviour |
| **hypnotism** | practice of inducing a hypnotic state in others (Greek *hypnos* sleep) |
| **idealism** | practice of living according to ideals |

**imperialism** principle of extending control over other nations' territory (Latin *imperium* sovereignty)
**Impressionism** artistic movement emphasizing artists' impressions of nature
**individualism** belief in individual freedom and self-reliance
**liberalism** belief in tolerance of different opinions or attitudes
**magnetism** state of possessing magnetic attraction
**mannerism** excessive use of an individual artistic style
**Marxism** philosophy that political change is brought about by struggle between social classes
**masochism** derivation of pleasure from one's own pain or suffering (named after the Austrian writer Sacher-Masoch)
**materialism** excessive interest in material possessions and financial success
**monarchism** support of the institution of monarchy
**monetarism** economic theory emphasizing the control of a country's money supply
**mysticism** practice of gaining direct communication with a deity through prayer and meditation (Greek *mystes* initiate)
**narcissism** excessive admiration for oneself or one's appearance
**nationalism** advocacy of national unity or independence
**naturalism** realistic and non-idealistic representation of objects
**nihilism** rejection of moral and religious principles (Latin *nihil* nothing)
**objectivism** tendency to emphasize what is objective
**opportunism** practice of taking advantage of opportunities regardless of principles
**optimism** tendency to expect the best possible outcome (Latin *optimus* best)
**pacifism** belief that violence and war are unjustified (Latin *pax* peace, and *facere* to make)
**paganism** belief in a religion which worships many gods (Latin *paganus* peasant, civilian)
**pantheism** doctrine that equates all natural forces and matter with god (Greek *pas* all, *theos* god)
**parochialism** practice of being narrow or provincial in outlook (Latin *parochia* parish)
**paternalism** practice of benevolent but over-protective management or government (Latin *pater* father)
**patriotism** devotion to one's country (Greek *patriotes* compatriot)
**pessimism** tendency to expect the worst possible outcome (Latin *pessimus* worst)
**plagiarism** practice of stealing an idea from another's work and presenting it as one's own (Latin *plagiarius* kidnapper)
**pluralism** co-existence of several ethnic and religious groups in a society (Latin *plus* more)
**pointillism** artistic movement using small dabs of unmixed colour to suggest shapes (French *pointille* dot)
**polytheism** belief in more than one god (Greek *polys* many, *theos* god)
**pragmatism** a practical, matter-of-fact approach to dealing with problems (Greek *pragma* deed)
**professionalism** practice of showing professional competence and conduct
**racism** *or* **racialism** discrimination on the grounds of ethnic origin
**realism** tendency to present things as they really are
**regionalism** devotion to or advocacy of one's own region
**sadism** derivation of pleasure from inflicting pain on others (named after the French writer the Marquis de Sade)
**Satanism** belief in and worship of the devil
**scepticism** tendency to question widely-accepted beliefs (Greek *skeptikos* thoughtful)
**sexism** discrimination on the grounds of sex
**socialism** doctrine that a country's wealth belongs to the people as a whole

| | |
|---|---|
| **spiritualism** | practice of communicating with the spirits of the dead through a medium |
| **stoicism** | tendency to accept misfortune or suffering without complaint (Greek *Stoa Poikile* Painted Porch, where Zeno taught) |
| **surrealism** | artistic movement emphasizing use of images from the unconscious |
| **symbolism** | use of symbols to express ideas or emotions |
| **terrorism** | practice of using violence to achieve political ends |
| **Thatcherism** | political system based on privatization and monetarism advocated by Margaret Thatcher |
| **tokenism** | practice of doing something once or with minimum effort to appear to comply with a law or principle |
| **tourism** | practice of travelling to and visiting places for pleasure and relaxation |
| **vandalism** | practice of inflicting indiscriminate damage on others' property |
| **vegetarianism** | practice of not eating meat or animal products |
| **ventriloquism** | practice of making one's voice appear to come from another source (Latin *ventri* belly, *loqui* to speak) |
| **voyeurism** | practice of watching private actions of others for pleasure or sexual gratification |

## PHOBIAS

A phobia is a fear, hatred or extreme dislike of something, especially an irrational one. The term comes from the Greek word *phobos* meaning 'fear'.

| Technical term | Everyday term |
|---|---|
| acerophobia | sourness |
| achluophobia | darkness |
| acrophobia | heights |
| aerophobia | draughts, air |
| agoraphobia | open spaces |
| aichmophobia | sharp or pointed objects |
| aichurophobia | points |
| ailurophobia | cats |
| akousticophobia | sound |
| algophobia | pain |
| amakaphobia | carriages |
| amathophobia | dust |
| androphobia | men |
| anemophobia | wind or draughts |
| anginophobia | narrowness |
| anthropophobia | people or society |
| antlophobia | flood |
| apeirophobia | infinity |
| apiphobia | bees |
| aquaphobia | water |
| arachnophobia | spiders |
| arithmophobia | numbers |
| asthenophobia | weakness |
| astraphobia, astrapophobia | lightning |
| atephobia | ruin |
| aulophobia | flutes |
| auroraphobia | Northern Lights |
| autophobia | being by oneself |
| bacilliphobia | microbes |

| Technical term | Everyday term |
|---|---|
| barophobia | gravity |
| basophobia | walking |
| bathophobia | falling from a high place |
| batrachophobia | frogs, toads, newts |
| belonephobia | needles |
| bibliophobia | books |
| brontophobia | thunder |
| cancerphobia, cancerophobia | contracting or having cancer |
| canophobia | dogs |
| cheimaphobia | cold |
| chionophobia | snow |
| chrometophobia | money |
| chronophobia | duration |
| chrystallophobia | crystals |
| claustrophobia | closed spaces |
| cnidophobia | stings |
| cometophobia | comets |
| cromophobia | colour |
| cyberphobia | computers |
| cynophobia | dogs |
| demonophobia | demons |
| demophobia | crowds |
| dermatophobia | skin |
| dikephobia | injustice |
| doraphobia | fur |
| dromophobia | crossing streets |
| dysmorphophobia | personal physical deformity |
| ecophobia | one's home surroundings |

| Technical term | Everyday term |
|---|---|
| eisoptrophobia | mirrors |
| electrophobia | electricity |
| eleutherophobia | freedom |
| emetophobia | vomiting |
| entomophobia | insects |
| eosophobia | dawn |
| eremophobia | solitude |
| eretephobia | pins |
| ereuthrophobia | blushing |
| ergasiophobia, ergophobia | work |
| erotophobia | sexual involvement |
| erythrophobia | blushing |
| euphobia | good news |
| genophobia | sex |
| geumaphobia | taste |
| graphophobia | writing |
| gymnophobia | nudity |
| gynophobia | women |
| hadephobia | hell |
| haematophobia | blood |
| hamartiophobia | sin |
| haphephobia | touch |
| harpaxophobia | robbers |
| hedonophobia | pleasure |
| helminthophobia | worms |
| herpetophobia | reptiles |
| hierophobia | sacred objects |
| hippophobia | horses |
| hodophobia | travel |
| homichlophobia | fog |
| hormephobia | shock |
| hydrophobia | water |
| hypegiaphobia | responsibility |
| hypnophobia | sleep |
| ideophobia | ideas |
| kakorraphiaphobia | failure |
| katagelophobia | ridicule |
| kenophobia | empty spaces, voids |
| keraunophobia | thunder |
| kinesophobia | motion |
| kleptophobia | stealing |
| kopophobia | fatigue |
| kristallophobia | ice |
| laliophobia | stuttering |
| linonophobia | string |
| logophobia | words |
| lyssophobia | insanity |
| maniaphobia | insanity |
| mastigophobia | flogging |
| mechanophobia | machinery |
| metallophobia | metals |
| meteorophobia | meteors |
| misophobia | contamination |
| monophobia | one thing, or being alone |
| musicophobia | music |
| musophobia | mice |
| mysophobia | contamination |
| necrophobia | corpses |
| nelophobia | glass |
| neophobia | newness, novelty |
| nephophobia | clouds |
| nosophobia | disease |
| nyctophobia | night or darkness |
| ochlophobia | crowds |
| ochophobia | vehicles |
| odontophobia | teeth |
| oikophobia | home |
| olfactophobia | smell |
| ommatophobia | eyes |
| oneirophobia | dreams |
| ophidiophobia, ophiophobia | snakes |
| ophthalmophobia | being stared at |
| ornithophobia | birds |
| ouranophobia | heaven |
| panphobia, pantophobia | everything |
| parthenophobia | girls |
| pathophobia | disease |
| patroiophobia | heredity |
| peniaphobia | poverty |
| phagophobia | eating |
| phasmophobia | ghosts |
| phengophobia | daylight |
| phobophobia | fears |
| phonophobia | noise or speaking aloud |
| photophobia | light |
| pnigerophobia | smothering |
| poinephobia | punishment |
| polyphobia | many things |
| potophobia | alcoholic drink |
| pteronophobia | feathers |
| pyrophobia | fire |
| rypophobia | soiling |
| satanophobia | the Devil |
| scopophobia, scoptophobia | being looked at |
| scotophobia | darkness |
| selaphobia | flashes |
| siderophobia | stars |
| sitophobia, sitiophobia | food |
| spermaphobia, spermatophobia | germs |

| Technical term | Everyday term |
|---|---|
| stasiphobia | standing |
| stygiophobia | hell |
| symmetrophobia | symmetry |
| syphilophobia | syphilis |
| tachophobia | speed |
| taphephobia, taphophobia | being buried alive |
| technophobia | technology |
| thaasophobia | sitting |
| thalassophobia | sea |
| thanatophobia | death |

| Technical term | Everyday term |
|---|---|
| theophobia | God |
| thermophobia | heat |
| tonitrophobia | thunder |
| toxiphobia, toxicophobia | poison |
| tremophobia | trembling |
| triskaidekaphobia, triskaidecaphobia | thirteen |
| xenophobia | strangers, foreigners |
| zelophobia | jealousy |
| zoophobia | animals |

## *Food Phobias*

One of the most famous, if perhaps medically uncommon, phobias is *arachibutyrophobia* – the fear of peanut butter sticking to the roof of one's mouth. Other food phobias that may or may not have a scientific basis are *ostraconophobia*, fear of shellfish, *lachanophobia*, fear of vegetables and *ichthyophobia*, fear of fish. Fear of food itself is called *sitophobia* or *sitiophobia*.

| Everyday term | Technical term |
|---|---|
| alcoholic drink | potophobia |
| animals | zoophobia |
| bees | apiphobia |
| being buried alive | taphephobia, taphophobia |
| being by oneself | autophobia |
| being looked at | scopophobia, scoptophobia |
| being stared at | ophthalmophobia |
| birds | ornithophobia |
| blood | haematophobia |
| blushing | ereuthrophobia, erythrophobia |
| books | bibliophobia |
| carriages | amakaphobia |
| cats | ailurophobia |
| closed spaces | claustrophobia |
| clouds | nephophobia |
| cold | cheimaphobia |
| colour | cromophobia |
| comets | cometophobia |
| computers | cyberphobia |
| contamination | misophobia, mysophobia |
| contracting or having cancer | cancerphobia, cancerophobia |
| corpses | necrophobia |
| crossing streets | dromophobia |
| crowds | demophobia, ochlophobia |
| crystals | chrystallophobia |
| darkness | achluophobia, scotophobia |

| Everyday term | Technical term |
|---|---|
| dawn | eosophobia |
| daylight | phengophobia |
| death | thanatophobia |
| demons | demonophobia |
| disease | nosophobia, pathophobia |
| dogs | canophobia, cynophobia |
| draughts, air | aerophobia |
| dreams | oneirophobia |
| duration | chronophobia |
| dust | amathophobia |
| eating | phagophobia |
| electricity | electrophobia |
| empty spaces, voids | kenophobia |
| everything | panphobia, pantophobia |
| eyes | ommatophobia |
| failure | kakorraphiaphobia |
| falling from a high place | bathophobia |
| fatigue | kopophobia |
| fears | phobophobia |
| feathers | pteronophobia |
| fire | pyrophobia |
| flashes | selaphobia |
| flogging | mastigophobia |
| flood | antlophobia |
| flutes | aulophobia |
| fog | homichlophobia |
| food | sitophobia, sitiophobia |
| freedom | eleutherophobia |
| frogs, toads, newts | batrachophobia |

| Everyday term | Technical term | Everyday term | Technical term |
|---|---|---|---|
| fur | doraphobia | personal physical deformity | dysmorphophobia |
| germs | spermaphobia, spermatophobia | pins | eretephobia |
| ghosts | phasmophobia | pleasure | hedonophobia |
| girls | parthenophobia | points | aichurophobia |
| glass | nelophobia | poison | toxiphobia, toxicophobia |
| God | theophobia | poverty | peniaphobia |
| good news | euphobia | punishment | poinephobia |
| gravity | barophobia | reptiles | herpetophobia |
| heat | thermophobia | responsibility | hypegiaphobia |
| heaven | ouranophobia | ridicule | katagelophobia |
| heights | acrophobia | robbers | harpaxophobia |
| hell | stygiophobia, hadephobia | ruin | atephobia |
| heredity | patroiophobia | sacred objects | hierophobia |
| home | oikophobia | sea | thalassophobia |
| horses | hippophobia | sex | genophobia |
| ice | kristallophobia | sexual involvement | erotophobia |
| ideas | ideophobia | sharp or pointed objects | aichmophobia |
| infinity | apeirophobia | shock | hormephobia |
| injustice | dikephobia | sin | hamartiophobia |
| insanity | lyssophobia, maniaphobia | sitting | thaasophobia |
| insects | entomophobia | skin | dermatophobia |
| jealousy | zelophobia | sleep | hypnophobia |
| light | photophobia | smell | olfactophobia |
| lightning | astraphobia, astrapophobia | smothering | pnigerophobia |
| machinery | mechanophobia | snakes | ophidiophobia, ophiophobia |
| many things | polyphobia | snow | chionophobia |
| men | androphobia | soiling | rypophobia |
| metals | metallophobia | solitude | eremophobia |
| meteors | meteorophobia | sound | akousticophobia |
| mice | musophobia | sourness | acerophobia |
| microbes | bacilliphobia | speed | tachophobia |
| mirrors | eisoptrophobia | spiders | arachnophobia |
| money | chrometophobia | standing | stasiphobia |
| motion | kinesophobia | stars | siderophobia |
| music | musicophobia | stealing | kleptophobia |
| narrowness | anginophobia | stings | cnidophobia |
| needles | belonephobia | strangers, foreigners | xenophobia |
| newness, novelty | neophobia | string | linonophobia |
| night or darkness | nyctophobia | stuttering | laliophobia |
| noise or speaking aloud | phonophobia | symmetry | symmetrophobia |
| Northern Lights | auroraphobia | syphilis | syphilophobia |
| nudity | gymnophobia | taste | geumaphobia |
| numbers | arithmophobia | technology | technophobia |
| one thing, or being alone | monophobia | teeth | odontophobia |
| one's home surroundings | ecophobia | the Devil | satanophobia |
| open spaces | agoraphobia | thirteen | triskaidekaphobia, triskaidecaphobia |
| pain | algophobia | thunder | brontophobia, keraunophobia, tonitrophobia |
| people or society | anthropophobia | | |

| Everyday term | Technical term | Everyday term | Technical term |
|---|---|---|---|
| touch | haphephobia | weakness | asthenophobia |
| travel | hodophobia | wind or draughts | anemophobia |
| trembling | tremophobia | women | gynophobia |
| vehicles | ochophobia | words | logophobia |
| vomiting | emetophobia | work | ergasiophobia, ergophobia |
| walking | basophobia | worms | helminthophobia |
| water | aquaphobia, hydrophobia | writing | graphophobia |

## MANIAS

A mania is an abnormal and obsessive desire or inclination, or an extreme enthusiasm, for something. The term comes from the Greek word *mania* meaning 'madness'.

| Technical term | Everyday term | Technical term | Everyday term |
|---|---|---|---|
| ablutomania | personal cleanliness | methomania | alcohol |
| acronymania | forming acronyms | metromania | writing verse |
| ailuromania | cats | monomania | single thought, idea or activity |
| anthomania | flowers | morphinomania | morphine |
| arithmomania | numbers | mythomania | lying or exaggerating |
| balletomania | ballet | narcomania | drugs |
| bibliomania | books | necromania | dead bodies |
| cleptomania | stealing | nostomania | returning to familiar places |
| cynomania | dogs | nymphomania | sexual desire |
| demomania | crowds | oenomania | alcohol |
| demonomania | being possessed by devils | opsomania | special kind of food |
| dipsomania | alcohol | orchidomania | orchids |
| egomania | oneself | potichomania | imitating Oriental porcelain |
| eleutheromania | freedom | pteridomania | ferns |
| ergomania | work | pyromania | fire-raising |
| erotomania | sexual passion | technomania | technology |
| etheromania | taking ether | thanatomania | death |
| flagellomania | beating and flogging | theatromania | play-going |
| graphomania | writing | theomania | God, religion |
| hedonomania | pleasure | tomomania | surgery |
| hippomania | horses | toxicomania | poison |
| hydromania | water | trichotillomania | pulling out tufts of one's own hair |
| infomania | gathering information | tulipomania | tulip-growing |
| kleptomania | stealing | xenomania | foreign things |
| logomania | talking | | |
| megalomania | power | | |
| melomania | music | | |

| Everyday term | Technical term | Everyday term | Technical term |
|---|---|---|---|
| alcohol | dipsomania, methomania, oenomania | books | bibliomania |
| ballet | balletomania | cats | ailuromania |
| beating and flogging | flagellomania | crowds | demomania |
| being possessed by devils | demonomania | dead bodies | necromania |
| | | death | thanatomania |
| | | dogs | cynomania |
| | | drugs | narcomania |

| Everyday term | Technical term | Everyday term | Technical term |
|---|---|---|---|
| ferns | pteridomania | poison | toxicomania |
| fire-raising | pyromania | power | megalomania |
| flowers | anthomania | pulling out tufts of one's own hair | trichotillomania |
| foreign things | xenomania | religion | theomania |
| forming acronyms | acronymania | returning to familiar places | nostomania |
| freedom | eleutheromania | sexual desire | nymphomania |
| gathering information | infomania | sexual passion | erotomania |
| God | theomania | single thought, idea or activity | monomania |
| horses | hippomania | special kind of food | opsomania |
| imitating Oriental porcelain | potichomania | stealing | kleptomania, cleptomania |
| lying or exaggerating | mythomania | surgery | tomomania |
| morphine | morphinomania | taking ether | etheromania |
| music | melomania | talking | logomania |
| numbers | arithmomania | technology | technomania |
| oneself | egomania | tulip-growing | tulipomania |
| orchids | orchidomania | water | hydromania |
| personal cleanliness | ablutomania | work | ergomania |
| play-going | theatromania | writing | graphomania |
| pleasure | hedonomania | writing verse | metromania |

## COLLECTIVE NAMES FOR ANIMALS

| Collective name | Animal | Collective name | Animal |
|---|---|---|---|
| ambush | tigers | colony | ants, bees, penguins, rats |
| army | caterpillars, frogs | company | parrots |
| bale | turtles | congregation | plovers |
| band | gorillas | convocation | eagles |
| bask | crocodiles | covey | partridges, quail |
| bed | clams, oysters | crash | rhinoceros |
| bevy | larks, pheasants, quail, swans | cry | hounds |
| bloat | hippopotami | descent | woodpeckers |
| bouquet | pheasants | dole | doves, turtles |
| brace | ducks | down | hares |
| brood | chickens, hens | draught | fish |
| building | rooks | dray | squirrels |
| bury | rabbits | drift | hogs, swine |
| busyness | ferrets, flies | drove | cattle, horses, oxen, sheep |
| cackle | hyenas | erst | bees |
| cast | hawks | exaltation | larks |
| cete | badgers | fall | woodcocks |
| charm | finches, goldfinches | family | otters |
| chirm | goldfinches | flight | birds |
| cloud | gnats | flock | birds, ducks, geese, sheep |
| clowder | cats | gaggle | geese |
| clutch | chickens | gam | whales |

# COLLECTIVE NAMES FOR ANIMALS

| Collective name | Animal | Collective name | Animal |
|---|---|---|---|
| gang | buffalo, elk | rafter | turkeys |
| grist | bees | romp | otters |
| herd | buffalo, cattle, deer, elephants, goats, horses, kangaroos, oxen, seals, whales | rookery | rooks, seals |
| | | rout | wolves |
| | | route | wolves |
| | | safe | ducks |
| hive | bees | school | dolphins, fish, porpoises, whales |
| horde | gnats | | |
| host | sparrows | scurry | squirrels |
| hover | trout | sedge | cranes |
| husk | hares | shiver | sharks |
| intrusion | cockroaches | shoal | fish |
| kennel | dogs | shrewdness | apes |
| kindle | kittens | siege | cranes, herons |
| knot | toads | skein | geese |
| labour | moles | skulk | foxes |
| leap | leopards | sleuth | bears |
| leash | foxes | sloth | bears |
| litter | kittens, pigs | smack | jellyfish |
| mob | kangaroos | sounder | swine |
| murder | crows | span | mules |
| murmuration | starlings | spring | teal |
| muster | peacocks, penguins | stable | horses |
| mustering | storks | stand | flamingos |
| mute | hares, hounds | stare | owls |
| nest | ants, bees, pheasants, vipers | streak | tigers |
| | | string | horses, ponies |
| nid | pheasants | swarm | ants, bees, flies, locusts |
| nide | pheasants | team | ducks, horses |
| nye | pheasants | tiding | magpies |
| obstinacy | buffalo | tittering | magpies |
| ostentation | peacocks | tower | giraffes |
| pace | asses | tribe | goats |
| pack | dogs, grouse, hounds, wolves | trip | goats, sheep |
| | | troop | baboons, kangaroos, monkeys |
| paddling | ducks | | |
| pandemonium | parrots | turmoil | porpoises |
| parade | elephants | turn | turtles |
| parcel | penguins | unkindness | ravens |
| parliament | owls, rooks | volery | birds |
| plague | locusts | watch | nightingales |
| pod | seals, whales | wedge | swans |
| pounce | cats | wing | plovers |
| prickle | porcupines | yoke | oxen |
| pride | lions | zeal | zebras |

## Collective Imagination

Some people enjoy inventing new and creative collective nouns for professions or other groups of people. Suggestions have included an *audit* of bookkeepers, a *complex* of psychologists, an *eloquence* of lawyers, a *flush* of plumbers, a *giggle* of girls, an *intrigue* of politicians, a *ponder* of philosophers, a *superfluity* of nuns and a *tedium* of golfers.

## ANIMAL ADJECTIVES

| Animal | Adjective | Animal | Adjective | Animal | Adjective |
|---|---|---|---|---|---|
| ape | simian | ferret | viverrine | peacock | pavonine |
| ass | asinine | finch | fringilline | pig | porcine, suilline |
| badger | musteline | fish | piscine, ichthyic, chthyoid | rabbit | oryctolagine |
| bear | ursine | fowl | gallinaceous | rattlesnake | crotaline |
| bee | apian | fox | vulpine | red deer | elaphine |
| bird | avian, avine, volucrine, ornithoid | goat | caprine, hircine | seal | phocine, otarine |
| buffalo | bubaline | goose | anserine | sheep | ovine |
| bull | taurine | gull | larine | shrew | soricine |
| butterfly | papilionaceous, rhopalocerous | hare | leporine | slug | limacine |
| calf | vituline | hawk | accipitrine | snake | anguine, colubrine, ophidian, serpentine |
| camel | cameline | horse | equine, caballine, hippic | squirrel | sciurine |
| cat | feline | kite | milvine | swallow | hirundine |
| cattle | bovine | lemur | lemurine | thrush | turdine |
| civet | viverrine | leopard | pardine | tiger | tigrine |
| crow | corvine | lion | leonine | tortoise | chelonian |
| deer | cervine | lizard | lacertilian, saurian | turtle | chelonian |
| dog | canine | mite | acarine | viper | viperine |
| donkey | asinine | monkey | simian | vulture | vulturine |
| dove | columbine | mouse | murine | wasp | vespine |
| eagle | aquiline | otter | musteline | weasel | musteline |
| elephant | elephantine | ox | bovine | wolf | lupine |
| falcon | falconine | parrot | psittacine | zebra | sebrine |

## EATING ADJECTIVES

| Adjective | Feeds on ... | Adjective | Feeds on ... |
|---|---|---|---|
| anthropophagous | humans (cannibalism) | ichthyophagous | fish |
| apivorous | bees | insectivorous | insects |
| autophagous | itself | lignivorous | wood |
| baccivorous | berries | meliphagous | honey |
| carnivorous | flesh | mellivorous | honey |
| carpophagous | fruit | merdivorous | dung |
| coprophagous | dung | myristicivorous | nutmegs |
| creophagous | flesh | myrmecophagous | ants |
| entomophagous | insects | necrophagous | carrion |
| fructivorous | fruit | nucivorous | nuts |
| frugivorous | fruits or seeds | omnivorous | both animal and vegetable food |
| fucivorous | seaweed | omophagous | raw flesh |
| geophagous | soil | ophiophagous | snakes |
| graminivorous | grass, cereals, etc | ossivorous | bones |
| granivorous | seeds, grain | ostreophagous | oysters |
| haematophagous | blood | pantophagous | both animal and vegetable food |
| herbivorous | grass or herbage | phyllophagous | leaves |
| hippophagous | horses | | |
| hylophagous | wood | | |

| Adjective | Feeds on ... | Adjective | Feeds on ... |
|---|---|---|---|
| phytophagous | plants | sarcophagous | flesh |
| piscivorous | fish | sarcosaprophagous | decaying flesh |
| radicivorous | roots | scatophagous | dung |
| ranivorous | frogs | theophagous | gods |
| rhizophagous | roots | toxicophagous | poison |
| sanguivorous, sanguinivorous | blood | vermivorous | worms |
| | | xylophagous | wood |
| saprophagous | decaying organic matter | zoophagous | animals |

## *Wonderful Words*

Often words like *myristicivorous*, feeding on nutmegs, become people's favourite words simply because we don't expect such a word to exist. Other delightful oddities include *callipygous*, having beautiful buttocks, *genethliac*, relating to a birthday, *leiotrichy*, straight-hairedness, *mallemaroking*, the carousing of seamen in icebound ships, *paneity*, the state of being bread and *pogonotomy*, a wonderful word for shaving.

## DIVINATION TECHNIQUES

**Divination is seeking to know the future or hidden things by supernatural means, instinctive prevision and prediction.**

| Term | Divination by ... |
|---|---|
| aeromancy | atmospheric phenomena |
| axinomancy | the motions of an axe poised upon a stake, or of an agate placed upon a red-hot axe |
| belomancy | means of arrows |
| bibliomancy | opening the bible or other book at random |
| botanomancy | means of plants, especially the leaves of sage and fig |
| capnomancy | smoke |
| cartomancy | playing cards |
| ceromancy | dropping melted wax in water |
| chiromancy | reading the hand |
| cleromancy | lot |
| coscinomancy | a sieve and pair of shears |
| crithomancy | strewing meal over sacrificial animals |
| crystallomancy | transparent bodies |
| dactyliomancy | means of a ring |
| gastromancy | sounds from the belly, or by large-bellied glasses |
| geomancy | shapes formed, eg when earth is thrown down onto a surface |
| gyromancy | walking in a circle and falling from giddiness |
| hepatoscopy | inspection of the livers of animals |
| hieromancy | observing the objects offered in sacrifice |
| hydromancy | water |
| lampadomancy | flame |
| lithomancy | stones |
| myomancy | observing the way in which mice move when released from a cage |
| oenomancy | from the appearance of wine poured out in libations |

| Term | Divination by ... |
| --- | --- |
| omoplatoscopy, scapulomancy | observing the cracks appearing in a burning shoulder blade |
| omphalomancy | the knots in the umbilical cord, to tell the number of future children |
| oneiromancy | dreams |
| onychomancy | the fingernails |
| ornithomancy | means of birds, by observing their flight, etc |
| pyromancy | fire |
| rhabdomancy | rod, especially divining for water or ore |
| sortes | chance opening of the bible, homer, virgil, etc |
| sortilege | drawing lots |
| spodomancy | means of ashes |
| taghairm | lying in a bullock's hide behind a waterfall |
| tephromancy | ashes, especially those left after a sacrifice |
| theomancy | means of oracles, or of persons directly inspired immediately by some divinity |
| tripudium | the hopping of birds feeding, or the dropping of scraps from their bills |
| zoomancy | observation of animals |

## COLLECTORS AND ENTHUSIASTS

| Devotee | Item or activity |
| --- | --- |
| ailurophile, ailourophile | cats |
| antiquary | antiques |
| arachnologist | spiders/arachnids |
| arctophile | teddy bears |
| audiophile | broadcast sound |
| balletomane | ballet |
| bibliophile | books |
| campanologist | bell-ringing |
| canophilist, cynophilist | dogs |
| cartophile, cartophilist | cigarette cards |
| chirographist | handwriting |
| chrysophilite | gold |
| cinephile | cinema |
| conservationist | countryside |
| Dantophilist | Dante |
| deltiologist | postcards |
| discophile | gramophone records |
| entomologist | insects |
| environmentalist | the environment |
| ephemerist | ephemera |
| ex-librist | bookplates |
| gastronome | good living |
| gourmet | good food |
| hippophile | horses |
| incunabulist | early printed books |
| lepidopterist | butterflies |
| logophile | words |
| monarchist | the monarchy |
| neophile | novelty and new things |
| notaphilist | banknotes, cheques |
| numismatist | coins/medals |

### Curious Collections

People collect almost anything. Guinness World Records® includes people with the largest collections of airsickness bags, autographed drum sticks, beer bottles, belly button fluff, chamber pots, coloured vinyl records, 'do not disturb' signs, four-leaf clovers, garden gnomes, golf balls, hair from historical figures, handcuffs, nail clippers, piggy banks, spoon rests and weighing scales.

| Devotee | Item or activity |
|---|---|
| oenophile, oenophilist | wine |
| ophiophilist | snakes |
| ornithologist | birds |
| paroemiographer | proverbs |
| philatelist, timbrophilist | stamps |
| phillumenist | matches/matchboxes |
| philomath | learning |
| pteridophilist | ferns |
| scripophile, scripophilist | bond and share certificates |
| stegophilist | climbing buildings for sport |
| stigmatophilist | tattooing or body piercing |
| technophile | technology |
| tegestollogist | beer mats |
| toxophilite | archery |
| xenophile | foreigners |
| zoophile | animals |

## FAMOUS LAST WORDS

### Prince Albert (1819–61)

I have had wealth, rank and power, but, if these were all I had, how wretched I should be.
**Attributed.**

### Anonymous

My mother thinks Vietnam is somewhere near Panama.
**c.1968, A US soldier fatally wounded during the Vietnam War, quoted by Australian film-maker John Pilger in his 1978 film *Do you remember Vietnam?***

### Augustus (63BC–AD14)

The play is over.
**Attributed.**

### Béla Bartók (1881–1945)

The trouble is that I have to go with so much still to say.
**Quoted in David Pickering *Brewer's Twentieth Century Music* (1994).**

### Ludwig van Beethoven (1770–1827)

I shall hear in heaven.
**Attributed. Quoted in Ian Crofton and Donald Fraser *A Dictionary of Musical Quotations* (1985).**

### Julius Caesar (100 or 102–44BC)

*Et tu, Brute?*
You too, Brutus?
**Attributed, when struck by his murderers, Cassius and Brutus.**

### Sir Winston Churchill (1874–1965)

I am so bored with it all.
**Attributed.**

### Dame Gladys Cooper (1888–1971)

If this is what virus pneumonia does to one, I really don't think I shall bother to have it again.

### Bing Crosby (1904–77)

That was a great game of golf.
**As he finished play at the 18th hole before suffering a heart attack.**

### Emily Dickinson (1830–86)

Let us go in; the fog is rising.
**Attributed.**

### Johann Wolfgang von Goethe (1749–1832)

More light!

### Henrik Ibsen (1828–1906)

On the contrary!
**Refuting a nurse's suggestion that he was feeling better.**

### Lord Horatio Nelson (1758–1805)

Kiss me, Hardy.
**Attributed, as he lay dying in the cockpit of the Victory during the Battle of Trafalgar.**

### Lawrence Oates (1880–1912)

I am just going outside and may be some time.

### William Pitt (1759–1806)

I think that I could eat one of Bellamy's veal pies.
**Attributed.**

### William Saroyan (1908–81)

Now what?

### Tom Simpson (1938–67)

Put me back on my bike.
**He died from heart failure during the Tour de France.**

### Lytton Strachey (1880–1932)

If this is dying, then I don't think much of it.
**Attributed.**

### Dylan Thomas (1914–53)

I've had 18 straight whiskies. I think that's the record.
**Attributed, before lapsing into his final coma.**

### Oscar Wilde (1854–1900)

Either that wallpaper goes or I do.
**Attributed, as he lay dying in a Paris hotel bedroom.**

## ARABIC ALPHABET

| Letter | Name | Usual transliteration |
|---|---|---|
| ا | *'alif* | ' |
| ب | *ba* | *b* |
| ت | *ta* | *t* |
| ث | *tha* | *th* |
| ج | *jim* | *j* |
| ح | *ha* | *h* |
| خ | *kha* | *kh* |
| د | *dal* | *d* |
| ذ | *dhal* | *dh* |
| ر | *ra* | *r* |
| ز | *za* | *a* |
| س | *sin* | *s* |
| ش | *shin* | *sh* |
| ص | *sad* | *s* |

| Letter | Name | Usual transliteration |
|---|---|---|
| ض | *dad* | *d* |
| ط | *ta* | *t* |
| ظ | *za* | *z* |
| ع | *'ain* | ' |
| غ | *ghain* | *gh* |
| ف | *fa* | *f* |
| ق | *qaf* | *q* |
| ك | *kaf* | *k* |
| ل | *lam* | *l* |
| م | *mim* | *m* |
| ن | *nun* | *n* |
| ه | *ha* | *h* |
| و | *waw* | *w* |
| ي | *ya* | *y* |

## CYRILLIC ALPHABET

| Letter | Usual transliteration |
|---|---|
| А а | a |
| Б б | *b* |
| В в | *v* |
| Г г | g |
| Д д | *d* |
| Е е | e (*ye*) |
| Ё ё | e (*yŏ*) |
| Ж ж | *zh* |
| З з | z |
| И и | *i* (*ē*) |
| Й й | (consonantal *y* sound; only used as the second letter of a diphthong) |
| К к | *k* |
| Л л | *l* |
| М м | *m* |
| Н н | *n* |
| О о | *o* |
| П п | *p* |
| Р р | *r* |

| Letter | Usual transliteration |
|---|---|
| С с | *s* |
| Т т | *t* |
| У у | *u* |
| Ф ф | *f* |
| Х х | *kh* |
| Ц ц | *ts* |
| Ч ч | *ch* |
| Ш ш | *sh* |
| Щ щ | *shch* (often pronounced rather as *sh* followed by consonantal *y*) |
| Ъ ъ | (hard sign; used to separate in pronunciation a following palatalized vowel from a preceding consonant either palatalized or unpalatalized) |
| Ы ы | *i* (a sound similar to *i* ) |
| Ь ь | (soft sign; used after a consonant to indicate palatalization, a sound like consonantal y) |
| Э э | e (*e*) |
| Ю ю | *u* (*yoo*) |
| Я я | *ya* (*yä*) |

## GREEK ALPHABET

| Letter | Name | Usual transliteration |
|---|---|---|
| Α α | *alpha* | *a* |
| Β β | *bēta* | *b* |
| Γ γ | *gamma* | *g* |
| Δ δ | *delta* | *d* |
| Ε ε | *epsīlon* | *e* |
| Ζ ζ | *zēta* | *z* |
| Η η | *ēta* | *ē* |
| Θ θ | *thēta* | *th* |
| Ι ι | *iōta* | *i* |
| Κ κ | *kappa* | *k* |
| Λ λ | *lambda* | *l* |
| Μ μ | *mū* | *m* |
| Ν ν | *nū* | *n* |
| Ξ ξ | *xī* | *x* |
| Ο ο | *omicron* | *o* |
| Π π | *pī* | *p* |
| Ρ ρ | *rhō* | *r* |
| Σ σ ς | *sigma* | *s* |
| Τ τ | *tau* | *t* |
| Υ υ | *upsīlon* | *u* or *y* |
| Φ φ | *phī* | *ph* |
| Χ χ | *chī* | *kh* or *ch* |
| Ψ ψ | *psī* | *ps* |
| Ω ω | *ōmega* | *ō* |

## HEBREW ALPHABET

| Letter | Name | Usual transliteration |
|---|---|---|
| א | *aleph* | ’ |
| ב | *beth* | *b* |
| ג | *gimel* | *g* |
| ד | *daleth* | *d* |
| ה | *heh* | *h* |
| ו | *vav* | *w* |
| ז | *zayin* | *z* |
| ח | *cheth* | *h* |
| ט | *teth* | *t* |
| י | *yod* | *y, j* |
| כ ך | *kaph* | *k* |
| ל | *lamed* | *l* |
| נ ן | *nun* | *n* |
| ס | *samekh* | *s* |
| ע | *ayin* | ‘ |
| פ ף | *peh* | *p, f* |
| צ ץ | *sadhe* | *s* |
| ק | *koph* | *q* |
| ר | *resh* | *r* |
| ש | *sin* | *sh, s* |
| ת | *tav* | *t* |

### *St Cyril's Alphabet*

The Cyrillic alphabet is used for Russian, Ukrainian, Serbian and Bulgarian. It is so-called because it is traditionally attributed to St Cyril (827–69), a Greek Christian missionary known as the Apostle of the Slavs, who made Slav translations of the Scriptures and whose feast day is still a national holiday in some Eastern European countries. Based on the Greek alphabet, the Cyrillic includes extra symbols to represent Slavic sounds not found in Greek.

## RUNIC ALPHABET

The runic alphabet, known as *futhark*, was made up of 24 basic symbols, although there was considerable regional variation in the overall number of symbols and symbol shapes used. Around 4 000 runic inscriptions and a few manuscripts survive, principally made by the early Scandinavians and Anglo-Saxons.

## *Pictography*

A *pictograph* is a picture used as a symbol for a word or phrase. Pictographs do not relate to the sounds of language, as in most modern writing systems, but represent an abstract idea related to a concrete object, and then the name for that object. In China pictographs developed into a complex system where the written symbol represents a complete word, or part of a word, meaning that in writing modern Chinese a knowledge of 2 000 characters is required, and in Japanese, where the writing system developed from the Chinese one, 1 850 characters are considered essential for everyday use. In contrast, most sound-based alphabets can manage with 30 or fewer symbols.

## PHONETIC ALPHABET

The phonetic alphabet, also known as the NATO alphabet, is a system used in international radio communication in which letters of the alphabet are identified by means of code words.

| | | | | | | | | | | | |
|---|---|---|---|---|---|---|---|---|---|---|---|
| **A** | Alpha | **F** | Foxtrot | **K** | Kilo | **P** | Papa | **U** | Uniform | **Z** | Zulu |
| **B** | Bravo | **G** | Golf | **L** | Lima | **Q** | Quebec | **V** | Victor | | |
| **C** | Charlie | **H** | Hotel | **M** | Mike | **R** | Romeo | **W** | Whiskey | | |
| **D** | Delta | **I** | India | **N** | November | **S** | Sierra | **X** | X-ray | | |
| **E** | Echo | **J** | Juliet | **O** | Oscar | **T** | Tango | **Y** | Yankee | | |

## BRAILLE

Braille is a system of printing for the blind, in which printed characters are represented by raised dots which can be read by touch. Each character is formed by a different combination taken from a basic six-dot matrix. It was invented in 1829 by the Frenchman Louis Braille (1809–52), who was blind from the age of three.

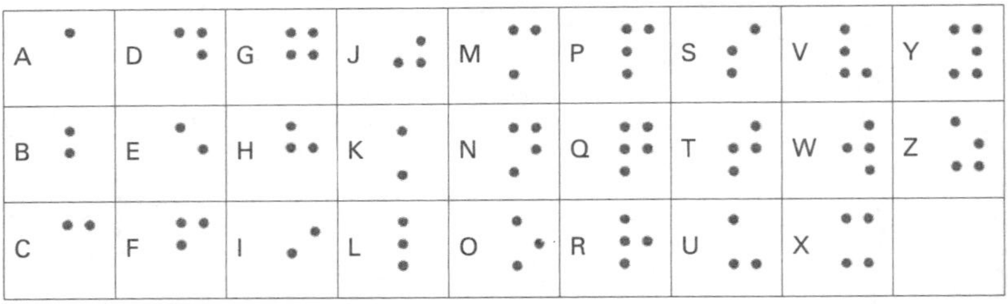

## MORSE CODE

Morse is a method of signalling by a code in which each letter is represented by a combination of dashes and dots or long and short light flashes, sound signals, etc. In the spoken form of Morse code, the word *dah* represents the dash and the word *dit* represents the dot. It was invented by Samuel F B Morse (1791–1872), a US inventor. Morse created one of the first telegraph lines between Washington and Baltimore as an experiment, and developed 'Morse code' (originally called the 'Morse alphabet') for use with it.

| | | | | | | | | | |
|---|---|---|---|---|---|---|---|---|---|
| A | •— | G | ——• | M | —— | S | ••• | Y | —•—— |
| B | —••• | H | •••• | N | —• | T | — | Z | ——•• |
| C | —•• | I | •• | O | ——— | U | ••— | | |
| D | —•• | J | •——— | P | •——• | V | •••— | | |
| E | • | K | —•— | Q | ——•— | W | •—— | | |
| F | ••—• | L | •—•• | R | •—• | X | —••— | | |

### SOS

SOS is an appeal for help or rescue, especially at sea. It is popularly believed to stand for 'Save Our Ship' or even 'Save Our Souls', but the truth is much simpler: it doesn't stand for anything. In fact, it was chosen for ease and clarity of transmission by Morse code (· · · – – – – – · · ·). The signal was adopted internationally in 1908; since 1999 the International Maritime Organization's new Global Maritime Distress and Safety System (GMDSS) for distress calls has led to SOS becoming almost obsolete, on larger ships at least.

## SEMAPHORE

Semaphore was widely used in visual telegraphy, especially at sea, before the advent of electricity. Old-style railway signals are a simple form of semaphore, with a single arm having two positions to indicate 'stop' and 'go'.

## SIGN LANGUAGE: FINGERSPELLING

Sign language is a means of communication using finger and hand movements, in which signs represent whole words or phrases. Fingerspelling uses the movements to represent letters of the alphabet, enabling words to be spelled letter by letter.

**British**

### *Silent Talking*

*Dactylology* is the art of talking with the fingers using sign language. The word comes from an ancient Greek word, *daktylos*, which means 'finger'.

**US**

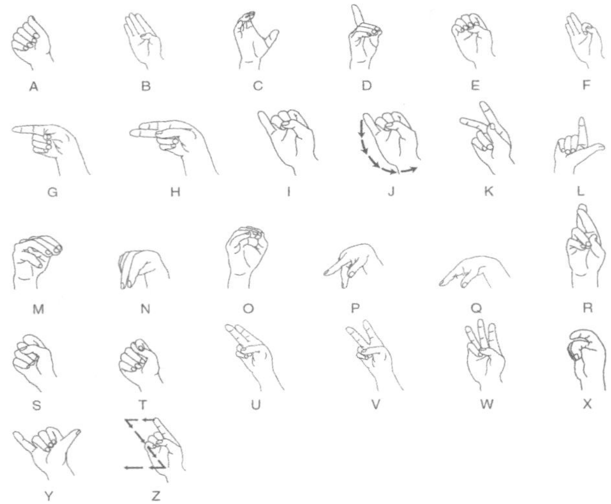

## KEYBOARD LAYOUT

The standard arrangement of keys on an English-language computer keyboard is known as *qwerty*, from the letters at the top left-hand side of the keyboard.

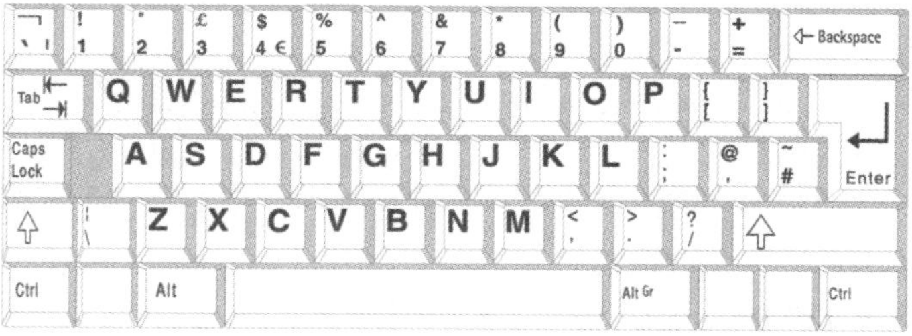


### *Quirky Qwerty*

It is widely believed that the arrangement of the letters on the qwerty keyboard was designed to slow typists down. But although it is true that the layout was designed to prevent jamming on the early typewriters, it wasn't achieved by slowing the fingers down. Instead the keys for common letter patterns, such as *sh*, are arranged so as to be far enough apart to prevent the typebars clashing when the keys were hit in rapid succession. An interesting side effect of the qwerty layout is that all the letters for the word *typewriter* are found on the keyboard's top row.

## DEWEY DECIMAL CLASSIFICATION

Dewey decimal classification is a system of library classification, based on the division of books into numbered classes, with further subdivision shown by numbers following a decimal point. The system was invented by Melvil Dewey (1851–1931), a US librarian, who designed the system for the Amherst College Library in 1876.

| | | | |
|---|---|---|---|
| 000 | Generalities | 500 | Natural sciences and mathematics |
| 100 | Philosophy and psychology | 600 | Technology (applied sciences) |
| 200 | Religion | 700 | The arts |
| 300 | Social sciences | 800 | Literature and rhetoric |
| 400 | Language | 900 | Geography and history |

### *Dewey Worldwide*

The Dewey system is used in 135 countries. It has been modified and updated many times, has had 22 major editions published and is capable of being infinitely expanded to allow new subject areas to be included. Current topics of concern to librarians using the Dewey system include where to classify books about Quidditch, the sport played in the Harry Potter novels by J K Rowling (under 823.914, apparently).

# INTERNET SUFFIXES

## General suffixes

| | |
|---|---|
| .ac.uk | UK academic institution |
| .aero | aviation industry |
| .biz | business |
| .com | commercial |
| .comp | newsgroup about computers |
| .coop | business co-operative |
| .co.uk | UK commercial |
| .edu | US educational institution |
| .gov | US government |
| .info | general information |
| .int | international organization |
| .mil | US military |
| .museum | museum |
| .name | individual |
| .net | major service provider |
| .org | non-profit organization |
| .pro | professional |
| .sci | newsgroup about science |
| .soc | newsgroup about society |

## Geographical suffixes

For suffixes listed by country see the individual entries in the **Countries A–Z** section of **Human Geography**.

| | |
|---|---|
| .ac | Ascension Island |
| .ad | Andorra |
| .ae | United Arab Emirates |
| .af | Afghanistan |
| .ag | Antigua and Barbuda |
| .ai | Anguilla |
| .al | Albania |
| .am | Armenia |
| .an | Netherlands Antilles |
| .ao | Angola |
| .aq | Antarctica |
| .ar | Argentina |
| .as | American Samoa |
| .at | Austria |
| .au | Australia |
| .aw | Aruba |
| .az | Azerbaijan |
| .ba | Bosnia and Herzegovina |
| .bb | Barbados |
| .bd | Bangladesh |
| .be | Belgium |
| .bf | Burkina Faso |
| .bg | Bulgaria |
| .bh | Bahrain |
| .bi | Burundi |
| .bj | Benin |
| .bm | Bermuda |
| .bn | Brunei Darussalam |
| .bo | Bolivia |
| .br | Brazil |
| .bs | The Bahamas |
| .bt | Bhutan |
| .bv | Bouvet Island |
| .bw | Botswana |
| .by | Belarus |
| .bz | Belize |
| .ca | Canada |
| .cc | Cocos (Keeling) Islands |
| .cd | Congo, Democratic Republic of |
| .cf | Central African Republic |
| .cg | Congo, Republic of |
| .ch | Switzerland |
| .ci | Côte d'Ivoire |
| .ck | Cook Islands |
| .cl | Chile |
| .cm | Cameroon |
| .cn | China |
| .co | Colombia |
| .cr | Costa Rica |
| .cu | Cuba |
| .cv | Cape Verde |
| .cx | Christmas Island |
| .cy | Cyprus |
| .cz | Czech Republic |
| .de | Germany |
| .dj | Djibouti |
| .dk | Denmark |
| .dm | Dominica |
| .do | Dominican Republic |
| .dz | Algeria |
| .ec | Ecuador |
| .ee | Estonia |
| .eg | Egypt |
| .eh | Western Sahara |
| .er | Eritrea |
| .es | Spain |
| .et | Ethiopia |
| .eu | European Union (*proposed*) |
| .fi | Finland |
| .fj | Fiji |
| .fk | Falkland Islands |
| .fm | Micronesia, Federated States of |
| .fo | Faroe Islands |
| .fr | France |
| .ga | Gabon |
| .gd | Grenada |
| .ge | Georgia |
| .gf | French Guiana |
| .gg | Guernsey |
| .gh | Ghana |
| .gi | Gibraltar |
| .gl | Greenland |
| .gm | The Gambia |
| .gn | Guinea |
| .gp | Guadeloupe |
| .gq | Equatorial Guinea |
| .gr | Greece |
| .gs | Georgia and the South Sandwich Islands |
| .gt | Guatemala |
| .gu | Guam |
| .gw | Guinea-Bissau |
| .gy | Guyana |
| .hk | Hong Kong |
| .hm | Heard and McDonald Islands |
| .hn | Honduras |
| .hr | Croatia |
| .ht | Haiti |
| .hu | Hungary |
| .id | Indonesia |
| .ie | Ireland |
| .il | Israel |
| .im | Isle of Man |
| .in | India |
| .io | British Indian Ocean Territory |
| .iq | Iraq |
| .ir | Iran |
| .is | Iceland |
| .it | Italy |
| .je | Jersey |
| .jm | Jamaica |
| .jo | Jordan |
| .jp | Japan |
| .ke | Kenya |
| .kg | Kyrgyzstan |
| .kh | Cambodia |
| .ki | Kiribati |

| | |
|---|---|
| .km | Comoros |
| .kn | St Kitts and Nevis |
| .kp | Korea, Democratic People's Republic |
| .kr | Korea, Republic of |
| .kw | Kuwait |
| .ky | Cayman Islands |
| .kz | Kazakhstan |
| .la | Laos |
| .lb | Lebanon |
| .lc | St Lucia |
| .li | Liechtenstein |
| .lk | Sri Lanka |
| .lr | Liberia |
| .ls | Lesotho |
| .lt | Lithuania |
| .lu | Luxembourg |
| .lv | Latvia |
| .ly | Libya |
| .ma | Morocco |
| .mc | Monaco |
| .md | Moldova |
| .mg | Madagascar |
| .mh | Marshall Islands |
| .mk | Macedonia |
| .ml | Mali |
| .mm | Myanmar (Burma) |
| .mn | Mongolia |
| .mo | Macau |
| .mp | Northern Mariana Islands |
| .mq | Martinique |
| .mr | Mauritania |
| .ms | Montserrat |
| .mt | Malta |
| .mu | Mauritius |
| .mv | Maldives |
| .mw | Malawi |
| .mx | Mexico |
| .my | Malaysia |
| .mz | Mozambique |
| .na | Namibia |
| .nc | New Caledonia |
| .ne | Niger |
| .nf | Norfolk Island |
| .ng | Nigeria |
| .ni | Nicaragua |
| .nl | The Netherlands |
| .no | Norway |
| .np | Nepal |
| .nr | Nauru |
| .nu | Niue |
| .nz | New Zealand |
| .om | Oman |
| .pa | Panama |
| .pe | Peru |
| .pf | French Polynesia |
| .pg | Papua New Guinea |
| .ph | Philippines |
| .pk | Pakistan |
| .pl | Poland |
| .pm | St Pierre and Miquelon |
| .pn | Pitcairn Islands |
| .pr | Puerto Rico |
| .ps | Palestinian Territories |
| .pt | Portugal |
| .pw | Palau |
| .py | Paraguay |
| .qa | Qatar |
| .re | Réunion |
| .ro | Romania |
| .ru | Russia |
| .rw | Rwanda |
| .sa | Saudi Arabia |
| .sb | Solomon Islands |
| .sc | Seychelles |
| .sd | The Sudan |
| .se | Sweden |
| .sg | Singapore |
| .sh | St Helena |
| .si | Slovenia |
| .sj | Svalbard and Jan Meyen Islands |
| .sk | Slovakia |
| .sl | Sierra Leone |
| .sm | San Marino |
| .sn | Senegal |
| .so | Somalia |
| .sr | Suriname |
| .st | São Tomé and Príncipe |
| .sv | El Salvador |
| .sy | Syria |
| .sz | Swaziland |
| .tc | Turks and Caicos Islands |
| .td | Chad |
| .tf | French Southern and Antarctic Territories |
| .tg | Togo |
| .th | Thailand |
| .tj | Tajikistan |
| .tk | Tokelau |
| .tm | Turkmenistan |
| .tn | Tunisia |
| .to | Tonga |
| .tp | East Timor |
| .tr | Turkey |
| .tt | Trinidad and Tobago |
| .tv | Tuvalu |
| .tw | Taiwan |
| .tz | Tanzania |
| .ua | Ukraine |
| .ug | Uganda |
| .uk | United Kingdom |
| .um | US Minor Outlying Islands |
| .us | United States |
| .uy | Uruguay |
| .uz | Uzbekistan |
| .va | Vatican |
| .vc | St Vincent and the Grenadines |
| .ve | Venezuela |
| .vg | Virgin Islands (British) |
| .vi | Virgin Islands (US) |
| .vn | Vietnam |
| .vu | Vanuatu |
| .wf | Wallis and Futuna Islands |
| .ws | Samoa |
| .ye | Yemen |
| .yt | Mayotte |
| .yu | Serbia and Montenegro |
| .za | South Africa |
| .zm | Zambia |
| .zw | Zimbabwe |

## Tuvalu TV

The internet domain name .tv is highly desirable to television and media companies. Tuvalu, a small island group in the south-west Pacific Ocean approximately 1 050km/650mi north of Fiji, realized its good fortune and leased the rights to its domain name for $50 million in royalties over a ten year period.

# TRANSPORT

## INTERNATIONAL VEHICLE REGISTRATION (IVR) CODES

| | |
|---|---|
| A | Austria |
| AFG | Afghanistan |
| AL | Albania |
| AN | Angola |
| AND | Andorra |
| AUS | Australia[1] |
| AZ | Azerbaijan |
| B | Belgium |
| BD | Bangladesh[1] |
| BDS | Barbados[1] |
| BF | Burkina Faso |
| BG | Bulgaria |
| BH | Belize |
| BIH | Bosnia and Herzegovina |
| BOL | Bolivia |
| BR | Brazil |
| BRN | Bahrain |
| BRU | Brunei Darussalam[1] |
| BS | The Bahamas[1] |
| BY | Belarus |
| C | Cuba |
| CAM | Cameroon |
| CDN | Canada |
| CH | Switzerland |
| CI | Côte d'Ivoire |
| CL | Sri Lanka[1] |
| CO | Colombia |
| CR | Costa Rica |
| CY | Cyprus[1] |
| CZ | Czech Republic |
| D | Germany |
| DK | Denmark |
| DOM | Dominican Republic |
| DY | Benin |
| DZ | Algeria |
| E | Spain |
| EAK | Kenya[1] |
| EAT | Tanzania[1] |
| EAU | Uganda[1] |
| EC | Ecuador |
| ES | El Salvador |
| EST | Estonia |
| ET | Egypt |
| ETH | Ethiopia |
| F | France |
| FIN | Finland |
| FJI | Fiji[1] |
| FL | Liechtenstein |
| FO | Faroe Islands |
| G | Gabon |
| GB | UK[1] |
| GBA | Alderney[1] |
| GBG | Guernsey[1] |
| GBJ | Jersey[1] |
| GBM | Isle of Man[1] |
| GBZ | Gibraltar |
| GCA | Guatemala |
| GE | Georgia |
| GH | Ghana |
| GR | Greece |
| GUY | Guyana[1] |
| H | Hungary |
| HK | Hong Kong[1] |
| HKJ | Jordan |
| HN | Honduras |
| HR | Croatia |
| I | Italy |
| IL | Israel |
| IND | India[1] |
| IR | Iran |
| IRL | Ireland[1] |
| IRQ | Iraq |
| IS | Iceland |
| J | Japan[1] |
| JA | Jamaica[1] |
| K | Cambodia |
| KS | Kyrgyzstan |
| KWT | Kuwait |
| KZ | Kazakhstan |
| L | Luxembourg |
| LAO | Laos |
| LAR | Libya |
| LB | Liberia |
| LS | Lesotho[1] |
| LT | Lithuania |
| LV | Latvia |
| M | Malta[1] |
| MA | Morocco |
| MAL | Malaysia[1] |
| MC | Monaco |
| MD | Moldova |
| MEX | Mexico |
| MGL | Mongolia |
| MK | Macedonia |
| MOC | Mozambique[1] |
| MS | Mauritius[1] |
| MW | Malawi[1] |
| MYA | Myanmar (Burma) |
| N | Norway |
| NA | Netherlands Antilles |
| NAM | Namibia[1] |
| NAU | Nauru[1] |
| NEP | Nepal[1] |
| NGR | Nigeria |
| NIC | Nicaragua |
| NL | The Netherlands |
| NZ | New Zealand[1] |
| P | Portugal |
| PA | Panama |
| PE | Peru |
| PK | Pakistan[1] |
| PL | Poland |
| PNG | Papua New Guinea[1] |
| PY | Paraguay |
| Q | Qatar |
| RA | Argentina |
| RB | Botswana[1] |
| RC | Taiwan |
| RCA | Central African Republic |
| RCB | Congo |
| RCH | Chile |
| RG | Guinea |
| RH | Haiti |
| RI | Indonesia[1] |
| RIM | Mauritania |
| RL | Lebanon |
| RM | Madagascar |
| RMM | Mali |
| RN | Niger |
| RO | Romania |
| ROK | Korea, Republic of |
| ROU | Uruguay |
| RP | Philippines |
| RSM | San Marino |
| RU | Burundi |
| RUS | Russia |
| RWA | Rwanda |
| S | Sweden |
| SA | Saudi Arabia |
| SCN | St Kitts and Nevis[1] |
| SD | Swaziland[1] |
| SGP | Singapore[1] |

| | | | | | |
|---|---|---|---|---|---|
| SK | Slovakia | TN | Tunisia | WL | St Lucia[1] |
| SLO | Slovenia | TR | Turkey | WS | Samoa |
| SME | Suriname[1] | TT | Trinidad and Tobago[1] | WV | St Vincent and the Grenadines[1] |
| SN | Senegal | UA | Ukraine | YAR | Yemen |
| SO | Somalia | UAE | United Arab Emirates | YU | Serbia and Montenegro |
| ST | São Tomé and Príncipe | USA | United States of America | YV | Venezuela |
| SUD | The Sudan | UZ | Uzbekistan | Z | Zambia[1] |
| SY | Seychelles[1] | V | Vatican | ZA | South Africa[1] |
| SYR | Syria | VN | Vietnam | ZRE | Congo, Democratic Republic of |
| T | Thailand[1] | WAG | The Gambia | ZW | Zimbabwe[1] |
| TCH | Chad | WAL | Sierra Leone | | |
| TG | Togo | WD | Dominica[1] | | |
| TJ | Tajikistan | WG | Grenada[1] | | |
| TM | Turkmenistan | | | | |

[1] *In countries so marked, the rule of the road is to drive on the left; in others, vehicles drive on the right.*

## LONDON UNDERGROUND LINES

An underground railway system for London was first proposed in 1843, and construction work began on the Metropolitan Railway in 1860. The line opened between Farringdon and Paddington in 1863 using steam locomotives to pull trains. However, the first electrically-hauled underground line was the City and Southern which opened in 1890, the year in which London's new underground railway first became known as the Tube.

| Line | Colour | Line | Colour |
|---|---|---|---|
| Bakerloo | brown | Jubilee | grey |
| Central | red | Metropolitan | maroon |
| Circle | yellow | Northern | black |
| District | green | Piccadilly | navy blue |
| East London | orange | Victoria | sky blue |
| Hammersmith and City | pink | Waterloo and City | sea green |

### Tracing the Tube

The standard London Underground map that we know today was designed by Harry Beck (1903–1974) back in the early 1930s. He abandoned the complicated geographic style of early Tube maps, instead creating a simple plan that was based on electrical circuit diagrams. It clearly showed the various lines (each a different colour) joining the stations. Beck's diagram – with some updates and modifications – is still in use today, more than 70 years after it was first published in 1933.

### Rush Hour

The busiest station on the London Underground system is Victoria – London Underground estimate that 76.5 million passengers pass through it annually. Britain's busiest railway station is Clapham Junction, in the London borough of Wandsworth.

## MOTORWAYS (UK)

The first British motorway was the M6 Preston Bypass, which opened in Dec 1958.

## ROAD DISTANCES (UK)

Road distances between British centres are given in statute miles, using routes recommended by the Automobile Association based on the quickest travelling time. *To convert to kilometres, multiply the number given by 1.6093.*

### *Roman Roads*

The first people to construct surfaced roads on a large scale were the Romans. The total distance of the roads built by the Romans has been estimated at a lengthy 85 000km/53 000mi, and their road network covered the whole of the Roman Empire, circling the Mediterranean and extending deep into Asia and northwards across Europe. A traveller in late Roman times could make the entire journey from York to Jerusalem on good, safe roads – something that wasn't possible again until the 20c.

| | Birmingham | Bristol | Cambridge | Cardiff | Dover | Edinburgh | Exeter | Glasgow | Holyhead | Hull | Leeds | Liverpool | Manchester | Newcastle | Norwich | Nottingham | Oxford | Penzance | Plymouth | Shrewsbury | Southampton | Stranraer | York | London |
|---|---|---|---|---|---|---|---|---|---|---|---|---|---|---|---|---|---|---|---|---|---|---|---|---|
| Aberdeen | 430 | 511 | 468 | 532 | 591 | 130 | 584 | 149 | 457 | 361 | 336 | 361 | 354 | 239 | 501 | 402 | 497 | 696 | 624 | 412 | 571 | 241 | 325 | 543 |
| Birmingham | | 85 | 101 | 107 | 202 | 293 | 157 | 291 | 151 | 136 | 115 | 98 | 88 | 198 | 161 | 59 | 63 | 272 | 199 | 48 | 128 | 307 | 128 | 118 |
| Bristol | | | 156 | 45 | 198 | 373 | 81 | 372 | 232 | 227 | 216 | 178 | 167 | 291 | 217 | 151 | 74 | 195 | 125 | 128 | 75 | 386 | 221 | 119 |
| Cambridge | | | | 191 | 121 | 337 | 233 | 349 | 246 | 157 | 143 | 195 | 153 | 224 | 62 | 82 | 82 | 346 | 275 | 142 | 133 | 361 | 153 | 60 |
| Cardiff | | | | | 234 | 395 | 119 | 393 | 209 | 246 | 236 | 200 | 188 | 311 | 252 | 170 | 109 | 232 | 164 | 110 | 123 | 406 | 241 | 155 |
| Dover | | | | | | 457 | 248 | 490 | 347 | 278 | 265 | 295 | 283 | 348 | 167 | 202 | 148 | 362 | 290 | 243 | 155 | 503 | 274 | 77 |
| Edinburgh | | | | | | | 446 | 45 | 325 | 229 | 205 | 222 | 218 | 107 | 365 | 268 | 361 | 561 | 488 | 276 | 437 | 130 | 191 | 405 |
| Exeter | | | | | | | | 444 | 305 | 297 | 288 | 250 | 239 | 361 | 295 | 222 | 152 | 112 | 45 | 201 | 114 | 457 | 291 | 170 |
| Glasgow | | | | | | | | | 319 | 245 | 215 | 220 | 214 | 150 | 379 | 281 | 354 | 559 | 486 | 272 | 436 | 88 | 208 | 402 |
| Holyhead | | | | | | | | | | 215 | 163 | 104 | 123 | 260 | 309 | 174 | 218 | 419 | 347 | 104 | 296 | 332 | 190 | 263 |
| Hull | | | | | | | | | | | 59 | 126 | 97 | 121 | 153 | 92 | 188 | 411 | 341 | 164 | 253 | 259 | 38 | 215 |
| Leeds | | | | | | | | | | | | 72 | 43 | 91 | 173 | 73 | 171 | 401 | 328 | 116 | 235 | 232 | 24 | 196 |
| Liverpool | | | | | | | | | | | | | 34 | 170 | 232 | 107 | 164 | 366 | 294 | 64 | 241 | 234 | 100 | 210 |
| Manchester | | | | | | | | | | | | | | 141 | 183 | 71 | 153 | 355 | 281 | 69 | 227 | 226 | 71 | 199 |
| Newcastle | | | | | | | | | | | | | | | 258 | 156 | 253 | 477 | 410 | 216 | 319 | 164 | 83 | 280 |
| Norwich | | | | | | | | | | | | | | | | 123 | 144 | 407 | 336 | 205 | 192 | 393 | 185 | 115 |
| Nottingham | | | | | | | | | | | | | | | | | 104 | 336 | 265 | 85 | 171 | 295 | 86 | 128 |
| Oxford | | | | | | | | | | | | | | | | | | 265 | 193 | 113 | 67 | 371 | 185 | 56 |
| Penzance | | | | | | | | | | | | | | | | | | | 78 | 315 | 227 | 572 | 406 | 283 |
| Plymouth | | | | | | | | | | | | | | | | | | | | 242 | 155 | 502 | 340 | 215 |
| Shrewsbury | | | | | | | | | | | | | | | | | | | | | 190 | 287 | 144 | 162 |
| Southampton | | | | | | | | | | | | | | | | | | | | | | 447 | 252 | 76 |
| Stranraer | | | | | | | | | | | | | | | | | | | | | | | 228 | 419 |
| York | | | | | | | | | | | | | | | | | | | | | | | | 209 |

## AIR DISTANCES

Air distances between some major cities, given in statute miles.
*To convert to kilometres, multiply the number given by 1.6093.*

| | Amsterdam | Beijing | Buenos Aires | Cairo | Chicago | Delhi | Hong Kong | Honolulu | Istanbul | Johannesburg | Lagos | London | Los Angeles | Mexico City | Montreal | Moscow | Nairobi | Paris | Perth | Rome | Santiago | Sydney | Tokyo |
|---|---|---|---|---|---|---|---|---|---|---|---|---|---|---|---|---|---|---|---|---|---|---|---|
| Beijing | 6566 | | | | | | | | | | | | | | | | | | | | | | |
| Buenos Aires | 7153 | 12000 | | | | | | | | | | | | | | | | | | | | | |
| Cairo | 2042 | 6685 | 7468 | | | | | | | | | | | | | | | | | | | | |
| Chicago | 4109 | 7599 | 5587 | 6135 | | | | | | | | | | | | | | | | | | | |
| Delhi | 3985 | 2368 | 8340 | 2753 | 8119 | | | | | | | | | | | | | | | | | | |
| Hong Kong | 5926 | 1235 | 3124 | 5098 | 7827 | 2345 | | | | | | | | | | | | | | | | | |
| Honolulu | 8368 | 6778 | 8693 | 9439 | 4246 | 7888 | 5543 | | | | | | | | | | | | | | | | |
| Istanbul | 1373 | 4763 | 7783 | 764 | 5502 | 2833 | 5998 | 9547 | | | | | | | | | | | | | | | |
| Johannesburg | 5606 | 10108 | 5725 | 4012 | 8705 | 6765 | 6728 | 12892 | 4776 | | | | | | | | | | | | | | |
| Lagos | 3161 | 8030 | 4832 | 2443 | 7065 | 5196 | 7541 | 10367 | 3207 | 2854 | | | | | | | | | | | | | |
| London | 217 | 5054 | 6985 | 2187 | 3956 | 4169 | 5979 | 7252 | 1552 | 5640 | 3115 | | | | | | | | | | | | |
| Los Angeles | 5559 | 6349 | 6140 | 7589 | 1746 | 8717 | 7231 | 2553 | 6994 | 10443 | 7716 | 5442 | | | | | | | | | | | |
| Mexico City | 5724 | 7912 | 4592 | 7730 | 1687 | 9806 | 8794 | 4116 | 7255 | 10070 | 7343 | 5703 | 1563 | | | | | | | | | | |
| Montreal | 3422 | 7557 | 5640 | 5431 | 737 | 7421 | 8564 | 4923 | 4795 | 8322 | 5595 | 3252 | 2482 | 2307 | | | | | | | | | |
| Moscow | 1338 | 3604 | 8382 | 1790 | 5500 | 2698 | 4839 | 8802 | 1089 | 6280 | 4462 | 1550 | 6992 | 6700 | 4393 | | | | | | | | |
| Nairobi | 4148 | 8888 | 7427 | 2203 | 8177 | 4956 | 7301 | 11498 | 2967 | 1809 | 2377 | 4246 | 9688 | 9949 | 7498 | 3951 | | | | | | | |
| Paris | 261 | 5108 | 6892 | 1995 | 4140 | 4089 | 5987 | 7463 | 1394 | 5422 | 2922 | 220 | 5633 | 5714 | 3434 | 1540 | 4031 | | | | | | |
| Perth | 9118 | 4987 | 9734 | 7766 | 11281 | 5013 | 3752 | 7115 | 7846 | 5564 | 10209 | 9246 | 9535 | 11098 | 12402 | 8355 | 7373 | 12587 | | | | | |
| Rome | 809 | 5306 | 6931 | 1329 | 4828 | 3679 | 5773 | 8150 | 852 | 4802 | 2497 | 898 | 6340 | 6601 | 5431 | 1478 | 3349 | 688 | 8309 | | | | |
| Santiago | 7714 | 13622 | 710 | 8029 | 5328 | 12715 | 3733 | 8147 | 10109 | 5738 | 6042 | 8568 | 5594 | 4168 | 5551 | 10118 | 7547 | 461 | 15129 | 7548 | | | |
| Sydney | 1039 | 5689 | 7760 | 9196 | 9324 | 6495 | 4586 | 5078 | 9883 | 7601 | 11700 | 10565 | 7498 | 9061 | 9980 | 9425 | 9410 | 10150 | 2037 | 10149 | 13092 | | |
| Tokyo | 6006[1] | 1313 | 13100 | 6362 | 6286 | 3656 | 1807 | 3831 | 5757 | 8535 | 9130[1] | 6218 | 5451 | 7014 | 6913 | 4668 | 8565 | 6208[1] | 4925 | 6146 | 11049 | 4640 | |
| Washington | 3854 | 7930 | 6097 | 5859 | 590 | 7841 | 8385 | 4822 | 5347 | 8199 | 5472 | 3672 | 2294 | 1871 | 493 | 4884 | 7918 | 3843 | 11829 | 4495 | 5061 | 9792 | 6763 |

[1] *Shortest route.*

# FAMOUS TRANSPORTATIONS

| | |
|---|---|
| **Argo** | The ship that carried Jason and the Argonauts on the quest to bring back the Golden Fleece in Greek mythology. |
| **Ark** | The ship that saved Noah, his immediate family and a selection of animals from a widespread flood over the Earth (the Bible, Genesis 6–9). |
| **HMS Beagle** | The ship on which Charles Darwin (1809–82) sailed as naturalist (from 1831). |
| **Black Bess** | The horse that supposedly carried highwayman Dick Turpin (1705–39) on a famous ride to York (18c). |
| **Bluebird** | The hydroplane used in Donald Campbell's (1921–67) attempt to become the first man to break 300mph on water (1967). |
| **HMS Bounty** | The ship onboard which there was a mutiny on 28 Apr 1789, led by Fletcher Christian, in which Captain William Bligh (1754–c.1817) and 18 men were cast adrift in an open boat without charts. |
| **Chitty Chitty Bang Bang** | The flying car in the film *Chitty Chitty Bang Bang* (1968), based on Ian Fleming's 1964 novel. |
| **Copenhagen** | The chestnut stallion that carried the Duke of Wellington (1769–1852) at the Battle of Waterloo (18 Jun 1815). |
| **Discovery** | The ship that carried Robert Scott (1868–1912) and his expedition exploring Antarctica (1901–04). |
| **Endurance** | The ship that carried Sir Ernest Henry Shackleton (1874–1922) in his Antarctic expeditions but was crushed in the ice on his 1914–16 expedition. |
| **Enola Gay** | The US Air Force B-29 Superfortress bomber, piloted by Paul Tibbets (born 1915), that dropped the world's first atomic bomb on Hiroshima, Japan, during World War II on 6 Aug 1945. |
| **Fram** | The purpose-built ship for Fridtjof Nansen's (1861–1930) scheme to reach the North Pole by getting frozen into the ice north of Siberia and drifting with currents towards Greenland (1893–5). |
| **Golden Hind** | Sir Francis Drake's (c.1540–96) ship in which he circumnavigated the globe (1577–80). |
| **Marengo** | The horse that carried Napoleon Bonaparte (1769–1821) at the Battle of Waterloo (18 Jun 1815). |
| **Mayflower** | The ship that carried the English religious dissenters the Pilgrim Fathers, who established Plymouth Colony in North America, across the Atlantic in 1620. |
| **Rainbow Warrior** | The direct action protest ship operated by envionmental charity Greenpeace (original ship 1978–85, current ship from 1989). |
| **Spirit of St Louis** | The monoplane in which Charles Lindbergh (1902–74) made the first solo transatlantic flight in 1927, flying from New York, USA to Paris, France, in 33½ hours. |
| **Victoria** | The ship that completed the first circumnavigation of the world (10 Aug 1519–6 Sep 1522), captained by Ferdinand Magellan (c.1480–1521), although Magellan himself was killed in the Philippines. |
| **HMS Victory** | The ship from which Lord Horatio Nelson (1758–1805) directed the engagement with the French and Spanish fleets at Trafalgar (21 Oct 1805). |
| **Wright Flyer** | The first heavier-than-air flying machine that Orville (1871–1948) and Wilbur (1867–1912) Wright flew on 17 Dec 1903 at Kill Devil Hills, Kitty Hawk, North Carolina, USA. |

## OLYMPIC GAMES

The modern Olympic Games first took place in 1896, and were founded by the French educationist Baron Pierre de Coubertin (1863–1937). In 1894 he helped set up the International Olympic Committee (IOC), which still formulates policy and decides on venues. The Olympics are held every four years; women first competed in 1900; the first separate Winter Games were held in 1924.

### Olympic venues

The host city of each Olympic Summer Games and Olympic Winter Games is chosen by the International Olympic Committee (IOC) seven years in advance.

#### Olympic Summer Games

| | | | |
|---|---|---|---|
| 1896 | Athens, Greece | 1952 | Helsinki, Finland |
| 1900 | Paris, France | 1956[2] | Melbourne, Australia |
| 1904 | St Louis, USA | 1960 | Rome, Italy |
| 1906[1] | Athens, Greece | 1964 | Tokyo, Japan |
| 1908 | London, UK | 1968 | Mexico City, Mexico |
| 1912 | Stockholm, Sweden | 1972 | Munich, West Germany |
| 1916 | *not held* | 1976 | Montréal, Canada |
| 1920 | Antwerp, Belgium | 1980 | Moscow, USSR |
| 1924 | Paris, France | 1984 | Los Angeles, USA |
| 1928 | Amsterdam, The Netherlands | 1988 | Seoul, South Korea |
| 1932 | Los Angeles, USA | 1992 | Barcelona, Spain |
| 1936 | Berlin, Germany | 1996 | Atlanta, USA |
| 1940 | *not held* | 2000 | Sydney, Australia |
| 1944 | *not held* | 2004 | Athens, Greece |
| 1948 | London, UK | 2008 | Beijing, China |

[1] *Special Olympic Games held to commemorate the tenth anniversary of the birth of the modern Games.*

[2] *The 1956 equestrian events were held at Stockholm, Sweden, due to quarantine laws in Australia.*

*Note: Nine cities have applied to host the Olympic Games in 2012: Havana (Cuba), Istanbul (Turkey), Leipzig (Germany), London (UK), Madrid (Spain), Moscow (Russia), New York City (USA), Paris (France) and Rio de Janeiro (Brazil). The host city will be announced in Jul 2005.*

### Olympic Mystery

One of the most unlikely Olympic champions of all time is a young French boy whose identity remains a complete mystery. At the 1900 Olympics in Paris, a pair of Dutch rowers grabbed a local boy to replace their coxswain, who had dropped out at the last minute – and the unlikely trio went on to win the race. The child took part in the ceremony and winning celebrations with the rowers, but then vanished without trace. Despite strenuous efforts to find out more in the century since the Games, neither his name, nor his age nor anything else about him is known.

### Olympic Winter Games

| | | | |
|---|---|---|---|
| 1924 | Chamonix, France | 1968 | Grenoble, France |
| 1928 | St Moritz, Switzerland | 1972 | Sapporo, Japan |
| 1932 | Lake Placid, New York, USA | 1976 | Innsbruck, Austria |
| 1936 | Garmisch-Partenkirchen, Germany | 1980 | Lake Placid, New York, USA |
| | | 1984 | Sarajevo, Yugoslavia |
| 1940 | *not held* | 1988 | Calgary, Canada |
| 1944 | *not held* | 1992 | Albertville, France |
| 1948 | St Moritz, Switzerland | 1994[1] | Lillehammer, Norway |
| 1952 | Oslo, Norway | 1998 | Nagano, Japan |
| 1956 | Cortina, Italy | 2002 | Salt Lake City, USA |
| 1960 | Squaw Valley, USA | 2006 | Turin, Italy |
| 1964 | Innsbruck, Austria | 2010 | Vancouver, Canada |

[1] *In 1994, the Olympic Winter Games celebrations were re-adjusted to take place every four years between the Olympic Summer Games years.*

## *Naked Olympics*

According to tradition, the Olympics began in 776BC, when a festival of athletic competitions began to be held at Olympia, in western Greece, to honour the god Zeus. The festival was held at the end of each period of four years (known as an *Olympiad*), and at its peak attracted entrants from all over the Greek world. Many of the events are still familiar to us today, including boxing, wrestling, long jump, discus and javelin. Others were a little different – for example, a foot race run in full armour and a fiercely competitive chariot race of around 14km/8.7mi. There were separate events for boys and men, who competed naked. The winners were crowned simply with an olive wreath, but would be rewarded by their home city with privileges, money and free food and drink for life. The games were eventually ended by order of the Emperor Theodosius I in AD393.

## Leading medal winners

### Olympic Summer Games

Includes medals won in 2000.

| | | Gold | Silver | Bronze | Total |
|---|---|---|---|---|---|
| 1 | USA | 862 | 652 | 576 | 2 090 |
| 2 | Russia[1] | 499 | 410 | 369 | 1 278 |
| 3 | Germany[2] | 217 | 258 | 286 | 761 |
| 4 | Great Britain | 180 | 233 | 222 | 635 |
| 5 | France | 172 | 182 | 200 | 554 |
| 6 | Sweden | 137 | 154 | 171 | 462 |
| 7 | Italy | 172 | 136 | 153 | 461 |
| 8 | Hungary | 148 | 130 | 153 | 431 |
| 9 | East Germany | 153 | 129 | 127 | 409 |
| 10 | Australia | 103 | 110 | 136 | 349 |

[1] *Includes medals won by the former USSR team, and by the Unified Team (Armenia, Azerbaijan, Belarus, Georgia, Kazakhstan, Kyrgyzstan, Moldova, Russia, Tajikistan, Turkmenistan, Ukraine and Uzbekistan) in 1992.*

[2] *Includes medals won as West Germany 1968–88.*

*Data source: International Olympic Committee.*

### Olympic Winter Games

Includes medals won in 2002.

| | | Gold | Silver | Bronze | Total |
|---|---|---|---|---|---|
| 1 | Russia[1] | 113 | 83 | 78 | 274 |
| 2 | Norway | 94 | 92 | 75 | 261 |
| 3 | USA | 69 | 72 | 51 | 192 |
| 4 | Germany[2] | 68 | 68 | 52 | 188 |
| 5 | Austria | 42 | 57 | 64 | 163 |
| 6 | Finland | 41 | 52 | 49 | 142 |
| 7 | East Germany | 39 | 36 | 35 | 110 |
| 8 | Sweden | 36 | 30 | 38 | 104 |
| 9 | Switzerland | 33 | 33 | 38 | 104 |
| 10 | Canada | 30 | 28 | 37 | 95 |

[1] *Includes medals won by the former USSR team, and by the Unified Team (Armenia, Azerbaijan, Belarus, Georgia, Kazakhstan, Kyrgyzstan, Moldova, Russia, Tajikistan, Turkmenistan, Ukraine and Uzbekistan) in 1992.*

[2] *Includes medals won as West Germany 1968–88.*

*Data source: International Olympic Committee.*

## PARALYMPIC GAMES

An Olympic-style competition for elite athletes with a disability. Summer Games first held in 1952 (solely for competitors from the UK and The Netherlands), then once every four years from 1960; Winter Games first held in 1976, then once every four years until 1992, after which they were held once every four years from 1994, to coincide with the Winter Olympic Games.

### Paralympic venues

Since 1988 (Summer Paralympic Games) and 1992 (Winter Paralympic Games) the Paralympics have taken place at the same venue as the Olympic Games; this will become obligatory for Olympic host cities from 2012 onwards.

#### Paralympic Summer Games

| | |
|---|---|
| 1952 | Stoke Mandeville, UK |
| 1960 | Rome, Italy |
| 1964 | Tokyo, Japan |
| 1968 | Tel Aviv, Israel |
| 1972 | Heidelberg, West Germany |
| 1976 | Toronto, Canada |
| 1980 | Arnhem, The Netherlands |
| 1984 | Stoke Mandeville, UK and New York City, USA |
| 1988 | Seoul, South Korea |
| 1992 | Barcelona, Spain |
| 1996 | Atlanta, USA |
| 2000 | Sydney, Australia |
| 2004 | Athens, Greece |
| 2008 | Beijing, China |

### Deaflympics

Deaf athletes are not usually involved in the Paralympic Games. Instead, the International Committee of Sports for the Deaf (CISS) holds World Games for the Deaf (known as *Deaflympics*). More than 2 400 athletes from 71 countries took part in the most recent Deaflympic Summer Games in 2001.

### Paralympic Winter Games

| | | | |
|---|---|---|---|
| 1976 | Örnsköldsvik, Sweden | 1998 | Nagano, Japan |
| 1980 | Geilo, Norway | 2002 | Salt Lake City, USA |
| 1984 | Innsbruck, Austria | 2006 | Turin, Italy |
| 1988 | Innsbruck, Austria | 2010 | Vancouver, Canada |
| 1992 | Albertville, France | | |
| 1994[1] | Lillehammer, Norway | | |

[1] *In 1994, the Paralympic Winter Games celebrations were re-adjusted to take place every four years between the Paralympic Summer Games years.*

## Leading medal winners

Totals are for the years 1984–2002.

### Paralympic Summer Games

| | | Gold | Silver | Bronze | Total |
|---|---|---|---|---|---|
| 1 | USA | 381 | 352 | 364 | 1 097 |
| 2 | Great Britain | 284 | 305 | 292 | 881 |
| 3 | Germany | 274 | 287 | 267 | 828 |
| 4 | Canada | 227 | 191 | 197 | 615 |
| 5 | France | 217 | 209 | 187 | 613 |
| 6 | Australia | 199 | 191 | 184 | 574 |
| 7 | Spain | 151 | 113 | 140 | 404 |
| 8 | Sweden | 145 | 123 | 80 | 348 |
| 9 | The Netherlands | 124 | 108 | 92 | 324 |
| 10 | Poland | 105 | 104 | 82 | 291 |

*Data source: International Paralympic Committee.*

### Paralympic Winter Games

| | | Gold | Silver | Bronze | Total |
|---|---|---|---|---|---|
| 1 | Germany | 89 | 80 | 78 | 247 |
| 2 | Austria | 92 | 76 | 76 | 244 |
| 3 | Norway | 102 | 74 | 62 | 238 |
| 4 | USA | 85 | 91 | 61 | 237 |
| 5 | Switzerland | 35 | 53 | 47 | 135 |
| 6 | Finland | 54 | 31 | 39 | 124 |
| 7 | France | 36 | 39 | 37 | 112 |
| 8 | Russia[1] | 39 | 39 | 27 | 105 |
| 9 | Canada | 19 | 30 | 33 | 82 |
| 10 | Sweden | 13 | 22 | 22 | 57 |

[1] *Includes medals won by the former USSR team, and by the Unified Team (Armenia, Azerbaijan, Belarus, Georgia, Kazakhstan, Kyrgyzstan, Moldova, Russia, Tajikistan, Turkmenistan, Ukraine and Uzbekistan) in 1992.*

*Data source: International Paralympic Committee.*

## COMMONWEALTH GAMES

Open to competitors from all Commonwealth countries, colonies and dependent or associated territories of a Commonwealth country. First held as the British Empire Games in 1930; take place every four years and between Summer Olympic celebrations; became the British Empire and Commonwealth Games in 1954; known as British Commonwealth Games from 1966 to 1974; current title adopted in 1978.

### Commonwealth Games venues

The host city of each Commonwealth Games is chosen by the Commonwealth Games Federation (CGF) seven years in advance.

| | | | |
|---|---|---|---|
| 1930 | Hamilton, Canada | 1974 | Christchurch, New Zealand |
| 1934 | London, England | 1978 | Edmonton, Canada |
| 1938 | Sydney, Australia | 1982 | Brisbane, Australia |
| 1942 | *not held* | 1986 | Edinburgh, Scotland |
| 1946 | *not held* | 1990 | Auckland, New Zealand |
| 1950 | Auckland, New Zealand | 1994 | Victoria, Canada |
| 1954 | Vancouver, Canada | 1998 | Kuala Lumpur, Malaysia |
| 1958 | Cardiff, Wales | 2002 | Manchester, England |
| 1962 | Perth, Australia | 2006 | Melbourne, Australia |
| 1966 | Kingston, Jamaica | 2010 | Delhi, India |
| 1970 | Edinburgh, Scotland | | |

### Leading medal winners

Includes medals won in 2002.

| | | Gold | Silver | Bronze | Total |
|---|---|---|---|---|---|
| 1 | Australia | 646 | 551 | 488 | 1 685 |
| 2 | England | 542 | 513 | 528 | 1 583 |
| 3 | Canada | 388 | 413 | 430 | 1 231 |
| 4 | New Zealand | 118 | 156 | 221 | 495 |
| 5 | Scotland | 71 | 87 | 142 | 300 |
| 6 | South Africa | 80 | 79 | 83 | 242 |
| 7 | India | 80 | 79 | 63 | 222 |
| 8 | Wales | 46 | 64 | 85 | 195 |
| 9 | Kenya | 53 | 42 | 49 | 144 |
| 10 | Nigeria | 35 | 41 | 50 | 126 |

### *Athletes' Villages*

At the first Commonwealth Games in Hamilton in 1930 the facilities were somewhat spartan: the 400-odd competitors slept at a school near the stadium, with up to 24 athletes sharing each classroom. In contrast, the Athletes' Village at the 2002 Games in Manchester included a bar, cinema, entertainment marquee, games room, gym, internet cafe, medical centre, religious centre and restaurant. The organizers estimated beforehand that the beds would be made 120 500 times, 530km/331mi of toilet roll would be used and a stack of towels 4km/2.4mi high would be needed to cater for the thousands of athletes attending.

## SPORTS INTRODUCTION

Sports results are listed for the last 25 years only. Where there are winners in a range of disciplines within one competition (for example Athletics), complete results are given for the last five competitions only. Exceptions exist (for example the FIFA World Cup) where all winners are listed.

*Note: For 1992 Summer Olympic events the designation (UT) is given for members of the Unified Team (Armenia, Azerbaijan, Belarus, Georgia, Kazakhstan, Kyrgyzstan, Moldova, Russia, Tajikistan, Turkmenistan, Ukraine and Uzbekistan).*

## AMERICAN FOOTBALL

Players wear heavy padding and helmets, and passing of the ball by hand, including forward passing, is permitted; played on a rectangular field, divided gridiron-like into segments; object is to score *touchdowns* by moving the ball into the opposing team's *end zone*, but progress has to be made upfield by a series of *plays*: a team must make 9.1m/10yd of ground within four plays, otherwise they lose possession of the ball. Six points are awarded for a touchdown. An extra point can then be gained by kicking the ball between the posts and over the crossbar – the equivalent of a conversion in rugby – or two points can be gained by advancing the ball (through play rather than kicking) from the two-yard line into the end zone in a *two-point conversion*. A goal kicked from anywhere on the field (a *field goal*) is worth three points. Teams consist of more than 40 members, but only eleven are allowed on the field at any one time; special units of players have different roles so they change, eg when the team changes from attacking to defending. First intercollegiate game 1869.

*Ruling body (USA): National Football League (NFL)*

### American football field

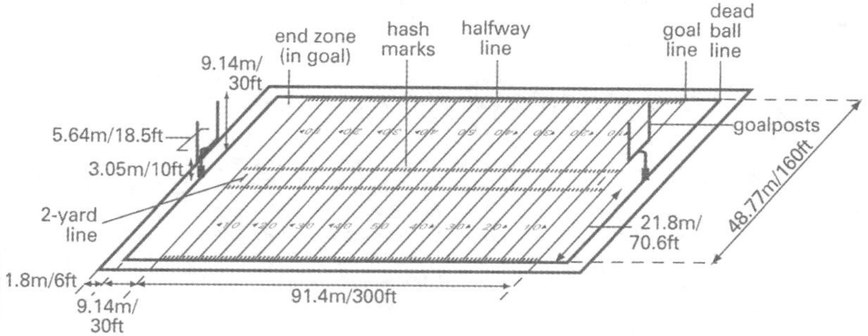

## Vikings and Giants

*NFL American football teams named after animals:* Bears (Chicago), Colts (Indianapolis), Dolphins (Miami), Eagles (Philadelphia), Falcons (Atlanta), Jaguars (Jacksonville), Lions (Detroit), Panthers (Carolina), Rams (St Louis), Ravens (Baltimore) and Seahawks (Seattle).

*Other NFL American football teams:* Bengals (Cincinnati), Bills (Buffalo), Broncos (Denver), Browns (Cleveland), Buccaneers (Tampa Bay), Cardinals (Arizona), Chargers (San Diego), Chiefs (Kansas City), Cowboys (Dallas), 49ers (San Francisco), Giants (New York), Jets (New York), Packers (Green Bay), Patriots (New England), Raiders (Oakland), Redskins (Washington), Saints (New Orleans), Steelers (Pittsburgh), Texans (Houston), Titans (Tennessee) and Vikings (Minnesota).

### Super Bowl

**First held in 1967; takes place each Jan; an end-of-season meeting between the champions of the National Football Conference (NFC) and the American Football Conference (AFC).**

| | |
|---|---|
| 1967 | Green Bay Packers (NFC) |
| 1968 | Green Bay Packers (NFC) |
| 1969 | New York Jets (AFC) |
| 1970 | Kansas City Chiefs (AFC) |
| 1971 | Baltimore Colts (AFC) |
| 1972 | Dallas Cowboys (NFC) |
| 1973 | Miami Dolphins (AFC) |
| 1974 | Miami Dolphins (AFC) |
| 1975 | Pittsburgh Steelers (AFC) |
| 1976 | Pittsburgh Steelers (AFC) |
| 1977 | Oakland Raiders (AFC) |
| 1978 | Dallas Cowboys (NFC) |
| 1979 | Pittsburgh Steelers (AFC) |
| 1980 | Pittsburgh Steelers (AFC) |
| 1981 | Oakland Raiders (AFC) |
| 1982 | San Francisco 49ers (NFC) |
| 1983 | Washington Redskins (NFC) |
| 1984 | Los Angeles Raiders (AFC) |
| 1985 | San Francisco 49ers (NFC) |
| 1986 | Chicago Bears (NFC) |
| 1987 | New York Giants (NFC) |
| 1988 | Washington Redskins (NFC) |
| 1989 | San Francisco 49ers (NFC) |
| 1990 | San Francisco 49ers (NFC) |
| 1991 | New York Giants (NFC) |
| 1992 | Washington Redskins (NFC) |
| 1993 | Dallas Cowboys (NFC) |
| 1994 | Dallas Cowboys (NFC) |
| 1995 | San Francisco 49ers (NFC) |
| 1996 | Dallas Cowboys (NFC) |
| 1997 | Green Bay Packers (NFC) |
| 1998 | Denver Broncos (AFC) |
| 1999 | Denver Broncos (AFC) |
| 2000 | St Louis Rams (NFC) |
| 2001 | Baltimore Ravens (AFC) |
| 2002 | New England Patriots (AFC) |
| 2003 | Tampa Bay Buccaneers (NFC) |

## Star-Spangled Super Bowl

The singing of the US National Anthem at the Super Bowl is a time-honoured tradition. While in the early years of the Super Bowl the anthem was often sung with great ceremony by bands or choirs (for example the Universities of Arizona and Michigan Bands in 1967, the US Air Force Academy Chorale in 1972 and the Little Angels of Holy Angels Church in 1973), in later years it has usually been the luminaries of US pop music who belt out the Banner. Thus, Super Bowl audiences have been treated to the patriotic warblings of Diana Ross (1982), Whitney Houston (1991) and Mariah Carey (2002), the country croonings of Garth Brooks (1993), Faith Hill (2000) and the Dixie Chicks (2003), plus the star-spangled likes of Barry Manilow (1984), Cher (1999) and the Backstreet Boys (2001).

## ATHLETICS

Tests of running, jumping, throwing and walking skills. The running or track events range from the 100m/328ft sprint to the 42km 195m/26mi 385yd marathon; jumping and throwing or field events consist of high jump, long jump, triple jump and pole vault, and the discus throw, shot put, javelin throw and hammer throw. Multi-event competitions are the decathlon (ten events) for men and the heptathlon (seven events) for women. Athletics dates to c.3800BC in Egypt; the International Amateur Athletic Federation was founded in 1912.

**high jump** Field event; competitors attempt to clear a bar without any aids; height increased gradually; three failed attempts means disqualification. The winner clears the greatest height, or has the fewest failures.

**long jump** Field event; contestant runs up to the take-off mark and leaps into a sandpit; length of the jump measured from front of take-off line to nearest break in the sand made by any part of the competitor's body; also called broad jump in North America.

**triple jump** Field event; takes place in the same part of the stadium as the long jump, governed by same rules. After the run-up, competitors must take off and hop on the same foot; second phase is a step onto the other foot, followed by a jump; previously called the hop, step and jump.

**pole vault** Field event; jumping contest for height using fibreglass pole for leverage to clear a bar, which is raised progressively; three attempts may be made to clear the height before attempting a new one.

**discus throw** Field event; uses a circular disc of wood with metal plates, weighing 2kg/4.4 lb for men and 1kg/2.2 lb for women. It is thrown with one hand from within the confines of a circle 2.5m/8ft 2in in diameter.

**shot put** Field event; the shot is a brass or iron sphere weighing 7.26kg/16 lb for men and 4kg/8 lb 13oz for women. It is propelled, using only one hand, from a starting position under the chin. The thrower must not leave the 2.1m/7ft diameter throwing circle. In competition six throws are allowed.

**javelin throw** Field event; throwing a spear-like javelin which consists of three parts: pointed metal head, shaft and grip; men's javelin is 2.6–2.7m/8ft 6in–8ft 10in in length and weighs 800g/1.8 lb; women's is 2.2–2.3m/7ft 2in–7ft 6in and weighs at least 600g/1.3 lb; the competitor runs to a specified mark with the javelin in one hand, and throws it; for throw to count, metal head must touch ground before any other part; first mark made by the head is the point used for measuring the distance achieved.

**hammer throw** Field event; hammer weighing 7.26kg/16 lb is thrown using one hand from within the confines of a circle 2.13m/7ft in diameter (protected by a wire cage). Six throws are allowed, the object being to attain the greatest distance.

**decathlon** Ten-event track-and-field competition held over two days, usually for men: 100m, long jump, shot put, high jump, 400m, 110m hurdles, discus, pole vault, javelin and 1 500m. Points are awarded in each event.

**heptathlon** Seven-event track-and-field competition held over two days, usually for women: 100m hurdles, shot put, high jump, 200m, long jump, javelin and 800m.

*Ruling body: International Association of Athletics Federations (IAAF)*

## World Championships

First held in 1983; since 1995 every two years.

### 1995

**Men**

| | |
|---|---|
| 100m | Donovan Bailey (Canada) |
| 200m | Michael Johnson (USA) |
| 400m | Michael Johnson (USA) |
| 800m | Wilson Kipketer (Denmark) |
| 1 500m | Noureddine Morceli (Algeria) |
| 5 000m | Ismael Kirui (Kenya) |
| 10 000m | Haile Gebrselassie (Ethiopia) |
| marathon | Martin Fiz (Spain) |
| 3 000m steeplechase | Moses Kiptanui (Kenya) |
| 110m hurdles | Allen Johnson (USA) |
| 400m hurdles | Derrick Adkins (USA) |
| 20km walk | Michele Didoni (Italy) |
| 50km walk | Valentin Kononen (Finland) |
| 4×100m relay | Canada |
| 4×400m relay | USA |
| high jump | Troy Kemp (Bahamas) |
| long jump | Iván Pedroso (Cuba) |
| triple jump | Jonathan Edwards (Great Britain) |
| pole vault | Sergei Bubka (Ukraine) |
| shot | John Godina (USA) |
| discus | Lars Riedel (Germany) |
| hammer | Andrei Abduvaliyev (Tajikistan) |
| javelin | Jan Zelezný (Czech Republic) |
| decathlon | Dan O'Brien (USA) |

**Women**

| | |
|---|---|
| 100m | Gwen Torrence (USA) |
| 200m | Merlene Ottey (Jamaica) |
| 400m | Marie-José Pérec (France) |
| 800m | Ana Fidelia Quirot (Cuba) |
| 1 500m | Hassiba Boulmerka (Algeria) |
| 5 000m | Sonia O'Sullivan (Ireland) |
| 10 000m | Fernanda Ribeiro (Portugal) |
| marathon | Manuela Machado (Portugal) |
| 100m hurdles | Gail Devers (USA) |
| 400m hurdles | Kim Batten (USA) |
| 10km walk | Irina Stankina (Russia) |
| 4×100m relay | USA |
| 4×400m relay | USA |
| high jump | Stefka Kostadinova (Bulgaria) |
| long jump | Fiona May (Italy) |
| triple jump | Inessa Kravets (Ukraine) |
| shot | Astrid Kumbernuss (Germany) |
| discus | Ellina Zvereva (Belarus) |
| javelin | Natalya Shikolenko (Belarus) |
| heptathlon | Natalya Shikolenko (Belarus) |

### 1997

**Men**

| | |
|---|---|
| 100m | Maurice Greene (USA) |
| 200m | Ato Boldon (Trinidad) |
| 400m | Michael Johnson (USA) |
| 800m | Wilson Kipketer (Denmark) |
| 1 500m | Hicham El Guerrouj (Morocco) |
| 5 000m | Daniel Komen (Kenya) |
| 10 000m | Haile Gebrselassie (Ethiopia) |
| marathon | Abel Antón (Spain) |
| 3 000m steeplechase | Wilson Kipketer (Denmark) |
| 110m hurdles | Allen Johnson (USA) |
| 400m hurdles | Stephane Diagana (France) |
| 20km walk | Daniel Garcia (Mexico) |
| 50km walk | Robert Korzeniowski (Poland) |
| 4×100m relay | Canada |

**Women**

| | |
|---|---|
| 100m | Marion Jones (USA) |
| 200m | Zhanna Pintussevich (Ukraine) |
| 400m | Cathy Freeman (Australia) |
| 800m | Ana Fidelia Quirot (Cuba) |
| 1 500m | Carla Sacramento (Portugal) |
| 5 000m | Gabriela Szabo (Romania) |
| 10 000m | Sally Barsosio (Kenya) |
| marathon | Hiromi Suzuki (Japan) |
| 100m hurdles | Ludmila Engquist (Sweden) |
| 400m hurdles | Nezha Bidouane (Morocco) |
| 10km walk | Annarita Sidoti (Italy) |
| 4×100m relay | USA |
| 4×400m relay | Germany |
| high jump | Hanne Haugland (Norway) |
| long jump | Lyudmila Galkina (Russia) |

**Men**

| | |
|---|---|
| 4×400m relay | USA |
| high jump | Javier Sotomayor (Cuba) |
| long jump | Iván Pedroso (Cuba) |
| triple jump | Yoelvis Quesada (Cuba) |
| pole vault | Sergei Bubka (Ukraine) |
| shot | Aleksandr Bagach[1] (Ukraine) |
| discus | Lars Riedel (Germany) |
| hammer | Heinz Weis (Germany) |
| javelin | Marius Corbett (South Africa) |
| decathlon | Tómas Dvorák (Czech Republic) |

**Women**

| | |
|---|---|
| triple jump | Sarka Kasparkova (Czech Republic) |
| shot | Astrid Kumbernuss (Germany) |
| discus | Beatrice Faumuina (New Zealand) |
| javelin | Trine Hattestad (Norway) |
| heptathlon | Sabine Braun (Germany) |

[1] *Stripped of gold medal following positive drugs test; medal awarded to John Godina (USA).*

### 1999

**Men**

| | |
|---|---|
| 100m | Maurice Greene (USA) |
| 200m | Maurice Greene (USA) |
| 400m | Michael Johnson (USA) |
| 800m | Wilson Kipketer (Denmark) |
| 1 500m | Hicham El Guerrouj (Morocco) |
| 5 000m | Salah Hissou (Morocco) |
| 10 000m | Haile Gebrselassie (Ethiopia) |
| marathon | Abel Antón (Spain) |
| 3 000m steeplechase | Christopher Koskei (Kenya) |
| 110m hurdles | Colin Jackson (Great Britain) |
| 400m hurdles | Fabrizio Mori (Italy) |
| 20km walk | Ilya Markov (Russia) |
| 50km walk | German Skurygin (Russia) |
| 4×100m relay | USA |
| 4×400m relay | USA |
| high jump | Vyacheslav Voronin (Russia) |
| long jump | Iván Pedroso (Cuba) |
| triple jump | Charles Michael Friedek (Germany) |
| pole vault | Maksim Tarasov (Russia) |
| shot | C J Hunter (USA) |
| discus | Anthony Washington (USA) |
| hammer | Karsten Kobs (Germany) |
| javelin | Aki Parviainen (Finland) |
| decathlon | Tomás Dvorák (Czech Republic) |

**Women**

| | |
|---|---|
| 100m | Marion Jones (USA) |
| 200m | Inger Miller (USA) |
| 400m | Cathy Freeman (Australia) |
| 800m | Ludmilla Formanova (Czech Republic) |
| 1 500m | Svetlana Masterkova (Russia) |
| 5 000m | Gabriela Szabo (Romania) |
| 10 000m | Gete Wami (Ethiopia) |
| marathon | Jong Song-Ok (North Korea) |
| 100m hurdles | Gail Devers (USA) |
| 400m hurdles | Daimi Pernia (Cuba) |
| 20km walk | Liu Hongyu (China) |
| 4×100m relay | The Bahamas |
| 4×400m relay | Russia |
| high jump | Inga Babakova (Ukraine) |
| long jump | Niurka Montalvo (Spain) |
| triple jump | Paraskevi Tsiamita (Greece) |
| pole vault | Stacy Dragila (USA) |
| shot | Astrid Kumbernuss (Germany) |
| discus | Franka Dietzsch (Germany) |
| hammer | Michaela Melinte (Romania) |
| javelin | Mirela Manjani-Tzelili (Greece) |
| heptathlon | Eunice Barber (France) |

## Running Records

The world record for the fastest time for the 100m for men was set by the US athlete Tim Montgomery in Paris in Sep 2002. Montgomery ran the distance – equivalent to 328ft – in just 9.78 seconds. This works out at 37kph, or 23mph. But even the fastest humans are slowcoaches compared with the fastest mammal, the cheetah, which can reach speeds of up to 100kph/62mph in short bursts.

## 2001

**Men**

| | |
|---|---|
| 100m | Maurice Greene (USA) |
| 200m | Konstantinos Kederis (Greece) |
| 400m | Avard Moncur (Bahamas) |
| 800m | André Bucher (Switzerland) |
| 1 500m | Hicham El Guerrouj (Morocco) |
| 5 000m | Richard Limo (Kenya) |
| 10 000m | Charles Kamathi (Kenya) |
| marathon | Gezahegne Abera (Ethiopia) |
| 3 000m steeplechase | Reuben Kosgei (Kenya) |
| 110m hurdles | Allen Johnson (USA) |
| 400m hurdles | Felix Sánchez (Dominican Republic) |
| 20km walk | Roman Rasskazov (Russia) |
| 50km walk | Robert Korzeniowski (Poland) |
| 4×100m relay | USA |
| 4×400m relay | Jamaica |
| high jump | Buss Martin (Germany) |
| long jump | Iván Pedroso (Cuba) |
| triple jump | Jonathan Edwards (Great Britain) |
| pole vault | Dmitry Markov (Russia) |
| shot | John Godina (USA) |
| discus | Lars Riedel (Germany) |
| hammer | Szymon Ziólkowski (Poland) |
| javelin | Jan Zelezný (Czech Republic) |
| decathlon | Tomás Dvorák (Czech Republic) |

**Women**

| | |
|---|---|
| 100m | Zhanna Pintusevich-Block (Ukraine) |
| 200m | Marion Jones (USA) |
| 400m | Amy Mbacke Thiam (Senegal) |
| 800m | Maria Mutola (Mozambique) |
| 1 500m | Gabriela Szabo (Romania) |
| 5 000m | Olga Yegorova (Russia) |
| 10 000m | Derartu Tulu (Ethiopia) |
| marathon | Lidia Simon (Romania) |
| 100m hurdles | Anjanette Kirkland (USA) |
| 400m hurdles | Nezha Bidouane (Morocco) |
| 20km walk | Olimpiada Ivanova (Russia) |
| 4×100m relay | USA |
| 4×400m relay | USA |
| high jump | Hestrie Cloete (South Africa) |
| long jump | Fiona May (Italy) |
| triple jump | Tatyana Lebedeva (Russia) |
| pole vault | Stacy Dragila (USA) |
| shot | Yanina Korolchik (Belarus) |
| discus | Natalya Sadova (Russia) |
| hammer | Yipsi Moreno (Cuba) |
| javelin | Osleidys Menéndez (Cuba) |
| heptathlon | Yelena Prokhorova (Russia) |

## 2003

**Men**

| | |
|---|---|
| 100m | Kim Collins (St Kitts and Nevis) |
| 200m | John Capel (USA) |
| 400m | Jerome Young (USA) |
| 800m | Djabir Saïd-Guerni (Algeria) |
| 1 500m | Hicham El Guerrouj (Morocco) |
| 5 000m | Eliud Kipchoge (Kenya) |
| 10 000m | Kenenisa Bekele (Ethiopia) |
| marathon | Jaoud Gharib (Morocco) |
| 3 000m steeplechase | Saif Saaeed Shaheen (Qatar) |
| 110m hurdles | Allen Johnson (USA) |
| 400m hurdles | Felix Sánchez (Dominican Republic) |
| 20km walk | Jefferson Pérez (Ecuador) |
| 50km walk | Robert Korzeniowski (Poland) |
| 4×100m relay | USA |
| 4×400m relay | USA |

**Women**

| | |
|---|---|
| 100m | Kelli White (USA) |
| 200m | Kelli White (USA) |
| 400m | Ana Guevara (Mexico) |
| 800m | Maria Mutola (Mozambique) |
| 1 500m | Tatyana Tomashova (Russia) |
| 5 000m | Tirunesh Dibaba (Ethiopia) |
| 10 000m | Berhane Adere (Ethiopia) |
| marathon | Catherine Ndereba (Kenya) |
| 100m hurdles | Perdita Felicien (Canada) |
| 400m hurdles | Jana Pittman (Australia) |
| 20km walk | Yelena Nikolayeva (Russia) |
| 4×100m relay | France |
| 4×400m relay | USA |
| high jump | Hestrie Cloete (South Africa) |
| long jump | Eunice Barber (France) |
| triple jump | Tatyana Lebedeva (Russia) |
| pole vault | Svetlana Feofanova (Russia) |

**Men**

| | |
|---|---|
| high jump | Jacques Freitag (South Africa) |
| long jump | Dwight Phillips (USA) |
| triple jump | Christian Olsson (Sweden) |
| pole vault | Giuseppe Gibilisco (Italy) |
| shot | Andrei Mikhnevich (Belarus) |
| discus | Virgilijus Alekna (Lithuania) |
| hammer | Ivan Tikhon (Belarus) |
| javelin | Sergey Makarov (Russia) |
| decathlon | Tom Pappas (USA) |

**Women**

| | |
|---|---|
| shot | Svetlana Krivelyova (Russia) |
| discus | Irina Yatchenko (Belarus) |
| hammer | Yipsi Moreno (Cuba) |
| javelin | Miréla Manjani (Greece) |
| heptathlon | Carolina Kluft (Sweden) |

### *Changing Flags*

Qatar won its first ever World Championships athletics medal in 2003 when Saif Saaeed Shaheen took the gold in the men's 3 000m steeplechase. But while Qatar celebrated, Kenya mourned: Shaheen, previously known as Stephen Cherono, was a Kenyan who had recently transferred his allegiance to run for Qatar for a reputed $1 000 a month for life plus large victory bonuses.

## AUSTRALIAN RULES FOOTBALL

A handling and kicking game with few rules, a cross between association football and rugby, with 18 players on an oval pitch. The object is to score by kicking the ball between the opponent's goal posts (six points). Smaller posts are positioned either side of the main goal: a ball kicked through that area scores one point; first recorded game played 1858.

*Ruling body: Australian Football League (AFL)*

### Australian Rules football pitch

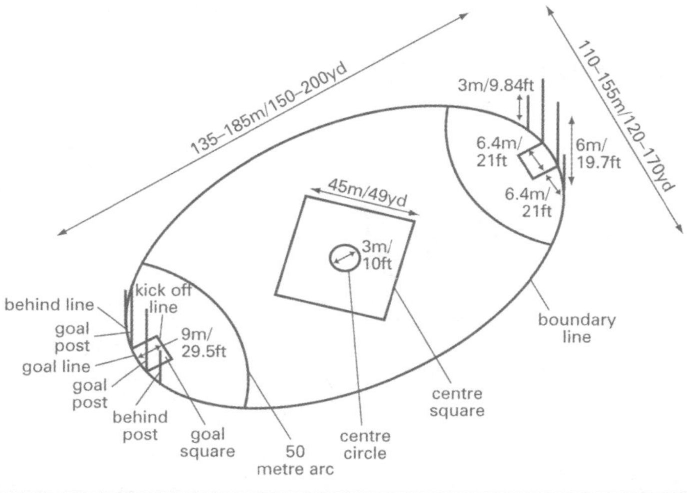

### Premiership Trophy

First held in 1897 as the Victorian Football League (1897–1989); inaugural winners were Essendon. In 1990 the Australian Football League replaced the Victorian Football League as the main governing body for the sport.

| | | | | | |
|---|---|---|---|---|---|
| 1979 | Carlton | 1988 | Hawthorn | 1997 | Adelaide |
| 1980 | Richmond | 1989 | Hawthorn | 1998 | Adelaide |
| 1981 | Carlton | 1990 | Collingwood | 1999 | North Melbourne |
| 1982 | Carlton | 1991 | Hawthorn | 2000 | Essendon |
| 1983 | Hawthorn | 1992 | West Coast | 2001 | Brisbane |
| 1984 | Essendon | 1993 | Essendon | 2002 | Brisbane |
| 1985 | Essendon | 1994 | West Coast | 2003 | Brisbane |
| 1986 | Hawthorn | 1995 | Carlton | | |
| 1987 | Carlton | 1996 | North Melbourne | | |

### *Rugby and Rules*

The game of Australian Rules football was concocted by Tom Wills, H C A Harrison, W J Hammersley and J B Thompson in the mid-1800s. Wills had been educated in the UK and was football captain at Rugby School. Upon his return to Australia he suggested that cricketers could keep fit during the winter by playing a version of rugby football. Wills worked out the rules for their new game, and the first ever Australian Rules match was held in 1858.

## BADMINTON

Indoor game, with two or four players, played on a court using rackets, a shuttlecock (cork or plastic half sphere with 'feathers') and a raised central net; object is to volley the shuttlecock over the net so that the opponent is unable to return it.

*Ruling body: International Badminton Federation (IBF)*

### Badminton court

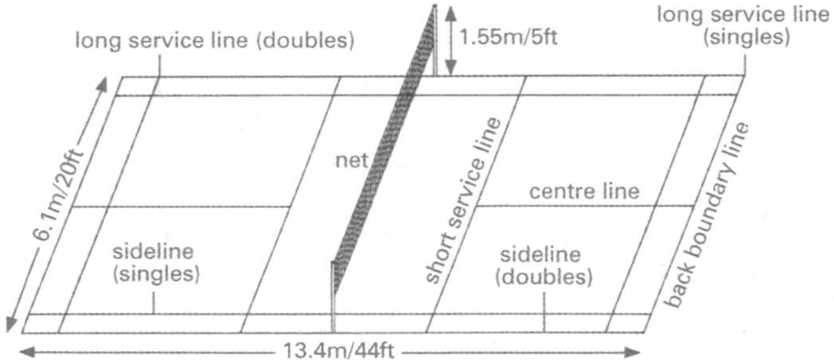

## World Championships

First held in 1977; initially took place every three years; since 1983 every two years.

**Men**

| | |
|---|---|
| 1977 | Flemming Delfs (Denmark) |
| 1980 | Rudy Hartono (Indonesia) |
| 1983 | Icuk Sugiarto (Indonesia) |
| 1985 | Han Jian (China) |
| 1987 | Yang Yang (China) |
| 1989 | Yang Yang (China) |
| 1991 | Zhao Jianhua (China) |
| 1993 | Joko Suprianto (Indonesia) |
| 1995 | Heryanto Arbi (Indonesia) |
| 1997 | Peter Rasmussen (Denmark) |
| 1999 | Sun Jun (China) |
| 2001 | Hendra Wan (Indonesia) |
| 2003 | Xia Xuanze (China) |

**Women**

| | |
|---|---|
| 1977 | Lene Køppen (Denmark) |
| 1980 | Verawaty Wiharjo (Indonesia) |
| 1983 | Li Lingwei (China) |
| 1985 | Han Aiping (China) |
| 1987 | Han Aiping (China) |
| 1989 | Li Lingwei (China) |
| 1991 | Tang Jiuhong (China) |
| 1993 | Susi Susanti (Indonesia) |
| 1995 | Ye Zhaoying (China) |
| 1997 | Ye Zhaoying (China) |
| 1999 | Camilla Martin (Denmark) |
| 2001 | Gong Ruina (China) |
| 2003 | Zhang Ning (China) |

### *Beaufort's Badminton*

The name *badminton* derives from Badminton House in Gloucestershire, the seat of the Duke of Beaufort, where the game was played by house guests in the 19c. However, the game actually originated in China over 2 200 years ago.

## Thomas Cup

An international team event for men's teams; inaugurated 1949; now held every two years.

| | | | | | |
|---|---|---|---|---|---|
| 1978–9 | Indonesia | 1988 | China | 1996 | Indonesia |
| 1981–2 | China | 1990 | China | 1998 | Indonesia |
| 1984 | Indonesia | 1992 | Malaysia | 2000 | Indonesia |
| 1986 | China | 1994 | Indonesia | 2002 | Indonesia |

## Uber Cup

An international event for women's teams; first held in 1957; now held every two years.

| | | | | | |
|---|---|---|---|---|---|
| 1980–1 | Japan | 1990 | China | 1998 | China |
| 1984 | China | 1992 | China | 2000 | China |
| 1986 | China | 1994 | Indonesia | 2002 | China |
| 1988 | China | 1996 | Indonesia | | |

## All-England Championship

Badminton's premier event prior to the inauguration of the World Championships; first held in 1900.

| Men | | Women | |
|---|---|---|---|
| 1979 | Liem Swie King (Indonesia) | 1979 | Lene Køppen (Denmark) |
| 1980 | Prakash Padukone (India) | 1980 | Lene Køppen (Denmark) |
| 1981 | Liem Swie King (Indonesia) | 1981 | Hwang Sun Ai (Korea) |
| 1982 | Morten Frost (Denmark) | 1982 | Zhang Ailing (China) |
| 1983 | Luan Jin (China) | 1983 | Zhang Ailing (China) |
| 1984 | Morten Frost (Denmark) | 1984 | Li Lingwei (China) |
| 1985 | Zhao Jianhua (China) | 1985 | Han Aiping (China) |
| 1986 | Morten Frost (Denmark) | 1986 | Yun-Ja Kim (Korea) |
| 1987 | Morten Frost (Denmark) | 1987 | Kirsten Larsen (Denmark) |
| 1988 | Ib Frederikson (Denmark) | 1988 | Gu Jiaming (China) |
| 1989 | Yang Yang (China) | 1989 | Li Lingwei (China) |
| 1990 | Zhao Jianhua (China) | 1990 | Susi Susanti (Indonesia) |
| 1991 | Ardi Wiranata (Indonesia) | 1991 | Susi Susanti (Indonesia) |
| 1992 | Liu Jun (China) | 1992 | Tang Jiuhong (China) |
| 1993 | Heryanto Arbi (Indonesia) | 1993 | Susi Susanti (Indonesia) |
| 1994 | Heryanto Arbi (Indonesia) | 1994 | Susi Susanti (Indonesia) |
| 1995 | Poul-Erik Hoyer-Larsen (Denmark) | 1995 | Lim Xiao Qing (Sweden) |
| 1996 | Poul-Erik Hoyer-Larsen (Denmark) | 1996 | Bang Soo Hyun (South Korea) |
| 1997 | Dong Jiong (China) | 1997 | Ye Zhaoying (China) |
| 1998 | Sun Jun (China) | 1998 | Ye Zhaoying (China) |
| 1999 | Peter Gade Christensen (Denmark) | 1999 | Ye Zhaoying (China) |
| 2000 | Xia Xuanze (China) | 2000 | Zichao Gong (China) |
| 2001 | Pulella Gopichand (India) | 2001 | Zichao Gong (China) |
| 2002 | Chen Hong (China) | 2002 | Camilla Martin (Denmark) |
| 2003 | Muhammad Hafiz Hashim (Malaysia) | 2003 | Mi Zhou (China) |

## BASEBALL

Team game played by two sides of 25 possible players on a diamond-shaped field which has bases at the corners. Essential pieces of equipment are long solid bats, the solid ball *pitched* from the *mound*, and the glove worn by each fielder; team *at bat* tries to score most runs by having its players circle the three bases and touch home plate before being put out by the team *in the field*; players out if their hit is caught, if they are tagged with the ball when *off-base*, if the base is touched by the ball before they arrive at it, or if they *strike out*, ie fail to hit the ball after three pitches have been judged strikes by the umpire; *home run* scored when player hits ball, circles all three bases and crosses home plate; game consists of nine innings; popularly believed to have been invented by Abner Doubleday (1819–93), at Cooperstown, NY in 1839, but it is now known that a game similar to baseball was played in the USA and England long before Doubleday's time.

*Ruling body: International Baseball Federation (IBAF)*

## Baseball field

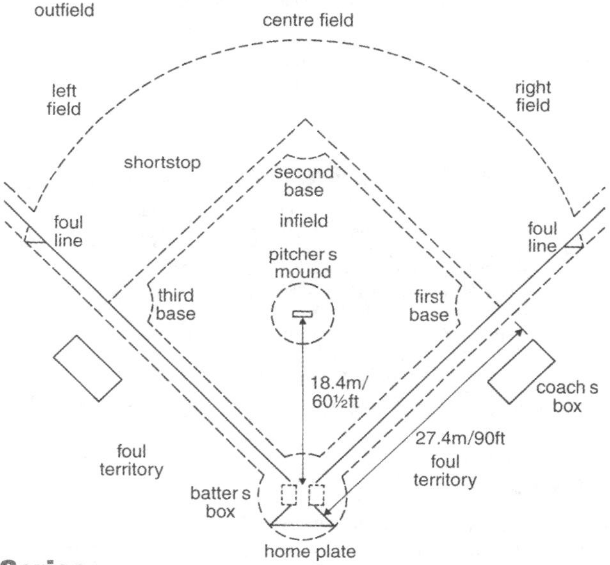


## World Series

First held in 1903; takes place each Oct, the best of seven matches; professional baseball's leading event, the end-of-season meeting between the winners of the two major baseball leagues in the USA, the National League (NL) and American League (AL).

| | | | |
|---|---|---|---|
| 1979 | Pittsburgh Pirates (NL) | 1992 | Toronto Blue Jays (AL) |
| 1980 | Philadelphia Phillies (NL) | 1993 | Toronto Blue Jays (AL) |
| 1981 | Los Angeles Dodgers (NL) | 1994 | *not held* |
| 1982 | St Louis Cardinals (NL) | 1995 | Atlanta Braves (NL) |
| 1983 | Baltimore Orioles (AL) | 1996 | New York Yankees (AL) |
| 1984 | Detroit Tigers (AL) | 1997 | Florida Marlins (NL) |
| 1985 | Kansas City Royals (AL) | 1998 | New York Yankees (AL) |
| 1986 | New York Mets (NL) | 1999 | New York Yankees (AL) |
| 1987 | Minnesota Twins (AL) | 2000 | New York Yankees (AL) |
| 1988 | Los Angeles Dodgers (NL) | 2001 | Arizona Diamondbacks (NL) |
| 1989 | Oakland Athletics (AL) | 2002 | Anaheim Angels (AL) |
| 1990 | Cincinnati Reds (NL) | 2003 | Florida Marlins (NL) |
| 1991 | Minnesota Twins (AL) | | |

### *Where Have You Gone, Joe DiMaggio?*

New York Yankees star Joe DiMaggio (1914–99) was a hit off the field as well as on, marrying actress Marilyn Monroe in 1954. He is also mentioned in the lyrics of Simon and Garfunkel's 1967 hit song *Mrs Robinson*.

## World Cup

Instituted in 1938; since 1990 held approximately every four years.

| | | | | | |
|---|---|---|---|---|---|
| 1980 | Cuba | 1988 | Cuba | 2001 | Cuba |
| 1982 | Korea | 1990 | Cuba | 2003 | Cuba |
| 1984 | Cuba | 1994 | Cuba | | |
| 1986 | Cuba | 1998 | Cuba | | |

### *What's in a Name?*

The Iron Horse, the Georgia Peach, Mr October and the Sultan of Swat are just some of the nicknames of major league baseball players (in reality Lou Gehrig (1903–41), Ty Cobb (1886–1961), Reggie Jackson (born 1946) and Babe Ruth (1895–1948) respectively). Joe DiMaggio (1914–99) was known as Joltin' Joe and the Yankee Clipper, while Hank Aaron (born 1934) was called Hammerin' Hank, Honus Wagner (1874–1955) was the Flying Dutchman and James Hunter (1946–99) was better known as Catfish.

## BASKETBALL

Five-a-side team ball game played on a hard surface court with a bottomless basket at each end; object is to move the ball by a series of passing and bouncing moves and throw it through the opponent's basket.

*Ruling body: International Basketball Federation (FIBA; Fédération Internationale de Basketball)*

## Basketball court

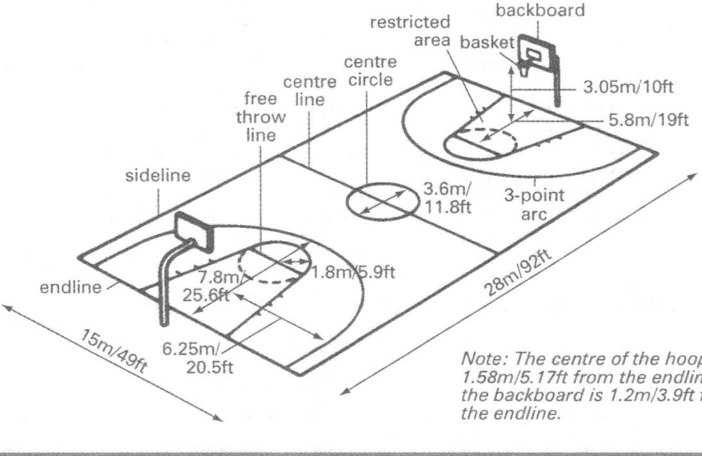


*Note: The centre of the hoop is 1.58m/5.17ft from the endline; the backboard is 1.2m/3.9ft from the endline.*

## World Championship

First held 1950 for men, 1953 for women; takes place approximately every four years.

| Men | | Women | |
|---|---|---|---|
| 1982 | USSR | 1979 | USA |
| 1986 | USA | 1983 | USSR |
| 1990 | Yugoslavia | 1986 | USA |
| 1994 | USA | 1990 | USA |
| 1998 | Yugoslavia | 1994 | Brazil |
| 2002 | Yugoslavia | 1998 | USA |
| | | 2002 | USA |

### Basketball's Beginnings

A Canadian, James Naismith (1861–1939), is regarded as being the originator of basketball. He invented the game in 1891 at the YMCA college in Springfield, Massachusetts, USA, using peach baskets on a gym wall. The game was originally designed merely to bridge the gap between the baseball and American football seasons, but it soon became popular in its own right. A similar game is believed to have been played in Mexico in the 10c.

## NBA Championship

First held in 1947; the major competition in professional basketball in the USA, held under the auspices of the US ruling body, the National Basketball Association (NBA); an end-of-season play-off involving the champion teams from the Eastern Conference (EC) and Western Conference (WC).

| | | | |
|---|---|---|---|
| 1979 | Seattle SuperSonics (WC) | 1992 | Chicago Bulls (EC) |
| 1980 | Los Angeles Lakers (WC) | 1993 | Chicago Bulls (EC) |
| 1981 | Boston Celtics (EC) | 1994 | Houston Rockets (WC) |
| 1982 | Los Angeles Lakers (WC) | 1995 | Houston Rockets (WC) |
| 1983 | Philadelphia 76ers (EC) | 1996 | Chicago Bulls (EC) |
| 1984 | Boston Celtics (EC) | 1997 | Chicago Bulls (EC) |
| 1985 | Los Angeles Lakers (WC) | 1998 | Chicago Bulls (EC) |
| 1986 | Boston Celtics (EC) | 1999 | San Antonio Spurs (WC) |
| 1987 | Los Angeles Lakers (WC) | 2000 | Los Angeles Lakers (WC) |
| 1988 | Los Angeles Lakers (WC) | 2001 | Los Angeles Lakers (WC) |
| 1989 | Detroit Pistons (EC) | 2002 | Los Angeles Lakers (WC) |
| 1990 | Detroit Pistons (EC) | 2003 | San Antonio Spurs (WC) |
| 1991 | Chicago Bulls (EC) | | |

### Magic and Mavericks

*NBA basketball teams named after animals:* Bobcats (Charlotte), Bucks (Milwaukee), Bulls (Chicago), Grizzlies (Memphis), Hawks (Atlanta), Hornets (New Orleans), Raptors (Toronto) and Timberwolves (Minnesota).

*Other NBA basketball teams:* Cavaliers (Cleveland), Celtics (Boston), Clippers (Los Angeles), Heat (Miami), Jazz (Utah), Kings (Sacramento), Knicks (New York), Lakers (Los Angeles), Magic (Orlando), Mavericks (Dallas), Nets (New Jersey), Nuggets (Denver), Pacers (Indiana), Pistons (Detroit), Rockets (Houston), 76ers (Philadelphia), Spurs (San Antonio), Suns (Phoenix), Supersonics (Seattle), Trail Blazers (Portland), Warriors (Golden State) and Wizards (Washington).

## BOXING

Fistfighting between two people, usually men, in a roped ring 4.3–6.1m/14–20ft square. Professional championship bouts constitute twelve three-minute rounds; amateur bouts three rounds, unless one fighter is knocked out or retires, the referee halts the fight, or a fighter is disqualified. There are 17 weight divisions (see below).

*Ruling bodies: International Boxing Federation (IBF), World Boxing Association (WBA), World Boxing Council (WBC), World Boxing Organization (WBO)*

### Butlers and Butchers

Boxing dates from Greek and Roman times. The first known match in Britain was in 1681 when the Duke of Albemarle organized a bout between his butler and his butcher in New Hall, Essex. The first rules were drawn up in 1743, when each round lasted until one fighter was knocked down; gloves and three-minute rounds were introduced in 1867.

### Boxing weight categories

| Category | Weight |
|---|---|
| mini flyweight, minimum weight or strawweight | under 48kg/105 lb |
| light flyweight or junior flyweight | maximum 49kg/108 lb |
| flyweight | maximum 51kg/112 lb |
| super flyweight/junior bantamweight | maximum 52kg/115 lb |
| bantamweight | maximum 54kg/118 lb |
| super bantamweight/junior featherweight | maximum 55kg/122 lb |
| featherweight | maximum 57kg/126 lb |
| super featherweight/junior lightweight | maximum 59kg/130 lb |
| lightweight | maximum 61kg/135 lb |
| super lightweight/junior welterweight | maximum 63.5kg/140 lb |
| welterweight | maximum 67kg/147 lb |
| junior middleweight, light middleweight or super welterweight | maximum 70kg/154 lb |
| middleweight | maximum 73kg/160 lb |
| super middleweight | maximum 76kg/168 lb |
| light heavyweight | maximum 79kg/175 lb |
| cruiserweight | maximum 86kg/190 lb |
| heavyweight | above 86kg/190 lb |

### Wilde in the Ring

In 1867 the 8th Marquis of Queensberry, Sir John Douglas (1844–1900), supervised the formulation of new rules to govern boxing, since known as the 'Queensberry Rules'. The same Marquis was unsuccessfully sued for criminal libel by Oscar Wilde in 1895; Queensberry disapproved of Wilde's friendship with his son, Lord Alfred Douglas, and it was Queensberry's allegations of homosexuality that led in turn to Wilde's trial and imprisonment.

## World heavyweight champions

The first world heavyweight champion under Queensberry Rules with gloves was James J Corbett in 1892.

| | | |
|---|---|---|
| 1979 | John Tate (USA) | WBA |
| 1980 | Mike Weaver (USA) | WBA |
| 1982 | Michael Dokes (USA) | WBA |
| 1983 | Gerrie Coetzee (South Africa) | WBA<br>WBA |
| 1984 | Tim Witherspoon (USA) | WBC |
| 1984 | Pinklon Thomas (USA) | WBC |
| 1984 | Larry Holmes (USA) | IBF |
| 1984 | Greg Page (USA) | WBA |
| 1985 | Tony Tubbs (USA) | WBA |
| 1985 | Pinklon Thomas (USA) | WBC |
| 1985 | Michael Spinks (USA) | IBF |
| 1986 | Tim Witherspoon (USA) | WBA |
| 1986 | Trevor Berbick (Canada) | WBC |
| 1986 | Mike Tyson (USA) | WBC |
| 1986 | James Smith (USA) | WBA |
| 1987 | Tony Tucker (USA) | IBF |
| 1987 | Mike Tyson (USA) | WBA/WBC |
| 1987 | Mike Tyson (USA) | UND |
| 1989 | Francesco Damiani (Italy) | WBO |
| 1990 | James (Buster) Douglas (USA) | WBA/WBC/IBF |
| 1990 | Evander Holyfield (USA) | WBA/WBC/IBF |
| 1991 | Ray Mercer (USA) | WBO |
| 1992 | Riddick Bowe (USA)[1] | WBA/WBC/IBF |
| 1992 | Michael Moorer (USA) | WBO |
| 1993 | Evander Holyfield (USA) | WBA/IBF |
| 1993 | Lennox Lewis (UK) | WBC |
| 1993 | Tommy Morrison (USA) | WBO |
| 1993 | Michael Bentt (USA) | WBO |
| 1994 | Herbie Hide (UK) | WBO |
| 1994 | Michael Moorer (USA) | WBA/IBF |
| 1994 | Oliver McCall (USA) | WBC |
| 1994 | George Foreman (USA)[2, 3] | WBA/IBF |
| 1995 | Riddick Bowe (USA) | WBO |
| 1995 | Bruce Seldon (USA) | WBA |
| 1995 | Frank Bruno (UK) | WBC |
| 1995 | Frans Botha (South Africa)[4] | IBF |
| 1996 | Mike Tyson (USA)[5] | WBA/WBC |
| 1996 | Henry Akinwande (UK) | WBO |
| 1996 | Michael Moorer (USA) | IBF |
| 1996 | Evander Holyfield (USA) | WBA |
| 1997 | Evander Holyfield (USA) | WBA/IBF |
| 1997 | Lennox Lewis (UK) | WBC |
| 1997 | Herbie Hide (UK) | WBO |
| 1999 | Vitali Klitschko (Ukraine) | WBO |
| 1999 | Lennox Lewis (UK)[6] | UND (WBA/WBC/IBF) |
| 2000 | Chris Byrd (USA) | WBO |
| 2000 | Evander Holyfield (USA) | WBA |
| 2000 | Lennox Lewis (UK) | WBC/IBF |
| 2001 | John Ruiz (USA) | WBA |
| 2000 | Wladimir Klitschko (Ukraine) | WBO |
| 2001 | Hashim Rahman (USA) | WBC/IBF |
| 2001 | Lennox Lewis (UK) | WBC/IBF |
| 2002 | Lennox Lewis (UK)[7] | IBF |
| 2002 | Chris Byrd (USA) | IBF |
| 2003 | Roy Jones Jr (USA) | WBA |
| 2003 | Corrie Sanders (South Africa)[8] | WBO |

[1] *Stripped of WBC title in 1992.*
[2] *Gave up IBF title in 1995.*
[3] *Stripped of WBA title in 1995.*
[4] *Stripped of IBF title in 1996.*
[5] *Gave up WBC title in 1996.*
[6] *Stripped of WBA title in 2000.*
[7] *Gave up IBF title in 2002.*
[8] *Gave up WBO title in 2003.*

*IBF* — *International Boxing Federation*
*UND* — *Undisputed Champion*
*WBA* — *World Boxing Association*
*WBC* — *World Boxing Council*
*WBO* — *World Boxing Organization*

## CHESS

Game of strategy for two players using chequered board of 64 squares. Each player has 16 pieces: eight pawns, two rooks, two knights, two bishops, queen and king; object is to capture or *checkmate* opponent's king; all pieces have set moves, queen is most versatile.

*Ruling body: World Chess Federation (FIDE; Fédération Internationale des Échecs)*

### World Champions

World Champions have been recognized since 1886; first women's champion recognized in 1927. In 1993 a new Professional Chess Association was created as a rival body to FIDE but it collapsed in 1996; replaced by the World Chess Council which also collapsed in 2000.

**Men**

| | |
|---|---|
| 1975–85 | Anatoly Karpov (USSR) |
| 1985–93 | Garry Kasparov (USSR)[1] |
| 1993–9 | Anatoly Karpov (Russia) |
| 1999 | Alexander Khalifman (Russia) |
| 2000 | Vishwanathan Anand (India) |
| 2001– | Ruslan Ponomariov (Ukraine) |

[1] *Continued as PCA World Champion to 2000.*

**Women**

| | |
|---|---|
| 1978–91 | Maya Chiburdanidze (USSR) |
| 1991–7 | Xie Jun (China) |
| 1997–9 | Zsuza Polgar (Hungary) |
| 1999–2000 | Xie Jun (China) |
| 2001– | Zhu Chen (China) |

### *Chaturanga and Chess*

Chess was played in ancient India as *chaturanga*, and the earliest reference to it dates from c.600AD. The current pieces have existed in standard form for over 500 years.

## CRICKET

Bat and ball eleven-a-side team game. A wicket consisting of three stumps (wooden sticks) surmounted by a pair of bails (smaller sticks) is placed at each end of a grassy pitch 20.1m/22yd in length. Each team takes it in turn to bat (with long flat-sided wooden bats) and bowl (with a solid ball), the object being to defend the two wickets while trying to score as many runs as possible. A bowler delivers an *over* of six balls to a batsman standing in front of one of the wickets before a different bowler attacks the other wicket. If the batsman hits a ball (and in certain other circumstances), he may exchange places with the other batsman, thus scoring at least one run. A ball reaching the boundary of the field scores four runs automatically, and six if it has not bounced on the way. A batsman can be got out by being *caught* (a fielder catches the ball before it reaches the ground), *bowled* (the ball from the bowler knocks the bails off the stumps), *stumped* (the wicketkeeper knocks the bails off the stumps with the ball while the defending batsman is standing outside his *safe ground* or *crease*), *run out* (the bails on the wicket towards which one of the batsmen is running are knocked off before the safe ground is reached), *leg before wicket* or *lbw* (when the lower part of the batsman's leg prevents the ball from the bowler reaching the wicket) and *hit wicket* (the batsman accidentally knocks the bails off the stumps). Once ten batsmen have been dismissed, the innings comes to a close, but a team can stop its innings or *declare* if it thinks it has made enough runs. In longer games each team has two innings, at the end of which the team with the greater number of runs at the end of the match wins. If both innings are not completed within the permitted time the match is declared a draw. Test matches usually last five days; county championship matches four, and limited-over competitions are normally concluded in one day, lasting for a specific number of overs per side.

*Ruling bodies: International Cricket Council (ICC), England and Wales Cricket Board (ECB), Marylebone Cricket Club (MCC)*

## Cricket fielding positions

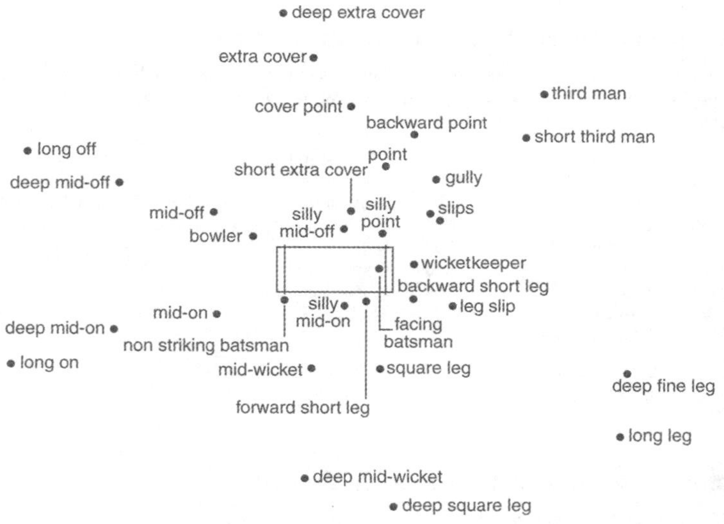


## World Cup

First played in England in 1975; usually held every four years; the 1987 competition, held in India and Pakistan, was the first to be played outside England.

| | | | | | |
|---|---|---|---|---|---|
| 1975 | West Indies | 1987 | Australia | 1999 | Australia |
| 1979 | West Indies | 1992 | Pakistan | 2003 | Australia |
| 1983 | India | 1996 | Sri Lanka | | |

## CRICKET

### County Championship

The oldest cricket competition in the world; first won by Sussex in 1827; not officially recognized until 1890, when a proper points system was introduced.

| | | | | | |
|---|---|---|---|---|---|
| 1979 | Essex | 1988 | Worcestershire | 1997 | Glamorgan |
| 1980 | Middlesex | 1989 | Worcestershire | 1998 | Leicestershire |
| 1981 | Nottinghamshire | 1990 | Middlesex | 1999 | Surrey |
| 1982 | Middlesex | 1991 | Essex | 2000 | Surrey |
| 1983 | Essex | 1992 | Essex | 2001 | Yorkshire |
| 1984 | Essex | 1993 | Middlesex | 2002 | Surrey |
| 1985 | Middlesex | 1994 | Warwickshire | 2003 | Sussex |
| 1986 | Essex | 1995 | Warwickshire | | |
| 1987 | Nottinghamshire | 1996 | Leicestershire | | |

### Norwich Union National Cricket League

First held in 1969; known as the John Player League until 1987, the Refuge Assurance League until 1991, the Axa Equity and Law League until 1999 and the CGU League until 2000.

| | | | | | |
|---|---|---|---|---|---|
| 1979 | Somerset | 1988 | Worcestershire | 1997 | Warwickshire |
| 1980 | Warwickshire | 1989 | Lancashire | 1998 | Lancashire |
| 1981 | Essex | 1990 | Derbyshire | 1999 | Lancashire |
| 1982 | Sussex | 1991 | Nottinghamshire | 2000 | Gloucestershire |
| 1983 | Yorkshire | 1992 | Middlesex | 2001 | Kent |
| 1984 | Essex | 1993 | Glamorgan | 2002 | Glamorgan |
| 1985 | Essex | 1994 | Warwickshire | 2003 | Surrey |
| 1986 | Hampshire | 1995 | Kent | | |
| 1987 | Worcestershire | 1996 | Surrey | | |

### Cheltenham and Gloucester Trophy

First held in 1963; known as the Gillette Cup until 1981 and the NatWest Bank Trophy until 2000.

| | | | | | |
|---|---|---|---|---|---|
| 1979 | Somerset | 1988 | Middlesex | 1997 | Essex |
| 1980 | Middlesex | 1989 | Warwickshire | 1998 | Lancashire |
| 1981 | Derbyshire | 1990 | Lancashire | 1999 | Gloucestershire |
| 1982 | Surrey | 1991 | Hampshire | 2000 | Gloucestershire |
| 1983 | Somerset | 1992 | Northamptonshire | 2001 | Somerset |
| 1984 | Middlesex | 1993 | Warwickshire | 2002 | Yorkshire |
| 1985 | Essex | 1994 | Worcestershire | 2003 | Gloucestershire |
| 1986 | Sussex | 1995 | Warwickshire | | |
| 1987 | Nottinghamshire | 1996 | Lancashire | | |

## Twenty20 Cup

First held in 2003.

| | |
|---|---|
| 2003 | Surrey |

## Benson and Hedges Cup

First held in 1972 and abolished in 2002.

| | |
|---|---|
| 1979 | Essex |
| 1980 | Northamptonshire |
| 1981 | Somerset |
| 1982 | Somerset |
| 1983 | Middlesex |
| 1984 | Lancashire |
| 1985 | Leicestershire |
| 1986 | Middlesex |
| 1987 | Yorkshire |
| 1988 | Hampshire |
| 1989 | Nottinghamshire |
| 1990 | Lancashire |
| 1991 | Worcestershire |
| 1992 | Hampshire |
| 1993 | Derbyshire |
| 1994 | Warwickshire |
| 1995 | Lancashire |
| 1996 | Lancashire |
| 1997 | Surrey |
| 1998 | Essex |
| 1999 | Gloucestershire |
| 2000 | Gloucestershire |
| 2001 | Surrey |
| 2002 | Warwickshire |

## Pura Cup

Australia's leading domestic competition; contested inter-state since 1892–3; known as the Sheffield Shield until 1999.

| | |
|---|---|
| 1979 | Victoria |
| 1980 | Victoria |
| 1981 | Western Australia |
| 1982 | South Australia |
| 1983 | New South Wales |
| 1984 | Western Australia |
| 1985 | New South Wales |
| 1986 | New South Wales |
| 1987 | Western Australia |
| 1988 | Western Australia |
| 1989 | Western Australia |
| 1990 | New South Wales |
| 1991 | Victoria |
| 1992 | Western Australia |
| 1993 | New South Wales |
| 1994 | New South Wales |
| 1995 | Queensland |
| 1996 | South Australia |
| 1997 | Queensland |
| 1998 | Western Australia |
| 1999 | Western Australia |
| 2000 | Queensland |
| 2001 | Queensland |
| 2002 | Queensland |
| 2003 | New South Wales |

### *Leather on Willow*

A similar game to cricket was played in the mid-16c. The first known county match was held in 1719, and the earliest known rules were drawn up in 1744; the august Marylebone Cricket Club (MCC) was founded in 1787. The first ever test match took place in Melbourne in 1877.

## CROSS COUNTRY RUNNING

An athletic running event using a predetermined course over natural terrain. The length of race varies, but world championships are over 12km/7.5mi for men and 5km/3.1mi for women. The first recorded international race was in May 1898, and covered a 14.5km/9mi course at Ville D'Avray near Paris, France.

*Ruling body: International Association of Athletics Federations (IAAF)*

### World Championships

First international championship held in 1903, but only included runners from England, Ireland, Scotland and Wales; recognized as an official world championship from 1973; first women's race in 1967.

**Individual – Men**

| | |
|---|---|
| 1979 | John Treacy (Ireland) |
| 1980 | Craig Virgin (USA) |
| 1981 | Craig Virgin (USA) |
| 1982 | Mohammed Kedir (Ethiopia) |
| 1983 | Bekele Debele (Ethiopia) |
| 1984 | Carlos Lopes (Portugal) |
| 1985 | Carlos Lopes (Portugal) |
| 1986 | John Ngugi (Kenya) |
| 1987 | John Ngugi (Kenya) |
| 1988 | John Ngugi (Kenya) |
| 1989 | John Ngugi (Kenya) |
| 1990 | Khalid Skah (Morocco) |
| 1991 | Khalid Skah (Morocco) |
| 1992 | John Ngugi (Kenya) |
| 1993 | William Sigei (Kenya) |
| 1994 | William Sigei (Kenya) |
| 1995 | Paul Tergat (Kenya) |
| 1996 | Paul Tergat (Kenya) |
| 1997 | Paul Tergat (Kenya) |
| 1998 | Paul Tergat (Kenya) |
| 1999 | Paul Tergat (Kenya) |
| 2000 | Mohammed Mourhit (Belgium) |
| 2001 | Mohammed Mourhit (Belgium) |
| 2002 | Kenenisa Bekele (Ethiopia) |
| 2003 | Kenenisa Bekele (Ethiopia) |

**Individual – Women**

| | |
|---|---|
| 1979 | Grete Waitz (Norway) |
| 1980 | Grete Waitz (Norway) |
| 1981 | Grete Waitz (Norway) |
| 1982 | Maricica Puica (Romania) |
| 1983 | Grete Waitz (Norway) |
| 1984 | Maricica Puica (Romania) |
| 1985 | Zola Budd (England) |
| 1986 | Zola Budd (England) |
| 1987 | Annette Sergent (France) |
| 1988 | Ingrid Kristiansen (Norway) |
| 1989 | Annette Sergent (France) |
| 1990 | Lynn Jennings (USA) |
| 1991 | Lynn Jennings (USA) |
| 1992 | Lynn Jennings (USA) |
| 1993 | Albertina Dias (Portugal) |
| 1994 | Helen Chepngeno (Kenya) |
| 1995 | Derartu Tulu (Ethiopia) |
| 1996 | Gete Wami (Ethiopia) |
| 1997 | Derartu Tulu (Ethiopia) |
| 1998 | Sonia O'Sullivan (Ireland) |
| 1999 | Gete Wami (Ethiopia) |
| 2000 | Derartu Tulu (Ethiopia) |
| 2001 | Paula Radcliffe (England) |
| 2002 | Paula Radcliffe (England) |
| 2003 | Werknesh Kidane (Ethiopia) |

**Team – Men**

| | |
|---|---|
| 1979 | England |
| 1980 | England |
| 1981 | Ethiopia |
| 1982 | Ethiopia |
| 1983 | Ethiopia |
| 1984 | Ethiopia |
| 1985 | Ethiopia |
| 1986 | Kenya |
| 1987 | Kenya |

**Team – Women**

| | |
|---|---|
| 1979 | USA |
| 1980 | USSR |
| 1981 | USSR |
| 1982 | USSR |
| 1983 | USA |
| 1984 | USA |
| 1985 | USA |
| 1986 | England |
| 1987 | USA |

**Team – Men**

| | |
|---|---|
| 1988 | Kenya |
| 1989 | Kenya |
| 1990 | Kenya |
| 1991 | Kenya |
| 1992 | Kenya |
| 1993 | Kenya |
| 1994 | Kenya |
| 1995 | Kenya |
| 1996 | Kenya |
| 1997 | Kenya |
| 1998 | Kenya |
| 1999 | Kenya |
| 2000 | Kenya |
| 2001 | Kenya |
| 2002 | Kenya |
| 2003 | Kenya |

**Team – Women**

| | |
|---|---|
| 1988 | USSR |
| 1989 | USSR |
| 1990 | USSR |
| 1991 | Ethiopia *and* Kenya *(shared)* |
| 1992 | Kenya |
| 1993 | Kenya |
| 1994 | Portugal |
| 1995 | Kenya |
| 1996 | Kenya |
| 1997 | Ethiopia |
| 1998 | Kenya |
| 1999 | France |
| 2000 | Ethiopia |
| 2001 | Kenya |
| 2002 | Kenya |
| 2003 | Ethiopia |

## CYCLING

Bicycle riding as a sport can take several forms: *time trials* are raced against the clock; *cyclocross* is a mixture of cycling and cross-country running, carrying the bike; *track racing* takes place on purpose-built concrete or wooden velodromes; *criteriums* are races around town or city centres; *road races* are normally in excess of 150km/93mi in length, between two points or several circuits of a predetermined course; *stage races* involve many days' racing over more than 150km/93mi. First cycle race Paris 1868, won by James Moore of England.

*Ruling body: International Cycling Union (UCI; Union Cycliste Internationale)*

### World Road Race Championships

Men's race first held in 1927; first women's race in 1958; takes place annually.

**Men**

| | |
|---|---|
| 1979 | Jan Raas (The Netherlands) |
| 1980 | Bernard Hinault (France) |
| 1981 | Freddy Maertens (Belgium) |
| 1982 | Giuseppe Saronni (Italy) |
| 1983 | Greg LeMond (USA) |
| 1984 | Claude Criquielion (Belgium) |
| 1985 | Joop Zoetemelk (The Netherlands) |
| 1986 | Moreno Argentin (Italy) |
| 1987 | Stephen Roche (Ireland) |
| 1988 | Maurizio Fondriest (Italy) |
| 1989 | Greg LeMond (USA) |
| 1990 | Rudy Dhaenens (Belgium) |
| 1991 | Gianni Bugno (Italy) |

**Women**

| | |
|---|---|
| 1979 | Petra De Bruin (The Netherlands) |
| 1980 | Beth Heiden (USA) |
| 1981 | Ute Enzenauer (West Germany) |
| 1982 | Mandy Jones (Great Britain) |
| 1983 | Marianne Berglund (Switzerland) |
| 1984 | *not held* |
| 1985 | Jeannie Longo (France) |
| 1986 | Jeannie Longo (France) |
| 1987 | Jeannie Longo (France) |
| 1988 | *not held* |
| 1989 | Jeannie Longo (France) |
| 1990 | Catherine Marsal (France) |
| 1991 | Leontien van Moorsel (The Netherlands) |

## CYCLING

| Men | | Women | |
|---|---|---|---|
| 1992 | Gianni Bugno (Italy) | 1992 | *not held* |
| 1993 | Lance Armstrong (USA) | 1993 | Leontien van Moorsel (The Netherlands) |
| 1994 | Luc Leblanc (France) | 1994 | Monica Valvik (Norway) |
| 1995 | Abraham Olano (Spain) | 1995 | Jeannie Longo (France) |
| 1996 | Johan Museeuw (Belgium) | 1996 | Barbara Heeb (Switzerland) |
| 1997 | Laurent Brochard (France) | 1997 | Alessandra Cappellotto (Italy) |
| 1998 | Oskar Camenzind (Switzerland) | 1998 | Diana Ziliute (Lithuania) |
| 1999 | Oscar Freire Gomez (Spain) | 1999 | Edita Pucinskaite (Lithuania) |
| 2000 | Romans Vainsteins (Latvia) | 2000 | Zinaida Stahurskaia (Belarus) |
| 2001 | Oscar Freire Gomez (Spain) | 2001 | Rosa Polikeviciute (Lithuania) |
| 2002 | Mario Cipollini (Italy) | 2002 | Susanne Ljungskog (Sweden) |
| 2003 | Igor Astarloa (Spain) | 2003 | Susanne Ljungskog (Sweden) |

### Tour de France

World's premier cycling event; first held in 1903.

| | | | |
|---|---|---|---|
| 1979 | Bernard Hinault (France) | 1991 | Miguel Indurain (Spain) |
| 1980 | Joop Zoetemelk (The Netherlands) | 1992 | Miguel Indurain (Spain) |
| | | 1993 | Miguel Indurain (Spain) |
| 1981 | Bernard Hinault (France) | 1994 | Miguel Indurain (Spain) |
| 1982 | Bernard Hinault (France) | 1995 | Miguel Indurain (Spain) |
| 1983 | Laurent Fignon (France) | 1996 | Bjarne Riis (Denmark) |
| 1984 | Laurent Fignon (France) | 1997 | Jan Ullrich (Germany) |
| 1985 | Bernard Hinault (France) | 1998 | Marco Pantani (Italy) |
| 1986 | Greg LeMond (USA) | 1999 | Lance Armstrong (USA) |
| 1987 | Stephen Roche (Ireland) | 2000 | Lance Armstrong (USA) |
| 1988 | Pedro Delgado (Spain) | 2001 | Lance Armstrong (USA) |
| 1989 | Greg LeMond (USA) | 2002 | Lance Armstrong (USA) |
| 1990 | Greg LeMond (USA) | 2003 | Lance Armstrong (USA) |

### Yellow Jerseys

The famous *yellow jersey* (or *maillot jaune*) is worn each day of the Tour de France by the race's overall leader. The jersey, which was first worn in 1919, gained its distinctive colour from the yellow pages of *Auto*, the magazine which instituted the Tour in 1903. The Belgian Eddy Merckx holds the record for wearing the jersey, having been yellow-clad for an impressive 96 days. The Tour's cyclists also compete to wear the *green jersey*, since 1953 the reward for the best sprinter, the *red polka-dot jersey*, worn since 1975 by the best mountain climber, and the *white jersey*, first awarded in 1975 to the leading young cyclist under 25 years.

## DARTS

Indoor game of throwing three 13cm/5in darts from a distance of 2.37m/7ft 9.25in at a circular board which has its centre 1.73m/5ft 8in from the floor. The standard board is divided into 20 segments numbered 1–20 (not in numerical order); each contains smaller segments which either double or treble that number's score if hit. The centre ring (the *bull*) is worth 50 points, and the area around it (the *outer*) is worth 25 points. Most popular game *501*: players start at that figure and deduct all scores from it, aiming to reduce the starting score exactly to zero; final shot must consist of a double.

*Ruling body: British Darts Organization (BDO), World Darts Federation (WDF)*

### Dartboard

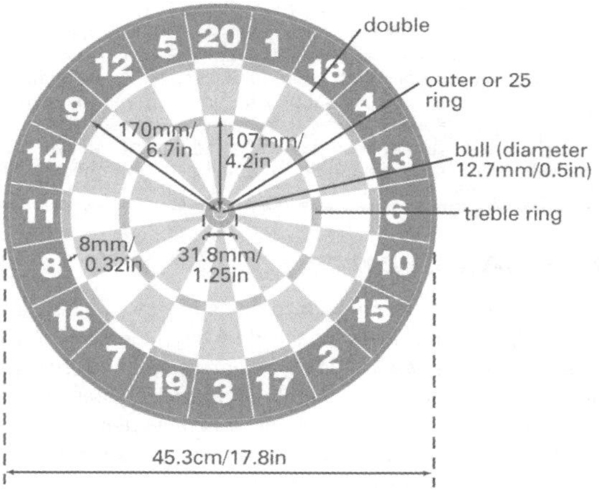


### Embassy World Darts Championship

First held at Nottingham in 1978. Women's championship introduced in 2001.

**Men**

| | |
|---|---|
| 1979 | John Lowe (England) |
| 1980 | Eric Bristow (England) |
| 1981 | Eric Bristow (England) |
| 1982 | Jocky Wilson (Scotland) |
| 1983 | Keith Deller (England) |
| 1984 | Eric Bristow (England) |
| 1985 | Eric Bristow (England) |
| 1986 | Eric Bristow (England) |
| 1987 | John Lowe (England) |
| 1988 | Bob Anderson (England) |
| 1989 | Jocky Wilson (Scotland) |
| 1990 | Phil Taylor (England) |
| 1991 | Dennis Priestley (England) |
| 1992 | Phil Taylor (England) |

**Women**

| | |
|---|---|
| 2001 | Trina Gulliver (England) |
| 2002 | Trina Gulliver (England) |
| 2003 | Trina Gulliver (England) |

**Men**

| | |
|---|---|
| 1993 | John Lowe (England) |
| 1994 | John Part (Canada) |
| 1995 | Richie Burnett (Wales) |
| 1996 | Steve Beaton (England) |
| 1997 | Les Wallace (Scotland) |
| 1998 | Raymond Barneveld (The Netherlands) |
| 1999 | Raymond Barneveld (The Netherlands) |
| 2000 | Ted Hankey (England) |
| 2001 | John Walton (England) |
| 2002 | Tony David (Australia) |
| 2003 | Raymond Barneveld (The Netherlands) |

### *Blowin' in the Wind*

When Mervyn King lost 5–2 to Raymond Barneveld in the semifinal of the Embassy World Darts Championship in 2003, the BBC reported that he blamed excessive air-conditioning for blowing his darts off course. Disgruntled King allegedly claimed that the air-conditioning 'was blowing [his] darts all over the shop', and reckoned that Barneveld was not affected because his darts were heavier. King reportedly threatened to boycott subsequent championships and was not swayed by organizers' protests that the air-conditioning had been switched off throughout.

## EQUESTRIAN EVENTS

Events in which riders on horseback compete in various disciplines: *dressage*, performance of set manoeuvres signalled by the rider; *three day event*, a competition in show jumping, cross-country riding and dressage; and *show jumping*, in which competitors take turns to jump a variety of obstacles, often against time; in most competitions, each pair of horse and rider has one attempt at clearing the fences; those that clear the fences and incur no penalty points are then involved in a *jump-off* against the clock, where speed as well as accuracy are important.

*Ruling body: International Equestrian Federation (FEI; Fédération Équestre Internationale)*

### World Equestrian Games

Show jumping championships first held in 1953 (for men) and 1965 (for women); since 1978 men and women have competed together and on equal terms; team competition introduced in 1978; three day event and dressage championships introduced in 1966; all three now held every four years. Formerly known as the World Championships.

#### Show jumping

| Individual | | Team | |
|---|---|---|---|
| 1982 | Norbert Koof (West Germany) | 1982 | France |
| 1986 | Gail Greenough (Canada) | 1986 | USA |
| 1990 | Eric Navet (France) | 1990 | France |
| 1994 | Franke Sloothaak (Germany) | 1994 | Germany |
| 1998 | Rodrigo Pessoa (Brazil) | 1998 | Germany |
| 2002 | Dermott Lennon (Ireland) | 2002 | France |

### Three day event

| Individual | | Team | |
|---|---|---|---|
| 1982 | Lucinda Green (Great Britain) | 1982 | Great Britain |
| 1986 | Virginia Leng (Great Britain) | 1986 | Great Britain |
| 1990 | Blyth Tait (New Zealand) | 1990 | New Zealand |
| 1994 | Vaughn Jefferis (New Zealand) | 1994 | Great Britain |
| 1998 | Blyth Tait (New Zealand) | 1998 | New Zealand |
| 2002 | Jean Teulere (France) | 2002 | USA |

### Dressage

| Individual | | Team | |
|---|---|---|---|
| 1982 | Reiner Klimke (West Germany) | 1982 | West Germany |
| 1986 | Anne Grethe Jensen (Denmark) | 1986 | West Germany |
| 1990 | Nicole Uphoff (West Germany) | 1990 | West Germany |
| 1994 | Anky van Grunsven (Holland) | 1994 | Germany |
| 1998 | Isabell Werth (Germany) | 1998 | Germany |
| 2002 | Nadine Capellmann (Germany) | 2002 | Germany |

## FENCING

Sword fighting, using a light *foil*, heavier *épée*, or *sabre* (curved handle, narrow blade). Different target areas exist for each weapon, and protective clothing registers hits electronically.

*Ruling body: International Fencing Federation (FIE; Fédération Internationale d'Escrime)*

### World Championships

Held annually since 1921 (between 1921–35, known as European Championships). Not held in Olympic years. Women's épée was introduced in 1989 and women's sabre in 1999.

#### 1998

| Men | | Women | |
|---|---|---|---|
| foil individual | Sergei Golubitsky (Ukraine) | foil individual | Sabine Bau (Germany) |
| foil team | Poland | foil team | Italy |
| épée individual | Hughes Obry (France) | épée individual | Laura Flessel (France) |
| épée team | Hungary | épée team | France |
| sabre individual | Luigi Tarantino (Italy) | | |
| sabre team | Hungary | | |

## FENCING

### 1999

| Men | | Women | |
|---|---|---|---|
| foil individual | Sergei Golubitsky (Ukraine) | foil individual | Valentina Vezzali (Italy) |
| foil team | France | foil team | Germany |
| épée individual | Arnd Schmitt (Germany) | épée individual | Laura Flessel (France) |
| épée team | France | épée team | Hungary |
| sabre individual | Damien Touya (France) | sabre individual | Elena Jemayeva (Azerbaijan) |
| sabre team | France | sabre team | Italy |

*Note: A World Championships for women's sabre was held in 2000; the individual contest was won by Elena Jemayeva (Azerbaijan) and the team event by the USA.*

### 2001

| Men | | Women | |
|---|---|---|---|
| foil individual | Salvatore Sanzo (Italy) | foil individual | Valentina Vezzali (Italy) |
| foil team | France | foil team | Italy |
| épée individual | Paulo Milanoli (Italy) | épée individual | Claudia Bokel (Germany) |
| épée team | Hungary | épée team | Russia |
| sabre individual | Stanislav Pozdniakov (Russia) | sabre individual | Anne Lise Touya (France) |
| sabre team | Russia | sabre team | Russia |

### 2002

| Men | | Women | |
|---|---|---|---|
| foil individual | Simone Vanni (Italy) | foil individual | Svetlani Bojko (Russia) |
| foil team | Germany | foil team | Russia |
| épée individual | Pavel Kolobkov (Russia) | épée individual | Hee Hyun (Korea) |
| épée team | France | épée team | Hungary |
| sabre individual | Stanislav Pozdniakov (Russia) | sabre individual | Xue Tan (China) |
| sabre team | Russia | sabre team | Russia |

### 2003

| Men | | Women | |
|---|---|---|---|
| foil individual | Peter Joppich (Germany) | foil individual | Valentina Vezzali (Italy) |
| foil team | Italy | foil team | Poland |
| épée individual | Fabrice Jeannet (France) | épée individual | Natalia Conrad (Ukraine) |
| épée team | Russia | épée team | Russia |
| sabre individual | Vladimir Lukashenko (Ukraine) | sabre individual | Dorina Mihai (Romania) |
| sabre team | Russia | sabre team | Italy |

### The Language of Fencing

Fencing can be traced back to Egypt in c.1300BC and was popular in the Middle Ages. It was first practised as a sport in Europe in the 14c–15c, and its many movements were originally named in 1570 by the Frenchman Henri Saint-Didier. Today fencing moves include the *appel*, the *botte*, the *flanconade*, the *imbroccata*, the *stoccado* or *stoccata* and the *tac-au-tac*. Fencing also provides the origin of the term *touché* (claiming or acknowledging a point scored in an argument) which originally referred to a fencing hit by an opponent.

## FOOTBALL

A field team game using an inflated ball, formally known as *association football*, and sometimes called *soccer*. An 11-a-side team game played on a grass or synthetic pitch; object is to move the ball around using the foot or head until it can be put into the net, thus scoring a goal. Only the goalkeeper within a specific area is allowed to touch the ball with the hand while it is in play.

*Ruling body: Fédération Internationale de Football Association (FIFA), Union of European Football Associations (UEFA), Confederación Sudamericana de Fútbol (CONMEBOL), Football Association (FA), Scottish Football Association (SFA)*

### Football pitch

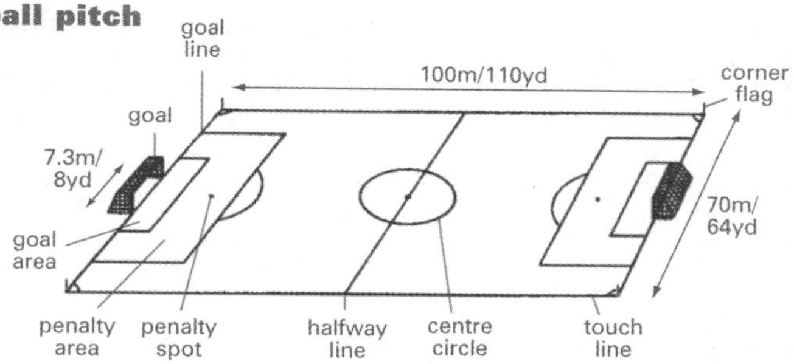


### FIFA World Cup

Football's premier event; first contested for the Jules Rimet Trophy in 1930; Brazil won it outright after winning for the third time in 1970; since then teams have competed for the FIFA World Cup; held every four years.

**Host countries**

| | |
|---|---|
| 1930 | Uruguay |
| 1934 | Italy |
| 1938 | France |
| 1942 | *not held* |
| 1946 | *not held* |
| 1950 | Brazil |
| 1954 | Switzerland |
| 1958 | Sweden |
| 1962 | Chile |
| 1966 | England |
| 1970 | Mexico |
| 1974 | West Germany |
| 1978 | Argentina |
| 1982 | Spain |
| 1986 | Mexico |
| 1990 | Italy |
| 1994 | USA |
| 1998 | France |
| 2002 | South Korea/Japan |
| 2006 | Germany |
| 2010 | *to be held in Africa* |

**Winners**

| | |
|---|---|
| 1930 | Uruguay |
| 1934 | Italy |
| 1938 | Italy |
| 1942 | *not held* |
| 1946 | *not held* |
| 1950 | Uruguay |
| 1954 | West Germany |
| 1958 | Brazil |
| 1962 | Brazil |
| 1966 | England |
| 1970 | Brazil |
| 1974 | West Germany |
| 1978 | Argentina |
| 1982 | Italy |
| 1986 | Argentina |
| 1990 | West Germany |
| 1994 | Brazil |
| 1998 | France |
| 2002 | Brazil |

## European Championship

Held every four years since 1960; qualifying group matches held over the two years preceding the final.

| | | | | | |
|---|---|---|---|---|---|
| 1960 | USSR | 1976 | Czechoslovakia | 1992 | Denmark |
| 1964 | Spain | 1980 | West Germany | 1996 | Germany |
| 1968 | Italy | 1984 | France | 2000 | France |
| 1972 | West Germany | 1988 | Netherlands | | |

## Copa América

First held in 1916 for South American national sides; there were two tournaments in 1959, won by Argentina and Uruguay; discontinued in 1967, but revived eight years later; since 1987 played every two years; frequency may change to every four years; to be held in Peru in 2004.

| | | | | | |
|---|---|---|---|---|---|
| 1979 | Paraguay | 1991 | Argentina | 1997 | Brazil |
| 1983 | Uruguay | 1993 | Argentina | 1999 | Brazil |
| 1987 | Uruguay | 1995 | Uruguay | 2001 | Colombia |
| 1989 | Brazil | | | | |

## European Champions League

The leading club competition in Europe; open to the leading teams of countries affiliated to the Union of European Football Associations (UEFA), the Cup's ruling body, on a quota basis; commonly known as the 'European Cup'; inaugurated in the 1955–6 season; played annually.

| | | | |
|---|---|---|---|
| 1979 | Nottingham Forest (England) | 1992 | Barcelona (Spain) |
| 1980 | Nottingham Forest (England) | 1993 | Olympique Marseille (France) |
| 1981 | Liverpool (England) | 1994 | AC Milan (Italy) |
| 1982 | Aston Villa (England) | 1995 | Ajax (The Netherlands) |
| 1983 | Hamburg (West Germany) | 1996 | Juventus (Italy) |
| 1984 | Liverpool (England) | 1997 | Borussia Dortmund (Germany) |
| 1985 | Juventus (Italy) | 1998 | Real Madrid (Spain) |
| 1986 | Steaua Bucharest (Romania) | 1999 | Manchester United (England) |
| 1987 | Porto (Portugal) | 2000 | Real Madrid (Spain) |
| 1988 | PSV Eindhoven (The Netherlands) | 2001 | Bayern Munich (Germany) |
| 1989 | AC Milan (Italy) | 2002 | Real Madrid (Spain) |
| 1990 | AC Milan (Italy) | 2003 | AC Milan (Italy) |
| 1991 | Red Star Belgrade (Yugoslavia) | | |

### *Football Firsts*

The Ancient Greeks, Chinese, Egyptians and Romans all played a form of football. It became an organized game in Britain in the 19c, and standard rules were drawn up in 1848. The Football Association (FA) was formed in 1863 and the first FA Cup final was played in 1872; the first World Cup was held in 1930.

## UEFA Cup

Held since 1958; originally the Fairs Cup, renamed the UEFA Cup in 1971; open to the runners-up in domestic championships, as well as to the winners of certain other domestic competitions.

| | |
|---|---|
| 1979 | Borussia Mönchengladbach (West Germany) |
| 1980 | Eintracht Frankfurt (West Germany) |
| 1981 | Ipswich Town (England) |
| 1982 | IFK Goteborg (Sweden) |
| 1983 | Anderlecht (Belgium) |
| 1984 | Tottenham Hotspur (England) |
| 1985 | Real Madrid (Spain) |
| 1986 | Real Madrid (Spain) |
| 1987 | IFK Goteborg (Sweden) |
| 1988 | Bayer 04 Leverkusen (West Germany) |
| 1989 | Napoli (Italy) |
| 1990 | Juventus (Italy) |
| 1991 | Inter Milan (Italy) |
| 1992 | Ajax (The Netherlands) |
| 1993 | Juventus (Italy) |
| 1994 | Inter Milan (Italy) |
| 1995 | Parma (Italy) |
| 1996 | Bayern Munich (Germany) |
| 1997 | Schalke 04 (Germany) |
| 1998 | Inter Milan (Italy) |
| 1999 | Parma (Italy) |
| 2000 | Galatasaray (Turkey) |
| 2001 | Liverpool (England) |
| 2002 | Feyenoord (The Netherlands) |
| 2003 | Porto (Portugal) |

## European Cup Winners Cup

Held since 1961 and abolished in 1999; for winners of European domestic cup competitions.

| | |
|---|---|
| 1979 | Barcelona (Spain) |
| 1980 | Valencia (Spain) |
| 1981 | Dynamo Tbilisi (USSR) |
| 1982 | Barcelona (Spain) |
| 1983 | Aberdeen (Scotland) |
| 1984 | Juventus (Italy) |
| 1985 | Everton (England) |
| 1986 | Dynamo Kiev (USSR) |
| 1987 | Ajax (The Netherlands) |
| 1988 | Mechelen (Belgium) |
| 1989 | Barcelona (Spain) |
| 1990 | Sampdoria (Italy) |
| 1991 | Manchester United (England) |
| 1992 | Werder Bremen (Germany) |
| 1993 | Parma (Italy) |
| 1994 | Arsenal (England) |
| 1995 | Real Zaragoza (Spain) |
| 1996 | Paris Saint-Germain (France) |
| 1997 | Barcelona (Spain) |
| 1998 | Chelsea (England) |
| 1999 | Lazio (Italy) |

### The Other Final

While the World Cup Final was being contested by Germany and Brazil in Jun 2002 in front of more than 69 000 spectators and millions of television viewers worldwide, another final was taking place rather more quietly at the Chlanglimithang Stadium in Thimphu, Bhutan. FIFA's two lowest ranked teams – Bhutan and Montserrat, rated 202 and 203 in the world – had been brought together by a couple of Dutch filmmakers to contest what became known as 'The Other Final' for the sheer love of football. The altitude (2 250m/7 380ft above sea level), stray dogs rambling across the pitch, torrential Himalayan rain and repeated choruses of Montserrat's only worldwide hit song 'Hot Hot Hot' all combined to create a unique match in a nation where the national sport is archery. Despite Montserrat's initial optimism, the end result was 4–0 to Bhutan.

## Football Association Challenge Cup (FA Cup)

The world's oldest club knockout competition held annually by the Football Association (FA); first contested in the 1871–2 season; first final at the Kennington Oval on 16 Mar 1872.

| | | | | | |
|---|---|---|---|---|---|
| 1979 | Arsenal | 1988 | Wimbledon | 1997 | Chelsea |
| 1980 | West Ham United | 1989 | Liverpool | 1998 | Arsenal |
| 1981 | Tottenham Hotspur | 1990 | Manchester United | 1999 | Manchester United |
| 1982 | Tottenham Hotspur | 1991 | Tottenham Hotspur | 2000 | Chelsea |
| 1983 | Manchester United | 1992 | Liverpool | 2001 | Chelsea |
| 1984 | Everton | 1993 | Arsenal | 2002 | Arsenal |
| 1985 | Manchester United | 1994 | Manchester United | 2003 | Arsenal |
| 1986 | Liverpool | 1995 | Everton | | |
| 1987 | Coventry City | 1996 | Manchester United | | |

## Football League

The oldest league in the world, and regarded as the toughest; founded in 1888, it has four divisions, with the Premiership (founded in the 1992–3 season) as the top division.

| | | | | | |
|---|---|---|---|---|---|
| 1979 | Liverpool | 1988 | Liverpool | 1997 | Manchester United |
| 1980 | Liverpool | 1989 | Arsenal | 1998 | Arsenal |
| 1981 | Aston Villa | 1990 | Liverpool | 1999 | Manchester United |
| 1982 | Liverpool | 1991 | Arsenal | 2000 | Manchester United |
| 1983 | Liverpool | 1992 | Leeds United | 2001 | Manchester United |
| 1984 | Liverpool | 1993 | Manchester United | 2002 | Arsenal |
| 1985 | Everton | 1994 | Manchester United | 2003 | Manchester United |
| 1986 | Liverpool | 1995 | Blackburn Rovers | | |
| 1987 | Everton | 1996 | Manchester United | | |

## Football League Cup (Carling Cup)

Founded 1961; open to the 92 members of the Football League; formerly known as the Milk Cup, Littlewoods Cup, Rumbelows Cup, Coca Cola Cup and Worthington Cup.

| | | | | | |
|---|---|---|---|---|---|
| 1979 | Nottingham Forest | 1987 | Arsenal | 1996 | Aston Villa |
| 1980 | Wolverhampton Wanderers | 1988 | Luton Town | 1997 | Leicester City |
| | | 1989 | Nottingham Forest | 1998 | Chelsea |
| 1981 | Liverpool | 1990 | Nottingham Forest | 1999 | Tottenham Hotspur |
| 1982 | Liverpool | 1991 | Sheffield Wednesday | 2000 | Leicester City |
| 1983 | Liverpool | 1992 | Manchester United | 2001 | Liverpool |
| 1984 | Liverpool | 1993 | Arsenal | 2002 | Blackburn Rovers |
| 1985 | Norwich City | 1994 | Aston Villa | 2003 | Liverpool |
| 1986 | Oxford United | 1995 | Liverpool | | |

## Scottish Football League

Organized in various divisions since 1891; in 1998 the top ten teams broke away to form the new independent Scottish Premier League, which was expanded to twelve teams in 2000.

| | | | | | |
|---|---|---|---|---|---|
| 1979 | Celtic | 1988 | Celtic | 1997 | Rangers |
| 1980 | Aberdeen | 1989 | Rangers | 1998 | Celtic |
| 1981 | Celtic | 1990 | Rangers | 1999 | Rangers |
| 1982 | Celtic | 1991 | Rangers | 2000 | Rangers |
| 1983 | Dundee United | 1992 | Rangers | 2001 | Celtic |
| 1984 | Aberdeen | 1993 | Rangers | 2002 | Celtic |
| 1985 | Aberdeen | 1994 | Rangers | 2003 | Rangers |
| 1986 | Celtic | 1995 | Rangers | | |
| 1987 | Rangers | 1996 | Rangers | | |

## Scottish FA Cup

Competition held by the Scottish Football Association (SFA); first contested in the 1873–4 season; first final held in 1874 at Hampden Park.

| | | | | | |
|---|---|---|---|---|---|
| 1979 | Rangers | 1988 | Celtic | 1997 | Kilmarnock |
| 1980 | Celtic | 1989 | Celtic | 1998 | Heart of Midlothian |
| 1981 | Rangers | 1990 | Aberdeen | 1999 | Rangers |
| 1982 | Aberdeen | 1991 | Motherwell | 2000 | Rangers |
| 1983 | Aberdeen | 1992 | Rangers | 2001 | Celtic |
| 1984 | Aberdeen | 1993 | Rangers | 2002 | Rangers |
| 1985 | Celtic | 1994 | Dundee United | 2003 | Rangers |
| 1986 | Aberdeen | 1995 | Celtic | | |
| 1987 | St Mirren | 1996 | Rangers | | |

## Scottish League Cup (CIS Insurance Cup)

Founded 1947 and open to the 42 members of the Scottish Football League.

| | | | | | |
|---|---|---|---|---|---|
| 1979 | Rangers | 1990 | Aberdeen | 2001 | Celtic |
| 1980 | Dundee United | 1991 | Rangers | 2002 | Rangers |
| 1981 | Dundee United | 1992 | Hibernian | 2003 | Rangers |
| 1982 | Rangers | 1993 | Rangers | | |
| 1983 | Celtic | 1994 | Rangers | | |
| 1984 | Rangers | 1995 | Raith Rovers | | |
| 1985 | Rangers | 1996 | Aberdeen | | |
| 1986 | Aberdeen | 1997 | Rangers | | |
| 1987 | Rangers | 1998 | Celtic | | |
| 1988 | Rangers | 1999 | Rangers | | |
| 1989 | Rangers | 2000 | Celtic | | |

## English Premiership and Football League clubs

| Club | Location | Stadium | Nickname |
|---|---|---|---|
| Arsenal | London | Highbury | The Gunners |
| Aston Villa | Birmingham | Villa Park | The Villains |
| Barnsley | Barnsley | Oakwell | The Bees |
| Birmingham City | Birmingham | St Andrews | The Blues |
| Blackburn Rovers | Blackburn | Ewood Park | The Rovers/ The Blue and Whites |
| Blackpool | Blackpool | Bloomfield Road | The Seasiders |
| Bolton Wanderers | Bolton | Reebok Stadium | The Trotters |
| Boston United | Boston | York Street | The Pilgrims |
| Bournemouth | Bournemouth | Fitness First Stadium | The Cherries |
| Bradford City | Bradford | Valley Parade[1] | The Bantams |
| Brentford | London | Griffin Park | The Bees |
| Brighton & Hove Albion | Brighton | Withdean Stadium | The Seagulls |
| Bristol City | Bristol | Ashton Gate | The Robins |
| Bristol Rovers | Bristol | Memorial Stadium | The Pirates |
| Burnley | Burnley | Turf Moor | The Clarets |
| Bury | Bury | Gigg Lane | The Shakers |
| Cambridge United | Cambridge | Abbey Stadium | The U's |
| Cardiff City | Cardiff | Ninian Park | The Bluebirds |
| Carlisle United | Carlisle | Brunton Park | The Cumbrians |
| Charlton Athletic | London | The Valley | The Addicks |
| Chelsea | London | Stamford Bridge | The Blues |
| Cheltenham Town | Cheltenham | Whaddon Road | The Robins |
| Chesterfield | Chesterfield | Saltergate[2] | The Spireites |
| Colchester United | Colchester | Layer Road | The U's |
| Coventry City | Coventry | Highfield Road | The Sky Blues |
| Crewe Alexandra | Crewe | Alexandra Stadium | The Railwaymen |
| Crystal Palace | London | Selhurst Park | The Eagles |
| Darlington | Darlington | Reynolds Arena | The Quakers |
| Derby County | Derby | Pride Park Stadium | The Rams |
| Doncaster Rovers | Doncaster | Belle Vue | The Rovers |
| Everton | Liverpool | Goodison Park | The Toffees |
| Fulham | London | Loftus Road Stadium[3] | The Cottagers |
| Gillingham | Gillingham | Priestfield Stadium | The Gills |
| Grimsby Town | Cleethorpes | Blundell Park | The Mariners |
| Hartlepool United | Hartlepool | Victoria Park | The Pool |
| Huddersfield Town | Huddersfield | The McAlpine Stadium | The Terriers |
| Hull City | Kingston upon Hull | Kingston Communications Stadium | The Tigers |
| Ipswich Town | Ipswich | Portman Road | The Tractor Boys |
| Kidderminster Harriers | Kidderminster | Aggborough Stadium | The Harriers |
| Leeds United | Leeds | Elland Road | The Whites |
| Leicester City | Leicester | The Walkers Stadium | The Foxes |
| Leyton Orient | London | The Matchroom Stadium | The O's |
| Lincoln City | Lincoln | Sincil Bank Stadium | The Red Imps |
| Liverpool | Liverpool | Anfield | The Reds |
| Luton Town | Luton | Kenilworth Stadium | The Hatters |
| Macclesfield Town | Macclesfield | The Moss Rose | The Silkmen |
| Manchester City | Manchester | City of Manchester Stadium | The Citizens |
| Manchester United | Manchester | Old Trafford | The Red Devils |
| Mansfield Town | Mansfield | Field Mill | The Stags |

| Club | Location | Stadium | Nickname |
|---|---|---|---|
| Middlesborough | Middlesborough | The Riverside Stadium | Boro |
| Millwall | London | The New Den | The Lions |
| Newcastle United | Newcastle upon Tyne | St James' Park | The Magpies |
| Northampton Town | Northampton | Sixfields Stadium | The Cobblers |
| Norwich City | Norwich | Carrow Road | The Canaries |
| Nottingham Forest | Nottingham | The City Ground | The Reds |
| Notts County | Nottingham | Meadow Lane | The Magpies |
| Oldham Athletic | Oldham | Boundary Park | The Latics |
| Oxford United | Oxford | The Kassam Stadium | The U's |
| Peterborough United | Peterborough | London Road | The Posh |
| Plymouth Argyle | Plymouth | Home Park | The Pilgrims |
| Portsmouth | Portsmouth | Fratton Park | Pompey |
| Port Vale | Stoke-on-Trent | Vale Park | The Valiants |
| Preston North End | Preston | Deepdale | The Lilywhites |
| Queen's Park Rangers | London | Loftus Road Stadium[3] | The R's |
| Reading | Reading | Madejski Stadium | The Royals |
| Rochdale | Rochdale | Spotland Stadium | The Dale |
| Rotherham United | Rotherham | Millmoor | The Merry Millers |
| Rushden & Diamonds | Irthlingborough | Nene Park | The Diamonds |
| Scunthorpe United | Scunthorpe | Glanford Park | The Irons |
| Sheffield United | Sheffield | Bramall Lane | The Blades |
| Sheffield Wednesday | Sheffield | Hillsborough | The Owls |
| Southampton | Southampton | Friends Provident St Mary's Stadium[4] | The Saints |
| Southend United | Southend | Roots Hall | The Shrimpers |
| Stockport County | Stockport | Edgeley Park | The Hatters |
| Stoke City | Stoke-on-Trent | The Britannia Stadium | The Potters |
| Sunderland | Sunderland | Stadium of Light | The Black Cats |
| Swansea City | Swansea | Vetch Field | The Swans |
| Swindon Town | Swindon | County Ground | The Robins |
| Torquay United | Torquay | Plainmoor | The Gulls |
| Tottenham Hotspur | London | White Hart Lane | Spurs |
| Tranmere Rovers | Birkenhead | Prenton Park | The Rovers |
| Walsall | Walsall | Bescot Stadium | The Saddlers |
| Watford | Watford | Vicarage Road | The Hornets |
| West Bromich Albion | West Bromwich | The Hawthorns | The Baggies/The Throstles |
| West Ham United | London | Upton Park[5] | The Hammers |
| Wigan Athletic | Wigan | JJB Stadium | The Latics |
| Wimbledon | Milton Keynes | National Hockey Stadium[6] | The Dons |
| Wolverhampton Wanderers | Wolverhampton | Molineux Stadium | Wolves |
| Wrexham | Wrexham | The Racecourse Ground | The Robins |
| Wycombe Wanderers | High Wycombe | Causeway Stadium[7] | The Chairboys/The Blues |
| Yeovil Town | Yeovil | Huish Park | The Glovers |
| York City | York | Bootham Crescent | The Minstermen |

[1] *Officially now The Bradford & Bingley Stadium.*

[2] *Officially The Recreation Ground.*

[3] *Fulham and Queen's Park Rangers share the stadium.*

[4] *Previous home ground was The Dell.*

[5] *Officially Boleyn Ground.*

[6] *Temporary; previous home ground was Selhurst Park.*

[7] *Previously known as Adams Park.*

## Scottish Premier League and Football League clubs

| Club | Location | Stadium | Nickname |
|---|---|---|---|
| Aberdeen | Aberdeen | Pittodrie Stadium | The Dons |
| Airdrie United | Airdrie | Excelsior Stadium | The Diamonds |
| Albion Rovers | Coatbridge | Cliftonhill Stadium | The Wee Rovers |
| Alloa Athletic | Alloa | Recreation Park | The Wasps |
| Arbroath | Arbroath | Gayfield Park | The Red Lichties |
| Ayr United | Ayr | Somerset Park | The Honest Men |
| Berwick Rangers | Berwick | Shielfield Park | The Borderers |
| Brechin City | Brechin | Glebe Park | The City |
| Celtic | Glasgow | Celtic Park | The Bhoys |
| Clyde | Cumbernauld | Broadwood Stadium | The Bully Wee |
| Cowdenbeath | Cowdenbeath | Central Park | The Blue Brazil |
| Dumbarton | Dumbarton | Strathclyde Homes Stadium | The Sons |
| Dundee | Dundee | Dens Park | The Dark Blues |
| Dundee United | Dundee | Tannadice Park | The Arabs/The Terrors |
| Dunfermline Athletic | Dunfermline | East End Park | The Pars |
| East Fife | Methil | Bayview Stadium | The Fifers |
| East Stirlingshire | Falkirk | Firs Park | The Shire |
| Elgin City | Elgin | Borough Briggs | City/Black and Whites |
| Falkirk | Falkirk | Ochilview Park[1] | The Bairns |
| Forfar Athletic | Forfar | Station Park | The Loons |
| Greenock Morton | Greenock | Cappielow Park | The Ton |
| Gretna | Gretna | Raydale Park | The Black and Whites |
| Hamilton Academical | Hamilton | New Douglas Park | The Accies |
| Heart of Midlothian | Edinburgh | Tynecastle Stadium | The Jam Tarts |
| Hibernian | Edinburgh | Easter Road Stadium | Hibees |
| Inverness Caledonian Thistle | Inverness | Caledonian Stadium | Caley Thistle |
| Kilmarnock | Kilmarnock | Rugby Park | Killie |
| Livingston | Livingston | City Stadium | The Livvy Lions |
| Montrose | Links Park | Montrose | The Gable Endies |
| Motherwell | Motherwell | Fir Park Stadium | The Well |
| Partick Thistle | Glsagow | Firhill Stadium | The Jags |
| Peterhead | Peterhead | Balmoor Stadium | The Blue Toon |
| Queen of the South | Dumfries | Palmerston Park | The Doonhamers |
| Queen's Park | Glasgow | Hampden Park | The Spiders |
| Raith Rovers | Kirkcaldy | Stark's Park | The Rovers |
| Rangers | Glasgow | Ibrox Stadium | 'Gers/Teddy Bears |
| Ross County | Dingwall | Victoria Park | The County |
| St Johnstone | Perth | McDiarmid Park | Saints |
| St Mirren | Paisley | St Mirren Park | The Buddies |
| Stenhousemuir | Stenhousemuir | Ochilview Park | The Warriors |
| Stirling Albion | Stirling | Forthbank Stadium | The Albion/The Reds/The Binos |
| Stranraer | Stranraer | Stair Park | The Blues |

[1] *Falkirk formerly played at Brockville Park; new ground at Westfield opening in 2004; in the interim the club is sharing Ochilview Park with Stenhousemuir.*

## Major European football clubs

| Club | City | Stadium |
|---|---|---|
| **Belgium** | | |
| Anderlecht | Brussels | Constant van den Stock Stadium |
| **France** | | |
| AS Monaco | Monaco | Stade Louis II |
| Paris Saint-Germain | Paris | Parc des Princes |
| **Germany** | | |
| Bayer 04 Leverkusen | Leverkusen | Ulrich Haberland Stadion/BayArena |
| Bayern Munich | Munich | Olympiastadion |
| Borussia Dortmund | Dortmund | Westfalenstadion |
| Borussia Mönchengladbach | Mönchengladbach | Der Bökelberg |
| Eintracht Frankfurt | Frankfurt | Waldstadion |
| Hamburg | Hamburg | AOL Arena |
| Schalke 04 | Gelsenkirchen | Parkstadion/Arena auf Schalke |
| **Italy** | | |
| AC Milan | Milan | Stadio Giuseppe Meazza |
| AS Roma | Rome | Stadio Olimpico |
| Inter Milan | Milan | Stadio San Siro |
| Juventus | Turin | Stadio Delle Alpi |
| Lazio | Rome | Stadio Olimpico |
| Napoli | Naples | Stadio San Paolo |
| Parma | Parma | Stadio Ennio Tardini |
| **The Netherlands** | | |
| Ajax | Amsterdam | Amsterdam ArenA |
| Feyenoord | Rotterdam | Stadion De Kuip |
| PSV Eindhoven | Eindhoven | Philips Stadion |
| **Portugal** | | |
| Benfica | Lisbon | Estádio da Luz |
| Porto | Porto | Estádio das Antas |
| Sporting Lisbon | Lisbon | Estádio José Alvalade |
| **Serbia and Montenegro** | | |
| Red Star Belgrade | Belgrade | Red Star Stadium ('Marakana') |
| **Spain** | | |
| Atletico Madrid | Madrid | Vicente Calderon |
| Barcelona | Barcelona | Camp Nou |
| Deportivo la Coruña | La Coruña | Estadio Municipal de Riazor |
| Real Madrid | Madrid | Santiago Bernabeu |
| Valencia | Valencia | Mestalla |
| **Turkey** | | |
| Fenerbahçe | Istanbul | Şükrü Saracoğlu |
| Galatasaray | Istanbul | Ali Sami Yen |

## GAELIC FOOTBALL

Mixture of rugby, soccer and Australian Rules football, played by teams of 15 on a rectangular pitch with goals resembling rugby posts with soccer-style nets attached; points scored by either putting the ball into the goal net (three), or over the crossbar and between the up-rights (one); first game resembling Gaelic football took place 1712 at Slane, Ireland.

*Ruling body: Gaelic Athletic Association (GAA)*

### Gaelic football pitch

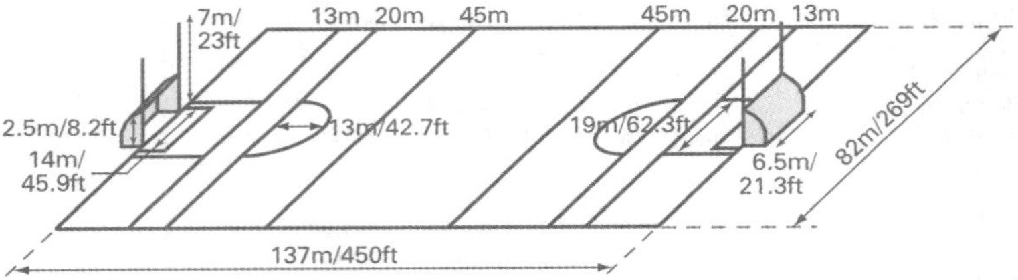


*Note: Pitch size is approximate (length minimum 130m/426.5ft, maximum 145m/475.7ft; width minimum 80m/262.5ft, maximum 90m/295.3ft). The goalpost height of 7m/23ft is the minimum permitted.*

### All-Ireland Championship

First held in 1887; takes place in Dublin on the third Sunday in Sep each year.

| | | | | | |
|---|---|---|---|---|---|
| 1979 | Kerry | 1988 | Meath | 1997 | Kerry |
| 1980 | Kerry | 1989 | Cork | 1998 | Galway |
| 1981 | Kerry | 1990 | Cork | 1999 | Meath |
| 1982 | Offaly | 1991 | Down | 2000 | Kerry |
| 1983 | Dublin | 1992 | Donegal | 2001 | Galway |
| 1984 | Kerry | 1993 | Derry | 2002 | Armagh |
| 1985 | Kerry | 1994 | Down | 2003 | Tyrone |
| 1986 | Kerry | 1995 | Dublin | | |
| 1987 | Meath | 1996 | Meath | | |

### *More Than Just Sport*

The Gaelic Athletic Association (GAA) was founded to support traditional Irish national sports, including Gaelic football, hurling and camogie, but also to nurture and protect Irish cultural heritage, a role that the GAA is proud to continue today. The GAA's rules state that it 'shall actively support the Irish language, traditional Irish dancing, music, song and other aspects of Irish culture', and through its Scór programmes of cultural competitions it endeavours to 'enrich the culture of the nation and further Gaelic ideals'.

## GOLF

Outdoor sport played on a course 4 500–6 500m/5 000–7 000yd long, usually with 18 but sometimes nine holes; object is to hit a small rubber-cored ball using a long-handled iron or wooden-faced club from a flat starting point or *tee* along a *fairway* to a hole positioned on an area of smooth grass or *green*; additional hazards: trees, bushes, streams, sand-filled *bunkers* and the *rough*, or uncut grass beside the fairway; winner completes the course using the lowest number of strokes. The *par* is the expected number of strokes a good player needs to complete a hole; one stroke above par is called a *bogey*; one stroke below par is a *birdie*; two strokes below an *eagle*; three strokes below an *albatross*; a hole completed in one stroke is a *hole in one*.

*Ruling body: Professional Golf Association (PGA), United States Golf Association (USGA), Ladies Professional Golf Association (LPGA), Royal and Ancient Golf Club of St Andrews (R&A)*

### British Open

First held at Prestwick in 1860; takes place annually; regarded as the world's leading golf tournament.

| | | | |
|---|---|---|---|
| 1979 | Severiano Ballesteros (Spain) | 1992 | Nick Faldo (Great Britain) |
| 1980 | Tom Watson (USA) | 1993 | Greg Norman (Australia) |
| 1981 | Bill Rogers (USA) | 1994 | Nick Price (Zimbabwe) |
| 1982 | Tom Watson (USA) | 1995 | John Daly (USA) |
| 1983 | Tom Watson (USA) | 1996 | Tom Lehman (USA) |
| 1984 | Severiano Ballesteros (Spain) | 1997 | Justin Leonard (USA) |
| 1985 | Sandy Lyle (Great Britain) | 1998 | Mark O'Meara (USA) |
| 1986 | Greg Norman (Australia) | 1999 | Paul Lawrie (Great Britain) |
| 1987 | Nick Faldo (Great Britain) | 2000 | Tiger Woods (USA) |
| 1988 | Severiano Ballesteros (Spain) | 2001 | David Duval (USA) |
| 1989 | Mark Calcavecchia (USA) | 2002 | Ernie Els (South Africa) |
| 1990 | Nick Faldo (Great Britain) | 2003 | Ben Curtis (USA) |
| 1991 | Ian Baker-Finch (Australia) | | |

### US Open

First Held at Newport, Rhode Island, in 1895; takes place annually.

| | | | |
|---|---|---|---|
| 1979 | Hale Irwin (USA) | 1992 | Tom Kite (USA) |
| 1980 | Jack Nicklaus (USA) | 1993 | Lee Janzen (USA) |
| 1981 | David Graham (Australia) | 1994 | Ernie Els (South Africa) |
| 1982 | Tom Watson (USA) | 1995 | Corey Pavin (USA) |
| 1983 | Larry Nelson (USA) | 1996 | Steve Jones (USA) |
| 1984 | Fuzzy Zoeller (USA) | 1997 | Ernie Els (South Africa) |
| 1985 | Andy North (USA) | 1998 | Lee Janzen (USA) |
| 1986 | Raymond Floyd (USA) | 1999 | Payne Stewart (USA) |
| 1987 | Scott Simpson (USA) | 2000 | Tiger Woods (USA) |
| 1988 | Curtis Strange (USA) | 2001 | Retief Goosen (South Africa) |
| 1989 | Curtis Strange (USA) | 2002 | Tiger Woods (USA) |
| 1990 | Hale Irwin (USA) | 2003 | Jim Furyk (USA) |
| 1991 | Payne Stewart (USA) | | |

## US Masters

First held in 1934; takes place at the Augusta National course in Georgia every Apr.

| | | | |
|---|---|---|---|
| 1979 | Fuzzy Zoeller (USA) | 1992 | Fred Couples (USA) |
| 1980 | Severiano Ballesteros (Spain) | 1993 | Bernhard Langer (Germany) |
| 1981 | Tom Watson (USA) | 1994 | José-María Olazábal (Spain) |
| 1982 | Craig Stadler (USA) | 1995 | Ben Crenshaw (USA) |
| 1983 | Severiano Ballesteros (Spain) | 1996 | Nick Faldo (Great Britain) |
| 1984 | Ben Crenshaw (USA) | 1997 | Tiger Woods (USA) |
| 1985 | Bernhard Langer (West Germany) | 1998 | Mark O'Meara (USA) |
| 1986 | Jack Nicklaus (USA) | 1999 | José-María Olazábal (Spain) |
| 1987 | Larry Mize (USA) | 2000 | Vijay Singh (Fiji) |
| 1988 | Sandy Lyle (Great Britain) | 2001 | Tiger Woods (USA) |
| 1989 | Nick Faldo (Great Britain) | 2002 | Tiger Woods (USA) |
| 1990 | Nick Faldo (Great Britain) | 2003 | Mike Weir (Canada) |
| 1991 | Ian Woosnam (Great Britain) | | |

## US PGA Championship

The last of the season's four 'Majors'; first held in 1916, and a match-play event until 1958; takes place annually.

| | | | |
|---|---|---|---|
| 1979 | David Graham (Australia) | 1992 | Nick Price (Zimbabwe) |
| 1980 | Jack Nicklaus (USA) | 1993 | Paul Azinger (USA) |
| 1981 | Larry Nelson (USA) | 1994 | Nick Price (Zimbabwe) |
| 1982 | Raymond Floyd (USA) | 1995 | Steve Elkington (Australia) |
| 1983 | Hal Sutton (USA) | 1996 | Mark Brooks (USA) |
| 1984 | Lee Trevino (USA) | 1997 | Davis Love III (USA) |
| 1985 | Hubert Green (USA) | 1998 | Vijay Singh (Fiji) |
| 1986 | Bob Tway (USA) | 1999 | Tiger Woods (USA) |
| 1987 | Larry Nelson (USA) | 2000 | Tiger Woods (USA) |
| 1988 | Jeff Sluman (USA) | 2001 | David Toms (USA) |
| 1989 | Payne Stewart (USA) | 2002 | Rich Beem (USA) |
| 1990 | Wayne Grady (Australia) | 2003 | Shaun Micheel (USA) |
| 1991 | John Daly (USA) | | |

### Greenland Golf

Every spring golfers converge from all over the world to compete in the World Ice Golf Championships, held in Uummannaq, Greenland. The green is the 'white', the ball is fluorescent pink or orange, the temperatures drop to –50°C/–58°F and the obstacles are icebergs and polar bears. The shape of the course, which is created anew each year, is dictated by the position of icebergs in the frozen fjord in which the Championships take place; however, the course changes constantly as the pack ice drifts and new icy outcrops are thrown up. It melts completely by May.

### Ryder Cup

The leading international team tournament; first held at Worcester, Massachusetts in 1927; takes place every two years between teams from the USA and Europe (Great Britain 1927–71; Great Britain and Ireland 1973–7).

| | | |
|---|---|---|
| 1979 | USA | 17–11 |
| 1981 | USA | 18½–9½ |
| 1983 | USA | 14½–13½ |
| 1985 | Europe | 16½–11½ |
| 1987 | Europe | 15–13 |
| 1989 | *Drawn* | 14–14 |
| 1991 | USA | 14½–13½ |
| 1993 | USA | 15–13 |
| 1995 | Europe | 14½–13½ |
| 1997 | Europe | 14½–13½ |
| 1999 | USA | 14½–13½ |
| 2002 | Europe | 15½–12½ |

**Kolf, Colf, Gouf and Golf**

A similar game to golf was played by the Dutch c.1300, and was known as *kolf* or *colf*. *Gouf* was definitely played in Scotland in the 15c, and the world's first golf club, the Gentleman Golfers of Edinburgh, was formed in 1744.

## GYMNASTICS

Physical exercises. Men compete on the parallel bars, pommel horse, high bar, rings, horse vault and floor exercise, and women on the asymmetrical bars, beam, horse vault and floor exercise. Judges award marks out of ten, looking for control, suppleness, balance and ingenuity. The ancient Greeks and Romans performed such exercises for health purposes; modern techniques date from late 18c Germany.

*Ruling body: International Gymnastics Federation (FIG; Fédération Internationale de Gymnastique)*

### World Championships

First contested in 1903; women's championships first held in 1934.

**Individual – Men**

| | |
|---|---|
| 1979 | Alexander Ditjatin (USSR) |
| 1981 | Yuri Korolev (USSR) |
| 1983 | Dmitri Belozerchev (USSR) |
| 1985 | Yuri Korolev (USSR) |
| 1987 | Dmitri Belozerchev (USSR) |
| 1989 | Igor Korobichensky (USSR) |
| 1991 | Vitaly Scherbo (USSR) |
| 1993 | Vitaly Scherbo (Belarus) |
| 1994 | Ivan Ivankov (Belarus) |
| 1995 | Li Xiaoshuang (China) |
| 1997 | Ivan Ivankov (Belarus) |
| 1999 | Nikolay Krukov (Russia) |
| 2001 | Jing Feng (China) |
| 2003 | Paul Hamm (USA) |

**Individual – Women**

| | |
|---|---|
| 1979 | Nelli Kim (USSR) |
| 1981 | Olga Bitscherova (USSR) |
| 1983 | Natalia Yurtschenko (USSR) |
| 1985 | Yelena Shoushounova (USSR) and Oksana Omeliantchuk (USSR) |
| 1987 | Aurelia Dobre (Romania) |
| 1989 | Svetlana Boginskaya (USSR) |
| 1991 | Kim Zmeskal (USA) |
| 1993 | Shannon Miller (USA) |
| 1994 | Shannon Miller (USA) |
| 1995 | Lilia Podkopayeva (Ukraine) |
| 1997 | Svetlana Khorkina (Russia) |
| 1999 | Maria Olaru (Romania) |
| 2001 | Svetlana Khorkina (Russia) |
| 2003 | Svetlana Khorkina (Russia) |

| Team – Men | |
|---|---|
| 1979 | USSR |
| 1981 | USSR |
| 1983 | China |
| 1985 | USSR |
| 1987 | USSR |
| 1989 | USSR |
| 1991 | USSR |
| 1993 | *no team prize* |
| 1994 | China |
| 1995 | China |
| 1997 | China |
| 1999 | China |
| 2001 | Belarus |
| 2003 | China |

| Team – Women | |
|---|---|
| 1979 | Romania |
| 1981 | USSR |
| 1983 | USSR |
| 1985 | USSR |
| 1987 | Romania |
| 1989 | USSR |
| 1991 | USSR |
| 1993 | *no team prize* |
| 1994 | Romania |
| 1995 | Romania |
| 1997 | Romania |
| 1999 | Romania |
| 2001 | Romania |
| 2003 | USA |

### Perfect Ten

One of the most famous gymnasts of all time is Nadia Comaneci (born 1961) from Romania. At the 1976 Olympic Games, at the age of just 14, Comaneci won gold medals in the parallel bars and beam disciplines, and a bronze in the floor, becoming the first gymnast to obtain a perfect score of 10 for her performance on the bars and beam. She also won a gold medal at the 1978 world championships and gold medals in the 1980 Olympics, later becoming an international judge and coach to the Romanian national team. In 1989 she defected to the USA.

## HOCKEY

**Stick-and-ball game played by two teams of eleven, the object being to move the ball around with the sticks until a player can score from within the semicircle in front of the opposing side's goal; game is split into two halves of 35 minutes. Also known in North America as *field hockey*.**

*Ruling body: International Hockey Federation (FIH; Fédération Internationale de Hockey)*

### Historic Hockey

The ancient Greeks played a game akin to hockey c.2500BC, and the ancient Egyptians are believed to have played an early version of it 4 000 years ago. The Romans, ancient Ethiopians and Aztecs are all thought to have played similar games.

## Hockey pitch

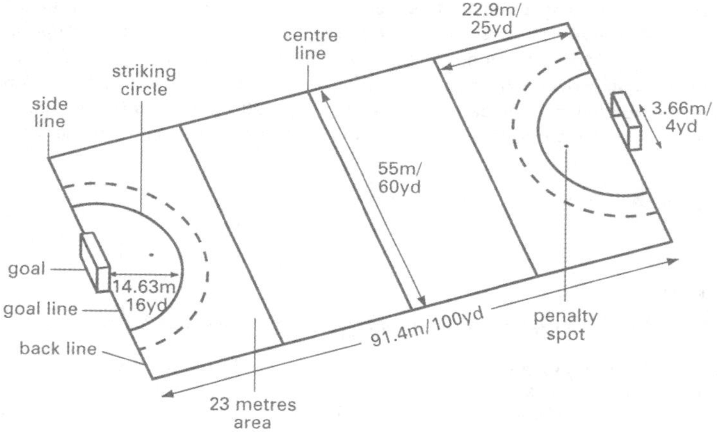


## World Cup

Men's tournament first held in 1971, and every four years since 1978; women's tournament first held in 1972, and now takes place every three or four years.

**Men**

| | |
|---|---|
| 1982 | Pakistan |
| 1986 | Australia |
| 1990 | The Netherlands |
| 1994 | Pakistan |
| 1998 | The Netherlands |
| 2002 | Germany |

**Women**

| | |
|---|---|
| 1981 | West Germany |
| 1983 | The Netherlands |
| 1986 | The Netherlands |
| 1990 | The Netherlands |
| 1994 | Australia |
| 1998 | Australia |
| 2002 | Argentina |

## Olympic Games

Regarded as hockey's leading competition; first held in 1908; included at every celebration since 1928; women's competition first held in 1980.

**Men**

| | |
|---|---|
| 1980 | India |
| 1984 | Pakistan |
| 1988 | Great Britain |
| 1992 | Germany |
| 1996 | The Netherlands |
| 2000 | The Netherlands |

**Women**

| | |
|---|---|
| 1980 | Zimbabwe |
| 1984 | The Netherlands |
| 1988 | Australia |
| 1992 | Spain |
| 1996 | Australia |
| 2000 | Australia |

## HORSE RACING

Racing of horses against one another, each ridden by a jockey. Two categories: flat racing for thoroughbred horses on a flat grass or dirt surface over a predetermined distance from 1–4km/5 furlongs–2.5mi, and national hunt racing in which the horses negotiate either movable hurdles or fixed fences over a distance up to 6.5km/4.5mi. The ancient Egyptians took part in horse races in c.1200BC; popularized in 12c England. Most monarchs have supported the sport, hence the name the 'sport of kings'.

*Ruling body (UK): British Horseracing Board (BHB)*

### The Derby

The 'Blue Riband' of the turf; run at Epsom over 1½ miles; first run in 1780.

| | Horse (Jockey) |
|---|---|
| 1979 | Troy (W Carson) |
| 1980 | Henbit (W Carson) |
| 1981 | Shergar (W Swinburn) |
| 1982 | Golden Fleece (P Eddery) |
| 1983 | Teenoso (L Piggott) |
| 1984 | Secreto (C Roche) |
| 1985 | Slip Anchor (S Cauthen) |
| 1986 | Shahrastani (W Swinburn) |
| 1987 | Reference Point (S Cauthen) |
| 1988 | Kahyasi (R Cochrane) |
| 1989 | Nashwan (W Carson) |
| 1990 | Quest For Fame (P Eddery) |
| 1991 | Generous (A Munro) |
| 1992 | Dr Devious (J Reid) |
| 1993 | Commander in Chief (M Kinane) |
| 1994 | Erhaab (W Carson) |
| 1995 | Lammtarra (W Swinburn) |
| 1996 | Shaamit (M Hills) |
| 1997 | Benny the Dip (W Ryan) |
| 1998 | High Rise (O Peslier) |
| 1999 | Oath (K Fallon) |
| 2000 | Sinndar (J Murtagh) |
| 2001 | Galileo (M Kinane) |
| 2002 | High Chaparral (J Murtagh) |
| 2003 | Kris Kin (K Fallon) |

### The Oaks

Run at Epsom over 1½ miles; for fillies only; first run in 1779.

| | Horse (Jockey) |
|---|---|
| 1979 | Scintillate (P Eddery) |
| 1980 | Bireme (W Carson) |
| 1981 | Blue Wind (L Piggott) |
| 1982 | Time Charter (W Newnes) |
| 1983 | Sun Princess (W Carson) |
| 1984 | Circus Plume (L Piggott) |
| 1985 | Oh So Sharp (S Cauthen) |
| 1986 | Midway Lady (R Cochrane) |
| 1987 | Unite (W Swinburn) |
| 1988 | Diminuendo (S Cauthen) |
| 1989 | Aliysa (W Swinburn) |
| 1990 | Salsabil (W Carson) |
| 1991 | Jet Ski Lady (C Roche) |
| 1992 | User Friendly (G Duffield) |
| 1993 | Intrepidity (M Roberts) |
| 1994 | Balanchine (F Dettori) |
| 1995 | Moonshell (F Dettori) |
| 1996 | Lady Carla (P Eddery) |
| 1997 | Reams of Verse (K Fallon) |
| 1998 | Shahtoush (M Kinane) |
| 1999 | Ramruma (K Fallon) |
| 2000 | Love Divine (R Quinn) |
| 2001 | Imagine (M Kinane) |
| 2002 | Kazzia (F Dettori) |
| 2003 | Casual Look (M Dwyer) |

## One Thousand Guineas

Run at Newmarket over 1 mile; for fillies only; first run in 1814.

| | Horse (Jockey) | | Horse (Jockey) |
|---|---|---|---|
| 1979 | One in a Million (J Mercer) | 1992 | Hatoof (W Swinburn) |
| 1980 | Quick As Lightning (B Rouse) | 1993 | Sayyedati (W Swinburn) |
| 1981 | Fairy Footsteps (L Piggott) | 1994 | Las Meninas (J Reid) |
| 1982 | On The House (J Reid) | 1995 | Harayir (R Hills) |
| 1983 | Ma Biche (F Head) | 1996 | Bosra Sham (P Eddery) |
| 1984 | Pebbles (P Robinson) | 1997 | Sleepytime (K Fallon) |
| 1985 | Oh So Sharp (S Cauthen) | 1998 | Cape Verdi (F Dettori) |
| 1986 | Midway Lady (R Cochrane) | 1999 | Wince (K Fallon) |
| 1987 | Miesque (F Head) | 2000 | Lahan (R Hills) |
| 1988 | Ravinella (G Moore) | 2001 | Ameerat (P Robinson) |
| 1989 | Musical Bliss (W Swinburn) | 2002 | Kazzia (F Dettori) |
| 1990 | Salsabil (W Carson) | 2003 | Russian Rhythm (K Fallon) |
| 1991 | Shadayid (W Carson) | | |

### *Charlotte and Wizard*

The very first One Thousand Guineas race in 1814 was won by a horse named Charlotte, owned by Christopher Wilson and ridden by Bill Clift. The same team of owner and jockey had also triumphed at the very first Two Thousand Guineas race in 1809 with a horse named Wizard.

## Two Thousand Guineas

Run at Newmarket over 1 mile; first run in 1809.

| | Horse (Jockey) | | Horse (Jockey) |
|---|---|---|---|
| 1979 | Tap On Wood (S Cauthen) | 1992 | Rodrigo de Traiano (L Piggott) |
| 1980 | Known Fact (W Carson) | 1993 | Zafonic (P Eddery) |
| 1981 | To-Agori-Mou (G Starkey) | 1994 | Mister Baileys (J Weaver) |
| 1982 | Zino (F Head) | 1995 | Pennekamp (T Jarnet) |
| 1983 | Lomond (P Eddery) | 1996 | Mark of Esteem (F Dettori) |
| 1984 | El Gran Senor (P Eddery) | 1997 | Entrepreneur (M Kinane) |
| 1985 | Shadeed (L Piggott) | 1998 | King of Kings (M Kinane) |
| 1986 | Dancing Brave (G Starkey) | 1999 | Island Sands (F Dettori) |
| 1987 | Don't Forget Me (W Carson) | 2000 | King's Best (K Fallon) |
| 1988 | Doyoun (W Swinburn) | 2001 | Golan (K Fallon) |
| 1989 | Nashwan (W Carson) | 2002 | Rock of Gibraltar (J Murtagh) |
| 1990 | Tirol (M Kinane) | 2003 | Refuse to Bend (P Smullen) |
| 1991 | Mystiko (M Roberts) | | |

### *Royal Racing*

The One Thousand Guineas and Two Thousand Guineas are raced on the Rowley Mile Racecourse in Newmarket. The course is named after King Charles II (1630–85) – one of whose nicknames was supposedly 'Old Rowley' – who encouraged horse racing in Newmarket in the 17c.

## St Leger

The oldest of the five English classics; first run in 1776; run at Doncaster annually over 1 mile 6 furlongs 127 yards.

| | Horse (Jockey) |
|---|---|
| 1979 | Son of Love (A Lequeux) |
| 1980 | Light Cavalry (J Mercer) |
| 1981 | Cut Above (J Mercer) |
| 1982 | Touching Wood (P Cook) |
| 1983 | Sun Princess (W Carson) |
| 1984 | Commanche Run (L Piggott) |
| 1985 | Oh So Sharp (S Cauthen) |
| 1986 | Moon Madness (P Eddery) |
| 1987 | Reference Point (S Cauthen) |
| 1988 | Minster Son (W Carson) |
| 1989 | Michelozzo (S Cauthen) |
| 1990 | Snurge (R Quinn) |
| 1991 | Toulon (P Eddery) |
| 1992 | User Friendly (G Duffield) |
| 1993 | Bob's Return (P Robinson) |
| 1994 | Moonax (P Eddery) |
| 1995 | Classic Cliche (F Dettori) |
| 1996 | Shantou (F Dettori) |
| 1997 | Silver Patriarch (P Eddery) |
| 1998 | Nedawi (J Reid) |
| 1999 | Mutafaweq (R Hills) |
| 2000 | Millenary (R Quinn) |
| 2001 | Milan (M Kinane) |
| 2002 | Bollin Eric (K Darley) |
| 2003 | Brian Boru (J Spencer) |

### Becher's Brook

When the first Grand National was run at Aintree competitors had to jump a stone wall and cross a ploughed field, as well as clearing two final hurdles. Today, the course includes a total of 30 fences (16 jumped on the first circuit and 14 on the second), described by the organizers as being some of 'the most testing fences in the world of jump racing'. The most famous is the sixth, Becher's Brook, renowned for its difficulty because of its average take-off height of just over 1.2m/4ft but steep drop of almost 2.2m/7ft on the landing side. The obstacle is named after one Captain Martin Becher (1797–1864). Becher was thrown from his horse at the fence during the first Aintree Grand National in 1839 and deposited unceremoniously in the water – he famously commented on 'how dreadful water tastes without the benefit of whisky'. It was his first and last Grand National appearance.

## Grand National

Steeplechasing's most famous race; first run at Maghull in 1836; at Aintree since 1839; wartime races at Gatwick 1916–18; run over 4½ miles.

| | Horse (Jockey) |
|---|---|
| 1979 | Rubstic (M Barnes) |
| 1980 | Ben Nevis (C Fenwick) |
| 1981 | Aldaniti (B Champion) |
| 1982 | Grittar (D Saunders) |
| 1983 | Corbiere (B de Haan) |
| 1984 | Hallo Dandy (N Doughty) |
| 1985 | Last Suspect (H Davies) |
| 1986 | West Tip (R Dunwoody) |
| 1987 | Maori Venture (S Knight) |
| 1988 | Rhyme 'N' Reason (B Powell) |
| 1989 | Little Polveir (J Frost) |
| 1990 | Mr Frisk (M Armytage) |
| 1991 | Seagram (N Hawke) |
| 1992 | Party Politics (C Llewellyn) |
| 1993 | *race declared void* Esha Ness (J White) first past the post |
| 1994 | Minnehoma (R Dunwoody) |
| 1995 | Royal Athlete (J Titley) |
| 1996 | Rough Quest (M Fitzgerald) |
| 1997 | Lord Gyllene (T Dobbin) |
| 1998 | Earth Summit (C Llewellyn) |
| 1999 | Bobbyjo (P Carberry) |
| 2000 | Papillon (R Walsh) |
| 2001 | Red Marauder (R Guest) |
| 2002 | Bindaree (J Culloty) |
| 2003 | Monty's Pass (B Geraghty) |

## Prix de l'Arc de Triomphe

The leading end of season race in Europe; raced over 2 400 metres at Longchamp; first run in 1920.

| | Horse (Jockey) |
|---|---|
| 1979 | Three Troikas (F Head) |
| 1980 | Detroit (P Eddery) |
| 1981 | Gold River (G Moore) |
| 1982 | Akiyda (Y Saint-Martin) |
| 1983 | All Along (W Swinburn) |
| 1984 | Sagace (Y Saint-Martin) |
| 1985 | Rainbow Quest (P Eddery) |
| 1986 | Dancing Brave (P Eddery) |
| 1987 | Trempolino (P Eddery) |
| 1988 | Tony Bin (J Reid) |
| 1989 | Caroll House (M Kinane) |
| 1990 | Suamarez (G Mosse) |
| 1991 | Suave Dancer (C Asmussen) |
| 1992 | Subotica (T Jarnet) |
| 1993 | Urban Sea (E Saint-Martin) |
| 1994 | Carnegie (T Jarnet) |
| 1995 | Lammtarra (F Dettori) |
| 1996 | Helissio (O Peslier) |
| 1997 | Peintre Celebre (O Peslier) |
| 1998 | Sagamix (O Peslier) |
| 1999 | Montjeu (M Kinane) |
| 2000 | Sinndar (J Murtagh) |
| 2001 | Sakhee (F Dettori) |
| 2002 | Marienbard (F Dettori) |
| 2003 | Dalakhani (C Soumillon) |

## Kentucky Derby

Run at Churchill Downs, Louisville, Kentucky, USA over 1¼ mile; first run in 1875.

| | Horse (Jockey) |
|---|---|
| 1979 | Spectacular Bid (R Franklin) |
| 1980 | Genuine Risk (J Vasquez) |
| 1981 | Pleasant Colony (J Velasquez) |
| 1982 | Gato Del Sol (E Delahoussaye) |
| 1983 | Sunny's Halo (E Delahoussaye) |
| 1984 | Swale (L Pincay, Jr) |
| 1985 | Spend a Buck (A Cordero, Jr) |
| 1986 | Ferdinand (W Shoemaker) |
| 1987 | Alysheba (C McCarron) |
| 1988 | Winning Colors (G Stevens) |
| 1989 | Sunday Silence (P Valenzuela) |
| 1990 | Unbridled (C Perret) |
| 1991 | Strike the Gold (C Antley) |
| 1992 | Lil E Tee (P Day) |
| 1993 | Sea Hero (J Bailey) |
| 1994 | Go for Gin (C McCarron) |
| 1995 | Thunder Gulch (G Stevens) |
| 1996 | Grindstone (J Bailey) |
| 1997 | Silver Charm (G Stevens) |
| 1998 | Real Quiet (K Desormeaux) |
| 1999 | Charismatic (C Antley) |
| 2000 | Fusaichi Pegasus (K Desormeaux) |
| 2001 | Monarchos (J Chavez) |
| 2002 | War Emblem (V Espinoza) |
| 2003 | Funny Cide (J Santos) |

### *Kentucky Colours*

If you're looking to win money at the Kentucky Derby, back a bay: by 2003 47 bay horses had won the race, compared to 42 chestnut horses, 28 dark bay or brown horses, eight grey or roan horses and four black horses. Another quirk of the Derby is that two anonymous horses have been entered – one in 1998 which never actually ran, and another which finished ninth in 1882.

## HURLING

Irish 15-a-side field game played with curved sticks (the *hurley* or *camán*) and a ball (the *sliothar*); object to hit ball into opposing team's goal: under the crossbar scores three points; above the crossbar but between the posts scores one.

*Ruling body: Gaelic Athletic Association (GAA)*

### Hurling pitch

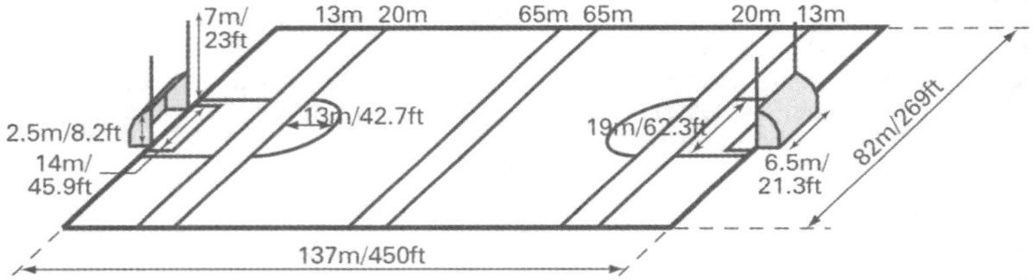


*Note: Pitch size is approximate (length minimum 130m/426.5ft, maximum 145m/475.7ft; width minimum 80m/262.5ft, maximum 90m/295.3ft). The goalpost height of 7m/23ft is the minimum permitted.*

### All-Ireland Championship

First contested in 1887; played on the first Sunday in Sep each year.

| | | | | | |
|---|---|---|---|---|---|
| 1979 | Kilkenny | 1988 | Galway | 1997 | Clare |
| 1980 | Galway | 1989 | Tipperary | 1998 | Offaly |
| 1981 | Offaly | 1990 | Cork | 1999 | Cork |
| 1982 | Kilkenny | 1991 | Tipperary | 2000 | Kilkenny |
| 1983 | Kilkenny | 1992 | Kilkenny | 2001 | Tipperary |
| 1984 | Cork | 1993 | Kilkenny | 2002 | Kilkenny |
| 1985 | Offaly | 1994 | Offaly | 2003 | Kilkenny |
| 1986 | Cork | 1995 | Clare | | |
| 1987 | Galway | 1996 | Wexford | | |

### *Hurling in History*

Hurling is thought to be the oldest field game in Europe. The Gaelic Athletic Association believes that it was brought to Ireland by the Celts, and that the game has been part of Irish culture for 2 000 years.

## ICE HOCKEY

Fast game played by two teams of six on an ice rink with sticks and a small rubber puck; aim is to score goals by using the stick to hit the *puck* into the opposing team's goal; players wear ice skates and protective clothing; possibly first played 1850s Canada.

*Ruling body: International Ice Hockey Federation (IIHF)*

### Ice hockey rink

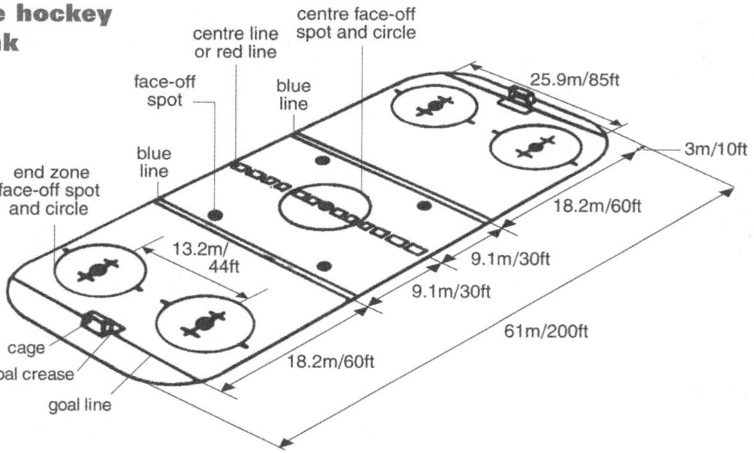


### World Championship

First held in 1920; takes place annually (except in the Olympic years 1980, 1984 and 1988); up to 1968 Olympic champions also regarded as world champions.

| | | | | | |
|---|---|---|---|---|---|
| 1979 | USSR | 1991 | Sweden | 2000 | Czech Republic |
| 1981 | USSR | 1992 | Sweden | 2001 | Czech Republic |
| 1982 | USSR | 1993 | Russia | 2002 | Slovakia |
| 1983 | USSR | 1994 | Canada | 2003 | Canada |
| 1985 | Czechoslovakia | 1995 | Finland | | |
| 1986 | USSR | 1996 | Czech Republic | | |
| 1987 | Sweden | 1997 | Canada | | |
| 1989 | USSR | 1998 | Sweden | | |
| 1990 | USSR | 1999 | Czech Republic | | |

### *No Pressure*

How would you like a job where, every time you make a mistake, a big red light goes on and 18 000 people boo?

**Jacques Plante (1929–86), Canadian ice hockey player and a leading goalkeeper. Attributed. Quoted in John Robert Colombo (ed) *Colombo's All-Time Great Canadian Quotations* (1994).**

## Stanley Cup

The most sought-after trophy at club level; the end-of-season meeting between the winners of the two conferences in the National Hockey League (NHL) in the USA and Canada; first held in 1893.

| | | | | | |
|---|---|---|---|---|---|
| 1979 | Montreal Canadiens | 1988 | Edmonton Oilers | 1997 | Detroit Red Wings |
| 1980 | New York Islanders | 1989 | Calgary Flames | 1998 | Detroit Red Wings |
| 1981 | New York Islanders | 1990 | Edmonton Oilers | 1999 | Dallas Stars |
| 1982 | New York Islanders | 1991 | Pittsburgh Penguins | 2000 | New Jersey Devils |
| 1983 | New York Islanders | 1992 | Pittsburgh Penguins | 2001 | Colorado Avalanche |
| 1984 | Edmonton Oilers | 1993 | Montreal Canadiens | 2002 | Detroit Red Wings |
| 1985 | Edmonton Oilers | 1994 | New York Rangers | 2003 | New Jersey Devils |
| 1986 | Montreal Canadiens | 1995 | New Jersey Devils | | |
| 1987 | Edmonton Oilers | 1996 | Colorado Avalanche | | |

# ICE SKATING

*Figure skating* is artistic dancing on ice for individuals and pairs; first known skating club formed mid-18c London; first artificial rink opened 1876 Baker Street.

*Ruling body: International Skating Union (ISU)*

## World Championships

First men's championships in 1896; first women's event in 1906; pairs first contested in 1908; Ice Dance officially recognized in 1952.

| **Men** | | **Women** | |
|---|---|---|---|
| 1979 | Vladimir Kovalev (USSR) | 1979 | Linda Fratianne (USA) |
| 1980 | Jan Hoffmann (East Germany) | 1980 | Anett Pötzsch (East Germany) |
| 1981 | Scott Hamilton (USA) | 1981 | Denise Biellmann (Switzerland) |
| 1982 | Scott Hamilton (USA) | 1982 | Elaine Zayak (USA) |
| 1983 | Scott Hamilton (USA) | 1983 | Rosalynn Sumners (USA) |
| 1984 | Scott Hamilton (USA) | 1984 | Katarina Witt (East Germany) |
| 1985 | Alexander Fadeyev (USSR) | 1985 | Katarina Witt (East Germany) |
| 1986 | Brian Boitano (USA) | 1986 | Debbie Thomas (USA) |
| 1987 | Brian Orser (Canada) | 1987 | Katarina Witt (East Germany) |
| 1988 | Brian Boitano (USA) | 1988 | Katarina Witt (East Germany) |
| 1989 | Kurt Browning (Canada) | 1989 | Midori Ito (Japan) |
| 1990 | Kurt Browning (Canada) | 1990 | Jill Trenary (USA) |
| 1991 | Kurt Browning (Canada) | 1991 | Kristi Yamaguchi (USA) |
| 1992 | Viktor Petrenko (CIS) | 1992 | Kristi Yamaguchi (USA) |
| 1993 | Kurt Browning (Canada) | 1993 | Oksana Baiul (Ukraine) |
| 1994 | Elvis Stojko (Canada) | 1994 | Yuka Sato (Japan) |
| 1995 | Elvis Stojko (Canada) | 1995 | Lu Chen (China) |
| 1996 | Todd Eldredge (USA) | 1996 | Michelle Kwan (USA) |
| 1997 | Elvis Stojko (Canada) | 1997 | Tara Lipinski (USA) |
| 1998 | Alexei Yagudin (Russia) | 1998 | Michelle Kwan (USA) |
| 1999 | Alexei Yagudin (Russia) | 1999 | Maria Butyrskaya (Russia) |
| 2000 | Alexei Yagudin (Russia) | 2000 | Michelle Kwan (USA) |

**Men**

| | |
|---|---|
| 2001 | Evgeny Plushenko (Russia) |
| 2002 | Alexei Yagudin (Russia) |
| 2003 | Evgeny Plushenko (Russia) |

**Women**

| | |
|---|---|
| 2001 | Michelle Kwan (USA) |
| 2002 | Irina Slutskaya (Russia) |
| 2003 | Michelle Kwan (USA) |

**Pairs**

| | |
|---|---|
| 1979 | Tai Babilonia/Randy Gardner (USA) |
| 1980 | Marina Cherkasova/Sergei Shakhrai (USSR) |
| 1981 | Irina Vorobieva/Igor Lisovski (USSR) |
| 1982 | Sabine Baess/Tassilo Thierbach (East Germany) |
| 1983 | Yelena Valova/Oleg Vasiliev (USSR) |
| 1984 | Barbara Underhill/Paul Martini (Canada) |
| 1985 | Yelena Valova/Oleg Vasiliev (USSR) |
| 1986 | Yekaterina Gordeeva/Sergei Grinkov (USSR) |
| 1987 | Yekaterina Gordeeva/Sergei Grinkov (USSR) |
| 1988 | Yelena Valova/Oleg Vasiliev (USSR) |
| 1989 | Yekaterina Gordeeva/Sergei Grinkov (USSR) |
| 1990 | Yekaterina Gordeeva/Sergei Grinkov (USSR) |
| 1991 | Natalya Mishkutienok/Artur Dmtriev (USSR) |
| 1992 | Natalya Mishkutienok/Artur Dmtriev (USSR) |
| 1993 | Isabelle Brasseu/Lloyd Eisler (Canada) |
| 1994 | Evgenia Shiskova/Vadim Naumov (Russia) |
| 1995 | Radka Kovarikova/Rene Novotny (Czech Republic) |
| 1996 | Marina Eltsova/Andrei Bushkov (Russia) |
| 1997 | Mandy Woetzel/Ingo Steuer (Germany) |
| 1998 | Elena Berezhnay/Anton Sikharulidze (Russia) |
| 1999 | Elena Berezhnay/Anton Sikharulidze (Russia) |
| 2000 | Maria Petrova/Alexei Tikhonov (Russia) |
| 2001 | Jamie Sale/David Pelletier (Canada) |
| 2002 | Hongbo Zhao/Xue Shen (China) |
| 2003 | Hongbo Zhao/Xue Shen (China) |

**Ice Dance**

| | |
|---|---|
| 1979 | Natalya Linichuk/Gennadi Karponosov (USSR) |
| 1980 | Krisztina Regoczy/Andras Sallay (Hungary) |
| 1981 | Jayne Torvill/Christopher Dean (Great Britain) |
| 1982 | Jayne Torvill/Christopher Dean (Great Britain) |
| 1983 | Jayne Torvill/Christopher Dean (Great Britain) |
| 1984 | Jayne Torvill/Christopher Dean (Great Britain) |
| 1985 | Natalya Bestemianova/Andrei Bukin (USSR) |
| 1986 | Natalya Bestemianova/Andrei Bukin (USSR) |
| 1987 | Natalya Bestemianova/Andrei Bukin (USSR) |
| 1988 | Natalya Bestemianova/Andrei Bukin (USSR) |
| 1989 | Marina Klimova/Sergei Ponomarenko (USSR) |
| 1990 | Marina Klimova/Sergei Ponomarenko (USSR) |
| 1991 | Isabelle and Paul Duchesnay (France) |
| 1992 | Marina Klimova/Sergei Ponomarenko (CIS) |
| 1993 | Maya Usova/Alexandr Zhulin (Russia) |
| 1994 | Oksana Gritschuk/Yevgeni Platov (Russia) |
| 1995 | Oksana Gritschuk/Yevgeni Platov (Russia) |
| 1996 | Oksana Gritschuk/Yevgeni Platov (Russia) |
| 1997 | Oksana Gritschuk/Yevgeni Platov (Russia) |
| 1998 | Anjelika Krylova/Oleg Ovsyannikov (Russia) |
| 1999 | Anjelika Krylova/Oleg Ovsyannikov (Russia) |

**Ice Dance**

| | |
|---|---|
| 2000 | Marina Anissina/Gwendal Peizerat (France) |
| 2001 | Barbara Fusar-Poli/Maurizio Margaglio (Italy) |
| 2002 | Irina Lobacheva/Ilia Averbukh (Russia) |
| 2003 | Shae-Lynn Bourne/Victor Kraatz (Canada) |

### *Skating Boxer*

US skater Tonya Harding (born 1971) gained notoriety when she won the US Figure Skating Championships in 1994. The favourite, Nancy Kerrigan, was unable to compete having been clubbed on the knee by a hitman while training, and Harding's ex-husband and her bodyguard were later given prison sentences for their role in the attack. Harding herself was later stripped of her skating title, banned for life from the US Figure Skating Association and fined $100 000 when she was found guilty of withholding information concerning Kerrigan's injury. Harding began a new career as a boxer, but lost her first professional fight – a show bout before a Mike Tyson fight in Memphis, Tennessee, USA, in early 2003.

## JUDO

Unarmed combat sport of late 19c Japanese origin. Contestants wear a *judogi* or loose-fitting suit and compete on a mat which breaks their falls. When one cannot break a hold, surrender is signalled by slapping the mat; ability is graded from fifth to first Kyu, and then first to 12th Dan – only Dr Jigoro Kano, who devised the sport, has been awarded 12th Dan. Different coloured belts indicate grades; eg white for novice, brown (three degrees) and black (nine degrees).

*Ruling body: International Judo Federation (IJF)*

### World Championships

First held in 1956, now contested every two years; current weight categories established in 1999; women's championship instituted in 1980.

#### 1995

**Men**

| | |
|---|---|
| open class | David Douillet (France) |
| over 95kg | David Douillet (France) |
| under 95kg | Pawel Nastula (Poland) |
| under 86kg | Jeon Ki Young (South Korea) |
| under 78kg | Toshihiko Koga (Japan) |
| under 71kg | Daisuke Hideshima (Japan) |
| under 65kg | Udo Quellmalz (Germany) |
| under 60kg | Nikolai Ojeguine (Russia) |

**Women**

| | |
|---|---|
| open class | Monique van der Lee (The Netherlands) |
| over 72kg | Angelique Seriese (The Netherlands) |
| under 72kg | Castellano Luna (Cuba) |
| under 66kg | Cho Min Sun (South Korea) |
| under 61kg | Jung Sung Sook (South Korea) |
| under 56kg | Driulis González (Cuba) |
| under 52kg | Marie-Claire Restoux (France) |
| under 48kg | Ryoko Tamura (Japan) |

## 1997

**Men**

| | |
|---|---|
| open class | Rafael Kubacki (Poland) |
| over 95kg | David Douillet (France) |
| under 95kg | Pawel Nastula (Poland) |
| under 86kg | Jeon Ki Young (South Korea) |
| under 78kg | Chul Cho In (South Korea) |
| under 71kg | Kenzo Nakamura (Japan) |
| under 65kg | Hyuk Kim (Korea) |
| under 60kg | Tadahiro Nomura (Japan) |

**Women**

| | |
|---|---|
| open class | Daina Beltran (Cuba) |
| over 72kg | Christine Cicot (France) |
| under 72kg | Noriko Anno (Japan) |
| under 66kg | Kate Howey (Great Britain) |
| under 61kg | Servenr Vandenhende (France) |
| under 56kg | Isabel Fernandez (Spain) |
| under 52kg | Marie-Claire Restoux (France) |
| under 48kg | Ryoko Tamura (Japan) |

## 1999

**Men**

| | |
|---|---|
| open class | Shinichi Shinohara (Japan) |
| over 100kg | Shinichi Shinohara (Japan) |
| under 100kg | Kosei Inoue (Japan) |
| under 90kg | Hidehiko Yoshida (Japan) |
| under 81kg | Graeme Randall (Great Britain) |
| under 73kg | Jimmy Pedro (USA) |
| under 66kg | Larbi Benboudaoud (France) |
| under 60kg | Manuelo Poulot (Cuba) |

**Women**

| | |
|---|---|
| open class | Daina Beltran (Cuba) |
| over 78kg | Beata Maksymow (Poland) |
| under 78kg | Noriko Anno (Japan) |
| under 70kg | Sibelis Veranes (Cuba) |
| under 63kg | Keiko Maedo (Japan) |
| under 57kg | Driulis González (Cuba) |
| under 52kg | Noriko Narasaki (Japan) |
| under 48kg | Ryoko Tamura (Japan) |

## 2001

**Men**

| | |
|---|---|
| open class | Alexandre Mikhaylin (Russia) |
| over 100kg | Alexandre Mikhaylin (Russia) |
| under 100kg | Kosei Inoue (Japan) |
| under 90kg | Frederic Demoutfaucon (France) |
| under 81kg | Chul Cho In (South Korea) |
| under 73kg | Vital Makarov (Russia) |
| under 66kg | Arash Miresmaeli (Iran) |
| under 60kg | Anis Lounifi (Tunisia) |

**Women**

| | |
|---|---|
| open class | Celine Lebrun (France) |
| over 78kg | Yuan Hua (China) |
| under 78kg | Noriko Anno (Japan) |
| under 70kg | Masae Ueno (Japan) |
| under 63kg | Gella van de Cayeve (Belgium) |
| under 57kg | Yourisledes Lupety (Cuba) |
| under 52kg | Sun Hui Kye (North Korea) |
| under 48kg | Ryoko Tamura (Japan) |

## 2003

**Men**

| | |
|---|---|
| open class | Keiji Suzuki (Japan) |
| over 100kg | Yauyuki Muneta (Japan) |
| under 100kg | Kosei Inoue (Japan) |
| under 90kg | Hee Tae Hwang (South Korea) |
| under 81kg | Florian Wanner (Germany) |
| under 73kg | Won Hee Lee (South Korea) |
| under 66kg | Arash Miresmaeli (Iran) |
| under 60kg | Min Ho Choi (South Korea) |

**Women**

| | |
|---|---|
| open class | Wen Tong (China) |
| over 78kg | Fuming Sun (China) |
| under 78kg | Noriko Anno (Japan) |
| under 70kg | Masae Ueno (Japan) |
| under 63kg | Daniela Krukower (Argentina) |
| under 57kg | Sun Hui Kye (North Korea) |
| under 52kg | Amarilis Savon (Cuba) |
| under 48kg | Ryoko Tamura (Japan) |

## KARATE

Martial art of unarmed combat, dating from 17c; developed Japan 20c; name adopted 1930s; aim is to be in total control of the body's muscular power, so it can be used with great force and accuracy at any instant. Experts may show their mental and physical training by eg breaking various thicknesses of wood, but in fighting an opponent blows do not actually make contact; levels of prowess symbolized by coloured belts.

*Ruling body: World Karate Federation (WKF)*

### World Championships

First held in Tokyo in 1970; has taken place every two years since 1980; today, there are team competitions plus individual competitions at Kumite and Kata.

#### Kumite

**Combined**

| | |
|---|---|
| 1980 | Spain |
| 1982 | Great Britain |
| 1984 | Great Britain |
| 1986 | Great Britain |
| 1988 | Great Britain |
| 1990 | Great Britain |

**Men**

| | |
|---|---|
| 1992 | Spain |
| 1994 | France |
| 1996 | France |
| 1998 | France |
| 2000 | France |
| 2002 | Spain |

**Women**

| | |
|---|---|
| 1992 | Great Britain |
| 1994 | Spain |
| 1996 | Great Britain |
| 1998 | Turkey |
| 2000 | France |
| 2002 | Spain |

#### Kata

**Men**

| | |
|---|---|
| 1986 | Japan |
| 1988 | Japan |
| 1990 | Italy |
| 1992 | Japan |
| 1994 | Japan |
| 1996 | Japan |
| 1998 | Japan |
| 2000 | Japan |
| 2002 | Japan |

**Women**

| | |
|---|---|
| 1986 | Taiwan |
| 1988 | France |
| 1992 | Japan |
| 1994 | Japan |
| 1996 | Japan |
| 1998 | Japan |
| 2000 | France |
| 2002 | France |

**Empty Hand**

*Karate* means 'empty hand' in Japanese.

## MARATHON

Long-distance running race, normally on open roads, over 42km 195m/26mi 385yd. In the 1980s the half marathon over 21km/13mi 194yd also became popular. For World Championship marathon results see **Athletics**.

*Ruling body: International Association of Athletics Federations (IAAF)*

### London Marathon

First run in 1981, when 6 255 people completed the course of 42km 195m/26mi 385yd. To date, over half a million people have completed the London Marathon.

**Men**

| | |
|---|---|
| 1981 | Dick Beardsley (USA)/Inge Simonsen (Norway) |
| 1982 | Hugh Jones (Great Britain) |
| 1983 | Mike Gratton (Great Britain) |
| 1984 | Charlie Spedding (Great Britain) |
| 1985 | Steve Jones (Great Britain) |
| 1986 | Toshihiko Seko (Japan) |
| 1987 | Hiromi Taniguchi (Japan) |
| 1988 | Henrik Jorgensen (Denmark) |
| 1989 | Douglas Wakiihuri (Kenya) |
| 1990 | Allister Hutton (Great Britain) |
| 1991 | Yakov Tolstikov (Russia) |
| 1992 | Antonio Pinto (Portugal) |
| 1993 | Eamonn Martin (Great Britain) |
| 1994 | Dionicio Ceron (Mexico) |
| 1995 | Dionicio Ceron (Mexico) |
| 1996 | Dionicio Ceron (Mexico) |
| 1997 | Antonio Pinto (Portugal) |
| 1998 | Abel Antón (Spain) |
| 1999 | Abdelkader El Mouaziz (Morocco) |
| 2000 | Antonio Pinto (Portugal) |
| 2001 | Abdelkader El Mouaziz (Morocco) |
| 2002 | Khalid Khannouchi (USA) |
| 2003 | Gezahegne Abera (Ethiopia) |

**Women**

| | |
|---|---|
| 1981 | Joyce Smith (Great Britain) |
| 1982 | Joyce Smith (Great Britain) |
| 1983 | Grete Waitz (Norway) |
| 1984 | Ingrid Kristiansen (Norway) |
| 1985 | Ingrid Kristiansen (Norway) |
| 1986 | Grete Waitz (Norway) |
| 1987 | Ingrid Kristiansen (Norway) |
| 1988 | Ingrid Kristiansen (Norway) |
| 1989 | Veronique Marot (Great Britain) |
| 1990 | Wanda Panfil (Poland) |
| 1991 | Rosa Mota (Portugal) |
| 1992 | Katrin Dorre (Germany) |
| 1993 | Katrin Dorre (Germany) |
| 1994 | Katrin Dorre (Germany) |
| 1995 | Malgorzata Sobanska (Poland) |
| 1996 | Liz McColgan (Great Britain) |
| 1997 | Joyce Chepchumba (Kenya) |
| 1998 | Catherina McKiernan (Ireland) |
| 1999 | Joyce Chepchumba (Kenya) |
| 2000 | Tegla Loroupe (Kenya) |
| 2001 | Derartu Tulu (Ethiopia) |
| 2002 | Paula Radcliffe (Great Britain) |
| 2003 | Paula Radcliffe (Great Britain) |

### Deciding Distance

The slightly unusual marathon distance of 42km 195m/26mi 385yd was first used at the London Olympics in 1908, so that competitors would finish exactly in front of the royal box. The race was introduced at the 1896 Olympic Games in Athens, Greece, to commemorate the run of the Greek courier (according to legend, Pheidippides) who ran the c.39km/24mi from Marathon to Athens in 490BC with the news of a Greek victory over the Persian army.

## MOTOR SPORTS

*Motor racing*: Racing finely-tuned motor cars, either purpose-built or modified production vehicles; season-long (Mar–Nov) *Formula One* world championship involves usually 16 races at different venues worldwide; other popular forms include *stock car racing*, *hill climbing*, *sports car racing* and *rallying*; first race 1894, between Paris and Rouen.

*Motorcycle racing*: Speed competitions for motorcycles which for the annual season-long grand prix are categorized by the engine sizes *80cc*, *125cc*, *250cc*, *500cc*, *Superbike* and *Sidecar*. Other forms include *speedway*, *moto-cross* and *motorcycle trials* riding.

*Ruling body: International Automobile Association (FIA; Fédération Internationale d'Automobile), International Motorcycling Federation (FIM; Fédération Internationale de Motocyclisme)*

### Formula One World Championship

A Formula One drivers' world championship instituted in 1950; constructor's championship instituted in 1958.

| | Drivers | Constructors |
|---|---|---|
| 1979 | Jody Scheckter (South Africa; Ferrari) | Ferrari |
| 1980 | Alan Jones (Australia; Williams) | Williams |
| 1981 | Nelson Piquet (Brazil; Brabham) | Williams |
| 1982 | Keke Rosberg (Finland; Williams) | Ferrari |
| 1983 | Nelson Piquet (Brazil; Brabham) | Ferrari |
| 1984 | Niki Lauda (Austria; McLaren) | McLaren |
| 1985 | Alain Prost (France; McLaren) | McLaren |
| 1986 | Alain Prost (France; McLaren) | Williams |
| 1987 | Nelson Piquet (Brazil; Williams) | Williams |
| 1988 | Ayrton Senna (Brazil; McLaren) | McLaren |
| 1989 | Alain Prost (France; McLaren) | McLaren |
| 1990 | Ayrton Senna (Brazil; McLaren) | McLaren |
| 1991 | Ayrton Senna (Brazil; McLaren) | McLaren |
| 1992 | Nigel Mansell (Great Britain; Williams) | Williams |
| 1993 | Alain Prost (France; Williams) | Williams |
| 1994 | Michael Schumacher (Germany; Benetton) | Williams |
| 1995 | Michael Schumacher (Germany; Benetton) | Benetton |
| 1996 | Damon Hill (Great Britain; Williams) | Williams |
| 1997 | Jacques Villeneuve (Canada; Williams) | Williams |
| 1998 | Mika Hakkinen (Finland; McLaren) | McLaren |
| 1999 | Mika Hakkinen (Finland; McLaren) | Ferrari |
| 2000 | Michael Schumacher (Germany; Ferrari) | Ferrari |
| 2001 | Michael Schumacher (Germany; Ferrari) | Ferrari |
| 2002 | Michael Schumacher (Germany; Ferrari) | Ferrari |
| 2003 | Michael Schumacher (Germany; Ferrari) | Ferrari |

## Le Mans 24-Hour Race

The greatest of all endurance races; first held in 1923.

| | |
|---|---|
| 1979 | Klaus Ludwig (West Germany)<br>Bill Whittington (USA)<br>Don Whittington (USA) |
| 1980 | Jean-Pierre Jaussaud (France)<br>Jean Rondeau (France) |
| 1981 | Jacky Ickx (Belgium)<br>Derek Bell (Great Britain) |
| 1982 | Jacky Ickx (Belgium)<br>Derek Bell (Great Britain) |
| 1983 | Al Holbert (USA)<br>Hurley Haywood (USA)<br>Vern Schuppan (Australia) |
| 1984 | Henri Pescarolo (France)<br>Klaus Ludwig (West Germany) |
| 1985 | Klaus Ludwig (West Germany)<br>'John Winter' (West Germany)<br>Paolo Barilla (Italy) |
| 1986 | Hans Stück (West Germany)<br>Derek Bell (Great Britain)<br>Al Holbert (USA) |
| 1987 | Hans Stück (West Germany)<br>Derek Bell (Great Britain)<br>Al Holbert (USA) |
| 1988 | Jan Lammers (Holland)<br>Johnny Dumfries (Great Britain)<br>Andy Wallace (Great Britain) |
| 1989 | Jochen Mass (West Germany)<br>Manuel Reuter (West Germany)<br>Stanley Dickens (Sweden) |
| 1990 | John Nielsen (Denmark)<br>Price Cobb (USA)<br>Martin Brundle (Great Britain) |
| 1991 | Volker Weidler (Germany)<br>Johnny Herbert (Great Britain)<br>Bertrand Gachot (Belgium) |
| 1992 | Derek Warwick (Great Britain)<br>Mark Blundell (Great Britain)<br>Yannick Dalmas (France) |
| 1993 | Geoff Brabham (Australia)<br>Christophe Bouchut (France)<br>Eric Helary (France) |
| 1994 | Yannick Dalmas (France)<br>Hurley Haywood (USA)<br>Mauro Baldi (Italy) |
| 1995 | Yannick Dalmas (France)<br>J J Lehto (Finland)<br>Masanori Sekiya (Japan) |
| 1996 | Manuel Reuter (Germany)<br>Davy Jones (USA)<br>Alexander Würz (Austria) |
| 1997 | Michele Alboreto (Italy)<br>Stefan Johansson (Sweden)<br>Tom Kristensen (Denmark) |
| 1998 | Allan McNish (Great Britain)<br>Laurent Aiello (France)<br>Stephane Ortelli (France) |
| 1999 | Pierluigi Martini (Italy)<br>Joachim Winkelhock (Germany)<br>Yannick Dalmas (France) |
| 2000 | Frank Biela (Germany)<br>Tom Kristensen (Denmark)<br>Emanuele Pirro (Italy) |
| 2001 | Frank Biela (Germany)<br>Tom Kristensen (Denmark)<br>Emanuele Pirro (Italy) |
| 2002 | Frank Biela (Germany)<br>Tom Kristensen (Denmark)<br>Emanuele Pirro (Italy) |
| 2003 | Tom Kristensen (Denmark)<br>Rinaldo Capello (Italy)<br>Guy Smith (Great Britain) |

### Driving into History

With his win in 2003, Tom Kristensen became the first driver to achieve four consecutive Le Mans wins. Kristensen moved into joint second place in the all-time winners table, joining Derek Bell with five wins apiece. The record for Le Mans wins is held by the Belgian racing driver Jacky Ickx, who won the race six times (in 1969, 1975, 1976, 1977, 1981 and 1982).

## Indianapolis 500

Often known as the Indy 500; first held in 1911; raced over the Indianapolis Raceway as part of the Memorial Day celebrations at the end of May each year.

| | | | |
|---|---|---|---|
| 1979 | Rick Mears (USA) | 1992 | Al Unser (USA) |
| 1980 | Johnny Rutherford (USA) | 1993 | Emerson Fittipaldi (Brazil) |
| 1981 | Bobby Unser (USA) | 1994 | Al Unser (USA) |
| 1982 | Gordon Johncock (USA) | 1995 | Jacques Villeneuve (Canada) |
| 1983 | Tom Sneva (USA) | 1996 | Buddy Lazier (USA) |
| 1984 | Rick Mears (USA) | 1997 | Arie Luyendyk (The Netherlands) |
| 1985 | Danny Sullivan (USA) | 1998 | Eddie Cheever (USA) |
| 1986 | Bobby Rahal (USA) | 1999 | Kenny Brack (USA) |
| 1987 | Al Unser (USA) | 2000 | Juan Montoya (Colombia) |
| 1988 | Rick Mears (USA) | 2001 | Helio Castroneves (Brazil) |
| 1989 | Emerson Fittipaldi (Brazil) | 2002 | Helio Castroneves (Brazil) |
| 1990 | Arie Luyendyk (The Netherlands) | 2003 | Gil de Ferran (Brazil) |
| 1991 | Rick Mears (USA) | | |

### *Winning by a Whisker*

Some Indy 500 races have been won by the slenderest of margins. The closest ever finish took place in 1992, when Al Unser beat Scott Goodyear by just 0.043 of a second. Other close races have been in 1982 (0.16 of a second separating the winner from the runner up), 1997 (0.57 of a second) and 1996 (0.695 of a second).

## World Rally Championship

First held in 1979; comprises a series of races in 16 different countries over a variety of terrains, between Jan and Nov.

| | | | |
|---|---|---|---|
| 1979 | Bjorn Waldegard (Sweden) | 1992 | Carlos Sainz (Spain) |
| 1980 | Walter Rohrl (West Germany) | 1993 | Juha Kankkunen (Finland) |
| 1981 | Ari Vatanen (Finland) | 1994 | Didier Auriol (France) |
| 1982 | Walter Rohrl (West Germany) | 1995 | Colin McRae (Great Britain) |
| 1983 | Hannu Mikkola (Finland) | 1996 | Tommi Makinen (Finland) |
| 1984 | Stig Blomqvist (Sweden) | 1997 | Tommi Makinen (Finland) |
| 1985 | Timo Salonen (Finland) | 1998 | Tommi Makinen (Finland) |
| 1986 | Juha Kankkunen (Finland) | 1999 | Tommi Makinen (Finland) |
| 1987 | Juha Kankkunen (Finland) | 2000 | Marcus Gronholm (Finland) |
| 1988 | Miki Biasion (Italy) | 2001 | Richard Burns (Great Britain) |
| 1989 | Miki Biasion (Italy) | 2002 | Marcus Gronholm (Finland) |
| 1990 | Carlos Sainz (Spain) | 2003 | Petter Solberg (Norway) |
| 1991 | Juha Kankkunen (Finland) | | |

## Motorcycling World Championships

First organized in 1949; current titles for Superbike, 500cc, 250cc, 125cc, 80cc and Sidecar; Formula One and Endurance world championships also held annually; the most prestigious title is the 500cc category, known as MotoGP.

**500cc**

| | | | |
|---|---|---|---|
| 1979 | Kenny Roberts (USA) | 1992 | Wayne Rainey (USA) |
| 1980 | Kenny Roberts (USA) | 1993 | Kevin Schwantz (USA) |
| 1981 | Marco Lucchinelli (Italy) | 1994 | Michael Doohan (Australia) |
| 1982 | Franco Uncini (Italy) | 1995 | Michael Doohan (Australia) |
| 1983 | Freddie Spencer (USA) | 1996 | Michael Doohan (Australia) |
| 1984 | Eddie Lawson (USA) | 1997 | Michael Doohan (Australia) |
| 1985 | Freddie Spencer (USA) | 1998 | Michael Doohan (Australia) |
| 1986 | Eddie Lawson (USA) | 1999 | Alex Criville (Spain) |
| 1987 | Wayne Gardner (Australia) | 2000 | Kenny Roberts (USA) |
| 1988 | Eddie Lawson (USA) | 2001 | Valentino Rossi (Italy) |
| 1989 | Eddie Lawson (USA) | 2002 | Valentino Rossi (Italy) |
| 1990 | Wayne Rainey (USA) | 2003 | Valentino Rossi (Italy) |
| 1991 | Wayne Rainey (USA) | | |

## Isle of Man TT Races

The most famous of all motorcycle races; take place each Jun; first held 1907; principal race is the Senior TT.

**Senior TT**

| | | | |
|---|---|---|---|
| 1979 | Mike Hailwood (Great Britain) | 1992 | Steve Hislop (Great Britain) |
| 1980 | Graeme Crosby (New Zealand) | 1993 | Phil McCallen (Ireland) |
| 1981 | Mick Grant (Great Britain) | 1994 | Steve Hislop (Great Britain) |
| 1982 | Norman Brown (Great Britain) | 1995 | Joey Dunlop (Ireland) |
| 1983 | Rob McElnea (Great Britain) | 1996 | Phil McCallen (Ireland) |
| 1984 | Rob McElnea (Great Britain) | 1997 | Phil McCallen (Ireland) |
| 1985 | Joey Dunlop (Ireland) | 1998 | Ian Simpson (Great Britain) |
| 1986 | Roger Burnett (Great Britain) | 1999 | David Jefferies (Great Britain) |
| 1987 | Joey Dunlop (Ireland) | 2000 | David Jefferies (Great Britain) |
| 1988 | Joey Dunlop (Ireland) | 2001 | *not held* |
| 1989 | Steve Hislop (Great Britain) | 2002 | David Jefferies (Great Britain) |
| 1990 | Carl Fogarty (Great Britain) | 2003 | Adrian Archibald (Great Britain) |
| 1991 | Steve Hislop (Great Britain) | | |

### *Road Racing*

The TT takes place over temporarily closed public roads in the Isle of Man. The island became the home of road racing in the early 1900s, when racing on public roads in the UK was forbidden by an Act of Parliament, and a strict 20mph, or 32kph, speed limit was enforced. However, the ban did not apply to the Isle of Man, and after a little persuasion by early racing enthusiasts, Tynwald – the island's Parliament – passed a Bill allowing road racing in 1904.

## ROWING

Propulsion of a boat by oars; involves two or more rowers, each with an oar, and often with a coxswain; sculling involves one rower with two oars; rowing as an organized sport dates from 1715 (first rowing of the Doggetts Coat and Badge race on the River Thames, London).

*Ruling body: International Rowing Federation (FISA; Fédération Internationale des Sociétés d'Aviron)*

### World Championships

First held for men in 1962 and for women in 1974; Olympic champions assume the role of world champion in Olympic years; principal event is the single sculls.

**Single sculls – Men**

| | |
|---|---|
| 1979 | Pertti Karpinnen (Finland) |
| 1980 | Pertti Karpinnen (Finland) |
| 1981 | Peter Michael Kolbe (West Germany) |
| 1982 | Reiche Rüdiger (East Germany) |
| 1983 | Peter Michael Kolbe (West Germany) |
| 1984 | Pertti Karpinnen (Finland) |
| 1985 | Pertti Karppinen (Finland) |
| 1986 | Peter Michael Kolbe (West Germany) |
| 1987 | Thomas Lange (East Germany) |
| 1988 | Thomas Lange (East Germany) |
| 1989 | Thomas Lange (East Germany) |
| 1990 | Yuri Janson (USSR) |
| 1991 | Thomas Lange (Germany) |
| 1992 | Thomas Lange (Germany) |
| 1993 | Derek Porter (Canada) |
| 1994 | Andre Wilms (Germany) |
| 1995 | Iztok Cop (Slovenia) |
| 1996 | Xeno Müller (Switzerland) |
| 1997 | Jamie Koven (USA) |
| 1998 | Rob Waddell (New Zealand) |
| 1999 | Rob Waddell (New Zealand) |
| 2000 | Rob Waddell (New Zealand) |
| 2001 | Olaf Tufte (Norway) |
| 2002 | Marcel Hacker (Germany) |
| 2003 | Olaf Tufte (Norway) |

**Single sculls – Women**

| | |
|---|---|
| 1979 | Toma Sanda (Romania) |
| 1980 | Toma Sanda (Romania) |
| 1981 | Toma Sanda (Romania) |
| 1982 | Irina Fetissova (USSR) |
| 1983 | Jutta Hampe (East Germany) |
| 1984 | Valeria Racila (Romania) |
| 1985 | Cornelia Linse (East Germany) |
| 1986 | Jutta Hampe (East Germany) |
| 1987 | Magdelena Georgieva (Bulgaria) |
| 1988 | Jutta Behrendt (East Germany) |
| 1989 | Elisabeta Lipa (Romania) |
| 1990 | Brigit Peter (East Germany) |
| 1991 | Silke Laumann (Canada) |
| 1992 | Elisabeta Lipa (Romania) |
| 1993 | Jana Phieme (Germany) |
| 1994 | Trine Hansen (Denmark) |
| 1995 | Maria Brandin (Sweden) |
| 1996 | Ekaterina Khodotovich (Belarus) |
| 1997 | Ekaterina Khodotovich (Belarus) |
| 1998 | Irina Fedotova (Russia) |
| 1999 | Ekaterina Karsten (Belarus) |
| 2000 | Ekaterina Karsten (Belarus) |
| 2001 | Katrin Rutschow-Stomporowski (Germany) |
| 2002 | Rumyana Neykova (Bulgaria) |
| 2003 | Rumyana Neykova (Bulgaria) |

### The Boat Race

An annual contest between the crews from the Oxford and Cambridge University rowing clubs; first contested in 1829; not held in some years in the early history of the race; held twice in 1849 (Mar/Dec); the current course is from Putney to Mortlake.

| | |
|---|---|
| 1829 | Oxford |
| 1836 | Cambridge |
| 1839 | Cambridge |
| 1840 | Cambridge |
| 1841 | Cambridge |
| 1842 | Oxford |
| 1845 | Cambridge |
| 1846 | Cambridge |
| 1849 | Cambridge |

| | |
|---|---|
| 1849 | Oxford |
| 1852 | Oxford |
| 1854 | Oxford |
| 1856 | Cambridge |
| 1857 | Oxford |
| 1858 | Cambridge |
| 1859 | Oxford |
| 1860 | Cambridge |
| 1861 | Oxford |
| 1862 | Oxford |
| 1863 | Oxford |
| 1864 | Oxford |
| 1865 | Oxford |
| 1866 | Oxford |
| 1867 | Oxford |
| 1868 | Oxford |
| 1869 | Oxford |
| 1870 | Cambridge |
| 1871 | Cambridge |
| 1872 | Cambridge |
| 1873 | Cambridge |
| 1874 | Cambridge |
| 1875 | Oxford |
| 1876 | Cambridge |
| 1877 | *dead heat* |
| 1878 | Oxford |
| 1879 | Cambridge |
| 1880 | Oxford |
| 1881 | Oxford |
| 1882 | Oxford |
| 1883 | Oxford |
| 1884 | Cambridge |
| 1885 | Oxford |
| 1886 | Cambridge |
| 1887 | Cambridge |
| 1888 | Cambridge |
| 1889 | Cambridge |
| 1890 | Oxford |
| 1891 | Oxford |
| 1892 | Oxford |
| 1893 | Oxford |
| 1894 | Oxford |
| 1895 | Oxford |
| 1896 | Oxford |
| 1897 | Oxford |
| 1898 | Oxford |
| 1899 | Cambridge |
| 1900 | Cambridge |
| 1901 | Oxford |
| 1902 | Cambridge |
| 1903 | Cambridge |
| 1904 | Cambridge |
| 1905 | Oxford |
| 1906 | Cambridge |
| 1907 | Cambridge |
| 1908 | Cambridge |
| 1909 | Oxford |
| 1910 | Oxford |
| 1911 | Oxford |
| 1912 | Oxford |
| 1913 | Oxford |
| 1914 | Cambridge |
| 1915 | *not held* |
| 1916 | *not held* |
| 1917 | *not held* |
| 1918 | *not held* |
| 1919 | *not held* |
| 1920 | Cambridge |
| 1921 | Cambridge |
| 1922 | Cambridge |
| 1923 | Oxford |
| 1924 | Cambridge |
| 1925 | Cambridge |
| 1926 | Cambridge |
| 1927 | Cambridge |
| 1928 | Cambridge |
| 1929 | Cambridge |
| 1930 | Cambridge |
| 1931 | Cambridge |
| 1932 | Cambridge |
| 1933 | Cambridge |
| 1934 | Cambridge |
| 1935 | Cambridge |
| 1936 | Cambridge |
| 1937 | Oxford |
| 1938 | Oxford |
| 1939 | Cambridge |
| 1940 | *not held* |
| 1941 | *not held* |
| 1942 | *not held* |
| 1943 | *not held* |
| 1944 | *not held* |
| 1945 | *not held* |
| 1946 | Oxford |
| 1947 | Cambridge |
| 1948 | Cambridge |
| 1949 | Cambridge |
| 1950 | Cambridge |
| 1951 | Cambridge |
| 1952 | Oxford |
| 1953 | Cambridge |
| 1954 | Oxford |
| 1955 | Cambridge |
| 1956 | Cambridge |
| 1957 | Cambridge |
| 1958 | Cambridge |
| 1959 | Oxford |
| 1960 | Oxford |
| 1961 | Cambridge |
| 1962 | Cambridge |
| 1963 | Oxford |
| 1964 | Cambridge |
| 1965 | Oxford |
| 1966 | Oxford |
| 1967 | Oxford |
| 1968 | Cambridge |
| 1969 | Cambridge |
| 1970 | Cambridge |
| 1971 | Cambridge |
| 1972 | Cambridge |
| 1973 | Cambridge |
| 1974 | Oxford |
| 1975 | Cambridge |
| 1976 | Oxford |
| 1977 | Oxford |
| 1978 | Oxford |
| 1979 | Oxford |
| 1980 | Oxford |
| 1981 | Oxford |
| 1982 | Oxford |
| 1983 | Oxford |
| 1984 | Oxford |
| 1985 | Oxford |
| 1986 | Cambridge |
| 1987 | Oxford |
| 1988 | Oxford |
| 1989 | Oxford |
| 1990 | Oxford |
| 1991 | Oxford |
| 1992 | Oxford |
| 1993 | Cambridge |
| 1994 | Cambridge |
| 1995 | Cambridge |
| 1996 | Cambridge |
| 1997 | Cambridge |
| 1998 | Cambridge |
| 1999 | Cambridge |
| 2000 | Oxford |
| 2001 | Cambridge |
| 2002 | Oxford |
| 2003 | Oxford |

## RUGBY LEAGUE

Team ball game played with oval ball; developed 1823 from football (supposedly when William Webb Ellis of Rugby school picked up the ball and ran with it); rugby league was formed by the breakaway Northern Union after a dispute with the Rugby Football Union about pay in 1895; object is to score a *try* by grounding ball in opposing team's scoring area behind goal line. The 13-a-side Rugby League game is now a professional game; scoring: try 4 points, conversion 2 points, penalty 2 points, drop goal 1 point.

*Ruling body: Rugby League (RL)*

### Rugby League pitch

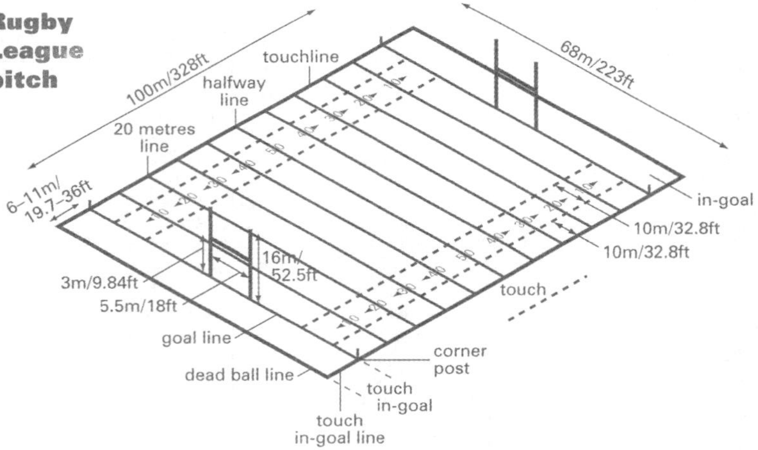


### World Cup

First held in 1954 between Great Britain, France, Australia and New Zealand; played intermittently since; will next be held in 2005.

| | | | | | |
|---|---|---|---|---|---|
| 1954 | Great Britain | 1970 | Australia | 1988 | Australia |
| 1957 | Australia | 1972 | Great Britain | 1992 | Australia |
| 1960 | Great Britain | 1975 | Australia | 1995 | Australia |
| 1968 | Australia | 1977 | Australia | 2000 | Australia |

### Tetley's Super League

First held in 1996. The top five teams in the league at the end of the season play off for the title; known as the JJB Super League from 1996 to 1999.

| | | | | | |
|---|---|---|---|---|---|
| 1996 | St Helens | 1999 | St Helens | 2002 | St Helens |
| 1997 | Bradford | 2000 | St Helens | 2003 | Bradford |
| 1998 | Wigan | 2001 | Bradford | | |

### Challenge Cup

First contested in 1897 and won by Batley; first final at Wembley Stadium in 1929.

| | | | | | |
|---|---|---|---|---|---|
| 1979 | Widnes | 1988 | Wigan | 1997 | St Helens |
| 1980 | Hull K R | 1989 | Wigan | 1998 | Sheffield |
| 1981 | Widnes | 1990 | Wigan | 1999 | Leeds |
| 1982 | Hull | 1991 | Wigan | 2000 | Bradford |
| 1983 | Featherstone | 1992 | Wigan | 2001 | St Helens |
| 1984 | Widnes | 1993 | Wigan | 2002 | Wigan |
| 1985 | Wigan | 1994 | Wigan | 2003 | Bradford |
| 1986 | Castleford | 1995 | Wigan | | |
| 1987 | Halifax | 1996 | St Helens | | |

## RUGBY UNION

Team ball game played with oval ball; developed 1823 from football (supposedly when William Webb Ellis of Rugby school picked up the ball and ran with it); object is to score a *try* by grounding ball in opposing team's scoring area behind goal line. The 15-a-side Rugby Union game is now a professional game; scoring: try 5 points, conversion 2 points, penalty 3 points, drop goal 3 points.

*Ruling body: Rugby Football Union (RFU), International Rugby Board (IRB)*

### Rugby Union pitch

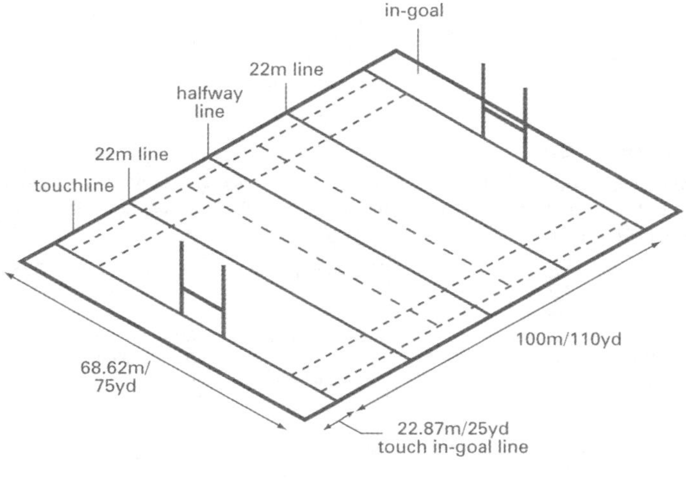

# RUGBY UNION

## World Cup

The first Rugby Union World Cup was staged in 1987 and now takes place every four years.

| | | | | | |
|---|---|---|---|---|---|
| 1987 | New Zealand | 1995 | South Africa | 2003 | England |
| 1991 | Australia | 1999 | Australia | | |

## Six Nations' Championship

A round robin competition involving England, Ireland, Scotland, Wales, France, and from 2000, Italy; first contested in 1882.

| | | | | | |
|---|---|---|---|---|---|
| 1979 | Wales | 1988 | France and Wales | 1997 | France |
| 1980 | England | 1989 | France | 1998 | France |
| 1981 | France | 1990 | Scotland | 1999 | Scotland |
| 1982 | Ireland | 1991 | England | 2000 | England |
| 1983 | France and Ireland | 1992 | England | 2001 | England |
| 1984 | Scotland | 1993 | France | 2002 | France |
| 1985 | Ireland | 1994 | Wales | 2003 | England |
| 1986 | France and Scotland | 1995 | England | | |
| 1987 | France | 1996 | England | | |

## County Championship

First held in 1889.

| | | | | | |
|---|---|---|---|---|---|
| 1979 | Middlesex | 1988 | Lancashire | 1997 | Cumbria |
| 1980 | Lancashire | 1989 | Durham | 1998 | Cheshire |
| 1981 | Northumberland | 1990 | Lancashire | 1999 | Cornwall |
| 1982 | Lancashire | 1991 | Cornwall | 2000 | Yorkshire |
| 1983 | Gloucestershire | 1992 | Lancashire | 2001 | *not held* |
| 1984 | Gloucestershire | 1993 | Lancashire | 2002 | Gloucestershire |
| 1985 | Middlesex | 1994 | Yorkshire | 2003 | Lancashire |
| 1986 | Warwickshire | 1995 | Warwickshire | | |
| 1987 | Yorkshire | 1996 | Gloucestershire | | |

## Powergen Cup

An annual knockout competition for English club sides; first held in the 1971–2 season; known as the John Player Special Cup until 1988, the Pilkington Cup until 1997, and the Tetley's Bitter Cup until 2000.

| | | | | | |
|---|---|---|---|---|---|
| 1979 | Leicester Tigers | 1988 | NEC Harlequins | 1997 | Leicester Tigers |
| 1980 | Leicester Tigers | 1989 | Bath | 1998 | Saracens |
| 1981 | Leicester Tigers | 1990 | Bath | 1999 | London Wasps |
| 1982 | Gloucester/Moseley | 1991 | NEC Harlequins | 2000 | London Wasps |
| 1983 | Bristol | 1992 | Bath | 2001 | Newcastle Falcons |
| 1984 | Bath | 1993 | Leicester Tigers | 2002 | London Irish |
| 1985 | Bath | 1994 | Bath | 2003 | Gloucester |
| 1986 | Bath | 1995 | Bath | | |
| 1987 | Bath | 1996 | Bath | | |

## English League (Zurich Premiership)

Known as the Courage League until 1997 and the Allied Dunbar Premier League until 2000.

| | | | | | |
|---|---|---|---|---|---|
| 1988 | Leicester Tigers | 1994 | Bath | 2000 | Leicester Tigers |
| 1989 | Bath | 1995 | Leicester Tigers | 2001 | Leicester Tigers |
| 1990 | London Wasps | 1996 | Bath | 2002 | Leicester Tigers |
| 1991 | Bath | 1997 | London Wasps | 2003 | London Wasps |
| 1992 | Bath | 1998 | Newcastle Falcons | | |
| 1993 | Bath | 1999 | Leicester Tigers | | |

## Welsh Rugby Union Challenge Cup (Principality Cup)

The knockout tournament for Welsh clubs; first held in 1971–2; formerly known as the Schweppes Welsh Cup and the Swalec Cup.

| | | | | | |
|---|---|---|---|---|---|
| 1979 | Bridgend | 1988 | Llanelli | 1997 | Cardiff |
| 1980 | Bridgend | 1989 | Neath | 1998 | Llanelli |
| 1981 | Cardiff | 1990 | Neath | 1999 | Swansea |
| 1982 | Cardiff | 1991 | Llanelli | 2000 | Llanelli |
| 1983 | Pontypool | 1992 | Llanelli | 2001 | Newport |
| 1984 | Cardiff | 1993 | Llanelli | 2002 | Pontypridd |
| 1985 | Llanelli | 1994 | Cardiff | 2003 | Llanelli |
| 1986 | Cardiff | 1995 | Swansea | | |
| 1987 | Cardiff | 1996 | Pontypridd | | |

## Welsh Premiership

Premiership begun in 1991 and revived in 1998; from 1992–7 title taken by Division 1 Welsh League champions.

| | | | | | |
|---|---|---|---|---|---|
| 1991 | Neath | 1996 | Neath | 2001 | Swansea |
| 1992 | Swansea | 1997 | Pontypridd | 2002 | Llanelli |
| 1993 | Llanelli | 1998 | Swansea | 2003 | Bridgend |
| 1994 | Swansea | 1999 | Llanelli | | |
| 1995 | Cardiff | 2000 | Cardiff | | |

## Scottish Club Championship (BT Premiership)

First held in 1973–4.

| | | | | | |
|---|---|---|---|---|---|
| 1979 | Heriot's FP | 1988 | Kelso | 1997 | Melrose |
| 1980 | Gala | 1989 | Kelso | 1998 | Watsonians |
| 1981 | Gala | 1990 | Melrose | 1999 | Heriot's FP |
| 1982 | Hawick | 1991 | Boroughmuir | 2000 | Heriot's FP |
| 1983 | Gala | 1992 | Melrose | 2001 | Hawick |
| 1984 | Hawick | 1993 | Melrose | 2002 | Hawick |
| 1985 | Hawick | 1994 | Melrose | 2003 | Boroughmuir |
| 1986 | Hawick | 1995 | Stirling County | | |
| 1987 | Hawick | 1996 | Melrose | | |

## SKIING

Propelling oneself along snow while standing on skis, aided by poles; named from Norwegian *ski*, 'snowshoe'; two forms of competition skiing: *alpine skiing*, consisting of the *downhill*, *slalom* (zigzag courses through markers) and *ski-jumping*, and *Nordic skiing* or *langlaufing* (on narrower skis to which only the toe is attached), incorporating cross-country skiing and the biathlon.

*Ruling body: International Ski Federation (FIS; Fédération Internationale de Ski)*

### World Cup

A season-long competition first organized in 1967; champions are declared in downhill, slalom, giant slalom and super-giant slalom, as well as the overall champion; points are obtained for performances in each category.

#### Overall winners

**Men**

| | |
|---|---|
| 1979 | Peter Luscher (Switzerland) |
| 1980 | Andreas Wenzel (Liechtenstein) |
| 1981 | Phil Mahre (USA) |
| 1982 | Phil Mahre (USA) |
| 1983 | Phil Mahre (USA) |
| 1984 | Pirmin Zurbriggen (Switzerland) |
| 1985 | Marc Girardelli (Luxembourg) |
| 1986 | Marc Girardelli (Luxembourg) |
| 1987 | Pirmin Zurbriggen (Switzerland) |
| 1988 | Pirmin Zurbriggen (Switzerland) |
| 1989 | Marc Girardelli (Luxembourg) |
| 1990 | Pirmin Zurbriggen (Switzerland) |
| 1991 | Marc Girardelli (Luxembourg) |
| 1992 | Paul Accola (Switzerland) |
| 1993 | Marc Girardelli (Luxembourg) |
| 1994 | Kjetil-Andre Aamodt (Norway) |
| 1995 | Alberto Tomba (Italy) |
| 1996 | Lasse Kjus (Norway) |
| 1997 | Luc Alphand (France) |
| 1998 | Hermann Maier (Austria) |
| 1999 | Lasse Kjus (Norway) |
| 2000 | Hermann Maier (Austria) |
| 2001 | Hermann Maier (Austria) |
| 2002 | Stephan Eberharter (Austria) |
| 2003 | Stephan Eberharter (Austria) |

**Women**

| | |
|---|---|
| 1979 | Annemarie Moser-Proell (Austria) |
| 1980 | Hanni Wenzel (Liechtenstein) |
| 1981 | Marie-Therese Nadig (Switzerland) |
| 1982 | Erika Hess (Switzerland) |
| 1983 | Tamara McKinney (USA) |
| 1984 | Erika Hess (Switzerland) |
| 1985 | Michela Figini (Switzerland) |
| 1986 | Maria Walliser (Switzerland) |
| 1987 | Maria Walliser (Switzerland) |
| 1988 | Michela Figini (Switzerland) |
| 1989 | Vreni Schneider (Switzerland) |
| 1990 | Petra Kronberger (Austria) |
| 1991 | Petra Kronberger (Austria) |
| 1992 | Petra Kronberger (Austria) |
| 1993 | Anita Wachter (Austria) |
| 1994 | Vreni Schneider (Switzerland) |
| 1995 | Vreni Schneider (Switzerland) |
| 1996 | Katja Seizinger (Germany) |
| 1997 | Pernilla Wiberg (Sweden) |
| 1998 | Katja Seizinger (Germany) |
| 1999 | Alexandra Meissnitzer (Austria) |
| 2000 | Renate Götschl (Austria) |
| 2001 | Janica Kostelic (Croatia) |
| 2002 | Michaela Dorfmeister (Austria) |
| 2003 | Janica Kostelic (Croatia) |

## SNOOKER

Indoor game played on a standard billiard table by two (or occasionally four) players; aim is to *pot* the 21 coloured balls (arranged on the table at the start) by hitting them with the white *cue ball*, itself hit using a tapered pole or *cue*. Fifteen of the balls are red; these must be potted alternately with the coloured ones. This sequence is called a *break* and continues until a mistake is made; reds remain in the pockets but coloured balls are returned to their designated *spots* on the table until no reds are left, when they are potted in ascending order; game ends when the black is finally potted. Points 1–7 relate to the colours, in order: red, yellow, green, brown, blue, pink, black. The maximum break possible is 147.

*Ruling body: International Billiards and Snooker Federation (IBSF), World Professional Billiards and Snooker Association (WPBSA)*

### Snooker table

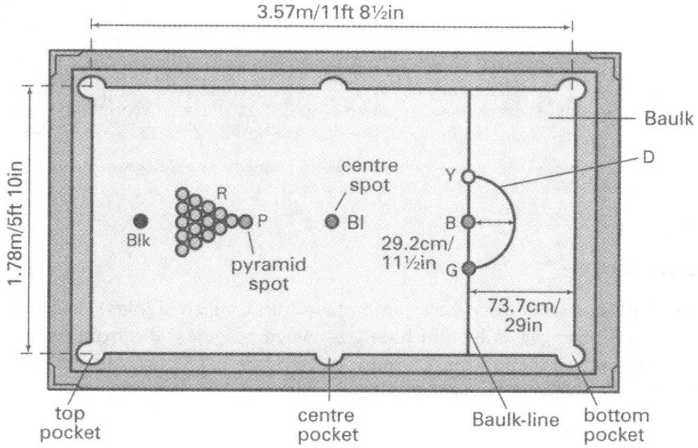


*Note: The snooker table is 85–88cm/2ft 9½in–2ft 10½in high.*

| | | | |
|---|---|---|---|
| Y | yellow | P | pink |
| G | green | R | red |
| Br | brown | Blk | black |
| Bl | blue | | |

### *Breaking the Bank*

Ronnie O'Sullivan made the fastest ever 147 break (at the 1997 World Championship), pocketing not only the balls but also £165 000 in bonus money. His maximum break took just 5 minutes and 20 seconds – working out at a cool £515 per second!

### World Professional Championships

Instituted in the 1926–27 season; a knockout competition open to professional players who are members of the World Professional Billiards and Snooker Association; played at the Crucible Theatre, Sheffield.

| | | | | | |
|---|---|---|---|---|---|
| 1979 | Terry Griffiths | (Wales) | 1992 | Stephen Hendry | (Scotland) |
| 1980 | Cliff Thorburn | (Canada) | 1993 | Stephen Hendry | (Scotland) |
| 1981 | Steve Davis | (England) | 1994 | Stephen Hendry | (Scotland) |
| 1982 | Alex Higgins | (Northern Ireland) | 1995 | Stephen Hendry | (Scotland) |
| 1983 | Steve Davis | (England) | 1996 | Stephen Hendry | (Scotland) |
| 1984 | Steve Davis | (England) | 1997 | Ken Doherty | (Ireland) |
| 1985 | Dennis Taylor | (Northern Ireland) | 1998 | John Higgins | (Scotland) |
| 1986 | Joe Johnson | (England) | 1999 | Stephen Hendry | (Scotland) |
| 1987 | Steve Davis | (England) | 2000 | Mark Williams | (Wales) |
| 1988 | Steve Davis | (England) | 2001 | Ronnie O'Sullivan | (England) |
| 1989 | Steve Davis | (England) | 2002 | Peter Ebdon | (England) |
| 1990 | Stephen Hendry | (Scotland) | 2003 | Mark Williams | (Wales) |
| 1991 | John Parrott | (England) | | | |

#### *Sinistral Snooker*

Lefties everywhere rejoiced when Mark Williams won the Championship in 2000, the first left-hander ever to do so.

## SQUASH

Strenuous indoor racket-and-ball game played (in English singles) on an enclosed court; small rubber ball is hit alternately by players against the front wall; object is to play so that the ball cannot be returned; developed 1817 from rackets at Harrow school. Also sometimes known as *squash rackets*.

*Ruling body: World Squash Federation (WSF)*

#### *Squash Worldwide*

The World Squash Federation keeps records of the number of squash courts worldwide; they estimate that there are more than 47 000 courts around the globe. They calculate that there are 6 169 courts in Africa, 6 299 in Asia, 22 955 in Europe, 7 902 in the Americas and 4 407 in Oceania. Squash-playing nations include Antigua (2 courts), Bhutan (1 court), Republic of Congo (2 courts), Kyrgyzstan (2 courts), Moldova (1 court) and Vanuatu (2 courts). Somewhat surprisingly, Papua New Guinea has no less than 30 courts.

## Squash court

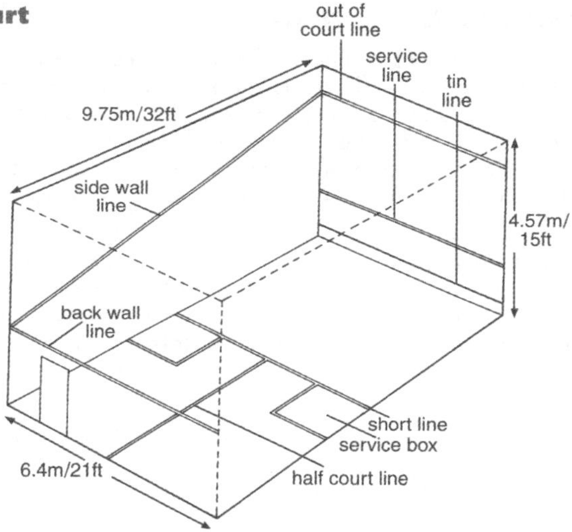


## World Open Championship

First held in 1976; takes place annually for men and women; women's event first held 1979; every two years for women until 1989.

**Men**

| | |
|---|---|
| 1979 | Geoff Hunt (Australia) |
| 1980 | Geoff Hunt (Australia) |
| 1981 | Jahangir Khan (Pakistan) |
| 1982 | Jahangir Khan (Pakistan) |
| 1983 | Jahangir Khan (Pakistan) |
| 1984 | Jahangir Khan (Pakistan) |
| 1985 | Jahangir Khan (Pakistan) |
| 1986 | Ross Norman (New Zealand) |
| 1987 | Jansher Khan (Pakistan) |
| 1988 | Jahangir Khan (Pakistan) |
| 1989 | Jansher Khan (Pakistan) |
| 1990 | Jansher Khan (Pakistan) |
| 1991 | Rodney Martin (Australia) |
| 1992 | Jansher Khan (Pakistan) |
| 1993 | Jansher Khan (Pakistan) |
| 1994 | Jansher Khan (Pakistan) |
| 1995 | Jansher Khan (Pakistan) |
| 1996 | Jansher Khan (Pakistan) |
| 1997 | Rodney Eyles (Australia) |
| 1998 | Jonathon Power (Canada) |
| 1999 | Peter Nicol (Great Britain) |
| 2000 | *not held* |
| 2001 | *not held* |
| 2002 | David Palmer (Australia) |
| 2003 | Amr Shabana (Egypt) |

**Women**

| | |
|---|---|
| 1979 | Heather McKay (Australia) |
| 1981 | Rhonda Thorne (Australia) |
| 1983 | Vicki Cardwell (Australia) |
| 1985 | Sue Devoy (New Zealand) |
| 1987 | Sue Devoy (New Zealand) |
| 1989 | Martine Le Moignan (Great Britain) |
| 1990 | Sue Devoy (New Zealand) |
| 1991 | *not held* |
| 1992 | Sue Devoy (New Zealand) |
| 1993 | Michelle Martin (Australia) |
| 1994 | Michelle Martin (Australia) |
| 1995 | Michelle Martin (Australia) |
| 1996 | Sarah Fitz-Gerald (Australia) |
| 1997 | Sarah Fitz-Gerald (Australia) |
| 1998 | Sarah Fitz-Gerald (Australia) |
| 1999 | Cassie Campion (Great Britain) |
| 2000 | Carol Owens (Australia) |
| 2001 | Sarah Fitz-Gerald (Australia) |
| 2002 | Sarah Fitz-Gerald (Australia) |
| 2003 | Carol Owens (New Zealand) |

## SWIMMING AND DIVING

*Swimming*: Propelling oneself through water without mechanical aids. Four strokes: *breast stroke*, the slowest stroke, developed in the 16c; *front crawl* or *freestyle*, the fastest stroke; *backstroke*; and *butterfly*, developed in the USA in the 20c. In competitions there are also relays, involving four swimmers, and medley races, combining all four strokes. Olympic-size pool is 50m/55yd long, with eight lanes; race lengths from 50m/55yd to 1 500m/1 640yd; earliest reference to swimming as a sport is 36BC Japan.

*Diving*: Jumping from an elevated rigid or sprung board into a swimming pool, often performing a variety of twists and somersaults. Style gains marks, as does successfully completing the dive, based on the level of difficulty of each attempt (which is used as a multiplying factor). Springboard events take place from a board 3m/9ft 10in above the water; platform diving from a rigid board 10m/32ft 10in above the water.

*Ruling body: International Swimming Federation (FINA; Fédération Internationale de Natation)*

### World Championships

First held in 1973 and again in 1975; from 1978 held approximately every four years; since 2001 held every two years.

#### 1991

**Men**

| | |
|---|---|
| 50m freestyle | Tom Jager (USA) |
| 100m freestyle | Matt Biondi (USA) |
| 200m freestyle | Giorgio Lamberti (Italy) |
| 400m freestyle | Joerg Hoffmann (Germany) |
| 1 500m freestyle | Joerg Hoffmann (Germany) |
| 100m backstroke | Jeff Rouse (USA) |
| 200m backstroke | Martín López-Zubero (Spain) |
| 100m breaststroke | Norbert Rózsa (Hungary) |
| 200m breaststroke | Mike Barrowman (USA) |
| 100m butterfly | Anthony Nesty (Suriname) |
| 200m butterfly | Melvin Stewart (USA) |
| 200m individual medley | Tamas Darnyi (Hungary) |
| 400m individual medley | Tamas Darnyi (Hungary) |
| 4×100m freestyle relay | USA |
| 4×200m freestyle relay | Germany |
| 4×100m medley relay | USA |
| 1m springboard diving | Edwin Jongejans (The Netherlands) |
| 3m springboard diving | Kent Ferguson (USA) |
| 10m platform diving | Sun Shuwei (China) |

**Women**

| | |
|---|---|
| 50m freestyle | Zhuang Yong (China) |
| 100m freestyle | Nicole Haislett (USA) |
| 200m freestyle | Hayley Lewis (Australia) |
| 400m freestyle | Janet Evans (USA) |
| 800m freestyle | Janet Evans (USA) |

**Women**

| | |
|---|---|
| 100m backstroke | Krisztina Egerszegi (Hungary) |
| 200m backstroke | Krisztina Egerszegi (Hungary) |
| 100m breaststroke | Linley Frame (Australia) |
| 200m breaststroke | Elena Volkova (Russia) |
| 100m butterfly | Qian Hong (China) |
| 200m butterfly | Summer Sanders (USA) |
| 200m individual medley | Lin Li (China) |
| 400m individual medley | Lin Li (China) |
| 4×100m freestyle relay | USA |
| 4×200m freestyle relay | Germany |
| 4×100m medley relay | USA |
| 1m springboard diving | Gao Min (China) |
| 3m springboard diving | Gao Min (China) |
| 10m platform diving | Fu Mingxia (China) |

## 1994

**Men**

| | |
|---|---|
| 50m freestyle | Alexander Popov (Russia) |
| 100m freestyle | Alexander Popov (Russia) |
| 200m freestyle | Antti Kasvio (Finland) |
| 400m freestyle | Kieren Perkins (Australia) |
| 1 500m freestyle | Kieren Perkins (Australia) |
| 100m backstroke | Martín López-Zubero (Spain) |
| 200m backstroke | Vladimir Selkov (Russia) |
| 100m breaststroke | Norbert Rózsa (Hungary) |
| 200m breaststroke | Norbert Rózsa (Hungary) |
| 100m butterfly | Rafal Szukala (Poland) |
| 200m butterfly | Denis Pankratov (Russia) |
| 200m individual medley | Jani Sievinen (Finalnd) |
| 400m individual medley | Tom Dolan (USA) |
| 4×100m freestyle relay | USA |
| 4×200m freestyle relay | Sweden |
| 4×100m medley relay | USA |
| 1m springboard diving | Evan Stewart (Zimbabwe) |
| 3m springboard diving | Yu Zhuocheng (China) |
| 10m platform diving | Dimitri Sautin (Russia) |

**Women**

| | |
|---|---|
| 50m freestyle | Le Jingyi (China) |
| 100m freestyle | Le Jingyi (China) |
| 200m freestyle | Franziska van Almsick (Germany) |
| 400m freestyle | Yang Aihua (China) |
| 800m freestyle | Janet Evans (USA) |
| 100m backstroke | He Cihong (China) |
| 200m backstroke | He Cihong (China) |
| 100m breaststroke | Sam Riley (Australia) |
| 200m breaststroke | Sam Riley (Australia) |
| 100m butterfly | Liu Limin (China) |
| 200m butterfly | Liu Limin (China) |
| 200m individual medley | Lu Bin (China) |
| 400m individual medley | Dai Guohong (China) |
| 4×100m freestyle relay | China |
| 4×200m freestyle relay | China |
| 4×100m medley relay | China |

**Women**

| | |
|---|---|
| 1m springboard diving | Chen Lixia (China) |
| 3m springboard diving | Tan Shuping (China) |
| 10m platform diving | Fu Mingxia (China) |

## 1998

**Men**

| | |
|---|---|
| 50m freestyle | Bill Pilczuk (USA) |
| 100m freestyle | Alexander Popov (Russia) |
| 200m freestyle | Michael Klim (Australia) |
| 400m freestyle | Ian Thorpe (Australia) |
| 1 500m freestyle | Grant Hackett (Australia) |
| 100m backstroke | Lenny Krayzelburg (USA) |
| 200m backstroke | Lenny Krayzelburg (USA) |
| 100m breaststroke | Fred Deburghgraeve (Belgium) |
| 200m breaststroke | Kurt Grote (USA) |
| 100m butterfly | Michael Klim (Australia) |
| 200m butterfly | Denys Sylantyev (Ukraine) |
| 200m individual medley | Marcel Wouda (The Netherlands) |
| 400m individual medley | Tom Dolan (USA) |
| 4×100m freestyle relay | USA |
| 4×200m freestyle relay | Australia |
| 4×100m medley relay | Australia |
| 1m springboard diving | Yu Zhuocheng (China) |
| 3m springboard diving | Dimitri Sautin (Russia) |
| 10m platform diving | Dimitri Sautin (Russia) |

**Women**

| | |
|---|---|
| 50m freestyle | Amy Van Dyken (USA) |
| 100m freestyle | Jenny Thompson (USA) |
| 200m freestyle | Claudia Poll (Costa Rica) |
| 400m freestyle | Yan Chen (China) |
| 800m freestyle | Brooke Bennett (USA) |
| 100m backstroke | Lea Maurer (USA) |
| 200m backstroke | Roxanna Maracineanu (France) |
| 100m breaststroke | Kristy Kowal (USA) |
| 200m breaststroke | Agnes Kovacs (Hungary) |
| 100m butterfly | Jenny Thompson (USA) |
| 200m butterfly | Susie O'Neill (Australia) |
| 200m individual medley | Wu Yanyan (China) |
| 400m individual medley | Yan Chen (China) |
| 4×100m freestyle relay | USA |
| 4×200m freestyle relay | Germany |
| 4×100m medley relay | USA |
| 1m springboard diving | Irina Lashko (Russia) |
| 3m springboard diving | Yulia Pakhalina (Russia) |
| 10m platform diving | Olena Zhupyna (Ukraine) |

## 2001

**Men**

| | |
|---|---|
| 50m freestyle | Anthony Ervin (USA) |
| 100m freestyle | Anthony Ervin (USA) |
| 200m freestyle | Ian Thorpe (Australia) |
| 400m freestyle | Ian Thorpe (Australia) |

**Men**

| | |
|---|---|
| 1 500m freestyle | Grant Hackett (Australia) |
| 100m backstroke | Matt Welsh (Australia) |
| 200m backstroke | Aaron Peirsol (USA) |
| 50m breaststroke | Oleg Lisogor (Ukraine) |
| 100m breaststroke | Roman Sloudnov (Russia) |
| 200m breaststroke | Brendan Hansen (USA) |
| 50m butterfly | Geoff Huegill (Australia) |
| 100m butterfly | Lars Frolander (Sweden) |
| 200m butterfly | Michael Phelps (USA) |
| 200m individual medley | Massimiliano Rosolini (Italy) |
| 400m individual medley | Alessio Boggiatto (Italy) |
| 4×100m freestyle relay | Australia |
| 4×200m freestyle relay | Australia |
| 4×100m medley relay | Australia |
| 1m springboard diving | Feng Wang (China) |
| 3m springboard diving | Dimitri Sautin (Russia) |
| 10m platform diving | Liang Tian (China) |

**Women**

| | |
|---|---|
| 50m freestyle | Inge de Bruijn (The Netherlands) |
| 100m freestyle | Inge de Bruijn (The Netherlands) |
| 200m freestyle | Giaan Rooney (Australia) |
| 400m freestyle | Yana Klochova (Ukraine) |
| 800m freestyle | Hannah Stockbauer (Germany) |
| 1 500m freestyle | Hannah Stockbauer (Germany) |
| 50m backstroke | Haley Cope (USA) |
| 100m backstroke | Natalie Coughlin (USA) |
| 200m backstroke | Diana Iuliana Mocanu (Romania) |
| 50m breaststroke | Luo Xuejuan (China) |
| 100m breaststroke | Luo Xuejuan (China) |
| 200m breaststroke | Agnes Kovacs (Hungary) |
| 50m butterfly | Inge de Bruijn (The Netherlands) |
| 100m butterfly | Petria Thomas (Australia) |
| 200m butterfly | Petria Thomas (Australia) |
| 200m individual medley | Martha Bowen (USA) |
| 400m individual medley | Yana Klochova (Ukraine) |
| 4×100m freestyle relay | Germany |
| 4×200m freestyle relay | Great Britain |
| 4×100m medley relay | Australia |
| 1m springboard diving | Blythe Hartley (Canada) |
| 3m springboard diving | Mian Xu (China) |
| 10m platform diving | Mian Xu (China) |

## 2003

**Men**

| | |
|---|---|
| 50m freestyle | Alexander Popov (Russia) |
| 100m freestyle | Alexander Popov (Russia) |
| 200m freestyle | Ian Thorpe (Australia) |
| 400m freestyle | Ian Thorpe (Australia) |
| 1 500m freestyle | Grant Hackett (Australia) |
| 100m backstroke | Aaron Peirsol (USA) |
| 200m backstroke | Aaron Peirsol (USA) |
| 50m breaststroke | James Gibson (Great Britain) |
| 100m breaststroke | Kosuke Kitajima (Japan) |

**Men**

| | |
|---|---|
| 200m breaststroke | Kosuke Kitajima (Japan) |
| 50m butterfly | Matthew Welsh (Australia) |
| 100m butterfly | Ian Crocker (USA) |
| 200m butterfly | Michael Phelps (USA) |
| 200m individual medley | Michael Phelps (USA) |
| 400m individual medley | Michael Phelps (USA) |
| 4×100m freestyle relay | Russia |
| 4×200m freestyle relay | Australia |
| 4×100m medley relay | USA |
| 1m springboard diving | Xiang Xu (China) |
| 3m springboard diving | Alexander Dobrosok (Russia) |
| 10m platform diving | Alexandre Despatie (Canada) |

**Women**

| | |
|---|---|
| 50m freestyle | Inge de Bruijn (The Netherlands) |
| 100m freestyle | Hanna-Maria Seppälä (Finland) |
| 200m freestyle | Alena Popchanka (Bulgaria) |
| 400m freestyle | Hannah Stockbauer (Germany) |
| 800m freestyle | Hannah Stockbauer (Germany) |
| 1 500m freestyle | Hannah Stockbauer (Germany) |
| 50m backstroke | Nina Zhivanevskaya (Spain) |
| 100m backstroke | Antje Buschschulte (Germany) |
| 200m backstroke | Katy Sexton (Great Britain) |
| 50m breaststroke | Luo Xuejuan (China) |
| 100m breaststroke | Luo Xuejuan (China) |
| 200m breaststroke | Amanda Beard (USA) |
| 50m butterfly | Inge de Bruijn (The Netherlands) |
| 100m butterfly | Jenny Thompson (USA) |
| 200m butterfly | Otylia Jedrzejczak (Poland) |
| 200m individual medley | Yana Klochova (Ukraine) |
| 400m individual medley | Yana Klochova (Ukraine) |
| 4×100m freestyle relay | USA |
| 4×200m freestyle relay | USA |
| 4×100m medley relay | China |
| 1m springboard diving | Irina Lashko (Australia) |
| 3m springboard diving | Guo Jingjing (China) |
| 10m platform diving | Emilie Heymans (Canada) |

## TENNIS

Properly lawn tennis. Racket-and-ball game for two or four players; net is stretched across centre; rackets have oval heads strung with nylon or gut; playing surface can be grass, clay, shale, concrete, wood, or other man-made materials; object is to play unreturnable strokes, thus scoring points; progression of scoring is 15, 30, 40, deuce if both reach 40, and game; set won by winning six games with a two game lead (or one in a 'short' set); a very close match can be decided using a tie-break. In doubles, players may hit the ball in any order, but must serve in rotation.

*Ruling bodies: International Tennis Federation (ITF), Lawn Tennis Association (LTA)*

## Tennis court

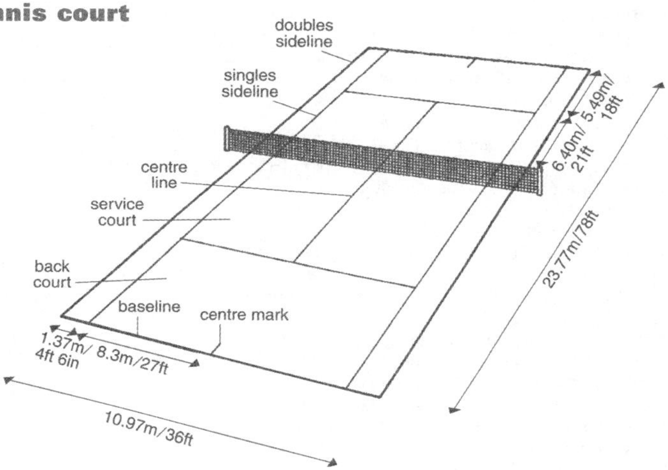


## All-England Championships at Wimbledon

The All-England Championships at Wimbledon are lawn tennis's most prestigious championships; first held in 1877.

**Men's singles**

| | |
|---|---|
| 1979 | Bjorn Borg (Sweden) |
| 1980 | Bjorn Borg (Sweden) |
| 1981 | John McEnroe (USA) |
| 1982 | Jimmy Connors (USA) |
| 1983 | John McEnroe (USA) |
| 1984 | John McEnroe (USA) |
| 1985 | Boris Becker (West Germany) |
| 1986 | Boris Becker (West Germany) |
| 1987 | Pat Cash (Australia) |
| 1988 | Stefan Edberg (Sweden) |
| 1989 | Boris Becker (West Germany) |
| 1990 | Stefan Edberg (Sweden) |
| 1991 | Michael Stich (Germany) |
| 1992 | André Agassi (USA) |
| 1993 | Pete Sampras (USA) |
| 1994 | Pete Sampras (USA) |
| 1995 | Pete Sampras (USA) |
| 1996 | Richard Krajicek (The Netherlands) |
| 1997 | Pete Sampras (USA) |
| 1998 | Pete Sampras (USA) |
| 1999 | Pete Sampras (USA) |
| 2000 | Pete Sampras (USA) |
| 2001 | Goran Ivanisevic (Croatia) |
| 2002 | Lleyton Hewitt (Australia) |
| 2003 | Roger Federer (Switzerland) |

**Women's singles**

| | |
|---|---|
| 1979 | Martina Navratilova (USA) |
| 1980 | Evonne Goolagong Cawley (Australia) |
| 1981 | Chris Evert Lloyd (USA) |
| 1982 | Martina Navratilova (USA) |
| 1983 | Martina Navratilova (USA) |
| 1984 | Martina Navratilova (USA) |
| 1985 | Martina Navratilova (USA) |
| 1986 | Martina Navratilova (USA) |
| 1987 | Martina Navratilova (USA) |
| 1988 | Steffi Graf (West Germany) |
| 1989 | Steffi Graf (West Germany) |
| 1990 | Martina Navratilova (USA) |
| 1991 | Steffi Graf (Germany) |
| 1992 | Steffi Graf (Germany) |
| 1993 | Steffi Graf (Germany) |
| 1994 | Conchita Martínez (Spain) |
| 1995 | Steffi Graf (Germany) |
| 1996 | Steffi Graf (Germany) |
| 1997 | Martina Hingis (Switzerland) |
| 1998 | Jana Novotna (Czech Republic) |
| 1999 | Lindsay Davenport (USA) |
| 2000 | Venus Williams (USA) |
| 2001 | Venus Williams (USA) |
| 2002 | Serena Williams (USA) |
| 2003 | Serena Williams (USA) |

**Men's doubles**

| | |
|---|---|
| 1979 | Peter Fleming/John McEnroe (USA) |
| 1980 | Peter McNamara/Paul McNamee (Australia) |
| 1981 | Peter Fleming/John McEnroe (USA) |
| 1982 | Peter McNamara/Paul McNamee (Australia) |
| 1983 | Peter Fleming/John McEnroe (USA) |
| 1984 | Peter Fleming/John McEnroe (USA) |
| 1985 | Heinz Gunthardt (Switzerland)/Balazs Taroczy (Hungary) |
| 1986 | Joakim Nystrom/Mats Wilander (Sweden) |
| 1987 | Ken Flach/Robert Seguso (USA) |
| 1988 | Ken Flach/Robert Seguso (USA) |
| 1989 | John Fitzgerald (Australia)/Anders Jarryd (Sweden) |
| 1990 | Rick Leach/Jim Pugh (USA) |
| 1991 | John Fitzgerald (Australia)/Anders Jarryd (Sweden) |
| 1992 | John McEnroe (USA)/Michael Stich (Germany) |
| 1993 | Todd Woodbridge/Mark Woodforde (Australia) |
| 1994 | Todd Woodbridge/Mark Woodforde (Australia) |
| 1995 | Todd Woodbridge/Mark Woodforde (Australia) |
| 1996 | Todd Woodbridge/Mark Woodforde (Australia) |
| 1997 | Todd Woodbridge/Mark Woodforde (Australia) |
| 1998 | Jacco Eltingh/Paul Haarhuis (The Netherlands) |
| 1999 | Mahesh Bhupathi/Leander Paes (India) |
| 2000 | Todd Woodbridge/Mark Woodforde (Australia) |
| 2001 | Donald Johnson/Jared Palmer (USA) |
| 2002 | Todd Woodbridge (Australia)/Jonas Bjorkman (Sweden) |
| 2003 | Todd Woodbridge (Australia)/Jonas Bjorkman (Sweden) |

**Women's doubles**

| | |
|---|---|
| 1979 | Billie Jean King/Martina Navratilova (USA) |
| 1980 | Kathy Jordan/Anne Smith (Australia) |
| 1981 | Martina Navratilova/Pam Shriver (USA) |
| 1982 | Martina Navratilova/Pam Shriver (USA) |
| 1983 | Martina Navratilova/Pam Shriver (USA) |
| 1984 | Martina Navratilova/Pam Shriver (USA) |
| 1985 | Kathy Jordan/Elizabeth Smylie (Australia) |
| 1986 | Martina Navratilova/Pam Shriver (USA) |
| 1987 | Claudia Kohde-Kilsch (West Germany)/Helena Sukova (Czechoslovakia) |
| 1988 | Steffi Graf (West Germany)/Gabriela Sabatini (Argentina) |
| 1989 | Jana Novotna/Helena Sukova (Czechoslovakia) |
| 1990 | Jana Novotna/Helena Sukova (Czechoslovakia) |
| 1991 | Natalya Zvereva/Larissa Savchenko (USSR) |
| 1992 | Gigi Fernandez (USA)/Natalya Zvereva (CIS) |
| 1993 | Gigi Fernandez (USA)/Natalya Zvereva (CIS) |
| 1994 | Gigi Fernandez (USA)/Natalya Zvereva (CIS) |
| 1995 | Arantxa Sanchez Vicario (Spain)/Jana Novotna (Czech Republic) |
| 1996 | Helena Sukova (Czech Republic)/Martina Hingis (Switzerland) |
| 1997 | Gigi Fernandez (USA)/Natalya Zvereva (Belarus) |
| 1998 | Jana Novotna (Czech Republic)/Martina Hingis (Switzerland) |
| 1999 | Lindsay Davenport/Corina Morariu (USA) |
| 2000 | Serena Williams/Venus Williams (USA) |
| 2001 | Lisa Raymond (USA)/Rennae Stubbs (Australia) |
| 2002 | Serena Williams/Venus Williams (USA) |
| 2003 | Kim Clijsters (Belgium)/Ai Sugiyama (Japan) |

**Mixed doubles**

| | |
|---|---|
| 1979 | Greer Stevens/Robert Hewitt (South Africa) |
| 1980 | Tracy Austin/John Austin (USA) |
| 1981 | Betty Stove (The Netherlands)/Frew McMillan (South Africa) |
| 1982 | Anne Smith (USA)/Kevin Curren (South Africa) |
| 1983 | Wendy Turnbull (Australia)/John Lloyd (Great Britain) |
| 1984 | Wendy Turnbull (Australia)/John Lloyd (Great Britain) |
| 1985 | Martina Navratilova (USA)/Paul McNamee (Australia) |
| 1986 | Kathy Jordan/Ken Flach (USA) |
| 1987 | Jo Durie/Jeremy Bates (Great Britain) |
| 1988 | Zina Garrison/Sherwood Stewart (USA) |
| 1989 | Jana Novotna (Czechoslovakia)/Jim Pugh (USA) |
| 1990 | Zina Garrison/Rick Leach (USA) |
| 1991 | Elizabeth Smylie/John Fitzgerald (Australia) |
| 1992 | Larissa Savchenko-Neiland (Latvia)/Cyril Suk (Czechoslovakia) |
| 1993 | Martina Navratilova (USA)/Mark Woodforde (Australia) |
| 1994 | Helena Sukova (Czech Republic)/Todd Woodbridge (Australia) |
| 1995 | Martina Navratilova/Jonathan Stark (USA) |
| 1996 | Helena Sukova/Cyril Suk (Czech Republic) |
| 1997 | Helena Sukova/Cyril Suk (Czech Republic) |
| 1998 | Serena Williams (USA)/Max Mirnyi (Belarus) |
| 1999 | Lisa Raymond (USA)/Leander Paes (India) |
| 2000 | Kimberly Po/Donald Johnson (USA) |
| 2001 | Daniela Hantuchova (Slovakia)/Leos Friedl (Czech Republic) |
| 2002 | Elena Likhovtseva (Russia)/Mahesh Bhupathi (India) |
| 2003 | Martina Navratilova (USA)/Leander Paes (India) |

## US Open

First held in 1891 as the United States Championship; became the United States Open in 1968.

**Men's singles**

| | |
|---|---|
| 1979 | John McEnroe (USA) |
| 1980 | John McEnroe (USA) |
| 1981 | John McEnroe (USA) |
| 1982 | Jimmy Connors (USA) |
| 1983 | Jimmy Connors (USA) |
| 1984 | John McEnroe (USA) |
| 1985 | Ivan Lendl (Czechoslovakia) |
| 1986 | Ivan Lendl (Czechoslovakia) |
| 1987 | Ivan Lendl (Czechoslovakia) |
| 1988 | Mats Wilander (Sweden) |
| 1989 | Boris Becker (West Germany) |
| 1990 | Pete Sampras (USA) |
| 1991 | Stefan Edberg (Sweden) |
| 1992 | Stefan Edberg (Sweden) |
| 1993 | Pete Sampras (USA) |
| 1994 | André Agassi (USA) |
| 1995 | Pete Sampras (USA) |
| 1996 | Pete Sampras (USA) |
| 1997 | Pat Rafter (Australia) |
| 1998 | Pat Rafter (Australia) |

**Women's singles**

| | |
|---|---|
| 1979 | Tracy Austin (USA) |
| 1980 | Chris Evert Lloyd (USA) |
| 1981 | Tracy Austin (USA) |
| 1982 | Chris Evert Lloyd (USA) |
| 1983 | Martina Navratilova (USA) |
| 1984 | Martina Navratilova (USA) |
| 1985 | Hana Mandlikova (Czechoslovakia) |
| 1986 | Martina Navratilova (USA) |
| 1987 | Martina Navratilova (USA) |
| 1988 | Steffi Graf (West Germany) |
| 1989 | Steffi Graf (West Germany) |
| 1990 | Gabriela Sabatini (Argentina) |
| 1991 | Monica Seles (Yugoslavia) |
| 1992 | Monica Seles (Yugoslavia) |
| 1993 | Steffi Graf (Germany) |
| 1994 | Arantxa Sanchez Vicario (Spain) |
| 1995 | Steffi Graf (Germany) |
| 1996 | Steffi Graf (Germany) |
| 1997 | Martina Hingis (Switzerland) |
| 1998 | Lindsay Davenport (USA) |

## TENNIS

**Men's singles**

| | |
|---|---|
| 1999 | André Agassi (USA) |
| 2000 | Marat Safin (Russia) |
| 2001 | Lleyton Hewitt (Australia) |
| 2002 | Pete Sampras (USA) |
| 2003 | Andy Roddick (USA) |

**Women's singles**

| | |
|---|---|
| 1999 | Serena Williams (USA) |
| 2000 | Venus Williams (USA) |
| 2001 | Venus Williams (USA) |
| 2002 | Serena Williams (USA) |
| 2003 | Justine Henin-Hardenne (Belgium) |

### *Anyone for Sphairistike?*

'Field tennis' was played in the 18c, but a game similar to the modern game was invented in Wales in 1873 by Walter Wingfield, who christened the new game *sphairistike*. He patented the game and it was quite widely known for a time by this name, which comes from the Greek *sphairistike techne* 'the art of playing ball', from *sphaira* 'ball'. The simpler term *tennis* is thought to come from the French word *tenez*, the imperative of *tenir* meaning 'to take or receive'.

### French Open

First held in 1891 as the French Championships, became an international competition in 1925, and was renamed the French Open in 1968 when professionals were first allowed to enter.

**Men's singles**

| | |
|---|---|
| 1979 | Bjorn Borg (Sweden) |
| 1980 | Bjorn Borg (Sweden) |
| 1981 | Bjorn Borg (Sweden) |
| 1982 | Mats Wilander (Sweden) |
| 1983 | Yannick Noah (France) |
| 1984 | Ivan Lendl (Czechoslovakia) |
| 1985 | Mats Wilander (Sweden) |
| 1986 | Ivan Lendl (Czechoslovakia) |
| 1987 | Ivan Lendl (Czechoslovakia) |
| 1988 | Mats Wilander (Sweden) |
| 1989 | Michael Chang (USA) |
| 1990 | Andres Gomez (Ecuador) |
| 1991 | Jim Courier (USA) |
| 1992 | Jim Courier (USA) |
| 1993 | Sergi Bruguera (Spain) |
| 1994 | Sergi Bruguera (Spain) |
| 1995 | Thomas Muster (Austria) |
| 1996 | Yevgeny Kafelnikov (Russia) |
| 1997 | Gustavo Kuerten (Brazil) |
| 1998 | Carlos Moya (Spain) |
| 1999 | André Agassi (USA) |
| 2000 | Gustavo Kuerten (Brazil) |
| 2001 | Gustavo Kuerten (Brazil) |
| 2002 | Albert Costa (Spain) |
| 2003 | Juan Carlos Ferrero (Spain) |

**Women's singles**

| | |
|---|---|
| 1979 | Chris Evert Lloyd (USA) |
| 1980 | Chris Evert Lloyd (USA) |
| 1981 | Hana Mandlikova (Czechoslovakia) |
| 1982 | Martina Navratilova (USA) |
| 1983 | Chris Evert Lloyd (USA) |
| 1984 | Martina Navratilova (USA) |
| 1985 | Chris Evert Lloyd (USA) |
| 1986 | Chris Evert Lloyd (USA) |
| 1987 | Steffi Graf (West Germany) |
| 1988 | Steffi Graf (West Germany) |
| 1989 | Arantxa Sanchez Vicario (Spain) |
| 1990 | Monica Seles (Yugoslavia) |
| 1991 | Monica Seles (Yugoslavia) |
| 1992 | Monica Seles (Yugoslavia) |
| 1993 | Steffi Graf (Germany) |
| 1994 | Arantxa Sanchez Vicario (Spain) |
| 1995 | Steffi Graf (Germany) |
| 1996 | Steffi Graf (Germany) |
| 1997 | Iva Majoli (Croatia) |
| 1998 | Arantxa Sanchez Vicario (Spain) |
| 1999 | Steffi Graf (Germany) |
| 2000 | Mary Pierce (France) |
| 2001 | Jennifer Capriati (USA) |
| 2002 | Serena Williams (USA) |
| 2003 | Justine Henin-Hardenne (Belgium) |

## Australian Open

First held in 1905 as the Australasian Tennis Championships; became the Australian Championships in 1927.

**Men's singles**

| | |
|---|---|
| 1979 | Guillermo Vilas (Argentina) |
| 1980 | Brian Teacher (USA) |
| 1981 | Johan Kriek (South Africa) |
| 1982 | Johan Kriek (South Africa) |
| 1983 | Mats Wilander (Sweden) |
| 1984 | Mats Wilander (Sweden) |
| 1985 | Stefan Edberg (Sweden) |
| 1986 | *not held* |
| 1987 | Stefan Edberg (Sweden) |
| 1988 | Mats Wilander (Sweden) |
| 1989 | Ivan Lendl (Czechoslovakia) |
| 1990 | Ivan Lendl (Czechoslovakia) |
| 1991 | Boris Becker (Germany) |
| 1992 | Jim Courier (USA) |
| 1993 | Jim Courier (USA) |
| 1994 | Pete Sampras (USA) |
| 1995 | André Agassi (USA) |
| 1996 | Boris Becker (Germany) |
| 1997 | Pete Sampras (USA) |
| 1998 | Petr Korda (Czech Republic) |
| 1999 | Yevgeny Kafelnikov (Russia) |
| 2000 | André Agassi (USA) |
| 2001 | André Agassi (USA) |
| 2002 | Thomas Johansson (Sweden) |
| 2003 | André Agassi (USA) |

**Women's singles**

| | |
|---|---|
| 1979 | Barbara Jordan (USA) |
| 1980 | Hana Mandlikova (Czechoslovakia) |
| 1981 | Martina Navratilova (USA) |
| 1982 | Chris Evert Lloyd (USA) |
| 1983 | Martina Navratilova (USA) |
| 1984 | Chris Evert Lloyd (USA) |
| 1985 | Martina Navratilova (USA) |
| 1986 | *not held* |
| 1987 | Hana Mandlikova (Czechoslovakia) |
| 1988 | Steffi Graf (West Germany) |
| 1989 | Steffi Graf (West Germany) |
| 1990 | Steffi Graf (Germany) |
| 1991 | Monica Seles (Yugoslavia) |
| 1992 | Monica Seles (Yugoslavia) |
| 1993 | Monica Seles (Yugoslavia) |
| 1994 | Steffi Graf (Germany) |
| 1995 | Mary Pierce (France) |
| 1996 | Monica Seles (USA) |
| 1997 | Martina Hingis (Switzerland) |
| 1998 | Martina Hingis (Switzerland) |
| 1999 | Martina Hingis (Switzerland) |
| 2000 | Lindsay Davenport (USA) |
| 2001 | Jennifer Capriati (USA) |
| 2002 | Jennifer Capriati (USA) |
| 2003 | Serena Williams (USA) |

## Davis Cup

International men's team competition organized on a knockout basis; first held in 1900; contested on a challenge basis until 1972.

| | |
|---|---|
| 1979 | USA |
| 1980 | Czechoslovakia |
| 1981 | USA |
| 1982 | USA |
| 1983 | Australia |
| 1984 | Sweden |
| 1985 | Sweden |
| 1986 | Australia |
| 1987 | Sweden |
| 1988 | West Germany |
| 1989 | West Germany |
| 1990 | USA |
| 1991 | France |
| 1992 | USA |
| 1993 | Germany |
| 1994 | Sweden |
| 1995 | USA |
| 1996 | France |
| 1997 | Sweden |
| 1998 | Sweden |
| 1999 | Australia |
| 2000 | Spain |
| 2001 | France |
| 2002 | Russia |
| 2003 | Australia |

### Grand Slam winners (singles)

Players who have won the Australian Open, the French Open, Wimbledon and the US Open in the same calendar year.

**Men**

| | |
|---|---|
| 1938 | Don Budge (USA) |
| 1962 | Rod Laver (Australia) |
| 1969 | Rod Laver (Australia) |

**Women**

| | |
|---|---|
| 1953 | Maureen Connolly (USA) |
| 1970 | Margaret Court (Australia) |
| 1988 | Steffi Graf (West Germany) |

## VOLLEYBALL

Indoor court game; two teams of six play on a court which has a raised net stretched across the centre; aim is to score points by grounding the inflated ball on opponent's side after hitting it over net with the arms or hands; ball may not be hit more than three times on one team's side of the net.

*Ruling body: International Volleyball Federation (FIVB; Fédération Internationale de Volleyball)*

### Volleyball court

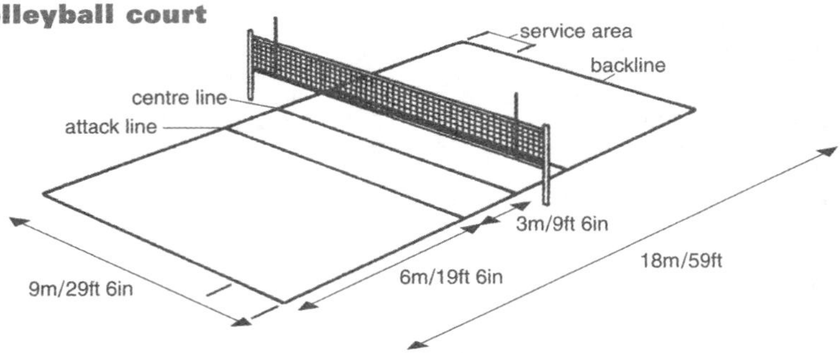


### World Championships

Inaugurated in 1949; first women's championships in 1952; now held every four years, but Olympic champions are also world champions in Olympic years.

**Men**

| | |
|---|---|
| 1980 | USSR |
| 1982 | USSR |
| 1984 | USA |
| 1986 | USA |
| 1988 | USA |
| 1990 | Italy |
| 1992 | Brazil |
| 1994 | Italy |
| 1996 | The Netherlands |
| 1998 | Italy |
| 2000 | Yugoslavia |
| 2002 | Brazil |

**Women**

| | |
|---|---|
| 1980 | USSR |
| 1982 | China |
| 1984 | China |
| 1986 | China |
| 1988 | USSR |
| 1990 | USSR |
| 1992 | Cuba |
| 1994 | Cuba |
| 1996 | Cuba |
| 1998 | Cuba |
| 2000 | Cuba |
| 2002 | Italy |

# WEIGHTLIFTING

Test of strength by lifting weights attached to both ends of a metal pole or *barbell*. Competitors have to make two successful lifts: the *snatch*, taking the bar to an outstretched position above the head in one movement (held for two seconds), and the *clean and jerk* or *jerk* which is achieved in two movements, first onto the chest, then above the head with outstretched arms; aggregate weight of the two lifts gives a competitor's total, and the weights are gradually increased. Another form is *powerlifting*, which calls for sheer strength rather than technique, and takes three forms: the *squat*, *dead lift* and *bench press*. Weightlifting was part of Ancient Olympic Games; introduced as sport c.1850.

*Ruling body: International Weightlifting Federation (IWF)*

## World Championships

First held in 1891; 11 weight divisions; the most prestigious is the 105kg-plus category (formerly known as Super Heavyweight, then 110kg-plus; in 1993 changed to 108kg-plus; in 1998 reduced to current weight); Olympic champions are automatically world champions in Olympic years. Women's World Championships instituted in 1987; the most prestigious of 7 weight divisions is the 75kg-plus category (formerly 82.5kg-plus; in 1993 changed to 83kg-plus; in 1998 reduced to current weight).

**Men 105kg-plus**

| | |
|---|---|
| 1979 | Sultan Rakhmanov (USSR) |
| 1980 | Sultan Rakhmanov (USSR) |
| 1981 | Anatoli Pisarenko (USSR) |
| 1982 | Anatoli Pisarenko (USSR) |
| 1983 | Anatoli Pisarenko (USSR) |
| 1984 | Dean Lukin (Australia) |
| 1985 | Antonio Krastev (Bulgaria) |
| 1986 | Antonio Krastev (Bulgaria) |
| 1987 | Aleksandr Kurlovich (USSR) |
| 1988 | Aleksandr Kurlovich (USSR) |
| 1989 | Stefan Botev (Bulgaria) |
| 1990 | Stefan Botev (Bulgaria) |
| 1991 | Aleksandr Kurlovich (USSR) |
| 1992 | Aleksandr Kurlovich (UT) |
| 1993 | Ronnie Weller (Germany) |
| 1994 | Aleksandr Kurlovich (Belarus) |
| 1995 | Andrey Chemerkin (Russia) |
| 1996 | Andrey Chemerkin (Russia) |
| 1997 | Andrey Chemerkin (Russia) |
| 1998 | Andrey Chemerkin (Russia) |
| 1999 | Andrey Chemerkin (Russia) |
| 2000 | Hossein Reza Zadeh (Iran) |
| 2001 | Saeed Salem Jaber (Qatar) |
| 2002 | Hossein Reza Zadeh (Iran) |
| 2003 | Hossein Reza Zadeh (Iran) |

**Women 75kg-plus**

| | |
|---|---|
| 1987 | Han Changmei (China) |
| 1988 | Han Changmei (China) |
| 1989 | Han Changmei (China) |
| 1990 | Li Yajuan (China) |
| 1991 | Li Yajuan (China) |
| 1992 | Li Yajuan (China) |
| 1993 | Li Yajuan (China) |
| 1994 | Karolina Lundahl (Finland) |
| 1995 | Erika Takacs (Hungary) |
| 1996 | Ni Wan (China) |
| 1997 | Ma Runmei (China) |
| 1998 | Tang Gonghong (China) |
| 1999 | Ding Meiyuan (China) |
| 2000 | Ding Meiyuan (China) |
| 2001 | Albina Khomich (Russia) |
| 2002 | Agata Wrobel (Poland) |
| 2003 | Ding Meiyuan (China) |

## WRESTLING

Fighting person to person without using fists; aim is to throw opponent to the ground; most popular forms are *freestyle*, where the legs can be used to hold and trip, and *Graeco-Roman* where holds below the waist are not allowed. Ten weight divisions, from 55kg to 120kg.

*Ruling body: International Federation of Associated Wrestling Styles (FILA; Fédération Internationale de Lutte Amateur)*

### World Championships

Graeco-Roman world championships first held in 1921; first freestyle championships in 1951; each style contests 10 weight divisions, the heaviest being the 120kg (formerly over 100kg, and until Dec 2001 130kg) category; Olympic champions become world champions in Olympic years.

#### Super-heavyweight/120kg

**Freestyle**

| | | | |
|---|---|---|---|
| 1979 | Salman Khasimikov (USSR) | 1992 | Bruce Baumgartner (USA) |
| 1980 | Soslan Andiev (USSR) | 1993 | Bruce Baumgartner (USA) |
| 1981 | Salman Khasimikov (USSR) | 1994 | Mahmut Demir (Turkey) |
| 1982 | Salman Khasimikov (USSR) | 1995 | Bruce Baumgartner (USA) |
| 1983 | Salman Khasimikov (USSR) | 1996 | Mahmut Demir (Turkey) |
| 1984 | Bruce Baumgartner (USA) | 1997 | Zekeriya Güclü (Turkey) |
| 1985 | David Gobedzhishvilli (USSR) | 1998 | Alexis Rodriguez (Cuba) |
| 1986 | Bruce Baumgartner (USA) | 1999 | Stephen Neal (USA) |
| 1987 | Aslam Khadartsev (USSR) | 2000 | David Moussoulbes (Russia) |
| 1988 | David Gobedzhishvilli (USSR) | 2001 | David Moussoulbes (Russia) |
| 1989 | Ali Reiza Soleimani (Iran) | 2002 | David Moussoulbes (Russia) |
| 1990 | David Gobedzhishvilli (USSR) | 2003 | Artur Taymazov (Uzbekistan) |
| 1991 | Andreas Schroder (Germany) | | |

**Graeco-Roman**

| | | | |
|---|---|---|---|
| 1979 | Alexander Tomow (Bulgaria) | 1992 | Aleksandr Karelin (UT) |
| 1980 | Alexander Ushakov (Russia) | 1993 | Aleksandr Karelin (Russia) |
| 1981 | Refik Memisevic (Yugoslavia) | 1994 | Aleksandr Karelin (Russia) |
| 1982 | Nikola Dinev (Bulgaria) | 1995 | Aleksandr Karelin (Russia) |
| 1983 | Jewgeni Artjuchin (Russia) | 1996 | Aleksandr Karelin (Russia) |
| 1984 | Jeffrey Blatnick (USA) | 1997 | Aleksandr Karelin (Russia) |
| 1985 | Igor Rostorotzki (USSR) | 1998 | Aleksandr Karelin (Russia) |
| 1986 | Thomas Johansson (Sweden) | 1999 | Aleksandr Karelin (Russia) |
| 1987 | Igor Rostorotzki (USSR) | 2000 | Rulon Gardner (USA) |
| 1988 | Aleksandr Karelin (USSR) | 2001 | Rulon Gardner (USA) |
| 1989 | Aleksandr Karelin (USSR) | 2002 | Dremiel Byers (USA) |
| 1990 | Aleksandr Karelin (USSR) | 2003 | Khassan Baroev (Russia) |
| 1991 | Aleksandr Karelin (USSR) | | |

### *Wrestling Around the World*

Other forms of wrestling include *sumo*, the national sport in Japan; *sambo* in Russia; *kushti* in Iran; *glima* in Iceland; *schwingen* in Switzerland; and *yagli*, the national sport in Turkey. There are also variations within the UK, such as *Devon and Cornwall* wrestling and *Cumberland and Westmoreland* wrestling.

## YACHTING

Travelling over water in a suitable craft, usually a small single or double-sided dinghy, often with outboard motor or auxiliary engine for use in no wind; yachting involves racing small, light sailing vessels with crews of one, two or three; large ocean-going yachts may be 25m/80ft or more in length; several classes of racing yacht in Olympic and international competitions – eg the Admiral's Cup and America's Cup.

*Ruling body: International Sailing Federation (ISAF); Royal Ocean Racing Club (RORC)*

### America's Cup

One of sport's famous trophies; first won by the schooner *Magic* in 1870; now held approximately every four years, when challengers compete in a series of races to find which of them races against the holder; all 25 winners up to 1983 were from the USA.

| | Winning Yacht (Nation) (Skipper) |
|---|---|
| 1980 | Freedom (USA) (Dennis Conner) |
| 1983 | Australia II (Australia) (John Bertrand) |
| 1987 | Stars & Stripes (USA) (Dennis Conner) |
| 1988 | Stars & Stripes (USA) (Dennis Conner)[1] |
| 1992 | America (USA) (Bill Koch) |
| 1995 | Black Magic (New Zealand) (Russell Coutts) |
| 2000 | Black Magic (New Zealand) (Russell Coutts) |
| 2003 | Alinghi (Switzerland) (Russell Coutts) |

[1] *Stars & Stripes won a special challenge match but on appeal the race was awarded to the New Zealand boat. However, the decision was reversed by the New York Appeals Court in 1989.*

#### The Auld Mug

Europe secured its first America's Cup victory in 2003 with a win for Switzerland, a landlocked country not usually known for its yachting prowess. However, the win is less surprising given that Alinghi's skipper was Russell Coutts, a Kiwi who had defected to the Swiss attempt with several key New Zealand team members. Coutts's victory also meant that he became the record holder for captaining the most America's Cup race wins, with 14 race victories under his belt. The America's Cup is affectionately known by those in the business as the 'Auld Mug'.

### Admiral's Cup

A two-yearly series of races, originally held in the English Channel, around Fastnet rock and at Cowes; originally four national teams of three boats per team, now nine teams of three boats per team; first held in 1957.

| | |
|---|---|
| 1979 | Australia |
| 1981 | Great Britain |
| 1983 | West Germany |
| 1985 | West Germany |
| 1987 | New Zealand |
| 1989 | Great Britain |
| 1991 | France |
| 1993 | Germany |
| 1995 | Italy |
| 1997 | USA |
| 1999 | The Netherlands |
| 2001 | *not held* |
| 2003 | Australia |

## CRUFTS WINNERS

Crufts is the world's largest dog show. It is held annually under the auspices of the Kennel Club UK. Named after the show's founder, Charles Cruft (1852–1938); first held in 1891.

| Year | Name | Breed |
|---|---|---|
| 1979 | Eng Am Ch Callaghan of Leander | Kerry Blue Terrier |
| 1980 | Ch Shargleam Blackcap | Retriever (Flat Coated) |
| 1981 | Ch Astley Portia of Rua | Irish Setter |
| 1982 | Ch Grayco Hazelnut | Toy Poodle |
| 1983 | Ch Montravia Kaskarak Hitari | Afghan Hound |
| 1984 | Ch Saxonsprings Hackensack | Lhasa Apso |
| 1985 | Ch Montravia Tommy-Gun | Standard Poodle |
| 1986 | Ch Ginger Xmas Carol | Airedale Terrier |
| 1987 | Ch Viscount Grant | Afghan Hound |
| 1988 | Sh Ch Starlite Express at Valsett | English Setter |
| 1989 | Ch Potterdale Classic of Moonhill | Bearded Collie |
| 1990 | Ch Olac Moon Pilot | West Highland White Terrier |
| 1991 | Sh Ch Raycrofts Socialite | Clumber Spaniel |
| 1992 | Ch Pencloe Dutch Gold | Whippet |
| 1993 | Sh Ch Danaway Debouair | Irish Setter |
| 1994 | Ch Purston Hit | Welsh Terrier |
| 1995 | Ch Starchelle Chicago Bear | Irish Setter |
| 1996 | Sh Ch Canigou Cambrai | Cocker Spaniel |
| 1997 | Ch Ozmilion Mystification | Yorkshire Terrier |
| 1998 | Ch Saredon Forever Young | Welsh Terrier |
| 1999 | Sh Ch Caspians Intrepid | Irish Setter |
| 2000 | Ch Torums Scarf Michael | Kerry Blue Terrier |
| 2001 | Ch Jethard Cidevant | Basenji |
| 2002 | Nord Ch Topscore Contradiction | Standard Poodle |
| 2003 | Ch Yakee A Dangerous Liaison | Pekingese |

*Note: In the names of pedigree dogs, Ch stands for Champion and Sh Ch for Show Champion.*

### Hound Heaven

More than 22 000 pedigree pooches were entered in competition at Crufts 2003, with retrievers, labradors and Cavalier King Charles spaniels bounding ahead with the highest number of dogs entered. Nipping at their heels were Border collies and Irish setters, which each had more than 400 entries. Languishing at the lonely end of the entry table were the Belgian Shepherd, the Greenland Dog, the Canadian Eskimo Dog and the foxhound with just a handful of dogs entered apiece. But just one dog in the competition was unique: the Hungarian Kuvasz. Unsurprisingly, Ashley Chase By Dreamcatcher won Best of Breed in her class.

## MONOPOLY® PROPERTY VALUES

Property values shown are for the standard British edition of the game.

| Property | Value | Colour |
|---|---|---|
| Old Kent Road | £60 | brown |
| Whitechapel Road | £60 | brown |
| Kings Cross Station | £200 | — |
| The Angel Islington | £100 | light blue |
| Euston Road | £100 | light blue |
| Pentonville Road | £120 | light blue |
| Pall Mall | £140 | pink |
| Electric Company | £150 | — |
| Whitehall | £140 | pink |
| Northumberland Avenue | £160 | pink |
| Marylebone Station | £200 | — |
| Bow Street | £180 | orange |
| Marlborough Street | £180 | orange |
| Vine Street | £200 | orange |
| Strand | £220 | red |
| Fleet Street | £220 | red |
| Trafalgar Square | £240 | red |
| Fenchurch Street Station | £200 | — |
| Leicester Square | £260 | yellow |
| Coventry Street | £260 | yellow |
| Water Works | £150 | — |
| Piccadilly | £280 | yellow |
| Regent Street | £300 | green |
| Oxford Street | £300 | green |
| Bond Street | £320 | green |
| Liverpool Street Station | £200 | — |
| Park Lane | £350 | navy blue/purple |
| Mayfair | £400 | navy blue/purple |

### *Monopoly® Money*

The game's makers estimate that more than 160 million copies of Monopoly® have been sold worldwide in 80 countries, and it has been translated into 26 languages. More than 20 million of those copies have been sold in the UK – manufacturers Hasbro estimate that is more than £302.8 billion in Monopoly® money, as a total of £15 140 in Monopoly® money is included in each game. Games have been played in the House of Commons, the London Stock Exchange and the Bank of England – where real money was used for the 1996 UK finals.

## BINGO CALLS

A selection of traditional bingo calls is given.

| | |
|---|---|
| 1 | Kelly's eye *or* Buttered scone *or* At the beginning |
| 2 | One little duck *or* Me and you *or* Little boy blue |
| 3 | Cup of tea *or* You and me |
| 4 | Knock at the door |
| 5 | Man alive |
| 6 | Half a dozen *or* Tom's tricks |
| 7 | Lucky |
| 8 | Garden Gate *or* One fat lady |
| 9 | Doctor's orders |
| 10 | Tony's Den[1] |
| 11 | Legs eleven |
| 12 | One dozen |
| 13 | Unlucky for some *or* Bakers dozen |
| 14 | Valentines Day |
| 15 | Young and keen *or* Rugby Team |
| 16 | Sweet sixteen *or* Never been kissed |
| 17 | Dancing queen |
| 18 | Coming of age *or* Now you can vote |
| 19 | Goodbye teens |
| 20 | One score |
| 21 | Key of the door |
| 22 | Two little ducks *or* All the twos |
| 23 | Thee and me *or* The Lord's My Shepherd |
| 24 | Two dozen |
| 25 | Duck and dive |
| 30 | Dirty Gertie |
| 40 | Naughty forty |
| 50 | Half a century |
| 60 | Five dozen |
| 70 | Three score and ten |
| 80 | Eight and blank |
| 90 | Top of the shop |

[1] *Name changes with the incumbent prime minister; for example, during Margaret Thatcher's time in office it would have been Maggie's Den.*

### Bingo Lingo

Other classic bingo calls include *Tweak of the thumb* (51), *Heinz varieties* (57), *Brighton line* (59), *Old age pension* (65), *Clickety click* (66), *Danny la Rue* (72), *Trombones* (76), *Torquay in Devon* (87), *Two fat ladies* (88) and *Nearly there* (89).

# INDEX

## A

## B

## C

## D

## F

## I

## J



## K

## L

## N

## O



## P

## Q

## U

## V



## W

## Y



## Z